The Sociology of Organizations

An Anthology of Contemporary Theory and Research

Amy S. Wharton
Washington State University

Roxbury Publishing Company
Los Angeles, California

Library of Congress Cataloging-in-Publication Data

The sociology of organizations : an anthology of contemporary theory and research / [edited by] Amy S. Wharton.
    p. cm.
Includes bibliographical references and index.
ISBN 1-933220-05-8 (alk. paper)
1. Organizational sociology. I. Wharton, Amy S.

HM786.S62 2007
302.3'5—dc22
                    2006017460
                    CIP

THE SOCIOLOGY OF ORGANIZATIONS: An Anthology of Contemporary Theory and Research

Publisher: Claude Teweles
Managing Editor: Dawn VanDercreek
Production Editor: Nina M. Hickey
Production Assistant: Sacha A. Howells
Proofreader: Renee Ergazos
Typography: Robert Leuze
Cover Artist: Marnie Kenney

Printed on acid-free paper in the United States of America. This book meets the standards for recycling of the Environmental Protection Agency.

ISBN 1-933220-05-8

ROXBURY PUBLISHING COMPANY
P.O. Box 491044
Los Angeles, California 90049-9044
Voice: (310) 473-3312 • Fax: (310) 473-4490
Email: roxbury@roxbury.net
Website: www.roxbury.net

Contents

Preface

This anthology provides an overview of contemporary theory and research in the sociology of organizations. The study of organizations is truly multidisciplinary. Many organizations courses are taught in business and a great deal of organizational research is generated by researchers in this area. The sociology of organizations overlaps somewhat with the business approach, but is not completely coincident with it. Within sociology, the study of organizations overlaps with the study of work, although there are some important distinctions between these two fields as they have evolved historically. In compiling this anthology, I have tried to acknowledge the multidisciplinarity and breadth of the organizations area, while at the same time giving primary emphasis to readings that reflect sociological (versus business) views of organizations (versus work).

In addition to the field's breadth, I considered the balance between classic and contemporary selections. The selections I included in this anthology primarily emphasize the latter. I have also tried to select papers that deal with issues that might appeal to advanced undergraduates. Most of the selections have an empirical component and together they show a range of methodological approaches.

The book is divided into three major parts—Understanding Organizations, In-side Organizations, and Organizations and Environments. The readings in Part I are designed to answer the following two questions: What is an organization? Why study this particular field? The readings in this section also examine alternative conceptions of organizations and organizational structure. They are fairly diverse, as they show some of the many vantage points from which sociologists have theorized about organizations.

Part II addresses the interrelated topics of culture, conflict, and control. We move "inside" organizations to examine these issues. The readings in this section explore the social relations of organizations from the perspective of demography, social networks, and inequality. Several chapters address topics of concern to policymakers and the public, such as racial and gender diversity in the workplace and work-family conflict.

In Part III we consider organizations in relation to their environments. This perspective is useful for examining issues relating to the emergence of new organizational forms and, more broadly, organizational change. The book concludes with two chapters on economic organizations and organizational theory in the twenty-first century. ✦

Acknowledgments

This anthology has been a long time coming. I am indebted to the many people who offered their assistance along the way. I am especially grateful to Claude Teweles and his staff at Roxbury Publishing for their patience and encouragement. I would also like to thank the following reviewers who read the prospectus and made many useful suggestions about the book's contents and organization: Matthew Archibald, Emory University; Donna C. Bird, University of Southern Maine; William Canak, Middle Tennessee State University; Carol Caronna, Towson University; William J. Kinney, University of St. Thomas; Peter Meiksins, Cleveland State University; Sue Monahan, Montana State University; and Joyce Tang, Queens College/CUNY. I extend my gratitude as well to all of the contributing authors. The most challenging part of compiling an anthology like this is deciding what should be left out when there is so much excellent scholarship to choose from.

Finally, and most of all, I thank my family for their unwavering love and support. I could not do this work without them.

—Amy S. Wharton
Washington State University

Contributing Authors

Catherine Alter is Professor and Dean of the Graduate School of Social Work at the University of Denver.

Stephen R. Barley is the Charles M. Pigott Professor of Management Science and Engineering and the co-director of the Center for Work, Technology, and Organization at the Stanford University School of Engineering.

Christine Beckman is the Assistant Professor of Organization and Strategy at the Paul Merage School of Business at the University of California, Irvine.

Robert J. Bies is the Professor of Organizational Behavior at Georgetown University's McDonough School of Business.

Glenn R. Carroll is the Laurence W. Lane Professor of Organizations in the Graduate School of Business at Stanford University.

Gerald F. Davis is the Sparks/Whirlpool Reseach Professor at the University of Michigan School of Business.

Paul J. DiMaggio is the Professor of Sociology and Business Administration at Princeton University.

Robin J. Ely is the Associate Professor of Organizational Behavior at Harvard Business School.

James A. Evans is the Assistant Professor of Sociology at the University of Chicago.

Cristina B. Gibson is a Research Associate Professor at the University of Southern California Center for Effective Organizations.

Mary Ann Glynn is the Professor of Organization and Management in the Goizueta School of Business at Emory University.

Jerry D. Goodstein is the Professor of Management and Operations at Washington State University, Vancouver.

Michael T. Hannan is the StrataCom Professor of Management in the Graduate School of Business at Stanford University.

Herminia Ibarra is a Professor of Organizational Behavior at the INSEAD Business School.

Robert Jackall is a Professor of Sociology and Public Affairs at Williams College.

Kathleen Knopoff is affiliated with the Center for Professional Development at Santa Clara University.

Gideon Kunda is an Associate Professor in the department of Labor Studies at Tel Aviv University.

Michael Lounsbury is an Associate Professor of Strategic Management and Organization at the University of Alberta.

Joanne Martin is the Fred H. Merrill Professor of Organizational Behavior at the Stanford University School of Business.

Doug McAdam is a Professor of Sociology at Stanford University.

John W. Meyer is a Professor Emeritus of Sociology at Stanford University.

J. Miller McPherson is a Professor of Sociology at the University of Arizona and Duke University.

Patrick H. Mooney is a Professor of Sociology at the University of Kentucky.

Calvin Morrill is a Professor and chair of Sociology at the University of California, Irvine.

William G. Ouchi is a Professor of Management at the University of California, Los Angeles.

Leslie A. Perlow is a Professor of Business Administration at the Harvard Business School.

Charles Perrow is a Professor Emeritus of Sociology at Yale University.

Pam Popielarz is an Associate Professor of Sociology at the University of Illinois, Chicago.

Walter W. Powell is a Professor of Education and an affiliated professor of Organizational Behavior, Sociology, and Communications at Stanford University.

Hayagreeva Rao is a Professor of Organizational Behavior in the Graduate School of Business at Stanford University.

Brian Rowan is the Burke A. Hinsdale Collegiate Professor of Education at the University of Michigan.

W. Richard Scott is a Professor Emeritus of Sociology at Stanford University.

Rachel Sherman is an Assistant Professor of Sociology at Yale University.

Brian H. Smith holds the Charles and Joan Van Zoeren Chair in Religion, Ethics, and Values at Ripon College, Wisconsin.

Lynn Smith-Lovin is a Professor of Sociology at Duke University.

Robert I. Sutton is a Professor of Management Science and Engineering in the Stanford University School of Engineering.

David A. Thomas is the Senior Associate Dean, the director of Faculty Recruiting, and the H. Naylor Fitzhugh Professor of Business Administration at Harvard Business School.

Tracy A. Thompson is an Associate Professor in the Milgard School of Business at the University of Washington, Tacoma.

Thomas M. Tripp is a Professor of Management and Operations at Washington State University, Vancouver.

Diane Vaughan is a Professor of International and Public Affairs at Columbia University.

Kim Voss is a Professor of Sociology at the University of California, Berkeley.

Mayer N. Zald is a Professor Emeritus of Business Administration, Sociology, and Social Work at the University of Michigan.

Mary E. Zellmer-Bruhn is an Assistant Professor of Strategic Management and Organization in the Carlson School of Management at the University of Minnesota. ✦

Part I

Understanding Organizations

Foundations of Contemporary

Organizational Sociology

Chapter 1
Reflections on a Half-Century of Organizational Sociology

W. Richard Scott

Organizations are a pervasive and enduring feature of contemporary society. Evidence of their significance can be found both in the sheer numbers of organizations, as well as their indisputably broad impact on individuals and social institutions. How can sociology help us make sense of organizations?

Like organizations themselves, which differ along many dimensions, there are multiple approaches to the study of organizations. Researchers focus on different kinds of organizations, at different levels of analysis, and employ diverse theoretical perspectives. In looking at the historical development of these differing perspectives, we see how the sociological study of organizations has been closely linked to larger societal developments and to practical problems. As you read this chapter and learn about the ways that sociological approaches to organizations have changed over the last century, consider how organizations and society are likely to develop in the century ahead. What new challenges and opportunities confront organizations, and how can sociologists help us understand these forces? What will the sociology of organizations look like at the dawn of the next century?

Introduction

I had the good fortune to grow up with the field of organizational sociology. When I was in graduate school during the 1950s, the field was just beginning to coalesce, and through the succeeding decades, I observed the broadening and deepening of theory and the widening flood of empirical studies. The overall history is, I believe, a positive one, beginning from a relatively barren landscape and developing into one of the most vigorous intellectual areas of the second half of the twentieth century. A challenge I confront throughout this essay is that the field of organizational sociology is hopelessly entangled with the larger area of organization studies. . . . The influences go in both directions, and it is often not possible to distinguish developments in the more circumscribed area of organizational sociology from those in the wider field. Nevertheless, on this occasion and in this venue, I feel justified in emphasizing sociological contributions. In this chapter, I review some of the major developments and trends. . . .

Crafting a New Field of Study

Field Foundations: Upon this Cleft Rock

Although it is possible to detect concepts and arguments relevant to the study of organizations throughout recorded history, the first systematic studies of organizational behavior occurred during the late decades of the nineteenth century. Spurred by changes in social structure associated with industrialization and bureaucratization, scholars from a number of disciplines began to pay closer attention to organizations and to their effects on social life. From the outset, however, the growing body of scholarship exhibited a polarity that has continued to the present.

The earliest approach, and one that is still active, featured an engineering orientation: How could work systems be designed to improve reliability and productivity? Engineers—most famously Taylor (1911)—proposed reforming work systems from the bottom up. They began with the standardization of nuts and bolts but gradually addressed the motions of workers, the sequencing of tasks, the packaging of tasks into jobs, and the arrangement of jobs into departments (Shenhav 1999). Industrial engineers and operations researchers continue to examine these issues. Managerial theorists, such as Fayol (1919/1949), proceeded from the top down, devising principles for subdividing and coordinating complex work systems. Much of this work was more prescriptive than empirical. Most early organization scholars passed over Weber's

(1924/1968) magisterial history of the transformation of administrative systems to concentrate on his ideal-type models of rational-legal administrative systems that, taken out of context, served to reinforce the prevailing design-driven, formalized, prescriptive approach to organizations.

In reaction to these technocratic versions, social scientists entered the workplace during the 1930s and 1940s, talked to and observed participants, and began to challenge the conception of organization as dominated by rational, instrumental behavior. The research of social psychologists uncovered more complex individual motives, and studies by anthropologists and sociologists revealed unofficial, informal patterns of cooperation, shared norms, and conflicts between and among managers and workers (Roethlisberger & Dickson 1939, Arensberg 1951, Roy 1952, Dalton 1959).

Absent from both of these early approaches was attention to organizations as of interest in their own right. The topics under examination were, variously, industrial design, management, employee psychology, or work groups. Organizations were viewed, at best, as settings within which work was carried out, not as themselves distinctive social systems, let alone collective actors. Barnard (1938) and Selznick (1948) were among the first scholars to focus primary attention on the organization as the unit of interest. Both viewed organizations not only as technical production systems but also as adaptive social systems attempting to survive in their environment.

Thus, Barnard and Selznick commenced the still-continuing task of synthesizing the conflicting views of organizations as production systems and adaptive social systems. Barnard devoted much attention to the interdependence of formal and informal structures within organizations and viewed the primary function of the executive not to design efficient systems—mere "managers" could do that—but to devise and promulgate moral visions of the organization's mission that would command commitment from participants. Selznick emphasized the "paradox" presented by organizations as, on the one hand, "formal structures subject to calculable manipulation" and, on the other, social structures "inescapably imbedded in an institutional matrix" (Selznick 1948, pp. 25–26). In a seminal essay, Gouldner (1959) codified these two linked but contrasting visions, identifying (*a*) a "rational system" perspective that regards organizations as instruments that can be consciously manipulated and molded to accomplish given ends; and (*b*) a "natural system" perspective that views organizations as organic systems seeking survival, as collectivities that evolve via spontaneous, indeterminate processes. Somewhat paradoxically, the explicit recognition of the conflicting assumptions on which previous work was based allowed scholars to see more coherence in the field than had been apparent previously. The growing awareness among scholars that there was a central debate with clearly defined positions and protagonists spurred a kind of unity: a cleft rock, perhaps, but nevertheless a rock on which to build.

Field Construction: Institutionalizing Dualism

Organizations emerged as a recognized field of social scientific study during the 1950s. The field was interdisciplinary from the outset. The two academic centers most critical in shaping this nascent discipline were the Carnegie Institute of Technology (now Carnegie-Mellon University) and Columbia University. The Carnegie group included political scientists, economists, and psychologists. Simon's earlier work (1945) focused attention on decisions and decision makers, but later collaborative work (March & Simon 1958) raised the level of analysis to the organization. The Columbia scholars, under the leadership of Merton, were all sociologists. Both sets of scholars embraced the paradox that had confounded and divided their predecessors. Simon and colleagues at Carnegie worked from a model—that of "bounded rationality"—that neatly linked arguments stressing purpose and intentionality with the recognition of cognitive and social constraints restricting such rational action (Simon 1945, March & Simon 1958, Cyert & March 1963). Merton (1949) at Columbia emphasized the "unintended consequences of purposive action," and his junior colleagues, who carried out early definitive studies of public and private organizations, each gave his own twist to the dual nature of organization. We have already noted Selznick's (1948, 1949) attention to "paradox." Blau (1955) focused on the "dilemmas" of bureaucracy, as formal structures designed to solve one problem give rise to others; and Gouldner (1954) wrote of the "Janus-faced" nature of organizations as systems of coercion and consent. And, in the United Kingdom, an eclectic collection of organizational scholars pursued a "socio-technical" model, insisting that organizations represented a "coupling of dissimilars" (Emery 1959).

As a student of Peter Blau during the mid-1950s at the University of Chicago, I was a second-generation witness to and beneficiary of these foundational studies. Our collaborative work—an early text-treatise—on organizations (Blau & Scott 1962/2003) reflected these conflicting currents as we gave equal attention to such topics as informal and formal structure, leadership and authority, and discretion and control.

The institutionalization of this duality is apparent up to the present. Although occasional scholars present purified models stressing either perfect rationality (posited by assumption) or unadulterated irrationality (viewing organizations as a modern curse), most contemporary scholars seem content to work somewhere within the space anchored by these two poles. Concepts as varied as "transaction costs" (Williamson 1975), "rational myths" (Meyer & Rowan 1977), the "social embeddedness of economic action" (Granovetter 1985), and the juxtaposition of logics of "instrumentality" and "appropriateness" (March & Olsen 1989) continue to reflect a fault line buried deeply within the field.

In this sense, the broader interdisciplinary field of organization studies and the more restricted arena of organizational sociology exhibit a common heritage and bear similar birthmarks. The field of organization studies has expanded rapidly. The range of disciplines involved includes all the social sciences—anthropology, communications, economics, political science, psychology, sociology—as well as selected branches of engineering, cognitive and decision sciences, and management studies such as organization behavior, strategy, and entrepreneurship. Sociologists have played a central role in shaping many aspects of this wide-ranging field, and I focus attention on these contributions.

During the formative period beginning in the 1950s and continuing into the 1980s, sociologists pursued a variety of topics, but their most distinctive and consistent focus was on the determinants of organization structure. How could one best describe the distinctive features of organizations, and what forces were at work in shaping these characteristics? For example, Blau's comparative research program, conducted with a number of collaborators, relentlessly examined the formal structures of contrasting types of organizations as systems "exhibiting regularities of [their] own" (Blau & Schoenherr 1971, p. 356). During the later period, from the 1980s to the present, these interests have been pursued at higher levels of analysis, as sociologists have led the way in examining the structural characteristics of collections of similar organizations—organizational populations—and collections of diverse, interdependent organizations—the structure of organizational fields and networks.

Simultaneously, sociologists have focused not only on the determinants but also on the consequences of organization structure, examining effects on organizational performance and participants and, at a broader level, on power and social inequality. In the following sections, I discuss these developments in more detail.

Field Transformation: Entry of Open System Models

Working at the same time as these pioneer organizational scholars, but independently, a motley collection of interdisciplinary scholars were crafting open (or general) system models, seeking to connect and renew parochial disciplines by focusing on commonalities in elements and processes across varied systems—ranging from biological cell to solar system (von Bertalanffy 1956). Although these ideas penetrated numerous fields of study, including sociology (Buckley 1967), nowhere did they have a larger impact than in organization studies. Before open system ideas, organizational scholars had concentrated on actors (workers, work groups, managers) and processes (motivation, cohesion, control) within organizations. Scant attention was accorded to the environment within which the organization operated. If noticed, the environment was too often depicted as the source of troubles. This myopic focus began to be replaced during the 1960s, spurred by the work of Katz & Kahn (1966), Lawrence & Lorsch (1967), Thompson (1967/2003), and Weick (1969). (Katz, Kahn, and Weick were social psychologists; Lawrence and Lorsch, students of management; Thompson, a sociologist.)

In important respects, much of the history of the development of organization studies during the last quarter of the twentieth century to the present reflects a growing recognition of the many and diverse ways in which the environment constitutes, influences, and penetrates organizations. A second theme has been a growing awareness of the ways in which organizations affect other vital societal processes and systems.

A Field Matures

A Frenzy of Theorizing Concerning Determinants

With the introduction of open system models, a field mired in shop-worn distinctions and unproductive debates suddenly surged to life. One after another, innovative theoretical frameworks and arguments were introduced, each of which afforded new insights into the determinants of organizational structure.

First to arrive was *contingency theory*, an approach that recognized that, although all organizations are dependent on their environment for resources and technical information, these environments vary in complexity and uncertainty, and, consequently, organization structures are expected to differ (Woodward 1958, Lawrence & Lorsch 1967, Galbraith 1973). Organizations were observed to vary as a function of their technical environments. Moreover, those organizations whose structures were best adapted to their specific environments were expected to perform best. Although contingency theory was the earliest formulation to appear in what we can term the "modern" era of organization studies, it remains the most influential (Donaldson 2001). No doubt this popularity partly reflects its applied appeal to practitioners who seek to improve their organizations.

A related approach—*transaction cost*—builds on the economic insight that all transactions (exchanges of goods and services) are costly, but some are more costly than others. Williamson (1975, 1985) pursued Coase's (1937) insight that organizations arise to deal with transaction costs that markets are ill-equipped to handle. Transactions that are relatively uncertain and complex call for more elaborate mechanisms of gov-

ernance to insure security for the parties involved. One such mechanism is the organization, which attempts to align interests and creates control systems to discourage opportunistic behavior. Note that this approach supplies a rational account for the existence of organizations. Also, because the types of transactions managed differ, organizational structures vary in the resources devoted to governance. Such arguments provide yet another explanation for organizational variety and another basis for designing organizations.

A third approach—*resource dependence theory*—also stresses the benefits of adaptation to the environment, but it conceives of environments as including political as well as economic systems. Building on Emerson's (1962) formulation of power-dependence relations, as developed by Pfeffer & Salancik (1978/2003), this framework recognizes that organizations must exchange resources to survive, but that such exchanges, if imbalanced, give rise to power differences. Hence, economic exchanges may create power differences, and economic dependency may spawn political solutions. Resource dependence scholars stress that managers must take steps to manage not only their structures but also their environments, reducing dependencies and seeking adequate power advantages.

Network theory had long been used by psychologists and sociologists to examine interpersonal relations, but during the 1970s and 1980s it was applied to the study of relations among organizations. Building on the foundational work of White et al. (1976), scholars moved to develop measures and methods appropriate to examining networks of organizations. An organization's location in a network of relations, as well as the structure of the network itself, were recognized to affect organizational behavior and outcomes. These network ties and structures have been pursued in studies of interlocking directorates (Mizruchi 1982), competitive exchange structures and profits (Burt 1983), interorganizational systems affecting policy setting at the national level (Laumann & Knoke 1987), and the formation and effects of strategic alliances (Powell et al. 1996). Because network theory emphasizes the relational aspects of environments, its development aided the study of resource dependence connections (Pfeffer 1987).

At about the same time, *organizational ecology* was developed as an alternative paradigm. Building on the work of Hawley (1950), Hannan & Freeman (1977) argued that previous theories exaggerated the extent to which it is possible for individual organizations to undergo fundamental change. They therefore argued that those interested in change should shift their attention from a focus on single organizations to "populations" of organizations—organizations of the same type—because fundamental change typically involves the replacement of one type of organization with another. Subsequent work has focused on population dynamics—on the ways in which new types of organizations arise, grow, compete, and decline over long periods of time (Hannan & Freeman 1989).

Also, during the same period, yet another approach—*institutional theory*—emerged that stresses the importance of the cultural features of environments. Building on the work of Berger & Luckmann (1967), institutional theorists argued that organizations must consider not only their technical environment but also their "institutional" environment: regulative, normative, and cultural-cognitive features that define "social fitness" (Meyer & Rowan 1977, DiMaggio & Powell 1983, Meyer & Scott 1983). Earlier theorists, such as Selznick (1949) and Parsons (1960), stressed the regulative and normative aspects of institutional systems. Later "neoinstitutionalists" recognized these as significant factors, but they also called attention to the role of symbolic elements—schemas, typifications, and scripts that perform an important, independent role in shaping organization structure and behavior (Scott 2001a).

Indeed, by insisting that cultural factors play an equal and independent role alongside structural and material factors, institutional theorists propose to push the origins of organizations back (from the conventionally accepted time of the latter stages of the industrial revolution) to the Enlightenment period of the seventeenth century. Meyer et al. (1987) and Pedersen & Dobbin (1997) argue that it was at this early time that philosophers and scientists began to codify first physical and then social phenomena into general types and subcategories, launching the project of societal rationalization. Gradually the idea was accepted that there are generic types of social structures—organizations—to be administered under a common body of knowledge—management—and containing recognized subcategories (firms, schools, agencies). The emergence of organization studies, which provide a scientific account of these phenomena, has served to underscore and advance this professional project.

These diverse theoretical developments followed one another in rapid succession during the 1960s and 1970s, as investigators began to recognize the richness of the environment and examine its importance for organizational structures and processes. Technical, economic, political, relational, ecological, and cultural factors were, one by one, theorized and examined. Of the six approaches, three of them—the ecological, relational, and institutional—were based on the work of sociologists, and a fourth—the political (resource dependence) perspective—drew heavily on sociologist Richard Emerson's formulation, applying it at the interorganization rather than the interpersonal level. It is noteworthy that the approaches using sociological arguments all reside on the natural side of the rational-natural continuum. Economists (espousing transaction costs) and selected management theorists (advocating contingency theory) anchor the rational end. (The important exception, sociologist Thompson, insisted that his contingency arguments applied only "under norms of rationality.")

Throughout this creative period, I was working at Stanford University, where I would remain throughout my career. By the mid-1970s, the collection of organizational scholars assembled at this place was unrivaled in the world. Three of the six major theories—resource dependence, organizational ecology, and institutional theory—were launched by members of the Stanford faculty. In my opinion, it was not simply the array of talent—the "density of competence," to quote my friend and colleague, Jim March—present at Stanford at this time but the type of collegial community we built together that helped to fuel this creative moment. In any event, the primary font of scholarly fecundity had migrated west from Columbia and Carnegie to Stanford.

Higher Levels

These theoretical developments not only enlarged our conception of the environment, as more and different facets were taken into account, but also raised the level at which organizations were analyzed. The earliest closed system approaches restricted attention to phenomena within the boundaries of a given organization. To the extent they were considered, organizational structures were the contexts within which individual and group behavior of interest occurred. Only with the advent of open system models did organizations themselves become the subject of investigation, viewed variously as responsive systems shaped by environments, as collective actors themselves shaping their context, or as component players in larger, more encompassing systems.

Beginning during the 1960s, scholars designed research in which organizations, their structures and processes, were the subject of study. Empirical studies gathered systematic information on samples of organizations—either of the same type (e.g., Blau & Schoenherr 1971) or of diverse types within the same area (e.g., Pugh et al. 1969). This mode of investigation continued through subsequent decades, but it was not until the mid-1990s that a study was conducted based on a representative sample of organizations in one society, the United States (Kalleberg et al. 1996). These studies, particularly those involving multiple types of organizations and societal contexts, reaffirmed the dualist nature of organizations—shaped in part by material-resource forces (technology, size, competition), and in part by social and cultural systems (norms and cultural beliefs) (e.g., Lincoln & Kalleberg 1990, Orrù et al. 1997).

Moving above the level of the individual organization, analysts focused on the *organization-set*: a focal organization and its significant exchange partners (Blau & Scott 1962/2003, Evan 1966). This approach allowed researchers to define more precisely the salient context at work for a given organization. Rather than assessing abstracted environmental dimensions such as "complexity" and "uncertainty," examination of a set fostered attention to particular resource and information flows, specific networks ties, and their consequences. This level of analysis was well suited to exploring resource dependence relations and questions of organization strategy.

Organizational ecologists have elected to work primarily at the level of the *organization population*, although this theoretical framework is applicable at multiple levels. A population is defined as consisting of all those organizations that compete for resources in the same environmental niche. Operationally, researchers typically examine organizations sharing the same form or archetype, exhibiting a similar structure, and pursuing similar goals. A given organizational form arises at a particular time, combining in a distinctive way existing technologies and types of social actors, and once created, it tends to persist with little change through time (Stinchcombe 1965). Studies of numerous, diverse populations reveal a similar empirical pattern of S-shaped growth and decline if the entire history of a form is examined (Hannan & Freeman 1989, Baum 1996). Hannan & Freeman argue that population density processes reflect the familiar dualistic tension between forces of legitimation that govern the early stages of growth but are eventually overcome by forces of competition.

Institutional influences operate at all levels, but researchers have accorded much attention to the *organization field* level—defined as a collection of both similar and dissimilar interdependent organizations operating in a functionally specific arena together with their exchange partners, funding sources, and regulators (DiMaggio & Powell 1983). Because the field, by definition, coincides with an institutionally defined area of social activity, this level has been favored as a site for the examination of structuration processes—both convergent and divergent change in the types of organizational actors and relations among them. Scholars have examined long-term changes in the rules and belief systems governing organization fields in contexts as diverse as international commercial arbitration (Dezalay & Garth 1996), Norwegian fisheries (Holm 1995), the largest U.S. industrial corporations (Fligstein 1990), petroleum and chemical industries as they adjusted to changes in environmental regimes (Hoffman 1997), and health care delivery systems (Scott et al. 2000). Each of these accounts underscores the complex interplay between material resource, competitive environments, and institutional environments.

Considering Consequences

The structure and functioning of organizations have consequences, both for the organizations themselves as well as for their wider host societies. Whereas economists and management theorists have focused on identifying organizational factors that affect performance and productivity, sociologists have raised questions about who benefits and who does not (or suffers) from these activities (Scott 1977, Perrow 1986). Sociologists have also raised troubling questions about tightly coupled, complex organizations touted for their fail-safe reliability, such as nuclear reactors and airline safety systems. Their complexity and interdependence of parts is such that accidents must be expected and, indeed, are "normal" (Perrow 1984; Vaughan 1996).

A concern for organizations as systems of power was eloquently reframed by Coleman (1974), who pointed out that organizations as collective actors develop interests and pursue goals distinct from those of their members, and that individuals regularly lose power, not just in relation to other individuals but in relation to organizations. Rather than organizations serving as agents under our control to assist us in pursuing our goals, we more often spend our time and energy serving as the agents of organizations as they pursue their specialized and limited ends. Organizations also increasingly affect social mobility and dispense life chances. Students of social stratification, long enamored of social classes, began to focus on the role of organizations as central mediators of mobility in modern societies. The "new structuralists" focus on the structure of work—now routinely embedded in firms and industries—and to the organizational processes—hiring, training, promotion, and dismissal—that govern status attainment (Baron & Bielby 1980). And a growing number of investigations demonstrate that these processes are not race or gender neutral (Reskin et al. 1999).

In sum, the history of organization studies generally and organizational sociology in particular has been dominated in recent decades by the logic of open systems, as theorists and investigators have expanded their purview to incorporate more and different facets of environments affecting organizations and elevated their designs to allow the study of larger, more encompassing systems in which organizations are central players (Scott 2003). And central topics of interest to sociologists—including the distribution of power and status—have been convincingly linked to organizational processes and structures.

Recent Trends

Although the most recent decades have not witnessed the same level of creative intensity, the field has continued to evolve in new directions. I consider, briefly, three ways in which organizations are undergoing change and a fourth way in which our ideas about organizations are being revised.

Changing Boundaries

Organizational boundaries have figured centrally in organizational analysis since the work of Weber (1924/1968). Weber defined organizations as social relations that are "closed," with access limited to specific individuals and the limits enforced by a chief or director assisted by an administrative staff. With the advent of open system conceptions, theorists recognized the dependence of organizations on managing resource flows and other exchanges with the environment, but continued to emphasize the need for organizations to "buffer" themselves from external influences, often by "sealing off" their technical core from environmental perturbations (Thompson 1967/2003). Scholars have proffered multiple conceptions and examined various indicators in their study of boundaries, including actors (distinctive roles, membership criteria, identity), relations (interaction frequency, communication patterns, networks), activities (tasks, routines, talk), and normative and legal criteria (ownership, contracts, legitimate authority).

There is no doubt, however, that in recent decades the boundaries of organizations have become more open and flexible. Although it seems premature to declare the advent of the "boundaryless" organization, as have some overenthusiastic observers, there are many indicators that boundaries have become more permeable and less fixed. Permanent workers are joined or replaced by temporary, part-time, and contract employees; teams and project groups often include members from multiple independent firms; and organizations downsize, add and sell off components, and enter into alliances with exchange partners and competitors that realign operational frontiers (Kanter et al. 1992). Today's production and service systems are increasingly likely to extend across networks of independent or semi-independent companies and agencies, as earlier craft production systems are joined by small-firm industrial districts, core-ring systems centered around big firms, and strategic alliances (Harrison 1994, DiMaggio 2001). However, such developments suggest not the disappearance of boundaries, but changes in their scope, composition, duration, and enforcement mechanisms. Symbolic signals increasingly replace materialist modes of boundary demarcation.

Changing Strategies

Closely related to changing conceptions of organizational boundaries are changes in views regarding how organizations relate to their environments. For most of the twentieth century, organizations pursued a grand strategy of *internalization*. As organizations confronted key challenges to their functioning, the likely responses were to absorb or to map them into their structure. "Absorption" entails bringing formerly external elements within one's boundaries. Organizations began by absorbing workers, technologies, and technical expertise, and, as the firm grew, shifted to a strategy of vertical integration, incorporating sources of inputs, marketing, and distribution systems (Chandler 1977). In cases in which internalization was unfeasible, organizations worked to "map" crucial aspects of the environment into their own structures, for example hiring persons with union experience to staff labor relations departments or lawyers to cope with the legal environment. It appeared, as Perrow (1991) alleged, that large-scale organizations would eventually absorb all aspects of society.

However, beginning during the latter decades of the twentieth century, a surprising and unpredicted turnaround occurred as organizations began to slough off various components and functions. The master strategy now pursued by an increasing number of organizations is one of *externalization*: disposing of internal units and contracting out functions formerly performed in-house. As already noted, organizations are applying these strategies to employees, divisions, and functions. As an indicator of how widespread this tendency is, Carroll & Hannan (2000) report that the average size of U.S. corporations has declined from about 60 employees in 1960 to around 34 employees in 1990. (This trend reflects not only the dis-

mantling of larger firms but also the growing importance of new, small firms in the economy.) The current mantra guiding managers is to "cultivate your core competence." These developments necessarily affect employees, who have discovered that the "implicit contract" guaranteeing job security in exchange for loyalty has been renegotiated, if not repealed. Sociologists have led the way in examining the implications—both positive and negative—of externalization for individual participants (Pfeffer & Baron 1988, Smith 2002).

Although a number of market-based, neoliberal explanations exist for the turn toward externalization, I believe an important unnoticed factor relates to changes occurring in wider societal systems. As more and more aspects of society become rationalized—organized as instrumental systems linking systematic means to ends—it becomes less necessary to buffer one's own system and more possible to consider connecting to "external" systems (governed by the same logics) to pursue objectives. In this sense, rather than organizations absorbing societies, as Perrow argues, it may rather be the case that societies are absorbing organizations (Meyer 1983; Scott & Meyer 1994, p. 4).

Changing Power Processes

The uses and modes of power and control are changing in organizations. The archetypical unitary hierarchy, which for so long has been the defining characteristic of organizations, is giving way to more decentralized and horizontal systems, particularly among organizations in the newer industries. When most of the important information needed to compete effectively is found at the boundaries of organizations rather than at the core, then centralized command/control structures become dysfunctional and obsolete. As the operational boundaries of firms and agencies extend outward to include temporary workers and contractors, managers are obliged to learn to manage horizontally (without authority) as well as vertically.

Externalization strategies represent a growing reliance on market mechanisms in contrast to internal organizational controls. They also reflect a growing realization among both private and public organizations that ownership does not guarantee control:

It is often the case that contracting provides leverage that is absent in ownership.

The emergence of new capital markets, dominated by institutional rather than individual investors, threatens the internal power structure of organizations, which during the past half-century had witnessed the ascendance of the professional manager. It may well be that the age of "managerial capitalism" has come to an end, although the declining power of the corporate elite may be offset by the rise in power of managers of pension funds and other institutional investors (Davis 1994, Useem 1996).

Corporations have long enjoyed substantial power in relation to the state. As sociologists from Mills (1956) to Mizruchi (1992) to Perrow (2002) have documented, economic wealth and power can readily translate into political influence. In the United States, corporations enjoy the advantage of being treated legally as persons with the right of free speech, expressed primarily through the medium of lobbies and financial campaign contributions. Corporate power and political influence have never been stronger.

Changing Conceptions

It would be surprising, indeed, if these quite fundamental changes in organizational structure and behavior were not reflected in the conceptions scholars employ to guide their work. I believe that important changes under way in our field are illuminated by trends described by Emirbayer (1997) in an essay on conceptions of social structure more generally. He points to a shift from reliance on substantialist to relational models of structure. A *substantialist* approach defines structures as things or entities. Emirbayer distinguishes between two subtypes of substantialist conceptions:

- *Substantialist self-action* definitions: As applied to organizations, such conceptions emphasize the independence of organizations and stress those features that distinguish organizations from other types of social structures. Such conceptions dominated organization studies in its formative period, including Weber, March and Simon, and Blau and Scott.

- *Substantialist interaction* definitions: Such conceptions emerged as organizational scholars embraced an open system perspective. Although organiza-

tions continue to be viewed as discrete units, they are thought to possess attributes that vary in response to changing circumstances, whether technical, political, transactional, or institutional.

Although still a minority position, a growing number of scholars have begun to embrace a *relational* or process conception of organizations. These views recognize that organizations are "inseparable from the transactional contexts in which they are embedded" (Emirbayer 1997, p. 287). In a relational conception, the meaning and identity of actors (including collective actors) arise from the roles they play in ongoing relations and encounters, a view elaborated by White (1992). Giddens' (1979) conception of structuration is the most influential general formulation of this perspective.

To my knowledge, the earliest organizational scholar to employ a relational view of organizations was Weick (1969), who advocated shifting from an entity conception—organizations—to a process conception—organizing. During recent decades, a wide variety of theorists have proposed relational formulations. However, once again, the old antinomy surfaces between those stressing more rational aspects—e.g., organization as a "nexus of contracts" (Jensen & Meckling 1976) or as a "portfolio of financial assets" (Fligstein 1990)—and those emphasizing more natural features—e.g., organization as a shifting collection of populations of participants (Bidwell & Kasarda 1985) or as constituted by stories or "narratives" (Czarniawska 1997). In general, however, relational approaches applied to organizations

> celebrate process over structure, becoming over being. What is being processed varies greatly. In some versions it is symbols and words, in others, relationships or contracts, in still others, assets. But in relational approaches, if structures exist it is because they are continually being created and recreated, and if the world has meaning, it is because actors are constructing and reconstructing intensions and accounts, and thereby, their own and others' identities (Scott 2001b, p. 10913).

Comments and Concerns

Perhaps it is apparent that I am enthusiastic about the progress made in constructing a vital field of organizational studies and about the contributions made by sociologists to this enterprise throughout the past half-century. In comparison to other areas of scientific study of which I am aware, none has been more vibrant or has made more progress in theorizing and documenting central developments in the phenomena of interest. Scholars in organizational sociology, like their counterparts in the broader field of organization studies, have not embraced a single, unifying paradigm. Rather, as Augier et al. (200[3], p. 21) conclude:

> [Our] progress is measured not by increasing convergence but by increasing diversity and complexity and by a shared sense of what is part of the history. The cannon changes by expansion and inclusion, by elaborating and adding perspectives. . . . There is change, but there is also continuity.

. . . Sociologists for many decades have been leading contributors to our understanding of organizations in modern society, and organizations remain one of the most influential actors of our time. The parts they play and the challenges they pose to every facet of social life have never been greater. It is inconceivable to me that our profession will not find a way to continue to play a leading role in understanding and guiding these developments.

Literature Cited

Arensberg CM. 1951. Behavior and organization: industrial studies. In *Social Psychology at the Crossroads*, ed. JH Rohrer, M Sherif, pp. 324–52. New York: Harper.

Augier M, March JG, Sullivan BN. 2003. *The evolution of a research community: organization studies in anglophone North America, 1945–2000*. Work. Pap., Sch. Educ., Stanford Univ.

Barnard CI. 1938. *The Functions of the Executive*. Cambridge, MA: Harvard Univ. Press.

Baron JN, Bielby WT. 1980. Bringing the firms back in: stratification, segmentation, and the organization of work. *Am. Sociol. Rev.* 45:737–65.

Baum JAC. 1996. Organizational ecology. In *Handbook of Organization Studies*, ed. SP Clegg, C Hardy, W Nord, pp. 77–114. London/Thousand Oaks, CA: Sage.

Berger PL, Luckman T. 1967. *The Social Construction of Reality*. New York: Doubleday.

Bidwell C, Kasarda JD. 1985. *The Organization and Its Ecosystem: A Theory of Structuring in Organizations*. Greenwich, CT: JAI.

Blau PM. 1955. *The Dynamics of Bureaucracy*. Chicago: Univ. Chicago Press.

Blau PM, Schoenherr RA. 1971. *The Structure of Organizations*. New York: Basic Books.

Blau PM, Scott WR. 1962/2003. *Formal Organizations: A Comparative Approach*. San Francisco: Chandler/Stanford: Stanford Univ. Press.

Buckley W. 1967. *Sociology and Modern Systems Theory*. Englewood Cliffs, NJ: Prentice-Hall.

Burt RS. 1983. *Corporate Profits and Cooptation*. New York: Academic.

Carroll GR, Hannan MT. 2000. *The Demography of Corporations and Industries*. Princeton, NJ: Princeton Univ. Press.

Chandler AD Jr. 1977. *The Visible Hand: The Managerial Revolution in American Business*. Cambridge, MA: Belknap of Harvard Univ. Press.

Coase RH. 1937. The nature of the firm. *Economica* 4:386–405.

Coleman JS. 1974. *Power and the Structure of Society*. New York: Norton.

Cyert RM, March JG. 1963. *A Behavioral Theory of the Firm*. Englewood Cliffs, NJ: Prentice-Hall.

Czarniawska B. 1997. *Narrating the Organization: Dramas of Institutional Identity*. Chicago/London: Univ. Chicago Press.

Dalton M. 1959. *Men Who Manage*. New York: Wiley.

Davis GF. 1994. The corporate elite and the politics of corporate control. In *Current Perspectives in Social Theory*, ed. C Prendergast, JD Knottnerus, Suppl. 1:215–39. Greenwich, CT: JAI.

Dezalay Y, Garth BG. 1996. *Dealing in Virtue: International Commercial Arbitration and the Construction of a Transnational Legal Order*. Chicago: Univ. Chicago Press.

DiMaggio PJ, ed. 2001. *The Twenty-First Century Firm: Changing Economic Organization in International Perspective*. Princeton, NJ: Princeton Univ. Press.

DiMaggio PJ, Powell WW. 1983. The iron cage revisited: Institutional isomorphism and collective rationality in organizational fields. *Am. Sociol. Rev.* 48:147–60.

Donaldson L. 2001. *The Contingency Theory of Organizations*. London/Thousand Oaks, CA: Sage.

Emerson RM. 1962. Power-dependence relations. *Am. Sociol. Rev.* 27:31–40.

Emery FE. 1959. *Characteristics of Socio-Technical Systems*. London: Tavistock.

Emirbayer M. 1997. Manifesto for a relational sociology. *Am. J. Sociol.* 103:962–1023.

Evan WM. 1966. The organization set: toward a theory of interorganizational relations. In *Approaches to Organizational Design*, ed. JD Thompson, pp. 173–88. Pittsburgh: Univ. Pittsburgh Press.

Fayol H. 1919/1949. *General and Industrial Management*. London: Pitman.

Fligstein N. 1990. *The Transformation of Corporate Control*. Cambridge, MA: Harvard Univ. Press.

Galbraith JR. 1973. *Designing Complex Organizations*. Reading, MA: Addison-Wesley.

Giddens A. 1979. *Central Problems in Social Theory*. Berkeley/Los Angeles: Univ. Calif. Press.

Gouldner AW. 1954. *Patterns of Industrial Bureaucracy*. Glencoe, IL: Free Press.

———. 1959. Organizational analysis. In *Sociology Today*, ed. RK Merton, L Broom, LS Cottrell Jr, pp. 400–28. New York: Basic Books.

Granovetter M. 1985. Economic action and social structure: the problem of embeddedness. *Am. J. Sociol.* 91:481–510.

Hannan MT, Freeman J. 1977. The population ecology of organizations. *Am. J. Sociol.* 82:929–64.

———. 1989. *Organizational Ecology*. Cambridge, MA: Harvard Univ. Press.

Harrison B. 1994. *Lean and Mean: The Changing Landscape of Corporate Power in the Age of Flexibility*. New York: Basic Books.

Hawley A. 1950. *Human Ecology*. New York: Ronald.

Hoffman AW. 1997. *From Heresy to Dogma: An Institutional History of Corporate Environmentalism*. San Francisco: New Lexington.

Holm P. 1995. The dynamics of institutionalization: transformation processes in Norwegian fisheries. *Admin. Sci. Q.* 40:398–422.

Jensen MC, Meckling WH. 1976. Theory of the firm: Managerial behavior, agency costs, and ownership structure. *J. Financ. Econ.* 3:305–60.

Kalleberg AL, Knoke D, Marsden PV, Spaeth JL. 1996. *Organizations in America: Analyzing their Structures and Human Resource Practices*. London/Thousand Oaks, CA: Sage.

Kanter RM, Stein BA, Jick TD. 1992. *The Challenge of Organizational Change: How Companies Experience It and Leaders Guide It*. New York: Free Press.

Katz D, Kahn RL. 1966. *The Social Psychology of Organizations*. New York: Wiley.

Laumann EO, Knoke D. 1987. *The Organizational State: Social Choice in National Policy Domains*. Madison: Univ. Wis. Press.

Lawrence PR, Lorsch JW. 1967. *Organization and Environment: Managing Differentiation and Integration*. Boston: Grad. Sch. Bus. Admin., Harvard Univ.

Lincoln JR, Kalleberg AL. 1990. *Culture, Control and Commitment: A Study of Work Organization and Work Attitudes in the United States and Japan*. Cambridge/New York: Cambridge Univ. Press.

March JG, Olsen JP. 1989. *Rediscovering Institutions: The Organizational Basis of Politics*. New York: Free Press.

March JG, Simon H. 1958. *Organizations*. New York: Wiley.

Merton RK. 1949. *Social Theory and Social Structure*. Glencoe, IL: Free Press.

Meyer JW. 1983. Conclusion: Institutionalization and the rationality of formal organization structure. See Meyer & Scott 1983, pp. 261–82.

Meyer JW, Boli J, Thomas GM. 1987. Ontology and rationalization in the Western cultural account. In *Institutional Structure: Constituting State, Society, and the Individual*, ed. GM Thomas, JW Meyer, FO Ramirez, J Boli, pp. 12–37. London/Newbury Park, CA: Sage.

Meyer JW, Rowan B. 1977. Institutionalized organizations: formal structure as myth and ceremony. *Am. J. Sociol.* 83:340–63.

Meyer JW, Scott WR. 1983. *Organizational Environments: Ritual and Rationality*. Beverly Hills, CA/London: Sage.

Mills CW. 1956. *The Power Elite*. New York: Oxford Univ. Press.

Mizruchi MS. 1982. *The American Corporate Network, 1904–1974*. Beverly Hills, CA: Sage.

———. 1992. *The Structure of Corporate Political Action*. Cambridge: Harvard Univ. Press.

Orrù M, Biggart NW, Hamilton GG. 1997. *The Economic Organization of East Asian Capitalism*. Thousand Oaks, CA: Sage.

Parsons T. 1960. *Structure and Process in Modern Societies*. Glencoe, IL: Free Press.

Pedersen JS, Dobbin F. 1997. The social invention of collective actors: on the rise of organizations. *Am. Behav. Sci.* 40:431–43.

Perrow C. 1984. *Normal Accidents: Living with High-Risk Technologies*. New York: Basic Books.

———. 1986. *Complex Organizations: A Critical Essay*. New York: Random House. 3rd ed.

———. 1991. A society of organizations. *Theory Soc.* 20:725–62.

———. 2002. *Organizing America: Wealth, Power, and the Origins of Corporate Capitalism*. Princeton, NJ: Princeton Univ. Press.

Pfeffer J. 1987. A resource dependence perspective on intercorporate relations. In *Intercorporate Relations: The Structural Analysis of Business*, ed. MS Mizruchi, M Schwartz, pp. 25–55. New York: Cambridge Univ. Press.

Pfeffer J, Baron JN. 1988. Taking the workers back out: recent trends in the structuring of employment. In *Research in Organizational Behavior*, ed. BM Staw, LL Commings, 10:257–303. Greenwich, CT: JAI.

Pfeffer J, Salancik G. 1978/2003. *The External Control of Organizations*. New York: Harper & Row/Stanford: Stanford Univ. Press.

Powell WW, Koput KW, Smith-Doerr L. 1996. Interorganizational collaboration and the locus of innovation: networks of learning in biotechnology. *Admin. Sci. Q.* 41:116–45.

Pugh DS, Hickson DJ, Hinings CR, Turner C. 1969. The context of organization structures. *Admin. Sci. Q.* 14:91–114.

Reskin B, McBrier DB, Kmec JA. 1999. The determinants and consequences of workplace sex and race composition. *Annu. Rev. Sociol.* 25:235–61.

Roethlisberger FJ, Dickson WJ. 1939. *Management and the Worker*. Cambridge: Harvard Univ. Press.

Roy D. 1952. Quota restriction and goldbricking in a machine shop. *Am. J. Sociol.* 57:427–42.

Scott WR. 1977. The effectiveness of organizational effectiveness studies. In *New Perspectives on Organizational Effectiveness*, ed. PS Goodman, JM Pennings, pp. 63–95. San Francisco: Jossey-Bass.

———. 2001a. *Institutions and Organizations*. London/Thousand Oaks, CA: Sage. 2nd ed.

———. 2001b. Organizations, overview. In *International Encyclopedia of the Social and Behavioral Sciences*, ed. NJ Smelser, PB Baltes, 16:10910–17. Amsterdam: Pergamon/Elsevier Sci.

———. 2003. *Organizations: Rational, Natural and Open Systems*. Upper Saddle River, NJ: Prentice-Hall. 5th ed.

Scott WR, Meyer JW. 1994. *Institutional Environments and Organizations: Structural Complexity and Individualism*. London/Thousand Oaks, CA: Sage.

Scott WR, Ruef M, Mendel PJ, Caronna CA. 2000. *Institutional Change and Healthcare Organizations: From Professional Dominance to Managed Care*. Chicago/London: Univ. Chicago Press.

Selznick P. 1948. Foundations of the theory of organizations. *Am. Sociol. Rev.* 13:25–35.

———. 1949. *TVA and the Grass Roots*. Berkeley/Los Angeles: Univ. Calif. Press.

Shenhav Y. 1999. *Manufacturing Rationality: The Engineering Foundations of the Management Revolution*. Oxford/New York: Oxford Univ. Press.

Simon H. 1945. *Administrative Behavior*. New York: Macmillan.

Smith V. 2002. *Crossing the Great Divide: Worker Risks and Opportunities in the New Economy*. Ithaca: Cornell Univ. Press/ILR Press.

Stinchcombe AL. 1965. Social structure and organizations. In *Handbook of Organizations*, ed. JG March, pp. 142–93. Chicago: Rand-McNally.

Taylor FJ. 1911. *The Principles of Scientific Management*. New York: Harper.

Thompson JD. 1967/2003. *Organizations in Action*. New York: McGraw-Hill/New Brunswick, NJ: Transaction.

Useem M. 1996. *Investor Capitalism: How Money Managers Are Changing the Face of Corporate America*. New York: Basic Books.

Vaughan D. 1996. *The Challenger Launch Decision: Risky Technology, Culture and Deviance at NASA*. Chicago: Univ. Chicago Press.

von Bertalanffy L. 1956. General systems theory. In *General Systems: Yearbook of the Society for the Advancement of General Systems Theory*, ed. L von Bertalanffy, A Rapoport, 1:1–10. Ann Arbor, MI: The Society.

Weber M. 1924/1968. *Economy and Society: An Interpretive Sociology*, ed. G Roth, C Wittich. New York: Bedminister.

Weick KE. 1969. *The Social Psychology of Organizing*. Reading, MA: Addison-Wesley.

White HC. 1992. *Identity and Control: A Structural Theory of Social Action*. Princeton: Princeton Univ. Press.

White HC, Boorman SA, Breiger RL. 1976. Social structure from multiple networks: II. Blockmodels of roles and positions. *Am. J. Sociol.* 81:730–80.

Williamson OE. 1975. *Markets and Hierarchies: Analysis and Antitrust Implications*. New York/London: Free Press.

———. 1985. *The Economic Institutions of Capitalism*. New York/London: Free Press.

Woodward J. 1958. *Management and Technology*. London: HMSO.

Chapter 2
Markets, Bureaucracies, and Clans

William G. Ouchi

Ouchi asks, "What is an organization, and why do organizations exist?" Under what conditions do people come together instead of going it alone? These are not easy questions to answer. Pursuing these questions is important, however, if we are to understand how and why organizations have become such a pervasive feature of modern life. In addition, the answers to these questions will help us make sense of the varieties of organizations and the tensions that sometimes arise within them. Although many factors must be addressed when considering the best way to organize or to accomplish a task, exploring answers to Ouchi's questions may also help us with these dilemmas.

This discussion requires us to consider issues that are at the core of social life. Cooperation, for example, is essential for accomplishing many of life's most critical tasks. Our interdependence makes cooperation necessary, but creating and sustaining cooperation are not automatic. In addition, for any given task, some forms of cooperation may be more effective than others.

Organizations can help solve some of the challenges of cooperation. In fact, this feature of organizations is one of the primary explanations for their existence. Ouchi explains, however, that exactly how organizations resolve issues of cooperation varies. Moreover, any particular organizational solution to the challenges of cooperation may not work in all circumstances. This helps us to understand both the variation and the regularities we see across the organizational landscape.

The Nature of Organizations

What is an organization, and why do organizations exist? Many of us would answer this question by referring to Barnard's (1968) technological imperative, which argues that a formal organization will arise when technological conditions demand physical power, speed, endurance, mechanical adaptation, or continuity beyond the capacity of a single individual (1968: 27–28). Yet when the stone is too large or the production facility too complex for a single person, what is called for is cooperation, and cooperation need not take the form of a formal organization. Indeed, grain farmers who need a large grain elevator do not form corporations which take over the farms and make the farmers into employees; instead, they form a cooperative to own and operate the elevator.

Others would refer to March and Simon's (1958) argument that an organization will exist so long as it can offer its members inducements which exceed the contributions it asks of them. While this position explains the conditions under which an organization may continue to exist, it does not explain how an organization can create a whole which is so much greater than the sum of its parts that it can give them more than they contribute.

Most of us, however, would refer to Blau and Scott's (1962) definition of a formal organization as a purposive aggregation of individuals who exert concerted effort toward a common and explicitly recognized goal. Yet we can hardly accept this definition whole, suspecting as Simon (1945: 257–278) has that individuals within organizations rarely have a common understanding of goals.

Another point of view on the question of why organizations exist began with an inquiry by Coase (1937) and has recently been developed by Williamson (1975). In this view, an organization such as a corporation exists because it can mediate economic transactions between its members at lower costs than a market mechanism can. Under certain conditions, markets are more efficient because they can mediate without paying the costs of managers, accountants, or personnel departments. Under other conditions, however, a market mechanism becomes so cumbersome that it is less efficient than a bureaucracy. This transactions cost approach explicitly regards efficiency as the fundamental element in determining the nature of organizations.

Markets, Bureaucracies, and Clans

Transactions costs are a solution to the problem of cooperation in the realm of economic activity. From the perspective of Mayo (1945) and Barnard (1968), the fundamental problem of cooperation stems from the fact that individuals have only partially overlapping goals. Left to their own devices, they pursue incongruent objectives and their efforts are uncoordinated. Any collectivity which has an economic goal must then find a means to control diverse individuals efficiently.

Many helpful ideas have flowed from this definition of the problem of cooperation. Some (e.g., Etzioni, 1965; Weick, 1969) have emphasized the tension between individual autonomy and collective interests which must attend cooperative action, while others (e.g., Simon, 1945) have emphasized the impossibility of achieving a completely cooperative effort. Our interest is in the efficiency with which transactions are carried out between individuals who are engaged in cooperative action.

Cooperative action necessarily involves interdependence between individuals. This interdependence calls for a transaction or exchange in which each individual gives something of value (for example, labor) and receives something of value (for example, money) in return. In a market relationship, the transaction takes place between the two parties and is mediated by a price mechanism in which the existence of a competitive market reassures both parties that the terms of exchange are equitable. In a bureaucratic relationship, each party contributes labor to a corporate body which mediates the relationship by placing a value on each contribution and then compensating it fairly. The perception of equity in this case depends upon a social agreement that the bureaucratic hierarchy has the legitimate authority to provide this mediation. In either case, individuals must regard the transaction as equitable: it must meet the standards of reciprocity which Gouldner (1961) has described as a universal requirement for collective life.

It is this demand for equity which brings on transactions costs. A transactions cost is any activity which is engaged in to satisfy each party to an exchange that the value given and received is in accord with his or her expectations.

Transactions costs arise principally when it is difficult to determine the value of the goods or service. Such difficulties can arise from the underlying nature of the goods or service or from a lack of trust between the parties. When a company is being sold by one corporation to another corporation, for example, it may not be unambiguously clear what the true value of that company is. If firms similar to the company are frequently bought and sold, and if those transactions occur under competitive conditions, then the market process will be accepted as a legitimate estimator of the true value. But if the company is unique, and there is only one potential buyer, then market forces are absent. How will the buyer and seller determine a fair price? They may call upon a third party to estimate the value of the company. Each party may in addition call upon other experts who will assist them in evaluating both the value of the company and the adequacy of the judgment of the third party. Each side may also require an extensive and complete contract which will describe exactly what is being bought and sold. Each of these activities is costly, and all of them are regarded here as transactions costs: they are necessary to create a perception of equity among all parties to the transaction.

This same argument applies to transactions in which a service, such as the labor of an individual, is the object of exchange. If one individual sells his or her services to another, it may be difficult to assess the true value of that labor. In particular, if the labor is to be used in an interdependent technology, one which requires teamwork, it may be difficult to assess the value contributed by one worker as opposed to another, since their joint efforts yield a single outcome in this case, or in a case where it is likely that task requirements will change, then the auditing and complex contracting required to create the perception of equity can become unbearably costly.

We have identified two principal mechanisms for mediating these transactions: a market and a bureaucracy. These alternatives have received the greatest attention from organization theorists (e.g., Barnard, 1968; Weber, 1968) and economists (e.g., Coase, 1937; Arrow, 1974). However, the paradigm also suggests a third mechanism: If the objectives of individuals are congruent (not mutually exclusive), then the conditions of reciprocity and equity can be met quite differently.

Both Barnard and Mayo pointed out that organizations are difficult to operate because their members do not share a selfless devotion to the same objectives. Mayo (1945) argued that organizations operated more efficiently in preindustrial times, when members typically served an apprenticeship during which they were socialized into accepting the objectives of the craft or organization. Barnard (1968: 42–43) posed the problem thus:

> A formal system of cooperation requires an objective, a purpose, an aim. . . . It is important to note the complete distinction between the aim of a cooperative effort and that of an individual. Even in the case where a man enlists the aid of other men to do something which he cannot do alone, such as moving a stone, the objective ceases to be personal.

While Barnard, like Arrow, views markets and bureaucracies as the basic mechanisms for achieving the continued cooperation of these individuals, he also allowed (1968: 141) for the possibility of reducing the incongruence of goals in a manner consistent with Mayo's view of the preindustrial organization:

> An organization can secure the efforts necessary to its existence, then, either by the objective inducement it provides or by changing states of mind. It seems to me improbable that any organization can exist as a practical matter which does not employ both methods in combination.

If the socialization of individuals into an organization is complete, then the basis of reciprocity can be changed. For example, Japanese firms rely to a great extent upon hiring inexperienced workers, socializing them to accept the company's goals as their own, and compensating them according to length of service, number of dependents, and other nonperformance criteria (see Abegglen, 1958; Dore, 1973; Nakane, 1973). It is not necessary for these organizations to measure performance to control or direct their employees, since the employees' natural (socialized) inclination is to do what is best for the firm. It is also unnecessary to derive explicit, verifiable measures of value added, since rewards are distributed according to nonperformance-related criteria which are relatively inexpensive to deter-

mine (length of service and number of dependents can be ascertained at relatively low costs). Thus, industrial organizations can, in some instances, rely to a great extent on socialization as the principal mechanism of mediation or control, and this "clan" form ("clan" conforms to Durkheim's meaning of an organic association which resembles a kin network but may not include blood relations, 1933: 175) can be very efficient in mediating transactions between interdependent individuals.

Markets, bureaucracies, and clans are therefore three distinct mechanisms which may be present in differing degrees, in any real organization.[1] Our next objective is to specify the conditions under which the requirements of each form are most efficiently satisfied.

The Market Failures Framework

We can approach this question most effectively by examining the markets and hierarchies approach provided by Williamson (1975), which builds upon earlier statements of the problem by Coase (1937) and others (for a more detailed description of the functioning of each mechanism, see Ouchi, 1979).

Market transactions, or exchanges, consist of contractual relationships. Each exchange is governed by one of three types of contractual relations, all of which can be specified completely. That is, because each party is bound only to deliver that which is specified, the contract must specify who must deliver what under every possible state of nature. The simplest form of contract is the "spot" or "sales" contract. This is what occurs when you walk up to a candy counter, ask for a candy bar, and pay the amount the salesperson asks. In such a transaction, all obligations are fulfilled on the spot. However, the spot market contract is, by definition, incapable of dealing with future transactions, and most exchange relationships involve long-term obligations.

A common device for dealing with the future is the "contingent claims contract," a document that specifies all the obligations of each party to an exchange, contingent upon all possible future states of nature. However, given a future that is either complex or uncertain, the bounded rationality of individuals makes it impossible to specify such a contract completely. Leaving such a contract incompletely specified is an alternative, but one that will succeed only if each party can trust the other to interpret the uncertain future in a manner that is acceptable to him. Thus, given uncertainty, bounded rationality, and opportunism, contingent claims contracting will fail.

Instead of trying to anticipate the future in a giant, once-and-for-all contract, why not employ a series of contracts, each one written for a short period within which future events can confidently be foreseen? The problem with such "sequential spot contracting" is that in many exchange relationships, the goods or services exchanged are unique, and the supplier requires specialized knowledge of how to supply the customer best and most efficiently. The supplier acquires this knowledge over time and in doing so gains a "first mover advantage," which enables him to bid more effectively on subsequent contracts than any potential competitor can. Knowing this, potential competitors will not waste their time bidding, thus producing a situation of "small numbers bargaining" or bilateral monopoly, in which there is only one buyer and seller. Under this condition, competitive pressures are absent, and each party will opportunistically claim higher costs or poor quality, whichever is in his or her interest. In order to maintain such an exchange, each party will have to go to considerable expense to audit the costs or performance of the other. If these transactions costs are too high, the market relationship will fail due to the confluence of opportunism with small numbers bargaining, even though the limitations of uncertainty and bounded rationality have been overcome.

Thus, under some conditions no completely contractual market relationship is feasible. Table 2.1 summarizes the conditions which lead to market failure. According to the paradigm, no one of the four conditions can produce market failure, but almost any pairing of them will do so.

The idea of market failure is an analytical device. Economists do not agree on a specific set of conditions that constitute the failure of a market; indeed one point of view argues that even monopolistic conditions may be competitive. However, the idea of market failure as expressed by Williamson (1975) is useful as a conceptual framework within which to compare the strengths of markets as opposed to bureaucracies. The technique is to contend that all transactions can be mediated entirely by market relations, and then ask what conditions will cause some of these market mechanisms to fail and be replaced by bureaucratic mechanisms. In this sense, every bureaucratic organization constitutes an example of market failure.

The bureaucratic organization has two principal advantages over the market relationship. First, it uses the employment relation, which is an incomplete contract. In accepting an employment relation, a worker agrees to receive wages in exchange for submitting to the legitimate right of the organization to appoint superior officers who can (1) direct the work activities of the employee from day to day (within some domain or zone of indifference), thus overcoming the problem of dealing with the future all at once and (2) closely monitor the employee's performance, thus minimizing the problem of opportunism.

Second, the bureaucratic organization can create an atmosphere of trust between employees much more readily than a market can between the parties to an exchange. Because members of an organization assume some commonality of purpose, because they learn that long-term relationships will reward good performance and punish poor performance, they develop some goal congruence. This reduces their opportunistic tendencies and thus the need to monitor their performance.

Bureaucracies are also characterized by an emphasis on technical expertise which provides some skill training and some socialization into craft or professional standards. Professionals within a bureaucratic setting thus combine a primary affiliation to a professional body with a career orientation, which increases the sense of affiliation or solidarity with the employer and further reduces goal incongruence.[2]

In summary, the market failures framework argues that markets fail when the costs of completing transactions become unbearable. At that point, the inefficiencies of bureaucratic organization will be preferred to the relatively greater costs of market organi-

Table 2.1
The Market Failures Framework*

Human factors		Environmental factors
Bounded rationality	←——→	Uncertainty/Complexity
Opportunism	←——→	Small numbers

* Adapted from Williamson (1975: 40).

zation, and exchange relationships move from one domain into the other.

Consider one example. The 10,000 individuals who comprise the workforce of a steel mill could be individual entrepreneurs whose interpersonal transactions are mediated entirely through a network of market or contractual relationships. Each of them could also have a market relation with yet another combine which owned the capital equipment and facilities necessary to produce steel. Yet steel mills are typically bureaucratic in form and each worker is in an employment, not market, relation with the corporation. Market forces have failed because the determination of value contributed by one worker is highly ambiguous in the integrated steelmaking process, which makes the transactions cost attendant upon maintaining a market too high.

Extending the Market Failures Framework: Clans

Bureaucracies can fail when the ambiguity of performance evaluation becomes significantly greater than that which brings about market failure. A bureaucratic organization operates fundamentally according to a system of hierarchical surveillance, evaluation, and direction. In such a system, each superior must have a set of standards to which he can compare behavior or output in order to provide control. These standards only indicate the value of an output approximately, and are subject to idiosyncratic interpretation. People perceive them as equitable only as long as they believe that they contain a reasonable amount of performance information. When tasks become highly unique, completely integrated, or ambiguous for other reasons, then even bureaucratic mechanisms fail. Under these conditions, it becomes impossible to evaluate externally the value added by any individual. Any standard which is applied will be by definition arbitrary and therefore inequitable.

If we adopt the view that transactions costs arise from equity considerations, then we can interpret Table 2.1 in a different light. Simon's work on the employment relation (1957: 183–195) shows that Table 2.1 contains some redundancy. He emphasized that under an employment contract, the employer pays a worker a premium over the "spot" price for any piece of work. From the point of view of the worker, this "risk premium" compensates him for the likelihood that he will be asked to perform duties which are significantly more distasteful to him than those which are implied in the employment contract. The uncertainty surrounding the likelihood of such tasks and the expectation that the employer will or will not ask them determines the size of the risk premium. If the employee agreed with all the employer's objectives, which is equivalent to completely trusting the employer never to request a distasteful task, then the risk premium would be zero.

The employment relation is relatively efficient when the measurement of performance is ambiguous but the employer's goals are not. In an employment relation, each employee depends on the employer to distribute rewards equitably; if employees do not trust the employer to do so, they will demand contractual protections such as union representation and the transactions cost will rise.

Thus, the critical element in the efficiency of market versus employment relations has to do with (1) the ambiguity of the measurement of individual performance, and (2) the congruence of the employees' and employer's goals. We can now reformulate the transactions cost problem as follows: in order to mediate transactions efficiently, any organizational form must reduce either the ambiguity of performance evaluation or the goal incongruence between parties. Put this way, market relations are efficient when there is little ambiguity over performance, so the parties can tolerate relatively high levels of opportunism or goal incongruence. And bureaucratic relations are efficient when both performance ambiguity and goal incongruence are moderately high.

What form of mediation succeeds by minimizing goal incongruence and tolerating high levels of ambiguity in performance evaluation? Clearly, it is one which embodies a strong form of the employment relation as defined by Simon (1945), which is a relationship in which the risk premium is minimized. The answer is what we have referred to as the clan, which is the obverse of the market relation since it achieves efficiency under the opposite conditions: high performance ambiguity and low opportunism.

Perhaps the clearest exposition of the clan form appears in what Durkheim (1933: 365) refers to as the case of organic solidarity and its contrast with contractual relations:

For organic solidarity to exist, it is not enough that there be a system of organs necessary to one another, which in a general way feel solidarity, but it is also necessary that the way in which they should come together, if not in every kind of meeting, at least in circumstances which most frequently occur, be predetermined. . . . Otherwise, at every moment new conflicts would have to be equilibrated. . . . It will be said that there are contracts. But, first of all, social relations are not capable of assuming this juridical form. . . . A contract is not self-sufficient, but supposes a regulation which is as extensive and complicated as contractual life itself. . . . A contract is only a truce, and very precarious, it suspends hostilities only for a time.

The solidarity to which Durkheim refers contemplates the union of objectives between individuals which stems from their necessary dependence upon one another. In this sense, any occupational group which has organic solidarity may be considered a clan. Thus, a profession, a labor union, or a corporation may be a clan, and the professionalized bureaucracy may be understood as a response to the joint need for efficient transactions within professions (clan) and between professions (bureaucracy). Goal congruity as a central mechanism of control in organizations also appears repeatedly in Barnard:

The most intangible and subtle of incentives is that which I have called the condition of communion. . . . It is the feeling of personal comfort in social relations that is sometimes called solidarity, social integration. . . . The need for communion is a basis of informal organization that is essential to the operation of every formal organization (1968: 148; see also pp. 89, 152, 169, 273).

Descriptions of organizations which display a high degree of goal congruence, typically through relatively complete socialization brought about through high inclusion (Etzioni, 1965), are also found in Lipset, Trow, and Coleman (1956: 79–80), Argyris (1964: 10, 175), Selznick (1966), and Clark (1970). In each case, the authors describe the organization as one in which it is difficult to determine individual performance. However, such organizations are not "loosely coupled" nor are they "organized anarchies" simply because they lack market and bureaucratic mechanisms. A clan, as Durkheim points out, provides great regularity of relations and may in fact be more directive than the other, more explicit mechanisms. That clans display a high degree of discipline is emphasized by Kanter (1972) in her study of utopian communities, some of which were successful businesses such as Oneida and Amana. According to Kanter, this discipline was not achieved through contractualism or surveillance but through an extreme form of the belief that individual interests are best served by a complete immersion of each individual in the interests of the whole (1972: 41).

More recently, Ouchi and Jaeger (1978) and Ouchi and Johnson (1978) have reported on modern industrial organizations which closely resemble the clan form. In these organizations, a variety of social mechanisms reduces differences between individual and organizational goals and produces a strong sense of community (see also Van Maanen, 1975; Katz, 1978). Where individual and organizational interests overlap to this extent, opportunism is unlikely and equity in rewards can be achieved at a relatively low transactions cost. Moreover, these organizations are typically in technologically advanced or closely integrated industries, where teamwork is common, technologies change often, and therefore individual performance is highly ambiguous.

When a bureaucracy fails, then due to excessively ambiguous performance evaluation, the sole form of mediation remaining is the clan, which relies upon creating goal congruence. Although clans may employ a system of legitimate authority (often the traditional rather than the rational-legal form), they differ fundamentally from bureaucracies in that they do not require explicit auditing and evaluation. Performance evaluation takes place instead through the kind of subtle reading of signals that is possible among intimate coworkers but which cannot be translated into explicit, verifiable measures. This means that there is sufficient information in a clan to promote learning and effective production, but that information cannot withstand the scrutiny of contractual relations. Thus, any tendency toward opportunism will be destructive, because the close auditing and hard contracting necessary to combat it are not possible in a clan.

If performance evaluation is so ambiguous and goals so incongruent that a clan fails, what then? We can only speculate, but it seems that this final cell may be the case discussed by Meyer and Rowan (1977) in which control is purely ceremonial and symbolic. School systems, like other organizations, do employ a variety of mechanisms. Yet if there is no effective mechanism of mediation between individuals, the perception of equity may be purely superstitious, based on a broad, community-based acceptance of the legitimacy of the institution.

Markets, Bureaucracies, and Clans: An Overview

Having distinguished three mechanisms of intermediation, we can now summarize them and attempt to set out the general conditions under which each form will mediate transactions between individuals most efficiently. Table 2.2 discriminates markets, bureaucracies, and clans along two dimensions: their underlying normative and informational requirements.

Normative requirements refer to the basic social agreements that all members of the transactional network must share if the network is to function efficiently, without undue costs of performance auditing or monitoring. A norm of reciprocity, according to Gouldner (1961), is one of only two social agreements that have been found to be universal among societies across time and cultures (the other is the incest taboo). If no such norm were widely shared, then a potential trader would have to consume so much energy in setting the contractural terms of exchange in advance and in auditing the performance of the other party afterwards that the potential transaction would cost too much. Under such conditions, a division of labor is unthinkable and social existence impossible. Therefore, a norm of reciprocity underlies all exchange mechanisms.

A norm of legitimate authority is critical for two reasons. As discussed above, it permits the assignment of organizational superiors who can, on an ad hoc basis, specify the work assignments of subordinates, thus obviating the need for a contingent claims employment contract which would be either so complex as to be infeasible or so simple as to be too confining or else incomplete. Legitimate authority also permits organizational superiors to audit the performance of subordinates more closely than is possible within a market relationship. In a bureaucracy, legitimate authority will commonly take the "rational/legal" form, whereas in a clan it may take the "traditional" form (see Blau and Scott, 1962: 27–38). Legitimate authority is not ordinarily created within the organization but is maintained by other institutions such as the church or the educational system (Weber, 1947; Blau and Scott, 1962; Barnard, 1968: 161–184). While the legitimacy of a particular organization may be greater or smaller as a result of its managerial practices, it is fundamentally maintained within a society generally.

Common values and beliefs provide the harmony of interests that erase the possibility of opportunistic behavior. If all members of the organization have been exposed to an apprenticeship or other socialization period, then they will share personal goals that are compatible with the goals of the organization. In this condition, auditing of performance is unnecessary except for educational purposes, since no member will attempt to depart from organizational goals.

A norm of reciprocity is universal, legitimate authority is accepted, though in varying degree, in most formal organizations, and common values and beliefs are relatively rare in formal organizations. Etzioni (1965) has described this last form of control as being common only to "total organizations" such as the military and mental hospitals, and Light (1972) describes its role in ethnically bound exchange relationships. However, we have also noted that a partially complete form of socialization, accompanied by market or bureaucratic mechanisms, may be effective across a wider range of organizations, Mayo (1945) contended that instability of employment, which upsets the long socialization period necessary, is the chief enemy of the development of this form of control.

Table 2.2
An Organizational Failures Framework

Mode of control	Normative requirements	Informational requirements
Market	Reciprocity	Prices
Bureaucracy	Reciprocity Legitimate authority	Rules
Clan	Reciprocity Legitimate authority Common values and beliefs	Traditions

The informational prerequisites of each form of control are prices, rules, and traditions. Prices are a highly sophisticated form of information for decision making. However, correct prices are difficult to arrive at, particularly when technological interdependence, novelty, or other forms of ambiguity obscure the boundary between tasks or individuals. Rules, by comparison, are relatively crude informational devices. A rule is specific to a problem, and therefore it takes a large number of rules to control organizational responses. A decision maker must know the structure of the rules in order to apply the correct one in any given situation. Moreover, an organization can never specify a set of rules that will cover all possible contingencies, Instead, it specifies a smaller set of rules which cover routine decisions, and refers exceptions up the hierarchy where policymakers can invent rules as needed. As Galbraith (1973) has pointed out, under conditions of uncertainty or complexity the number of exceptions becomes so great that the hierarchy becomes overloaded and the quality of decision making suffers.

Traditions are implicit rather than explicit rules that govern behavior. Because traditions are not specified, they are not easily accessible, and a new member will not be able to function effectively until he or she has spent a number of years learning them (Van Maanen and Schein, 1978). In terms of the precision of the performance evaluation they permit, traditions may be the crudest informational prerequisite, since they are ordinarily stated in a general way which must be interpreted in a particular situation. On the other hand, the set of traditions in a formal organization may produce a unified, although implicit philosophy or point of view, functionally equivalent to a theory about how that organization should work. A member who grasps such an essential theory can deduce from it an appropriate rule to govern any possible decision, thus producing a very elegant and complete form of control. Alternatively, a disruption of the socialization process will inhibit the passing on of traditions and bring about organizational inefficiency.

Some Concluding Thoughts

Under conditions of extreme uncertainty and opportunism, transactions cost may rise. Indeed, Denison (1978) has observed that net productivity declined in the United States between 1965 and 1975 due to changes in "the industrial and human environment within which business must operate" (1978:21). According to Denison, output per unit of input has declined for two reasons: 78 percent of the decline is due to increased costs of air, water, and safety on the job, and the remaining 22 percent is attributable to increased needs for surveillance of potentially dishonest employees, customers, contractors, and thieves. The resources put into improvements in air, water, and safety are not a net loss to society although they may reduce corporate profitability. The increased need for surveillance in business, however, may represent the fact that the cost of monitoring transactions has risen. Mayo (1945) might have predicted this change as an inevitable result of the instability which accompanies industrialization. In our framework, we could advance the following explanation: exchange relationships are generally subject to so much informational ambiguity that they can never be governed completely by markets. Consequently, they have been supplemented through cultural, clan mechanisms. As instability, heterogeneity, and mobility have intensified in the United States, however, the effectiveness of these cultural mechanisms has been vitiated and bureaucratic mechanisms of surveillance and control have increased. Although bureaucratic surveillance may be the optimal strategy under present social conditions, it is nonetheless true that the United States is devoting more of its resources to transactional matters than it did ten years ago, and that represents a net decline in its welfare.

The degree of uncertainty and opportunism that characterize American society may be such that no mechanisms of control ever function very well. We have already observed that the conditions necessary for a pure market, bureaucracy, or clan are rare. Even a combination of these control mechanisms may be insufficient in many cases, however. In organizations using new technologies or in the public sector, the rate of change, instability of employment, or ambiguity of performance evaluation may simply overwhelm all rational control attempts.

In these cases, exchange becomes institutionalized. Meyer and Rowan's (1977) central thesis is that school systems, by their nature, evade any form of rational control.

They have no effective price mechanism, no effective bureaucratic control, and no internally consistent cultures (see also Meyer et al., 1978). Thus school systems (as distinguished from education, which need not be done by large organizations) continue to grow and survive because the objectives which they are believed to pursue have been accepted as necessary by society. Since rational control is not feasible within the school, no one knows whether it is actually pursuing these goals, but an institutionalized organization (the church is another example) need not give evidence of performance (see also Ouchi, 1977: 97–98).

All work organizations are institutionalized in the sense that fundamental purposes of all viable organizations must mesh at least somewhat with broad social values (Parsons and Shils, 1951). This institutionalization permits organizations to survive even under conditions that severely limit their capacity for rational control. Ultimately, organizational failure occurs only when society deems the basic objectives of the organization unworthy of continued support.

What is an organization? An organization, in our sense, is any stable pattern of transactions between individuals or aggregations of individuals. Our framework can thus be applied to the analysis of relationships between individuals or between subunits within a corporation, or to transactions between firms in an economy. Why do organizations exist? In our sense, all patterned transactions are organized, and thus all stable exchanges in a society are organized. When we ask "why do organizations exist," we usually mean to ask "why do bureaucratic organizations exist," and the answer is clear. Bureaucratic organizations exist because, under certain specifiable conditions, they are the most efficient means for an equitable mediation of transactions between parties. In a similar manner, market and clan organizations exist because each of them, under certain conditions, offers the lowest transactions cost.

Notes

1. In the broader language necessary to encompass both economics and organization theory, an organization may be thought of as any stable pattern of transactions. In this definition, a market is as much an organization as is a bureaucracy or a clan. The only requirement is that, for the purposes of this discussion, we maintain a clear distinction between the idea of "bureaucracy" and the idea of "organization." Bureaucracy as used here refers specifically to the Weberian model, while organization refers to any

stable pattern of transactions between individuals or aggregations of individuals.

2. Despite these desirable properties, the bureaucratic type has continually been under attack and revision. As Williamson points out, the move from U-form (functional) to M-form (divisional) organization among many large firms has been motivated by a desire to simulate a capital market within a bureaucratic framework because of its superior efficiency. By regrouping the parts of the organization, it is possible to create subentities that are sufficiently autonomous to permit precise measurement and the determination of an effective price mechanism. Although each division may still operate internally as a bureaucracy, the economies which accrue from this partial market solution are often large, offsetting the diseconomies of functional redundancy which often accompany the separation of the organization into divisions.

References

Abegglen, James C. 1958. *The Japanese Factory Aspects of Its Social Organization*. Glencoe, IL: Free Press.

Argyris, Chris. 1964. *Integrating the Individual and the Organization*. New York: Wiley.

Arrow, Kenneth J. 1974. *The Limits of Organization*. New York: Norton.

Barnard, Chester I. 1968. *The Functions of the Executive*, 30th anniversary ed. Cambridge: Harvard.

Blau, Peter M., and W. Richard Scott. 1962. *Formal Organizations*. San Francisco: Scott, Foreman.

Clark, Burton R. 1970. *The Distinctive College: Antioch, Reed, and Swarthmore*. Chicago: Aldine.

Coase, R. H. 1937 "The nature of the firm." *Economica*, new series, 4: 386–405.

Denison, Edward F. 1978. *Effects of Selected Changes in the Institutional and Human Environment upon Output Per Unit of Input*. Brookings General Series Reprint #335. Washington: Brookings.

Dore, Ronald. 1973. *British Factory–Japanese Factory*. Berkeley: University of California.

Durkheim, Emile. 1933. *The Division of Labor in Society*. G. Simpson, trans. New York: Free Press.

Etzioni, Amitai. 1965. "Organizational control structure." In James G. March (ed.), *Handbook of Organizations*: 650–677. Chicago: Rand McNally.

Galbraith, Jay. 1973. *Designing Complex Organizations*. Reading, MA: Addison-Wesley.

Gouldner, Alvin W. 1961. "The norm of reciprocity." *American Sociological Review*, 25: 161–179.

Kanter, Rosabeth Moss. 1972. *Commitment and Community*. Cambridge: Harvard.

Katz, Ralph. 1978. "Job longevity as a situational factor in job satisfaction." *Administrative Science Quarterly*, 23: 204–223.

Light, Ivan H. 1972. *Ethnic Enterprise in America*. Berkeley: University of California.

Lipset, Seymour M., Martin A. Trow, and James S. Coleman. 1956. *Union Democracy*. Glencoe, IL: Free Press.

March, James G., and Herbert A. Simon. 1958. *Organizations*. New York: Wiley.

Mayo, Elton. 1945. *The Social Problems of an Industrial Civilization*. Boston Division of Research, Graduate School of Business Administration, Harvard University.

Meyer, John W., and Brian Rowan. 1977. "Institutionalized organizations: Formal structure as myth and ceremony." *American Journal of Sociology*, 83: 340–363.

Meyer, John W., W. Richard Scott, Sally Cole, and Jo-Ann K. Intili. 1978. "Instructional dissensus and institutional consensus in schools." In Marshall W. Meyer and Associates (eds.), *Environments and Organizations*: 233–263. San Francisco: Jossey-Bass.

Nakane, Chie. 1973. *Japanese Society*, rev. ed. Middlesex, England: Penguin.

Ouchi, William G. 1977. "The relationship between organizational structure and organizational control." *Administrative Science Quarterly*, 22: 95–113.

————. 1979. "A conceptual framework for the design of organizational control mechanisms." *Management Science*, 25: 833–848.

Ouchi, William G., and Alfred M. Jaeger. 1978. "Type Z organization: Stability in the midst of mobility." *Academy of Management Review*, 3: 305–314.

Ouchi, William G., and Jerry B. Johnson. 1978. "Types of organizational control and their relationship to emotional well-being." *Administrative Science Quarterly*, 23: 293–317.

Parsons, Talcott, and Edward A. Shils. 1951. "Values, motives, and systems of action." In Talcott Parsons and Edward A. Shils (eds.), *Toward a General Theory of Action*: 47–275. Cambridge: Harvard.

Selznick, Philip. 1966. *TVA and the Grass Roots* (orig. ed., 1949). New York: Harper Torchbooks.

Simon, Herbert A. 1945. *Administrative Behavior*. New York: Free Press.

————. 1957. *Models of Man*. New York: Wiley.

Van Maanen, John. 1975. "Police socialization: A longitudinal examination of job attitudes in an urban police department." *Administrative Science Quarterly*, 20: 207–228.

Van Maanen, John, and Edgar H. Schein. 1978. "Toward a theory of organizational socialization." Manuscript, Sloan School of Industrial Administration, Massachusetts Institute of Technology.

Weber, Max. 1947. *The Theory of Social and Economic Organization* (orig ed., 1925). A. M. Henderson and T. Parsons, trans. New York: Free Press.

————. 1968. *Economy and Society* (orig ed., 1925). G. Roth and C. Wittich, eds. New York: Bedminster Press.

Weick, Karl E. 1969. *The Social Psychology of Organizing*. Reading, MA: Addison-Wesley.

Williamson, O. E. 1975. *Markets and Hierarchies: Analysis and Antitrust Implications*. New York: Free Press.

William G. Ouchi, "Markets, Bureaucracies, and Clans." In *Administrative Science Quarterly* 25: 129–141. Copyright © 1980. Reprinted with permission. ✦

Chapter 3
Why Bureaucracy?

Charles Perrow

Bureaucracy is often depicted in negative terms. It is much more likely to be viewed as the problem, rather than the solution. If Max Weber, the foremost student of bureaucracy, were alive today, he could probably understand these perceptions, but his view of bureaucracy was much different. For Weber, bureaucracy—in its ideal form—had the potential to solve many of the more vexing challenges posed by large-scale administration and organization.

Perrow's discussion of work at General Gypsum Corporation reminds us why bureaucratic forms of organization continue to be embraced—especially when they replace more traditional ways of organizing. Tradition is a powerful way to legitimize a way of doing things, but it is rarely the most effective way of organizing work. In the gypsum plant, bureaucratic impersonality offered an alternative to the particularism and informality that once reigned supreme.

Weber's ideal bureaucracy has rarely been realized in practice, however. Perrow thus argues that many of the "sins" of bureaucracy can be traced to "a failure to bureaucratize properly." He urges us to appreciate the advantages of bureaucracy, while at the same time to be aware that many other aspects of society make these advantages difficult to achieve.

Several miles from a medium-sized city near one of the Great Lakes, there was a plant that mined gypsum rock, crushed it, mixed it with bonding and foaming agents, spread it out on a wide sheet of paper, covered it with another sheet, let it set a bit, sliced it into large but inedible sandwiches, and then dried them. The resulting material was sold as wallboard, used for insulation and for dividing up rooms in buildings. Plants such as this were scattered about the country, some of them owned, as was this one, by General Gypsum Corporation (a pseudonym). A book by Alvin Gouldner, *Patterns of Industrial Bureaucracy,* described the plant and the surrounding communities as they existed in 1950.[1]

The towns around the plant were small and had been settled about a century before. The people in the area generally knew one another well and regarded strangers with considerable misgiving. They led a peaceful, semirural life, with an emphasis upon farming, hunting, and fishing. They were conservative in their outlook, strait-laced in their behavior, and, according to one member, "thrifty, religious, God-fearing, and anti-Semitic."[2]

The gypsum plant fitted comfortably into the style of life in the area. Most of the men working at the plant, some 225 including the miners, had worked there for many years. They knew one another well on the job and visited outside the plant in the surrounding hamlets. Indeed, perhaps as many as one-half of the workers were related to others employed in the plant. The personnel man who hired and fired people argued that it was good to learn something about a prospective employee by asking others in the plant or community about him and his family. He did not want hostile employees or troublemakers. He also preferred farm boys over city boys. The former worked harder, he thought, and took greater pride in their work. The personnel man had few other rules for hiring, firing, or other matters with which he had to deal, however. He disliked paperwork and, as one employee said, "He regarded everything that happened as an exception to the rule." He had only an eighth-grade education, but since he relied so heavily on the community norms and his own rule-of-thumb methods, not much education seemed to be required. Apparently, hardly anyone was ever fired from the p1ant. Even those who left during the war years to work in defense plants paying much higher wages were welcomed back when those plants closed. A city boy, however, or a stranger laid off by a defense plant in the city had a hard time getting a job from this man.

In the plant itself, the workers had considerable leeway. The men were able to try different jobs until they found one that they liked, as long as they did so within the general limits of their union regulations. Moreover, they stretched out their lunch hours, were allowed to arrive late as long as they had some excuse, and were not required to keep busy. As long as their work was done, their time was their own. Production records were kept informally. The trouble was that the company management felt that not enough work was being done.

Further, the rhythm of the plant was, to some degree, determined by the men. During hunting season fewer showed up; the same thing sometimes occurred during planting season, since many employees farmed in their spare time. In co1d weather more of them complained of sprains or other ailments so they could be transferred to the "sample room," where the work was light and the room was warm, until they were feeling better. This was preferable to staying at home and using up sick leave or to living off unemployment compensation. Mining operations fell off considerably on Mondays because of hangovers among the heavy-drinking miners. As a mill foreman explained, "You can't ride the men very hard when they are your neighbors. Lots of these men grew up together."[3]

Many employees used the plant materials and services freely. Men took dynamite home with them to explode in ponds (an easy way to fish) and for construction. They appropriated quantities of wallboard, even truckloads, for their personal use. They brought in broken items such as furniture to be fixed by the carpenters. And both employees and farmers in the area brought in broken parts for free welding.

For the workers, the plant was a pleasant and comfortable operation. One could hardly "get ahead," but few desired to go wherever "ahead" was. Those who showed a desire to advance in the company got transfers to company plants in different areas. Others left for the big city.

But for other interested parties, the plant was not all that satisfying. A job seeker found it difficult to get work if he was not well knows, or did not measure up to the vague standards of the personnel man—which had little to do with the ability to do the job. Customers found deliveries erratic. They might have suspected that if all gypsum plants were run this way, they would be paying a surcharge to cover the purloined materials, free repair work, and general slack. Top managers in the company headquarters, faced with postwar competition from other companies and competing products, were apparently climbing the walls.

When the plant manager died ("Old Doug," he was affectionately called), head-quarters sent in an aggressive new manager with orders to tighten things up—increase productivity and cut costs. According to Gouldner's account, this man was not blessed with bountiful tact and insight, even though he was otherwise efficient. He cracked down rather hard and accumulated much ill will. He activated dormant rules, instituted new ones, demoted the personnel man, and brought in one who applied a "universalistic" standard—the only thing that counted was a person's ability to do the job. The new manager successfully "bureaucratized" the surface plant. (He was unable to bureaucratize the more dangerous mine, for there was too much uncertainty and unpredictability in the work, and teamwork was extremely important.) However, some time later he was faced with a wildcat strike.

What had been a "traditional" form of organization, or in the terms of Max Weber,[4] a "traditional bureaucracy," became a "rational-legal bureaucracy." A rational-legal bureaucracy is based on rational principles (rational in terms of management's interests, not necessarily the worker's), is backed by legal sanctions, and exists in a legal framework. A miner fired for taking a case of dynamite, for example, was unsuccessful in his appeal that "everyone did it" and that the foreman "told him he could." Tradition or precedent was not binding; the material belonged to the company, not to the miner or the foreman.

Most of the key elements of the rational-legal bureaucracy are represented in this brief case history. They include:

1. Equal treatment for all employees.
2. Reliance on expertise, skills, and experience relevant to the position.
3. No extraorganizational prerogatives of the position (such as taking dynamite, wallboard, etc.); that is, the position is seen as belonging to the organization, not the person. The employee cannot use it for personal ends.
4. Specific standards of work and output.
5. Extensive record keeping dealing with the work and output.
6. Establishment and enforcement of rules and regulations that serve the interests of the organization.
7. Recognition that rules and regulations bind managers as well as employees; thus employees can hold management to the terms of the employment contract.

The rational-legal form of bureaucracy developed over many centuries of Western civilization. It grew slowly and erratically, beginning in the Middle Ages, and reached its full form on a widespread basis only in the twentieth century.[5] Nearly all large, complex organizations in the United States, for example, are best classified as bureaucracies, though the degree and forms of bureaucratization vary.

Its "ideal" form, however, is never realized for at least three reasons. First, it tries to do what must be (hopefully) forever impossible—to eliminate all unwanted extra-organizational influences on the behavior of members. Ideally, members should act only in the organization's interests. The problem is that even if the interest of the organization is unambiguous, people do not exist just for organizations. They track all kinds of mud from the rest of their lives into the organization, and they have all kinds of interests that are independent of the organization.

Second, the ideal form also falls short of realization when rapid changes in some of the organizational tasks are required. *Bureaucracies are set up to deal with stable, routine tasks; that is the basis of organizational efficiency.* Without stable tasks there cannot be a stable division of labor, a prescribed acquisition of skills and experience, formal planning and coordination, and so on. But when changes come along, organizations must alter their programs; when such changes are frequent and rapid, the form of organization becomes so temporary that the efficiencies of bureaucracy cannot be realized. (The price of the product it delivers then goes up.) The gypsum mine could not be bureaucratized to the degree that the surface plant was because the unpredictability of the seams and the dangers and variability of the raw material made continual change and improvisation necessary.

Third, bureaucracy in its ideal form falls short of its expectations because people are only differently intelligent, prescient, all-knowing, and energetic. All organizations must be designed for the "average" person one is likely to find in each position, not the superhuman.

While bureaucracy always falls short of the ideal model that Weber outlined, neither Weber in his time nor many people today would be comfortable with the ideal. In fact, much can be said for the placid, community-oriented gypsum-plant organization before the owners decided it was not making enough money for them. There was job rotation and variability, consideration for special problems such as minor illnesses, and trust among the workers and between workers and management. Furthermore, to a small extent, workers could consider the resources of the organization (wallboard, the carpentry shop) to be theirs. Perhaps above all, they could farm and hunt and thus avoid complete dependence on wages paid by the gypsum plant. If all gypsum companies were like this, some of the "social costs" of bureaucracy—dependence on a wage, dull work, and inflexible demands—would be spread over all consumers of the product. But all companies are not like this, so this one could not compete and survive. In this sense, where all organizations strive toward efficiency as defined by the owners, the rational-legal form of bureaucracy is the most efficient form of administration known in industrial societies.

Weber claimed that all else is dilettantism, but the verdict is not yet in. Alternative forms of organization are being tried. Nevertheless, they have yet to do more than to humanize rigid bureaucracies and make them more adaptive to changes. They have not seriously challenged the wage system, which takes in about 85 percent of the gainfully employed who must work for someone else. Nor have they fully rejected the notion that the resources of the organization belong to the owners of private firms or the officials of state and voluntary organizations, rather than to all members. Without fundamental changes in the wage system and ideas of ownership, alternative forms of bureaucracy are likely to be expensive, unstable, brief, and rare.

In the rest of this chapter, I am going to illustrate the essentials of bureaucracy by showing what happens when they are violated (as they constantly are). The chapter will give us all an appreciation for bureaucracy as a remarkable product of gradual, halting, and often unwitting social engineering. As we shall see, many of the "sins" of bureaucracy really reveal the failure to bureaucratize sufficiently. But while I will defend bureaucracy from many of the attacks we all are prone to make, I will attack it much more severely on quite different grounds, grounds that social scientists have been reluctant to explore. Let me explain my puzzling position briefly.

Critics usually attack bureaucracy for two reasons—it is unadaptive, and it stifles the humanity of employees. Both are legitimate criticisms to a degree. But what the first avoids noticing is that another description of unadaptiveness might be stability, steadfastness, and predictability. If we want a particular change and fail to get it, we blame the unadaptive bureaucracy. If it changes in ways we do not like, though, we call for stability. The second criticism—that bureaucracies stifle spontaneity, freedom, and self-realization—is certainly true for many employees, but unfortunately, since they do not own what they produce and must work for someone else, expressions of spontaneity and self-realization are not likely to result in better goods and services for consumers. We have constructed a society where the satisfaction of our wants as consumers largely depends on restricting the employees who dot he producing. Bureaucracy cannot be faulted for society's demands; if blame is to be placed, it should fall on those elites who constructed bureaucracy over many generations and offered us no alternatives, a subject we will return to at the end of the book.

Most social scientists (almost all of them until the mid-1970s) have offered these two criticisms of bureaucracy—rigidity and employee discipline—if they have offered any. I would offer a third: bureaucracy has become a means, both in capitalist and noncapitalist countries, of centralizing power in society and legitimating or disguising that centralization. A full defense of this thesis is impossible here. But this book will sketch, through a critical review of historical and recent thought or organizational analysis, how social scientists have, until recently, avoided the "big" question of unregulated and unperceived power through bureaucratic organizations even though the research that has been done points in this direction.

Bureaucracy is a tool, a social tool that legitimizes control of the many by the few, despite the formal apparatus of democracy, and this control has generated unregulated and unperceived social power. This power includes much more than just control of employees. As bureaucracies satisfy, delight, pollute, and satiate us with their output of goods and services, they also shape our ideas, our very way of conceiving of ourselves, control our life chances, and even define our humanity. As employees, whether we see ourselves as exploited or as pursuing "careers," we may dimly perceive this fact; as citizens in a society of organizations, where large organizations have absorbed all that used to be small, independent, personal, communitarian, religious, or ethnic, it is rarely perceived. We grow up in organizations; to stand outside them is to see their effect on what we believe, what we value, and, more important, how we think and reason. . . .

At present, without huge, disruptive, and perilous changes, we cannot survive without large organizations. Organizations mobilize social resources for ends that are often essential and even desirable. But organizations also concentrate those resources in the hands of a few who are prone to use them for ends we do not approve of, for ends we may not even be aware of, and, more frightening still, for ends we are led to accept because we are not in a position to conceive alternative ones. The investigation of these fearful possibilities has too long been left to writers, journalists, and radical political leaders. It is time that organizational theorists began to use their expertise to uncover the true nature of bureaucracy. This will require a better understanding both of the virtues of bureaucracy and its largely unexplored dangers.

This chapter will examine the customary view of the sins of bureaucracy and then argue that these sins result largely from a failure to bureaucratize properly. If we must have bureaucracy, we must understand its many strengths. . . .

Purging Particularism

One of the many dilemmas of organizations is that they attempt to be efficient in producing their output of steel, court convictions, reformed delinquents, legislation, or whatever, and yet they seek to be quite particular about who shall enjoy the pay and the honor of doing the work. *Particularism* means that criteria irrelevant for efficient production (e.g., only relatives of the boss have a chance at top positions), in contrast to universalistic criteria (e.g., competence is all that counts), are used to choose employees. The criteria of efficiency and particularism are likely to clash since the most efficient workers may lack the particular social characteristics desired. For example, few Jews ever rise very high in such industries as steel;[6] few blacks have thus far been able to break into many skilled trades in the construction industry. In a study of one manufacturing firm, Melville Dalton found that membership in the Masons was a prerequisite to advancement in management. Even though it is hard to imagine what there is about Masonic membership that would increase managerial efficiency,[7] ambitious managers were smart enough to join the fraternal order. Some levels in organizations, some work groups, and even whole plants are uni-ethnic—that is, all Irish or all Polish. One of the distinctive characteristics of voluntary associations such as patriotic societies or clubs is that they often specify membership criteria openly, while economic or governmental organizations can only do so informally. The Daughters of the American Revolution was founded at a time when many native-born Anglo-Saxons had parents who had lived during the days of the Revolution; the unqualified, then, were conveniently all immigrants.

The development of bureaucracy has been in part an attempt to purge organizations of particularism. This has been difficult, because organizations are profoundly "social," in the sense that all kinds of social characteristics affect their operation *by intent*. Take the relatively trivial matters of nepotism (giving preferred treatment to relatives) and personal favoritism. Both are very common—and very annoying, unless you are a favored relative or friend of the boss. But both reflect social solutions to the organizational problems of members. One of the things that you can do with the power that a decent position in an organization gives you is to reward people whom you like or are related to you or who will help you in return. Families, for example, are a major resource in society; relatives who work for you can be expected to hide your mistakes and incompetence, warn you about threats to your position, and support you in conflicts with others. Similarly, subordinates are well advised to defer to their superior because they will be protected and rewarded for covering for their boss, warning her, and lightening her workload. Two or three levels above the boss, the higher-ups will try to measure objective competence, but it is both hard to determine competence and easy to disguise incompetence. Since the subordinate's career and even comfort are always at risk in organizations, we can hardly expect them always to put the abstract "interests of the organization" ahead of their own interests and those of the bosses who control their fate.

The social character of organizations goes deeper. In a society where organizations provide the livelihood of eight out of ten of the "economically active" and where organizations are necessary for most other interests, merely being allowed to be a member of an organization is critical for well-being, if not survival. Assiduous efforts are made to restrict access to this resource; organizations discriminate on social, rather than objective, grounds in letting people in.

We view these particularistic criteria with suspicion partly because of our democratic ideals of equality. But we also view them with suspicion because we dimly recognize that organizations draw on resources provided by society in general and thus are beholden to all of society. In spite of this fact, though, there is, for example, a flourishing and Byzantine structure of courts, laws, and law-enforcement facilities that is available to organizations to protect their interests. We support this structure through taxes. On campus, fraternities and sororities have special access to university facilities, receive special protection—and are tax-exempt. And private clubs that discriminate get quiet subsidies in one form or another. For example, in 1984 a county judge in Maryland ruled that an elite golf club, the Burning Tree Club, would lose its $186,000 real estate tax exemption because it would not admit women as members; indeed, even the kitchen staff had to be male. How could a club that charged an initiation fee of $12,000 and annual dues of $1,700 justify a yearly tax break of $186,000? Because the huge grounds preserved open spaces (in a suburb where the least expensive homes cost $400,000). The Burning Tree officials said they would appeal, cited the constitutional guarantee of freedom of association, and charged that the necessary increase in dues—about $292 per member—would turn the club into "a rich man's club."[8]

The factory is fairly free to pollute the air and water, to enforce its law through its own police force and its access to the courts, to hire and fire (and thus provide or deny livelihood), to utilize the services of the local chamber of commerce (which is tax-exempt and may even receive local tax support), and to draw upon tax-supported services of many state and federal agencies. These things cost all of us money. No matter that the factory pays taxes in return, or that the sorority provides housing and surveillance that the university might otherwise have to build and provide. Common resources are drawn from society, whatever the specific products returned. Thus, we feel the services should be common to all who desire them. Particularism or discrimination is frowned upon.

But these are political rather than bureaucratic reasons for distrusting particularism. The bureaucratic reason for frowning on particularism is that efficiency is forgone if recruitment or access is decided upon grounds that are not related to the members' performance in the organization. For most organizational goals or roles, social origins (race, ethnicity, and class) are not likely to be a measure of competence. The steel company or bank that bars Jews from middle management is possibly depriving itself of talent at the higher levels. The appointment of a large political campaign donor to the position of Ambassador to the Court of St. James suggests that the criteria are not knowledge of foreign affairs and skill in foreign diplomacy, but party loyalty and personal wealth. The son of the president of a corporation may well start out on the shop floor or as a sales trainee, but it is not his competence that moves him quickly to a vice-presidency. Moreover, the frequent practice of a professional person hiring staff members from the same university he or she attended suggests something other than universalistic criteria. One finds this in university departments ("only Eastern schools have a chance there," or "that's where Michigan sends its run-of-the-mill Ph.D.'s"), research and development labs ("someone from MIT doesn't stand a chance in that company"), social agencies ("they only give supervisory positions to Chicago graduates" [University of Chicago School of Social Work]), and hospital medical staffs ("that's a Johns Hopkins shop").

The problem with these practices is not only that there is little relationship between the social criteria for hiring or promoting people and the characteristics that affect performance in the organization. More serious, the particularistic criteria are likely to be *negatively* related to performance—the more these particularistic criteria are used, the poorer the performance. By hiring only Chicago graduates, one may have to take

some who were among the poorer students, missing out on the good Michigan graduates. More serious still, one may end up with only one way of seeing the world and only one way of approaching a problem. By using broad or universalistic hiring criteria; the chances of getting different perspectives, and thus more ideas, are increased.

That particularistic criteria are often equivalent to favoritism also means that corruption is a likely accompaniment. The agency head who hires or favors primarily people from her own region, state, or university may get subtle returns in the bargain. She may be favored as a consultant to her former university or to the state government and receive handsome fees; she may place herself at the head of the line for bigger and better appointments. Competence is hard to judge, so we rely on familiarity. The corruption may be less discreet, as in the political spoils system, whereby the elected official hires only people who are willing to contribute to his election campaign or to provide him with kickbacks.

Tenure and the Career Concept

Political patronage reached such a corrupting extreme in the late nineteenth century that the merit system and civil service examinations were instituted in the federal and most state governments. We now pay a price for that sweeping change, since merit systems may have little to do with merit. Once a civil service appointee receives "tenure," it is very hard to remove that employee for lack of competence. Over the years, as the organization changes and the demand for new skills increases, the person who may have once been a very competent employee may turn out to be quite incompetent. But the organization is stuck with him or her. One need look no further, for example, than university departments where skills change quickly, promise does not materialize into productivity, or people simply pass their prime. If research-oriented universities changed to the extent that teaching ability became a prime criterion for competence, rather than a secondary one, many tenured people might be found incompetent.

It is a tenet of the bureaucratic model of organizations that an employee is expected to pursue a "career" in the organization. Thus, if the person burns out too quickly or, more likely, if the skills demanded of the position change without the occupant changing (e.g., more emphasis on teaching and less on research), the organization is expected to retain him or her. The employee has tenure. Despite the frequency with which this annoyance is met in organizations, the career principle is a sound one. People would not be likely to master sets of skills through long technical training or experience in an organization if they knew they could not perpetually draw on the capital of their investment. There must be some guarantee that if the demands of the job change radically in the future, a person will still be credited with having met them in the present. Otherwise, personnel might be less willing to make large investments in skills.

In short, the benefits of universalistic standards clearly appear to exceed the costs; tenure may be a necessary inducement for mastering obscure skills and a necessary protection against arbitrary rulers. There are costs, but the alternatives are worse.

Universalism and Organizational Goals

Universalistic criteria, then, would appear to be a proper goal in organizations, and few would fault the bureaucratic model in this respect. But the situation is not that simple. To establish the standards, one has to know the real goals of the organization. Suppose a manufacturing firm favors members of a certain fraternal organization when it hires and promotes its managers. On the face of it, this sounds particularistic. Closer examination, though, might well reveal that the manufacturing organization receives a variety of tax benefits from the local government, and the local government is heavily loaded with Masons, Lions, Legionnaires, or whatever. If the firm gives preference to Masons, should they be the dominant group in the city government, it may avoid paying its fair share of the sewage system; it may get special arrangements for power supplies; zoning ordinances may be drafted so that it does not have to pay a heavy school tax; it may be able to get certain city streets closed to permit convenient expansion; and a good share of its security protection may come from the city's police department, rather than from plant guards. Furthermore, the local authorities may see that other plants are discouraged from coming in, through zoning ordinances or restrictions on transportation or available power supplies. Competing

industry, particularly, would up the demand for skilled labor in one field and drive up wages. Moreover, the city planning commission may ensure that a new superhighway comes close to the front gate of the plant, even at the expense of cutting a residential district in two.

Showing favoritism within the manufacturing company to this fraternal organization is hardly, then, a particularistic criterion from the *company's* point of view. Any loss in managerial competence that may result from using selective criteria is more than offset by the gain of having sympathetic friends in the city administration. For similar reasons, defense industries have a disproportionate number of former military officers in their top echelons, even though it is questionable whether former procurement or inspection officers are particularly good managers of large aerospace firms or conglomerates. For defense industries, political ties to the Pentagon are a universalistic criterion. Similarly, experience in the major corporations and investment houses is often crucial for top civilian positions in the State Department, the Defense Department, the CIA, and the Atomic Energy Commission; Richard Barnet found that seventy of the ninety-one top men in those agencies from 1940 to 1967 had such backgrounds.[9] The Polish foreman who favors Polish workers under him is acting no differently.

This reasoning also applies to voluntary associations such as fraternities and sororities. If the "real" goals of the Greek-letter societies were auxiliary support for the university, good fellowship, recreation, character building, and efficient housing, then discrimination against Jews and blacks would be unwarranted. However, if the goal of the fraternity or sorority also includes promoting social class and ethnic solidarity, ties that will lead to business or marital advantages, and reinforcement of religious, ethnic, and class sentiments, then the discrimination is certainly efficient. The Jew or the black is deemed an inappropriate resource for the organization; he or she does nothing for the group.

We may deplore the particularism of the Greek-letter society or the manufacturing firm and call for the universalism that is explicit in the bureaucratic model. There, at least, bureaucracy is virtuous in its impersonality. But to deplore particularism is only to advance an ideal and to neglect the reality of organizational affairs. The real cause for concern is not just the failure to apply universalism; rather it involves the uses the leaders make of the organization; these determine just what are universalistic or particularistic criteria. We are being naive when we deplore patronage, collusion, and snobbery in our political, economic, and voluntary organizations, as if those traits stemmed from a failure to apply sound organizational principles or even general moral principles. A more realistic view would question the uses to which owners and managers put these organizations, for these uses define what is efficient for those in control. Organizations are tools. The bureaucratic ideal assumes the uses are legitimate—that is, in society's interests. In doing so, it disguises some of the purposes to which people put organizations. Still, bureaucracy—with its ideals of clearly stated goals and rational instrumentation of legitimate purposes—is a clear advance over ancient satrapies, feudal domains, family dynasties, warlords and their retinues, and the autocracies of the past. At the least, since official goals are proclaimed, unofficial, unpublicized, and unlegitimated uses can be held up to scrutiny when they are found, and action can be taken. The hidden uses of organizations, always present, can be exposed and addressed.

The Contest for Control

Organizations generate power; control and use of that power are vital organizational issues. Particularism is a strategy to control and use that power, and it is not easily purged. It is a central theme of this book that organizations must be seen as tools, as having bundles of all sorts of resources that people inside and outside can make use of and try to control. Organizations are multipurpose tools because they can do many things for many people.

For example, regardless of their goals, organizations offer employment opportunities for friends and relatives, as well as for oneself. They also provide prestige and status for their members, as well as chances to make contacts and to strengthen social class ties. Obviously, there are opportunities for graft and corruption through organizations. But most important of all, *organizations are tools for shaping the world as one wishes it to be shaped.* They provide the means for impos-

ing one's own definition of the proper affairs of humankind on others. The person who controls an organization has power that goes far beyond that of those lacking such control. The power of the rich lies not in their ability to buy goods and services, but in their capacity to control the ends toward which the vast resources of large organizations are directed.

Such power is naturally contested. People attempt to achieve control of organizations or even parts of an organization in order to gain that power. "If I were in charge I would do it this way." "We really should be doing such and such." "Top management should never let the union [or suppliers, or customers, or medical staff, or the prison guards, or the government, or middle management, or whatever] get away with this." "The trouble with top management is that it is only interested in immediate profits and not in long-term growth; I want to see this organization strong over the long run." "This agency should be serving lower-class people, not the middle class." "Top management is too tied to the industry way of doing things; it is preoccupied with traditions that are no longer relevant, and it does not want to rock the boat." "We should be revolutionizing things in this industry." "We don't want people of *that sort* in our company." "Business has a responsibility to protect the American way of life. We should make it clear to these groups that they can't get away with this." These are statements about power and the uses to which it can be put.

Retaining or gaining power is difficult because it is almost always contested, and the contest is not decided by measuring the "efficiency" or "productivity" of the contenders. The criterion is not narrow and testable, but general and vague. The principles of bureaucracy have little to do with the contest. One decidedly unbureaucratic principle is crucial—personal loyalty or loyalty to a superior rather than to the organization and its goals. One of the best ways to seize or retain control is to surround oneself with loyal people. If a person has a certain charisma or force of personality, the loyalty may be freely given by strangers and acquaintances. If one lacks this rare quality, there are other means of ensuring loyalty. The most powerful is dependence. The subordinate who is a relative of a superior or a friend of the family is more dependent than one who is not; his or her superior has privileged access to "significant others" in the subordinate's social world. The marginally competent manager who is promoted over others is vulnerable and thus had better be loyal.

Of course, one purchases some inefficiency along with this loyalty. Inefficiency means that the costs of doing business are increased. But the difference between a small increase in the operating cost and a threat to losing control of all or some of the resources of the organization is enormous. In most cases, the exchange of loyalty for competence is in the executive's interest.

Even less-than-exemplary subordinates can perform very well for their superiors. A man may lack good judgment in setting policies, be inefficient in organizing his work and his staff, and even spend an excessive amount of time on the golf course or traveling at company expense. However, if he manages to sniff out potential sources of opposition within the organization, nominate loyal subordinates and identify those who cannot be trusted, and generally keep track of the activities of "internal enemies," he is worth a great deal to his boss. Such functions are commonplace in organizations of all types. As we have said, organizations are tools; they mobilize resources that can be used for a variety of ends. These resources and the goals of the organization are up for grabs, and people grab for them continually. Internecine warfare, often involving lawsuits, is a very prominent news item in the business press; it generally concerns the uses to which organizational power is to be put.

Viewing organizations as tools should reduce our tendency to cry incompetence when they do not do what we think they should. Incompetence certainly exists; organizations must contend with the distribution of incompetence in the general population, as well as the distribution of tendencies toward venality, stupidity, sycophancy, and so on, since they must draw upon the general population for employees. But a tool view alerts us to the possibility that what we see as incompetent performance or policy really reflects what some leaders wanted all along. A president will not announce that he or she intends to discipline labor and reduce inflation by creating a recession; it will be announced instead that the economy is not competitive enough. If an acquired firm goes downhill in performance, the new leaders need not be charged with incompetence in running the acquisition; they

may have decided to appropriate its available cash and other liquid assets, its unused tax credits, and its best personnel and use them where they will provide greater returns. The acquired firm may then be sold, or even scrapped, possibly with significant tax breaks. Before assuming that an outcome was unintended, it is best to see if someone in top management might not have had reason to have intended the outcome. Bureaucracy is not the breeder of incompetence, as we often would like to believe. Instead, bureaucratic organization allows leaders to achieve goals, some of which are unannounced and costly for the rest of us and are only *attributed* to incompetence.

In conclusion, we have explored particularism in organizations, indicating the desirability of the bureaucratic ideal of universalism—hiring and promoting on the basis of performance ability (skills, competence, diligence, etc.) rather than on agreement to support the goals of the organization. We deplore particularism for several reasons. It goes against the values of a liberal society—that is, it yields racial or religious discrimination; it involves using public resources for the advantage of specific groups; it promotes inefficiency in organizations. But we also have been suggesting that much of the particularism we frown on is particularistic only if we think the goals of an organization should be other than what they are; from the point of view of those who control the organization, the criteria may really be universalistic and promote the efficiency of the organization. Better personnel practices, or standards, or screening criteria are irrelevant when only changes in the uses to which the organization is put would meet the criticisms. This is because organizations are tools designed to perform work for their masters, and particularism or universalism is relative to the goals of the masters. Because organizations generate power to get a variety of things done, people contend for that power, and favoritism and nepotism help to ensure loyalty to the contenders.

We also briefly touched on one other characteristic of bureaucracy—tenure, or the career principle; we argued that the costs of this principle, as seen in the frustration of dealing with incompetent personnel who have civil service protection or incompetent tenured professors, are more than made up for by its advantages. These include freedom from arbitrary authority, protection from changes in skill demands and declining ability, and assurance that one's investment in skills and experience will be secure. The bureaucratic model emphasizes efficiency in the long run, not the short run.

It is a tribute to the bureaucratic model as it developed since the Middle Ages that it has at least partially answered the problem of particularism and pursued it with vigor. Loyalty to the king or lord or chief was once everything; incompetence counted for little. With the rise of the university-educated scribes, jurists, and mathematicians, a class of presumably professional, neutral, and loyal personnel arose, the business administration students of yore.[10] The kings and chiefs could use these and get both competence and loyalty (through dependence) in their administration. The eunuch in the harem is the prototype of the modern professional; he can be trusted with everything except that which really counts—the uses to which the masters put the organization. We have come so far from the particularism of medieval days that nepotism and favoritism today are frowned on as both subversive and inefficient. A substantial residue of these practices remains in organizations simply because organizations, then as now, are tools in the hands of their masters; thus, control over them is a prize that many people seek. Particularism is one weapon in that struggle, but its use must be masked.

Feathering the Nest

Organizations generate a great deal of power and leverage in the social world, power and leverage far beyond their ostensible goals. But one problem of organizations is that they are very leaky vessels. It is quite easy for a member of one to use some of his or her power and leverage for personal ends rather than for the ends of the organization. (The ends of the organization, we may say for the present, are those of a small group at the top of the organization or, in many cases, a small group outside the organization that controls those at the top.) In the ideal world of the ideal bureaucracy, it should be possible to calculate neatly, and thus control, the relationship between a person's contribution to an organization and the rewards he or she receives. Theoretically, too, the rewards the organization has to pay should not exceed the contribution of the person. In practice, this is very difficult because it is hard to

control people so closely and because organizations have permeable boundaries. People tend to act as if they own their positions; they use them to generate income, status, and other things that rightfully belong to the organization. Bureaucracy has made great strides in reducing the discrepancy between people's contributions, on the one hand, and the inducements necessary to keep them in the organization and make them work, on the other.[11] During the period when bureaucracies were just beginning to form, this problem was most acute.

During the late Middle Ages, the king who wanted revenues from the land and from the people he controlled would sell a tax franchise to someone, generally a nobleman. This official would agree to pay the king a set fee; he was then free to collect as much money as he could from the people and keep anything beyond the set fee. The king benefited because he did not have to organize and maintain a large bureaucracy to collect taxes. However, the collector might extract such a heavy toll that the subjects would revolt. Or the basis of the economy might be ruined so that fewer and fewer taxes could be collected. Or the collector might become so rich that he could challenge the power of the king. Eventually, the king or the state took control of taxation, centralized it, hired personnel on a salaried basis to run the system, and used the army to back up the collectors. In this way, the imbalance between the effort and reward of the tax collector was markedly reduced. The tax collectors were paid what they were worth on the labor market at that time.

Today, we do not find tax collectors paying a franchise fee to the state to collect as much as they can, but problems still remain because government units are empowered to force people to pay taxes. This power is a source of leverage for the officeholder. For example, local assessors (who determine the value of property for taxation purposes) have been known to make deals with business firms or other interests such that certain property is assessed at a lower value than it would normally be. Then the assessors receive a percentage of the reduction from the organization that is being assessed. Internal revenue agents have been known to make deals with taxpayers whereby the latter's taxes are reduced and the agents get a portion of the savings. The Internal Revenue Service spends a good deal of money on various forms of surveillance to minimize this practice and to keep the agent from using the power of that organization for his or her private purposes.

The medieval system of selling franchises is still legally practiced in some of the less-organized areas of our economy. For example, small businesspeople, particularly doctors and dentists, "sell" delinquent accounts to a tax-collecting firm; the tax-collecting firm gives the businessperson, say, 40 percent of the value of the account and then keeps anything above that amount, if it is able to collect. Most businesses are wary of using all the powers legally or illegally at hand to collect debts because they do not want to alienate people who might be future customers or clients. For the tax-collecting firm, however, this is not a constraint, so their methods of extracting money from debtors are more severe.[12] Of course, the agencies also do not care whether the debtors feel that the debt is unjust or not. It is irrelevant to the agency if the debtors failed to pay their full bill because they were overcharged or because they did not receive the goods or services. Furthermore, agencies stand to gain a great deal by collecting all or 70 percent of the debt rather than 40 percent, so they pursue their task with vigor. Agencies also find it easier to extract money from the poorer and less well-educated strata of society since those with few resources are more easily intimidated.

Another example of ancient practices in the less well-organized and rationalized sectors of our economy is the selling of professional services. Normally, one thinks that a client goes to a doctor, dentist, or lawyer on a voluntary basis. However, for a number of reasons, clients do not have effective choice in these matters. In varying degrees, professionals have captive clients. There is not much competition among doctors, for example, because clients have few ways to judge doctors and have to consider geographical accessibility; also, doctors have restricted entry to their profession to keep the numbers low. If the patient has been going to a particular doctor for any period of time at all, she has a "sunk cost" in this relationship—the doctor knows her and has X rays and other records. What happens, then, when a doctor or lawyer or dentist retires or moves away? If it is a sizable practice at all, it will be "sold" to another professional. Indeed, if the professional dies, his or her bene-

ficiaries can sell the practice. Patients are not literally sold to the new buyer, of course, but in fact the new buyer has quite privileged access to them. Practices are put up for competitive bidding and go to the highest bidder. Of course, there is no guarantee of any relationship between ability and reward, since an incompetent doctor, for example, may be able to pay more for a practice than a good one. Given the highly entrepreneurial, even medieval, character of our independent professions, little was done until recently to rationalize or bureaucratize them in order to control the relationship between effort and reward.

However, rationalization of medical and legal services is beginning to appear as the demand for service has increased. Walk-in storefront medical clinics and law offices are opening; psychological counselors have formal ties with medical and legal professionals. Shopping-center emporiums with doctors, dentists, opticians, lawyers, accountants, tax experts, counselors, chaplains, chiropractors, and fitness experts will probably soon provide one-stop service for every conceivable personal need. We seem to have survived the loss of a personal relationship with our grocer or barber; we will probably accept, though not welcome, taking a number and standing in line for the next available professional. This is an efficient use of work power for the organizers of such groups, as for-profit hospital chains and franchises have learned. (The Kentucky Fried Chicken organization, for instance, has branched off into hospital franchises.)

The rationalization of professional services also reduces the occasions for the individual professional to feather his or her nest, though very likely at the expense of individualized service. The relationship between the effort the professional puts in and the reward he or she receives, open to abuse before such rationalization, is greatly controlled. But note that the consumer's definitions of effort and reward are no longer as potent; it is the entrepreneur who runs the service or the emporium who now sets the definition. Bureaucracy requires standardized inputs and outputs; after taking your number and waiting your turn for whichever professional is free, the professional will take note of your need and sort it into the nearest appropriate box for standard treatment, no exceptions please, in the interest of low fees and quick turnover. The relationship between effort and reward for the employee may be very rational, but for the consumer, an individualized, personal definition is lost. Why bureaucracy in the area of personalized services? Because most of us cannot afford the personalized attention, and our key needs would remain untended. We should not blame bureaucracy for not providing the personal services available only to the wealthy.

Once professionals have been bureaucratized, they will, like everyone else, seek to feather their nests from the copious amounts of down floating around in most organizations. Generally, such uses are simply taken for granted, as if they were fringe benefits written into the employment contract. No professor in his right mind (and they all have right minds in this regard) would think of buying his own paper, pencils, carbon paper, and so on to write a book from which he hopes to gain substantial income in the form of royalty. It does not occur to many professors that they should pay for the privilege of using a huge library that caters to their exotic tastes and allows them to keep books out for months or years without paying fines. Nor do many universities question a professor's use of secretarial time that is officially budgeted as an educational expense. When pressed, professors may insist that while they draw royalties on their books (which range from a few dollars a year to over $100,000), they are really contributing to the educational resources of society and that this is an inexpensive way to produce knowledge and teaching materials. This is true enough, but it is still remarkable that very few universities have attempted to require professors to pay back to the school some percentage of any outside income that comes from exploiting resources that are tax exempt or derived from students and, in public universities, from the taxpayers. A few have tried, and fewer actually do it; it meets with considerable resistance. In addition to royalties from books, there are the matters of lecture engagements and consulting jobs. A professor at a prestigious university is able to demand very high fees for consulting and lecturing and will get many opportunities to do these things. Since few prepare for these tasks only on Saturdays and Sundays, spending the other five days of the week busily teaching, these activities undoubtedly divert one from teaching duties.

Virtually all organizations offer opportunities to feather one's nest. Recall the dynamite that was readily taken from the gypsum mine described at the opening of this chapter. A more dramatic example is the scandals in the Chicago police department and other police departments in the early 1960s that were referred to as the "cops and/or robbers" syndrome. These scandals involved police officers who, by knowing when people were going to be away and when on-duty officers were not likely to be around, were able to burglarize stores and homes.

We may not expect a great deal of rectitude in police departments, but we might in voluntary hospitals supported by government funds, private donations, community chest funds, and, of course, patient fees. Nevertheless, I was not surprised to find that in some voluntary hospitals it was the custom for top-level administrators, physicians, and surgeons to receive expensive filets and other food from the hospital kitchens for use at home. Also, the maintenance staff occasionally remodeled or maintained the private houses of key executives, doctors, or board members. These illustrations may be trivial, but the principle is not. Organizations generate surpluses and leverage in our world, and those who have any power in them can use these for their own ends. The device of bureaucracy was designed to prevent *any but the masters* of the organization from doing this.

We might think that the more bureaucratized and rationalized the organization is, the less nest feathering will occur. This may be so, at least at the lower levels, but we have no research on the subject. However, to the extent that business and industrial organizations are among the most bureaucratized and rationalized, the generalization probably would not stand. Highly placed executives of business and industrial firms sometimes profit handsomely from giving lucrative contracts to suppliers in which they have invested their personal funds. These arrangements rarely become public because it is very difficult to gain such information. One did become public in 1960, when an aggressive stockholder pursued the matter with the Chrysler Corporation. Eventually, the president of Chrysler resigned, and, after being sued by the corporation, returned $450,000 to the company. He allegedly favored suppliers in whose firm he had a personal financial interest. (It is not often, however, that a stockholder with only a pittance of stock can bring down the administrative head of a large corporation.) Perhaps the reason that such an "unbureaucratic" practice could occur in a highly bureaucratized firm is that, as Max Weber noted long ago, the top of an organization is never bureaucratized. It always belongs to somebody. In this case, though, the board of directors and stockholders insisted that the organization was also theirs; it did not belong just to the president.

The practice of feathering one's nest in large part reflects the problem of separating the interests of the person from the interests of the organization. In our organizational society, this becomes increasingly difficult. For example, to whom does the experience of an employee belong? Does it belong to him or her or to the organization in which that experience was acquired? The growth of bureaucracy was equivalent to putting a label of "company property" on the skills, experience, and creativity of the employee. It is a measure of our socialization into a society of bureaucratic organizations that we no longer question this extraction at all in the case of blue-collar workers and most white-collar ones. But consider industry at the turn of the century. Most of the work in the large, mass-producing factories and mills (except textiles, which had been "rationalized" long before) was done by work crews that were recruited, organized, and paid by independent contractors.[13] They used the company's facilities, supplies, and tools but worked under yearly contracts to produce so many rifle barrels or parts of sewing machines or whatever. The contractors sometimes made very large profits and paid their workers presumably what the market would bear, or more likely, what the local custom dictated. The system was apparently quite efficient—technological changes were rapidly introduced and were in the interests of the contractors. It flourished in factories producing highly engineered products on a mass basis. Owners supplied the capital and organized the final assembly and marketing.

The genius of F. W. Taylor and others in the scientific management movement . . . was to convince the owners that they should employ engineers to go around and find out how the men and women drilled the rifle barrels or made the gears for machine tools or cast the locomotive parts, centralize this information and study it, then break the tasks down into small parts so as to remove as much of the skill and accumulated experience as possible, hire a foreman who would supervise the crew for a wage, and assign the highly specialized "deskilled" tasks to the workers and pay them at a much lower wage rate. The owners "expropriated" the craft skills and craft system and designated as company property the ingenuity, experience, and creativity of the workers. Only now are we beginning to painfully rediscover and recommend giving back to the workers a small part of what had been their own property, in the form of such schemes as job enlargement, workers' participation, workers' autonomy, and group incentives.

What was settled for workers and most managers long ago (sometimes through bloody strikes)[14] still appears for top executives and scientists in new fields today. What happens when a team of researchers, or an executive and three or four subordinates who have been working together for a long time, leave the organization? At least two issues are involved. One is the charge that the leader raided the company by taking the subordinates along, since they had been trained by the organization; the other is the knowledge of the technology, business operations, market strategies, and so forth developed within the organization and now taken elsewhere. In both cases, the organization loses heavily. Such incidents have become frequent enough to produce a number of court rulings. The principles are still obscure, but in general the court has been ruling in favor of the former firm in requiring, for example, that the departing manager or scientist not work in the same product area for a period of five years. If he or she goes to work for firm B, after having worked in firm A, and firm B comes out with a product that is similar to the one he or she was working on in firm A, firm A can sue firm B on the grounds that the person left A with specific knowledge and gave it to B.

The executive and the subordinates need not go to another established firm, taking with them the fruit of years of experimentation, trial, gestation, and stimulation. They may start their own company. In one case, an engineer for IBM took thirty-six people with him and started a competing company that made integrated circuits for memory cores for large computers. IBM sued. Even if a large firm had little hope of winning such a suit, it could help persuade other employees that it is not wise to leave with so many company-provided resources in their hands. It is a measure of our organizational society that the courts are able to rule in favor of the organization rather than the creative individual.[15]

The case of the scientist who decides that what she has in her head belongs to her and not to the organization, even though organizational resources were used to develop it, is a borderline case in the basic question of who owns the office. As such it is illuminating. For there is no intrinsic difference between such a case and one in which an executive makes sure that the supplier in which he has a financial interest gets contracts from his company, even though that supplier's products may be inferior. In both cases, the organization provides a resource, which is then exploited by the individual for his or her own benefit and to the disadvantage of the organization. It does not matter whether the organization is considered a socially valuable one or whether the individual is moral or immoral. We are stuck with the organizational logic of our time; the official does not own his or her office—as Weber put it, and as the gypsum-plant employees and countless other workers discovered. The organization takes precedence over the individual.

Stated thusly, we are likely to deplore this concept. But as consumers of the goods and services of many organizations, we are likely to applaud it. Why bureaucracy if it takes precedence over the individual? Because our society has developed no alternative method of flooding us with goods and services just as cheaply.

"There Ought to Be a Rule"

We have looked at several criticisms of bureaucracy and argued that some of its supposed sins have more to do with the uses to which organizations are put than any inherent evil and others are only abuses from the point of view of special interests, not the organization as a whole. But the weaknesses of bureaucracy considered so far are rather minor. Rules and red tape, hierarchy, and conservatism are more frequently identified as sins and considered more serious. First let us take the criticism that bureaucracies have too many rules.

A multitude of rules and regulations appears to be the very essence of a bureaucracy.

The term "red tape" adequately conveys the problem. Rules govern everything; one cannot make a move unless one does it by the book or, to use military slang, by the numbers. Every office in every department has seen to it that its autonomy is protected by rules. An attempt to change one rule immediately runs into the problem that half a dozen other rules are connected to it; to change these, a geometric proportion of additional rules will be affected, and so on.

While it is obvious that some rules are needed in organizations, it is generally felt that most organizations have far too many rules. How might these be eliminated?

Reducing Rules

There are a number of ways to reduce the number of rules. One way is to mechanize as much as possible. A typewriter eliminates the need for rules about the size and clarity of script and the way letters will be formed. Rules on these matters were common before the appearance of typewriters. Any machine is a complex bundle of rules that are built into the machine itself. Machines ensure standardized products, thus eliminating rules regarding dimensional characteristics. They ensure even output time; they also indicate precisely what kind of material can be fed into them. The larger the machine, the more people it presumably replaces, and this eliminates rules about how workers are to interact, cooperate, and coordinate their activities. The thoroughly automated factory, of which we have none as yet, would be one with few or no written rules or regulations.

Another way to cut down on the number of rules is to insist on near uniformity of personnel in an organization. If we could hire people with the same physical characteristics, intelligence, amount of self-discipline, personality traits, and so on, we would need far fewer rules to govern the range of differences that we usually observe among personnel. If none of them had families, ever got sick, or needed vacations, and if all were thoroughly trained before they arrived at the office, plant, or agency, matters would also be simplified greatly. But, for the lack of a robot, we have people and thus rules.

If we could seal the organization off from its environment so that nothing ever affected it, we would need very few rules regarding relationships with the environment. We would also need few or no rules regarding changes in procedures—because nothing would change. Once things were started in the proper manner, they could run that way forever. Finally, if we could produce only simple products in our organizations, rather than complex ones in various sizes, shapes, and colors and with a lot of custom-made attributes, this would eliminate the need for a lot of rules.

As these comments suggest, we might not care for organizations that eliminate the need for rules—they would be rather dull, mechanized, and inflexible. Rules are needed in organizations when complexity increases due to variability in personnel, customers, environment, techniques of producing the goods and services, and so on. When these matters are complex, it is not possible to allow personnel to "do their own thing," no matter how much we might prefer that. And every time variability in handling personnel is introduced by these complexities, rules are required to limit the discretion of those with power to handle people under them. There will be rules about favoritism and nepotism and discrimination on irrelevant grounds, rules about transferring people, rules about expectations regarding pay, promotion, accrued leave, and so on.

Of course, rules in the sense of formal written procedures can be essentially eliminated, thus giving the impression of a place that operates with few rules, even though the impression is bound to be mistaken. Wilfred Brown, an experienced and successful manager, discussed this matter at some length in connection with the English industrial firm of which he was president:

> Many managers feel that "freedom" lies in the sort of situation where their supervisor says to them: "There are not many regulations in this place. You will understand the job in a month or two, and you make your own decisions. No red tape—you are expected to take command; make the decisions off your own bat as they arise I am against a lot of rules or regulations, and we do not commit too much to paper." In my experience a manager in such a situation has virtually no "freedom to act" at all. He starts making decisions and his boss sends for him to say: "Look here, Jones, I am sorry to tell you that you have made two rather serious mistakes in the course of reorganizing your work. You have promoted one man to supervisor who is not the next man due for promotion in the factory, and you

have engaged five additional machinists, a decision you should have referred to me because we have some surplus men in this category in an adjacent factory." Now Jones might well say: "You said there were no regulations but, in fact, you have already mentioned the existence of two; one concerned with promotion and the other with increase of establishment. Please detail these regulations to me precisely, so that I can work to them in future, and let me know now of any further regulations which bear upon my work."

In practice, Jones probably says nothing of the kind, because he does not think in this way; to him regulations are stumbling blocks in the path of those wishing to display initiative. He will proceed, over the years, to learn, by making mistakes, of the whole array of regulations which, by the very nature of Executive Systems, do in fact exist. His boss will have to say to him frequently: "Yes, Jones, freedom for subordinates to act on their own is the policy here, but surely it must have been obvious that you should have seen me before doing *that*." Jones is thus in a situation where he does not know what decisions he can or cannot make, and when in doubt he is likely to follow a course of doing nothing at all. In three years he will have got through this difficult period; he will know when he can or cannot act, because he has learn[ed] by testing what his boss was unable to give him in writing—*the prescribed component of his job*. Thereafter, Jones will be a staunch supporter of the "no-red-tape" policy, and so the situation will continue.

It is much more efficient to delineate as precisely as possible to a new subordinate all of the regulations he must observe and then say: "You must take all the decisions that seem to you to be required, so long as you keep within the bounds of that policy. If, keeping within those bounds, you take decisions which I think you should have referred to me, then I cannot criticize; for such a happening implies that some part of the policy [by] which I wish you to operate has not been disclosed to you. I must, then, formulate that policy and add it to the prescribed content of your job." If, in addition, the manager can give his subordinate a rounded idea of the discretionary component of his job by stating the types of decisions which he must make, then that subordinate is in a real position to act on his own initiative in the prescribed area.

I have found, however, particularly in discussing jobs with external applicants, that the array of policy represented by our Policy Document, Standing Orders and Directives, causes people to assume the precise opposite of the real situation, i.e., that this extant written policy will deprive them of the right to make decisions. In fact, it is only by delineating the area of "freedom" in this way that a subordinate knows when he can make decisions. The absence of written policy leaves him in a position where any decision he takes, however apparently trivial, may infringe [upon] an unstated policy and produce a reprimand.[16]

Professionalization and Rules. Buying and installing machines, as indicated above, is one way to reduce the number of rules in an organization. The rules are built into the machine itself, and the organization pays for those rules when it buys the machine. A quite similar means to reduce the number of written rules is to "buy" personnel who have complex rules built into them. We generally call these people professionals. Professionals, such as engineers and scientists, psychiatrists, doctors, social workers, teachers, and professors, are trained on the outside, usually at great public expense, and a large number of rules are inculcated into them. They bring these to the organization and are expected to act on them without further reference to their skills. While accounting practices differ more widely than some might expect, accountants in general are expected to be familiar with the rules and techniques of accounting. Doctors know when they should give certain drugs or what kinds of drugs should not be given to certain kinds of people; medicine is a complex body of rather imperfect rules. Professors, through long, arduous, and heroic training, learn rules about plagiarism in their writing, truth in their teaching, and deference to their more senior colleagues.

Professionals, like machines, cost a lot of money. There is a high initial investment in training that someone must pay, and the care and feeding of machines and professionals is expensive. Therefore, we tend to use them only when the economies are apparent or when there is no real choice. We charge more for services produced by complex machines or professionals than simple ones— other things, such as volume of production, being equal. It costs more to go to Harvard or to an outstanding hospital than it does to attend a city college or go to a substandard hospital. Were we able to thoroughly routin-

ize the tasks performed by professionals and get around the restrictions that professionals are able to place on their positions, we would substitute machines for them. We are trying, for better or worse, with computerized teaching.

Expressive Groups. One other example of a way to avoid rules in an organization is rare but interesting. This involves organizations where all members agree on the goals of the organization (or, to put it more accurately, where the goals of the individual members are identical) and the techniques for achieving these goals are within the ability of all members. In such cases, few or no rules are required. Each will do his or her own thing, but this will fit with the thing of all other members. Such organizations are generally quite small and usually oriented around expressive needs. Few organizations have members solely on this basis. Most of the so-called voluntary associations rely on services to the members for which members pay in one form or another through dues, allowing their name to be used, or doing some work.[17] Since most voluntary associations provide services to members, they, like other organizations, also have a proliferation of rules and regulations.

Interdepartmental Regulations

So far we have been talking about rules with respect to the whole organization. A quite different dimension of rules appears when we examine the relationships among units in an organization. Here many rules are clearly the basis of self-protection, predictability, and autonomy. Take the matter of distribution requirements in a university. The rule that students shall take a certain number of credits in various departments exists because students are not homogeneous when they enter the university; all cannot be expected to "know their own best interests." Only some would be motivated enough, the argument goes, to sample the sciences if they are majoring in the humanities or to sample the humanities if they are in the sciences, so a rule is promulgated. However, the matter does not end there. Departments, knowing there will be a big influx of students into their courses, want to control which courses the students come into. So they set rules regarding which courses are to be utilized for distribution requirements. This protects departmental autonomy and provides scheduling benefits and staffing economies. To change these rules when the characteristics of students or advances of knowledge have changed may prove to be quite difficult because a host of other practices have grown up in the department that depend on the designation of certain courses appropriate for distribution requirements. For example, perhaps only instructors and assistant professors are assigned to teach these courses. Also, majors may be steered into more high-level courses where enrollment is kept down. A dean who attempts to force the department to make what seems to be eminently sensible changes from her point of view, or the point of view of the students or other departments, may run into serious opposition from the department. The change would threaten the department's whole fragile structure of work assignments and course requirements. The department might turn around in retaliation and change some of its rules on its own. For example, it might limit the enrollment in certain courses. Soon, if not immediately, a first-class *political* situation has evolved that has little to do with the original problem and can be solved only by bargaining. But bargaining threatens the status quo, involves other departments, and ramifies the changes. Because rules protect interests, and groups are interdependent, changing the rules is difficult.

Rules are like an invisible skein that bundles together all the technological and social aspects of organizations. As such, rules stem from past adjustments and seek to stabilize the present and future. When things are different in the future, an attempt to change these tough, invisible threads means that all kinds of practices, bargains, agreements, and payoffs will tumble out of the web and must be stuffed back in again. As a result of these kinds of interdependencies, changes in organizational rules (which go on continuously, if only informally)[18] are generally incremental—a little bit here and there. The hope is that somehow the whole structure of the organization will gradually, painlessly, and, most of all, *covertly* change over time. It generally does.

In sum, rules protect those who are subject to them. Rules are means of preserving group autonomy and freedom; to reduce the number of rules in an organization generally means to make it more impersonal, more inflexible, more standardized. But even given this, rules are still a bore. We would all prefer to be free of them, or so it would seem. Actually, only *some* rules are bores. The good, effective rules are rarely noticed; the bad ones stand out. Bad rules are inevitable. Some merely reflect the fact that people make rules, and people are not generally geniuses. The problem is not rules in general, but particular ones that need changing.

Rules as Scapegoats

Rules are the scapegoats for a variety of organizational problems. Complaints about excessive rules or bad rules generally are symptomatic of more deep-seated problems that cannot be solved by changing rules. During the unhappy days of the breakdown in telephone service in New York in 1969–1970, a number of "stupid" rules surfaced and were held to have caused the difficulties. Actually, the difficulties appeared to be that the system was designed so that it would operate with a good deal of inefficiency and slack. Such an operation is easy when an organization has a monopoly and, despite the lack of risk, a guaranteed high rate of return. Savings from technical advances need not result in significant rate decreases, but simply in more inefficient ways of doing business—which is, after all, the easiest route. No one in the company gets upset, and since the public is uninformed and the rate-setting agencies are weak and generally captives of the utilities, the lack of rate reduction is not noticed. (The same appears to be true for the gas and electric utilities, which also are very profitable, inefficiently regulated monopolies.) When greater demands were made on the company than it could fulfill, it became apparent that, for example, the business-office side of the company in the New York area was not talking to the plant or operations side; both hid under a complex set of rules and regulations that governed their interrelationship and the operations within each of the divisions. As long as there was sufficient "fat," or surplus, in the system, it did not matter; when more efficiency was needed to meet demand for services, these inefficiencies surfaced, and rules got the blame. The rules were not bad in themselves. For example, they probably reduced contact and thus antagonisms between the operations and customer-service branches. A more efficient operation would require more contact, however, and under these situations the rules were inappropriate. But the whole premise on which the system operated would have to be changed; rules would be only one aspect that would be changed.

In a similar fashion, hidebound government bureaucracies are not unresponsive to their clients because of their rules but because of the premises they operate on and the system designed around those premises. The New York public school system[19] and the Bureau of Indian Affairs are two outstanding examples. In both cases, professionals have captured the organization and made it too difficult or expensive for policy makers—board members, staff of the Secretary of the Interior, politicians, and the like—to wrest control and change practices. The incredible rules of these agencies are only by-products and symptoms of a commonplace fact of organization life: those who can will seize control of an organization and use it for their own ends—in these cases security, power, and expansion.

As we noted above, good rules are often those that are rarely noticed. They may be written down or just a matter of custom, but they are rarely challenged. They simply make sense. Some other good rules are those that cut the Gordian knots that inevitably bind organized endeavors of any complexity. Frequently, there is no clear ground for doing A instead of B; both will have unpleasant outcomes. Rather than agonize over a decision, a rule cuts the knot. Another function of good rules is to justify unpleasant decisions or actions. "Sorry, old boy, but I will have to discipline you for that." "I know it's not fair, from your point of view, but it's the rule." "It took a lot of extra work, and I made some enemies in the agency, but the rule is that these kinds of clients are entitled to more service." Without the rules, these necessary but unpleasant actions might not be taken.

The greatest problem with rules is that organizations and their environments change faster than the rules. Most bad rules were once good, designed for a situation that no longer exists. Nepotism was apparently a problem in university departments of the past, when they were dominated by one man who made all the decisions as to what the courses would be, what texts would be used, who was to be hired and who promoted. It was easy to extend this power by putting one's wife on the staff. Today, departmental chairpersons have much less power, and there are more finely graded criteria for per-

formance. Yet, as more women once again come into the academic job market and have husbands who are also teachers, the nepotism rule becomes more burdensome and discriminatory. It is often stoutly defended, though, by those who resent women professors anyway, since they are a threat to male hegemony.

In sum, "there ought to be a rule" is as valid as saying "there are too damn many rules around here." Rules do a lot of things in organizations: they protect as well as restrict; coordinate as well as block; channel effort as well as limit it; permit universalism as well as provide sanctuary for the inept; maintain stability as well as retard change; permit diversity as well as restrict it. They constitute the organizational memory and the means for change. As such, rules in themselves are neither good nor bad, nor even that important. It is only because they are easy scapegoats for other problems that are more difficult to divine and analyze that we have to spend this much time on them. Social scientists, no less than the person in the street, love to denounce them and to propose ruleless organizations. But ruleless organizations are likely to be either completely automated, if they are efficient and have much output, or completely professionalized, turning out expensive and exotic services. Only a tiny fraction of organizations fit either case.

"Who's in Charge Around Here?"

For many social scientists, rules are a nuisance, but the existence of a hierarchical ordering of offices and authority is a barely tolerable evil. The principle of hierarchical ordering of offices and authority says that for every person there shall be one person above to whom he or she primarily reports and from whom he or she primarily receives direction. The organization is structured in the form of a pyramid, with the top controlling everything. Power is centralized. Though all aspects of bureaucracy—rules, universalism, impersonality, tenure, and stability—are criticized, hierarchy, the most characteristic aspect of bureaucracy, is judged its worst. It is the negation of individual autonomy, freedom, spontaneity, creativity, dignity, and independence.

The Collegial University

When we think of organizations with elaborate hierarchies, we often have the government and its bureaus in mind, or perhaps the large corporation. Professional organizations, according to theory, are not so arranged—colleagues are at more or less the same level.[20] I would probably be considered a professional, being a full professor of sociology in a university, so let us see what I might have had to go through at the University of Wisconsin in 1970 order to make a suggestion, take up an issue, make a complaint, or whatever, if I wished to touch all bases. Theoretically, I would first go to the assistant chairman of my department, who would send the matter on to the chairman. The chairman might wish to consult with the departmental executive committee to be on "solid ground" before proceeding. The departmental chairman would then take it up with one of the appropriate assistant deans (there were eight to choose from) in the College of Letters and Science, who would refer it to one of the associate deans (there were four of them), who would take it up with the dean of the College of Letters and Science (there are Colleges of Agriculture, Engineering, etc., each of which has its dean and associate and assistant deans). If the matter involved the graduate program at all, it would next go to one of the two assistant deans, and then to one of the five associate deans of the Graduate School; then it would be taken up with the dean of the Graduate School (who would, of course, confer with the dean of the pertinent college). The Graduate School dean might consult with a student-faculty committee in the process. After that, it would be taken up by one of the two assistants to the chancellor, who would refer it to one of the two vice-chancellors, who would take it up with the chancellor of the Madison campus (there are other campuses—Milwaukee, Green Bay, and Parkside among them). The chancellor of the Madison campus would send it along to one of the vice-presidents of the university (he had seven to choose from), who would take it up with the president of the university. If the matter were still unresolved and had not lost its power of ascent, the president would take it up with the university's regents. They, in turn, might have to refer to the State Coordinating Council for Higher Education (which has several staff layers of its own). It, though, receives its power from the legislature, whose actions can be vetoed by the governor. Were the matter important enough to go as far as the Coordinating Council, it would have gone through five major levels of authority, each with about three internal levels of authority, for a total of at least fifteen steps in the staircase.

Of course, it is not that simple. We have assumed that the matter did not involve any of the numerous other fiefdoms in the university, which is highly unlikely. There are numerous councils, committees, divisional organizations (e.g., a chairman of social studies), administrative units (such as the admissions office with its director, associate director, and four assistant directors), the libraries (an Egyptian-sized pyramid in itself), a jumble of business offices, the computing center, counseling services, and offices concerned with public relations, parking, physical plant, protection and security, purchasing, registration, student affairs, and so on—each of which could be involved. A professor has occasion to deal with all of these at times. In addition, much power is exercised by the campus university committee, the senate, the all-university faculty assembly, the university faculty council, the course committee, the divisional executive committee, the social studies committee of the graduate school, the research committee, the honors committee, various student-faculty committees (at the time an area of exponential growth in form, though with little substance), and various all-university committees. These committees plug the interstitial areas of the fifteen levels above me very effectively and relieve all the assistant deans or whatever of their backbreaking loads.

Of course, even with fifteen levels of authority and a tropical jungle of committee growth to go through to get to the top, I would not be at the bottom of the heap. Below me are strung out the associate professors, assistant professors, instructors, lecturers, teaching assistants, graduate students, and, somewhere down there, undergraduates. This is not a chain of command; undergraduates have been known to talk directly to full professors without going through a teaching assistant, for example. But these levels come into operation in numerous ways. For example, if two full professors desire the same office, the one who has been "in rank" longer will generally get it. We cannot really add six more levels below a full professor in terms of authority, though we can in terms of status.

In addition, I might have a secretary, research assistant, undergraduate workstudy assistants, and graduate student trainees in a training program—that is, another little empire. (I have left out the enormous informal power of the head secretary of the department, other directors of training programs or of the graduate program, renowned colleagues, and those who somehow just manage to amass power.) Just to grasp this social structure intellectually, let alone maneuver it, is a demanding task.[21]

So much for the myth that the university is a collegial body having a minimum of hierarchy and status difference. Nor should one assume that other professional bodies, such as the medical staff of a hospital or the U.S. Senate, also enjoy the advantages of lack of hierarchy. The medical personnel in hospitals are generally highly organized in a structure that parallels that of the administrative staff of the hospital. The medical staff has its own nursing committee, outpatient department committee, pharmacy committee, and so forth, and in between the major ranks of junior and senior attending staff are several clear distinctions in grade, with appropriate powers and entrance criteria.[22] The U.S. Senate is also more highly structured than one would expect on the basis of the contrast between bureaucratic and professional organizations, and it takes a new senator a long time to learn all the aspects of this structure. Even law firms are highly structured.[23] Indeed, any group with a division of labor, professional or not, will be hierarchically structured.

The Sins of Hierarchy

What is the consequence of this ubiquitous structuring of even "professional" organizations? For the critics of bureaucracy, the consequence is that the bulk of people in the lower and middle levels are prevented from really giving their all for goal achievement; they turn, instead, into infantile, fearful robots. The argument runs like this:

The hierarchy promotes rigidity and timidity. Subordinates are afraid of passing bad news up the ladder[24] or of suggesting changes.[25] (Such an action would imply that their superiors should have thought of the changes and did not.) They also are more afraid of new situations than of familiar ones, since with the new situations, those above them might introduce new evils, while the old ones are sufficient. The hierarchy promotes delays and sluggishness; everything must be kicked upstairs for a decision either because the boss insists or because the subordinate does not want to risk making a poor decision. All this indecision exists at the same time that superiors are being authoritarian, dictatorial, and rigid, making snap judgments that they refuse to reconsider, implementing on-the-spot decision without consulting their subordinates, and generally stifling any independence or creativity at the subordinate levels. Subordinates are under constant surveillance from superiors; thus they often give up trying to exercise initiative or imagination and instead suppress or distort information. Finally, since everything must go through channels, and these are vertical, two people at the same level in two different departments cannot work things out themselves but must involve long lines of superiors.

At this point one may wonder how organizations can function at all, but it becomes even more alarming when we consider a contrasting series of complaints frequently made by members of a hierarchy. These are complaints about people in one department making decisions that affect other units without checking first with their respective superiors, and about the *lack* of clear lines of authority, the *failure* to exercise authority or to be decisive, and the *lack* of accountability. Some typical complaints:

1. Who's in charge here? Who am I supposed to take this matter to?

2. That bureau gets away with murder; no one will exercise authority over it, and it is not clear what their authority is supposed to be.

3. Some technician in engineering went ahead and made these design changes in conjunction with a department head in production, but they never bothered to check with the sales manager or the account supervisor in finance.

4. We make changes, and before we can see how well they are working out, we are making more changes.

5. What this place lacks is decisive leadership.

6. No one told me.

In such cases we hear of too much flexibility, too little attention to the hierarchy, too little forceful decision making. According to one survey,[26] managers in industrial firms are decidedly in favor of more, rather than less, clarity in lines of authority, rules, duties, specification of procedures, and so on. Only when the structure is clear can authority be delegated, they indicate, as did Wilfred Brown (see p. [37]).

If both the presence and the absence of hierarchy can be faulted, and if authority can be both excessive and absent, change too rapid and too infrequent, employees both fearful and aggressive, gutless and crafty, and flexible and rigid, the problem may not lie in hierarchy per se. Some degree of hierarchy is needed in any organized endeavor, but how much and in what kinds of endeavors? We are only beginning to phrase the problem in this fashion, and to get a glimpse of how hierarchies actually work.

Research on Span of Control

Take the matter of "span of control"—the number of subordinates whom a superior directly controls. This is the building block of hierarchy. If each superior controls few people—has a narrow span of control—there will be many levels in the organization; if he or she controls many, there will be few. For twenty to thirty years, social scientists and management theorists debated regarding the optimum span of control—was it four, six, eight, or what? If only we knew, we could design our organizations properly. Embedded in this discussion was the assumption that if a manager had many people under her, she could not supervise them closely, and thus they would have more autonomy.[27] This assumption was furthered in an influential piece of reporting by a personnel officer with Sears Roebuck who described how morale and efficiency improved when the number of levels in the organization was reduced.[28]

Of course, as is true of most "principles" of organization, there was an alternative view—rarely stated as a principle, but acted on by management consulting firms. This principle said that if a manager had a lot of people reporting to him, he was centralizing power and would not want to give it up. Such a manager should establish an intermediate level in order to give his subordinates some leeway. A wide span of control meant reluctance to delegate, rather than delegation.

Few theorists took the rule-of-thumb wisdom of the management consultants seriously, however. One of the best theorists, for example, is Peter Blau. He and his associates conducted a study of 156 public personnel agencies, starting with "a few plausible considerations" that led to inferences "which appeared straightforward and perhaps even self-evident." They reasoned that if a person was well trained, he or she would need little supervision. The span of control would be wide. If personnel were not well trained, they would need more supervision, and the span of control would be narrow and the hierarchy higher. (In the language of journal articles, it reads like this: The inferences suggested, "as an initial hypothesis, that expert requirements decrease the ratio of managerial to nonsupervisory personnel in organizations, which widens the average span of control."[29])

To the admitted surprise of Blau and associates, the hypothesis was found to be incorrect. The more qualified the people, the *less* the span of control. They then suggested that the explanation might be that a narrow span of control—only two or three subordinates per superior—allows easy consultation on difficult problems and permits common problem solving. Though they did not state it directly, this would suggest that wide spans of control could mean close supervision but little consultation.

Actually, as is so true in much of organizational research, the resolution of the dilemma lies in distinguishing different types of organizations or situations. In some cases, a span of control of ten can mean close supervision through highly routinized controls over people performing routine tasks; in others, it can mean very little supervision, with the ten subordinates working out things with each other and only occasionally seeking the advice or direction of the boss.[30] The span of control, then, can be independent of the closeness of supervision. Supervision can be direct or indirect with either a wide or a narrow span of control.

The span of control, in turn, affects the degree of hierarchy, or the number of levels of supervision in an organization. Where spans of control are wide, the organization tends to be "squat"—there are not many levels of authority. Where spans of control are narrow, the organization tends to have a narrow, "tall" hierarchy, with many levels of authority. But we have argued that a squat organization does not necessarily mean either close or distant supervision. There are a number of factors that might affect the closeness of supervision (beyond, of course, the personality and leadership style of a manager), and they are worth listing to indicate the complexity of the matter:

1. The degree to which tasks are routine or nonroutine.

2. The difference between the expertise of the manager and that of his or her subordinates; the amount of interdependence among tasks under one manager; and the interdependence of these tasks with those performed under different managers.

3. The interdependence of the department as a whole with other departments in the organization, and the varying kinds of routine and nonroutine mixes of the departments.

4. The degree to which written rules and regulations or machines can reduce the need for personal supervision.

5. The extent to which flexibility and rapid response is necessary to the organization.

Given these relevant sources of variation, it remains to be seen whether, as Blau maintains, the relationship they suggested between span of control and supervision is likely to hold in all organizations.

Using the same data, Marshall Meyer concludes that there are two strategies available to organizations—control through direct supervision, utilizing a wide span of control, which promotes flexibility of response since the manager can change things quickly; and control through rules, regulations, and professional expertise, utilizing a greater number of hierarchical levels with a narrow span of control, which promotes more "rational" administration and more stable operations.[31] Blau also concludes that there are two types of organizations, but he labels the first the "old-fashioned bureaucracy." It has a "squat hierarchy with authority centralized at the top," little automation, and personnel rules that emphasize managerial discretion, seniority, and personal judgment. The second he calls the "modern organization" with a "tall, slim

hierarchy with decentralized authority," relying upon experts, automation, and universalistic personnel procedures (objective merit standards).[32]

Meyer's data show only weak support for Blau's conclusions; the differences between the two types of strategies are in the predicted direction but are quite small. The important thing, however, is that they are *not* in the *opposite* direction; that is, the usual view of hierarchy would indicate that the higher the degree of hierarchy the greater the centralized control.[33] But that does not hold here. If anything, the greater hierarchy is associated with decentralization. Blau handles his data somewhat differently and finds somewhat stronger relationships, but more important, he finds the relationships consistent over three types of organizations: personnel departments, finance departments, and state employment agencies. Thus, even though the differences may not be large in any one sample, the consistency over the three is impressive.

Furthermore, a quite independent and large study in England, generally referred to as the Aston study because the team, headed by Derek Pugh, was then at the University of Aston in Birmingham, came to very similar conclusions.[34] In the Blau and the Aston studies, the gap between the indicators used and the concepts these indicators were supposed to represent is often very large. For example, the items that are used to measure the degree of delegation of authority, or decentralization, refer only to decisions that are visible, binary (either-or), and capable of clear statement in official rules, such as the level at which a certain amount of money can be spent without prior authorization. More subtle, basic, and certainly more powerful decisions are not measured; these may be quite centralized. We refer to this as the problem of "operationalization," or making the measurement of concepts operational. The operationalization of the concept of hierarchy in the Aston study was particularly controversial. Nevertheless, one can have some confidence in the findings of the Blau and Aston studies for three important reasons: (1) they are independently arrived at, using different measures; (2) they were unexpected by both research teams; and (3) they are counterintuitive.

In short, we cannot assume that the more hierarchical the organization, the more centralized it is. If the limited data show anything, they indicate an inverse relationship. More important, the very characteristics that both Blau and Meyer ascribe to their tall, hierarchical, and decentralized organizations are those that Weber stressed in his bureaucratic model: expertise, written rules and regulations, clear ordering of positions, and hierarchy. The characteristics of the squat centralized organization are personal rule, personal evaluations, and low expertise. These are closer to the traditional model, which the development of bureaucracy attempted to supplant.

Hierarchy and Timidity

Another attribute often associated with tall hierarchies is timidity and caution on the part of subordinates who fear criticism from superiors and thus hesitate to pass unpleasant information up the line. That such an attitude exists in bureaucracies is clear, but that it is an inevitable concomitant of hierarchy, and thus its product, is far from evident. Timidity and caution appear to vary greatly among bureaucracies, on the basis of casual impressions. Peter Blau, in his study of two government agencies, commented that he found little evidence of this behavior.[35] It certainly does not show up among the more successful managers in Dalton's study,[36] nor among all managers in Gouldner's study.[37] Why, then, the variation?

It would seem that tendencies toward conservatism and self-protective behavior are natural outcomes of all organized activity that is not spontaneously coordinated and based on wholehearted cooperation. But it also would appear that organizations have mechanisms to minimize the danger and even reverse these tendencies. For example, people can be rewarded for passing critical items of information up the hierarchy; the reward may have to be high if it reflects on one's superior, but if it is that important to the organization it can be done. Actually, the opposite is sometimes a problem—a person gets ahead by showing up the superior. Between these two instances—timidity and cunning—there is the far more usual situation in which constructive criticisms are encouraged and rewarded because the boss can take the credit. Accounting departments are generally rewarded for critical information, which is why, in the organization Dalton studied, it was so essential for aggressive managers to neutralize or bribe the accountants. Innovative and risk-taking behavior may be harder to reward than conservative behavior, but it is possible to do it.

Timidity and caution appear to be functions of the technology and market of organizations, rather than of their degree of hierarchy. In some market situations—for example, Social Security administration, aid to dependent children, railroads, public utilities, mining (especially in such oligopolistic situations as sulfur mining)—there is little perceived need for risk taking. In other large and equally bureaucratic organizations—the Agency for International Development in its golden days of the late 1950s and early 1960s, the federal rehabilitation agencies during the 1950s and early 1960s, which used the money dumped on them by an uncomprehending Congress to upgrade physically healthy but untrained blacks, and the electronics and chemical industries—risk taking is much more in evidence. There is no evidence that these organizations had fewer levels of authority than more conservative organizations.

Still, problems remain. Some officials do insist that a great many minor matters be brought to their attention before action is taken. The explanation may be that they are poor or insecure administrators or have incompetent subordinates. This happens all the time, but it can hardly be attributed to hierarchy alone. Sometimes it is impossible to get an answer out of a higher officer; the explanation may simply be that he does not know and unfortunately will not admit it, or that he is still searching, or that he is perhaps hoping that the lower officer will go ahead and make the decision (and take the blame if it is wrong). But someone has to decide, and the principle of hierarchy at least specifies *who* should decide if ambiguity exists. Wilfred Brown observes that the principal function of a hierarchy is to resolve disputes or uncertainties; things go on well enough without slavishly going through channels if there is no dispute and no uncertainty.[38]

The Official and the Unofficial Hierarchical Order

One of the true delights of the organizational expert is to indicate to the uninitiated the wide discrepancy between the official hierarchy (or rules, for that matter) and the unofficial one. It is a remarkable phenomenon in many cases and well known to most people who spend their working lives as managers in organizations. Departmental secretaries in many universities have power far beyond their status. David Mechanic's well-known essay, "Sources of Power of Lower Participants in Complex Organization," touches on this and other examples.[39] Melville Dalton, in his excruciatingly unsettling study of a manufacturing plant, reveals top people with no power and those three or four levels below with extensive power.[40] Sociologists have been particularly fond of the contrast between the official and the unofficial because it indicates that organizations are natural systems rather than artificial or mechanistic ones—living things that the people within them create out of their own needs, rather than rational tools in the hands of a master. They are right, of course: between the conception and the reality, as the poet tells us, falls the shadow. The first thing the new employee should learn is who is really in charge, who has the goods on whom, what are the major debts and dependencies—all things that are not reflected by the neat boxes in the organization chart. With this knowledge he or she can navigate with more skill and ease.

For the organizational theorists, however, a different kind of question is required: What are the systematic bases for the deviations? We should not expect the official map to be completely accurate because:

1. It is never up-to-date—it does not reflect the growing power of a subordinate who will be promoted over his or her boss in a year or two, or the waning power of a boss who has been passed by because of changes in technology or markets.

2. It does not pretend to make the finely graded distinctions that operating personnel have to live by—for example, three departments may be on the same official level, but one of them is three times the size of the other two and may carry commensurately more power.

3. It does not reflect all transactions in the organization, but primarily those disputes that can be settled formally.

4. Most important, the hierarchy functions primarily for routine situations; when new ones come along, someone two levels down may have more say for this or that situation, but unless the new situation itself becomes the persistent or frequent one, his or her authority will only be temporary. If it persists, that person may well move up fast.

5. Finally, hierarchical principles are sometimes violated intentionally. When, for example, the head office cannot get enough information about a division's operation, it sends in a spy. Dalton describes such a case. The man involved had a relatively unimportant job of manager of industrial relations, but his power over many other aspects of the organization was substantial because everyone knew that he was there to find out what was going on.

Few organizations keep an official chart of offices ranked by authority for very long or, if they do, such charts are rarely referred to. (Some organizations even refuse to draw them up.) Positions and units move up and down in authority over time, and the lag with the official chart is always there. Thus, we should not be surprised at the discrepancy, nor should we assume that the unofficial is necessarily a more accurate rendition than the official. The two are just different and only briefly join hands in their mutual evolution. While the "natural" or "living" system is important, it may only be a wistful and touching part of a rather mechanical and imperative whole. The fact that the dean and I (or the chancellor and I, or the president and I) are both professors in a collegial body of equals is as much a romance of the actual situation as the view that only the yeasty, vital, living, informal system counts in an organization. The official hierarchy is there, and no one who has both eyes open forgets it. One must know the hierarchy to survive it. . . .

Professionalism and Discipline

The final criticism of bureaucracy that we shall consider is one of the most widespread. It concerns the discrepancy between the expertise of the subordinate and that of the superior. That is to say, it involves the manager or official who knows less about things than the people that work for him or her yet who exercises authority over them. Virtually every discussion of bureaucracy mentions this point. It is an attractive criticism because we all resent, more or less, those who have authority over us when we suspect that we know more about life on the firing line than they do. The outstanding example of this concerns professionals in organizations. The manager of professionals often simply cannot be as well informed as highly trained subordinates. Social scientists have always been preoccupied with the plight of professionals and have defended their interests extensively.

This whole line of thought started with a footnote in Talcott Parsons' introduction to his translation of parts of Weber's *Economy and Society*. Weber, Parsons said, confused two types of authority in his discussion—the authority that is based on "technical competence," and the authority based on "incumbency of a legally defined office."[41] Could there not be a discrepancy between the two? Could there not be officials who were not experts but who directed the work of those who were? Indeed, there were examples, asserted Parsons. Unfortunately, his main example had little to do with organizations, and his second example was something less than relevant. But since this is possibly the most important footnote in the history of organizational theory, it is worth digging into at some length.

Parson's main example was the physician whose "authority rests fundamentally on the belief on the part of the patient that the physician has and will employ for his benefit a technical competence adequate to help him in his illness." The trouble with the example is that in this role the physician does not function in an organization. Parsons recognizes this, but adds that where the physician does function in an organization, "instead of a rigid hierarchy of status and authority [hierarchies are always rigid, one gathers] there tends to be what is roughly, in formal status, a 'company of equals,' an equalization of status which ignores the inevitable gradation of distinction and achievement to be found in any considerable group of technically competent persons."[42] However, the evidence from studies of hospitals indicates that medical staffs are quite bureaucratic in their organizational functioning, with hierarchies that are apparent; moreover, they are quite sensitive to "inevitable gradations of distinction and achievement."[43]

His other example concerns "powers of coercion in case of recalcitrance." It is not logically essential, he says, that the person with this power "should have either superior knowledge or superior skill as compared to those subject to his orders. Thus, the treasurer of a corporation is empowered to sign checks disbursing large funds. There is no implication in this 'power' that he is a more competent signer of checks than the bank clerks or tellers who cash or deposit them for the recipient."[44] The example is irrelevant because the power of the treasurer rests in his knowledge that certain checks should be made out and sent, not in his ability to sign his name.

Nevertheless, despite these two quite weak illustrations, the idea took immediate root. (Many earlier writers had noted the possible discrepancy between authority and expertise, of course, but Parsons made it famous.) Everyone, it appears, could think of superiors who were less competent than their subordinates, and the bureaucratic dilemma of expertise and discipline was firmly established. Alvin Gouldner used it as the organizing basis for his previously mentioned study of a gypsum plant, *Patterns of Industrial Bureaucracy*.[45] In his hands, it became the explanation for two contrasting bureaucratic patterns—representative bureaucracy, which relied on expertise "based on rules established by agreement, rules which are technically justified and administered by specially qualified personnel, and to which consent is given voluntarily," and punishment-centered bureaucracy, "based on the imposition of rules, and on obedience for its own sake."[46] He, too, thought that Weber saw things two ways; in one, administration was based on expertise, and in the other "Weber held that bureaucracy was a mode of administration in which obedience was an end in itself."[47] (That Weber held nothing of the sort regarding obedience is not important here; it is the distinction that is. Gouldner's representative pattern, incidentally, is based on the slim reed of a safety rule.)

Stanley Udy, studying records of organizations in primitive societies, and Arthur Stinchcombe, in his discussion of the organization of the construction industry, come to much the same conclusion—that there are two fundamentally different forms of organizations, rational or professional organizations and bureaucratic ones.[48] But data on primitive organizations, and the statistics from the construction industry, have dubious relevance for modern large-scale organizations, though both of these studies are excellent for other purposes. The next use of the distinction is by Peter Blau in the article cited above, where it sets the stage for his analysis.[49] But it is apparent that the professionalized (and more hierarchical) organizations are the closest to the Weberian ideal, as we have seen. Blau's data thus support the opposite conclusion—professionalism is consistent with bureaucracy. While Weber asserted the importance of strict discipline, he was much more emphatic about the critical importance of expertise.[50]

But the most extensive use of this distinction has been in the voluminous literature on professionals in organizations; it was the hottest single topic in the field of organizational analysis during the early 1960s and continues to be discussed. With the increasing importance of university-trained scientists and engineers in organizations, the expense of these people, and the need to keep their morale high in a highly competitive employment market, a number of social scientists began to study their adjustment to industrial organizations. Some of these studies were concerned mostly with research laboratories, where the work was complex, innovative, unstructured, and unpredictable. These were truly new organizations that were difficult to cut to the bureaucratic pattern. Some sense of the enormous importance of charismatic leadership, individual autonomy, and serendipity can be gleaned from the fascinating account of the way J. Robert Oppenheimer directed the large Los Alamos laboratory, where the first atomic bombs were built, during World War II.[51] The efforts of General Groves (under whom Oppenheimer worked) to bureaucratize the enterprise—to treat it as if it were turning out Sherman tanks—had disastrous effects on morale and productivity. This example is more pertinent for understanding professionals than, say, studies of such research labs as Bell Laboratories or the DuPont experimental station, since in the Los Alamos case a single product was turned out—a bomb. In the labs, the administrative organization is an umbrella over scores of individual or small-group projects that produce diverse outputs unrelated to one another. To generalize from this highly decentralized type of operation to the usual case of large groups of professionals working on various aspects of one problem or product is misleading.

Many of the studies of scientists in industry, however, did deal with actual industrial organizations with a common problem focus rather than with university-like basic research labs. They revealed, in keeping with antibureaucratic views, that scientists did indeed resent the constraints placed on them by the organization in general, and by their superiors in particular, and preferred the luxuries of academic life such as flexible schedules, few deadlines, uninhibited bull sessions, conference going, freedom to publish, and so on. This is not surprising. If you present yourself as a sociologist or a psychologist from a university and ask if these things are not valued more than profits, production deadlines, and restrictions on publications and inability to study whatever problem one is interested in, the answer is very likely to be yes. The hypothesis is confirmed: there is a conflict between professional values and bureaucratic ones.

However, if one asked a question such as the following, the answer might be quite different: "Would you sooner spend most of your time working on a basic problem that might result in an academic journal publication, but be of little value to the company, or on a problem the company is interested in which might bring you a handsome bonus and a promotion?" Such a question has not been asked, but it poses the dilemma in realistic terms. I suspect that the majority of scientists and engineers in industry would choose the profitable project. The reasons are close at hand. The education these people receive in a university is from departments that are vocationally oriented.[52] Engineering departments and such science departments as chemistry and geology are designed to meet industrial needs, at least at the undergraduate level, and in many places at the graduate levels. Professors in these departments judge the quality of their teaching by the status of the companies in which their students obtain jobs. The professors also consult with industrial firms. The curriculum is designed to be relevant to industrial employment. The large majority of the students go into industry. Once there, they find that the route to power, prestige, and money is through serving the company and, in particular, through getting out of technical work and into management. Dalton has observed that the action and the rewards are in line positions rather than in staff (professional) positions.[53] A study by Fred Goldner and R. R. Ritti of recent engineering graduates, conceived without a bias in favor of a conflict between scientists and managers, found that "from the start of their business careers many engineers have personal goals that coincide with the business goals of the corporations."[54] Business-oriented goals, dealing with power and participation in the affairs of the company, were ranked far above professional goals.

Furthermore, although it is rarely noted, managers also are usually college-trained—for example in law, business administration, and economics. Are they not professionals, too? Presumably they would prefer to work in a university-like atmosphere if they could have the power and the income provided by industry at the same time. They, too, resent supervision and discipline and if asked the proper questions would probably question the profit goal of business even as do scientists. In fact, the student with a master's degree in business administration will hear more about the "social responsibilities" of business than the scientist.

Finally, the distinction made by Parsons and invoked by so many since then fails to recognize the *technical* character of administration. That is, though the scientist promoted to a supervisory position will soon lose some of her *scientific* technical competence (she cannot keep up with the field; the new graduates know the latest things in some cases; she loses touch with the practical, daily problems), she is probably promoted on, and expected to exercise and increase, her *administrative* technical competence. The job of the scientific manager is to manage, not to do research. It is a very common observation in industry that the best scientists do not make the best managers; the skills required are quite different, even though the manager of scientists must know a good bit about the technical work of these specialists. The same is true of the manager in marketing, finance, personnel, and even production. By assuming that official incumbency of a supervisory role has no relationship to expertise (expertise in management, in this case), it is possible for critics of the bureaucratic model to suggest a hiatus between expertise and occupancy of an official position. It was Weber's simple but enduring insight to see how crucial expertise was as a requirement for holding office throughout the hierarchy. The critics of bureaucracy have failed to utilize that simple insight when they propose that the official is not an expert in anything but survival. Far more damning would be the criticism that bureaucracy, by enfeebling so many workers, has made management a specialized skill demanding expertise.

Summary

When we attribute the ills of organizations and those of our society to the bureaucratization of large-scale organizations, as we are so wont to do, we may be only fooling ourselves. We may be talking about specific instances of maladministration, of which there will naturally be many since people are more or less imperfect, or we are talking about the causes to which the power generated by organizations is put. The presence of hierarchy, rules, division of labor, tenure provisions, and so on can hardly be blamed for maladministration or abuses of social power. Indeed, the bureaucratic model provides a greater check on these problems than do nonbureaucratic or traditional alternatives once you have managerial capitalism. Critics then of our organizational society, whether they are the radicals of the Left emphasizing spontaneity and freedom, the New Right demanding their own form of radical decentralization, or the liberals in between speaking of the inability of organizations to be responsive to community values, had best turn to the key issue of who controls the varied forms of power generated by organizations, rather than flail away at the windmills of bureaucracy. If we want our material civilization to continue as it is and are not ready to change the economic system drastically, we will have to have large-scale bureaucratic enterprises in the economic, social, and governmental areas. The development of industrialization has made this the most efficient way to get the routine work of a society done. If we were prepared to engineer a modest change in our economy, we could even reap more of the advantages of bureaucracy. Our present system of huge, inflexible firms dominating markets in highly concentrated industries costs us dearly. Large size distorts bureaucracy, encouraging the problems of outdated rules, improperly invoked hierarchies, particularism, and favoritism. If all but the few industries where capital investment must be enormous were limited to modest-sized firms of, say, less than 1,000 employees, they could be efficient, flexible, and limited in their market power. . . .

Endnotes

1. Alvin Gouldner, *Patterns of Industrial Bureaucracy* (New York: Free Press, 1954).

2. Ibid., p. 35.

3. Ibid., p. 65.

4. The famous German sociologist, writing in the early decades of this century, laid out the model of bureaucracy and described and explained its origins. Weber's writings on bureaucracy appear in two different parts of an uncompleted draft of his opus, *Economy and Society*. The first part is presented in Max Weber, *The Theory of Social and Economic Organization*, trans. A. M. Henderson and Talcott Parsons (New York: Oxford University Press, 1947), pp. 324–340. The second part, which was actually written first and is a more discursive section, appears in Max Weber, *From Max Weber, Essays in Sociology*, trans. and ed. by Hans Gerth and C. Wright Mills (New York: Oxford University Press, 1946), pp. 196–244. The corresponding pages in the 1968 translation of Weber's work, *Economy and Society*, ed. Guenther Roth and Claus Wittich (New York: Irvington Publications, 1968), are vol. 1, pp. 212–225 and vol. 3, pp. 956–1001.

5. See Reinhard Bendix, "Bureaucracy," in *International Encyclopedia of the Social Sciences* (New York: Free Press, 1977).

6. And not just steel, of course. In Detroit, only two-thirds of 1 percent of the white-collar jobs at the three major auto companies are filled by Jews. A 1960 study of 1,500 U.S. corporations showed that although Jews made up 8 percent of all college graduates and, even more important, 15 percent of the graduates of professional and business schools, they account for only 0.5 percent of management. See "Has Bias Locked Up the Room at the Top?" *Business Week*, January 24, 1970.

7. Melville Dalton, *Men Who Manage* (New York: Wiley, 1959).

8. *New York Times*, September 14, 1984, p. 1.

9. Richard Barnet, *Economy of Death* (New York: Atheneum House, 1969).

10. As Lewis Coser notes in *Greedy Institutions* (New York: Free Press, 1974), slaves, Jews, and others excluded from society could also be used because they owed to their lord their promotion from nonpersons to quasipersons.

11. The contributions-inducements theory of organizations was first formulated by Chester Barnard in the late 1930s and subsequently greatly refined by James G. March and Herbert A. Simon in their book, *Organizations* (New York: Wiley, 1958). Their contributions are cited as landmarks in organizational theory, despite the simplicity of the idea or perhaps because of it. . . .

12. One of the most frequent consumer fraud devices is for a collection agency to send a fake social survey questionnaire out. Along with the usual attitude questions ("How do you feel about law and order?"), unsuspecting debtors are asked about their place of employment, the value of their car and other property, and whether their spouse works or not. The agencies also send letters on official-looking stationery saying that a heavily insured package is being held for them by the post office, and they should fill out the identification papers and mail them in to receive the package. Debtors thus disclose the information that the collection agency can use as leverage. Both practices are forbidden by law but are very hard to police.

13. Dan Clawson, *Bureaucracy and the Labor Process: The Transformation of U.S. Industry: 1860–1920* (New York: Monthly Review Press, 1980). See also the more general discussion of this issue in Harry Braverman, *Labor and Monopoly Capital* (New York: Monthly Review Press, 1975).

14. Katherine Stone, "The Origins of Job Structures in the Steel Industry," *Radical America* 7, no. 6 (November/December 1973): 19–64, describes the process and conflicts for the steel industry. See also the seminal piece by Steven Marglin, "What Do Bosses Do?" *Review of Radical Political Economics* 6, no. 2 (Summer 1974): 33–60, and the book by Richard Edwards, *Contested Terrain: The Transformation of the Workplace in the Twentieth Century* (New York: Basic Books, 1979).

15. But on the other hand, it is striking that few creative individuals appear to start on their own, forming their own companies. Generally, they work first for a large firm. Only then can they attract the necessary capital from those arbitrators of the business scene, the banks.

16. Wilfred Brown, *Exploration in Management* (New York: Wiley, 1960), pp. 97–98.

17. Charles Perrow, "Members as a Resource in Voluntary Organization," in *Organizations and Clients*, ed. W. Rosengren and M. Lefton (Columbus, Ohio: Charles E. Merrill, 1970), pp. 93–116.

18. Peter M. Blau, *The Dynamics of Bureaucracy*, 2nd rev. ed. (Chicago: University of Chicago Press, 1973).

19. David Rogers, *110 Livingstone Street* (New York: Random House, 1968).

20. Talcott Parsons, "Introduction," in Max Weber, *The Theory of Social and Economic Organization*, pp. 58–60. Amitai Etzioni, *A Comparative Analysis of Complex Organizations* (New York: Free Press, 1961), pp. 218–261.

21. I wish to thank Robert Taylor, former vice-president of the University of Wisconsin, for constructive comments on this material. As he points out, the chain of command works in a variety of ways, depending on who or what is involved. "Very little (maybe no) 'traffic' moves up or down this chain in this fashion. The fact is that most of it moves as your letter [to me] did—from professor to vice-president and back with all the other levels left in blessed ignorance. And, of course, no modern student would countenance such a chain for a moment—he'd pick up the phone and call the president or the president of the board of regents, if he thought either of these officials capable of acting on his request." (Private correspondence.) This is true, but in a crunch, the chain is there for those higher up to use it. As we shall see, much short-circuiting of the chain occurs in organizations that are not made up of "professionals."

22. Charles Perrow, "Goals and Power Structures: A Historical Case Study," and Mary E. W. Goss, "Patterns of Bureaucracy Among Hospital Staff Physicians," in *The Hospital in Modern Society*, ed. Eliot Freidson (New York: Free Press, 1963).

23. Erwin O. Smigel, *Wall Street Lawyer*, rev. ed. (Bloomington, Ind.: Indiana University Press, 1970).

24. Harold L. Wilensky, *Organizational Intelligence: Knowledge and Policy in Government and Industry* (New York: Basic Books, 1969), pp. 42–48.

25. Victor A. Thompson, *Modern Organization*, 2nd ed. (University, Ala.: Univ. of Alabama Press, 1977), Chapter 8.

26. Charles Perrow, "Working Paper on Technology and Structure," mimeographed, February 1970.

27. William F. Whyte, "Human Relations—A Progress Report," in *Complex Organizations, A Sociological Reader*, ed. Amitai Etzioni (New York: Holt, Rinehart & Winston, 1962), pp. 100–112.

28. James C. Worthy, "Organizational Structure and Employee Morale," *American Sociological Review* 15 (1950): 169–179.

29. Peter Blau, "The Hierarchy of Authority in Organizations," *American Journal of Sociology* 73 (January 1968): 453–457.

30. See, for example, the various discussions by Joan Woodward, *Industrial Organization: Theory and Practice* (London: Oxford University Press, 1965). In discussing span of control, Jay Lorsch generally finds a broad span is associated with nonroutine tasks, contrary to Blau. But on the other hand, in the routine production department of one of his companies, Lorsch also finds a broad span of control. See Jay W. Lorsch, *Product Innovation and Organization* (New York: Macmillan, 1965), p. 53. For a good discussion and additional evidence supporting Blau's view see Gerald Bell, "Determinants of Span of Control," *American Journal of Sociology* 73, no. 1 (July 1967): 90–101.

31. Marshall Meyer, "Two Authority Structures of Bureaucratic Organizations," *Administrative Science Quarterly* 13 (September 1968): 211–228.

32. Blau, "Hierarchy." There are complex problems here of different degrees of "tallness" in different units of an organization that are not relevant for these agencies, but would be for most organizations.

33. See, for example, Worthy, "Employee Morale." It is noteworthy that in a study of school teachers that used, by and

large, unloaded questions to tap bureaucracy, it was found that, quite contrary to the authors' expectations, "Teachers in highly bureaucratic systems had a significantly higher, not lower, sense of power than those in less bureaucratic systems." See Gerald H. Moeller and W. W. Charters, "Relation of Bureaucratization to Sense of Power Among Teachers," *Administrative Science Quarterly* 10, no. 4 (March 1966): 457. These authors were as surprised as Blau and his associates but fell back upon the influence of other factors that might have clouded or reversed a relationship predicted by most schools of thought.

34. The best summary and introduction to these studies is that of John Child, "Predicting and Understanding Organization Structure," *Administrative Science Quarterly* 18, no. 2 (June 1973): 168–185. For a sample of the criticisms of this important survey see Howard Aldrich, "Technology and Organizational Structure: A Reexamination of the Findings of the Aston Group," *Administrative Science Quarterly* 17, no. 1 (March 1972): 26–43; Sergio E. Mindlin and Howard Aldrich, "Interorganizational Dependence: A Review of the Concepts and Reexamination of the Findings of the Aston Group," *Administrative Science Quarterly* 20, no. 3 (September 1975): 382–392; and especially William Starbuck, "A Trip to View the Elephants and Rattlesnakes in the Garden of Aston," in *Perspectives on Organization Design and Behavior*, ed. Andrew H. Van de Ven and William F. Joyce (New York: Wiley, 1981), pp. 167–199.

35. Blau, *Dynamics*.

36. Dalton, *Men Who Manage*.

37. Gouldner, *Industrial Bureaucracy*.

38. Wilfred Brown, *Exploration in Management*.

39. David Mechanic, "Sources of Power of Lower Participants in Complex Organization," *Administrative Science Quarterly* 7, no. 4 (December 1962): 349–364.

40. Dalton, *Men Who Manage*, Chapter 2.

41. Parsons, "Introduction," in Weber, *The Theory of Social and Economic Organizations*, p. 59.

42. Ibid., p. 60.

43. Perrow and Goss in *The Hospital in Modern Society*.

44. Parsons, "Introduction," in Weber, *The Theory of Social and Economic Organizations*, p. 60.

45. Gouldner, *Industrial Bureaucracy*.

46. Ibid., p. 24.

47. Ibid., p. 22.

48. Stanley H. Udy, Jr., " 'Bureaucracy' and 'Rationality' in Weber's Organization Theory," *American Sociological Review* 24 (1959): 591–595; Arthur L. Stinchcombe, "Bureaucratic and Craft Administration of Production," *Administrative Science Quarterly* 4 (1959): 168–187.

49. Blau, "Hierarchy."

50. See Weber, *The Theory of Social and Economic Organizations*, pp. 337–339, for the following: "The primary source of bureaucratic administration lies in the role of technical knowledge.... Bureaucratic administration means fundamentally the exercise of control on the basis of knowledge. This is the feature of it which makes it specifically rational. ... Bureaucracy is superior in knowledge, including both technical knowledge and knowledge of the concrete fact."

51. Nuel Pharr Davis, *Lawrence and Oppenheimer* (New York: Simon & Schuster, 1968), Chapters 6 and 7. General Groves is reported to have said, "Here at great expense the government has assembled the world's largest collection of crackpots" (pp. 173–174). He proceeded to run it like an asylum as well as a factory. Group leaders were required to turn in reports on the daily hours worked by Nobel laureates and other top scientists. The purpose, which they did not know, was to keep down absenteeism. "The payroll office did not know what to do with work reports ranging up to a preposterous and unreimbursable eighteen hours a day." The military police closed up the labs at five o'clock every afternoon. Said a physicist, "Apparently they didn't have orders to throw us out, but they did have orders to lock up the supplies. We sawed around the locks on the stockroom doors and just stayed and worked. We kept a refrigerator full of sandwich stuff because everybody was pretty hungry by four in the morning, our usual quitting time. After a while, whoever was directing the M.P.'s caught the spirit of the thing and stopped replacing the locks" (p. 181). Another scientist contrasted the University of California lab at Berkeley, run by Ernest Lawrence, with the Los Alamos complex. They were similar only in the long hours put in. "The difference was the atmosphere. There you did whatever task they assigned you and learned not to ask why. Here (Los Alamos) you asked what you liked and at least thought you did what you liked. There the pressure came from outside. Here there didn't seem to be any pressure" (pp. 181–182).

52. See Harold L. Wilensky, "The Professionalization of Everyone?" *American Journal of Sociology* 70 (September 1964): 137–158, for a discussion of the role of the training institution in the process of professionalization.

53. Dalton, *Men Who Manage;* see also "Conflicts Between Staff and Line Managerial Officers," *American Sociological Review* 15 (1950): 342–351.

54. Fred Goldner and R. R. Ritti, "Professionalization as Career Immobility," *American Journal of Sociology* 73 (March 1967): 491. This article contains a good discussion of the issues raised here, as well as citations and review of the literature that views the goals of professionals and managers (or the company) as in conflict. See also the critical review of the literature in Norman Kaplan, "Professional Scientists in Industry," *Social Problems* 13 (Summer 1965): 88–97.

Chapter 4
The Social Structure of Managerial Work

Robert Jackall

Hierarchy is a distinguishing feature of bureaucracy. Because hierarchy implies an unequal distribution of power and authority, it is the aspect of bureaucracy that is most often a source of complaints and criticism. But how do hierarchies work in practice? What is the relationship between the "official" hierarchical structure in an organization and the "unofficial" lines of communication, authority, and power?

In order to explore these questions, Robert Jackall takes us inside the managerial ranks of an American corporation. His focus is on the social structures that emerge out of any hierarchical system. These structures are revealed in the worldviews and psychological makeup of individual managers as they devise strategies for career success and advancement. They can also be seen in the social relations and interactions between individuals and groups within the managerial ranks. In Jackall's view, managerial hierarchies are essentially political systems, characterized by a jockeying for resources, position, and power.

I

The hierarchical authority structure that is the linchpin of bureaucracy dominates the way managers think about their world and about themselves. Managers do not see or experience authority in any abstract way; instead, authority is embodied in their personal relationships with their immediate bosses and in their perceptions of similar links between other managers up and down the hierarchy. When managers describe their work to an outsider, they almost always first say: "I work for [Bill James]" or "I report to [Harry Mills]" or "I'm in [Joe Bell's] group,"[1] and only then proceed to describe their actual work functions. Such a personalized statement of authority relationships seems to contradict classical notions of how bureaucracies function but it exactly reflects the way authority is structured, exercised, and experienced in corporate hierarchies.

American businesses typically both centralize and decentralize authority. Power is concentrated at the top in the person of the chief executive officer (CEO) and is simultaneously decentralized; that is, responsibility for decisions and profits is pushed as far down the organizational line as possible. For example, Alchemy Inc., . . . is one of several operating companies of Covenant Corporation. When I began my research, Alchemy employed 11,000 people; Covenant had over 50,000 employees and now has over 100,000. Like the other operating companies, Alchemy has its own president, executive vice-presidents, vice-presidents, other executive officers, business area managers, staff divisions, and more than eighty manufacturing plants scattered throughout the country and indeed the world producing a wide range of specialty and commodity chemicals. Each operating company is, at least theoretically, an autonomous, self-sufficient organization, though they are all monitored and coordinated by a central corporate staff, and each president reports directly to the corporate CEO. Weft Corporation has its corporate headquarters and manufacturing facilities in the South; its marketing and sales offices, along with some key executive personnel, are in New York City. Weft employs 20,000 people, concentrated in the firm's three textile divisions that have always been and remain its core business. The Apparel Division produces seven million yards a week of raw, unfinished cloth in several greige (colloquially gray) mills, mostly for sale to garment manufacturers; the Consumer Division produces some cloth of its own in several greige mills and also finishes—that is, bleaches, dyes, prints, and sews—twelve million yards of raw cloth a month into purchasable items like sheets, pillowcases, and tablecloths for department stores and chain stores; and the Retail Division operates an import-export business, specializing in the quick turnaround of the fast-moving cloths desired by Seventh Avenue designers. Each division has a president who reports to one of several executive vice-presidents, who in turn report to the corporate CEO. The divisional structure is typically less elaborate in its hierarchical ladder than the framework of independent operating companies; it is also somewhat more dependent on corporate staff for essential services. However, the basic principle of simultaneous centralization and decentralization prevails and both Covenant and Weft consider their companies or divisions, as the case may be, "profit centers." Even Images Inc., while much smaller than the industrial concerns and organized like most service businesses according to shifting groupings of client accounts supervised by senior vice-presidents, uses the notion of profit centers.

The key interlocking mechanism of this structure is its reporting system. Each manager gathers up the profit targets or other objectives of his or her subordinates and, with these, formulates his commitments to his boss; this boss takes these commitments and those of his other subordinates, and in turn makes a commitment to his boss.[2] At the top of the line, the president of each company or division, or, at Images Inc., the senior vice-president for a group of accounts, makes his commitment to the CEO. This may be done directly, or sometimes, as at Weft Corporation, through a corporate executive vice-president. In any event, the commitments made to top management depend on the pyramid of stated objectives given to superiors up the line. At each level of the structure, there is typically "topside" pressure to achieve higher goals and, of course, the CEO frames and paces the whole process by applying pressure for attainment of his own objectives. Meanwhile, bosses and subordinates down the line engage in a series of intricate negotiations—managers often call these "conspiracies"—to keep their commitments respectable but achievable.

This "management-by-objective" system, as it is usually called, creates a chain of commitments from the CEO down to the lowliest product manager or account executive. In practice, it also shapes a patrimonial authority arrangement that is crucial to defining both the immediate experiences and the long-run career chances of individual managers. In this world, a subordinate owes fealty principally to his immediate boss. This means that a subordinate must not over-commit his boss, lest his boss "get on the hook" for promises that cannot be kept. He must keep his boss from making mistakes, particularly public ones; he must keep his boss informed, lest his boss get "blindsided."

If one has a mistake-prone boss, there is, of course, always the temptation to let him make a fool of himself, but the wise subordinate knows that this carries two dangers—he himself may get done in by his boss's errors, and, perhaps more important, other managers will view with the gravest suspicion a subordinate who withholds crucial information from his boss even if they think the boss is a nincompoop. A subordinate must also not circumvent his boss nor ever give the appearance of doing so. He must never contradict his boss's judgment in public. To violate the last admonition is thought to constitute a kind of death wish in business, and one who does so should practice what one executive calls "flexibility drills," an exercise "where you put your head between your legs and kiss your ass goodbye." On a social level, even though an easy, breezy, first-name informality is the prevalent style of American business, a concession perhaps to our democratic heritage and egalitarian rhetoric, the subordinate must extend to the boss a certain ritual deference. For instance, he must follow the boss's lead in conversation, must not speak out of turn at meetings, must laugh at his boss's jokes while not making jokes of his own that upstage his boss, must not rib the boss for his foibles. The shrewd subordinate learns to efface himself, so that his boss's face might shine more clearly.

In short, the subordinate must symbolically reinforce at every turn his own subordination and his willing acceptance of the obligations of fealty. In return, he can hope for those perquisites that are in his boss's gift—the better, more attractive secretaries, or the nudging of a movable panel to enlarge his office, and perhaps a couch to fill the added space, one of the real distinctions in corporate bureaucracies. He can hope to be elevated when and if the boss is elevated, though other important criteria intervene here. He can also expect protection for mistakes made, up to a point. However, that point is never exactly defined and depends on the complicated politics of each situation. The general rule is that bosses are expected to protect those in their bailiwicks. Not to do so, or to be unable to do so, is taken as a sign of untrustworthiness or weakness. If, however, subordinates make mistakes that are thought to be dumb, or especially if they violate fealty obligations—for example, going around their boss—then abandonment of them to the vagaries of organizational forces is quite acceptable.

Overlaying and intertwined with this formal monocratic system of authority, with its patrimonial resonance, are patron-client relationships. Patrons are usually powerful figures in the higher echelons of management. The patron might be a manager's direct boss, or his boss's boss, or someone several levels higher in the chain of command. In either case, the manager is still bound by the immediate, formal authority and fealty patterns of his position but he also acquires new, though more ambiguous, fealty relationships with his highest ranking patron. Patrons play a crucial role in advancement, a point that I shall discuss later.

It is characteristic of this authority system that details are pushed down and credit is pulled up. Superiors do not like to give detailed instructions to subordinates. The official reason for this is to maximize subordinates' autonomy. The underlying reason is, first, to get rid of tedious details. Most hierarchically organized occupations follow this pattern; one of the privileges of authority is the divestment of humdrum intricacies. This also insulates higher bosses from the peculiar pressures that accompany managerial work at the middle levels and below: the lack of economy over one's time because of continual interruption from one's subordinates, telephone calls from customers and clients, and necessary meetings with colleagues; the piecemeal fragmentation of issues both because of the discontinuity of events and because of the way subordinates filter news; and the difficulty of minding the store while sorting out sometimes unpleasant personnel issues. Perhaps more important, pushing details down protects the privilege of authority to declare that a mistake has been made. A high-level executive in Alchemy Inc. explains:

> If I tell someone what to do—like do A, B, or C—the inference and implication is that he will succeed in accomplishing the objective. Now, if he doesn't succeed, that means that I have invested part of myself in his work and I lose any right I have to chew his ass out if he doesn't succeed. If I tell you what to do, I can't bawl you out if things don't work. And this is why a lot of bosses don't give explicit directions. They just give a statement of objectives, and then they can criticize subordinates who fail to make their goals.

Moreover, pushing down details relieves superiors of the burden of too much knowledge, particularly guilty knowledge. A superior will say to a subordinate, for instance: "Give me your best thinking on the problem with [X]." When the subordinate makes his report, he is often told: "1 think you can do better than that," until the subordinate has worked out all the details of the boss's predetermined solution, without the boss being specifically aware of "all the eggs that have to be broken." It is also not at all uncommon for very bald and extremely general edicts to emerge from on high. For example, "Sell the plant in [St. Louis]; let me know when you've struck a deal," or "We need to get higher prices for [fabric X]; see what you can work out" or "Tom, I want you to go down there and meet with those guys and make a deal and I don't want you to come back until you've got one." This pushing down of details has important consequences.

First, because they are unfamiliar with—indeed deliberately distance themselves from—entangling details, corporate higher echelons tend to expect successful results without messy complications. This is central to top executives' well-known aversion to bad news and to the resulting tendency to kill the messenger who bears the news.

Second, the pushing down of details creates great pressure on middle managers not only to transmit good news but, precisely because they know the details, to act to protect their corporations, their bosses, and themselves in the process. They become the "point men" of a given strategy and the potential "fall guys" when things go wrong. From an organizational standpoint, overly conscientious managers are particularly useful at the middle levels of the structure. Upwardly mobile men and women, especially those from working-class origins who find themselves in higher status milieux, seem to have the requisite level of anxiety, and perhaps tightly controlled anger and hostility, that fuels an obsession with detail. Of course, such conscientiousness is not necessarily, and is certainly not systematically, rewarded; the real organizational premiums are placed on other, more flexible, behavior.

Credit flows up in this structure and is usually appropriated by the highest ranking officer involved in a successful decision or resolution of a problem. There is, for instance, a tremendous competition for ideas in the corporate world; authority provides a license to steal ideas, even in front of those who originated them. Chairmen routinely appropriate the useful suggestions made by members of their committees or task forces; research directors build their reputations for scientific wizardry on the bricks laid down by junior researchers and directors of departments. Presidents of whole divisions as well are always on the lookout for "fresh ideas" and "creative approaches" that they can claim as their own in order to put themselves "out in front" of their peers. A subordinate whose ideas are appropriated is expected to be a good sport about the matter; not to balk at so being used is one attribute of the good team player. The person who appropriates credit redistributes it as he chooses, bound essentially and only by a sensitivity to public perceptions of his fairness. One gives credit, therefore, not necessarily where it is due, although one always invokes this old saw, but where prudence dictates. Customarily, people who had nothing to do with the success of a project can be allocated credit for their exemplary efforts. At the middle levels, therefore, credit for a particular idea or success is always a type of refracted social honor; one cannot claim credit even if it is earned. Credit has to be given, and acceptance of the gift implicitly involves a reaffirmation and strengthening of fealty. A superior may share some credit with subordinates in order to deepen fealty relationships and induce greater efforts on his behalf. Of course, a different system obtains in the allocation of blame.

Because of the interlocking character of the commitment system, a CEO carries enormous influence in his corporation. If, for a moment, one thinks of the presidents of operating companies or divisions as barons, then the CEO of the corporation is the king. His word is law; even the CEO's wishes and whims are taken as commands by close subordinates on the corporate staff, who turn them into policies and directives. A typical example occurred in Weft Corporation a few years ago when the CEO, new at the time, expressed mild concern about the rising operating costs of the company's fleet of rented cars. The following day, a stringent system for monitoring mileage replaced the previous casual practice. Managers have a myriad of aphorisms that refer to how the power of CEOs, magnified through the zealous efforts of subordinates, affects them. These range

from the trite "When he sneezes, we all catch colds" to the more colorful "When he says 'Go to the bathroom,' we all get the shits."

Great efforts are made to please the CEO. For example, when the CEO of Covenant Corporation visits a plant, the most significant order of business for local management is a fresh paint job, even when, as in several cases, the cost of paint alone exceeds $100,000. If a paint job has already been scheduled at a plant, it is deferred along with all other cosmetic maintenance until just before the CEO arrives; keeping up appearances without recognition for one's efforts is pointless. I am told that similar anecdotes from other corporations have been in circulation since 1910, which suggests a certain historical continuity of behavior toward top bosses.

The second order of business for the plant management is to produce a book fully describing the plant and its operations, replete with photographs and illustrations, for presentation to the CEO; such a book costs about $10,000 for the single copy. By any standards of budgetary stringency, such expenditures are irrational. But by the social standards of the corporation, they make perfect sense. It is far more important to please the king today than to worry about the future economic state of one's fief, since, if one does not please the king, there may not be a fief to worry about or indeed vassals to do the worrying.

By the same token, all of this leads to an intense interest in everything the CEO does and says. In all the companies that I studied, the most common topic of conversation among managers up and down the line is speculation about their respective CEOs' plans, intentions, strategies, actions, style, public image, and ideological leanings of the moment. Even the metaphorical temper of a CEO's language finds its way down the hierarchy to the lower reaches of an organization. In the early stages of my fieldwork at Covenant Corporation, for example, I was puzzled by the inordinately widespread usage of nautical terminology, especially in a corporation located in a landlocked site. As it happens, the CEO is devoted to sailboats and prefers that his aides call him "Skipper." Moreover, in every corporation that I studied, stories and rumors circulate constantly about the social world of the CEO and his immediate subordinates—who, for instance, seems to have the CEO's ear at the moment; whose style seems to have gained approbation; who in short seems to be in the CEO's grace and who seems to have fallen out of favor. In the smaller and more intimate setting of Images Inc., the circulation of favor takes an interesting, if unusual, tack. There, the CEO is known for attaching younger people to himself as confidants. He solicits their advice, tells them secrets, gets their assessments of developments further down in the, hierarchy gleans the rumors and gossip making the rounds about himself. For the younger people selected for such attention, this is a rare, if fleeting, opportunity to have a place in the sun and to share the illusion if not the substance of power. In time, of course, the CEO tires of or becomes disappointed with particular individuals and turns his attention to others. "Being discarded," however, is not an obstacle to regaining favor. In larger organizations, impermeable structural barriers between top circles and junior people prevent this kind of intimate interchange and circulation of authoritative regard. Within a CEO's circle, however, the same currying and granting of favor prevails, always amidst conjectures from below about who has edged close to the throne.

But such speculation about the CEO and his leanings of the moment is more than idle gossip, and the courtlike atmosphere that I am describing more than stylized diversion. Because he stands at the apex of the corporation's bureaucratic and patrimonial structures and locks the intricate system of commitments between bosses and subordinates into place, it is the CEO who ultimately decides whether those commitments have been satisfactorily met. The CEO becomes the actual and the symbolic keystone of the hierarchy that constitutes the defining point of the managerial experience. Moreover, the CEO and his trusted associates determine the fate of whole business areas of a corporation.

Within the general ambiance established by a CEO, presidents of individual operating companies or of divisions carry similar, though correspondingly reduced, influence within their own baronies. Adroit and well-placed subordinates can, for instance, borrow a president's prestige and power to exert great leverage. Even chance encounters or the occasional meeting or lunch with the president can, if advertised casually and subtly, cause notice and the respect among other managers that comes from uncertainty. Knowledge of more clearly established relationships, of course, always sways behavior, A middle manager in one company, widely known to be a very close personal friend of the president, flagged her copious memoranda to other managers with large green paperclips, ensuring prompt attention to her requests. More generally, each major division of the core textile group in Weft Corporation is widely thought to reflect the personality of its leader—one hard-driving, intense, and openly competitive; one cool, precise, urbane, and proper; and one gregarious, talkative, and self-promotional. Actually, market exigencies play a large role in shaping each division's tone and tempo. Still, the popular conception of the dominance of presidential personalities not only points to the crucial issue of style in business, a topic to be explored in depth later, but it underlines the general tendency to personalize authority in corporate bureaucracies.

Managers draw elaborate cognitive maps to guide them through the thickets of their organizations. Because they see and experience authority in such personal terms, the singular feature of these maps is their biographical emphasis. Managers carry around in their heads thumbnail sketches of the occupational history of virtually every other manager of their own rank or higher in their particular organization. These maps begin with a knowledge of others' occupational expertise an specific work experience, but focus especially on previous and present reporting relationships, patronage relationships, and alliances. Cognitive maps incorporate memories of social slights, of public embarrassments, of battles won and lost, and of people's behavior under pressure. They include as well general estimates of the abilities and career trajectories of their colleagues. I should mention that these latter estimates are not necessarily accurate or fair; they are, in fact, often based on the flimsiest of evidence. For instance, a general manager at Alchemy Inc. describes the ephemeral nature of such opinions:

> It's a feeling about the guy's perceived ability to run a business—like he's not a good people man, or he's not a good numbers man. This is not a quantitative thing. It's a gut feeling that a guy can't be put in one spot, but he might be put in another spot. These kinds of informal opinions about others are the lifeblood of an orga-

nization's advancement system. Oh, for the record, we've got the formal evaluations; but the real opinions—the ones that really count in determining people's fates—are those which are traded back and forth in meetings, private conferences, chance encounters, and so on.

Managers trade estimates of others' chances within their circles and often color them to suit their own purposes. This is one reason why it is crucial for the aspiring young manager to project the right image to the right people who can influence others' sketches of him. Whatever the accuracy of these vocabularies of description, managers' penchant for biographical detail and personal histories contrasts sharply with their disinclination for details in general or for other kinds of history. Details, as I have mentioned, get pushed down the ladder; and a concern with history, even of the short-run, let alone long-term, structural shifts in one's own organization, constrains the forward orientation and cheerful optimism highly valued in most corporations. Biographical detail, however, constitutes crucial knowledge because managers know that, in the rough-and-tumble politics of the corporate world, individual fates are made and broken not necessarily by one's accomplishments but by other people.

One must appreciate the simultaneously monocratic and patrimonial character of business bureaucracies in order to grasp the personal and organizational significance of political struggles in managerial work. As it happens, political struggles are a constant and recurring feature in business, shaping managers' experience and outlooks in fundamental ways. Of course, such conflicts are usually cloaked by typically elaborate organizational rhetorics of harmony and teamwork. However, one can observe the multiple dimensions of these conflicts during periods of organizational upheaval, a regular feature of American business where mergers, buyouts, divestitures, and especially "organizational restructuring" have become commonplace occurrences. As Karl Mannheim, among others, has pointed out, it is precisely when a social order begins to fall apart that one can discern what has held it together in the first place. A series of shake-ups that occurred in Covenant Corporation, all within a period of a few years, present a focused case study of political processes basic to all big corporations.

II

In 1979, a new CEO took power in Covenant Corporation. The first action of most new CEOs is some form of organizational change. On the one hand, this prevents the inheritance of blame for past mistakes; on the other, it projects an image of bare-knuckled aggressiveness much appreciated on Wall Street. Perhaps most important, a shake-up rearranges the fealty structure of the corporation, placing in power those barons whose style and public image mesh closely with that of the new CEO and whose principal loyalties belong to him. Shortly after the new CEO of Covenant was named, he reorganized the whole business, after a major management consulting firm had "exhaustively considered all the options," and personally selected new presidents to head each of the five newly formed companies of the corporation—Alchemy, Energy, Metals, Electronics, and Instruments. He ordered the presidents to carry out a thorough reorganization of their separate companies complete with extensive "census reduction," or firing as many people as possible. The presidents were given, it was said, a free hand in their efforts, although in retrospect it seems that the CEO insisted on certain high-level appointments.

The new president of Alchemy Inc.—let's call him Smith[3]—had risen from a marketing background in a small but important specialty chemicals division in the former company. Specialty chemicals are produced in relatively small batches and command high prices, showing generous profit margins; they depend on customer loyalty and therefore on the adroit cultivation of buyers through professional marketing. Upon promotion to president, Smith reached back into his former division, indeed back to his own past work in a particular product line, and systematically elevated many of his former colleagues, friends, clients, and allies. Powerful managers in other divisions, particularly in a rival process chemicals division, whose commodity products, produced in huge quantities, were sold only by price and who exemplified an old-time "blood, guts, and courage" management style were: forced to take big demotions in the new power structure; put on "special assignment"—the corporate euphemism for Siberia, sent to a distant corner office where one looks for a new job (the saying is: "No one ever comes back from special assignment"); fired; or given "early retirement," a graceful way of doing the same thing. What happened in Alchemy Inc. was typical of the pattern in the other companies of the conglomerate. Hundreds of people throughout the whole corporation lost their jobs in what became known as "Bloody Thursday," the "October Revolution," or in some circles, the "Octoberfest." I shall refer back to this event as the "big purge."

Up and down the chemical company, former associates of Smith were placed in virtually every important position. Managers in the company saw all of this as an inevitable fact of life. In their view, Smith simply picked those managers with whom he was comfortable. The whole reorganization could easily have gone in a completely different direction had another CEO been named, or had the one selected picked someone besides Smith, or had Smith come from a different work group in the old organization. Fealty is the mortar of the corporate hierarchy, but the removal of one well-placed stone loosens the mortar throughout the pyramid. And no one is ever quite sure, until after the fact, just how the pyramid will be put back together.

The year after the "big purge," Alchemy prospered and met its financial commitments to the CEO, the crucial coin of the realm to purchase continued autonomy. Smith consolidated his power and, through the circle of the mostly like-minded and like-mannered men and women with whom he surrounded himself, further weeded out or undercut managers with whom he felt uncomfortable. At the end of the year, the mood in the company was buoyant not only because of high profits but because of the expectation of massive deregulation and boom times for business following President Reagan's first election. On the day after the election, by the way, managers, in an unusual break with normal decorum, actually danced in the corridors.

What follows might be read as a cautionary tale on the perils of triumph in a probationary world where victory must follow victory. Elated by his success in 1980, and eager to make a continued mark with the CEO vis-à-vis the presidents of the other four companies, all of whom were vying for the open presidency of Covenant Corporation, Smith became the victim of his own upbeat marketing optimism. He overcommitted

himself and the chemical company financially for the coming year just as the whole economy began to slide into recession. By mid-1981, profit targets had to be readjusted down and considerable anxiety pervaded Smith's circle and the upper-middle levels of management, whose job it became both to extract more profits from below and to maintain a public facade of cheerful equanimity. A top executive at Alchemy Inc. describes this anxiety:

> See, the problem with any change of CEO is that any credibility you have built up with the previous guy all goes by the board and you have to begin from scratch. This CEO thinks that everybody associated with the company before him is a dummy. And so you have to prove yourself over and over again. You can't just win some and lose some. You have to keep your winning record at least at 75 percent if not better. You're expected to take risks. At least the CEO says that, but the reality is that people are afraid to make mistakes.

Toward the end of the year, it became clear that the chemical company would reach. only 60 percent of its profit target and that only by remarkable legerdemain with the books. Publicly, of course, managers continued to evince a "cautious optimism" that things would turn around; privately, however, a deepening sense of gloom and incipient panic pervaded the organization. Stories began to circulate about the CEO's unhappiness with the company's shortfall. To take but one example, managers in chemical fertilizers were told by the CEO never again to offer weather conditions or widespread farmer bankruptcy as excuses for lagging sales. Rumors of every sort began to flourish, and a few of these are worth recounting.

Smith was on his way out, it was feared, and would take the whole structure of Alchemy Inc. with him. In fact, one of the CEO's most trusted troubleshooters, a man who "eats people for breakfast," was gunning for Smith and his job. (This man distinguished himself around this time by publicly accusing those who missed a 9:00 A.M. staff meeting, held during one of the worst snowstorms in two decades, of being disloyal to Covenant.)

Smith would survive, it was said, but would be forced to sacrifice all of his top people, alter his organization's structure, and buckle under to the increasingly vigorous demands of the CEO.

The CEO, it was argued, was about to put the whole chemical company on the block; in fact, the real purpose of creating supposedly self-contained companies in the first place might have been to package them for sale. At the least, the CEO would sell large portions of Alchemy Inc., wreaking havoc with its support groups at corporate headquarters.

There were disturbing rumors too about the growth of personal tension and animosity between Smith and the CEO. The CEO was well-known for his propensity for lording it over his subordinates, a behavioral pattern that often emerges in top authority figures after years of continual suppression of impulses. He was now said to have targeted Smith for this kind of attention. Managers up and down the line knew instinctively that, if the personal relationship between Smith and the CEO were eroding, the inevitable period of blame and retribution for the bad financial year might engulf everyone, and not just well-targeted individuals. Managers began to mobilize their subordinates to arrange defenses, tried to cement crucial alliances, and waited. In the meantime, they joked that they were updating their résumés and responding graciously to the regular phone calls of headhunters.

While reorganizations by CEOs have the broadest impact in a corporation, such shake-ups are not made by CEOs alone. Shake-ups are in fact the first line of defense against a CEO's demands by presidents of operating companies or divisions in trouble. At Alchemy Inc., invoking a commissioned study by management consultants, Smith eliminated a layer of top management early in 1982 to give himself and his top aides "greater access to the business areas." In the process, he got rid of Brown, the chemical company's executive vice-president. Brown was an anomaly in the higher circles of the company. Although his formal training had been in marketing, he had ended up performing a financial function in the executive vice-president slot—that is, riding herd on business managers about costs. His principal rise had been through the old specialty chemicals division; however, his original roots in the corporation were in the Energy Division where he had been a friend and close associate of the man who later rose to the presidency of that company in the "big

purge." This biographical history made Brown suspect, especially when the tension between the CEO and Smith intensified and some of the presidents of the other companies were thought to be seizing the chance to extend their own influence. Brown's straitlaced personal style was also out of keeping with the back-slapping bonhomie that marked Smith's inner circle. Managers often note that one must stay at least three drinks behind one's boss at social functions; this meant that Brown's subordinates might never drink at all on such occasions. As it happens, however, the CEO, himself a financial man, saved Brown and appointed him an executive vice-president of the Electronics company, in charge of what had become known as the "corporate graveyard," a place with decaying businesses that one buries by selling off.

Many managers were amused at Brown's reassignment. They felt that, as soon as he had succeeded in disposing of the unwanted businesses, he would be out of a job. He was, in effect, being told to dig his own grave in an appropriate location. Some managers, however, were more wary; they saw the move as a complicated gambit, in fact as a cover-up by the CEO himself who had invested heavily in several businesses in the electronics area only to have them expire. In any case, Brown had not been popular at Alchemy and his departure was greeted, as one manager describes it, "by a lot of people standing on the sidelines, hooting, and hollering, and stamping our feet. We never thought we'd see old [Brown] again."

In Brown's place, Smith appointed two executive vice-presidents, one a trusted aide from his favorite product group in the old specialty chemicals division and the other an outsider whose expertise was, it was said, in selling off commodity businesses, that is, what was left of the old process chemicals division. Though badly scarred, Smith managed to deflect blame for the bad year onto the heads of a few general managers, all from the old process division, whom he fired. One ominous note was Smith's loss of administrative control of the corporate headquarters site, a function that had fallen to the chemical company during the "big purge." A fundamental rule of corporate politics is that one never cedes control over assets, even if the assets are administrative headaches. More ominous was the CEO's gift of responsibility for headquarters to the man "who eats people for breakfast," mentioned earlier. On the whole, however, managers felt that not only had Smith reasserted the supremacy of his own alliances but that he had in the bargain bought himself eight months—time enough perhaps for the economy to turn around.

As it happened, however, the economy continued to worsen and the CEO's pressure on Smith increased. In the late spring of 1982, the CEO began sending a series of terse notes to company executives accompanied by photocopied articles written by a well-known management consultant in *The Wall Street Journal* about the necessity of trimming staff to streamline operations. Only companies that aggressively cut staff during the recession, the articles argued, would emerge lean and poised for the economic recovery. The CEO's notes usually said simply: "This article merits your careful attention." Smith's aides privately referred to the CEO as a "tinhorn tyrant" and muttered about his "henchmen" being sent to extract information from them to be used against Smith. One executive describes the chemical company's growing feeling toward corporate staff: "The boys he [the CEO] has over there are not very nice . . . they never miss a chance to stomp on you when you're down." As time passed, this feeling became more acerbic. Another executive describes how he sees "internal auditors," that is, the CEO's people who were overlooking Alchemy's operations:

> Have I ever told you my definition of an auditor? An auditor is someone who situates himself up on a hill overlooking a battle, far from the noise of the guns and the smoke of the explosions. And he watches the battle from afar, and when it is over and the smoke is cleared, he goes down onto the battlefield and walks among the wounded. And he shoots them.

Finally, in the early summer, the CEO demanded a 30 percent cut in staff in the chemical company, even asking for the names of those to be terminated. Smith had little choice but to go along and he fired 200 people. Most of these, however, were technical support people, Indians rather than chiefs. Smith was thus able to maintain a basic rule of management circles, namely that management takes care of itself, at least of other known managers, in good times and bad.

As the economy continued to flounder throughout the summer, Alchemy's earnings dipped even further, and the CEO's demands on Smith became relentless. By this point, the watchword in the corporation had become "manage for cash" and the CEO wanted some businesses sold, others cut back, still others milked, and costs slashed. Particular attention began to be focused on the chemical company's environmental protection staff, a target of hostility not only from the CEO's people but from line managers within Alchemy itself. In response to an environmental catastrophe in the late 1970s, and to the public outrage about chemical pollution in general, Smith had erected, upon his ascendancy to the presidency, an elaborate and relatively free-roaming environmental staff. Though costly, Smith felt that this apparatus was the best defense against another severely embarrassing and even more expensive environmental debacle. The company had, in fact, won an industrial award and wide public recognition for its program; the CEO himself, of course, had been a principal beneficiary of all this public praise and he basked in that attention. But, as the political atmosphere in the country changed with the conservative legislative, budgetary, and regulatory triumphs after President Reagan's election, line managers in Alchemy began chafing under staff intrusions. They blamed the environmental staff for creating extra work and needless costs during a period of economic crisis. The CEO agreed with these sentiments, and his opinion helped deepen the splits in the chemical company. In the early fall, faced with unremitting pressure because of the company's declining fortunes internal warring factions, and, worse, the prospect of public capitulation to the CEO on the structure of his supposedly autonomous company, Smith chose to resign to "pursue other interests," pulling the cord on his "golden parachute" (a failsafe plan ensuring comfortable financial landing) as he left.

His parting letter to the company typifies the peculiar combination of in-house humor, personal jauntiness in the face of adversity, and appeals to some of the classical legitimations of managerial work that one may observe among high-ranking managers. It reads in part:

> Hi!
>
> Someone from the stockroom just called and said there were reams of my stationery left downstairs—what did I want to

do with it? Not only have I relocated my-self to a distant corner office, but it appears that I've also freed up space on the stockroom shelves as well! Since I will be leaving on October 15, I want to take this opportunity to thank each and every one of you for the never-failing support and understanding you have given me through-out my years with [Alchemy]. I have had the privilege of knowing many of you personally, and the greatest satisfaction in my job here has been, throughout the years, to be able to walk down the hall and have so many of you say "Hi, [Joe]."

I would like to invite you to have a drink with me after work on October 6th. My first inclination was that it would be great to pitch a tent in the front parking lot and have hotdogs, too, but somehow I don't think that one would fly. So the [nearby hotel] it is, and I promise you—no speeches, no presentations, no formalities. Just a chance to personally say thank you for being part of a great team—one that I will never forget.

It is important to note that many managers were deeply moved by Smith's letter and particularly by the social occasion to which he invited them. It became not only a fare-well party for a fallen leader, but was seen as a small act of rebellion against the CEO. Alchemy Inc. went into a state of shock and paralysis at Smith's resignation, and the rumor mills churned out names of possible replacements, each tied to a scenario of the future. Once again, the mortar of fealty loos-ened throughout the pyramid even as it bound managers to their pasts. Managers know that others' cognitive maps afford little escape from old loyalties, alliances, and associations. At the same time, they realize that they must be poised to make new alliances in a hurry if their areas get targeted for "restructuring."

As things turned out, a great many managers found themselves in exactly that position. To almost everyone's astonishment, and to the trepidation of many, the CEO brought Brown back from the electronics graveyard after a "thorough assessment of all the candidates," which took two days, and made him the new president of Alchemy. No laughter or jeering was heard in the corridors, although some wags suggested nominating Brown as the "Comeback Player of the Year." Whatever Brown's previous affiliations, there was no doubt about where his fealty now lay. He became known throughout

the corporation as the "CEO's boy" and everyone recognized that he had a mandate to "wield a meat axe" and to wreak whatever mayhem was necessary to cut expenditures. At every level of the company, managers began furiously to scramble—writing position papers, holding rushed meetings, making deals—to try to secure their domains against the coming assault. Within a short time, Brown had fired 150 people, mostly at the managerial level, focusing particular attention on "streamlining" the environmental staff, slashing it by 75 percent. The survivors from the environmental staff were "moved close to the action," that is, subordinated to the business units, each of which was made more "free-standing," and thus the staff was effectively neutralized. The official rationale was as follows. The company had gone through an extraordinary learning experience on environmental issues and had bene-fited greatly from the expertise of the environmental staff. It had, however, by this point fully integrated and institutionalized that knowledge into its normal operations. Moreover, since there were no longer any environmental problems facing the company, a modest reduction in this area made good business sense. Privately, of course, the assessments were different. Brown himself said at a managerial meeting that good staff simply create work to justify their own existence. Many line managers echoed this opinion. More to the point, the feeling was that work on environmental issues had lost any urgency in the Reagan era. The Environmental Protection Agency (EPA) was dead. Moreover, the only real threat to corporations on environmental issues was in the courts, which, however, judge past actions, not present practices. By the time the courts get to cases generated by contemporary practices, typically in fifteen years, those executives presently in charge will have moved on, leaving any problems their policies might create to others. Managers noted, some ruefully, some with detached bemusement, the irony of organizational reform. The public outcry against Covenant after the environmental disaster of the late 1970s produced thorough-going internal reform designed to ward off such incidents in the future. But the reforms also unintentionally laid down the bases of resentment among managers who did not benefit from the staff increase. During a crisis, these managers grasped the chance to clamor for dismantling the safeguards that might prevent future catastrophes.

Brown's "housecleaning" created extreme anxiety throughout Alchemy. Even managers who agreed with Brown's attack on the staff and his wholesale pruning of other areas expressed astonishment and sometimes outrage that mostly persons of managerial rank had been fired. This seemed an ominous violation of the managerial code. Those that survived were "looking over their shoulders" and "listening for footsteps behind them." Bitter jokes circulated freely, like: "Opening Day at the chemical company; Brown comes in and throws out the first employee." Some managers even passed around among their colleagues a list of thirteen tough questions to throw at Brown at an internal news conference.

Throughout this entire period, the CEO had been pursuing an aggressive policy of acquisitions, picking up small and medium-sized companies and adding them to one or another of the operating companies' holdings. No one could discern the pattern of the acquisitions. High-technology industries with rapid growth potential were the officially stated targets; in fact, however, mostly mature businesses were purchased and unsuccessful bids were made for several others. Suddenly, in the midst of Alchemy's crisis, the CEO announced the acquisition, publicly called a merger, of another major corporation with mostly mature businesses and large, complicated corporate and company staffs. The announcement precipitated both consternation and excitement throughout Covenant Corporation; up and down the ladder of every company both line and staff managers began to mobilize their forces and to gear their troops for the inevitable and dangerous showdown with the personnel of the newly acquired firm. Showdowns following the acquisition of a smaller company are wholly predictable and are virtually no contest. The apprehension of Covenant managers in this case stemmed from their wariness of the bureaucratic battle skills of their opposite numbers in the firm acquired. Everything, of course, would depend on which leaders emerged from the crucible.

In the meantime, Alchemy Inc. staggered into the following year. Six months after the national economy took an upswing, its own fortunes began to improve, a typical pattern for industrial supply companies. Suddenly, in the spring of 1983, the CEO announced another major reorganization in order to integrate the newly acquired corporation, citing yet another thorough appraisal by a management consulting firm. Once again the entire corporation was divided into several "sectors," each section with different companies. This time, the Industrial Supplies Sector incorporated Alchemy, Metals, and Plastics. Brown did not get the call to head the whole Industrial Supplies Sector but remained as the president of Alchemy. The leadership of the whole sector fell instead to a man who had emerged out of the Metals company where he had been president in the old order. He in turn gave the presidencies of Metals and Plastics to metals people, and a new cycle of ascendancy with its own patterns of fealty, patronage, and power cliques began. Managers noted, with some satisfaction, the irony of Brown being passed over by the CEO for the sector presidency after performing the CEO's dirty work. Their satisfaction was short-lived. After a stint at the helm of chemicals, Brown returned to his original home in the corporation as the aide-de-camp of the president of the new Energy Sector—his old mentor. When the latter retired, Brown assumed control of that sector.

III

This sequence of events is remarkable only for its compactness. One need only regularly read *The Wall Street Journal*, the business section of *The New York Times*, any of the leading business magazines, let alone more academic publications, to see that these sorts of upheavals and political struggles are commonplace in American business. In Weft Corporation, one could observe exactly similar patterns, though played out over a much longer period of time. For instance, more than a decade ago, a new CEO was brought into the company to modernize and professionalize what had been up to that point a closely held family business. His first act was to make a rule that no executives over sixty years old could hold posts above a certain high-ranking management grade. In one stroke, he got rid of a whole cohort of executives who had ruled the company for a generation. He then staffed all key posts of each division, as well as his own inner circle, either with people who had served under him in the Army during World War II, or with whom he had worked in another corporation, or with former consultants who had advised him on how to proceed with the re-organization, or with people from the old organization with whom he felt comfortable. All of these managers in turn brought in their own recruits and protégés. They established a corporate order notable for its stability for many years. As the CEO and his subordinates grew older, of course, he eliminated the rule governing age. Eventually, however, retirement time did come. The new CEO was handpicked by the outgoing boss from the high reaches of another corporation where he had been vice-chairman and thus effectively dead-ended. He graciously bided his time until the old CEO had entirely left the scene and then moved decisively to shape the organization to his liking. The most important move in this regard was the rapid elevation of a man who had been a mere vice-president of personnel, normally the wasteland of the corporate world. Within a year of the new CEO's ascendancy, this manager was given control over all other staff functions. He then moved into an executive vice-president post as the closest aide and confidant of the CEO on the Central Management Committee, with decisive say-so over financial issues and thus over operations. Tough, seasoned managers in the operating divisions—men and women of great drive and ambition—began to see their own chances for future ascendancy possibly blocked. Many began to depart the corporation. The posts of those who left were filled by men and women whose loyalties and futures lay with the new regime. Thus, the compressed sequence of events at Covenant Corporation simply allows one to be particularly attentive to ongoing, and usually taken for granted, structural and psychological patterns of corporate life.

Here I want to highlight a few of these basic structures and experiences of managerial work, those that seem to form its essential framework. First of all, at the psychological level, managers have an acute sense of organizational contingency. Because of the interlocking ties between people, they know that a shake-up at or near the top of a hierarchy can trigger a widespread upheaval, bringing in its wake startling reversals of fortune, good and bad, throughout the structure. Managers' cryptic aphorism, "Well, you never know . . . ," repeated often and regularly, captures the sense of uncertainty created by the constant potential for social reversal. Managers know too, and take for granted, that the personnel changes brought about by upheavals are to a great extent arbitrary and depend more than anything else on one's social relationships with key individuals and with groups of managers. Periods of organizational quiescence and stability still managers' wariness in this regard, but the foreboding sense of contingency never entirely disappears. Managers' awareness of the complex levels of conflict in their world, built into the very structure of bureaucratic organizations, constantly reminds them that things can very quickly fall apart.

The political struggles at Covenant Corporation, for instance, suggest some immediately observable levels of conflict and tension.

First, occupational groups emerging from the segmented structure of bureaucratic work, each with different expertise and emphasis, constantly vie with one another for ascendancy of their ideas, of their products or services, and of themselves. It is, for instance, an axiom of corporate life that the greatest satisfaction of production people is to see products go out the door; of salesmen, to make a deal regardless of price; of marketers, to control salesmen and squeeze profits out of their deals; and of financial specialists, to make sure that everybody meets budget. Despite the larger interdependence of such work, the necessarily fragmented functions performed day-to-day by managers in one area often put them at cross purposes with managers in another. Nor do competitiveness and conflict result only from the broad segmentation of functions. Sustained work in a product or service area not only shapes crucial social affiliations but also symbolic identifications, say, with particular products or technical services, that mark managers in their corporate arenas. Such symbolic markings make it imperative for managers to push their particular products or services as part of their overall self-promotion. This fuels the constant scramble for authoritative enthusiasm for one product or service rather than another and the subsequent allocation or re-allocation of organizational resources.

Second, line and staff managers, each group with different responsibilities, different pressures, and different bailiwicks to protect, fight over organizational resources and over the rules that govern work. The very definition of staff depends entirely on one's vantage point in the organization. As one manager points out: "From the perspective of the guy who actually pushes the button to make the machine go, everyone else is staff." However, the working definition that managers use is that anyone whose decisions directly affect profit and loss is in the line; all others in an advisory capacity of some sort are staff. As a general rule, line managers' attitudes toward staff vary directly with the independence granted staff by higher management. The more freedom staff have to intervene in the line, as with the environmental staff at Alchemy or Covenant's corporate staff, the more they are feared and resented by line management. For line managers, independent staff represent either the intrusion of an unwelcome "rules and procedures mentality" into situations where line managers feel that they have to be alert to the exigencies of the market or, alternatively, as power threats to vested interests backed by some authority. In the "decentralized" organizations prevalent today in the corporate world, however, most staff are entirely dependent on the line and must market their technical, legal, or organizational skills to line managers exactly as an outside firm must do. The continual necessity for staff to sell their technical expertise helps keep them in check since line managers, pleading budgetary stringency or any number of other acceptable rationales, can thwart or ignore proffered assistance. Staff's dependent position often produces jealous respect for line management tinged with the resentment that talented people relegated to do "pine time" (sit on the bench) feel for those in the center of action. For instance, an environmental manager at Weft Corporation comments on his marginal status and on how he sees it depriving him of the recognition he feels his work deserves:

> I also want recognition. And usually the only way you get that is having a boss near you who sees what you do. It rubs me raw in fact.... For instance, you know they run these news releases when some corporate guy gets promoted and all? Well, when I do something, nothing ever gets said. When I publish papers, or get promoted, and so on, you never see any public announcement. Oh, they like me to publish papers and I guess someone reads them, but that's all that's ever said or done.... I can get recognition in a variety of arenas, like professional associations, but if they're going to recognize the

plant manager, why not me? If we walked off, would the plants operate? They couldn't. We're *essential*.

This kind of ambivalent resentment sometimes becomes vindictiveness when a top boss uses staff as a hammer.

Staff can also become effective pitchmen; line managers' anxious search for rational solutions to largely irrational problems, in fact, encourages staff continually to invent and disseminate new tactics and schemes. Alternatively, social upheavals that produce rapid shifts in public opinion—such as occurred in the personnel or environmental areas in the aftermath of the 1960s—may encourage proliferation of staff. In either circumstance, staff tend to increase in an organization until an ideological cycle of "organizational leanness" comes around and staff, at least those of lower rank, get decimated.

Third, powerful managers in Alchemy Inc., each controlling considerable resources and the organizational fates of many men and women, battle fiercely with one another to position themselves, their products, and their allies favorably in the eyes of their president and of the CEO. At the same time, high-ranking executives "go to the mat" with one another striving for the CEO's approval and a coveted shot at the top. Bureaucratic hierarchies, simply by offering ascertainable rewards for certain behavior, fuel the ambition of those men and women ready to subject themselves to the discipline of external exigencies and of their organization's institutional logic, the socially constructed shared understanding of how their world works. However, since rewards are always scarce, bureaucracies necessarily pit people against each other and inevitably thwart the ambitions of some. The rules of such combat vary from organization to organization and depend largely on what top management countenances either openly or tacitly.

Nor are formal positions and perquisites the only objects of personal struggle between managers. Even more important on a day-to-day basis is the ongoing competition between talented and aggressive people to see whose will prevails, who can get things done their way. The two areas are, of course, related since one's chances in an organization depend largely on one's "credibility," that is, on the widespread belief that one can act effectively. One must therefore prevail regularly, though not always, in small things to have any hope of positioning oneself for big issues. The hidden agenda of seemingly petty disputes may be a struggle over long-term organizational fates.

At the same time, all of these struggles take place within the peculiar tempo and framework each CEO establishes for an organization. Under an ideology of thorough decentralization—the gift of authority with responsibility—the CEO at Covenant actually centralizes his power enormously because fear of derailing personal ambitions prevents managers below him from acting without his approval. A top official at Alchemy comments:

> What we have now, despite rhetoric to the contrary, is a very centralized system. It's [the CEO] who sets the style, tone, tempo of all the companies. He says: "Manage for cash," and we manage for cash. The original idea . . . was to set up free-standing companies with a minimum of corporate staff. But . . . we're moving toward a system that is really beyond what we used to have, let alone modeled on a small corporate staff and autonomous divisions. What we used to have was separate divisions reporting to a corporate staff. I think we're moving away from that idea too. I think what's coming is a bunch of separate businesses reporting to the corporation. It's a kind of portfolio management. This accords perfectly with [the CEO's] temperament. He's a financial type guy who is oriented to the bottom line numbers. He doesn't want or need intermediaries between him and his businesses.

In effect, the CEO of Covenant, who seems to enjoy constant turmoil, pits himself and his ego against the whole corporation even while he holds it in vassalage. Other CEOs establish different frameworks and different tempos, depending on self-image and temperament. The only firm rule seems to be that articulated by a middle-level Covenant manager: "Every big organization is set up for the benefit of those who control it; the boss gets what he wants."

Except during times of upheaval, the ongoing conflicts that I have described are usually hidden behind the comfortable and benign social ambiance that most American corporations fashion for their white-collar personnel. Plush carpets, potted trees, burnished oak wall paneling, fine reproductions and sometimes originals of great art, mahogany desks, polished glass tables and ornaments, rich leather upholstery, perfectly coiffured, attractive and poised reception-

ists, and private, subsidized cafeterias are only a few of the pleasant features that grace the corporate headquarters of any major company. In addition, the corporations that I studied provide their employees with an amazing range and variety of services, information, and social contacts. Covenant Corporation, for instance, through its daily newsletter and a variety of other internal media, offers information about domestic and international vacation packages; free travelers' checks; discounted tickets for the ballet, tennis matches, or art exhibits; home remedies for the common cold, traveling clinics for diagnosing high blood pressure, and advice on how to save one's sight; simple tests for gauging automotive driving habits; tips on home vegetable gardening; advice on baby-sitters; descriptions of business courses at a local college; warning articles on open fireplaces and home security; and directions for income tax filing. The newsletter also offers an internal market for the sale, rental, or exchange of a myriad of items ranging from a Jamaican villa, to a set of barbells, to back issues of *Fantasy* magazine. Covenant offers as well intracompany trapshooting contests, round-robin tennis and golf tournaments, running clinics, and executive fitness programs. Weft Corporation's bulletin is even more elaborate, with photographic features on the "Great Faces" of Weft employees; regular reports on the company's 25- and 50-year clubs; personal notes on all retirees from the company; stories about the company's sponsorship of art exhibits; human-interest stories about employees and their families—from a child struggling against liver cancer to the heroics of a Weft employee in foiling a plane hijacker; and, of course, a steady drumbeat of corporate ideology about the necessity for textile import quotas and the desirability of "buying American."

My point here is that corporations are not presented nor are they seen simply as places to work for a living. Rather the men and women in them come to fashion an entire social ambiance that overlays the antagonisms created by company politics; this makes the nuances of corporate conflict difficult to discern. A few managers, in fact, mistake the first-name informality, the social congeniality, and the plush exterior appointments for the entire reality of their collective life and are surprised when hard structural jolts turn their world upside down. Even battle-scarred veterans evince, at times, an ambivalent half-belief in the litany of rhetorics of unity and cohesive legitimating appeals. The latter are sometimes accompanied by gala events to underline the appeal. For instance, not long after the "big purge" at Covenant Corporation when 600 people were fired, the CEO spent $1 million for a "Family Day" to "bring everyone together." The massive party was attended by over 14,000 people and featured clowns, sports idols, and booths complete with bean bag and ring tosses, foot and bus races, computer games, dice rolls, and, perhaps appropriately, mazes. In his letter to his "Fellow Employees" following the event, the CEO said:

> I think Family Day made a very strong statement about the [Covenant] "family" of employees at [Corporate Headquarters]. And that is that we can accomplish whatever we set out to do if we work together; if we share the effort, we will share the rewards. The "New World of [Covenant]" has no boundaries only frontiers, and each and everyone can play a role, for we need what *you* have to contribute.

The very necessity for active involvement in such rituals often prompts semicredulity. But wise and ambitious managers resist the lulling platitudes of unity, though they invoke them with fervor, and look for the inevitable clash of interests beneath the bouncy, cheerful surface of corporate life. They understand implicitly that the repression of open conflict simply puts a premium on the mastery of the socially accepted modes of waging combat.

The continuous uncertainty and ambiguity of managerial hierarchies, exacerbated over time by masked conflict, causes managers to turn toward each other for cues for behavior. They try to learn from each other and to master the shared assumptions, the complex rules, the normative codes, the underlying institutional logic that governs their world. They thus try to control the construction of their everyday reality. Normally, of course, one learns to master the managerial code in the course of repeated, long-term social interaction with other managers, particularly in the course of shaping the multiple and complex alliances essential to organizational survival and success.

Alliances are ties of quasiprimal loyalty shaped especially by common work, by common experiences with the same problems, the same friends, or the same enemies, and by favors traded over time. Although alliances are rooted in fealty and patronage relationships, they are not limited by such relationships since fealty shifts with changing work assignments or with organizational upheavals.

Making an alliance may mean, for instance, joining or, more exactly, being included in one or several of the many networks of managerial associates that crisscross an organization. Conceptually, networks are usually thought of as open-ended webs of association with a low degree of formal organization and no distinct criteria of membership. One becomes known, for instance, as a trusted friend of a friend; thought of as a person to whom one can safely refer a thorny problem; considered a "sensible" or "reasonable" or, especially, a "flexible" person, not a "renegade" or a "loose cannon rolling around the lawn"; known to be a discreet person attuned to the nuances of corporate etiquette, one who can keep one's mouth shut or who can look away and pretend to notice nothing; or considered a person with sharp ideas that break deadlocks but who does not object to the ideas being appropriated by superiors.

Alliances are also fashioned in social coteries. These are more clublike groups of friends that, in Weft Corporation, forge ties at the cocktail hour over the back fence on Racquet Drive, the road next to the company's tennis courts where all important and socially ambitious executives live; or in Friday night poker sessions that provide a bluff and hearty setting where managers can display their own and unobtrusively observe others' mastery of public faces, a clue to many managerial virtues. In other companies, coteries consist of "tennis pals" who share an easy camaraderie over salad and yogurt lunches following hard squash games or two-mile jogs at noon. They are also made up of posthours cronies who, in midtown watering holes, weld private understandings with ironic bantering, broad satire, or macabre humor, the closest some managers ever get to open discussion of their work with their fellows; or gatherings of the smart social set where business circles intersect with cliques from intellectual and artistic worlds and where glittering, poised, and precisely vacuous social conversation can mark one as a social lion. In one company, a group of "buddies" intertwine their private lives with their organizational fates in the most complete way by, for example, persuading an ambitious younger colleague to provide a woodsy cabin retreat and local girls for a collegial evening's entertainment while on a business trip. At the managerial and professional levels, the road between work and life is usually open because it is difficult to refuse to use one's influence, patronage, or power on behalf of another regular member of one's social coterie. It therefore becomes important to choose one's social colleagues with some care and, of course, know how to drop them should they fall out of organizational favor.

Alliances are also made wholly on the basis of specific self-interests. The paradigmatic case here is that of the power clique of established, well-placed managers who put aside differences and join forces for a "higher cause," namely their own advancement or protection. Normally, though not always, as Brown's case at Covenant shows, one must be "plugged into" important networks and an active participant in key coteries in order to have achieved an organizational position where one's influence is actively counted. But the authority and power of a position matter in and of themselves. Once one has gained power, one can use one's influence in the organization to shape social ties. Such alliances often cut across rival networks and coteries and can, in fact, temporarily unite them. Managers in a power clique map out desired organizational tacks and trade off the resources in their control. They assess the strengths and weaknesses of their opponents; they plan coups and rehearse the appropriate rationales to legitimate them. And, on the other hand, they erect requisite barriers to squelch attempted usurpations of their power. Cliques also introduce managers to new, somewhat more exclusive networks and coteries. Especially at the top of a pyramid, these social ties extend over the boundaries of one's own corporation and mesh one's work and life with those of top managers in other organizations.

I shall refer to all the social contexts that breed alliances, fealty relationships, networks, coteries, or cliques, as circles of affiliation, or simply managerial circles. Now, the notion of "circles," as it has been used in sociological literature, as well as colloquially, has some drawbacks for accurately delineating the important features of the web of managerial interaction. Specifically, a circle

suggests a quasiclosed social group made up of members of relatively equal status without defined leadership and without formal criteria for membership or inclusion. In a bureaucratic hierarchy, nuances of status are, of course, extremely important. Moreover, since business cannot be conducted without formal authorization by appropriate authorities, one's formal rank always matters even though there is ample scope for more informal charismatic leadership. Finally, the most crucial feature of managerial circles of affiliation is precisely their establishment of informal criteria for admission, criteria that are, it is true, ambiguously defined and subject to constant, often arbitrary, revision. Nonetheless, they are criteria that managers must master. At bottom, all of the social contexts of the managerial world seek to discover if one "can feel comfortable" with another manager, if he is someone who "can be trusted," if he is "our kind of guy," or, in short, if he is "one of the gang." The notion of gang, in fact, insofar as it suggests the importance of leadership, hierarchy, and probationary mechanisms in a bounded but somewhat amorphous group, may more accurately describe re1ationships in the corporation than the more genteel, and therefore preferable, word "circle." In any event, just as managers must continually please their boss, their boss's boss, their patrons, their president, and their CEO, so must they prove themselves again and again to each other. Work becomes an endless round of what might be called probationary crucibles. Together with the uncertainty and sense of contingency that mark managerial work, this constant state of probation produces a profound anxiety in managers, perhaps the key experience of managerial work. It also breeds, selects, or elicits certain traits in ambitious managers that are crucial to getting ahead.

Endnotes

1. Brackets within quotations represent words or phrases changed or added by the author, either to protect identity or to provide grammatical fluency.
2. Henceforth, I shall generally use only "he" or "his" to allow for easier reading.
3. All personal names in the field data throughout the [chapter] are pseudonyms.

Chapter 5
Institutionalized Organizations

Formal Structure as Myth and Ceremony

John W. Meyer and Brian Rowan

What accounts for the formal structures that make up an organization? In this classic article, Meyer and Rowan argue that formal structures "dramatically reflect the myths of their institutional environments instead of the demands of their work activities." For Meyer and Rowan, these myths take the form of "institutionalized rules" that surround organizations and are embraced by the people who manage and work in them.

Meyer and Rowan's claim that we should look outside, rather than inside, organizations to understand their structures and practices has had a profound influence on organizational theory. In particular, researchers began to view organizations as embedded within society, rather than as set apart from it. This approach provided a new vantage point from which to understand organizations, and it gave analysts new tools to explain organizational structures and processes. We will see these tools at work in forthcoming chapters, as researchers examine the cultural, social, political, and economic forces that shape organizations.

Formal organizations are generally understood to be systems of coordinated and controlled activities that arise when work is embedded in complex networks of technical relations and boundary-spanning exchanges. But in modern societies, formal organizational structures arise in highly institutionalized contexts. Professions, policies, and programs are created along with the products and services that they are understood to produce rationally. This process permits many new organizations to spring up and forces existing ones to incorporate new practices and procedures. That is, organizations are driven to incorporate the practices and procedures defined by prevailing rationalized concepts of organizational work and institutionalized in society. Organizations that do so increase their legitimacy and their survival prospects, independent of the immediate efficacy of the acquired practices and procedures.

Institutionalized products, services, techniques, policies, and programs function as powerful myths, and many organizations adopt them ceremonially. But conformity to institutionalized rules often conflicts sharply with efficiency criteria; conversely, to coordinate and control activity in order to promote efficiency undermines an organization's ceremonial conformity and sacrifices its support and legitimacy. To maintain ceremonial conformity, organizations that reflect institutional rules tend to buffer their formal structures from the uncertainties of technical activities by becoming loosely coupled, building gaps between their formal structures and actual work activities.

This chapter argues that the formal structures of many organizations in post-industrial society (Bell 1973) dramatically reflects the myths of their institutional environments instead of the demands of their work activities. The first part describes prevailing theories of the origins of formal structures and the main problem the theories confront. The second part discusses an alternative source of formal structures: myths embedded in the institutional environment. The third part develops the argument that organizations reflecting institutionalized environments maintain gaps between their formal structures and their ongoing work activities. The final part summarizes by discussing some research implications.

Throughout the chapter, institutionalized rules are distinguished sharply from prevailing social behaviors. Institutionalized rules are classifications built into society as reciprocated typifications or interpretations (Berger and Luckmann 1967:54). Such rules may be simply taken for granted or may be supported by public opinion or the force of law (Starbuck 1976). Institutions inevitably involve normative obligations but often enter into social life primarily as facts which must be taken into account by actors. Institutionalization involves the processes by which social processes, obligations, or actualities come to take on a rulelike status in social thought and action. So, for example, the social status of a doctor is a highly institutionalized role (both normative and cognitive) for managing illness as well as a social role made up of particular behaviors, relations, and expectations. Research and development is an institutionalized category of organizational activity which has meaning and value in many sectors of society; it is also a collection of actual research and development activities. In a smaller way, a No Smoking sign is an institution with legal status and implications as well as an attempt to regulate smoking behavior. Fundamental to the argument of this chapter is that institutional rules may have effects on organizational structures and their implementation in actual technical work which are very different from the effects generated by the networks of social behavior and relationships which compose and surround a given organization.

Prevailing Theories of Formal Structure

A sharp distinction should be made between the formal structure of an organization and its actual day-to-day work activities. Formal structure is a blueprint for activities which includes, first of all, the table of organization: a listing of offices, departments, positions, and programs. These elements are linked by explicit goals and policies that make up a rational theory of how, and to what end, activities are to be fitted together. The essence of a modern bureaucratic organization lies in the rationalized and impersonal character of these structural elements and of the goals that link them.

One of the central problems in organization theory is to describe the conditions that give rise to rationalized formal structure. In conventional theories, rational formal structure is assumed to be the most effective way to coordinate and control the complex relational networks involved in modern technical or work activities (see Scott 1975 for a review). This assumption derives from Weber's (1946, 1947, 1952) discussions of the historical emergence of bureaucracies as consequences of economic markets and centralized states. Economic markets place a premium on rationality and coordination. As markets expand, the relational networks in a given domain become more complex and differentiated, and organizations in that domain must manage more internal and boundary-spanning interdependencies. Such factors as size (Blau 1970) and technology (Woodward 1965) increase the complexity of internal relations, and the division of labor among organizations increases boundary-spanning problems (Aiken and Hage 1968; Freeman 1973; Thompson 1967). Because the need for coordination increases under these conditions, and because formally coordinated work has competitive advantages, organizations with rationalized formal structures tend to develop.

The formation of centralized states and the penetration of societies by political centers also contribute to the rise and spread of formal organization. When the relational networks involved in economic exchange and political management become extremely complex, bureaucratic structures are thought to be the most effective and rational means to standardize and control subunits. Bureaucratic control is especially useful for expanding political centers, and standardization is often demanded by both centers and peripheral units (Bendix 1964, 1968). Political centers organize layers of offices that manage to extend conformity and to displace traditional activities throughout societies.

The problem: *Prevailing theories assume that the coordination and control of activity are the critical dimensions on which formal organizations have succeeded in the modern world.* This assumption is based on the view that organizations function according to their formal blueprints: coordination is routine, rules and procedures are followed, and actual activities conform to the prescriptions of formal structure. But much of the empirical research on organizations casts doubt on this assumption. An earlier generation of researchers concluded that there was a great gap between the formal and the informal organization (e.g., Dalton 1959; Downs 1967; Homans 1950). A related observation is that formal organizations are often loosely coupled (March and Olsen 1976; Weick 1976): structural elements are only loosely linked to each other and to activities, rules are often violated, decisions are often unimplemented, or if implemented have uncertain consequences, technologies are of problematic efficiency, and evaluation and inspection systems are subverted or rendered so vague as to provide little coordination.

Formal organizations are endemic in modern societies. There is need for an explanation of their rise that is partially free from the assumption that, in practice, formal structures actually coordinate and control work. Such an explanation should account for the elaboration of purposes, positions, policies, and procedural rules that characterizes formal organizations, but must do so without supposing that these structural features are implemented in routine work activity.

Institutional Sources of Formal Structure

By focusing on the management of complex relational networks and the exercise of coordination and control, prevailing theories have neglected an alternative Weberian source of formal structure: the legitimacy of rationalized formal structures. In prevailing theories, legitimacy is a given; assertions about bureaucratization rest on the assumption of norms of rationality (Thompson 1967). When norms do play causal roles in theories of bureaucratization, it is because they are thought to be built into modern societies and personalities as very general values, which are thought to facilitate formal organization. But norms of rationality are not simply general values. They exist in much more specific and powerful ways in the rules, understandings, and meanings attached to institutionalized social structures. The causal importance of such institutions in the process of bureaucratization has been neglected.

Formal structures are not only creatures of their relational networks in the social organization. In modern societies, the elements of rationalized formal structure are deeply ingrained in, and reflect, widespread understandings of social reality. Many of the positions, policies, programs, and procedures of modern organizations are enforced by public opinion, by the views of important constituents, by knowledge legitimated through the educational system, by social prestige, by the laws, and by the definitions of negligence and prudence used by the courts. Such elements of formal structure are manifestations of powerful institutional rules which function as highly rationalized myths that are binding on particular organizations.

In modern societies, the myths generating formal organizational structure have two key properties. First, they are rationalized and impersonal prescriptions that identify various social purposes as technical ones and specify in a rulelike way the appropriate means to pursue these technical purposes rationally (Ellul 1964). Second, they are highly institutionalized and thus in some measure beyond the discretion of any individual participant or organization. They must, therefore, be taken for granted as legitimate, apart from evaluations of their impact on work outcomes.

Many elements of formal structure are highly institutionalized and function as myths. Examples include professions, programs, and technologies:

Large numbers of rationalized professions emerge (Wilensky 1965; Bell 1973). These are occupations controlled not only by direct inspection of work outcomes but also by social rules of licensing, certifying, and schooling. The occupations are rationalized, being understood to control impersonal techniques rather than moral mysteries. Further, they are highly institutionalized: the delegation of activities to the appropriate occupations is socially expected and often legally obligatory over and above any calculations of its efficiency.

Many formalized organizational programs are also institutionalized in society. Ideologies define the functions appropriate to a business—such as sales, production, advertising, or accounting; to a university—such as instruction and research in history, engineering, and literature; and to a hospital—such as surgery, internal medicine, and obstetrics. Such classifications of organizational functions, and the specifications for conducting each function, are prefabricated formulas available for use by any given organization.

Similarly, technologies are institutionalized and become myths binding on organizations. Technical procedures of production, accounting, personnel selection, or data processing become taken-for-granted means to accomplish organizational ends. Quite apart from their possible efficiency, such institutionalized techniques establish an organization as appropriate, rational, and modern. Their use displays responsibility and avoids claims of negligence.

The impact of such rationalized institutional elements on organizations and organizing situations is enormous. These rules define new organizing situations, redefine existing ones, and specify the means for coping rationally with each. They enable, and often require, participants to organize along prescribed lines. And they spread very rapidly in modern society as part of the rise of postindustrial society (Bell 1973). New and extant domains of activity are codified in institutionalized programs, professions, or techniques, and organizations incorporate the packaged codes. Some examples are the following.

The discipline of psychology creates a rationalized theory of personnel selection and certifies personnel professionals; personnel departments and functionaries appear in all sorts of extant organizations, and new, specialized personal agencies also appear.

As programs of research and development are created and professionals with expertise in these fields are trained and defined, organizations come under increasing pressure to incorporate R & D units.

As the prerational profession of prostitution is rationalized along medical lines, bureaucratized organizations—sex-therapy clinics, massage parlors, and the like—spring up more easily.

As the issues of safety and environmental pollution arise, and as relevant professions and programs become institutionalized in laws, union ideologies, and public opinion, organizations incorporate these programs and professions.

The growth of rationalized institutional structures in society makes formal organizations more common and more elaborate. Such institutions are myths which make formal organizations both easier to create and more necessary. After all, the building blocks for organizations come to be littered around the societal landscape; it takes only a little entrepreneurial energy to assemble them into a structure. And because these building blocks are considered proper, adequate, rational, and necessary, organizations must incorporate them to avoid illegitimacy. Thus, the myths built into rationalized institutional elements create the necessity, the opportunity, and the impulse to organize rationally, over and above pressures in this direction created by the need to manage proximate relational networks:

Proposition 1. *As rationalized institutional rules arise in given domains of work activity, formal organizations form and expand by incorporating these rules as structural elements.*

Two distinct ideas are implied here: (1A) As institutionalized myths define new domains of rationalized activity, formal organizations emerge in these domains. (1B) As rationalizing institutional myths arise in existing domains of activity, extant organizations expand their formal structures so as to become isomorphic with these new myths.

To understand the larger historical process it is useful to note that:

Proposition 2. *The more modernized the society, the more extended the rationalized institutional structure in given domains and the greater the number of domains containing rationalized institutions.*

Modern institutions, then, are thoroughly rationalized, and these rationalized elements act as myths giving rise to more formal organization. When propositions 1 and 2 are combined, two more specific ideas follow: (2A) Formal organizations are more likely to emerge in more modernized societies, even with the complexity of immediate relational networks held constant. (2B) Formal organizations in a given domain of activity are likely to have more elaborated structures in more modernized societies, even with the complexity of immediate relational networks held constant.

Combining the ideas above with prevailing organization theory, it becomes clear that modern societies are filled with rationalized bureaucracies for two reasons. First, as the prevailing theories have asserted, relational networks become increasingly complex as societies modernize. Second, modern societies are filled with institutional rules which function as myths depicting various formal structures as rational means to the attainment of desirable ends. Figure 5.1 summarizes these two lines of theory. Both lines suggest that the postindustrial society—the society dominated by rational organization even more than by the forces of production—arises both out of the complexity of the modern social organizational network and, more directly, as an ideological matter. Once institutionalized, rationality becomes a myth with explosive organizing potential, as both Ellul (1964) and Bell (1973)—though with rather different reactions—observe.

Figure 5.1

The origins and elaboration of formal organizational structures.

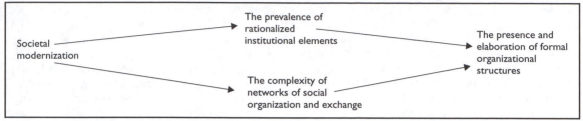

The Relation of Organizations to Their Institutional Environments

The observation is not new that organizations are structured by phenomena in their environments and tend to become isomorphic with them. One explanation of such isomorphism is that formal organizations become matched with their environments by technical and exchange interdependencies. This line of reasoning can be seen in the works of Aiken and Hage (1968), Hawley (1968), and Thompson (1967). This explanation asserts that structural elements diffuse because environments create boundary-spanning exigencies for organizations, and that organizations which incorporate structural elements isomorphic with the environment are able to manage such interdependencies.

A second explanation for the parallelism between organizations and their environments—and the one emphasized here—is that organizations structurally reflect socially constructed reality (Berger and Luckmann 1967). This view is suggested in the work of Parsons (1956) and Udy (1970), who see organizations as greatly conditioned by their general institutional environments and therefore as institutions themselves in part. Emery and Trist (1965) also see organizations as responding directly to environmental structures and distinguish such effects sharply from those that occur through boundary-spanning exchanges. According to the institutional conception as developed here, organizations tend to disappear as distinct and bounded units. Quite beyond the environmental interrelations suggested in open-systems theories, institutional theories in their extreme forms define organizations as dramatic enactments of the rationalized myths pervading modern societies rather than as units involved in exchange—no matter how complex—with their environments.

The two explanations of environmental isomorphism are not entirely inconsistent. Organizations both deal with their environments at their boundaries and imitate environmental elements in their structures. However, the two lines of explanation have very different implications for internal organizational processes, as is argued below.

The Origins of Rational Institutional Myths

Bureaucratization is caused in part by the proliferation of rationalized myths in society, and this in turn involves the evolution of the whole modern institutional system. Although the latter topic is beyond the scope of this chapter, three specific processes that generate rationalized myths of organizational structure can be noted.

The Elaboration of Complex Relational Networks. As the relational networks in societies become dense and interconnected, increasing numbers of rationalized myths arise. Some of them are highly generalized; for example, the principles of universalism (Parsons 1971), contracts (Spencer 1897), restitution (Durkheim 1933), and expertise (Weber 1947) are generalized to diverse occupations, organizational programs, and organizational practices. Other myths describe specific structural elements. These myths may originate from narrow contexts and be applied in different ones. For example, in modern societies the relational contexts of business organizations in a single industry are roughly similar from place to place. Under these conditions a particularly effective practice, occupational specialty, or principle of coordination can be codified into mythlike form. The laws, the educational and credentialing systems, and public opinion then make it necessary or advantageous for organizations to incorporate the new structures.

The Degree of Collective Organization of the Environment. The myths generated by particular organizational practices and diffused through relational networks have legitimacy based on the supposition that they are rationally effective. But many myths also have official legitimacy based on legal mandates. Societies that, through nation building and state formation, have developed rational-legal orders are especially prone to give collective (legal) authority to institutions which legitimate particular organizational structures. The rise of centralized states and integrated nations means that organized agents of society assume jurisdiction over large numbers of activity domains (Swanson 1971). Legislative and judicial authorities create and interpret legal mandates; administrative agencies—such as state and federal governments, port authorities, and school districts—establish rules of practice; and licenses and credentials become necessary in order to practice occupations. The stronger the rational-legal order, the greater the extent to which rationalized rules and procedures and personnel become institutional requirements. New formal organizations emerge, and extant organizations acquire new structural elements.

Leadership Efforts of Local Organizations. The rise of the state and the expansion of collective jurisdiction are often thought to result in domesticated organizations (Carlson 1962) subject to high levels of goal displacement (Clark 1956; Selznick 1949; Zald and Denton 1963). This view is misleading: organizations do often adapt to their institutional contexts, but they often play active roles in shaping those contexts (Dowling and Pfeffer 1975; Parsons 1956; Perrow 1970; Thompson 1967). Many organizations actively seek charters from collective authorities and manage to institutionalize their goals and structures in the rules of such authorities.

Efforts to mold institutional environments proceed along two dimensions. First, powerful organizations force their immediate relational networks to adapt to their structures and relations. For instance, automobile producers help create demands for particular kinds of roads, transportation systems, and fuels that make automobiles virtual necessities; competitive forms of transportation have to adapt to the existing relational context. But second, powerful organizations attempt to build their goals and procedures directly into society as institutional rules. Automobile producers, for instance, attempt to create the standards in public opinion defining desirable cars, to influence legal standards defining satisfactory cars, to affect judicial rules defining cars adequate enough to avoid manufacturer liability, and to force agents of the collectivity to purchase only their cars. Rivals must then compete both in social networks or markets and in contexts of institutional rules which are defined by extant organizations. In this fashion, given organizational forms perpetuate themselves by becoming institutionalized rules. For example, school administrators who create new curricula or training programs attempt to validate them as legitimate innovations in educational theory and governmental requirements. If they are successful, the new procedures can be perpetuated as authoritatively required or at least satisfactory. New departments within business enterprises, such as personnel, advertising, or research and development departments, attempt to professionalize by creating rules of practice and personnel certification that are enforced by the schools, prestige systems, and the laws. Organizations under attack in competitive environments—small farms, passenger railways, or Rolls Royce—attempt to establish themselves as central to the cultural traditions of their societies in order to receive official protection.

The Impact of Institutional Environments on Organizations

Isomorphism with environmental institutions has some crucial consequences for organizations: (*a*) they incorporate elements which are legitimated externally, rather than in terms of efficiency; (*b*) they employ external or ceremonial assessment criteria to define the value of structural elements; and (*c*) dependence on externally fixed institutions reduces turbulence and maintains stability. As a result, it is argued here, institutional isomorphism promotes the success and survival of organizations. Incorporating externally legitimated formal structures increases the commitment of internal participants and external constituents. And the use of external assessment criteria—that is, moving toward the status in society of a subunit rather than an independent system—can enable an organization to remain successful by social definition, buffering it from failure.

Changing Formal Structures. By designing a formal structure that adheres to the prescriptions of myths in the institutional environment, an organization demonstrates that it is acting on collectively valued purposes in a proper and adequate manner (Dowling and Pfeffer 1975; Meyer and Rowan 1978). The incorporation of institutionalized elements provides an account (Scott and Lyman 1968) of activities that protects the organization from having its conduct questioned. The organization becomes, in a word, legitimate, and it uses its legitimacy to strengthen its support and secure its survival.

From an institutional perspective, then, a most important aspect of isomorphism with environmental institutions is the evolution of organizational language. The labels of the organization chart as well as the vocabulary used to delineate organizational goals, procedures, and policies are analogous to the vocabularies of motive used to account for the activities of individuals (Blum and McHugh 1971; Mills 1940). Just as jealousy, anger, altruism, and love are myths that interpret and explain the actions of individuals, the myths of doctors, of accountants, or of the assembly line explain organizational activities. Thus, some can say that the engineers will solve a specific problem or that the secretaries will perform certain tasks, without knowing who these engineers or secretaries will be or exactly what they will do. Both the speaker and the listeners understand such statements to describe how certain responsibilities will be carried out.

Vocabularies of structure which are isomorphic with institutional rules provide prudent, rational, and legitimate accounts. Organizations described in legitimated vocabularies are assumed to be oriented to collectively defined, and often collectively mandated, ends. The myths of personnel services, for example, not only account for the rationality of employment practices but also indicate that personnel services are valuable to an organization. Employees, applicants, managers, trustees, and governmental agencies are predisposed to trust the hiring practices of organizations that follow legitimated procedures—such as equal opportunity programs, or personality testing—and they are more willing to participate in or to fund such organizations. On the other hand, organizations that omit environmentally legitimated elements of structure or create unique structures lack acceptable legitimated accounts of their activities. Such organizations are more vulnerable to claims that they are negligent, irrational, or unnecessary. Claims of this kind, whether made by internal participants, external constituents, or the government, can cause organizations to incur real costs. For example, with the rise of modern medical institutions, large organizations that do not arrange medical-care facilities for their workers come to be seen as negligent—by the workers, by management factions, by insurers, by courts which legally define negligence, and often by laws. The costs of illegitimacy in insurance premiums and legal liabilities are very real. Similarly environmental safety institutions make it important for organizations to create formal safety rules, safety departments, and safety programs. No Smoking rules and signs, regardless of their enforcement, are necessary to avoid charges of negligence and to avoid the extreme of illegitimation: the closing of buildings by the state. The rise of professionalized economics makes it useful for organizations to incorporate groups of economists and econometric analyses. Though no one may read, understand, or believe them, econometric analyses help legitimate the organization's plans in the eyes of investors, customers (as with Defense Department contractors), and internal participants. Such analyses can also provide rational accountings after failures occur: managers whose plans have failed can demonstrate to investors, stockholders, and superiors that procedures were prudent and that decisions were by rational means.

Thus, rationalized institutions create myths of formal structure which shape organizations. Failure to incorporate the proper elements of structure is negligent and irrational; the continued flow of support is threatened and internal dissidents are strengthened. At the same time, these myths present organizations with great opportunities for expansion. Affixing the right labels to activities can change them into valuable services and mobilize the commitments of internal participants and external constituents.

Adopting External Assessment Criteria. In institutionally elaborated environments, organizations also become sensitive to and employ external criteria of worth. Criteria include, for instance, such ceremonial awards as the Nobel Prize, endorsements by important people, the standard prices of professionals and consultants, or the prestige of programs or personnel in external social circles. For example, the conventions of modern accounting attempt to assign value to particular components of organizations on the basis of their contribution—through the organization's production function—to the goods and services the organization produces. But for many units—service departments, administrative sectors, and others—it is utterly unclear what is being produced that has clear or definable value in terms of its contribution to the organizational product. In these situations, accountants employ shadow prices: they assume that given organizational units are necessary and calculate their value from their prices in the world outside the organization. Thus modern accounting creates ceremonial production functions and maps them onto economic production functions: organizations assign externally defined worth to advertising departments, safety departments, managers, econometricians, and occasionally even sociologists, whether or not these units contribute measurably to the production of outputs. Monetary prices, in postindustrial society, reflect hosts of ceremonial influences, as do economic measures of efficiency, profitability, or net worth (Hirsch 1975).

Ceremonial criteria of worth and ceremonially derived production functions are useful to organizations: they legitimate organizations with internal participants stockholders, the public, and the state, as with the IRS or the SEC. They demonstrate socially the fitness of an organization. The incorporation of structures with high ceremonial value, such as those reflecting the latest expert thinking or those with the most prestige, makes the credit position of an organization more favorable. Loans, donations, or investments are more easily obtained. Finally, units within the organization use ceremonial assessments as accounts of their productive service to the organization. Their internal power rises with their performance on ceremonial measures (Salancik and Pfeffer 1974).

Stabilization. The rise of an elaborate institutional environment stabilizes both external and internal organizational relationships. Centralized states, trade associations, unions, professional associations, and coalitions among organizations standardize and stabilize (see the review by Starbuck 1976).

Market conditions, the characteristics of inputs and outputs, and technological procedures are brought under the jurisdiction of institutional meanings and controls. Stabilization also results as a given organization becomes part of the wider collective system. Support is guaranteed by agreements instead of depending entirely on performance. For example, apart from whether schools educate students or hospitals cure patients, people and governmental agencies remain committed to these organizations, funding and using them almost automatically year after year.

Institutionally controlled environments buffer organizations from turbulence (Emery and Trist 1965; Terreberry 1968). Adaptations occur less rapidly as increased numbers of agreements are enacted. Collectively granted monopolies guarantee clienteles for organizations like schools, hospitals, or professional associations. The taken-for-granted (and legally regulated) quality of institutional rules makes dramatic instabilities in products, techniques, or policies unlikely. And legitimacy as accepted subunits of society protects organizations from immediate sanctions for variations in technical performance. Thus, American school districts (like other governmental units) have near monopolies and are very stable. They must conform to wider rules about proper classifications and credentials of teachers and students, and of topics of study. But they are protected by rules which make education as defined by these classifications compulsory. Alternative or private schools are possible, but must conform so closely to the required structures and classifications as to be able to generate little advantage. Some business organizations obtain very high levels of institutional stabilization. A large defense contractor may be paid for following agreed-on procedures, even if the product is ineffective. In the extreme, such organizations may be so successful as to survive bankruptcy intact—as Lockheed and Penn Central have done—by becoming partially components of the state. More commonly, such firms are guaranteed survival by state-regulated rates which secure profits regardless of costs, as with American public utility firms. Large automobile firms are a little less stabilized. They exist in an environment that contains enough structures to make automobiles, as conventionally de-fined, virtual necessities. But still, customers and governments can inspect each automobile and can evaluate and even legally discredit it. Legal action cannot as easily discredit a high school graduate.

Organizational Success and Survival. Thus, organizational success depends on factors other than efficient coordination and control of productive activities. Independent of their productive efficiency, organizations which exist in highly elaborated institutional environments and succeed in becoming isomorphic with these environments gain the legitimacy and resources needed to survive. In part this depends on environmental processes and on the capacity of given organizational leadership to mold these processes (Hirsch 1975). In part it depends on the ability of given organizations to conform to, and become legitimated by, environmental institutions. In institutionally elaborated environments, sagacious conformity is required: leadership (in a university, a hospital, or a business) requires an understanding of changing fashions and governmental programs. But this kind of conformity—and the almost guaranteed survival which may accompany it—is possible only in an environment with a highly institutionalized structure. In such a context an organization can be locked into isomorphism, ceremonially reflecting the institutional environment in its structure, functionaries, and procedures. Thus, in addition to the conventionally defined sources of organizational success and survival, the following general assertion can be proposed:

Proposition 3. *Organizations that incorporate societally legitimated rationalized elements in their formal structures maximize their legitimacy and increase their resources and survival capabilities.*

This proposition asserts that the long-run survival prospects of organizations increase as state structures elaborate and as organizations respond to institutionalized rules. In the United States, for instance, schools, hospitals, and welfare organizations show considerable ability to survive, precisely because they are matched with—and almost absorbed by—their institutional environments. In the same way, organizations fail when they deviate from the prescriptions of institutionalizing myths: quite apart from technical efficiency, organizations which innovate in important structural ways bear considerable costs in legitimacy.

Figure 5.2 summarizes the general argument of this section, alongside the established view that organizations succeed through efficiency.

Institutionalized Structures and Organizational Activities

Rationalized formal structures arise in two contexts. First, the demands of local relational networks encourage the development of structures that coordinate and control activities. Such structures contribute to the efficiency of organizations and give them competitive advantages over less efficient competitors. Second, the interconnectedness of societal relations, the collective organization of society, and the leadership of organizational elites create a highly institutionalized context. In this context rationalized structures present an acceptable account of organizational activities, and organizations gain legitimacy, stability, and resources.

All organizations, to one degree or another, are embedded in both relational and institutionalized contexts and are therefore concerned both with coordinating and controlling their activities and with prudently accounting for them. Organizations in highly institutionalized environments face internal and boundary-spanning contingen-

Figure 5.2

Organizational survival.

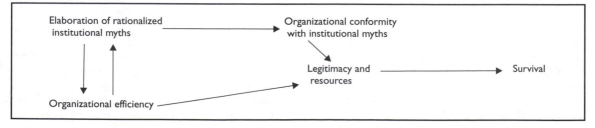

cies. Schools, for example, must transport students to and from school under some circumstances and must assign teachers, students, and topics to classrooms. On the other hand, organizations producing in markets that place great emphasis on efficiency build in units whose relation to production is obscure and whose efficiency is determined not by a true production function, but by ceremonial definition.

Nevertheless, the survival of some organizations depends more on managing the demands of internal and boundary-spanning relations, while the survival of others depends more on the ceremonial demands of highly institutionalized environments. The discussion to follow shows that whether an organization's survival depends primarily on relational or on institutional demands determines the tightness of alignments between structures and activities.

Types of Organizations

Institutionalized myths differ in the completeness with which they describe cause and effect relationships, and in the clarity with which they describe standards that should be used to evaluate outputs (Thompson 1967). Some organizations use routine, clearly defined technologies to produce outputs. When output can be easily evaluated, a market often develops, and consumers gain considerable rights of inspection and control. In this context, efficiency often determines success. Organizations must face exigencies of close coordination with their relational networks, and they cope with these exigencies by organizing around immediate technical problems.

But the rise of collectively organized society and the increasing interconnectedness of social relations have eroded many market contexts. Increasingly, such organizations as schools, R & D units, and governmental bureaucracies use variable, ambiguous technologies to produce outputs that are difficult to appraise, and other organizations with clearly defined technologies find themselves unable to adapt to environmental turbulence. The uncertainties of unpredictable technical contingencies or of adapting to environmental change cannot be resolved on the basis of efficiency. Internal participants and external constituents alike call for institutionalized rules that promote trust and confidence in outputs and buffer organizations from failure (Emery and Trist 1965).

Thus, one can conceive of a continuum along which organizations can be ordered. At one end are production organizations under strong output controls (Ouchi and Mcguire 1975) whose success depends on the management of relational networks. At the other end are institutionalized organizations whose success depends on the confidence and stability achieved by isomorphism with institutional rules. For two reasons it is important not to assume that an organization's location on this continuum is based on the inherent technical properties of its output and therefore permanent. First, the technical properties of outputs are socially defined and do not exist in some concrete sense that allows them to be empirically discovered. Second, environments and organizations often redefine the nature of products, services, and technologies. Redefinition sometimes clarifies techniques or evaluative standards. But often organizations and environments redefine the nature of techniques and output so that ambiguity is introduced and rights of inspection and control are lowered. For example, American schools have evolved from producing rather specific training that was evaluated according to strict criteria of efficiency to producing ambiguously defined services that are evaluated according to criteria of certification (Callahan 1962; Tyack 1974; Meyer and Rowan 1978).

Structural Inconsistencies in Institutionalized Organizations

Two very general problems confront an organization if its success depends primarily on isomorphism with institutionalized rules. First, technical activities and demands for efficiency create conflicts and inconsistencies in an institutionalized organization's efforts to conform to the ceremonial rules of production. Second, because these ceremonial rules are transmitted by myths that may arise from different parts of the environment, the rules may conflict with one another. These inconsistencies make a concern for efficiency and tight coordination and control problematic.

Formal structures that celebrate institutionalized myths differ from structures that act efficiently. Ceremonial activity is significant in relation to categorical rules, not in its concrete effects (Merton 1940; March and

Simon 1958). A sick worker must be treated by a doctor using accepted medical procedures; whether the worker is treated effectively is less important. A bus company must service required routes whether or not there are many passengers. A university must maintain appropriate departments independent of the departments' enrollments. Activity, that is, has ritual significance: it maintains appearances and validates an organization.

Categorical rules conflict with the logic of efficiency. Organizations often face the dilemma that activities celebrating institutionalized rules, although they count as virtuous ceremonial expenditures, are pure costs from the point of view of efficiency. For example, hiring a Nobel Prize winner brings great ceremonial benefits to a university. The celebrated name can lead to research grants, brighter students, or reputational gains. But from the point of view of immediate outcomes, the expenditure lowers the instructional return per dollar expended and lowers the university's ability to solve immediate logistical problems. Also, expensive technologies, which bring prestige to hospitals and business firms, may be simply excessive costs from the point of view of immediate production. Similarly, highly professionalized consultants who bring external blessing on an organization are often difficult to justify in terms of improved productivity, yet may be very important in maintaining internal and external legitimacy.

Other conflicts between categorical rules and efficiency arise because institutional rules are couched at high levels of generalization (Durkheim 1933), whereas technical activities vary with specific, unstandardized, and possibly unique conditions. Because standardized ceremonial categories must confront technical variations and anomalies, the generalized rules of the institutional environment are often inappropriate to specific situations. A governmentally mandated curriculum may be inappropriate for the students at hand, a conventional medical treatment may make little sense given the characteristics of a patient, and federal safety inspectors may intolerably delay boundary-spanning exchanges.

Yet another source of conflict between categorical rules and efficiency is the inconsistency among institutionalized elements. Institutional environments are often pluralistic (Udy 1970), and societies promulgate sharply inconsistent myths. As a result, organizations in search of external support and stability incorporate all sorts of incompatible structural elements. Professions are incorporated although they make overlapping jurisdictional claims. Programs are adopted which contend with each other for authority over a given domain. For instance, if one inquires who decides what curricula will be taught in schools, any number of parties from the various governments down to individual teachers may say that they decide.

In institutionalized organizations, then, concern with the efficiency of day-to-day activities creates enormous uncertainties. Specific contexts highlight the inadequacies of the prescriptions of generalized myths, and inconsistent structural elements conflict over jurisdictional rights. Thus the organization must struggle to link the requirements of ceremonial elements to technical activities and to link inconsistent ceremonial elements to each other.

Resolving Inconsistencies

There are four partial solutions to these inconsistencies. First, an organization can resist ceremonial requirements. But an organization that neglects ceremonial requirements and portrays itself as efficient may be unsuccessful in documenting its efficiency. Also, rejecting ceremonial requirements neglects an important source of resources and stability. Second, an organization can maintain rigid conformity to institutionalized prescriptions by cutting off external relations. Although such isolation uphold ceremonial requirements, internal participants and external constituents may soon become disillusioned with their inability to manage boundary-spanning exchanges. Institutionalized organizations must not only conform to myths but must also maintain the appearance that the myths actually work. Third, an organization can cynically acknowledge that its structure is inconsistent with work requirements. But this strategy denies the validity of institutionalized myths and sabotages the legitimacy of the organization. Fourth, an organization can promise reform. People may picture the present as unworkable but the future as filled with promising reforms of both structure and activity. But by defining the organization's valid structure as lying in the future, this strategy makes the organization's current structure illegitimate.

Instead of relying on a partial solution, however, an organization can resolve conflicts between ceremonial rules and efficiency by employing two interrelated devices: decoupling and the logic of confidence.

Decoupling. Ideally, organizations built around efficiency attempt to maintain close alignments between structures and activities. Conformity is enforced through inspection, output quality is continually monitored, the efficiency of various units is evaluated, and the various goals are unified and coordinated. But a policy of close alignment in institutionalized organizations merely makes public a record of inefficiency and inconsistency.

Institutionalized organizations protect their formal structures from evaluation on the basis of technical performance: inspection, evaluation, and control of activities are minimized, and coordination, interdependence, and mutual adjustments among structural units are handled informally.

Proposition 4. *Because attempts to control and coordinate activities in institutionalized organizations lead to conflicts and loss of legitimacy, elements of structure are decoupled from activities and from each other.*

Some well-known properties of organizations illustrate the decoupling process: (1) Activities are performed beyond the purview of managers. In particular, organizations actively encourage professionalism, and activities are delegated to professionals. (2) Goals are made ambiguous or vacuous, and categorical ends are substituted for technical ends. Hospitals treat, not cure, patients. Schools produce students, not learning. In fact, data on technical performance are eliminated or rendered invisible. Hospitals try to ignore information on cure rates, public services avoid data about effectiveness, and schools deemphasize measures of achievement. (3) Integration is avoided, program implementation is neglected, and inspection and evaluation are ceremonialized. (4) Human relations are made very important. The organization cannot formally coordinate activities because its formal rules, if applied, would generate inconsistencies. Therefore individuals are left to work out technical interdependencies informally. The ability to coordinate things in violation of the rules—that is, to get along with other people—is highly valued.

The advantages of decoupling are clear. The assumption that formal structures are really working is buffered from the inconsistencies and anomalies involved in technical activities. Also, because integration is avoided, disputes and conflicts are minimized and an organization can mobilize support from a broader range of external constituents. Thus, decoupling enables organizations to maintain standardized, legitimating, formal structures while their activities vary in response to practical considerations. The organizations in an industry tend to be similar in formal structure—reflecting their common institutional origins—but may show much diversity in actual practice.

The Logic of Confidence and Good Faith. Despite the lack of coordination and control, decoupled organizations are not anarchies. Day-to-day activities proceed in an orderly fashion. What legitimates institutionalized organizations, enabling them to appear useful in spite of the lack of technical validation, is the confidence and good faith of their internal participants and their external constituents.

Considerations of face characterize ceremonial management (Goffman 1967). Confidence in structural elements is maintained through three practices—avoidance, discretion, and overlooking (Goffman 1967: 12–18). Avoidance and discretion are encouraged by decoupling autonomous subunits; overlooking anomalies is also quite common. Both internal participants and external constituents cooperate in these practices. Assuring that individual participants maintain face sustains confidence in the organization and ultimately reinforces confidence in the myths that rationalize the organization's existence.

Delegation, professionalization, goal ambiguity, elimination of output data, and maintenance of face are all mechanisms for absorbing uncertainty while preserving the formal structure of the organization (March and Simon 1958). They contribute to a general aura of confidence within and outside the organization. Although the literature on informal organization often treats these practices as mechanisms for the achievement of deviant and subgroup purposes (Downs 1967), such treatment ignores a critical feature of organization life: effectively absorbing uncertainty and maintaining confidence requires people to assume that everyone is acting in good faith. The assumption that things are as they seem, that employees and managers are performing their roles properly, allows an organization to perform its daily routines with a decoupled structure.

Decoupling and maintenance of face, in other words, are mechanisms that maintain the assumption that people are acting in good faith. Professionalization is not merely a way of avoiding inspection—it binds both supervisors and subordinates to act in good faith. So in a smaller way does strategic leniency (Blau 1956). And so do the public displays of morale and satisfaction which are characteristic of many organizations. Organizations employ a host of mechanisms to dramatize the ritual commitments which their participants make to basic structural elements. These mechanisms are especially common in organizations which strongly reflect their institutionalized environments.

Proposition 5. *The more an organization's structure is derived from institutionalized myths, the more it maintains elaborate displays of confidence, satisfaction, and good faith, internally and externally.*

The commitments built up by displays of morale and satisfaction are not simply vacuous affirmations of institutionalized myths. Participants not only commit themselves to supporting an organization's ceremonial facade but also commit themselves to making things work out backstage. The committed participants engage in informal coordination that, although often formally inappropriate, keeps technical activities running smoothly and avoids public embarrassments. In this sense the confidence and good faith generated by ceremonial action is in no way fraudulent. It may even be the most reasonable way to get participants to make their best efforts in situations made problematic by institutionalized myths at odds with immediate technical demands.

Ceremonial Inspection and Evaluation. All organizations, even those maintaining high levels of confidence and good faith, are in environments that have institutionalized the rationalized rituals of inspection and evaluation. And inspection and evaluation can uncover events and deviations that undermine legitimacy. So institutionalized organizations minimize and ceremonialize inspection and evaluation.

In institutionalized organizations, in fact, evaluation accompanies and produces ille-

gitimacy. The interest in evaluation research by the U.S. federal government, for instance, is partly intended to undercut the state, local, and private authorities which have managed social services in the United States. The federal authorities, of course, have usually not evaluated those programs which are completely under federal jurisdiction; they have only evaluated those over which federal controls are incomplete. Similarly, state governments have often insisted on evaluating the special fundings they create in welfare and education but ordinarily do not evaluate the programs which they fund in a routine way.

Evaluation and inspection are public assertions of societal control which violate the assumption that everyone is acting with competence and in good faith. Violating this assumption lowers morale and confidence. Thus, evaluation and inspection undermine the ceremonial aspects of organizations.

Proposition 6. *Institutionalized organizations seek to minimize inspection and evaluation by both internal managers and external constituents.*

Decoupling and the avoidance of inspection and evaluation are not merely devices used by the organization. External constituents, too, avoid inspecting and controlling institutionalized organizations (Meyer and Rowan 1978). Accrediting agencies, boards of trustees, government agencies, and individuals accept ceremonially at face value the credentials, ambiguous goals, and categorical evaluations that are characteristic of ceremonial organizations. In elaborate institutional environments these external constituents are themselves likely to be corporately organized agents of society. Maintaining categorical relationships with their organizational subunits is more stable and more certain than is relying on inspection and control. Figure 5.3 summarizes the main arguments of this section of our discussion.

Summary and Research Implications

Organizational structures are created and made more elaborate with the rise of institutionalized myths, and, in highly institutionalized contexts, organizational action must support these myths. But an organization must also attend to practical activity. The two requirements are at odds. A stable solu-

Figure 5.3

The effects of institutional isomorphism on organizations.

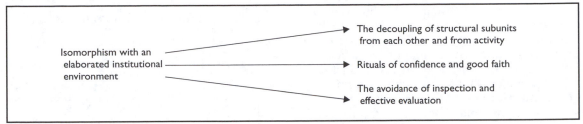

tion is to maintain the organization in a loosely coupled state.

No position is taken here on the overall social effectiveness of isomorphic and loosely coupled organizations. To some extent such structures buffer activity from efficiency criteria and produce ineffectiveness. On the other hand, by binding participants to act in good faith and to adhere to the larger rationalities of the wider structure, they may maximize long-run effectiveness. It should not be assumed that the creation of microscopic rationalities in the daily activity of workers effects social ends more efficiently than commitment to larger institutional claims and purposes.

The argument presented here generates several major theses that have clear research implications. The first thesis is that environments and environmental domains which have institutionalized a greater number of rational myths generate more formal organization. This thesis leads to the research hypothesis that formal organizations rise and become more complex as a result of the rise of the elaborated state and other institutions for collective action. This hypothesis should hold true even when economic and technical development are held constant. Studies could trace the diffusion to formal organizations of specific institutions—professions, clearly labeled programs, and the like. For instance, the effects of the rise of theories and professions of personnel selection on the creation of personnel departments in organizations could be studied. Other studies could follow the diffusion of sales departments or research and development departments. Organizations should be found to adapt to such environmental changes, even if no evidence of their effectiveness exists.

Experimentally, one could study the impact on the decisions of organizational managers in planning or altering organizational structures, of hypothetical variations in environmental institutionalization. Do managers plan differently if they are informed about the existence of established occupations or programmatic institutions in their environments? Do they plan differently if they are designing organizations for more or less institutionally elaborated environments?

Our second thesis is that organizations which incorporate institutionalized myths are more legitimate, successful, and likely to survive. Here, research should compare similar organizations in different contexts. For instance, the presence of personnel departments or research and development units should predict success in environments in which they are widely institutionalized. Organizations which have structural elements not institutionalized in their environments should be more likely to fail, as such unauthorized complexity must be justified by claims of efficiency and effectiveness.

More generally, organizations whose claims to support are based on evaluations should be less likely to survive than those which are more highly institutionalized. An implication of this argument is that organizations existing in a highly institutionalized environment are generally more likely to survive.

Experimentally, one could study the size of the loans banks would be willing to provide organizations which vary only in (1) the degree of environmental institutionalization, and (2) the degree to which the organization structurally incorporates environmental institutions. Are banks willing to lend more money to firms whose plans are accompanied by econometric projections? And is this tendency greater in societies in which such projections are more widely institutionalized?

Our third thesis is that organizational control efforts, especially in highly institutionalized contexts, are devoted to ritual conformity, both internally and externally. Such organizations, that is, decouple structure from activity and structures from each other. The idea here is that the more highly institutionalized the environment, the more time and energy organizational elites devote to managing their organization's public image and status and the less they devote to coordination and to managing particular boundary-spanning relationships. Further, the argument is that in such contexts managers devote more time to articulating internal structures and relationships at an abstract or ritual level, in contrast to managing particular relationships among activities and interdependencies.

Experimentally, the time and energy allocations proposed by managers presented with differently described environments could be studied. Do managers, presented with the description of an elaborately institutionalized environment, propose to spend more energy maintaining ritual isomorphism and less on monitoring internal conformity? Do they tend to become inattentive to evaluation? Do they elaborate doctrines of professionalism and good faith? The arguments here, in other words, suggest both comparative and experimental studies examining the effects on organizational structure and coordination of variations in the institutional structure of the wider environment. Variations in organizational structure among societies, and within any society across time, are central to this conception of the problem.

References

Aiken, Michael, and Jerald Hage. 1968. Organizational Interdependence and Intraorganizational Structure. *American Sociological Review* 33:912–30.

Bell, Daniel. 1973. *The Coming of Post-Industrial Society.* New York: Basic Books.

Bendix, Reinhard. 1964. *Nation-Building and Citizenship.* New York: Wiley.

———. 1968. Bureaucracy. In *International Encyclopedia of the Social Sciences*, ed. David L. Sills, 206–19. New York: Macmillan.

Berger, Peter L., and Thomas Luckmann. 1967. *The Social Construction of Reality.* New York: Doubleday.

Blau, Peter M. 1956. *Bureaucracy in Modern Society.* New York: Random House.

———. 1970. A Formal Theory of Differentiation in Organizations. *American Sociological Review* 35:201–18.

Blum, Alan F., and Peter McHugh. 1971. The Social Ascription of Motives. *American Sociological Review* 36:98–109.

Callahan, Raymond E. 1962. *Education and the Cult of Efficiency.* Chicago: University of Chicago Press.

Carlson, Richard O. 1962. *Executive Succession and Organizational Change.* Chicago: Midwest Administration Center, University of Chicago.

Clark, Burton R. 1956. *Adult Education in Transition.* Berkeley: University of California Press.

Dalton, Melville. 1959. *Men Who Manage.* New York: Wiley.

Dowling, John, and Jeffrey Pfeffer. 1975. Organizational Legitimacy: Social Values and Organizational Behavior. *Pacific Sociological Review* 18:122–36.

Downs, Anthony. 1976. *Inside Bureaucracy.* Boston: Little, Brown.

Durkheim, Émile. 1933. *The Division of Labor in Society.* New York: Macmillan.

Ellul, Jacques. 1964. *The Technological Society.* New York: Knopf.

Emery, Fred L., and Eric L. Trist. 1965. The Causal Texture of Organizational Environments. *Human Relations* 18:21–32.

Freeman, John H. 1973. Environment, Technology, and Administrative Intensity of Manufacturing Organizations. *American Sociological Review* 38:750–63.

Goffman, Erving. 1967. *Interaction Ritual.* Garden City, N.Y.: Anchor.

Hawley, Amos. 1968. Human Ecology. In *International Encyclopedia of the Social Sciences*, ed. David L. Sills, 328–37. New York: Macmillan.

Hirsch, Paul M. 1975. Organizational Effectiveness and the Institutional Environment. *Administrative Science Quarterly* 20:327–44.

Homans, George C. 1950. *The Human Group.* New York: Harcourt, Brace.

March, James G., and Johan P. Olsen. 1976. *Ambiguity and Choice in Organizations.* Bergen: Universitetsforlaget.

March, James G., and Herbert A. Simon. 1958. *Organizations.* New York: Wiley.

Merton, Robert K. 1940. Bureaucratic Structure and Personality. *Social Forces.* 18:560–68.

Meyer, John W., and Brian Rowan. 1978. The Structure of Educational Organizations. In *Environments and Organizations*, ed. Marshall W. Meyer et al., 78–109. San Francisco: Jossey-Bass.

Mills, C. Wright. 1940. Situated Actions and Vocabularies of Motive. *American Sociological Review* 5:904–13.

Ouchi, William, and Mary Anne Maguire. 1975. Organizational Control: Two Functions. *Administrative Science Quarterly* 20:559–69.

Parsons, Talcott. 1956. Suggestions for a Sociological Approach to the Theory of Organizations, Parts I and II. *Administrative Science Quarterly* 1:63–85, 225–39.

———. 1971. *The System of Modern Societies.* Englewood Cliffs, N.J.: Prentice-Hall.

Perrow, Charles. 1970. *Organizational Analysis: A Sociological View.* Belmont, Calif.: Wadsworth.

Salancik, Gerald R., and Jeffrey Pfeffer. 1974. The Bases and Use of Power in Organizational Decision Making. *Administrative Science Quarterly* 19:453–73.

Scott, Marvin B., and Stanford M. Lyman. 1968. Accounts. *American Sociological Review* 33:46–62.

Scott, W. Richard. 1975. Organizational Structure. *Annual Review of Sociology* 1:1–25.

Selznick, Philip. 1949. *TVA and the Grass Roots.* Berkeley: University of California Press.

Spencer, Herbert. 1897. *Principles of Sociology.* New York: Appleton.

Starbuck, William H. 1976. Organization and Their Environments. In *Handbook of Industrial and Organizational Psychology*, ed. Marvin D. Dunnette, 1069–1123. New York: Rand McNally.

Swanson, Guy. 1971. An Organizational Analysis of Collectivities. *American Sociological Review* 36:607–623.

Terreberry, Shirley. 1968. The Evolution of Organizational Environments. *Administrative Science Quarterly* 12:590–613.

Thompson, James D. 1967. *Organizations in Action.* New York: McGraw-Hill.

Tyack, David. 1974. *The One Best System: A History of American Urban Education.* Cambridge: Harvard University Press.

Udy, Stanley, H., Jr. 1970. *Work in Traditional and Modern Society.* Englewood Cliffs, N.J.: Prentice-Hall.

Weber, Max. 1930. *The Protestant's Ethic and the Spirit of Capitalism.* New York: Scribner's.

———. 1946. *Essays in Sociology.* New York: Oxford University Press.

———. 1947. *The Theory of Social and Economic Organization.* New York: Oxford University Press.

Weick, Karl E. 1976. "Educational Organizations as Loosely Coupled Systems." *Administrative Science Quarterly* 21 (March): 1–19.

Wilensky, Harold L. 1965. "The Professionalization of Everyone?" *American Journal of Sociology* 70 (September): 137–58.

Woodward, Joan. 1965. *Industrial Organization, Theory and Practice.* London: Oxford University Press.

Zald, Mayer N., and Patricia Denton. 1963. From Evangelism to General Service: The Transformation of the YMCA. *Administrative Science Quarterly* 8:214–34.

Part I

Understanding Organizations

Varieties of Organizations

Chapter 6
Organizing America

Wealth, Power, and the Origins of Corporate Capitalism

Charles Perrow

Large, bureaucratic organizations are a ubiquitous feature of life in our global society and have been part of the social landscape in the United States for at least a century. Their influence is growing, however. In fact, Perrow suggests that large organizations increasingly resemble "societies" in themselves, "providing, on their own terms, the cradle-to-grave services that communities and small organizations used to provide." The problem, as Perrow sees it, is that size does matter. Small organizations, even highly bureaucratic ones, are not as troubling to him as large ones that are private, largely unregulated, and ever-expanding in scope and power. Perrow urges us to view organizations as powerful social actors and to consider them as key independent variables in our search to understand the factors that are shaping life in the twenty-first century.

This [chapter] seeks to tell us how and why it happened that the most important feature of our social landscape is the large organization, public or private. Americans celebrate individualism and entrepreneurship, and some see organizations as getting smaller or more decentralized; so concern with bigness and bureaucracy may have abated. But we should be reminded that today, well over 90 percent of the work force works for someone else—as wage and salary employees—up from 20 percent in 1800; over half of the gainfully employed people in the country work for organizations with 500 or more employees, up from 0 percent in 1800. Today, although establishments have an average size of about thirty employees, organizations can own and control many separate establishments. And control is the important factor, not the size of the branch bank or the factory site or the fast food outlet or the service franchise. The truly big organizations, public and private, have come to define and even absorb much of our society. Despite all the talk of downsizing, our organizational population has not become perceptibly thinner; the Fortune 500 industrials have declined in size by about 8 percent in a decade, but their average size changed little, from about 3,000 employees in 1979, the peak year, to 2,750 in 1993. That is still very big. Meanwhile, the average size of the 500 largest service corporations rose from 1,700 in 1982 to 2,750 in 1993, making them as big as the industrials (Useem 1996, 165). Even with the government contracting out many activities to private firms (generally large ones), government has not shrunk appreciably.

The American population increases, and so does the number of big organizations. More and more they have come to constitute societies in themselves, providing, on their own terms, the cradle-to-grave services that communities and small organizations used to provide. We could not have our level of affluence without organizations, of course, and some of them, including certain government organizations such as the armed forces or the social security administration, are bound to be huge.

But most do not need to be very large, and their size and power is troubling. Our economic organizations—business and industry—concentrate wealth and power; socialize employees and customers alike to meet their needs; and pass off to the rest of society the cost of their pollution, crowding, accidents, and encouragement of destructive life styles. In the vaunted "free market" economy of the United States, regulation of business and industry to prevent or mitigate this market failure is relatively ineffective, as compared to that enacted by other industrialized countries.

Big noneconomic organizations also trouble me. Big churches and school systems and local, state, and federal governments also centralize power, socialize employees to bureaucratic values, "de-skill" them unnecessarily, and generate their own "externalities"—the costs of doing their business that are shifted onto a fragile environment or fragile groups within the polity.

Increasingly, especially since the mid-twentieth century, politicians and government leaders have tried to ameliorate these problems, saying that we need big organizations but that they need to be more responsive to citizens. In this area we have made some progress. But perhaps not enough. Antitrust enforcement has waxed and waned; conceptions of unfair competition are relaxed; big organizations and their masters dominate campaign financing and shape regulatory procedures. Cleaning up after the economic organizations has generated more big organizations to do the clean up, and they bring more externalities, and more incorporation of social functions that once were filled by small groups, families, neighborhoods, and small local governmental units. . . .

Only two things are more basic to the structure of our society than organizations: basic demographic forces and cognitive structures of the mind. Acknowledging these, I will make the following grand claim for organizations:

> Bureaucratic organizations are the most effective means of unobtrusive control human society has produced, and once large bureaucracies are loosed upon the world, much of what we think of as causal in shaping our society—class, politics, religion, socialization and self-conceptions, technology, entrepreneurship—becomes to some degree, and to an increasing degree, and a largely unappreciated degree, shaped by organizations. . . .

Organizations as the Independent Variable

The impact of large organizations on society has not been fully appreciated. The story of organizations in the United States can be found in works by historians, but quite a bit of digging is required. Even in the other social sciences, organizations appear as dependent variables, created by other forces, rather than as independent variables, as actors in themselves. In many accounts of social change, wealth and power are not associated with organizations; wealth is resident in an individual, a family, or a class, and power is resident in persons or ideologies. Organizations are at best unproblematic resources for other expressions of wealth and power (W & P). This interpretation may occasionally be true, but I wish to explore the extent to which organizations may not only back up these sources of W & P, but shape them because of the characteristics of the organizations themselves, independent of persons, classes, and ideologies. To the extent that organizations are considered in discussions of W & P, they are often merely the suitcases that carry more important variables, and have no distinctive properties of their own. But I argue that organizations produce more than their marketed goods and services, and will shortly list some of these products.

The passive role of organizations in most accounts is suggested by the following familiar formulations, true but incomplete: Politicians "use" organizations; culture is "expressed" through organizations; organizations are "designed" for the efficient production of goods and services. When people do comment on particular organizational characteristics, the comments are generally limited to their imperfections as vessels, as in discussions of their best form or structure or of the leadership qualities required of their managers. But rarely do these discussions take into account any of the many characteristics of organizations that shape society. In this book, however, we shall see the effects of internal properties such as size, degree of centralization, skill requirements, and labor policies; the effect of environmental relations such as network properties, political power and the corruption of officials, and the ability to ignore social costs and pass them off to the weaker parts of society.

We hear that culture shapes our behavior, and because organizations are made up of behaving people, organizations therefore must be shaped by culture. They are shaped by culture, but they also shape culture. Or we hear that efficient forms prevail over inefficient forms, and so we think that the prevailing organizations must be reflections of this efficiency. True, in general and in a largely tautological sense, but whose efficiency is being realized; for whom is it inefficient? Organizational forms or structures may be chosen for ideological reasons by the masters and locked in by group interests; not all the stakeholders such as employees, their families, the community, and the natural environment, see their own efficiency realized by the same form that benefits the masters. Or we hear that political parties or Congress is the means of mobilizing political values or the political will, and thus politics is what we should study—this is the "independent variable." But while it is commonplace that large organizations fund the politicians, and it is noted that, for example, the sizable percentage of the U.S. senators who are millionaires a few times over have their millions invested in particular organizations, political scientists do not then turn toward the characteristics of these politics-shaping organizations. Furthermore, the political parties and Congress and the executive branch are all large organizations in themselves, with interests that are independent of any individual members and certainly the public, and thus can have a large say about which values will be offered and about the terms for mobilizing the "public will." The examination of governmental organizations has been largely limited to the inefficiency or efficiency of their services, not focusing on the way in which their properties as organizations shape our considerations of legitimate services and even hide the source of problems that require services.

What Do Organizations Do?

I am concerned with what organizations do, beyond producing goods and services. As I said, organizations are more important than most theories allow, and their importance has not been fully realized. . . .

What do organizations do, beyond producing goods and services, that makes them so protean? Drawing on Karl Marx, Max Weber, and numerous modern theorists, we can be reminded of the following:

Wage Dependence. Organizations generate wage dependence—a condition where you have to work to create the surplus value that will be used by someone else as wealth, prestige, or power, or you won't survive. The condition of wage dependence at first was resisted, but it gradually changed our stratification system and centralized social and economic power in society. Dependence on a wage or salary for survival was not taken for granted in the nineteenth century, but was characterized in negative terms referring to the only two institutions that had such complete control—"wage slavery" and "the industrial army." A democratic society could not experience much centralization of wealth and power if wage dependence were not extensive; it permits the accumulation of wealth from productive activity. Thus, wage dependency *centralizes surpluses.*

Centralization of Surpluses. If you work for only yourself, accumulation is limited to

your own surplus or profit, not that of all your employees. If your employees can freely choose another employer or get part of their livelihood on their own, the employees can extract a larger share of the surplus, limiting accumulation by the boss. If the organizations are large, the mounting surplus means that wealth (or prestige and power for noneconomic organizations) is increasingly centralized, and this concentration can lead to power. Those with great wealth and power can shape ideologies and values and thus shape the culture.

Socialization. Organizations socialize us to fit their needs. From working in organizations, we get organizationally friendly habits of the heart and organizationally friendly cognitive patterns of the mind, stemming from unobtrusive controls over, and extensive socialization of, personnel and even customers. Among working adults in the nineteenth century, roughly three quarters of their waking time was spent in settings that had an interest in shaping their behavior; in the twentieth century, nearly half of their waking hours were so spent. This amount of exposure to conditions controlled by the organization helps transmit the culture favored by the masters.

Divisions. Modern organizations use and shape ethnic, racial, and gender differences and divisions, acting on group identities and family structures, thus affecting much of what we call culture, and shaping the stratification system and political dynamics. They also have the power to reduce the divisions that exist in the society. In either case they are exercising power in society. We will see that in the nineteenth century large organizations used existing divisions and magnified them, reinforcing prejudices in most cases. In the twentieth century this continued, but using and creating divisions increasingly interfered with efficiency as skill levels rose and women were needed for the work force. The most striking case is that of gender divisions, as explored by Robert Max Jackson (1998), where hiring practices promoted more gender equality. Frank Dobbin and John Sutton (1998) document how human resource divisions in corporations, set up in response to federal prodding, developed justification for fair treatment that top management could accept, and thus fostered employment rights, thereby reducing divisions more than top management would have desired. Michael Burawoy (1985, 99–

100) and others have noted that in modern organizations the internal divisions of seniority and skill can cut across divisions sustained outside of the organizations, such as race and gender, and thus reduce their salience; John Meyer and associates (1994) even go so far as to argue that large bureaucracies "rationalize" the world and in the process eliminate the "nonrational" divisions and distinctions that I find magnified in the nineteenth century. We know little about the circumstances that encourage the exploitation of division versus those under which organizations would ignore divisions recognized outside of the workplace. I belatedly discovered, too late for serious incorporation, the magnificent and award-winning book by Charles Tilly, *Durable Inequality* (1998), which has a great discussion of what I call "divisions," which goes far beyond my own formulation.

Structural Interests. Organizations have a "life of their own," in that maintenance and stability requirements, as well as group interests, form around their structure and activities. These two set systemic limits on elite intentions. The usual emphasis in "neoinstitutional" theory and population-ecology theory is on the way practices become valued for their own sake and thus locked in—a cultural view. I would emphasize instead the interests served by practices, an "interests and power" view. Departments and divisions will have interests that thwart those of the masters. Organizations are tools, but only "recalcitrant tools" (Perrow 1986). . . . (The interests that groups can realize are small compared to those that the masters realize; masters generally get what they want. But at times groups can be quite consequential, greatly limiting theories of rationality and efficiency.) These requirements and interests are conceptually distinct from the interests of the masters; they are organizational rather than part of the elite / class / family / person interests of the masters. Of course, in practice, the interests of groups in the organization and those of the masters are most often overlapping and conflated.

The term "structural interests" hardly captures the notion of the organization as an agent, an actor with needs and preferences, but it will have to serve. The organization is structured into groups, which develop interests in survival, growth, sexism, liberalism, and so on. The expression of these interests born of the organizational structure constitutes a part of "organizational behavior." Structural interests affect the socialization, divisions, and externalities of the organization.

Externalities. Organizations shape the external environment of neighborhood, community, and government at all levels. Some of the shaping is what economists describe as "negative externalities," or an unobtrusive transfer of wealth from communities and employees to the masters of the organizations. I have in mind such obvious things as pollution, the exhaustion of natural resources, and workplace accidents, but also the externalities of urban crowding, the failure to smooth production resulting in boom-and-bust cycles and layoffs, and some of our military adventures to secure investments and markets abroad. Since these are not included in the price of the goods or services, they are borne by everyone rather than just those that purchase the goods and services.

Concentration of Wealth and Power. The things that organizations do, beyond producing goods and services, combine to produce inequalities in the distribution of wealth and power. A system with many small organizations deconcentrates wealth and power; a system with a few big ones concentrates it (Perrow 1992). I am ignoring the positive externalities here. Life would be shorter, nastier, and more brutish if it were not for the enormous productivity and efficiency of organizations, some of which may necessarily be large and bureaucratic. Organizations generate wealth and power; we need them. But large organizations make it possible to centralize the wealth and power they generate. . . . The point, necessarily oversimplified here, is that most of the negative externalities we have experienced were not necessary; with the abundance of this continent and the skills of its conquerors, we could have made far less of a mess of it had it not been for the particular conflux of events that generated our form of organizations. But there is more to this story than the concentration of wealth and power; there are general systemic effects that manifested themselves in the middle and late twentieth century. This is a period beyond the scope of this work, so I will mention them only briefly at this point.

System Accidents. One is the systemic impact of the distinctive dynamics of social systems in which large organizations are tightly coupled to each other so that unanticipated interactions create system-wide disturbances, such as stock market crashes, interruptions of service, widespread contamination, and opportunities for fraud and corruption. . . .

Absorption of Society. Another systemic effect, increasingly apparent in the second half of the twentieth century, is that large organizations wittingly and unwittingly absorb the functions performed by smaller autonomous units of society such as families, kinship networks, local churches, and small governmental units and businesses, weakening those parts of society that are not governed by an employment contract, and creating a "society of organizations" (Perrow 1991, 1996). . . .

Conclusion

The nineteenth century is the prelude to our market society with its distinctive form of capitalism. There was nothing inevitable about the turn that the century took. It was the product, first, of the "initial conditions": a lightly populated land of great natural resources, a fear of a strong state, and a powerful industrial revolution in Europe, and second, it was shaped by the decisions of organizational leaders and a supporting cast of elected and appointed government servants. Many conditions were in place to grow a society of well-regulated and moderate-sized firms focused upon regional economic development; at various points in the century many citizens argued for this. But other conditions made a quite different society possible and it was the one we got—an economy with lightly regulated, very large firms focused upon national economic development, with all the attendant social costs that accompanied the concentration of wealth and power this allowed. My argument is that while culture, politics, technology, efficiency concerns, and entre-

preneurship all played a role, the most neglected and the most significant role was played by formal organizations. Organizations are more than the shadow of the entrepreneur. Their shape affects working conditions and points of community access; their size affects their ability to control competition and control politics and regulation; the density and concentration of their employees in a community determines the degree of wage dependence, and thus power over employees and the community. And when organizations grow large enough there is the possibility of significant internal interest groups whose concern for stability and internal power deflects the direction of the organization from the path the leaders prefer. . . .

References

Burawoy, Michael. 1985. *The Politics of Production.* London: Verso.

Dobbin, Frank, and John Sutton. 1998. "The Strength of a Weak State: The Employment Rights Revolution and the Rise of Human Resources Management." *American Journal of Sociology* 104:441–76.

Jackson, Robert Max. 1998. *Destined for Equality: The Inevitable Rise of Women's Status.* Cambridge: Harvard University Press.

Meyer, John. 1994. "Rationalized environments." In *Institutional Environments and Organizations*, edited by W. Scott and J. Meyer. Newbury Park: Sage.

Perrow, Charles. 1986. *Complex Organizations: A Critical Essay.* 3rd ed. New York: Random House.

———. 1991. "A Society of Organizations." *Theory and Society* 20:725–62.

———. 1992. "Small Firm Networks." In *Networks and Organizations*, edited by N. Nohria and R. G. Eccles. Boston: Harvard Business School Press.

———. 1996. "The Bounded Career and the Demise of Civil Society." In *Boundaryless Careers: Work, Mobility, and Learning in the New Organizational Era*, edited by Michael B. Arthur and Denise M. Rousseau. New York: Oxford University Press.

Tilly, Charles. 1998. *Durable Inequality.* Berkeley: University of California Press.

Useem, Michael. 1996. *Investor Capitalism: How Money Managers Are Changing the Face of Corporate America.* New York: Basic Books.

Chapter 7
Bureaucracy and Democracy in Organizations

Revisiting Feminist Organizations

Catherine Alter

Sociologists of organizations and students of bureaucracy have devoted much of their attention to profit-making organizations. Catherine Alter takes the discussion in a different direction by considering the implications of bureaucracy for nonprofit, voluntary associations. Democracy and social equality occupy a larger role in these organizations than in those designed to produce goods and services for profit. Alter suggests, however, that many nonprofit, voluntary organizations experience a gradual process of bureaucratization that challenges, if not eliminates, their commitments to equality and democracy. What does it take for a nonprofit, voluntary organization to resist these challenges? Are some kinds of organizations better positioned to accomplish this than others? As she explores these questions, Alter examines the unique strengths and weaknesses of feminist forms of organization.

We assume that the bureaucratic form of organization is necessary for the delivery of human services and for reform efforts which aim to change or ameliorate large-scale social problems. Bureaucracy, a hierarchical form of organization, is virtually the only type of organizational form used in the public sector through which health and welfare benefits are dispensed to large populations. Even in the private sector, in which nonprofit organizations are smaller and client populations more localized than in the public sector, hierarchy is the typical form of or-

ganizing. Given such widespread use, it is a puzzle, then, why bureaucracies engender widespread dissatisfaction among clients and consumers, staff and administrators.

The bureaucratic form is recognized for its efficiency and ability to formalize and routinize vast amounts of work (Weber 1946); it is also, however, notorious for its negative effects on organizational members—alienation, antipathy, and burnout (Crozier 1964). In the public sector, there have been experiments and much research in the area of organizational development demonstrating alternatives to bureaucracy which draw on contemporary organizational theory and practice. There has been precious little of this type of development among voluntary associations.

The democratic form of organization has always been viewed as appropriate to voluntary associations given their nature and aims but seldom has it been consistently implemented in health and welfare organizations. Although historians and students of government have studied democracy in political systems, it has not been a primary focus of those interested in the development and improvement of voluntary associations and welfare systems.

Classical thinking has always assumed the presence of democracy in voluntary associations, however. Alexis de Tocqueville, during his travels in the young America, observed firsthand that *men*, escaping the despot, want to be in control of their social relations and will share power with others rather than return to the tyranny of a king. Of course, in de Tocqueville's age, *all others* were defined as white, landowning males. Nineteenth-century philosophers could not view democratic aspirations as inherent to all human beings, and neither could they foresee the rich variety of organizational forms, processes, and transformations necessary to realize these aspirations. The twenty-six-year-old Comte de Tocqueville during his trip to America in 1831, expressed his contemporaries' concept of democracy: "The principle of equality, which makes *men* independent of each other, gives them a habit and a taste for following in their private actions no other guide than their own will. This complete independence . . . tends to make [man] look upon all authority with a jealous eye . . . and value that government whose head he has himself elected and whose administration he may control" (emphasis added). The principle of equality is the basic concept of democracy, an inherited truth upon which Western society has built its institutions and voluntary associations.

It is ironic, then, that 150 years later, it is feminist organizations that most clearly exemplify democratic principles in their construction and day-to-day operations, in spite of the fact that feminists themselves have seldom used the concept of democracy as the defining variable of their distinctive nonnative type of organization (one exception is Brown 1992). Feminist and women's organizations were formed and continue to be formed as a democratic alternative to contemporary bureaucracy—an organizational form that, they assert, is hierarchical, authoritarian, and discriminatory.

Although suffrage organizations are credited with achieving significant political, legal, and workplace advances for women, and feminist movement organizations are believed to have been responsible for further pushing gender-based discrimination and oppression into the national agenda, the feminist organization as an ideal type has been ignored, if not discounted.

As an oppositional form, the distinctive characteristic of feminist organizations is that they are collectives, whereby all members have equal voice in the decisions of the organization, and the organization proceeds only after consensus is reached. They are nonhierarchical and function by means of processes that attempt to preserve nondifferentiation, collaboration among all members, and equal attention to means and ends. Because feminist organizations are almost always formed as small, voluntary associations with clearly articulated ideology and member commitment they are an overlooked test case of the iron law of oligarchy.

The question of whether health and welfare organizations can be established and maintained through the democratic form is especially important for nonprofit organizations that are confronted today with increases in the intensity and scope of social problems. The study of feminist organizations shows that the strength of ideological commitment, organizational goals, political resistance, and resource dependency are factors which can inhibit or promote the development of either democratic or bureaucratic processes, depending on how they combine over time. Given that many feminist organizations have survived relatively intact for more than two decades and that the problems of many mainstream nonprofit organizations are reaching crisis proportions, it may be that the lesson learned by feminists in resisting elite rule and hierarchy has application today in a wide range of voluntary associations.

Social Equality or Technical Efficiency

By law, nonprofit voluntary associations must be democratically constituted to be tax-exempt. To obtain status under section 503 of the United States Internal Revenue Code, a voluntary organization must be nonprofit, serve a public purpose, be governed by its membership, and maintain financial records that are open to public scrutiny. These formal requirements are, of course, minimal, but they establish the basic tenet that the public interest, as opposed to private interests, can be achieved only by structures designed to ensure the principle of *social equality*.

Although nonprofits are legally constituted as democratic organizations, Internal Revenue Service regulations do not ensure democracy in organizations in any substantial sense. The basic, or inherent, character of an organization is defined by a much wider range of processes and practices which, by the tenets of substantive democracy, guarantee that all members of the organization be able to hold office and have a voice in all important decisions affecting the organization (Hage 1980). Substantive democracy thus requires additional rules beyond the basic requirements of legal or formal construction. At a minimum, organizational bylaws must establish a rotation schedule for directors, the tenure of directors, the maximum number of consecutive terms that may be served by directors, procedures for election by secret ballot or by mail ballot, the requirement of at least two nominees for each office from a nominating committee, and the election of the nominating committee (Cafferata 1982). All of these rules, established to prevent individual privilege and the development of status groups, are institutionalized by means of the organization's bylaws and serve to maximize *equality of opportunity*.

All nonprofit organizations, then, meet the criteria of social equality by virtue of their Internal Revenue status, and many achieve substantive democracy via bylaws which incorporate the principle of equality of opportunity. Thus, higher levels of democracy are achieved by rules which govern internal processes of decision making and operations. It is perhaps ironic that rules are necessary for preserving democracy; yet, they are a two-edged sword. On one hand, rules protect minority interests and opinion within the organization and ensure the maintenance of social equality and equal opportunity. On the other hand, rules can be used to establish elite governance and bureaucratic processes and, in excess, they can stultify and rigidify an organization. Contrary to what the critics of public bureaucracy (and many feminists) assert, it is not rules themselves that are inherently nondemocratic. It is their number and how they are used by the men and women of an organization that determine whether they yield democratic or bureaucratic governance. Many nonprofit organizations, although democratic in their infancy, tend to become oligarchical and bureaucratic as they develop. The central task of this chapter is to describe the factors which enable organizations to reverse this bureaucratization process.

The term *bureaucracy* generally describes an organization in which all important decisions are made by an individual or small group at the top of a hierarchical, pyramidal structure. The operational definition used here, however, is Max Weber's (1946); a bureaucracy is an organization that maximizes *technical efficiency* through a large number of administrative rules, horizontal differentiation, complexity, span of control, permanent administrators, exclusivity of membership and promotion within the organization, vertical differentiation of the authority structure/centralization of decision making, and specialization of roles/divisions of labor (Cafferata 1982, p. 302). The requirements of technical efficiency also involve a large number of rules which are intended to narrow decision-making authority rather than broaden it.

The relationship between democratic rule and bureaucracy was the essence of the dispute between Weber and Robert Michels (Nyden 1985). The two theorists agreed that bureaucracy always accompanies the struggle to achieve democracy. Further, they agreed that as organizations begin to fulfill their intended purpose, they tend to grow, requiring increased specialization of func-

tion and expert leadership and reducing grassroots control of important decisions. They disagreed, however, over the question of whether growth, and its companion, bureaucracy, spells the end of democracy. Whereas Michels believed that "every system of leadership is incompatible with the most essential postulates of democracy" (1959, 400), Weber thought that some level of equality could be maintained via rules which work to prevent the development of an inaccessible status group and to expand the sphere of influence of the total membership (Weber 1968, 985). For Weber, it cannot be assumed that the appearance of elite or expert leadership eliminates all possibility of democracy (Scaff 1981). If we take Weber's view that the "iron law of oligarchy" is not inevitable, then we can view any organization as more or less democratic and bureaucratic. Because of the legal mandates for nonprofits, we also assume that organizations serving the public interest, in comparison with organizations operated for profit, will be more democratic and less bureaucratic—and have more rules ensuring social equality and fewer implementing technical efficiency. This conception of democracy is not that of a static form of organization; rather, it is one that acknowledges democracy as a developmental process which results in a wide range of organizational types with differing degrees of democracy and bureaucratic rule. Nonprofits, starting with the same degree of formal democracy, may take various developmental paths, depending on many internal and external factors.

The relationship of democracy to bureaucracy in nonprofits is of interest not just to academics; it continues to attract public and media attention. The national press in 1992, for example, extensively covered revelations that the United Way of America had for some time been ruled by elites who were serving their own private interests and not fulfilling the public mission for which United Way was created. In spite of its altruistic mission, elitist and autocratic governance in United Way took control, and the organization was severely damaged in the process.

The press is also quick to point out, however, that the process can go in the opposite direction. For example, the Forest Service was described in a recent article as a rule-bound bureaucracy which, thanks to participatory decision making and quality circles, has been transformed into an agency

Figure 7.1

Bureaucratization and Democratization in Nonprofit Organizations

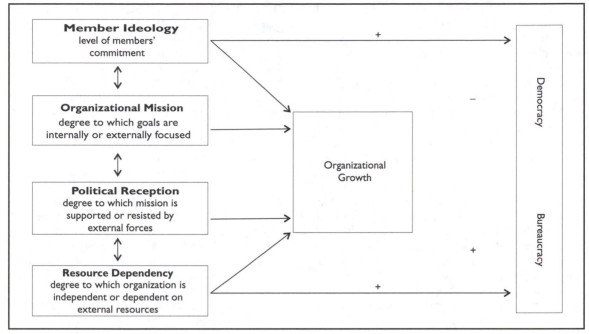

Democratic and Bureaucratic Processes

with full worker participation (McKenna 1993). Likewise, the once mob-ruled and highly oligarchical Teamsters union was reported to have been remade by means of court orders which mandated unionwide elections (Bernstein 1991). The point is that nonprofit organizations are perceived as being capable of wide swings between democratic and bureaucratic forms and are not necessarily stuck in unchanging patterns of governance (for a counter view, see Cafferata 1982). This observation concerning the processes of democratization and bureaucratization is illustrated by the theoretical model described below.

Democratic and Bureaucratic Processes

For many decades, the study of organizations has been, in effect, the study of bureaucracy in its many variations. Based on Weber's assertion that hierarchical organizations are the most efficient way to accomplish goals, very little attention has been paid to alternative forms of organization—how they develop, how they maintain themselves in the face of strong and subtle environmental forces, and whether, given different circumstances, they are actually less efficient. Also, for many decades, one of the crucial issues in social development has

been the role of voluntary organizations and their ability to adjust to changing organizational conditions while remaining true to their mission (Zald 1970). What has not been explored fully are organizational forms that allow nonprofits to adjust to internal and external forces and yet remain congruent with the values and ideology upon which they were founded. It is often assumed that growth is accompanied by a parallel increase in bureaucratic structure and process, but little attention has been paid to the factors which sustain self-rule against totalitarian incursions and which minimize the degree to which development imposes stultifying rules, processes, and values.

In this section I describe briefly a theoretical model intended to explain why some organizations may be capable of achieving this improbable feat. The model is described first in general terms, with a brief explanation of the factors which push and pull against democratic rule. I hypothesize that four factors can largely explain democratization and bureaucratization in voluntary associations: ideology (Zald 1970), organizational goals (Etzioni 1964; Hage 1980), the need for resources to implement goals (McCarthy and Zald 1977; Benson 1975), and outside oppositional forces (Hyde 1992; Rodriguez 1988). These four factors have direct and indirect effects on the development of both democracy and bureaucracy, and together they have a wide range of consequences for the organization. The effect of these four factors on organizational growth and subsequently on the tendency toward democracy or oligarchy in organizations is illustrated in figure 7.1.

Voluntary associations differ in the nature and strength of their ideological commitment to the mission of the organization. The nature of ideology is shaped by many forces, among them the historical epoch and popular culture of the time and the socialization and personal histories of the members of the collective (or dominant group) (Etzioni 1988). The nature of ideology is, of course, based on deeply held cultural and religious values which produce a system of beliefs. A voluntary association, created to be an instrument of collectively held beliefs, develops in direct response to the nature and intensity of the membership's tightly linked beliefs and values. There are many dimensions of ideology which could be cited here; the one most important in terms of organizational development is the level of member commitment (Brown 1992). Commitment determines the persistence and obstinacy with which members pursue the organization's objectives in the face of resource shortages, market changes, and political opposition (Zald 1970). Commitment stems from the degree to which the members' ideological system is clearly articulated and zealously held.

Nonprofit organizations also vary widely in the mission and goals which operationalize their organizational ideologies. As a description of the idealized future which the organization is striving to achieve, goals guide and justify the activities and efforts of the membership. Goals, therefore, have enormous influence on the internal processes of organizations. If they are related to social change and development and are externally focused, then the membership will be forced, over time, to expand the organization's size in order to achieve its global mission. If, on the other hand, the organization's mission is related to members' self-improvement or to bettering the collective in some way, then members will find it less necessary to become dependent on external resources.

Voluntary associations also differ in the degree to which their goals are supported or resisted by major actors in their environ-

ment. If there is widespread approval for the aims, then political and social support will accrue to the organization and it will expand to whatever size is necessary. If, on the other hand, the objectives engender opposition and resistance, then the opposite may well be the case. Opposition, of course, may vary in intensity, ranging from political methods which subtly undermine the organization's ability to function, to extremely acrimonious attacks which wreck havoc. The most visible forms of resistance have been the violent physical acts against women's health clinics, ranging from harassment and blockades to gas and fire bombings. In some cases, attacks against abortion clinics and their physicians have caused the temporary suspension of services, but they have not been successful in permanently closing clinics. It is clear that a high level of commitment by the membership, accompanied by some measure of organizational self-sufficiency and combined with support for the clinic's mission by other external constituencies, has resulted in the survival, if not the growth, of reproductive rights groups and women's health services.

Last, voluntary associations vary in the degree to which they remain independent of external influence (Pfeffer and Salancik 1978). There are social, religious, and special interest organizations which have survived for long periods of time as essentially self-sufficient bodies requiting no resources outside the association—voluntary associations and cooperatives which fulfill a need of their members and which rely solely on the resources and efforts of members. On the other hand, some organizations, in their desire to seek social change and altruistic goals, expand their scope and size so as to reach a greater audience or geographic area or to pursue greater effectiveness and efficiency. In order to acquire the information and technologies needed to achieve these objectives, voluntary associations may become dependent on extreme public and private resources (Kramer and Grossman 1987). This fourth factor, resource dependency, has a strong impact on the operations of an organization, as has been pointed out by a long line of organizational theorists (Benson 1975; Brown 1992; Smith and Lipsky 1992). When a voluntary association adopts goals whose accomplishment requires concerted action in the larger environment, then the organization becomes necessarily more dependent on its environment for resources because the membership itself does not have the resources necessary to achieve its goals.

These, then, are four potential forces which have a direct effect on growth and which, in turn, drive democratic or bureaucratic processes. The intervening variable, organizational growth, is the strongest force pushing against democratic rule and toward technical efficiency. The effect of an organization's size on the operations of profit-making firms has been widely researched; it has received far less attention in the literature on voluntary organizations.

When it becomes necessary because of increasing organizational size to differentiate between types of members and to control increasingly chaotic organizational activities, then more rules are promulgated to balance power between directors and staff and among staff and the clients, patients, or service consumers. There are two basic dynamics arising out of growth and expansion which tip the balance of nonprofit development toward bureaucracy.

The first is an internal dynamic set in motion by efforts to bring order to out-of-control conditions associated with growth. This balance of power is achieved through requirements that make distinctions between organizational members and by structures that segment members into different operating units—for example, those governing operations, finance, personnel promotion and evaluation, and marketing. The more that organizational members are placed in different roles, with different functions and tasks, the greater the likelihood that status differences will develop and that those in control of the whole will have more power and authority.

The second dynamic is the effect asserted by external forces needed for growth. The bureaucratizing influence of government funding on voluntary associations is well documented (Kramer and Grossman 1987; Morgan 1986; Rodriguez 1988). The quid pro quo of state funding is accountability, which can mean everything from requiring staff to be professionally trained to double entry fund accounting procedures to limitations on the scope and duration of the organization's activities. The potential results of utilizing external resources are incremental steps toward rationalization and formalization of the operations of the organization and of the interactions among its members. Those voluntary associations which abstain or minimize their reliance on outside resources retain a far greater measure of internal autonomy.

Maintaining social equality and equality of opportunity in a nonprofit organization is probably difficult in the best of circumstances. Endurance requires, at a minimum, abiding organizational goals, stable and supportive environments, and abundant internal resources. In less nurturing circumstances, decisions by organizational members can move the organization in opposite directions. In sum, democracy and bureaucracy are opposite poles of the same controlling mechanism, two potentials which exist simultaneously in all organizations and which point toward diverging organizational objectives—social equality or technical efficiency—both of which are necessary if a nonprofit organization is to sustain democratic rule in a turbulent environment and during periods of organizational expansion. Under these circumstances, organizational members are required to make continually occurring choices, each of which nudges or propels the organization in one direction or the other, each of which either resists oligarchical tendencies or sustains democratic rule. If voluntary associations are incubators of democratic rule, as proposed by de Tocqueville, then it is important to understand what factors enable organizational members to withstand nondemocratic forces (and thus prove Weber to be right and Michels to be wrong). The important question here is the membership's ability or willingness to steadfastly pursue its goals in spite of market constraints, regulations, and ideological assault. There are many descriptions in the academic literature as well as in the popular press of organizations that have abandoned their ideology or displaced their goals because of internal change or external pressure. There are also a large number of organizations that have survived for a considerable period of time and been able to resist encroachments upon their autonomy. Feminist organizations are a class of nonprofits which fall into the latter category.

Feminist Organizations

Feminist and women's organizations today exist around the world in great profusion. They are created for many purposes and causes and are dedicated to innumerable goals in their attempt to better the lives of women and children. In the West, these organizations had their genesis in earlier suffrage movements, which, after forty years of dormancy, gathered force again in the late 1960s as the women's movement. These organizations have survived twenty to twenty-five years, and, although they are highly diverse in some aspects, they have much in common. In the mid-1990s, they engender curiosity but to date, little research (exceptions are Bordt 1990; Hyde 1992). In that they represent alternative forms of organizing and that they have survived for a quarter century or more they are useful for investigating the relation between organizational growth and the processes of democratization and bureaucratization. I shall examine these organizations through the lens of the model described above, framing the analysis in terms of ideology, goals, resource dependency, and environmental resistance or support as antecedents of organizational size.

It is difficult to use these organizations as an explicit category of alternative organization because we immediately encounter definitional problems. Although the feminist organization is an ideal type that differs from the traditional organization in very significant ways, it is also, in reality, part of a continuum which displays significant within-group differences. A range of organizations promote the interests of women, reflecting differences in the degree to which their agendas advocate reform of the status quo or more basic structural change in gender and sexual roles. Other women's organizations attempt to co-opt the feminist movement in order to advocate traditional gender role relationships in home, work, and political life. Although these organizations call themselves women's organizations and advance the traditional ideals of "total women" and "feminism" (Kaminer 1994), they are in many cases part of fundamentalist religious movements or radically conservative political parties with broader agendas and therefore cannot be understood as feminist organizations.

Of the organizations that do advocate reform or structural change, the mainline women's organizations were formed to challenge discrimination in a wide range of arenas, and they focus on problems of exclusion of women from political, commercial, social, and artistic life. The oldest of these organizations date from the suffrage movement, and they include such national organizations as the American Association of University Women and the League of Women Voters as well as many state and community voluntary associations which have survived as democratic organizations in which important decisions are made by consensus. The newer of these organizations, those arising out of the women's movement, are national feminist organizations which advocate profound change and community organizations which are collectivist but focused on a narrower set of issues. An example of the former is the National Organization for Women; examples of the latter are battered women's shelters, women's health clinics, and artists' cooperatives. These are explicitly self-styled feminist organizations whose members challenge not only discrimination and exclusion, but the assumptions and personal behaviors which undergird them. They require individual change of both men and women as well as social change in society.

An interesting recent development—on a theme that seems to unite the disparate range of women's and feminist organizations, including perhaps even those I term bogus feminists—is a belief that female-oriented organizations meet female needs better than traditional organizations do. There is a growing sense that assimilation into male-dominated organizations will not advance the cause of women as much as activism within a feminist organization. This is the old separatist versus integrationist argument, but now there is evidence that women in feminist organizations do better than those in male-dominated ones: girls who attend girls' schools score higher in mathematics and science; women who graduate from women's colleges reach higher levels in politics and corporations (Estrich 1994); women who avail themselves of domestic violence shelters and women's health clinics experience more empowerment and have a much better sense of their potential (Rodriguez 1988). To a greater or lesser degree, the belief in the efficacy of women's organizations is based on women's negative perceptions of and experiences in male organizations.

Feminist Critiques of Traditional Organizations

The postmodern feminist critique asserts that modern organizations are dependent upon a specific configuration of gender relations. This assertion is arrived at through historical study, linguistic analysis, and organizational research. Feminist historians, for example, have analyzed the development of bureaucracy in the nineteenth century. The classic case studies are the reform of the British Civil Service (Corrigan and Sayer 1985) and the Post Office (Zimmeck 1988), and they provide specific evidence of the development of the hierarchical distinction between mechanical and intellectual labor (Savage and Witz 1992). These analyses show that the rapid growth of bureaucratic organizations was made possible by the so-called White Blouse Revolution, which employed women for routine work, institutionalizing them as subordinate workers in both white- and blue-collar organizations and freeing men to do the cognitive work. This gendered structure of work within organizations had a series of important effects. First, because they did the commonplace, day-to-day work, women made it possible for organizations to promote male employees more quickly into positions of authority, for male workers to gain the knowledge necessary to do administrative work through education and training rather than by learning the business as they rose through the ranks, and for men to have careers because women, of course, were not eligible for promotion (Compton 1986; Compton and Jones 1984). Thus, as organizations grew larger, differentiation increased proportionately. Women were denied status and power because of their housekeeping roles within organizations and because of their exclusion from the networks through which men gained knowledge and political resources. Rosabeth Kanter (1977) offered this process and its outcome, male homosocial reproduction, as one explanation for the patriarchal culture and structure of bureaucracy. Until very recently, job classification and promotion structures have remained gender-based—women and men recruited into different job tracks, with different salary structures and promotion prospects (Kanter 1977).

More recently, the critique of organizations has been extended by postmodern feminist scholars who analyze the discourse and linguistic patterns of organizations to identify the institutional practices that maintain gender and organizational identity. For example, K. E. Ferguson (1984) described bureaucratic discourse as male-dominated, linking this observation to the historical fact that women have been excluded while men have been included in the public realm. Women's exclusion has enabled them to develop a "submerged" voice, one characterized by expressive modes of action and discourse. When women do enter the public realm, they are disadvantaged, being unfamiliar and unschooled in the "rational" and "instrumental" modes of male discourse.

Focusing on the nature of organizational discourse, feminist scholars postulate that when family ties were completely removed from work and replaced with highly bureaucratic and professional structures, then organizational goals and purposes completely dominated discourse within the organization (Hearn, Sheppard, Tancred-Sheriff, and Burrell 1989). The dominance of bureaucratic and professional culture purged organizational life of all emotional content and strengthened "the process in which men become associated (in location) with rationality/instrumentality and women with emotionality/expressiveness" (Burrell 1984, 104; Miles 1988). If this is the case, then it follows that decision making in organizations separates mind and body by isolating and suppressing the emotional and physical self from the process of organizing (Mumby and Putnam 1992):

> Researchers using the bounded rationality concept treat emotional experience (defined as feelings, sensations, and affective responses to organizational situations) as either a weak and handicapped appendage to reason or as another "means" to serve organizational ends. In the former case, emotions are devalued, trivialized, or treated as inappropriate at work. For example, decisions based on "gut feelings," emotions, or intuition, must be rationalized through satisficing and alignment with organizational values and goals. . . . In the latter case, emotions are ways to achieve such organizational ends as efficiency, profit, and productivity. As such, the emotional realm is co-opted and alienated in a form known as *emotional labor*. (Mumby and Putnam 1992, 472)

Emotional labor is a central concept of postmodern feminist scholars because it is viewed as the means by which organizations remain undemocratic and male-dominated in spite of legislation that equalizes spending by gender in college athletics, affirmative action, and the strivings of individual women. Emotional labor is a form of organizational control of the emotions whereby feelings are treated as organizational commodities, as when employees are forced to be nice, to use phony smiles, to suppress anger, and to tolerate sexual harassment (Hochschild 1989). Thus, feminists see emotional labor as just another means of socially constructing roles which force women to make an unfair choice (Schwartz, Gottesman, and Perlmutter 1988). They can either adopt the role and thus fail to achieve an integrated self or they can differentiate themselves and be seen as not fitting in or as insubordinate (Ferguson 1984).

Other feminist scholars, using standpoint methodology, have extended these ideas to describe the distinctive ways in which women engage in daily life at home and within patriarchal organizational structures. By describing the systematically different structure of male and female life activity, these scholars understand women's lives as being shaped by the sexual division of labor. Dorothy Smith (1987), for example, sees the development of bureaucracy as the emergence of an abstracted conceptual mode of organizing society and rational administrative practice. By making this distinction between the conceptual mode and the concrete mode, she is able to describe the fundamentally relational difference between the male and female mode of action and discourse:

> If men are to participate fully in the abstract, conceptual mode of action, they must be liberated from having to attend to their needs in the concrete and particular. . . . The place of women, then, in relation to this mode of action is where the work is done to facilitate men's occupation of the conceptual mode of action. . . . At almost every point women mediate for men the relation between the conceptual mode of action and the actual concrete forms in which it is and must be realized, and the actual material conditions upon which it depends. (Smith 1987, 90)

Women, then, are concerned with "the concrete underbelly of conceptual activities" (Savage and Witz 1992, 25), whether they are in the organization or in the home, and are ordering and organizing the real world. From standpoint theory emerges the conclusion that men, who dominate the conceptual and thus authoritarian mode, are privileged at the expense of, but only because of, women. In their review of the feminist literature, Savage and Witz (1992) rightly point out that "the whole concept of 'dependency' within the context of gender relations acquires an interesting new twist, for it is men who are dependent upon the concretizing activities of women in order to sustain their involvement in the everyday world of, for example, bureaucratic administration (Savage and Witz 1992, 27).

One current conclusion of this stream of scholarship is that the powerless position of women in bureaucratic organizations is not just an outcome of historical events that can be fixed by reform activity which aims to removes the "glass ceiling." Rather, exploitation based on gender is an inherent property of modern organizations; bureaucracy is possible as a form because of the exclusion of women from the conceptual and symbolic organization of activity and thus from public life altogether. This "sexual division of labor" pushed women outside the realm of authority and *distributed organizational power by gender.*

Most recently, feminist scholars have disagreed with the view that gender and organizational power are inseparable (Pringle 1989a, 1989b). There has been a shift from the gender paradigm to one of sexuality; the root cause of the dispossession of women is believed to be the power of sexuality. In fact, by this view, *sexuality is power is organization*—three properties which are inseparable and intertwined. No longer are male-female differences thought to account for power differentials; rather, organizational structure and discourse account for male-female differences. It is organization itself which rests on sexuality. Seen in this light, the current campaign against sexual harassment in the workplace is the most important step toward equity within organizations that has been taken in decades.

By these views, bureaucratic organizations are the primary means by which women's oppression has been sustained over the past century and a half. Political and sexual domination of females by males is perpetuated by organizational structures which place power and control in the hands of a few male elites. The suppression of emotionality in favor of rationality and instrumentality—or its use only in service of organizational goals—is the means by which oppression of women continues. The continuation of male domination via hierarchical forms and processes, freed from a need to attend to the concrete necessities of daily life at home and work, is made possible by a continued toleration of male use of sex as power. It is to be expected, therefore, that feminists would strive for alternative means of organizing. Although feminists continue to support actions to reform public and private bureaucracies, the separatist orientation has been adopted by many women who wish to live their ideology within their own organizations.

Feminist Ideology as the Basis for Feminist Organizing

Women who experience themselves as different from their socially prescribed roles have always come together to protest and give mutual support. In the nineteenth and twentieth centuries, women have created formal organizations to accomplish these goals, and their organizations were structured and operated as alternatives to what they perceived to be mere extensions of a society that was patriarchal and discriminatory. Feminists, viewing organizations through the lens of feminist ideology, perceive traditional organizations as extending, perpetuating, and strengthening the inequities of male domination—and eventually of such "-isms" as racism, homophobism, capitalism, and imperialism. Unlike social anarchists and other utopian activists before them, feminists have developed their opposition into a clearly articulated belief system which is the basis for an oppositional ideology of organizing (Brown 1990). Feminist organizing, then, is a self-conscious method of protest itself because feminist organizations are an oppositional alternative—based on principles of social equality, wholism, nondifferentiation, collectivist rule, and, of course, nonhierarchical form. Because of these principles, made explicit by the feminist movement, the ideal of the feminist organization is easily described in terms of a normative model.

At the heart of feminist ideology is the belief that people can work together for common purposes without resorting to a highly structured, pyramidal hierarchy to control internal processes and order decision making. The ideal of cooperation within a collective of like-minded individuals has seldom had as clear, conscious, and long-lasting an expression by a social movement (Bouchier 1983), in spite of the fact that in its application, many differences across the political continuum have appeared (Kaminer 1993).

Feminist organizations, because they share an opposition to traditional power structures, share a commitment to egalitarianism. As a reaction to and cure for the injustices perpetuated by male political domination of organizations, feminist organizations aim to be universally and explicitly egalitarian regardless of the degree to which they have a revolutionary or reformist orientation. Social equality is an intrinsic characteristic which defines the feminist organization.

The capability of feminist organizations to operationalize cooperative collective behavior is due, in part, to their understanding of the interconnection between individuals and the structures within which they exist;

Table 7.1

Goals, Resource Dependency, and Political Resistance to Feminist Organizations

	Consciousness-Raising/ Self-Help Groups	Service Organizations	Social Movement Organization
Goals	To facilitate members' individual change	To facilitate change in specific groups of women and/or to create change in community structures that discriminate or oppress them	To promote change in community or societal structures that discriminate or oppress women
Resource dependency	Isolated from established political and cultural structures	Moderately interactive with established political and cultural structures	Highly interactive with established political and social structures
	Little or no need for financial resources	Highly dependent for resources	Ranges from self-sufficient to highly dependent
		Acquisition tactics require professional skill and persuasion	Acquisition tactics include both professional skill and political action
Political resistance	Low	Moderate	High

or, to put it a different way, the degree to which *the personal is political* (Friedan 1981; Steinem 1982). This concept encapsulates a wholistic approach to viewing organizations, one which stipulates that process and means are every bit as important as ends and that the structure of organizations should be derived from the process of organizing. Thus, another concept of feminist organizations is that both process and form must be congruent with the tenets of the ideology, and the construction of both is a conscious political act. Feminist organizations strive to pay as much attention to the content of everyday life and to the interactions of members as to daily tasks.

Feminist organizations aim not to differentiate between participants; or at the least, differentiation is minimized to the greatest extent possible. Differences between members—for example, in social status, access to information and resources, and skills—are not acknowledged in work processes; thus all tasks are performed by all members through sharing of jobs or job rotation. Having no leaders, who in traditional bureaucracies have authority to make most or all of the important decisions, feminist organizations require the membership to be actively involved in decision making and to make all decisions collectively. Full participation in all aspects of the organization, from decision making to work processes, is believed to be what makes the feminist organization powerful and empowering.

Given their rejection of hierarchy and a wholistic orientation, feminist organizations operate ideally without leadership, which is possible because of widespread agreement about underlying values and principles among members. Collaborative participation is the means by which nonhierarchy is made to work. Because of the existing consensus over organizational processes, feminist organizations can govern either intraorganizational or interorganizational activity with very few rules and methods of coordination. This characteristic was described by Anna Coote and Beatrix Campbell (1987) in their documentation of the dissolution of the National Coordinating Committee, an early women's movement organization in London in 1971:

> Most women were confident that the movement would hang together without a coordinating committee—and it has remained a loose federation of small groups, linked chiefly by a sense of involvement and a common cause. That it has survived nearly two decades was a measure of the strength of the *idea* that held it together. It was also due to the fact that the movement's lack of formal structure was a positive, not a negative feature. (Coote and Campbell 1987, 27, quoted in Brown 1992, 9)

The belief that hierarchies result in self-defeating traps for those at the bottom (women) is a central tenet of feminist organizations. Hierarchies are inimical to women who struggle for autonomy and fulfillment in positions that are subordinate and disadvantaged, and they symbolize all that is discriminatory and unjust in traditional organizations. The feminist movement is noteworthy for its ability to critique hierarchical organizations and for its success in constructing a positive alternative form of organization. That any women's organizations have survived more than a quarter of a century is evidence that they can work effectively.

Feminist Goals, Political Resistance, and Resource Dependency

Although feminist organizations share a core of beliefs and values, their goals and the level of resource dependency necessary for implementing them can vary substantially. To capture these differences one must start with the purpose for which the organizations were formed; their missions are, of course, tightly tied to their ideology (Clemens 1989, 1993; Hyde 1992; Leidner 1991; Rodriguez 1988).

One useful way of classifying the diversity of feminist organizations is in terms of their orientation. At one end of the spectrum are organizations that focus inwardly and aim to change some aspect of their members' lives. At the other end are those that focus outwardly on other groups of women or on changing some aspect of society at large. The table below is inclusive of this variation and describes feminist organizational goals as well as the parallel variation in resource dependency and political resistance.

The cells in this table are not mutually exclusive; many organizations have multiple goals and thus include self-improvement goals as well as service or social action goals or both within their mission. There are innumerable small women's groups, for example, which were formed for social or intellectual pursuits but which eventually adopted service goals. Likewise, there are service organizations that expand the geographic reach of their mission so far beyond their communities that they link or merge with other, similar organizations, become national in scope, and take on additional policy and legislative change goals. For analysis, however, it is useful to distinguish between self-centered and other-centered goals.

When a feminist organization adds an other-centered goal, it expands its mission in terms of scope or geography. Expansion—in response to additional feminist issues or the need to reach greater numbers of women—requires the organization to grow in size, and this it will do unless it meets with resistance either from unresponsive funding bodies or political foes. If there is substantial opposition, its growth may be slowed or halted and its organizational properties may remain unchanged. If, however, this expanding feminist organization overcomes resistance and its growth is bolstered by financial and political support, then its trajectory toward bureaucratization is guaranteed. As described earlier (see fig. 7.1), the coordinating of activities which serve multiple goals or supervising of operations across vast geographic distances makes it difficult to avoid bureaucratic processes and procedures. In these situations, the strength of the members' ideological commitment to egalitarian and collective processes may enable them to avert a bureaucratic outcome.

The hypothesis represented in figure 7.1 is that every time there is a change in any of the four variables that precede growth—member ideology, goals, environmental resistance, and resource needs—the organization will shift toward greater democratic or bureaucratic governance, depending on how the combination has changed. The reason that feminist organizations are a good test of the hypothesis is that when they are founded they are usually small and have a strong ideological foundation. The question, therefore, is whether their members' commitment is strong enough to overcome political obstruction while simultaneously resisting the corrupting influences of success. The answer, of course, is that it depends on what type of feminist organization it is.

Self-Help Groups and Organizations.
Women have always formed cells for protest and support, but the late 1960s and 1970s were a time when consciousness-raising, support, and mutual aid groups became vehicles to aid women in developing the personal strength to overcome discrimination and oppression. These groups were purposely focused on the individuals involved, and their mission was to facilitate change in members (Rothschild-Whitt 1979). Most of the groups formed originally for support have survived as collectives which use group process to enable members to meet their personal psychosocial needs. Many, in addition, have expanded their goals in order to meet members' needs for labor and financial resources. Because they are small and devoted almost exclusively to facilitating personal change or meeting their members' needs, they exist independently of other community political and cultural organizations, which they do not need to survive.

These small organizations are so numerous and private, they are almost invisible. Many—for example, support groups for single mothers, childless women, lesbians, displaced homemakers, minority women, union members, businesswomen—are informal arid are organized to facilitate individual change through group processes, give friendship and emotional support, and provide peer counseling. But many are formal nonprofit and profit-making organizations which, in addition to carrying out the functions of the informal groups, exchange and sell labor or commodities. There are cooperatives of women artists, quilt makers, and dairy farmers; there are cooperatives for child care, food procurement, and English language tutoring. There are organizational networks of working-class women, businesswomen, and professional women, who together provide mutual support or attempt to create new products or establish new markets. The list is endless, and all have two characteristics in common: they tend to have relatively small memberships and they are self-sufficient. Because their goal is self-centered—personal change, interpersonal support, or financial gain—they usually do not interact with their environment (unless interaction is necessary to market a product).

Feminist organizations that remain small over long periods of time can maintain democratic governance fairly easily as long as this is the will of their membership. Because they do not have to depend on resources other than their own, they do not have to be accountable to anybody but themselves. Because they do not aim to affect anyone other than themselves, they generally do not engender opposition that can threaten their survival.

Service Organizations. Another expression of the feminist movement looks outwardly and provides assistance to the many groups of women who are victimized in various areas of contemporary life. These organizations offer services or interventions which focus on the social, emotional, health, or welfare problems of women, although the problems are viewed as originating in the larger systems and structures of which the women are a part. Such organizations reject theories based on the medical model; which diagnose or label women's problems in terms of mental illness and social dysfunction (individual pathology) or as intergenerational transference (family pathology). Thus, many of these service organizations aim to empower individual women to change their victimizing circumstances, while at the same time they work on behalf of women in efforts to change the informal and formal organizational systems in which the oppression originates.

Medium- and large-size communities typically have many feminist or women's service organizations today. Some of the oldest provide shelter services to battered women and their children. These domestic violence programs (DVPs) tend to limit the use of professional staff, emphasize self-help and peer counseling, and incorporate a political analysis of battering into their programs (Dobash and Dobash 1978). One DVP in Hawaii is typical:

> It has an egalitarian organizational structure run by a non-professional staff of former residents who earn equal pay, make decisions by consensus, and operate a program in which residents actively participate in running the shelter. . . . [I]t prefers an open-door policy, sets no limits on how long residents may stay, and encourages nonprofessional, egalitarian, and informal relationships within the organization. Because their goal is to have women achieve self-development, politicization, and liberation, they strive to have the battered women actively participate in running the shelter along with the staff and volunteers. (Rodriguez 1988, 236–37)

The goal of this DVP is to help women avoid returning to abusive relationships and enable them to achieve self-sufficiency for themselves and their children. This goal is common to many types of feminist service organizations. There are women's health care organizations that promote self-care within a self-affirming and wholistic lifestyle. There are rape counseling services that support victims so they can confront their attackers and thus regain their self-confidence. There are business training programs that teach welfare recipients the skills and courage necessary to start small-scale enterprises and thus become self-employed. There are substance abuse programs that afford women a safe place to recover while they care for their children.

Feminist service organizations, however, live with a constant dilemma. On one hand, they strive to meet the needs of all the women in their communities needing their service, a goal which, even with participant and paraprofessional staff, requires substantial financial resources. The operation of one shelter for just a dozen women with children or of a health clinic for a few hundred women requires a hundred thousand dollars a year or more. Feminist organizations do not want to seek government funding or even voluntary dollars, however, because they know it will subject them to many regulations and forms of accountability. Funding bodies, especially public ones, often demand professional expertise in the name of effectiveness and accountability. They require an administrative hierarchy, job descriptions, differential salary structures, limits on duration or intensity of service, and extensive financial reporting.

These requirements, however, are not consistent with egalitarian processes, rotation of members, and consensus decision making. When a feminist organization decides to broaden its goals to reach more women or women with different types of problems, it puts its ideology to the test. The challenge becomes finding ways to maintain operating methods consistent with their beliefs and values while at the same time satisfying outside demands. In addition, the maintenance of internal processes is made even more difficult when the organization experiences political or physical opposition from activists with different ideological commitments. Resistance, however, can have a strengthening effect. Some women's health clinics which perform abortions are stronger because their members' resolve hardened as physical violence escalated. Others closed or stopped performing abortions because their physicians were unwilling to risk their physical safety.

Since the 1970s, some feminist service organizations have become moderately self-sufficient (because they have limited the size of their service populations), while others have grown large and become highly dependent on resource allocation bureaucracies. In the latter case, co-optation has pushed some formerly democratic organizations into bureaucratic processes and structures. This fact raises the question of how a highly dependent social service organization can remain democratic with internal egalitarianism. Can it have both formal structures that are highly bureaucratic to satisfy external forces and day-to-day operations that are highly democratic and non-hierarchical (Bordt 1990)? The model described above suggests that one necessary (but not sufficient) element for overcoming this dilemma is clearly articulated values which govern day-to-day operations. M. Lipsky and S.R. Smith summarize this dilemma: "Ultimately, our argument that developments in government contracting with non-profit organizations vitally affect the future of the welfare state depends upon recognizing that these organizations have traditionally played a role in integrating the individual into community-sponsored activities (as client, donor, or volunteer) and in offering *an alternative* to public policies derived from governmental power and coercion" (Lipsky and Smith 1989–90, 646) (emphasis added).

Social Movement Organizations. The range of feminist social movement organizations is very wide, and they differ in the degree to which they view women's problems through the single lens of gender or through the multiple lenses of gender, class, race, and sexual orientation. They differ also in the degree to which they are reformist or oppositional, using tactics that range from persuasion to confrontation to combat. Finally, they differ greatly in the size of their infrastructure and the resulting level of bureaucracy needed to carry out large-scale public education and political campaigns. They are all at least moderately democratic, however, and usually use memberwide elections, consensus decision making on at least

the policy level, and, although they may have to become somewhat hierarchichal, their form is as flat as possible.

Today, it is easy to forget the enormous impact that suffrage movement organizations had on political processes as well as on women's issues, and that their methods—personal discourse, social research, policy advocacy, and lobbying—became standards for all political organizing after 1920 (Clemens 1989, 1993). Also often overlooked is that the suffrage organizations were transformed, after 1920, into a second generation of organizations that survive today in relatively good health: for example, the National Association of University Women, the Junior League, and many national sororities. The League of Women Voters, for example, has chapters that work directly on women's issues in every state and in many cities and towns and well. The league membership, using the methods of its predecessor as well as media and public relations techniques, adopts study items at the local, state, and national levels each year and then reaches a consensus on collective action to be taken to implement its positions. The league is credited with numerous child labor, welfare, environmental, and political reforms. It and other women's membership organizations are self-sufficient but are limited in their reformist agenda by the middle-class values of their members.

There are, of course, more oppositional women's organizations like the National Organization for Women, Title VII monitoring organizations, and the Guerrilla Girls. The latter, an organization of women artists, campaigns to open up the male-dominated art industry through the use of nonviolent guerrilla tactics, including sophisticated graffiti placed in strategic locations, boycotts, and cooperatives. There are local and national organizations that work to end discrimination against lesbians and gays and that demand increased research on HIV and support for its victims.

The factor that differentiates these feminist social movement organizations is the scope and reach of their missions. Those that focus on the discriminatory institutions and structures within their own neighborhoods and communities may use their own labor and resources to achieve their agendas, although if it is an effort that must be sustained for a long time then additional resources are probably essential. Those that go beyond their own reach in attempts to change larger societal systems and structures cannot rely only on what they bring to the effort, but must acquire substantial resources.

The larger the scope and reach, the larger the organization, the more difficult it is to maintain social equality, collectivist rule, nondifferentiation, and nonhierarchical forms. The reasons are many. It is very difficult to achieve and maintain a sense of social equality among members of a group who must live within a broader society in which social equality does not exist. It takes continual face-to-face interaction among members, time to break down social barriers and to construct new ways of relating and doing. Personal interaction among members of a group becomes increasingly difficult as group size gets larger, and impossible as members are physically distant from one another.

Democracy also takes time. Reaching consensus is extremely time-consuming, especially in the beginning, when nonnative roles and behaviors are being worked out. It is far more efficient for a supervisor to hand down an order or circulate a directive than for a group to reach agreement on an issue. In addition, members have to be willing to give their time consistently or power and status will devolve to those who are constant in their involvement. Further, even if the organization does not need to expand to achieve its mission, it must constantly search for new members to replace those who drop out from fatigue or who leave because of waning interest.

When a single social movement organization expands its scope beyond its community to the state or regional level, it soon bumps into the limits of voluntary association. If there is to be concerted and consistent action across a wide geographic area, then coordination is necessary. Unless volunteers are willing to assume this time-consuming task, then paid staff is necessary, and this introduces differentiation and status differences into the collective based on educational level and technical skill. Further, if the organization must use education and public relations methods to persuade and influence, then professional communication skills and new technologies are needed for the organization to be effective; this acts as another assault upon social equality and nondifferentiation. There are many national organizations in which local cells are collectivist in structure, but in which the centralized state or national coordinating unit is staffed by paid professional staff. This arrangement allows the community organization to operate without a hierarchy but is sure to engender tension and conflict between the two levels. An alternative is the British model described above, a network of small local women's groups without a formal structure or centralized coordinating capability (Brown 1992). To effect change in federal legal or administrative systems is difficult, however, without a central coordination.

To return, then, to the central question of this paper: Are feminist organizations especially successful in using democratic forms of governance, and, if so, how have they been able to sustain nonhierarchical forms of organization and resist the encroachment of bureaucracy as they mature through time? One simple answer to the first part of this question is to recount the achievements of the feminist movement since the late 1960s. Most, if not all, of these gains could not have been made by individual women acting alone; concerted actions by voluntary associations over long periods of time have changed American society. Domestic violence, sexual assault and harassment, and women's health problems—to name only a few—are now recognized by large segments of the population as major problems and are now on the nation's agenda; to a lesser extent, child care, equal pay for equal work, and the Equal Rights Amendment have been given the priority they require.

The question, however, is to what extent feminist organizations have been successful *because* they used processes that were true to their original organizing ideology. This question cannot be answered, of course, without more research, but theory and anecdotal evidence provide guidance for that research.

Clearly, the 1960s adage Small Is Beautiful has merit in this context. Small feminist organizations which stay within their own space and do not evolve much beyond their original purposes (either self-centered or other-centered or both) are more likely to remain nonhierarchical if their members are highly committed to the feminist belief system. Even if they meet with political resistance, this experience often strengthens their resolve. For example, members of one well-known women's health cooperative in the Midwest have often responded to actions by Operation Rescue, an antiabortion group, by saying, "The bad news is our entrances were blockaded again last week; the good news is we have twenty-five new members." It is clear that the intensity of members' ideology is the most important variable in resisting the effects of both attack and the more subtle forms of bureaucratic co-optation.

Ideology is easy to espouse; it is very difficult to enact. For two decades, democratic feminist organizations have used many of the practices that are only now being espoused in the for-profit world, and, as a result, their members have a sense of control and autonomy, feel a sense of personal responsibility for their involvement, have an opportunity to develop personally in concert with the group and the organization, and are able to integrate their work and development with other aspects of their lives. As has been pointed out by organizational theorists from Tom Burns and G.M. Stalker (1961) to Thomas Peters (1987), a work group with these qualities makes for an organization that is flexible, innovative, adaptive, and capable of accomplishing its goals. If democratic feminist organizations have survived with nonhierarchical processes intact, then this fact argues for the conclusion that democracy has evolutionary advantages. Democracy may be less efficient than bureaucracy but effectiveness may be more important in the long run for nonprofit organizations.

It is also clear that many service and social movement organizations must go beyond their original space, either in terms of agenda or locality or both. If they are service organizations and wish to increase their service capacity, they obtain financial support from funding bureaucracies and hire paraprofessional and professional staff. If they are social movement organizations and they must compete with oppositional voices and interests, they need to acquire technology with which to reach and influence larger audiences. To withstand invasion and preserve democratic life within their organizations, feminist organizations then need to consciously and explicitly invent two versions of their reality—their internal collective culture and their worldly personae. Successful attempts at sustaining this dual personality should be documented, so that it

can become a technology by which increasing numbers of voluntary associations may preserve their commitment to themselves and their communities.

The model described in figure 7.1 suggests that the level of ideological commitment is the most important factor affecting the degree to which an organization will sustain democratic governance because it has both a direct effect of supporting democratic practices and an indirect effect of sustaining goals that are congruent with the internal belief system. It is perhaps an obvious observation, but nevertheless true, that the most potent remedy for drift toward bureaucratic tendencies is a continual clarification of the ideology as well as of the processes which reinforce it. Many feminist organizations consider their belief system to be organic, and in applying themselves to its continual development, they are keeping their organizational life congruent with their values and their changing environment.

References

Alter, C., and J. Rage. 1993. *Organizations Working Together.* Newbury Park: Sage.

Benson, J. 1975. "The Interorganizational Network as a Political Economy." *Administrative Science Quarterly* 20(2):229–49.

Bernstein, A. 1991. "The Teamsters Try Something New: Democracy." *Business Week,* December 9.

Bordt, R. L. 1990. "The Diversity of Women's Organizations: A Survey of New York City." Unpublished report of preliminary findings of dissertation research. New Haven: Yale University.

Brown, R. 1992. *Women Organising.* London: Routledge.

Burns, T., and G. M. Stalker. 1961. "The Management of Innovation." London: Tavistock.

Burrell, G. 1984. "Sex and Organizational Analysis." *Organization Studies* 5(2):97–118.

Cafferata, G. L. 1982. "The Building of Democratic Organizations: An Embryological Metaphor." *Administrative Science Quarterly* 27:280–303.

Clemens, E. S. 1989. "Gender, Class and Political Identity: Progressivism and the Politics of Representation." Later version of a paper presented at the Social Science History Meeting, November, Washington, D.C.

———. 1993. "Organizational Repertoires and Institutional Change: Women's Groups and the Transformation of U.S. Politics, 1890–1920." *American Journal of Sociology* 98(4):755–98.

Compton, R. 1986. "Women and the Service Class." In *Gender and Stratification,* ed. R. Crompton and M. Mann. Cambridge; Polity.

Corrigan, P., and D. Sayer. 1985. *The Great Arch.* Oxford: Blackwells.

Crompton, R., and G. Jones. 1984. *A White Collar Proletariat? Deskilling and Gender in Clerical Work.* Basingstoke: Macmillan.

Crozier, M. 1964. *The Bureaucratic Phenomenon.* London: Tavistock.

Dobash, R. E., and R. P. Dobash. 1978. "Wife Beating: The Victims Speak." *Victimology: An International Journal* 2:608–22.

Etzioni, A. 1964. *Modern Organizations.* Englewood Cliffs: Prentice-Hall.

———. 1988. *The Moral Dimension: Toward a New Economics.* New York: Free Press.

Ferguson, K. E. 1984. *The Feminist Case Against Bureaucracy.* Philadelphia: Temple University Press.

Friedan, B. 1981. *The Second Stage.* New York: Summit Books.

Hage, J. 1980. *Theories of Organization.* New York: John Wiley.

Hearn, J., D. Sheppard, P. Tancred-Sheriff, and G. Burrell. 1989. *The Sexuality of Organizations.* Newbury Park, Calif.: Sage Publications.

Hochschild, A. R. 1979. "Emotion Work, Feeling Rules and Social Structure." *American Journal of Sociology* 85:551–75.

———. 1989. *The Managed Heart.* Berkeley: University of California Press.

Hyde, C. 1992. "The Ideational System of Social Movement Agencies: An Examination of Feminist Health Centers." In *Human Services as Complex Organizations,* ed. Y. Rasenfeld, 121–44. Newbury Park, Calif.: Sage Publications.

Kaminer, W. 1993. "Feminism's Identity Crisis." *Atlantic Monthly,* October.

Kanter, R. M. 1977. *Men and Women of the Organization.* New York: Basic Books.

Kramer, R., and B. Grossman. 1987. "Contracting for Social Services: Process Management and Resource Dependences." *Social Service Review* 61:33–55.

Leidner, R. 1991. "Stretching the Boundaries of Liberalism: Democratic Innovation in a Feminist Organization." *Signs: Journal of Women in Culture and Society* 16(2):263–89.

Lipsky, M. and S. R. Smith. 1989–90. "Nonprofit Organizations, Government, and the Welfare State." *Political Science Quarterly* 104(4):625–48.

McCarthy, I. C., and M. N. Zald. 1977. "Resource Mobilization and Social Movements: A Partial Theory." *American Journal of Sociology* 82:1212–41.

McKenna, I. F. 1993. "Empowerment Thins a Forest of Bureaucracy." *Industry Week* 242(7):64.

Michels, R. 1959. *Political Parties.* New York: Dover.

Miles, A. I. 1988. "Organization, Gender and Culture." *Organization Studies* 9(3):351–69.

Morgan, G. 1986. *Images of Organisation.* London: Sage.

Mumby, D. K., and L. L. Putnam. 1992. "The Politics of Emotion: A Feminist Reading of Bounded Rationality." *Academy of Management Review* 17(3):465–86.

Nyden, P. W. 1985. "Democratizing Organizations: A Case Study of a Union Reform Movement." *American Journal of Sociology* 90(6):1179–1203.

Perrow, C. 1961. "The Analysis of Goals in Complex Organizations." *American Sociological Review* 26:854–66.

Peters, T. I. 1987. *Thriving on Chaos: Handbook for a Management Revolution.* New York: Knopf.

Pfeffer, I., and G.R. Salancik. 1978. *The External Control of Organizations: A Resource Dependence Perspective.* New York: Harper and Row.

Pringle, R. 1989a. *Secretaries Talk: Sexuality, Power and Work.* London: Verso.

———. 1989b. "Bureaucracies, Rationality and Sexuality: The Case of Secretaries." In *The Sexuality of Organization,* ed. J. Hearn et al. London: Sage.

Rodriguez, N. M. 1988. "A Successful Feminist Shelter: A Case Study of the Family Crisis Shelter in Hawaii." *Journal of Applied Behavioral Science* 24(3):235–50.

Rothschild-Whitt, J. 1982. "The Collectivist Organization: An Alternative to Bureaucratic Models." In *Workplace Bureaucracy and Social Change,* ed. F. Lidenfield and I. Rothschild-Whitt. Boston: Porter Sargent.

Savage, M., and A. Witz. 1992. "Gender and Bureaucracy." *Sociological Review.* Oxford: Blackwells.

Scaff, L. 1981. "Max Weber and Robert Michels." *American Journal of Sociology* 86:1269–86.

Schwartz, A. Y., E.W. Gottesman, and F.D. Perlmutter. 1988. "Blackwell: A Case Study in Feminist Administration." *Administration in Social Work* 12(2):5–15.

Smith, S. R., and M. Lipsky. 1992. "Privatization in Health and Human Services: A Critique." *Journal of Health Politics, Policy and Law* 17(2):133–253.

Smith, D. E. 1987. *The Everyday World as Problematic.* Milton Keynes: Open University.

Steinem, G. 1983. *Outrageous Acts and Everyday Rebellions.* New York: Holt, Rinehart and Winston.

Tocqueville, A. de. [1835] 1958. *Democracy in America,* ed. P. Bradley. New York: Vintage Books.

Weber, M. 1946. "Bureaucracy." In *From Max Weber: Essays in Sociology,* ed. H. Gerth and C.W. Mills, 196–244. New York: Oxford University Press.

———. 1968. *Economy and Society,* ed. F. Roth and C. Wittich. Reprint. New York: Bedminster.

Zald, M. N. 1970. *Organizational Change: The Political Economy of the YMCA.* Chicago: University of Chicago Press.

Zimmeck, J. 1988. "The New Women and the Machinery of Government: A Spanner in the Works." In *Government and Expertise: Specialists, Administrators and Professionals, 1860–1919,* ed. R. McLeod. Cambridge: Cambridge University Press.

Chapter 8
Nonprofit Organizations in International Development

Agents of Empowerment or Preservers of Stability?

Brian H. Smith

We continue our examination of nonprofits by exploring their role in international development efforts. Smith's chapter underscores the message of earlier readings: Large organizations play an ever-increasing role in the world, including the administration of large-scale development efforts. In certain respects, nonprofits participating in development initiatives across the globe are very different from the smaller, more local voluntary associations that Catherine Alter examines in the previous chapter. Despite these differences, Smith's discussion of the tensions between bureaucracy and political empowerment echoes some of Alter's concerns.

In the past two decades nonprofit organizations (NPOs) have significantly expanded their involvement in international development. In 1970 American, Canadian, and European NPOs transferred $2.7 billion to developing countries, and by 1990 the amount totaled $7.2 billion (in constant 1986 dollars). The Organization for Economic Cooperation and Development (OECD) listed 1,600 North Atlantic NPOs involved in foreign assistance in 1980, 2,500 in 1989, and more than 4,000 in 1996. Their aid now reaches approximately 250 million people, or about one in five of the 1.3 billion people living in absolute poverty in developing countries (Clark 1990, 40; OECD 1981, 1988, 1989, 1996; UNDP 1993, 88; Smilie 1993, 3).

Funds for NPO development work originate primarily from two sources: individual private donations and grants from the foreign assistance ministries of North Atlantic governments. Over the past two decades not only has the total amount from these two sources dramatically increased (as indicated above), but the proportion contributed by each has changed significantly. In 1970, of the $2.7 billion given to NPOs, only 1.5 percent ($40 million) originated from governments, but by 1988 public subsidies counted for 34.6 percent of the total ($1.8 billion of $5.2 billion) (Clark 1990, 40).

Thus, although (in constant terms) private donations increased 25.9 percent (from $2.7 billion to $3.4 billion), government support grew 4,400 percent (from $40 million to $1.8 billion) during this eighteen-year period. The major factor, therefore, in the expansion of NPOs' international commitments since the 1970s has been increases in public, not private, aid.

Indigenous nonprofit organizations in developing countries at the national and regional levels act as intermediaries in channeling this international assistance to the poor in their own societies. They have also grown in number significantly over the past two decades. It is estimated that there are now at least 30,000 to 35,000 intermediary nonprofit development organizations at the national and regional levels in Asia, Africa, and Latin America.

These intermediary NPOs sometimes carry out projects but more frequently act as brokers between local groups at the grassroots level who have formed their own smaller NPOs. The intermediary NPOs offer these smaller grassroots NPOs both technical assistance in drawing up project proposals for foreign NPO funding and advice in the implementation and evaluation of the actual projects that receive funding from abroad. The smaller grassroots NPOs presently number in the hundreds of thousands (Fisher 1993, 5, 23; Durning 1989, 55).

Thus, there is a clear hierarchy in the transnational nonprofit aid network: NPOs in the North Atlantic countries raise private and public funds for development projects overseas. National and regional NPOs in developing countries receive these funds from abroad and disperse them on a project-by-project basis. Finally, local NPOs in these same societies run the actual projects at the grassroots level among the poor.

The indigenous NPOs in developing countries—national, regional, and local—have been able to function under different types of governmental regimes. Democracies and authoritarian governments alike have allowed them to support projects in their territories even though NPO foreign assistance is not dispersed through their own public agencies.

In this chapter I discuss why this cooperation among governments and NPOs has grown so significantly in recent decades. I also compare the intentions of the North Atlantic donors with the actual projects funded in developing societies and assess if empowerment is occurring for the grassroots poor abroad as a result of this assistance. Finally, some challenges facing the transnational NPO network in the future will be identified.

NPO-Government Cooperation

The American Experience

Many large NPOs currently engaged in foreign assistance originated as relief agencies to alleviate the effects of wars and other disasters. During both world wars many American humanitarian organizations were formed to assist refugees, orphans, and other victims of conflicts in Europe. All received strong encouragement from the U.S. government to undertake relief work, and some were given public subsidies even during the early years of the respective world wars when the United States was technically neutral (Curti 1963; Ringland 1954).

During the early 1950s, with the reconstruction of Europe winding down, American relief NPOs, rather than disband their sizable institutional networks, searched for a new mission and turned their attention to Asia, Africa, and Latin America—an illustration of the "garbage can" theory of organizational goal expansion (see Chaves, in this volume). In the mid-1950s, the U.S. government expanded its purchase of surplus wheat and dairy products from American farmers and began employing American relief NPOs to dispose of such commodities abroad so as not to depress American food prices at home.

As the Cold War continued, the U.S. government and private citizens alike shared an interest in keeping newly merging nations from opting for alliances with the Soviet Union. Accordingly, the creation of private institutions to alleviate poverty and stimulate popular participation in the civic life of these societies became a major objective of U.S. foreign policy.

In 1966, Congress mandated that some U.S. foreign aid be channeled through American credit unions, cooperatives, and savings and loans associations to help create similar institutions in developing societies abroad. The new focus on private institution building in American foreign aid in turn stimulated the creation of new American NPOs to carry out such tasks. It also encouraged older NPOs engaged in relief and food distribution to begin to include a technical focus in their work abroad. This role expansion by NPOs is another illustration of the garbage can theory of organizational growth.

The growing alliance between NPOs and the American government advanced to another plateau in the early 1970s. Congress was becoming increasingly dissatisfied with the inability of U.S. economic aid to alleviate poverty abroad. A series of studies at the time criticized American assistance for not reaching the poorest sectors abroad, claiming much of it was being siphoned off by corrupt or inept government bureaucracies or spent on projects benefiting the minority of middle- and upper-income groups (Goulet and Hudson 1971; Adelman and Taft Morris 1973; Paddock and Paddock 1973). The failed war in Vietnam was winding down, and various attempts by the Central Intelligence Agency to undermine legitimate governments abroad were coming to light. Americans were becoming increasingly cynical about American foreign policy and unenthusiastic about foreign aid.

Reacting to these criticisms, Congress in 1973 mandated "new directions" for U.S. foreign aid that were to give it a more humanitarian focus by concentrating on basic needs of the poor abroad—food production, nutrition, health, education, and rural development. Representatives of some of the large American NPOs like CARE, Catholic Relief Services, and Church World Service testified on behalf of this legislation at congressional hearings. They argued that the focus of American nonprofits abroad now included just such an emphasis and that NPOs should be given increasing amounts of government assistance to expand their new development projects overseas among the poor.

In its final form, the Foreign Assistance Act of 1973 praised NPOs for "embodying the American spirit of self-help" and for "mobilizing private American financial and human resources to benefit poor people in developing countries." The new law stipulated that NPOs receive additional public funds to accomplish these goals abroad more effectively (U.S. Congress 1973).

In succeeding years, a steady increase in U.S. government subsidies to American NPOs leveled off by the late 1980s at about the 25 percent level of overall NPO budgets. The U.S. government continued to rely on American NPOs as a means to dispose of surplus food commodities abroad, and as of 1992, food and food-related aid constituted nearly one-third (32 percent) of all public subsidies to NPOs (USAID 1992, 82).

American NPOs engaged in foreign assistance have proven to be strong domestic advocates of economic assistance to developing countries in an era when foreign aid has continued to remain unpopular among most Americans. NPOs regularly testify in support of increased foreign assistance at congressional hearings and are among the most reliable lobby groups the State Department has to support foreign aid. Many also have begun development education programs at home since the mid-1980s (some with government grants) to make their donors and other citizens more aware of the needs of developing countries, thus hopefully enlarging the constituency for American aid to such societies.

The European and Canadian Experiences

In Europe, similar factors have accounted for the emergence of close working relationships between governments and NPOs in foreign assistance. Many European NPOs were founded earlier in this century to alleviate the destruction caused by major wars in their societies. After World War II, they, like their American counterparts, moved abroad to find new tasks rather than dismantle their operations.

NPOs proved useful to such governments as Britain, France, Belgium, and the Netherlands as alternate means of maintaining cultural influence in territories in which home-country colonial offices were being phased out during the era of political independence. In Sweden and Canada, where no colonial heritage existed, and in the Federal Republic of Germany, where such a heritage had not existed for more than a generation, NPOs pioneered in setting up new ties between the home country and newly emerging societies that set the stage for later commercial and investment relations.

Newer NPOs were also formed during the 1960s, when pressures were building on a by-then economically recovered Europe to do more for developing countries. Often European governments found that channeling of public aid through NPOs rather than government agencies was more cost-effective because the overhead expenses in these smaller private agencies were lower.

The use of NPOs became increasingly attractive by the mid-1970s. During those years, left-of-center coalitions were in power in Canada and most of Western Europe, and they sympathized with the New International Economic Order (NIEO) endorsed by the United Nations General Assembly, which called for very substantial increases of economic aid to developing countries targeted at the basic needs of the poorest sectors. Given the impact of two major oil price rises in the 1970s, however, these governments were not able to take on significant new commitments in foreign aid. But they did begin to increase their grants to NPOs. Such subsidies were small compared to the massive new commitments called for by the NIEO, but Canadian and European governments could claim that they were meeting some NIEO objectives because the small-scale development projects of NPOs almost all reached the grassroots poor in developing countries.[1]

Thus, between 1973 and 1983 public subsidies to NPOs in Europe and Canada more than quadrupled (in constant 1986 dollars). They jumped from $160 million to $680 million in this ten-year period as governments channeled increasing amounts of their own foreign assistance through NPOs that sponsored projects abroad among some of the poorest sectors of the populations. Government subsidies to NPOs in Europe and Canada, in fact, grew much faster than private contributions during these years; the percentage of overall NPO revenues that such subsidies comprised increased from 16 percent in 1973 ($160 million of $998 million) to 36 percent in 1983 ($680 million of $1.9 billion).

Some important differences exist between American NPOs and those in other

North Atlantic countries. One is the smaller amount of food aid channeled through NPOs by the European and Canadian as compared to the American governments. The discrepancy is attributable to the types of farm subsidy programs that exist in each area. The European and Canadian governments do not buy and store excess food from farmers and thus do not rely on NPOs as conduits for disposing of it abroad. Almost all government aid to European and Canadian NPOs is in the form of cash grants for development projects, not of commodities to alleviate hunger.

In addition, many of the Canadian and European NPOs created in the post–World War II era were formed by groups who had close ties to labor organizations, professional associations, and leftist political parties. These ties have continued, and many large Canadian and European NPOs continue to attract executives and staff with similar ties. Unlike the American NPOs, which have no close links to domestic political movements and tend to avoid partisan issues, European and Canadian NPOs include in their fund-raising and development education programs criticisms of home-country policies they feel harm developing countries in the areas of tariffs, immigration quotas, investment priorities, and weapons transfers. They are thus far more political in their style than their American counterparts (see Ullman, in this volume). They thus view development not merely as an economic issue but one requiring a redress of power imbalances between rich and poor nations and between elites and masses in developing countries (a perspective shared by proponents of the NIEO agenda).

Experiences of Developing Countries

NPOs in developing countries date back to charitable organizations started by Christian missions in the sixteenth century in Latin America and in the following three centuries in Asia and Africa. In the post–World War II era, and especially in the 1960s, these missionary groups shifted their focus from relief to development as they began to emphasize as part of their work long-term strategies to attack poverty—literacy and job training, formation of production and consumer, cooperatives, primary health care, water development, and support for small-scale farming (Smith 1990, 232–33; Landim 1987, 31).[2]

By the 1970s, however, two major factors in developing countries stimulated the expansion of church-related service organizations and the creation of a series of new secular NPOs focusing on similar small-scale development projects among the grassroots poor. One was the cutback in public services by governments in the 1970s and 1980s, and the other was the disenchantment of middle-class professionals with the public sector as a means to help the poor.

Governments in the non–oil producing countries of Asia, Africa, and Latin America began to cut back educational and health services to the poor after rises in petroleum prices in 1973 and 1978. Many governments borrowed from private international banks that were glutted with investments from the oil-producing countries of the Middle East, and this led to ever-increasing debts. By the early 1980s, they had difficulty meeting even interest payments on such loans, and a new round of cuts in central government spending on social services occurred. This left the bottom 40 percent of their populations in even more dire straits than before (George 1990).

The austerity measures adopted by many third world governments precipitated a search among middle-class professionals in these countries for alternate strategies to assist the poor. Government corruption and policies geared to the preservation of elite interests had begun to sour idealistic professionals in many developing countries as early as the 1960s. Once substantial numbers had lost their jobs in governments or national universities owing to cutbacks in public expenditures, they began looking for new employment opportunities that would also realize their ideals for service. This combination of factors gave rise to the creation of a series of new NPOs staffed by these professionals to assist urban and rural poor in their countries (Fisher 1993, 77; Bratton 1989, 570–71; Garilao 1987, 114).

Many new NPOs were also created in Africa and Latin America in the late 1960s and early 1970s, when authoritarian regimes replaced elected democracies. This change of regimes (especially in Latin America) created new cadres of unemployed professionals or former party activists who had lost their jobs for political reasons under newly established military governments. These

NPOs often took the form of research organizations aimed at keeping alive alternate perspectives on development, and some became technical assistance organizations for self-help projects among the grassroots poor. A series of new private organizations was also created, many under the auspices or protection of the churches, to assist victims of human rights violations and to provide needed social services no longer available from governments (Smith 1990, 236–37; Landim 1987, 31–32; Smith, 1980).

A final factor which made intermediary NPOs attractive to those seeking alternate means of helping the poor and oppressed in Africa, Asia, and Latin America was the availability of new funds from international NPOs. From the mid1970s on (as described earlier), American, Canadian, and European NPOs received increasing amounts of home-government subsidies, and they found ready recipients in newly created intermediary NPOs in developing countries—many of which could neither have begun nor continued without foreign NPO assistance (Fisher 1993, 174).

Some of these intermediary NPOs brokered resources from northern NPOs to local development projects carried out by grassroots groups in their own societies. Others acted as support institutions offering their technical expertise to these local groups in such areas as primary health care, small-scale agricultural development, prefabricated housing, credit management, production and marketing cooperatives, and environmental preservation. Still others focused on policy research and dissemination of information on alternate strategies for attacking poverty, and some of these also provided training in community development to rural and urban grassroots leaders.

Hence, crises in public sector service institutions in developing countries that came to a head in the 1970s stimulated the proliferation of nonprofit organizations. It was not so much that governments reached out to embrace NPOs, as they did in the North Atlantic countries. It was rather an opportunity seized by NPOs when state budgets shrank (as has been the case recently in Eastern Europe—see Anheier and Seibel, in this volume) or when state repression increased. This new opening for NPOs in Asia, Africa, and Latin America occurred at the very time that North Atlantic NPOs were coming into a windfall of new resources from their govern-

ments and were looking for private clients abroad to disperse the funds and materials. Thus, the transnational NPO network for development was forged.

Intentions of Donors Vs. Character of the Projects

In spite of this convergence of factors that stimulated the growth of NPOs both north and south of the equator in the 1970s and 1980s, questions arise as to why governments, private donors, and NPOs would continue to collaborate even though they had differing interests. Some northern NPOs are staffed by persons who articulate strong criticisms of home-country foreign policies, and who advocate changes that will cost private citizens in increased taxes or higher prices for imported goods. Abroad, those staffing intermediary NPOs often criticize their government's policies toward the poor. Some are former activists in political movements that openly opposed governments, and others support projects that assist those suffering from some of the worst effects of government repression.

One might expect, given these differences, that cooperation between governments and NPOs might break down at both the sending and receiving ends of the international NPO network and that private donors in the north would soon stop supporting organizations that threatened some of their economic interests. What keeps the system functioning, however, are a sufficient number of overlapping interests among all the partners, despite some diverging objectives each espouses. Moreover, the actual projects among the grassroots poor abroad do not threaten either developing country governments or the interests of North Atlantic public and private donors.

Citizens in North Atlantic countries tend to give the most to NPOs during times of well-publicized disasters like famines, earthquakes, migration of refugees in civil wars, and so forth, and the large North Atlantic NPOs still act as major conduits of relief aid to the victims of such disasters when they occur. In spite of the shift to long-term development as the first objective of many North Atlantic NPOs since the 1960s, many still operate as short-term relief agencies—even the Canadian and European NPOs that do not receive substantial food aid from their respective governments. This continued humanitarian focus maintains strong credibility for all NPOs among private donors at home. It also gives them added legitimacy with governments of different ideologies, all of whom need immediate relief assistance whenever natural or human-made crises occur.

Although some North Atlantic NPOs, especially in Canada and Europe, engage in education and lobbying campaigns at home that challenge some of the interests of their governments and private citizens alike, their influence in effecting policy changes in these areas has been minimal (Smith 1990, 215). Their dissent is thus tolerated even by parliaments dominated by right of center coalitions. Such criticisms actually find some support among leftist parties in parliaments. Whether they wield executive power or not, leftists often favor liberalization of trade, aid, and immigration policies but are not in a position to implement them owing to a lack of public support.

The airing of criticisms by NPOs thus is accepted as part of the political debate in countries with a much wider ideological spectrum than the United States. Citizens in Europe do not view the call for significant political changes as beyond the legitimate purview of NPOs. French NPOs, for example (see Ullman, in this volume), have been significant lobbyists in domestic welfare reform over the past decade.[3]

More so than American NPOs, Canadian and European ones tend to favor political change as a major goal of the projects they sponsor abroad. This is evident in table 8.1, which is based on a survey I conducted in 1982 and 1983 among American, Canadian, and European NPOs.[4] The Americans rated as their top objectives the improvement of technical skills and the increasing of job opportunities. The Canadians and Europeans ranked their main priorities as the building of institutions run by the poor themselves and empowering of the poor to challenge dominant power structures in their environment.

Notwithstanding this sharp difference of objectives among North Atlantic NPOs, the kind of development projects they sponsor abroad do not differ significantly. These tend to cluster around skill- and resource-enhancement programs that generate *new* income and social opportunities among the poor rather than challenge dominant elites to surrender some of their *existing* privileges or power.

Although intermediary NPOs in developing countries are frequently staffed by persons critical of their governments for not adequately addressing the needs of the poor, they do not normally espouse as part of their goals a redistribution of wealth or political power. Under authoritarian regimes in Latin America in the 1970s and early 1980s some NPOs carried out legal assistance to victims of oppression or offered economic assistance to those ostracized for political reasons, but they did not engage in popular mobilization to thwart government policies or to stimulate open political opposition (Smith 1990, 267–69; Smith 1980). The evidence presented by L. David Brown in his chapter in this book indicates that the development projects of NPOs in military or single-party states in Asia and Africa (including Bangladesh, Indonesia, Pakistan, and Zimbabwe) were also no threat to regime stability. In fact, he shows that some of these

Table 8.1
Weighted Priorities of American, Canadian, and European NPOs (1982–1983)

Priorities	U.S. (N = 13) Rank (Score)	Canadian (N = 5) Rank (Score)	European (N = 19) Rank (Score)
Immediate relief of suffering (hunger, sickness, etc.)	4 (48)	6 (5)	5 (37)
Increasing income and employment	2 (53)	5 (12)	6 (28)
Improving skills, capacities to solve problems	1 (57)	3 (20)	4 (71)
Building institutions and networks of participation operated by the poor	3 (49)	1 (26)	1 (99)
Enhancing bargaining power of poor with merchants, landlords, governments	5 (41)	4 (18)	3 (76)
Empowerment of poor to challenge and change dominant political and economic structures in their environment	6 (22)	2 (24)	2 (80)

governments either sought the cooperation of NPOs or listened seriously to their advice in learning how to provide needed services to the poor in the areas of immunization, irrigation, sanitation, and credit management.

In some democratic countries, NPOs sometimes take more openly critical stances toward government policy. For example, AWARE, an NPO in the state of Andhra Pradesh in India, has orchestrated a series of public demonstrations by grassroots groups it assists to pressure the local government to implement land reform legislation promulgated by the central government but largely ignored thereafter. It has also encouraged members of local groups to run for election to the local parliament, and forty of the two hundred seats are now held by AWARE local groups. NPOs in neighboring Bangladesh have urged the same strategy for landless groups they have been assisting (Clark 1990, 98–99).

NPOs rarely seek, however, to replace political parties or to act primarily as partisan political groups themselves. Some rather tend to use political structures that are responsive to public pressures as conduits for furthering their causes within the rules of the system (Clark 1990, 99).[5]

In democratic regimes throughout Asia, Africa, and Latin America, however, most NPOs focus on supporting economic projects that have some impact on enhancing skills or resources rather than aiming at political participation of the poor (Smith 1990; Fisher 1993; Clark 1990). These national and regional NPOs work closely with self-help organizations (grassroots NPOs) formed by the poor themselves to gain some well-defined improvement in their lives.

Some of the more innovative and extensive activities have been in areas of basic health and family planning, credit and management training for small businesses, small-scale agriculture and water development that is linked with environmental preservation, and production and consumer cooperatives. All of these have included both technical assistance and financial help from intermediary NPOs, but individuals and groups at the local level manage the projects themselves through their local NPOs. These have also been some of the areas in which techniques have been replicated through dissemination of information by intermediary and northern NPOs, and (as Brown also shows in his chapter) sometimes govern-

ments have adapted these into their own public service programs (Fisher 1993, 119–28, 202–03; Clark 1990, 86, 110–11; Smith 1990, 241–47).

The poorest of the poor (the landless, the sick, the elderly, the handicapped) usually do not directly benefit from all of these grassroots associations because many grassroots NPOs—especially those that are cooperatives or credit unions—require a minimum of resources and skills to participate. Many local projects tend to miss the poorest 5 to 10 percent in their regions. The reach of grassroots NPOs, however, clearly extends beyond that of most government agencies, which do not go below the bottom 20 percent of the poor in service delivery. Moreover, even the poorest groups benefit from the activities of those grassroots NPOs that are multiservice organizations and include as part of their mission nutrition and health assistance to all in need (Carroll 1992, 67–69; UNDP 1993, 96).

Thus, most governments in developing countries, regardless of their political ideology, find NPOs at the intermediary and local levels useful. Although public officials normally do not have access to NPO funds, NPOs leverage new international resources for their societies not available to the governments themselves. Sometimes local development projects such as those sponsored by private agencies act as surrogates for social services formerly provided by the governments facing shrinking resources; or they pioneer in delivering new cost-efficient services later to be adapted by public institutions (see Brown, in this volume). By acting as important gap-fillers and troubleshooters, NPOs shore up social stability, head off potential unrest, and sometimes pave the way for governments to learn better techniques of reaching isolated regions or marginalized groups. Even authoritarian governments have tolerated NPO activities so long as they operate within the boundaries of relief assistance or economic development—which the vast majority do.

Are the Poor Empowered?

In spite of the above caveats and limitations on the *political* power of NPOs in developing countries, there clearly have been some forms of empowerment of the poor as a result of their activities. A United Nations report of 1993 on the work of NPOs in development underscores the *economic* empowerment countless people have experienced because of NPO work:

> Many people judge NGOs [nongovernmental organizations, or NPOs] primarily by their success in improving the living standards of the poor, and there are plenty of individual success stories. The landless have obtained land. Farmers are growing more food. Wells and boreholes have been sunk. Children have been inoculated against killer diseases. In these and countless other ways, NGOs have transformed the lives of millions of people all over the world. (UNDP 1993, 94)

The same report also cites other studies that point to the *social* empowerment of the poor resulting from their participation in NPO projects:

> How far NGOs really enhance participation is impossible to say. But one recent Dutch study [1992]—with evidence from Brazil, Burkina Faso, Chile, Indonesia and Zimbabwe—concluded that NGOs had broadly increased empowerment, even if it could not offer quantitative evidence. It reported that people in target groups now ". . . act more often as partners in discussions with organizations outside the village, have the courage to lodge complaints with civil servants of the local government, move freer and travel more." These are seemingly small changes but of essential importance for the people themselves. (UNDP 1993, 94)

Grassroots NPOs of all types have been particularly helpful to women in their efforts to advance their social power throughout developing countries. Health and family planning NPOs have not only given women more security and choice, but they have often been run by women themselves, thus enhancing their own self-esteem and their stature in their respective communities. Revolving credit funds have given rise to many new small businesses run by women in regions where such projects have been created. Buying and selling of cooperatives have enabled women to supplement their family incomes through more effective linkages to markets for the labor-intensive goods they produce. Through all of these new roles women collectively have begun to erode some of the stereotypes in their respective countries, stereotypes that assume that male leadership is essential for the implementation of effective development (Clark 1990, 101; UNDP 1993, 96–97).

Linking all of these dimensions of social empowerment are the new organizations operated by the poor themselves.[6] Although not financially autonomous, thus far they have operated with some autonomy from governments and political and economic elites in their societies. This has given the participants increased control over their immediate environment and a sense of group awareness that they can do things for themselves. Moreover, their benefactors—that is, intermediary NPOs, international NPOs, foreign private donors, and foreign governments—have allowed them a range of freedom to define their own objectives so long as they stay within broad parameters of economic development. If these grassroots NPOs can maintain their relative autonomy and continue to set their own economic goals, the social empowerment of their members is likely to grow.

L. David Brown, building on the work of Robert Putnam, identifies the greatest contribution of NPOs as expanding the "social capital" of the poor—structural arrangements of voluntary cooperation that nurture attitudes of trust, self-confidence, tolerance, and hope for a better future (Brown, in this volume). These new collective experiences and the gradual attitudinal changes they foster do not translate into an immediate increase of political power for the poor—more voice in governments, more parties responsive to their interests, more effective laws protecting their rights, and so on. But the expansion of social capital is laying the groundwork for a different type of future society in which the poor will have enhanced capacities to articulate, pursue, and realize some important interests on their own. Eventually, if such capital continues to accrue it cannot help but have a positive impact on political systems. Growing numbers of the poor are coming to believe that they have a stake in society and that they can make institutions work in their favor and for the good of others—one basis for healthy democratic politics.[7]

Currently, NPOs in developing countries are not a serious threat to established economic and political elites. As indicated above, they serve some important interests of governments in developing countries, and their existence makes it possible for other actors in the transnational NPO network to achieve some of their objectives. In the north and south alike, therefore, NPOs enable groups in both public and private spheres to achieve a variety of objectives that would not be as easily realized if the transnational NPO network were not in place.

Challenges for the Future

Despite overlapping interests in the transnational NPO network, there are some emerging trends that may create serious problems for its future stability. Governmental pressures on northern NPOs to professionalize and specialize, the increasing competence of southern NPOs vis-á-vis their northern NPO funders, the shrinking state in developing countries searching for private contractors for public services, and the latent political potential of grassroots NPOS in poor countries—all of these factors are creating challenges for the transnational NPO network in the future.

Pressures on Northern NPOs to Professionalize and Specialize

North Atlantic governments are beginning to demand higher standards of performance from NPOs to whom they make grants. They are asking for more systematic evaluation procedures to determine conditions of project success and to generate more systematic information on what has been learned from failures. They are also urging NPOs to upgrade their managerial skills and are offering grants for NPO institutional development (Smith 1990, 165–66, 199, 211).

Canadian and European governments have recently created funds for more specialized NPO projects in regions that are foreign policy priorities of home governments (for example, former colonies) or in policy areas of domestic political concern (for example, AIDS prevention, women in development, support for democracy) (Smilie 1993, 12, 20). The U.S. government in the post–Cold War era has become particularly interested in focusing more of its foreign aid on those countries and subregions of nations that have the greatest possibility of expanding markets for U.S. products or providing more needed raw materials for its domestic consumption. The U.S. Agency for International Development (AID) has begun to view American NPOs as contractees performing specific services for clients and in the process is imposing more stringent administrative restrictions on NPO operations. It is also urg-

ing them to convince NPOs in developing countries to charge "user fees" for services rendered to the poor as a way of cutting project costs (ACVFA 1993, 13; Smith 1993, 33–32), a trend now also occurring among domestic U.S. NPOs.

These growing pressures for professionalization, specialization, and efficiency can have positive effects in improving NPO project quality and focus. Such demands can also limit NPOs' flexibility in breaking new ground, their autonomy in setting their own agendas in response to developing country needs, and the variety of activities they can sponsor abroad.

Craig Jenkins warns (in this volume) that donor pressures for increased professionalization in NPOs can curtail support for grassroots movements. This probably will not occur because grassroots NPOs abroad will still be necessary to implement projects. Nevertheless, if these suggestions are implemented they could eliminate some poor people from participating if they do not live within the particular countries or regions identified by foreign governments as priorities, or if they cannot afford to shoulder more of the costs—for example, pay user fees for services received.

Shrinking government budgets for public services in North Atlantic countries are creating demands on state-subsidized private organizations to become more cost-efficient (Hyde 1993). These same pressures to cut and monitor more carefully public expenditures are now beginning to affect North Atlantic NPOs using governmental resources for international development. Responding to these pressures without losing some of their independence and range of action will be a critical challenge for NPOs in the years ahead.[8]

Expanded Capacities of Intermediary NPOs in Developing Countries

Just as increased professionalization may be a mixed blessing for NPOs in North Atlantic countries, expanding institutional capacities of intermediary NPOs which administer the funds in developing countries can create new challenges. Many intermediary NPOs are reaching a stage where they can act as significant agents in the development process—screening and evaluating increasing numbers of projects, assisting in the creation, expansion, and coordination of grassroots NPOs, formulating micro-policy recommendations for their governments, creating consortia among themselves at the regional and international levels to share experiences (Korten 1987; Stremlau 1987).

These growing professional skills are increasing NPOs' capacities to manage more funds, make decisions more effectively, and wield some influence in public policy making (see Brown, in this volume). Intermediary NPOs are also asking northern NPOs for block grants and greater discretion over use of funds; at present, most northern NPOs make all the decisions on a project-by-project basis. They are also approaching northern governments on their own with funding requests, bypassing northern NPOs, and some have had success in leveraging direct government aid from abroad (Smilie 1993, 22–23; Smith 1993, 334–37).

These are signs of institutional maturity and growing professionalization among intermediary NPOs. They may, however, create some serious tensions with northern NPOs who will have to surrender some of their power and deal with southern NPOs more as partners than as clients. This will require some readjustment in attitude and style of operation and a letting go of some northern NPO prerogatives.

Some northern NPOs may have to scale down their operations or expand in other areas to maintain their institutional size—for example, by increasing their advocacy at home for more equitable governmental policies toward developing countries. A time of uneasy readjustment of the relationships among northern and southern NPOs may lie ahead.

Increasing Ties between Intermediary NPOs and Home Governments

A more serious challenge to southern NPOs' professionalization, however, is the increasing incidence of offers from their governments to act as government contractors. As the reputation of intermediary NPOs grows, there is an effort by governments to incorporate them into public social service systems as they privatize their economies and cut back on state expenditures. This trend has existed for some time in parts of Africa and now is expanding rapidly in Latin America.

Newly constituted Latin American democratic governments, some of whose policymakers worked for intermediate NPOs during previous military regimes, are setting up special funds for private service programs (Carroll 1992, 177–78). There are popular expectations that a return to democracy will better the economic situation of the poor, who suffered both political repression and economic austerity under previous military regimes. Newly elected civilians, however, are also under continuing pressures from international lending institutions (to whom large debts still are owed) to continue privatizing their economies. They need to find ways to increase social services for the poor but do not have adequate resources or delivery mechanisms to do so.

The World Bank, the Inter-American Bank, and AID are all providing these countries with additional loans and grants to help meet these service needs. Because NPO administrative costs in Latin America are still lower than those of the state—a situation that does not hold in North Atlantic countries (see Ullman, in this volume)—and because NPOs can leverage additional foreign money on their own through the transnational NPO network, Latin American governments are seeking them out as new partners to meet public needs.[9]

If such funds grow and NPOs take increasing advantage of them, it could help them expand and scale up considerably their service delivery capabilities to meet the ever-growing demands of the poor. Moreover, moving into a closer association with the public sector might result in governments adopting innovative NPO techniques in their own service agencies (see Brown, in this volume). Some of the recent literature on NPOs in developing countries, in fact, has been urging that they extend their reach, seek to have their projects replicated on a wider scale, and search for more effective ways to impact on public policy making (Fisher 1993, 209; Clark 1990, 78–79; UNDP 1993, 98; Carroll 1992, 179–80).

Developing country governments, however, will likely place more stringent conditions on their contracts with intermediate NPOs than do current international NPOs on their grants. If this occurs, the danger of being co-opted to serve government interests will grow, and NPOs' ability to serve as independent advocates for the poor will decline (Smith 1993, 341). In fact, such co-optation is already happening to those NPOs in advanced capitalist societies that, as government contractors, are suffering the effects of the welfare state crisis (Hyde 1993).

If such controls emerge in developing countries, the credibility of intermediary NPOs in the eyes of grassroots NPOs and the poor whom they now serve could be significantly diminished. They could become parastatal organizations, thus losing their capacity for innovation and flexibility. More research is needed on how local government funding is affecting the autonomy and performance of those intermediary NPOs because the implications of such arrangements have yet to be explored in developing countries.

The Growing Political Potential of Grassroots NPOs

Just as there is a tendency for intermediary NPOs to establish federations, networks among grassroots NPOs are now emerging. Some are regional organizations (cooperatives), some informal economic networks (bartering systems), and other, more heterogeneous groupings combining grassroots NPOs and social movements seeking redress of grievances for their members (for example, peasant unions, tribal organizations, environmental groups) (Fisher 1993, 57–74). As a result of such coordination, the political potential of grassroots NPOs (as discussed earlier) may be increasingly realized in the years ahead. Strategies deployed in India and Bangladesh, where some NPOs are encouraging participants to run for local office, may evolve into trends in other contexts as NPOs become more coordinated.

This scenario is fraught with both positive and negative implications. On the one hand, if grassroots NPOs establish closer bonds with one another at the regional and national levels in their societies and also forge closer links with popular protest movements, they might be able to create new political organizations (or reform existing ones) that are truly representative of the interests of the poor. These, in turn, may then be able to shift some political power away from landed, industrial, and commercial elites in these societies. This would please many European and Canadian NPOs (as reflected in their responses in table 8.1).

On the other hand, greater involvement in politics could divert the energies of grassroots NPOs away from some of the solid economic and social accomplishments they have achieved thus far and embroil them in debilitating partisan battles. Governments could begin to resent those who link closely with social protest movements and remove their nonprofit status. Others might gradually take on the characteristics of parties, which they currently criticize, if they eventually decide to compete in the electoral arena—exaggerated campaign promises that outrun performance in office, leaders who become enamored of power and lose their interest in caring for the needs of their clientele, compromises with other parties that sacrifice principle for expediency.

In sum, the world of politics could have more of an impact on NPOs than vice versa, and, if so, they would lose some of their comparative advantage in development. Ironically, the closer NPOs come to assisting the poor toward political empowerment, the more jeopardized is their viability. Whether grassroots NPOs can join forces with other social movements of the poor to exert more coherent pressure on governments for equitable public policies while avoiding the debilitating effects of partisan politics remains to be seen.

The choices open to NPOs in the north and south as they face all of these new challenges will not be easy. Managing new opportunities will require adjustments in their interrelationships and in their linkages with public and private donors if the transnational NPO system is to continue to operate as an important instrument for global equity.

Author's Note

This chapter draws on some of the material in my book (Smith 1990). In its present form, it has greatly benefited from the constructive criticisms of Elisabeth Clemens, Woody Powell, and Debra Minkoff.

Notes

1. Claire Ullman . . . argues that limitations in state bureaucracies led policymakers in North Atlantic countries to reach out to NPOs as conduits for public service delivery. A similar phenomenon of government limits (particularly incapacities of developing country bureaucracies to administer foreign aid efficiently) made NPOs attractive conduits of foreign economic assistance for European governments by the 1970s. An added attraction was that overhead costs of transnational NPOs were also considerably cheaper than those of home-government foreign aid ministries.

2. Mark Chaves . . . sees this as part of a wider trend emerging among Christian organizations in Western societies over the past generation. He believes these are increasingly shifting from religious to secular functions as a means to

maintain a service ideal in the face of the declining attraction of their religious ministries.

3. A sizable proportion of the population in Europe views development problems abroad as requiring political, not merely economic, solutions. This segment is not upset by NPOs that call for major changes in power relations between rich and poor nations and inside poor nations. A random survey of more than 9,700 persons in ten West European countries in 1983 indicated that 60.6 percent believed that rich countries (including their own) exploited poor countries, and 83.3 percent felt that within developing countries a rich minority exploits the rest of the population—in contrast to only 6 percent of Americans who viewed the poor in such societies as victims of unjust systems (Rabier, Riffault, and Inglehart 1985, 81, 84, 92, 93, 96; Contee 1987, 49; Laudicina 1973, 11).

4. In my sample of interviews I included persons in administrative positions in forty-five of the largest American, Canadian, and European NPOs. All respondents were asked to rank order the six goals, and I weighted the priorities according to how often they were mentioned to come up with a composite score: first choice, six points; second choice, five points; third choice, four points; fourth choice, three points; fifth choice, two points; sixth choice, one point; not applicable, or not ranked, no points (Smith 1990, 133–34). Although these data are more than a decade old, the same patterns have continued. American agencies still tend to stress technical and economic issues and shy away from the espousal of confrontation. Canadians and Europeans continue to emphasize in their literature the necessity to change political structures so as to alleviate poverty abroad (Smilie 1993, 18–20; ACVFA 1990, 1993).

5. I found this to be the case in Colombia, where I studied a variety of intermediary NPOS (thirty-six in all) in 1984. Although the activities of some of their staff included political tactics (e.g., petitioning local government agencies to implement land reform already required by law), the NPOs to which they belonged did not become competitors of political parties in their respective regions (Smith 1990, 255–56).

6. John Friedmann (1990) has defined the social power that is accruing to various low-income groups through grassroots NPO projects as greater control over their "life space," their economic resources, social networks, and autonomous organizations.

7. Daniel Levine makes a similar argument based on behavioral and attitudinal changes he observed among those participating in new local communities sponsored by the Catholic Church in Latin America, many of which function as grassroots NPOs. These organizations foster attitudes of respect and cooperation among their members in carrying out needed social services and act as training grounds for potential new community leaders among the poor (Levine 1992, 319–20, 340–44).

8. An alternative for North Atlantic NPOs would be to expand their sources of private funding and thus cut their dependence on governmental subsidies to maximize their autonomy. Private funding of NPOs, however, is still not increasing except in time of disasters. In 1992, for example, donations for all international causes were a very small part of overall American philanthropy, amounting to only 1.4 percent of total U.S. charitable contributions—$1.7 billion of $124 billion—and that was $40 million *less* for all foreign causes than in 1991 (Teltsch 1993).

9. The governments of Colombia, Peru, Bolivia, Chile, Guatemala, Honduras, and Mexico all now have social investment funds. These pay private agencies to deliver needed social services to the poor. The funds range in amounts from $20 to $60 million (Colombia, Bolivia, Chile, Guatemala), to $100 million to $200 million (Peru and Honduras), to $2 billion (Mexico). Telephone interview and correspondence with Dr. Charles A. Reilly, Thematic Studies Officer, Office of Learning and Dissemination, Inter-American Foundation, Alexandria, VA, October 1993.

References

Advisory Council on Voluntary Foreign Aid (ACVFA). 1990. *Responding to Change: Private Voluntarism and Interna-*tional Development. Washington, D.C.: U.S. Agency for International Development (USAID).

———. 1993. *International Development and Private Voluntarism: A Maturing Partnership*. Washington, D.C.: USAID.

Adelman, Irma, and Cynthia Taft Morris. 1973. *Economic Growth and Social Equity in Developing Countries*. Stanford: Stanford University Press.

Bratton, Michael. 1989. "The Politics of Government-NGO Relations in Africa." *World Development* 17:569–87.

Carroll, Thomas F. 1992. *Intermediary NGOs: The Supporting Link in Grassroots Development*. West Hartford, Conn.: Kumarian Press.

Clark, John. 1990. *Democratizing Development: The Role of Voluntary Organizations*. West Hartford, Conn.: Kumarian Press.

Contee, Christine E. 1987. *What Americans Think: Views on Development and U.S.-Third World Relations*. Washington, D.C.: Interaction and the Overseas Development Council (ODC).

Curti, Merle. 1963. *American Philanthropy Abroad: A History*. New Brunswick: Rutgers University Press.

Durning, Alan B. 1989. "Action at the Grassroots: Fighting Poverty and Environmental Decline." Worldwatch Paper No. 88. Washington, D.C.: Worldwatch Institute.

Fisher, Julie. 1993. *The Road from Rio: Sustainable Development and the Nongovernmental Movement in the Third World*. Westport, Conn.: Praeger.

Fleet, Michael, and Brian H. Smith. 1997. *The Catholic Church and Democracy in Chile and Peru*. Notre Dame, Ind.: University of Notre Dame Press.

Friedmann, John. 1990. "Empowerment: The Politics of an Alternative Development." Graduate School of Architecture and Urban Planning, University of California at Los Angeles. Mimeographed.

Garilao, Ernesto D. 1987. "Indigenous NGOs as Strategic Institutions: Managing the Relationship with Government and Resource Agencies." *World Development* 15:113–20.

George, Susan. 1990. *A Fate Worse than Debt: The World Financial Crisis and the Poor*. Rev. ed. New York: Grove Weidenfeld.

Goulet, Denis, and Michael Hudson. 1971. *The Myth of Aid: The Hidden Agenda of Development Reports*. New York: International Documentation (IDOC) North America.

Hyde, Cheryl. 1993. "Class Stratification in the Nonprofit Sector." Paper presented at the conference Private Action and the Public Good. Indiana University Center on Philanthropy, Indianapolis, November 4–6, 1993.

Korten, David C. 1987, "Third Generation NGO Strategies: A Key to People-Centered Development." *World Development* 15:145–59.

Landim, Leilah. 1987. "Non-Governmental Organizations in Latin America." *World Development* 5:29–38.

Laudicina, Paul A. 1973. *World Poverty and Development: A Survey of American Public Opinion*. Washington, D.C.: Overseas Development Council (ODC).

Levine, Daniel H. 1992. *Popular Voices in Latin American Catholicism*. Princeton: Princeton University Press.

Organization for Economic Cooperation and Development (OECD). 1981. *Collaboration Between Official Development Cooperation Agencies and Nongovernmental Organizations*. Paris: OECD.

———. 1988. *Voluntary Aid for Development: The Role of Nongovernmental Organizations*. Paris: OECD.

———. 1989. *Directory of Nongovernmental Organizations in OECD Member Countries Active in Development Cooperation*. 2 volumes. Paris: OECD.

———. 1996. *Directory of Nongovernmental Organizations Active in Sustainable Development, Part I: Europe*. Paris: OECD.

Paddock, William, and Elizabeth Paddock. 1973. *We Don't Know How: An Independent Audit of What They Call Success in Foreign Assistance*. Ames: Iowa State University Press.

Putnam, Robert D. 1993. *Making Democracy Work: Civic Traditions in Modern Italy*. Princeton: Princeton University press.

Rabier, Jacques-Rene, Helene Riffault, and Ronald Inglehart. 1985. *Euro-Barometer 20: Aid to Developing Nations, Octo-*

ber 1983. Ann Arbor: Inter-University Consortium for Political and Social Research, University of Michigan.

Ringland, Arthur C. 1954. "The Organization of Voluntary Foreign Aid, 1939–1953." *Department of State Bulletin* 30:383–93.

Smilie, Ian. 1993. "Changing Partners: Northern NGOs, Northern Governments." Paris: OECD Development Center. Mimeographed.

———.1995. *The Alms Bazaar: Altruism under Fire—Nonprofit Organizations and International Development.* Ottawa: International Development Research Centre.

Smith, Brian H. 1980. "Churches and Human Rights in Latin America: Recent Trends in the Subcontinent." In *Churches and Politics in Latin America,* ed. Daniel H. Levine. Beverly Hills: Sage Publications.

———. 1990. *More than Altruism: The Politics of Private Foreign Aid.* Princeton: Princeton University Press.

———. 1993. "Nongovernmental Organizations in International Development: Trends and Future Research Priorities." *Voluntas* 4:326–44.

Stremlau, Carolyn. 1987. "NGQ Coordinating Bodies in Africa, Asia, and Latin America." *World Development* 15:213–25.

Teltsch, Kathleen. 1993. "Despite Slump, Giving to Charities Rose 6.4% in '92." *New York Times,* May 26, A8.

United Nations Development Program (UNDP). 1993. *Human Development Report 1993.* New York: Oxford University Press.

United States Agency for International Development (USAID). 1992. *Voluntary Foreign Aid Programs 1992.* Washington, D.C.: Bureau for Food and Humanitarian Assistance, Office of Private and Voluntary Cooperation, USAID.

U.S. Congress. 1973. *Mutual Development and Cooperation Act of 1973: Hearings before the Committee on Foreign Affairs.* 93d Congress, 1st session. Washington, D.C.: Government Printing Office.

Chapter 9

Homophily in Voluntary Organizations

Status Distance and the Composition of Face-to-Face Groups

J. Miller McPherson and Lynn Smith-Lovin

Voluntary associations are an important feature of the organizational landscape and participation in these groups is seen as important to a healthy civil society. In this chapter, McPherson and Smith-Lovin explore some of the consequences of this participation. Specifically, they examine how individuals' friendship choices are shaped by the characteristics of the groups to which they belong. The more heterogeneous the membership, the more likely group members are to associate with people who differ from them in some way. Likewise, when people belong to voluntary associations comprised of others similar to themselves, their friendship choices are similarly constrained. Our group memberships thus create an "opportunity structure" for our interactions with others.

Researchers recognized *homophily*, the tendency of people in friendship pairs to be similar, in their work before the turn of the century (Galton, cited in Byrne 1971). Research by sociologists and social psychologists has since found homophily on a wide variety of characteristics in many different settings.[1] In this paper, we are interested in the effects of face-to-face groups on homophily. In particular, we want to show how a group's composition sets the stage for homophilous friendship tie formation.[2]

Since groups provide opportunity structures for tie formation, the nature and extent of homophily is related to these social origins of the association. The composition, size, and structure of groups determine the types of opportunities they offer for network contacts (McPherson 1982, 1983; McPherson and Smith-Lovin 1982, 1986). Ties formed in work-related groups, for example, are likely to be homophilous on socioeconomic status (Fischer, Jackson, Srueve, Gerson, and Jones 1977). Feld (1982) called the social entities around which activities were organized "foci" and derived three propositions about them. First, most relationships will originate in foci—since we must meet to associate, centers of our activity will lead us to contact others, Second, foci tend to be homogeneous.[3] Third, the more homogeneous are foci, the more homogeneous are the ties that are created there. This argument, which appears in many places in the literature (e.g., Blau 1977), is the main theme of our paper.

Induced Homophily and Choice Homophily

To illustrate the effect of group homogeneity on homophily, we contrast two poles of the influence of groups on friendship ties. First, consider entirely homogeneous groups within which random pairing occurs. In this form, which we call the "focus" model after Feld (1981, 1982, 1984), the character of the organization dictates the nature of the friendship tie completely. Groups account for all of the similarity in friendship pairs; the composition of the group dictates that all pairs will be homophilous. We call the type of homophily produced by group composition *induced homophily*.

On the other hand, in the "network" model all groups are maximally heterogeneous (reflecting the composition of the total population), and pairs within groups are formed purely on the basis of dyadic similarity. In this model, none of the similarity among pairs is an effect of group composition; groups merely provide a local arena for the formation of friendship ties. We term the type of homophily produced by individual choices *choice homophily*.[4] In this pure case, there is no effect of group composition on homophily; friendship dyads are as heterogeneous as if the pairs were formed in the population at large, with no opportunity structure created by organized social groups.

Clearly then, there are two basic features of the system which govern the amount of observed homophily: the individual-level propensity to choose similar others (choice homophily) and the composition of the groups in the system, which dictate the possibilities for friendship choice (induced homophily). If there is only between-group (as opposed to within-group) variance in social characteristics, then induced homophily must dominate, since all members of the group have the same values on social characteristics. If there is only within-group variance, then choice homophily dominates and the network model is true by definition, since group composition cannot have an effect. If there is an intermediate level of between- versus within-group variance, then there could be a mixture of the types of homophily.

Blau (1977) called our distinction between between-group and within-group variance "penetrating differentiation." According to Blau, "the further society's differentiation penetrates into successive subunits of its structural components, the more it promotes the integration of groups and strata by increasing the social associations among their members" (1977, p. 175). The greater the diversity within groups, the greater the status diversity of pairs of friends in the groups. The basic idea in Blau's work is that social associations develop from opportunities generated by the structure of the group. Blau's (1977) concerns with heterogeneity and homogeneity led him to derive from his theory a theorem (T-1.2) exactly analogous to Feld's proposition from his focus approach: "Increasing status diversity increases the probability of association among persons whose status differs."

This study tests Blau's theorem and Feld's focus proposition with a unique body of data on the members of 304 face-to-face organizations to show how dyadic homophily is conditioned by the opportunity structure of social organizations.[5] Our form of this relationship is:

HYPOTHESIS 1. *The greater the diversity within an organization, the greater the dyadic status distance between friends within the organization.*

Now, if dyadic similarity is attributable mostly to organizational homogeneity, then the focus model and its induced homophily are supported. On the other hand, if choice homophily is very strong, the hypothesis is false. If people within organizations make homophilous choices, they produce similar pairings even in cases of high group diversity. For example, perfectly homophilous sex pairings can be made in both an organization with 50 men and 50 women—high sex diversity—in an organization with 10 men and 90 women—low sex diversity—and, of course, in an organization with 100 women—zero sex diversity. Moderate levels of choice homophily produce moderate support for the hypothesis, and a complete absence of choice homophily produces friendship dyads that are completely explained by the opportunity structure of the group (because they are random within the group). Therefore, the level of support for Hypothesis 1 is related to the level of choice homophily.

Multidimensional Status Structure and Homophily

So far, we have treated status distance on a single dimension as though it existed in isolation. Blau (1977) developed his theory to deal with the influence of multiple status dimensions, arguing that the correlations among the status dimensions affect the similarity of ties in the group. These correlations among status dimensions are the subject of four of Blau's key theorems about association:

T-12.2. Intersecting graduated parameters [uncorrelated continuous variables] integrate different strata by raising the rates of social association among them.

T-12.21. Consolidated graduated parameters attenuate the rates of social associations among different strata and thus weaken their integration.

T-12.3. The intersection of nominal [categorical] by graduated parameters integrates groups and strata by raising the rates of social associations among them.

T-12.31. The more consolidated are group differences with correlated status differences, the less frequent are integrative social relations among groups and strata. (p. 108)

Our form of this set of propositions is:

HYPOTHESIS 2. *Correlated status dimensions reduce dyadic social distance.*

This hypothesis is strongly related to Hypothesis 1 in that correlations among the dimensions force persons who are status distant (or close) to ego on a single dimension to be status distant (or close) on several dimensions. When this is true, dissimilarity tends to be minimized because of the cumulative impact of several dimensions on choices. Obversely, when correlations are weak, then a similarity on one dimension does not imply similarity on another; people are faced with a system in which most choices imply dissimilarity on some dimension. The extent of correlation among dimensions constrains the kind of choices that are possible in the system in much the same way that the simple presence or absence of diversity does in Hypothesis 1.

Hypothesis 2 is one of Blau's most appealing ideas in that it gets to the heart of the social environment provided by the group. Correlated dimensions constrict and simplify social space; dimensions become more and more interchangeable the more they are correlated. At the limit, when all dimensions are perfectly correlated, there is only a single axis of social differentiation—all of the poor are also black, uneducated, female, and so on. At the other extreme, when dimensions are uncorrelated, then people are scattered randomly through the multidimensional space defined by the status characteristics. A person similar to ego on one dimension is unlikely to be similar on others. The correlations of the dimensions define a form of multivariate diversity which is a logical extension of the univariate diversity of Hypothesis 1.

Hypothesis 2 is logically tied to the distinction between induced and choice homophily. If only induced homophily is operating (that is, if choices are random within the group), then the correlation of traits within the group does not influence dyadic status distance. If the homophily is being imposed upon the dyad by group composition, there is no effect of correlated characteristics on homophily, since the choices made are independent of the individuals' location on a given dimension. It is only when there is choice homophily that a dimension's correlation with other dimensions can affect homophily.

Consider, for example, Dimensions A and B in a group, where Dimension A (e.g., eye color) does not produce choice homophily and Dimension B (e.g., race) does. If A and B are not correlated, there is no homophily on A above and beyond the amount dictated by the composition of the group. If A and B are correlated, A shows what will appear to be choice-homophilous effects in direct proportion to the correlation between A and B. At the limit, when they are perfectly correlated, there appears to be exactly as much choice homophily on A as on B.

Therefore, the amount of support for Hypothesis 2 tells us how strong the choice homophily in the system is. The hypothesis will be supported most strongly in situations where a characteristic without choice homophily is the variable of interest and is correlated with a characteristic with strong choice homophily. In the absence of choice homophily, the hypothesis should be falsified.

Group Size and Homophily

One variable with substantial impact on almost all organizational variables is the size of the group (McPherson 1983b). Two factors lead us to suspect that larger groups might create more homophilous pairings. First, there is a substantial literature indicating that size is related to internal differentiation: larger groups are more differentiated into subparts (see review in Kasarda 1974). Because of their greater differentiation, larger groups should have more homophily at a given level of diversity. Dissimilar others may be in the same umbrella organization, but they may be segregated into I separate subparts of that group. For example, the PTA may include both males and females, but if the females are all on the bake sale committee and the males are on the fund-raising committee, then the organization will not integrate the sexes to the degree that its overall sex diversity would indicate. In a small bridge club with three couples, such differentiation would be unlikely to occur.

If groups are arenas for tie formation, large groups should produce more homophily, even net of diversity. At a given level of diversity, there will be more potential matches for each individual. For example, a group with a two-to-one male/female split at size six there are only four men and two women; to make a sex-homophilous choice, each woman has only one other woman to choose, who may differ in other important respects such as age. However, in a group of size 60 there are 40 men and 20 women; each woman would have 19 alters to choose to make a sex-homophilous choice. If there is choice homophily on many characteristics (and the literature strongly indicates that there will be), then the smaller group is more likely to produce a non-sex-homophilous choice because some other aspect of the match is not appealing. The larger group offers many opportunities for making a sex-homophilous choice that is also acceptable on other dimensions.

Both the size-differentiation relationship and the unmeasured choice homophily argument lead us to our third hypothesis:

HYPOTHESIS 3. *Group size is positively related to homophily.*

Data and Methods

The data were collected in a three-stage probability sample in 10 communities in the state of Nebraska. This location was chosen for a variety of reasons, including the proximity of the Bureau of Sociological Research at the University of Nebraska, an organization that has had extensive experience in studies of voluntary organization. The citizens of the area have a history of cooperating with projects of this type. In addition, more is known about the voluntary sector of this population than virtually any other, because of several major studies done here. These include panel studies (Babchuk and Booth 1969; McPherson 1981, 1983), ongoing trend studies (McPherson 1982; McPherson and Smith-Lovin 1982), and a variety of other projects.

One goal of the project was to obtain a probability sample of the face-to-face voluntary organizations in a set of communities. We began with a probability sample of individuals and then sampled their organizations. The methods and the rationale for this procedure appear in McPherson (1982). The 10 communities chosen were (nominal population size in parentheses): Omaha (311,681), Lincoln (171,932), Grand Island (33,180), Columbus (17,328), Seward (12,891), York (7,743), Beatrice (5,713), West Point (3,609), Geneva (2,400), and Pender (1,318).

A total of 656 respondents (a minimum of 54 to a maximum of 88 per community) were contacted in the first stage. The refusal rate (including those too sick or disabled to interview) was less than 24 percent. A list of the organizations to which these respondents belonged provided the sampling framework for the second stage. These lists produced from 67 to 114 eligible organizations in each community. From each of these 10 lists, approximately 45 organizational leaders were interviewed (total of 457 respondents in the second stage), to provide information on interorganizational relationships, organizational structure, and most importantly for this paper, to get permission to interview members at a meeting of the group. The refusal rate for this stage was less than 5 percent.

The groups for the third stage were selected from the 10 lists by a probability process based on McPherson (1982). Over 75 percent of the organizations contacted (311 of 413) allowed our interviewers access to meetings for the third-stage interviews. This rate of cooperation substantially exceeded the expected rate of 60 percent. The pattern of refusals suggests that fraternal groups have a slightly lower chance of appearing in the sample, but an analysis in which weights were used to correct this tendency suggests no substantive differences between our sample and a perfectly representative one for this paper.

The number of members of the 311 groups interviewed in the third stage varied from 2 to 88, for a total sample size of respondents in this stage of 5,860. Several smaller groups were eliminated for this analysis, leaving a sample of 304 groups with a total of 5,842 members. Those 304 groups are the focus of this paper. For a detailed analysis of the response rates and other characteristics of the sample, see McPherson (1984).

The status dimensions with which we are most concerned are age, sex, education, and occupational status. Respondents provided this information in response to a four-page questionnaire administered at a meeting of the group. Respondents were also asked to choose the person at the meeting whom they knew best, excluding relatives. The person's first name and initial provided a means of matching respondents and their choices.

The occupation of the respondent and friend are coded with Duncan's socioeconomic index (1962). Education and age are in years, and sex is a binary variable. The group is the unit of analysis because the hypotheses apply at the group level (Blau 1977, pp. 48–49). Each of the 304 groups is characterized by its size, its diversity (the mean absolute difference among. members on each of the status dimensions), the correlations among the status dimensions, and the mean status distance between friendship pairs on each status dimension. The correlations among dimensions range from –1.0 to +1.0, with an unsurprising tendency for the smaller groups to have more extreme correlations.[6] We use generalized least squares for our multivariate analyses to weight by size of group. (The differences among the weighted and unweighted results are minimal. The weighted results are reported, unless otherwise noted.)

Results

One of the best established findings in the literature is that friends tend to be similar. In Blau's work, this basic finding appears as an axiom, A-l: "Social associations are more prevalent among persons in proximate than between those in distant social positions" (1977, p. 36). Since Blau's predictions (and therefore our Hypotheses 1 and 2) depend logically on this axiom, we must confirm that this pattern exists in our own data on ties within groups.

To establish the presence of homophily, we compare our observations to a model of chance pairing, in which all possible pairs of individuals are equally likely to associate (Mayhew 1984; Verbrugge 1977, pp. 580–82). We apply this baseline model both to the general population and to the face-to-face groups. Column I of the top panel in Table 1 gives the mean distance between all possible pairs of individuals in the population. The column II gives the mean distance between all pairs within groups. The column III gives the distance between dyads of friends. For each of the four dimensions, the average distance in friendship pairs is much smaller than random choice in the population would produce. The ratios of actually observed dyadic status distance to the distance produced by random choice within the population (the first column of the lower panel) range from .68 for education to .15 for sex. This result means that, taking sex as an example, the observed friendship pairs in our groups are only 15 percent as heterogeneous as they would be if random choice were occurring. Clearly, friendships form, and/or are maintained among, pairs which are much more similar than chance within these voluntary groups. The ratios in the bottom panel of Table 9.1 tell us how salient each di-

Table 9.1
Summary of Status Differences in the Population, within Organizations, and in Observed Dyads

Status Dimension	I Status Difference in Population[a]	II Status Difference in Organizations[b]	III Status Difference in Dyads[c]
Education[d]	2.63	2.33	1.76
Occupation[e]	24.67	17.18	14.49
Age[d]	22.35	11.80	7.58
Sex[f]	.48	.17	.07
Ratio	III/I	II/I	III/II
Education	.68	.89	.75
Occupation	.59	.70	.84
Age	.34	.53	.64
Sex	.15	.35	.43

a Status differences in the population are the average distance (e.g., the mean absolute differences in years of education) between all possible pairs of a representative sample from the population. This sample of 656 individuals was obtained in the first stage of the study.

b Status differences in the organizations are the average distance between all possible pairs within each of the 304 organizations.

c Status differences in pairs are the average distance between the reported friendship pairs in organizations (N = 4,827).

d Education and Age are in years.

e Occupation is measured in Duncan's socioeconomic index (Duncan 1962).

f Comparisons for sex may be interpreted as the proportion of pairs (both potential and observed) which differ in sex. Thus, 48 percent of possible pairs in the population differ in sex (column I), while only 7 percent of observed friendship pairs in organizations differ in sex (column III).

mension is; the smaller the ratio, the more salient the dimension. As in earlier research, the homophily effects in our data for the ascribed statuses age and sex (.34 and .15) are much more pronounced than those for education and occupation (.68 and .59).[7]

Choice Homophily and Induced Homophily

Data in the bottom panel of Table 9.1 allow us to address a question central to our argument: how much of the observed homophily is due to the composition of the organization ("induced," in our terms), and how much is due to choice? That is, we would like to know whether the organization is producing the observed pair homophily through restricting choice or there is substantial pair homophily beyond that produced by restricted choice.

Unsurprisingly, there is evidence for both types. There is a great deal of homophily observed among friendship pairs (first column of rates in Table 9.1). Organizations are considerably more homogeneous than random selection would produce on all four dimensions, indicating induced homophily (second column of ratios). However, homophilic selection is still taking place inside the groups; the observed homophily in friendship pairs is somewhat greater than would be expected by chance even within the groups (third column of ratios). For example, the ratios in the second column show that about 35 percent of the population heterogeneity in sex exists inside the groups, while 43 percent of the group heterogeneity in sex was reflected within actually observed friendship pairs. For three of the variables (occupation, age, and sex), induced homophily is greater than choice homophily. For education, the pattern is reversed. Thus, the observed pair homophily is due partly, but not entirely, to group composition. We have a mixture of the network and focus models.

The Influence of Group Structure on Homophily

The above discussion underlines the importance of considering the impact of status diversity in groups on the similarity of friendship pairs, since there is substantial induced homophily. This topic, the subject of Hypothesis 1, is addressed in Table 9.2. The correlation of status diversity with the mean status distance between observed friendship dyads within the group is shown in the first column. Again, status diversity is measured by the mean absolute difference among all members of the group on a status characteristic. The correlations are significant and consistent, ranging from .595 for occupational prestige to .630 for education. Groups with low status diversity provide restricted opportunity structures for friendship choice. These four bivariate correlations support the idea that diversity decreases homophily, as stated in Hypothesis 1.

In Table 9.2, the regressions of group size, diversity, and consolidation[8] on mean status difference between friends clearly support Hypothesis 1; diversity has very strong effects. Hypothesis 2, on the other hand, receives mixed support. The hypothesis predicts that correlated status dimensions reduce dyadic social distance. In the first column, the correlations of consolidation and mean status distance are weak and nonsignificant; the correlation with mean status difference in occupational prestige is in the wrong direction. (Breaking the consolidation measure into its constituent correlations does not improve the situation; five of the correlations are significant, but four are in the wrong direction.) In the regression analyses (second column), coefficients for consolidation are all in the predicted direction, but only one of them is statistically significant in its equation.[9] Even the significant coefficient, that for education, is not as large as the coefficient for diversity.

An inspection of regressions with the consolidation measure disaggregated into its constituent correlations (not presented) shows that the correlations have extremely varied effects on the status distance variables. In fact, only about half of the correlations have effects in the correct direction.[10] Given this inconsistent result, we tried a very large number of alternative specifications, including signed correlations, alternative indices based on the correlations, and several other forms. None of these specifications produced support for the influence of correlated status dimensions on homophily.[11]

The idea that social groups shape friendship patterns receives strong support from results for Hypothesis 3, which argues that group size should increase homophily. The pattern that emerges in the table is quite striking; homophily is greater in larger groups. Apparently, larger groups provide a

Table 9.2
Correlation and Regression of Mean Status Differences among Observed Friendship Pairs on Status Diversity in 304 Groups

Dependent Variable	Independent Variables		
Mean Status Distance between Friends in:		Zero-Order Correlations	Standardized Regressions
Years of education	Group size	−.068	−.153*
	Diversity(educ)	.630*	.569*
	Consolidation(educ)	−.103	−.144*
	[r (educ age)]	−.020	
	[r (educ occ)]	.103	
	[r (educ sex)]	−.041	
	R^2		.421
Years of age	Group size	−.055	−.107*
	Diversity(age)	.613*	.559*
	Consolidation(age)	−.013	−.012
	[r (age educ)]	−.000	
	[r (age occ)]	.019	
	[r (age sex)]	−.135*	
	R^2		.409
Occupational prestige	Group size	−.141*	−.088*
	Diversity(occ)	.595*	.647*
	Consolidation(occ)	.044	−.092
	[r (occ educ)]	.185*	
	[r (occ age)]	−.055	
	[r (occ sex)]	.002	
	R^2		.479
Sex	Group size	−.055	−.119*
	Diversity(sex)	.613*	.631*
	Consolidation(sex)	−.013	−.007
	[r (sex educ)]	.284*	
	[r (sex age)]	.332*	
	[r (sex occ)]	.364*	
	R^2		.591

* Coefficient exceeds twice its standard error.

Notes: Abbreviations: educ—years of education; age—years of age; sex—sex of respondent; occ—occupational prestige in SEI scores (Duncan 1962). Variables: Diversity(x)—mean absolute difference among all members of group in status dimension x; [r(x y)]—absolute value of Pearson correlation between variables x and y for the group; Consolidation(x)—average Pearson correlation between all status dimensions within the group (see text).

larger absolute number of people with similar characteristics to choose from; that is, at a given level of group diversity, a larger group will provide more people who are near in status to choose from. On the other hand, small groups provide fewer people to choose from who are status equals. If idiosyncratic criteria (or unmeasured status dimensions) rule out the nearest status equal, then a distant status choice is forced. Another possible explanation for this finding is that the greater structural differentiation of large groups produces subgroups more homogeneous than the overall group diversity measure indicates.

Summary and Conclusions

The strongest predictor of homophily in our data is group diversity; the more diverse the group, the greater the average status distance between friendship dyads. Clearly, group composition has a very substantial effect on the amount of homophily in friendship networks. Less satisfactory were our results for the correlated dimension hypothesis (2). Blau's prediction here seems to offer little in the way of explanatory power. The relationships tend to be in the predicted direction, but they are not statistically significant. We would be hard pressed to argue that our sample size of over 300 did not offer enough statistical power to detect even moderate effects. We suspect that Hypothesis 2, if true for face-to-face groups, is fairly weak.

Our analysis has the advantage of being a representative sample of naturally occurring groups. Thus, we can weigh the relative amount of induced and choice homophily in natural settings. Our data suggest a greater amount of induced than choice homophily for friendship dyads inside naturally occurring groups. Both the stronger effects of group diversity in the regressions and the relative absence of effects of correlated dimensions seem to point this way. The only result that seems to favor choice homophily is the presence of more homophily in larger groups. This result could be due to the operation of choice homophily in that larger groups allow individuals to minimize distance on several dimensions at once. Even here, however, all induced-homophily explanation is available: greater differentiation of larger groups may structure friendships to a greater degree than the diversity measure indicates.

There are two limitations of our research design. First, since our respondents were limited to choices inside our groups, we were not able to estimate directly what proportion of all friendship ties actually originated in such groups. Fortunately, Feld (1982) has data that bear on this question; groups such as these form the third most important source of these nonkin ties, after work and neighborhood.

Second, we could actually be overestimating the amount of choice homophily in that the ties that appear to us to be affected by variables unrelated to group composition could be due to the effects of some other group. That is, friendship ties that appear to be based on choice rather than induced through group structure could have actually been induced in another group setting. In fact, Feld (1982) argues that most ties occur in such settings.

Our results clearly support the idea that face-to-face groups have substantial effects on tie formation in social networks. We find very strong effects of diversity, consistent but smaller effects of group size, and almost no effects of correlated social characteristics on the formation of dyadic relationships. We expect that our results will encourage further exploration of the idea that face-to-face groups and social networks are coevolutionary social forms.

Endnotes

1. Homophily has been found among all age groups, from schoolchildren (Billy, Rodgers, and Udry 1984; Gerard and Miller 1975; Hargreaves 1972; Kandel 1978; St. John and Lewis 1975; Singleton and Asher 1977; Tuma and Hallinan 1979) to the elderly (Nahamow and Lawton 1975; Riley and Foner 1968; Rosow 1967). It occurs on many dimensions, including basic sociodemographic characteristics such as age and sex (Lazarsfeld and Merton 1954; Tuma and Hallinan 1977; Verbrugge 1977, 1979), acquired characteristics like education, prestige, and social class (Barnes 1954; Coleman 1957; Curtis 1963; Domhoff 1970; Ellis 1957; Gans 1962, 1967; Garrison 1979; Greer 1956; Kahl and Davis 1955; Laumann 1966, 1973; Lincoln and McBride 1985; Lincoln and Miller 1979; Lipset, Trow, and Coleman 1956; Loomis 1946; Lundberg and Steele 1938; Michaelson 1970; Suttles 1968; Verbrugge 1977, 1979), personal attributes like attitudes and beliefs (Ajzen and Fishbein 1980; Berscheid 1985; Byrne 1971; Hallinan 1974; Richardson 1940; Williams 1959; Zander and Havelin 1960), aspirations (Cohen 1977, 1983) and social behavior (Billy et al. 1984; Berkum and Meeland 1958).

2. Social psychologists have long recognized that availability is an important factor in attraction and association (Festinger, Schachter, and Back 1950; Kerchoff 1974; Nahaynow and Lawton 1975; Newcomb 1961; Segal 1974; Verbrugge 1977). One of the most important arenas for the formation and maintenance of social networks is social groups (Feld 1981, 1982, 1984; Fischer et al. 1977; Fischer 1982; Verbrugge 1979). Indeed, Feld (1982) argued that almost all social ties are formed in some type of organized activity.

3. Since organizational homogeneity and heterogeneity are so important to our argument, we should briefly outline why groups tend to be homogeneous. First, voluntary groups often recruit through friendship networks (Babchuk and Booth 1969; Booth and Babchuk 1969). Dyadic homogeneity in friendships across the organizational boundary is translated directly into organizational homogeneity when the friend is brought into the organization. Some recent results in the social network literature suggest that cliques and informal groups create and maintain their homogeneity primarily through recruitment (Cohen 1977). Second, ecological selection at the level of the population of organizations probably favors homogeneous organizations. Indirect evidence for this proposition comes from Newcomb (1961), who found that groups marked by internal differences are most likely to dissolve. Some important theoretical work such as that of Davis (1963) suggests that intraorganizational diversity leads to dissension and division. If groups are subject to differential mortality by level of homogeneity, the groups that survive will be more homogeneous. Third, organizations are likely to become homogeneous through the competition of other groups for members (McPherson 1983). Organizations tend to develop distinctive social niches. Competitive pressures from other groups tend to sharpen and focus the compositional features of the group, resulting in organizational homogeneity. Finally, groups tend to become homogeneous because the tasks performed are related to the social positions of the members. Unions are occupationally homogeneous; Parent Teacher Associations (PTAs) are

homogeneous with respect to age and marital status, and so forth.

4. Skvoretz (1983) has called this tendency "tau bias," the probability that a homophilous choice will be made, over and above the probability of such a choice by chance under random pairing.

5. Blau's major test of the theory (Blau and Schwartz 1984) uses "groups" that are actually statistical aggregates. We think that our face-to-face groups actually provide a stronger test for the theory, as well as allowing a generalization of Blau's theory to more concrete networks.

6. We view the statistical instability of correlations among dimensions for smaller groups as a reflection of the very real effect of group size on social interaction. Smaller groups constrain choice much more than large groups, in both a univariate and multivariate sense. For more on the effects of group size, see the results section. Note that we use unsigned correlations for this analysis.

7. In one of the earliest of the modern studies of friendship, Lazarsfeld and Merton (1954, p. 22) found that status similarity varied from very strong for ascribed variables such as race and sex to "entirely negligible" similarity in achieved characteristics such as educational status. Similarly, Verbrugge (1977) found that sex and age were the most salient dimensions for friendship choice. Tuma and Hallinan (1979) found that sex was the only social characteristic that affected both the formation and maintenance of friendships among schoolchildren; other characteristics produced homophily by affecting the survival of the tie. Blau (1977, p. 39) incorporated this consistent strength of ascribed (and often visible) characteristics into his theoretical statement.

8. Consolidation is the average (absolute value of) produce-moment correlations among all status dimensions for each group. Blau and Schwartz (1984) use factor analysis to construct a scale for consolidation from the set of correlations Since we have four status dimensions, producing six correlations, we use a simple average. Note that the average is taken across all possible correlations; when a correlation is undefined, as in the case of correlations involving sex for single sex groups, we take the average among the reduced number of correlations.

9. Of course, since these four equations are separate tests of the hypothesis, the fact that all four coefficients are in the same direction provides stronger support for the hypothesis than the comparison of coefficients with their standard errors would suggest.

10. The differences between the strength of our support for Hypothesis 2 and the corresponding results in Blau and Schwartz (1984) may be due to the fact that they threw out correlations which had low loadings on their factors. We speculate that this procedure effectively eliminates the correlations that have the wrong sign.

11. A status dimension cannot be correlated with another if it has no diversity. Since groups that are homogeneous on some dimension are not uncommon (McPherson and Smith-Lovin 1986), this issue deserves discussion. If diversity is very low (or zero) on a characteristic, then induced homophily will explain all homophily on that characteristic (e.g., if there are only women in the groups discussed above, then the age distribution will have no effect on sex homophily). Therefore, one could argue that the impact of a correlation between traits would be greatest when the diversity on the characteristic was high. Interestingly, Fararo and Skvoretz (1984) derive exactly such a specification from a mathematical formalization of Blau's propositions. They predict (equation 23, p. 241) an interaction effect between the correlation and diversity, such that the greater the product of diversity and correlation, the greater the homophily. Their model predicts only an interaction effect between structural consolidation (correlated variables) and diversity: the greater the variance in a characteristic, the greater the effect of consolidation. There is no main effect of consolidation in their model. The results from this alternative specification are mixed. Nine of the 12 coefficients are in the correct direction, but only 2 are significant; 1 coefficient is significant in the wrong direction. In three of the four dependent variables, using the Fararo and Skvoretz specification results in larger coefficients for the diversity variable, and in larger R-squares. Another specification is one in which the main effects of the correlations are added to the Fararo and Skvoretz

model. When this model is run, none of the correlations has significant coefficients singly or setwise, and only 7 of 12 have the correct sign. Another model includes all types of diversity in each equation, rather than just diversity in the primary dimension. Only the primary dimension (e.g., diversity in education when education is the dependent variable) is significant in this model. We also tried models that included many more of the possible combinations and permutations of variables, with no important differences from the reported results.

References

Ajzen, I. and Martin Fishbein. 1980. *Understanding Attitudes and Predicting Social Behavior*. Englewood Cliffs, NJ: Prentice-Hall.

Babchuk, Nicholas and Alan Booth. 1969. "Voluntary Association Membership: A Longitudinal Analysis." *American Sociological Review* 34:31–45.

Barnes, J.A. 1954. "Class and Communities in a Norwegian Island Parish." *Human Relations* 7:39–58.

Berkun, M. and T. Meeland. 1958. "Sociometric Effects of Race and of Combat Performance." *Sociometry* 21:145–49.

Berscheid, Ellen. 1985. "Interpersonal attraction." Pp. 413–84 in *The Handbook of Social Psychology, Vol. 2*. edited by Gardner Lindsey and Elliot Aronson. New York: Random House.

Billy, John O.G., Joseph Lee Rodgers and J. Richard Udry. 1984. "Adolescent Sexual Behavior and Friendship Choice." *Social Forces* 62:653–78.

Blau, Peter M. 1977. *Inequality and Heterogeneity*. New York: Free Press.

———. 1978. "A Macrosociological Theory of Social Structure." *American Journal of Sociology* 83:26–54.

Blau, Peter M., Carolyn Beeker, and Kevin M. Fitzpatrick. 1984. "Intersecting Social Affiliations and Intermarriage." *Social Forces* 62:585–606.

Blau, Peter M., Terry C. Blum, and Joseph E. Schwartz. 1982. "Heterogeneity and Intermarriage." *American Sociological Review* 47:45–62.

Blau, Peter M. and Joseph E. Schwartz. 1984. *Crosscutting Social Circles: Testing a Macrostructural Theory of Intergroup Relations*. New York: Academic Press.

Blum, Terry C. 1984. "Racial Inequality and Salience: An Examination of Blau's Theory of Social structure." *Social Forces* 62:607–17.

———. 1985. "Structural Constraints on Interpersonal Relations. A Test of Blau's Macrosociological Theory." *American Journal of Sociology* 91:511–20.

Boissevain, Jeremy. 1968. "The Place of Non-Groups in the Social Sciences." *Man* 3:542–56.

Booth, Alan and Nicholas Babchuk. 1969. "Personal Influence Networks and Voluntary Association Affiliation." *Sociological Inquiry* 39:179–88.

Bott, Elizabeth. 1957. *Family and Social Network*. London: Tavistock.

Byrne, D. 1971. *The Attraction Paradigm*. New York: Academic Press.

Cohen, Jere M. 1977. "Sources of Peer Group Homogeneity." *Sociology of Education* 50:227–341.

———. 1983. "Peer Influence on College Aspirations." *American Sociological Review* 48:728–34.

Coleman, James S. 1957. *Community Conflict*. New York: Free Press.

Collins, Randall. 1981. "On the Microfoundations of Macrosociology." *American Journal of Sociology* 86:984–1014.

Curtis, R.F. 1963. "Differential Association and the Stratification of the Urban Community." *Social Forces* 42:68–77.

Davis, James A. 1963. "Structural Balance, Mechanical Solidarity, and Interpersonal Relations." *American Journal of Sociology*, 68:444–62.

Domhoff, G. William. 1970. *The Higher Circles*. New York: Random House.

Duncan, O. Dudley. 1962. "A Socioeconomic Index for all Occupations." Pp. 109–38 in *Occupation and Social Status*, edited by Albert J. Riess. Glencoe, IL: Free Press.

Ellis, R.A. 1957. "Social Stratification and Social Relations: An Empirical Test of the Disjunctiveness of Social Classes." *American Sociological Review* 22:570–78.

Fararo, Thomas J. and John V. Skvoretz. 1984. "Biased Networks and Social Structure Theorems: Part II." *Social Networks* 6:223–58.

Feld, Scott L. 1981. "The Focused Organization of Social Ties." *American Journal of Sociology* 86:1015–35.

———. 1982. "Structural Determinants of Similarity among Associates." *American Sociological Review* 47:797–801.

———. 1984. "The Structured Use of Personal Associates." *Social Forces* 62:640–52.

Festinger, Leon, S. Schachter, and Kurt Back. 1950. *Social Pressures in Informal Groups: A Study of Human Factors in Housing.* Stanford, CA: Stanford University Press.

Fischer, Claude S. 1982. *To Dwell among Fiends: Personal Networks in Town and City.* Chicago: University of Chicago Press.

Fischer, Claude S., Robert M. Jackson, C. Ann Srueve, Kathleen Gerson, and Lynne M. Jones. 1977. *Networks and Places.* New York: Free Press.

Gans, H. 1962. *The Urban Villagers.* New York: Free Press.

———.1967. *The Levittowners.* New York: Pantheon.

Garrison, Howard H. 1979. "Education and Friendship Choice in Urban Zambia." *Social Forces* 57:1310–24.

Gerard, H.B. and N. Miller. 1975. *School Desegregation.* New York: Plenum.

Greer, S. 1956. "Urbanism Reconsidered: A Comparative Study of Local Areas in a Metropolis." *American Sociological Review* 21:19–25.

Hallinan, Maureen T. 1974. *The Structure of Positive Sentiment.* New York: Elsevier.

Hargreaves, David H. 1972. *Interpersonal Relations and Education.* Boston: Routledge & Kegan Paul.

James, John. 1951. "Clique Organization in a Small Industrial Plant." *Research Studies* 19:125–30.

Kahl, J.A. and J.A. Davis. 1955. "A Comparison of Indexes of Socio-Economic Status." *American Sociological Review* 20:317–25

Kandel, Denise B. 1978. "Homophily, Selection and Socialization in Adolescent Friendships." *American Journal of Sociology* 84:427–36.

Kasarda, John D. 1974. "The Structural Implications of Social System Size. A Three Level Analysis. " *American Sociological Review* 39:19–28.

Kerchoff, A.C. 1974. "The Social Context of Interpersonal Attraction." In *Foundations of Interpersonal Attraction,* edited by T.L. Huston. New York. Academic Press.

Laumann, Edward O. 1966. *Prestige and Association in an Urban Community.* Indianapolis: Bobbs-Merrill.

———. 1973. *Bonds of Pluralism: The Forms and Substance of Urban Social Networks.* New York: Wiley.

Lazarsfeld, Paul F. and Robert K. Merton. 1954. "Friendship as Social Process: A Substantive and Methodological Analysis." Pp 18–66 in *Freedom and Control in Modern Society,* edited by Monroe Berger, Theodore Abel, Charles H. Page. New York: Octagon Books.

Lincoln, James R. and Kerry McBride. 1985. "Resources, Homophily and Dependence: Organizational Attributes and Asymmetric Ties in Human Service Networks." *Social Science Research* 14:1–30.

Lipset, Seymour Martin, M.A. Trow, and James S. Coleman. 1956. *Union Democracy.* Glencoe, IL: Free Press.

Loomis, C.P. 1946. "Political and Occupational Cleavages in a Hanoverian Village." *Sociometry* 9:316–33.

Lundberg, G.A. and M. Steele. 1938. "Social Attraction Patterns in a Village." *Sociometry* 1:375–419.

Mayhew, Bruce H. 1984. "Baseline Models of Social Phenomena." *Journal of Mathematical Sociology.*

McCallister, Lynn and Claude S. Fischer. 1978. "A Procedure for Surveying Personal Networks." *Sociological Methods and Research* 7:131–48.

McPherson, J. Miller. 1981. "A Dynamic Model of Voluntary Affiliation." *Social Forces* 59:705–28.

———. 1982. "Hypernetwork Sampling: Duality and Differentiation in Voluntary Organizations." *Social Networks* 3:225–49.

———. 1983. "An Ecology of Affiliation." *American Sociological Review* 48:519–32.

———. 1984. "Sampling Populations of Organizations: Final Report on National Science Foundation Grant SES-8120666." Mimeographed.

McPherson, J. Miller and Lynn Smith-Lovin. 1982. "Women and Weak Ties: Differences by Sex in the Size of Voluntary Organizations." *American Journal of Sociology* 87:883–904.

———. 1986. "Sex Segregation in Voluntary Associations." *American Sociological Review* 51:61–80.

Michaelson, W. 1970. *Man and His Environment.* Reading, MA: Addison-Wesley.

Nahamow, L. and M.P. Lawton. 1975. "Similarity and Propinquity in Friendship Formation." *Journal of Personality and Social Psychology* 2:205–13.

Newcomb, T.M. 1961. *The Acquaintance Process.* New York: Holt, Rinehart and Winston.

Richardson Helen M. 1940. "Community of Values as a Factor in Friendships of College and Adult Women." *Journal of Social Psychology* 11:303–12.

Riley, M.W and A. Foner. 1968. *Aging and Society. Vol. 3. An Inventory of Research Findings.* New York: Russell Sage.

Rosow, I. 1967. *Social Integration of the Aged.* New York. Free Press.

St. John, N.H. and R.G. Lewis 1975. "Race and the Social Structure of the Elementary Classroom." *Sociology of Education* 48:346–68.

Sampson, Robert I. 1984. "Group Size, Heterogeneity and Intergroup Conflict. A Test of Blau's Inequality and Heterogeneity." *Social Forces* 62:618–39.

Segal, M.W. 1974. "Alphabet and Attraction: An Unobtrusive Measure of the Effect of Propinquity in a Field Setting." *Journal of Personality and Social Psychology* 30:654–57.

Singleton, L.C. and S.R. Asher. 1977. "Peer Preference and Social Interaction among Third-Grade Children in an Integrated School District." *Journal of Educational Psychology* 69:330–36.

Skvoretz, John V. 1983. "Salience, Heterogeneity, and Consolidation of Parameters: Civilizing Blau's Primitive Theory." *American Sociological Review* 48:360–75.

South, Scott, Charles Bonjean, William T. Markham, and Judy Corder. 1982. "Social Structure and Intergroup Interaction." *American Sociological Review* 47:587–99.

Suttles, G. 1968. *The Social Order of the Slum.* Chicago: University of Chicago Press.

Tuma, Nancy Brandon and Maureen T. Hallinan. 1979. "The Effects of Sex, Race and Achievement on Schoolchildren's Friendships." *Social Forces* 57:1265–85.

Verbrugge, Lois M. 1977. "The Structure of Adult Friendship Choices." *Social Forces* 56:576–97.

———. 1979. "Multiplexity in Adult Friendships." *Social Forces* 57:1286–1309.

Williams, R.M. 1959. "Friendship and Social Values in a Suburban Community: An Exploratory Study." *Pacific Sociological Review* 2:3–10.

Zander, A. and A. Havelin. 1960. "Social Comparison and Interpersonal Attraction." *Human Relations* 13:21–32.

J. Miller McPherson and Lynn Smith-Lovin, "Homophily in Voluntary Organizations: Status Distance and the Composition of Face-to-Face Groups." In *American Sociological Review* 52: 370–379. Reprinted with permission. ✦

Chapter 10
Democratizing Rural Economy

Institutional Friction, Sustainable Struggle and the Cooperative Movement

Patrick H. Mooney

The tensions between democracy and bureaucracy are freshly explored in this chapter on the cooperative movement in agriculture. Agricultural cooperatives in the United States have been around a long time and remain a force in the agricultural marketplace. What accounts for the longevity and economic success of this form of organization, especially in light of the rise of corporate agriculture? What role do agricultural cooperatives play today?

Patrick Mooney answers these questions through a close look at the economic and political forces that have shaped the cooperative movement over time. He explores the tensions between the democratic political structures of cooperatives and the economic structures of capitalism. Despite attempts to weaken or transform them, cooperatives remain an important force in sustaining democratic principles within organizations and in the society at large.

In the early 20th century, North Dakota farmers staged one of the most serious challenges to the emergent monopoly capitalist economy when they gained control over the state legislature on the basis of an agrarian socialist agenda. However, they faced a dilemma. Should they use the state to build state-owned enterprises (e.g., banks, elevators, insurance) or should they use the state to lay the foundations of a cooperative economy? Following the dominant socialist framings of the time, they emphasized the creation of state socialist institutions rather than cooperative socialist institutions.

Within a decade, their political power was severely eroded, and in that process, much of the institutional structure they created was subverted (Morlan 1955). The prophetic warnings of their allies were realized: political power alone was insufficient to sustain an opposition to the power of monopoly capitalism. Only a broader and more tightly woven cooperative commonwealth based on a tension-filled balance of both political power and economic interest could sustain their struggle.

Introduction

As we entered the 21st century, *sustainability* became a keyword in development discourse. This ambiguous term, claimed by many interests, might be understood as a disputed frame (Benford 1993). Sociologically, sustainability does not reduce to its narrower ecological framing. Rather, sustainable development entails what Buttel (1997:348) has referred to as "socio-ecological contradictions and limits" in the broader system of social, political, and economic institutions that structure our relationship with the physical environment. Development, sustainable or otherwise, will always entail the pursuit of distinct material and ideal interests between antagonistic opposing social forces. Given the necessity and ubiquity of such struggle, it is important that sustainable development be built upon institutions that can also sustain forms of struggle coincident with the value premises of our cultural heritage. Following Redclift (1997), it has been argued: "We should be spending more time sorting out the institutional fabric that might keep open sustainability options, so bequeathing institutions rather than environment to future generations" (LeHeron and Roche 1997:366). This is perhaps the most valuable contribution sociologists can make to the creation of a sustainable future.

Rather than a utopian vision of an ultimate end to struggle between social groups, what is needed are mechanisms and institutions that permit the sustainability of struggle in legitimate institutions. In the United States, one of the most important and commonly proclaimed values is that of democratic forms of participation. It is argued here that formal cooperation privileges a democratic structure within an economy that is generally driven by quite different social forces and forms of organization. In this sense, cooperatives can potentially pave the bridge between polity and economy with a democratic ethos. This corresponds to Busch's (2000:3) recent call to "extend networks of democracy to the workplace" as a means by which we can begin to "reclaim our moral responsibility . . . " from what he calls the Leviathans of statism, scientism, and, especially in this case, marketism.

This argument derives from two primary concerns. One concern follows Verta Taylor's (1989) interest in the need to understand mobilization as a long-term form of struggle, rather than the episodic manner in which it is often treated by both sociologists as well as historians (Mooney and Majka 1995; Mooney and Hunt 1996). A second concern involves the economic reductionism in most contemporary modeling of formal agricultural cooperation. Together, these form a point of departure for an original, alternative approach to the analysis of cooperatives. This framework emphasizes cooperatives' capacity to generate a flexible and sustainable form of struggle by focusing on the importance of retaining a sense of contradiction and tension, even paradox, within the theorization of cooperation. The focus is on institutionalized cooperation in U.S. agriculture. The use of the term "institutionalized cooperation" is intended as a somewhat broader definition of cooperative than a purely legalistic conception would provide. Thus, to adapt Cobia's (1989) definition, we are speaking of patterned, formal or informal, economic activity that is user-owned, user-controlled, and distributes benefits on the basis of use. Implicit in this definition is the contention that retaining ownership, control, and benefit for the user-members is also an inherently political action in the context of a developed capitalist economy.

Background: The Significance of Cooperation in U.S. Agriculture

The cooperative movement in U.S. agriculture is well over one hundred years old, although its firm institutionalization might be established as just less than the century mark, coinciding with the achievements attained in the early 20th century and perhaps consolidated with the passage of the Capper-Volstead Act in 1922. By almost any definition, the cooperative movement in agriculture must be regarded as an eminently successful form of enterprise in terms of economic performance. Though not the dominant form of agribusiness (except in a few commodities) in the late 20th century, the cooperative market share is usually about one-third of marketed goods, and over one-fourth of input supplies (USDA-RD 1998). By 1999 U.S. cooperatives had a total net worth of $20 billion (USDA-RBCS 1999). From an historical point of view, this must be recognized as success, given the origins of the movement as a form of resistance to the oppressive conditions of monopoly and oligopoly at local, regional, and national levels faced by farmers at the end of the 19th century. Despite the hopes of cooperative theorists, such as Nourse, that cooperatives would simply rise, correct market imbalances, and then disappear after performing this function, such conditions have not disappeared in the face of cooperative development but have continued to provide the basis for sustaining a strong cooperative movement (Coffey 1992; Torgerson, Reynolds, and Gray 1997:3).

Toward a Political Economy of Agricultural Cooperation

Where North Dakota's Non-Partisan League mistakenly relied on an overly politicized cooperative strategy, most contemporary models, under the dominance of neo-classical economic theory, assume away the political element. Mooney, Roahrig, and Gray (1996) provided a critique of this reductionist economic theorization of cooperation and called for a need to incorporate political elements. This paper aspires to take up that latter task: to simultaneously theorize cooperatives in terms of both their political as well as their economic functions. Recognizing that cooperatives are, of course, also economic entities means that the objective is not a purely political theorization of cooperation, but rather a political economy of agricultural cooperation. This addresses recently expressed interests in the need to redefine the relationship between "economy and society, institutions and markets, moral commitments and the rational pursuit of self-interest" (Society for the Advancement of Socio-Economics 1999:1–2). This is in contrast to the predominant theorization of cooperation by neo-classical agricultural economics which has been directed toward eliminating paradoxical or contradictory qualities in the cooperative movement, primarily by redefining or theorizing cooperation from a purely economic and individually rational or "asocial" point of view. As Hendrickson et al. (2001:18) argue: "A growing chorus of voices . . . is beginning to challenge the ideology—the assumptions, beliefs and values—of neoclassical economic theory . . . Many feel that the loss of economic democracy may also lead to a loss of political democracy—and nowhere is that more apparent than in food."

This approach highlights and focuses on contradiction, rather than assuming it away by theorizing only one line of rationality in the sphere of cooperative action. To the contrary, it is contended that some tension within cooperatives has been a positive force in their development, an advantage rather than a liability, and that a new theorization of cooperation is needed that embraces, rather than fears, the existence of such tensions in cooperatives.

Levine (1985:8–9) has argued:

In their quest for precision, social scientists have produced instruments that represent the facts of human life in one-dimensional terms. . . . Investigations that rely on such instruments produce representations of attitudes and relations that strike us time and again as gratuitously unrealistic. For the truth of the matter is that people have mixed feelings and confused opinions, and are subject to contradictory expectations and outcomes, in every sphere of existence.

Indeed, just as individuals embody contradiction and paradox, so do the institutions that we construct. Formal agricultural cooperation is a particularly significant and revealing site of such tensions. As Mooney, Roahrig, and Gray (1996) argued, by stripping away all but the economic interest of cooperators, economists have built elaborate but insular models of cooperation, even when they transcend their inclination toward the individual as the only unit of analysis. In these models, other motives are absent and with them go the contradictions, the tensions, and the paradox of this form of collective action. Again, it is important to embrace such tensions, not only because they exist in the lived experience of cooperative members, but also because the theorization along a single dimension is the point of departure for the sort of rationalization process that ultimately leads to substantive irra-

tionality. In this sense, the elaboration of the political dimension provides a check on the development of a substantive irrationality of economic rationalization, just as an exclusive focus on only the political dimension would lead to a substantive irrationality in relation to the economic interest also deeply embedded in cooperatives. Recent calls for interdisciplinary approaches to the study of cooperatives (Cook, et al. 1997) and various feminist demands for more holistic theorization suggest that we not seek to escape the ambiguities by the use of simplifying assumptions that "discipline" the reality. This theoretical disciplining of paradox emanates from a desire to be rid of such "troubling" empirical matters. To the extent that the disciplines have been successful in this expulsion, there has been a loss of integrity and holistic perspective.

This view of cooperatives has a unique potential to examine a variety of tensions that are captured in the cooperative form of interaction. Recent work by Flora et al. (1998:31) anticipate the significance of this tension when they observe that the new generation cooperatives "work best" as a form of community self-development when decision-making processes are "based on both substantive and formal rationality." I share a similar understanding of this notion of contradiction in that such oppositions are not mutually exclusive but in fact, form a unified, dynamic whole.

In an attempt to develop a political economy of the cooperative movement there is an overriding interest in the tensions present in the economic and political elements of cooperatives. As a **capitalist** economic form usually governed by a **democratic** principle, we immediately find two qualities that do not easily co-exist. In a related manner, the internal governance of cooperatives contains tensions between **democratic** impulses and **bureaucratic** tendencies in, for example, the need to accommodate the diversity of membership interests and the interest in developing a more governable homogeneous membership. In the realm of social relations, cooperatives provide an interesting site for the exploration of tensions noted by Friedmann (1995) and others in current work on the social relations of **production** and social relations of **consumption.** In terms of spatial relations, cooperatives may illuminate the paradox associated with tensions between the **global** and the **local.**

From an interest in collective action, the predominant representation of cooperatives would lead us to classify them as **traditional social movements.** However, there are at least latent elements of **"new" social movements** within even the most traditional cooperatives. In these and other ways, the cooperative organizational form encompasses those tensions that are often modeled in neo-classical economic analysis as obstacles to the pursuit of a single-minded economic interest (Torgerson, Reynolds, and Gray 1997). In contrast, the point made here is that those very tensions may, in fact, be a wellspring of strength, innovation, and flexibility that, in the long run, serve multiple and sometimes apparently contradictory functions quite well.

Grabher and Stark's (1998:55) recent work on "organizing diversity" argues that such "institutional friction" is a means of preserving diversity that:

> . . . might later be recombined in new organizational forms. . . . Institutional legacies embody not only the persistence of the past but also resources for the future. Institutional friction that blocks transition to an already designated future keeps open a multiplicity of alternative paths to further exploration.

The function of such tensions is indicated by the relative success of the cooperative movement in agriculture when examined over the course of the 20th century. Retention of this institutional friction in cooperative organizations may prove a valuable resource for the 21st century.

The objective of this paper is to explore these sites of contradiction under the premise that contradiction is not necessarily dysfunctional. Instead, it is held that democratic relations may enable each of these sites of contradiction to generate functional adaptations in response to the tensions of

Table 10.1
Contradictions within Cooperatives as Institutional Frictions

Level of Contradiction	Site of Institutional Friction
Capitalism/Democracy	Political economy
Production/Consumption	Social relations
Global/Local	Spatial relations
Traditional/New social movements	Collective action

paradoxical demands. Democratic relations within the cooperative movement function as a means of resisting the homogenization associated with the singular rationality of the neoclassical economic model. As Buttel (1997:347) has argued: "Modern social science has accordingly tended to conjure up a highly dematerialized view of agro-food realities—a view that tends to regard the natural environment of agriculture as being essentially epiphenomenal." Similarly, neoclassical economics has constructed a highly deinstitutionalized view that treats the institutional context as merely epiphenomenal. The present model not only brings the institutional context back in, but recognizes that context as heterogeneous and permeated with tensions. Again, to follow Grabher and Stark (1998:54): although "institutional homogenization might foster *adaptation* in the short run, the consequent loss of institutional diversity will impede *adaptability* in the long run." Sustainable development demands this long-term adaptability of political and economic relations.

Democratic Capitalism in a Capitalist Democracy?

Referring to the late 20th century U.S. as a capitalist democracy, Cohen and Rogers (1983: 49–50) argue that:

> Capitalist democracy is not a system in which a capitalist economy persists alongside a democratic political system, each unaffected by the other . . . Capitalist democracy is neither just capitalism, nor just democracy, nor just some combination of the two that does not change its component parts. Indeed, even to think of such separate parts is to miss the vital integrity of the system.

Cohen and Rogers argue (1983:169) that these two forms are, in the last instance, incompatible: "For its realization, democracy requires the abolition of capitalism." Until that last instance comes, however, there is a need for mechanisms that can sustain democratic relations and processes. Thus, I focus on tensions that exist *within* this system of capitalist democracy with a view toward exploring the generation of cooperatives as institutions of democratic capitalism.

Perhaps the most apparent manner in which cooperatives reveal a contradictory tension is in the interface between the economic and political elements. As economic entities, cooperatives are capitalist enterprises created, in part, to meet needs (e.g., rural electrification) that are simply not met by the larger capitalist sector or, to compete with other, especially monopoly capitalist, enterprises. The historical conditions that gave rise to agricultural cooperatives in the U.S. led to a strong, though perhaps sometimes merely formal, democratic structure in their organization. Thus, unlike other capitalist enterprises, cooperatives have traditionally incorporated a democratic political principle (one member, one vote) with respect to their internal governance. Most agricultural cooperatives in the U.S. have historically used the "one member, one vote" principle in which "all members have equal voting power, regardless of their investment in the cooperative" (Barton 1989:15). This aspect has always stood in contrast to the proportional voting typical of most "investor-oriented firms" (IOFs) in which voting privileges are based directly on levels of equity or shares of common stock owned.

The early cooperative associations of U.S. agriculture (e.g., Grange, Northern and Southern Alliance) were heavily grounded in the political sphere as well as the economic. Indeed, the economic and political functions were not clearly distinguished. Cooperation and "pooling" were economic class practices that complemented political class practices in opposing monopoly capital. The Alliance curriculum encouraged members to "assume political responsibility for the nation." To neglect the political sphere would lead to the loss of "individuality, influence, and power in our political institutions, and be wholly at the mercy of the soulless corporations that are now wielding such an influence over our government" (Mitchell 1987:79). In the populist era, this conflation of economic and political class interest was strong, extreme and radical (in the sense of getting at the root). Some of the early post Civil War political parties that were the predecessors of the Populist Party were self-identified as "Anti-Monopoly" parties (Saloutos and Hicks 1951). In the context of failing to establish successful cooperatives (due primarily to lack of economic resources to resist capital's opposition), the movement increasingly turned from the economic solution and temporarily elevated the political element, culminating in the Populist political campaigns of the 1890s, the defeat of which led back to an economic focus and the

development of cooperatives in the agricultural prosperity of the early 20th century.

Viewed from an historical perspective, the continuities at some levels are quite interesting. Mitchell (1987:82) quotes one late 19th century Alliance lecturer as contending that: "capitalism places property above life, thereby declaring war on humanity. This war must not cease until capitalism is vanquished and property becomes the servant, not the master of man." More than a century later, we find Harriet Friedmann (1995) viewing broad historical cycles as a pendulum swinging back and forth between self-regulation by markets and subsequent self-protection by society in light of the economic and ecological crises that follow, making a statement which resonates with that Populist framing. As the pendulum is now swinging back toward self-regulation (from New Deal protections), she writes: "A new era is being constructed, in which people and the earth are forced to 'adjust' to the 'market', and it is the markets, not people, that require freedom." Today, of course, cooperatives are subject to this historical force.

The vast majority (93%) of agricultural cooperatives are still formally run by democratic principles (Reynolds, Gray, and Kraenzle 1997). However, this democratic quality is increasingly coming into question. Two forces seem to be largely responsible for this challenge. First, some cooperative theorists find cooperatives' democratic element to be at odds with purely economic interests and call for either wholesale restructuring of cooperatives as IOFs or for the elimination of the "one member, one vote" principle and for the substitution of proportional (to capital investment) representation (Schrader 1989; Smith 1988). Here the needs of capital are privileged relative to the needs of members of the cooperative. The path of conversion to an IOF is indicated by an analysis that reifies a formal rationality oriented toward exchange value as against a substantive rationality centered on use value (Collins 1991a, 1991b). Such an orientation toward cooperation contradicts traditional core cooperative principles that emphasize use value: *user-ownership, user-control, and user-benefit* (Barton 1989). The principle of democratic governance is, of course, the mechanism by which the centrality of such use value is secured against its usurpation by exchange value. The substitution of proportional voting (based on levels of financial investment) clearly subverts the democratic character of the cooperative form of organization and, with that erosion, other fundamental principles of cooperation are also threatened.

The second force opposing the democratic principle is the increasing bureaucratization of ever larger and more complex cooperative organizations. Control is usurped by management as members are increasingly defined as incapable of making decisions on "technical" matters that only experts are qualified to evaluate. Drawing on Lasley's (1981) analysis of cooperatives' inherent "dual objectives," Seipel and Heffernan (1997) argue that maintaining member involvement and the generation of profit necessary for survival in the economic marketplace are inherently contradictory. They contend that as authority has increasingly been delegated to hired management and staff, the formal rationality of the economic function has come to dominate the substantive rationality of democratic participation in cooperative decision making. It is this bureaucratic erosion of the democratic element that may be more threatening. The fact that cooperatives are not converting in droves to IOFs but are instead primarily simply consolidating or merging with other cooperatives constantly adds to the very complexity and scale of cooperative organizations (Wadsworth 1998; Mooney and Gray 2002). This consolidation encourages structural conditions under which the bureaucratic subversion of the democratic element takes place. The complexity and diversity of forms of consolidation both among co-ops as well as between co-ops and IOFs, force Hendrickson et al. (2001:8) back to the fundamental question of such hybrids: "What is the management unit?"

Further, Seipel and Heffernan (1997:5–6) argue that cooperative management may develop a set of interests that are quite distinct from the interests of the cooperatives' members. Cooperative managers may tend to administer the cooperative as an IOF, single-mindedly focusing on "earnings or sales growth" to the "neglect of other activities that could enhance member service or meet other member goals" in order, for example, to enhance their own individual marketability as business managers. Monitoring this potentially autonomous interest is more difficult in the case of cooperatives than in IOFs where there is a more clearly defined and singular objective, and the stock market value provides a fundamental regulatory role. Since cooperatives have dual, if not multiple, objectives, the evaluation of managerial performance is rendered problematic. Further, as cooperatives "pursue business activities that are increasingly removed from their members' and directors' agricultural experience, oversight is weakened" (Seipel and Heffernan 1997:6). Thus, the board of directors, whose expertise is in production agriculture, may be subordinated to the expertise of management. In the extreme case, the board may become a "rubber stamp for management decisions" (Seipel and Heffernan 1997:6).

Active democratic participation is the means by which this autonomous interest of management can be countered. Democratic participation may ensure that multiple objectives, if they exist, remain "on the table" and are not reduced to single objectives. Retention of democratic principles facilitates the institutional friction which managerial interests tend to work against in the process of rationalization along singular dimensions.

The Social Relations of Production and Consumption

In arguing that power in the food system is increasingly shifting from the manufacturing sphere to the retailing sphere of the food system, Hendrickson et al. (2001), among others, raise questions concerning the place of both the farmer and the consumer in the emerging system. By this account, these seemingly fundamental actors in the food system appear to be increasingly marginalized in terms of their power in the agro-food complex. The distinctive rationalization of production and consumption spheres is driven by capitalist economies in terms of antagonistic interests in the realm of exchange. The paradox here is that this antagonism is also a relation of interdependency in which these interests can be viewed as unitary. Indeed, each sphere can only be meaningfully understood in relation to its other.

The pluralist political arena replicates this distinctive rationalization of an antagonistic economic relationship in its formulation of "producer groups" and "consumer groups" who simply carry on the battle in another sphere. The historical origins of the co-operative movement reflect an interest in overcoming this division. The vision of a co-operative commonwealth was one that recognized both the distinctive interests as well as the common interests of producers and consumers, seeking to create an organizational structure that unified these interests.

Voorhis (1961:83) expressed this long-standing desire to link production and consumption through cooperative structures: "... if a considerable proportion of farm crops could be sold directly by farmer-owned enterprises to consumer-owned ones, the 'spread' between what farmers receive and what consumers pay would amount simply to the costs of processing, transportation and sale." Further, Voorhis (1961:150) argued strongly for the development of consumer cooperatives:

> But only as major consumer needs are met cooperatively, only as the people come into ownership of businesses supplying the things on which their big expenditures are made—only then can the full influence of cooperative enterprise upon a nation's economy be brought to bear. Only then can "consumer preference" begin to have any meaning. And only then can the consumer interest begin to be asserted and defended as a salutary countervailing force to the overweening power of highly organized producers.

Even more recently, Friedmann's (1995) examination of the social relations of production and consumption allows us to advance an argument that the cooperative form is well suited to confront certain problems that she raises. Friedmann (1995:30) suggests that the real alternative to the dichotomy in production and consumption is "democratic regulation of regional food economies."

> If food is to be susceptible to democratic regulation, the links in the food chain must first be made visible. An environmentally and socially sensitive agriculture presupposes consumers whose food needs are effectively transmitted to farmers, as well as citizens whose environmental needs are effectively transmitted to farmers.

In this case, co-ops may have an advantage over IOFs. Cooperatives are characterized by a structural form that can encompass both the social relations of production (producer cooperatives) and consumption (supply cooperatives) and share the capability of democratizing both spheres. While purely market driven social relations of production and consumption tend toward inequalities and hierarchal structures, cooperative structures that retain the democratic principle would have the potential to reduce the unequal economic influences on food production and consumption by elevating people's needs and desires, or substantive use values, perhaps even minimizing the process by which consumers' "minds are 'colonized' through advertising and merchandising" (Friedmann 1995:25). This is at least implicit in the cooperative movement's tradition of envisioning a cooperative commonwealth and in the principle of cooperation among cooperatives.

Friedmann (1995:21) also asks if there is some happy medium "between public regulation and private power." I suggest that the cooperative form has the advantage of providing a middle course in which regulation lies neither purely in the economic sphere (market regulation, or in a private, corporate regulation to be enforced by emergent transnational institutions) nor in the public sphere of state regulation. Rather, cooperative regulation would entail control by producers and consumers of food in economic organizations whose internal political structure is democratized. In this sense, again, the cooperative has the advantage, not the liability, of synthesizing the two spheres.

At the present moment, however, Friedmann (1995:24) argues that "strategic power has shifted from farmers to corporations." She contends that:

> Economists and corporate managers, who have considerable clout in setting political agendas, count the human costs of hunger and the ecological costs of monocultural farming as "external." Agricultural policy is at an impasse because it cannot address these social problems. New agents can in principle find unity through redefinition of issues centered on the production and consumption of food.

Community supported agriculture (CSA) groups might be seen as an embryonic form that overcomes this disjuncture and, in so doing, addresses many of the issues raised here. Most CSAs are effectively, if informally, a synthesis of production cooperative and consumer cooperative. Further, most CSAs contain mechanisms, again either formal or informal, for directly transmitting information between producers and consumers. CSAs also tend to be tied to place, rendering an affinity with Friedmann's argument that only food economies that are geographically bounded, i.e., regional, can be democratically regulated. She argues that "to create regional food economies requires politics that re-embed land and labor in the needs and capacities of communities" (1995:30).

Even democratization via distinct (producer and consumer) cooperative structures would ameliorate the tendency to view many of the "costs" of the current food production and consumption as external costs. To the extent that co-ops are wedded to place more than IOFs, democratically organized co-ops would be more effective in dealing with these externalities; i.e., to those members in the cooperative community, health issues, environmental issues, and land use issues are **not** external, but constitute part of their everyday lifeworld.

This leads to a third site of contradictory tensions in which cooperatives share a unique position—spatial relations—particularly that tension that characterizes the relationship between the local and the global.

Local and Global

In the context of the globalization process, a parallel and contradictory process of "localization" also develops in the interstices (see, for example, McMichael 1996; Giddens 2002). Cooperatives have a distinct quality in terms of their spatial tensions. The equity retention principle in cooperatives effectively functions (though perhaps in latent, rather than manifest form) to tie the cooperative to a particular place. From the standpoint of capital, this may appear as an unnecessary constraint. Paradoxically, from the standpoint of the cooperator and the local community, it may be seen as a means of preventing the "problem" of capital flight which capital wishes to enjoy. Rationalization along the singular lines of economic logic at the level of the individual actor leads to calls for freeing this equity from its presumed "inefficient" lack of mobility. However, a more historical and holistic view reveals this as a long-term functional adaptation (an efficiency of a different sort) that shields cooperatives and the communities to

which they are tied from those recessions that would drive private capital from the region.

Seipel and Heffernan (1997) argue that cooperatives' attempts to compete with investor-oriented transnational corporations (TNCs) in the global market are characterized by both specific constraints as well as unique opportunities. In addition to the bureaucratic hierarchy and technocratic tendencies that threaten member governance of cooperatives, so too does the possibility of overseas investment in which members are also separated by physical distance. Seipel and Heffernan's (1997) examination of recent efforts by several large cooperatives to operate globally reveals some interesting tensions.

Land O' Lakes, for instance, purchased a feed manufacturing plant in Poland which markets both through privately owned local farm supply stores as well as through remnants of Poland's dairy cooperatives. At the time of Seipel and Heffernan's writing, Land o' Lakes was "grappling internally with the issue of whether or not the customers of the Polish feed mill should become members of the cooperative" (1997:7). Of course, the very purchase of such a plant in Poland immediately raises questions about how this provides a service to cooperative members or expands markets for members' products. Seipel and Heffernan conclude that management enjoyed considerable autonomy in making this investment decision on the basis of interests in growth and profitability, acting much as an IOF would in a similar situation. Should the Polish farmer-customers become members of the cooperative, we would have an interesting challenge to cooperatives' traditional identification with the boundaries of the nation state. Hendrickson et al. (2001) raise many questions concerning the economic and political relationship between the producer and the cooperative when cooperative enterprises expand beyond the locale of origin. Nevertheless, even if cooperatives are merely to be the Noursian cure for "market failure," to the extent that markets are global and thus subject to global failure, perhaps cooperatives must also be global. Analogous to the vision of labor unions uniting across state boundaries, transnational cooperative organization presents some very interesting issues with respect to state policy.

Hassanein (1999) has argued for the importance of developing local knowledge in response to processes of globalization. She details the advantages that can be obtained by familiarity with a locale and its specificity in competition with the forces of globalization and their inevitable demands for standardization and the subordination of unique local qualities. Hassanein shows clearly that democratic forms of organization are far more capable of retaining and even producing such indigenous or local knowledge related to agricultural production than the bureaucratically organized, hierarchical forms of knowledge production and exchange employed by IOFs or the public land grant college complex. It is perhaps especially in the alliance of the latter two institutional interests that we see the way in which the rationalization of production centers on the elimination of that local knowledge as both capital and science seek more universal conditions (see also Busch 2000).

Hassanein's analysis of the emergence of rotational grazing networks in the Wisconsin dairy sector reveals a weak role played by the cooperative sector as a whole (though she does note the role of one small, locally controlled cooperative performing this function) in facilitating this counterhegemonic production technique. Even though such cooperatives have both the "netness" (network) as well as the "catness" (category inclusiveness) that Tilly (1978) points to as significant mechanisms of mobilization, these cooperatives apparently did not function to enhance the development of rotational grazing, instead forcing farmers to develop new, parallel networks to learn this technique. One must consider that the "interests of the cooperative" lay with more traditional high input, capital intensive production. For example, production cooperative management might desire higher volumes of product while service cooperative management would not wish to see sales volume cut into by this lower input cost form of production. This does not, of course, imply that cooperatives are necessarily driven to such responses. Again, the condition is that of democratic control by members or bureaucratic control by management. Under democratic principles, the cooperative would be structurally quite capable of facilitating the production and exchange of knowledge related to local production conditions. Indeed, such a function would be an advantage to the cooperative form that would be difficult for IOFs to duplicate, but one that also increases in importance with new interests in a decentralized agriculture as a defense against bioterrorist threats to our food security.

Seipel and Heffernan (1997:15) recognize this general cooperative advantage and that such innovation "may require flattening hierarchical managerial structures and returning more operational autonomy to local affiliates." They argue that: the federated structure of many regional cooperatives offers a model which could facilitate such decentralization but it will take a conscious effort by the upper levels of management to make it a reality. Relinquishing such control is difficult and often goes against the historical tendency toward centralization of decision making in cooperatives (1997:15).

In Seipel and Heffernan's (1997:15) account, this decentralization of control is predicated on high member involvement, i.e., the practice of democratic principles. Its promise is high in terms of developing the "permanent innovation," flexible specialization, and quality that "health- and food-safety-conscious consumers" are expected to demand in the future. Finally, Seipel and Heffernan (1997:15) contend that cooperatives may have an advantage in the development of "new, customized products . . . marketed outside of traditional channels." Their suggestion that cooperatives seek out "new alliances with consumer groups" relates back to our previous discussion of the cooperative commonwealth vision of bridging social relations of production and consumption. Once again, CSAs may represent a prototype or possible embryonic form of this synthesis.

Hassanein's treatment of these forms of development of local knowledge is tied to issues raised by the literature on what are often referred to as the "new social movements." This brings us to a consideration of a fourth site of contradiction upon which cooperatives seem uniquely situated: the tension between the "old" or traditional forms of social movements and the new social movements.

New and Traditional Social Movements

Beuchler (1995:442) notes that new social movement models look for "other logics of action . . . based in politics, ideology and culture." Given our interest in the dual, if not multiple, purposes of cooperatives, the new social movement model provides a useful heuristic device for allowing us to examine some tensions within the cooperative movement regarding its paradoxical orientation as simultaneously both a new and a traditional social movement.

Castells (1983) resists the tendency to dichotomize the new and traditional social movements, pointing instead to the dialectical interplay between these forms. In this sense, I am arguing that cooperatives contain both orientations simultaneously. As a traditional social movement, cooperatives are readily viewed along class lines as a means of surplus value retention by direct producers. However, co-ops also have inherent structural qualities that permit a resistance to the process of its continued rationalization along purely class lines. The above discussion of the interest in eliminating cooperatives' democratic principle in favor of proportional voting exemplifies this drive toward eliminating diverse, competing class interests *within* the membership by rendering it more purely a class instrument of larger sized farm operations. Nevertheless, prior to such a decisive moment in the process of its rationalization along economic lines, cooperative forms of organization still retain characteristics of the new social movements or at least as potential incubators of new social movements. In this sense, the site of collective action reflects tensions within the cooperative movement that are indicated by contrasting models of new social movements and traditional social movements. We can look for forms of conflict within the cooperative movement that challenge the predominant economistic rationality or, in Melucci's (1994:103) terms: "engage the constitutive logic of the system."

Melucci (1994:123) argues that "the features that render the challenge to the system most visible are organizational structure and internal power relations." The principle of "one member, one vote" is one such feature of cooperative organizational structure that democratizes the internal power relations of cooperatives in contradistinction to the "constitutive logic" of most business enterprises in advanced capitalism. Indeed, Melucci (1994:103) points out that: "the ability of collective demands to expand and to find expression depends on the way in which

political actors are able to translate them into democratic guarantees." This structuring of cooperative internal power relations is characteristic of what Johnston, Larana, and Gusfield (1994:7) note as the new social movements' interest in searching for "institutional reforms that enlarge the systems of members' participation in decision making." Following Castells (quoted in Beuchler 1995:298), this democratic extension structures the possibility of institutional friction functioning as a mechanism of resistance to "the standardization and homogenization associated with bureaucratic forms of organization by establishing and defending genuine forms of community." On the one hand, that resistance may take place, as we have noted earlier, as a defense of self-management and autonomy in the cooperatives' unique ties to place or locale. This, in turn, lends to the decentralization, diffuseness, and segmentation (Johnston, Larana, and Gusfield 1994) also said to be characteristic of the new social movements. Further, to the extent that cooperatives retain an emphasis on providing services to a community of members, rather than providing simply an investment function, this follows Castells' emphasis on the new social movements' challenge to the singular capitalist logic of exchange value by emphasizing a plurality of use values in the context of a diverse community.

This sphere of use values determined by democratic relations opens the door to the "other logics of action" that characterize new social movements. This may be especially important in new social movements' tendency toward what Boggs (1986) calls "prefigurative action" (or what Melucci refers to as prophecy). Here the new social movements perspective calls attention to the possibility that cooperation might be valued for its own sake. No longer seen as merely a means to a given end, the means and ends of cooperation are understood as fused; or stated differently, the process of cooperation prefigures an interest or value in the cooperation itself as an objective that inheres in the very process of cooperating. Similarly, we can conceive of the democratic principle being valuable in itself, rather than being subordinated to its relative instrumental utility in obtaining economic rewards. Not unlike the economistic model, the rationalization of cooperation along traditional movement lines as only a class interest eliminates the possibility of understanding cooperative members' interest in democracy or cooperation as forms of interaction that might be valued for their own sake. For that matter, any other value-based or substantive rationality that might contradict this singular interest is excluded from consideration. In this manner, we see that while some co-ops may be more oriented toward the new social movement model than the traditional social movement model, the contrasting conceptualizations permit an hypothesis that stresses the potential role of postmaterialist, or other than materialist, values in opposition to a reduction of the movement to a concern with only economic matters.

Following Touraine (1988), it might be argued that cooperatives present an antagonism that corresponds with what he sees as the predominant conflict in contemporary society: i.e., that conflict between consumer/clients as the popular class and managers/technocrats as the dominant class. Seipel and Heffernan (1997) noted this same tension in the conflict within cooperatives between principals and agents. For Touraine, the new social movements are located between these two logics: "a system seeking to maximize production, money, power, and information and that of subjects seeking to defend and expand their individuality." Similarly, Habermas examines the extent to which those forces that contribute to the development of new social movements will condition the resistance to the colonization of the instrumental logic of the system "that detaches media of money and power from any responsibility or accountability" (quoted in Beuchler 1995:445).

Resistance to the concentration of decision-making and control in the hands of experts and administrative apparatus would reflect a new social movement influence within the cooperative movement. Cooperatives uniquely sit "at the seams between system and lifeworld" where managerial interests reflecting systemic demands of growth conflict with lifeworld interests of members in their own goals of service and participation. In this sense, cooperatives would seem to be a site for a new social movement defensive posture. Yet the dual objectives of the cooperative also suggest that the continued role of "the system" should exist alongside and in tension with other demands or interests given by the members' lifeworld. Only in the context of continued democratic governance, however, is it possible to conceive of cooperatives holding this tension. Melucci's approach suggests that those cooperatives reflecting new social movement interests in conflict with this instrumental rationality will increasingly render visible the power structure and managerial/administrative interests of the rest of the cooperative movement. Inherent in cooperatives' organizational structure is a mechanism that "prevents the channels of representation and decision making in pluralist societies from adopting instrumental rationality as the only logic with which to govern complexity" (Melucci 1994:102). The retention and practice of the democratic principle in cooperative organizations permits the possibility of revealing that "the neutral rationality of means masks interests and forms of power" (Melucci 1994:102). Indeed, there is perhaps no better example of the colonization of the cooperative lifeworld by systemic interests than in demands for the elimination of this democratic principle.

Undoubtedly, if cooperatives are to rejuvenate any such oppositional force as existed in their historical origins, there is a good deal of identity work to be done. This would involve, as suggested by Torgerson, Reynolds, and Gray (1997), an amplification of traditional cooperative values and beliefs as a means of enhancing cooperative members' identification with cooperative history as an alternative economic institution with an explicit political agenda. As Johnston et al. (1994:8) note, new social movements involve the "emergence of new or formerly weak dimensions of identity . . . They are associated with a set of beliefs, symbols, values, and meanings related to sentiments of belonging to a differentiated social group." Once again, the democratic reclamation is key to this boundary maintenance insofar as collective identity results from a process of "negotiation and 'laborious adjustment' of different elements relating to the ends and means of collective action and its relation to the environment . . . by this process of interaction, negotiation and conflict over the definition of the situation, and the movement's reference frame, members construct the collective 'we'" (Johnston et al. 1994:14). In this process, as in new social movements, "the relation between the individual and the collective is blurred" (Johnston et al. 1994:8) and to the extent that this occurs, the individually rational actor at the center of neo-classical economic models becomes even less adequate for explaining the uniqueness of cooperative forms of organization.

Conclusion

This analysis was guided by an interest in the process of institutional democratization. The democratic tradition of cooperatives is threatened. This is related, in part, to the eclipse of institutional economic analysis of cooperatives by the neo-classical economic tradition. The predominance of this theorization is recognized in its practical effects. This unidimensional modeling creates a vacuum that gives rise to critique of its narrow rationality, as in Etzioni's (1993:27) complaint that: "The moral patrimony of the eighties has been the proliferation of cost-benefit analysis into realms in which it has no place. . . ." Further, all of this comes at a time when political and sociological theorists and practitioners are increasingly decrying the absence of just such kinds of associations in terms of their function in building both community and a more democratic civil society. . . .

. . . I have focused on the democratic aspect of cooperatives as a principle that is fundamental to the continued success of cooperatives both internally with respect to effective management and externally with respect to the role that various associations can play in revitalizing and sustaining a democratic society and culture. Cooperatives may function as a form of sustainable struggle insofar as it bridges political and economic interests, if not broader social and cultural concerns, with the amplification of democracy as a common value. In short, it is difficult to envision the construction of such a democratic society while the economy sits outside of that structure governed by antithetical social relations in production and consumption. . . .

Note

The author would like to acknowledge helpful comments from Thomas W. Gray; Wynne Wright; Jess Gilbert; faculty and students at the University of Kentucky and at Cornell University, who patiently listened to early formulations of these ideas; anonymous reviewers for this journal; and the various authors whose work I have tried to synthesize here. Direct correspondence to: Patrick H. Mooney, 1537 Patterson Office Tower, Department of Sociology, University of Kentucky, Lexington, KY 40506-0027. Email: SOC168@uky.edu.

References

Barton, D.G. 1989. "What is a Cooperative?" Pp. 1–20 in *Cooperatives in Agriculture*, D. Cobia, Editor. Englewood Cliffs, N.J.: Prentice-Hall.

Benford, R.D. 1993. "Frame Disputes in the Nuclear Disarmament Movement." *Social Forces* 71(3):677–701.

Boggs, C. 1986. *Social Movements and Political Power: Emerging Forms of Radicalism in the West*. Philadelphia: Temple University Press.

Beuchler, S.M. 1995. "New Social Movement Theories." *The Sociological Quarterly* 36(3):441–464.

Busch, L. 2000. *The Eclipse of Morality: Science, State and Market*. Hawthorne, NY: Aldine De Gruyter.

Buttel, F.H. 1997. "Some Observations on Agro-Food Change and the Future of Agricultural Sustainability Movements." Pp. 344–365 in *Globalizing Food: Agrarian Questions and Global Restructuring*, edited by D. Goodman and M. J. Watts. London: Routledge.

Castells, M. 1983. *The City and the Grassroots*. Berkeley: University of California Press.

Cobia, D. (Ed.). 1989. *Cooperatives in Agriculture*. Englewood Cliffs, N.J.: Prentice-Hall.

Coffey, J.D. 1992. "Comment: Edwin Nourse's 'The Place of the Cooperative in Our National Economy.' " *Journal of Agricultural Cooperation* Volume 7:111–114.

Cohen, J. and J. Rogers. 1983. *On Democracy*. New York: Penguin.

Collins, R.A. 1991a. "The Conversion of Cooperatives to Publicly Held Corporations: A Financial Analysis of Limited Evidence." *Western Journal of Agricultural Economics* 16(2):326–330.

Collins, R.A. 1991b. *Analysis of Economic Motives for Cooperative Conversions to Corporations*. University of California: Center for Cooperatives.

Cook, M., R. Torgerson, T. Sporleder, D. Padberg. 1997. *Cooperatives: Their Importance in the Future Food and Agricultural System*. Washington, D.C.: National Council of Farmer Cooperatives and The Food and Agricultural Marketing Consortium.

Flora, J.L., and C. Flora, H. Hansen, J.S. Sharp. 1997. "New Cooperatives, Community, and Entrepreneurial Social Structure." Paper presented at the Rural Sociological Society annual meetings. Toronto, Ontario. August.

Friedmann, H. 1995. "Food Politics: New Dangers, New Possibilities." In *Food and Agrarian Orders in the World Economy*, P. McMichael, editor. Westport, CT: Praeger Publishing.

Giddens, A. 2002. *Runaway World: How Globalization is Reshaping Our Lives*. London: Profile Books.

Grabher, G., and D. Stark. 1998. "Organizing Diversity: Evolutionary Theory, Network Analysis and Post-Socialism." Pp. 54–75 in *Theorising Transition: The Political Economy of Post-Communist Transformation*, edited by J. Pickles and A. Smith. London: Routledge.

Hassanein, N. 1999. *Changing the Way America Farms: Knowledge and Community in the Sustainable Agriculture Movement*. Lincoln: University of Nebraska Press.

Hendrickson, M., and W.D. Heffernan, P.H. Howard, J.B. Heffernan. 2001. *Consolidation in Food Retailing and Dairy: Implications for Farmers and Consumers in a Global Food System*. University of Missouri Department of Rural Sociology: Report to the National Farmers Union. January 8.

Johnston, H., E. Larana, and J. Gusfield. 1994. "Identities, Grievances, and New Social Movements." Pp. 3–35 in *New Social Movements: From Ideology to Identity*. Philadelphia: Temple University Press.

Lasley, R.P. 1981. "Organizational Structure and Membership Participation in Farmer Cooperatives." Ph.D. Dissertation, Department of Sociology, University of Missouri-Columbia.

LeHeron, R. M. Roche. 1997. "Sustainability and Institution Building: Issues and Prospects as Seen from New Zealand." Pp. 366–374 in *Globalizing Food: Agrarian Questions and Global Restructuring*, edited by D. Goodman and M. J. Watts. London: Routledge.

Levine, D.N. 1985. *The Flight from Ambiguity: Essays in Social and Cultural Theory*. Chicago: University of Chicago Press.

McMichael, P. 1996. "Globalization: Myths and Realities." *Rural Sociology* 61(1):25–55.

Melucci, A. 1994. "A Strange Kind of Newness: What's 'New' in the New Social Movements." Pp. 101–130 in *New Social Movements: From Ideology to Identity*. Philadelphia: Temple University Press.

Mitchell, T. 1987. *Political Education in the Southern Farmers Alliance, 1887–1900*. Madison: University of Wisconsin Press.

Mooney, P.H., J. Roahrig, and T.W. Gray. 1996. "The De/Repoliticization of Cooperation and the Discourse of Conversion." *Rural Sociology* 61(4):559–576.

Mooney, P.H. and T.J. Majka. 1995. *Farmers and Farm Workers Movements: Social Protest in American Agriculture*. New York: Twayne.

Mooney, P.H. and S.A. Hunt. 1996. "A Repertoire of Interpretations: Master Frames and Ideological Continuity in U.S. Agrarian Mobilization." *The Sociological Quarterly* 37(1):177–197.

Mooney, P.H. and T.W. Gray. 2002. *Cooperative Restructuring in Theory and Practice*. Washington: D.C.: United States Department of Agriculture, Rural Business and Cooperative Service: Research Report #185.

Morlan, R. 1955. *Political Prairie Fire: The Non-Partisan League, 1915–1922*. Minneapolis: University of Minnesota Press.

Redclift, M. 1997. "Sustainability and Theory: An Agenda for Action." Pp. 333–343 in *Globalizing Food: Agrarian Questions and Global Restructuring*, edited by D. Goodman and M. J. Watts. London: Routledge.

Reynolds, B.J., T.W. Gray, and C.A. Kraenzle. 1997. "Voting and Representation Systems in Agricultural Cooperatives." *RBS Research Report 156*. June.

Saloutos, T. and J.D. Hicks. 1951. *Twentieth Century Populism: Agricultural Discontent in the Middle West, 1900–1939*. Lincoln: University of Nebraska Press.

Schrader, L. 1989. "Equity Capital and Restructuring of Cooperatives as Investor-Oriented Firms." *Journal of Agricultural Cooperation* Volume 4:41–53.

Seipel, M. and W.D. Heffernan. 1997. *Cooperatives in a Changing Global Food System*. Washington, D.C.: USDA Rural Business-Cooperative Service. Research Report 157.

Smith, F.J. 1988. Review of D.W. Cobia (ed.), *Cooperatives in Agriculture*. In *Journal of Agricultural Cooperation* 3(1):107–109.

Society for the Advancement of Socio-Economics. 1999. *Madison Declaration on the Need for Socio-Economic Research and Theory*. The Society for the Advancement of Socio-Economics. Website: http://www.sase.org/conf99/declaration.html.

Taylor, V. 1989. "Social Movement Continuity: The Women's Movement in Abeyance." *American Sociological Review* 54:761–75.

Tilly, C. 1978. *From Mobilization to Revolution*. Reading, MA: Addison-Wesley.

Touraine. A. 1988. *The Return of the Actor: Social Theory in Post-Industrial Society*. Minneapolis: University of Minnesota Press.

Torgerson, R.C., B.J. Reynolds, and T.W. Gray. 1997. "Evolution of Cooperative Thought, Theory and Purpose." Pp. 3–20 in D. Padberg (ed.) *Cooperatives: Their Importance in the Future of the Food and Agricultural System*. College Station, Texas: Texas A&M University.

United States Department of Agriculture: Rural Development. 1998. "Co-ops Break Supply Sales Record." *Rural Cooperatives* 65(6):4–6. November/December.

United States Department of Agriculture: Rural Business Cooperative Service. 1999. *Farmer Cooperative Statistics* RBS Service Report #59.

Voorhis, J. 1961. *American Cooperatives: Where They Come From, What They Do, Where They Are Going*. New York: Harper and Brothers.

Wadsworth, J.J. 1998. *Cooperative Restructuring, 1989–1998*. USDA Rural Business-Cooperative Service. Service Report #57. November.

Part II

Inside Organizations

Culture and Control

Chapter 11
Boundary Control

The Social Ordering of Work and Family Time in a High-tech Corporation

Leslie A. Perlow

All organizations have an interest in controlling the behavior and activities of their members. Control can be exercised in different ways, however, depending on the type of organization and the characteristics of organizational members. In this chapter, Leslie Perlow examines what she calls "boundary control," referring to the ways that organizations seek to regulate the boundary between employees' work and nonwork lives.

This type of control is more salient in some kinds of organizational settings than others. Perlow's research focuses on "knowledge workers"—well-educated software engineers employed by a high-tech firm. By most accounts, these employees have a great deal of autonomy and flexibility at work. They have no set starting or ending times and are given a high degree of discretion on the job about the best way to carry out their work assignments. Despite this appearance of control, however, the engineers Perlow studied worked extremely long hours with little ability to resist demands on their time. As a result, their ability to have a life outside of work was significantly eroded. What are the consequences of this form of boundary control for employees and their families? Perlow raises important questions for us to consider as boundaries between work and nonwork continue to change.

Introduction

The industrial revolution marked a fundamental change in the separation of work and family life. On the farm, families worked together from dawn until dusk, intermingling work and family responsibilities, subject to the particular demands of the day. Similarly, although work and family constituted distinct spheres of life, skilled artisans did not have an externally defined, rigid temporal framework that determined when the responsibilities of either sphere had to be handled (Rock, 1988). For both farmers and artisans, tasks, rather than the clock or cultural pressures, determined the length of their work days. As workers entered factories, they faced external control not only over their activities at work but also over how much time they spent working (Owen, 1979; Landes, 1983). Employees' work schedules became regulated by the technical control exerted by the production process (Bendix, 1956). The later development of bureaucracies led to control embedded in social relations and social structure (Etzioni, 1961). A system of rules emerged governing when employees were to be at work and what types of absences were excused.

More recently, it has become difficult to design jobs as a series of explicit tasks to be performed, with appropriate incentives to ensure adequate output from qualified employees. We are told with increasing frequency that organizational culture, built from underlying values and beliefs about what is important. valued, and rewarded within an organization, assumes and carries crucial control functions (Ouchi, 1980; Wilkins and Ouchi, 1983; Van Maanen and Kunda, 1989). This seems especially true in so-called knowledge organizations, where the work to be performed is of an open-ended, creative, individually styled, and highly demanding sort that cannot be standardized or fully planned out in advance (Bell, 1973). In such work settings, attempts are made to elicit and direct the required efforts of members by controlling the experiences, thoughts, and feelings that guide their actions (Hochschild, 1983; Van Maanen and Kunda, 1989). The intent is for workers to be driven by internal commitment, strong identification with company goals, and intrinsic satisfaction from work (Kunda, 1992). This type of control compels employees not only to do what is expected at work but to conform to norms at work that determine how they lead their lives both in and out of the workplace.

Each of these types of control involves managers governing the temporal boundary between employees' work and their lives outside of work. I refer to the various ways in which managers in organizations cajole, encourage, coerce, or otherwise influence the amount of time employees physically spend in the workplace as "boundary control." As I define this term, boundary control refers to managers' ability to affect how employees divide their time between their work and nonwork spheres of life.

Forms of Boundary Control

The nature of control itself has varied with the social class of workers as much as with the dominant structure of work. In a study of department stores, Ouchi and Maguire (1975) found that people at lower hierarchical levels experience more personal surveillance, or "behavior control," whereas people at higher hierarchical levels experience more measurement of outputs, or "output control." Moreover, the overall amount of control ("behavior" and "output" control combined) people experience decreases as they move up the hierarchy. One can also safely assume, however, that increased work hours are expected of those higher in the hierarchy. While people at the bottom of organizational hierarchies are more closely monitored at work, their time is reckoned by the clock rather than by their activities (Thompson, 1967; Clark, 1985); the length of their work day is fixed rather than driven by demands of the job. As a result, people at the bottom of the hierarchy surrender control over when they work and what they do at work, exchanging control for predictability in their work lives.

Although many studies have examined employees' loss of control over their time at work as they moved from the farm to the factory and later to the office (Edwards, 1979; Owen, 1979; Barley and Kunda, 1992), an important but often overlooked effect of these changes for people low in occupational hierarchies was the significant increase in predictability that they experienced over the temporal boundary between work and life outside of work. As Zerubaval (1981: 166) has asserted, "The very same institutions that are directly responsible for much of the rigidification of our life—namely the schedule and the calendar—can also be seen as being among the foremost liberators of the modern individual."

People higher in the hierarchy, i.e. managers, professionals, and technical workers, did not experience the same degree of loss of control over what they did at work nor the same increased predictability in their work schedules. In his description of work life in the 1950s, Whyte (1956) labeled senior executives "non-well-rounded men," to characterize his finding that senior executives typically worked nine and a half hours in the office on weekdays, four out of five weeknights, and part of most weekends and therefore had no time for anything else. Kanter (1977: 65), like Whyte, documented the blurring of the boundary between work and life outside of work for people at the top of organizational hierarchies: "*Question:* How does the organization know managers are doing their jobs and that they are making the best possible decisions? *Answer:* Because they are spending every moment at it and thus working to the limits of human possibility. *Question:* When has a manager finished the job? *Answer:* Never. Or at least, hardly ever. There is always something more that could be done."

Boundary control can be represented as a spectrum ranging from the imposition of constrained work schedules characteristic of blue-collar work to the all-encompassing schedules characteristic of senior management. In this paper, I focus on the boundary control exerted on the higher echelons, which results in long and often unpredictable hours of work. While this form of boundary control has always been familiar to senior executives, its prevalence is growing rapidly as we approach the twenty-first century.

Boundary Control and Knowledge Work

Since the 1950s, a demand for increasingly complex, analytic, and even abstract work has shifted the division of labor in the United States away from blue-collar work toward technical and professional work (Bell, 1973; Stehr, 1994). The number of professional and technical jobs has increased 300 percent since 1950 (Barley and Orr, 1997). A quarter of all new jobs currently being created in the United States are either professional or technical (Silvestri and Lukasiewicz, 1991). According to management scholars, these new jobs result from a transition from an industrial era to a knowledge era. Savage (1990) claimed that networking enterprises are replacing steep hierarchies, complex, unpredictable work tasks are displacing routines, and functions performed concurrently and more wholistically have eclipsed sequential processing. Some of the names for this new organizational form include the post-industrial firm (Bell, 1973), the information-based organization (Zuboff, 1988), the human networking enterprise (Savage, 1990), and the high-involvement organization (Lawler, 1986). However it is labeled, the new firm is said to process information and knowledge, in contrast to the industrial enterprise, which fabricated goods. Using General Motors to illustrate the resulting shift in expectations, Bennis (1985: vii) wrote: "It used to be that the old fashioned GM philosophy of management could be summed up by this phrase: 'DON'T THINK, DUMMY—DO WHAT YOU'RE TOLD.' Now, . . . there is a new and very different credo which goes: 'THINK! I'M NOT GOING TO TELL YOU WHAT TO DO.' " Jobs therefore demand workers with capacities for planning, judgment, collaboration, and analyzing complex systems (Dertouzos et al., 1989).

Scholars claim that the people—knowledge workers—who fill these jobs cannot be managed like blue-collar workers. Dertouzos et al. (1989) warned that compulsion will not effectively generate the commitment, responsibility, and knowledge necessary to be effective in highly cerebral organizations. Lawler (1986) and Walton (1985) have advocated, instead, for a new high-involvement management, which gives knowledge workers broader responsibilities, encourages them to contribute, and helps them to derive satisfaction from their work. Drucker (1989) suggested that these employees must be treated as specialists who direct and discipline themselves. Handy (1989) therefore encouraged managers to reinforce, motivate, teach, and counsel knowledge workers, while giving them room to make mistakes. Savage (1990) holds managers responsible for creating an environment of trust and openness.

At the same time, managers are held accountable by senior executives for the performance of the knowledge workers under their command. Because managers cannot easily or directly measure the work output or involvement of knowledge workers, they turn to work hours as an indicator of both productivity and commitment. Moreover, managers recognize that knowledge work is both interdependent and open-ended and that those they manage often need each other to complete their work on time. Managers therefore assume it is best for everyone to be present as much of the time as possible and judge knowledge workers accordingly. As a result, the managerially valued knowledge worker in today's world—a world that demands responsiveness, adaptability, flexibility, and creativity in responding to global markets and to customers—demonstrates total devotion to work. The grueling schedules that used to be typical only of top corporate management and self-employed people are becoming common in one occupation after another. Corporate lawyers, investment bankers, computer programmers, and many other professionals are now expected to work seventy- or eighty-hour weeks routinely, with extra effort during particularly hectic times (Kidder, 1981; Schor, 1991).

Current workplace structures, practices, and expectations surrounding knowledge work are based on the notion that employees are willing and able to make work their priority over and above their family, community, or other concerns in their private lives (Christopherson, 1991; Bailyn, 1993). People are consumed by what Coser (1974) referred to as the "greedy institution." This notion is clearly problematic for anyone who has responsibilities outside of work. And, as the demographics of the work force continue to change, more and more employees have such outside commitments. In 1960, for example, 61 percent of married couples had a relationship in which the husband worked and the wife was a full-time homemaker; in contrast, by 1990 this number had dropped to 25 percent of married couples. During the same period, the number of couples in which both spouses worked increased from 28 percent to 54 percent (Hayghe and Cromartie, 1991). Moreover, the number of working women in managerial and professional occupations increased dramatically. From 1972 to 1990, the percentage of women working in executive, administrative, and managerial occupations grew from 20 percent to 40 percent; the proportion of women in professional specialty occupations rose from 44 percent to 51 percent. In particular, the percentage of physicians increased from 10 percent to 19 percent; lawyers from 4 percent to 21 percent, and computer programmers from 20 percent to 26 percent (Hayghe and Cromartie, 1991). Thus, women are not only entering the labor force, creating dual-earner couples. but large numbers of women are entering the professional and managerial ranks and therefore must confront the long and unpredictable hours seemingly inherent in these positions. Furthermore, most women who work outside the home have primary responsibility for the "second shift," as Hochschild (1989) referred to child care and household chores. The demands on their time are therefore exceedingly high. Some men share the responsibilities at home and also suffer from the burden of trying to meet the demands of both work and family. Even those men in dual-earner couples who do not share equally in the responsibilities at home experience much marital stress and demands to help at home (Hochschild, 1989).

In the remainder of the paper, I explore in-depth one high-technology organization's use of boundary control and engineers and their spouses' responses to it. Much research on engineers has focused on the degree to which engineers have autonomy at work (Zussman, 1985; Whalley, 1986; Meiskins and Watson, 1989). I focus, instead, on engineers' lack of autonomy across the boundary between their work and life outside of work.

Methods

Research Site

I studied a product development team at Ditto (a pseudonym), a large, high-tech corporation.[1] I chose Ditto because of its reputation as a leading-edge firm in terms of awareness of employees' work-family concerns. A corporation concerned with these issues provided the potential opportunity to observe a wide spectrum of accepted work-family arrangements.

Ditto employs 100,000 people worldwide, 3,000 of them at the site I studied, which is Ditto's primary site for design and manufacturing. The team I studied was developing PEARL (a fictitious product name), a color laser printer positioned to sell for $10,000. Prior to PEARL, this team made much larger electronic machines that sold for closer to $100,000. It was hoped that PEARL would not only prove profitable but would also position Ditto in this new market. There were plans to follow PEARL with a whole product family.

The PEARL product development team consisted of 45 people. The product manager reported to one of Ditto's seven division vice presidents. In turn, eight managers, including a software manager, reported to the product manager. I focused my data collection on the seventeen members of the software group—the software manager, three project team leaders, an individual contributor, and twelve software engineers—and their three senior managers: the product manager, the senior software manager, and the division vice president. The status of these twenty people is hierarchically organized as follows: the twelve software engineers report to the three project team leaders. In turn, the three project team leaders and the individual contributor report to the software manager. He, in turn, reports to both the product manager and the senior software manager, both of whom report to the division vice president. Figure 11.1 shows this reporting structure. In this paper, I refer to everyone above the software manager as "senior managers." I refer to the software manager and the three project team leaders as managers. I refer to the software manager and everyone below him as part of the "software group."

Table 11.1 shows the demographics of the software group and its senior managers. The software group consists of four women and thirteen men. All of the women are married with children. Eight of the men are married, and seven of them have at least one child. The average age in the software group is 32 years old. The seventeen members of the software group are highly experienced. They have been at the company for an average of seven years. The shortest period of time that anyone of them has been at the company is three and one-half years, and all three engineers who arrived at that time came from other software development jobs. Furthermore, over half the group has Masters in computer science or related fields, and four were pursuing Master's degrees part-time at the time of the study.

The members of the software group have a high degree of control over their time at work. They are free to come and go as they please. They do not have to report to anyone if they leave for a few hours to attend to personal issues such as automobile maintenance, a dentist or doctor's appointment, or a child's Little League game. If they are absent for a whole day, they merely have to inform a more senior member of the group. There is no set limit on the number of personal days that individuals may take. Rather, on an ad hoc basis, absence from the office for accommodation to demands outside of work is tolerated.

Beyond what I refer to as "ad hoc flexibility," the members of the software group also have a high degree of operational autonomy, although not strategic autonomy. Bailyn (1985) differentiated between operational autonomy—freedom to attack a designated problem by means determined by oneself within given organizational constraints—and strategic autonomy—freedom to set one's own research agenda. The twelve engineers each have a list of deliverables for which he or she is personally responsible, and each of the three project team leaders is further responsible for the output and integration of the work of the four engineers he or she manages. Engineers and project team leaders, therefore, are provided with a clear sense of what they have to do (low strategic autonomy) but have freedom in how they accomplish these goals (high operational autonomy).

I did not choose to study this software group because it is typical in terms of the autonomy its members have at work. Rather, managers of the division chose the group for me, based on my desire to study a small group of engineers with a large number of seasoned employees in a mix of family situations. I expected to find variability among successful employees in terms of how they managed work and life outside of work, especially given the apparent ad hoc flexibility and operational autonomy. Instead, I found a group of engineers all under enormous pressure and with little choice about how they allocated time between their work and their lives outside of work.

Data Sources

My field work at Ditto took place over a complete product development cycle. My aim was to develop an understanding of how a small group of individuals manage demands at work and outside of work. I collected data from participant observation, interviews, "shadowing" employees, yearly performance evaluations, and interviews with employees' spouses.

Participant observations. I observed the software group for nine months, from the date funding was committed to PEARL in September until PEARL launched in June. I spent an average of four days a week on site observing members of the software group at

Figure 11.1

Organization chart of Ditto division.

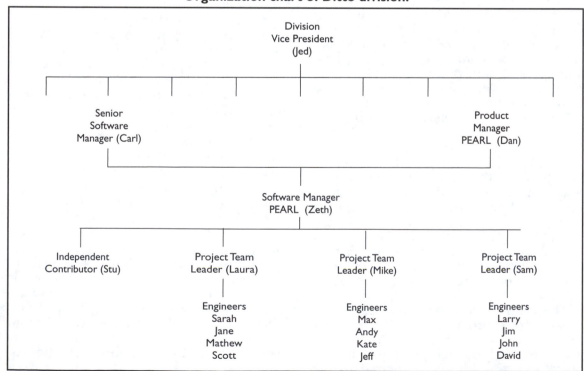

Table 11.1
Employee Demographics of Ditto Software Group and Its Senior Managers

Title	Employee (sex)	Marital status	Children under 18
Division vice president	Jed (m)	M	—
Product manager	Dan (m)	M	—
Sr. software manager	Carl (m)	M	—
Software manager	Zeth (m)	M	3
Independent contributor	Stu (m)	M	1
Project team leader	Mike (m)	M	1
Project team leader	Laura (f)	M	3
Project team leader	Sam (m)	M	4
Engineer	Mathew (m)	M	1
Engineer	Max (m)	S	—
Engineer	Andy (m)	S	—
Engineer	Jane (f)	M	1
Engineer	Sarah (f)	M	1
Engineer	Larry (m)	M	—
Engineer	Scott (m)	M	2
Engineer	Kate (f)	M	3
Engineer	Jim (m)	M	4
Engineer	David (m)	S	—
Engineer	John (m)	S	—
Engineer	Jeff (m)	S	—

work in their cubicles, in the labs, in meetings, and in hallway conversations. I also engaged in social activities with the group members: I regularly ate lunch with them, attended many company parties, joined in several "happy hours" at a local bar, and traveled with them on a two-day bus trip to New York City to take part in the unveiling of their product. When I was on site, I typed field notes throughout the day (as time permitted) and for several hours each night. I recorded all observations and reactions to the day's events.

Interviews. I engaged each of the seventeen members of the software group in an interview lasting one to two hours. These interviews provided background information about group members and allowed me to gain an understanding of their perceptions about the demands they face at work. I conducted an additional fifteen interviews with other members of the division. These interviews served a dual purpose: as with the interviews of the members of the software group, I asked questions about these individuals' backgrounds and about their perceptions of their own work demands. I also asked questions about these individuals' relationships with members of the software group and their perceptions of whether the expectations of the software group are similar to or different from the rest of the members of the division. The people interviewed included the product manager and the division vice president. I also interviewed three of the eight direct reports to the product manager (in addition to the software manager). I further interviewed two mechanical engineers and three system engineers on the product team. Finally, I interviewed five software engineers who were in the division but did not work on the PEARL product team.

Shadowing. I "shadowed" all seventeen members of the software group for at least half a day. I observed everything the individual did, and I wrote down each activity as it occurred. Shadowing group members provided me with an in-depth understanding of how these people spend their time at work. I shadowed one member of the team for three days, five members for one day, and eleven members for half a day.

Performance evaluations. At the end of each year, Ditto senior managers decide the categories of possible raises for that year and the percentage of employees who should be placed in each category. The year I was on site, Ditto senior managers determined that the top 10 percent of employees would receive a 6-percent raise, the middle 70 percent would receive a 3-percent raise, and the bottom 20 percent would receive no raise. The division managers then decided how to put their employees into these categories. They first ranked their employees and then determined each individual's raise. I had access to this information.

Managers are subject to a different system of reward and recognition. The year I was at Ditto, it was decided that due to the company's poor earnings that year, managers would not receive a raise. The top 10 percent of managers, however, would receive a one-time, 10-percent, lump-sum bonus. I had access to information on whether each of the managers I studied received this bonus.

Family interviews. Since I wished to understand spouses' responses to the repercussions of work demands on them as well as the effects of their responses on the employees to whom they were married, I requested to go to the homes of each of the married group members and interview their spouses. Most of the engineers met my request with enthusiasm. Of the twelve software engineers I studied, seven are married, and five of the seven allowed me to interview their spouses. Furthermore, the three project team leaders, the independent contributor, and the software manager are married, and all five of them welcomed me into their homes to interview their spouses. I also visited the homes and interviewed the spouses of the product manager and the division vice president.

I made a total of twelve home visits. Each visit lasted from two to six hours. In the case of the male Ditto employees, I visited all of their homes, except one, in the afternoon and interviewed their wives before the employee came home. In two of those cases, I joined the families for dinner after the interview. In the case of the four female Ditto employees, all of their husbands work full-time; and I therefore went home with the women after work, took part in picking up their children from day care, preparing and eating dinner, and putting their children to bed. I interviewed these spouses while the women were home but conducted the interviews in another room. In the case of the seven homes I visited where both spouses were present at the end of the interview, I also engaged in three-way discussions with the couple about work-family trade-offs they were each making. These discussions gave me (and them) an opportunity to hear and respond to each other's opinions.

Analyses

. . . At the conclusion of field work, I analyzed transcripts and field notes to address the following three questions: (1) How is boundary control maintained by managers? (2) How do employees respond to these controls? and (3) How do spouses respond to the resulting demands on them? . . .

Maintaining Boundary Control

Three techniques are used by managers to pressure individuals to work long hours. Senior managers *impose* demands on both project team leaders and engineers, *monitor* the work of project team leaders and engineers, and act in the desired ways, *modeling* the behavior that they expect from more junior managers and engineers. It is those who are most responsive to the demands put on them, demonstrating that work is their first priority at whatever cost to their lives outside of work, who are highly rewarded.

Imposing Demands

Although there are no set times at which work officially begins or ends, senior managers impose demands on more junior managers and engineers which ensure that these people are at work during certain hours. The ways in which managers impose demands take a variety of forms.

Meetings. Scheduling meetings is a prime example of the imposition of boundary control. If meetings occur, individuals are expected to be present. Yet there is no thought about the implications of scheduling meetings early in the morning, late at night, or over the weekend. Every morning at 8:30 there is a "Sunrise" meeting. If the agenda involves a topic relevant to an individual's work, he or she is expected to be present and often must attend a pre-sunrise meeting to prepare for the subsequent meeting. Similarly, when senior managers feel that a weekend meeting is necessary, they do not ask their subordinates about their availability but, rather, inform them that a meeting will take place. As one engineer explained, "You can only say no so many times. You need to think carefully before you say the word 'no.' And when you do, it had better be for a good reason."

The engineers and project team leaders may be asked for their input as to the time of a meeting, but even those responses are hardly taken into account. One Thursday afternoon, the software manager informed his direct reports that they would meet the following Saturday. He asked if anyone had a preference for the time. One employee said that he would prefer the afternoon. The software manager responded, "Oh, you have baby-sitting responsibility in the morning?" The employee answered, "This is true," and then immediately added, "Don't worry about my preference, I can easily hire a baby-sitter." He seemed embarrassed that he had expressed a preference. In the end, his request was ignored, and the meeting was set for 8 A.M. on Saturday morning, which is exactly when the employee's wife worked.

Another common phenomenon is for meetings to run late. During one meeting I attended, it became clear around 4:30 P.M. that they would never be able to get through all of the agenda items by 5 P.M. At this point the manager leading the meeting suggested that they extend the meeting until 7 P.M. He asked the obligatory "Will that be OK with everyone?" One woman agreed but then left the room immediately following the decision, to make alternative arrangements for her children. When these situations arise, sometimes employees can make alternative arrangements at home at the last minute. Other times, however, they simply cannot and must leave as planned, risking the consequences at work, both in terms of negative stereotypes and missed information or decisions that may affect them.

Requests to individuals. Sometimes, an employee is requested to work extra hours. When managers make these requests, employees have little choice but to agree if they want to be perceived as productive and committed. Managers become familiar with those who respond to such requests and return to them with future requests.

Managers register the conditions under which their subordinates are most likely to consent but also expect them to respond whenever they are needed. For example, one engineer will work all night any week night but prefers not to work on the weekends. According to his manager: "I try to monopolize on [this engineer's] willingness to work during the week. . . . I don't refrain from asking over the weekend. . . . I just know that it is better not to. . . . Recently, I called him at home on a Saturday and had to go through the third degree from his wife before she would even put him on the phone . . . but he still helped. . . . In general, it is easier to ask on a weekday, but he will always say yes if I need him." Such willingness to respond characterizes the organizationally successful Ditto employee. Employees tend to get caught in a cycle either spiraling upward or downward: the more often one accepts managers' requests, the more one is asked to do; the less often one accepts these requests, the less one is asked to do. Typically, only those who accept extra work are rewarded.

Reviews and internal deadlines. A less direct way of imposing control on engineers and project team leaders is through the scheduling of reviews and release dates to assesses progress. Managers at the division level and above set a series of reviews for the product. The threat to group members is that if they fail a review, the product may be canceled and their employment may be subject to question. Beyond the reviews for the product, the software group also has a set of internal deadlines for which it is supposed to release portions of the software for further development by other members of the product team. Failure to meet one of these deadlines results in a highly visible failure to meet expectations.

Prior to both reviews and internal deadlines, managers expect employees to increase their work hours. Usually, an extra investment of time is required because employees are worried about falling short of the goals they are expected to achieve. Even if they, personally, are on schedule, however, employees are expected to put in extra effort around these times. One project team leader said about an engineer, "He may have been done with his work, but the expectation is that he . . . help the group during a crunch time. Before a major release we are all supposed to pitch in." Engineers seem to agree that if there is a deadline that involves their work, it is their responsibility to stay late. As one engineer put it, "When it is crunch time, no one refuses. You know you just have to do it."

Managers tend to take advantage of this norm. They perpetuate what can be labeled a crisis mentality to appeal to individuals' sense that they must be present under these circumstances. Referring to the software manager, one engineer said, "If the work is due in two days he will tell us it is due in one, just to ensure we get it done." If the team slips behind schedule, additional reviews and deadlines are often inserted in the schedule to further intensify the pressure on group members. As the division vice president reckoned at one point in the product's development, "I fear we are slipping behind schedule so I added a review. . . . This will give me a better sense of what is going on. . . . It also makes people work harder. People work harder when there are deadlines coming up." Also common is for managers to assign work based on a "real" deadline, but if the deadline changes, managers do not inform their subordinates. Rather, managers leave engineers under the impression that the original deadline remains intact, to ensure that the work is completed. One engineer spoke about a project he worked on:

> Monday morning we were given notice that something was due for a senior manager at 3 P.M. on Tuesday. Three of us stayed all night. I grabbed the output from the printer and ran to our 12 P.M. meeting on Tuesday, only to find out that yesterday afternoon our 3 P.M. deadline had been indefinitely delayed. . . . When I asked why no one had told us, he [referring to his manager] just said, "We are going to have to do the work some time, so it is better to have gotten it done."

Managers use deadlines as a way of maintaining a high level of work intensity. They set dates on which work is due without consulting the engineers, who often regard these dates as arbitrary and unfair.

Restricting vacations. Another way of imposing boundary control is to limit the times during which it is acceptable for employees to take vacations. Despite the three to six weeks of vacation that group members are entitled to each year, few of them use all of their vacation time. Managers pressure subordinates not to take vacation during periods of crisis. Yet slow periods are rare and hard to predict. As one engineer explained, "I would like to take a vacation. . . . I have not had a vacation in a year. But to take a vacation would require I plan ahead, and with a sense of urgency, that is impossible . . . vacations are not the norm around here."

Vacations, if planned, tend to be delayed, canceled, or aborted. Employees try to plan vacations strategically to follow major deadlines. The expectation is that, following a deadline, the demands at work should temporarily slow down. The schedule tends to slip, however, and well-planned vacations often end up occurring at critical times, making them highly problematic from managers' perspectives. As a result, employees feel they must cancel their vacations at the last minute. According to one engineer, his manager told him, "If I insisted on going, I should consider shortening my vacation by a week." This engineer further explained, "When you are told to think about something, that means you better do it. If you decide not to listen, you risk being scorned by your manager and may even be called back early." One engineer's experience exemplifies the reality of this assessment. He, his wife, and their two young children scheduled a family trip four months in advance. Although they were supposed to leave Thursday night for ten days, crises at work prevented them from leaving until Saturday afternoon, by which time the engineer's wife had grown impatient. On Sunday, the engineer received a call that he was needed back in the office. Someone else on the project team could have solved the problem, but since everyone was dealing with crises, it was more efficient, from his manager's perspective, to bring this engineer back rather than use anyone else's time. He took the first plane back Monday morning. He spent three days in the office, while his wife vacationed with their two young children. According to the engineer, "Luckily, she was at home with her parents, who could help with the children . . . otherwise, I would have had a real dilemma leaving her to return to work. . . . She certainly would have made it more difficult for me to go."

Training. Requiring that engineers spend extended periods in training to advance their careers is a further way of imposing control on their time. For example, after receiving a promotion from engineer to project team leader, one is expected to attend a two-week management training course seven hundred miles away from the Ditto site I studied. Several years ago, one of the engineers in the software group declined the "opportunity" to attend training because she, her husband, and their three children (all under five years of age) were moving during that same two-week period. She requested to attend a training session at a later date. She has never been given the opportunity , nor has she ever been forgiven for missing training. Managers still refer to the fact that she declined training. They never mention her reason, only that she did not attend and, therefore, implicitly, that she did not display the expected devotion to Ditto. A second engineer who was recently promoted to project team leader was told that to continue her rapid career progress she would have to get an MBA degree. She was given two choices. She could spend six weeks at an intensive management training program off-site, close to six hundred miles from home. Or she could go to school part-time for the next two years, taking two classes a semester on top of her job at Ditto and her responsibilities at home for three young children. Clearly, it would have been more efficient for her to accept the six-week intensive program and finish sooner, but this option would have involved leaving her family for an extended period of time, and her husband was unwilling to take on this responsibility. Consequently, the woman enrolled at the local business school, and she struggles to manage her increased load.

Monitoring

In addition to imposing demands on subordinates, managers monitor subordinates' presence in a range of ways, including standing over them trying to "help," constantly checking their status and their plans, and standing back and observing the hours that they work.

Standing over. The most visible form of monitoring occurs when managers stay late at work to "assist" the engineers and therefore ensure that the engineers themselves stay late. One day, two engineers were struggling to solve a critical problem. They stayed late to work on it. The software manager also stayed late. According to the software manager, he stayed to help the engineers get the work done, but one of the two engineers explained: "He [the software manager) was slowing down the process. He should have gone home. It doesn't help us get the work done to have someone constantly standing over us. . . . We work best when we are left alone. . . . The managers just don't get it. They stand over us constantly asking how they can be of help. All they are doing is distracting us. They can help the most by not trying to help at all." On a different night, an engineer and his manager stayed late to solve a critical

problem. According to the engineer, "Around 9 P.M. when I complained I had a sore throat, he [his manager] encouraged me to work another hour. At 10 P.M., again I mentioned not feeling well, but it wasn't until 11:30 P.M. he suggested I go home and get some rest." To ensure that the work gets done, managers stand over their engineers continually asking about their status, offering to help, but pressuring them to keep on working.

Checking up. Managers also monitor engineers by frequently asking for a progress report, both verbally and in writing. Early each week, engineers must submit an oral update on their progress to their project team leaders. In turn, each Wednesday, the project team leaders present a written status report on their engineers' progress to the software manager. The software manager then provides a written status report to the senior software manager on Fridays and to the product manager on Mondays. In addition, the software manager asks people how they are doing every time he sees them. If he is concerned about their progress, he often seeks them out and inquires multiple times in a given day. As one engineer put it, "He [the software manager] increases the stress level by constantly asking how we are doing."

Furthermore, when managers are concerned about the progress of their engineers, they often question the engineers about their recovery action plans. For example, when one group was two days behind schedule, members were asked to write a memo explaining the slippage and stating their plan for recovery. After a 45-minute discussion with his four engineers, the project team leader drafted a memo that identified the cause of the delay and simply stated as a plan of recovery, "We will work two days overtime." The recovery action steps never involve rethinking the work processes but merely state plans to work more hours.

Checking-up provides managers with information on where engineers are and further pressures the engineers to work long hours. Moreover, engineers often end up feeling that they must commit to finishing work by dates and times that they know are unrealistic. In one example of checking-up, the software manager called one of his engineers at home. He wanted to know what had happened that night at work and when the engineer would be in the next morning. The engineer recounted:

> I would not have gone in until probably close to 9 A.M., but after he [the software manager] called I made sure to be there by 7 A.M. . . . What he said to me last night was: "I want to make sure we have our release ready for Sunrise in the morning," which is at eight-thirty, "because I want to be able to go in and say 'you're wrong, we have our release ready.'" . . . He [the software manager] always assumes that everything is going to go OK. And nothing ever goes perfectly smooth, especially when you try to rush something and get it done really quick. Then you always fuck it up and have to do it again. I don't think he realizes that. So he just assumed that if I came in real early and gave the code to John, and he made the proms, and we plugged them into the machine, and then they would be ready to go, and he could go to Sunrise at eight-thirty and say, "Here's the release." But, it turns out that we didn't have it working until when? . . . Eleven thirty or something like that. I knew it would never be ready by eight thirty—that would have taken a miracle.

This engineer, however, never mentioned his well-founded doubts to his manager. Rather, he simply agreed to arrive early, give it his best effort, and thereby display the expected level of commitment to the project.

Observing. Managers also monitor by standing back and taking note of the hours that engineers work. Engineers are well aware that they are being observed. They note that the division vice president walks around conducting "bed checks" to see who is still around at night. Moreover, managers themselves stress the importance of perception. According to one of the project team leaders, the senior software manager told him: "There is an advantage of being perceived as really killing yourself when you are first on a project. . . . He told me about the importance of perception. . . . He said perceptions mean a lot around here. It is important to be perceived as a person who will sacrifice personal life for work. . . . He specifically mentioned sacrificing family time for work as an indication of commitment." According to another manager, "A star performer is one who doesn't know enough to go home at night." One woman embodies the star performer. One day each week, she arrives at 2 A.M. and works straight through the day until 5:30 P.M. She does this because it impresses her manager. She explained: "[He] was really impressed when he ran into me at 2 A.M. one morning. . . . I used to just go to the kitchen table and use my PC, but after the reaction I got from my manager I decided it was important to do that early morning work in the office. . . . It is better to be seen here if you are going to work in the middle of the night."

At the other extreme, not being present usually creates a bad impression. With ten days to go on a major software release, two engineers stayed late one night. Their project team leader's boss, the software manager, stayed late to help as well. Even the senior software manager stopped in as he was leaving work around 6:30 P.M. to check on the team's progress. The project team leader, however, left at 6:00 P.M. His parents were visiting, and a family gathering was planned. He felt that it was unnecessary for him to stay at work: "There was nothing that I could do to help. I lacked the technical expertise that was necessary . . . so I left." According to the engineers, their project team leader's departure presented no problem to the team: "There is nothing that he could have done to help out. . . . His presence would have been more of a hindrance than anything." Nonetheless, the project team leader was accosted the next morning by the senior software manager, who questioned him about why he had not stayed late the night before to support his engineers. His response to the censure was not anger or defensiveness but, rather, guilt. He offered the senior software manager an apology. He remarked to me, "I am such a schmuck. I should have stayed around and done busy work. It is terrible that I left. It looks really bad. . . . If I had stayed, he [the senior software manager] would have seen me here." To the engineers, "being present" has little to do with performance or substantive output. All of the engineers felt there was no practical reason for their project team leader to have stayed. In fact, had he stayed, his presence might have slowed the team's progress. Still, from his perspective, leaving constituted a grave mistake. He feared that he would now have to live with an image of lacking commitment to the team—"I left them in a time of crisis," he said.

At the end of the calendar year the managers ranked software engineers to determine individuals' raises. The names of each member of the software group were listed, followed by a comment explaining each ranking. The comment following the engineer ranked first on the list read: "works 80–100 hours/week, top quality work." Similarly, the second on the list was noted for working 80–100 hours a week. Comments about others in the top included: "works days and nights" and "works 80 hours per week." In contrast, the comments about those at the bottom of the list included: "average contribution," "light work load," and "minimal contribution." Senior managers clearly notice the hours that the engineers work and use these observations as a criterion for ranking them. Moreover, the engineers know the range of raises given and therefore get a relative sense of where they stand in their managers' eyes.

Modeling Behavior

Managers expect the same behavior of themselves as they expect of their engineers. They work long hours, in most cases, longer hours than the engineers. Managers come in early, stay late, and work most weekends. The senior software manager, for example, typically works from 6 A.M. to 7 P.M. five days a week, plus at least six hours on both Saturday and Sunday. He makes it clear, "No one works harder than I do." Furthermore, when managers put in the time, they publicize their hours. They often refer to the hour at which they have done a certain piece of work or had a certain thought. The product manager, for example, will often refer to a thought he had at 4 A.M., when he was on the treadmill in his personal gym. The senior software manager often refers to the early morning and weekend hours he was in the office and remarks that no one else was there. One project team leader told a story about his chats with the senior software manager at 6 A.M. He emphasized that he, too, is in by 6 A.M. every morning. Managers point with pride to the long hours that they work. They often say, "I would never ask for anything I wouldn't do myself." This expectation translates into a tremendous number of hours spent at work.

Employee and Spouse Responses

All employees face boundary control, but analysis of the data reveals that their responses to it vary. Not all employees accept the boundary control imposed on them. Some resist it. Moreover, many employees

are married, and the demands of their work have consequences for their spouses. Spouses' reactions to the demands that ultimately affect them further influence how employees respond to boundary control. For married employees, it is not clear whether their own reaction comes first and in turn affects their spouse's reaction or whether their spouse's reaction influences their own initial reaction. What is clear is that different employees expect their spouses to play very different roles, and some spouses accept and others resist this role. Below I provide a description of employees who are "acceptors" and "resisters" of boundary control, as well as spouses who are "acceptors" and "resisters" of the role that results for them at home. Table 11.2 summarizes the responses of employees and the spouses I interviewed.

Employee Responses

Acceptors. Employees who accept boundary control make work their first priority, always trying to meet work expectations. One acceptor said: "The work is crucial, and I am willing to put in whatever hours the work demands." He continued, "It is not the company's job to manage crises. It is the individual's responsibility to accommodate." When confronted with a crisis, he commits all his waking hours to finding a solution. He arrives at work early in the morning and stays until 10 or 11 P.M. It is not unusual for him to work an 85- or 90-hour week. The stash of food, candy, and tea found throughout his office testify to his habit of sacrificing meals to enable extra periods of work. Another engineer characterized as an acceptor further exclaimed, "Right now at work, I need to be single-minded. . . . I must dedicate my life to this battle . . . and only when it is over can I celebrate."

Although the quintessential acceptor is one who commits fully to work, some are in dual-career relationships and have responsibilities at home. One woman does everything she can to care for her home and family without failing to meet the demands at work. During one two-week period when her husband was away, she was assigned to a short-term, high-visibility project. The project demanded extraordinary hours. For two straight weeks, she would leave work every evening at 5:30 P.M., pick up the kids from day care, feed them, play with them, and put them to bed. She said she would then take a

Table 11.2
Employee and Spouse Responses

Title	Employee (sex)	Acceptor/Resister	Spouse (sex)	Acceptor/Resister
Division vice president	Jed (m)	Acceptor	Pat (f)	Acceptor
Product manager	Dan (m)	Acceptor	Kaye (f)	Acceptor
Sr. software manager	Carl (m)*	Acceptor	—	—
Software manager	Zeth (m)	Acceptor	Pam (f)	Acceptor
Independent contributor	Stu (m)	Acceptor	Natalie (f)	Acceptor
Project team leader	Mike (m)	Acceptor	Kim (f)	Acceptor
Project team leader	Laura (f)	Acceptor	Rick (m)	Resister
Project team leader	Sam (m)	Resister	Betsy (f)	Acceptor
Engineer	Mathew (m)*	Acceptor	—	—
Engineer	Max (m)	Acceptor	NA	NA
Engineer	Andy (m)	Acceptor	NA	NA
Engineer	Jane (f)	Resister	Dan (m)	Acceptor
Engineer	Sarah (f)	Resister	Tom (m)	Acceptor
Engineer	Larry (m)	Resister	Lisa (f)	Resister
Engineer	Scott (m)	Resister	Heather (f)	Resister
Engineer	Kate (f)	Resister	Paul (m)	Resister
Engineer	Jim (m)*	Resister	—	—
Engineer	David (m)	Resister	NA	NA
Engineer	John (m)	Resister	NA	NA
Engineer	Jeff (m)	Resister	NA	NA

* Indicates married person whose spouse I did not interview.

short nap and get up around 12 A.M. to start the next day's work. She worked at home until 5 A.M. and then would get the kids up, dressed, fed, and off to day care before coming into the office to work until 5:30 P.M. She did this repeatedly, never mentioning to her manager that her husband was away. Such behavior is characteristic of acceptors.

Resisters. In contrast to acceptors, who may never get away from their work, employees who resist boundary control make themselves unavailable to work at certain times. Some who resist boundary control do so because they simply do not have a burning desire to succeed, like one of the male engineers. who is single and has few responsibilities outside of work. He works regularly from 7:30 A.M. to 4:30 P.M. with a half-hour for lunch. He is very focused on his work while he is at work and spends little time conversing with colleagues, but he leaves regularly at 4:30 P.M. He is not on the fast track, nor does he aspire to be. For him, work is a job, not a step on a career ladder.

Others who resist boundary control do so because they have demands on their time outside of work that they consider more im-

portant. According to one female engineer, "I work because I want to be intellectually stimulated during the day. . . . I want to have colleagues to talk to. . . . I would go crazy staying home all the time." Her primary commitment, however, is to her family. She will not work unlimited hours. She takes her work seriously and will occasionally stay late if the situation is desperate, but in general she works a 45-hour week. As she says, "Family is my first priority."

In contrast to resisters like these engineers, who make sacrifices at work to have more time outside of work but resign themselves to the consequences, some employees resist boundary control because they perceive that they have no choice, yet they express frustration about their situations. These engineers often search for alternative ways of working, to make it possible to meet the demands of both a successful career and their responsibilities outside of work. One male engineer must leave work three days a week by 4:30 P.M. His wife works evenings, and she insists that he be home to care for their son before she leaves. When he is behind schedule, he works Saturdays instead of Mondays to increase his productivity. According to this man, "Saturdays are at least twice as productive as Mondays . . . there are no interruptions." One female engineer also tried to create an alternative way of working so that she could limit her hours and still meet her work demands. Six months before I arrived, she was a project team leader. She created a rotating position such that one day a week one of her engineers would fill in for her. This enabled her to work from home on this day, saving two and one-half hours of commuting and providing her with uninterrupted time during which to work. Moreover, her group members each had the unusual opportunity to act as project team leader while she was home. As a result, they developed managerial skills, and the project did not suffer. Her six-month performance review noted that her group was on schedule. Managers, however, never acknowledged her innovation. Instead, just before I arrived, she was reassigned to a position as an engineer working with confidential data that could not leave the lab. She could no longer work from home.

At the end of the year, the two engineers who sacrificed work for family without trying to compensate each received a 3-percent raise, with which they were satisfied. The male engineer who tried to make a small change also received a 3-percent raise, although he had hoped for higher. In contrast, the female engineer who opted to use a flexible work schedule dropped from a rating in the top 10 percent of employees the previous year to the bottom 20 percent in the year of the study. She ended up receiving no raise. The major difference between her resistance and that of the male engineer was that he framed his change as temporary and benefiting the work, whereas she framed her change as permanent and benefiting herself and her family. Resistance, especially when motivated by a need to meet family obligations, hinders employees' recognition and promotability. These findings reveal the entrenched nature of boundary control and the costs to employees who try to go against the flow, Satisfying output requirements simply is not enough.

Classification of employees. Of the twenty employees I studied, ten accept boundary control, while ten resist it. Of the ten who accept it, nine are male, seven of them married, and the other is a married woman. Moreover, of the eight individuals in the top four levels of hierarchy (project team leader and above), only one is a resister. These numbers make sense. To succeed, one must accept boundary control; therefore, those who accept boundary control would be expected to be the most successful.

In contrast to the ten acceptors, ten employees resist boundary control. Of these ten, seven have resigned themselves to the fact that they must selectively resist certain of their managers' expectations if they are to restrict the time they spend at work. Five of them are men, three of them single and two married, and the other two are married women. The priority for three of these employees is family, for one it is other work responsibilities outside of Ditto, and for three it is simply lack of commitment to spending time at work. In contrast, the three other resisters (two men and one woman, all married) are more frustrated by the tradeoffs they must make. They want to succeed at work, but they cannot put in the necessary time. Two of these employees have family responsibilities, and the third is investing much of his time pursuing a Master's degree.

All acceptors share an ambition to succeed but not all of those with this ambition are acceptors. The frustrated resisters share this ambition, but they are unable to live up to the associated work demands. Neither ambition, nor gender, nor marital status, nor the existence of children can therefore explain whether an engineer accepts or resists boundary control. All of the acceptors and three of the resisters share an ambition to succeed. Nine of the acceptors and seven of the resisters are male. Eight of the acceptors and seven of the resisters are married. And four of the acceptors and eight of the resisters have children under eighteen.

To understand individuals' responses, it is important to consider the demands on their time outside of work. The five single employees I studied were male. Three lived alone, one had roommates, and one lived with his parents. Only one had a serious girlfriend. Although none of these single men felt major obligations to anyone else, it certainly could be the case that a single person would have such responsibilities (i.e. child care or elder care). For married employees, the division of labor at home has a profound impact on their ability to meet work demands. Some are married to a spouse who expects minimal amounts of help at home. Other spouses expect the responsibilities at home to be shared. I refer to spouses who accept the demands put on them at home, at whatever level those demands may be, as "acceptor" spouses. I refer to spouses who resist the demands placed on them as "resister" spouses. A full understanding of married employees' responses to boundary control requires considering the reactions of their spouses to maintaining the home and caring for children.

Spouse Responses

Acceptor spouses. One female spouse embodies the definition of an acceptor spouse. She is the mother of two and has a part-time job (three days a week) as a social worker at the university hospital. When asked what role her husband plays at home, she can tell many stories' about events her husband has missed, responsibilities he has shirked, and tasks she would like him to do. She says: "He used to be responsible to empty the dishwasher in the morning before he went to work. Now, even that is more than he can handle. . . . I used to try to force him to help around the house, but it would always result in an argument. Now, I don't even try. . . . I have decided it is just easier to do things myself rather than getting angry." Despite her resentment, she accepts these demands. This behavior is common for acceptor spouses. They accommodate the chaotic schedules of their spouses but harbor resentment with the distribution of tasks that results at home.

Although more acceptor spouses are female than male, not all are female. One man, for example, picks up his daughter from the baby-sitter, brings her home, makes dinner, feeds her, bathes her, plays with her, and puts her to bed, while his wife works. He loves his daughter and appears to be a committed, caring father, but he notes, "It gets hard having to be a single parent every night of the week." He says: "I love her [his daughter] and spending time with her, but sometimes it just gets to be too much. Sometimes I want some time to myself, time in the yard, time to finish all the projects that I want to do. . . . Sometimes I just feel cheated that I don't have a wife who has dinner on the table when I get home. . . . I don't really understand what she [his wife] is doing, but I always give her the benefit of the doubt."

Resister spouses. In contrast to acceptor spouses, who enable employees to accommodate boundary control, some spouses exacerbate the difficulty faced by employees who attempt to manage both work and family responsibilities. For example, one female spouse has two children, and she works part time. She expects her husband to be home at night and to do his share of the household chores and child care. "If he isn't paid for overtime," she insists, "he should not work it." Although both husband and wife agreed that her job was secondary, this assessment did not translate into his work ruling their lives. On the contrary, she established strict constraints on what she was willing to accept in terms of his work demands. In the odd crisis, he accommodates work, but he does not regularly make the accommodations made by other employees who are eager to succeed at work. Several male spouses set similar limits for their wives. One male spouse says:

> After 7:30 I am too tired to deal with the kids. I find being with them very stressful. I pick them up from day care and bring them home. I spend time with them until she [his wife] gets home but bed time is her responsibility. . . . I can do the things I do for the kids, but I am not their mother. These things should be a mother's responsibility. When she is not around I do them out of necessity. But when she's around she does them. . . . She makes sure to be home by 6 P.M. every night . . . otherwise we have a fight.

The female engineer in this case gets her children up, dressed, and ready for school. She also does all of the evening chores. Still, her husband resents that he is left to drive the children to school, pick them up, and spend an hour with them each night before she arrives home and takes over.

Employee Responses Revisited

Employees may be categorized as acceptors or resisters. Their spouses also may be categorized as acceptors or resisters. It is important to note, however, that the categorizations of employees and their spouses are not independent. For example, a married engineer may be a resister precisely because his or her spouse resists anything less than a major commitment of time at home. Similarly, a spouse may be an acceptor because his or her spouse, the engineer, already resists boundary control and helps at home to a level of satisfaction. Of the twelve spouses interviewed, eight were acceptors and four were resisters. Of the eight acceptors, six were female. Of the four resisters, two were female.

Employees and their spouses. Putting together the employees with their spouses, four types of married employees result, as shown in figure 11.2. I term them careerists, compromisers, jugglers, and rejecters. When both employees and their spouses are acceptors, I refer to the employees as careerists. The employee accepts the demands at work, and his or her spouse perpetuates this acceptance of boundary control by assuming much responsibility for household chores and child care. These spouses' responses enable the employees to devote themselves fully to their work. For example, one male engineer's wife supports his work and tolerates the burdens that result from his erratic work schedule. She goes out of her way to care for the home and asks nothing of him in return. Her response alleviates much pressure for him, allowing him to accommodate work demands. In fact, he is so caught up in responding to the demands of his work and the effects it has on him that he fails to notice the burden he puts on his wife. All careerists in this study are male and occupy the level of project team leader or above. Women employees who had an accepting spouse and themselves accepted work demands would fall into this category, as well, but there were no such women in this study, nor is this scenario common in our society.

Figure 11.2

Employee's experiences of boundary control.*

		Employee Response	
		Acceptor	Resister
Spouse Response	Acceptor	Careerist 5 Male 0 Female	Compromiser 1 Male 2 Female
	Resister	Juggler 0 Male 1 Female	Rejector 2 Male 1 Female

* The twelve employees represented in this figure include the ten married members of the software group whose spouses I interviewed, plus the product manager and the division vice president.

In contrast to the five careerists, who are in relationships in which both members accept boundary control and its repercussions, in three relationships, the spouse accepts boundary control, but the employee resists it. In two of these three couples, the employee is female; in the third, the employee is male. I refer to these employees as compromisers. It is possible that these spouses would accept the demands on them regardless of the response of their partners, the employees, to boundary control. Listening to these acceptor spouses, however, it sounds as if they accept boundary control precisely because their partners resist it and if their partners, the employees, did not resist it, the spouses would not accept their current set of responsibilities. It therefore seems not only to be employees' willingness to participate at home, but their spouses' expectation that they participate at home that results in employees becoming compromisers. For example, one of the male engineers accepts that he will have to make trade-offs at work if he wants to be with his family. His wife accepts the demands at home that result for her. She willingly takes care of much of the child care and household chores, but she says, "I know he [her husband) will always come home when I need him." She told a story about one day when she felt depressed because of a recent death in her family. She called her husband at the office, and he came home immediately to comfort her. She says, "I treasure the security of knowing he will always be there when I need him."

The compromisers all seem to experience pressure from their spouses not to work all of the time. Their responsiveness to these expectations helps alleviate ill feelings at home. Their responsiveness, however, may also negatively affect their career potential. A project team leader is the highest-ranked employee in this category, and he acknowledges his expectation that he will stop climbing the organizational hierarchy as a result. He says, "I would never be able to work these reduced hours if I still wanted to be a success at work . . . but I am happy at the level I have achieved." As would be expected, he did not receive a bonus given to top managers. The other two compromisers were engineers who both ranked in the middle 70 percent of employees.

In contrast to the eight employees married to acceptor spouses, four employees are married to spouses who resist the demands placed on them. One of the four employees married to a resister spouse still tries to accept boundary control. I refer to this type of individual as a "juggler," because the employee must balance a spouse's resistance and the responsibilities at work. This is a demanding position to put oneself into and leads to a high degree of anxiety about the trade-offs one must continually make. This employee's husband expects her to maximize her time at home and to assume primary responsibility for their children's care. She tries to appease him while also meeting and exceeding work demands. One weekend she had to finish some work, but she did not want to leave her husband at home with the children because, she says, "He would have been resentful." Therefore, she played outdoors with her children Saturday morning and afternoon, fed them dinner, bathed them, and put them to bed. Once the children were asleep (and her husband was sitting happily in front of the TV watching a hockey game), she felt she could go to work. As she recalled, it was about 8 P.M. She worked throughout the night and said she felt good about the work, since she had accomplished it without "sacrificing . . . her family." But she is tormented by the trade-offs that she must constantly make. She describes her priorities as:

> . . . wishy washy . . . I want both a successful career, and quantity time with my children. . . . I worry that I am not spending enough time with my kids. I am with them after work, but the time is so pressured. I feel like I need more time, more time at home and more time at work. . . . If I truly thought we had enough money on one salary, I would quit working, at least for a few years. But I am afraid that I would never get the same opportunities again. . . . Family is my first priority. My heart is at home and, as a result, my work is suffering. . . . I wake up often in the middle of the night and think to myself, it does not matter if you're a superstar; if you are not a premium employee. . . . I want to be less stressed and more happy. I just want to be average.

But then she admits, "I am too internally competitive for that. I cannot stand not being at the top." At the same time that she struggles to manage responsibilities at home, she achieved a lump-sum bonus at work, placing her among the top 10 percent of managers at Ditto.

Women who strive for success at work are expected to be a man's equal in a man's world (Gordon, 1991: 7). These women must be acceptors. At the same time, they are expected to do the majority of the second shift (Hochschild, 1989), which means that they likely have a resister spouse. Women striving for success therefore tend to be jugglers. The fact that only one woman in my sample was a juggler is not indicative of how common this scenario is among professional women in our society who strive for success (Swiss and Walker, 1993); however, it is indicative of how difficult it is to manage both a career and family and of the reason many employees search for alternatives.

I refer to the last category of employees as "rejecters." In these couples, both the engineer and the spouse resist boundary control. I found three rejecters in my sample, two male and one female. All three of these employees did more than just resist boundary control; they each tried to create an alternative way to accomplish work within constrained amounts of time. Two of their change efforts were described above. One of the male engineers worked Saturdays instead of Mondays in an attempt to accommodate his own ambition to succeed and his wife's expectation that he be home at night. Another engineer worked from home one day a week to balance work, a long commute to work, and her husband's resistance to family responsibilities. The frustration the three rejecters experienced led each of them to create new ways of working that enabled them to do the same work, or sometimes even more, in constrained amounts of time but none of them benefited from these efforts in terms of career progress, I found no rejecters in managerial ranks or headed toward such a position. Moreover, each of the three rejecters received little or no increase in pay.

Gender explanations. A further examination of the four types of married employees by gender reveals that all five careerists are male and that the only juggler is female. These findings corroborate the theory of gender ideology proposed by Hochschild (1989): men strive for success, and women reinforce their husband's effort by accepting responsibility at home. From Hochschild's theory, however, one would expect all men to be careerists and women who are ambitious enough to endure the responsibility and the stress of managing both a home and a career to be jugglers. All other female employees would be expected to resist boundary control. Despite some support for gender identity theory, not all of the data are consistent. Three of the six married male employees are resisters. Furthermore, of the four male spouses married to female Ditto employees, three would be classified as resisters to their own organizational demands, if one were to classify the men instead of their spouses (the employees). Of the twelve men included in this sample of married couples, half are resisters of work demands and therefore not careerists.

Moreover, as more married women enter the work force, the number of employees who are careerists will likely continue to decline, both because married women themselves are not likely to have an accepting husband and because as more married women are working, men are less likely to have a wife who assumes most of the responsibility for the household chores and child care. This inference is substantiated by the fact that the average age of the careerist in my study is 42 years old, compared with the average age of the non-careerist, which is 31 years old. While it could be the case that the careerists were themselves non-careerists when they were 31, evidence from them and their spouses suggests they have always been careerists. This implies that younger employees are not following in the footsteps of their seniors in terms of the roles they and their spouses play. Currently, men are more likely than women to be acceptors, not just because they are men but also because they are more likely to have an accepting spouse who makes it easier for them to be an acceptor. Marriage to an acceptor spouse—which currently is highly characteristic of men—is a critical factor in determining how one responds to boundary control. With the changing nature of relationships at home, there will likely be a shift in response to boundary control, with more individuals, both men and women, resisting it.

Discussion and Conclusion

This study describes a form of boundary control that has long been in existence but is becoming increasingly prominent and problematic. This form of control is best adapted to by employees who are either single with no responsibilities outside of work or are married to a spouse who takes care of the responsibilities outside of work. For these employees, all of whom were men at Ditto, the choice at least exists as to how they want to respond to boundary control. Most employees, however, do not even have this choice. Rather, they are married to a spouse who also works and will not relieve them of all of the home and child care responsibilities. These employees feel pressured from both sides: pressured to put more time into their work and pressured to share more responsibility at home.

There is some room for resistance at work. Those who resist, within reason, do not lose their jobs, but they do sacrifice reward and recognition at work. Nippert-Eng (1995) documented two strategies available to employees struggling to balance work and life outside of work: one strategy is to physically separate work and home life ("segmenting"); the other strategy is to intertwine work and home ("integrating"). In my study, resisters quite clearly adopt a segmenting strategy, conducting work at the office but not from home. Resisters often make statements such as: "I leave work behind me when I pass the guard booth on the way out the door. I have twenty minutes on the drive home to transition into family life. I don't think about work again until I pass the guard booth in the morning." In contrast, the married acceptors (although not the single ones) follow an integrating strategy: they describe working from home late at night after their children have gone to bed and on weekends. The evidence suggests, however, that regardless of how individuals organize their lives, only a relatively small number are in life situations that enable them to comply fully with work demands. . . .

To alter a control system so deeply ingrained in the work culture requires challenging widely shared assumptions. Senior managers who work long hours because they assume that long hours lead to better performance might alter their behavior if provided with enough compelling evidence to convince them that their current actions do not lead to the best performance, by themselves or those they manage. They would likely be difficult to convince, however, given that they have climbed to the top by acting in the very way that is suddenly being subject to question. Moreover, at lower levels, where long hours are not only considered important in and of themselves but are perceived as a requirement of interdependent work and as an indicator of productivity, change would be even more difficult. Elsewhere, I have described exploratory studies with software engineers that indicate that despite the interdependent nature of their work, they don't all need to be present all the time to facilitate each other's work. I found that structuring work so that large blocks of time are set aside for individuals to work independently improved the organization's productivity (Perlow, 1999). For these blocks of time, it should not matter where individuals work or when they put in this time. To address the requirement that everyone doing interactive and collaborative work be present at all times, therefore, should not involve changing the nature of the work but, rather, only the perception that to best complete this type of work everyone needs to be present at all times. Changing the way people are evaluated, however, would be more complicated. Alternative ways of assessing people's output would need to be established. If further evidence is found to support the claim that long hours hinder productivity (Perlow, 1997), then at least managers should have an incentive to help identify these alternatives.

Finally, while altering boundary control would require deep-seated cultural change, such change would have potential implications for resolving conflicts between work and family (Rapoport and Bailyn, 1996; Perlow, 1997). Because work-family conflict is usually conceptualized as an individual-level problem of managing work and family responsibilities, solutions provide ways to help individuals cope. Increasing numbers of corporations are implementing work-family policies (e.g., flex-time, flex-place, job sharing, and part-time work) to ease the burden for those who are trying to balance work and family (Levitan and Conway, 1990; Ferber and O'Farrell, 1991; Schwartz, 1992). These policies help employees manage the demands resulting from boundary control. Ditto, as a company, has a set of progressive human resource policies that provides employees with opportunities to alter their work schedules in multiple ways. Yet, despite the best of intentions, knowledge workers who take advantage of these policies often suffer in terms of career progress (Shamir and Salomon, 1985; Perin, 1991; Bailyn, 1993). The problem is that these options enable knowledge workers to resist boundary control, but they do nothing to change managers' perceptions about employees who do resist.

Note

1. This research was conducted in conjunction with a larger project sponsored by the Ford Foundation. Team members included Lotte Bailyn, Deborah Kolb, Susan Eaton, Joyce Fletcher, Maureen Harvey, Robin Johnson, and Rhona Rapoport, as a consultant.

References

Bailyn, Lotte. 1985. "Autonomy in the industrial R&D lab." *Human Resource Management*, 24: 129–146.

———. 1993. *Breaking the Mold*. New York: Free Press.

Bailyn, Lotte, Rhona Rapoport, Deborah Kolb, and Joyce Fletcher. 1996. "Relinking work and family: A catalyst for change." Sloan School of Management Working Paper #3892–96.

Barley, Stephen R. 1988. "On technology, time and social order: Technically induced change in the temporal organization of radiological work." In Frank Dubinskas (ed.), *Making Time*: 123–169. Philadelphia: Temple University Press.

Barley, Stephen R., and Gideon Kunda. 1992. "Design and devotion: Surges of rational and normative ideologies of control in managerial discourse." *Administrative Science Quarterly*, 37: 363–399.

Barley, Stephen R., and Julian Orr. 1997. *Between Craft and Science: Technical Work in the United States*. Ithaca, NY: ILR Press.

Bell, Daniel. 1973. *The Coming of Post Industrial Society*. New York: Basic Books.

Bendix, Reinhard. 1956. *Work and Authority in Industry*. Berkeley: University of California Press.

Bennis, Warren. 1985. "Foreword." In Douglas McGregor (ed.), *The Human Side of Enterprise*: iv–viii. New York: McGraw-Hill.

Bluedorn, Allen C., and Robert B. Denhardt. 1988. "Time and organizations." *Journal of Management*, 14: 299–320.

Christopherson, Susan. 1991. "Trading time for consumption: The failure of working hours reduction in the United States." In Karl Hinrichs, William Roche, and Carmen Sirianni (eds.), *Working Time in Transition*, 7: 171–187. Philadelphia: Temple University Press.

Clark, Peter. 1985. "A review of the theories of time and structure for organizational sociology." In S. B. Bacharach and S. M. Mitchell (eds.), *Research in the Sociology of Organizations*, 4: 35–79. Greenwich, CT: JAI Press.

Coser, Lewis A. 1974. *Greedy Institutions*. New York: Free Press.

Czarniawska-Joerges, Barbara. 1989. *Economic Decline and Organizational Control*. New York: Praeger.

Dertouzos, Michael L., Richard K. Lester, Robert M. Solow, and the MIT Commission on Industrial Productivity. 1989. *Made in America*. Boston: MIT Press.

Drucker, Peter F. 1989. *The New Realities*. New York: Harper & Row.

Edwards, Richard C. 1979. *Contested Terrain*. New York: Basic Books.

Etzioni, Amitai. 1961. *A Comparative Analysis of Complex Organizations*. New York: Free Press.

Ferber, Marianne A., and Brigid O'Farrell. 1991. *Work and Family: Policies for a Changing Work Force*. Washington, DC: National Academy Press.

Fine, Gary A. 1990. "Organizational time: Temporal demands and the experience of work in restaurant kitchens." *Social Forces*, 69: 95–114.

Gordon, Suzanne. 1991. *Prisoners of Men's Dreams*. Boston: Little, Brown.

Handy, Charles. 1989. *The Age of Unreason*. Boston: Harvard Business School Press.

Hayghe, Howard V., and Stella W. Cromartie. 1991. "Working woman. A chart book." U.S. Department of Labor, Bureau of Labor Statistics, August, Bulletin 2385.

Hochschild, Arlie R. 1983. *The Managed Heart*. Berkeley: University of California Press.

———. 1989. *The Second Shift*. New York: Avon Books.

Kanter, Rosabeth M. 1977. *Men and Women of the Corporation*. New York: Basic Books.

Kidder, Tracy. 1981. *The Soul of a New Machine*. New York: Avon Books.

Kunda, Gideon. 1992. *Engineering Culture*. Philadelphia: Temple University Press.

Landes, David S. 1983. *Revolution in Time*. Cambridge, MA. Harvard University Press.

Lawler, Edward E., III. 1986. *High Involvement Management*. San Francisco: Jossey-Bass.

Levitan, Sar A., and Elizabeth A. Conway. 1990. *Families in Flux: New Approaches to Meeting Workforce Challenges for Child, Elder, and Health Care in the 1990s*. Washington, DC: Bureau of National Affairs.

Meiskins, Peter F., and James M. Watson. 1989. "Professional autonomy and organizational constraint: The case of engineers." *Sociological Quarterly*, 30: 561–585.

Nippert-Eng, Christina E. 1995. *Home and Work*. Chicago: University of Chicago Press.

Ouchi, William G. 1977. "The relationship between organizational structure and organizational control." *Administrative Science Quarterly*, 22: 95–113.

———1980. "Markets, bureaucracies, and clans." *Administrative Science Quarterly*, 25: 129–141.

Ouchi, William G., and Mary Ann Maguire. 1975. "Organizational control: Two functions." *Administrative Science Quarterly*, 20. 559–569.

Owen, John D. 1979. *Working Hours*. Lexington, MA: Lexington Books.

Perin, Constance. 1991. "The moral fabric of the office: Panopticon discourse and schedule flexibilities." P.S. Tolbert and S.R. Barley (eds.), *Research in the Sociology of Organizations*, 8: 241–268. Greenwich, CT: JAI Press.

Perlow, Leslie A. 1997. *Finding Time: How Corporations, Individuals and Families Can Benefit from New Work Practices*. Ithaca, NY: Cornell University Press.

———. 1999. "The time famine: Towards a sociology of work time." *Administrative Science Quarterly*, vol. 44 (forthcoming).

Rapoport, Rhona, and Lotte Bailyn. 1996. *Relinking Life and Work: Toward a Better Future*. New York: Ford Foundation.

Rock, Howard. 1988. "Independent hours: Time and the artisan in the new republic." In Gary Cross (ed.), *Worktime and Industrialization: An International History*, 2: 21–39. Philadelphia: Temple University Press.

Savage, Charles M. 1990. *Fifth Generation Management*. Digital Press.

Schor, Juliet B. 1991. *The Overworked American*. Basic Books.

Schwartz, Felice N. 1992. *Breaking with Tradition*. New York: Warner Books.

Shamir, Boas, and Irving Salomon. 1985. "Work at home and the quality of working life." *Academy of Management Review*, 10: 455–464.

Silvestri, George, and John Lukasiewicz. 1991. "Occupational employment projections." *Monthly Labor Review*, November: 64–94.

Stehr, Nico. 1994. *Knowledge Societies*. London: Sage.

Swiss, Deborah J., and Judith P . Walker. 1993. *Women and the Work/Family Dilemma: How Today's Professional Women Are Finding Solutions*. New York: Wiley.

Thompson, E. P. 1967. "Time, work-discipline and industrial capitalism." *Past and Present*, 38: 56–97.

Van Maanen, John, and Gideon Kunda. 1989. "Real feelings: Emotional expression and organizational culture." In L. L. Cummings and B. M. Staw (eds.), *Research in Organizational Behavior*, 11: 43–103. Greenwich, CT: JAI Press.

Walton, Richard E. 1985. "From control to commitment in the workplace." *Harvard Business Review*, March-April: 77–84.

Whalley, Peter. 1986. *The Social Production of Technical Work*. Albany: State University of New York Press.

Whyte, William H., Jr. 1956. *The Organization Man*. New York: Simon and Schuster.

Wilkins, Alan L., and William G. Ouchi. 1983. "Efficient cultures. Exploring the relationship between culture and organizational performance." *Administrative Science Quarterly*, 28: 468–481.

Zerubaval, Eviater. 1981. *Hidden Rhythms*. Chicago: University of Chicago Press.

Zuboff, Shoshana. 1988. *In the Age of the Smart Machine*. New York: Basic Books.

Zussman, Robert. 1985. *Mechanics of the Middle Class*. Berkeley: University of California Press.

Chapter 12
An Alternative to Bureaucratic Impersonality and Emotional Labor

Bounded Emotionality at The Body Shop

Joanne Martin, Kathleen Knopoff, and Christine Beckman

Issues of control and coordination of work are central themes in this study of The Body Shop International, a multinational cosmetics giant. The authors explore whether it is possible to sustain a successful organization on the basis of principles that run counter to traditional bureaucratic methods of administration. Are true alternatives confined to small, nonprofit organizations, or can they also be successful in a large, for-profit company?

The Body Shop was founded by a woman and had a disproportionately high percentage of women in its managerial ranks. In addition, its core values included a commitment to doing business differently. All of these factors were key ingredients in the company's ability to eschew the norms of impersonality that mark most large, bureaucratic enterprises and replace them with what the authors refer to as "bounded emotionality." Does bounded emotionality represent a positive alternative to traditional bureaucratic forms of organization or does it signify the possibility of even greater degrees of control over employees?

People constantly experience emotions, yet in organizational theory, as in organizational life, the exploration of emotions has been largely deemphasized, marginalized,

or ignored. Impersonal criteria for making decisions and restraints on emotional expression at work have long been the hallmarks of bureaucracy (e.g., Weber, 1946, 1981). Recent work has broken this emotional taboo: explaining how certain organizations require the expression of particular emotions at work to maximize organizational productivity, an aspect of job performance that has been labeled emotional labor (Hochschild, 1983). Van Maanen and Kunda (1989) and Turner (1986) have described the displays of enthusiasm and loyalty required in some corporate cultures. Hochschild (1983) and Sutton and his colleagues (e.g., Sutton and Rafaeli, 1988; Sutton, 1991) have explored discrepancies between outward behavior and inward feelings experienced by smiling flight attendants and nasty bill collectors. In contrast, feminist organizational theorists have taken a focus on emotions one step closer to a kind of personal authenticity, arguing that expression of a wider range of emotions at work (labeled bounded emotionality) is desirable, not to enhance productivity but to foster the psychological well-being of organizational members and their families (Mumby and Putnam, 1992; Putnam and Mumby, 1993; Meyerson, 1998).

This paper explores this last, feminist approach to emotional expression in organizations. While these ideas have emerged from the study of small, usually nonprofit organizations, we examine whether bounded emotionality is feasible in the large, for-profit firms that dominate contemporary industrialized societies. We also ask if bounded emotionality in these contexts is desirable, from employees' points of view, or if it is yet another, more intimate and powerful form of organizational control. More generally, as the bureaucratic form proliferates across the industrialized landscape (e.g., DiMaggio and Powell, 1983), these organizations seek to enhance their efficiency and chances for survival through such mechanisms as hierarchy, division of labor, and impersonal, apparently unemotional, and deindividualized "rule by rules" (Weber, 1946, 1981; Ritzer, 1996). This paper focuses on one of these mechanisms, the management of emotion, and asks whether it is possible for a large organization, struggling to profit and grow in a highly competitive marketplace, to find new ways of incorporating emotional expression into organizational life. In the domain of emotions, is the isomorphism of bureau-

Table 12.1

Comparison of Traditional Bureaucratic, Normative, and Feminist Types of Organizations

Dimensions—Degree to which:	Traditional bureaucratic	Normative	Feminist*
Hierarchy is emphasized	High: Hierarchical; authority at the top.	Low: Relatively egalitarian; authority within collective.	Low: Egalitarian; authority dispersed throughout organization.
Division of labor is formal and specialized	High: Formalized; specialized.	Low: Informal; nonspecialized.	Low: Informal; nonspecialized.
Employment is based on expertise	High: Employment based on technical qualifications; previous thorough training in a specialized area; little or no job rotation.	Low: Employment based on skills and knowledge; training on the job; job rotation.	Low: Employment based on commitment to feminist agenda; training on the job; job rotation.
Jobs are segregated by gender	High: Not explicitly addressed, but norm is high segregation by job title; women clustered at bottom.	High: Not explicitly addressed, but norm is high segregation by job title; women clustered at bottom.	Low: Goal is minimal segregation; many feminist organizations all female.
Leadership style is authoritarian	High: Authoritarian leadership emphasized; autocratic.	Moderate-low: Authoritarian leadership de-emphasized; participative.	Low: Authoritarian leadership de-emphasized; participative.
Control is direct	High: Control is direct.	Low: Control unobtrusive, through internalized values.	Low: Control unobtrusive, through internalized values reflecting feminist ideology.
Decision making centralized and concentrated at high levels	High: Centralized decision making at higher levels; decisions final.	Moderate: Consensual decision making within groups; open to renegotiation.	Low: Decentralized decision making; open to renegotiation.
Corporate culture emphasizes competition	High: Competitive culture; status, rewards based on individual achievement.	Moderate: Cooperative culture; fewer status differences; rewards distributed across collective.	Low: Cooperative culture; status differences minimized; rewards somewhat equalized.
Work behavior determined by impersonal rules	High: Impersonal decisions; based on formal rules, applied consistently.	Moderate-low: Group-specific decisions based on group norms rather than formal rules.	Low: Individuated decisions, based on personal relations and formal rules that are open to renegotiation.
Emotion treated as acceptable form of expression	Low: Emotional expression generally discouraged, devalued as irrational.	Moderate: Emotion sometimes expressed, primarily for instrumental purposes.	High: Emotion openly expressed, personal and work related.
Work and private life regarded as separate	High: Private life presumed to be separate from work activity; private adapted to work.	High: Private life presumed to be separate from work activity; private adapted to work.	Low: Private life concerns are primary; work adapted to private rhythms.

* Feminist organizations share some, but not all characteristics of collectivist organizations (e.g., Mansbridge, 1973; Gamson and Levin, 1984; Jackall and Levin, 1984; Rothschild and Whitt, 1986; Whyte and Whyte, 1991).

cracy an iron cage, or is it possible to find ways of doing business differently, on a large scale?

Control in Three Ideal Types of Organizations

The process of organizing requires the coordination of employees' behavior. Because coordination may be imperfect (e.g., because of miscommunication or conflicts of interest), organizational members engage in various control strategies. Perrow (1986: 129–131) distinguished three types of control:(1) direct and fully obtrusive, such as giving orders, surveillance, and rules; (2) bureaucratic and somewhat less obtrusive, such as division of labor and hierarchy; and (3) fully unobtrusive control of the cognitive premises underlying action, in which the employee voluntarily restricts the range of behaviors considered appropriate. We draw on and extend this conceptualization of control to distinguish three ideal types of organizations: traditional bureaucratic, normative, and feminist. Table 12.1 summarizes the characteristics of each of these ideal types. As ideal types, these categories are theory-derived; actual organizations, including the organization studied in this paper, The Body Shop International, are expected to exhibit a mix of these characteristics.

The traditional bureaucracy described in table 12.1 is derived from a Weberian model, combining Perrow's first two, relatively obtrusive forms of control, direct and bureaucratic (e.g., Barnard, 1938; Rushing, 1966; Hall, 1968; Ouchi, 1977; Weed, 1993; Adler and Borys, 1996). Contrary to Weber's ideal type formulation, the expression of certain emotions (e.g., anger and competitiveness), is often condoned in traditional bureaucracies. The second, normative type of organization is characterized by Perrow's third, unobtrusive form of control, in which management has shifted limited powers to lower-level employees through such strategies as participative management, team-based production, less specialized division of labor, job rotation, consensual decision making, and an emphasis on cooperation (e.g., Tompkins and Cheney, 1985; Soeters, 1986; Bartunek and Moch, 1991; Eccles and Nohria, 1992; Barker and Tompkins, 1994). Normative organizations rely less on control by formal authorities and more on the internalization of values; control is achieved by employees' self-policing. Members actively take up management's or a group's decision premises and make them their own, seeing their own goals and those of the organization as coinciding (e.g., Ouchi, 1980; Perrow, 1986; Cheney and Tompkins, 1987). As table 1 shows, normative strategies preserve, in a modified fashion, many of the major dimensions of traditional bureaucracies. For example, the verticality of a hierarchy is somewhat flattened, while preserving many of the prerogatives of management's formal authority, and the division of labor between lower-level employees and top management is largely preserved, while at lower levels, some forms of specialization and direct supervision are reduced or eliminated. In a study particularly relevant to a subset of the data presented in this paper, Barker (1993) traced how teams of employees created a distinctive set of norms that were eventually transformed into formal, standardized rules of behavior.

Researchers disagree about the desirability of normative forms of control. Some praise the harmony, loyalty, and productivity that are seen to issue from value congruence (e.g., Ouchi, 1980; Schein, 1985), while others argue that normative control strategies, in spite of their apparent emphasis on more egalitarian, participative ways of doing business, are in fact dangerously effective ways of asserting and enforcing managerial control of employees' behavior through cooptation and false consciousness (e.g., Van Maanen and Barley, 1984; Tompkins and Cheney, 1985; Calas and Smircich, 1987; Alvesson and Berg, 1992). Willmott (1993: 541) argued that "under the guise of giving more autonomy to the individual than in organizations governed by bureaucratic rules, corporate culture threatens to promote a new, hypermodern neo-authoritarianism which, potentially, is more insidious and sinister than its bureaucratic predecessor."

Feminist theorists have challenged the assumptions of traditional forms of bureaucracy and proposed a variant of the normative approach. This feminist organizational form is outlined in the right-hand column of table 12.1. Feminist organizations seek to foster employee well-being, rather than to maximize efficiency or performance. They deemphasize hierarchy, preferring relatively egalitarian modes of organizing and consensual modes of decision making; leadership responsibilities are shared, often on a rotating basis; and specialized divisions of labor are either avoided or circumvented by the use of task rotation and training (e.g., Ferguson, 1984; Iannello, 1992; Eisenstein, 1995; Ferree and P. Martin, 1995). Many of these attributes of feminist organizations are shared by nonfeminist cooperative organizations (e.g., Gamson and Levin, 1984; Jackall and Levin, 1984; Rothschild and Whitt, 1986; Whyte and Whyte, 1991). Feminist organizations, however, rely on a specialized form of unobtrusive control that places unique emphasis on emotional expression and the primacy of private, as opposed to work, concerns.

Feminist Perspectives

Although The Body Shop International exhibits only a small subset of the attributes of a feminist organization, feminist theory elucidates the theoretical implications of our choice of organization for study and provides a critical theoretical context for our focus on bounded emotionality. . . .

In this paper, we draw on a positional version of feminist theory (Alcoff, 1988), according to which the socially constructed viewpoints of those who are not members of a dominant group in society can yield insights that are often inaccessible from other positions. Most organizations, particularly in the private sector, are dominated by men. Positional feminism suggests that if an organization has an unusual prevalence of women, this might make visible some phenomena that would surface less frequently and less obviously in a more conventional, male-dominated setting. Research on segregation by race in schools and by gender in organizations (see Pettigrew and Martin, 1987, for a review) suggests that approximately 15–22 percent minority membership is a minimum prerequisite for systemwide change, e.g., significant numbers of blacks elected to student council, women promoted to high-level positions. Because women are often clustered in lower-status positions, with little formal authority, we believe that in an organizational context, the presence of significant numbers of women in relatively high-status positions would be necessary to overcome the usual conformity pressures placed on a few token, high-ranking women executives. In addition, the support of men who share aspects of feminist ideology would be important. Thus, if an organization had unusually large numbers of women at the upper and middle levels of a hierarchy, and at least 15–22 percent at the highest levels, a different set of emotional norms might emerge. Alternatively, if bureaucratic norms of impersonality and emotional restraint are indeed inescapable elements of any large, hierarchical organization, then simply adding a larger proportion of women ("add women and stir"), even with a substantial proportion in high-ranking positions, is unlikely, by itself, to produce different emotional norms.

Traditional sex differences research has produced findings relevant to this argument. For example, women are more likely than men to engage in self-disclosure, express a wider range of emotions, and seek ways to acknowledge the inseparability of work and personal lives without letting work concerns take priority over family needs (e.g., Allen and Haccoun, 1976; Eagly and Johnson, 1990; Ely, 1995; Fletcher, 1995). A few researchers attribute such differences to biology, but most argue they are an effect of socially or culturally constructed differences, for example, differential socialization of men and women or differential recruitment and control mechanisms (e.g., Ekman, 1973; Acker and Van Houten, 1974; Zajonc, 1985; Harding, 1993; Kitayama and Markus, 1996). Positional feminism does not assume that all women fit the pattern of behavior found in these studies or that men do not. Rather, a positional feminism postulates that an unusual prevalence of women in an organization might constitute a promising milieu for innovative, self-disclosing emotional management practices to emerge among both men and women. Furthermore, such studies suggest that a woman leader might be somewhat more likely than a man to advocate and support the emergence of such innovative emotional practices.

Focus on Emotions

Traditional bureaucratic, normative, and feminist organizations differ regarding their orientations toward emotional issues (see table 12.1, last three dimensions of comparison: impersonality, emotional expression, and work-private life). Traditional bureaucratic organizations echo Weber in emphasizing control by impartial and impersonal rules that eschew the personal favoritism that can come with individuating solutions to problems (e.g., Hellriegel and Slocum, 1979). Traditional bureaucracies also attempt to keep the public domain of work and the private domain of personal and family life separate, so that if an employee experiences difficulties balancing work and family demands, responsibility for the problem and the solution lies with the individual employee, not the employing firm.

Critical studies of traditional bureaucracies have noted that although not all interactions are impersonal or unemotional, some emotions, such as anger and competitiveness, are generally condoned in bureaucratic organizations, while others, such as sadness, fear, some forms of sexual attraction, and vulnerability are taboo (e.g.,

Cockburn, 1983; Burrell, 1984; Stearns and Stearns, 1986; Adler and Adler, 1988; Van Maanen, 1991; Hearn, 1993). Further, different types of emotional expression are condoned in different contexts (e.g., around the coffee pot) at some times and not others (Fineman, 1993), When emotions are displayed for instrumental purposes, this is termed emotional labor. For example, gossiping hairdressers, deferential flight attendants, smiling retail clerks, and nasty bill collectors control their emotional expression to improve productivity, customer satisfaction, efficiency, and even profitability (e.g., Hochschild, 1983; Sutton and Rafaeli, 1988; Rafaeli, 1989; Rafaeli and Sutton, 1989, 1990, 1991; Sutton, 1991).

In some cases, emotional labor is subject to traditional bureaucratic forms of control, for example, when it is carefully monitored by supervisors. Emotional labor can also be monitored by customers, as when passengers ask flight attendants, "Why aren't you smiling?" (Hochschild, 1983: 127). When the need for emotional labor is internalized, it also functions as an unobtrusive normative control, particularly for employees who work outside the purview of supervisors. For example, Mary Kay beauty consultants were told, "You've got to fake it until you make it—that is—act enthusiastic and you will become enthusiastic" (Rafaeli and Sutton, 1989: 14). In these latter examples of emotional labor, normative control of expressed and felt emotion breaches the putative public and private divide—in the interest of the organization, not the individual.

Critical studies of emotional labor have decried the personal costs of this commercialization of emotion, particularly when what is felt is decoupled from what is expressed (e.g., Willmott, 1993; Fineman, 1996). Hochschild (1983: 20) drew attention to the loss of the ability to recognize private feelings that were not subject to instrumental demands for public emotional display. Flight attendants used the phrase "go robot" to describe the deadened emotional state they sometimes adopted when their private feelings and public behavior were strongly divergent. Van Maanen and Kunda (1989) discussed individual distancing, burnout, and phoniness, while Waldron and Krone (1991) found evidence of suppressed disagreements. reduced upward information flow, and loss of "voice." Despite this awareness of the personal costs of emotional con-

trol, an alternative to emotional labor has not been developed within this stream of research.

In contrast, feminist scholars have developed an idealized view of the role of emotions in organizations, unencumbered, for the most part, by concerns about productivity, customer satisfaction, or profitability (e.g., Marshall, 1984; Calas and Smircich, 1989; Hearn et al., 1989; Mills and Tancred, 1992; Wharton and Erickson, 1993; Meyerson, 1998). . . .

According to these feminist scholars, relatively unbounded emotionality at work should be enacted not for the instrumental gain of the organization (although this may happen) but to enhance the well-being of the individual organizational members (e.g., Hearn and Parkin, 1987; Hearn et al. 1989; Morgen, 1994; Gherardi, 1995). Some argue that work stress, for example, should not be viewed as an individual problem but, rather, as a political, organizational, and community issue that must be approached collectively, even if at some cost to the employing organization (Newton, 1995; Meyerson, 1998). This relatively unbounded feminist approach to emotional expression, we believe, would be difficult to implement in large organizations subject to the efficiency pressures of the competitive marketplace in which both for-profit and nonprofit organizations must operate.

Bounded Emotionality

Putnam and Mumby (1993) offered a modification of the feminist position on these emotional issues. They introduced bounded emotionality as a limited and pragmatic approach to the problem of emotional control in organizations (see Pauchant and Mitroff, 1992, for a different formulation of bounded emotionality). Mumby and Putnam (1992: 471) focused on work-related emotions, which they defined as "feelings, sensations, and affective responses to organizational situations," although they acknowledged that such work feelings stem from and affect emotions arising from one's personal history and home life. Bounded emotionality encourages the expression of a wider range of emotions than is usually condoned in traditional and normative organizations, while stressing the importance of maintaining interpersonally sensitive, variable boundaries between what is felt and what is expressed. At the risk of extending Mumby and Putnam's (1992: 471) ideas with a specificity they did not intend, bounded emotionality has six defining characteristics: intersubjective limitations, emergent (rather than organizationally ascribed) feelings, tolerance of ambiguity, heterarchy of goals and values, integrated self-identity, and community building.

Intersubjective limitations. Emotional expression in organizations should be bounded, Mumby and Putnam argued, because individuals should constrain emotional expression in order to function effectively in interpersonal relationships in ways that are sensitive to other people's emotional needs and competencies. In work settings, bounded emotionality should begin with a recognition of another person's subjectivity, acknowledging potential differences as well as commonalities and working within whatever emotional limitations both individuals bring to the relationship (Mumby and Putnam, 1992: 478; see also Putnam and Mumby, 1993: 51–52; Meyerson, 1998). Such limitations would include an individual's preferred modes and range of emotional expression. For example, one person might have a hot temper, needing to express anger before calming down, while another might be more restrained and self-contained, preferring public expression of a narrower range of emotions. Intersubjective responsiveness to such individual limitations, or preferred modes of emotional expression, would presumably require as a prerequisite some intimate knowledge of the other obtained through careful observation and voluntary self-disclosure.

Bounded emotionality presents a stark contrast to bounded rationality (e.g., Meyerson, 1998). Emotions are to be bounded voluntarily, to protect interpersonal relationships, while rationality is bounded (e.g., Simon, 1976) because of inevitable human limitations in information processing ability producing such shortcuts as cognitive heuristics, satisficing, and standard operating procedures. Mumby and Putnam's formulation of the bounding of emotional expression at work drew on feminist deconstructions of the false dichotomy between rationality and emotionality and delineated ways organizational theory and research has privileged cognitive functioning, leading to a neglect of emotional issues and an overemphasis on cognitive aspects of decision mak-

ing. To highlight these issues, Mumby and Putnam chose to frame bounded emotionality as a concept of resistance to bounded rationality.

Spontaneously emergent work feelings. The goal of bounded emotionality is to build interpersonal relationships though improved mutual understanding of work-related feelings, to foster community rather than to further the efficiency or productivity goals of the organization. Work feelings should emerge spontaneously from the performance of tasks; they should not be organizationally ascribed. Several studies show how emergent work feelings can surface in a manner that is not controlled by an organization's management or initiated primarily for the organization's benefit. For example, Morgen (1994, 1995) found that staff in feminist health clinics emphasized self-disclosure and openly discussed work-related and personal feelings. Cohen and Sutton (1998) found that, for their own enjoyment, hairstylists encouraged salon clients to talk about personal matters.

Mumby and Putnam (1992: 479) acknowledged that emotions can sometimes be bounded, both for intersubjective reasons and to serve the organization's instrumental purposes, simultaneously: "Organizations do not need to sacrifice or lose sight of technical efficiency, but they should embed instrumental goals within a larger system of community and inter-relatedness." This means that, in spite of their conceptual distinctiveness, bounded emotionality and emotional labor may be empirically difficult to distinguish. It may be that bounded emotionality will be more situationally variable, as the need to exercise respect for intersubjective limitations may vary depending on the individual and the context while emotional labor norms (e.g., you should smile) may be more stable. When instrumental concerns foster emotional labor, Mumby and Putnam argued, resulting felt emotions such as anxiety or frustration are to be expected and should, within intersubjective limits, be expressed in accord with bounded emotionality.

Tolerance of ambiguity. Tolerance of ambiguity is an essential component of bounded emotionality because it permits contradictory feelings, positions, and demands to coexist. Given the discussion above regarding the complex mix of feelings likely to emerge in situations in which emotional labor is required, the enactment of bounded emotionality necessarily entails some tolerance of ambiguity, including contradictions and irresolvable tensions (Meyerson, 1998).

Heterarchy of values. A heterarchy of goals and values is the opposite of a hierarchical ordering of value preferences. It suggests that no one set of values, even one that gives organizational priority to profit seeking, should take precedence over all others. Enacting value priorities must according to bounded emotionality, depend on individual preferences and context.

Integrated self-identity and authenticity. Mumby and Putnam conceptualized self-identity in integrated terms, assuming that a person has a single self that transcending context can be known. Without such a concept of self, the idea that bounded emotionality can facilitate the experience of being "authentically oneself" at work would be meaningless. This conceptualization of a unified self supersedes notions of mind-body dualism and, presumably, alienated or fragmented labor.

Community. One purpose of enacting bounded emotionality is to facilitate strong feelings of community among organizational members. Evidence supporting this contention has been found in a series of studies of bounded emotionality in feminist organizations, including a record company (Lont, 1988), a female weaver's guild (Wyatt, 1988), and dyadic tutoring teams at a university (Nelson, 1988). Studies such as these, of organizations exhibiting norms of bounded emotionality, have all focused on relatively small, usually nonprofit organizations.

Exploring the bounds of bounded emotionality. Rather than referring to an integrated self, we argue, drawing on post-structuralism and social psychological research (e.g., Flax, 1990; Kitayama and Markus, 1996), that the self is fragmented, composed of overlapping, nested identities that become activated in a context-specific manner, without assuming clarity or consistency over time. Definitions of the self and the potential for authenticity are important, particularly because this paper addresses questions of diversity in emotional preferences. Mumby and Putnam seemed to advocate bounded emotionality as a singular and more desirable alternative to the usual ways of organizing work, remaining silent about how to treat diversity. This silence raises

some questions. How does a group or an organization foster bounded emotionality without creating conformity pressures that undermine or counteract commitment to being sensitive to individual limitations and respecting a heterarchy of values? Some people prefer more impersonality and emotional reserve. If an ideal bounded emotionality is enacted, such differing subjectivities should be recognized, listen to, and treated particularistically, so that multiple patterns of reaction to bounded emotionality are treated as normal and acceptable (Meyerson, 1998). Alternatively, those who differ could simply be pressured to conform to accepted, bounded emotional behavior, suppressing, repressing, or subordinating their subjectivities. This would entail a departure from authenticity, whether one defines this in integrated or fragmented terms. Without enacting respect for those who differ, bounded emotionality may carry the risk of becoming simply a revised claim for conformity, albeit with a different definition of what is desirable. Further, if more women than men have been socialized to prefer emotional expressiveness and self-disclosure, then bounded emotionality may become a claim for conformity to reversed gendered standards of behavior that disproportionately disadvantage men. . . .

Method

The Organization and Its Employees

As part of a larger project, we studied a large, for-profit organization that had an unusual prevalence of women employees in the managerial ranks and endorsed an ideology that supports a subset of the elements of bounded emotionality. The Body Shop International, a publicly owned multinational firm in the cosmetics industry, is known for its commitment to using naturally based products, protecting the environment, and promoting various social and political causes. This paper is based on data collected between December 1992 and November 1993; during this interval The Body Shop employed over 6,000 people internationally. At that time there were just under 1,000 retail outlets in 42 countries, with new stores, both franchised and company-owned, opening every two to three days. Between March 1, 1990 and February 28, 1992, total revenues had risen from £208.1 million to £265.4

Table 12.2
Summary of Participants Interviewed

Area	Number interviewed	Status level	Gender
Body Shop International			
Board	3	3 Upper mgmt.	2 Female, 1 male
Environment	1	1 Upper mgmt.	1 Male
R & D	2	2 Mgmt.	1 Female, 1 male
Tours	1	1 Mgmt.	1 Female
Other	4	3 Mgmt., 1 clerical	2 Female, 2 male
Body Shop UK			
Retail	1	1 Upper mgmt.	1 Male
Retail operations (London)	2	1 Mgmt., 1 clerical	2 Female
Communications/BSTV	5	3 Mgmt., 2 clerical	2 Female, 3 male
Supply Company			
Board	6	6 Upper mgmt.	6 Male
Warehouse	7	2 Upper mgmt., 1 mgmt., 4 line	2 Female, 5 male
Human resources	1	1 Upper mgmt.	1 Female
Filling	4	1 Upper mgmt., 2 mgmt., 1 line	2 Female, 2 male
Colourings	3	2 Upper mgmt., 1 clerical	3 Female
Body Shop retail outlets			
Shops—franchise U.S.	6	1 Upper mgmt., 2 mgmt., 3 clerks	6 Female
Shops—company U.S.	4	2 Mgmt., 2 clerks	3 Female, 1 male
U.K. company shops	7	2 Upper mgmt., 4 mgmt., 1 clerk	6 Female, 1 male
Total	57	20 Upper mgmt., 21 mgmt., 5 clerical, 6 clerks, 5 line	33 Female, 24 male

million (Body Shop memo dated 9/16/92). This, then, is a large and successful private sector organization. Recent growth had been so rapid that current structures, job definitions, employee statistics, and even records of names and telephone numbers were unavailable or seriously out of date. Because rapid change both preceded and extended beyond the period of investigation, this study is an in-depth snapshot of a particular period in the company's life cycle, rather than a longitudinal study.

The Body Shop had recently been split into five separate "companies," with considerable decentralization of policies and control, to counteract perceptions that the company was becoming too large, impersonal, and bureaucratic. The five companies were: The Body Shop International (BSI), which oversaw much of the headquarters work as well as the international shops; Body Shop U.K. (BSUK), which was responsible for the retail shops in the U.K. and internal communications (such as weekly videos, public relations); Supply Company, which handled both production and distri-

bution; Colourings, which designed and marketed makeup products; and CosTec, which manufactured the makeup line. We studies parts of all five sectors, in the U.S. and England. . . . As described in . . . table 12.2, we conducted in-depth structured interviews with 57 employees, representing all five parts of the firm, including most levels of management; 16 (28 percent) of these interviewees held nonmanagerial positions. . . .

Although a detailed description of The Body Shop's formal structure and administrative policies is beyond the scope of this paper, some background will prove useful. Each of the five companies, at the time of the study, had its own board of directors, management structure, and personnel policies. The formal structure of each of the five units seemed, on the surface, to be traditionally bureaucratic, with superior-subordinate relationships, division of labor, and a few unit-specific standardized rules and procedures, most notably group interviews of job applicants, some form of performance appraisal, and some attempt to standardize rewards, holidays, and vacation policies, etc. It would be misleading, however, to delineate aspects of the formal structure of The Body Shop without also noting (here and in the data that follow) the extent to which these traditional bureaucratic controls were subjected to ridicule, disregarded, outdated, and subverted on a regular basis—by Anita Roddick, the company's founder and chief executive officer in 1993, her husband, Gordon Roddick, the chairman of the board in 1993, and other employees at all levels of the hierarchy in all five companies. Even counting employees was seen by some as bureaucratic; titles, lists, and employee statistics were often viewed as a low priority, so these kinds of information were difficult to find, often out of date, and sometimes in error. . . .

Several limitations of our focus merit mention. This is a study of a single organization. The company is similar to many others in its large size, financial solvency, international scope, and rapid growth. We also chose it because of the distinctiveness of its ideology and the proportion of women in its managerial ranks. Our goal was to examine an outlier—an unusual corporation—that would help us define the limits of what is organizationally possible given the efficiency pressures of a competitive marketplace. In addition, this is a cross-sectional study, rather than a longitudinal account that would permit us to address questions about the origin and evolution of bounded emotionality.

Participants

We gained entry into this organization through Anita Roddick. The lead investigator approached Ms. Roddick, suggesting an academic study of her organization, in part because it was so rare to find a large, successful, for-profit firm founded, managed, and staffed by such a comparatively large proportion of women. After an exchange of letters, we obtained permission and arranged the study. . . .

Data Collection

The first and second coauthors collected data from a variety of sources:

1. Archival materials. Prior to and simultaneous with data collection, we studied publications about the company, including *Body and Soul* (Roddick, 1991), numerous magazine and newspaper articles, teaching cases from various business schools, and scholarly writings (e.g., Gaines, 1993; Shrivastava, 1996). We also studied memos and other documents produced by the company, including both publicly and internally distributed materials. . . .

2. Observation. Observation took place in office spaces, manufacturing and distribution plants, and on shopfloors. We also attended "values meetings," a recent innovation designed to bring together employees from all levels of the company to discuss a perceived erosion of commitment to the values in the company's charter. . . .

3. Participant observation. One of the researchers worked without payment from The Body Shop as a short-term participant-observer in three different contexts. . . .

4. On-site structured interviews. In both the U.K. and the U.S., we prepared a list of people/job titles whom we wished to interview. We asked to meet employees from a wide range of areas of the company, requesting both highranking managers and nonmanagerial employees in each area. . . .

5. Informal conversations. More informal, less lengthy (less than one hour) conversations with the investigators occurred constantly on site—during tea breaks, in the cafeteria, and while informants were en route to other appointments. . . .

6. Lectures and seminars. Investigators attended various lectures and seminars given by Ms. Roddick and other Body Shop employees on visits to business schools and academic conventions in the U.S. These events included guest lectures in MBA courses, public lectures at conventions and at a university, and doctoral student/faculty seminars. . . .

Data Analysis

This data collection effort was part of a larger study of the internal functioning of The Body Shop. We began the data analysis by sorting the more than 400 pages of transcribed notes and documents by abstract, theoretically derived categories: the founders' histories, values, and goals; employees' attitudes about commercial issues, such as profits and stock price; political action campaigns locally and internationally; environmental issues; reactions to traditional bureaucratic policies and procedures, particularly regarding human resources issues; international practices; gender, including sexuality, bodies, beauty, and family issues; and a catch-all category focusing on contradictions regarding egalitarianism, hierarchy, and styles of management. We then worked, first separately and then jointly, sorting the data and inductively developing new and subdividing or discarding old categories, as suggested by proponents of grounded theory (Glaser and Strauss, 1967). One of the first new categories to emerge, unanticipated when we planned our study, was the topic of this paper, the management of emotions. . . .

Emotion at the Body Shop

Although the origins of a company's emotional management practices cannot be attributed solely, or perhaps even substantially, to a leader's actions or preferences, these can be contributing factors. For this reason, it is important to include in this account, as a piece of the puzzle, a statement from The Body Shop's founder, Ms. Roddick, on the company's goals and values, which were institutionalized in the form of the company's charter. Focusing on emotional values, Ms. Roddick, (1991: 17) explained:

> I am mystified by the fact that the business world is apparently proud to be seen as hard and uncaring and detached from human values . . . the word "love" was as threatening in business as talking about a loss on the balance sheet. Perhaps that is why using words like "love" and "care" is so difficult in today's extraordinarily macho business world. No one seems to know how to put the concept into practice. . . . I think all business practices would improve immeasurably if they were guided by "feminine" principles— qualities like love and care and intuition.

Ms. Roddick's use of the word feminine in conjunction with qualities like love and care signals an attempt to revalue emotionally expressive characteristics, such as caring, stereotypically associated with women. She does not explicitly endorse bounded emotionality, although love and caring are congruent with it. Her language, however, intertwines instrumental objectives with emotional concerns, making it difficult to determine if she is giving priority to emotional labor over bounded emotionality. Because a leader's rhetoric and employees' reality can differ, it is essential to examine how and if these ideas are enacted.

Enacting Bounded Emotionality

Although the company does not explicitly advocate discussing home, family, and friendship concerns at work, Body Shop employees switched easily between task-oriented concerns and the more intimate self-disclosures that provide a basis for bounded emotionality. This shifting, which blurred distinctions between public and private concerns, was evident in observations of employees at all levels of The Body Shop, in the relative privacy of tête à têtes and in the more public arenas of meetings, casual conversations among tour guides, or chatter in a manufacturing plant, as is evident in this field note:

> A woman [on the bottling line for Fuzzy Peach Gel Shampoo] who seemed relatively senior began telling me that her son had his Ph.D. in computer science. She described how hard he had worked to get it. She seemed very proud of him. She had been at The Body Shop for more than five years, but didn't seem very interested in discussing the company. She talked a bit about the washout [of the bottles] and how it was important not to get parts mixed up, but mostly we talked about her son. (Field notes, participant-observation on the bottling line, supply, U.K.)

Although the conversation described above was not deeply intimate or unusual, we regularly heard employees openly discussing a wide range of emotional topics, such as sexual orientation, violence in the home, sadness and joy about work related matters, as well as fears and psychiatric difficulties. Nonverbal communication was affectionate and intimate (although seldom obviously sexual), with hugs, kisses, and touching evident in both public and private settings, to an extent that surprised us. Although we cannot offer verbal quotations of this more intimate, individualized material because of our promises of anonymity, the following quote from a shop clerk suggests that intimacy was a way of life at work for many Body Shop employees: "There's lots of gay men and women in the company. In all the shops we know the ins and outs of each other's personal lives" (Frederick, company shop, U.K.).

Such self-disclosure provides a basis for assessing the subjective state of an individual. The next step in enacting bounded emotionality, according to Putnam and Mumby, is to take that information into account and adjust one's taskrelated interaction to fit the other's emotional preferences and limitations. At The Body Shop, for example, one employee was having trouble being filmed for a Body Shop video, "He fucked it up half way through, but he was so stressed out, I couldn't ask him to do it again. Really, I thought he would burst into tears" (Ursula, lower management, headquarters, U.K.). Some Body Shop employees described their working relationships in terms that suggested that such interpersonal emotional calibration was a habit. Sally, a middle manager in the marketing division (a pseudonym) in the U.K. showed her understanding of one of her coworkers: "William works in [our group]. He sees things in terms of right and wrong, numbers, prices, quantities. There is no middle ground. Figures are either right or wrong. A staff situation right now, however, has William agonizing. Difficult feedback is needed. It will hurt a person. William worries; should he give feedback now, before his vacation? He worries that he wouldn't be there after the feedback, when the pieces will need picking up. William has a high degree of sensitivity for a man." Ms. Roddick, known for her emotional exuberance, also understood the need for intersubjective sensitivity and sometimes restrained herself with particular employees, much to their relief. For example, at one of the values meetings, employees were discussing the ways Ms. and Mr. Roddick expressed appreciation for particularly good work, ranging from pats on the back to "Bravo-grams," which said simply, "Well done" and were signed by both Roddicks. One participant in the values meeting added, "There are also Bravo sweatshirts. Anita bounded up to me. I was afraid she'd embarrass me. But she never did. She'd give it [the sweatshirt] to you. Brilliant" (Paula, values meeting, headquarters, U.K.).

Another aspect of bounded emotionality involves recognizing a heterarchy of values, by allowing others to have a different set of values, or a different priority of values, than oneself not giving precedence to either person's view. This is a difficult objective to attain and even more difficult for a researcher to see. We did note, repeatedly, that Body Shop employees of both sexes tended to portray men and women as having stereotypically different emotional preferences and styles of interaction, differences that they tried to be sensitive to: "There are differences between men and women. Women have more emotion; [it's] not just hidden in some corner. Guys use delaying tactics while women say, 'Let's just go for it.' A complete over-balance either way is a problem" (Winston, upper management, headquarters, U.K.).

Strong emphasis was placed, throughout the company, on informal subjective assessments of performance, sometimes supplemented by more formal evaluation procedures. Managers, in particular, were assessed on their emotional competency, which included letting work-related feelings emerge spontaneously. Here, too, sex, or sexual stereotypes, were seen as creating a heterarchy of values and goals in the emotional domain: "I manage an all-female team. I was appraised as keeping well with women's emotions; I use empathy. Women have more tears, sensitivities, PMS [premenstrual syndrome], more personal conflicts" (Tim, middle management, headquarters, U.K.). Other, more individuated or less stereotypical ways of respecting a heterarchy of values reflected sensitivities to differences in job responsibilities, age, and personal circumstances.

According to Mumby and Putnam, these practices of intimate self-disclosure, blurring boundaries between public and private, showing sensitivity to another person's subjective state, allowing work feelings to emerge spontaneously, and respecting a heterarchy of values and goals should allow employees to feel a kind of authenticity at work. Some Body Shop employees reported such feelings:

> The Body Shop is nice because I don't feel like I have to fit some kind of mold. At The Body Shop I feel I can be more myself. (Lorie, shop clerk, company shop, U.S.)

> Emotion is not frowned on. People have no separate work personality. You are accepted as who you are. A "normal" corporate culture requires that you put on the personality of the company while you are at work. Not here. There are negatives [associated with this]; it makes management more difficult. There is no instant obedience. People debate, then agree about what needs to be done. There are also positive [effects]; people own the decision. Emotional work is sometimes a negative. There are always compromises.

It would be bad not to have it, though. (Winston, upper management, headquarters, U.K.)

It is difficult to discern from such remarks whether these feelings of authenticity are, as Mumby and Putnam asserted, reinforcing a sense of an integrated self. The prevalence of sex stereotyping suggests that it may be difficult to express some aspects of a fragmented self, particularly those aspects that contradict existing sex stereotypes. Taken as a whole, the data presented above suggest that many but not all elements of bounded emotionality were enacted at The Body Shop.

Co-existence of Emotional Labor and Bounded Emotionality

The presence of bounded emotionality does not mean that emotional labor was eschewed at The Body Shop. As suggested by many of the quotes above, as well as the theorizing of Mumby and Putnam, at The Body Shop, emotion was frequently managed for instrumental purposes, although whether such instrumentality took priority was often difficult to decipher. For example, shop staff were well trained to hide emotions that might impede a sale, using emotional labor techniques similar to those in previous studies of cashiers, flight attendants, and bill collectors:

A customer wanted to buy two identical baskets of Body Shop products. Two similar baskets had already been made up, but they were not exactly the same; the washcloths were different colors. Karen said, "OK, I'll make you one exactly the same." As Karen turned away from the customer, she rolled her eyes and smiled at the observing researcher. (Field notes, observation in franchise shop, U.S.)

Although this behavior could indicate bounded emotionality if the shop clerk were worried that the customer might find it difficult to deal with the clerk's feelings about the extra work being required, the researcher observing this incident was assured, in a subsequent conversation, that the clerk was simply feeling impatient with the customer's demands.

The emotionally charged atmosphere of The Body Shop, combined with the firm's attempt to avoid bureaucratic modes of operation, caused severe confusion. In this ambiguous environment employees had to show extreme forms of emotion, positive and negative, to complete essential tasks. As one manager told us, "It's amazing because there are loads of things that stink. It's not a sharp organization. You can't get things done easily. You don't just make a proposal. You have to pitch it—be emotional and argue it. There aren't clear channels and structure" (Martha, upper management franchise and company shops, U.K.).

Emotional, as well as financial rewards were used to express personal appreciation for work well done. Emotional rewards at The Body Shop were not just verbal; they were also physical: "Rewards are not just money. You can't bribe people. You'll lose it all. [People need] strokes, cuddles, hello, little things" (Diane, values meeting, headquarters, U.K.).

Emotional labor at The Body Shop was used to further the firm's political and environmental objectives, as well as its productivity-related concerns. For example, Ms. Roddick (1991: 170–171) explained how she used emotions to encourage employees to join in the company's various community and political action projects:

Whenever we wanted to persuade our staff to support a particular project we always tried to break their hearts. At the next franchise holders' meeting we put on a real tear-jerking audio-visual presentation, with wonderful slides of the children against a background of Willie Nelson's version of "Bridge over Troubled Water." And to enable members of staff to experience what we had experienced, the next edition of "Talking Shop," the monthly video distributed throughout The Body Shop organization, was devoted to Boys' Town and what we could do there. The response was a joy. Everyone wanted to get involved in raising money and sponsoring boys, and from that moment onwards the International Boys' Town Trust more or less became an integral part of The Body Shop's extended family.

Ms. Roddick also encouraged employees to use emotional expression for more conventional instrumental purposes: "Sally doesn't support women much. But she's the one who breaks down in tears with frustration. She can cry so easily. I told her it has to be used. I said, 'Here, cry at this point in the . . . meeting'" (Ms. Roddick, interview, researcher's house, November 17, 1993). Thus, Ms. Roddick and other Body Shop employees frequently and self-consciously used emotion management techniques for instrumental organizational purposes. This combination of emotional labor and bounded emotionality created a close knit, intimate community in which employees were deeply involved with each other and passionately committed to their work.

Impediments to the Implementation of Bounded Emotionality

Several factors made it difficult to enact bounded emotionality consistently at The Body Shop. Some of these factors stemmed from corporate policies, such as pursuing rapid international expansion, while others were environmental causes, such as characteristics of the labor market. Other difficulties stemmed from employees' internal states and preferences, which, in turn, were affected by their home circumstances.

Effects of growth. Expanding into 42 countries in a short time created enormous logistical problems that strained the company's ability to enact bounded emotionality. This can be seen in a conversation among employees at a values meeting in the U.K. headquarters:

> "We have no time to meet. The department is run by phone and deadlines."

> "You can find time."

> "We don't have time. We don't."

> "Individuals are islands, sidetracked because we're so busy. Sad."

> "This is a normal effect of quick growth."

> "In the old days, we were moving just as fast."

> "Everyone had the same pressure then."

> " And cared for each other more."

> "Where do the franchisees fit in?"

> "Who are they?" (*Laughter*)

> "We have to include them as part of the family."

The company's commitment to avoiding bureaucratic red tape exacerbated the confusion caused by growth. New hires proliferated, jobs were changed; and office-and desks were shuffled. Emotional sensitivity to another's emotional needs or work feelings required, at the very least, a knowledge of who people were and what they were supposed to be doing. This crucial information sometimes was hard to find. "[We need] pictures and names in departments. They would help us know who people are. Now we're so big we don't know the people in our own department" (Lisa, values meeting, headquarters, U.K.). Sometimes the open expression of emotion, in the midst of all this ambiguity, was clearly insensitive to employees' emotional need, as one employee reported: "I got called a fucking dick head the other day. I don't know people anymore. There's less friendliness. I'm scared that I know less than half the people. We need a system to build social introductions to know people—not just a voice on the phone, but a person" (Chris, values meeting, headquarters, U.K.). Under such conditions, face-to-face interactions among all or even many employees were impossible and knowledge of the subjectivities of others was scarce, as so many of the others were now strangers. The lack of interpersonal closeness due to the company's growth made it more difficult to follow through on commitment to the company's espoused values of caring and nurturance, creating instead conditions that fostered impersonality.

Time and financial pressures, caused in part by growth, began to erode many of the company's social rituals, which had provided occasions for building and enjoying a sense of community within the company. These events were important to the employees not only for their symbolic value but also as a way to renew connections with other employees not seen on a daily basis, as can be seen in the following discussion at a values meeting in the U.K. headquarters:

> "It's a shame that company day was canceled due to money, but if directors want to be close to average workers, they shouldn't cancel these things."

> "First thing we're knocked on the head when there are cuts."

> "There's a rumor that the Xmas party will be canceled; it's bad for morale."

> "Are social events important to our company?"

> "They would be better if people mixed up and do not stay with their own group."

> "We tried it both ways; staying with people you know is best. People change places anyway."

"Can I be mouthy again? Again on the friendliness issue. By doing it [socializing] by department we stay separate."

"It's easier to manage that way."

Although it is an achievement to enact the goal of bounded emotionality, even partially, in a large, for-profit organization, it is clear that The Body Shop's rapid growth placed strains on its ability to do so.

Limitations of the labor market. These problems were exacerbated by the influx of new hires. Growth created a need to expand the managerial staff at the headquarters in Littlehampton, on the coast of southern England. There was a shortage of qualified candidates with the requisite managerial-level retailing experience who lived within commuting distance. Experienced female managers were said to be especially hard to find. And, given that employment at The Body Shop entailed showing evidence of prior deep commitment to the company's political, community, and environmental agendas, the local labor market had been exhausted. Some of the new hires, especially at the managerial level, were criticized as lacking some of the political commitments, gender sensitivity, and emotional management skills of the "old guard" employees. When some employees complained about a growing lack of community at The Body Shop, they attributed it not to a lack of time or to the pressure of work to be done, nor to growth per se but, rather, to the influx of high-ranking men hired from more traditional retailing organizations:

> Now more senior males have been brought in [from the outside] and it is more male macho, more "go get it." Some individuals and some of these outside hires do not have empathy. [In contrast] take George [an old guard employee]. Janet says, "He's an honorary female." As the company has grown, gender comes in. Men haven't got the feminine instinct that the company was founded on. They are brought up through the company by osmosis. Caring and sharing are expressed physically in the company. People give a hug and a kiss. This is anathema for certain individuals; they tend to be those who were brought in during the last couple of years. (Tim, middle management, headquarters, U.K.)

Dealing with emotional diversity. Those Body Shop employees who found intimate self-disclosure and emotional expressiveness at work to be comfortable and desirable were often unsympathetic when other employees, such as some new hires, had different emotional preferences. For example, in response to an observation about managers at other companies, who avoided getting really personal or emotional at work, Sally objected: "That's a cop out. It's like refusing to love if you've been hurt once. Don't let anyone get too close? This is crazy. If good friends can and do work together, tough stuff comes up. It's something we can handle" (Sally, middle management, marketing division, U.K.). Those who had difficulty complying with demands for emotional openness encountered verbal hints or informal requests for conformity; threats of punishment for refusing to comply were usually latent, such as the tacit threat of withdrawn warmth and friendliness. There were also a few formal bureaucratic procedures that encouraged compliance. For example, part of the job application process at The Body Shop was a group interview by a panel of current employees who sought evidence of the applicant's commitment to Body Shop values and its political agendas. Morris was a Body Shop manager who had suggested that one of his acquaintances be interviewed for a managerial job. According to Morris, the panel members interviewing his acquaintance had asked, "If The Body Shop doesn't offer you a job, would you take a job elsewhere if you didn't know the company's policies on human rights and the environment?" When the applicant answered affirmatively, the panelists rejected him, in part, according to Morris, because they thought that if he were really committed to The Body Shop values, he would not accept a job anywhere without investigating the company's policies in these key areas. But Morris knew that his friend was too emotionally reserved to reveal that he would accept the other job because he needed money badly to support his wife and child. The child had a severe disability and needed constant, expensive care.

Weber's emphasis on unemotional impersonality in bureaucracies is premised on a deindividualized "rule by rules." In the case of the rejected job applicant, his apparently unemotional preference for impersonality was caused by intense emotions about his son and his desire to keep these feelings private. The panelists, in contrast, chose to apply their deindividualized rules regarding the paramount importance of any applicant's political commitments, so that self-disclosure about this intimate problem became an essential prerequisite for Morris's friend becoming a Body Shop employee. Morris's friend's silence was congruent with his individual emotional limitations, but he was not hired. Emotional diversity entails a contradiction for bounded emotionality. If compliance pressures are used to support bounded emotionality, by sanctioning or excluding those uncomfortable with its tenets, this process contradicts bounded emotionality by requiring acts of intolerance that fail to recognize as legitimate the emotional preferences of people with differing subjectivities and values.

Resistance. Some Body Shop employees enacted bounded emotionality yet simultaneously expressed some limited discomfort with it. For example, some expressed impatience with the time required to respond to the needs of others:

> At an afternoon meeting in Supply, a male warehouse packer complained passionately about PZP's [peak zone pallets].[1] His manager responded, "Don't get emotional; let's just deal with it." (Mike, warehouse manager, supply, U.K.)

> Sometimes there is too much talk about emotion. Right now [I wish I could say], "Let's get on with it," but I don't. Usually people use their boss as a confidant. They aren't constrained by [the lack of privacy in an office with] open space and desks. (Tim, middle management, headquarters, U.K.)

Sometimes employees questioned whether intense emotional expression was authentic: "A supervisor apologized for a mistake and his supervisor responded, 'Don't get overcontrite' " (Field notes, observation, supply, U.K.). Other employees expressed discomfort with emotional practices by joking about them. At an afternoon coordination meeting, one man's complaint was countered with an unsympathetic, "I'm an emotional man here; I'm welling up," as the speaker pretended to wipe an imaginary tear from his eye. These signs of resistance were observed most frequently among men, both nonmanagerial employees and high-ranking managers.

Attempts to separate public and private. The company's emotional practices, including its advocacy of merging personal and working life, met with some opposition from the families of some Body Shop employees. Theresa, a middle manager in U.K. retail operations, told us, "And my Mom said, 'Don't let [The Body Shop job] change your character.' " Jeff, a manager of a company shop in the U.K., had a similar reaction: "When I started work [at The Body Shop] my brother said, 'Don't bring your leftist vegetarian bullshit home.' " An employee's home situation may have important implications for how work life should be structured, and vice versa, but it is difficult to enact the slogan "the personal is political" when members of a family have differing opinions about what is personally and politically desirable and when some members want to separate home and work concerns.

Stress at work. Whenever private emotional concerns are mixed with an organization's instrumental objectives, there is a danger—particularly in a firm struggling to survive in a highly competitive market—that instrumental concerns will take priority over an individual's personal or family needs. Rhonda, a manager of a franchise shop in the U.S., permitted shop staff to engage in personal talk and phone calls during the day, but stressed that personal talk must take place in a separate emotional zone, away from customers, so it would not interfere with selling: "When you're on the floor, you're at work. It's important to be there for each other. You can talk, but not on the shop floor. If you've had a hard day discuss it in the back [of the shop], off the shop floor."

Signs of physical and emotional stress were evident at The Body Shop, particularly in some parts of the headquarters, where claims of being understaffed and overworked were common. Bonnie, a secretary who had a temporary position at the company's U.K. headquarters, expressed it this way:

> This is the hardest temping assignment I've ever had. I am looking forward to my next assignment. The phones never stop ringing and I am expected keep track of too many things. The job is not delineated enough; it's unclear to me from moment to moment what I am to be doing. I would never work here as a regular employee. People are too hyper and stressed out. The hours they work are much too long. I have become more sullen and moody from working here. The people are nice, but the pace is too crazy.

Although we heard similar complaints throughout the company, the problems of stress were particularly visible among the tour guides who scheduled and delivered tours of the headquarters. Their feet hurt, their necks ached, the phones were ringing off the hook, visitors were clamoring for attention, and everyone was very busy. Several tour guides talked openly about the physical and emotional effects of work stress. One told us: "I was on the phone 22 hours between Monday morning and Wednesday night. Betty [a new employee] told another Body Shop employee to piss off, and she's only been here [a very short time]." Another reported, "Nadine is the third person to hurt her foot. You get tired and fall over—just not concentrating." Some employees felt that working very long hours, rather than demands for emotional expressiveness and self-disclosure, made their personal and work lives merge, to the detriment of the former. This problem was evident in some shops, as well as in headquarters and some other working sites. For example:

I have no personal life. . . . Each of [these particular] shops is evacuated two times a week due to terrorist threats. Each time this happens I get phone calls. It's hard on marriage. There's no way I could do my job with a child. . . . To do this you need a partner who understands. The quality of life is ridiculous. At 4 A.M. I'm up north; at 11 P.M. I come home, but then I have two more hours of work to do at home. I work like a maniac during the week. On Saturday I watch [Body Shop videos) at home and go through the postal. I put aside one hour for the post. Sunday I do my weekly report. I try to ignore it and keep clear, but I live with a dread of the phone because I'm always on call. . . . When I'm in Littlehampton [headquartersl I can't get over their hours. It seems more relaxed. I resent it a bit. (Martha, upper management, franchise and company shops, U.K.)

Recognizing that job demands affect home life, The Body Shop was one of the few U.K. companies to provide on-site childcare. Although the facility was beautiful, no child could attend more than 42 hours a week, far short of the long hours many headquarters employees worked. Further, childcare provisions of any kind were available only at the headquarters, excluding the employees who worked in the shops throughout the world and elsewhere in the company's scattered of-fices. Employees with children who worked outside headquarters were stressed by balancing childcare needs on their own.

The company's concern about stress was sufficiently strong that the headquarters provided (anonymous) counseling for those employees who wished to take advantage of this resource. As noted in Meyerson's (1994) analysis of the work stress literature, however helpful such a counselor may be, the implicit message is that the work stress is an abnormal response that must be controlled, with the blame for the problem and the responsibility for fixing it resting primarily with the individual experiencing the stress. Such an analysis overstates the case in The Body Shop example, as the company took the initiative to relieve the organizational sources of stress, offering paid leave to some employees and reallocating work and working hours for others, Allocation of these sources of help was facilitated by the company's norms of emotional openness and self-disclosure:

People know if you are sick [from stress] or depressed from nervous exhaustion. Someone is off the team now from stress and depression. The reaction was "Take whatever time you need to re-evaluate your life." [*Question:* "Is she paid?"] Of course. Another company might say, "If you can't take the heat get out of the kitchen." We [at The Body Shop] have a full-time counselor for us overworked people. (Tim, middle management headquarters, U.K.)

Ms. Roddick openly and repeatedly discussed, with evident worry, signs of stress among Body Shop employees. She was particularly concerned about the disturbing number of female employees who reported violence at home. Whereas the employees generally attributed their stress to long hours of work, Ms. Roddick stressed that the company had provided an exciting, aesthetically pleasing, and emotionally supportive environment that empowered employees, and in this, most of them agreed. Ms. Roddick believed that the empowerment of female employees—economically and personally—upset the balance of power at home:

The company talks about the body, having relaxed forms of interaction. [People are] frisky, touch, hug, kiss. Women are so excited by their work. They have an emotional support system. They are valued. They have new ways of communicating. The company counselor says that employees' worst problem is domestic violence. Littlehampton is a working class town, where there are few college degrees. The men aren't prepared for the changes their wives go through after working for us. After a full day of being valued and listened to at work, they want to be valued and listened to at home. I don't know what to do about it. What is never said: do women really need a domestic relationship? (Ms. Roddick, interview, researcher's house, November 17, 1993)

Whether caused by overwork or a discrepancy between an exciting, empowering work environment and a more mundane, less empowered home life, both male and female employees of The Body Shop sometimes reported considerable emotional and physical work stress. Although The Body Shop emphasized integrating emotional concerns into the working environment, in ways that were unusual and went beyond the usual "act nice" or "act tough" demands of instrumental emotional display, their version of bounded emotionality provided little protection from the experience of aversive emotional stress on the job.

Loss of Bounded Emotionality: Work Feelings Become Norms

So far, this description has presented The Body Shop's approach to emotionality at work in unitary terms, but we also found some variation across different parts of the company. For example, a marketing division (a pseudonym) had evolved a distinctive approach to managing emotion. This division had been geographically and structurally separate for some time and was managed and staffed almost exclusively by women. Although it was not clear whether this division's distinctive approach to emotion had its origins in geographical and structural isolation or the preferences of its employees, at the time our study was conducted, all levels of employees in the division articulated and enforced compliance with a clearly defined set of emotional norms that offered a complex mixture of some elements of bounded emotionality and a preponderance of emotional labor.

Defining the norms. In this section we rely heavily on quotations from Moira, an upper-level manager, because she was excep-

tionally articulate regarding the marketing division's emotional norms and especially active in reinforcing them. When asked about her management style, Moira said she tried to keep a balance, illustrating that balance by drawing a continuum. She labeled the left end of the continuum "insensitive" and wrote under it: "Management is all about getting a task done." She labeled the other end of the continuum "hypersensitive" and described it as "Out of balance. Highly strung. Like when a person feels it is easier to write a memo than discuss a problem face to face." Moira then labeled the center of the continuum "sensitive." She said, "We talk about it openly. We need to be sensitive to each other's moods." This statement retains bounded emotionality's sensitivity to intersubjective limitations, but quotations below suggest that spontaneous emergence of context-specific, personally authentic work feelings were not encouraged. Instead, emotional "face work" was required. Employees were encouraged to express particular emotions and suppress others in all work contexts, no matter how they were privately feeling. These expectations were explicitly articulated and repeatedly communicated, using feedback and catchy slogans, so they would be internalized by division employees. As Moira told us:

> In front of a crowd, we put on a different face in front of people from The Body Shop [headquarters] and [other parts of the company]: everything's cool. We don't like an atmosphere of chaos and aggression and stress. . . . [The division] is perceived as laid back, casual, laughing. Here's why we do it. If a person is frowning or gets no exercise, they feel sluggish and depressed. If a person is laughing, it gets adrenaline going. So: act cheerful. I've never worked with such busy, contented people. We have time for people. We enjoying doing things.

This emphasis on enacting approved emotional behavior included clear expectations for nonverbal as well as verbal emotional expression. Moira described her reaction to a new hire: "Technically, she's the best in the business. In meetings I counted the times she didn't respond when I made eye contact and smiled. If she were my new staff member, right after the meeting I would ask, 'Is anything wrong?' The vibes you give off are important. A smile is endearing. People feel snubbed if you don't smile." Morale in the division appeared to be quite high, in accord with bounded emotionality's emphasis on community. In both public and quite private contexts, employees expressed enthusiasm about working in the division. They were, with very few exceptions, apparently happy with and proud of their division's distinctive norms, considering the emotional face work required to be worth the effort. For example, Tina, a clerical employee said, "It seems relaxed at the [division], but we try hard to make it that way. I am a professional. We all are. Professionals get it done without being frazzled and bothered. I love it here. It is always so friendly." This then was a part of the company with distinctive emotional norms: appearing laid back, being cheerful, and smiling. These norms were apparently enforced to foster employee well-being and productivity.

Treatment of emotional diversity in the division. In spite of an appearance of looking "laid back," marketing division employees took pride in how hard they worked—harder, they claimed, than the rest of The Body Shop. This demanding work ethic entailed a self-conscious component of emotional labor. Those who did not abide by the emotional norms of the marketing division were pressured to reform. In describing reactions to emotionally nonconforming employees, division members revealed contradictions and stress:

> One manager at [the marketing division] let her stress level spill over to other people. Most of us are stressed. We are very stressed. . . . We stamp out a person who becomes turbulent because it makes the atmosphere turbulent. We give such a person serious counseling, focusing on why she behaves this way. We must apply the rule to old as well as new people: it's not just doing the job; it's how you do the job. This stressed woman affected her whole team. Team members asked, "Can I see my manager today or will she be in a bad mood?" She had extreme highs. She gave people flowers for their desks, praise. She was extravagant with words—over the top. Then she had black lows. No one could cope. Kathy had to be confrontational. We must cut off problems early and see warning bells. (Sally, middle management marketing division, U.K.)

Tina, a clerical employee, also emphasized the norms: "John worked at another company, where he was a project manager. People there lied, cheated, banged on desks to get what they wanted. After two or three weeks at [the division], John learned that is not how we achieve results here." Inappropriate gender-related behavior was also quickly punished, as Moira reported: "We hired a guy from a traditional company. He tried a bit of inappropriate behavior [demeaning to women]. The women just ripped him, took the mickey out of him—not with heavy confrontation. Here we never say, directly and seriously, 'I was really offended.' It's not done that way. Any problem should be dealt with at the time, lightheartedly." When division employees failed to conform to any of these emotional norms, they were asked to change their behavior, as above, or encouraged to leave. Sally, a middle manager in the division, related the story of one man hired at the division: "He had a bad attitude. He thought it was easy [to fit in]. He arrived the first day in shorts. He seemed to have the attitude, 'Aren't you glad I'm here? Don't you all love me?' You earn the right to be liked. You don't just get it automatically. He left in two weeks."

Division employees were judged by the extent to which they engaged in specified emotional displays. Some of these displays were congruent with bounded emotionality, for example, an off-again, on-again emphasis on intersubjective sensitivity and a strong sense of community. Other elements of bounded emotionality, particularly the spontaneous expression of personally authentic work feelings and a respect for a heterarchy of values (as illustrated by treatment of emotional nonconformists), were enacted inconsistently and rarely in this division. This, then, was a division in which traditional bureaucratic (e.g., firing) and normative mechanisms of control (e.g., negative feedback about inappropriate emotional behavior) were freely used to ensure compliance with clearly defined emotional norms. Although the patterns of behavior found in the marketing division could be found elsewhere in The Body Shop, these patterns were more firmly codified and compliance more strictly enforced by superiors in the marketing division, making the distinctiveness of this division a question of degree. In this division, forced compliance with emotional norms eroded a subset of the components of bounded emotionality and began to take on more of the overtones of emotional labor in contexts in which the two approaches to emotional expression were in conflict.

Conclusion

Enacting Bounded Emotionality

We found considerable evidence of the enactment of bounded emotionality. The employees of The Body Shop frequently discussed intimate personal issues with coworkers. Work feelings emerged spontaneously, often with no apparent instrumental motivation. Sensitivity to the emotional limitations of coworkers tempered the expression of these emotions, as did respect for a heterarchy of values. Ambiguity primarily caused by the firm's disdain for standardized bureaucratic procedures, was tolerated, if not enjoyed, and ensuing feelings of frustration were freely expressed. Employees often expressed delight at the extent they felt they could "be themselves at work," reflecting a sense of personal authenticity, although we could not determine from our data whether this reflected an integrated or fragmented self. Although morale varied across individuals, across time, and across parts of the organization, most employees shared a strong sense of being part of The Body Shop community. Thus, we found all six of the elements of bounded emotionality enacted regularly in a large, for-profit organization. This approach to the management of emotion, then, is not too idealistic for implementation in a highly competitive, large-scale business context.

Conformity Pressures

This enactment of bounded emotionality, however, fell short of the ideal Putnam and Mumby described. Sometimes employees failed to listen to each other's emotional concerns or expressed impatience with emotional needs, thereby eroding mutual understanding and perhaps, to some extent undermining the company's well-developed sense of community. Such shortfalls, we believe, are inevitable in any interpersonal context and are especially likely to occur in a task-oriented context such as a corporation. Of greater theoretical interest are the ways in which success in enacting bounded emotionality carried the seeds of its own erosion, in that pressure to conform to the ideals of bounded emotionality paradoxically undermined some of its premises. . . .

Although bounded emotionality requires respect for individuals whose values differ, employees who preferred more restrained forms of emotion management were sometimes pressured to display more open emotionality. Sometimes these conformity pressures were relatively subtle (e.g., gentle jokes), but in other cases, the pressures were enforced by formal procedures. It was difficult for Body Shop employees to find a balance between commitment to a form of bounded emotionality and the needs of some employees who preferred more emotional distance. These conformity demands present a dilemma that is perhaps inherent in bounded emotionality: How can a variety of emotional preferences be honored in a heterarchy of values, without eroding bounded emotionality itself?

Co-existence of Bounded Emotionality and Emotional Labor

Bounded emotionality did not displace more conventional forms of emotion management at The Body Shop. Employees also freely and frequently engaged in emotional labor, for example, smiling to increase productivity or using tears to help get a task completed. In addition: even apparently noninstrumental behavior at The Body Shop may have indirectly served instrumental organizational purposes, for example, by increasing loyalty and commitment to the firm or by reinforcing the sense that this was a uniquely desirable place to work. In addition, it is likely that feelings of authenticity created productivity benefits for the company because of reactions such as, "I can do my best work when I can be myself." Although the bounded emotionality model draws a conceptual distinction between instrumental emotional labor and noninstrumental work feelings, in practice it is virtually impossible to maintain such separation, particularly in a high commitment organization like The Body Shop, where many employees expressed a deep satisfaction with their work and saw congruence between their values and those of the company. Mumby and Putnam drew attention to the possibility of such congruence, and in most parts of The Body Shop we found that emotional labor and bounded emotionality were indeed hard to separate.

Emotional labor was seen most clearly in the marketing division, where emotional norms were defined with unusual explicitness; employees were required to seem relaxed, cheerful, and happy, even when they felt otherwise, to get work done in a more efficient, less turbulent fashion. These norms were enforced with a variety of direct and unobtrusive controls. Finding a part of an organization that differs from the rest is not unexpected; organizational culture research, for example, has generally found differentiation and fragmentation, rather than uniformity, across various parts of an organization (e.g., Frost et al., 1991; Alvesson and Berg, 1992; Kunda, 1992; Martin, 1992). This division's emphasis on emotional labor shows how informal self-policing of innovative practices can evolve and be replaced by formal rules and procedures (Barker, 1993). Although emotional labor was easy to see in the marketing division, it was also evident, to a lesser extent, throughout The Body Shop, intertwined with evidence of bounded emotionality.

Bounded Emotionality: A More Dangerous Form of Control?

The Body Shop represents a mixture of the three ideal types of organization described in table 12.1 above. Its mixture of bounded emotionality and emotional labor is enacted primarily, but not exclusively, through normative self-policing, although some traditional bureaucratic means of control are also evident, particularly in the marketing division. Although The Body Shop did not exhibit most of the characteristics of a feminist organization, it did de-emphasize impersonality, encourage the open expression of emotion, and acknowledge the inseparability of "private" and work concerns; bounded emotionality did sometimes take precedence over emotional labor when needs conflicted. In these ways, The Body Shop represents an innovative mix of all three of these ideal types of organization, offering a distinctive way for large corporations to manage emotions at work. Because this firm is, to a large extent, successful in enacting bounded emotionality, it provides an opportunity to question the desirability of this approach to managing emotions: Is bounded emotionality a better way of doing business, from employees' points of view, or is it a more effective, more invasive, and therefore potentially more dangerous control mechanism?

Answers to this question represent a matter of opinion, and opinions will differ.

Those advocating the pro-bounded-emotionality position would echo Mumby and Putnam's enthusiasm for the advantages of personal authenticity at work. Generally, most Body Shop employees appreciated the chance to be themselves at work, to share their personal joys and sadnesses, and to join in a community with others who shar.ed their political and communitarian convictions, as well as intimate knowledge of their personal lives and emotional ups and downs. . . .

Those advocating the anti-bounded-emotionality position would note that when organizational commitments to profit making conflicted with individual interests or other organizational interests that had been democratically chosen by employees, work often took precedence over personal concerns. . . .

There is no conclusive empirical means of disconfirming or supporting one of these interpretations at the expense of the other. As the authors of this paper, we differ in our opinions. One of us worries that while most people at The Body Shop sincerely believed in the company's espoused values, the rhetoric may have been stronger than the implementation. . . . The other two coauthors of this paper take these signs of stress very seriously and see them as an area meriting serious ameliorative action but nevertheless believe that this company was trying hard to enact its ideals, including bounded emotionality. . . .

Obstacles to Implementing Bounded Emotionality

Several factors threatened The Body Shop's ability to continue implementing bounded emotionality. The organization's increased size had detrimental effects because it increased both the amount of work and the number of employees who did not know each other or each other's job responsibilities. The company's growth also made it more difficult to hire and retain a demographically and ideologically homogeneous group of employees from the local labor market. Many job applicants with the requisite retailing experience came from more traditional organizations, lacked an intense commitment to The Body Shop's political agenda, and were uncomfortable with the emotional expressiveness required by bounded emotionality. In addition, most of these job applicants were men, making it more difficult to maintain the company's commitment to providing opportunities for managerial positions to women. Further, many of The Body Shop's long-term employees, who had been hired when they were young and single, were now married and anticipating caring for children or aging parents. The goals and attributes of an aging workforce didn't mesh easily with the company's predilection for extremely long working hours and high-pressure performance. Many of the long-term employees were women, a fact that exacerbated these anticipated difficulties, because so much of the dependent care within the family would be done by women. Such difficulties were intensified by the fact that The Body Shop was subject to the pressures of a highly competitive marketplace. The Body Shop's financial success and public stock offering created demands for rapid growth, and that growth exacerbated the effects of local labor market limitations. The Body Shop was in danger of losing its distinctiveness and becoming imprisoned, with so many other formerly innovative organizations, in the iron cage of bureaucracy, with its traditional and normative emphases on impersonality and emotional labor.

Despite the obstacles, however, the company had so far managed to maintain two distinguishing features that may have facilitated the continued implementation of bounded emotionality: a relatively high proportion of women employees, some with high-Ievel managerial positions, and a relatively strong ideological commitment to finding ways of doing business differently. The presence of one or both of these factors may be key to resisting bureaucratic isomorphism, at least in the domain of bounded emotionality. In large for-profit organizations would the presence of a high proportion of women, with a significant minority at the highest ranks, be enough to sustain bounded emotionality? Or would ideology alone suffice, perhaps in the firms that have joined the Social Venture Network, a network of organizations with ideologies similar in some ways to that of The Body Shop? Or, because so many women do not seek to do business differently, must both factors be present? If studies addressing questions such as these could show that bureaucratic isomorphism is less pervasive

than we thought, or need not be as pervasive as it is, they would make an important contribution to organizational theory and practice. . . .

Note

1. Peak zone pallets containing high-turnover products are more readily accessible in the warehouse than pallets holding other products.

References

Acker, Joan, and Donald R. Van Houten. 1974. "Differential recruitment and control: The sex structuring of organizations." *Administrative Science Quarterly*, 19: 152—163.

Adler, Patricia A., and Peter Adler. 1988. "Intense loyalty in organizations: A case study of college athletics." *Administrative Science Quarterly*, 33: 401–417.

Adler, Paul S., and Bryan Borys. 1996. "Two types of bureaucracy: Enabling and coercive." *Administrative Science Quarterly*, 41: 61–89.

Alcoff, Linda. 1988. "Cultural feminism versus poststructuralism: The identity crisis in feminist theory." *Signs*, 13: 405–436.

Allen, Jon G., and Dorothy Markiewicz Haccoun. 1976. "Sex differences in emotionality: A multidimensional approach." *Human Relations*, 29:711–722.

Alvesson, Mats, and Per Olaf Berg. 1992. *Corporate Culture and Organizational Symbolism*. New York: de Gruyter.

Barker, James R. 1993. "Tightening the iron cage: Concertive control in self-managing teams." *Administrative Science Quarterly*, 38: 408–437.

Barker, James, and Phillip Tompkins. 1994. "Identification in the self-managing organization: Characteristics of target and tenure." *Human Communication Research*, 21: 223–240.

Barnard, Chester I. 1938. *The Functions of the Executive*. Cambridge, MA: Harvard University Press.

Bartunek, Jean M., and Michael K. Moch. 1991. "Multiple constituencies and the quality of working life intervention at FoodCom." In Peter J. Frost, Larry F. Moore, Meryl Reis Louis, Craig C. Lundberg, and Joanne Martin (eds.), *Reframing Organizational Culture*: 104–114. Newbury Park: CA: Sage.

Bernard, Jessie. 1982. *The Future of Marriage*, 2d ed. New Haven, CT: Yale University Press.

Burrell, Gibson. 1984. "Sex and organizational analysis." *Organization Studies*, 5: 97–118.

Calas, Marta, and Linda Smircich. 1989. "Using the f-word: Feminist theories and the social consequences of organizational research." Paper presented at the annual meeting of the Academy of Management, Washington, DC.

———. 1992. "Re-writing gender into organization theorizing: Directions from feminist perspectives." In M. Reed and M. Hughes (eds.), *Re-thinking Organizations: New Directions in Organizational Research and Analysis*: 227–253. London: Sage.

Cheney, George, and Phillip Tompkins. 1987. "Coming to terms with organizational identification and commitment." *Central States Speech Journal*, 38:1–15.

Cockburn, Cynthia. 1983. *Brothers: Male Dominance and Technological Change*. London: Pluto Press.

Cohen, Randi C., and Robert I. Sutton. 1998. "Clients as a source of enjoyment on the job: How hair stylists shape demeanor and personal disclosures." In J. A. Wagner (ed.), *Advances in Qualitative Organization Research*, 1: 1–32. Greenwich, CT: JAI Press.

Collinson, David L., David Knights, and Margaret Collinson. 1990. *Managing to Discriminate*. New York: Routledge.

DiMaggio, Paul J., and Walter W. Powell. 1983. "The iron cage revisited: Institutional isomorphism and collective rationality in organizational fields." *American Sociological Review*, 48: 147–160.

Eagly, Alice H., and Blair T. Johnson. 1990. "Gender and leadership style: A meta-analysis." *Psychological Bulletin*, 108: 233–256.

Eccles, Robert G., and Nitin Nohria. 1992. *Beyond the Hype: Rediscovering the Essence of Management.* Cambridge, MA: Harvard Business School Press.

Eisenstein, Hester. 1995. "The Australian femocratic experiment: A feminist case for bureaucracy." In Myra Marx Ferree and Patricia Yancey Martin (eds.), *Feminist Organizations*: 69–83. Philadelphia: Temple University Press.

Ekman, Paul. 1973. "Cross cultural studies of facial expression." In Paul Ekman (ed.), *Darwin and Facial Expression: A Century of Research in Review*: 169–222. New York: Academic Press.

Ely, Robin J. 1995. "The power of demography: Women's social constructions of gender identity at work." *Academy of Management Journal*, 38: 589–634.

Ferree, Myra Marx, and Patricia Yancey Martin (eds). 1995. *Feminist Organizations.* Philadelphia: Temple University Press.

Fineman, Stephen. 1993. "Emotions as organizational arenas?" In Stephen Fineman (ed.), *Emotions in Organizations*: 9–35. London: Sage.

———. 1996. "Emotion and organizing." In Stewart Clegg (ed.), *Handbook of Organization Studies*: 543564. London: Sage.

Flax, Jane. 1990. *Thinking Fragments: Psychoanalysis, Feminism, and Postmodernism in the Contemporary West.* Berkeley: University of California Press.

Fletcher, Joyce K. 1995. "Radically transforming work for the 21st century: A feminist reconstruction of 'real' work." *Academy of Management Best Papers Proceedings*: 448–452.

Fraser, Nancy. 1989. *Unruly Practices: Power, Discourse and Gender in Contemporary Social Theory.* Minneapolis: University of Minnesota Press.

Frost, Peter J., Larry F. Moore, Meryl Reis Louis, Craig C. Lundberg, and Joanne Martin (eds.). 1991. *Reframing Organizational Culture.* Newbury Park, CA: Sage.

Gaines, Jeannie. 1993. " 'You don't necessarily have to be charismatic. . . .' An interview with Anita Roddick and reflections on charismatic processes in the Body Shop International." *Leadership Quarterly*, 4: 347–359.

Gamson, Z., and H. Levin. 1984. "Obstacles to survival for democratic workplaces." In Robert Jackall and Henry Levin (eds.), *Worker Cooperatives In America*: 219–245. Berkeley: University of California Press.

Gherardi, Silvia. 1995. *Gender, Symbolism and Organizational Cultures.* London: Sage.

Glaser, Barney, and Anselm Strauss. 1967. *The Discovery of Grounded Theory: Strategies for Qualitative Research.* Chicago: Aldine.

Hall, Richard H. 1968. "Professionalization and bureaucratization." *American Sociological Review*, 33: 92–104.

Harding, Sandra. 1993. "Rethinking standpoint epistemology: What is 'strong objectivity'?" in Linda Alcoff and Elizabeth Potter (eds.), *Feminist Epistemologies*: 49–82. New York: Routledge.

Harlan, A., and C. Weiss. 1982. "Sex differences in factors affecting managerial career advancement." In Phyllis Ann Wallace (ed.), *Women in the Workplace*: 59–100. Boston: Auburn House.

Hearn, Jeff. 1993. "Emotive subjects: Organizational men, organizational masculinities and the (de)construction of 'emotions'." In Stephen Fineman (ed.), *Emotion in Organizations*: 142–167. Newbury Park, CA: Sage.

Hearn, Jeff, and Wendy Parkin. 1987. *'Sex' at 'Work': The Power and Paradox of Organization Sexuality.* New York: St. Martin's.

Hearn, Jeff, Deborah L. Sheppard, Peta Tancred-Sheriff, and Gibson Burrell (eds.). 1989. *The Sexuality of Organization.* Newbury Park, CA: Sage.

Hellriegel, Don, and John Slocum. 1979. *Organizational Behavior.* St. Paul: West.

Hochschild, Arlie Russell. 1983. *The Managed Heart: The Commercialization of Human Feeling*: Berkeley, CA: University of California Press.

———. 1989. *The Second Shift.* New York: Avon Books.

Iannello, Kathleen P. 1992. *Decisions Without Hierarchy.* New York: Routledge.

Jackall, Robert, and Henry Levin (eds.). 1984. *Worker Cooperatives in America.* Berkeley: University of California Press.

Kanter, Rosabeth. 1977. *Men and Women of the Corporation.* New York: Anchor Press.

Kitayama, Shinobu, and Hazel Rose Markus (eds.). 1996. *Emotion and Culture: Empirical Studies of Mutual Influence.* Hyattsville, MD: American Psychological Association.

Kunda, Gideon. 1992. *Engineering Culture: Control and Commitment in a Hightech Corporation.* Philadelphia: Temple University Press.

Leidner, Robin. 1991. "Serving hamburgers and selling insurance: Gender, work, and identity in interactive service jobs." *Gender and Society*, 5: 154–177.

Lont, C. 1988. "Redwood Records: Principles and profit in women's music." In Barbara Bate and Anita Taylor (eds.), *Women Communicating: Studies of Women's Talk*: 233–250. Norwood, NJ: Ablex.

Mansbridge, Jane. 1973. "Time, emotion and inequality: Three problems of participatory groups." *Journal of Applied Behavioral Science*, 9: 351–368.

Marshall, Judi. 1984. *Women Managers: Travelers in a Male World.* New York: Wiley.

Martin, Joanne. 1990. "Deconstructing organizational taboos: The suppression of gender conflict in organizations." *Organization Science*, 1: 339–359.

———. 1992. *Cultures in Organizations: Three Perspectives.* New York: Oxford University Press.

Martin, Joanne, and Kathleen Knopoff. 1998. "The gendered implications of apparently gender-neutral theory: Re-reading Weber." In E. Freeman and A. Larson (eds.), *Business Ethics and Women's Studies*, vol. 3. Oxford: Oxford University Press (forthcoming).

Meyerson, Debra E. 1994. "Interpretations of stress in institutions: The cultural production of ambiguity and burnout." *Administrative Science Quarterly*, 39: 628–653.

———. 1998. "Feeling stressed and burned out: A feminist reading and re-visioning of stressed-based emotions within medicine and organizational science." *Organization Science*, 9: 103–118.

Mills, Albert J., and Peta Tancred (eds.). 1992. *Gendering Organizational Analysis.* Newbury Park, CA: Sage.

Morgen, Sandra. 1994. "Personalizing personnel decisions in feminist organizational theory and practice." *Human Relations*, 47: 665–683.

———. 1995. " 'It was the best of times, it was the worst of times': Emotional discourse in the work cultures of feminist health clinics." In Myra Marx Ferree and Patricia Yancey Martin (eds.), *Feminist Organizations*: 234–247. Philadelphia: Temple University Press.

Morrison, Ann M., Randall P. White, Ellen Van Velso, and the Center For Creative Leadership. 1987. *Breaking the Glass Ceiling: Can Women Reach the Top of America's Largest Corporations?* Menlo Park, CA: Addison-Wesley.

Mumby, Dennis K., and Linda L. Putnam. 1992. "The politics of emotion: A feminist reading of bounded rationality." *Academy of Management Review*, 17: 465–485.

Nelson, M. 1988. "Women's ways: interactive patterns in predominantly female research teams." In Barbara Bate and Anita Taylor (eds.), *Women Communicating: Studies of Women's Talk*: 199–232. Norwood, NJ: Ablex.

Newton, Tim. 1995. *'Managing' Stress: Emotion and Power at Work.* London: Sage.

Ouchi, William. 1977. "The relationship between organizational structure and organizational control." *Administrative Science Quarterly*, 22: 95–113.

———. 1980. "Markets, bureaucracies, and clans." *Administrative Science Quarterly*, 25: 129–141.

Pauchant, Thierry C., and Ian Mitroff. 1992. *Transforming the Crisis-Prone Organization: Preventing Individual, Organizational, and Environmental Tragedies.* San Francisco: Jossey-Bass.

Perrow, Charles. 1986. *Complex Organizations: A Critical Essay*, 3rd ed. New York: Random House.

Pettigrew, Thomas F., and Joanne Martin. 1987. "Shaping the organizational context for black American inclusion." *Journal of Social Issues*, 43: 41–78.

Putnam, Linda L., and Dennis K. Mumby. 1993. "Organizations, emotion and the myth of rationality." In Stephen Fineman (ed.), *Emotion in Organizations*: 36–57. London: Sage.

Rafaeli, Anat. 1989. "When cashiers meet customers: An analysis of the role of supermarket cashiers." *Academy of Management Journal*, 32: 245–273.

Rafaeli, Anat, and Robert I. Sutton. 1989. "The expression of emotion in organizational life." in L. L. Cummings and B. M. Staw (eds.), *Research in Organizational Behavior*, 11: 1–42. Greenwich, CT: JAI Press.

———. 1990. "Busy stores and demanding customers: How do they affect the display of positive emotion?" *Academy of Management Journal*, 33: 623–637.

———. 1991. "Emotional contrast strategies as means of social influence: Lessons from criminal interrogators and bill collectors." *Academy of Management Journal*, 34: 749–775.

Ritzer, George. 1996. *The McDonaldization of Society: An Investigation into the Changing Character of Contemporary Social Life*. Thousand Oaks, CA: Pine Forge Press.

Roddick, Anita. 1991. *Body and Soul*. New York: Crown.

Rothschild, Joyce, and Alan Whitt. 1986. *The Cooperative Workplace*. Cambridge: Cambridge University Press.

Rushing, William A. 1966. "Organizational rules and surveillance: Propositions in comparative organizational analysis." *Administrative Science Quarterly*, 10: 423–443.

Schein, Edgar H. 1985. *Organizational Culture and Leadership*. San Francisco: Jossey-Bass.

Shrivastava, Paul. 1996. *Greening Business: Profiting the Corporation and the Environment*: Cincinnati, OH: Thompson Executive Press.

Simon, Herbert Alexander. 1976. *Administrative Behavior*, 3d ed. New York: Free Press.

Soeters, Joseph L. 1986. "Excellent companies as social movements." *Journal of Management Studies*, 23: 299–312.

Spivak, Gayatri Chakrovorty. 1987. *In Other Worlds: Essays in Cultural Politics*. New York: Methuen.

Stearns, Carol Zisowitz, and Peter N. Stearns. 1986. *Anger: The Struggle for Emotional Control in America's History*. Chicago: University of Chicago Press.

Sutton, Robert I. 1991. "Maintaining norms about expressed emotions: The case of bill collectors." *Administrative Science Quarterly*, 36: 245–268.

Sutton, Robert I., and Anat Rafaeli. 1988. "Untangling the relationship between displayed emotions and organizational sales: The case of convenience stores." *Academy of Management Journal*, 31: 461–487.

Tompkins, Phillip K., and George Cheney. 1985. "Communication and unobtrusive control in contemporary organization." In Robert D. McPhee and Phillips K. Tompkins (eds.), *Organizational Communication: Traditional Themes and New Directions*: 179–210. Newbury Park, CA: Sage.

Turner, Barry A. 1986. "Sociological aspects of organizational symbolism." *Organization Studies*, 7: 101–115.

Van Maanen, John. 1991. "The smile factory: Work at Disneyland." In Peter J. Frost, Larry F. Moore, Meryl Reis Louis, Craig C. Lundberg, and Joanne Martin (eds.), *Reframing Organizational Culture*: 58–76. Newbury Park, CA: Sage.

Van Maanen, John, and Stephen R. Barley. 1984. "Occupational communities: Culture and control in organizations." In Barry M. Staw and L. L. Cummings (eds.), *Research in Organizational Behavior*, 6: 287–366. Greenwich, CT: JAI Press.

Van Maanen, John, and Gideon Kunda. 1989. "Real feelings: Emotional expression and organizational culture." In L. L. Cummings and B. M. Staw (eds.), *Research in Organizational Behavior*, 11: 43–103. Greenwich, CT: JAI Press.

Waldron, Vincent, and Kathleen Krone. 1991. "The experience and expression of emotion in the workplace: A study of a corrections organization." *Management Communication Quarterly*, 4: 287–309.

Weber, Max. 1946. "Bureaucracy." In Hans H. Gerth and C. Wright Mills (eds. and trans.), *From Max Weber: Essays in Sociology*: 196–244. New York: Oxford University Press.

———. 1981. "Bureaucracy." In Oscar Grusky and George A. Miller (eds.), *The Sociology of Organizations: Basic Studies*: 7–36. New York: Free Press.

Weed, Frank J. 1993. "The MADD Queen: Charisma and the founder of Mothers Against Drunk Driving." *Leadership Quarterly*, 4: 329–346.

Wharton, Amy S., and Rebecca J. Erickson. 1993. "Managing emotions on the job and at home: Understanding the consequences of multiple emotional roles." *Academy of Management Review*, 18: 457–486.

Whyte, William, and Kathleen Whyte. 1991. *Making Mondragon*, 2d ed. Ithaca, NY: ILR Press.

Willmott, Hugh. 1993. "Strength is ignorance; slavery is freedom: Managing culture in modern organizations." *Journal of Management Studies*, 30: 515–552.

Wyatt, N. 1988. "Shared leadership in the Weavers Guild." In Barbara Bate and Anita Taylor (eds.), *Women Communicating: Studies of Women's Talk*: 147–175. Norwood, NJ: Ablex.

Zajonc, Robert B. 1985. "Emotion and facial efference: An ignored theory reclaimed." *Science*, April 5: 15–21.

Chapter 13
Maintaining Norms About Expressed Emotions

The Case of Bill Collectors

Robert I. Sutton

Norms about appropriate emotional expression permeate everyday life. From an early age, children are socialized in the proper display of emotion—from the solemnity required at a funeral to the spontaneous laughter at a birthday party. Organizations also have norms about emotional expression, and this is increasingly the case in a service economy like our own. But how do organizations enforce these norms? And how do employees manage to comply with them, while at the same time attending to their own emotions on the job?

Robert Sutton examines these issues as they play out among workers and managers employed by a bill collection agency. Bill collection is not a typical service job in which "the customer is always right" and emotion norms emphasize friendliness and hospitality. Instead, collectors aim to create a sense of urgency and fear in debtors, and, thus, routinely interact with people who are angry and uncooperative. Although the setting may be unusual, Sutton's arguments have much broader implications for the management of emotion and emotional expression in organizations.

The notion that organizations have strong norms about the emotions that members ought to display to others is the central theme of an emerging body of theory and research. This literature has focused on service employees who are expected to convey good cheer, including flight attendants (Hochschild, 1983), Disney employees (Van Maanen and Kunda, 1989), and convenience store clerks (Sutton and Rafaeli, 1988). Researchers also have described roles such as those of physicians (Smith and Kleinman, 1989), in which a neutral demeanor is normative, and bill collectors (Hochschild, 1983), in which members are expected to display negative emotions. Other studies have described employees who are expected to adjust their demeanor to different categories of persons encountered on the job, like the police detectives studied by Stenross and Kleinman (1989), who were expected to convey negative emotions to suspected criminals and warmth to victims.

These norms, or organizational "display rules" (Ekman, 1973), usually are espoused by managers because they believe that expressing required emotions will help employees gain control over others in ways that promote organizational goals. These expectations are termed norms, however, not because they are accurate descriptions of how members usually behave (Bettenhausen and Murnighan, 1985), but because more powerful organization members believe that less powerful members ought to engage in such behaviors. Despite their presumed importance, such norms are not all-powerful determinants of the emotions that members convey to others. Evidence gathered thus far suggests that employees' inner feelings are among the most important additional determinants of their expressed emotions (Hochschild, 1983; Rafaeli and Sutton, 1989; Van Maanen and Kunda, 1989). Organizations often go through considerable effort to help ensure that employees (especially those in boundary roles) will be inclined to experience normative emotions. These organizations appear to do so because if employees feel the same emotions that they are expected to express, then norms can be maintained more easily and consistently.

Selection and socialization appear to be the primary means that organizations use to fill positions with employees who feel emotions that are congruent with norms (Rafaeli and Sutton, 1987). Hochschild (1983) reported that Delta Airlines used extensive interviews to help ensure that flight attendants were upbeat people. Delta also used a trial period to determine if new attendants had the "emotional stamina" to exude good cheer during long, crowded flights. Socialization practices help ensure that, even if employees aren't initially disposed to experience required emotions, they will internalize display rules and learn to experience such feelings. Mary Kay Ash, president of Mary Kay Cosmetics, insists that her beauty consultants act enthusiastic and asserts that even if this emotion is not felt, they should offer fake enthusiasm until it becomes a genuine feeling (Ash, 1984).

Despite such efforts to staff organizations with members who will tend to feel (and thus display) normative emotions, employees' feelings still may clash with norms. Existing research focuses on how pressure generated by interactions with customers or clients can cause service employees who are expected to display pleasant emotions to experience conflicting unpleasant inner feelings. These negative feelings are often successfully concealed from clients or customers. Mars and Nicod's (1984) ethnographic research suggests that waiters in fancy restaurants routinely convey the required polite demeanor while simultaneously feeling angry toward rude patrons. Hochschild (1983: 90) labelled such a clash between inner feelings and norms about expressed emotions as "emotive dissonance."

In other cases, despite organizational rewards and punishments supporting displayed positive emotions, pressure from clients or customers can cause negative feelings to leak or gush out. Van Maanen and Kunda (1989) reported that Disney cast members occasionally conveyed negative, esteem-degrading emotions to guests who angered them with personal insults. Research in convenience stores found that the pressure of long lines of customers provoked unpleasant feelings in clerks. These unpleasant feelings helped explain why line length was negatively related to clerks' compliance with organizational norms requiring friendly greetings, smiles, eye contact, and thanks to customers (Sutton and Rafaeli, 1988).

Thus, bits and pieces of evidence have been reported about how organizations seek to maintain norms about the emotions their members ought to express in light of the influence of members' inner feelings. This literature also provides some hints about the limits of such efforts to control members' expressed emotions. The investigation reported here explores these issues explicitly. I conducted a qualitative and inductive study of a bill-collection organization. These data are used to describe how this organization tried to maintain norms about the emotions bill collectors ought to express to debtors, given that such expressions were influenced simultaneously by collectors' (sometimes conflicting) inner feelings, especially feelings provoked by debtors.

Methods

The Research Site

I conducted this study at a collection facility that specialized in obtaining overdue credit-card payments. Typically, payments on one-sixth to one-third of the millions of credit cards the parent corporation issued were 30 or more days overdue. The facility made collections by telephone and wrote letters only to debtors who could not be reached by phone. Collectors made calls every three days to debtors they were unable to reach and every seven days to debtors they had reached in the prior call, the maximum allowed by law. The facility made about 800,000 calls, and collectors spoke with about 200,000 debtors each month. About 200 of the 350 employees were bill collectors. Collectors were paid salaries and could earn incentive pay and prizes (e.g., a VCR or $100 cash) from contests, but such incentives rarely composed more than 10 percent of their pay. There was much differentiation and specialization among collectors, whom the facility grouped primarily by stages of debtor delinquency, known as "buckets": bucket two = 35 to 64 days delinquent; bucket three = 65 to 94 days delinquent; bucket four = 95 to 124 days delinquent; bucket five = 125 to 154 days delinquent; and bucket six = 155 to 184 days delinquent.

Collectors in earlier buckets were younger, less experienced, and less well-paid and often did not view collecting as a career. Collectors in later buckets were older, more experienced, and better paid and thought of debt collection as a career. Other groups of collectors included those who dealt with debtors who held multiple charge cards and with "recovery," where payments were sought from the most recalcitrant debtors who, after day 185 of delinquency, had their loans written off as corporate losses. Other groups handled skiptracing (finding debtors who had "disappeared"), computer support, training, and legal work.

Conversations between collectors and debtors were similar across buckets, although the complexity and intensity increased in later buckets. Typically, a collector began by using a friendly, informal style to disguise the purpose of the call (e.g., "Hi, is Andy around? This is Janet."). If the debtor answered the phone, the collector introduced him- or herself ("Hi, this is Bill calling from your bank."), asked about the late payment ("According to our records, your account is $800 past due."), and pressed for a promise to pay a specific amount by a specific day.

Collectors had instant access to eight "screens," or computerized pages of information, about each debtor. These screens had hundreds of bits of information, including account status (open or closed and why), amount owed, payment history , notes summarizing each past call about the account, how long the person had held the card, total lifetime charges, and payment histories for other cards the debtor held. Collectors in buckets two and three and about half those in bucket four had machine-paced jobs. An automatic dialing system presented them with a stream of debtors (or answering machines) to speak with, in concert with screens summarizing each account. In contrast, collectors in later buckets chose the order in which to call their portfolio of debtors. Bucket-two collectors were expected to speak with about 15 debtors an hour. Fewer "connects" were expected in later buckets because calls were dialed manually, debtors were more difficult to find, and conversations were longer. For example, bucket-five collectors were expected to make about 35 "connects" a day.

Collectors had much success in convincing debtors to pay. Data from a one-month period showed that they had obtained substantial payments from about 60 percent of debtors in bucket two (35 to 64 days late) and from 25 percent of the few recalcitrant debtors (about 1 percent) who, despite the prior efforts of collectors in buckets two through five, reached bucket six (155 to 184 days late).

Data Sources

I gained entry into this organization after a former student was hired there as a management trainee. She arranged a meeting with the facility manager, during which he gave me permission to conduct this study. I gathered these data over a three-month period. I made about 25 visits to the site and had about 20 telephone conversations with facility employees. I typed field notes after each visit and tape-recorded semistructured interviews. I used seven methods:

1. Interacting with a key informant. . . .
2. Training as a collector. . . .
3. Working as a collector. . . .
4. Group interviews. . . .
5. Supervisor interviews. . . .
6. Observing collectors. . . .
7. Written materials. . . .

Analyses

. . . I followed the guidelines suggested by Glaser and Strauss (1967) and Miles and Huberman (1984) to develop an empirically grounded set of insights. The analyses conducted during data collection that are pertinent to the present paper focused on organizational norms about expressed emotions. . . .

More systematic qualitative analyses were conducted after the data gathering was complete. These analyses began by focusing on norms about emotional expression and the means of maintaining such norms. I found a general norm for conveying urgency to the debtor and five norms that were contingent on the debtor's demeanor: (1) displaying warmth to extremely anxious debtors, (2) showing irritation, even anger, to indifferent debtors, (3) showing irritation, even anger, to friendly debtors, (4) showing irritation, even anger, to sad debtors, and (5) remaining calm with angry debtors. Norms were maintained through the selection of new collectors, the socialization of these newcomers, and rewards and punishments. . . .

I then focused on the feelings that collectors had about debtors. I identified six kinds of debtor demeanor that usually generated different kinds of inner feelings in bill collectors: (1) mildly irritated and mildly anxious debtors elicited mild irritation, (2) extremely anxious debtors elicited warmth, possibly sympathy, (3) indifferent debtors elicited irritation, possibly anger, (4) friendly debtors elicited neutrality, possibly sympathy, (5) sad debtors elicited neutrality, possibly sympathy, and (6) angry debtors elicited irritation, possibly anger. . . .

Maintaining Organizational Norms About Expressed Emotions

The data analyses led me to four interrelated findings about this organization's efforts to maintain norms for bill collectors. First, new collectors were selected and socialized to have inner feelings congruent with the general norm of conveying urgency (high arousal with a hint of irritation) to typical debtors. And all collectors were monitored by managers, who used information about whether or not urgency was conveyed as one basis for dispensing rewards and punishments. Second, urgency was the normative starting point for most calls, but collectors were further expected to follow five contingent norms about adjusting their expressed emotions to the debtor's demeanor. Third, contingent norms for extremely anxious and indifferent debtors were easily maintained because they matched collectors' usual feelings toward such debtors. Fourth, contingent norms for friendly, depressed, and angry debtors were relatively difficult to maintain because they clashed with collectors' usual feelings toward such debtors. In addition to means used to maintain other norms, collectors were taught to use cognitive appraisals that helped them to become emotionally detached from friendly, depressed, and angry debtors. Further, to cope with the especially pronounced tension resulting from the norm that calmness be conveyed to angry debtors, collectors were taught and encouraged to release anger without communicating it to debtors.

These four insights focus on similarities rather than differences across the groups of collectors I studied. As in contrasting studies that focus on differences rather than similarities, this was done to develop a sufficiently parsimonious perspective. There were some differences in the expected demeanor in different buckets: collectors in later buckets expected to be somewhat less pleasant and more assertive than in earlier buckets. But the norm of urgency and the contingent norms were generally evident in both earlier and later buckets, as were the patterns of emotive dissonance and of acceptable and unacceptable means of coping with such dissonance.

Maintaining the Urgency Norm

The collection organization presented debtors with a stream of unpleasant interruptions and information. Debtors were interrupted at regular intervals with collection calls. The unpleasant information that collectors conveyed to debtors ranged from the threatened loss of the credit card (in bucket two) to loss of major assets such as a house (in buckets five and six and recovery). Regardless of the stage of delinquency, managers believed that this negative reinforcement scheme (Rachlin, 1976) was effective, because most debtors could only escape this aversive onslaught by paying their bills. Our class was told during training:

> We're absolutely relentless. The squeaky wheel gets the grease. Well, in our case the squeaky wheel gets the cash first. We absolutely don't leave people alone. The only way to make us go away—to stop calling every three days if they won't talk or every seven days if they will talk—is to pay the bill.

Collectors were generally expected to coat such unpleasant information in a tone labelled by managers as "urgency," or, less often, "intensity" or "firmness." This tone entails conveying high arousal with a hint of irritation or disapproval. Collectors were also expected to convey urgency during the "talk-off," with vague, yet alarming, phrases. The organization sometimes struck me as a sea of emphatic and slightly irritated people repeating phrases such as "It is imperative that you pay us today," and "This account has reached a critical stage."

Managers and collectors used two primary justifications for the urgency norm. First, because encounters with an intense and slightly irritated person are aversive, they believed that debtors would pay their bills to escape from unpleasant people as well as from unpleasant information. Second, they believed that concrete warnings of unpleasant consequences coated in an emphatic and somewhat unpleasant tone (in concert with alarming phrases) would be taken more seriously—a belief congruent with psychological theory (Swanson, 1989). An experienced collector summarized this justification for the urgency norm as follows:

> If the warnings alone were enough to make them pay, we wouldn't need to call

them. Letters would work just as well. But when you get them on the phone, the firmness of your voice makes them realize that we mean business. and they damn well better pay us.

Similarly, a manager and skilled collector asserted:

You can tell I have a big mouth, my voice carries, people probably think I'm seven feet tall. So that comes across. That's a big part of collections, how you come across on the phone. I know when I talk that way, my voice, it does project urgency, and that makes things happen. When I say that I'm going to do an asset search, they believe me. When I say that legal action will begin, they believe me.

Urgency was even the expected demeanor when a message was left for a debtor with a family member, coworker, or friend. The law mandates that collectors may discuss the account only with persons responsible for the debt. But vague messages in an urgent tone can be left with anyone. By doing so, managers believed that collectors could create alarm among the members of a debtor's social network that, in turn, would be conveyed to the debtor. This use of urgency is illustrated by the following call that I listened to in bucket two:

Collector (friendly voice): Hello, is Tom around? This is Andy.
Debtor's Mother (friendly voice): Sorry, Tom is not around. Would you like to leave a message? This is his mother.
Collector (urgent voice): Yes, please ask Tom to call me at [gives toll free number]. Please tell him it is *very important* that he call me tonight.
Debtor's Mother (worried voice): What is this regarding?
Collector (urgent voice): It is a personal banking matter.
Debtor's Mother (even more worried voice): You can tell me. I'm his mother.
Collector (maintaining urgency): I'm sorry, I can't. But please leave him a message that it is *imperative* that he call me by nine tonight.
Debtor's Mother (still worried): I'll tell him the minute he walks in. I hope he isn't in serious trouble.

Rafaeli and Sutton (1987) contended that organizational norms for emotional expression can be maintained through selection, socialization, and rewards and punishments. The bill collection organization used all of these means in efforts to maintain the norm of urgency. The organization used selection and socialization in an effort to fill positions with collectors who were apt to feel and express urgency, along with rewards and punishments to persuade collectors to convey urgency regardless of their inner feelings.

Selection. Data from five sources suggested that the organization tried to select collectors who seemed disposed to feel (and thus display) arousal and a bit of irritation. Like researchers and clinicians who attempt to measure feelings ranging from transient moods (e.g., Isen, 1970) to dispositional affect (e.g., Staw, Bell, and Clausen, 1986), managers could not assess such internal states directly. Judgments about potential collectors' dispositional affect were based on observing candidates during interviews, training, and the trial period and on descriptions by others who knew candidates. Managers looked for "intensity," "fire in the belly," "aggressiveness," and "firmness." One manager also sought candidates who were "a bit snide."

These informal criteria were used in hiring both collectors who were new to the occupation and those with prior collection experience. Nonetheless, consistent with findings that selection interviews are poor predictors of behavior on the job (Arvey and Campion, 1982), managers placed greater emphasis on emotions displayed during the trial period. Collectors who were new to the occupation typically worked in bucket two because less skill was required there than in later buckets. Turnover among new collectors in bucket two was over 50 percent a year. An experienced collector described a key difference between those who quit or were fired versus those who stayed: "The first thing I watch for is to see if there is firmness in their voice, the urgency that creates alarm. If they've got it, then they usually stick around awhile." Similarly, I asked the manager of a later bucket what he looked for during the trial period with collectors hired from outside agencies. He responded:

You can't really be a laid-back type of person because you won't get the results. If you see somebody sitting on the phone like *this* [demonstrates collector leaning back in chair. looking very relaxed], that comes across in your tone of voice on the phone. "Wellll, how ya doin today, Joeeee? You didnnnn't pay your accounttttt" But when somebody is like *this* [demonstrates a collector leaning forward, with tension in the body] on the phone in front of the tube, they're *intense* enough. You can see that those people probably have something that makes them the best collector. I guess that would be about it because everybody can learn from there.

Thus, regardless of the degree that expressed emotions are determined by dispositions (Staw, Bell, and Clausen, 1986) or organizational arrangements (Davis-Blake and Pfeffer, 1989), these managers behaved as if affectivity were a trait. But they didn't believe that it was sufficient to attract and hire employees who seemed disposed toward high arousal (with perhaps a touch of grouchiness). Instead, they believed that such employees could learn and internalize norms about expressed emotion more easily, would not need to be monitored as closely or cajoled as frequently, and would suffer less from the "leakage" of inner feelings (Ekman, 1985) that often occurs when people try to express emotions that clash with their inner feelings.

Socialization. . . . The handbook for new collectors indicated that an "urgent" and "concerned" style was expected from bucket two onward. This norm was also made explicit in training when my class was told:

> We are proud of the quality of our customer service, and we insist that you protect the company's good name by being courteous to customers. But that doesn't mean we are friendly doormats. Let them hear the firmness in your voice. Tell them "Mr. Smith, it is imperative that we resolve this matter *today*."

Supervisors and experienced collectors coached newcomers to use urgency. A supervisor told me that my tone was too tentative, and I had to learn to "talk like you mean business." The collector I sat with my first day on the phones scolded me (in an intense and somewhat irritated tone, of course) after I failed to get a promise to pay from a debtor: "Come on, don't be such a wimp. You've got to be more intense—where is that urgency in your voice?"

Collectors' socialization led them to internalize this norm and thus experience as well as express arousal and mild irritation. After a week of training and a week on the phones, I found that, rather than the sympathy and fear I felt at first, I reacted to most debtors with feelings of intensity and vague irritation. I heard similar assertions from experienced collectors and their supervisors. . . .

Rewards and punishments. Collectors were rewarded and punished for the outcomes of their work. Raises, promotions, cash prizes, gifts, and praise were used to encourage collectors to get many "connects," promises to pay, and dollars in payments. Criticism, warnings, demotions, and firings were used to sanction collectors who had far fewer connects, promises to pay, or dollars in payments than expected. Collectors also were rewarded and punished for how they handled calls. Managers could use the spy-and-tell system to monitor any collector from any computer terminal in the facility. Collectors were monitored routinely and then were provided with written feedback. Managers also monitored new and poorly performing collectors and, often at the collector's request, calls with troublesome debtors. This information was used as a basis for praise and criticism and to help make decisions about raises, promotions, and firings.

Managers used the spy-and-tell system as the primary basis for praising collectors who followed the urgency norm and for criticizing those who did not. . . . On one occasion, when a supervisor and I monitored calls, she became upset at an experienced collector who spoke in a flat tone because "She isn't conveying any urgency at all. She won't get a dime." A few minutes later, the supervisor gave another collector a standing ovation and said, "She is so good! Oh is she wonderful!" for using a firm tone to reinforce a warning that legal action would begin if the bill was not paid. Both collectors received such feedback later that day. The constant monitoring and associated consequences meant that, even if selection and socialization worked imperfectly and collectors weren't aroused and slightly irritated, they had incentives for conveying urgency.

Maintaining the Contingent Norms

Managers expected urgency to be the starting point in most calls and contended that it was the best demeanor for getting money from the typical debtor. But contingent norms about how collectors ought to adjust the emotions they conveyed to different kinds of debtors also were present. The contingent norms considered here concern variations in debtor demeanor because this was one of the primary features collectors were expected to use when making adjustments in conveyed emotions, and consistent patterns were evident across buckets and data sources.

. . . Both the general norm of urgency and the contingent norms were justified by beliefs that anxious debtors were likely to pay their bills quickly to escape from such unpleasant feelings. Managers and experienced collectors asserted that if a debtor sounded anxious, then conveying urgency was sufficient for maintaining and amplifying such anxiety. Contingent norms reflected beliefs that collectors ought to express stronger irritation, even anger, to indifferent, friendly, and sad debtors because they were not sufficiently aroused and worried about their late payments. Contingent norms also reflected beliefs that some debtors were too upset to focus on their debts: Warmth was thought best for relaxing extremely anxious debtors, calmness best for cooling off angry debtors. The ease or difficulty of maintaining each contingent display rule depended heavily on whether it was congruent with collectors' feelings about debtors. I first describe how the organization supported the two norms that were congruent with collectors' usual feelings and then turn to the more complex means used to support the three norms that clashed with collectors' usual feelings.

For extremely anxious and indifferent debtors, collectors were expected to express emotions that were congruent with the inner feelings usually provoked by such debtors: warmth, possibly sympathy, to extremely anxious debtors, and irritation, possibly anger, to indifferent debtors. These norms were made explicit during training, and collectors were rewarded (typically by being praised) for compliance. Managers mentioned few difficulties in maintaining these norms and no collector reported or demonstrated struggling to comply.

Extremely anxious debtors. Collectors were often discouraged from getting "too chummy" with debtors. But managers expected collectors to treat extremely anxious debtors with warmth, especially if they were first-time debtors who had paid bills promptly in the past. The justification was that because such debtors were sufficiently aroused and worried, the collector's task was

to calm them enough so they could process information about how to pay the bill. Collectors also were told by trainers, supervisors, and coworkers to be kind, because such people were loyal customers. While observing in bucket two, I listened to Tom, one of the collectors, speak to a woman who sounded terrified that her credit rating would suffer. Tom was very sweet to her. After the call he said to me, "You've got to be nice to folks like that. They want to pay their bills." He showed me that her payment record indicated that, as the debtor had claimed, she had never been late or missed a payment before. Most collectors felt warmly toward extremely anxious debtors who had histories of paying bills on time. This norm was easy to maintain because, once it was taught, most collectors only had to remember to turn off the usual urgency and to convey genuine warmth. . . .

Indifferent debtors. Managers believed that debtors who sounded indifferent were not sufficiently aroused and worried about their bills. Collectors were expected to express strong irritation, and even anger, to such debtors. A supervisor asserted that it was important to make sure that debtors who "didn't care" had an "unpleasant experience" during the call to get them to "make the payment to make you go away even if they don't care about protecting their credit rating." I asked another supervisor how he would treat a debtor who responded with an indifferent tone:

> **Supervisor:** I slam 'em. I slam 'em against the wall.
> **Interviewer:** What does "slam 'em" mean?
> **Supervisor:** I don't yell at them. You're not supposed to yell at them. I just get real tough with them.

When I asked him to explain what he meant by getting "real tough," he abruptly shifted from a friendly to an agitated and hostile tone of voice, in which he said:

> I want the payment today, express mail. I don't care how or where they are going to get it, short of telling them to go stand down on the street corner. If I can hear television in the background, I tell them, "Why don't you go sell your television?" If they have call waiting, I tell them, "You can't pay your bills, but you have call waiting, which is five dollars more. Turn off your call waiting and send me the five dollars."

Six of the seven data sources indicated that collectors felt irritation, even anger, toward indifferent debtors because, as one collector put it: "Dealing with people who don't give a shit is tough. It frustrates the hell out of me." Similarly, members of both groups of collectors I interviewed agreed that debtors who "didn't care" were the most frustrating to deal with. And the members of the group of collectors from buckets four, five, and six and recovery all agreed when one member said, "But the wonderful thing is that those people make us mad and we are supposed to let them know we are mad at them!" As a result, this norm was easily maintained by teaching collectors to convey their inner feelings to such debtors and praising them occasionally for doing so.

Contingent display rules for friendly, sad, and angry debtors clashed with collectors' usual feelings toward such debtors. As Figure 13.1 summarizes, collectors usually felt neutral or even sympathetic toward friendly and sad debtors but were expected to convey strong irritation, even anger. Angry debtors, however, generally provoked strong irritation and anger, but collectors were expected to convey neutrality and calmness. Conver-

Figure 13.1

Bill collectors' feelings about debtors versus organizational norms about emotions that ought to be expressed to debtors.

	Bill Collector's Feelings	Organizational Norms about Expressed Emotion
Friendly or Sad Debtors	Neutrality, Possibly Sympathy	Irritation, Even Anger
Angry Debtors	Irritation, Anger	Neutrality, or Calmness

sations with such debtors often created the dilemma for collectors of enduring the strain of emotive dissonance versus expressing genuine, but forbidden feelings.

The organization dealt with these pressures on collectors in several ways. First, newcomers were told repeatedly that, no matter how they felt, compliance to these norms was essential for job performance. Second, collectors were monitored especially closely (and rewarded and punished) to help maintain these norms. Third, trainers, supervisors, and experienced collectors provided newcomers with cognitive appraisals that helped them to define these debtors in ways that reduced the gap between emotions felt and emotions feigned. These appraisals were variations of the classic Freudian defense mechanism of "intellectualization," which Frijda (1986:423) defined as "detachment when it is achieved more cognitively by coding the event in an impersonal, factual, or harmless manner." Collectors were encouraged to attain emotional detachment from friendly, sad, and angry debtors by telling themselves that these conversations concerned impersonal, factual matters. They were further encouraged to tell themselves that required emotional displays were in the debtor's best interest and that a debtor's unpleasant words or tone could do them no harm.

Friendly debtors. The organization relied on socialization, rewards, and punishments to maintain the contingent norm of treating debtors with irritation, even anger. We were told in training not to reciprocate a debtor's kindness with a friendly tone because it signalled that the overdue payment wasn't important and that the threatened negative consequences weren't genuine. Instead, rather than just using urgency, we were told to get "especially tough with the buddy-buddy types to let them know you are not their friend."

Once newcomers began making collection calls, managers and experienced collectors warned them about the risks of dealing with "nice" debtors. While I was working on the phones, several collectors urged me to "get nasty" with debtors who "acted like your friend" because it conveyed that the overdue payment was a serious matter, and even if it seemed likely that a "nice" debtor would pay, such unpleasantness encouraged them to "get off the phone and stop wasting your time." For example, I called a woman who was stuck at home with a broken leg. She seemed pleased to hear from me and started chatting in a warm, friendly way about how she would get around to paying the bill soon and about how boring it was to have a broken leg. I was friendly in return and was enjoying the conversation, until the collector I was sitting with reached over, pressed the mute button, and scolded me: "You've got to get her upset! Say 'Excuse me, but don't you even care about losing your credit card? Don't you care about your credit rating?' " . . .

Sad debtors. Compared with expectations about friendly debtors, managers and veteran collectors were even more emphatic that strong irritation, even anger, should be conveyed to debtors who sounded depressed. They believed that a tired, lethargic-sounding debtor was likely to feel unwilling or unable to take the steps required to pay the bill, even if he or she had the money or could borrow it. Collectors were encouraged to go beyond urgency and convey strong irritation, even anger, to such debtors. Managers and collectors believed that this demeanor would create motivation to pay the bill. Yet collectors often felt neutral or warm feelings toward such people, thus setting the stage for emotive dissonance. My field notes indicate that I was criticized for expressing my feelings to a sad debtor rather than following the organization's display rules:

> I talked to a woman who sounded very depressed and lethargic. I was nice to her. She promised to put the check in the mail tomorrow. My supervisor told me that I should have been much firmer. When I talked to another collector about the call, he told me, "You've got to lean on folks like that, be a little nasty to get their attention, to get them motivated."

Even experienced collectors reported that they sometimes felt conflicting emotions that made it difficult to express irritation to depressed debtors, especially to debtors who suffered financial problems through no fault of their own. As a bucket-four collector put it:

> The sob stories make it hard sometimes. especially for new collectors, and especially when they seem to be telling the truth. But you've got to get tough with them when they sound down. If you don't get the money, another creditor will.

Like the norm for dealing with friendly debtors, in addition to emphasizing this norm during training and using rewards and punishments to maintain it, managers and experienced collectors encouraged newcomers to use cognitive appraisals to reduce the gap between their inner feelings and the expected display. A supervisor reported that she constantly reminded collectors that no matter how sad the debtor sounded and no matter how heart-wrenching the reasons for financial problems, they had to focus on the task of collecting the money. Another supervisor said:

> Remember, even if they have to get tough to get the payment, the collector is helping the debtor. The collector has to tell himself: "I'm helping this person to save their credit rating. If they don't pay me, they may never be able to buy a car or a house."

Cognitive appraisals of this kind apparently were intended to help collectors convey required emotions to depressed debtors by thinking of them impersonally and by thinking of displayed irritation as helpful to debtors in the long run.

Angry debtors. The expectation that collectors ought to convey a calm or neutral tone to angry debtors was the most frequently discussed—and struggled with—of the five contingent norms. Managers' justification for this norm was that angry debtors were too upset about the collection call, and thus the problem was to calm them so that their attention could be turned away from the debt collector and toward the debt. For example, a supervisor recommended this approach for dealing with irate debtors:

> I would listen. I would say in a soft voice, "Mr. Jones, calm down. Excuse me." If you can't cut the person off, then you should just let them blow their smoke, and then when your chance comes, try and be positive with them. Say, "Look. I know you've got a problem. I hope nothing I did set you off, because neither of us is going to benefit if we don't resolve this thing."

Similarly, another supervisor asserted that following this norm prevented a vicious circle of hostility between collector and debtor:

> If you talk softer and softer and softer, they're going to have to stop to listen or they're not going to hear anything you're

saying. The louder you get, the louder they get. And if you start to tone it down, they start to tone it down.

The organization went to great lengths to maintain this norm. New collectors were selected partly with this norm in mind. Those with reputations as "screamers" weren't hired from outside agencies. Newcomers who responded to nasty debtors with anger were reprimanded and, if they didn't learn to control their tempers, often were fired. My class was told repeatedly that "slamming" irate debtors was a mistake because it would only escalate their anger. During my work on the phone, a collector told me: "If they are nasty, motivation isn't the problem—then you've got to be neutral." Rewards and punishments were also used to maintain this norm among all collectors. And even experienced collectors occasionally were fired because they could not control their tempers.

At the same time, however, as all seven data sources indicated, rude, loud, cussing, or insulting debtors generated anger in collectors. This pattern is consistent with findings that aggression provokes the "fight" response (Frijda, 1986) and that anger is a contagious emotion (Schacter and Singer, 1962; Baron, 1977). Moreover, anger is an especially difficult emotion to conceal from others (Ekman, 1985). These pressures may explain why I observed or was told of numerous incidents in which collectors conveyed anger to nasty debtors. My field notes describe the following incident:

> Something happened at the next cubicle that caused the collector to blow her top. I heard her shout very loudly, "Well, congratulations on your new card. I'm very happy for you." And then she slammed down the phone—I mean slammed it down so loud that I could feel the floor shake from where I was sitting. Then she ran around screaming about what an asshole this guy was, how nasty he had been, how he had lied continually, and so on. Then, five minutes later, I heard her talking to the guy again. He apparently had called her back to "rub in" the fact that the bank had sent him a new credit card. She started out by sitting down. But about a minute later, I saw a move out of the corner of my eye that I'd witnessed perhaps three times during my field work: She jumped into the air, which sent her chair rolling (it ended up 10 feet behind her). She then started screaming at the debtor: "You lied to me. Why did you

lie to me? Don't talk to me like that. What? How dare you say that? I'm not your honey."

There was a flurry of gossip among nearby collectors after this incident. They all agreed that the debtor was a "jerk," but they were critical of this collector for her loss of emotional control, for not being "tough enough" to "keep her cool." Collectors usually viewed episodes in which anger was expressed to nasty debtors as failures in others and in themselves. They were selected and socialized carefully enough—and subjected to enough sanctions—that most believed that they should convey calm to angry debtors, even if it was a struggle to do so. As a manager put it, "When collectors do lose control and start hollering back at a debtor, you usually hear them say later, 'I blew it. I lost control of that one'." Similarly, my field notes describe an experienced collector's struggle to convey the normative calm demeanor:

> He said that if you can control your temper, and help them calm down, then you might be able to reach the point where you can say to them, "What can we work out so that we don't have to call you any more?" He did admit that there were times when he had "lost it" because the debtor was "such an asshole that I couldn't take it any more." But he said that was a mistake. "It is better to be reasonable. There is no need to yell."

Episodes in which collectors responded to angry debtors with hostility were among the most public (it is obvious when a person is standing and shouting), vivid, and widely discussed reactions to debtors. Nonetheless, I was struck by how often collectors tolerated emotive dissonance and conveyed the expected calmness. The selection, socialization, reward, and punishment practices described above helped in this regard. In addition, as in dealing with friendly and sad debtors, newcomers were taught by trainers, supervisors, and fellow collectors how to use cognitive appraisals to reduce or eliminate feelings about angry debtors that clashed with the norm. For example, after presenting a calm demeanor to an irate, insulting debtor, a collector explained to me, "I always tell myself, 'He isn't mad at me. Maybe he is just having a bad day.' Or 'He just can't take being called by one bill collector after another.' I keep reminding myself that it is nothing personal."

Moreover, because pressure for emotive dissonance was so pronounced with angry debtors, collectors learned and were encouraged (often subtly) by management and other collectors to use two coping mechanisms to release their tension without communicating it to angry debtors. The first is a variation of the Freudian defense mechanism, displacement aggression (Freud, 1946; Berkowitz, 1962), in which anger is expressed but deflected away from the person or object that provoked such unpleasant feelings. After calls with nasty debtors were over, collectors often pounded their desks and cussed about that "idiot" or "jerk." I didn't observe or hear of a single case in which a collector was criticized by managers or other collectors for doing so. Collectors sitting nearby usually offered social support, as did managers who happened to be walking by. I heard one manager congratulate a collector for cussing-out a debtor after (rather than during) the call, because it made the collector feel better "without having the debtor sue our deep pockets." The most interesting displacement strategies that collectors were allowed to use, however, were employed during calls. My field notes from a side-by-side describe the following method:

> One of the first debtors was quite abusive. Jack warned him about his credit rating being at risk. The debtor told Jack: "My credit rating is better than yours, buddy." Jack told him "That is not the issue. Your credit rating has suffered, and it will get worse if you don't start paying these bills on time. And we are on the verge of taking your card away." When the guy started cussing again, Jack then hit the "mute" button and said some words that he would have been fired for if the debtor could hear them: "You asshole my credit card never looked that bad. I'm not a deadbeat like you."

Similarly, collectors sometimes made obscene gestures at the phone while speaking to a hostile debtor, and I never observed them being sanctioned for doing so.

Joking was the second coping mechanism that collectors were allowed and subtly encouraged to use to release tension caused by angry debtors. The idea that joking and laughter help release tension was proposed by Freud (1960) and elaborated by Berlyne (1969), who asserted that creates an "arousal jag" in which, after a brief and sharp crease in arousal while laughing, tension then decreases dramatically. The jokes about debtors and associated laughter I often heard after conversations with nasty debtors appeared to be a safety valve that enabled collectors to release their anger rather than directing it at the nasty debtor or at the next debtor. After a conversation with a mean-spirited debtor, for example, one collector provoked widespread laughter by joking that she was going to "get that guy's first-born son."

Finally, because conveying anger to nasty debtors was officially disapproved, collectors were taught in training, reminded by supervisors, and encouraged each other to hang up if they were about to holler back. But I noticed that collectors were tacitly allowed to convey their anger to at least two kinds of nasty debtors. In both cases, collectors were allowed to holler back to gain revenge after displaying calm had proven fruitless. First, when a collector had exhausted all reasonable efforts to calm an irate debtor, it seemed to be acceptable to holler back. A manager reported: "When you have lost control of the conversation, and you're mad at them for yelling at you and wasting your time, you might as well yell back at them." Second, after "wasting" time and enduring emotive dissonance to calm a nasty debtor, a collector occasionally judged that the debtor was unable to pay. Giving the debtor a blast of anger at the end of such an exacting call was generally not punished by supervisors, apparently because collectors who had worked hard to follow norms were thought to "deserve" revenge if there was apparently no money to get. A manager and experienced collector reported that with such debtors: "Sometimes I slam them. I might as well get some satisfaction out of the call."

Just because a collector judged that a debtor had no money did not mean that collectors who handled the account in later buckets believed that the debtor could not pay. I observed a collector convince a broke 28-year-old man who was a year behind in his payments to borrow several thousand dollars from his mother. The debtor's mother called the collector, and she sent the money directly to the collection organization. What seemed to make it acceptable for collectors to holler back at such debtors was that they had a justifiable belief that they had done all that they could to make the debtors pay and, up to that point, had followed organizational norms.

Discussion and Conclusions

This qualitative study revealed how one organization sought to maintain norms about expressed emotions in light of the simultaneous influence of members' inner feelings. A persistent theme in this study is that managers put forth greater effort to maintain norms that clashed with collectors' inner feelings about debtors than to maintain norms that were congruent with collectors' inner feelings about debtors. Managers did so because they believed that the feelings evoked by collectors' experiences on the job were a powerful constraint on the emotions collectors conveyed to others, a constraint that could overwhelm any espoused norm. And these managers understood the pressures on bill collectors. because all had years of experience as collectors and most still made collection calls as part of their jobs. If the observed patterns are descriptive of large numbers of organizations rather than idiosyncratic features of a single case, then this study suggests several useful pathways for theory building and research on how organizations shape the emotions expressed by their members, as well as the consequences of such expressed emotions. . . .

Another persistent theme in this study is that if employees in boundary roles can be convinced to comply with norms that clash with their inner feelings, they will suffer from emotive dissonance. Yet little is known about the prevalence, consequences, or varieties of such dissonance. . . .

Finally, in contrast to Delta Airlines, the Disney Corporation, and the bill-collection organization I studied, many organizations ignore or pay only lip service to their employees' expressed emotions. Hochschild's (1983) perspective suggests that such lack of attention may have benefits, because efforts to maintain norms about expressed emotions can lead to exploitation when employees are robbed of their right to display, and even feel, genuine emotions. But such lack of attention may also harm employees, as well as their clients and organizations. For example, experiences at the departments of motor vehicles in several states suggest that at these agencies no efforts, or at least no successful efforts, are made to maintain norms about the expression of pleasant emotions. Employees are rarely pleasant to clients, and expressions of disdain and hostility are common. The perspective developed here suggests that these employees could be selected to be at least mildly upbeat people who have the stamina to maintain this demeanor during a long day at work. In addition to espousing a norm of displaying mildly pleasant emotions, formal and informal employee training could focus on teaching these boundary employees various means for coping with the unpleasant feelings evoked by rude or otherwise difficult clients. And extrinsic rewards could be provided for employees who are consistently pleasant or, at least, who are rarely unpleasant. Employees would have the benefits of feeling and expressing positive emotions on the job and of avoiding vicious circles in which mutually reinforcing anger is conveyed by both employee and client. Employees would also be equipped to cope with emotive dissonance when it arises. Clients would be spared the distress of watching nasty public servants and nasty taxpayers do battle while they wait in line, dreading their own unpleasant interactions. The agencies might benefit because a better fit between person and job could reduce the costs of employee turnover, absenteeism, and, as a result of decreased stress, reduce health insurance costs. And greater client satisfaction could enhance the reputations of these organizations. This scenario may sound excessively optimistic. But the bill-collection organization described here suggests that even when a job entails repeated contact with unpleasant clients, organizations can successfully maintain norms about expressed emotions through the use of selection, socialization, and rewards.

References

Arvey, Richard D., Thomas J. Bouchard, Jr., Nancy L. Segal, and Lauren M. Abraham. 1989. "Job satisfaction: Environmental and genetic components." *Journal of Applied Psychology*, 74: 187–192.

Arvey, Richard D., and James E. Campion. 1982. "The Employment interview: A summary and review of recent research." *Personnel Psychology*, 35: 281–322.

Ash, Mary Kay. 1984. *Mary Kay on People Management*. New York: Warner Books.

Baron, Robert. 1977. *Human Aggression*. New York: Plenum.

Berkowitz, Leonard. 1962. *Aggression: A Social Psychological Analysis*. New York: McGraw-Hill.

Berlyne, D. E. 1969. "Laughter, humor and play." In Gardner Lindzey and Elliot Aronson (eds.), *Handbook of Social Psychology*: 795–852. Reading, MA. Addison-Wesley.

Bettenhausen, Kenneth, and J. Keith Murnighan. 1985. "The emergence of norms in competitive decision-making groups." *Administrative Science Quarterly*, 30: 350–372.

Caplan, Robert D. 1983. "Person-environment fit: Past, present and future." In Cary L. Cooper (ed.), *Stress Research: Issues for the Eighties*: 35–77. New York: Wiley.

Davis-Blake, Allison, and Jeffrey Pfeffer. 1989. "Just a mirage: The search for dispositional effects in organizational research." *Academy of Management Review*, 14: 385–400.

Ekman, Paul. 1973. "Cross culture studies of facial expression." In Paul Ekman (ed.), *Darwin and Facial Expression: A Century of Research in Review*: 169–222. New York: Academic Press.

———. 1985. *Telling Lies*. New York: Berkley Books.

Franks, David D., and E. Doyle McCarthy (eds.). 1989. *The Sociology of Emotions: Original Essays and Research Papers*. Greenwich, CT: JAI Press.

Freud, Sigmund. 1946. *The Ego and Mechanisms of Defense*. New York: International University Press.

———. 1960. *Jokes and Their Relation to the Unconscious*. London: Pergamon Press.

Frijda, Nico H. 1986. *The Emotions*. Cambridge, MA: Cambridge University Press.

Glaser, Barney G., and Anslem L. Strauss. 1967. *The Discovery of Grounded Theory: Strategies for Qualitative Research*. New York: Aldine.

Hochschild, Arlie Russell. 1983. *The Managed Heart*. Berkeley and Los Angeles, CA: University of California Press.

Isen, Alice M. 1970. "Success, failure, attention, and reaction to others: The warm glow of success." *Journal of Personality and Social Psychology*, 15: 294–301.

Mars, Gerald, and Michael Nicod. 1984. *The World of Waiters*. London: Allen and Unwin.

Miles, Matthew B., and A. Michael Huberman. 1984. *Qualitative Data Analysis*. Beverly Hills, CA: Sage.

Rachlin, Howard. 1976. *Introduction to Modern Behaviorism*. San Francisco: Freeman.

Rafaeli, Anat, and Robert I. Sutton 1987 "Expression or emotion as part of the work role." *Academy of Management Review*, 12: 23–37.

———. 1989 "The expression of emotion in organizational life." In L. L. Cummings and Barry M. Staw (eds.), *Research in Organizational Behavior*, 11: 1–42. Greenwich, CT: JAI Press.

Schacter, Stanley, and Jerome E. Singer. 1962. "Cognitive, social, and psychological determinants of emotional state." *Psychological Review*, 69: 379–399.

Smith, Allen C., III, and Sherryl Kleinman. 1989 "Managing emotions in medical school: Students' contacts with the living and the dead." *Social Psychology Quarterly*, 52: 56–69.

Staw, Barry M., Nancy E. Bell, and John A. Clausen. 1986. "The dispositional approach to job attitudes: A lifetime longitudinal test." *Administrative Science Quarterly*, 31: 56–77.

Stenross, Barbara, and Sherryl Kleinman. 1989. "The highs and lows of emotional labor. Detectives' encounters with criminals and victims." *Journal of Contemporary Ethnography*, 17: 435–452.

Sutton, Robert I., and Anat Rafaeli. 1988. "Untangling the relationship between displayed emotions and organizational sales: The case of convenience stores." *Academy of Management Journal*, 31: 461–487.

Swanson, Guy E. 1989. "On the motives and motivation of selves" In David D. Franks and E. Doyle McCarthy (eds.), *The Sociology of Emotions: Original Essays and Research Papers*, 3–32. Greenwich, CT: JAI Press.

Van Maanen, John, and Gideon Kunda. 1989. "Real feelings: Emotional expression and organizational culture." In L. L. Cummings and Barry M. Staw (eds.), *Research in Organizational Behavior*, 11 43–104. Greenwich, CT: JAI Press.

Chapter 14
Metaphors and Meaning

An Intercultural Analysis of the Concept of Teamwork

Cristina B. Gibson and
Mary E. Zellmer-Bruhn

What does it mean to be part of a team? What metaphors best capture these meanings? Does the concept of a team invoke images of sports? The military? Family? How do these metaphors vary depending upon a person's cultural background? The authors of this chapter examine these questions. Their analyses are based on interviews they conducted with employees from ten organizations distributed across the United States, Puerto Rico, the Philippines, and France.

Gibson and Bruhn's finding that definitions of teamwork are strongly "culturally contingent" raises questions about how best to encourage teamwork among workers from different cultural backgrounds. Their research also helps to explain the sources of such differences in teamwork metaphors. These issues have practical significance as more employers adopt team-based systems and as organizations and their workforces continue to spill across national boundaries.

The past two decades have witnessed a steady increase in research investigating differences in teamwork across cultures. This research has identified variance across cultural contexts in team processes, such as social loafing and conflict (Cox, Lobel, and McLeod, 1991; Earley, 1994; Oetzel, 1998), team leadership (Ayman and Chemers, 1983; Pillai and Meindl, 1998), goal setting (Earley and Erez, 1987; Erez and Somech, 1996), teams' beliefs about performance (Gibson, 1999), and employees' receptivity to working in teams (Kirkman and Shapiro, 2001; Kirkman, Gibson, and Shapiro, 2001). Taken to-gether, these studies suggest important differences in teamwork across cultures, yet the cross-cultural literature on teams lacks a comprehensive framework for understanding why these differences occur (Earley and Gibson, 2001). In this paper, we attempt to fill this gap by exploring the underlying differences in the definition of teamwork that people hold, represented by the metaphors they use to describe their teams. Verifying that national and organizational cultures are sources of variance in conceptualizations of teamwork has the potential to provide insight into the differences in preferred practices that have been noted across cultural contexts in other empirical research and challenges scholars to build specific theories of teamwork that incorporate these differences.

Even if the specific content of teamwork conceptualizations varies across cultures, at a general level, most definitions are likely to include what a team does (activity scope), who is on the team (roles) and why (nature of membership), and why the team exists (objectives) (e.g., see reviews of team definitions in Cohen and Bailey, 1997; Sundstrom et al., 1999). For example, when some people think of a team, they picture a project team whose activity is limited to the time during which members work on the project, whereas others may picture a team more like a family whose activity is broad and extends across a number of domains in life (McGrath, 1984). Likewise, some concepts of teamwork may include clearly differentiated roles, such as leaders and members, whereas others may be less structured (Cohen and Bailey, 1997). When some people think about teamwork they picture voluntary membership, whereas for others membership is not necessarily a matter of choice (Bar-Tal, 1990). Finally, some people define teamwork by clear outcomes; others have argued that multiple, sometimes implicit benefits can be derived (McGrath, 1984).

Previous empirical demonstrations of differences in team processes and practices across cultures may be due to these different mental pictures (or definitions). Ayman and Chemers (1983) found that sensitivity to group norms was a more important element of leader behavior in Iran and Mexico than in the U.S. This may be true because team members in Iran and Mexico had a conception of teamwork that included clear leader roles, while team members in the U.S. may have had a less role-oriented conception and thus expected the leader to pay less attention to role-related elements such as norms. In a similar vein, Pillai and Meindl (1998) demonstrated that charismatic group leadership is more prevalent in collectivistic (e.g., group-oriented) cultures. This could be due to a conception of a team as a broad, encompassing entity that exists for multiple benefits. Members that have these team conceptions might be more responsive to charismatic leadership that emphasizes vision and emotion. In contrast, less collectivistic team members may hold a task-focused conception of teams and thus be less receptive to non-task-oriented leader behavior. Similarly, another stream of research has demonstrated that teams high in collectivism behave more cooperatively than individualistic teams (Cox, Lobel, and McLeod, 1991) and that collectivistic groups have fewer conflicts, more cooperating tactics, and less competitive tactics than individualistic teams (Oetzel, 1998). This may be because of the individualistic tendency to have an underlying definition of a team as a task-oriented entity, focused on a specific activity, with formal roles and deliverables. When teams are defined as such, team members are likely to be highly concerned with performance and behave so as to maximize the accomplishment of specific objectives.

Different underlying definitions of teams may help explain findings on teams not fully accounted for in the past. For example, collectivism has been positively associated with self-efficacy for teamwork (Eby and Dobbins, 1997) and people's receptivity to teams and team-based rewards (Kirkman and Shapiro, 2001). It may be that collectivists have a concept of teamwork that is broader and less task-focused than that of individualists, one that assumes social motivations for membership. This concept is similar to naturally occurring groups in society, and thus, teams may come as second nature for the collectivists, while they represent a major shift in focus and process for individualists. If this is true, one would expect differences in the ease with which teams are implemented and accepted. Although we do not test the impact of these different mental pictures (or definitions) of teamwork in this study, we offer an initial attempt at identifying them and sources of variance in them by examining the metaphors that members use to describe their teams and showing how these metaphors are based on national and organizational culture.

Metaphors allow us to understand abstract subject matter in terms of more concrete, familiar terms. In a technical sense, metaphors are "mappings across conceptual domains" (Lakoff, 1993: 245), and metaphor is evoked whenever a pattern of inferences from one conceptual domain is used in another domain. In this way, metaphors are a key mechanism through which we comprehend abstract concepts and perform abstract reasoning. Our behavior reflects our metaphorical understanding of experience. The importance of metaphor for understanding experience is evident in the metaphors embedded in the following comments we heard in studying U.S. teams: "Among the sales people on our team, Jack is the star quarterback"; and "Our team leader acts more like a coach than a referee." One can understand these statements to the extent that one identifies with the metaphor "Workteam-as-sports-team," which involves understanding one (target) domain of experience (work teams) in terms of a very different (source) domain of experience (sports teams). There are ontological correspondences between entities in the domain of a sports team (the coach, the players, the players' positions, the team's field position, the score, etc.) and entities in the domain of work teams (e.g., the leader, the team members, their roles, their progress, their objectives). It is via such mappings that an individual in the U.S. is likely to project sports-domain inferences (e.g., expectations about sports teams) onto the work-team domain (Lakoff, 1993: 245).

Furthermore, the metaphor is a source of cognitive priming in that it brings forth semantic, behavioral, and affective responses (Blair and Banaji, 1996) that are characteristic of the source domain. Examples of this phenomenon are evident in stories in the U.S. popular press. At Eastman Chemical, leaders are called "coaches," and their main role is to help teams set performance goals, assist teams in resolving personnel problems, and manage upsets and emergencies. At Wilson Corporation, during the annual rewards and recognition dinner, gold, silver, and bronze achievement medals are awarded to winning teams based on process improvements. At Sabre, Inc. North America, team training is administered through the "Tour de Teams" program, in which teams progress along a route of programs, pass various milestones, and receive a "yellow jersey" if they are ahead of other teams. These practices are consistent with the work-team-as-sports-team metaphor. Team members are likely to respond to such a metaphor to the extent that they make sense of their work team in terms of a sports team.

At the same time, metaphors for teamwork serve as cognitive reference points for team members. They are similar to internalized behavioral routines, or scripts, and the mental models that team members hold about team structure and process (Cannon-Bowers, Salas, and Converse, 1993; Orasanu and Salas, 1993). They aid members in predicting the behavior or needs of other members and provide a structure for working together as a team. In particular, given their etic nature, it is likely that teamwork metaphors contain essential information about expectations regarding scope, roles, membership, and objectives. For example, the work-team-as-sports-team metaphor conveys such expectations. Sports teams tend to have a narrow scope, with activity limited to the time during which players practice and compete (and an occasional social event). Sports teams typically have fairly clear roles and little hierarchy, and membership is highly voluntary. Finally, objectives are specific, with clear consequences (win or lose). People who describe their work team with a sports metaphor are likely to hold these expectations. This implies that understanding the use of a given metaphor hinges on clarifying the expectations about scope, roles, membership, and objectives that the metaphor represents and identifying the context in which such expectations are likely to be held. For example, why might people hold expectations about their work team that are similar to those embedded in the sports-team metaphor, in which scope is limited, hierarchy is minimal, membership is voluntary, and objectives are clear and consequential? To answer this, we must integrate linguistics and cross-cultural psychology to make specific predictions about sources of variation in metaphors.

Variation in Teamwork Metaphors

Over the course of our lives, the requirements for spoken communication foster selectivity in metaphors, forcing us more frequently to use metaphors that have cul-

tural currency, so that their meaning will be intersubjectively shared with those to whom we talk, and they will hence be useful in clarifying our point (Quinn, 1997). Some experiences may be widely shared, by members of a national culture, while other experiences may be limited to members of a restricted group, such as members of an organizational culture.

National Culture

Individuals bring cultures of origin to work (Brannen, 1994) that reflect their particular ongoing histories in various cultural contexts, such as national cultures. Cross-cultural research has established that national culture explains between 25 and 50 percent of variation in attitudes (see Gannon et al., 1994, for a review) and is also related to social behaviors such as aggression, conflict resolution, social distance, helping, dominance, conformity, and obedience (see Triandis, 1994, for a review), as well as decision-making and leadership behaviors (Hofstede, 1980; Schneider and De Meyer, 1991; Shane, 1994). In cognitive terms, national culture is viewed as a set of shared meanings transmitted by a set of mental programs that control responses in a given context (Hofstede, 1980; Shweder and LeVine, 1984). The basic thesis of a cognitive - approach to culture is that processing frameworks acquired in one culture persist and influence behavior even though contextual circumstances change. In this manner, culture guides our choices, commitments, and standards of behavior (Erez and Earley, 1993). Team collaboration requires information exchange and collective information processing (Gibson, 2001) and is therefore rich in cognitive content; however, since cultural contexts around the globe are infused with very different cognitive frameworks, teamwork metaphors are likely to vary across national cultures. Based on this theory, we propose the following general hypothesis:

H1: The use of a given metaphor for teamwork is likely to vary across nations.

Contemporary cross-cultural theorists argue that it is not enough to observe that behaviors differ across national cultures, we must be able to understand how and why they differ (e.g., Earley and Singh, 1995). Cross-cultural researchers commonly argue that most cultural differences are due to variations in cultural values. Although variations within countries do exist, people within a given country often share common values and these values can be used to distinguish one country's culture from another (e.g., Hofstede, 1980; Shweder and LeVine, 1984; Triandis, 1989). Although there are numerous cultural frameworks (see Erez and Earley, 1993, for a review), the two key cultural values that have received the most attention in the organizational literature and are the most likely to influence teamwork are power distance and individualism. Power distance is the degree to which members of a culture accept and expect that power in society is unequally distributed (Hofstede, 1980). Cultures low in power distance minimize inequalities, favor less autocratic leadership, and favor less centralization of authority. Cultures high in power distance are characterized by a greater acceptance of inequalities and preference for authoritarianism, Power distance is likely to influence people's expectations about roles in teams. Specifically, in high power-distance cultures, team members are likely to use teamwork metaphors containing clear information about hierarchical role relationships. The following hypothesis captures this argument:

H2: The higher the power distance, the more likely it is that teamwork metaphors with clear roles will be used.

A second important element of national culture for teamwork is the value of individualism, defined as the degree of social connectedness among individuals (see Hofstede, 1980; Earley and Gibson, 1998, for reviews). In a highly individualistic society there are weak connections among individuals, the self-concept is defined in terms of the individual or traits, and personal identity is derived from individual achievement. In contrast, in less individualistic (i.e., collectivistic) societies, there are many and varied strong connections among people, self-concept is defined with reference to a societal and cultural context, and personal identity is derived through the ingroup and its successes (Earley and Gibson, 1998). Furthermore, those high in individualism tend to view group membership as task-specific and transitory, whereas those low in individualism view group membership as more long term, permanent, and far reaching. When individualism is low, work group membership is highly integrated into a person's life. For in-

stance, workers with extremely low individualism in Asia tend to eat evening meals together as a team and will often vacation together as an extension of their life within an organization (Earley and Gibson, 1998). Thus, in highly individualistic cultures team members should be less likely to use metaphors involving broad activity scope:

H3: Individualism decreases the likelihood that teamwork metaphors that are broad ill scope will be used.

Organizational Culture

A second important force likely to shape teamwork metaphors is organizational culture, defined as an identifiable set of beliefs and norms shared by members of an organization or subunit (Schein, 1993; Trice and Beyer, 1993). Organizational culture is a source of shared understanding and sense-making and shapes the behaviors of organizational members (Smirich and Calas, 1987; Schein, 1993; Trice and Beyer, 1993). A number of researchers have demonstrated that organizational and national cultures are not simply parallel constructs at two levels of analysis; rather, they have distinct contents and influences (e.g., Bartunek, 1984; Hofstede et al., 1990; Sackman, 1992; Chatman and Jehn, 1994). For example, Hofstede et al. (1990) found evidence for this distinction in a combined qualitative and quantitative study across 20 Danish and Dutch organizational units. National culture was a source of pervasive underlying values that guided priorities, whereas organizational culture was more context-specific, pertaining to preferred practices and orientations.

Because language is an element of organizational culture (Trice and Beyer, 1993), organizational culture is likely to play a role in the development of common teamwork metaphors in an organization. Empirical evidence indicates that organizational culture affects meaning structures in the form of perceptions about behavioral norms held by organizational members (Gundry and Rousseau, 1994). Without common language and cognitive views among at least some members of the organization, the link between comprehension and action would have to be continually renegotiated (Langfield-Smith, 1992; Laukkanen, 1994). Given that organizational cultures are likely to influence members' preferences and expectations, we propose:

H4: The use of a given metaphor for teamwork is likely to vary across organizations.

It is not enough to simply suggest that concepts vary across organizational cultures; it is also important to examine systematic variation due to specific aspects of culture. Researchers have demonstrated that patterns of orientations (O'Reilly, Chatman, and Caldwell, 1991; Kabanoff, Waldersee, and Cohen, 1995; Kabanoff and Holt, 1996) and practices (Hofstede et al., 1990) can be used to explain differences in organizational cultures. Kabanoff and colleagues (Kabanoff, Waldersee, and Cohen, 1995; Kabanoff and Holt, 1996) identified a set of nine orientations—performance, reward, authority, leadership, teamwork, commitment, normative orientation, participation, and affiliation—that can be discerned from organizational documents such as annual reports and demonstrated that different patterns of orientations were associated with different ways of portraying and communicating change. Several of the nine orientations provided in Kabanoff's work overlap conceptually with national culture, however, and many researchers recommend distinguishing between national culture and organizational culture (e.g., Hofstede et al., 1990). For example, the authority, leadership, normative, and commitment dimensions capture content similar to power distance, and teamwork, participation, and affiliation are conceptually similar to collectivism. In light of this overlap, we focus here on two orientations identified by Kabanoff and colleagues—performance and rewards—that have the least conceptual overlap with national cultural values as portrayed in the intercultural literature and thus clear distinctions between the two constructs. In addition these two dimensions have strong implications for the elements of teamwork that are embedded in metaphors. The first dimension, performance, captures the degree to which an organization emphasizes achievement, service, and efficiency and has been related to differences in attitudes toward change across organizations (Kabanoff and Holt, 1996), This dimension is likely related to the extent to which members of the organization will define teamwork in terms of clear consequences of activity in teams; thus, we propose:

H5: An organizational emphasis on performance increases the likelihood that teamwork metaphors implying clear outcomes will be used.

The second dimension, rewards, captures the degree to which an organization emphasizes inducements to participate and perform, including remuneration, bonus, compensation, and salary (Kabanoff and Holt, 1996), Kabanoff, Waldersee, and Cohen (1995) found different levels of emphasis on rewards across the organizations in their sample, and an emphasis on rewards was related to the tendency to view change as positive. In organizations that emphasize rewards, team members are likely to use metaphors that imply membership as induced by rewards rather than voluntary membership. The following hypothesis captures this idea:

H6: An organizational emphasis on rewards decreases the likelihood that teamwork metaphors implying voluntary membership will be used.

A separate stream of research has identified differences in practices across organizations. Hofstede et al. (1990) identified six fundamental practices in organizations: results orientation, degree of control, employee orientation, degree of professionalism, openness of systems, and normative orientation. Professionalism overlaps conceptually with power distance, and openness is similar to collectivism. Furthermore, results orientation and normative orientation are conceptually similar to Kabanoff's performance orientation. In light of this, we focused on two dimensions—degree of control and employee orientation—that are clearly distinct from national cultural characteristics, distinct from Kabanoff's two dimensions described above, and the most clearly related to conceptualizations of teamwork. Degree of control captures the extent to which people take organizational membership seriously and with reverence, the degree to which members of an organization are expected to follow rules and procedures, the extent to which punctuality is emphasized, and the degree to which the organization is cost-conscious (Hofstede et al., 1990). These practices should be related to concepts of teamwork that contain clear role information. Thus, we hypothesize:

H7: An organizational emphasis on tight control increases the likelihood that teamwork metaphors with clear roles will be used.

Employee orientation concerns the degree to which the organization decentralizes decision making, focuses on the employees as people, and shows concern for people beyond simply the organizational roles they play or the specific jobs they hold (Hofstede et al., 1990). In organizations with high employee orientation, members should use teamwork metaphors that emphasize involvement beyond a limited role:

H8: The greater the organization's emphasis on employee orientation, the likelier it is that teamwork metaphors that are broad in scope will be used.

Methods

Sample and Interview Procedures

Given our hypotheses about national cultural values, we selected the national contexts for our research—Puerto Rico, the Philippines, France, and the U.S.—to maximize differences on power distance and individualism (Erez and Earley, 1993; Earley and Gibson, 1998). Previous research (Hofstede, 1980; Erez and Earley, 1993) indicates that Puerto Rico is high on power distance and very low on individualism, with strong familial ties, extended family, common values, and a recognition of tradition. The Philippines is also high on power distance and low on individualism, but the key affiliation is to one's entire village or barrio, and social ties are often regional. Filipinos are also more formal, emphasizing respect for elders and authority figures. The French are unique in that they are more individualistic than workers in Latin or Asian countries, focusing on individual achievement, but, like Puerto Ricans or Filipinos, they are high on power distance and have a strong sense of hierarchy and adherence to the chain of command. Finally, although the U.S. comprises many subcultures, the dominant values are individualism and egalitarianism, with a strong tendency to circumvent hierarchy and tradition. Although a long history of research supports these differences, we conducted analyses to verify them in our sample, as described below.

We used four guidelines to select the organizations: (1) to control for industry-related effects, they all are in the same general industry; (2) they have facilities in each of our four country settings; (3) they exhibit extensive use of teams; and (4) they illustrate differences on the organizational culture dimensions we identified in our hypotheses; We selected the pharmaceutical and medical products industry and used the *Corporate Families and International Affiliates Directory* to identify specific organizations and their countries of operation. Ten organizations operated in all four of our country settings. We contacted each organization, provided a brief introduction to the research, and screened for their use of teams. Only six of the ten organizations used a variety of team types, including management teams, human resource project teams, marketing teams, sales and service delivery teams, production teams, and finance teams. As demonstrated in the descriptions taken from the popular press and summarized in table 14.1, these six organizations also varied in terms of performance and reward orientations and in terms of tight control and employee focus. We conducted an additional analysis, described below, however, to verify that this was the case in our sample. Organizations are disguised with pseudonyms throughout the paper.

We contacted human resource professionals in each organization and asked for assistance in identifying individuals from a variety of team functions, levels in the organization, and both high- and low-performing teams. We traveled to each nation and conducted in-depth personal interviews with one to five members in each team, ultimately totaling 107 individuals representing 52 teams, with 44 interviewees in the U.S., 16 in France, 23 in Puerto Rico, and 24 in the Philippines. A total of 30 interviews were conducted at Photoco, 6 at Chemco, 32 at Biomedco, 13 at Pharmco, 8 at Healthco, and 18 at Medco. Rank ranged from hourly employees to general managers. About half were women, and respondents' average age was 36 years; there were no significant differences in age, gender, or rank across nations or organizations, Teams were homogeneous in terms of organization and nationality.

We asked general questions about teamwork and examined the interview texts for the language that our subjects naturally used in the process of answering our questions. As a result, the data can be considered more "natural" than evoked (Kabanoff, 1997). Evoked data have a direct source and result from transparent questioning, while, with natural data, the interviewees have no way of knowing how the text data will be used. Interviews were conducted in the native language of the interviewees, with the assistance of a team of bilingual interviewers. The interview questions are provided in the Appendix [at the end of the chapter].

Analysis

Our analyses had four objectives. First, we used computer-assisted text analysis to identify metaphorical language used by our interviewees to describe teamwork. We used this information to create dependent variables for our statistical tests. Second, we ensured that the countries and organizations represented in our interview sample differed empirically as expected in terms of national culture and organizational culture. Third, we developed a quantitative database from our interviews. Finally, we conducted statistical analyses to test our hypotheses....

Identifying teamwork metaphors. For any qualitative analysis, a key challenge is to develop a word list to capture the constructs of interest (Gephart and Wolfe, 1989; Gephart, 1993; Jehn and Doucet, 1997). Thus, our first step in identifying teamwork metaphors was to develop a list of words that capture how people conceptualize teamwork....

Next, we printed the words onto cards and asked five raters from each country involved in the study to sort them into groups they felt represented metaphors for teamwork. The raters had themselves been members of work teams in their native countries, had some work experience together, were similar to each other, and resembled the interviewees in terms of demographic characteristics. They were told to define "teamwork" broadly but were not given a definition of teamwork....

... Through a process of discussion, negotiation, and elimination, the raters arrived at five piles, each of which they characterized by a different metaphor: family, sports, community, associates, and military. These five metaphor piles contained an average of 100 unique words each and included both English and non-English words (i.e., words that were not translatable into English). The raters defined the metaphors broadly and placed words in them that they felt elaborated the metaphor from their native-language point of view....

By way of illustration, one respondent in the Philippines drew a hut on a piece of paper when asked what mental images come to mind regarding his team and then explained:

The hut illustrates community. It's called a *nipa* hut. Sometimes you do require that the hut be moved from one location to another. And in the old days, *nipa* huts would probably be located along the safe side of a river because there's water there, fish would be there. Some erosion could happen and you would need to relocate the hut to a safer ground. In the Philippines, you would gather your neighbors, call them and you would put handles and literally lift the house—in one, big haul, the house as one big piece, and move it to a new location. And that's called the *bayanihan* spirit. I think that would best describe in my culture, how teams can work.

This excerpt is an example of the community metaphor. The respondent utilized three words from the community word list: community, neighbors, and *bayanihan* (literally, a Filipino word for team). Illustrating the sports metaphor, a respondent in the U.S. said the following in response to a question about rewards:

I also think it's easy to have individual recognition within the team and still have a clear direction, but the team results are what's important. We have outstanding individuals on the team. And, very similar to a sports team, somebody needs to hit the home run; somebody needs to stop the ball. You know, somebody needs to catch'm and drag'm out. So I think it's a combination, but I think it's very difficult to play together as a team now. You know, we have bench players too. And we need bench players. We need the people that can get up and go fix the equipment every day.

In this excerpt, the respondent explained the tendency for teams to struggle with roles and the recognition process, using several words from the sports word list. The sports metaphor helps to graphically depict the process of "backing each other up" on a team, similar to the support provided by bench players to the rest of the players on the field in a baseball game. Using a different metaphor (the military) to describe a related phenomenon, a respondent in the Philippines stated:

I am supposed to be an active shooter in terms of assisting and liasoning with the people and making sure that [the organization's] kinds of problems are run at sort of a management level. At the moment it's very [prevalent in the] rank and file. We have not really gone to the reduction of a lot of employees. So I'm helping to do that. Right now we're having to think in terms of manpower in the trenches. . . .

Here, the respondent illustrated what he viewed as the benefits of a militaristic approach to using teams, in that responsibilities and direction are clear. A respondent in

Table 14.1
Organizational Descriptions

Firm	Reward emphasis	Performance emphasis	Employee orientation	Tight control	Description
Photoco	Moderate	High	Moderate	Low	The mission of Photoco is to become a world-class, results-oriented organization with many product options, differentiated and cost-effective solutions, quick market responsiveness, and flawless quality through a diverse team of employees. Photoco has been struggling in recent years, fragmented as a result of divestiture, and recent emphasis has been on cost reduction and reinforcing traditional products.
Chemco	Low	Low	Moderate	High	Chemco's mission focuses on innovation in health care products. Chemco has had a half century of steady sales increases and attributes these results to long-term investment in people and processes, claiming an "unrelenting attention to focus, innovation and effectiveness" enables it to "navigate successfully through challenging times in the short term, while simultaneously strengthening our position for the long term."
Biomedco	High	Moderate	High	High	Biomedco describes its competitive advantage as its people and its values of customers, innovation, integrity, and people. Company documents state that it is "people with a purpose, working together to make the lives of people everywhere healthier, striving in everything we do to become simply better as judged by all those we serve: customers, shareholders, employees and the global community." Personal commitment, team spirit, and the creation of a strong common culture around the world are central.
Pharmco	High	High	High	High	Pharmco is a research-driven company with a mission to provide society with superior products and services and innovations that improve quality of life. Pharmco emphasizes a meaningful work environment and advancement opportunities for employees and superior rate of return for investors. Core values include the integrity, knowledge, imagination, diversity, and teamwork of employees.
Healthco	Moderate	Low	Moderate	Low	Healthco is the most comprehensive producer of health care products and services in the sample, serving consumer, pharmaceutical, and professional markets. Healthco's credo focuses on ethics, social responsibility, local responsiveness, and flexibility. Management of each franchise, or group of product categories, is led by a general manager who reports directly to a company group chairman.
Medco	Moderate	Moderate	Low	Low	Medco is focused on learning, excellence, and new frontiers and is characterized by an intolerance of bureaucracy and emphasis on boundarylessness. Global intellectual capital and best practices are prized. Diverse teams are used to maximize innovation and to support a decentralized structure. Company documents describe the "right" leadership teams as those with "the agility and speed to seize the big opportunities we know this changing world will present us."

the U.S. expressed a contrasting expectation using the associates metaphor:

> The responsibilities which we ask of each team make them function as if they were a franchise organization, a group of franchise associates. They are given as much autonomy and freedom and empowerment as we possibly can, to make decisions at the local level.

In this excerpt, the respondent used two words from the associates word list—franchise and associates—to convey the practice of allowing teams the autonomy to make their own decisions. As yet another contrast, a Puerto Rican respondent said, "Every family has to take care of the team work. Every family has to work together. If we consolidate that feeling. . . . A team is a family." Using the family metaphor, this respondent captured the expectation that teamwork involves elements of nurturing and support.

Constructing dependent variables. We used the results of our text searches for the five metaphors to create the dependent variables for our hypothesis tests. The level of analysis for our hypothesis tests is the metaphor. Each occurrence of a metaphor is considered an event, for a total of 462 occurrences. The metaphors—sports, military, family, community, and associates—represent five options from which a given interviewee could choose when discussing teamwork. Thus, our first dependent variable, choice of metaphor, has five possible values (sports, military, family, community, or associates). This variable was used in tests of H1 and H4 described below.

Each of the five metaphors both illustrates the mental picture the respondent has of teamwork and expresses certain expectations of team practices, particularly with regard to roles, scope, objectives, and membership. To test our hypotheses about these expectations, we created four additional dependent variables, one for each category of expectations (roles, scope, objectives, and membership). We independently compared the content of the excerpts for each metaphor to better understand these expectations and then categorized the family and military metaphors as containing more information about hierarchical roles than the community, associates, or sports metaphors. For example, the family metaphor excerpts contained information about identifiable roles, like mother, father,

brother, and sister, each with varying levels of authority. We used this information to create a dependent variable called *roles*, which was coded 1 in our analysis if the metaphor occurrence was family or military, or 0 for any other metaphor.

We categorized the family and community metaphors as broader in scope than the sports, military, and associates metaphors, primarily because many of the family and community excerpts expressed far-reaching boundaries, suggestive of broader activity domains, such as a cultural community or entire province. We used this information to create the variable *scope*, which was coded 1 in our analysis if the metaphor occurrence was family or community, or 0 for any other metaphor.

We categorized the sports and associates metaphors as implying more voluntary membership than the family, military, or community metaphors. In excerpts using sports and associates language, respondents frequently mentioned that members have the choice to participate on teams; this rarely occurred in conjunction with the other metaphors. Thus, we used this information to create the variable *membership*, which was coded 1 in our analysis if the metaphor was sports or associates, or 0 for any other metaphor.

Finally, we categorized the sports and military metaphors as containing more information about objectives than the family, associates, or community metaphors, due to the common presence of concepts such as winning, losing, performance, goals, and survival in the military and sports excerpts; these were rare in the other excerpts. We used this information to create the variable *objectives*, which was coded 1 in our analysis if the metaphor was sports or military, or 0 for any other metaphor.

Confirming national and organizational differences in culture. Before testing the hypotheses, we verified that the nations and organizations in our sample differed along the dimensions of culture we anticipated and developed the independent variables for power distance, individualism, performance emphasis, reward emphasis, tight control, and employee orientation. . . .

. . . Table 14.2 contains some sample terms.

Hypothesis testing. In testing H1 and H4, that the use of a given metaphor is likely to vary across nations and organizations, the dependent variable is the choice of metaphor from five possible types, and each occurrence of a metaphor in the interviews is treated as one event. Because the dependent variable can take on multiple forms that are not ordered, we used multinomial logit (Aldrich and Nelson, 1984) to test these hypotheses. Multinomial logit estimates the probability of choice among a set of $J - 1$ categories in a dependent variable (in our case $J - 1 = 4$); the omitted category is like an omitted dummy variable and serves as the comparison. The independent variables in this model are three dummy variables for country and five dummy variables for organization. We also included a number of control variables. First, we controlled for gender, which may affect how people think about teams and the language they use to describe them. Gender was coded 1 for female and 0 for male. Second, team function may also influence metaphor choice. From self-reports of function in the interviews, we created five dummy variables to capture six categories of function: finance, production/engineering, marketing, human resources, management, and sales/service. Finally, because interviews varied in length, we included the total number of words in the interview as a final control. Upon entering these variables, we conducted a Wald test (Judge et al., 1985) to examine the joint hypothesis across all equations that the country dummies (H1) taken together are statistically significant and the joint hypothesis across all equations that the

organization dummies (H4) taken together are statistically significant.

We used logistic regression to test the hypotheses on the relationship between dimensions of national and organizational culture and the use of metaphors containing certain expectations about clarity of roles, breadth of team scope, the nature of membership, and objectives. The four metaphor category variables—*roles, scope, membership,* and *objectives*—served as dependent variables in four separate regression equations. The independent variables for these models were power distance, individualism, performance emphasis, reward emphasis, tight control, and employee orientation. As in the model above, we included gender, function, and number of words as controls. . . .

Results

Variation in Teamwork Metaphors

Mean frequencies for each metaphor by country and organization appear in table 14.3. Parameter estimates and model statistics are presented in table 14.4. The Wald test for the effect of country on choice of metaphor was statistically significant ($\chi^2 = 42.80$, $p < .001$), supporting H1, that the use of a given metaphor is likely to vary across countries. The Wald test for the effect of organization on choice of metaphor was also statistically significant ($\chi^2 = 47.98$, $p < .001$), supporting H4, that the use of a given metaphor is likely to vary across organizations.

Table 14.2
Search Terms for Cultural Values

Dimension	Definition	Sample search terms
Power distance	The degree to which members of a culture accept and expect that power in society is unequally distributed (Hofstede, 1980)	Hierarchy, respect, control, rank, subordinate, superior, authority, stratified, reverence
Individualism	The degree of social connectedness (Earley and Gibson, 1998)	Individual, self-interest, own, personal freedom, independence, self-reliance, self-emphasis, alone
Employee orientation (based on survey items from Hofstede et al., 1990)	A concern for people	Employees, individuals, union, community, personal
Tight control (based on survey items from Hofstede et al., 1990)	Amount of internal structuring in the organization	Tight, cost conscious, punctual, well-groomed, serious
Rewards (Kabanoff, Waldersee, & Cohen, 1995)	Concern with organizational rewards	Bonus, compensation, salary, reward
Performance (Kabanoff, Waldersee, & Cohen, 1995)	Concern with performance	Achievement, performance, service, efficiency

National and Organizational Culture and Metaphor Use

H2 predicted that greater power distance would increase the likelihood that metaphors containing clear role content would be used. Contrary to this, the logistic regression results on model 1 presented in table 14.5 show that the coefficient for power distance is negative and statistically significant. H3 predicted that individualism would decrease the likelihood that metaphors that are broad in scope would be used. In support of this hypothesis, the coefficient for individualism was negative and statistically significant in model 2, in which scope is the dependent variable.

H5 predicted that the emphasis an organization places on performance would increase the likelihood that metaphors containing clear objectives and outcomes would be used. This hypothesis was supported. The coefficient for performance emphasis in model 3 was positive and statistically significant, using objectives as the dependent variable. H6, predicting that an organization's emphasis on rewards would decrease the likelihood of using metaphors concerning voluntary membership was marginally supported, as shown by the results of model 4. H7, predicting that the extent to which an organization emphasizes tight control would increase the likelihood of using metaphors containing clear roles, was supported (model 1). Finally, H8 predicted that the extent to which an organization emphasizes employee orientation would increase the likelihood that metaphors broad in scope would be used. Contrary to this hypothesis, the relationship in model 2 was negative and significant.

Discussion

This study demonstrated that people around the globe hold different definitions of teamwork, as indicated by the metaphors they use when they talk about their teams. Furthermore, this variance is systematic across nations and organizations, with sev-

Table 14.3

Mean Frequency of Occurrence of Metaphors by Organization and Country*

Metaphor	Organization					
	Photoco	Chemco	Biomedco	Pharmco	Healthco	Medco
Sports						
Puerto Rico	.00	.50	.00	2.33	NA	NA
Philippines	1.50	NA	.33	1.33	.75	1.33
France	.00	.00	NA	NA	3.25	2.33
U.S.	.64	NA	1.06	.86	NA	2.44
Military						
Puerto Rico	.00	.50	.00	1.00	NA	NA
Philippines	.13	NA	.17	.33	.25	1.33
France	.25	.00	NA	NA	.00	.00
U.S.	.27	NA	.12	.29	NA	.67
Family						
Puerto Rico	.00	2.50	.33	.33	NA	NA
Philippines	.50	NA	1.5	1.33	.75	3.67
France	.00	1.50	NA	NA	1.75	.50
U.S.	.18	NA	.76	.57	NA	1.33
Community						
Puerto Rico	.14	.50	.56	.67	NA	NA
Philippines	1.13	NA	2.33	3.0	.50	4.33
France	.00	.50	NA	NA	1.75	.83
U.S.	1.09	NA	1.23	.29	NA	.44
Associates						
Puerto Rico	.29	.75	.11	.00	NA	NA
Philippines	.13	NA	1.0	1.33	3.50	1.67
France	1.50	4.50	NA	NA	1.25	1.33
U.S.	.91	NA	.53	1.14	NA	4.56

* The total number of interviewees included 30 from Photoco, 6 from Chemco, 32 from Biomedco, 13 from Pharmco, and 18 from Medco. "NA" indicates countries in which we conducted no interviews for a particular organization.

Table 14.4
Multinomial Regression Results (N = 462)*

Variable	Sports	Family	Military	Community
Gender	.53	1.42••••	0.74	1.22•••
	(.40)	(.44)	(.66)	(.41)
Number of words	0.00	0.00	−.00	0.00
	(.00)	(.00)	(.00)	(.00)
Finance (omitted function = Sales & Service)	−.97	−.94	.99	.51
	(1.53)	(1.63)	(.17)	(1.42)
Production/engineering	−1.72•••	−1.68•••	−1.65•	−1.06
	(.60)	(.64)	(.92)	(.75)
Marketing	−.90	−.54	−.86	.05
	(.70)	(.74)	(1.10)	(.82)
HR	−.72	−2.35••••	−.96	−.48
	(.56)	(.64)	(.91)	(.72)
Management	−1.40•	−2.91••	−0.44	−0.26
	(.72)	(1.22)	(1.08)	(.84)
Puerto Rico (omitted category = U.S.)	2.09•••	2.55•••	2.31••	2.84••••
	(.79)	(.86)	(1.10)	(.80)
Philippines	0.10	1.91••••	0.39	1.51•••
	(.50)	(.56)	(.79)	(.50)
France	.76	.49	−1.53	.77
	(.54)	(.65)	(1.23)	(.59)
Photoco (omitted org. = Medco)	3.04••••	−.84	.83	2.33•••
	(.93)	(.91)	(1.29)	(.89)
Chemco	2.61•••	.37	.12	2.35•••
	(.98)	(.85)	(1.29)	(.91)
Biomedco	2.15••	−1.49•	.66	
	(.98)	(.88)	(1.15)	(.93)
Pharmco	1.54•	−.93	−.60	.50
	(.90)	(.80)	(1.57)	(.87)
Healthco	2.11••	−.07	.89	1.00
	(.86)	(.74)	(1.21)	(.83)
Log likelihood	−620.23			
Model χ^2	162.75••••			
H1† (country) χ^2	42.80••••			
H4‡ (organization) χ^2	47.98••••			

• *p* < .10; •• *p* < .05; ••• *p* < .01; •••• *p* < .001; based on Wald chi-square tests.

* Standard errors are in parentheses. The omitted category for metaphors is associates.

† Test for H1 is Wald test for the joint hypothesis for the country dummy variables across all equations.

‡ Test for H4 is Wald test for the joint hypothesis for the organization dummy variables across all equations.

eral predictable differences based on values, orientations, and practices. If the national context is individualistic, for example, then sports or associates metaphors are likely to resonate. If the organization emphasizes tight control, then a military or family metaphor is likely to resonate. Because they represent mappings from a source domain (e.g., military) to a target domain (e.g., the work team), these metaphors carry with them expectations for how teams will be managed and how team processes will unfold. For example, employees who use the military metaphor are likely to have strong expectations about clarity of objectives and performance indicators.

Our use of in-depth interviews covering a variety of topics concerning teamwork broadened our analysis, and we made every attempt to be sensitive to intercultural variation. Had we not conducted our analyses with the assistance of researchers from each nation, our results may have represented a North American bias. Instead, through a careful, culturally sensitive process, we were able to identify metaphors that are relevant across cultures and organizations. Furthermore, we used an iterative process, moving back and forth between qualitative and quantitative data, as has been recommended for early stages of research (e.g., Kabanoff, Waldersee, and Cohen, 1995).

Table 14.5
Logistic Regression Results (N = 462)[*]

Variable	Model 1 Clear roles	Model 2 Broad scope	Model 3 Clear objectives	Model 4 Voluntary membership
Gender	−.66•••	−.99•••	.38•	.97••••
	(.30)	(.27)	(.28)	(.28)
Number of words	−.00	.00	−.00	−.00
	(.00)	(.00)	(.00)	(.00)
Finance	−.38	.20	−.30	−.61
	(.97)	(.95)	(.95)	(.97)
Production/engineering	−.65•	−.50	−.64•	.62•
	(.45)	(.44)	(.43)	(.43)
Marketing	−.24	.20	−.76•	−.02
	(.53)	(.51)	(.52)	(.51)
Human resources	−1.37•••	−.95•••	.04	1.01•••
	(.45)	(.43)	(.41)	(.42)
Management	−1.38••	−.32	−.28	.25
	(.67)	(.55)	(.52)	(.52)
National culture				
Power distance	−1.72••••	−1.71••••	.99••	2.06••••
	(.57)	(.48)	(.50)	(.48)
Individualism	−52.64•••	−87.30••••	36.85••	86.36••••
	(18.71)	(17.86)	(18.14)	(17.66)
Organizational culture				
Performance emphasis	−.15	−.12	.36•••	.05
	(.15)	(.13)	(.14)	(.13)
Reward emphasis	−.26•	1.12••	.28	−.88•
	(.66)	(.60)	(.70)	(.61)
Tight control	19.22•••	19.22•••	−17.97	−19.83•••
	(8.23)	(7.47)	(9.12)	(7.51)
Employee emphasis	−1.41•	−1.89•••	.87	1.88•••
	(.93)	(.81)	(.83)	(.80)
Likelihood ratio χ^2 (d.f. = 13)	37.53••••	72.98••••	25.40•••	70.88••••

• $p < .10$; •• $p < .05$; ••• $p < .01$; •••• $p < .001$; one-tailed and based on Wald chi-square tests.
[*] Standard errors are in parentheses.

The strengths of our study must be tempered with a recognition of its limitations. Conceptually, a frequent criticism of attempts to capture the gestalt of a phenomenon as rich and full as national or organizational culture is that the researchers may be "guilty" of using or promoting stereotypes. From the perspective of cognitive psychology, applying the concept of stereotypes to our understanding of the impact of culture is indeed appropriate (Gannon et al., 1994); more recently, however, the term stereotype has been used in a pejorative way. Adler (1991) argued persuasively that it is legitimate to use stereotypes in cross-cultural contexts if they are descriptive rather than evaluative, substantiated, and subject to change when new information merits it. Thus, while this study supports the linguistic approach to describing the impact of culture, clearly, culturally determined metaphors should be used with caution. They do not pertain to every individual or even to every subgroup within a society. Rather, they highlight cultural differences in an easily understood way that provides a rich vocabulary for discussion. . . .

Our research . . . has direct practical application. A strong implication of these findings is that multinational managers cannot assume that their own conceptualization of teamwork will be shared. Team members in different nations or organizational contexts are likely to have different expectations for how the team will be managed. Imagine a scenario in which team members define teamwork using a family metaphor that includes clear parental roles. A manager who defines teamwork more like a community or a circle of associates is not likely to meet the members' expectations for parental guidance and support. Or imagine a situation in which team members picture their team like a sports team, with clear, competitive objectives for a specific task. If their manager holds a conception of teamwork similar to a family that is less task focused, he or she is likely to be deemed ineffective in accomplishing objectives. A similar scenario could play out in a cross-organizational team, such as one representing a merger among two very different organizational cultures. If some of the team members picture their team as doing battle with fierce competitors, while others view the team as a loosely connected open community, conflict regarding a preferred structure, process, and deliverables is likely to ensue.

In these scenarios, it would be helpful for those involved to identify the language being used to talk about their team, share the expectations that map to the target domain from the source domain, and negotiate to resolve the potentially conflicting preferred practices in a mutually agreeable manner. Metaphor provides a very potent and graphic tool for doing so. Taken as a whole, our results do not suggest that any given metaphor is good or bad but, rather, that metaphor use varies across cultural settings and should be considered explicitly by managers and researchers. While different teamwork metaphors among team members or between members and the organization could be a source of conflict, metaphorical assessment may also help facilitate greater understanding among coworkers when the metaphors are discussed and explained and can be used to manage effectively in multinationals.

In conclusion, our research challenges the assumption that the meaning of teamwork is commonly held across contexts and thus represents a first step toward a cultural contingency framework for the meaning of teamwork. Because empirical research on teams across cultures has been limited, leaders within multinational organizations have been forced to make educated guesses about the most appropriate methods to manage teams across geographic facilities. This research provides insight into variation in teamwork metaphors that can help team members, managers, and researchers identify their common understandings as well as their cultural differences.

References

Abrahamson, E., and D. Hambrick. 1997. "Attentional homogeneity in industries: The effect of discretion." *Journal of Organizational Behavior*, 18: 513–532.

Adler, N. J. 1991. *International Dimensions of Organizational Behavior*, 2d ed. Boston: PWS Kent.

Aldrich, J. H., and F. D. Nelson. 1984. *Linear Probability, Logit, and Probit Models*. Newbury Park, CA: Sage.

Ayman, R., and M. M. Chemers. 1983. "Relationship of supervisory behavior ratings to work group effectiveness and subordinate satisfaction among Iranian managers." *Journal of Applied Psychology*, 68: 338–341.

Bar-Tal, D. 1990. *Group Beliefs*. New York. Springer-Verlag.

Bartunek, J. M. 1984. "Changing interpretive schemes and organizational restructuring: The example of a religious order." *Administrative Science Quarterly*, 29: 355–373.

Blair, I. V., and M. R. Banaji. 1996. "Automatic and controlled processes in stereotype priming." *Journal of Personality and Social Psychology*, 70: 1142–1163.

Brannen, M. Y. 1994. "Your next boss is Japanese: Negotiating cultural change at a Western Massachusetts paper plant." Unpublished doctoral dissertation, University of Massachusetts, Amherst.

Cannon-Bowers, J. A., E. Salas, and S. Converse. 1993. "Shared mental models in expert team decision making." In N. J. Castellan (ed.), *Individual and Group Decision Making*, 221–246. Hillsdale, NJ: Lawrence Erlbaum.

Chatman, J., and K. Jehn. 1994. "Assessing the relationship between industry characteristics and organizational culture: How different can you be?" *Academy of Management Journal*, 37: 522–553.

Cohen, S. G., and D. E. Bailey. 1997. "What makes teams work: Group effectiveness research from the shop floor to the executive suite." *Journal of Management*, 23: 239–290.

Cox, T. H., S. A. Lobel, and P. S. McLeod. 1991. "Effects of ethnic group cultural differences on cooperative and competitive behavior on a group task." *Academy of Management Journal*, 34: 827–847.

Earley, P. C. 1994. "Self or group? Cultural effects of training on self-efficacy and performance." *Administrative Science Quarterly*, 39: 89–117.

Earley, P. C., and M. Erez. 1987. "Comparative analysis of goal-setting strategies across cultures." *Journal of Applied Psychology*, 72: 658–665.

Earley, P. C. and C. B. Gibson. 2001. *Multinational Teams: A New Perspective*. Lawrence Erlbaum.

Earley, P. C., and H. Singh. 1995. "International and intercultural management research: What's next?" *Academy of Management Journal*, 38: 327–340.

Eby, L. T., and D. H. Dobbins. 1997. "Collectivistic orientation in teams: An individual and group-level analysis." *Journal of Organizational Behavior*, 18: 275–295.

Edmondson, A. 1999. "Psychological safety and learning behavior in work teams." *Administrative Science Quarterly*, 44: 350–383.

Erez, M., and P. C. Earley. 1993. *Culture, Self-identity, and Work*. New York: Oxford University Press.

Erez, M., and A. Somech. 1996. "Is group productivity loss the rule or the exception? Effects of culture and group-based motivation." *Academy of Management Journal*, 39: 1513–1537.

Gannon, M. J., and Associates. 1994. *Understanding Global Cultures: Metaphorical Journeys Through 17 Countries*. Thousand Oaks, CA: Sage.

Gephart, R. P. 1993. "The textual approach: Risk and blame in disaster sense-making." *Academy of Management Journal*, 36: 1465–1514.

Gephart, R. P., and R. Wolfe. 1989. "Qualitative data analysis: Three microcomputer-supported approaches." Academy of Management Best Paper Proceedings: 382150386.

Gibson, C. B. 1994. "The implications of culture for organization structure: An investigation of three perspectives." In J. L. C. Cheng and R. B. Peterson (eds.), *Advances in International Comparative Management*, 9: 3–38. Greenwich, CT: JAI Press.

———. 1999. Do they do what they believe they can? Group-efficacy beliefs and group performance across tasks and cultures." *Academy of Management Journal*, 42: 138–152.

———. 2001. "From knowledge accumulation to transformation: Phases and cycles of collective cognition in workgroups." *Journal of Organizational Behavior*, 22: 121–134.

Gundry, L. K., and D. M. Rousseau. 1994. "Critical incidents in communicating culture to newcomers: The meaning in the message." *Human Relations*, 46: 1063–1087.

Hofstede, G. 1980. *Culture's Consequences: International Differences in Work-related Values*. Beverly Hills, CA: Sage.

Hofstede, G., B. Neuljen, D. D. Ohayv, and G. Sanders. 1990. "Measuring organizational cultures: A quantitative study across twenty cases." *Administrative Science Quarterly*, 35: 286–316.

Jehn, K. S., and L. Doucet. 1997. "Analyzing hard words in a sensitive setting American expatriates in communist China." Unpublished working paper, the Wharton School, University of Pennsylvania.

Judge, G. G., W. E. Griffiths, R. C. Hill, H. Lütkepohl, and T. C. Lee. 1985. *The Theory and Practice of Econometrics*, 2d ed. New York: Wiley.

Kabanoff, B., and J. Holt. 1996. "Changes in the espoused values of Australian organizations 1986–1990." *Journal of Organizational Behavior*, 17: 201–219.

Kabanoff, B., R. Waldersee, and M. Cohen. 1995. "Espoused values and organizational change themes." *Academy of Management Journal*, 38: 1075–1104.

Kirkman, B. L., and D. L. Shapiro. 2001. "The impact of cultural values on job satisfaction and organizational commitment in self-managing work teams. The mediating role of employee resistance." *Academy of Management Journal*, 44: 557–569.

Kirkman, B. L, C. B. Gibson, and D. L Shapiro. 2001. "Exporting teams: Enhancing the implementation and effectiveness of work teams in global affiliates." *Organizational Dynamics*, vol. 29 (in press).

Lakoff, G. 1993. "The contemporary theory of metaphor." In A. Ortony (ed.), *Metaphor and Thought*: 202–252. Cambridge: Cambridge University Press.

Langfeld-Smith, K. 1992. "Exploring the need for a shared cognitive map." *Journal of Management Studies*, 29: 349–368.

Laukkanen, M. 1994. "Comparative cause mapping of organizational cognitions." *Organization Science*, 5: 322–343.

McGrath, J. E. 1984. *Groups, Interaction and Performance*. Englewood Cliffs, NJ: Prentice-Hall.

Oetzel, J. G. 1998. "Culturally homogeneous and heterogeneous groups: Explaining communication processes through individualism-collectivism and self-construal." *International Journal of Intercultural Relations*, 22: 135–161.

Orasanu, J., and E. Salas. 1993. "Team decision making in complex environments." In G. A. Klein, J. Orasanu, R. Calderwood, and C. E. Zsambok (eds.), *Decision Making in Action: Models and Methods*: 327–345. Norwood, NJ: Ablex.

O'Reilly, C. A., III., J. Chatman, and D. F. Caldwell. 1991. "People and organizational culture: A profile comparison approach to assessing person-organization fit." *Academy of Management Journal*, 34: 487–516.

Pillai, R., and J. R. Meindl. 1998. "Context and charisma: A 'meso' level examination of the relationship of organic structure, collectivism, and crisis to charismatic leadership." *Journal of Management*, 24: 643–871.

Qualitative Solutions and Research. 1997. *QSR*NUDIST*. Scolari Sage Publication Software. Thousand Oaks, CA: Sage.

Quinn, N. 1997. "Research on shared task strategy." In C. Strauss and N. Quinn (eds.), *A Cognitive Theory of Cultural Meaning*: 137–189. Cambridge, Cambridge University Press.

Sackman, S. A. 1992. "Culture and subcultures: An analysis of organizational knowledge." *Administrative Science Quarterly*, 37: 140–162.

Schein, E. H. 1993. *Organizational Culture and Leadership*, 2d ed. San Francisco: Jossey-Bass.

Schneider, S., and A. DeMeyer. 1991. "Interpreting and responding to strategic issues: The impact of national culture." *Strategic Management Journal*, 12: 307–320.

Shane, S. 1994. "The effect of national culture on the choice between licensing and direct foreign investment." *Strategic Management Journal*, 15: 627–642.

Shweder, R. A., and R. A. LeVine. 1984. *Culture Theory: Essays on Mind, Self, and Emotion*. New York: Cambridge University Press.

Smirich, L, and M. Calas. 1987. "Organizational culture: A critical assessment." In F. M. Jablin, L. L. Putnam, and L. W. Porter (eds.), *Handbook of Organizational Communication*: 228–263. Newbury Park, CA: Sage.

Sundstrom, E., and Associates. 1999. *Supporting Work Team Effectiveness*. San Francisco: Jossey-Bass.

Triandis, H. C. 1989. "The self and social behavior in differing cultural contexts." *Psychological Review*, 96: 506–520.

Triandis, H. C. 1994. "Cross-cultural industrial and organizational psychology." In H. C. Triandis, M. D. Dunnette, and L. Hough (eds.), *Handbook of Industrial and Organizational Psychology*, 2d ed., 4: 103–172. Palo Alto, CA: Consulting Psychologists Press.

Trice, H., and J. Beyer. 1993. *The Cultures of Work Organizations*. Englewood Cliffs, NJ: Prentice-Hall.

APPENDIX: Interview Protocol

1. Could you tell us a little about what you do and the teams you work with?

2. Who is on the teams? How are these members selected? How are responsibilities divided?

3. What is the function of the teams [what outputs do they provide]?

4. Who is the team's "customer" [internal or external]?

5. Who receives the teams' work [who is directly downstream in the process]?

6. How is performance monitored and rewarded?

7. What kind of feedback do teams receive about performance?

8. How do you know when you have done a good job?

9. Do you believe the teams are effective? Why or why not?

10. Do the teams have leaders? What are the responsibilities of the leader?

11. Who does the team report to? Does it interact with other teams?

12. Would the teams benefit from more direction? Who should provide it? In what format?

13. What are the key factors that contribute to and/or inhibit the success of the teams?

14. How are practices shared in this organization?

15. To what extent does headquarters dictate practices?

16. Is individual achievement or collective achievement more important in this organization?

17. Is individual achievement or collective achievement more important in this country?

18. What facets of the culture here impact teams, either positively or negatively?

19. What mental images do people use for teams in this country?

20. Do you have anything else you would like to add?

Cristina B. Gibson and Mary E. Zellmer-Bruhn, "Metaphors and Meaning: An Intercultural Analysis of the Concept of Teamwork." In *Administrative Science Quarterly* 46: 274–303. Copyright © 2001. Reprinted with permission. ✦

Chapter 15
Beach Time, Bridge Time, and Billable Hours

The Temporal Structure of Technical Contracting

James A. Evans, Gideon Kunda, and Stephen R. Barley

How do people escape organizational control? According to conventional wisdom, the way to accomplish this is to become a "free agent" and move from the organization directly to the marketplace. As Evans, Kunda, and Barley explain, recent years have seen a virtual explosion of career advice advocating the advantages of freelancing, consulting, and other short-term employment contracts. These employment activities are touted as enhancing personal freedom and flexibility, while making it possible to shed organizational obligations and constraints.

These researchers' study of technical contractors challenges this conventional wisdom. Although contractors gain greater freedom and flexibility in some areas, they are often unable to take advantage of these aspects of their work life. Moreover, in many ways, contractors experienced even less control and greater constraints than they might have had they been employed by organizations. Organizations control their members, but can also shelter them from some of the time demands engendered by the marketplace.

Feeling overworked and pressed for time have become familiar complaints among members of the American middle class. Managers and professionals routinely commiserate about working long hours and what those hours cost them and their families. The booming market for advice on managing time effectively and the popularity of ac-ademic treatises with titles like *The Overworked American* (Schor, 1991) and *The Time Bind* (Hochschild, 1997) attest to the issue's resonance. In most accounts, temporally greedy organizations are to blame for the "time famine" (Perlow, 1999), and recommended solutions usually involve organizational policies that strike a compromise over how many and which hours employers can lay claim- Some commentators, however, have suggested that employees can gain temporal control by leaving organizational employment for a life in the labor market (Handy, 1989; Kanter, 1989, 1995; Bridges, 1994; Pink, 1998, 2001). The theme of liberation through markets is also found in the recent literature on boundaryless, project-based and portfolio careers, which unfold across rather than within organizations (Faulkner and Anderson, 1987; Mirvis and Hall, 1994; Arthur and Rousseau, 1996; Jones, 1996; Weick, 1996; Gold and Fraser, 2002). Although scholars have noted a rise in market-oriented careers, they have yet to investigate whether such careers actually grant incumbents more control over their time.

The idea that organizations make unreasonable demands on people's time revolves around two issues: how many and which hours people work. The first issue, how many hours people work, is most fully explored in the literature on "overworked Americans." Interest in the topic burgeoned after Schor (1991) claimed that American men and women were working considerably more hours in the mid-1980s than they had in the 1960s and that growth in the number of weeks that people devote to work explained most of this increase, Although some researchers have disputed Schor's findings on methodological grounds (Robinson and Godbey, 1997), a general consensus has emerged: workers at the lower end of the income distribution often have difficulty finding enough work, while people with higher incomes, especially those in professional and managerial jobs, work more hours than ever before (Coleman and Pencavel, 1993a, 1993b; Bluestone and Rose, 1997, 1998; Jacobs and Gerson, 1998; Reynolds, 2003).

Scholars have offered several explanations for why professionals and managers work so many hours. These explanations range from norms about work (Kunda, 1992; Blair-Loy and Wharton, 2002) and rampant consumerism (Schor, 1991) to the notion that work offers an escape from stressful homes (Hochschild, 1997). Most frequently, however, scholars indict managers and organizations. Schor (1991) and others (Maume and Bellas, 2001) have argued that instead of hiring new employees, organizations prefer to extract longer hours from salaried workers because doing so reduces labor costs. Bluestone and Rose (1997) and Hecksher (1995) claimed that rampant downsizing and increasing job insecurity have led white-collar employees to work longer hours in the hope of avoiding layoffs. Long hours signal the kind of commitment and visibility that employees believe firms demand in return for raises, promotions, and continued employment (Bailyn, 1993; Perlow, 1997).

The second issue, which hours people work, is addressed in the literature on work-family balance under the banner of flexibility. Flexibility can mean many things. Although Kickert (1984) discussed flexibility in the context of strategic planning, he captured flexibility's allure, calling it "the magic word." In the context of dual-career issues, the term usually suggests ceding control to workers over the circumstances of their work by enabling them to vary those circumstances to address personal and family needs and uncertainties (Golden, 2001). The circumstance most often implied in flexibility programs is time. In this paper, flexibility always means temporal flexibility, the ability to determine which and how many hours one works.

Flexibility first became an issue in the mid-1970s when enough middle-class women had entered the managerial and professional workforce to generate concern over dual-career families (e.g., Bailyn, 1970; Rapoport and Rapoport, 1978). In such families, men and women discovered that it was difficult to rear children when both spouses worked more than forty hours a week and when neither could accommodate their work schedules to family needs. As a result, both family and work suffer. When work spills over into the home, workers are more likely to experience marital conflict, withdraw from their families, and neglect domestic responsibilities (Bolger, Delongis, and Kessler, 1989; Barnett, 1994; Paden and Buehler, 1995; Repetti and Wood, 1997; Bumpus, Crouter, and McHale, 1999). When home spills into the workplace, job satisfaction falls while absenteeism and turnover in-

crease (Goff, Mount, and Jamison, 1990; Higgins, Duxbury, and Irving, 1992; Forthofer et al., 1996). Commentators have argued that in the face of such difficulties, men and women need leeway to adjust their schedules to meet simultaneously the needs of their employers and the needs of their families (Bailyn, 1993; Tausig and Fenwick, 2001).

While American employers have generally resisted calls to limit the number of hours that employees work, since the 1970s they have gradually adopted a variety of programs designed to provide employees with more control over which hours they work. Between two-thirds and four-fifths of all employers report offering flextime programs that allow employees to vary the start and end of their workday and to leave work for family obligations (Osterman, 1995; Daniels, 1997; McShulskis, 1997; Galinsky and Bond, 1998; Greenwald, 1998; Saltzstein, Ting, and Saltzstein, 2001). Yet despite the popularity of flextime, accumulating evidence suggests that no more than a quarter of all eligible employees take advantage of the offering (Galinsky, Bond, and Friedman, 1993; Bond, Galinsky, and Swanberg, 1998; Eaton, 2000; Mead et al., 2000; Golden, 2001; Blair-Loy and Wharton, 2002). Employees are even less likely to use other programs that support greater temporal flexibility, such as the option to work from home or take maternity or paternity leave (Bond, Galinsky, and Swanberg, 1998; O'Mahony and Barley, 1999; Mead et al., 2000).

The discrepancy between employees' professed desire for greater flexibility and their relatively low rates of using flextime has puzzled researchers and policy makers. Some analysts maintain that the gap simply indicates that people are unable to afford time off from work because of debt, low salaries, and norms of consumption (Schor, 1991). Most researchers, however, explain low utilization in terms of organizational pressures similar to those that account for why employees work long hours. Respondents and informants usually say that managers and peers interpret the use of flexibility programs as evidence of a lack of commitment, motivation, and productivity and that supervisors and mid-level managers routinely deny requests for more flexible work schedules (Bailyn, 1993; Perlow, 1997; Clarkberg and Moen 2001; Meiksins and Whalley, 2002; Blair-Loy and Wharton, 2002; McBride,

2003). Moreover, in many firms, flexibility programs are stigmatized as women's programs (Schwartz, 1989; Mead et al., 2000; Meiksins and Whalley, 2002), and managers themselves admit that they hesitate to grant employees flexibility because they anticipate shirking (Olson, 1987; Perm, 1991; Kurland and Egan, 1999). In short, commentators argue that firms subject employees to informal pressures and tacit threats of sanction that discourage then from using the flexibility programs formally offered.

Etzioni (1961) and Schein (1972) have argued that organizations bring three types of control to bear on employees to ensure that they fulfill managerial expectations: coercive, remunerative, and normative control. Coercive control rests on the organization's ability to extract compliance by threat, especially the threat of termination or withholding promotions. Remunerative control rests on management's ability to elicit compliance by setting the terms for dispensing salaries, raises, and bonuses. Normative control, the most diffuse of the three, elicits compliance through sustained social and interpersonal pressures to internalize and conform to managerially defined norms and values. Whereas traditional bureaucracies relied primarily on coercive and remunerative control encoded in rules and procedures (Edwards, 1979), contemporary organizational theorists generally concur that normative control dominates traditional controls in postindustrial organizations, especially high-technology and professional firms (Kunda, 1992; Barker, 1993; Perlow, 1997).

Policies of flexibility explicitly loosen coercive and remunerative control over the employee's time: the firm promises, within reasonable limits, to neither terminate the employee nor withhold recompense and promotions for adopting a more flexible schedule. But these policies do not necessarily remove normative pressures. Managers and coworkers may continue to insist that employees work to expectations that undermine customized schedules. Most explanations for why employees fail to take advantage of flexibility programs, therefore, highlight normative pressures that make it difficult for employees to control their time. Perlow (1999) demonstrated that engineers on development teams feel considerable pressure from management to remain visible by working long and inflexible hours.

Similarly, Barker (1993) showed how members of self-managed teams pressure fellow members to disregard family obligations and to work longer hours to finish a job. The unstated proposition in such studies is that more people would avail themselves of flexibility programs, and perhaps even limit the time they spend working, if they could free themselves from the normative control endemic to permanent employment.

Theorists have suggested that one way to escape organizational control is to move into the market. In markets, selling skills to multiple clients, rather than a long-term affiliation with one employer, guarantees a living (Handy, 1989; Kanter, 1989, 1995; Arthur, 1994). Career theorists interested in the notion of boundaryless careers have explored this theme in the academic literature (Arthur, 1994; Mirvis and Hall, 1994; Arthur and Rousseau, 1996). These theorists have accepted the idea that firms can no longer guarantee employment as they once did and that internal labor markets are disintegrating. Drawing inspiration from Hollywood (Jones, 1996), software development (Kanter, 1995), and other project-oriented industries, they have argued that workers in the new economy can attain greater security as well as greater autonomy by configuring their careers around skills that allow them to move freely between organizations.

A popular literature on employability and free agency has advocated an even more extreme movement into the market (Beck, 1992; Bridges, 1994; Caulkin, 1997; Darby, 1997; Pink, 2001). The doctrine of employability exalts consultants, contractors, freelancers, and other free agents who have jettisoned permanent employment in favor of temporary engagements mediated by the market. Like the scholars of boundaryless careers, advocates of free agency claim that markets liberate workers from the shackles of organizational control. Both literatures hold that markets grant considerable flexibility, including the ability for workers to control their time. Writing about boundaryless careers in the software industry where people can easily change employers, Kanter (1995: 56) noted,

> Often no more than buzzwords, flexibility and empowerment take on meaning in software companies where people feel they have real control. . . . Managers can authorize any schedule . . . for people whose knowledge is valuable—for exam-

ple, having a new mother work two days a week. . . . Employees can design their own three-day, four-day or five-day altered-schedule work weeks.

To support the promise of temporal freedom advocates of free agency routinely offer readers stories of freelancers who work when they want to work and vacation when they please. "Free agents have less time anxiety than the typical worker," wrote Pink (2001: 109–115). "Independent workers may log about forty hours every week, but how they configure those forty hours is highly fluid. Unlike employees, free agents mostly control the faucet. . . . The free agent way is as much vacation as you can afford and as much work as you need." As these passages illustrate, advocates of boundaryless careers and free agency assert that markets give people control over both how many and which hours they work. They also suggest that temporal flexibility applies to multiple units of time: free agents can choose how to deploy hours within a day, days within a week, or months within a year.

The underlying assumption, in both the academic and popular literatures, is that markets offer individuals greater control over their time because they reduce the relationship between employers and workers to a simple economic exchange between buyers and sellers of skill and time. . . . But market relationships are neither as simple nor as context free as the advocates of boundaryless careers and free agency suggest with their images of frictionless supply and demand for labor (Hirsch and Shanley, 1996). . . .

. . . [T]he rhetoric of markets and free agency inflates the worker's individual freedom and may therefore overestimate the temporal control that workers can achieve by leaving organizations for the market. To explore how workers experience time when they leave permanent employment and how much control they actually achieve over how many and which hours they work, we need to study a population of workers oriented primarily to markets rather than organizations. Technical contractors are one such population.

Technical contractors are the epitome of free agents. They include engineers, software developers, technical writers, and information technology (IT) specialists who sell their services to firms on a project-by-project basis for an hourly wage or a set fee. Their contracts typically last from three to eighteen months. When a contract expires, they move on to another client organization. Although researchers have paid little attention to technical contracting, several recent studies suggest that contractors seek and may even enjoy temporal flexibility. Meiksins and Whalley (2002) reported that technical professionals often turn to contracting because they want more control over their time. Matusik and Fuller (2002) showed that when contractors' skills are in sufficiently high demand, they experience more control over their time. Technical contracting, therefore, appears to offer an ideal context for determining whether and how workers experience flexibility in the absence of organizational control. An even stronger test would be to examine technical contracting during a tight labor market when contractors' bargaining power is enhanced. It was during just such a period that we set out to study the experience of highly skilled technical contractors.

Methods

In the fall of 1997 we embarked on a two-and-a-half year study of how the labor market for technical contractors operates and how participants in that market experience and structure their work and lives. We began with a year of ethnographic observation in three staffing agencies that brokered technical contractors. From this vantage point, we could not only study the agents who brokered the market for contractors, we could also encounter contractors who were seeking jobs and the managers who hired them. Over the course of the year, we developed a substantive understanding of how the market for technical contractors operates, as well as an initial appreciation for the issues that contractors and their clients face.

Legal institutions and court rulings have shaped the market for technical contractors. In the U.S., employment and tax law are tied to permanent employment. During the 1980s, many firms, including Microsoft, tried to skirt employment taxes and avoid paying benefits by replacing employees with contractors. The Internal Revenue Service (IRS) successfully challenged the practice by taking Microsoft to court. Microsoft subsequently rehired many contractors as permanent employees and let others go. Those who were dismissed sued Microsoft for back benefits and stock options in *Vizcaino v. Microsoft* (97F.3d. 1887, 9th Circuit Court, 1996). In 1996, after years of litigation, the court determined that Microsoft had failed to distinguish adequately between contractors and employees and required the firm to pay millions of dollars retroactively for the benefits that contractors would have received had they been employees. The ruling forced other employers to become more cautious about how they played this game. Firms began to differentiate contractors from employees by requiring them to wear special badges, assigning them to less desirable workspaces, and avoiding the appearance of directing contractors' work. To achieve the latter, employers shifted from hiring independent contractors to hiring contractors through staffing agencies. As employers-of-record, staffing agencies shielded companies from legal responsibility for contractors by withholding the contractors' state and federal taxes and thereby appearing, at least on paper, to direct the contractors' work.

Thus, by the time we began collecting data, there were two markets for technical contractors: one for independents who negotiated directly with clients and another for contractors brokered by staffing agencies (commonly called W2s, after the IRS tax form that makes a person an employee in the eyes of the law). Independents and W2s both billed by the hour, but the W2s' bill rate included the agency's markup, which averaged about 30 percent of the total charge.

Although clients rarely hesitated to renew their independent contractors' contracts, they often restricted the duration of a W2's engagement to eighteen months to avoid the appearance of being their employer. Regardless of employment status however, all contractors' careers were cyclical: all contracts were sooner or later followed by a return to the labor market in search of the next contract. This structure sensitized contractors to both a coarse- and fine-grained flow of time. The coarse grain was defined by the contract cycle and the contractor's choice of how to sequence and space contracts, while the fine grain was measured by the hours of a day and week that contractors worked while on contract.

It was the coarse-grain structure that most clearly set contracting's dynamics apart from permanent employment. Entering the labor market repeatedly to secure new assignments defined the essence of contracting. Both contractors and agents parsed the contractors' time into periods of employment and unemployment, but neither used these terms. Instead, they talked about "being on contract" or "having downtime." "Being on contract" referred to periods when one or more clients compensated a contractor for work. Downtime—also called "beach time," "bench time," or "dead time"—referred to periods between contracts. What distinguished downtime from the notion of unemployment was that downtime was considered normal and inherent to contracting. As the connotative distinction between beach and bench time suggests, downtime could be viewed as a luxury, a time for pleasure and relaxation, for going to the beach. At other times, downtime was equivalent to sitting on the bench out of play, waiting to return to the game. Coarse-grained flexibility entailed decisions about when and how much downtime to allow and, hence, whether downtime would be spent on the beach or the bench.

Agents and contractors also had a vocabulary for talking about the types of hours that defined the fine-grained flow of a contractor's time. Like lawyers and accountants they spoke of "billable hours," hours of work for which they could charge clients. Hours worked but not billed were known as "unbillable" hours. Unbillable hours were of two types: hours that contractors could have billed but didn't and hours that were necessary for completing the work, but for which they could not ethically or practically bill. Fine-grained flexibility entailed decisions about how many billable and unbillable hours a contractor would accrue in the course of a day or week and when they would work billable hours.

As we learned more about the market for technical contractors, we decided to explore the contractors' experience in depth. Conversations with contractors who were seeking jobs through the agencies we studied suggested that their career histories, their work and business practices, their perceptions of the social world of contracting, and how contracting meshed with their personal and family life were crucial areas of study. To elicit this information, we developed an interview guide . . . consisting of open-ended questions designed to structure our conversations with contractors.

Because there was no representative enumeration of individuals, who work as technical contractors, all options for selecting informants posed limitations. We could have convinced a staffing firm to make available the names of the people in its databases, sampled from one of several resume databanks on the Internet, or sought subscription records from magazines targeted at contractors. All of these would have yielded samples biased in different ways. We chose to use a modified snowball sample (Faugier and Sargeant, 1997). . . .

Table 15.1 reports the distribution of informants across age, marital status, citizenship, residency, experience as a contractor, career structure, and occupation. Our informants ranged from 25 to 68 years of age, although most were over forty. Most had a college education, and 25 percent were women. The majority were U.S. citizens, but only 55 percent resided in the Silicon Valley. Informants represented a variety of occupations and skill levels, from software and hardware engineers to technical writers and quality assurance technicians. The demographic and occupational patterns in table 1 are nearly identical to those reported in Black and Andreini's (1997) survey of IT contractors in the Silicon Valley. . . .

The Contractor's Temporal Experience

Organizational Independence

Before turning to the question of how much control markets give contractors over their time, we must first establish that contractors actually perceive themselves to be free from the normative and coercive shackles of organizational life. Otherwise, we cannot reasonably claim that movement into the market largely restricts clients to using remunerative control. In our interviews, we systematically asked informants why they became contractors. Although their reasons ranged from making more money to escaping boredom, 54 percent told us that they had gradually become frustrated with organizational politics, incompetent management, and inequities in the employment relationship (Kunda, Barley, and Evans, 2002). Our informants eventually turned to contracting to escape organizational control and gain professional autonomy. As one programmer put it:

> [As an employee] I couldn't push back if somebody asked me to do something that was—from an engineering point of view—just clearly stupid. . . . As a contractor I can say, "This is dumb. I'm not going to do it." "This is dumb, I'm not going to do it" is not something you can say as an employee. They basically get to tell you what you do and don't do. They hold the whip hand over you. Being able to walk away, being independent, having autonomy adds authenticity to your judgment in their eyes.

A majority of informants (70 percent) explicitly told us that they enjoyed considerably more autonomy than they had experienced as permanent employees. In fact, some (35 percent) felt that their freedom from the organization was so great that they sometimes felt like outsiders in the firms where they worked. For many contractors, freedom from organizational control translated directly into the perception of temporal autonomy. They recognized, often in retrospect, just how much of their time employers had extracted for reasons unrelated to the actual requirements of work. A verification engineer recounted:

> When I was a permanent employee I worked a lot of long hours. It was for politics. It wasn't for getting the project done. It was like I was doing this for somebody else's ego, or somebody else's personal or career goals. They could check off, they got this or that done based on my work. . . . There seemed to be this rush to impress people. You were there on the weekends or you came in on a holiday. Like when I worked at Motorola last time, people actually went in on 4th of July—the actual 4th of July!—where they could sign in, and people saw they signed in. I don't see that happening as a contractor.

While gaining control over time was not the primary reason our informants became contractors, over a third (38 percent) told us that being able to control their time was a significant unanticipated benefit. The benefit covered both how many and which hours they worked. Moreover, our informants felt that they had control over both the coarse-and fine-gained flow of their lives. Contractors claimed that the cyclic structure of con-

Table 15.1
Descriptive Statistics for Informants*

Characteristic	Mean	N	S.D.	Min.	Max.
Demographic					
Mean age[†]	43 yrs.		10	25	68
Mean years of post-high-school education[†]	4.2 yrs.		1.4	0	8
Pay rate (in $/hour)[‡]	$68		27	20	125
Male	75%	(49)			
Married[§]	63%	(34)			
With children[‡‡]	50%	(26)			
Caucasian	75%	(49)			
U.S. citizens	83%	(54)			
California residents	69%	(45)			
Silicon Valley residents	55%	(36)			
Career					
Mean years contracted[†]	6.8 yrs.		4.9	0.5	21
Mean years worked[†]	17.9 yrs.		8.5	3	44
Mean years contracted / mean years worked[†]	.41 yrs.		.26	0	1
Independent contractors or corps.	33%	(21)			
On first contract[#]	7%	(5)			
Always contracted[#]	11%	(7)			
Left permanent employment behind[#]	54%	(35)			
Moved back and forth to contracting[#]	25%	(16)			
Technical specialties					
Software developers	29%	(19)			
Hardware designers	8%	(5)			
Database programmers and administrators	18%				
Systems administrators	12%	(8)			
Project managers	5%	(3)			
Technical writers	11%	(7)			
Quality assurance technicians	11%	(7)			
Multimedia (Web)	3%	(2)			
Others	3%	(2)			

* N = 65 individuals. Numbers are drawn from semistructured interview data, and so all of the information is not available on all cases. Numbers in parentheses are the actual number of cases for dummy-variable tabulation.

† Only includes data on 64 cases.

‡ Only includFes data on 41 cases.

§ Only includes data on 54 cases.

‡‡ Only includes data on 52 cases.

Only includes data on 63 cases.

tracting gave them more options than they had as permanent employees. For instance, a quality control technician explained how contractors could construct a lifestyle unknown to most workers by deciding about how many and which weeks they would work:

I think contracting gives me the sense of freedom, I feel like if I need to take a lot of time off for something, I can just do it. Finish up what I am doing and just take a lot of time off and not feel obligated to anything. Whereas I think if I worked full time for a company, I would feel like I only have two to three weeks vacation. You know, plan it carefully instead of just like deciding I am going to Mexico and just going and having fun and stuff. I don't like that obligation I guess. I have a lot of obligations being a contractor because I have a lot of responsibility, but at the same time, I know that if I need to leave, I can leave.

Contractors also told us that they were free to set limits on how many and which hours of a day or week they worked. One software engineer testified to his freedom to choose the number of hours he worked:

As a consultant . . . I'm completely autonomous. I can say, "I really can't do that. I have to leave." As an employee I might find an employer who would be so far thinking as to say, "This employee is going to work 30 hours a week and he's going to get a full salary, maybe even a big salary." Let's say they do that. And then let's say the project is push coming to shove. What are they going to do? "Well, I'm sorry. We really do need you to come in." So they own your ass, and I'm not into that.

A database programmer used the occasion of the interview to make the point that he could decide what he would do with each hour of his day: "I can blow off the afternoon and sit down and talk to you. If I had a real job, I'd have to get an okay from the boss . . . and he's gotta worry about, 'Do we do this against your vacation time' or whatever. Heck, we just do it! The good news is I've got a lot more flexibility in my hours." One of the most accomplished software developers we interviewed made a similar point with respect to her family:

I can spend time with the kids. I know that we need to get this done, so I'll take the morning and do it. If my husband needs to be someplace, I don't have to be at work at any particular time and I don't have to stay at work for any particular length of time, since the object is getting the job done, not how many hours you're there. So it allows me a lot of flexibility in terms of scheduling. My husband says I'm a much calmer person, because I really don't care that much anymore.

Although, most of our informants perceived themselves to be politically and temporally independent of organizations' control and, hence, able to decide how many and which hours they would devote to work, as researchers have shown (Tausig and Fenwick, 2001; Gareis and Barnett, 2002) there is an important distinction between perceiving that one has temporal flexibility and making use of it. Employees who believe they have temporal flexibility nevertheless work as if they did not. The difference hinges, in part, on organizational pressures but also on how employees make sense of time in the larger context of their lives and careers. To determine whether contractors deploy their flexibility as market advocates predict, we examined how they interpreted the meaning of time as well as the choices they made about its use.

The Coarse Grain: Contract Cycles and Vacations

The coarse-grained structure of contractors' time is bound to repeated cycles of contracts and downtime. The essence of coarse-grained choice is how contractors use the time between contracts. The choices that our informants made rested on differences in how they experienced and interpreted that time.

Every informant we interviewed spoke of downtime as an inherent risk of contracting. A few told us that they found the possibility of downtime stressful, if not downright frightening. These tended to be individuals who were new to contracting, who worried about the effect of economic insecurity on their family, or whose spouses were uncomfortable with contracting's risks. One was a young Indian programmer who had recently come to the U.S. to be with her husband. When asked where she "saw herself in a couple of years," she replied, "Two years down the road is too far; I am still thinking, 'Do I have a contract next month?' . . . I stress a lot over whether I will have a job after this. I mean, it is OK to say that the market is good and there is no need to worry. But you do." Another was a technical writer who had experienced several months of downtime that coincided with his wife being laid off from her job. Earlier in his career he had been laid off from a permanent job and was out of work for several months. At the time we interviewed him, he was considering returning to full-time employment because he feared what might happen to his family if he had difficulty maintaining steady work. As he put it, "Say something turns bad and my contract at Cisco is terminated, so what happens? I have my $860 a month mortgage, my $300 a month car payment, my $300 a month food bill, I don't know what else, you know, utilities, electric, gas, water." Ultimately, he did return to full-time employment.

Most contractors, however, took downtime for granted. Although they never scoffed at its possibility, they minimized its threat and spoke as if it were a normal event. These contractors gradually came to accept downtime because experience had taught them that it was rare and that if it occurred, they could generally weather the storm. A programmer who had worked for ten years as a contractor was typical of those whose experience allowed them to come to terms with the possibility of downtime.

> I used to get really nervous. The six months hiatus [that he once experienced] was really hard on my psyche. I would go into any contract or any job—I had some permanent jobs after that—with fear and trembling. Anytime the boss would say "Hi," I was afraid I was about to get fired. I still have a tiny bit of that. Since then I have never had more than a two-week gap. I have learned that I can make it. If something happens and there is a larger gap, I know that I will make it work out somehow and, second of all, it generally won't be that long.

Perhaps because of the tight labor market, some contractors with substantial experience even treated the possibility of downtime cavalierly, characterizing the process of finding a new job as trivial. "Around here," said one technical writer about life in the Silicon Valley, "If you have seven years experience, you can work literally all the time. You can literally finish a contract at noon and start the next one an hour later. Eat lunch and then go to your next one."

Most of the contractors we interviewed expected that periods of unwanted downtime would last no more than a few weeks, and their experience generally supported that stance. . . . If one assumes that unwanted downtime was not salient enough for these informants to have mentioned it explicitly, then one is left with the conclusion that at least among the contractors we interviewed, unwanted downtime was rare and of relatively short duration. When facing downtime, contractors took one of three general approaches: they scheduled it, embraced it as an unanticipated gift, or minimized it.

Scheduling downtime. One approach to controlling downtime was to plan it and use it for one's own purposes. A handful of contractors scheduled downtime when they wanted to devote a continuous block of time to learning a new technology or skill. They might use this time for taking formal courses or for studying on their own. Others planned downtime to pursue an avocation. For instance, we interviewed one contractor who sailed with his wife and son on their yacht six months of every year. Another contracted for six to eight months and then turned his attention to photography and scuba diving, which took him to Malaysia and other exotic locations. He had published several books of underwater photography.

Embracing downtime. A second group of informants embraced unanticipated downtime as a spontaneous opportunity for a much-needed break. "It is not uncommon," explained a multimedia designer, "to have a couple of weeks off. But that's OK! Part of the reason I like contract work is that you work on something and when you get done, you get to take a break for a while if you made enough money. It is almost like you can go off on an adventure of some sort." An Oracle database administrator saw downtime in much the same way:

> I knew when a contract was coming to an end or, more often, I saw that my contribution was trailing off. So I would tell the client, "I am costing you money and I am really not doing you any good, so why don't we do some documentation and I will hand whatever I am responsible for over to someone else who will be here for a little longer." And then I look at that as a vacation. And that is another reason, why the money issue isn't just to buy cool toys. It is so I don't have to work 12 months out of the year.

Minimizing downtime. Most informants, however, sought to minimize downtime. They reported that they began searching for a new job as soon as the current contract began to wind down. Usually contractors could anticipate the end of a job by the terms of the contract itself or by the amount of work that was left to do. Experienced contractors pointed to more subtle social cues that allowed them to anticipate even unscheduled terminations. As one systems administrator told us:

> And then one day, there's nothing for you to do. You can feel it coming. At one point the manager is around all the time and is really excited. Then the manager just kind of ignores you. Then you know that

you have a couple of weeks left. That's when you know they will fire you. Things start slowing down first, although I usually end before they end.

Most informants argued that if they began searching for a new job two to three weeks before the end of their contract they could almost always secure another in time to avoid downtime. To increase the odds of finding work in such a short period of time, informants employed a number of tactics. One was to work more or less exclusively with a staffing firm that was committed to keeping its contractors employed, A completely different tactic was to play one agency off against another, especially if one's current agency refused to line up a new job until it was clear that the client would not renew. A systems administrator remarked:

> What I've encountered is that when I'm nearing the end of a job, the headhunters want me to stay 'til the end of the job. Of course, what that means is that I'll be sitting for a couple of weeks without a paycheck. So I have been forced in most cases to switch to a different headhunter at the end of one particular job so that I can get another lined up before I'm just sitting around for a couple of weeks.

Other contractors employed their personal and professional networks to generate opportunities. Still others made use of the Internet, knowing that staffing firms routinely trolled online job listings in search of possible candidates for openings they were trying to fill. As one quality assurance technician told us, this tactic worked particularly well when contractors had skills that were in very high demand, such as the ability to write COBOL during the Y2K scare:

> So anyway, I ended up leaving Toyota. The first thing I did was put my name out on the Internet. Let's see, they sent me home at 12, was on the Internet by 1:30 and I had my first offer by 4 o'clock. It's not hard. Put your name out there. Let 'em know that you can do COBOL and you'll have 500 offers by tomorrow morning.

A final tactic, employed by some contractors, was to work several contracts simultaneously. In fact, one contractor reported having six contracts in play at once. Typically, contractors who held multiple concurrent contracts were software developers and technical writers who worked a significant number of hours from home. These individuals tried to stagger their contracts' end times so that they were never without compensation.

Although none of the informants explicitly gave a name to the period of time at the end of one contract when they began to search for the next, a potentially useful name for this period might be bridge time. With this concept, one can explicitly outline how contractors who sought to minimize downtime understood the temporal structure of contract work, They saw downtime as a problem instead of an opportunity. Their objective was to incur no downtime involuntarily. They used bridge time to unite two periods of contract time so that they could, in essence, skip over downtime and ensure continued employment.

The strategies of scheduling, embracing, and minimizing downtime represented different interpretations of the contract cycle. Most informants used one strategy or another. Those who sought to schedule or embrace downtime saw contracting as an opportunity to live a different lifestyle. For schedulers, downtime was a resource to save or spend as they saw fit. For embracers it was a windfall. Those who preferred to minimize downtime, despite how cavalierly they might otherwise talk, implicitly saw the contract cycle as a threat. Their notion of control entailed regaining the security of continual employment by lining up the next contract before the current contract ended so that they could move from one job to the next without incurring time on the bench.

Among our informants, schedulers and embracers were far less common than minimizers. A total of 17 contractors (25 percent) said that they routinely scheduled or embraced downtime for breaks, vacations, or hobbies, even though the vast majority of our informants claimed that the freedom to do so was one of contracting's primary benefits. Yet almost as many informants (13, or 20 percent) said that they had not taken a vacation for a number of years, while another 23 (35 percent) took no more than one or two weeks a year. One technical writer described his summer vacation as a single day between contracts spent going on amusement park rides, interrupted with cell phone calls to his recruiter. A software engineer, when asked what she did outside work, responded, "I've been married for 18 years, and I must say our honeymoon was the last time we took a vacation." A firmware engineer admitted, without regret, "I'm not a real big vacation person. It's not like the family goes for a week someplace twice a year. We don't do that."

In short, even though most contractors felt that contracting offered them more control over their time than did permanent employment, relatively few used this freedom to harness the contract cycle to pursue an alternative lifestyle. Natural breaks between contracts made it possible for contractors to take more time off, but a desire to control the contract cycle led most to avoid doing so. For them, not only were there no paid vacations, but vacations bore a suspicious resemblance to unwanted downtime and what they saw as its consequences: increased expenses, decreased income, and an uncomfortable sense of insecurity and failure.

The Fine Grain

The daily and weekly organization of hours exerted an even more immediate pressure on contractors' temporal choices. Almost every contractor we encountered sold his or her services by the hour. After accounting for the cost of benefits, a contractor's hourly wage was usually 1.5 to 3 times higher than his or her permanent counterparts. Contracts might specify the number of hours per week that contractors would devote to the contract, but they rarely precluded working additional hours or dictated when hours would be spent. Contractors therefore had considerable leeway in choosing how many and which hours to work. A woman who specialized in technical marketing spoke for many of our informants:

> Usually the hours are flexible, so there's a feeling of control. Even though you're working at midnight, you're the one who decided you wanted to work at midnight. I mean I know some companies are flexible anyway, but when they know you're consulting they're usually more open about you being flexible because they just want the job done. They don't care that you're not there 8:00 to 5:00, they just want results.

Some contractors, like this marketing specialist, used their flexibility to work non-traditional hours. Others exercised flexibility on a weekly basis. These informants valued the freedom to take a day off, and some aspired to work four-day weeks.

Yet, because contractors bore much of the responsibility for deciding when to work and how much to work, they became acutely conscious of how they spent their time. Every hour was a form of capital, which the contractor could invest in a variety of ways. Contractors could invest hours in doing directly compensated work for a client. They could invest hours in unbillable activities that ensured long-term employability: managing their business, developing new skills or maintaining their networks. Contractors could also invest hours in their families, hobbies, or leisure. The need to make these tradeoffs, often on a daily basis, led contractors to develop an accountant's appreciation for the microeconomics of time. Some contractors set annual targets for the number of billable hours they wanted to work. The baseline was usually a 40-hour week, the standard for a permanent job. A technical writer made the calculations for us:

> Normally, most people work about 2,000 hours a year. Forty-hour weeks, fifty weeks a year. But last year I did about 2,300 hours. We all keep log books of our hours, so it's pretty easy for us to know how many hours we bill. Like lawyers or CPAs, we all know, "Oh, you did 2,400 hours last year," and stuff like that. So then you take 60 times 2,300, you come up with an idea of how much someone makes.

Most informants also worked a sizable number of unbillable hours. Sometimes jobs simply required more time than the terms of the contract allowed. Contractors worked these additional hours because they agreed to provide a deliverable by a certain date, because they could not always estimate the amount of time the work required, or because they felt they needed to adhere to their own standard of excellence. One software developer explained his rationale:

> I end up working more than I charge. Maybe 10 percent more. I usually bill for eight hours a day, but there is so much more you do: you try things, you think. If it doesn't work, you try new things. I guess it averages out to 50 hours a week. Sometimes you need to take an extra week, and often you need to work weekends. . . . You have to meet milestones, show progress. If you haven't, you can't bill.

Contractors also logged unbillable hours because they wanted to make a good impression on the client. By working more hours than they billed or by attending meetings and engaging in other unpaid activities, contractors hoped to signal a level of dedication that would preclude them from being terminated early and ensure a positive recommendation from the client. A project manager explained the tactic:

> I want to make sure that when they are laying off contractors, I am the last one they look at on the list. So I do a lot of things, like when I came on board for the first two weeks, I probably worked 70 hours a week and billed them for 40. . . . I had been there a week when they noticed that I was there at 6:00 in the morning until 6:00 at night.

In addition to unbillable hours worked for clients, contractors invested considerable time in support activities such as learning new skills, maintaining their professional network, and managing the business aspects of contracting. Contractors realized that they were marketable only to the degree that their skills were in demand. In our informants' occupations, technology changed quickly. New programming languages, new applications, and new hardware were continually making older approaches and technologies obsolete. The majority of informants spoke of the necessity of allocating time to remaining up to date. Contractors employed a wide range of strategies for acquiring new knowledge: they read technically oriented journals and books, they took classes from community colleges and universities, they sought industry certifications, they made use of the Internet, they bought software packages and taught themselves the packages at home, they attended users' groups, and availed themselves of the expertise of other technical specialists in their personal networks. As a mechanical engineer explained, each of these activities absorbed time.

> I need to know what's going around, what's in demand, what's developing, how the software is changing, how the hardware is changing. It takes a lot of research everyday, trying to stay ahead. But it's all worth it. I spend at least an hour a day. Maybe 20 minutes at work and about an hour at home—sometimes even two, three, four hours at home—trying to call people, other agencies, job shops, software, hardware companies. I'll ask questions and talk to them: how is the

software changing and what's the new version coming out?

In addition to acquiring new skills, all contractors devoted time to business activities. Even contractors who worked primarily through staffing firms actively marketed themselves. Marketing activities ranged from maintaining one's network of contacts to developing brochures, attending meetings of users' groups, going to career fairs, talking to recruiters, and revising résumés and posting them on the Web. In addition, contractors who worked from home typically had a considerable amount of computer equipment to maintain and upgrade. Independent contractors had the additional burden of maintaining tax records and doing other bookkeeping chores. A software developer nicely summarized the amount of time contractors spend in support activities and how these activities inflate the number of hours worked, while decreasing the proportion of hours billed:

> I read an article one time, where a good consultant should spend 50 percent of their time learning, and that's what I've been doing lately. I'm spending almost 50 percent of my time trying to keep current—reading the trade magazines, going to the meetings and stuff. You figure I spend 10–15 percent of my time to do marketing, another 10–15 percent of my time to do the housekeeping chores when you've got your own office. Gee, that leaves maybe 15–20 percent of the time that's billable. Think about the rate I'd have to charge if I was working only twenty hours a week. Nobody's going to spend $400 an hour for me, I'm not that good. So, how do you juggle all this?

In short, the fine-grained temporal structure of contracting differed substantially from most permanent employment. First, contractors had to balance more kinds of time use than their full-time counterparts. Because contractors went to the labor market more frequently, they felt more persistent pressure to invest substantial time in unbillable and support activities than they had as permanent employees. Second, contractors enjoyed more control than most full-time workers over how many and which hours to work. In fact, they confronted an ever-present choice of how to spend every hour. Third, unlike salaried employees, contractors could put a precise value on every hour of the day—their hourly wage. When choosing how to spend their time, contractors could calculate to the penny the opportunity costs of every unbilled or leisure hour.

Finally, unlike employees whose jobs buffer them from the hour-to-hour implications of how they spend their time, contractors were immediately exposed to the consequences of their temporal choices. The number of billable hours that contractors worked translated directly into income. Their investments in unbillable hours affected the probability that clients would extend their contract by making the contractor appear more diligent and by increasing the quality of their work. In this way, unbillable hours increased the odds that a client would provide glowing recommendations. Hours spent in support activities shored up contractors' reputations, skills, and networks, which in turn shaped the outcome of their next encounter with the labor market. These distinctive aspects of the fine-grained structure of contracting combined to focus contractors on the tradeoff between different ways of spending an hour. Generally speaking, contractors approached the tradeoff in two ways. One group evaluated time solely by economic criteria, while another evaluated it more broadly.

Economic evaluators. The temporal logic of contracting conditioned many of our informants to equate time with money. For these contractors, the temptation to maximize income by working as many hours as possible was considerable. As a software developer exclaimed, "When you're a consultant, all you have is your time. You use it or lose it! You can only sell your time, so you need to . . . figure out how to sell the most time! Cause when it's gone, it's gone." Informants reported that they were acutely aware that every hour they failed to work was lost compensation. Another software engineer, who attributed his divorce to contracting, described the experience of wasting time and feeling money pass through his hands: "The funny thing about contracting—I find myself doing this and talking to people [who do it as well]—you develop this mentality. I was one of those guys that said, 'I take a day off—I'm losing 800 dollars, Oh my gosh!' "

A number of informants reported that equating time and money was so ingrained that they could no longer enjoy leisure. One software engineer described taking time off in the middle of the day to chaperone a youth group around San Francisco's Fisherman's Wharf. He described how he lost patience when the children misbehaved. Rather than bemoan his loss of control, he complained about wasted time: "They were really terrible. They spread out in all directions and I ended up with the other chaperone—just the two of us walking around. I was counting those dollars going off. I was really upset about that." He summed up his experience by admitting that as a contractor, "there is a huge temptation to work every hour of the day." Another contractor, a business applications specialist who worked simultaneously for multiple clients, made it abundantly clear that his time was his most valuable resource: "You can do a lot of things to me: you can call me names; you can throw rocks at me; you can shoot at me, and I won't care. Waste my time and I'll drive over you in the parking lot."

In short, many contractors were continuously concerned with the opportunity costs they would incur if they took advantage of the flexibility they perceived themselves to have. As a result, many felt guilty about taking time off. A software developer detailed the experience of doing such a cost/benefit analysis:

> [Contracting] is like being a stockbroker. It's not about the fact that you made a million dollars today on your portfolio, it's about the fact that you left 200,000 dollars on the table. If you didn't sell today and waited until tomorrow, or sold earlier, you could have made that 200,000. So this is the lingering thought in your head as a fund manager. . . . The same thing is true in consulting. Time becomes money. When time becomes money, management of that time becomes a critical asset.

A quality assurance technician put the point more succinctly, "I was always hoping that if I could earn more money, I could cut down the number of hours. But because the money is good, I find it very difficult to turn it down."

When contractors used an economic metric as the sole measure of time, they often discounted the worth of other activities whose economic value was difficult to calculate. This was especially true for leisure. When a systems programmer who specialized in mainframes was asked about her life outside work she responded, "What life? I mean I work three weekends out of the month. I work most holidays. I've put in an average of twelve hours a day for the last four years. I work overtime because I want the extra money." When contractors billed 70 or 80 hours a week, they simply had little time left with which to be flexible.

Broad evaluators. Another group of contractors measured time more broadly. They too took economic criteria into account and valued contracting's high wages, but, unlike the economic evaluators, they used contracting's flexibility to set aside time for other purposes. These purposes varied widely. Some sought greater balance between work and family. They spoke about the importance of being available for their children and budgeted their time accordingly. For these informants, flexibility meant not only choosing which hours to work, but also limiting those hours. As one software developer said, "I now am a father. I have two children. And now job one for me is managing my time myself. And that means making the income that I need to make in as little time as possible and not working 40 hours. So I like to work as little as possible. And I don't think employee situations afford that. I work generally 30 hours a week, but I can work 20 hours some weeks. And I like that." For other broad evaluators work was a necessary evil to be avoided whenever possible. For example, an accomplished programmer remarked candidly when asked why he typically worked only 30 hours a week, "I'm a goof off. . . . I mean I like the rest of my life. It's very important to me. I've adapted to working less than full time." This contractor used the time he bought for himself to write science fiction, pursue his interests in dance and hang out at the beach. Although he didn't regret his lifestyle, he was fully aware of its cost. "You know," he confided, "Every so often kick myself 'cause if I'd have put in sixty hours a week for the last five years at these rates I'd have at least a house to my name."

Still other broad evaluators used opportunities for flexibility spontaneously. Like embracers, they valued both work and leisure but did not routinely plan for one or the other. Without reneging on their obligations, they took advantage of possibilities to redefine their schedules as they arose. A business application specialist described this stance:

> I try to maintain some kind of a pattern with clients, because it helps them. But at the same time, I shift my schedule to meet my needs. If we're going to have a couple of days of very good weather, and there are no major conflagrations burning at a client, I'll decide that maybe what I want to do is pack my cameras and get on the road, I'll say "Hey look, I've got other things going on and instead of me being in on Tuesday and Wednesday, I'm going to be in on Thursday and Friday. I'll see you then unless you have a problem with that." That's what I do usually, 90 percent of the time. Also, if I'm being nonproductive. . . . One day last week was just one of those days where I went to press the "n" on the keyboard and pressed the "q," you know, 37 times in a row—one of those bumble-finger days. My heart wasn't in it that day. I just told the client, "Look, I can stay here and send you a bill, or I can take the afternoon off, go throw rocks at the pigeons in the park or whatever I'm going to go do, and I'll be in better shape tomorrow and you'll get more for your money." And that's the way it is.

Even though broad evaluators had different reasons for doing so, as a group, they did not allow contracting's economic logic to squeeze out the other parts of their lives, They could therefore use the market's flexibility to create temporal rhythms that were consistent with their daily needs and values. On the face of it, broad evaluators had achieved precisely the lifestyle that the free agency literature promises. But broad evaluators were few in number (9, or 14 percent). Most informants worked extremely long hours. In the course of our interviews, three-quarters of our informants estimated the number of hours that they worked each week. Twenty-six percent of the men and 18 percent of the women who estimated their time reported working over 55 hours a week. These figures can be compared with data for full-time technicians, computer scientists, and programmers drawn from the U.S. Department of Labor's Current Population Survey. Hecker (1998) reported that in 1997, only 7 and 3 percent of permanently employed male and female computer scientists, respectively, worked 55 or more hours weekly. Only 4 and 2 percent of male and female technicians worked as long. Even among permanently employed male programmers, a group known for working long hours, only 5 percent worked 55 hours or more each week. . . .

Why Do Contractors Make Such Little Use of Flexibility?

Researchers have repeatedly shown that demographic characteristics play a role in determining the number of hours that people work and whether they make use of flexibility programs (Schor, 1991; Jacobs and Gerson, 1998; Mead et al. 2000; Golden, 2001). One would expect a similar phenomenon among contractors. For example, one might argue that because women assume more family obligations than men, female contractors might structure their time more flexibly than male contractors. One might also expect differences between those who have children and those who do not, although scholars could disagree on the direction of the effect. People with children might exhibit more temporal flexibility because they need to take care of their children; conversely, they might show less temporal flexibility because of the need to maximize family income. The structure of contractors' careers might also matter. For instance, experienced contractors might use their time differently than newcomers because they are less likely to worry about job security and, therefore, have less anxiety about taking vacations and hours off.

Panels A and B of table 15.2 compare the demographic attributes and careers of informants who had some flexibility, either coarse- or fine-grained, with those who had neither. These data suggest that demographic differences do not provide much leverage in predicting whether our informants made use of their opportunities for temporal control. Only four demographic differences were significant. Contractors who exhibited temporal flexibility were more commonly highly paid Caucasians and independent contractors with more years of contracting experience. These results point to differences in market power (higher wages, Caucasians, and independent contractors) and to the importance of experience in handling the uncertainties of contracting. Notably, sex, marital status, and the presence of children did not seem to distinguish how our informants used their time.

Professional identities and norms of quality offer another plausible explanation for why most contractors did not use the temporal control they perceived themselves to have. Occupational sociologists have shown that professionals are strongly committed to their work (Hughes, 1958; Bucher and Stelling, 1977). Because the professional's identity is tied to his or her work and because professionals typically find their work intrinsically interesting, they tend to work long hours and have a craftsperson's orientation to quality. Moreover, professional norms extend well beyond the confines of organizations: they influence practitioners regardless of work context (Van Mannen and Barley, 1984). Accordingly, one might argue that contractors work long hours and take little time off because they view themselves as committed technical professionals for whom work is a central life interest (Dubin, 1956; Orzack, 1959). But our data do not support this interpretation. We examined all the passages in our transcripts in which contractors explained why they worked long hours for evidence of professional identities and appeals to intrinsic motivation for work. We also searched the transcripts for all mentions of profession and similar words (professionalism, professional, etc.). Only six of our informants voiced such motives as part of their account for why they worked long hours or eschewed vacations. Professional identities and norms, therefore, did not appear to play a significant role in how the majority of our informants allocated their time. Far more important were the nature of our informants' work and their view of the exchange relationship.

Technical contractors were almost always hired onto a project. Not only did projects have discrete beginnings and endings, but their pace was also patterned. Typically, a project started off slowly and eventually accelerated. By the final third of a project, participants realized that they were running out of time, and the pace became frantic (Gersick, 1988, 1989). This occurred when projects had crises and managers strove to "put out fires" by "throwing bodies at the problem." The bodies usually belonged to contractors. Consequently, contractors typically entered projects precisely when demands on the team's time were greatest. Contractors were expected and paid to do whatever it took to finish the job. Several contractors compared their work with that of a mercenary, entering battle after battle, with heavy expectations balanced by high rewards. Most of our informants agreed with the sentiments expressed by a quality assurance technician, whose avocation was competitive dancing:

Table 15.2
Attributes of Informants with and without Flexibility*

Characteristic	Some flexibility	No flexibility	t-stat.
A. Demographic			
Mean age (in years)†	42.5 yrs.	42.2 yrs.	−.11
Mean education (in post-high-school years)†	4.3 yrs	4.0 yrs.	−.68
Mean pay rate (in $/hour)‡	$78	$58	−2.10•
Male	74%	74%	.01
Married§	47%	71%	1.65
With children‡‡	50%	52%	.10
Caucasian	95%	67%	−2.s43••
U.S. citizens	89%	80%	.82
California resident	74%	67%	−.54
Bay Area resident	58%	55%	−.22
B. Career structure			
Mean years contracted†	8.5 yrs.	6.1 yrs.	−1.78•
Mean years worked†	18.1 yrs.	17.2 yrs.	−.37
Years contracted / years worked†	.47 yrs.	.40 yrs.	−1.04
Independent contractors or corps.†	47%	25%	−1.73
On first contract#	11%	7%	−.40
Have always contracted#	12%	11%	.18
Left permanent employment behind#	58%	51%	−.47
Moved back and forth to contracting#	21%	27%	.47
C. Technical specialty (percentage)			
Software developers	42%	21%	−1.68•
Hardware designers	11%	7%	−.44
Database programmers and administrators	26%	17%	−.87
Systems administrators	0%	17%	1.92•
Project managers	0%	7%	1.19
Technical writers	11%	10%	−.12
Quality assurance technicians	11%	12%	.15
Multimedia (Web)	0%	5%	.95
Others	0%	5%	.96

•p < .05; ••p < .01; one-tailed test.

* N = 60 individuals. Numbers are drawn from semistructured interview data. Thus, some comparisons are based on a subset of the cases. Five informants did not give any information on time use . . . and were excluded from this table. Contractors with "some flexibility" had fine-, coarse-grained, or both types of flexibility.

† Only includes data on 59 cases.

‡ Only includes data on 36 cases.

‡ Only includes data on 36 cases.

§ Only includes data on 50 cases.

‡‡ Only includes data on 48 cases.

Only includes data on 58 cases.

There are times when the job is pretty stressful, especially when they come up on their deadlines and they're expecting you to put in 50 plus hours a week and there's problems with the project. They're falling behind. Things aren't going the way they're supposed to. Almost invariably that's what happens. . . . Now [the team's] under the gun. It's like, "We have till January 1, and who knows if we're gonna make it on time." . . . And I think if I weren't doing this, I would go out dancing a lot more often, I would be competing more. . . . But it certainly puts a Kibosh on that because by the time I get home, and I talk [to my wife] about the bills and whose birthday's coming up next month, very little energy is left for dancing.

The pressure to work long hours created by the fact that contractors usually arrived at "crunch time" was sometimes exacerbated by the nature of the work itself. For example, quality assurance technicians were responsible for running tests on hardware and software. Complex testing could require constantly monitoring the computers on which the tests were running. When running tests, quality assurance technicians would sometimes need to work for stretches of 10 to 15 hours at a time. Systems administrators had responsibility for maintaining networks, the infrastructures whose continual operation was critical to a client's ability to do business. When networks failed or servers crashed, systems administrators had little choice but to work until they fixed the problem. When writing code, software developers, Web designers, and database developers lived in micro-worlds defined entirely by the parameters of the programs they were writing (cf. Kidder, 1981). Writing high-quality, efficient code requires absorption of consciousness that makes designers oblivious to the flow of time. Programmers experience this state as a kind of fixation. A Web designer explained how coding binges sucked up time: "It is very easy for me to become obsessive when it comes to this stuff. I can sit there and do this stuff until 2 A.M. Wake up, go to work, come back and do it until 2 A.M. again. You know, for at least a few days straight. . . . It's something I can't really quit."

Panel C in table 15.2 suggests how occupations and the tasks they encompass can constrain temporal flexibility. The panel displays the percentage of those with some or no flexibility in eight occupational groups. Compared with contractors with flexibility, contractors without flexibility are more likely to be systems administrators (0 percent vs, 17 percent, $p < .05$), most likely for the reasons discussed above. Despite the fact that software developers could become lost in their work for significant periods of time, they were the most likely occupational group to have some type of temporal flexibility (42 percent vs. 21 percent, $p < .05$). This freedom reflected the fact that coding tasks could be modularized, which freed programmers from a ceaseless temporal regimen and also allowed them to work from home. If the developer was an independent contractor, clients would often require only that he or she deliver completed code by a specified date. How the contractor spent time was irrelevant, so long as he or she delivered the code on time.

Contractors, however, felt that the nature of their work was not nearly as important for how they their allocated time as the exigencies of the exchange relationship. Contractors understood that selling time and skills to a client meant entering a relationship with reciprocal obligations. Clients were obligated to pay contractors but, in return, contractors were obligated to do more than complete a piece of work. They also had to satisfy the client. In the role of customer, clients could make demands that went beyond the letter of the contract, which often translated into demands for additional time. It was precisely because the exchange beneath the contract relationship was remunerative and because current exchanges affected future exchanges that contractors had both immediate and long-term reasons for keeping clients happy, even when this limited contractors' temporal flexibility.

Because contractors sold expertise, the exchange between clients and contractors had overtones of a professional engagement. The ethos of ministering to a client's needs, much as would a doctor or lawyer, was exaggerated by the short-term nature of the contract. Realizing that they hired contractors as experts allowed clients, as one female software developer put, to adopt an attitude of "OK, you're a consultant. Our employees aren't carrying the load. We're paying you so you do this, this, this, and that." Independent contractors, in particular, found that their obligation to serve clients was broad. Like many independents, an experienced database developer told us he felt he had to be on-call 24 hours a day: "I've had phone calls at 3:00 in the morning. You know, the phone's ringing by the bed at 3:00 in the morning every day because somebody's operation is more important than my life." Contractors who worked several contracts simultaneously found it even more difficult to maintain control over their time while also meeting clients' expectations. A software developer explained:

On a project it'll be "We need this done. How soon can we get it done?" If I've only got one or two projects, then it's just "Gee, I'm spending all my time working on your project. We'll have it out in a couple weeks." Right now, I've gotten myself into a bind where I've got all these projects. One of them should have been done six months ago. Another's due out March 31. A couple others are expecting stuff in the next two weeks and that's not gonna happen. . . . When I'm concentrating on one project, customers will phone up, "Gee, it broke," and I have to go out and fix it. . . . I don't have 240 percent time.

Even more important than immediate pressures to please the client was the shadow of the future: the fact that contractors relied on clients for referrals and references. Contractors understood that having a reputation as a reliable expert enabled them to negotiate their next contract quickly and successfully. Contractors therefore had incentives to exceed the terms of the contract and to meet clients' demands to protect their reputation and guarantee good references. Informants repeatedly told us that they worked in "small worlds," in which word of performance traveled quickly. A workstation technician, who worked as a W2 and who was moving into quality assurance, explained how concern for her reputation led her to sacrifice her temporal flexibility:

> We're kind of in a heavy point right now. The thing I like about contracting is that it's voluntary. I mean if I don't want to go in, I don't go in. Nobody's telling me to do anything. Nobody's saying, "You have to do this. You have to be here at a certain time." But, say it was a real critical part of the project that needed to be done by Monday, and I decided "Oh, I'm not coming in," and I didn't have a really good reason. I'm still not dinged, but it's filed in the back of somebody's mind and they'll say, "Well, she's not as dependable as we thought she would be" or something like that.

The independent contractor cited above who worked multiple contracts echoed those sentiments: "You must always take responsibility for your projects. If you do a bad job, it will get around and people will stop calling you. When I hear people saying that they want to be a contractor because they want to make lots of money, I think, it's more than that. You have to have a knack for it, and you have to be willing to work weird hours."

Contractors quickly learned that market-based remunerative relationships came with more strings attached than they had originally anticipated. Where they once may have had an employer who could exercise control they now had clients who had the prerogatives of customers. As in all markets for expertise, reputations built at least partially on client satisfaction lubricated the flow of work. The need to keep clients happy meant that once contractors accepted a contract, they also experienced constraints on contracting's promise of fine-grained flexibility. Although clients had little normative control over how contractors allocated their hours and their days, they owned part of the contractors' reputations. This gave them a kind of coercive control in the present because of the possibility that they could exact retribution in the future when asked by potential employers to provide references. Contractors therefore found exercising fine-grained flexibility more costly than using coarse-grained flexibility. Unlike insisting on temporal autonomy within a contract, taking time off between contracts might lower contractors' annual incomes and deplete their savings, but it did not jeopardize their reputations. For this reason, contractors were more likely to take advantage of the market's coarse-grained flexibility than they were to enjoy its promise of fine-grained freedom.

Discussion

Scholars who study time and flexibility in organizations routinely find that employees feel overworked and desire greater control over their time but take little advantage of the flextime programs available to them. Researchers usually blame this paradox on the normative pressures of organizational life (Kunda, 1992; Barker, 1993; Perlow, 1997). Advocates of employability and free agency contend that people can escape these pressures and regain temporal control by leaving permanent employment for market-based careers that span organizations (Kanter, 1989; Arthur, 1994; Pink, 2001). Our study suggests otherwise. Moving from organizations to markets created new time binds for technical contractors. As the literature would predict, contractors believed they had more control over their time than they had as full-time employees, but this belief rarely led them to limit their hours or schedule their time more flexibly. Few took advantage of contracting's greater opportunity for breaks and vacations, and most worked such long hours each day that there was little time left with which to be flexible, even if they so desired. Thus, despite the absence of normative pressures, our informants exhibited a disjuncture between perceived and realized flexibility similar to that documented by researchers among employees in firms with flexibility programs (Tausig and Fenwick, 2001; Gareis and Barnett, 2002).

The reasons for the disjuncture lay in how the market influenced our informants' interpretations of time and their subsequent choices. First, the contract cycle repeatedly exposed contractors to the possibility of downtime, periods without work and pay. The majority of contractors saw downtime primarily as a period without pay, as opposed to a period without work, and hence sought to avoid or minimize downtime. Second, the market's high wages, which were paid by the hour, led contractors to equate time with money and allowed them to calculate precisely the cost of an hour of leisure or family time. By contrast, the opportunity cost of spending an additional hour at work was more difficult to calculate. Contractors therefore gravitated toward working more rather than fewer hours. Third, the demand for contractors was marked by crisis. The tendency for firms to hire contractors into troubled projects at the last minute exacerbated the contractors' proclivity to work long and inflexible hours. Finally, because reputations were crucial for securing a steady stream of contracts, many contractors put in long, even unbillable hours to ensure solid references and referrals. . . .

Ultimately, our research raises doubts about whether organizational life is really as troublesome for workers' ability to control their time as the literature suggests. Although organizations expose workers to mechanisms of control that contractors appear to escape, organizations also buffer employees from repeated encounters with the labor market. As we have seen, the structure of the labor market constrained most contractors from choosing to work fewer and more flexible hours. Our evidence suggests that contractors may actually work more hours than their full-time counterparts in the same occupations. Our study implies that organizations may conceivably consume less of a worker's time than do markets. Organizational employment may also offer at least as much, if not more, fine-grained control over which hours one works. Were studies to confirm these conjectures, they would not only challenge notions of free agency's promised benefits, they

would warrant rethinking a key assumption behind the literature on time binds, namely, that organizations offer only constraints. At the very least, our investigation casts doubt on the claim that market-based careers give workers greater flexibility and control over time. Free agency may lead people to perceive that they have more temporal flexibility, but aside from longer vacations, most will likely never use it. Like bureaucracies, markets are also cages, but cages of a different material. Contractors' choices about beach time, bridge time, and billable hours in the context of work may make it difficult for them to see this.

References

Arthur, M. B. 1994. "The boundaryless career: A new perspective for organizational inquiry." *Journal of Organizational Behavior*, 15: 295–306.

Arthur, M. B., and D. M. Rousseau. 1996. *The Boundaryless Career: A New Employment Principle for a New Organizational Era*. New York: Oxford University Press.

Bailyn, L. 1970. "Career and family orientations of husbands and wives in relation to marital happiness." *Human Relations*, 23: 97–113.

———. 1993. *Breaking the Mold: Women, Men, and Time in the New Corporate World*. New York: Free Press.

Barker, J. R. 1993. "Tightening the iron cage: Concertive control in self-managing teams." *Administrative Science Quarterly*, 38: 408–437.

Barnett, R. C. 1994. "Home-to-work spillover revisited: A study of full-time employed women in dual-earner couples." *Journal of Marriage and the Family*, 56: 647–656.

Beck, N. 1992. *Shifting Gears: Thriving in the New Economy*. Toronto: Harper Collins.

Black, D. S., and R. C. Andreini. 1997. *The Information Elite: The Future of the Independent Information Technology Consultant*. Redwood Shores, CA: Advanced Technology Staffing.

Blair-Loy, M. and A. Wharton. 2002. "Employees' use of family-responsive policies and the workplace social context." *Social Forces*, 80: 813–845.

Bluestone, B., and S. Rose. 1997. "Overworked and underemployed: Unraveling an economic enigma." *American Prospect*, 31: 58–69.

———. 1998 "The macroeconomics of time." *Review of Social Economy*, 56: 425–441.

Bolger, N. A. Delongis, and R. C. Kessler. 1989. "The contagion of stress across multiple roles." *Journal of Marriage and the Family*, 51: 175–183.

Bond, J. T., E. Gelinsky, and J. E. Swenberg. 1998. *The 1997 National Study of the Changing Workforce*. New York: Families and Work Institute.

Bridges, W. 1994. *Job Shift: How to Prosper in the Workplace without Jobs*. Reading, MA: Addison Wesley.

Bucher, R., and J. G. Stelling. 1977. *Becoming Professional*. Beverly Hills, CA: Sage.

Bumpus, M. F., A. C., Crouter, and S. M. McHale. 1999. "Work demands of dual-earner couples: Implications for parents' knowledge about children's daily lives in middle childhood." *Journal of Marriage and the Family*, 61: 465–475.

Caulkin, S. 1997. "Skills, not loyalty, are new key if you want job security." *San Francisco Sunday Examiner and Chronicle*, September 7(4): 2.

Clarkberg, M., and P. Moen. 2001. "Understanding the time squeeze: Married couples' preferred and actual work-hour strategies." *American Behavioral Scientist*, 44: 1115–1135.

Coleman, M. T., and J. Pencavel. 1993a. "Trends in market work behavior of women since 1940." *Industrial and Labor Relations Review*, 46: 653–676.

———. 1993b. "Changes in work hours of male employees, 1940–1988." *Industrial and Labor Relations Review*, 46: 262–283.

Daniels, S. 1997 "Flexible hours, telecommuting increasing." *National Underwriting*, September 1: 23.

Darby, J. B. 1997 "The ultimate contractor: Lessons from a parallel universe." *Contract Professional*, 2: 27–32.

Dubin, R. 1956. "Industrial workers' worlds: A study of the 'central life interests' of industrial workers." *Social Problems*, 3: 131–142.

Eaton, S. C. 2000. "Work and family integration in the biotechnology industry: Implications for employers and firms." Unpublished Ph.D. dissertation, Sloan School of Management, Massachusetts Institute of Technology.

Edwards, R. 1979. *Contested Terrain*. New York: Basic Books.

Etzioni, A. 1961. *A Comparative Analysis of Complex Organizations: On Power, Involvement and Their Correlatives*. New York: Free Press.

Faugier, J., and A. Sargeant. 1997. "Sampling hard to reach populations." *Journal of Advanced Nursing*, 26: 790–797.

Faulkner, R. R., and A. B. Anderson. 1987. "Short-term projects and emergent careers: Evidence from Hollywood." *American Journal of Sociology*, 92: 879–909.

Finlay, W., and J. E. Coverdill. 2002. *Headhunters: Matchmaking in the Labor Market*. Ithaca, NY; Cornell University Press.

Forthofer, M. S., H. J., Merkmen, M. Cox, S. Stanley, and R. C. Kessler. 1996. "Associations between marital distress and work loss in a national sample." *Journal of Marriage and the Family*, 58: 597–605.

Galinsky, E., and J. T. Bond. 1998. *The 1998 Business Work-Life Study: A Sourcebook*. New York: Families and Work Institute.

Galinsky, E., J. T. Bond, and D. E. Friedman. 1993. *National Study of the Changing Workforce*. New York: Families and Work Institute.

Gareis, K. C., and R. C. Barnett. 2002. "Under what conditions do long work hours affect psychological distress: A study of full-time and reduced-hours female doctors." *Work and Occupations*, 29: 483–497.

Gersick, C. J. 1988. "Time and transition in work teams: Toward a new model of group development." *Academy of Management Journal*, 31: 9–41.

———. 1989. "Marking time: Predictable transitions in task groups." *Academy of Management Journal*, 32: 274–309.

Goff, S., J., M. K., Mount, and R. L. Jamison. 1990. "Employer supported child care, work/family conflict, and absenteeism: A field study." *Personnel Psychology*, 43:793–809.

Gold, M., and J. Fraser. 2002. "Managing self-management: Successful transitions to portfolio careers." *Work, Employment and Society*, 16: 579–598.

Golden, L. 2001. "Flexible work schedules: Which workers get them?" *American Behavioral Scientist*, 44 1157–1178.

Gonos, G. 1997. "The contest over employer status in the postwar United States: The case of temporary help firms." *Law and Society Review*, 31: 81–110.

Greenwald, J. 1998. "Employers warming up to flexible schedules." *Business Insurance*, June 15: 3–6.

Handy, C. 1989. *The Age of Unreason*. Boston: Harvard University Press.

Hecker, D. 1998. "How hours of work affect occupational earnings." *Monthly Labor Review*, October: 8–18.

Heckscher, C. 1995. *White-Collar Blues*. New York: Basic Books.

Higgins, C. A., L. E. Duxbury, and R. H. Irving. 1992. "Work-family conflict in the dual-career family." *Organizational Behavior and Human Decision Processes*, 51: 51–75.

Hirsh, P. M., and M. Shanley. 1996. "The rhetoric of boundaryless—Or how the newly empowered managerial class bought into its own marginalization." In M. B. Arthur and D. M. Rousseau (eds.), *The Boundaryless Career: A New Employment Principle for a New Organizational Era*, 218–234, New York: Oxford University Press.

Hochschild, A. 1997. *The Time Bind: When Work Becomes Home and Home Becomes Work*. New York: Metropolitan Books.

Hughes, E. C. 1958. *Men and Their Work*. Glencoe, IL: Free Press.

Jacobs, J. A., and K. Gerson. 1998. "Who are the overworked Americans?" *Review of Social Economy*, 56: 422–459.

Jones, C. 1996. "Careers in project networks: The case of the film industry." In M. B. Arthur and D. M. Rousseau (eds.), *The Boundaryless Career: A New Employment Principle for a New Organizational Era*: 58–75. New York: Oxford University Press.

Kanter, R. M. 1989. *When Giants Learn to Dance: Mastering the Challenge of Strategy, Management, and Careers in the 1990s*. New York: Simon and Schuster.

———. 1995. "Nice work if you can get it: The software industry as a model for tomorrow's jobs." *American Prospect*, 23: 52–58.

Kickert, W. J. M. 1984. "The magic word *flexibility*." *International Studies of Management and Organization*, 14(4): 8–31.

Kidder, T. 1981. *The Soul of a New Machine*. New York: Avon Books.

Kunda, G. 1992. *Engineering Culture Control and Commitment in a High Tech Corporation*. Philadelphia: Temple University Press.

Kunda, G., S. R. Barley, and J. A. Evans. 2002. "Why do contractors contract? The experience of highly skilled technical professionals in a contingent labor market." *Industrial and Labor Relations Review*, 55: 234–261.

Kurland, N. B., and T. D. Egan. 1999. "Telecommuting: Justice and control in the virtual organization." *Organization Science*, 10: 500–513.

Matusik, S., and S. R. Fuller. 2002. "The nexus of work arrangement preferences and demand for skills: An exploratory examination of alternative work." Paper delivered at the Academy of Management Meeting, Denver.

Maume, D.J., and M. L. Bellas. 2001. "The overworked American or the time bind?: Assessing competing explanations for time spent in paid labor." *American Behavioral Scientist*, 44: 1137–1156.

McBride, A. 2003. "Reconciling competing pressures for working-time flexibility: An impossible task in the National Health Service." *Work, Employment and Society*, 17: 159–170.

McShulskis, E. 1997. "Work and family benefits increasingly popular?" *HR Magazine*, July: 26–29.

Mead, R. J., S. McConville, P. Harmer, M. Lubin, A. Linsley, J. Chang, and J. McMahon. 2000. *The Struggle to Juggle Work and Family*. Los Angeles: Center for Labor Research and Education, School of Public Policy and Social Research, UCLA.

Meiksins, P., and P. Whalley. 2002. *Putting Work in Its Place: A Quiet Revolution*. Ithaca, NY: Cornell University Press.

Mirvis, P. H., and D. T. Hall. 1994. "Psychological success and the boundaryless career." *Journal of Organizational Behavior*, 15: 365–380.

Olson, M. H. 1987. "Telework: Practical experience and future prospects." In R. E. Kraut (ed.), *Technology and the Transformation of White-Collar Work*: 135–152. Hillsdale, NJ: Lawrence Erlbaum.

Osterman, P. 1995. "Work/family programs and the employment relationship." *Administrative Science Quarterly*, 40: 681–700.

O'Mahony, S., and S. R. Barley. 1999. "Do digital telecommunications affect work and organization? The state of our knowledge." In R. I. Sutton and B. M. Staw (eds.), *Research in Organizational Behavior*, 21: 125–161. Stamford, CT: JAI Press.

Orzack, L. H. 1959. "Work as a central life interest of professionals." *Social Problems*, 7: 125–132.

Paden, S. L., and C. Buehlel. 1995. "Coping with the dual-income lifestyle." *Journal of Marriage and the Family*, 57: 101–110.

Parker, R. E. 1994. *Flesh Peddlers and Warm Bodies: The Temporary Help Industry and Its Workers*. New Brunswick, NJ: Rutgers University Press.

Perin, C. 1991. "The moral fabric of the office: Panopticon discourse and schedule flexibilities." In P. S. Tolbert and S. R. Barley (eds.), *Research in the Sociology of Organizations*, vol. 8: *Organizations and Professions*: 241–268. Greenwich, CT: JAI Press.

Perlow, L. A. 1997. *Finding Time*. Ithaca, NY: Cornell University Press.

———. 1999 "The time famine: Toward a sociology of work time." *Administrative Science Quarterly*, 44: 57–81.

Pink, D. H. 1998 "Free agent nation." *Fast Company*, December/January: 131–147.

———. 2001. *Free Agent Nation: How America's New Independent Workers Are Transforming the Way We Live*. New York: Warner Business Books.

Rapoport, R., and R. Rapoport. 1978. *Working Couples*. New York: Harper.

Repetti, R. L., and J. Wood. 1997. "Effects of daily stress at work on mothers' interactions with preschoolers." *Journal of Family Psychology*, 11: 90–108.

Reynolds, J. 2003. "You can't always get the hours you want: Mismatches between actual and preferred work hours in the U.S." *Social Forces*, 81: 1171–1199.

Robinson, J., and G. Godbey. 1997. *Time for Life: The Surprising Ways Americans Use Their Time*. University Park, PA: Pennsylvania State University.

Saltzstein, A. L., Y. Ting, and G. H. Saltzstein. 2001. "Work-family balance and job satisfaction: The impact of family-friendly policies on attitudes of federal government employees." *Public Administration Review*, 61: 452–467.

Schein, E. H. 1972. *Organizational Psychology*, 2d ed. Englewood Cliffs, NJ: Prentice-Hall.

Schor, J. B. 1991. *The Overworked American: The Unexpected Decline of Leisure*. New York: Basic Books.

Schwartz, F. 1989. "Management women and the new facts of life." *Harvard Business Review*, January/February: 68.

Smelser, N. J., and R. Swedberg. 1994. *The Handbook of Economic Sociology*. New York: Princeton University Press.

Tausig, M. and R. Fenwick. 2001. "Unbinding time: Alternate work schedules and work-life balance." *Journal of Family and Economic Issues*, 22: 101–119.

Van Maanen, J. and S. R. Barley. 1984. "Occupational communities: Culture and control in organizations." In B. M. Staw and L. L. Cummings (eds.), *Research in Organizational Behavior*, 6: 287–365. Greenwich, CT: JAI Press.

Weick, K. E. 1996. "Enactment and the boundaryless career: Organizing as we work." In M. B. Arthur and D, M Rousseau (eds.), *The Boundaryless Career: A New Employment Principle for a New Organizational Era*: 40–57. New York: Oxford University Press.

Part II

Inside Organizations

Power and Conflict

Chapter 16
Covert Political Conflict in Organizations
Challenges from Below

Calvin Morrill, Mayer N. Zald, and Hayagreeva Rao

The sociology of organizations does not exist in a vacuum, divorced from other areas of sociological theory and research. One of the most productive dialogues in recent years has been between organizational sociologists and students of social movements. Social movement theory has helped researchers better understand many types of organizations and aspects of organizational life. In this chapter, we explore issues of conflict in organizations and examine how theory and research by social movement scholars can help us make sense of this issue. By looking more closely at organizational conflict, particularly covert political conflict, we can better grasp the "dark, informal side" of organizations and consider issues of power, conflict, and change.

Introduction

During the past decade, sociologists increasingly drew on social movement theory to understand change in a broad array of organizations: economic corporations (Davis & Thompson 1994, McCann 1994, Scully & Segal 2002), governmental bureaucracies (Katzenstein 1998, Zhou 1992), interest groups and political parties (Clemens 1997, Zhou 1992), religious institutions (Ammerman 1990, Chaves 1997, Kurzman 1997), emergent professional associations (Morrill 2003, Morrill & Owen-Smith 2002), and consumer agencies (Rao 1998). Zald & Berger (1978) provided an early exemplar with their analyses of "mass movements," "bureaucratic insurgencies," and "coup d'etats" in American corporations. More recently, Davis & McAdam (2000) argued that the globalized decline of the mass production paradigm and economies rooted in managerialist ideology renders conventional organization theory inadequate by itself for investigating how contemporary social forces have transformed workplaces. Social movement theory, they maintain, offers a useful conceptual vocabulary for understanding the new social structures wrought by transitory global production, volatile financial markets, and transnational collective action and governance. Rao et al. (2000) build on these insights by demonstrating the role of collective action and social movements in the creation of new organizational forms and fields of practice.

Bringing social movement theory into organizational research has yielded undeniably useful insights into organizations. Yet, this theoretical innovation suffers from a narrow focus on open confrontation that overlooks a range of political action simmering beneath the surface of mass mobilizations and other movementlike phenomena. Conflict of this sort is often overlooked because it is usually not viewed as "politics" in the conventional sense, instead it is labeled as opportunistic criminal behavior (Taylor & Walton 1971) or the work of isolated, disgruntled individuals (Jermier 1988). Moreover, the injustices that fuel such conflict typically fall outside the realms of legal and conventional extrajudicial complaint handling mechanisms (e.g., Nader 1980). Yet, as Scott (1989; for organizations, see Kolb & Putnam 1992, Lammers 1969) vividly demonstrates for covert political conflict, more generally, such action is a "vital means" by which subordinated groups express their political grievances against superiors, displaying tacit, if not explicit, coordination and various forms of group solidarity. By contrast, organizational elites and superiors typically deploy formally structured instruments of control as they engage in political struggles with subordinates (Arvey & Jones 1985, Baumgartner 1984).

What is missing in the literature is a more coherent vision of covert political conflict with regards to its conceptual foundations, empirical findings, and linkages to overt political voice in organizations. In the ensuing pages, we address these shortcomings with particular reference to challenges by subordinates in capitalist workplaces where the bulk of research on covert conflict has been conducted. We organize our review around three broad questions: First, how can covert political action be conceptualized such that it aids research on political processes of organizational change? To answer this question, we briefly outline the constitutive elements that define covert political opposition. Second, what variable aspects of covert political action have been identified? We answer this question by discussing material and symbolic forms of covert political action, as well as variation in social visibility, collective dimensions, and outcomes. Third, under what conditions will covert political conflict occur? Here we explore explanations for covert conflict at the micro, organizational, field, and macro levels of analysis. This last section comes full circle as we link covert political conflict with explicit voice, thus deepening the sense of complex organizations as "contested terrains" (Edwards 1982) over control and broadening the processes through which social power can be expressed. This last section also leads to a final summary and a brief outline of implications and potentially fruitful areas for future inquiry.

Constitutive Elements of Covert Political Conflict

We define political conflict as a form of "contentious politics" in which challengers contest authorities over the "shape" and governance of "institutionalized systems of power" (McAdam et al. 2001, pp. 342–43). This definition focuses on how the dynamics of interaction constitute political conflict and recognizes that such opposition in organizations need not directly involve states but can challenge authority based in formal authority structures, culture, or other social arrangements (Snow 2002). Such challenges are often embedded, either implicitly or explicitly, in broad social cleavages and power inequities, including those between capital and labor, shareholders and managers, members of different status and identity groups (e.g., women and men, gays, ethnic minorities), and elites vying for power (Jermier et al. 1994b). At the same time, research on covert conflict resonates with earlier organizational approaches to "micro politics" (Burns 1955, 1961; Mechanic 1962), organizational "trouble" (Emerson & Messinger 1977), coalition formation (Dal-

ton 1959), and decision-making power (Petigrew 1973, Pfeffer 1981, Zald 1970). Most importantly, the study of covert dissent underscores Zald & Berger's (1978) conceptualization of organizations as "polities" with interest groups, distributions of right and duties, and governance systems.

The presence of enduring cleavages in organizational polities, however, is insufficient to define or fuel conflict without some sense of collective injury (Tucker 1993) or "justice motive" (Nader 1980). The meanings that such perceptions can carry are nearly always negotiated in informal and unseen ways by participants and various social audiences. At the outset, actors may have difficulty locating the sources of their injuries, assessing blame, or making claims about appropriate remedies (Felstiner et al. 1980/1981) and may turn to collective action "master frames" for help in making sense of their troubles (Snow & Benford 1992). Moreover, blurred boundaries can exist between covert conflict in terms of its pro- and/or anti-organizational footings. Meyerson's (2001, see also Meyerson & Scully 1995) work on "tempered radicals" illustrates this tendency. Tempered radicals are individuals who "contribute and succeed at their jobs . . . but who are considered outsiders because they represent ideals or agendas that are . . . at odds with the dominant culture" (Meyerson 2001, p. 5). Tempered radicals thus uphold their identities as insiders but push hard to change the system that casts them as outsiders. Once blame is subjectively assessed, there can still be enormous gulfs between perception, collective action, and identifiable outcomes as social movement theory underscores (Snow & Benford 1992). Organizational authorities can directly interrupt this process, should they discover it, by suppressing would-be activists as deviants (Taylor & Walton 1971). Moreover, covert conflict can become implicated in interpersonal squabbles (Clarke 1988, Greenhalgh 1987) and the broader "underlife" of organizations, as Goffman (1962) called it, creating further ambiguities about its scope and nature.

In addition to the elements discussed above, covert political conflict must avert the detection and direct engagement of various social audiences, especially elites and other authorities. By remaining veiled, such action can appear nonthreatening or may even be ignored by elites until its impacts become undeniably apparent. As a result, covert political conflict can remain hidden for long periods of time, offering relative safety for those involved, thus enabling its diffusion and development. The occluded nature of covert political conflict is particularly salient because such opposition typically involves strategies to pursue grievances that are unprecedented or forbidden by the organization in question. Beyond these constitutive elements, covert political conflict also varies in terms of its forms, social visibility, collective dimensions, and outcomes. We discuss these features in the next section.

Variable Features of Covert Political Conflict

Material and Symbolic Forms

By form, we mean the general properties inherent in a pattern of covert opposition, with particular emphasis placed on the primary means and aspects of an organization targeted for subversion. Scott (1989) provides a suggestive lead for classifying covert political conflict by drawing attention to whether it focuses on the material or symbolic aspects of social institutions. In organizations, "material" forms focus on the subversion (and often the destruction, hampering, or appropriation) of organizational technologies and resources, whereas "symbolic" forms attempt to subvert dominant meanings, ideologies, and discourses.

In practice, the material and symbolic aspects of covert forms can be intertwined and negotiated among various constituencies over time (Bayat 1997). The meanings of a single act of sabotage can sometimes take years to fully unfold or be recognized. Similarly, different kinds of accounts can emerge to explain an act of covert conflict before, during, and after its occurrence. As a result, it may be more appropriate to conceive of material and symbolic forms as existing in overlapping Venn diagrams, with most forms exhibiting tendencies toward one side of the diagram or the other. In fact, many studies of covert conflict reviewed here find that participants tend to accent the material or symbolic aspects of their actions. We follow this tendency in our discussion in this section, although we note along the way forms that tend to mix the material and the symbolic.

Material Forms. Sabotage and theft have dominated covert conflict research agendas. Some researchers define sabotage as any behavior that deliberately undermines organizational goals (Brown 1977) or restricts output and/or reduces the quality of goods (Dubois 1979). LaNuez & Jermier (1994, p. 221) more precisely characterize sabotage as "any deliberate action or inaction that is intended to damage, destroy, or disrupt some aspect of the workplace environment, including the organizations's property, product, or reputation." LaNuez & Jermier (1994, p. 241) offer an additionally useful distinction between "sabotage by direct action" and "sabotage by circumvention." The former describes behaviors that directly "damage or destroy organizational property or products," whereas the latter refers to actions that facilitate other events or situations that eventually harm an organization.

Of these two subtypes, sabotage by direct action in mass production factories is the most commonly studied, especially those drawing from neo-Marxist perspectives to study resistance in the labor process (LaNuez & Jermier 1994). Examples of direct sabotage include misassembling and omitting parts to produce high numbers of "reject" engines in a Detroit automobile factory (Watson 1971), damaging parts in a San Francisco–area automobile manufacturer (King 1978), breaking tools and machinery in a Midwestern electronic components factory (Fennell 1976), "arranging" machine breakdowns in a commercial bakery (Ditton 1979), breaking conveyor belts in a slaughterhouse (Thompson 1983), and surreptitiously breaking machines and electronic components in Japanese-owned Malaysian factories (Ong 1987). Historically, both the Luddites and the Wobblies engaged in direct material sabotage of manufacturing plants. In all of these cases, authors report some sense of collective injury held by saboteurs. Such injuries range from being collectively ignored in crucial decisions at the point of production (Watson 1971) to being denied basic human comforts on the shop floor (Ong 1987) or having an entire way of life destroyed by changes in the labor process (Jermier 1988). Although the material aspects of direct sabotage are emphasized in these works, some studies demonstrate how sabotage acts as a "symbolic gesture against the brutality of factory life" (LaNuez & Jermier 1994, p. 224) by asserting the dignity and self-worth of workers. Among these works are participant observation studies of slaughterhouse workers (Thompson 1983) and brewery workers (Molstad 1986).

Other types of organizations and work, however, are not immune to direct sabotage. Computerization provides a myriad of opportunities for direct sabotage, including unleashing computer viruses, erasing files, or not saving files appropriately (Gialcone & Greenberg 1997, Gilliom 1997, Gottfried & Fasenfest 1984). Researchers also report mental health workers defacing and debilitating property in mental wards to "protest" managerial practices (Spector 1975), construction workers breaking tools on construction sites to express their discontent with their working conditions (Tucker 1993), and civil servants in public bureacracies who subvert various policies (Brehm & Gates 1997).

Forced labor in a variety of historical and cultural contexts provides the occasion for direct sabotage as well. A case in point comes from indentured servants in seventeenth-century New England households who resisted their master's impositions by defiling food and other goods (Morgan 1966). Aggrieved peasants on eighteenth-century Polish manors reduced the "intensity" of their work and intentionally built structures that collapsed once completed (Kochanowicz 1989). North and South American slaves in the seventeenth through nineteenth centuries engaged in collective destruction of valued resources—including killing fellow slaves—as a means to resist their masters' domination (Baumgartner 1984). In the European-held colonies of the nineteenth and twentieth centuries, Guha (1989) reports the destruction of resources by indigenous peoples "statutorily" required to work under horrid conditions in colonial organizations.

Noncooperation with respect to organizational rules and procedures and/or superiors is perhaps the most common technique of sabotage by circumvention (Prasad & Pushkala 1998, Rusbult & Lowry 1985, Rusbult et al. 1988). Eldrige (1968), for instance, reports patterns of strategic "inaction" among British steelworkers intended to counter technologically reduced worker control and decision making at the point of production. So subtle were their actions that management blamed the new technology, rather than the workers, for production

snafus. Poignant historical illustrations of noncooperation can be found among early twentieth-century English day laborers (Howkins 1977), Polish workers in Nazi-run organizations during World War II (Gross 1979), farm hands on government-owned Nicaraguan farms (Colburn 1989), factory workers during August Pinochet's Chilean regime (J. Stillerman 1998, unpublished dissertation), and migrant workers in the aftermath of the Iranian revolution in the 1970s (Bayat 1997). All of these types of noncooperation involve not meeting organizational or overseer expectations. A more subtle type involves "working to rule" in which workers meet official procedures to the letter without exercising necessary discretion. Their actions in turn lead to production breakdowns and/or compromises in product quality (Eldrige 1968, Gottfried 1994).

Sabotage by circumvention, however, is not confined to lower-status members of organizations. A nonrandom survey from the late 1980s of 400 American managers found that one third of those surveyed admitted to withholding information needed for key decision making or not including key personnel in decision making in order to deleteriously affect the quality of the choices made (LaNuez & Jermier 1994). "Open mouth" sabotage is yet another type of sabotage by circumvention that can be directed to a number of constituencies, including competitors, customers, employees, and regulators (Knights & McCabe 1998a, LaNuez & Jermier 1994). Among the examples found in the literature are incidents of workers leaking information about "shoddy" production to the press or managers passing proprietary secrets to competitors (Jermier 1988).

Whereas sabotage involves harming organizational resources in direct and/or indirect ways, theft requires the appropriation of property by aggrieved parties. Justice-motivated sabotage and theft also differ in their underlying logics. Sabotage often carries a "penal" logic in which harming the organization punishes superiors for their transgressions, whereas theft compensates subordinates for wages and other material resources they believe superiors have unjustly denied them (Baumgartner 1984, Tucker 1989). In a survey of 5000 respondents across retailing, health, and manufacturing industries, Hollinger & Clark (1982, p. 142) found that "employees who felt exploited by their company or by their superiors" used theft as one of their prime strategies to right such injustices. Theft of this sort has been documented among a wide range of occupations, including dockworkers (Mars 1974, 1982), miners (Gouldner 1954), sales personnel (Zeitlin 1971), accountants (Cressey 1953), and managers (Willis 1986). At the same time, the boundaries between legitimate property appropriation and theft can be ambiguous: Pilfering is sometimes officially built into organizational control systems to make up for wage deficiencies (Ditton 1977, p. 48).

Compensatory theft not ordained by organizations has also been studied across occupations and organizations in a broad range of historical contexts. Hall (1952), for instance, recounted Aristotle's complaints about Athenian road commissioners who embezzled funds when they believed they were cheated by their superiors. Hanawalt (1979, p. 179) describes a thirteenth-century English case in which four peasants stole grain from the Abbot of Ramsey's barn. They believed their theft compensated them for the insufficient bread the Abbot supplied them while working on his land. Similar episodes can be found in "filching" by eighteenth-century Russian house serfs against "unfair" masters (Blum 1961), "swindling" committed by Danish peasants against landlords (Rockwell 1974), and theft by workers in nineteenth-century English cotton mills (Tobias 1972). Forced labor in countries militarily occupied also provides moral justifications for theft by workers (Gross 1979).

Symbolic Forms. Scholars have devoted less attention to the symbolic side of covert political conflict in organizations, although there is little evidence to suggest that symbolic forms occur less frequently than material forms (Goffman 1967, Scott 1989). Some of the reasons why fewer scholars have studied symbolic covert conflict include difficulties in its definition and detection, as well as difficulties in gauging its outcomes. Although an act of property destruction can provoke deliberations about its meaning (e.g., "Was it sabotage, incompetence, unavoidable, or some combination of all three?"), one is left with a damaged machine or depleted resources as a clue to what happened. The residue of symbolic covert conflict can be more subtle and thus harder to identify and analyze. Another limiting factor

may be the inordinate attention devoted to factory workers on assembly lines by labor process scholars who regard material sabotage as a key resistance strategy to capitalist discipline (Jermier 1988).

Consider Goffman's (1967, p. 58) observations on subversion in face-to-face interaction: "By easily showing a regard that he does not have, the actor can . . . insinuate all kinds of disregard by carefully modifying intonation, pronunciation, pacing, and so forth." Such processes can certainly express personal enmity that is decoupled from political grievances. Yet they can also feed into subtle, parallel lines of individual political action as Martin & Meyerson (1997, 1999) demonstrate in their research on "disorganized coaction." Female managers in the firm they studied rarely confronted male colleagues with grievances regarding their treatment as women in a masculine working environment. Instead, they adhered to masculine norms of interaction but sometimes engaged in acts of nonconformity that subverted the masculine interaction order. Men found these acts difficult to read because they were embedded in conformity to the dominant norms of interaction. Covert conflict of this sort has also been noted in service occupations (Paules 1991), mental hospitals (Goffman 1962), and among lower-status male executives in American corporations (Morrill 1995).

Another symbolic form—which we call symbolic escape—includes acts that aggrieved parties use to remove themselves from official organizational authority by carving out psychological, social, temporal, or physical niches in organizations. Symbolic escapists seek to reintroduce a measure of control into their lives that is beyond the reach of official routines they deem unfair or intolerable. Although these activities can be individualistic, such as daydreaming (Cohen & Taylor 1993), they more often than not take on a collective nature. A prime example is taking extra break time to protest organizational policies while a colleague covers one's actions (Gottfried 1994, Knights & McCabe 1998b). One of the most intriguing types of symbolic escape unfolds among Malaysian women working in Japanese-owned factories who "succumb" to mysterious "spirit possession" in the presence of overseers. Ong (1987) argues that women use these bouts of "hysteria" to escape capitalist discipline in the labor process. Earlier, Lewis (1971) argued that spirit possession thwarts male domination of Malaysian women's occupational and sexual identities by disrupting capitalist-patriaichal control systems and discourses. The aftermath of spirit possession can lead to managerial fears of contagion among women, costly factory shut downs, and hastily hired exorcists to perform "preventive" rites. It is unclear, however, how spirit possession leads to social change or how it affects the life chances and political consciousness of women.

Less ambiguous (at least to participants) are hidden transcripts that dissident subcultures generate (Scott 1989, 1990). Hidden transcripts develop backstage in the autonomous social spaces created by symbolic escape. In these spaces, subordinates spin tales of revenge, celebrate hero myths of those who stood up to exploitive superiors, and engage in discourses that underscore the inherent dignity of subordinates (Kanter 1977, Kunda 1992). Bies & Tripp (1998, p. 213) provide a dramatic case-in-point in their study of workplace "carnivals" that employees hold in response to organizational "tyranny." At carnivals, "employees would demonize their bosses—that is, vent their frustrations, assign blame, call the bosses names (e.g., Beezelbub), and generally bad-mouth their bosses." Although not as colorful as carnivals, gossip functions as a hidden transcript that evaluates the normative behavior of absent individuals (Merry 1982). In some instances, gossip can even act as a symbolic "trial in absentia" of authority figures in which blame and remedies are assigned (Tucker 1993, p. 31). Gossip also strengthens the boundaries of backstage groups relative to other social actors (Wittek & Wieiers 1998), which in turn protects the development of future hidden transcripts (Hodson 1991). Hidden transcripts can also occur in the presence of superiors. Gottfried (1994, p. 119), for example, describes how female temporary workers interpret dress codes by wearing slacks rather than skirts to "resist prepackaged gendered identities" regarding secretarial support staff, all the while claiming ignorance about the rules.

A final symbolic form is illustrated by ritualized confrontation, which feminist scholars argue carries the capacity to open up small fissures in male-dominated organizational power relations. For example, Martin & Meyerson (1997, 1999) documented a case of ritualized confrontation in which a female executive in an American high-tech firm conformed to the masculine norms of direct confrontation by telling her boss "to go to hell" and, at the same time, disrupted "expectations of appropriate 'feminine' behavior, such as deference and avoidance of conflict" (1999, p. 336). Yet another example of ritual confrontation comes from Van Mannen's (1992) ethnography of an English police department. In the midst of pub parties, verbal ripostes between higher and lower ranks can take on a stylistic character and touch highly charged personal and policy issues. The covert nature of these conflicts occurs in their aftermath—the next day—as participants (especially lower ranks) claim they "were out of their minds" with alcohol (1992, pp. 50–51). The mixture of confrontation and occlusion in ritualized confrontation points to a second variable aspect of covert political conflict: social visibility.

Social Visibility

Social visibility can be thought of as the degree to which opposition political interests and actions (including the participants' identities) are known (especially to authorities). In the upper left quadrant of Figure 16.1, as illustrated by union strikes, participants and their interests are typically well-known to broad social audiences. In political conflict, collective interests are always something of a moving target, with their dynamics occurring on back and front stages. In covert politics, such interplay largely occurs behind the scenes (Haldeman 1994, Mahmood 2001). Perhaps the most common configuration of visibility with respect to covert conflict is represented by the lower left quadrant of Figure 16.1, where the collective interests and intents of participants are known, but the times and places of their actions are unknown. As Scott (1989, p. 27) points out, covert actions of this sort send a signal of protest, yet are often concealed behind public conformity, as the nineteenth-century Luddite sabotage campaigns against English mills illustrate. Luddites maintained their daily work schedules while engaging in sabotage at night, which constrained authorities from learning when they would act or their individual identities (Jermier 1988).

Figure 16.1

Social visibility covert political conflict in organizations. (Each quadrant contains a relevant illustration.)

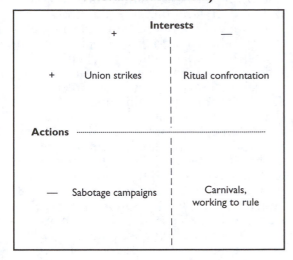

As illustrated by ritualized confrontation (upper-right quadrant of Figure 16.1), the undercover nature of covert conflict can unfold through ambiguous actions that occur directly in the presence of the authorities without the latter knowing the interests involved. Finally, there are actions (represented in the lower-right quadrant of Figure 16.1), such as working to rule or employee carnivals, in which both interest and action are largely unseen by all except direct participants. Even if authorities discover such acts, their significance may be regarded as blowing off steam without their political implications being comprehended.

Collective Dimensions

Closely related to the social visibility of covert political conflict are its collective dimensions. Although some popular and industrial pundits (Crino & Leap 1988, Curtius 1998, Vinzant 2000) and business scholars (Gialcone & Greenberg 1997, Gialcone & Knouse 1990) portray covert political conflict in organizations, especially sabotage, as the work of isolated misfits, much of the empirical research reviewed above suggests otherwise. Figure 16.2 represents the range of variation in the collective dimensions of covert political conflict. Close to the individualistic end of the continuum are seemingly solitary acts that nonetheless involve subtle collective aspects, as illustrated by disorganized coaction. At the opposite end of the

continuum are formally coordinated actions, which are illustrated by the command and control structures in the Luddite sabotage campaigns (Jermier 1988). Far more prevalent are studies of covert conflict that fall somewhere between these two extremes. At one point is action in which colleagues tacitly comply with those engaged in covert activities, as illustrated by much of the justice-motivated theft discussed previously. As early as the eighteenth century, Jonathan Swift (quoted in Thomas 1999, p, 553), in his sardonic *Directions to Servants*, recognized this collective dimension of covert conflict among English servants: "If you see your master wronged by any of your fellow-servants, be sure to conceal it." Even more prevalent within the literature is informally coordinated resistance networks (Fennell 1976) or "virtual groups" (Stephenson 1990) within and across organizations. Much of the material sabotage and hidden transcripts discussed previously are supported by networks and groups of these kinds.

Outcomes

A fourth way covert conflict varies is in terms of its outcomes. Few studies of covert opposition systematically conceptualize or measure its outcomes. Instead, researchers focus on the psychological relief enjoyed by participants or examine interpersonal "micro emancipation" that "break[s] away from diverse forms of oppression" (Alvesson & Wilmott 1992, p. 447). Some studies, however, report the role of covert conflict in organizational change, including the disruption of unfair organizational routines (LaNuez & Jermier 1994) and dominant gender identities (Martin & Meyerson 1999, Sotirin & Gottfried 1999). These studies suggest that covert conflict leads toward informal gains in which inequitable organizational practices and routines are questioned or

Figure 16.2

Collective dimensions of covert political conflict in organizations.

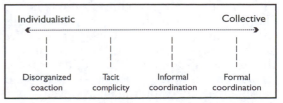

subverted and constrained, rather than transformed.

Scott (1989) is perhaps the most optimistic about the outcomes covert conflict can produce in wider society, although he does not directly address his comments to organizations. He argues covert conflict can subtly prepare the way for largescale transformations " . . . just as millions of anthozoan polyps create, willy-nilly, a coral reef, thousands upon thousands of petty acts of insubordination and evasion create a political and economic barrier reef of their own" (p. 20). This barrier reef is often constructed from the cultural transformation of understandings about what is unjust, what changes are possible, and how people can fight back covertly against injustice (Rochon 1997, p. 239). Applied to organizations, the long-term cultural readiness for overt political conflict may ultimately prove to be the most documented outcome of covert conflict even though the latter can ironically reproduce hegemony in the short term because its participants must cloak their activities in outward conformity to official policies and everyday routines.

Despite these speculations, the conditions under which covert collective action results in intensified mobilization among potential partisans, public voice, or significant changes in organizations remains an open question. Moreover, it is unclear, aside from some intriguing speculations, how covert political opposition in organizations is influenced by broad social movements or covert conflict (e.g., terrorist attacks) that become highly publicized.

Explaining Covert Conflict in Organizations

We turn now to a discussion of the conditions that influence the occurrence and patterning of covert conflict. Researchers often downplay explanations for covert conflict, instead concentrating on thick descriptions of its existence and vibrance. This trend is understandable given the relative lack of visibility of covert conflict both empirically and in the literatures on organizational conflict, change, and collective action. As a result, theoretical explanations for covert conflict are fragmented across an array of work at the micro, organizational, field, and macro levels of analysis. The most developed perspectives focus on the micro level.

Micro Level

Social Psychological Perspectives. Among the most prominent factors studied at the micro level are perceptions of declining control and frustration over the workplace. These factors operate as the chief social psychological mechanisms in research ranging from neo-Marxist studies of resistance in the labor process (Jermier et al. 1994a) to survey research on sabotage (Allen & Greenberger 1980). Proponents of this approach argue that organizational members whose perceptions of their task control have dipped below preexisting, desired levels are most likely to engage in covert opposition (Greenberger et al. 1989). Such control can involve an array of issues, including planning (Eldridge 1968, Watson 1971), compensation systems (Edwards & Scullion 1982), and temporal aspects of work, such as pace (Watson 1971) or break times (Ditton 1976, Gottfried & Fasenfest 1984). Frustration associated with a declining sense of control has also been found to precede and/or correlate with organizational sabotage (LaNuez & Jermier 1994, p. 225; Spector 1975).

Perhaps the most systematic program of social psychological research relevant to covert conflict draws from Hirschman's (1970) classic "exit, voice, and loyalty" typology (see the review in Dowding et al. 2000). Hirschman argued that people can either withdraw (exit) or express their grievances (voice) to a social organization (e.g., a market, a firm, a state) they define as deteriorating or unjust. One's commitment (loyalty) to the offending source modifies the choice between exit and voice, compelling people to withstand egregious conditions. In a series of studies, Farrell, Rusbult, and colleagues found loyalty (which they label investment) predicts voice, but that neglect (a form of noncooperation) is more likely when employees have long-term dissatisfaction with their jobs but little loyalty to their organizations (Farrell 1983, Farrell & Rusbult 1992, Rusbult & Lowery 1985, Rusbult et al. 1988). All these formulations portray exit as covert (relative to voice) and more likely when loyalty is low and alternative organizational membership is possible. Hirschman (1993) has questioned this characterization in light of highly visible mass exits from Eastern Europe during the late 1980s and well-known schisms in religious organizations.

Social Interaction, Identity, and Interpersonal Networks. Social interaction and social identities significantly influence how people define conflict, the repertoires they have for handling conflict, and the outcomes they expect (Barley 1991, p. 175; Kolb 1987; Morrill 1995). LaNuez & Jermier(1994, pp. 238–39), for instance, argue that middle managers who socially interact and identify more with superiors tend to develop "corporate social identities" with "low sabotage" potential. Managers who identify with their subordinates develop "worker identities" with "high sabotage potential."

The contents and forms of social networks can also influence covert opposition. Superiors and subordinates who enjoy social relationships with multiple substantive contents such as friendship and religion reduce the likelihood for covert conflict because they are more likely to identify with each other and develop trust that increases the likelihood of open negotiation (Morrill 1995, pp. 92–140). Intraorganizational social networks with dense-knit forms (in which organizational members interact with each other a great deal) can lead to overt conflict expressions, whereas loosely knit networks are associated with organizational exit and various forms of escape (Morrill 1991). Fennell (1976) reported that loosely knit networks across organizations can diffuse information about worker grievances and sustain covert sabotage.

Organizational Level

Formal Structure and Authority. At the organizational level, researchers have explicitly investigated the trade-offs between formal structures that encourage voice and those that discourage it. Zald & Berger (1978, see also Morrill 1995), for example, argue that formal organizational hierarchies limit the opportunities for voice when compared to professional, voluntary, and federated associations. Such organizations contain flatter organizational structures that encourage various forms of voice in open polities, thus reducing covert political action. The relationship between formal structure, voice, and covert conflict is sometimes framed in terms of two competing predictions: the "substitution" ("balloon") or the "complimentarity" ("iceberg") hypothesis (Sapsford & Turnbull 1994). The substitution hypothesis predicts formal structures

that facilitate voice will reduce covert conflict (i.e., squeeze a filled balloon in one place and the air inside it expands outward in another location). The complementarity hypothesis predicts that formally enabling voice is associated with "corresponding increases in other forms of . . . [submerged] conflict" (Sapsford & Turnbull 1994, p. 250). Empirical research reveals support for the substitution hypothesis (Hebdon & Stern 1998, Sapsford & Turnbull 1994).

These perspectives also link concretely with various approaches to organizational power. As we noted at the outset of this essay, one of the core assumptions in the literature on covert conflict is that subordinates—particularly the disenfranchised—are the most likely to engage in hidden political opposition. However, power and resources do not simply affect whether one is able to express voice or not: They also shape definitions of what is and is not objectionable. Studies of interactions between professionals and nonprofessionals, for example, find that nonprofessionals tend to adopt the definition of conflict proffered by the professional. Hence, whether one defines a situation as injurious can be a function of one's relative social power in an organization either defined by bureaucratic or professional status (Barley 1991, p. 181). Institutional theories of organizational power go one step further by underscoring how elite-enforced "conceptions of control" set the agenda for processes and outcomes of political contestations among organizational managers by demarcating the boundaries of legitimate conflict (Fligstein 1990, Ocasio & Kim 1999).

Organizational Culture. Martin's (1992) multiperspective analysis of organizational culture provides a useful lens to examine how theory influences the study of covert conflict. She argues that organizational culture approaches emphasize "integrationist," "differentiation," or "fragmented" assumptions. Integrationist approaches prize organization-wide consensus that largely exclude dissent. Differentiation approaches (the literature on collective action in organizations resonates with this view) focus on subcultural conflicts that turn on overt, rather than covert, opposition. The study of covert conflict is therefore more likely in approaches based in fragmented assumptions that direct attention to how ambiguity veils dissent and blunts punishment. As long as researchers tacitly or explicitly draw from integrationist or differentiation perspectives, covert conflict will be elided or ignored. In this sense, theories silence dissent.

Field Level

From the perspective of practice theory and institutionalist approaches, fields refer to social domains bounded by their expertise and legitimacy, distinctive interpersonal and interorganizational networks, hierarchical relationships, distributions of material resources, and institutional logics (Bourdieu & Waquant 1992, pp. 94–100; Friedland & Alford 1991). To date, there has been relatively little systematic research that explains covert conflict at the field level. However, studies of other phenomena provide clues to the potential payoffs of this approach.

One such clue can be found in Jackall (1988), who notes that managers in large corporations use moral codes that vary across the fields in which their organizations operate. Such codes define appropriate conflict processes and issues as well as appropriate sources of authorities that can be mobilized to settle disputes within firms. Another clue with regards to the role of fields in covert conflict can be found in the literature on field change and emergence. Field-level changes can generate new formal structures and technologies that profoundly affect "the way business is done" within and across existing organizations (Fligstein 2001, Rao et al. 2000, Scott et al. 2000). Katzenstein's (1998) analysis of the impact of the women's movement on the U.S. military offers an illustration. She documents how the women's movement moved into multiple organizational fields and provided various kinds of material and symbolic resources to women that enabled them to take clandestine struggles to the front stage of military politics.

Yet another field-level approach can be found in Black (1993), who conceives of social fields as "geometries" of social and normative statuses, material resources, relational and network connections, and cultural properties that are associated with particular conflict forms and processes. This approach is intended as a general perspective on conflict, rather than only political conflict in organizations, and has been used to investigate interpersonal and intergroup conflict in a variety of settings (Baumgartner 1988, Cooney 1998), including organizations

(Morrill 1995, Morrill et al. 1997, Tucker 1999). Within this tradition, Baumgartner (1984, p. 306) argues that covert political conflict—such as noncooperation and sabotage—is more likely in hierarchical social fields as the number and organization of aggrieved subordinates decrease. Senechal de la Roche (1996, 2001; see also Black 2002) observes that violent covert collective action, such as terrorism, thrives in polarized social fields where subordinates have long-standing grievances against their superiors, high solidarity, and a lack of ties to and extreme cultural distance from their superiors, and practice collective liability.

Macro Level

The restructuring of organizations and the emergence of transnational social movements compose a double-edged sword at the macro level with regard to covert political conflict in organizations. On the one hand, economic organizational restructuring of U.S. industries has altered traditional managerial ideologies and structures, as well as mass production processes (Smith 1990). On a global scale, restructuring has led to complex transnational networks of finance and governance as well as dispersals of organizations to far flung regions around the world (Davis & McAdam 2000). Nongovernmental organizations outside of the corporate sphere have also proliferated across national boundaries to add to the complexity of transnational organizational networks (Boli & Thomas 1999). Such conditions would seem conducive to decreased perceptions of control among organizational members of all statuses as sources of organizational authority are transferred to positions that appear ever more physically and politically remote from the locations where organizational work is conducted. Moreover, restructuring and globalization has meant the increasing flight of organizations from those countries with developed trade unions and other protections to those where organizational members have little or no experience with manufacturing and sparse histories of collective action within organizations (Ong 1987).

The other side of the macro coin is the emergence of transnational contentious politics constructed on social terrains built by states and linked to domestic political contention (Tarrow 2001). "Master" collective action frames that emphasize injustice and/or rights (Snow & Benford 1992) and "rationalized" accounts for political action (Meyer et al. 1997) are also in play across a wide variety of contexts and issues. These developments can supply material resources, models of collective action, rhetorical language, and legitimacy for those engaged in covert political action in organizations that span great geographical and cultural distances (McAdam et al. 1996). They may even facilitate the conditions that transform covert action into overt voice.

Conclusion

We raise three orienting questions at the outset of this review. With regard to our first question, we argue that covert conflict encompasses four interrelated elements: contestation of institutionalized power and authority, perceptions of collective injury, social occlusion, and officially forbidden forms of dissent. To answer our next question, we discuss several variable features of covert conflict, including its material and symbolic forms, social visibility, collective dimensions, and outcomes. We then tackle existing explanations of covert political conflict by examining perspectives at the micro, organizational, field, and macro levels of analysis. Using our review as a point of departure, we end by discussing the implications the study of covert conflict holds for organizational analysis, social movement research, and avenues of future inquiry.

The analysis of covert political conflict deepens our understanding of the dark, informal side of organizations (Vaughan 1999). Rather than only characterizing covert political conflict as a source of deviance or irrational opportunistic behavior, many studies suggest that it can act as a mechanism through which subordinated and disenfranchised organizational members defend their dignity and challenge dominant categorizations (Lamont 2000). Some covert conflict, especially that which occurs at the tops of organizations among elites, can act as a direct "check" on institutionalized authority (e.g., Dalton 1959, Morrill 1995). Second, analyses of covert political conflict sensitizes researchers to less-visible "repertoires of contention" in organizations, as well as broader society, thus expanding sociological knowledge about how collective action and social movements can develop

from and impact everyday life (e.g., McAdam et al. 2001). Such research also underscores the dynamic and, under some conditions, tenuous character of employee commitment to formal and informal organizational routines (Burawoy 1979, Collinson 1994). Finally, the study of covert conflict moves beyond perspectives of organizational change that emphasize managerially planned action, placing more emphasis on unplanned and unintended sources of change, especially from marginalized groups. Indeed, covert political conflict can draw from or activate informal social circuits of interaction and exchange (Zelizer 2003) in the pursuit of organizational change. Taken together, these points suggest the need to re-imagine forms of collective agency in organizations (and broader society) with respect to conflict, power, and change. . . .

Literature Cited

Allen V.L., Greenberger D.B. 1980. Destruction and perceived control. In *Advances in Environmental Psychology*, ed. A. Baum, J.E. Singer, pp. 85–109. Hillsdale, NJ: Earlbaum.

Alvesson M., Willmott H. 1992. On the idea of emancipation in manager and organization studies. *Acad. Manag. Rev.* 17:432–64.

Ammerman N.T. 1990. *Baptist Battles: Social Change and Religious Conflict in the Southern Baptist Convention*. New Brunswick, NJ: Rutgers Univ. Press.

Arvey R.D., Jones A.P. 1985. The use of discipline in organizational settings: a framework for future research. *Res. Organ. Behav.* 7:367–408.

Barley S.R. 1991. Contextualizing conflict: notes on the anthropology of disputes and negotiations. In *Research on Negotiation in Organizations*, ed. M.H. Bazerman, R.J. Lewicki, B.H. Sheppard, pp. 165–99. Greenwich, CT: JAI Press.

Baumgartner M.P. 1984. Social control from below. In *Toward a General Theory of Social Control, Vol. 1: Fundamentals*, ed. D. Black, pp. 303–45. Orlando, FL: Academic.

Baumgartner M.P. 1988. *The Moral Order of a Suburb*. NY: Oxford Univ. Press.

Bayat A. 1997. Un-civil society: the politics of the 'informal people.' *Third World Q.* 18:53–72.

Benford R.D., Snow D.A. 2000. Framing processes and social movements: an overview and assessment. *Annu. Rev. Sociol.* 26:611–39.

Bies R.J., Tripp T.M. 1998. Two faces of the powerless: coping with tyranny in organizations. In *Power and Influence in Organizations*, ed. R.M. Kramer, M.A. Neal, pp. 203–19. Thousand Oaks, CA: Sage.

Black D. 1993. *The Social Structure of Right and Wrong*. San Diego, CA: Academic.

Black D. 2002. Terrorism as social control. Part I: The geometry of destruction. *Am. Sociol. Assoc. Crime Law Deviance News:* Spring:3–5.

Blum J. 1961. *Lord and Peasant in Russia: From the Ninth to the Nineteenth Century*. Princeton, NI: Princeton Univ. Press.

Boli J., Thomas G.M., eds. 1999. *Constructing World Culture: International Non-Governmental Organizations Since 1875*. Stanford, CA: Stanford Univ. Press.

Bourdieu P., Wacquant L.J.D. 1992. *An Invitation to Reflexive Sociology*. Chicago: Univ. Chicago Press.

Brehm J., Gates S. 1997. *Working, Shirking, and Sabotage: Bureaucratic Response to a Democratic Public*. Ann Arbor, MI: Univ. Michigan Press.

Brown G. 1977. *Sabotage: A Study of Industrial Conflict.* Nottingham, Engl.: Spokesman Books.

Burawoy M. 1979. *Manufacturing Consent: Changes in the Labor Process Under Monopoly Capitalism.* Chicago: Univ. Chicago Press.

Burns T. 1955. The reference of conduct in small groups: cliques and cabals in occupational milieux. *Hum. Relat.* 8:467–86.

Burns T. 1961. Micro-politics: mechanisms of institutional change. *Admin. Sci. Q.* 3:257–81.

Calas M.B., Smircich L. 1996. From 'the woman's point of view': feminist approaches to organization studies. In *Handbook of Organization Studies,* ed. S. Klegg, C. Hardy, W.R. Nord, pp. 218–57. London: Sage.

Carroll G.T., Hannan M.T. 2000. *The Demography of Corporations and Industries.* Princeton, NJ: Princeton Univ. Press.

Clarke J. 1988. Presidential address on the importance of understanding organizational conflict. *Soc. Q.* 29:149–61.

Chaves M. 1997. *Ordaining Women: Culture and Conflict in Religious Organizations.* Cambridge, MA: Harvard Univ. Press.

Clemens E.S. 1997. *The People's Lobby: Organizational Innovation and the Rise of Interest Group Politics in the United States, 1890–1925.* Chicago: Univ. Chicago Press.

Cohen S., Taylor L. 1993. *Escape Attempts: The Theory and Practice of Resistance in Everyday Life.* London: Routledge. 2nd ed.

Cooney M. 1998. *Warriors and Peacemakers: How Third Parties Shape Violence.* NY: NYU Press.

Colburn F. 1989. Foot dragging and other peasant responses to the Nicaraguan revolution. In *Everyday Forms of Peasant Resistance,* ed. F.D. Colbum, pp. 175–97. Annonk, NY: M.E. Sharpe.

Collinson D. 1994. *Strategies of resistance: power, knowledge and subjectivity in the workplace.* See Jermier, Knights, Nord 1994b, pp. 25–68.

Cressey D.R. 1953. *Other People's Money: A Study in the Social Psychology of Embezzlement.* Glencoe, IL: Free Press.

Crino M.D., Leap T.L. 1988. Sabotage: Protecting your company means dealing with the dark side of human nature. *Success* 35:52–55.

Curtius M. 1998. Sure, workers get mad, but more getting even. *Los Angeles Times,* Oct. 31, p. C1.

Dalton M. 1959. *Men Who Manage: Fusions of Feeling and Theory in Administration.* NY: Wiley.

Davis G.F., McAdam D. 2000. Corporations, classes, and social movements after managerialism. *Res. Organ. Behav.* 22:193–236.

Davis G.F., Thompson A. 1994. A social movement perspective on corporate control. *Admin. Sci. Q.* 39:141–73.

Ditton J. 1976. Moral horror versus folk terror: output restriction, class, and the social organization of exploitation. *Sociol. Rev.* 24:519–44.

Ditton J. 1977. Perks, pilferage, and the fiddle: the historical structure of invisible wages. *Theory Soc.* 4:39–71.

Ditton J. 1979. Baking time. *Soc. Rev.* 27:157–67.

Dowding K., John P., Mergoupis T., Van Vugt M. 2000. Exit, voice and loyalty: analytic and empirical developments. *Eur. J. Polit. Res.* 37:469–95.

Dubois P. 1979. *Sabotage in Industry.* Harmondsworth, Engl.: Penguin Books.

Earl J. 2000. Methods, movements, and outcomes: methodological difficulties in the study of extra-movement outcomes. *Res. Soc. Mov. Confl. Change* 22:3–25.

Edwards P.K., Scullion H. 1982. *The Social Organization of Industrial Conflict: Control and Resistance in the Workplace.* Oxford: Basil Blackwell.

Edwards R. 1982. *Contested Terrain: The Transformation of the Workplace in the Twentieth Century.* NY: Basic Books.

Eldridge J.E.T. 1968. *Industrial Disputes.* London: Routlege & Kegan Paul.

Emerson R.E., Messinger S.L. 1977. The micropolitics of trouble. *Soc. Probl.* 25:121–34.

Farrell D. 1983. Exit, voice, loyalty, and neglect as responses to job dissatisfaction: a multidimensional scaling study. *Acad. Manag. J.* 26:596–606.

Farrell D., Rusbult C.E. 1992. Exploring the exit voice, loyalty, and neglect typology: the influence of job satisfaction, quality of alternatives, and investment size. *Empl. Responsib. Rights* 1.5:201–18.

Felstiner W.L.F., Abel R.L., Sarat A. 1980/1981. The emergence and transformation of disputes: naming, claiming, and blaming. *Law & Soc. Rev.* 15:631–54.

Fennell D. 1976. Beneath the surface. *Radic. Am.* 10:15–29.

Fligstein N. 1990. *The Transformation of Corporate Control.* Cambridge, MA: Harvard Univ. Press.

Fligstein N. 2001. Social skill and the theory of fields. *Soc. Theory* 19:105–25.

Friedland R., Alford R.A. 1991. Bringing society back in: symbols, practices, and institutional contradictions. In *The New Institutionalism in Organizational Analysis,* ed. W.W. Powell, P.I. DiMaggio, pp. 232–63. Chicago: Univ. Chicago Press.

Gamson W.A. 1990. *The Strategy of Social Protest.* Belmont, CA: Wadsworth. 2nd ed.

Gialcone R.A., Greenberg I., eds. 1997. *Anti-Social Behavior in Organizations.* Thousand Oaks, CA: Sage.

Gialcone R.A., Knouse S.B. 1990. Identifying wrongful employee behavior: the role of personality in organizational sabotage. *J. Bus. Ethics* 9:55–61.

Gilliom J. 1997. Everyday surveillance, everyday resistance: computer monitoring in the lives of the Appalachian poor. In *Studies in Law Politics and Society, Vol. 16,* ed. A. Sarat, S. Silbey, pp. 275–97. Greenwich, CT: JAI Press.

Giugni M. 1999. How social movements matter: past research, present problems, future problems. In *How Social Movements Matter,* ed. M. Giugni, D. McAdam, C. Tilly, pp. xiii–xxxiii. Minneapolis, MN: Univ. Minn. Press.

Goffman E. 1962. *Asylums: Essays on the Social Situation of Mental Patients and Other Inmates.* Garden City, NY: Anchor Books.

Goffman E. 1967. *Interaction Ritual: Essays on Face-to-Face Behavior.* NY: Pantheon Books.

Gottfried H. 1994. Learning the score: the duality of control and everyday resistance in temporary-help service industry. See Jermier, Knights, Nord 1994b, pp. 102–27.

Gottfried H., Fasenfest D.1984. The role of gender in class formation: a case of female clerical workers. *Rev. Radic. Polit. Econ.* 16:89–104.

Gouldner A.W. 1954. *Patterns of Industrial Democracy.* New York: Free Press.

Greenberger D., Strasser S., Cummings L., Dunham R. 1989. The impact of personal control on performance and satisfaction. *Organ. Behav. Hum. Decis. Processes* 43:29–51.

Greenhalgh L. 1987. Interpersonal conflict in organizations. In *International Review of Industrial and Organizational Psychology,* ed. C.L. Cooper, L.T. Robertson, pp. 229–71. NY: Wiley.

Gross J.T. 1979. *Polish Society Under German Occupation: The Generalgouvernement, 1939–1944.* Princeton, NJ: Princeton Univ. Press.

Guha R. 1989. Saboteurs in the forest: colonialism and peasant resistance in the Indian Himalaya. In *Everyday Forms of Peasant Resistance,* ed. F.D. Colbum, pp. 64–92. Armonk, NY: M.E. Sharpe.

Haldeman H.R. 1994. *The Haldeman Diaries: Inside the Nixon White House.* NY: G.P. Putnam's.

Hall J. 1952. *Theft, Law, and Society.* Indianapolis, IN: Bobbs-Merrill.

Hannan M.T., Freeman J.F. 1989. *Organizational Ecology.* Cambridge, MA: Harvard Univ. Press.

Hanawalt B.A. 1979. *Crime and Conflict in English Communities, 1300–1348.* Cambridge, MA: Harvard Univ. Press.

Hebdon R.P., Stern R.N. 1998. Tradeoffs among expressions of industrial conflict: Public sector strike bans and grievance arbitrations. *Ind. Labor Relat. Rev.* 51:204–21.

Hirschman A.O. 1970. *Exit, Voice, & Loyalty.* Cambridge, MA: Harvard Univ. Press.

Hirschman A.O. 1993. Exit, voice, and the fate of the German Democratic Republican essay in conceptual history. *World Polit.* 45:173–202.

Hodson R. 1991. The active worker: compliance and autonomy at the workplace. *J. Contemp. Ethnogr.* 20:47–78.

Hollinger R.C., Clark J.P. 1982. Employee deviance: a response to the perceived quality of the work experience. *Soc. Q.* 23:333–43.

Howkins A. 1977. Structural conflict and the farm worker: Norfolk, 1900–1920. *J. Peasant Stud.* 4:217–29.

Jackall R. 1988. *Moral Mazes: The World of Corporate Managers.* NY: Oxford Univ. Press.

Jermier J. 1983. Labor process control in modern organizations: subtle effects of structure. *J. Bus. Res.* 11:317–32.

Jermier J. 1988. Sabotage at work: a rational view. In *Research in the Sociology of Organizations,* ed. N. DiTomaso, S.B. Bacharach, pp. 101–34. Greenwich, CT: JAI Press.

Jermier J., Knights D., Nord W.R. 1994a. Resistance and power in organizations: agency, subjectivity and the labor process. See Jermier, Knights, Nord 1994b, pp. 1–24.

Jermier J., Knights D., Nord W.R., eds. 1994b. *Resistance and Power in Organizations.* London: Routledge.

Kanter R.M. 1977. *Men and Women of the Corporation.* NY: Basic Books.

Katzenstein M.F. 1998. *Faithful and Fearless: Moving Feminist Protest Inside the Church and the Military.* Princeton, NI: Princeton Univ. Press.

King R. 1978. In the sanding booth at Ford. In *Social Problems in Today's World,* ed. I. Perry, E. Perry, pp. 199–205. Boston: Little, Brown.

Knights D., McCabe D. 1998a. When "life is but a dream": obliterating politics through business process re-engineering? *Hum. Relat.* 51:761–98.

Knights D., McCabe D. 1998b. What happens when the phone goes wild? Staff, stress and spaces for escape in a BPR telephone banking work regime. *J. Manag. Stud.* 35:163–94.

Kochanowicz I. 1989. Between submission and violence: peasant resistance in the Polish manorial economy of the Eighteenth century. In *Everyday Forms of Peasant Resistance,* F.D. Colbum, ed. pp. 33–63. Armonk, NY: M.E. Sharpe.

Kolb D.M. 1987. Corporate ombudsmen and organizational conflict. *J. Confl. Resolut.* 31:673–92.

Kolb D.M., Putnam L.L. 1992. Introduction: The dialectics of disputing. In *Hidden Conflict in Organizations: Uncovering Behind-the-Scenes Disputes,* ed. D.M. Kolb, J.M. Bartunek, pp. 1–31. Thousand Oaks, CA: Sage.

Kunda G. 1992. *Engineering Culture: Control and Commitment in a High-Tech Corporation.* Philadelphia, PA: Temple Univ. Press.

Kurzman C. 1998. Organizational opportunity and social movement mobilization: a comparative analysis of four religious movements. *Mobilization* 3:23–49.

Lammers C. 1969. Strikes and mutinies: a comparative study of organizational conflicts between rulers and ruled. *Admin. Sci. Q.* 14:558–72.

Lamont M. 2000. *The Dignity of Working Men: Morality and the Boundaries of Race, Class, and Immigration.* Cambridge, MA and NY: Harvard Univ. Press and Russell Sage Found.

LaNuez D., Jermier J.M.1994. Sabotage by managers and technocrats: Neglected patterns of resistance at work. In *Resistance and Power in Organizations,* ed. J.M. Jermier, D. Knights, W.R. Nord, pp. 219–51. London: Routledge.

Lewis I.O. 1971. *Ecstatic Religion: An Anthropological Study of Spirit Possession and Shamanism.* Harmondsworth, Engl.: Penguin.

Mahmood C.K. 2001. Terrorism, myth and the power of ethnographic praxis. *J. Contemp. Ethnogr.* 20:520–45.

Martin J. 1990. Deconstructing organizational taboos: the suppression of gender conflict in organizations. *Organ. Sci.* 4:339–59.

Martin J. 1992. *Cultures in Organizations: Three Perspectives.* NY: Oxford Univ. Press

Martin J., Meyerson D. 1997. Executive women at Link.com [Teaching Cases]. Cambridge, MA: Harvard Bus. Sch. Press.

Martin J., Meyerson D. 1999. Women and power: conformity, resistance, and disorganized coaction. In *Power and Influence in Organizations,* ed. R.M. Kramer, M.A. Neale, pp. 311–48. Thousand Oaks, CA: Sage.

Mars G. 1974. Dock pilferage. In *Deviance and Social Control,* ed. P. Rock, M. McIntosh, pp. 209–228. London: Tavistock.

Mars G. 1982. *Cheats at Work: An Anthropology of Workplace Crime.* London: George Allen & Unwin.

McAdam D., McCarthy J.D., Zald M.N. 1996. Introduction: opportunities, mobilizing structures, and framing processes—toward a synthetic, comparative perspective on social movements. In *Comparative Perspectives on Social Movements: Political Opportunities, Mobilizing Structures, and Cultural Framings,* ed. D. McAdam, J.D. McCarthy, M.N. Zald, pp. 1–20. Cambridge, UK: Cambridge Univ. Press.

McAdam D., Tarrow S., Tilly C. 2001. *Dynamics of Contention.* Cambridge, UK: Cambridge Univ. Press.

McCann M.W. 1994. *Rights at Work: Pay Equity and the Politics of Legal Mobilization.* Chicago: Univ. Chicago Press.

Mechanic D. 1962. Sources of power in lower participants in complex organizations. *Am. J. Sociol.* 7:349–64.

Merry S.E. 1982. Rethinking gossip and scandal. In *Toward a General Theory of Social Control, Volume 1: Fundamentals,* ed. D. Black, pp. 271–302. Orlando, Fl: Academic.

Meyer D.S., Staggenborg S. 1996. Movements, counter-movements, and the structure of political opportunity. *Am. J. Sociol.* 101:1628–60.

Meyer J.W., Boli J., Thomas G.M., Ramirez F.M. 1997. World society and nation state. *Am. J. Sociol.* 103:144–81.

Meyerson D.E. 2001. *Tempered Radicals: How People Use Difference to Inspire Change at Work.* Boston: Harvard Bus. School Press.

Meyerson D.E., Scully M. 1995. Tempered radicalism and the politics of ambivalence and change. *Organ. Sci.* 6:585–600.

Molstad C. 1986. Choosing and coping with boring work. *Urban Life* 15:215–36.

Morgon E.S. 1966. *The Puritan Family: Religion and Domestic Relations in Seventeenth-Century New England.* New York: Harper & Row.

Morrill C. 1991. The customs of conflict management among corporate executives. *Am. Anthropol.* 94: 871–93.

Morrill C. 1995. *The Executive Way: Conflict Management in Corporations.* Chicago: Univ. Chicago Press.

Morrill C. 2003. Institutional change through interstitial emergence: the growth of alternative dispute resolution in American law, 1965–1995. In *How Institutions Change,* ed. W.W. Powell. Chicago: Univ. Chicago Press. In press.

Morrill C., Snyderman E., Dawson E. 1997. It's not what you do, but who you are: informal social control, social status, and normative seriousness in organizations. *Sociol. Forum* 12:519–43.

Morrill C., Owen-Smith J. 2002. The rise of environmental conflict resolution: Subversive stories and the construction of collective action frames and organizational fields. In *Organizations, Policy, and the Natural Environment: Institutional and Strategic Perspectives,* ed. M. Ventresca, A. Hoffman, pp. 90–119. Stanford, CA: Stanford Univ. Press.

Nader L. 1980. Alternatives to the American judicial system. In *No Access to Law: Alternatives to the American Judicial System,* ed. L. Nader, pp. 3–55. NY: Academic.

Ocasio W., Kim H. 1999. The circulation of corporate control: selection of functional backgrounds of new CEOs in large U.S. manufacturing firms, 1981–1992. *Admin. Sci. Q.* 44:532–562.

Ong A. 1987. *The Spirits of Resistance and Capitalist Discipline: Factory Women in Malaysia.* Albany, NY: SUNY Press.

Paules G.F. 1991. *Dishing it Out: Power and Resistance Among Waitresses in a New Jersey Restaurant.* Philadelphia: Temple Univ. Press.

Petigrew A. 1973. *The Politics of Organizational Decision-Making.* London: Tavistock.

Pfeffer J. 1981. *Power in Organizations.* Boston: Pitman.

Powell W.W., DiMaggio P.J., eds. 1991. *The New Institutionalism in Organizational Analysis.* Chicago: Univ. Chicago Press.

Powell W.W., Jones D., ed. 2003. *How Institutions Change.* Chicago: Univ. Chicago Press. In press.

Prasad A., Pushkala P. 1998. Everyday struggles at the workplace: The nature and implications of routine resistance in contemporary organizations. *Res. Sociol. Organ.* 15:225–57.

Rao H. 1998. Caveat emptor: the construction of nonprofit consumer watchdog organizations. *Am. J. Sociol.* 103:912–61.

Rao H., Morrill C., Zald M.N.2000. Power plays: how social movements and collective action create new organizational forms. *Res. Organ. Behav.* 22:237–81.

Rockwell J. 1974. The Danish peasant village. *J. Peasant. Stud.* 1:409–61.

Rochon T.R. 1997. *Culture Moves: Ideas, Activism, and Changing Values.* Princeton, NJ: Princeton Univ. Press.

Rusbult C., Lowery D. 1985. When bureaucrats get the blues: responses to dissatisfaction among federal employees. *J. Appl. Soc. Pyschol.* 15:80–103.

Rusbult C., Farrell D., Rogers G., Mainous A.G. III. 1988. Impact of exchange variables on exit, voice, loyalty, and neglect: an integrative model of responses to declining job satisfaction. *Acad. Manag. Rev.* 31:599–627.

Sapsford D., Turnbull P. 1994. Strikes and industrial conflict in Britain's docks: balloons or icebergs? *Oxford Bull. Econ. Stat.* 56:249–65.

Scott J.C. 1989. Everyday forms of resistance. In *Everyday Forms of Peasant Resistance*, F.D. Colbum, ed. pp. 3–33. Armonk, NY: M.E. Sharpe.

Scott J.C. 1990. *Domination and the Arts of Resistance: Hidden Transcripts.* New Haven, CT: Yale Univ. Press.

Scott W.R., Ruef M., Mendel P.J., Caronna C. 2000. *Institutional Change and Healthcare Organizations: From Professional Dominance to Managerial Care.* Chicago: Univ. Chicago Press.

Scully M., Segal A. 2002. Passion with an umbrella: grassroots activists in the workplace. *Soc. Struct. Organ. Revisit.* 19:125–68.

Senechal de la Roche R. 1996. Collective violence as social control. *Soc. Forces* 11:97128.

Senechal de la Roche R. 2001. Why is collective violence collective? *Soc. Theory* 19:126–44

Smith V. 1990. *Managing in the Corporate Interest: Control and Resistance in an American Bank.* Berkeley, CA: Univ. Calif. Press.

Snow D.A. 2002. *Social movements as challenges to authority: resistance to an merging conceptual hegemony.* Auth. Contention, Collect. Behav./Soc. Mov. Conf., Notre Dame Univ., South Bend, Indiana.

Snow D.A., Benford R.D. 1992. Master frames and cycles of protest. In *Frontiers in Social Movement Theory*, A.D. Morris, C.M. Mueller, pp. 133–55. New Haven, CT: Yale Univ. Press.

Soeters J.L. 1986. Excellent companies as social movements. *J. Manag. Stud.* 23: 299–312.

Sotirin P., Gottfried H. 1999. The ambivalent dynamics of secretarial 'bitching': control, resistance, and the construction of identity. *Organization* 6:57–80.

Spector P.E. 1975. Relationships of organizational frustration with reported behavioral reactions of employees. *J. Appl. Psychol.* 60:635–37.

Stephenson K. 1990. The emergence of virtual groups. *Ethnology* 29:279–96.

Stryker R. 2002. A political approach to organizations and institutions. *Res. Sociol. Organ.* 19:171–93.

Tarrow S. 2001. Transnational politics: contention and institutions in international politics. *Annu. Rev. Polit. Sci.* 4: 1–20.

Taylor L., Walton P. 1971. Industrial sabotage: motives and meanings. In *Images of Deviance*, ed. S. Cohen. pp. 219–45. Harmondsworth, Engl.: Penguin Books.

Thomas K., ed. 1999. *The Oxford Book of Work.* Oxford, Engl.: Oxford Univ. Press.

Thompson W.E. 1983. Hanging tongues: a sociological encounter with the assembly line. *Qual. Sociol.* 6:215–37.

Tilly C. 1999. Conclusion: From interactions to outcomes in social movements. In *How Social Movements Matter*, ed. M. Giugni, D. McAdam, C. Tilly, pp. 253–70. Minneapolis, MN: Univ. Minn. Press.

Tobias J.J. 1972. *Crime in Industrial Society in the Nineteenth Century.* Harmondsworth, Engl.: Penguin.

Tucker J. 1989. Employee theft as social control. *Deviant Behav.* 10:319–34.

Tucker J. 1993. Everyday forms of employee resistance: how temporary workers handle conflict with their employers. *Soc. Forum* 8:25–45.

Tucker J. 1999. *The Therapeutic Corporation.* NY: Oxford Univ. Press.

Van Mannen J. 1992. Drinking our troubles away: managing conflict in British police agency. In *Hidden Conflict in Organizations: Uncovering Behind-the-Scenes Disputes*, ed. D.M. Kolb, J.M. Bartunek, pp. 32–62. Thousand Oaks, CA: Sage.

Vaughan D. 1999. The dark side of organizations: mistake, conduct, and disaster. *Annu. Rev. Sociol.* 25:271–305.

Vinzant C. 2000. Messing with the boss's head. *Fortune*, May 1, pp. 329–31.

Watson B. 1971. Counter-planning on the shop floor. *Radic. Am.* 5:77–85.

Willis R. 1986. White-collar crime: the threat from within. *Manag. Rev.* 5:22–32.

Wittek R., Wielers R. 1998. Gossip in organizations. *Comput. Math. Organ. Theory* 4:189–204.

Zald M.N. 1970. *Organizational Change: The Political Economy of the YMCA.* Chicago: Univ. Chicago Press.

Zald M.N. 2002. Spinning disciplines: critical management studies in the context of the transformation of management education. *Organization* 9:365–85.

Zald M.N., Berger M.A. 1978. Social movements in organizations: Coup d'etat, insurgency, and mass movements. *Am. J. Sociol.* 83:823–61.

Zald M.N., Morrill C., Rao H. 2002. *How do social movements penetrate organizations? Environmental impact and organizational response.* Michigan Conf. Organ. Theory/Soc. Mov. Theory, Ann Arbor.

Zelizer V.A. 2003. Circuits within capitalism. In *The Economic Sociology of Capitalism*, ed. V. Nee, R. Swedberg. Cambridge, UK: Cambridge Univ. Press.

Zeitlin L.R. 1971. A little larceny can do a lot for employee morale. *Psychology Today* 5:22–26, 64.

Zhou X. 1992. Unorganized interests and collective action in communist China. *Am. Soc. Rev.* 58:54–73.

Chapter 17
A Social Movement Perspective on Corporate Control

Gerald F. Davis and
Tracy A. Thompson

Social movement theory and research have implications for many aspects of organizations. This chapter applies these ideas to the topic of corporate control. Issues relating to the ownership and control of large corporations are topics that are often understood through the lenses of political sociology or even political science. But corporate politics take place within and between organizations, and, thus, organizational factors cannot be left out of the analysis.

Davis and Thompson are especially interested in one area of corporate control: the rise of shareholder activism. Activist shareholders are becoming an influential force in corporate governance. This chapter helps us understand the conditions that have made such influence possible and the factors that have contributed to activists' power in the corporate arena.

Who owns and controls large corporations in the United States has changed significantly over the course of the twentieth century. Historically, firms were run primarily by founder-owners and their descendants, and ownership and control thus rested in the same hands. As firms grew large, the managerial revolution led to a separation of ownership and control in most large corporations. where control of the firm shifted from entrepreneurs to professional managers while ownership became dispersed among thousands of unorganized stockholders who were removed from the day-to-day management of the firm (Berle and Means, 1932). More recently, a parallel shift has occurred as ownership of the corporation has become concentrated in the hands of institutional investors rather than individual stockholders. Where corporate managers once faced a dispersed and relatively powerless set of stockholders, they now confront an increasingly organized social movement of fund trustees and advisors that share a common ideology of shareholder activism as well as the power to vote a substantial chunk of the largest firms' equity. Moreover, activist shareholders have expanded their demands from the circumscribed realm of shareholder rights to issues of how successors to the chief executive officer (CEO) are chosen, how much executives are paid, and even which compensation consultant is used, and they have influenced sympathetic regulators in Washington to increase the legitimate scope of their authority in corporate governance. Where shareholders were once disenfranchised outsiders in corporate governance, institutional investors are now members of the polity, and their concerns are routinely taken into account in decision-making processes in firms and in governmental policy making.

The rise of shareholder activism in the U.S. has forced a reassessment of the origins of the managerialist corporation. Recently, legal scholars have provided compelling arguments that the initial separation of ownership and control was not the inevitable consequence of large-scale enterprise, as portrayed by Berle and Means, but resulted from legal and regulatory constraints that originated in populist political pressures and were sustained by politically influential corporate managers (Roe, 1991). Management's control within the firm is contingent on rules determined externally by state and federal governments. and the allocation of corporate control thus depends on political struggles among management, capital, and various governmental bodies.

According to this view, corporate control is decidedly political, and at least since the 1930s, the rules of the game have been rigged in management's favor. Managers benefited from a regime of dispersed and powerless shareholders. and an extensive array of securities regulations historically made it difficult for institutional investors—pension funds, mutual funds, banks, and insurance companies—to own significant blocks of stock or to engage in collective action to influence management, despite their financial capacity to do so (Black, 1990). Thus, the fact that a social movement industry of activist shareholder organizations mushroomed in such an inhospitable environment is impressive, and the success of the movement at gaining influence over both firms and the state is remarkable.

The reassessment of the separation of ownership and control reflects a broader transition in thinking about the large corporation in law and economics—away from the efficiency orientation associated with the nexus of contracts (or agency theory) approach to the firm and toward the view that "the public corporation is as much a political adaptation as an economic or technological necessity" (Roe, 1991: 10). Several commentators have noted the need for a political theory of the corporation more sensitive to the role of the state (Black, 1990; Grundfest, 1990; Roe, 1991), but the methodological individualism of the nexus of contracts approach, which has dominated economic and policy discourse on the corporation since the early 1980s, limits its ability to make sense of the politics of corporate control. Politics, like other social action, is embedded in social structures that link actors and influence whether, when, and how collective action is accomplished (Granovetter, 1985; Laumann and Knoke, 1987). A political approach to the corporation therefore requires an explicit framework for analyzing the process by which those who run organizations—in particular. corporations and institutional investors—recognize or construct common interests, form coalitions, and press their views on the state or on each other.

Organization theory, broadly construed, is uniquely suited to contribute to a political theory of the corporation. A large body of organizational research analyzes the conditions facilitating unified corporate political action and demonstrates the embeddedness of organizational politics in social structures (Useem, 1984; Laumann and Knoke, 1987). Corporate managers attempting to influence the state are neither as parochial and fragmented as pluralists imply nor as unified and all-powerful as elite theorists suggest. Rather, unified corporate political action is contingent on a number of factors, some economic and some social (Mizruchi, 1992). Social movement theorists have demonstrated that collective action by individuals

and organizations is not a simple function of incentives and overcoming free-rider problems but depends on mutually acquainted actors sharing interpretations of events and seizing political opportunities (McCarthy and Zald, 1977; Tilly, 1978; McAdam, 1982). Meyer and Zucker (1989) and Kanter (1991) have noted the relevance of social movement theory for the types of corporations observed today. Owners of poorly performing firms for example, may have strong incentives to close them' down but may be unable to do so because of political efforts by organized alliances among groups that benefit in different ways from maintaining the firm—managers and other employees, as well as dependent organizations (Meyer and Zucker, 1989). Class theorists argue that there is no single logic of collective action that applies generally to all actors but that different classes, such as shareholders and managers, have different requirements for joint political action (Offe and Wiesenthal, 1980). We draw on each of these theories in outlining an organizational approach to the politics of corporate control. We illustrate this approach in describing the rise and entry into the polity of a social movement industry, demanding shareholder rights in corporate governance during the late 1980s and early 1990s, and efforts by corporate managers to resist this movement. . . .

A Social-Movement Approach to Corporate Control

Corporate control is inherently political, and politics is accomplished by coalitions of mutually acquainted actors that recognize or construct a common interest. Social movement theory adds insight into the process by which actors translate shared interests into collective action. Modern social movement theory developed in response to frustrations with conventional explanations of collective action, which emphasized incentives to the virtual exclusion of social structures (Tilly, 1978). Key insights of the resource mobilization school are that discontent sufficient to provide a basis for collective action is a constant feature of social life, that social movement activity does not correlate well with variation in levels of grievances, and thus that "grievances and discontent may be defined, created, and manipulated by issue entrepreneurs and organizations" (McCarthy and Zald, 1977: 1215).

Incentives are neither necessary nor sufficient for collective action. Instead, movement activity flows from effective social organization among actors, typically drawing on preexisting social structures. Thus, for example, the Black civil rights movement was built on an indigenous organizational network prominently featuring Black churches in the South (McAdam, 1982).

The political process model of social movements emphasizes the role of opportunities provided by the political climate, particularly major disruptions in the political status quo, and the role of insurgent consciousness flowing out of a shared interpretation that a political system has lost legitimacy and is vulnerable to new demands for rights from the aggrieved population (McAdam, 1982). In this situation, many formal social movement organizations commonly emerge to construct and press the movement's agenda—forming a "social movement industry" (McCarthy and Zald, 1977: 1219). Challengers, groups whose interests are not considered in the decision-making processes, seek through social movements to gain membership in the polity and thus have their interests routinely taken into account (McAdam, 1982). Because organizations are the critical units in governmental policymaking, creating formal organizations to represent the movement is in effect the price of admission to the polity (Laumann and Knoke, 1987).

All these elements fit well with the history of shareholder collective action. Those with an efficiency orientation might argue that the shareholder-rights movement arose to take up the slack in governance left by the stagnant takeover market; when one efficiency mechanism fails, another rises to take its place, thus ensuring an efficient allocation of corporate control. But this characterization would greatly distort the historical record. Shareholder grievances in general are as old as Adam Smith's famous treatise. One constant grievance is that executives in managerialist firms overpay themselves, which also concerned legislators constructing the Securities Exchange Act of 1934 (Conard, 1988: fn. 123). The shareholder-rights movement did not arise in response to a stagnant takeover market or even in response to particularly widespread managerial misdeeds. When the Council of Institutional Investors (CII), the most prominent shareholder-rights organization, was founded in January 1985 only a tiny minority of firms had poison pills, the U.S. Supreme Court had not yet handed down the 1987 *CTS Corp. v. Dynamics Corp. of America* decision legalizing significant state antitakeover laws, and large American firms thus were more vulnerable to hostile takeover than at any time before or since. Rather, Jesse Unruh, an "issue entrepreneur" and treasurer of California, recognized that greenmail by corporate management—paying raiders a premium to buy back their stock and thus avoid takeover—although relatively rare, was "an issue that, in political terms, could be sold in Pasadena," and Unruh thus used it as a basis for organizing public pension funds (Monks and Minnow, 1991: 213).

Given that corporate managers were vulnerable and that the Reagan administration's strong proshareholder stance indicated a tolerant ideological climate, the political opportunity structure was ripe for a shareholder-rights movement. Many movement organizations—including CII, United Shareholders Association (USA), founded by raider T. Boone Pickens in 1986 for individual shareholders, and Institutional Shareholders Services (ISS), formed by Robert A. G. Monks in 1985—were founded at roughly the same time, creating a social movement industry within two years. Proponents of the movement argued that the system of corporate governance had lost legitimacy because the interests of shareholders were organized out of policy deliberations, and they demanded rights to greater voice in decision making, which the creation of formal organizations facilitated. As SEC Chairman John Shad put it at the CII's first meeting in 1985, "We've never before been able to turn to a group that represents purely the shareholders' point of view," the class that is "the principal constituency the commission was created to serve" (*Atlanta Constitution*, October 30, 1985). Ultimately, the movement gained sufficient access to the polity that the chairman of the SEC used the 1990 annual meeting of the CII to announce the commission's initiation of a major review of the proxy rules (*Federal Register*, 56: 28987), which led to substantial changes in shareholders' ability to engage in firm-level collective action in October 1992.

Below we provide a brief history of the rise of this shareholder activism and then a more detailed framework outlining the mechanisms of collective action for shareholders and managers. The sources we used are listed in the Appendix [at the end of this chapter].

The Rise of Institutional Investor Activism in the 1980s

The initial rise of the shareholder-rights movement resulted from three trends: (1) the increasing concentration of corporate ownership in the hands of institutional investors, particularly public pension funds; (2) the elaboration and enforcement of standards of fiduciary responsibility for private pension funds; and (3) a set of grievances sufficiently accessible to unite investors, i.e., the spread of antitakeover activities among large corporations.

The proportion of the average firm's equity controlled by institutional investors has increased substantially in the past three decades, from 15.8 percent in 1965 to 42.7 percent in 1986 (Useem, 1993). This trend has been even more pronounced among the largest firms, where over 50 percent of the average firm's common shares are held by institutions. While institutional investors are a broad category that includes banks, insurance companies, investment companies, and others, pension funds are among the largest. In 1960, pension funds held a 4-percent stake in the Standard and Poor's 500; in 1970 it was 9.4 percent; and by 1988 it had increased to 23.2 percent. Pension fund assets are expected to grow to $3.5 trillion in the year 2000, representing 50 percent of all corporate equity. The ten largest pension funds alone hold 6 percent of the U.S. equities market. Thus, there has been an ongoing trend in which large firms are increasingly owned by institutions, rather than individuals. and by a relatively small number of pension funds in particular. This trend shows every sign of continuing into the future. Much as who manages the corporation shifted from entrepreneurs to professional managers during the managerial revolution, who owns the corporation shifted from individuals to professional investors.

The increased size of institutional investors' holdings limited their ability to divest from firms with which they were dissatisfied. Previously, institutions that were dissatisfied with management would typically do the Wall Street Walk and sell their stake rather than confront management. When one's stake is large enough, however, selling out depresses the share price and harms the seller; in addition, for the largest funds, the number of alternative investments is limited. Faced with such a high cost of exit, voice—shareholder activism—became more appealing. In addition, pension funds, and particularly private funds, which are subject to regulation under ERISA (the Employment Retirement Income Security Act, passed in 1974), faced greater demands during the 1980s to fulfill their fiduciary duty, that is, to act for the exclusive benefit of the plan's participants and beneficiaries. This emphasis on fiduciary responsibility was interpreted to include a demand to vote proxies in the interests of shareholders. Coupled with the difficulties of exit for the largest funds, this increased the attractiveness of voice.

The potential power of pension funds has been recognized for years (Drucker, 1976), but it took the wave of large takeovers in the 1980s to provide the political opportunity structure and specific grievances salient enough to activate the funds' latent potential for control. The takeover market exacerbated the conflicts between owners and managers. Shareholders almost inevitably gain from takeovers because raiders generally have to pay a premium to convince owners to sell their shares, white professional managers lose their position of control, and often their jobs, following a successful takeover. Thus, the takeover wave of the 1980s set the stage for overt conflicts between managers, who sought to maintain and expand their control by protecting their firm from unwanted takeovers, and institutional investors, who sought to retain their rights to benefit from takeover bids.

Managers of most large corporations responded to the threat to their control posed by the takeover wave by adopting devices to make it more difficult for outsiders to take over the firm without management's consent, including shark repellents, which require shareholder approval, and poison pills, which do not (see Walsh and Seward, 1990, for descriptions). These devices have two attributes that make them objectionable to institutional investors: First, their adoption tends to depress a firm's share price, and second, they reduce shareholders' discretion with respect to takeover bids. The poison pill has the additional feature of being adopted without shareholder consent; thus, it was perceived by many institutional investors as a technique for managers to entrench themselves and increase their own power at the expense of the shareholders, appropriating control rights that should belong to owners (Davis, 1991).

Another practice that investors found objectionable was greenmail, in which a firm would buy back a raider's shares at a premium to avoid being taken over, while other shareholders gained no such premium (Kosnik, 1987). The specific incident that sparked the formation of the Council of Institutional Investors was Texaco's payment of $1.3 billion to the Bass brothers to avoid takeover—at $55 per share, a $20 per share premium over the price available to other shareholders. In response to this incident, Jesse Unruh, treasurer of California and a trustee of CalPERS (the largest public pension fund) and the California State Teachers' Retirement Fund, founded the CII in January 1985. Originally composed of 19 of the largest pension funds, controlling $100 billion in assets, its membership increased to over 80 funds with over $500 billion in assets by 1993, including 24 union pension funds and 10 corporate pension funds. CII's agenda was broadly defined by a "Shareholder Bill of Rights" it endorsed in 1986, which was intended to give investors a new voice in all "fundamental decisions which could affect corporate performance and growth," including requiring shareholder approval of greenmail, poison pills, golden parachutes, selloffs, and issuance of excessive debt.

The effects of this nascent social movement were realized both in opposition to management proposals that increased management's power at the expense of owners (Brickley, Lease, and Smith, 1988) and in support for antimanagement proposals. Investor activism, as measured by shareholder resolutions proposed by institutional investors, grew dramatically during the late 1980s. The number of antimanagement shareholder resolutions increased from less than 40 in 1987 to 153 in 1991. Support for such proposals also greatly increased. Shareholder support for anti-poison-pill proposals increased in the average firm from 29.4 percent in 1987 to 44.8 percent in 1991. Of more long-lasting importance is activist investors' success in changing the rules by which they may influence corporate governance. The SEC systematically increased the range of issues open to shareholder vote on proxy issues. Of substantial symbolic importance is the fact that SEC Chairman Breeden announced the review leading to the most significant proxy reform of the early 1990s at a CII meeting. Shareholder activism thus achieved a degree of success unprecedented since the dawn of the managerial revolution, primarily as a result of a social movement of institutional investors.

The Politics of Corporate Control

The three primary elements that determine a group's capacity to act are interests, social infrastructure, and mobilization processes (Tilly, 1978). A group's *interests* are defined by the gains and losses resulting from its interaction with other groups; *social infrastructure* concerns the degree of common identity and social ties linking the individuals or organizations in a group that most affect the group's capacity to act on its interests; and *mobilization* is the process by which a group acquires collective control over resources needed for collective action. The fourth element of collective action, *political opportunity structure*, concerns the set of power relationships in the political environment and, in particular, the degree to which disruptions and instability undermine the status quo and therefore increase the chances for successful insurgency (McAdam, 1982). Collective action can be analyzed as a function of the changing combinations of these components.

Conflicts over corporate control occur at three levels, firm, state government, and federal government. Each level presents distinctive impediments and facilitators of collective action by shareholders and managers. *Distributive* conflicts concern particular concrete outcomes and occur primarily at the firm level, while *definitional* conflicts are over the rules of the game that influence the ability of actors to mobilize effectively and thus occur at state and federal levels (Offe and Wiesenthal, 1980). These definitional conflicts at higher levels provide the context for the conflicts at lower levels. For example, management can exclude matters of "ordinary business" from shareholder votes at the annual meeting, thereby limiting the influence of activist investors, but the definition of ordinary business is determined by state and federal law and interpreted by the SEC. Thus, the definition of ordinary business is contested by shareholders and managers and is susceptible to change by the SEC.

Shareholders influence the governance of individual firms both formally, through the proxy system where they can initiate and vote on proposals, and informally, through negotiations with corporate management. Public corporations hold annual meetings open to shareholders where votes on significant issues of corporate governance are taken. The vast majority of shareholders that vote do so by proxy, sending in a paper ballot. Votes are counted by management or a firm hired by management and normally are not anonymous. Management typically knows how the firm's shareholders voted, and because proxy votes are revocable up to the time of the annual meeting, management can lobby to change the votes of shareholders who vote contrary to its wishes. The primary issues formally considered include who sits on the board of directors, which accounting firm will audit the firm's books, major changes in governance rules, and shareholder proposals. The scope of issues open to proxy votes is primarily determined by the legal standards of the company's state of incorporation and by the SEC, which has broad authority to regulate the proxy system. Stock exchanges and Internal Revenue Service regulations also influence proxy issues. While the range of issues that management can propose for shareholder votes is quite broad, the topics deemed appropriate for shareholder proposals are somewhat limited, although lobbying by investor groups has expanded them recently. Management has broad control over what comes to a vote on the proxy ballot, including, most importantly, who is nominated to the board of directors. Shareholder organizations have been able to mobilize influence outside the proxy system, however, through private meetings (e.g., CII's request that General Motors executives come to Washington to explain to its members why General Motors paid several hundred million dollars to get rid of Ross Perot in 1986) and public pressure (e.g., USA's public targeting of highly paid executives, such as Steven Wolf at United Airlines).

Conflicts over control at the state level are primarily over the laws of incorporation specific to each state. Firms may incorporate in any state, and their choice reflects several factors, of which headquarters location is only one (Easterbrook and Fischel, 1991).

State laws of incorporation determine the issues open to shareholder vote, the scope of authority granted to the board of directors, the standards that apply to compensation and other arrangements between corporations and their officers, and the items that can appear in the corporate charter. Most states grant the board broad power to manage and direct the corporation, although such power is often subject to specific limitations provided in the governing instruments of the corporation. In addition, many state laws prohibit shareholder initiatives that compel directors to take action, thus, only those proposals that are in a precatory form (i.e., are phrased as requests or are advisory only) may be viewed as proper subjects for shareholder vote. State laws also regulate mergers and takeovers of firms incorporated in the state. While there is substantial evidence that state law, particularly takeover law, is tilted in management's favor, federal law is preemptive; notably, the 1982 *Edgar v. MITE* decision by the U.S. Supreme Court struck down antitakeover laws in 37 states, and "Congress could displace the states and enact all corporate law if it wanted" (Roe, 1993: 334). Thus, the federal government sets limits within which states can maneuver.

Conflicts at the federal level are primarily over the regulations concerning shareholder involvement in the proxy system—over what issues do shareholders have legitimate influence and by what process may they exercise it? When a shareholder seeks to have an initiative included on a company's proxy statement, management can either voluntarily include the initiative or petition the SEC to exclude it. The SEC permits exclusion of a proposal under two conditions: (1) the proposal is not considered a proper subject for action by shareholders under state law, or (2) the proposal relates to the ordinary business operations of the company. Activist shareholders' agenda at the federal level, therefore, was to lobby for changes in the SEC's interpretation of what constitutes ordinary business and to reduce the legal impediments to collective action described above.

Factors Influencing Collective Action by Corporate Managers and Institutional Investors

The elements of collective action—political opportunity structure, interests, social infrastructure, and mobilization—differ for corporate managers and shareholders and have different influences on each group's actions, both at the firm level and at the governmental level.

Political opportunity structure. Social movements thrive in times of social or political instability because the status quo is more vulnerable to successful challenge by outsiders to the polity. Disruptions change power relations and thus create opportunities for insurgency (McAdam, 1982). The 1980s takeover wave disrupted the managerialist status quo by subjecting roughly 29 percent of the *Fortune* 500 to takeover attempts by outsiders seeking to buy corporate control from shareholders, often against resistance by management. While takeovers of large firms were not unheard of prior to the 1980s, the stability of managerial control within the firm had never been threatened on such a grand scale (Davis and Stout, 1992). Management's vulnerability to takeover benefited shareholders of target firms—an outsider seeking to buy control typically ends up paying them a 30–50 percent premium—but threatened to leave managers of targets unemployed. This tension between the interests of managers and shareholders provided much of the drive behind the shareholder-rights movement.

The takeover wave of the 1980s was nurtured by the free-market regulatory stance of the Reagan administration, whose politics were aligned with the Chicago School of law and economics. The general thrust of this school is that, in the absence of egregious market failure, markets are better than governments at regulating economic exchange to maximize social benefit. Efficient capital markets and the protection of property rights (i.e., those of shareholders) are of central importance to this approach. Sympathizers with this position were appointed to the Federal Trade Commission, which substantially reduced its antitrust oversight and allowed a torrent of intraindustry mergers; the SEC, which consistently took strong protakeover positions in public debates and avoided regulation of the market for corporate control; the federal judiciary, which tilted proshareholder in numerous decisions; the Council of Economic Advisors, whose *1985 Economic Report of the President* sang the praises of the market for corporate control in promoting economic efficiency; and the Department of Labor's Pension and

Welfare Benefits Administration, which held fiduciaries of private pension plans responsible for their proxy voting under ERISA. The implications of these policies for takeovers were played out with the aid of new financial instruments, notably, junk bonds issued to underwrite large hostile takeovers.

Perhaps the most remarkable manifestation of the political climate for corporate control in the 1980s was the fact that while nearly one-third of the *Fortune* 500 changed hands and the Business Roundtable and other constituencies called for federal regulation of takeovers, almost no significant new federal antitakeover restrictions appeared during the takeover wave. Countless congressional hearings on hostile takeovers were held, and at least 60 bills to regulate takeovers were introduced between 1984 and 1987. But nothing of consequence came out of these efforts because of opposition by the Reagan administration and its protakeover SEC, the agency most likely to have been charged with implementing any takeover regulation (Romano, 1988).

It was this political climate that encouraged the "insurgent consciousness' that underlay the shareholder-rights movement (McAdam, 1982: 49). Shareholders (and raiders) had sympathizers in critical regulatory and judicial positions, and management's position of hegemony in corporate governance was vulnerable. Thus, although shareholders were still outside the polity, the fact that no federal takeover regulation was forthcoming provided the best opportunity for shareholders to assert power in the corporation since the securities regulations of the early 1930s. The political climate in the Reagan years, far more than any radically altered incentives for collective action, explains the rise of organized shareholder activism in the mid-1980s. It was not the failure of the market for corporate control but its success that promoted shareholder activism.

While regulation of takeovers was stagnant at the federal level, most state governments were decidedly antitakeover. The reasons are straightforward: Managers of large firms that may be threatened by takeover typically have long-term relationships with their local legislatures, and they have influence or control over resources that are consequential to state legislators, including plant and headquarters locations and political contributions. The clear winners from takeovers are shareholders of target firms, who tend to be nationally dispersed, whereas the clear losers are target executives and managers, who tend to be concentrated locally. Moreover, many state legislatures consist of part-time representatives who may be more susceptible to lobbying by local chambers of commerce than to the arguments of academic economists and institutional investors. All of these factors give corporate managers an advantage at the state level, except in Delaware (Romano, 1987, 1988; Roe, 1993).

Management also has a privileged power position at the level of the firm by virtue of its control over the proxy machinery. Because proxy voting is generally not anonymous it leaves institutional investors open to pressure by managers who are able to determine who voted with them and against them. Certain institutional investors are particularly susceptible to this sort of pressure because they are actual or potential business associates of the firm. Thus, to the extent that the political opportunity structure at the level of the firm has changed, it is due to changes at the federal level.

Interests. The degree to which the interests of a set of actors are small in number, shared, and readily recognized determines the likelihood of a group forming around those interests. Institutional investors are uniquely advantaged over corporate managers in this regard. The interests of corporate managers are numerous. diverse, and often contradictory. Vogel (1978) argued that, when it comes to governmental policy, the single underlying master interest that unites American corporate managers is how the policy affects the autonomy of management and, thus, their ability to allocate economic resources without interference from government or labor. On other dimensions, managerial interests are fragmented and diverse. Thus, to the extent that businesses have organized nationally around common political interests. their organizations have been narrowly focused, typically by industry in response to a regime of industry-specific regulation (see Hollingsworth, 1991). One standout from this tendency is the Business Roundtable (BR), chartered in 1972 to promote the broad interests of business in response to federal regulation in the early 1970s that cut across industries (McQuaid, 1980), but diverse interests often prevent the BR from constructing a unified position.

Tensions within the organization between labor-intensive companies and high-tech, low-labor-cost firms were a problem when the BR was fighting a labor reform bill in 1978 (McQuaid, 1980), and failure to reach consensus on tax reform in 1988 left the BR out of the policy debate.

Corporate managers have fragmented interests when it comes to takeovers. They generally favor having the ability to initiate takeovers or engage in voluntary mergers, yet they want to avoid challenges to their own control. The irony of this position was not lost on critics of big business such as raider (and USA founder) T. Boone Pickens (Pickens, 1988: 54), who pointed out that "the Business Roundtable says takeovers are hurting the U.S. economy, yet 76 percent of its member companies have carried out takeovers in the last three years. How hypocritical can you get?" Active participation by large firms would have been essential to any collective action aimed at federal regulation of takeovers, but large firms were least likely to face hostile takeover and most likely to make acquisitions in the 1980s. Thus, AT&T was at the center of the corporate establishment, yet its acquisition of NCR was the largest hostile takeover of the early 1990s, making AT&T an unlikely candidate to lead the charge against takeovers. Except in Delaware this problem was lessened at the state level, where potential targets greatly outnumber active raiders, which makes constructing a common business interest in regulating takeovers less problematic.

In contrast to professional managers, the interests of institutional investors are small in number, easy to define, and to some extent enforced by external regulatory bodies. Interests are operationally defined by market returns, that is, the percentage returned from holding an investment resulting from dividends and changes in share price.

Moreover, an enormous academic industry within financial economics has been built around event studies, which allow researchers to isolate the effect on share price of the public revelation of events relevant to a firm's value (e.g., the adoption of a poison pill, the firing of the CEO). Event studies can provide a quantitative basis for collective action by estimating such things as the amount of money that shareholders lose when a state adopts an antitakeover law (Karpoff and Malatesta, 1989) and therefore how much opposing such laws is worth. More broadly, event studies can provide a quasi-scientific guide to good corporate governance by rendering summary judgments about whether proposed actions are likely to affect snare price positively or negatively (see Altman, 1992). While discretion over the choice of sample, time frame, and method for calculating changes in share price allow different researchers to draw different conclusions about the effects of the same event, such studies have clearly influenced policy debates and provide a quantitative indicator of common interests among shareholders. SEC Chairman Richard Breeden at his Senate confirmation hearings said that golden parachutes "that might reasonably be expected to have a material impact on the value of a corporation's shares" should be subject to shareholder vote rather than excluded as ordinary business (Kanter and Bickford, 1990: 49). If significant changes in share price were the standard used by the SEC to define ordinary business (and thus the issues open to shareholder vote), then event studies would equate shareholder interests with shareholder capacities.

Although changes in share price are reflected directly in the value of an institutional investor's portfolio, the interests of different funds with respect to activism in corporate governance are not identical. Public pension funds, private pension funds, mutual funds, banks, and insurance companies face somewhat different pressures, and although public and private funds do not report following different proxy voting policies (Romano, 1993), evidence on actual voting on shark repellents suggests that they do (Brickley, Lease, and Smith, 1988). Private funds, the largest category of institutional investor, are primarily funds set up by corporations to provide for the retirement of their employees. Private funds commonly are run by trustees who are either top managers of the firm or members of the board of directors; in either case, choosing the portfolio is typically entrusted to professional fund managers, as is voting the proxies. Private-fund managers have been relatively passive because of a variety of pressures that make opposition to management in portfolio companies unpalatable. Corporate managers are unlikely to entrust their firm's pension fund to a fund manager that had previously voted against them. Corporate managers also have a history of influencing their firm's fund to vote with their management counterparts in

companies in which the fund owns shares, often in response to direct pressures or requests from portfolio firm management. In 1986 the CEO of GTE wrote to the CEOs of a number of large firms requesting that they instruct their firms' pension funds to vote in favor of antitakeover measures proposed by GTE management. Less visible pressures on proxy voting were reportedly common (Heard and Sherman, 1987), but some of them were curtailed under the authority of ERISA, which outlines the fiduciary responsibilities of corporate pension executives. In 1988. ERISA was interpreted by the Department of Labor's Pension and Welfare Benefits Administration to include a responsibility to treat proxy voting rights as plan assets, to be voted for the exclusive benefit of plan beneficiaries. This interpretation was meant to rule out conflicted voting resulting from overt pressures by corporate managers but left open subtler means of influence.

Banks, insurance companies, and mutual funds face similar conflicts of interest with respect to voting proxies. Because voting is not normally anonymous, fund managers are subject to implicit or explicit pressure to vote with management to the extent that they have current or potential business dealings with management (cf. Brickley, Lease, and Smith, 1988). This explains why banks and insurance companies have a virtually unblemished history of passivity. Some mutual funds have been active, but their potential conflict of interest "is illustrated by episodes such as the decision by Armstrong World Industries, a principal supporter of the [1990] Pennsylvania antitakeover law, to switch its $180 million employee savings plan to Fidelity Investments from Vanguard Group, after Fidelity withdrew its opposition to the new law" (Black, 1990: 602).

Pension funds for public employees do not do business directly with management that might affect their willingness to oppose managers, and thus they have been the most active institutional investors. Public funds are not regulated by ERISA but commonly have similar mandates. But while public pension funds are less susceptible to pressures by management than other institutional investors; they are not immune, because they themselves are highly politicized (Romano, 1993). Most members of the boards of public pension funds are political appointees or other officeholders (National

Association of State Retirement Administrators, 1989), who may be directly or indirectly subject to pressure by corporate managers who have discretion over plant location decisions and political action committee (PAC) contributions. When California governor Pete Wilson attempted to gain tighter control of CalPERS, many suspected that he was responding to pressures by big business to limit CalPERS' activism. A more direct instance of pressure by corporate managers occurred in 1987, when executives of General Motors paid visits to the governor of Wisconsin and the Wisconsin Investment Board to persuade the board to withdraw its shareholder proposal on stock buybacks, such as the costly one paid to Ross Perot to remove him from the board. The governor was seeking General Motors plants for the state; the proposal was withdrawn (Conard, 1988: 150; Monks and Minnow, 1991: 186).

CREF, a private fund for college professors and other employees of nonprofits, stands in a class by itself. It is by far the largest pension fund and owns stakes in roughly 2,400 corporations, where it is often one of the ten largest shareholders. While it was not a member of the CII by mid-1993, it was nonetheless one of the earliest activists in corporate governance, sponsoring annual resolutions opposing poison pills at many corporations beginning in 1987. Executives of CREF determined that the benefits of such activism outweighed the costs: Hundreds of firms in CREF's portfolio, collectively worth several billion dollars, adopted poison pills, which reduce share prices by about 1 percent on average, while CREF's 1987 campaign against pills cost less than $10,000 (Conard, 1988: fn. 94).

Social infrastructure. The recognition of a shared identity, coupled with previously existing social ties, greatly increases the ability of a group to translate common interests into mobilization toward a common objective (Tilly, 1978). A large body of research demonstrates that those most central in social networks are most likely to join social movements or otherwise become politically active and that social connections are the conduits through which individuals join movements (Knoke, 1990). Thus, denser networks increase the likelihood of the formation of a movement. On this dimension, managers of large corporations originally held a distinct advantage over investors.

The corporate elite forms an identifiable category of actors connected by extensive formal and informal social ties. Of most interest for corporate governance is the interlock network formed by overlapping membership on boards of directors. Most large corporations are linked into a single network by sharing directors with other firms. This network, which existed before the takeover wave, can serve as a basis for cohesion and collective action among professional managers (Useem, 1984) as well as a latent structure for spreading techniques for expanding corporate control. Because the board has ultimate authority within the firm in matters of governance, sharing directors provides a mechanism for innovations in governance to spread from board to board, as demonstrated by the spread of the poison pill by interlocking directors (Davis, 1991). Interlocks also influence common political actions such as PAC contributions (Mizruchi, 1992).

Informal networks among managers were also activated by the takeover wave. Top officers from International Paper and NCR initiated letter-writing campaigns to executives of other companies urging them to instruct their pension fund managers to vote against antimanagement shareholder resolutions, and it was common for managers to pressure representatives of institutions with actual or potential business relationships to vote in management's favor on antitakeover proxy issues (Brickley, Lease, and Smith, 1988).

While formal and informal networks linking corporate managers had a demonstrable impact on management's efforts at maintaining control at the firm level (by spreading poison pills and shark repellents) and at the state level (by pushing antitakeover laws), the indigenous organizational network necessary for effective political action at the federal level was less well developed. The Business Roundtable supported relatively mild restrictions on hostile takeovers and, in light of the failure of federal takeover regulation, had no perceptible impact on national policy. Because the most central firms in the corporate elite network, such as AT&T, were also the most prone to engage in takeovers (Haunschild, 1992), the network provided little basis for antitakeover political action at the national level.

Institutional investors, and public pension funds in particular, also form a recognized category based on common interests and had a moderate indigenous organizational network prior to the takeover wave. Two national organizations of public pension funds and their administrators existed before the takeover wave and provided potential social bases for activist funds, the National Council of Public Employee Retirement Systems (NCPERS), with over 400 members, and the National Association of State Retirement Administrators (NASRA), whose members include the administrators of funds from every state, the District of Columbia, and the American territories. NASRA collects and disseminates information about the structure of its members' funds and their relevant legislative changes and litigation and holds annual meetings for members. Members of the CII were also a social network prior to the formation of their organization—authorities of funds from three states (Jesse Unruh of California, Harrison J. Goldin of New York, and Roland Machold of New Jersey) knew each other well enough to meet informally and eventually create the CII in January 1985. As described above, a variety of legal restrictions previously prevented the formation of connections among institutional investors for the purpose of influencing corporate governance, but because of the relative transparency of the common interests of shareholders, social infrastructure was perhaps less necessary.

Mobilization. Homogeneous interests and dense social networks increase a group's capacity to mobilize its resources. These factors in turn determine the associational processes necessary for effective collective action. For the American corporate elite, the inability to act collectively for political gain seems to be a congenital defect. Early on, a succession of legal restrictions, particularly the Sherman Antitrust Act of 1890, prevented the formation of cartels and trusts and unintendedly promoted mergers within industries. Under these legal restrictions, mechanisms for collective action by corporate managers were left markedly underdeveloped, particularly relative to other advanced capitalist nations where corporatist arrangements entailing formalized contacts between business and state are common (Hollingsworth, 1991). To the extent that they exist in the U.S., such mechanisms tend to be localized in scope, either geographically or by industry, where common interests are more readily recognized.

Where corporate managers were historically restricted in their capacity for collec-

tive action by antitrust considerations, institutional investors were held back by securities regulations that made joint efforts at influence legally problematic (see Black, 1990; Roe, 1991). In particular, prior to October 1992, shareholders became subject to extensive regulations if ten or more of them communicated outside the proxy system in order to decide how to vote. For some purposes, this difficulty was easy to overcome in principle: If CREF, for example, sponsored a shareholder resolution against a firm's poison pill, other shareholders need only know that pills tend to reduce share prices to decide how to vote. But the long-term success of a social movement requires that more formal organizations be created "to assume the centralized direction of the movement previously exercised by informal groups" (McAdam, 1982: 54). Social movement organizations are capable of furthering the movement's agenda even if particular members drop out, and the formation of such organizations represents a critical turning point in American corporate governance. Such was the case for the national controversy over executive pay during the early 1990s, which provides a good context for demonstrating how a social movement can have an effect on issues of corporate control.

Social Movements in Action: The Fight Over Proxy Reform and Executive Pay

The question of how the nation should deal with "runaway executive pay," as a U.S. Senate hearing dubbed the issue, is a particularly telling one because it shows how activist shareholders have made a differenc in policy even in the face of a relatively high level of resistance by corporate managers. Managers were virtually unanimous in their sentiments against allowing significant shareholder influence over how and how much they are paid, whereas shareholders had somewhat weak incentives for activism against overpaying executives. But activist shareholders were relatively better organized around issues of proxy reform at the national level and were able to use the issue of executive pay to advance a more consequential agenda of proxy reform. Because the important outcomes were decided at the federal level by the SEC rather than at the state level, organized shareholders were more effective than organized managers at getting the policy outcomes they favored. Thus, through activism, shareholders gained considerably more influence over executive pay and other issues than they would have otherwise.

Incentives alone do not explain how the controversy over executive pay arose or how it was resolved. The notion that executives in managerialist firms may be unjustly over-rewarding themselves is neither a new grievance nor one that has much impact on the well-being of shareholders, because such compensation is a small factor in very large firms (Conard, 1988). It is far from obvious what appropriate levels of compensation are, and although there is some evidence that linking executive pay to stock market performance is helpful for share prices (Abowd, 1990), it is not sufficiently well established to provide a strong foundation for shareholder activism, particularly in comparison with other aspects of corporate governance. For example, a $10 million per year CEO of a $10 billion company could surrender his or her entire salary to the shareholders and it would have far less impact than rescinding a poison pill that raised the stock price by 1 percent. From the perspective of shareholders, then, the problem of overpaid executives is at most a minor nuisance with no obvious cost-effective solution. In contrast, managers care dearly about preserving the autonomy of their pay from shareholder influence, and they are more unanimous about this issue than almost any other, including that of hostile takeovers. The National Association of Corporate Directors in 1991 found that only 8 percent of the 4,600 executives it surveyed favored granting shareholders a role in determining their pay, and the Business Roundtable has consistently opposed efforts to increase shareholder voice in the proxy system. According to former SEC Chairman Joseph A. Grundfest, "The Business Roundtable has made it seem like the proxy rules are up there with the Ten Commandments, and any small modification is a threat to the world as we know it" (*Business Week*, June 15, 1992: 40).

But the salience of excessive executive pay as a populist issue indicated that the political opportunity structure was ripe for shareholder activism on corporate governance reform. The popular press published numerous stories exposing excessive executive compensation and the weak link between executive pay and corporate performance, as well as on the disparity between the incomes of top executives and other employees. The trade talks between the U.S. and Japan in 1991 invoked unflattering comparisons of executive pay practices in the two nations. *Business Week* reported that in 1990 the average U.S. CEO made eighty-five times the pay of a typical factory worker, whereas the comparable ratio in Japan was seventeen to one. Politicians and candidates eager to attract support explicitly addressed the issue of executive pay. Presidential candidate Bill Clinton suggested changing the tax code to curb high salaries, and Vice President Dan Quayle criticized excessive salaries as a drag on American competitiveness (Brownstein and Penner, 1992). Several pieces of legislation geared toward limiting executive pay surfaced in Congress. In 1992, Representative Martin Sabo proposed a bill to prevent companies from taking a tax deduction for the portion of executive pay that is more than 25 times the amount paid to the lowest-paid workers; Senator Carl Levin proposed the Corporate Pay Responsibility Act that would allow shareholders to compel proxy votes on how executives are paid; and Representative Dan Rostenkowski proposed a cap of $1 million on the annual deduction a company could take for an executive's compensation, a proposal that was ultimately included in the Omnibus Budget Reconciliation Act of 1993 with modifications that allowed pay over the cap if it was contingent on performance (see House Report No. 103-111).

Furthermore, compared with the pro-management bias informing legislative action at the state level, which facilitated the rapid spread of state antitakeover laws, the SEC had officials who were sympathetic to governance reform in general and shareholder voice in executive compensation in particular. SEC Commissioner Mary Schapiro stated "I find it hard to fathom what arguments can be made that executive compensation shouldn't be voted on when it is reaching into the $10 million or $15 million range and is being covered in every newspaper in the country. I don't think the average citizen would view it as ordinary business anymore" (*Wall Street Journal*, February 3, 1992: A3). The SEC's policies and interpretations evolve partly in response to concerns or pressures from the public, Congress, and shareholders, To the extent that shareholder activists can direct that pressure through organizations regarded as the legitimate voice of shareholder concerns, their influence is enhanced.

Shareholder organizations made the best of this opportunity by sending representatives to appear before Congress, sponsoring research to identify overpaid executives, and developing boilerplate shareholder proposals. Excessive compensation was what Congress and the public were buying, so that's what activist shareholders were selling in an effort to push a broader agenda of shareholder rights. The attention they got could then be turned to more consequential aspects of the shareholder rights agenda by proposing proxy reform as the solution to the general problem represented by runaway pay. This effort was evident in the testimony of several representatives of shareholder groups at a Senate hearing on "The SEC and the Issue of Runaway Executive Pay." "The promiscuity of present CEO compensation levels is the *smoking gun* that proves the lack of meaningful accountability of managements of large American corporations today," according to shareholder activist and ISS founder Robert Monks (U.S. Senate, 1991: 99; emphasis in original). Ralph Whitworth, president of USA, outlined a set of broad proxy reforms proposed to the SEC by USA and CalPERS and testified that "compensation is just one symptom of the bankrupt corporate governance system. That is where everything should be focused. . . . Forget what these people get paid. We would rather let them have it if you could get the process fixed so this country could become competitive again" (U.S. Senate, 1991: 17). Thus, the appropriate solution to the problem of excessive executive pay, the lack of American corporate competitiveness, and perhaps an essential step to safeguard the future of democracy in America (Monks and Minnow, 1991: 238) was to increase management's accountability to shareholders by giving shareholders greater voice in corporate governance. As Sarah Teslik, CII's executive director, put it, "Executive pay is becoming the shield for the SEC to do proxy reform" (*Pensions & Investments*, February 3, 1992: 27).

The results of the campaign for governance reform during the early 1990s show that activist shareholders made a difference in policy outcomes, When the SEC initially reviewed the shareholder proposal rule in the early 1980s, including how it applied to executive compensation, it did not generate much comment from parties interested in changing how pay was handled, and the SEC continued to exclude pay proposals as ordinary business (U.S. Senate, 1991, testimony of Linda C. Quinn, director of the SEC's Division of Corporate Finance). Ten years later, after the shareholder-rights movement became organized, proposed changes requiring proxy disclosure of a three-year summary of executive pay and a five-year graphic comparison of the firm's performance relative to that of an index of large firms generated more than 900 letters of comment, most from individual and institutional shareholders (*Federal Register*, 57: 48127). SEC proposals initiated by CalPERS and USA to allow communications among more than ten shareholders outside the proxy system also received hundreds of comment letters—500 from USA members alone. Although the rule changes were opposed by the Business Roundtable, the American Society of Corporate Secretaries, and the Business Council of New York, they were adopted in October 1992 along with the executive pay disclosure rule (*Federal Register*, 56: 28988).

The cumulative changes have been impressive, both in terms of the rules of the game and in terms of outcomes at specific firms. Prior to 1990, shareholders had very little formal influence in determining executive compensation. Between 1990 and 1992, shareholders gained the right to vote on golden-parachute pay packages, to request more detailed information on executive pay, to seek the creation of shareholder advisory committees to advise the board on various issues, to seek changes in company bylaws affecting executive pay, to initiate proposals relating to the appointment of compensation committees and consultants, and to initiate an advisory vote on executive pay. Whereas in 1990 all shareholder proposals on executive pay were excluded by the SEC as ordinary business, by 1993 the SEC allowed 47 of the 85 proposals on executive pay to go to a vote, with one (proposing that the CEO's salary be limited to 150 percent of that of the president of the U.S.) garnering 31 percent of the votes cast. Most importantly, shareholders gained the right to communicate with each other outside the management-dominated proxy system, opening up individual firms to much more effective shareholder collective action in the future.

At the firm level, a number of large corporations have been successfully pressured by shareholder groups outside of the proxy system to change their executive compensation arrangements. In 1991 CalPERS cited research showing that Rand Araskog, CEO of ITT, was paid 102 percent over the market rate despite the company's rating in the bottom 30 percent in performance and that Araskog's pay package was insensitive to changes in the company's performance—earnings per share dropped five times in the prior nine years, while Araskog's total compensation dropped only once. Thus, CalPERS submitted a proposal for the 1991 proxy asking for a bylaw amendment mandating that an independent board committee would evaluate management performance and establish executive compensation and that the committee would have access to independent outside counsel. ITT agreed to these terms, and CalPERS thus withdrew the proposal. When ITT's proxy statement subsequently revealed that Araskog's pay had gone up again, CalPERS and two other pension funds voted their shares against incumbent directors. In response to the negative publicity, Araskog met with CalPERS and agreed to ask his board to make the requested changes in the bylaws. Araskog also met with the president of USA in response to being placed on USA's Target 50 list, stating "I'm tired of being the poster boy for executive compensation," and assured the group that ITT's board was working to link executive pay with performance in line with USA's criteria (*Wall Street Journal*, April 27, 1992: A1). Similar stories can be told for W. R. Grace, Ryder, and several other corporations pressured by shareholders. Moreover, in light of the October 1992 rule changes, well-organized shareholders are likely to have much greater behind-the-scenes influence with management because of their enhanced ability to coordinate campaigns.

Conclusion

As the different patterns revealed by the policy debates over regulation of takeovers and excessive compensation show, the corporate elite doesn't always get the governmental policies it wants, nor do shareholders; in fact, they don't always have consistent interests or agree among themselves on what their interests are. There is interesting variation in the outcomes of struggles over corporate control that is contingent on a variety of factors (cf. Mizruchi, 1992), including the political level of the conflict and the social structures in which the players are embed-

ded. This paper has outlined an approach to identifying the factors that can explain this variation using theory about organizations, social movements, and classes. Our approach recognizes that the structure of large corporations is not strictly determined by capital market pressures but results from political struggles that implicate managers and owners as well as social structures extending beyond the firm. We have focused on the shareholder-rights movement of the late 1980s and early 1990s, but our approach could be elaborated and extended to consider other conflicts over corporate control, both at different times and with actors other than managers and shareholders. . . .

In contrast with functionalist approaches, a social movement perspective does not presume a strong push toward equilibrium in struggles over corporate control. The balance of power in the corporation is largely contingent on historical factors outside the direct control of shareholders and managers—notably the business cycle and incumbent presidential administration—which implies that no fixed regime of corporate control is likely to emerge. Neither managerialism nor the shareholder-rights movement were inevitable, and the range of governance regimes that could yet emerge is broad. We have tried to provide an orienting framework useful for understanding the American case that takes seriously the social and political structures in which these regimes evolve.

References

Abowd, John M. 1990. "Does performance-based managerial compensation affect corporate performance?" *Industrial and Labor Relations Review*, 43(3): 52–73.

Altman, Richard M. 1992. *Investor Response to Management Decisions: A Research-Based Analysis of Actions and Effects*. New York: Quorum.

Berle, Adolph, Jr., and Gardiner C. Means. 1932. *The Modern Corporation and Private Property*. New York: Macmillan.

Black, Bernard S. 1990. "Shareholder passivity reexamined." *Michigan Law Review*, 89: 520–608.

Brickley, James A., Ronald C. Lease, and Clifford W, Smith, Jr. 1988. "Ownership structure and voting on antitakeover amendments." *Journal of Financial Economics*, 20: 267–291.

Brownstein, Andrew R., and Morris J. Penner. 1992. "Who should set CEO pay? The press? Congress? Shareholders?" *Harvard Business Review*, 70(3): 28–38.

Conard, Alfred F. 1988. "Beyond managerialism: Investor capitalism?" *University of Michigan Journal of Law Reform*, 22: 117–178.

Davis, Gerald F. 1991. "Agents without principles? The spread of the poison pill through the intercorporate network." *Administrative Science Quarterly*, 36: 583–613.

———. 1993. "Who gets ahead in the market for corporate directors. The political economy of multiple board memberships." *Academy of Management Best Papers Proceedings*, 1993: 202–206.

Davis, Gerald F., and Suzanne K. Stout. 1992. "Organization theory and the market for corporate control: A dynamic analysis of the characteristics of large takeover targets, 1980–1990." *Administrative Science Quarterly*, 37: 605–633.

Drucker, Peter F. 1976. *The Unseen Revolution: How Pension Fund Socialism Came to America*. New York: Harper.

Easterbrook, Frank H., and Daniel R. Fischel. 1991. *The Economic Structure of Corporate Law*. Cambridge, MA: Harvard University Press.

Granovetter, Mark. 1985. "Economic action and social structure: The problem of embeddedness." *American Journal of Sociology*, 91: 481–510.

Grundfest, Joseph A. 1990. "Subordination of American capital." *Journal of Financial Economics*, 27: 89–114.

Haunschild, Pamela R. 1992. "The social bases of corporate acquisition activity." *Academy of Management Best Papers Proceedings*, 1992: 175–179.

Heard, James E., and Howard D. Sherman. 1987. *Conflicts of Interest in the Proxy Voting System*. Washington, DC: Investor Responsibility Research Center.

Hollingsworth, J. Rogers. 1991. "The logic of coordinating American manufacturing sectors." In John L. Campbell, J. Rogers Hollingsworth, and Leon N. Lindberg (eds.), *Governance of the American Economy*: 35–73. New York: Cambridge University Press.

Jensen, Michael C. 1986. "Agency costs of free cash flow, corporate finance and takeovers." *American Economic Review* (Papers & Proceedings), 76: 323–329.

Kanter, Jeffrey M., and Lawrence C., Bickford. 1990. "To the ballot box for golden parachutes." *Directors and Boards*, 14(3): 48–50.

Kanter, Rosabeth Moss. 1991. "The future of bureaucracy and hierarchy in organizational theory: A report from the field." In Pierre Bourdieu and James S., Coleman (eds.), *Social Theory for a Changing Society*: 63–87. Boulder, CO: Westview.

Kaplan, Steven N. and David Reishus. 1990. "Outside directorships and corporate performance." *Journal of Financial Economics*, 27: 389–410.

Karpoff, Jonathon M., and Paul H. Malatesta. 1989. "The wealth effects of second-generation state takeover legislation." *Journal of Financial Economics*, 25: 291–322.

Knoke, David. 1990. *Political Networks: The Structural Perspective*. New York: Cambridge University Press.

Kosnik, Rita D. 1987. "Greenmail: A study of board performance in corporate governance." *Administrative Science Quarterly*, 32: 163–185.

Laumann, Edward O., and David Knoke. 1987. *The Organizational State: Social Choice in National Policy Domains*. Madison, WI. University of Wisconsin Press.

McAdam, Doug. 1982. Political Process and the Development of Black Insurgency 1930–1970. Chicago: University of Chicago Press.

McCarthy, John D. and Mayer N. Zald. 1977. "Resource mobilization and social movements: A partial theory." *American Journal of Sociology*, 82: 1212–1241.

McQuaid, Kim. 1980. "Big business and public policy in the contemporary United States." *Quarterly Review of Economics and Business*, 20: 57–88.

Mergers and Acquisitions. 1992. "Endangered species of the M&A market: With the slide of public deals, tender offers got few calls in 1991." *Mergers and Acquisitions*, 26(6): 25–26.

Meyer, Marshall W. and Lynne G. Zucker. 1989. *Permanently Failing Organizations*. Newbury Park, CA: Sage.

Mizruchi, Mark S. 1992. *The Structure of Corporate Political Action: Interfirm Relations and Their Consequences*. Cambridge, MA: Harvard University Press.

Monks, Robert A. G., and Neil Minnow. 1991. *Power and Accountability*. New York: HarperBusiness.

National Association of State Retirement Administrators. 1989. *Survey of Systems*. Salt Lake City: NASRA.

Offe, Calus, and Helmut Wiesenthal. 1980. "Two logics of collective action: Theoretical notes on social class and organizational form." *Political Power and Social Theory*, 1: 67–115.

Pickens, T. Boone. 1988. "Takeovers: A purge of poor managements." *Management Review*, 77: 52–55.

Roe, Mark J. 1991. "A political theory of American corporate finance." *Columbia Law Review*, 91: 10–67.

———. 1993. "Takeover politics." In Margaret M. Blair (ed.), *The Deal Decade: What Takeovers and Leveraged Buyouts Mean for Corporate Governance*: 321–380. Washington, DC: Brookings Institution.

Romano, Roberta. 1985. "Law as product: Some pieces of the incorporation puzzle." *Journal of Law, Economics, and Organization*, 1: 225–283.

———. 1987. "The political economy of takeover statutes." *Virginia Law Review*, 73: 111–199.

———. 1988. "The future of hostile takeovers: Legislation and public opinion." *Cincinnati Law Review*, 57: 457–505.

———. 1993. "Public pension fund activism in corporate governance reconsidered." *Columbia Law Review*, 93: 79–53.

Snow, David A., and Robert D. Benford. 1992. "Master frames and cycles of protest." In Aldon D. Morris and Carol McClurg Mueller (eds.), *Frontiers in Social Movement Theory*: 133–155. New Haven, CT: Yale University Press.

Tilly, Charles. 1978. *From Mobilization to Revolution*. New York: Random House.

U.S. Senate. 1991. "The SEC and the issue of runaway executive pay." Hearing before the Subcommittee on Oversight of Government Management of the Committee on Governmental Affairs, United States Senate, One Hundred Second Congress, First Session, May 15.

Useem, Michael. 1984. *The Inner Circle*. New York: Oxford University Press.

———. 1993. *Executive Defense: Shareholder Power and Corporate Reorganization*. Cambridge, MA: Harvard University Press.

Vogel, David Zald, Mayer N., and Michael A. 1978. "Why businessmen distrust their state: The political consciousness of American corporate executives." *British Journal of Political Science*, 8: 45–78.

Walsh, James P., and James K. Seward. 1990. "On the efficiency of internal and external corporate control mechanisms." *Academy of Management Review*, 15: 421–458.

Zald, Mayer N., and Michael A. Berger. 1978. "Social movements in organizations: Coup d'etat, insurgency, and mass movements." *American Journal of Sociology*, 83: 823–861.

Appendix

Atlanta Constitution, 1985: October 30.

Barron's, 1990: December 24.

Business Month, 1987: April.

Business Week, 1987: April 27, May 18; 1988: February 8, October 21; 1991: June 6; 1992: June 4, June 15.

Chemical Week, 1990: August 1; 1991: July 31, November 21.

Chicago Tribune, 1991: June 19, October 14, November 21; 1992: February 14, 16, 24; October 16; 1993: June 1.

Chief Executive, 1992: January/February.

Dun's Review, 1976: December.

Economist, 1989: June 17; 1991: June 12, July 13.

Federal Register, 1991: 56 (June 25, July 10); 1992: 57 (October 21).

Financial World, 1991: October 1.

Fortune, 1987: April 13; 1988: September 12; 1989: June 5, 21; 1990: June 15.

Industry Week, 1990: June 18; 1991: April 15.

Institutional Investor, 1987: May; 1990: June.

Investor Responsibility Research Center, *Issues in Corporate Governance Background Report J*, 1991.

Los Angeles Times, 1992: February 16.

New York Times, 1988: July 5; 1990: March 30; 1991: June 6, 13; 1992: February 13, 25; March 21, June 24.

Pensions & Investments, 1990: April 16, November 11; 1991: February 18, April 16, October 14; 1992: March 16, 30.

Pension and Investment Age, 1985: December 9; 1988: November 28.

Time, 1986: April 21; 1992: May 4.

Wall Street Journal, 1986: July 13, December 15; 1990: February 28; 1991: May 16, June 21, November 18; 1992: January 10, 15, 21; February 3, 13, 14; April 1, 22, 27; May 1, 22; June 23, August 27, September 22, October 25.

Washington Post, 1985: January 25.

Chapter 18
Two Faces of the Powerless

Coping With Tyranny in Organizations

Robert J. Bies and
Thomas M. Tripp

For many people, organizational power is primarily a matter of human behavior. In particular, it involves the experience and exercise of power and control in organizational hierarchies. Bies and Tripp examine one extreme here: the "abusive boss." They describe their research as a study of "tyranny in the workplace," and are interested in people who exercise their power ruthlessly and without regard for others' well-being. Bies and Tripp also want to understand the victims of these abusive workplace tyrants. How do people cope with abuse and what are the implications for organizations?

> I dread each day coming to work. Once inside the door, I feel "chained" to my desk like a prisoner. My boss is the "prison warden" who delights in "torturing" me with a daily barrage of public criticism and ridicule. I feel so powerless, like a "pawn" being played in one of his power games. My friends ask me why I just don't quit? . . . Why do I stay and take that abuse? I don't know why . . . I guess I hope things will change, even though they don't. So I stay . . . hating him, and hating myself.
>
> —Manager, global telecommunication company

> I do not try to justify [Fletcher Christian's] crime, his mutiny, but I condemn the tyranny that drove him to it.
>
> —Roger Byam (from the movie *Mutiny on the Bounty*, 1935)

The words persecution, oppression, and tyranny conjure up terrifying images of evil dictators, such as Hitler and Stalin, who employed brutal and ruthless methods to dominate nations and people. Indeed, these words bring to mind the frightening vision of a totalitarian world in which those in power are obsessed with controlling the hearts and minds of people through fear and intimidation (Orwell, 1949).

Although political scientists and sociologists study the dynamics of tyranny (Gilliom, 1997; Scott, 1990), there is little, if any, mention of tyranny in the dominant models of leadership and power (Pfeffer, 1992). As the introductory quotation to this chapter suggests, however, people can and do describe their work experiences in those exact terms (see Shorris, 1981, for additional examples). Moreover, the popular press has provided ample anecdotal evidence of tyranny in organizations in articles on the "intolerable boss" (Lombardo & McCall, 1984), the "unbearable boss" (Goleman, 1986), and the "psycho boss from hell" (Dumaine, 1993). Ironically, these types of bosses, which are celebrated on business magazine covers, are deeply resented and scorned by their employees, who nickname them "Captain Bligh" (Nordhoff & Hall, 1932) and "Captain Queeg" (Wouk, 1951)—names that have become synonymous with tyranny in the workplace.

Although contemporary academics have been silent on tyranny by leaders and those in power, the most important and influential organizational theorist, Max Weber, was not. Weber (1946) worried about the potential for tyranny when he wrote about the concentration of power in the hands of a few masters in bureaucracy, which would imprison humanity in an "iron cage" (p. 228). Although our paradigms of leadership and power have ignored a discussion and analysis of tyranny (Treviño & Bies, 1997), there has been episodic scholarly interest in the phenomenon—for example, the sociological analysis by Miller, Weiland, and Couch (1978) and Ashforth's (1994) social psychological analysis of "petty tyranny." In addition, Hornstein (1996) provides some empirical evidence of the dynamics and consequences of tyranny in his analysis of the "brutal boss."

In acknowledging the existence of tyranny in the workplace, the important theoretical (and practical) question is raised as to how people cope with tyranny (Bies, in press).

History is filled with inspiring examples of people under the oppression of tyranny who, through creativity and the sheer will to live, have invented coping strategies to maintain their dignity (Scott, 1990) and sustain them in their pursuit of freedom (Havel, 1985). Although recent research in organizational settings provides some illustrative findings of how people cope with tyranny (Bies & Tripp, 1996; Tripp & Bies, 1997), there is clearly a large gap in our knowledge of how people cope with tyranny in the workplace.

The purpose of this chapter is threefold. First, we present the results of an empirical study of tyranny in the workplace, thus adding to a much needed empirical foundation for analyzing this phenomenon. In our study, we chose to focus on tyranny as manifested in the "abusive boss." The abusive boss is one whose primary objective is the control of others, and such control is achieved through methods that create fear and intimidation (Hornstein, 1996).

Second, we present data on how people cope with the tyranny of an abusive boss in the workplace. Our study finds evidence of a variety of coping responses, ranging from resignation to resistance. Finally, we explore implications of our findings and conclude with reflections on the academic silence—if not suppression—with respect to the study of tyranny in organizations.

The Abusive Boss: Profiles in Tyranny

In this study, we surveyed working managers about their experiences with the tyranny of abusive bosses. The respondents were participants in an Executive MBA program, a group that included 30 men and 17 women that had an average of 12 years of work experience. In the survey, we asked respondents to think of a specific boss for whom they had worked whom they would label as an abusive boss or a boss from hell. They were asked to describe the boss in as much detail as possible and then to identify how they coped with that boss.

The unit of analysis was the profile or description of the particular boss for whom the respondent had once worked. Respondents described the behaviors and characteristics of the abusive boss and how they coped with the abuse. The analysis strategy followed the grounded theory approach outlined by Glaser and Strauss (1967). In general, the method entails continually comparing theory and data until adequate conceptual categories are developed. To ensure accuracy and reliability of the coding process, the same data were coded independently by two raters.

The data suggest that the abusive boss engages in specific behaviors that comprise tyranny. Specifically, the abusive boss displays one or more of the following behaviors: acts as a "micromanager," provides inexplicit direction with decisive delivery, exhibits "mercurial" mood swings, demonstrates an obsession with loyalty and obedience, derogates the status of employees, is capricious, exercises raw power for personal gain, obsesses on gathering personal information about employees, and at times uses coercion to corrupt employees. A more detailed discussion of each of these aspects of the abusive boss is presented.

Micromanager

In describing the abusive boss as a micromanager, respondents agreed on two key characteristics of a micromanager: an obsession with details and an obsession with perfection.

Obsession With Details. One of the signature features of abusive bosses is that they must have "their hands in everything." One respondent described her boss as follows: "He had to attend every meeting, and then he had to review and sign off on *every* piece of paper produced by the group." Indeed, as another respondent reported, "No detail was too small for his [boss's] concern or inspection." The obsession with details also abusive bosses to want to know every movement and action of employees. For example, one respondent described his boss as "demanding knowledge of everybody's calendars 2 months in advance." Another respondent described her boss as "wanting to know my whereabouts *to the minute*, even when I was in the bathroom."

Obsession With Perfection. In almost "Queeg-like" fashion, our respondents reported the abusive boss has an obsession with perfection. This obsession manifests itself in the setting of unreasonably high performance expectations and, at the same time, being impatient with, and unforgiving of, any mistakes. Also, not surprisingly, it was never the boss's fault for performance failures; blame was always assigned to the subordinates. As one respondent described her boss, "No excuses was his motto." The obsession with perfection was also manifest in the "second-guessing" of employees' actions and decisions. One respondent reported, "No matter what I did, he second-guessed me. He was so pathological that he was even 'second-guessing' his second guesses!"

Inexplicit Direction With Decisive Delivery

The abusive boss created a "double bind" for many respondents because, although they were asked to provide high-quality performance, the abusive boss would never define what "quality" meant. One respondent described his boss as one who demanded quality "with precision in his commands, but precisely what he meant by quality was never clear. What it meant, ultimately, was what we did not do to his satisfaction." In a similar fashion, abusive bosses usually articulate no priorities because "everything is a priority," as one respondent described her boss's motto. As a result, many respondents felt they received "inexplicit direction with decisive delivery."

What further heightened the vagueness of directions was when the boss would send conflicting signals and messages. One method of sending conflicting signals was playing a question "cat-and-mouse" game. In this game, one respondent described her difficulty in reading "my boss's mind and anticipating his every need" because she typically had no clue about the boss's intentions.

Mercurial Mood Swings

Several respondents reported that the abusive boss exhibited volatile mood swings, which were mercurial in nature and often for no apparent reason. One manager reported that his boss had a "Dr. Jekyll and Mr. Hyde" personality. This meant that in one moment the boss could be very calm, peaceful, and satisfied; then, without any warning, the boss would erupt into a loud, angry, temper tantrum, a public tirade directed at one or all employees. Moreover, the intensity of the mood swings did not vary as a function of the seriousness of the triggering event—that is, the tirades were always loud and emotional.

Tirades were not limited to emotional outbursts. Respondents reported tirades that included the destruction of physical property (e.g., throwing telephones at the wall) or threatening, and occasionally even using, physical violence (e.g., shoving an employee). One respondent stated that when "he [the boss] went ballistic, we went for cover."

Obsession With Loyalty and Obedience

Much like a dictator, the abusive boss exhibits an obsession with loyalty and obedience. This obsession manifests itself in punishing those employees who dissented with the boss's viewpoint or position. For example, one manager, who challenged her boss' decision on technical and ethical grounds, received a strong negative performance appraisal, even though her record heretofore had been exemplary.

In another form of punishment, the abusive boss would often stigmatize any dissenter with pejorative labels (e.g., "traitor" and "troublemaker"). As loyal "subjects," employees were expected to humbly submit to and endure the public tirades and other punishments meted out by the boss.

Finally, abusive bosses may also test the loyalty of employees in an almost *1984*-like (Orwell, 1949) fashion by demanding that employees bring gossip and rumors about other employees. Respondents reported of bosses who would use their secretaries as "spies" to ferret out the " disloyal."

Status Derogation

Another signature feature of the abusive boss was the boss's willingness and ability to derogate employees in public. An example, shared by several respondents, is the boss who publicly criticizes the performance and character of an employee, even to the point of ridiculing him or her. Also, on more than one occasion, such actions would "bring men and women to tears," reported one respondent. Another respondent described his boss as the "master of sarcasm" who delighted in "putting people down" in public.

Capricious Actions

The abusive boss is also noted for arbitrariness and hypocrisy. For example, one respondent described how, when the sales group was just about to reach their target for the year (a record level), the boss raised the sales target, without any justification, causing the group to lose their bonus. Indeed, making arbitrary decisions, with no justification, was a common behavior of abusive bosses.

Hypocrisy took the form of employing double standards in dealing with employees. One example of hypocrisy was the boss "who left work early to run personal errands, but chastised me for attempting to do the same," as reported by one respondent. When she brought the hypocrisy to the boss's attention, she was told by the boss to "do as I say not as I do."

Exercises Raw Power for Personal Gain

For several respondents, it was in the use of "raw power" that defined the essence of tyranny. One example of raw power was the boss who "held up my approved job transfer because he wanted me to stay to serve his interests," reported one respondent. Another respondent reported an example of the boss who kept employees waiting for 3 hours into the early morning after their job was completed satisfactorily just because the boss had not finished his job. Raw power also took the form of blatantly stealing credit for a subordinate's idea.

In some cases, raw power took the form of coercion. Two stories illustrate this coercion. First, an employee was told that he had to fire one of his own subordinates, even though that subordinate was a good performer. The boss, however, did not personally like that subordinate and implied that if the employee did not fire his subordinate, it may reflect adversely on his managerial capabilities and limit his future at this company. This employee, being young and recently married with a newborn, submitted and terminated the employee, even though he knew it was wrong.

Second, one boss forced an employee to add a fourth vendor to a competitive bidding process, even though the vendor had failed to meet the requirements. Then, after one of the original three vendors technically won the competition, the employee was told to give it to the fourth vendor, with whom the boss had connections.

The Social Toxins of Tyranny: Poisoning the Mind, Body, and Spirit

There can be no darker or more devastating tragedy than the death of

man's faith in himself and in his power to direct his future.
  —Alinsky (1971, p. xxvi)

In describing abusive bosses, respondents provided us with some insight on how they "experienced" the effects of tyranny. Specifically; they outlined some effects of tyranny in cognitive, affective, and physiological terms. Often, these effects were lingering and interrelated. Furthermore, the effects went beyond mere issues of dissatisfaction and lower productivity; indeed, tyranny was viewed by many of our respondents as a "social toxin," poisoning their professional and personal lives.

Common responses to tyranny were the thoughts and feelings of betrayal, distrust, resentment, frustration, and mental exhaustion. In addition, several respondents reported a variety of physiological reactions to tyranny, including uncontrollable crying, "knots in the stomach," and physical exhaustion.

According to the respondents in our study, the bosses' actions were oriented toward one primary goal—control. Control was achieved through creating fear and intimidation and creating confusion and disorientation. Indeed, several respondents reported feeling "paranoid," and a few reported feeling "terror-stricken" and, at times, "paralyzed." One person reported that "I would stay at my desk and not even go to the bathroom, for the fear, if I was away from my desk, my boss would 'hammer' me in public." Not surprisingly, such people reported feeling vulnerable and powerless because the boss's tyranny had "broken the spirit and willingness to fight back," as described by one respondent.

Responses to Tyranny: Coping Strategies

Society is a very mysterious animal with many faces and hidden personalities, and . . . it's extremely short-sighted to believe that the face of society that happens to be presenting to you at a given moment is its only true face. None of us knows all the potentialities that slumber in the spirit of the population.
  —V. Havel (May 31,1990)

Our analysis of the data suggests that responses to tyranny can be fruitfully explored in a framework that has two dimensions. The first dimension is the persona or face that we project to the public. The second dimension is the persona or face that we keep private or hidden to ourselves—one that reflects our true beliefs and attitudes.

With respect to the tyrant boss, people can present two faces—one that consents to or agrees with the boss and the other that dissents from or disagrees with the boss. In this framework, then, the public persona mayor may not be consistent with the private face, resulting in a two-by-two framework for analysis. Table 18.1 presents this framework, and in the following sections we describe the more specific coping strategies as reflected in this framework.

Table 18.1
Responses to Tyranny

	Public Face	
Private Face	*Consent*	*Dissent*
Consent	Surrender	Disguise
Dissent	Disguise	Confrontation

Public Consent, Private Consent: Surrender

For some of our respondents, coping with their tyrant bosses was made "easy" by changing their own private beliefs to be consistent with those of the boss. A few respondents coped by realigning their private beliefs with their boss's beliefs and policies. Such realignment, they reported, resolved the conflict they had with their bosses. In other words, they "surrendered" and "gave up" completely.

Similarly, other respondents reported coping by loyally following orders or by simply accepting the tyranny as social reality. By accepting their "fate," it made the tyranny less oppressive. One respondent described her position as follows: "Once I gave in, and stopped trying to fight it, it became easier."

Public Consent, Private Dissent: Disguise

When the great lord passes, the wise peasant bows deeply and silently farts.

—Ethiopian proverb (as cited in Scott, 1990, p. v)

Several respondents reported that they coped with their tyrannical bosses by only appearing to change their own private beliefs. That is, respondents would publicly espouse their bosses' beliefs and support the bosses' policies but privately vehemently disagree with their bosses' beliefs and policies. In other words, our respondents reported disguising their true feelings by presenting a public face that was quite different than their private beliefs.

The acts of disguise can take a variety of forms, according to our respondents. One common form of disguise is in how people "manage" their bosses. For many respondents, efforts to better manage their bosses included keeping their bosses informed of all details, better preparing for meetings with their bosses, and better determining their bosses' needs and goals. Respondents also reported that they mirrored their bosses' working styles to avoid criticisms of their own work styles.

Managing the boss also included the strategic use of information. For example, one respondent reported how he "told the boss just enough information to avoid trouble, and reported successes, not failures." Most respondents noted that they managed their relationships with their bosses not because they liked their bosses but because they viewed it as "a personally effective survival strategy," as one respondent reported. They did not believe it was in their own best interests to make their bosses aware of the depth of their disaffection, so they hid their true feelings and tried to work with their bosses.

A second form of disguise involved keeping a "low profile." This meant " offering no challenges or criticisms," in the words of one respondent. Other respondents kept a low profile by minimizing contact with their bosses—an "evade and avoid" strategy. While keeping a low profile, respondents also secretly documented their bosses mistakes and transgressions, predicting that such documentation might become beneficial in the future.

A third form of disguise occurred in one's head. For example, many respondents highlighted the value of "revenge fantasies" in which they dreamed of getting even with their bosses but they projected the public face of "getting along" with the bosses. Relying on revenge fantasies was viewed by one respondent as a "mental survival" strategy. Another respondent described his perspective as follows: "While he plays his mind games with me, I play my own mind games."

As another enactment of disguise, some respondents acted out their revenge fantasies, but in ways that could not be recognized as getting even or as any kind of challenge. For example, some respondents reported withholding support from their bosses at critical times, resulting in failures for the bosses. Others reported following all orders, no matter how stupid some orders might be. Also, with those bosses who were obsessed with details and information, some respondents would deliberately feed their bosses so much information as to overload them while appearing as "dutiful subordinates keeping the boss informed," as one respondent stated.

A fifth form of disguise was "carnival" techniques. By carnival, respondents meant a festive gathering held at the boss's expense but without the boss knowing. For example, in small private gatherings, employees would demonize their bosses—that is, vent their frustrations, assign blame, call the bosses names (e.g., "Beelzebub"), and generally bad-mouth their bosses. In one case, subordinates used humor to ridicule their boss by holding an initiation ceremony for a new employee who had just had his first abusive encounter with the boss.

Finally, some respondents reported creating "refuges" from the boss for other subordinates. These people acted as buffers between the boss and the other subordinates. The buffer worked in two directions: It shielded the subordinates from the boss's tantrums and confusing edicts and shielded the boss from the subordinates' dissent.

Public Dissent, Private Dissent: Confrontation

> *Progressive forces need trumpets, not farts.*
> —Handler (1992, p. 727)

More than a few respondents reported engaging in confrontation in which they openly challenged their bosses. Some would directly confront their bosses, challenging them on their decisions in an open, public forum. Others would take the public challenge even further by openly ridiculing the boss. In a few cases, public challenges involved acts of insubordination, such as making decisions without the boss's knowledge or approval.

Confrontation also took the form of going around the boss to deal with the boss. Examples of such an "end-runs" around the boss included talking to the boss's boss, involving a third party such as a representative from human resources or legal departments, and consulting a lawyer. As part of these strategies, any private documentation of the boss's actions was brought to public light.

A final act of confrontation involved exiting the situation. Exit took the form of quitting or leaving the organization but with "a little panache" in the words of one respondent. For example, one respondent stated that her exit was done with a "blaze of glory, distributing e-mail and hard copy documentation with a list of her boss's crimes."

Public Dissent, Private Consent: Disguise

Our data did not reveal any direct evidence of this form of disguised behavior. Indirect evidence, however, was provided by a few respondents in their examples of secretaries and other employees acting as spies for the boss. In this role of the "mole" for the boss, secretaries would express their public disaffection with the boss as a means of disarming other employees to become more forthcoming about their true negative feelings about the boss. This intelligence gathered by the spies was then fed back to the boss. In other words, the secretaries hid or disguised their true loyalty to the boss by pretending to be dissatisfied with the boss.

Beyond the Data: Impressions and Implications

In interpreting these data, some interesting, albeit preliminary; conclusions emerge. First, even though our sample is small, leading us to be reasonably tentative, the findings are strikingly similar to descriptions made by other researchers, such as Hornstein (1996) and Ashforth (1994). They identified dimensions to describe tyranny in organizations similar to those found in our study (e.g., micromanagers, obsession with protection, and exercise of raw power). This convergence with the findings of other researchers suggests that we are capturing the essence and dynamics of tyranny in organizations, particularly in the form of the abusive boss.

Second, our data shed additional light on the dark side of power and politics in organizations. Indeed, it is very clear that in the use of power there can be the abuse of power (Bies & Tripp, 1995). Also, abuse does not take its toll in only economic terms; it also has a toxic effect and impact on the human lives of people who work in organizations. Any complete analysis of power can not only focus on its functional rationality in achieving organizational goals and objectives but also must account for the dysfunctional and irrational consequences of its use.

What distinguishes our research from the work of Hornstein (1996) and Ashforth (1994) is the identification of a broader range of coping strategies, and particularly how individuals manage and even manipulate their public persona as central to coping with tyranny. The most intriguing finding to us was people's rather extensive use of disguise and, in particular, the use of carnival techniques.

Although this "two-faced" approach can be difficult because employees are "living within a lie" (Havel, 1985), our respondents reported that the use of disguise can, in fact, be a rational and functional coping strategy. It is functional because it protects them to some extent from the unbridled wrath of a tyrant bent on harming those who disagree or dislike the tyrant. In addition, it is functional because it provides the employee with some measure of control and efficacy with respect to his or her environment (Bies & Tripp, 1996, in press; Tripp & Bies, 1997).

In particular, two aspects of the use of disguise proved especially interesting to us. First, respondents reported that through their acts of disguise they led the tyrant bosses to believe that they have a more supportive and submissive group of employees than was actually true. In other words, bosses, based on their observations of the employees' loyal and obedient behavior, made inferences that led to a false consciousness and a false consensus as to the level of affection or disaffection with their leadership (Nord & Doherty, 1994). In that sense, duplicity was central to managing conflict.

Indeed, in our data, there is clear evidence of a rich "underground" in organizations. In this underground world, people share common experiences and provide social support in a rich, liturgical fashion. They often engage in party-like social gatherings with initiation rites and storytelling. The evidence of this underground is strikingly similar to that found in research on how citizens cope with repressive political regimes (Scott, 1990) and quite consistent with evidence of the "everyday resistance" by those under the scrutiny of surveillance and regulation (Gilliom, 1997).

Beyond the Sounds of Silence: The Study of Tyranny in Organizations

An emerging body of research on tyranny and its consequences leads us to ask the following question: Why are our organization and management theories so silent on the abuse of power by leaders? One answer could be that researchers are simply unaware of the existence of the social phenomenon of tyranny in organizations. Given a growing body of empirical evidence of tyranny and its consequences, however, this answer is not persuasive.

A more likely answer to the question is found in the prevailing ideological assumptions of organization and management theory—the organizational imperative (Scott & Hart, 1979). The organizational imperative is based on a primary and absolute proposition, "Whatever is good for the individual can only come from the modern organization" (p. 43), and the related secondary proposition, "Therefore, *all behavior must enhance the health of such organizations* (italics added)" (p. 43). Indeed, as Scott and Hart conclude, "The organizational imperative is the sine qua non of management theory and practice . . . the metaphysic of management: absolute and immutable" (p. 46).

The ideology of the organizational imperative has important implications for the study of tyranny because, as is known, ideological assumptions shape theory building and empirical research (Barley & Kunda, 1992; Hatch, 1997; Scott & Hart, 1971). The ideology of organizational imperative has resulted in "blinding" people from "seeing" tyranny and its consequences (Bies & Tripp, in press; Treviño & Bies, 1997). As the empirical evidence continues to grow, however, ignoring or failing to see tyranny will become harder to do. Thus, the "defenders" of the ideology will be faced with the task of inventing new responses to legitimate the ideology.

One likely response will be "reframing" the methods and consequences of tyranny. That is, while acknowledging tyranny, it will be argued that although such methods may be harsh or even cruel, they are absolutely necessary and essential for creating high-performance organizations. In other words, the survival of the organization demands tyranny!

A second possible response will be to shift the focus away from the tyrant and the agents of tyranny and to highlight—and "condemn"— the actions of those who fight back against oppression in the workplace. No longer will the initial harmdoer be wrong because it will be the initial victim who is wrong! In other words, in an Orwellian twist the harmdoer becomes the victim, and the victim becomes the harmdoer.

This move to "blaming the victim" also results in a biased punctuation of the research problem because the focus will not be on the situational events or organizational practices that can precipitate, or even justify, a victim's response to harm and wrongdoing (Bies & Tripp 1996, in press; McLean Parks, 1997; Tripp & Bies, 1997). This biased punctuation of the problem should not be surprising because it follows from the ideology of the organizational imperative that any response to tyranny that attacks the interest of the organization—as articulated by its leaders—is by definition "wrong," "bad," and "deviant" (Robinson & Bennett, 1995).

To counteract the ideological bias of the organizational imperative, Treviño and Bies (1997) "nailed" a normative manifesto to the doors of the academy in an open challenge to the defenders of the ideology of the organizational imperative. In this manifesto, they argue that many organizational theorists and researchers assumed the roles of apologists and excuse-makers for management and its interests. As a result, theory and research have excluded the voices of a large group of people in organizations—those who are relatively powerless. Moreover, the efforts of many researchers may have contributed to perpetuating the use of dehumanizing or exploitative management practices (Scott & Hart, 1979).

For those theorists and researchers who have the courage to study tyranny—let alone speak out against it—your role will be that of a social critic: on the margin, not in the mainstream, motivated by what Beaney (1966) calls "a never-ending quest to increase the respect of all . . . for the essential values of human life" (p. 271). The choice to join this quest is yours. It always has been.

References

Alinsky, S. D. (1971). *Rules for radicals: A pragmatic primer for realistic radicals.* New York: Random House.

Ashforth, B. (1994). Petty tyranny in organizations. *Human Relations*, 47, 755–778.

Barley, S. R., & Kunda, G. (1992). Design and devotion: Surges of rational and normative ideologies of control in managerial discourse. *Administrative Science Quarterly*, 37, 363–399.

Beaney, W. M. (1966). The right to privacy and American law. *Law and Contemporary Problems*, 31, 253–271.

Bies, R. J. (in press). Interactional (in)justice: The sacred and the profane. In J. Greenberg & R. Cropanzano (Eds.), *Advances in organizational behavior.* San Francisco: New Lexington.

Bies, R. J., & Tripp, T. M. (1995). The use and abuse of power: Justice as social control. In R. Cropanzano & M. Kacmar (Eds.), *Organizational politics, justice, and support: Managing social climate at work* (pp. 131–145). New York: Quorum.

Bies, R. J., & Tripp, T. M. (1996). Beyond distrust: "Getting even" and the need for revenge. In R. M. Kramer & T. Tyler (Eds.), *Trust in organizations* (pp. 246–260). Thousand Oaks, CA: Sage.

Bies, R. J., & Tripp, T. M. (in press). Revenge in organizations: The good, the bad, and the ugly. In R. W. Griffin, A. O'Leary Kelly, & J. Collins (Eds.), *Dysfunctional behavior in organizations, Vol. 1: Violent behaviors in organizations.* Greenwich, CT: JAI.

Dumaine, B. (1993, October 18). America's toughest bosses. *Fortune*, 39–50.

Gilliom, J. (1997). Everyday surveillance, everyday resistance: Computer monitoring in the lives of the Appalachian poor. In A. Sarat & S. S. Silbey (Eds.), *Studies in law, politics, and society* (Vol. 16, pp. 275–297). Greenwich, CT: JAI.

Glaser, B. G., & Strauss, A. L. (1967). *The discovery of grounded theory: Strategies for qualitative research.* New York: Aldine.

Goleman, D. (1986, December 28). When the boss is unbearable. *New York Times*, Section 3, pp. 1,29.

Handler, J. F. (1992). Postmodernism, protest, and the new social movements. *Law and Society Review*, 26, 697–732.

Hatch, M. J. (1997). *Organization theory: Modern, symbolic, and postmodern perspectives.* Oxford, UK: Oxford University Press.

Havel, V. (1985). The power of the power less. In J. Keane (Ed.), *The power of the powerless: Citizens against the state in central-eastern Europe.* Armonk, NY: M. E. Sharpe.

Hornstein, H. A. (1996). *Brutal bosses and their prey.* New York: Riverhead Books.

Lombardo, M. M., & McCall, M. W., Jr. (1984, January). The intolerable boss. *Psychology Today*, 44–48.

McLean Parks, J. (1997). The fourth arm of justice: The art and science of revenge. Lewicki, R. J. Bies, & B. H. Sheppard (Eds.), *Research on negotiation in organizations* (Vol. 6, pp. 113–144). Greenwich, CT: JAI.

Miller, D. E., Weiland, M. W., & Couch, C. J. (1978). Tyranny. In N. Denzin (Ed.), *Studies in symbolic interaction* (Vol. 1, pp. 267–288). Greenwich, CT: JAI.

Nord, W. R., & Doherty, E. M. (1994). Toward an improved the conflict process. In R. J. Lewicki, B. H. Sheppard, & R. J. Bies (Eds.), *Research on negotiation in organizations* (pp. 173–240). Greenwich, CT: JAI.

Nordhoff, C., & Hall, J. N. (1932). *Mutiny on the bounty.* Boston: Little, Brown.

Orwell, G. (1949). *1984.* New York: Harcourt Brace.

Pfeffer, J. (1992). *Managing with power.* Cambridge, MA: Harvard Business School.

Robinson, S. L., & Bennett, R. J. (1995). A typology of deviant work place behaviors: A multidimensional scaling study. *Academy of Management Journal*, 38, 555–572.

Scott, J. C. (1990). *Domination and the arts of resistance.* New Haven, CT: Yale University Press.

Scott, W. G., & Hart, D. K. (1971). The moral nature of man in organizations: A comparative analysis. *Academy of Management Journal*, 14, 255.

Scott, W. G., & Hart, D. K. (1979). *Organizational America: Can individual freedom survive within the security it promises?* Boston: Houghton Mifflin.

Shorris, E. (1981). *The oppressed middle: Politics of middle management (scenes from corporate life).* Garden City, NY: Anchor/Doubleday.

Treviño, L. K., & Bies, R. J. (1997). Through the looking glass: A normative manifest of organizational behavior. In C. L. Cooper & S. E. Jackson (Eds.), *Creating tomorrow's organizations: A handbook for future research in organizational behavior* (pp.439–452). London: Wiley.

Tripp, T. M., & Bies, R. J. (1997). What's good about revenge? The avenger's perspective. In R. J. Lewicki, R. J. Dies, & B. H. Sheppard (Eds.), *Research on negotiation in organizations* (Vol. 6, pp. 145–160). Greenwich, CT: JAI.

Weber, M. (1946). *From Max Weber: Essays in sociology* (H. H. Gerth & C. W. Mills, Eds.). New York: Oxford University Press.

Wouk, H. (1951). *The Caine mutiny.* Garden City, NY: Doubleday.

Chapter 19
When Cymbals Become Symbols

Conflict Over Organizational Identity Within a Symphony Orchestra

Mary Ann Glynn

Organizations, like individuals, have identities. Identities—in both instances—are the product of an interplay between how we are seen by others and how we see ourselves. Unlike individuals, however, who are the sole "owners" of their identities, an organizational identity belongs to all of its members; therefore, organizational identities may be contested or disputed in ways that an individual's identity is not.

Identity conflict in organizations is experienced at the level of individuals and groups, as each may champion a different view of what the organization is and should be, and make claims premised on those assumptions. These processes can be seen in this chapter, which looks at organizational identity conflict within a symphony orchestra. Glynn shows that, just as people's identities shape their actions and perceptions of the world, organizational identities influence how members experience their organization. Though intangible, organizational identity is an important ingredient in understanding organizational behavior and change.

Introduction

Symphony orchestras are "ensembles whose primary mission is public performance of those orchestral works generally considered to fall within the standard symphonic repertoire and whose members are compensated nontrivially for their services" (Allmendinger and Hackman 1996, p. 340). Orchestras are particularly important cultural institutions because they are one of the early organizational forms that produced and delivered art to the public (*Americanizing the American Orchestra* 1993, p. 2). However, while orchestras may be singular in their cultural contribution, they are multiprofessional in their identity.

Most cultural institutions have identities composed of contradictory elements because they contain actors (artisans and administrators) within the organization who come from different professions; as a result, different groups of actors cherish and promote different aspects of the organization's identity (Albert and Whetten 1985, Golden-Biddle and Rao 1997). Central identity elements in cultural institutions—artistic and utilitarian—hybridize the organization's identity because they colocate "two or more types that would not normally be expected to go together" (Albert and Whetten 1985, p. 270). Consequently, tension and conflict can erupt when, in response to environmental change or organizational retrenchment, one identity element is emphasized over another.

It is through their particular identity lens (artistic or utilitarian) that organizational actors, by virtue of their organizational position and/or professional affiliation, craft their particular definitions of institutional resources and core capabilities. The result is to problematize the definition of core capabilities for multiprofessional institutions. Resource-based analyses of the strategy formulation process routinely exhort managers to identify core capabilities and match them to available environmental opportunities (Prahalad and Hamel 1990). Typically, the definition of core capabilities is portrayed as rational, analytical, and impersonal (e.g., Amit and Shoemaker 1993), but this has often proven to be a mirage in practice. Wide variation exists in executives' perceptions of an organization's distinctive capabilities (Stevenson 1976); my research illuminates how identity dynamics within a cultural institution can account for such perceptual variations.

In this qualitative study, I investigate how discrete identity fields, i.e., sets of actors clustered around "socially constructed identities" (Hunt et al. 1994), affect the construction of an organization's resources and problematize the definition of core capabilities. I conducted fieldwork research at the Atlanta Symphony Orchestra (ASO), where latent rifts between musicians and administrators culminated in a pivotal event, the 1996 musicians' strike. Strikes by professionals in organizations constitute "environmental jolts" and reveal ". . . properties that were not so visible during more tranquil periods" (Meyer 1982, p. 516). While disharmonious elements of utility and ideology may coexist in "collaborative evolution" in the orchestra (*Americanizing the American Orchestra* 1993, p. 67), environmental jolts awaken slumbering differences, which become expressed as discord, conflict, and strife. . . .

Organizational Identity

Organizational identity is a key intangible aspect of any institution. It affects not only how an organization defines itself, but also how strategic issues and problems, including the definition of firm capabilities and resources, are defined and resolved (e.g., Dutton and Dukerich 1991, Dutton et al. 1994, Dutton 1997). A statement of organizational identity consists of three *claims:* "the criterion of *claimed* central character . . . the criterion of *claimed* distinctiveness . . . [and] the criterion of *claimed* temporal continuity" (Albert and Whetten 1985, p. 265, emphases added). Developing an organization's identification can be construed as a *claim-making process* about those organizational attributes that are central, distinctive and enduring. Lending support to this perspective are Ashforth and Mael's (1996) notion that "claim" relates organizational identity to strategy, and Porac et al.'s (1999) definition of identity construction as "an explicit claim that an organization is of a particular type."

Research on the sociology of social problems reveals how claim-making activities construct problems, particularly when problems are contentious. Spector and Kitsuse (1977) conceive of social problems as claim-making activities, such that claims are definitional activities that arise around issues that groups of people find troublesome. Claim-making is a rhetorical activity, typically conducted by a group of social actors to persuade an audience to accept their construction of a problem as legitimate and, thus, their proffered solution (Best 1989). Claims derive from an underlying ideological script (Wolfgang 1996) which is reinforced in language and by the mass media, both of which are important devices in articulating claims (Fritz and Altheide 1987).

In the sociological literature, claim-making has been studied in a wide variety of contexts. For instance, Gerber and Short (1986) demonstrate how activists used the press to problematize a previously nonproblematic issue, i.e., the marketing of infant formula in less developed countries; public claims from organizational outsiders gained attention and generated pressure on corporations to change. In studying the emergence of child custody laws, Coltrane and Hickman (1992, p. 400) investigated how the claim-making of fathers' rights groups evoked counterclaims by mothers' groups; they found that claim-making activities of both groups involved rhetorical strategies that included "horror stories, numeric estimates, and an implied social consensus." Mulcahy (1995) investigated the 1981 Northern Irish hunger strike as a claim-making activity in which prisoners constructed their identities as legitimate political actors rather than terrorists. Goodrick et al. (1997) examined the role of physicians' claims in hospitals' ideological shift from social welfare to business-management.

As is evident from this research, claims can originate from social actors who coalesce around an issue, and/or from professional (or occupational) groups who may have a vested interest in an issue. The role of professional groups in making claims on organizations has been recognized (e.g., Goodrick et al. 1997). Professionals institutionalize expertise in a bid to garnish legitimacy through the formalization of work (Abbott 1991). In other words,

> At the simplest level, institutionalization of expertise means the emergence of a set of rules for handling it, a set of roles to play relative to it, and arrangements of those norms and roles into larger structures—organizations for delivering expert services, hierarchies of types of expertise, routines for reproducing expertise, and so on. (Abbott 1991, p. 20)

Logical systems, ideological values, and knowledge stores that attempt to monopolize a body of cultural capital govern professions or expertise from which rents can be extracted (Abbott 1991, p. 28). Thus, professionals have a stake in maintaining their identity in a professional field, and claiming a set of identity attributes that can be used to their advantage in society and/or in the marketplace of business.

When an organization is characterized by multiprofessionality (Abbott 1991) and multiplicity in identity, intergroup conflict often emerges; claims and counterclaims over the organization's identity are made in an effort to legitimate certain groups over others, thereby defining firm capabilities in ways that advantage them. Identity dynamics are wedded to the social context in which such groups situate their claims (Markson 1989). This sociological perspective on claim-making, when applied to cultural institutions, potentially offers an explanation as to why variations in the construction of core capabilities exist within organizations. More than that, it raises interesting questions concerning how core capabilities and resources may be contested and changed over time.

The identity of cultural organizations is specialized or ideographic; contradictory identity elements—normative artistry and utilitarian economics—coexist and are claimed by different units within the organization (Albert and Whetten 1985, p. 271). In the symphony orchestra, for instance, musicians enact the normative identity and administrators (managers and board members) enact the utilitarian identity, which is "governed by values of economic rationality, the maximization of profit, and the minimization of cost" (Albert and Whetten 1985, pp. 281–282). The multifaceted, complex nature of the symphony's identity is further elaborated in, and reinforced by, the existence of different professional groups within the orchestra. Musicians have a professional identity as performance artists and union members (The American Federation of Musicians, AFM); orchestra executives are somewhat under-professionalized, lacking certification (but seeking it), and trying to combine both business skills and artistic training, since many are former musicians. For board members, the symphony board is largely a secondary affiliate, following after their primary occupation (e.g., law, business, medicine).

The pluralism of the organization's identity is encoded institutionally, in both symbol and structure. Symbolically, utilitarian values are encoded in the bottom line, and ideological values are encoded in musical icons—cymbals—that are potent reminders of the orchestra's normative identity. For instance, the Boston Symphony Orchestra, as part of its identity, adopted a logo featuring a stylized gold horn (Selame and Selame 1985). The symbolic differences are further reinforced by the symphony's structure, which has been characterized as rigid, isolating orchestra members from each other

(*Americanizing the American Orchestra* 1993, p. 177). Its organization has been likened to a three-legged stool, consisting of the executive director, board chair, and music director/conductor. The musicians have no formal role in the leadership structure, and their voices often emerge through other institutional forms, such as the union.

Given the differences that exist structurally and symbolically in the orchestra, conflict between ideological elements in the organization's identity seems almost inevitable. Particularly during periods of organizational retrenchment or crisis, latent identity conflicts erupt (Albert and Whetten 1985). This occurs because groups resist attempts to label their particular function or activity as peripheral, preferring instead to champion their own group's identity and, indirectly, to promote selected elements of the hybrid organizational identity to the exclusion of others. I argue that the ideology embedded in identity claims filters organizational members' perceptions of firm resources, and thus affords a partial explanation for the observed variations in the definition of core capabilities that can be used for competitive advantage.

Research Methodology

Research Setting

The Atlanta Symphony Orchestra (ASO) was founded in 1947. For its first quarter-century, it grew in prominence as a regional orchestra and is today ranked among the top 10 orchestras in the United States. The ASO is housed under a cultural umbrella, the Woodruff Arts Center (which also encompasses the High Museum of Art, the Atlanta College of Art, and the Alliance Theater Company), whose founding concept was "not just to advance the arts, but to use the arts to advance Atlanta" (Rice 1994, p. 17). From early in its history, the dual chords of artistry and utility have resonated within the ASO.

The ASO consists of 95 full-time musicians and a conductor/artistic director, a 72-member board of directors (58% male), and a 44-member administration, which includes administration (16), artistic administration (6), development (11), and marketing and public relations (9). The 1996 musicians' strike took place over a 10-week period (September 22–December 4). This year was "an unusually stormy year for orchestras nationally" (Gay 1997, p. 1). Although the issues were different for every orchestra—in Philadelphia, it was recording contracts; in San Francisco, health benefits; and in Atlanta, wages and weeks of employment—the form these disagreements between musicians and administrators took was the same: a musicians' strike.

The ASO strike centered on the terms of a new musicians' contract and, in particular, on salary and working conditions. A key event precipitating the strike was management's decision not to tenure six probationary ASO musicians due to lack of finances, in spite of their having satisfied tenure standards of musical quality. The board, in explaining its decision, emphasized elements of the orchestra's economic identity (i.e., budget constraints and financial resources) at the expense of musical standards. In opposing the decision, musicians emphasized the normative identity, citing the need to improve artistic quality by playing challenging pieces which necessitated more, rather than fewer, players. When musicians' claims failed to persuade the board to change their decision, they initiated a strike to make their claims clearer and more unavoidable. A chronology of the strike and the precipitating and ensuing events is depicted in the Appendix.

Data Collection

An in-depth, qualitative methodology was used because it is effective in investigating sensitive matters, such as conflict (Kumar et al. 1993, Mouly and Sankaran 1997). Guided by earlier research (Mulcahy 1995, Coltrane and Hickman 1992, Allmendinger and Hackman 1995), two data sources were used: (1) semistructured interviews and (2) archival documents and press accounts.

Semistructured Interviews. Thirteen interviews were conducted (ten during the strike and three within the three months afterward), with the following individuals: three musicians, three board members, two managers, three audience members/subscribers, a music critic (who regularly reported on the ASO), and an industry expert and member of the American Symphony Orchestra League. . . .

Archival Sources. Published information about the ASO was reviewed, including materials generated by the musicians (e.g., ASOPA News, official bulletin of the Atlanta

Symphony Orchestra Players Association), press releases, leaflets/pamphlets distributed to audiences and the public, and materials generated by management and the board (i.e., reports, press releases, and advertising). . . .

The Atlanta Symphony Orchestra Strike

1. Backdrop for the Strike: The Conflicting Identities of Artistry and Utility

ASO Artistic Identity. Musicians felt that there were two sets of claims on the ASO identity: one which they claimed to espouse ("a world-class orchestra in a world-class city") and another which they claimed to be espoused by management ("the best orchestra *we can afford*"). Implied in these identity claims are technological competency and orchestral excellence in the former and financial capabilities in the latter.

Several musicians opined that, over the last 30 years, they had witnessed increasing polarization between management and musicians. Musicians acknowledged that the orchestra needed to negotiate a balance between an "idealistic, musical vision-driven perspective" (theirs) and the "revenue-driven, fiscally realistic view" (claimed to be management's). They testified to an ever-widening gulf in the aesthetic orientation of the two groups. Twenty or 30 years ago, the ASO board consisted largely of an "old guard" of doctors and lawyers who were not necessarily "big money" but were "lovers of music." More recently, the board shifted to embody a "corporate mentality," seemingly driven by increasing numbers of business people who became members. As a result, musicians claimed that there was an increasing focus on bottom-line expenditures with a fondness for what musicians described, in derogatory tones, as "McKinsey-like" presentations, briefings, reports, and "indoctrination." An article in the local press expressed the views of an ASO violinist, who spoke for many musicians:

> [ASO management is] looking at the orchestra like it was a potato chip factory. . . . A potato chip factory can have a good product with fewer workers, with automation and all. But in an orchestra, the product is the sum of the musicians. . . . I'm not even sure management knows what quality is. Otherwise, they

wouldn't be playing Russian roulette with us. (Kindred 1996, p. C3).

Themes of mistrust, disillusionment, and hurt resonated through the musicians' rhetoric. To the musicians, the orchestra's artistic identity did not seem to be appreciated or understood by the board; their musical prowess ("skilled as surgeons") was not acknowledged as a key and unique resource which could be claimed by no other group, and especially not by the board. As one musician put it: "I don't know anyone who has ever bought a ticket to attend a board meeting" (*Americanizing the American Orchestra* 1993, p. 67). One ASO player summed it up:

[Board members] are not really interested in socializing with us. Their level of wealth and power, community stature is so high. It's a whole 'nother world that isn't going to let us in. They're not interested in bringing us into that world. We're musicians, we play music. We make it look easy—only 20 hours a week and 8 weeks vacation—but they have no understanding of what it took to get here, the level of commitment it takes to continue here.

While contesting the control that the ASO administration held over their artistry, the musicians felt they controlled an important intangible resource: board members' reputations.

The musicians had something the board wanted—their reputation as altruistic people. [Board members] hate being made to look bad; that's why they're on the board—to look good.

Thus, with their rhetoric, the musicians claimed the artistic identity of the ASO, while downplaying (and often denigrating) its utilitarian or economic identity. Commensurate with their identity claims, they defined core capabilities and resources in terms of intangibles, i.e., musical talent and artistic enterprise, which in turn would draw board members who wanted to identify themselves as patrons of the arts. As Becker (1953) noted, within the musical profession there is inherent conflict between aesthetic autonomy and employment opportunities. At the ASO, professional tensions over identity were exacerbated in the contest for organizational identity.

ASO Economic Identity. To a person, administrators expressed enthusiasm and support for the musical caliber of the orchestra,

and were confident that musical performance was on a very high level. In spite of this, however, they cautioned that musical excellence alone would not overcome budgetary problems; finances were key, they claimed.

Board members emphasized that they did not take the attitude of "play well and (the audience) will come." Said one board member: "It will take more than great playing to get ASO into financial shape." They pointed out several environmental changes that would affect ongoing financial support for the ASO (for example, an industry in decline, a "graying" audience base, decreasing recording contract opportunities, and diminishing government funding for the arts). These perceptions were substantiated in an external research report, *The Financial Condition of Symphony Orchestras*, distributed to board members, which noted that "sustaining the economic vitality of orchestras has become a growing and difficult problem for the field" (*Americanizing the American Orchestra* 1993, pp. 4–5). Like other orchestras, the ASO had been accumulating a significant structural deficit. According to one board member:

The amount of money available from the endowment, coupled with the usual fund giving, coupled with ticket sales, coupled with extraordinary incidental items that come up, year in, year out, run half a million dollars. And had done so eight out of the last nine years.

Compounding these financial issues were concerns that musicians were insular and ignorant of such environmental changes. Administrators felt musicians needed to temper their view of ASO as a "world-class orchestra" and, instead, condition their expectations on what *"we can afford."* Administrators claimed that musicians were suspicious and mistrustful about the financial picture; musicians counterclaimed that the orchestra had received a multimillion dollar grant and had done costly but largely cosmetic (and unaesthetic) renovations to the symphony hall. This was money they felt could have been put directly into musical development. The board rebutted by giving limited financial information; any more, they claimed, would be "too complex" for musicians to understand. More generally, the board seemed to resent musicians' inquiry into the financial picture because they felt this questioned their province of professional expertise, as well as their motives. In the words of one board member:

> We serve selflessly . . . what do we get out of it? We're looking out for their best interests. The musicians got the details (on financial issues) but they lacked the expertise to understand it. The (financial) information was out there; I felt my questions were answered and nothing left room for suspicion, but the musicians were suspicious. Musicians had an inability to accept that the money had to have come from somewhere. Musicians didn't want to understand the financial picture because then they couldn't make the demands they were making.

Overall, musicians and administrators claimed different elements of the orchestra's identity while simultaneously and emphatically downplaying other elements. The construction of organizational resources and capabilities was shaped and articulated by their identity claims. Each group made resource claims consonant with their capabilities: musicians claimed to control intangible, reputational resources and administrators claimed tangible, financial resources. These differing identity claims embedded and fueled the dynamics of the musicians' strike.

2. The 1996 Musician's Strike: Conflict Over Identity

The rhetoric surrounding the contest for institutional identity and resources is outlined in Table 1, which presents the perspectives of musicians and administrators, respectively.

"Keep Your Symphony World Class." The musicians claimed that the issue of vision or identity was central to the strike, and described ASO as lacking' 'a common vision." When striking musicians rejected a "final" contract proposed by ASO management, the ASO Players' Association president, Doug Sommer explained their rationale:

> We are happy that management has finally chosen after nine months to engage in meaningful negotiations. However, we cannot accept management's proposal because it does not satisfy our vision of the public's vision for the future of the ASO (Kindred 1996).

Thus, musicians' rhetoric invoked the ideology of musical excellence, as well as their alignment with the music-loving public, which had important cultural capital and consequence.

Musicians claimed that their strike was lofty and ambitious; they were striking for "the future of the orchestra, the future of collective bargaining processes." They felt it absurd to believe the strike was about money; they insisted it was about working conditions, wage scales, and season length. They were skeptical about the administration's ability to meet their needs, claiming that "if we had negotiated the contract, management would ask for a salary freeze." Moreover, if they waited until they had sufficient funding for salary increases, musicians would never get raises.

My interviews with musicians uncovered strong emotions in their rhetoric. Musicians claimed management portrayed them as "money-grubbing weasels" who played the "union card," an image that they felt management pushed hard because it was unattractive. The musicians countered by saying "we do our job" but that management didn't do theirs; ironically, the musicians claimed, administrators "needed incentives to raise money." Thus, implicit in their logic of identity were not only the capabilities they claimed, but also those that they distinctively disavowed; for the musicians, this was fundraising. More than that, in claiming their identity, musicians seemed to deny ASO administrators theirs.

The musicians claimed to be driven by ideals and an "incredibly unified Orchestra." What few differences there were among the musicians were at the fringe; some musicians became more militaristic or more managerially oriented, while others withdrew from the conflict. The musicians described several tactics they used to keep their membership of a singular mind: one involved collecting and disseminating information (updates, surveys, etc.) and another involved playing music. They gave free, impromptu concerts on the streets, in malls, and in public places in the city; they also joined with players from other orchestras (Philadelphia, Pittsburgh, Baltimore, and Montreal) who came to Atlanta to play. One musician explained: "We're musicians and we need to play." This helped to maintain their professional identity, and to alleviate feelings of isolation, idleness, and frustration ("keep the members busy"), thus decreasing the chance that musicians might

Table 19.1
Claims of Organizational Identity, Resources, and Core Capabilities: 1996 Atlanta Symphony Orchestra Strike

	Organizational Identity	Resources Emphasized	Claims of What Core Capability Is	Claims of What Core Capability Is Not
Part A: The Musicians' Perspective				
Claims Made	Normative: "Idealistic, music-driven" "Musicians wanted to take a stand for American orchestras"	Aesthetic vitality of the orchestra: —increased size —more tenured musicians —"top ten" orchestra quality	Producer of high-quality classical music	
Conflict with Management	"(ASO management is) looking at the orchestra like it was a potato chip factory"			Not in business of fund-raising, marketing, etc.
Part B: The ASO Management and Board Perspective				
Claims Made	Utilitarian: "Organization of an orchestra is not dissimilar from business. The product is music . . . fiscal stability is crucial." "The issue is always money."	Major donors and foundations Subscribers and consumers Community Recording Contracts Volunteers	Low-cost, community responsive producer of classical music	
Conflict with Musicians	"It's not just that we're having a test of wills, we are talking about whether or not you could write a prospectus about this organization that says it's a going concern."	"It will take more than great playing to get ASO into financial shape."		Not adaptive to a changing, uncertain environment

migrate to management's view. In many ways, these tactics seemed to be deliberate identity strategies employed by musicians to keep their professional ideology intact, particularly in the absence of the usual behavioral cues (e.g., playing as an orchestral member in concert). Such identity-preserving strategies helped to solidify their framing of the strike as an ideological issue, one that involved musical quality rather than financial concerns. Furthermore, it also increased their emphasis on resources consonant with this identity.

Receiving neither resources nor other support from administrators, the musicians reached out to their audience. When tensions began in early spring, with negotiations underway and musicians upset about the firing of six of them, they began to "leaflet" audiences at concerts. The musicians hired a public affairs consultant, partly to counter the in-house public relations staff that worked with ASO management, but more importantly, to get their views out to the local press. They ran this outreach like a political campaign, concentrating on getting the attention of the mayor of Atlanta to help salvage "Gospel Christmas" and raising concerns about the possibility of canceling popular holiday concerts (at which point, musicians claimed, the administration would look like "grinches"). In addition, the musicians helped to find the first 20 members for a public support group, which became an energetic and committed force on behalf of the musicians.

The many free public concerts offered around Atlanta (for example, lunch hour concerts at a local food court, and others at different local performing arts centers) garnered a favorable response from the press:

The Atlanta Symphony Orchestra musicians have not sat idly by during their current strike for a new and better contract. They've given the public a chance to hear them at sites other than Symphony

Hall. . . . And they've afforded an opportunity to showcase just how good individual players in the orchestra are (Henry 1996).

Thus, by invoking their professional identity, the musicians were able to present their views favorably and find support and credibility with the community. They appeared somewhat successful in persuading audiences to see the strike from their ideological perspective and in framing the strike as artistry versus economics. Thus, they seemed to be seeking the power that came from the sanctioning of their values and the legitimation of their ideology (Clegg 1987). Embedded within the identity conflict were conflicts over status and power, and implicitly, control over the resources that would confer such status and power.

"The issue is always money." The board rationalized its decision not to tenure the six musicians as "a very tough business decision . . . (we) didn't have any criticism of the players, (we) just didn't have the funds to tenure." In general, the board and management construed the strike as a business event, with money as the bottom line:

> The reason finances were the issue, and they were always the issue, and they were always the only issue, was because that was the problem (interview with board member).

The ASO president and CEO likened the orchestra to a business, where "the product is music; PR, marketing, development, finance, (special events)—all are different departments. The President reports to the board and the music director reports to the board," and there is a creative tension between balancing the budget and "creating the most excellent artistic production" that permeates the management of the orchestra. The rhetoric of administrators was couched in the language of business (Fine 1996), where efficiency was the coin of the realm. Administrators repeatedly stated that the strike was about management–labor relationships.

Administrators felt that musicians succeeded in their attempts to solicit sympathy from the public. One board member described newspaper articles as being "detrimental, biased, and misrepresenting the facts." The ASO president said she gave the musicians an "A" for press, for presenting a very elegant, unTeamsterlike image on the picket line, playing the French horn in fine attire. The board viewed the public support group (CSASO) as "labor agitators," a "union tool" that exerted an antagonistic, polarizing force in the strike.

While management could not voice the ideological rhetoric of musicians in their claims, they used a different tactic to legitimate their position. Management invoked prestigious expertise to lend credence to their perspective on ASO's identity. In one letter to subscribers, representatives wrote that from the board and management, the guardianship identity was invoked:

> It's not the board's responsibility (to protect the endowment and not use it as a cash fund). Yale Professor James Tobin said it best: "The trustees of an endowed institution are the guardians of the future against the claims of the present." (ASO open letter to all subscribers)

Overall, both the board and management seemed to see the conflict as a choice between collaboration and confrontation; they felt that musicians chose the latter because it was the one choice that would secure them the most money and a better contract. It is interesting to note that the board imputed their motives to musicians and saw the players as being "in it for the money." Thus, as much as the conflict was about claiming a particular identity and issue, it was about disclaiming another; the board disavowed the notion that musical quality was the *real* issue and the musicians correspondingly disavowed that finances were the *real* issue. As much, then, as this was a conflict over claims, it was also about disclaims, or claiming what the institution's core capabilities were *not*. The strike was ultimately settled in December 1996, when both sides agreed to a new contract and a new set of working conditions; in the end, both sides claimed victory.

3. Aftermath of the Strike: Negotiated and Reclaimed Identities

The strike inflicted several organizational wounds; however, its resolution created an overall desire for healing. As a result, some of the initial reaction following the strike was to unify the entire membership—musicians, managers, and board members—and claim a new, integrated, negotiated identity. A harpist for the ASO (one of the six newest tenured members) reflected this in her statement:

> I think the strike was a huge growing experience that forced us to crystallize our vision as an orchestra and how we want to be seen in the community. It sharpened my awareness of what it means to be a musician and what my responsibilities are (Henry 1997a).

In December, the holiday concerts resumed their schedule. The music director, Yoel Levi, expressed his relief that the strike was over and his hope that "now we can go back and be again a great orchestra and do what we are supposed to do, which is (perform) great music" (Henry 1997b).

However, there were lingering divisions. Each group, while affirming the newly negotiated reunification of the ASO, also reclaimed its own professional identity with its associated resources and capabilities. Nowhere was this more evident than in poststrike press coverage. One pediatrician who has been a subscriber and contributor for nearly three decades expressed his nonsupport for the perspective of ASO administrators:

> I feel the strike should have been settled earlier. Money was coming in from the public, and the orchestra had done a wonderful job, and deserved more (money). I feel the board was very cavalier (in its handling of the situation). (Henry 1997b).

Musicians returned to work a bit more wise, if not a bit more wary. For their part, management and board members also found support in the press, which helped them to reclaim their custodial and financial identities. Scathing criticism of musicians and orchestral strikes in general was evidenced in one *Wall Street Journal* article, where the author argued that support from the National Endowment for the Arts (NEA) has actually had destructive effects on symphonies. He perceived that musicians benefit from a pro-union bias in NEA's grant-making procedures:

> . . . musicians' unions may be less visible in direct NEA lobbying efforts, but they are ever more powerful in the industry generally. Union ideology—the idea that only those who join the club should be paid to perform—pervades all big-city music establishments and the entire grant-giving culture, including that of the NEA. The American Federation of Musicians (slogan: "We're the Professionals!") has a cartel-like lock on music performance in most major cities. Woe to those who are not members. (Ritenour 1997)

Identity conflicts were still much in evidence, even after the strike concluded. Newly negotiated contracts and ideologies of artistic excellence did not fully bridge the gap between the discordant identity elements.

> The symphony also has had to contend with unseemly contract negotiations last year with music director Yoel Levi that ended with a three-year contract renewal but an understanding that it would be his last—a termination widely understood to be not of Levi's choice. (Schwartz 1998a).

Ten months subsequent, "(in) a move almost without precedent in the history of American orchestras" (Schwartz 1998b), Levi withdrew his resignation and asked to continue beyond his current contract. Eventually acknowledging that the board forced Levi's resignation as a condition of renewing his contract (Schwartz 1998b), the board members voted not to accept his resignation withdrawal, ironically citing artistic issues.

How Identity Shapes Resource Claims

The ASO's ideographic identity, that of two seemingly incompatible dimensions of artistic excellence (at any cost) and fiscal solvency (at the expense of musical development), was claimed by two distinct ASO units, musicians and administrators, respectively. By implication, these claims on the organization's identity also claimed very different sets of resources. Claims on the aesthetic identity evoked resource claims consonant with artistry (e.g., expanding the size of the orchestra, tenuring more musicians, investing in more complex musical pieces, touring worldwide, hiring guest conductors, etc.); claims on the economic identity argued for a pecuniary strategy of resource deployment (e.g., cutting costs, increasing ticket prices, raising funds, growing the endowment, limiting the number of costly orchestra performances, etc.).

To explain how these different claim-making processes between units within the symphony orchestra shape the contest over core capabilities and account for variations in resource definition within the institution, I propose a model, presented in Figure 19.1.

The four elements that comprise the identity and strategic resource definition are: (1) professional or occupational identity in which professional and occupational memberships are differentiated only by degree of exclusivity and use of abstract knowledge (Abbott 1991), dimensions not significant for this study and thus not differentiated herein, (2) organizational identity, (3) strategic issue definition, and (4) claimed resources. Together, these four elements affect the definition of core organizational capabilities through two joint and interactive processes: *identification processes*, which bridge between professional identity (i.e., Who am I? What kind of professional role/position do I play in this organization?) and organizational identity (i.e., What kind of organization is this?), and *interpretative processes*, which relate the perception of strategic issues (e.g., fiscal crisis versus music quality) to the resources claimed to address these issues (e.g., cost-cutting versus orchestral development).

The Role of Identification Processes. It is through their professional and/or occupational affiliations that musicians and managers/board members *identify* with different elements of the organization's identity. Since identification is predicated on a perception of oneness between the self and the collective (Ashforth and Mael 1989), the process of identifying enables organizational members to reinforce their professional identity by advancing claims on the organization's identity elements that are congruent with their expertise and capabilities. For musicians, this involves emphasizing the aesthetic over the economic; as Becker (1951, p. 136) noted: "The most distressing problem in the career of the average musician is the necessity of choosing between conventional success and his 'artistic' standards." Identification is stronger when organizational members perceive a large overlap between those attributes that characterize their professional identity and those that characterize the organizational identity (Dutton et al. 1994).

Professions seek legitimacy in order to establish the "cultural authority" of their work; as Abbott (1991, p. 187) illustrates: "some professions employ the economic legitimations of profit, security, and economic growth. . . . Others legitimize their work with values like happiness, self-actualization, personal culture . . . beautiful music." To establish their legitimacy, administrators as a professional group tend to place more worth on economic values, while musicians as a professional group tend to place more worth on less tangible values. Thus, as evidenced in this study, within professional groups shared values and identities develop and are mutually reinforced through social interactions, the language of the professions, and the rhetoric of claim-making. However, across professional groups, the construction of organizational problems may not be clear and uncontested, but rather marked by divergent and sometimes contentious claims, which spring from different ideologies held by groups who occupy different institutional positions (Trice 1993, Weick 1995). Thus, different professional groups are likely to claim as legitimate different types of organizational problems; the type of problem they claim is likely to be one they can solve, thereby increasing their own legitimacy and prestige.

Evident in these identity dynamics are sociopolitical processes. Disputes over what type of organization this is—and thus, what type of solution remedies a problem—are resolved politically (Walsh and Fahey 1986). Whichever professional group has the power to resolve a problem comes to the fore (Pfeffer and Salancik 1978) and, with their expertise valued and ideology accepted, gains power and political clout (Clegg 1989). Armed with such political advantage, the group regulates meaning—and conveys this meaning in their rhetoric (Clegg 1987)—to claim identity elements valued by the group. Thus, professional and occupational rhetoric frames and

Figure 19.1

Identity, Resources, and Core Capabilities

voices identity claims for the institution (Fine 1996). Fiscal crises tend to empower those groups who traffic in the rationale of business, i.e., administrators (Fine 1996); crises of musical quality, however, shift power towards those musicians who can play better and more complex orchestral pieces. Thus, crises can prompt a shift in the perceived legitimacy of a professional group and its claimed ideology; as a result, the relative emphasis on one element of the organization's identity may shift to the direction of the claims made by those who can resolve the crisis.

The Role of Interpretive Processes. How strategic issues become noticed and associated with a set of resources is the process of *interpretation*. Interpretive or sense making processes give meaning to individual perceptions and behavior (Weick 1995), as well as direction to strategic initiatives (Dutton 1997; Gioia and Chittepeddi 1991). Once strategic issues are framed and categorized (Jackson and Dutton 1988), resources are aligned accordingly. In the ASO, strategic issues were perceived to be one of two types: musical quality or financial solvency. Depending upon which of these was invoked, different resources were emphasized; clearly, artistic growth would require more talent, more touring, more exposure to challenging musical works, and thus more funding. Conversely, making an organization fiscally viable, particularly in the short term, would argue against such an investment of resources and for taking more aggressive cost-cutting measures. Claiming concerns about "generational equity," one board member described his interpretation of issues and how that dictated the management of resources:

> You're not buying music for yourself. What you're trying to do is provide music for your grandchildren. And the idea that you're just going to invade the trust and go take the money out of the endowment because you want to pay the musicians now is really stealing from the musicians of tomorrow.... If you try that (and people have), your orchestra goes out of business.

How issues are defined affects resource definition. A few months before the strike, the ASO board developed a set of long-range projections and options for the orchestra. The board mapped the following three possible strategic options, estimated their costs, and planned to choose one of them:

1. *World-market focus*, a 105-member orchestra. This was the most expensive option (more than $100 million); one musician described it as "pie in the sky."

2. *Atlanta-market focus*, or the status quo, a 92-member orchestra, with a cost of approximately $30 million.

3. *Fiscally conservative*, with tight fiscal controls, players cut to 80, and reputation enhanced by innovative music and marketing.

Strategic issue options for the ASO, ranging from world-class to more limited status, were tightly linked to resource availability and support. One board member put it succinctly: These three options had "price tags" of "More, Same, or Less." The language of the board in framing these options (as different possibilities for *market* focus, rather than different possibilities for *musical* focus) seemed to reflect its interpretation of the issues.

The model proposed (Figure 19.1) depicts how the contest over core capabilities lies at the intersection of identification and interpretative processes in the orchestra. It is through one's identification of self and one's organization that interpretations are made about strategic issues and sets of resources. It was through their professional identities as musicians that ASO players sought to define the central issues as aesthetic and seek resources to invest in developing artistic tradition and excellence. Conversely, the ASO board identified themselves as selfless guardians who sought to preserve the ASO for future generations; thus, they defined issues such as financial viability for the long term and emphasized resources that were monetary, not musical.

Each of the four elements (professional identity, organizational identity, strategic issue definition, and emphasized resources) affects and is affected by the others to create a set of conditions that make it ripe for cultural institutions to experience conflict and contest over claims to the organization's core capabilities. Such a conflict over claims about identity, resources, and core capabilities was very much evident in the ASO musicians' strike.

Conclusions

This study of the 1996 musician's strike at the Atlanta Symphony Orchestra revealed that the definition of organizational identity has a significant effect on the perceptions of its core competencies. Like most cultural institutions, the ASO displayed a specialized or ideographic identity, whose dual elements of economic utility (where financial return symbolizes success) and normative ideology (where artistic creativity and excellence symbolize success) came into conflict during organizational retrenchment. The crisis engendered by the strike made manifest the latent identity claims that characterized the different units in the organization, as well as the professional status they embodied. Thus, the multifaceted identity of the symphony, reinforced by the organization's multi-professionality, evoked variations in the way that firm capabilities and resources were defined and problematized.

The professional ideologies of musicians and administrators were at odds over the orchestra's allocation of resources; consistent with the legitimating values of their profession, the musicians emphasized investment in artistry, and administrators, seeking a demonstration of fiscal responsibility, emphasized cost containment. Each group felt that their prestige, legitimization, and power to influence others rested on their ability to realize such outcomes. The inherent conflict between these two processional groups was reinforced by the formal organizational design at the symphony.

This study extends theories on the resource-based view of the firm to account for variations in the construction of core capabilities. The dynamics of institutional identity claims, which reflect the social identities of professional groups, were found to account for differentiation in resource definitions. Resource-based views of the firm presume that resource definition is nonproblematic (Prahalad and Hamel 1990). By showing how resource definition and core capabilities are problematized by identity conflicts, this study illustrates how resource identification is neither impersonal nor rational (Amit and Shoemaker 1993) but, rather, closely tied to the sociopolitical dynamics embedded within actors' identity spheres. When actors with multiple and divergent identities exist within the same institution, different resources can become defined as core competencies, and strategic decision making can become increasingly contentious; thus, conflicts of strategic definition and resolution can stem from conflicts over identity.

Strategic issue definitions emerged from distinct "identity fields" (Hunt et al. 1994). For the symphony, these corresponded to organizational roles and professional occupations. Competing resource claims premised on the different logics underlying different identity elements led to conflict, especially during organizational crisis. When competing claims on organizational identity and, by implication, resource definition are advanced, conflict can be resolved through the logic of aggregation (bargaining) or the logic of integration (where parties learn from each other) (March and Olsen 1995). At the ASO, when integration failed, aggregation ensued, and its failure resulted in the musicians' strike. This research demonstrates how organizational identity can frame the manner in which resources become emphasized, prioritized, and deployed, and how perceptions of core capabilities can become constructed for the institution. Just as important, perhaps, was the insight that the same dynamics also determined perceptions of what the core capabilities were *not*.

Furthermore, this work suggests how an organization's identity may not be grounded simply in organizational images of what is central, enduring, and distinctive (Albert and Whetten 1985), but may also incorporate the identity dynamics of professional and occupational groups. Thus, identities of those individuals in key organizational roles (e.g., players, administrators, and board members) shape and construct the hybrid identities of the symphony. Because it incorporates such professional groups, the identity of this cultural institution is emergent from, and attenuated by, the interests that spring from these group identities. It is through the processes of identification, where professionals perceive an overlap between the profession's attributes and those of the organization, that group memberships affect the construction of core capabilities. Commensurately, these professional identity groups also direct attention towards particular definitions of strategic issues and resources and away from others; interpretative processes at the interface between issue definition and resource foci construct an institution's core capabilities.

Identity conflicts can occur among many issues in a wide variety of organizational contexts, but the conflict tends to be more salient in cultural organizations, often leading to polarization between professional groups. In other words, tension over identity conflict is more common among firms in cultural industries. . . .

Appendix
Chronology of the 1996 Musicians' Strike at the Atlanta Symphony Orchestra

Date	Description of Event and Impact
2/6/96	Six probationary ASO musicians not tenured for financial reasons; season cut to 48 weeks. Musicians feel this reflects management's "idiotic lack of understanding" and creates atmosphere of mistrust.
5/15/96	In response to infusion of new funds (gift of $4 million, with a $5 million challenge gift) and community outrage, the board recants and grants the six probationary musicians tenure. Negotiations for renewal of contract begin.
8/24/96	Musicians' contract expires.
Early Fall	Musicians hire a new attorney, who has a long history and strong reputation with union negotiations. Management and board view this as a strong signal of intent from the musicians.
9/21–9/23/96	Musicians vote to strike, walk out of negotiations, and begin to picket.
9/26/96	Last day musicians receive salary from ASO. ASO staff and the musical director are paid for the duration of the strike; striking musicians receive union compensation (initially, $150/week for not more than 15 weeks; increased to $300/week on Oct. 23, with a scheduled increase to $450/week when the strike enters the ninth week).
10/23/96	Offer and counteroffers made, as follows: *By management:* 1) 95 players minimum; 2) tenure trial of two years; and 3) new three-year contract with freeze in year one, and 2% raises for years two and three (0,2,2). *By musicians:* New four-year contract with a 3% raise years one and two, and a 4% raise in years three and four (3,3,4,4).
11/26/96	Musicians offer to return to work on condition that both sides submit to binding arbitration; board rejects their offer.
12/3/96	Proposal for new contract sent to board, with following terms: 1) 95 tenured orchestral positions, 2) outreach to metro Atlanta schools (with no additional compensation), 3) pension plan changed from an ASO managed plan to one managed by the union, and 4) new four-year contract with a wage freeze in the first year, a 2% increase for the second and third years, and 4% increase in the fourth year (0,2,2,4); in the final year, the lowest salary will be $62,500.
12/2/96	Musicians and management/board meet, without attorneys.

Date	Description of Event and Impact
12/4/96	Board votes to accept. The ten-week strike is settled and musicians return to work in time for the holiday events.
4/24/97	ASO musical director, Yoel Levi, negotiates a three-year extension on his contract, to expire the summer of 2000.
4/27/97	Yoel Levi announces his resignation in 2000, at the conclusion of his contract.
2/27/98	Yoel Levi asks to withdraw his resignation and stay beyond his contract.
3/10/98	At special meeting of the board of directors, the board votes not to accept Levi's resignation withdrawal, citing artistic issues.

References

Abbott, A. 1991. The future of professions: Occupation and expertise in the age of organization. In *Research in the Sociology of Organizations*, Vol. 8. JAI Press, Greenwich, CT, 17–42.

Albert, S., D. A. Whetten. 1985. Organizational identity. B. M. Staw, L.L. Cummings, eds. *Research in Organizational Behavior*, Vol. 7. JAI Press, Greenwich, CT, 263–295.

Allmendinger, J., J. R. Hackman. 1995. The more, the better? A four-nation study of the inclusion of women in symphony orchestras. *Social Forces* 74: 423–460.

——. 1996. Organizations in changing environments: The case of East German Symphony Orchestras. *Admin. Sci. Quart.* 41: 337–389.

The American Symphony Orchestra League. 1993. *Americanizing the American Orchestra, Report of the National Task Force for the American Orchestra: An initiative for change.* Washington, DC.

Amit, R., P. J. H. Shoemaker. 1993. Strategic assets and organizational rent. *Strategic Management J.* 14: 33–46.

Ashforth, B.E., F. E. Mael. 1989. Social identity theory and the organization. *Acad. Management Rev.* 14: 20–39.

——. 1996. Organizational identity and strategy as a context for the individual. J. A. C. Baum, J. E. Dutton, eds. *Advances in Strategic Management*, vol. 13. JAI Press, Greenwich, CT, 19–64.

Becker, H. S. 1951. The professional dance musician and his audience. *Amer. J. Soc.* 57: 136–144.

——. 1953. Some contingencies of the professional dance musician's career. *Human Organ.* Spring 22–26.

Best, J., ed. 1989. *Images of Issues: Typifying Contemporary Social Problems.* de Gruyter, Hawthorne, NY.

Clegg, S.R. 1987. The language of power and the power of language. *Organ. Stud.* 861–70.

——. 1989. Radical revisions: Power, discipline and organizations. *Organ. Stud.* 1097–115.

Coltrane, S., N. Hickman. 1992. The rhetoric of rights and needs: Moral discourse in the reform of child custody and support laws. *Social Problems* 39: 400–420.

Dutton, J. E. 1997. Strategic agenda building in organizations. S. Zur, ed. *Organizational Decision Making.* Cambridge University Press, Cambridge, U.K.

Dutton, J. E., J. M. Dukerich. 1991. Keeping an eye on the mirror: Image and identity in organizational adaptation. *Acad. Management J.* 34: 517–554.

Dutton, J. E., J. M. Dukerich, C. V. Harquail. 1994. Organizational images and member identification. *Admin. Sci. Quart.* 39: 239–263.

Fine, G. A. 1996. Justifying work: Occupational rhetorics as resources in restaurant kitchens. *Admin. Sci. Quart.* 41: 90–115.

Fritz, N. J., D. L. Altheide. 1987. The mass media and the social construction of the missing children problem. *Soc. Quart.* 28: 473–492.

Gay, W. L. 1997. Back in harmony: The Fort Worth Symphony and its musicians have settled their differences and are ready to get on with the future. *The Fort Worth Star-Tele-gram*, January 12.

Gerber, J., J. F. Short. 1986. Publicity and the control of corporate behavior: The case of infant formula. *Deviant Behavior.* 7 195216.

Gioia, D.A., K. Chittipeddi. 1991. Sensemaking and sensegiving in strategic change initiation. *Strategic Management J.* 12: 433–448.

Golden-Biddle, K., H. Rao. 1997. Breaches in the boardroom: Organizational identity and conflicts of commitment in a nonprofit organization. *Organ. Sci.* 8: 593–611.

Goodrick, E., J. R. Meindl, A. B. Flood. 1997. Business as usual: The adoption of managerial ideology by U.S. hospitals. *Res. Soc. Health Care* 14: 27–50.

Henry, D. 1996. Music of striking ASO players resounds outside Symphony Hall. *The Atlanta Journal and Constitution.* Oct. 20.

———. 1997a. Carnegie gig focuses ASO on its mission. *The Atlanta Journal and Constitution.* February 5.

———. 1997b. June 1 is ASO deadline for refunds, exchanges. *The Atlanta Journal and Constitution.* April 10.

Hunt, S.A., R. D. Benford, D. A. Snow. 1994. Identity fields: Framing processes and the social construction of movement identities. E. Larene, J. Johnston, R. Gurfield, eds. *New Social Movements: From Ideology to Identity.* Temple University Press, Philadelphia, PA, 185–207.

Jackson, S., J. E. Dutton. 1988. Discerning environmental threats and opportunities. *Admin. Sci. Quart.* 33: 370–387.

Kindred, D. 1996. Violinist tries to keep her chin up. *The Atlanta Journal and Constitution.* Oct. 9.

Kumar, N., L. W. Stern, J. C. Anderson. 1993. Conducting interorganizational research using key informants. *Acad. Management J.* 36: 1633–1651.

March, I. G., J. P. Olsen. 1995. *Rediscovering Institutions.* Free Press, New York.

Markson, S.L. 1989. Claims-making quasi-theories and the social construction of the rock and roll menace. Paper presented at the American Sociological Association, San Francisco, CA.

Meyer, A.D. 1982. Adapting to environmental jolts. *Admin. Sci. Quart.* 27: 515–537.

Mouly, V.S., J. K. Sankaran. 1997. On the study of settings marked by severe superior-subordinate conflict. *Organ. Stud.* 18: 175–192.

Mulcahy, A. 1995. Claims-making and the construct of legitimacy: Press coverage of the 1981 Northern Irish hunger strike. *Social Problems* 42: 449–467.

Pfeffer, J., G. R. Salancik. 1978. *The External Control of Organizations: A Resource Dependence Perspective.* Harper and Row, New York.

Porac, J. F., J. B. Wade, T. G. Pollock. 1999. Categorization and identity in CEO compensation: The politics of the comparable firm. *Admin. Sci. Quart.* 44: 112–144.

Prahalad, C.K., G. Hamel. 1990. The core competence of the corporation. *Harvard Bus. Rev.* 68 (May–June) 79–91.

Rice, B. R., ed. 1994. *Atlanta History: A Journal of Georgia and the South.* Special issue: A History of the Woodruff Arts Center, 38 (1–2).

Ritenour, S. 1997. How subsidiaries kill symphonies. *The Wall Street Journal,* April 8.

Saporta, M. 1997. Arts chief ready to wear his "change agent" hat. *The Atlanta Journal and Constitution.* March 25.

Schwartz, J. 1998a. Classical contrast: As popularity of opera soars, symphony sales doggedly decline. *The Atlanta Journal-Constitution.* January 4.

———. 1998b. ASO's Levi asks to stay. *The Atlanta Journal-Constitution.* February 27.

Selame, J., E. Selame. 1985. Corporate identity: Fund raising marketing tool. *Fund Raising Management.* 16: 96, 98.

Spector, M., J. Kitsuse. 1987. *Constructing Social Problems.* Aldine de Gruyter, Hawthorne, NY.

Stevenson, H. 1976. Defining corporate strengths and weaknesses. *Sloan Management Rev.* 17 (Spring) 51–68.

Trice, H.M. 1993. *Occupational Subcultures in the Workplace.* ILR Press, Ithaca, NY.

Walsh, J., L. Fahey. 1986. The role of negotiated belief structures in strategy making. *J. Management* 12: 325–338.

Weick, K.E. 1995. *Sensemaking in Organizations.* Sage, Thousand Oaks, CA.

Wolfgang, W. 1996. Family values: The construction of an intellectual movement. Paper #96S32529, American Sociological Association, New York.

Part II

Inside Organizations

Demography, Inequality, and Social Networks

Chapter 20
Cultural Diversity at Work

The Effects of Diversity Perspectives on Work Group Processes and Outcomes

Robin J. Ely and
David A. Thomas

How does diversity impact the functioning of a work group? Organizational researchers from many different disciplines have sought an answer to this question and have concluded that the best one is "it depends." Diversity takes many forms and its impact depends in part on what kind of diversity is being examined. In addition, research suggests that how diversity shapes work groups depends on several other aspects of the work group and the organization of which it is a part.

Ely and Thomas draw on this research as a way to identify the factors that best explain the conditions under which work group diversity will enhance or detract from group functioning. They are less interested in one specific form of diversity (e.g., racial diversity, gender diversity, etc.) than they are in understanding the impact of the more general category of "cultural diversity." Based on their analyses of culturally diverse work groups in three firms, Ely and Thomas conclude that work groups often have different orientations to diversity and that these orientations greatly affect its impacts on the group.

American management literature, both popular (e.g., Thomas, 1991; Morrison, 1992) and scholarly (e.g., Jackson et al., 1992; Cox, 1993), is rife with advice that managers should increase workforce diversity to enhance work group effectiveness. Empirical research on whether and how diversity is actually related to work group functioning is limited, however, and the evidence is mixed, depending in part on what kinds of differences constitute the "diversity" in question (see Milliken and Martins, 1996; Pelled, 1996, for reviews). Researchers have examined the impact of diversity in identity group memberships, such as race and sex (e.g., Cox, 1993; Jackson and Ruderman, 1995); organizational group memberships, such as hierarchical position or organizational function (e.g., Bantel and Jackson, 1989; Ancona and Caldwell, 1992); and individual characteristics, such as idiosyncratic attitudes, values, and preferences (e.g., Hoffman, 1959; Meglino, Ravlin, and Adkins, 1989; Bochner and Hesketh, 1994). Although certain types of diversity appear to be beneficial, studies focused on race and gender have demonstrated both positive and negative outcomes (see Williams and O'Reilly, 1998, for review), suggesting that certain conditions may moderate these outcomes. To date, however, most scholars have only speculated as to what these conditions might be. As a result, consultants and managers interested in diversity have had to rely largely on some combination of common sense and good faith for the rationales they advance about why and how companies should address the issue.

We set out to develop theory, grounded in people's experiences in culturally diverse work groups, about the conditions under which diversity enhances or detracts from work group functioning. From our research, we identified three different perspectives on workforce diversity that people embrace, each with different implications for a work group's ability to realize the benefits of its cultural diversity. We use these observations here to examine critically some of the themes and basic assumptions of previous research and to propose new directions for both researchers and practitioners interested in diversity.

Diversity is a characteristic of groups of two or more people and typically refers to demographic differences of one sort or another among group members (McGrath, Berdahl, and Arrow, 1995). Researchers have generated numerous dimensions for classifying demographic differences, often positing different outcomes for people and work groups, depending on the degree and nature of those differences. Pelled (1996) made one set of predictions about the impact of racial diversity among group members and another about the impact of functional background diversity, based on the visibility of race and the job-relatedness of functional background. Others have distinguished among the effects of diversity depending on whether differences are cultural (Cox, 1993; Larkey, 1996), physical (Strangor et al., 1992), inherent and immutable (Maznevski, 1994), or role-related (Maznevski, 1994; Pelled, 1996).

Perhaps more importantly, researchers' predictions about any one diversity variable differ depending on which of its dimensions they see as critical to determining its impact. Pelled (1996) predicted that racial diversity, as a source of visible differences, would incite intergroup bias and lead to negative outcomes for work groups, while Cox, Lobel, and McLeod (1991) predicted that racial diversity, as a source of cultural differences, would enhance creative problem solving and lead to positive outcomes for work groups. Maznevski (1994) suggested that racial diversity, as a source of inherent and immutable differences would provide groups with different kinds of information from which they could potentially benefit, but such differences would often be difficult for parties to understand and accept. As these examples illustrate, both the types and dimensions of demographic variables in which one is interested shape one's inquiry.

In this research, the demographic variables in which we were interested include race, ethnicity, sex, social class, religion, nationality, and sexual identity, all of which contribute to cultural identity. According to Cox (1993), cultural identities stem from membership in groups that are socioculturally distinct. They are often associated with particular physical (e.g., skin color), biological (e.g., genitalia), or stylistic (e.g., dress) features, though these may be more or less identifiable, depending in part on people's choices about whether and how they wish to be identified by others. Members of a cultural identity group tend to share certain worldviews (Alderfer and Smith, 1982); norms, values, goal priorities, and sociocultural heritage (Cox, 1993). The cultural markers of such groups can be communicated through communication style, rules, shared meaning, and even dialects or languages, which others may or may not recognize as culturally linked (Larkey, 1996). The degree to which one personally identifies with one's cultural identities and the value one places on them vary across cultural groups and across members within cultural groups (Cox, 1993; Thomas, 1993; Ely, 1995; Ragins 1997). Moreover, a person may vary in the degree to which he or she identifies with, values, or expresses a particular cultural identity at any given time, depending on the salience and meaning of that identity in the context within which he or she is operating (Ely, 1995; Larkey, 1996). Hence, cultural identity, as we understand it, is socially constructed, complex, and dynamic.

In addition, cultural identities are associated in the larger society with certain power positions, such that some cultural identity groups have greater power, prestige, and status than others (e.g., Ridgeway and Berger, 1986; Nkomo, 1992; Ragins, 1997). In Western society, men as a group are more powerful—have higher status and hold more positions of formal organizational and political power—than women as a group; similarly, whites are more powerful than people of color; Christians are more powerful than Jews; presumed heterosexuals are more powerful than gays, lesbians, and bisexuals; and the middle, upper-middle, and upper classes are more powerful than the working and lower classes.

There is much theoretical and empirical support for the notion that paying attention to differences in power and status is critical for understanding diversity in organizations. In Alderfer's (1987) theory of intergroup relations, for example, the distribution of power among cultural identity groups, both inside the organization and in the larger society, is key to how people think, feel, and behave at work. Similarly, proponents of status characteristics theory (Ridgeway, 1988; 1991) argue that much of what we think of as the effects of membership in particular identity groups, such as race or sex, are in fact produced by the status value our society ascribes to those groups. In organizations, status differentials are reinforced when higher-status identity groups are disproportionately represented in positions of organizational authority and are challenged when they are not (Alderfer, 1987; Lau and Murnighan, 1998). Perceptions of one's relative status in the organization, in turn, influence one's expectations and behaviors. Empirical evidence showing differential impacts of race and sex as a function of the social status accorded different race and sex groups supports the general position these theories advance that to understand the impact of cultural diversity in work groups, one must consider the relative power positions of cultural groups both in and outside of the organization (e.g., Ruhe and Eatman, 1977; Zimmer, 1988; Tsui, Egan, and O'Reilly, 1992).

By casting the demographic variables of interest in this study as aspects of cultural identity, the meaning and consequences of which are socially constructed and dynamic, we were well positioned to consider the role that different work group conditions might play in shaping whether and how cultural diversity influences work group functioning. This approach, together with attention to organizational and societal power differences between cultural identity groups, structured our conceptual framing of diversity.

Diversity and Work Group Functioning

Researchers interested in the impact of demography on individual and group behavior in organizations have taken several different approaches, two of which are especially relevant to our work. The first involves research on how the proportional representation of certain demographic groups influences those traditionally in the minority. The second involves research on the effects of group composition on outcomes related to work group effectiveness.

Effects of proportional representation. Much of the literature on proportional representation has focused on the question of whether increasing the number of traditionally underrepresented groups, such as white women and people of color, has a positive or negative impact on members of those groups. Some theorists have argued that increased numbers of women, for example, should lead to greater contact between men and women (Blau, 1977), less stereotyped perceptions of women (Kanter, 1977), and less spillover from sex roles to work roles (Gutek, 1985); hence, discrimination against women should subside as their numbers increase. This line of reasoning suggests that increasing the numbers of people in traditionally underrepresented groups in organizations will ultimately enhance a work group's effectiveness by removing the barriers associated with minority status and thereby enabling all people to be maximally productive (Cox, 1993; Larkey, 1996). Blalock (1957) has argued, alternatively, that numeric increases in the representation of groups traditionally in the minority threaten

the majority. Hence, men, for example, should react to increasing numbers of women in the workplace with heightened levels of discriminatory behavior, to limit women's power gains. Yoder (1991) described this response as "backlash" from the majority. Proponents of this view have argued that balancing numbers as a strategy to end discrimination is by itself insufficient; it is also necessary to attend to the ongoing relationships between groups, particularly to intergroup status and power differentials that would otherwise remain intact (Zimmer, 1988; Alderfer, 1992). . . .

Effects of group composition. The second approach to understanding how demographic diversity might influence work groups is predicated on the notion that demographic diversity increases the available pool of resources—networks, perspectives, styles, knowledge, and insights—that people can bring to bear on complex problems. Some have speculated as to what those new resources might be, focusing on the potential contributions that traditionally underrepresented people, such as women and people of color, may have to offer work groups. Others have examined empirically the link between group diversity and group outcomes, focusing on the potential contributions that diverse groups have to offer relative to those that are more homogeneous.

Those interested in the contributions of traditionally underrepresented groups have argued that the cultural styles and perspectives of these people, although typically ignored or devalued, are in fact valuable assets to work groups. The most vocal proponents of this point of view are those who contend that women's difference from men, particularly their relationship orientation, which has traditionally marked them as ill-suited for the hard-driving, task orientation of the workplace, in fact constitutes an effective and much-needed management style. Hence, they argue, gender diversity in managerial ranks would serve the group's needs better than most current arrangements, in which men are numerically dominant at those levels (Helgesen, 1990; Rosener, 1990). . . .

The parallel case for racial diversity in organizations is less well developed. It is based on research that documents cultural differences between whites and blacks in communication styles. Some have used this research to suggest that black cultural values such as assertiveness and forthrightness, and language patterns, such as verbal inventiveness, may be beneficial in workplace interactions and represent positive attributes rather than deficiencies in need of remediation (Foeman and Pressley, 1987), but we know of no empirical work that examines this hypothesis directly.

The skepticism as well as mixed results concerning intergroup differences in organizational behavior diminish the potential value of this line of research for elucidating the relationship between cultural diversity and work group effectiveness. Women and people of color may well bring different perspectives and styles to the workplace, but research has yet to demonstrate whether, under what conditions, and with what consequences they actually express them.

Others interested in group compositional effects have taken a different tack, focusing on the impact of diversity in the work group, rather than on the merits of newcomers who make the work group diverse. Here again, the argument for diversity is based on the notion that members of heterogeneous groups have different points of view, but instead of identifying what those points of view are and who holds them, these scholars contend that what is important is the diversity itself: heterogeneous groups are more likely to generate a diverse set of recommended approaches to tasks or solutions to problems; this in turn stimulates effective group discussion, which leads ultimately to high quality decisions (Wanous and Youtz, 1986). For groups that are heterogeneous on the cultural identity variables in which we are interested, the evidence for this hypothesis is mixed. Mixed-sex groups have performed both better (Hoffman and Maier, 1961; Ruhe, 1978; Wood, 1987) and worse (Ziller and Exline, 1958; Kent and McGrath, 1969; Clement and Schiereck, 1973; Murnighan and Conlon, 1991) than single-sex groups. Similarly, groups that are racially, ethnically, and/or nationally diverse have demonstrated both positive outcomes (Fiedler, 1966; Ruhe and Eatman, 1977; Watson, Kumar, and Michaelsen, 1993; Cox, Lobel, and McLeod, 1991) and negative outcomes (Fiedler, Meuwese, and Oonk, 1961; Shaw, 1983; Tsui, Egan, and O'Reilly, 1992) relative to groups that are homogenous on these dimensions.

Recent studies of factors that moderate the relationship between cultural diversity and work group effectiveness have begun to make some sense of these findings, suggesting that when group members share common goals and values, cultural diversity leads to more beneficial outcomes (Chatman et al., 1998; Jehn, Northcraft, and Neale, 1999). We elaborate this moderator strategy in our paper by suggesting that the impact of cultural diversity on group functioning is influenced by what we call the group's "diversity perspective": group members' normative beliefs and expectations about cultural diversity and its role in their work group. . . .

We studied three professional services firms, each of which had significant success in recruiting and retaining a culturally diverse workforce. Two had reputations for being high-functioning, multicultural firms; the third was experiencing conflicts and had concerns about the quality of its performance. This variability gave us an opportunity to investigate in the field what conditions foster more positive work relationships and outcomes in some instances and less positive outcomes in others. Although we were interested in examining diversity across a range of cultural differences, we focus our analysis in this paper primarily on race, because, even though the organizations in our study were all culturally diverse, different kinds of cultural differences were salient in each. In one, salient cultural differences included race, social class, and sexual orientation; in another, they were race, gender, and social class; and in the third, they were race, gender, religion and nationality. We focused on race because it was the aspect of diversity that was salient in all three and would allow us to make work group comparisons across firms. Although different cultural identity groups are associated with different sociocultural patterns and intergroup relations, because they share many of the basic features we outlined above, we should be able to generalize much of what we learn from our analysis of race to diversity on other aspects of cultural identity. . . .

Method

We studied a consulting firm, a financial services firm and a law firm. We based the research in all three sites on Alderfer and Smith's (1982; Alderfer, 1987) embedded intergroup theory, which delineates a method for researching intergroup relations

Figure 20.1

Relationship between cultural identity diversity and work group functioning.

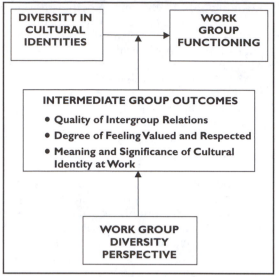

in organizations. The method involves a three-phase process of entering the organization and negotiating the terms of the inquiry, collecting data, and providing feedback (see Alderfer, 1980, for details). Each phase is designed to maximize understanding of how cultural-identity-group memberships influence people, their relationships, and their work.

The Law Firm

The law firm is a small, nonprofit public-interest law firm whose mission is to protect and advance the rights and well-being of economically disadvantaged women. Founded about 20 years earlier, the firm had undergone a transition over the previous ten years from a professional staff composed entirely of whites to one that included a program staff that was at least half people of color. Although the senior management positions of the firm were still held by whites, we included the firm in our study because people of color held positions of significant authority in the firm. This firm had a reputation for being a high-functioning, multicultural organization. It had 12 employees at the time of our study; six were white, six were people of color, and all participated in this research. This included the executive and associate directors of the firm (both white), the managing attorney (white), five program/professional staff (two white, two

Latinas, and one Asian American), and four support staff (one white, two Latinas, and one African Caribbean). We also interviewed three former members of the program staff. One, a Latina, had been the first woman of color to join the professional staff. Another, a white woman, had witnessed the demographic change from an all-white professional staff to a multicultural one. The third was an African American woman who had recently left the professional staff after six years.

The Financial Services Firm

The financial services firm is a for-profit company whose mission is to develop and revitalize the economy of the largely poor, African American urban community in which it is situated. In the course of the firm's 20-year history it had changed from a predominantly white professional and managerial staff to one that included about 40 percent people of color, mostly African Americans. Like the law firm, this firm had a reputation for being a high functioning, multicultural organization. We interviewed 29 employees or about 24 percent of the firm. We began by interviewing all seven members of the management committee (four whites and three African Americans) and two senior human resources managers (one white and one African American) and then focused the remainder of our data collection in the loan department and in the two departments of the Sales Division. According to the management committee, these departments together represented a range of the firm's diversity-related experiences. We interviewed all members of the loan department and the smaller department in the Sales Division (seven whites and five African Americans) and eight members, or about two-thirds, of the larger department in the Sales Division (all African Americans).

The Consulting Firm

The consulting firm is a nonprofit, international planning and consulting company that focuses on foreign and domestic urban economic development. Having operated for many years as a predominantly white organization, over the 15-year period prior to our data collection, it had implemented an aggressive affirmative action plan designed to increase the number of white women and people of color in the organization, especially in professional positions. At the time of our study, 40 percent of the firm's professional and managerial staff were people of color. Unlike the other two firms, this one was struggling to sustain its diversity in the face of a series of conflicts and performance concerns. We interviewed 37 employees or about 30 percent of the firm. This included nine members of the management committee (six white and three African American), 16 project leaders/middle managers (nine white, five African American, and two Latina), and 12 support staff (five white and seven African American). This interviewee group was proportionately representative of the four work groups that constituted the firm's structure: Administrative Support. Research and Development. North American Operations, and International Development. The latter two groups were the largest and accounted for over 90 percent of the firm's fee-for-service work.

Data Collection

We collected data primarily through interviews with participants and by observing between two and six staff meetings in each organization. We tape-recorded and transcribed the interviews, which lasted between one and two hours each took detailed notes during staff meetings, and made field notes after each site visit. . . .

Data Analysis

The authors independently read all of the transcripts and field notes from each organization to identify themes that might explain similarities and differences within and across firms' experiences of their diversity, in particular, how and under what conditions diversity enhanced or detracted from their effective functioning. We then met to discuss our observations and discovered that we had seized on the same insight: there seemed to be three different perspectives that governed how members of work groups created and responded to diversity, and these perspectives seemed to have important implications for how well the groups functioned (Thomas and Ely, 1996). This then became our working hypothesis, which framed and guided the remainder of our data analysis. . . .

Work Group Perspectives on Diversity

Our analysis supported our argument that the perspective that governed workgroups' orientation toward diversity was associated with different levels of individual and group functioning. We identified three diversity perspectives that appeared to have different implications for how well people functioned in their work groups and, therefore, how likely their work groups were to realize the benefits of their diversity: the integration-and-learning perspective, the access-and-legitimacy perspective, and the discrimination-and-fairness perspective. Each provides a rationale for why the work group should increase its cultural diversity, yet only the first was associated with what appeared to be sustainable performance gains attributable to diversity. Retrospective data from participants suggested that work groups' perspectives could develop and change over time, but, at the time of our data collection; a single, dominant perspective on diversity prevailed in each group we studied. If there were dissenting views within the group, they came from a small minority who expressed concerns privately that certain aspects of the group's perspective on diversity were problematic. The prevailing perspective in the group nevertheless shaped members' experiences in predictable ways. Although there was within-firm variability in the diversity perspectives work groups held, each perspective seemed to be best illustrated in one of the three firms.

Integration-and-Learning Perspective

According to the integration-and-learning perspective on diversity, the insights, skills, and experiences employees have developed as members of various cultural identity groups are potentially valuable resources that the work group can use to rethink its primary tasks and redefine its markets, products, strategies, and business practices in ways that will advance its mission. This perspective links diversity to work processes—the way people do and experience the work—in a manner that makes diversity a resource for learning and adaptive change. The integration-and-learning perspective and the outcomes associated with it were evident in the program function of the law firm, which included the attorneys and policy analysts in the firm, and in the management committee of the financial services firm. We focus our description on the program function in the law firm, however, because people there were especially articulate about how and with what consequences this perspective evolved over the course of their efforts to diversify their workforce, in particular, their program staff. Where this perspective was evident in the financial services firm, It was associated with the same kinds of processes and outcomes we observed in the law firm.

The law firm had developed a successful practice in its first ten years, representing a largely white female clientele in employment-related disputes. Nevertheless, in light of their mandate to protect and advance the economic rights and interests of low-income women, the firm's attorneys viewed their inability to attract women clients of color as a significant shortcoming, To address this problem, they decided to diversify their all-white program staff. They began by hiring a Latina attorney to head what they called the "women-of-color project." The project's purpose was to expand their work into the Latina community and demonstrate their commitment to advocacy on behalf of low-income women. By virtually all accounts, however, this change in staff composition moved them far beyond that original goal. Over the next ten years, they underwent a transition from a staff composed entirely of whites to one that included a program staff that was at least half people of color. More importantly, however, this change in the demographic composition of the program staff entirely reshaped the character and priorities of the firm's work in unanticipated ways as members learned from their diversity and integrated what they had learned into the core work of the organization. Several staff members, both current and former, described the change as follows:

> Our mission is still the same—the economic empowerment of women, but our strategies or how we define them have radically changed from a fairly straight feminist approach. We're still talking about sexual harassment, comparable worth [Title VII cases], those are the same. But our diversity made us look at the organization's program and how we had to change the work that we do—the substantive legal stuff that we do. So now

we're looking at minimum wage, manufacturers' liability.... That's not traditional sex discrimination, but these are primarily women workers who are affected by these things.

> At first, we were like, "[industry name] workers? That's men and women. Where's the gender discrimination?" And [the Latina attorney] was beating us over the heads with a stick and saying, "Hey, most of these folks in this industry are women; most of them are women of color; most of them are non-English-speaking women. What better place for us to be?" And eventually the staff said, "Right, you're right, that does make sense. That is a way for us to go."

Associated with this transformation in the firm's work was a shift in its perspective on its program staffs diversity. No longer was its diversity confined to a particular project: "Our women-of-color project became integrated in such a way that it was no longer this special little program off to the side," one program staff member explained. "It now just permeates the whole picture," added another. Their new perspective on diversity—an integration-and-learning perspective—was grounded in the notion that cultural identity shapes how people experience, see, and know the world. Hence, cultural differences can be a source of insight and skill that can be brought to bear on the organization's core tasks. This discovery enabled staff members to see their diversity not only as a resource through which they could gain entree into previously inaccessible niche markets but, more importantly, as a resource from which they could learn new ways of reconceiving and reconfiguring their work as well. As one white woman attorney explained, "[Diversity] means differences in terms of how you see the issues, who you can work with, how effective you are, how much you understand what's going on.... There's not a sense of 'you're just like me.'" And although several people spoke to the discomfort that often comes with such differences, they also emphasized the need to look "beyond feeling comfortable . . . to the different types of skills people bring."

This perspective on cultural differences required that program staff members place a high value on process—on time spent exploring their different points of view and deliberating about whether and how they should inform the work. Describing herself as "the process queen," the executive director stressed the importance of "learning how to not be afraid of the differences, learning about conflict, and learning to be willing to go toward it and trying to talk about hard things." Similarly, a former program staff member explained that "process is critical":

> [There has to be] a kind of group process of making sure that there's the time and a safe situation and that people are gonna be encouraged to say what they're worried about, even if it's not politically correct. . . . You need to provide, to whatever degree possible, permission for people to say what's on their mind and struggle through the consequences and inner personal dynamics of saying those things. . . . People have to be willing to take risks. You have to be willing to be wrong. It's not something lawyers do easily. I'm not sure anybody does. But lawyers especially just *hate* to be wrong. And a bunch of white liberal women lawyers *hate* to be politically incorrect.

Recognizing that people from different cultural backgrounds might bring different sets of experiences and skills to work did not dictate a cultural-identity-based division of labor among the program staff. Several people felt strongly, for example, that one need not be "gay to raise gay issues" nor "a person of color to raise issues of concern to women of color." A white attorney explained that although she could not be the founder of a Latina organization begun in her office, she would work with the group eventually. She talked about diversity as a learning experience: "I've learned a lot about things that just weren't in my background. I don't mean about salsa or whatever, but about . . . what life experiences are like in other places." As this woman suggests, the program staff's diversity was to serve as a resource on which all members could draw to expand their knowledge base as well as their networks. This meant a deep commitment to educating and learning from each other and reflects a central premise of the integration-and-learning perspective on diversity: while there may be certain activities at certain times that are best performed by particular people because of their cultural identities, the competitive advantage of a multicultural workforce lies in the capacity of its members to learn from each other and develop within each other a range of cultural competencies that they can all then bring to bear on their work.

As a result, white members of the program staff had to learn to make up, on their own, the issues and concerns that might initially have been raised by their colleagues of color so that certain tasks did not always fall to one group or another. As one white employee put it, "It's important that people of color coming into the organization don't see themselves as coming in and just educating a bunch of white folks; you have to demonstrate in a real way that you've been educated when you come back." Virtually everyone, both white and of color, commented on the personal and professional growth the staff's diversity had afforded them. As one white attorney reflected, "I think about things differently. Things I've taken for granted I can no longer take for granted. My sensitivities are just different."

To facilitate this kind of learning, the program staff had to organize their work differently. Whereas traditionally a case would have been staffed by a single attorney, it now would be staffed by at least two. This enabled people to engage more easily in the kind of cross-cultural learning and exposure that had become so central to the way they operated and, more importantly, demonstrated how, with this perspective on diversity, their work processes, as well as their work, were open to change.

According to this perspective, one measures progress in efforts to diversify by the degree to which newly represented groups have the power to change the organization and traditionally represented groups are willing to change. The executive director of the law firm described her litmus test of how well an organization is managing its diversity as how much change there is in the power structure:

> Is the organization trying to assimilate people into what already exists? Or do they want to create something that's different from what was there before—and maybe not know what that means? If you want people to be part of an organization and have ownership in the organization then they have to have power and some control. I think the way that we successfully did it here was in terms of the program. The power and who is in control of our program has really changed. . . . You can't assume that what's traditionally been done is the right way to go.

Access-and-Legitimacy Perspective

An access-and-legitimacy perspective on diversity is based in a recognition that the organization's markets and constituencies are culturally diverse. It therefore behooves the organization to match that diversity in parts of its own workforce as a way of gaining access to and legitimacy with those markets and constituent groups. Work groups in which this perspective prevails use their diversity only at the margins, to connect with a more diverse market; they do not incorporate the cultural competencies of their diverse workforces into their core functions. This perspective constitutes the rationale behind the now popularly touted business case for diversity (Cox and Blake, 1991). The access-and-legitimacy perspective guided the law firm's initial efforts to diversify its program staff and continued to provide the rationale for the cultural composition of its administrative and management staff. It was most vivid, however, in parts of the financial services firm, which we focus on here for our description. In each instance it was associated with similar kinds of outcomes.

In the financial services firm, the access-and-legitimacy perspective was especially evident in the diversification that occurred in two departments of the Sales Division—Retail Operations and External Deposits. Retail Operations was responsible for servicing the banking needs of a predominantly black, working-class, urban clientele to whom the firm marketed its services locally, in the surrounding neighborhood. External Deposits was responsible for servicing the banking needs of a predominantly white, affluent clientele to whom the firm marketed its services nationally. Mirroring the racial and class composition of these markets were the predominantly black, working-class employees who staffed Retail Operations and the predominantly white, middle- and upper-middle-class employees who staffed External Deposits. This staffing pattern characterized these departments from the lowest- to the highest-ranking employees. Members of both Retail Operations and External Deposits readily acknowledged the importance of their racial make-up as a way of gaining access to and legitimacy with their respective clientele. Explaining the role of the black staff in Retail Operations, the white manager of External Deposits explained:

> If [the firm] were all white, our relationships with the community would be extremely strained. And our retail deposit base would be very much threatened. [The community] would be saying, "What are these white people doing running a bank in the middle of *our* community?" And they'd be right. We've operated in black communities for 20 years. If we aren't fully integrated ourselves, it's pretty hypocritical.

This manager's black counterpart in Retail Operations commented similarly:

> For management to come into a black neighborhood and undertake [this mission], they would be remiss not to think we have to get some different color people in here to help us do this. It would give the community a level of comfort that there are people in the organization who actually know how to relate to . . . the people that are in the neighborhood, and what they actually *feel*, and, you know, how they actually communicate with one another, and those kinds of things. . . . I mean, we are in the heart of the black community.

This perspective provided a similar though less elaborate rationale for the predominantly white staff in External Deposits. Several people commented that External Deposits' white clientele were probably "more comfortable" with the white staff who served them. One staff member summarized the importance of having both white and black staff:

> I think if we were all black, we'd have a lot of obstacles. We wouldn't have access to a lot of the resources that we do. Minority-owned banks that are almost exclusively minority have really struggled because they're not as connected to those [white-controlled] resources. I think it could still be done, but it would be a harder task. If we were all white, I think we'd be in as bad or worse shape [as if we were all black], just because of the discomfort with the community, or not being able to relate to the borrowers or stand in their shoes so to speak.

Despite this apparent symmetry, however, the access-and-legitimacy perspective in fact defined a much more circumscribed role for blacks than for whites, limiting the contributions of blacks to just that—access and legitimacy—whereas the contributions of whites were more widely evident. For example, a white employee in External Deposits described the overall culture of the firm as much more consistent with the culture of her predominantly white department than with the culture of Retail Operations, which was predominantly black:

> . . . if you perform and exceed expectations, regardless of color, you are acknowledged and recognized. . . . The problem is that what is expected of senior management here has a cultural bias towards whites. And . . . if you're in that cultural modus, you don't understand why it's exclusionary. . . . Everyone is expected to work a lot of hours. There is this emphasis on perfectionism, this emphasis on sort of intellectual discussion and debate. People are very, very mission-driven. And that's not to say that African Americans aren't also able to do all that. But because of historical racial issues they have been limited. . . . So there aren't a lot of people from the neighborhood that would be senior management level, and there are an awful lot who would be in those low-paying, pretty routine, white-collar jobs.

Hence, although cultural identity in these two departments was clearly a legitimate resource to be used in service of the Sales Division's work, the access-and-legitimacy perspective provided a relatively narrow definition of the value black cultural identity had to offer, relative to white cultural identity. Blacks in Retail Operations were invited to use their cultural identity, but only at the boundaries between the organization and its black market. By contrast, there was a perception among employees in these departments that whites' cultural identity shaped how the Sales Division functioned more broadly, with middle- and upper-middle-class white culture in particular dictating the work norms and standards most valued.

With the access-and-legitimacy perspective, one measures progress in diversification efforts by whether there is sufficient representation either in those boundary positions or in visible positions that would enhance the legitimacy of the organization from the perspective of its outside markets. Although this raised the question of how many whites would be too many, as well as the converse, how many blacks would be enough, this perspective provided no clear answers. Rather, as one participant surmised,

It may be a function of the inner workings of the manager's mind that it's time for me to hire a minority or something. And that's legitimate in this organization. While it seems unfair that maybe the most qualified person or the best person for the job might not get that position, maybe the best qualified person isn't the right person for the organization, and maybe it's time to hire a minority.

Discrimination-and-Fairness Perspective

The discrimination-and-fairness perspective is characterized by a belief in a culturally diverse workforce as a moral imperative to ensure justice and the fair treatment of all members of society. It focuses diversification efforts on providing equal opportunities in hiring and promotion, suppressing prejudicial attitudes, and eliminating discrimination. A culturally diverse work group, therefore, is meant to be evidence of just and fair treatment of employees. In contrast to the previous two perspectives, in the discrimination-and-fairness perspective there is no instrumental link between diversity and the group's work. Work groups in the consulting firm provided the best illustration of this perspective and the processes and outcomes associated with it. In fact, there was very little evidence of any other perspective in the consulting firm, and this perspective was largely absent in the other two firms we studied.

Consulting firm employees expressed this perspective most clearly in their statements about why the firm's affirmative action program was important. One white manager explained, "The firm created a community that is diverse based on a very clear sense that there should be equality and justice." Similarly, an African American manager described the firm's philosophy as "everyone being equal or justice for all, being fair in regards to hiring, treating staff the same." A white manager elaborated as follows:

> I think [the firm], from my vantage point, has made tremendous progress in its commitment to build both a just society inside, as well as a just society outside the organization. . . . I think the organization has committed itself to restructuring its population, its personnel makeup, in order to right some of the wrongs caused by racism and sexism in our society. . . . And the cost has been to turn down a lot of good, qualified white people for jobs, which we've had to do in order to make

this program work. There's simply no way around it. . . . The other side of it is that the people of color in this organization have added immensely to it, I believe. . . . They have enriched the organization; they have helped us live up to our ideals of equality and justice.

According to this perspective, cultural diversity, as an end in itself, was not to influence the organization's work in any fundamental way. Although the firm established two committees whose mandate was to "infuse the firm's activities" with a "feminist" and "racial" perspective, respectively, in practice, these committees had virtually no impact on the firm's work. Instead, consistent with their discrimination-and-fairness perspective, they served a policing and advocacy function, scrutinizing the firm's treatment of women and people of color for evidence of sexism and racism and advocating on behalf of those groups when they deemed necessary. To the extent that these committees did influence the firm's program-related work, many employees were critical: "These committees tend to sometimes have more leverage, more power than perhaps they ought to have in decision making," one white manager lamented. "They are sometimes allowed to make interventions and judgments of certain programs based on their [political clout] rather than on their knowledge and information." Another repudiated any attempts the committees might make to influence programmatic decisions or directions "on racial grounds," arguing that they should have no role in the "normal decision-making process of the organization."

Many members of the organization, both white and of color, prided themselves on being blind to cultural differences. Although each group questioned the other's ability to uphold this virtue, members of both groups equated the organization's philosophy of justice with its commitment to the notion that "everyone is the same," "everyone is just a human being here; it doesn't matter what color he is." As one African American claimed, "I don't see people in color, I treat them all the same." Consistent with this insistence that everyone is the same, there were at least two norms that operated to suppress any differences that did exist. The first was to avoid conflict wherever possible. Many reported having received a clear and consistent message from management that

to express conflict was "potentially dangerous," as it "might do more damage than good." The second was a norm requiring assimilation to a white cultural standard. As one white manager explained, while the goal was to be "entirely race blind" in personnel decisions, the "expectation is still that people will speak in normal English and write the way white people write." Although some people complained about management's enforcement of these norms, they saw no inconsistency between their commitment to "color-blindness" and their concerns that these norms were oppressive. Similarly, the small minority of professional staff in the program areas who felt that incorporating relevant, race-based insights into their work was important nevertheless tended to espouse many of the norms and values associated with the discrimination-and-fairness perspective, which mitigated against their being able to do so.

According to the discrimination-and-fairness perspective, one measures progress in diversity by how well a work group achieves its recruitment and retention goals, As one African American executive explained, "a systematic monitoring of numbers" was a key indicator of whether or not "things are going along smoothly." A Latina manager expressed a similar sentiment about the importance of numbers: "A significant number of people of color is a sign of something good about the organization."

Table 20.1 summarizes the characteristics of the three work group perspectives on diversity. Each of the three different sets of expectations and beliefs that people held about cultural diversity and its role at work shaped individual experiences and group processes in different ways, which had implications for individual and group functioning.

Intermediate Group Outcomes

Quality of Intergroup Relations

The integration-and-learning perspective is predicated on the notion that a diverse group of people comes together for the express purpose of learning from one another how best to achieve the work group's mission, but that often meant tension-filled discussions in which people struggled to hear each other's points of view before resolving how to proceed with the work. As one white program staff member in the law firm ex-

Table 20.1
Summary of Work Group Diversity Perspectives

Characterization of perspective	Integration-and-learning	Access-and-legitimacy	Discrimination-and-fairness
Rationale for diversifying	To inform and enhance core work and work processes	To gain access to and legitimacy with diverse markets and clients	To ensure justice and equality and eliminate discrimination
Value of cultural identity	High; a resource for learning, change, and renewal; should integrate cultural differences into core work and work processes as appropriate	Moderate; a resource only at the interface between organization and markets/clients; should differentiate to gain access and legitimacy; otherwise, assimilate to dominant white culture	Low; it is a basis for unjust discrimination; should assimilate to dominant white culture
Connection between cultural diversity and work	Direct; incorporated throughout the work	Indirect; race-based division of labor to enhance access and legitimacy	Limited; norms against a connection
Indicators of progress	Increased representation of traditionally underrepresented groups that have power to change organization; process and product innovation; shared sense that cultural diversity is resource for learning	Increased representation of traditionally underrepresented groups, especially in boundary or visible positions	Increased representation of traditionally underrepresented groups

plained, "Cross-race discussions occur with some frequency and sometimes with some tension, because it's hard. There are real differences here. And that stuff is being discussed. It's not hidden under a rock." One former attorney of color described her particular experience of working through differences in point of view with the executive director:

> I would take on the executive director, and she and I would go *at* it. But . . . we'd really hear each other, and I think we learned a lot from one another. And you can come at her. And she can come back at you with reason, using the history of the organization, why that won't work. . . . And I'd remind her that the point of the organization was to let go of that history and only hold on to it where it makes sense. . . . I would . . . just hang in there until I was sure that she was really rejecting an idea or my client on its merits. Not because it was new or unsettling. And sometimes she'd really convince me that the rejection was based on merit. And sometimes, there were some things I should have let go earlier I'm sure.

Certain kinds of problems were inevitable, and they seemed to result from the fact that the program staff were not immune to the way race relations were structured in the larger culture. Two kinds of tensions in par-

ticular arose in the program staff's race relations as a result, and, although we viewed each as stemming from the difficulty of living up to the vision of diversity set forth, the kinds of relationships and processes the vision encouraged were precisely the mechanisms that eased those tensions and helped people work toward resolution. Hence, the perspective seemed to contain a self-correcting mechanism that both reinforced the vision and maintained its usefulness to the organization.

The first tension concerned the twin problems of burnout for the attorneys of color, who sometimes felt called upon to do more than their fair share of the work, and marginalization of white attorneys, who sometimes felt less central to the firm's work as a result. People attributed both of these problems to the "reality of the world out there," yet they seemed manageable largely because people were able to discuss them. As one white attorney explained, "we're pretty open about talking about those things here, so it's not like this unspoken thing." She elaborated:

> Like sometimes people are putting together panels and for good reasons they want a diverse panel. So I'll be the last one they'd ask, even if I'm the person who's done the most work in the area, be-

cause they'd prefer to have [one of the women of color]. And then we would talk about how it would be strange that organizations that I work with would call up [a black attorney] and ask her to be on a panel. So that both put a burden on her and kind of made me feel strange about being excluded. But it was something we understood because we thought the role model and the diversity aspect of the panel was an important thing to do.

The second kind of tension was the disappointment everyone felt when people's failure to use their own or to seek others' cross-cultural knowledge threatened to compromise the program staff's effectiveness. One such incident occurred during a staff meeting we observed, which the executive director afterward told us was "a very good view of what goes on here—people engaging in what is not always the easiest conversation and being really willing to take the time to challenge each other and to be educated by each other." A local Latino community group had invited the firm to join in a fund-raising event involving a Latino theater group. The executive and associate directors, unaware of the importance of the group in the community, decided to decline the invitation, without consulting program staff, on the grounds that it would interfere with a larger fund-raising event already scheduled. When one of the Latina program staff was informed of the decision, she felt that the directors' lack of cultural knowledge had led them to a hasty and costly decision, and she placed it on the agenda for the next staff meeting. At that staff meeting, the Latinas, across hierarchical lines, expressed unified disagreement with the decision, describing the event as "an important vehicle for us to do our work with this community." The staff seemed to have difficulty resolving the conflict until everyone was able to see the decision as more properly program-related than administrative. The administrative function in the firm had yet to develop an integration-and-learning perspective on diversity. With no clear sense of how racial diversity might enhance that function, managers had not sought and were initially resistant to hearing different perspectives on the usefulness of the event. As soon as the event was successfully recast as outreach, however, a program-related activity, they were able to see the relevance of race and the importance

of hearing a specifically nonwhite perspective.

Our direct queries about the quality of race relations in the Sales Division of the financial services firm, in which employees held an access-and-legitimacy perspective on their diversity, revealed few problems and a general sense that black and white employees experienced little tension in their crossrace interactions. As one white participant said, "It's not to say there's never any discomfort, but I've been very surprised—I've never run across an uncomfortable situation here." Similarly, a black employee described interactions "between everyone" as "really good" and a general sense that people ask questions about those from other cultures in a way that does not offend. "People are different," another explained, "but when the need arises they can work together." The dynamics within the Sales Division between Retail Operations and External Deposits, however, revealed a more complicated story.

The racial differentiation between these two departments, both in their staffing and in their clientele, resulted quite clearly in a two-tiered system in which the white department received better treatment and higher status relative to its black counterpart. Participants had much to say about this, and what they said did not reflect the sanguine sentiments we heard when we asked about race relations more directly. Yet there were unequivocal racial overtones, as well as explicit references to race, in their discussions of the relationship between these two departments. And despite the symmetry between blacks and whites in positions of authority, the relationship between these two departments seemed to reproduce the asymmetric division of power and status within the Sales Division that characterizes societal race relations more generally.

Most people agreed that there were very few differences between the kinds of tasks the two departments performed. Nevertheless, more than one participant referred to the fact that there were "two banks" within the firm: Retail Operations and External Deposits. One participant from External Deposits explained that, in her view, this had come about because the previous manager, who had an ambitious agenda and insisted on providing the highest quality services, duplicated functions that already existed in Retail whenever she encountered a level of quality that she judged as too low:

And so you had this sort of cracker-jack group of people who worked for her . . . that were in the absolute perfect job for the sort of white, smart, dedicated, loyal workaholic. And not the perfect job for the sort of black, hard-working, needs a salary, will do a good job, but not that kind of worker . . . and there was absolutely no time for people who wanted a 9-to-5 job.

This status differential between the two departments and the resentments it fostered were palpable. There was a perception among those in Retail Operations that management looked more favorably on External Deposits, that External Deposits got "special privileges" and was "more prestigious," and that people there were paid more "because they're white, even though the work is the same." By contrast, participants in both departments referred to Retail Operations as "the other side" of the firm, "the dark side." One black participant, now an officer in Retail Operations, described an experience he had when he was the lone black member of External Deposits several years earlier. This experience illustrates how racial stereotypes shaped interactions between blacks and whites in a manner that may have reinforced, at least for some, the appropriateness of the racial division of labor between the two departments:

> We were at a staff meeting talking about the problems we were having as a department trying to be all things to all people. And I remembered this thing my boss had said about a year earlier that we have to select the battles that we want to fight, and I took that to mean that we have to decide strategically what we will pursue and what we won't pursue. And I just happened to think about that quote, and so I said, "I think that we ought to be real careful not to bite off more than we can chew." . . . I got a response where the person said, "Well, what do you propose? We do nothing?" So I saw right then and there that I was misunderstood. I said, "No, of course not. I'm saying that we need to select the battles we want to fight and fight those." . . . And being pretty new to the organization then, I felt that it wasn't the right time for me to be forthright about what I meant. . . . [W]hen a white man disagrees, he's being strong. He's being taken with respect. When a black man disagrees, he's being negative and whiny, militant and kind of like Malcolm X. So you have to be really careful about

how you walk that line so that you don't get labeled and you don't sabotage your career.

In this story, the white employee interpreted her black colleague's comments as consistent with the view that blacks were not a good cultural fit with the aggressive, workaholic norms of this department. Concerned that his objections to her interpretation might reinforce additional negative racial stereotypes about him, the black colleague remained silent. Thus, race-based stereotypes imported from the larger culture shaped these employees' interpersonal interactions in a way that reinforced a view of this department as appropriately culturally white and elite.

This particular manifestation of the access-and-legitimacy perspective, in which two racially segregated, parallel entities were formed to service different racial and economic segments of the market, fostered a good deal of resentment and competitiveness between the two departments, which was often expressed explicitly in racial terms. One participant described the senior officer in charge of Retail Operations as "a little bit resentful when his territory is encroached on by white people [i.e., External Deposits]." Another described the "cultural barriers" to integrating the two departments, or even to fostering a more cooperative spirit, which might replace the "distrust" that seemed to characterize their relationships. Still another attributed "the tensions between the two sides" to "the logistics, the race, the professional mix, and just the nature of how the departments are compiled." Hence, although these participants often spoke positively of race relations in the firm, the racial segregation inside the Sales Division mirrored hierarchical race relations and racial tensions in the wider culture.

Participants' descriptions of race relations in the consulting firm, in which all work groups held a discrimination-and-fairness perspective on diversity, were nearly unanimously negative. People of all races described relationships between white and African American employees, who made up the majority of the nonwhite staff, as "tense," "cynical," "hostile" and "distrustful," and described their own feelings as "disappointed," "hopeless," "helpless," and "powerless."

Differences in people's characterizations of the problem tended to fall along a combination of racial and hierarchical lines. Black executives and whites across the hierarchy tended to agree that employees of color were too quick to bring charges of racism against white people. One African American executive was frustrated by her observation that any time management met to discuss a problem concerning an employee of color "people [of color] are up in arms and saying it's racism." A white manager voiced the same sentiment: "Whenever a person of color loses his job, there is an immediate perception that the decision to terminate the employee was a racist one."

At the same time, there was a widely shared fear among whites that any form of conflict or confrontation, especially if perceived as instigated by a white person in relation to a person of color, would automatically implicate the white person as racist. One white manager explained, "I would find it difficult to challenge a person of color because I like to think of myself as not being prejudiced and would hate to be said to be prejudiced." Another described the mounting pressure he felt, as a white male, "to show the correct attitudes towards race relations," which he believed meant he was expected to agree with everything people of color said: "There is a level of psychological intimidation; you don't question decisions or performance." As a result, white managers felt it had become "increasingly difficult for supervisors to provide firm, fair, constructive supervision to people of color, who are prone to charge racism if they are criticized." Where he "once felt that the firm's commitments to fight racism were honorable," one white manager now felt they were "getting to the point where we're not just fighting racism; we're setting up other standards for letting people get away with whatever bullshit they want to get away with."

On the flip side, middle- and lower-level staff of color resented their white colleagues' conflict-avoidant stance and fears of confrontation, as the cynical tone of the following comment illustrates: "There is a real sense on the part of some white people that whatever they're going to do they're going to get in trouble. They're going to get accused of being a racist which is almost the worst possible thing that could happen to a white person here, short of dismemberment." Many people of color argued that by keeping them from receiving honest feedback and getting the kind of supervision they de-

served, this stance was itself racist. They felt that, as a result, they never knew when the "hammer may fall," when "the trap door will drop." In a recent incident, a black woman, who had been an employee at the firm for ten years, was summarily fired for poor work performance and required to vacate the premises that afternoon. Though many conceded that her performance was problematic, people of color nevertheless organized a formal protest of management's failure to "confront her [early on] with her poor performance and treat her as if she were a normal, equal person." In another incident, many employees of color signed a petition to protest the disciplinary action taken against a black employee who was held responsible for money stolen from his department, arguing that the theft had occurred only because inadequate supervision had prevented him from taking the necessary precautions. As one black executive explained, these kinds of events "confirmed people's worst fears about the insensitivity of management to the well-being of employees of color." Both the white staff and the black executives in the firm emphasized privately the complicity of people of color in these incidents. One African American executive lamented that people of color, once fired or disciplined, become "purer than snow" and often fail to recognize that their own behavior "is not always so desirable." Another was more cynical, arguing that "blacks know they can milk these [white] people because they [white people] are so afraid of confrontation."

When the disciplining supervisor in such incidents was a person of color, other people of color often interpreted his or her actions as the result of manipulation and corruption by white management. Several black participants described times when they believed whites had purposely used black managers to handle problems with black staff to avoid having their own confrontations. Two invoked a plantation metaphor to capture this dynamic, in which the "owners" (executives) used the "house niggers" (black managers) to look after the "field niggers" (black support and technical staff). Interestingly, the ultimate oppressors in this metaphor—the "owners"—were black as well as white in this firm. This is consistent both with the similarity in views we found between black executives, on the one hand, and whites, on the other, and with the perception many black employees shared that black executives "must have sold out in some way" and did not identify with the blacks they supervised.

Finally, we were struck by the fact that most of the public debates about "racial incidents" at this firm centered on the treatment of people of color rather than on the work-related problems that instigated that treatment. For example, many people, both white and black, believed that the woman who was fired in the incident above had routinely and inappropriately biased affirmative action searches in favor of candidates of color in her role as an administrator in the Affirmative Action department. And the man who was disciplined for the theft ran a function within a department that had long been losing money for the firm through inefficiencies and poor management. Neither the quality of her performance, nor the efficiency of his department, however, was central to the public debates that ensued, leaving important questions about these aspects of their work unanswered.

That the tensions in race relations in this firm would be played out around charges and countercharges of racism and intimidation seemed ironic in light of work groups' diversity perspective in this firm, which emphasized fair treatment as its primary goal. Yet because it provides only a fairness-unfairness lens for viewing differences in point of view that fell, for whatever reasons, along race lines, this perspective seemed to foster the very kinds of tensions it sought to quell. Differences in work-related points of view were seen as a problem of primarily moral and ethical dimensions. This in turn limited the kind of discourse in which people could engage, especially across races. Finally, the perception that upper-level blacks identified more with whites in the firm than with blacks fueled tensions between upper- and lower-level people of color, mitigating against constructive intragroup relations as well.

Feeling Valued and Respected

Employees in work groups that held an integration-and-learning perspective on diversity reported feeling valued and respected by their colleagues. This was the case to a person for both current and past program staff in the law firm, where there was a sense that the firm "placed a value on the whole person." As one attorney of color put it, "The assumption about you is that you are competent." Other program staff of color corroborated this view. One said, "There is a lot of support for me to achieve. They really support and respect their staff of color in a way that I have not seen at other women's public interest law firms." To the extent that white people reported feeling marginalized at times from the central work of the organization, they also reported that "it isn't so bad." As one woman explained, "it doesn't consume me in the way that I think it would if I felt out of place here and questioned whether the organization really wanted me. I don't feel like that. I feel like there's enough support, and I have enough self-confidence about my role here that it doesn't consume me."

There was also a general feeling of well-being and a sense of having the respect of one's colleagues among employees of both Retail Operations and External Deposits in the Sales Division of the financial services firm, where an access-and-legitimacy perspective prevailed. "I get appreciation here," explained one black participant." People always check in, and it makes me feel warm inside. It's nice to know someone is recognizing what you do; and what you do, no matter how small, makes a difference." Another black participant said, "I talk to these individuals as people, regular people, and they talk to me as a regular person, not like I belong to a particular racial group." In a similar vein, other black participants felt that "most dismissals have been legitimate" and that "if you do your job well, you'll be recognized and promoted for it." As with race relations, however, these accounts of how people felt and were treated as individuals in their interpersonal interactions with others did not square with many of the things they said about how they felt and were treated as members of their respective departments. Whites in External Deposits had a clear sense of their privilege and the value they brought to the firm. Blacks in Retail Operations, however, were less sure about where they stood. As one black officer in Retail Operations said, "the jury is still out." He explained,

> One of the things that I take a measure of pride in is the fact that we can all live and work together. And that's OK. But I think where sometimes the problem comes in is in the division of the duties. You know, how do you perceive me? Do you perceive

me as someone who brings something to the able, who is a decision maker? Someone who understands our Customer base and whose thoughts should be taken seriously? Or do you see me as someone who is good at operationally making things work and making sure that the paperwork is together and making sure that the files are in order and making sure that the report is complete and typed and photocopied and all that stuff?

Although many described opportunities for promotion regardless of race, the division of labor in the Sales Division which followed directly from its access-and-legitimacy perspective on diversity, again made it clear to members that there were two tracks—one for whites and one for blacks. In fact, when one senior black officer on the retail side of the firm realized that he had no black male officers, he "pulled [the lone black member of External Deposits] out of there and made him an officer over on the retail side," with a sense that his career would otherwise have stagnated. When asked about the challenges and opportunities afforded by a diverse workforce this new officer in Retail Operations described the difficulties' he had faced in External Deposits in getting recognized for his contribution to doubling the department's portfolio in two years: only the two whites heading the department were promoted. When he finally received his own promotion two years later, it was on the retail side, where his supervisor more easily recognized and more readily rewarded his talents and skills. He accepted it with gratitude and excitement at the opportunities that lay ahead for him but nevertheless voiced his concerns about the lower status his new departmental affiliation now conferred. Thus, the message about the degree to which people felt valued and respected in these two departments was a complicated one. Although uniformly positive for the whites in External Deposits, the experience was mixed among blacks.

In work groups holding a discrimination-and-fairness perspective on their diversity, people of color reported more directly negative experiences in this regard. In the consulting firm, every one of the program and support staff members of color we interviewed reported feeling undermined, devalued, or disrespected in one way or another. The sense of having been denied honest, trustworthy feedback, for example, which led to a perception of standards as ambiguous and management as capricious, was the source of these feelings for many, One black support staff member felt that incidents such as the abrupt firing of her black colleague sent a clear message: "We are not going to make an attempt to orient ourselves to you or deal with you like you are a woman or intelligent being, but when we get tired of you we are going to get rid of you however we decide."

It was the belief that their competence was underestimated or overlooked, however, that produced by far the greatest sense of injury for most of the people of color we interviewed. They described being passed over for jobs they felt more qualified to do than the white candidates who were ultimately hired, ignored when they felt they had knowledge or skills to offer, and presumed automatically to lack the skills required to do their jobs competently. One black support staff member observed, "There's just no way that you can be black and just know what you're talking about or be able to learn something well enough for them to say, 'go ahead, try it and we'll see how it works.' " Another explained, "There's a tendency to put more credence in what is said by white people, not to act on something, till it's confirmed by a white voice." A Latina who worked on the program staff described her experience with lack of respect: "I find to this day that I'm treated with condescension on issues that I may know more about than they do. . . . Until [white people] discover [an idea], until they express it with their own words and their own style, it's as if it doesn't exist."

Many shared the sense of having either to be white or to act white to be taken seriously. For example, several attributed what they perceived to be the unfair discipline of the black man held responsible for the stolen money to the fact that he "is black—his attire, his mannerisms—he has a street style. I don't think they can really see past that." As one Latina explained, "A lot of the tensions have to do with a difficulty in recognizing that the habits, the ways of doing things have been set by white people. And there hasn't been enough recognition that just to include people of color isn't really enough." Because of their color-blind ideology, however, racial differences were taboo subjects for discussion, and it was therefore illegitimate to recognize, solicit, or offer work-related perspectives that Were informed by differences in people's cultural backgrounds. A number of the participants of color also described feeling "depressed" and "dispirited" at what they felt was the "paternalistic" or "patronizing" attitude toward people of color generally and themselves in particular. About the white program staff members who do economic development in Africa, for example, one black manager said, "They treat black people like they're little pygmy children."

The paternalism that staff of color perceived in their white colleagues' attitudes toward them appeared to stem at least in part from whites' belief that the firm should uphold its moral commitment to affirmative action, even if it meant lowering standards for employees of color. One white manager explained that he was "leaning over backward to be generous and fair and understanding." In doing so, he felt it was incumbent upon him to excuse staff of color for problems like tardiness, recognizing "that it may be far easier for me given my particular circumstances, living in the suburbs, to be able to maintain a schedule than it is for one with multiple pressures of being black and inner city." Contrary to this man's intentions, it was precisely this kind of charitable view that many blacks in the firm resented. It is consistent with a discrimination-and-fairness perspective on diversity in which whites interpret and respond to their perceptions of cultural differences within a moral frame: blacks were to be forgiven for their deviations from (white cultural) norms of acceptable behavior, as these deviations were merely understandable reactions to the unjust circumstances of their lives.

We heard comparatively little from black executives or from whites in any position about the ways in which they might have felt devalued in the organization. Black executives tended to comment on how blacks lower down felt devalued but said little about their own feelings in this regard. This is consistent with the fact that they were generally aligned with their white counterparts in their perceptions of the firm and its problems. And although one white male described feeling "denigrated" for being perceived as "not living up to the affirmative action goals of the firm," whites did not register complaints about the level of respect accorded to them.

Significance of Cultural Identity

Consistent with the integration-and-learning perspective's emphasis on cultural identity as a potential source of insight and skill, both current and past program staff of color in the law firm described their racial group membership as a significant factor in shaping how they approached and carried out their work. One Asian American attorney explained, "I have a different perspective on the work because I'm a woman of color, and I am interested in cases that, for example, would open doors to women of color that have traditionally been open only to white women. A white woman is naturally less likely to consider those cases." Program staff of color also routinely related stories about how their cultural knowledge and skills enhanced their ability to do their work by, for example, helping them to establish rapport with clients. One Latina described how she had convinced a reluctant Mexican woman, who was a key witness in a case, to testify:

> It was partly that I spoke the language, but I don't think it could have happened with an Anglo who spoke Spanish, because it had so much to do with understanding what was going on in this woman's mind. And being able to anticipate and just plug into what was happening with her. . . . It was a tense situation, but I was not afraid of her anger.

White program staff also described their racial identity as having a significant impact on them at work, but in different ways from their colleagues of color. Whites did not see their race as a source of skill or insight into their work; nevertheless, they were both aware of and articulate about how being white influenced them. "I think that all of us who are white here do think about being white," one attorney explained. Some spoke of the opportunities being white afforded them at work. Because of "people's racism," one white woman explained, "it's probably easier being white in settings that are often predominantly white." She had observed, for example, that in meetings outside the firm, lawyers would immediately assume that she was the lawyer and that her Asian American colleague was not, when the reverse was true; she attributed this to the greater authority and status they automatically attributed to her as a white person. A number of whites also commented on how diversity in the program staff, in particular, moving the women-of-color project from the periphery to the center of their work, had affected their own sense of what it means to be white. One white attorney felt that it had changed the way she thought about herself as a white middle-class woman and forced her to examine her own racism and stereotypes. Another commented on how diversifying the staff as they had had made her "less defensive" about being white because race issues were open to discussion. She explained, "I think before the change [in racial composition] if you'd asked me these [interview] questions I . . . [think] I would have felt more defensive. Like 'Oh God, she's trying to find out if I really am a racist or something like that. . . .' "

More generally, employees of all races reported feeling they could show more of who they were at work than had been able to do in other work settings. A Latina of the program staff told us, "It's my first work experience where the different perspectives I bring are not the only ones in the office, and they are appreciated and accepted. Talking about my life or bringing those perspectives is not something that I have to worry about."

Racial identity among people of color in work groups with an access-and-legitimacy perspective on diversity, in contrast, was full of contradiction and ambivalence. In her advice to other firms wishing to become more racially diverse, one young black financial services employee in Retail Operations summarized the quandary of being black in this setting: "Try not to let the race thing be an issue," she urged. "I know that's just like asking an elephant not to be gray. . . . I really don't know how that could work, but it just needs to happen, is all I can say." At the same time, she advised blacks in particular to "just remember who you are, and believe in yourself and where you stand." Her advice was thus paradoxical: erase the reality of race yet hold onto your black identity. We suspect that in this kind of setting, in which racial diversity assumes a highly circumscribed role—it has positive value only insofar as it provides access to and legitimacy with a diverse clientele—there is a mixed message about what it means to be black. On the one hand, it bestows value on blacks; on the other hand, it upholds an essentially assimilationist vision in which white culture remains the dominant culture. This mixed message raised concerns about losing one's

identity as a black person despite its avowed value in the group.

In light of the mixed message the access-and-legitimacy perspective sends about the value and significance of being black, it is not surprising that the meanings that black employees in Retail attributed to their racial group membership were often contradictory. When we asked black employees about the salience or significance to them of their identity group memberships at work, they typically responded by saying that "race is not a problem." The notion that their racial group membership might have had a positive impact on their work or their experiences at work, as it did for program staff of color in the law firm, was conspicuously absent in their responses, although they clearly understood the importance of having black employees in Retail to provide credibility with the firm's black clientele. For example, when asked about the impact of her own racial identity at work, one black employee was adamant that race was irrelevant. She also remarked later in her interview, however, that "if they put all of [External Deposits] down here [in Retail] for a week . . . they would be really whipped and surprised, and they would probably run back to their department and never look back . . . because that's an all white department." Her reaction to an incident in a staff meeting we had witnessed, in which a white male manager expressed strong disagreement with a position that senior management endorsed, also belied her declarations of racial equity: "I think that there are a lot of people who wish they could have been that outspoken," she said, "and the discussion [among black managers] was that had there been a black person he probably would not be here today." Her statements taken together thus were contradictory: race is irrelevant, but blacks are better suited to the work in Retail, and whites enjoy greater freedom of expression. These kinds of contradictions suggested that racial identity may well have been a source of ambivalence for blacks.

Unlike white program staff in the law firm, white employees in External Deposits had little consciousness of their racial identity at work. With the exception of the white manager who attributed her "fit" with the culture of the firm to her race, no whites in External Deposits reported their racial group membership as salient in shaping their experiences or how they expressed themselves at work. One white employee who now worked for External Deposits, but who had for many years been either the only white or one of a few in Retail, said that she was "never conscious that no one was white on the first floor [where Retail is located]. [Until a black colleague suggested it,] it never occurred to me that I might have been transferred to [External Deposits] because I'm white." That racial identity figured prominently in black Sales Division employees' reports of their experience and seemingly little in white employees' reports is predictable given the precepts of the access-and-legitimacy perspective, which minimize people's experience of diversity while seeking to gain its most immediate and instrumental benefits.

Consistent with other outcomes that were associated with the discrimination-and-fairness perspective, people of color across work groups in the consulting firm typically characterized membership in their racial group as a source of powerlessness and disenfranchisement. One black manager explained, "It's like a struggle between good white people and bad white people, and basically we're observers, and we just are rooting for good white people to win." Consistent with this observation, several described feelings of self-doubt they often experienced as people of color and even questioned whether their apparent failings might be due to their own shortcomings as members of their racial groups. As one Latina explained, "So many of us find that it's a sink-or-swim situation... . And I think that those of us who are part of the minority here feel that because of our temperament we're not strong enough, so that in the sink-or-swim, we sink." Similarly, another felt that her boss ignored her completely, and she questioned whether "that's a reflection on me as a Puerto Rican, or something I myself have made easy, you know, sort of like my personality gives room for him to feel comfortable doing that."

Although many employees of color, particularly members of the support staff, wished that they were not seen as "black, Hispanic, or whatever," but were instead seen simply for who they are," there were a few members of the program staff who saw their racial group membership as a source of cultural values for which they wished to be recognized. Nevertheless, because they felt that whites were "afraid to recognize that there are differences in culture" and would find such expressions "very problematic," these employees, who were, in any case, rare in this firm, typically did not express their cultural differences. Some employees of color resent this, accusing their seniors of "just becoming carbon copies of [whites] and . . . not really giving [whites] . . . a sense of the feelings of a person of color." Despite these criticisms and the similarities in points of view we found between white executives and executives of color, it was clear from our interviews whether there were any people of color in the organization who, in fact, felt assimilated.

Most white employees, to the extent that they discussed the significance of their racial group membership at all, discussed it only as a basis for feeling intimidated, apprehensive, or reluctant to speak out about race-related issues. They tended to describe themselves as "oblivious" to what people of color were experiencing, "perplexed" by their complaints. Others were somewhat more reflective. The white executive director, for example, recognized that in race relations, "although there is a wish to say that everybody starts out in the same place, and you should just deal as one infinitely valuable human being to another . . . all kinds of power stuff gets in there." Yet she had little to say about how she, as a white person in charge, might intervene to make race relations in the firm better. "There are only so many things somebody who's white and in a leadership position can do directly on that subject," she said. "[You just have to] be the best person you can be in terms of trying to make the program go the best way you can make it go." Although she recognized that this was "not sufficient," it was "about all I know to do." Consistent with the discrimination-and-fairness perspective, she was, as a white person, limited to the moral realm as a way of understanding the role her racial identity might play in her ability to address racial issues.

Work Group Functioning

We found that the perspective on diversity a group of people held influenced how they expressed and managed tensions related to diversity, whether those traditionally underrepresented in the organization felt respected and valued by their colleagues, and how people valued and expressed themselves as members of their cultural identity groups; these, in turn, influenced people's sense of self-efficacy and work group functioning. All three types of work group diversity perspectives were successful in motivating managers to diversify their staffs, but only the integration-and-learning perspective provided the kind of rationale and guidance people needed to achieve sustained benefits from diversity.[1] Table 20.2 summarizes the intermediate group outcomes of the three diversity perspectives and their effects on group functioning as detailed below.

Work groups with an integration-and-learning perspective were high functioning. At the law firm, all of the staff we interviewed described the firm's program as successful and virtually all attributed at least part of its success to program staff's ability and willingness to bring the interests and perspectives of people of color "into the centerpiece of the organization." As one woman explained, "[Diversity in the program staff] has affected the work in terms of expanding notions of what are women's issues and taking on issues and framing them as women's issues in creative ways that would have never been done [with an all-white staff] and doesn't get

done by other women's organizations. It's really changed the substance and in that sense enhanced the quality of our work." This result clearly hinged on the open and direct way in which the staff managed racial differences and conflicts, the fact that they respected people and sought their contributions as members of their respective racial groups, and the fact that both white employees and employees of color were able to consider and share with their colleagues how their experiences as members of those groups influenced them at work. This approach to diversity encouraged and enabled program staff of color to bring skills and capacities to the firm that gave them access to important information in their own communities and helped them build rapport with clients, thereby helping to expand the firm's client base. Equally important, however, was the emphasis on cross-cultural exposure and education so that staff members were continually expanding their own capacities. The integration-and-learning perspective made identity a source of insight that was transferable to a broad range of employees, not just to those who were members of "diverse"

Table 20.2
Intermediate Outcomes Mediating Effects of Diversity Perspectives on Group Functioning

Mediators	Integration-and-learning	Access-and-legitimacy	Discrimination-and-fairness
Quality of intergroup relations	Conflict resulting from cultural differences in point of view; different groups accorded equal power and status; open discussion of differences and conflict	Conflict resulting from differential power and status accorded different races/functions; little open discussion of conflict	Intractable race-related conflict stemming from entrenched, undiscussible status and power imbalances; no open discussion of conflict or differences
Feeling valued and respected	All employees feel fully respected and valued for their competence and contributions to the organization	Employees of color question whether they are valued and respected equally; perceive devaluation of functions staffed predominantly by people of color	Employees of color feel disrespected and devalued as members of minority racial/ethnic groups
Significance of own racial identity at work	Source of value for people of color, a resource for learning and teaching; a source of privilege for whites to acknowledge	Source of ambivalence for employees of color; whites not conscious	Source of powerlessness for people of color; source of apprehension for whites
Group functioning			
	Enhanced by cross-cultural exposure and learning and by work processes designed to facilitate constructive intergroup conflict and exploration of diverse views	Enhanced by increased access and legitimacy; inhibited by lack of learning and exchange between racially segregated functions	Inhibited by low morale of employees, lack of cross-cultural learning, and the inability of employees of color to bring all relevant skills and insights to bear on work

groups. Diversity, thus, was a resource on which all program staff could draw.

In addition, by incorporating diversity into the core work of the organization, this perspective afforded all employees some measure of access to and legitimacy with their clients, regardless of employees' respective cultural identities. One white member of the program staff for example, explained that the firm's reputation as a racially integrated firm had increased her credibility in minority communities and her ability to work in them. Similarly, a former member of the program staff who is African American felt that she personally gained credibility with the firm's Asian clients when a Japanese American attorney joined the staff. This credibility allowed staff members to network much more widely across communities, which provided them with a much richer, broader base of information; this, in turn, gave them a better perspective on the problems they were addressing, enhancing the quality of their analyses. Finally, this perspective created a model of working in coalition with a number of public interest, civil rights, and other "people-of-color" groups, which helped to facilitate a series of mutually beneficial, cross-organizational collaborations.

Our data suggested that while the access-and-legitimacy perspective enhanced a work group's ability to reach more diverse market, it was limiting in other ways. The financial service firm's goals were to make a profit for the company and to develop and revitalize the economy of the local community within which it was situated. The Sales Division's access-and-legitimacy perspective on diversity had indeed advanced these goals by giving members some measure of access to and legitimacy with both the local community to whom they appealed for personal investments and commercial ventures, as well as the national community to whom they appealed for socially responsible investments and the purchase of other kinds of competitive money-management products. And most informants agreed that External Deposits had grown the firm's assets well beyond expectations. Nevertheless, many were concerned that Retail Operations had thus far been unable to reach its growth potential in the local community and that External Deposits' capacity to sustain its growth would be severely limited by increasing competition in its national markets. Our

data suggested that, despite the benefits the access-and-legitimacy perspective had garnered for the Sales Division, this perspective also contributed to the problems Division employees faced in at least three ways, all of which were related to the racial division of labor it seemed inevitably to create.

First, some participants reported that Retail Operations' lower status in the organization compromised the quality of service Retail clients received. One woman who had worked in both departments speculated that the reason for making the two departments separate in the first place was to draw "a very distinct line" between their respective customers. Whether the result of fewer resources in Retail such as time, or Retail employees' diminished sense of entitlement for their clients, most people acknowledged, often with clear racial overtones, that Retail clients received a lower quality of service than clients in External Deposits: "Customers in Retail don't get that special touch that External Deposits' rich white clients get," one customer service agent in Retail lamented. Reiterating these concerns, the manager of Retail Operations provided anecdotal evidence to suggest that her customers were "overshadowed by the hoity-toity treatment" others got and were taking their business elsewhere as a result.

Second, referring to the duplication of efforts in the two departments—a direct result of how the access-and-legitimacy perspective was manifest in this division—the manager of External Deposits explained, "It's really inefficient to have what are essentially two banks here." It could take one of her employees "seven hours to do something himself that he could have taken to Retail and gotten done much more quickly," she explained, but for "the competitiveness and animosity between the two departments." Moreover, she felt that this competitiveness threatened to compromise the quality of service some customers received. Referring to the recent addition of a corporate banking function in Retail designed to service corporate accounts citywide, together with her own department's recent efforts to develop socially responsible investments within the city, the manager of External Deposits was concerned that the line between their client bases would become increasingly blurred: "Historically, the Retail side has been defined as [the neighborhoods]. Anything else in the city by rights should be mine if we use that definition. Right? So what happens if I get a law firm downtown that needs corporate banking services, and I bring them in? Whose account is that? I really can't service it, but Retail that's their stock and trade." It was her feeling that with better relationships and less disparity between the two departments, these kinds of conflicts could be avoided and customers would receive the quality of services that was their due, rather than being caught up in a battle over whose account was rightfully whose.

Finally, there were inefficiencies in the perfectionist "white" culture that had come to characterize External Deposits because they were unable to learn from Retail Operations. Critical of the culture her predecessor had built in her efforts to service the needs of her more affluent, more demanding clientele, the current manager of External Deposits explained,

> It's very hard to make money with all that perfectionism. A letter would be edited four times before it went out the door. . . . In my opinion, that just isn't necessary. . . . [T]he average bank customer, I think, wants somebody who's steady, loyal, knows their business inside and out and works hard. I don't necessarily want someone who, every time a customer calls they'll design a new product for them. . . . And we did an awful lot of that.

This manager felt strongly that in this respect, among others, there might be something to learn from the way Retail Operations functioned, but the "cultural barriers," created by their longstanding differences made it difficult for them to collaborate. "They're very guarded," she explained. "They don't believe that I really want to know what they're saying."

The discrimination-and-fairness perspective appeared to have a negative effect on work group functioning in a variety of ways. In the consulting firm, although different groups laid blame in different places for the fact that whites were reluctant to disagree with people of color, challenge them, or provide feedback to them, most agreed that it compromised both their own and their department's ability to reach their potential. "Because a lot of the problems here have not dealt with openly," a white manager explained, "they have been allowed to fester, and people who are incompetent remain incompetent." In a similar vein, a black support staff member lamented her inability to get "corrective criticism" from her white supervisor, "which would only further my desire, not only to do my job well, but also to gain as much knowledge about my job and any other technical skills as might be necessary to enhance my work."

The numerous "racial" incidents and subsequent organizing, memo-writing, and meeting cost the organization not only the time and energy of the people of color who engaged in these activities on company time but the morale of everyone who suffered from the tense work environment as a result. As one white manager explained, "the tension [over the firing of the black employee] was palpable in the organization, which made it harder to come in to work bounding with enthusiasm. These incidents affect everyone's morale; you bounce back, but only until the next one erupts." In response to a different incident, another described the whole organization as "grinding to a halt because of the morale problem."

People of color also found it draining and time-consuming always to have to wonder whether their treatment was race-related or not. As one woman explained, "It really hampered me in the beginning, and I started to question myself all the time." Others described how management's apparent lack of interest in their ideas not only made them feel devalued but was potentially costly to their departments as well. One mid-level manager said he "had a vision" for the function he supervised but found it difficult to get the ear of "the people who can make a difference." He said that although he tried to look past "the possibility that this was because of race," it was difficult. He found management's inattention both perplexing and depressing and, as a result, had decided no longer to offer his point of view.

To the extent that whites associated diversity with positive outcomes, it tended to be because they felt they had "learned an immense amount about race" or that the presence of people of color had helped them attain their "ideals of equality and justice." There were a few white program staff, however, who also felt that diversity had had a positive impact on their programs because members of other cultural groups were able to assist them in their program work with culturally similar client groups. One person, for example, saw the value of involving Latino staff in the firm's Central American work because they had useful insights into race relations there. Those program staff of color who also saw the possibility of such connections, however, typically described their colleagues' resistance to their using insights derived from their particular cultural perspectives. Moreover, when they did try to make such connections, they, like their white counterparts, would adopt the discrimination-and-fairness moral framing of differences in the ensuing debate, which was ultimately unproductive. An African American program manager who headed economic development activities in Eastern Europe tried to get his colleagues to consider reorganizing the firm's development work according to similarities in countries' development experiences rather than geographical area. Poland, he argued, had more in common with certain African and Latin American countries than with other European countries and therefore could benefit more from expertise developed in Africa and Latin America than in Europe. As an African American, he felt he was perhaps less committed to the firm's "Eurocentric" orientation, which he believed led his colleagues to assume erroneously—and to the firm's detriment—that white countries have more in common with each other than with nonwhite countries. He never succeeded in generating a constructive discussion of this idea, however, because the exchange quickly degenerated into a debate about which view—the firm's or his—was more racially motivated and therefore racist. This framing, in which he participated, foreclosed opportunities for learning about how his department might do its work more effectively.

Discussion

Our research showed how three diversity perspectives differentially affected the functioning of culturally diverse work groups. The crucial dimension along which the three diversity perspectives varied was whether and how cultural diversity was linked to the group's work and work processes. In the integration-and-learning perspective, cultural diversity is a potentially valuable resource that the organization can use, not only at its margins, to gain entree into previously inaccessible niche markets, but at its core, to rethink and reconfigure its primary tasks as well. It is based on the assumption that cultural differences give rise to different life experiences, knowledge, and insights, which

can inform alternative views about work and how best to accomplish it. In the work groups we studied that embraced this perspective, this view of the role of racial diversity encouraged group members to discuss openly their different points of view because differences—including those explicitly linked to cultural experience—were valued as opportunities for learning. This process communicated to all employees that they were valued and respected and encouraged them to value and express themselves as members of their racial identity groups. These aspects of the way they functioned afforded opportunities for cross-cultural learning, which enhanced the group's work.

In the access-and-legitimacy perspective, cultural diversity is a potentially valuable resource, but only at the organization's margins and only to gain access to and legitimacy with a diverse market. In the work groups we studied that embraced this perspective, this view of the role of racial diversity led to race-based staffing patterns that matched the racial make-up of the markets they served. This fostered perceptions of white-staffed functions as higher status than functions staffed by people of color; racially segregated career tracks and opportunities, which fostered concerns among staff of color about the degree to which they were valued and respected; and ambivalence on the part of people of color about the meaning and significance of their racial identity at work. The resulting interracial/interfunctional tensions appeared to inhibit learning and people's ability to be maximally effective in their work.

Finally, in the discrimination-and-fairness perspective, diversity is a mechanism for ensuring equal opportunity, fair treatment, and an end to discrimination; it articulates no link at all between cultural diversity and the group's work and, in fact, espouses a color-blind strategy for managing employees and employee relations. In the work groups that embraced this perspective, this view of the role of racial diversity restricted the discourse about race to one in which employees negotiated the meaning of all race-related differences on moral grounds. Questions and concerns about fairness led inevitably to strained race relations characterized. by competing claims of innocence, with each group assuming a defensive posture in relation to the other (Steele, 1990). Racial identity thus became a source of apprehension for white people and feelings of powerlessness for many people of color. This made it difficult for people to bring all relevant skills and insights to bear on their work, thus compromising their ability to learn from one another and to be maximally effective. . . .

Note

1. This is not to say that concerns about discrimination are unimportant nor that using cultural diversity to gain access to and legitimacy with different market segments is illegitimate; rather, our research suggests that these alone as the primary basis for a group's diversity strategy will likely undercut the group's effectiveness.

References

Alderfer, C. P. 1980. "The methodology of organization diagnosis." *Professional Psychology*, 11: 459–468.

———. 1987. "An intergroup perspective on group dynamics." In J. Lorsch (ed.), *Handbook of Organizational Behavior*: 190–219. Englewood Cliffs, NJ: Prentice-Hall.

———. 1992. "Changing race relations embedded in organizations. Report on a long-term project with the XYZ Corporation." In S. E. Jackson and Associates (eds.), *Diversity in the Workplace: Human Resources Initiatives*: 138–166. New York: Guilford Press.

Alderfer, C. P., and K. K. Smith. 1982. "Studying intergroup relations embedded in organizations." *Administrative Science Quarterly*, 27: 35–65.

Alderfer, C. P., R. Tucker, C. Alderfer, and L. Tucker. 1980. "Diagnosing race relations in management," *Journal of Applied Behavioral Science*, 16: 135–166.

Ancona, D. Gladstein, and D. F. Caldwell. 1992. "Demography and design: Predictors of new product team performance" *Organization Science*, 3: 321–341.

Bailyn, L. 1993. *Breaking the Mold: Women, Men, and Time in the New Corporate World*. New York: Free Press.

Bantel, K. A., and S. E. Jackson. 1989. "Top management and innovations in banking: Does the composition of the top team make a difference?" *Strategic Management Journal*, 10: 107–124.

Blalock, H. M., Jr. 1957. "Percent non-white and discrimination in the South." *American Sociological Review*, 22: 677–682.

Blau, P.M. 1977. *Inequality and Heterogeneity*. New York: Free Press.

Bochner, S., and B. Hesketh. 1994. "Power distance, individualism/collectivism, and job-related attitudes in a culturally diverse work group." *Journal of Cross-Cultural Psychology*, 25: 233–257.

Chatman, J. A., J. T. Polzer, S. G. Barsade, and M. A. Neale. 1998. "Being different yet feeling similar. The influence of demographic composition and organizational culture on work processes and outcomes." *Administrative Science Quarterly*, 43: 749–780.

Clement, D. E., and J. J. Schiereck. 1973. "Sex composition end group performance in a visual signal detection task." *Memory and Cognition*, 1: 251–255.

Cox, T. H., Jr. 1993. *Cultural Diversity in Organizations: Theory, Research, and Practice*. San Francisco: Berrett-Koehler.

Cox, T. H., Jr., and S. Blake. 1991. "Managing cultural diversity: Implications for organizational competitiveness." *Academy of Management Executive*, 5(3): 45–56.

Cox, T. H., Jr., S. A. Lobel, and P. L. McLeod. 1991. "Effects of ethnic group cultural differences on cooperative and competitive behavior on a group task." *Academy of Management Journal*, 34: 827–847.

Ely, R. J. 1994. "The effects of organizational demographics and social identity on relationships among professional women." *Administrative Science Quarterly*, 39: 203–238.

———. 1995. "The power in demography: Women's social constructions of gender identity at work." *Academy of Management Journal*, 38: 589–634.

Ely, R. J., and D. E. Meyerson. 2000. "Theories of gender in organizations: A new approach to organizational analysis and change." In B. M. Staw and R. I. Sutton (eds.), *Research in Organizational Behavior*, 22: 105–153. New York: Elsevier science/JAI.

Epstein, C. F. 1988. *Deceptive Distinctions*. New Haven, CT: Yale University Press.

Fiedler, F. E. 1966. "The effect of leadership and cultural heterogeneity on group performance: A test of the contingency model." *Journal of Experimental Social Psychology*, 2: 237–264.

Fiedler, F. E., W. A. T. Meuwese, and S. Oonk. 1961. "Performance on laboratory tasks requiring group creativity." *Acta Psychologica*, 18: 100–119.

Foeman, A. K., and G. Pressley. 1987. "Ethnic culture and corporate culture: Using black styles in organizations." *Communication Quarterly*, 35: 293–307.

Gutek, B. A. 1985. *Sex and the Workplace*. San Francisco: Jossey-Bass.

Harding, S. 1986. *The Science Question in Feminism*. Ithaca, NY: Cornell University Press.

Helgesen, S. 1990. *The Female Advantage: Women's Ways of Leadership*. New York: Doubleday.

Hoffman, L. R. 1959. "Homogeneity of member personality and its effect on group problem-solving." *Journal of Abnormal and Social Psychology*, 58: 27–32.

Hoffman, L. R., and N. R. F. Maier. 1961. "Quality and acceptance of problem solutions by members of homogeneous and heterogeneous groups." *Journal of Abnormal and Social Psychology*, 62: 401–407.

Jackson, S. E., and Associates. 1992. *Diversity in the Workplace: Human Resources Initiatives*. New York: Guilford Press.

Jackson, S. E., and M. N. Ruderman (eds.). 1995. *Diversity in Work Teams*. Washington, DC: American Psychological Association.

Jehn, K. A. 1997. "A qualitative analysis of conflict types and dimensions in organizational groups." *Administrative Science Quarterly*, 42: 530–557.

Jehn, K. A., G. B. Northcraft, and M. A. Neale. 1999. "Why differences make a difference: A field study of diversity, conflict, and performance in workgroups." *Administrative Science Quarterly*, 44: 741–763.

Kanter, R. M. 1977. *Men and Women of the Corporation*. New York: Basic Books.

Kent, R. N., and J. E. McGrath. 1969. "Task and group characteristics as factors influencing group performance." *Journal of Experimental Social Psychology*, 5: 429–440.

Larkey, L. K. 1996. "Toward a theory of communicative interactions in culturally diverse workgroups." *Academy of Management Review*, 21: 463–491.

Lawrence, B. S. 1997. "The black box of organizational demography." *Organization Science*, 8: 1–22.

Martin, P. Y. 1985. "Group sex composition in work organizations. A structural-normative model." In S. B. Bacharach and S. M. Mitchell (eds.), *Research in the Sociology of Organizations*, 4: 311–349. Greenwich, CT: JAI press.

Maznevski, M. L. 1994. "Understanding our differences. Performance in decision-making groups with diverse members." *Human Relations*, 47: 531–552.

McGrath, J. E., J. L. Berdahl, and H. Arrow. 1995. "Traits, expectations, culture, and clout: The dynamics of diversity in work groups." In S. E. Jackson and M. N. Ruderman (eds.), *Diversity in Work Teams*: 17–45. Washington, DC: American Psychological Association.

Meglino, B. M., E. C. Ravlin, and C. L. Adkins. 1989. "A work values approach to corporate culture: A field test of the value congruence process and its relationship to individual outcomes." *Journal of Applied Psychology*, 74: 424–432.

Milliken, F. J., and L. L. Martins. 1996. "Searching for common threads: Understanding the multiple effects of diversity in organizational groups." *Academy of Management Review*, 21: 402–433.

Morrison, A. M. 1992. *The New Leaders: Guidelines on Leadership Diversity in America*. San Francisco: Jossey-Bass.

Murnighan, J. K., and D. E. Conlon. 1991. "The dynamics of intense work groups: A study of British string quartets." *Administrative Science Quarterly*, 36: 165–186.

Nkomo, S. M. 1992. "The emperor has no clothes: Rewriting 'race' in organizations." *Academy of Management Review*, 17: 487–513.

Pelted, L. H. 1996. "Demographic diversity, conflict and work group outcomes. An intervening process theory." *Organization Science*, 7: 615–631.

Ragins, B. R. 1997. "Diversified mentoring relationships in organizations: A power perspective." *Academy of Management Review*, 22: 482–521.

Ridgeway, C. L. 1988. "Gender differences in task groups: A status and legitimacy account." In M. Webster, Jr. and M. Foschi (eds.), *Status Generalization: New Theory and Research*: 188–206. Stanford, CA: Stanford University Press.

——. 1991. "The social construction of status value: Gender and other nominal characteristics." *Social Forces*, 70: 367–386.

Ridgeway, C. L., and J. Berger. 1986. "Expectations, legitimation, and dominance behavior in task groups." *American Sociological Review*, 51: 603–617.

Rosener, J. 1990. "Ways women lead." *Harvard Business Review*, Nov–Dec: 119–125.

Ruhe, J. A. 1978. "Effect of leader sex and leader behavior on group problem-solving." Proceedings of the American Institute for Decisions Sciences, Northeast Division, May: 123–127.

Ruhe, J. A., and J. Eatman. 1977. "Effects of racial composition on small groups." *Small Group Behavior*, 8: 479–486.

Shaw, M. E. 1983. "Group composition." In H. H. Blumberg, A. P. Hare, V. Kent, and M. Davies (eds.), *Small Groups and Social Interaction*, 1: 89–96. Chichester, UK: Wiley.

Steele, S. 1990. *The Content of Our Character*. New York: St. Martin's.

Strangor, C., L. Lynch, C. Duan, and B. Glass. 1992. "Categorization of individuals on the basis of multiple social features." *Journal of Personality and Social Psychology*, 62: 207–218.

Thomas, D. A. 1993. "Racial dynamics of cross-race developmental relationships." *Administrative Science Quarterly*, 38: 169–194.

Thomas, D. A. 1999. "Beyond the simple demography-power hypothesis: How blacks in power influence white-mentor-black-protégé developmental relationships." In A. J. Murrell, F. Crosby, and R. J. Ely (eds.), *Mentoring Dilemmas: Developmental Relationships within Multicultural Organizations*: 157–170. Ogden, UT: Erlbaum.

Thomas, D. A., and R. D. Ely. 1996. "Making differences matter: A new paradigm for managing diversity." *Harvard Business Review*, Sept.–Oct.: 79–90.

Thomas, R. R., Jr. 1991. *Beyond Race and Gender*. New York: American Management Association.

Tsui, A. S., T. D. Egan, and C. A. O'Reilly III. 1992. "Being different: Relational demography and organizational attachment." *Administrative Science Quarterly*, 37: 549–579.

Valian, V. 1998. *Why So Slow? The Advancement of Women*. Cambridge, MA: MIT Press.

Wanous, J. P., and M. A. Youtz. 1986. "Solution diversity and the quality of group decisions." *Academy of Management Journal*, 29: 149–159.

Watson, W. E., K. Kumar, and L. K. Michaelsen. 1993. "Cultural diversity's impact on interaction process and performance: Comparing homogeneous and diverse task groups." *Academy of Management Journal*, 36: 590–602.

Williams K. Y., and C. A. O'Reilly III. 1998. "Demography and diversity in organizations." In B. M. Staw and R. I. Sutton (eds.), *Research in Organizational Behavior*, 20: 77–140. Stamford, CT: JAI Press.

Wood, W. 1987. "Meta-analytic review of sex differences in group performance." *Psychological Bulletin*, 102: 53–71.

Yoder, J. D. 1991. "Rethinking tokenism. Looking beyond numbers." *Gender and Society*, 5: 179–192.

Ziller, R. C., and R. V. Exline. 1958. "Some consequences of age heterogeneity in decision-making groups." *Sociometry*, 21: 198–211.

Zimmer, L. 1988. "Tokenism and women in the workplace. The limits of gender-neutral theory." *Social Problems*, 35: 64–77.

Chapter 21
Race, Opportunity, and Diversity of Social Circles in Managerial Networks

Herminia Ibarra

Organizations are made up of people and people in organizations are connected to one another in various ways. Some relationships are formalized by reporting lines or work assignments. Other relationships are much more informal and consist of the relationships people form as they look to others for information, professional advice, friendship, or support. The web of these informal ties make up a person's personal network. Of interest to organizational researchers are the properties of these networks and their relationship to career outcomes.

Just as family and friends outside organizations can provide social support and other forms of assistance to people, personal networks within organizations are a crucial social resource. Being "well-connected" can enhance career success, while people with less-developed or less-powerful networks may not fare as well. Organizational researchers interested in understanding racial, gender, and other forms of inequality suspect that differences in personal networks may help explain why some groups do better than others at work.

Herminia Ibarra takes up this issue by focusing on differences in the personal networks of a racially diverse group of middle managers. She finds that minority and white managers' networks differed in a variety of ways and that these differences could be partly explained by differences in the overall percentages of white and minority managers in the organization as a whole. Ibarra's research also reveals some important differences in social networks within racial groups.

A central theme that has emerged in the organizational literature on racial minorities in corporate settings is the difficulties members of minority groups experience gaining significant social and instrumental support in the workplace (Thomas & Alderfer, 1989). Many have argued that exclusion from social networks explains the failure of minority managers to advance more rapidly in their careers and organizations (Dickens & Dickens, 1982; DiTomaso, Thompson, & Blake, 1988; Fernandez, 1991; Irons & Moore, 1985; Morrison & Von Glinow, 1990), yet network differences by race are rarely examined empirically. Further, the scant existing literature offers contradictory recommendations: an assimilation paradigm suggests that members of racial minorities should develop interpersonal networks that are similar to those of their successful white peers. In contrast, a pluralist perspective implies that because of different circumstances, minority members must use different approaches to achieve similar ends (Cox, 1991; Nkomo, 1992; Thomas, 1993). Given the importance of informal networks for career success (Brass, 1985; Burt, 1992), investigating them may shed light on the nature of the obstacles racial minorities face in the workplace and strategies for overcoming those obstacles.

The reported study drew from social network and race relations theories to illuminate relationships among race, career outcomes, and network interaction patterns. My central thesis was twofold: the racial composition of a managerial network is highly constrained by the macro context in which interpersonal interaction is embedded, and decisions about network composition constitute the central strategic choice made at the individual level. Macrocontext, or the pattern of different racial groups' representation in organizational and societal power elites, produces systematic differences in network structure that factors such as "human capital" investment or position power cannot explain. Microlevel factors, however, particularly variables that shape individuals' goals and network development strategies (Wharton, 1992). also produce network differences. To investigate the role of these macro and micro factors and the relative explanatory values of the assimilation and pluralist perspectives, I compared the structures of the informal networks of white and minority middle managers and explored explanations for intraminority group variance in network patterns.

Recent research (Burt, 1992) further suggests that exclusive focus on the presence or absence of network differences may be misleading since similar networks may not necessarily provide similar benefits to members of different groups. Since individuals' views about what constitutes a useful network may affect their network strategies. the match between network structure and perceptions of network utility warrants exploration. The discovery of conditional effects would provide additional evidence of network development trade-offs that result from macrostructural factors and are unique to minorities. Thus, I also investigated the extent to which the relationship between network characteristics and managers' assessments of the utility of their networks varied by race.

Effects of Race on Managerial Networks

Networks as Social Resources

An informal managerial network is defined here as the set of job-related contacts that a manager relies on for access to task-related, career, and social support. In the sociological literature, a network's instrumental utility is viewed as a function of two dimensions: the network's range, which refers to the diversity of group affiliations encompassed and the potential access to information and resources from diverse and distant subgroups afforded by the network (Burt, 1992; Campbell, Marsden, & Hurlbert, 1986; Granovetter, 1973), and its status, which refers to the positions of network contacts in the relevant status hierarchy (Lin, 1982). Range provides both useful information and bargaining opportunities based on individuals' control over their contacts. Thus, people whose network contacts extend beyond their required work flow interactions and immediate work groups or units tend to be more powerful (Blau & Alba, 1982; Brass, 1984). Reaching diverse others, how-

ever, is not sufficient if few contacts are high enough in status to be instrumentally useful (Campbell et al., 1986; Lin, 1982); access to peers, superiors, and an organization's "dominant coalition" are critical for power and advancement (Brass, 1984; Kotter, 1982).

The organizational literature has additionally emphasized the importance of close informal bonds of trust and loyalty that ensure reliability under conditions of uncertainty (Kanter, 1977). Although range and status pertain to the probable instrumental value of what maybe exchanged, the closeness of a relationship determines the propensity of the contact to transmit a benefit to a particular individual and not to another (Burt, 1992). From a career development perspective, close relationships are more likely to fulfill psychosocial functions (Kram, 1988). Psychosocial functions are aspects of a relationship that enhance an individual's sense of competence, identity, and effectiveness in a professional role; they include serving as a role model, acceptance, and friendship. Psychosocial functions are distinguished from purely instrumental functions, such as providing exposure to senior management and advocacy for promotion, in that they involve benefits that stem from the nature of the relationship rather than the positional power of the contact.

Multiplexity is defined as the degree to which network relationships are multidimensional or, at an aggregate level, the extent to which network circles formed for different purposes overlap (have common members; Granovetter, 1973). The classic manifestation of a multiplex tie is socializing outside of work between co-workers; multiplex relationships are also associated with high trust and reliability since both parties have had the opportunity to interact and get to know each other in a variety of contexts. The career benefits of a particular type of strong, multiplex tie, the mentor-protégé relationship, are well documented (Kram, 1988: Thomas, 1990).

A network characteristic that tends to be overlooked in discussions of networks as social resources is homophily, defined as the degree to which pairs of individuals who interact are similar in identity or organizational group affiliations (Marsden, 1988; Rogers & Kincaid, 1981). Its relevance to the study of access to instrumental resources derives from findings that interpersonal similarity increases ease of communication, improves predictability of behavior, and fosters relationships of trust and reciprocity (Kanter, 1977: Lincoln & Miller, 1979). Consequently, explanations of network obstacles must consider the consequences of a defining feature of corporate life for minorities: the scant availability of similar—same-race—others for informal contact (Ibarra, 1993).

Macrostructural Constraints on Network Structure

A central tenet of social network theory is that any set of social relationships is embedded within a larger structural context that precludes or makes possible various kinds of social contacts; organizational demography, intergroup relations, and the distribution of valued resources within a social system constrain the development of informal relationships between individuals (Alderfer, 1986; Blau, 1977). In the United States, African Americans, Hispanics, and Asian Americans are underrepresented in private-sector managerial positions, particularly at the highest levels (Cox, 1991; Fernandez, 1991; Morrison & Von Glinow, 1990). The representation of minorities in the ranks of managers in the *Fortune* 500, for example, averages less than 12 percent, and gaps of 15 to 30 percentage points commonly exist between the proportions of minority members in the overall managerial ranks and in middle and higher levels of management in those companies (Cox, 1991).

Workplace information interaction, in turn, is embedded in a broader structure of social relations that extends beyond the boundaries of a firm. By virtue of societal patterns such as institutional segregation, members of minority groups often develop relationships within and across nonoverlapping social circles. The concept of biculturalism has been used to explain the experience of African Americans, who require access to both the black community and the dominant culture in order to obtain social support and job-related resources (Bell, 1990; Thomas & Alderfer, 1989). The immediate consequences of such a structural context for a managerial network are threefold. First, minority managers have a much smaller set of same-race others with whom to have informal interaction (Marsden, 1988). In contrast to white managers, minority managers will have the majority of their informal encounters with dissimilar others.

Hypothesis 1: Minority managers will have a smaller proportion of homophilous (same-race) ties in their personal networks than will their white counterparts.

Second, homophily strengthens interpersonal bonds (Kanter, 1977; Lincoln & Miller, 1979). An important component of tie strength is intimacy, that is, the interpersonal closeness of a network relationship (Granovetter, 1973). Cross-race relationships tend to be weaker than same-race ties (Thomas, 1990), and informal social relations (friendship ties) tend to develop between people who share commonalities, including race and gender (Ibarra, 1992; Lincoln & Miller, 1979; Tsui & O'Reilly, 1989). Thomas (1990) found that racial difference was often an obstacle for white mentors in identifying positively with their African American proteges, and Tsui and O'Reilly (1989) reported that demographic similarity affected superiors' personal attraction to and identification with subordinates. In research on peer relations, South, Bonjean, Markham, and Corder (1982) found that homophilous relationships provided individuals with greater social support from co-workers than did heterophilous relationships.

Hypothesis 2: Minority managers will have a smaller proportion of intimate ties in their personal networks than will their white counterparts.

Third, weaker cross-race relationships, coupled with nonoverlapping social circles outside the workplace, may produce nonoverlapping social and work-related circles in the workplace. Qualitative reports have suggested that racial minorities feel excluded from a variety of social activities that take place after working hours (e.g., Davis & Watson, 1982; Fernandez, 1991); demographically different individuals have also been found to be the least socially integrated within their groups (Kanter, 1977; O'Reilly, Caldwell, & Barnett, 1989). Further, minority group members often manage two different social circles in the workplace, developing both minority networks, which provide social support and information or advice on unique issues faced by minorities, and ties to the majority group, which provide access to important resources (Dickens & Dickens, 1982; Thomas, 1990). The net structural effects are race differences in multiplexity (the degree to which managerial networks include distinct circles that serve different purposes).

Hypothesis 3: Minority managers will have fewer multiplex network ties than their white counterparts.

As discussed in more detail below, differences in the range and status of contacts are not hypothesized to arise directly from macrostructural constraints; rather, they are expected to vary as a function of purposive network development strategies.

Microstrategies: Homophily, Career Success, and Identity

Despite the presence of significant structural constraints, people play an active role in structuring their social networks to achieve their goals. Their implicit or explicit strategies are based on theories of action, or "sets of guiding assumptions about situated orientations toward one another and the world" (DiMaggio, 1992: 118). Thomas (1993) argued that one important set of assumptions concerns appropriate and preferred ways of addressing race-related matters in the workplace. This article's argument is that for minority managers, such assumptions are reflected in the extent to which they develop informal ties to other minority group members, a central strategic choice in network development. Two different theoretical perspectives offer contrasting hypotheses about homophily within a minority group.

The "deficit hypothesis" posits that minority managers tend to have less instrumentally useful networks because they are less politically savvy in the ways of the white corporate world (Nkomo, 1992). This hypothesis implies assimilation, defined as "a unilateral process by which minority culture members adopt the norms and values of the dominant group in the organization" (Cox, 1991: 35). For network development, it suggests that if racial minorities developed networks structured like those of their successful white counterparts, they would reap similar instrumental benefits. In particular, given the distribution of power and resources within most organizations and in society at large, an informal network that is predominantly composed of majority group contacts will be most beneficial for instru-

mental purposes (Lin, 1982). This would be true for both functional and symbolic reasons: Majority group members have greater access to power and resources through their formal positions and informal network connections, and informal contact with the majority group may be viewed as evidence of assimilation and conformity to corporate norms and culture. The implication for the present study is that minority managers who have been assessed as having greater potential for further advancement would be expected to evidence more network contact with the majority group than less mobile minority group members.

The alternative perspective, advocated in this study, is based on theories of pluralism, racial identity, and intergroup relations. A pluralist perspective suggests that for a minority manager, a critical task is developing a positive sense of racial identity while at the same time adopting those aspects of the dominant culture necessary to be effective (Fernandez, 1990; Thomas, 1993). Racial identity theory (Davis & Watson, 1982; Dickens & Dickens, 1982) posits that the process of coming to grips with one's racial identity follows several phases, from efforts to be accepted within the dominant culture, to a rejection or avoidance of contact with the dominant culture beyond that necessary for "getting the job done," to a final stage in which the individual develops a style that is consistent with corporate norms but maintains his or her own uniqueness or sense of self. Each stage represents a dominant stance toward one's own racial group and the dominant group; each has a behavioral component: the individual's seeking to develop relationships primarily within the dominant culture, primarily within the minority group, or with people in both groups. Finally, according to intergroup theory (Alderfer, 1986), racial division and domination in organizations and society require minorities to use means that differ from those that are effective for majority group members to attain similar results. Following recent reviews of the empirical literature (Cox & Nkomo, 1990a), I develop a pluralist perspective on the relationship between network structure and career outcomes.

With regard to homophily, a pluralist perspective suggests that work-related informal contact across and within majority and minority groups is critical for career success. Minority managers provide each other with mutual support. But the role of these homophilous ties is not exclusively expressive; instrumental benefits include learning from other minority group members about interpersonal and behavioral strategies, such as strategies for managing racial barriers (Davis & Watson, 1982; Dickens & Dickens, 1982; Thomas, 1990, 1993). More generally, minority contacts function as necessary channels for accurate information, cooperation in getting things done, and career development functions, including rolemodeling. Cross-race contacts, on the other hand, are necessary for functioning effectively in a white-dominated context and also provide a variety of instrumental and psychosocial supports (Thomas, 1993). Thus, this stream of research and theorizing suggests that minorities with greater potential for advancement will develop a mix of same-race and cross-race relationships, in contrast to both their white and less mobile minority counterparts, who are expected to have networks dominated by ties within the majority group.

Hypothesis 4: Minority group members with high potential for organizational advancement will have a higher proportion of minority contacts in their informal networks than both their white counterparts and less mobile minority counterparts.

Cox and Nkomo (1990b) suggested that since minorities are still not accepted in corporate inner circles, mainstream strategies for networking may backfire for them. The arguments above suggest that homophily will be the principal indicator of alternative, nonassimilationist network strategies; however, organizational characteristics of a network, such as its range and status, also indicate strategies that are expected to differentiate high-potential minority group members from their white peers and less mobile minority counterparts. This argument is based on two notions. The first, directly related to homophily, reflects the fact that macrostructure constrains microstrategies: Since the number of minority managers is low in most organizations, a network high in its proportion of minorities will differ in other ways from a set of contacts predominantly drawn from the majority group. Second, as discussed below, homophily is only one indicator of a broader underlying strategy, one that emphasizes access to a diversity of social circles, defined on the basis

of both identity and organizational group memberships.

With respect to network range, if racial minorities seek ties to members of their identity groups, they are likely to have to reach out further in their organizations, beyond their immediate peers and superiors or functional areas. Thomas (1990), for example, found that black managers had more extradepartmental relationships and broader support networks than whites, as a result of their relationships with other blacks who were located outside their departments. Although partially a product of homophily, a strategy of developing a high proportion of extradepartmental contacts may indicate a cosmopolitan orientation that also leads to the development of other types of extragroup relationships. Beyond the benefits of access to same-race others, widely ranging networks may contribute more generally to career success by providing links to alternative positions and opportunities (Burt, 1992; Granovetter, 1982; Lin, 1982). Cross-boundary mobility may be more important for minority group members than for whites, since the former are more likely to encounter racial barriers (Morrison & Von Glinow, 1990).

Hypothesis 5: Minority group members with high potential for organizational advancement will have networks with wider range than both their white counterparts and less mobile minority counterparts.

Second, if minorities are disproportionately located in the lower echelons of most corporations, a network with a large proportion of minority members will be lower in status than a network with a different demographic composition (Thomas, 1990). Thus, although status is generally expected to bear a positive association to career success (see Burt [1992] for a review), the low number of minorities in top decision-making positions in predominantly white corporations means that, for minority managers, the benefits of having high-status contacts are likely to be in direct competition with the psychosocial benefits that are more easily obtained in interaction with like others (Thomas, 1993). Alternatives include peer networks, which also serve as sources of psychosocial support (Kram & Isabella, 1985). Again, membership in a network whose members have lower status implies that an individual has made a strategic trade-off to gain a balance of instrumental and psychosocial benefits and emphasizes using a diversity of groups as social resources.

Hypothesis 6: Minority group members with high potential for organizational advancement will have lower-status network contacts than both their white counterparts and less mobile minority counterparts.

Network Structure and Perceived Access to Network Resources

The discussion above implies that similar network characteristics may not provide access to the same benefits for members of different identity groups. For example, if racial dissimilarity means that relationships with people of higher rank are unlikely to provide sufficient psychosocial support (Thomas, 1993), minority managers may not view high status as being as useful as a white a manager would view it. Similarly, observers may not view a broad network that provides access to other minorities as providing the necessary internal information and sponsorship within a manager's subunit. In brief, because minority managers face trade-offs that their white counterparts do not confront, network characteristics that are associated with career success may not necessarily lead the minority members to view their networks as useful or adequate. Perceptions of what makes for a useful network are important because they are likely to affect network strategies for balancing competing network requirements.

Consistent with the pluralist perspective outlined above, my expectation was that the relationship between network characteristics and perceptions of having a useful network would differ, by race, in three ways. First, although a network that is broad in range may be necessary for access to instrumental resources, broad networks may not be as useful to individuals from groups lacking in "systemic legitimacy" (Burt, 1992; Granovetter, 1982). As Burt argued, when the legitimacy of an individual's position in a power structure is implicitly questioned, as is often the case for minorities, the information and brokerage benefits of broad networks become less important than the necessity of becoming a "known quantity," a goal often achieved through local sponsorship. Assuming that an individual has limited time and energy for network development, attenuation of the time available

for building within-group support may offset the advantages of a widely ranging network. This time effect is exacerbated when a lack of homophily poses barriers to the development of trust and attachment (Thomas, 1993; Thomas & Alderfer, 1989). Thus, for reasons other than the positive association between network range and career success for minorities discussed above, white managers with broad networks may be expected to view their networks as more instrumentally useful than minority managers with broad networks.

Hypothesis 7: Having a broad range of network contacts will be more predictive of perceived network utility for white than for minority managers.

Second, to the extent that minority group members' relationships with superiors are the ties most likely to be cross-racial, the benefits of sharing a common background are forfeited. Further, network relationships between people who are doubly dissimilar are more difficult to develop (Kaplan, 1984; Lin, 1982): A relationship with a superior may be heterophilous with respect to both identity (race) and organizational (rank) groups for a minority manager (Alderfer, 1986), but for a white manager, it may only be dissimilar on one dimension. Homophilous ties may not, however, provide access to an organization's power structure. One way minority managers manage these competing requirements is to establish dual support structures. Thomas (1990) found, for example, that black managers often relied on peer mentors because senior blacks were unavailable in their firms. Thus, the relationship between the status of contacts and perceptions of having a useful network is expected to be stronger for white managers.

Hypothesis 8: Having high-status contacts will be more predictive of perceived network utility for white than for minority managers.

Third, although a high proportion of intimate relationships among network contacts may be detrimental for managers from traditional insider groups, such as white men, because it can curtail their autonomy, for those outside organizational inner circles, such as members of racial minorities, intimate relationships may help signal legitimacy in the power structure (Burt, 1992). This hypothesis is consistent with research indicating that stereotypes and attribution biases are most prevalent in the absence of information obtained through personal experience (Berger, Fisek, Norman, & Zelditch, 1977) and that there is greater potential for bias and stereotyping in superficial relationships (Allport, 1954). Consequently, intimate relationships are expected to have greater instrumental value for minority than for white managers. Multiplex ties should have a similar effect since having informal contact in multiple contexts may reduce the uncertainty associated with cross-racial interaction.

Hypothesis 9: Having a high proportion of intimate and multiplex ties will be more predictive of perceived network utility for minority than for white managers.

Methods

Research Sites and Respondents

This research was conducted as part of a larger study of the informal networks of middle managers in four *Fortune* 500 firms. The four sites were divisions or business units of large, mature bureaucratic organizations operating in different industries (telecommunications and pharmaceutical, automotive, and photographic products) and geographical regions.

Respondents were 63 middle-level managers. Given previous research indicating that most identity-group differences in informal networks disappear when structural variables such as occupation and hierarchical rank are held constant (Ibarra, 1992; Moore, 1990), I chose individuals occupying equivalent middle management ranks as potential respondents. Since each company had a different grade-level structure, I tried to ensure comparability across companies by matching respondents on specific responsibilities and distance from the bonus-eligible, executive ranks of their divisions or business units.

A second selection criterion was demographic diversity. The group was selected to be balanced by race and gender rather than to reflect the demographic composition of the organizations. The final set of respondents included 46 white managers, 20 of whom were women, and 17 members of minority groups, 5 of whom were women. The minority group included 12 African Americans, 3 Hispanics, and 2 Asian Americans.

Third, in order to include a proxy for advancement opportunity, I asked the participating firms to "oversample" managers who had been placed in a fast-track or high-potential program. The high-potential programs are a critical part of each firms' formal succession planning processes: Supervisors and subunits' human resource management staffs nominate managers for advancement to the executive ranks on the basis of performance and potential, making final selections in consultation with division executive committees. Membership in the high-potential group indicated both an individual's perceived effectiveness to date and the likelihood of future advancement to a rank several levels higher than his or her present rank. The high-potential subgroup included 27 white and 9 minority managers.

Finally, although the group represented a mix of staff and line managerial jobs, care was taken to avoid selecting a group in which minorities were overrepresented in staff positions and whites in line jobs or in which non–high-potential managers were overrepresented in staff positions and high-potential managers held primarily line jobs (48 percent of non–high-potential managers and 47 percent of high-potential managers held line jobs; 47 percent of the minorities and 48 percent of whites held line jobs). . . .

My original plan was to include 12–18 managers from each of four research sites; the actual numbers were 18, 18, 11, and 16 from companies 1, 2, 3, and 4, respectively. Of these, the proportion of minority respondents from each firm was .28, .33, .33, and .25. Participation was voluntary; all managers who were identified agreed to participate in the study. The companies did not differ significantly with regard to the racial composition of their managerial ranks: Approximately 10–12 percent of each site's managers were members of racial minority groups, a figure consistent with current assessments of *Fortune* 500 demographics (Cox, 1991). Information on the proportion of African American managers (who composed the majority of the minority group in this study) was also available for three of the four companies: it was 9.9, 8.7, and 6.7 for companies 1, 2, and 3, respectively. Similar data were not available for company 4, but my observation was that the percentage was nearest that of company 3. Overall, there were no race-based differences between the minority and white managers in age (38.9 vs. 40.0, $t =$

–0.62, n.s.), tenure (12.4 vs. 15.8, $t = -1.6$, n.s.), or type of job (47 vs. 48 percent in line jobs, $t = -0.05$, n.s.). A significant difference did exist with regard to education, with minority managers more likely than whites to hold graduate degrees (76 vs. 46 percent, $t = 2.23$, $p < .05$), but there were no race-based differences in having a master's of business administration degree ($t = 0.45$, n.s.).

Data Collection

Data collection involved administering two segments of a sociometric questionnaire and conducting an approximately one-hour-long interview based on a semistructured interview guide. Participants were assured that their responses would be kept confidential. The interview began with preliminary questions about respondents' current jobs, followed by administration of the first segment of the questionnaire, which consisted of five network, or "name generator," questions. These questions asked respondents to list their contacts in five domains: (1) information—people "who have been valuable sources of information for you in your current job"; (2) advice—people who are "important sources of professional advice, whom you approach if you have a work-related problem or when you want advice on a decision you have to make"; (3) friendship—people "whom you consider to be personal friends, that is, those people you see most frequently for informal social activities such as going out to lunch, dinner, drinks, visiting one another's homes, and so on"; (4) career—people "who you feel have contributed most to your professional growth and development. Please include people who have taken an active interest in and concerted action to advance your career"; and (5) cooperation—"people whose help, support or cooperation you have successfully enlisted towards the accomplishment of your objectives."

These responses were then used as a basis for open-ended interview questions about the respondents' network development strategies and approaches. . . .

Measures

Network characteristics. Four indicators of the *range* of an individual's network. or the diversity of ties across organizational boundaries (Campbell et al., 1986), were computed: the proportion of total ties to people outside the manager's business unit or di-

vision, the proportion of total ties to people outside the company, the density of the network, and the average frequency of interaction. Network density was measured as the proportion of possible ties among a focal individual's network contacts that were present, with 0 indicating that none of an individual's contacts know each other and 1 indicating that each contact knew all the others (Marsden, 1990). Frequency was measured as the average frequency with which the managers talked to each of their contacts: "daily," "weekly," "monthly," or "less often." . . .

Status of contacts was defined as the average rank (superior, peer, or subordinate) of each respondent's network contacts. . . .

Intimacy measures were derived from reports of whether respondents felt "very close," "close," "less than close," or "distant" from each contact (Burt, 1992); since the variance was largely at the extremes, I defined intimacy as the proportion of very close relationships. . . .

Multiplexity was assessed by examining respondents' responses to the five network questions in "pairwise" fashion to determine the degree of overlap between any two lists. The number of common contacts for any two network questions was multiplied by two and divided by the total (nonredundant) number of names listed for the two questions. . . .

Homophily was measured as the proportion of same-race contacts mentioned among total citations across the five network questions. In keeping with the focus on network strategies, I also searched the qualitative interview data for evidence of choice patterns within the minority group. Thus, an additional, qualitative indicator of homophily consisted of coded responses to the interview question, Do you seek out other minorities as network contacts? Respondents's answers fell into two discrete categories. One subgroup of the minority managers talked about actively seeking relationships with other minorities and about the importance of support networks composed of both majority and minority group members. The second subgroup reported that they did not develop minority contacts and tended to devalue or even explicitly avoid minority networks.

Thus, I created two categories for statements that reflected similarities across cases (Kram & Isabella, 1985; Mainiero, 1986): in the first type, a manager stated that minority network contact was important or useful and reported seeking out network contact with other minorities; and in the second, the manager stated that he or she did not seek out minority network contact and did not think such contact useful. Qualitative analysis consisted simply of coding each response as falling into category 1, 2, or a default category for missing data. . . .

Career and task utility. . . . [I]ndividuals' perceptions of the usefulness of their networks were measured as two separate variables. These were derived from responses to questionnaire items asking respondents to rate the following on a five-point scale (1 = not at all, 5 = to a very great extent): "To what extent would you say that *your* network has been useful to you on these dimensions?" Items composing the task dimension included "helping me learn the ropes," "providing access to important information," and "providing access to resources and support." The career dimension included "gaining access to good opportunities," "as a signal that I am well connected," and "helping my career advancement." Coefficient alpha was .77 for each factor.

Race. Race was a dummy variable with a value of 1 assigned to white managers. African American, Asian American, and Hispanic managers were grouped in the minority category, which was assigned a value of 0.

Advancement potential. Since being in a fast-track or high-potential program in the four companies implied a positive judgment had been made about the managers' potential to advance to the executive ranks, I used inclusion in such a program as a proxy for opportunity for further advancement. Potential was a dummy variable with a value of 1 assigned to non–high-potential managers.

Control variables. Gender was a dummy variable with a value of 1 assigned to men. Education was also coded as a dummy variable (0 = bachelor's degree, 1 = graduate degree) and included as a control because educational level has been widely reported as having a great impact on managerial career advancement opportunities (Harlan & Weiss, 1982). Organization tenure was measured in years and included as a control because individuals' length of service with a firm can be expected to affect their informal networks. A set of three dummy variables was used to control for company-specific effects since the four firms differed in a variety

of ways, including industry, performance, and organizational culture; I included these variables to ensure that network effects could be observed net of company effects not measured directly.

Data Analysis

Ordinary-least-squares regression models were the principal form of data analysis. Each regression included the control variables, gender, education, tenure, and company. To show that significant differences did not exist where they were not hypothesized to exist, I computed results for all the network characteristics considered in this investigation and present results in the tables. . . .

Results

Main Effects for Race

Table 21.1 reports variable means, standard deviations, and correlations, and Table 21.2 provides t-test results and regression coefficients for race in models for each network characteristic dependent variable. Consistent with Hypothesis 1, minority managers differed from their white peers in that the former had significantly fewer homophilous contacts. Minorities also tended to have fewer intimate relationships (Hypothesis 2), but the significance level of that relationship dropped to .10 once controls were introduced. Hypothesis 3, however, was not supported: no race-based differences were observed in any of the three multiplexity regression models. As noted below, the observed range effect disappears once the interaction of race and potential is considered. . . .

Interactions of Race and Potential

Table 21.3 reports the regression models that result from adding interaction terms crossing race by potential to the models reported in Table 21.2. The homophily results support Hypothesis 4. Although minorities' networks in general evidenced significantly lower levels of homophily than those of their white counterparts, the regression coefficient for potential ($b = 0.22, p < .01$) indicates that the minority group members with high potential for advancement had a significantly higher proportion of same-race ties than the non-high-potential minorities. The regression coefficient for race ($b = 0.52, p < .001$) also indicates that white high-potential managers had more homophilous ties than their minority high-potential counterparts.

These results were paralleled in the qualitative responses to the interview question, "Do you seek out other minorities as network contacts?" The majority of the high-potential minority managers reported that they sought out and valued network contact with

Table 21.1
Means, Standard Deviations, and Correlations

Variables	Means	s.d.	1	2	3	4	5	6	7	8	9	10	11	12	13
1. Gender	0.60	0.49													
2. Race[a]	0.73	0.45	−.13												
3. Potential	0.57	0.50	−.11	.05											
4. Education	0.54	0.50	−.03	−.27*	.10										
5. Tenure	14.85	7.49	.15	.20	−.06	−.28*									
6. Homophily	0.77	0.32	−.19	.90**	.14	−.32*	.11								
7. Status	2.15	0.34	.11	−.06	−.02	.03	.06	−.03							
8. Range	0.00	1.00	.01	−.31*	.22	.10	.00	−.11	.04						
9. Intimacy	0.21	0.16	−.11	.28*	−.03	−.23	.08	.22	−.12	−.18					
10. Multiplexity, social	0.00	1.00	.05	.16	.04	−.04	−.02	.08	.13	−.10	.23				
11. Multiplexity, career	0.00	1.00	.17	−.02	.00	−.20	−.17	.06	.09	.06	−.08	.21			
12. Multiplexity, task	0.00	1.00	.03	.22	−.03	−.20	.13	.25	−.02	−.15	.25*	.22	.41**		
13. Task utility	0.00	1.00	−.09	.13	.06	.08	.03	.04	−.18	−.42***	.21	.14	.00	.24	
14. Career utility	0.00	1.00	−.21	.04	.11	.11	−.14	.03	.09	−.02	−.10	.08	.20	.16	.43***

[a] Race is coded as 0 = minority, 1 = white.

*p < .05
**p < .01
***p < .001

Table 21.2
Differences Between Whites and Minorities in Network Characteristics[a]

Dependent Variables	Means		t	b	s.e.
	Whites	Minorities			
Homophily	0.94	0.30	−15.96***	0.62***	.04
Range	−0.17	0.55	2.46*	−0.85**	.29
Status	2.14	2.17	0.28	0.02	.10
Intimacy	0.24	0.14	−2.30*	0.08[†]	.05
Multiplexity, social	−0.27	0.09	−1.26	0.44	.31
Multiplexity, career	0.04	−0.01	0.19	−0.01	.29
Multiplexity, task	−0.37	0.13	−1.75[†]	0.45	.30

[a] For whites, N = 46; for minorities, N = 17. Control variables were included in the models but results are not reported.

†p < .10
* p < .05
** p < .01
*** p < .001

other minorities. . . . In contrast, a majority of the non-high-potential managers, 57 percent, responded to the same question by stating that they did not seek out minority ties. . . .

The results in Table 21.3 also offer support for Hypothesis 5 and partial support for Hypothesis 6. The potential coefficients in the models having range and status as dependent variables indicate that, relative to their non–high-potential minority peers, high-potential minorities had networks that were broader in range ($b = -1.23, p < .05$) and lower in status ($b = 0.34, p < .05$). Relative to their high-potential white counterparts, however, high-potential minorities also had significantly ($b = -1.28, p < .001$) broader networks, but there was no difference in the status of the two subgroups' contacts ($b = 0.18$, n.s.). A noteworthy unhypothesized result was that high-potential minorities evidenced less social multiplexity than high-potential white managers ($b = 0.92, p < .05$).

Race and Network Utility

The final analyses explored the relationship between network characteristics and perceptions of network utility for task-related and career advancement purposes. The first model in Table 21.4 provides the analyses testing Hypotheses 7–9 for career utility. Hypotheses 7 and 8 were supported: Adding the interactions crossing race by range and race by status added .11 ($p < .05$) in variance explained. As Figures 21.1 and 21.2 illustrate, these significant relationships indicate that organizational range increases perceptions of networks' career utility for whites but decreases perceptions of their career utility for minority group members and that a modest increasing trend ($p < .10$) in perceived career utility is associated with having higher-ranking contacts for whites but is not present for minorities. Hypothesis 9, however, was not supported

Table 21.3
Analysis of Race by Potential Interaction Effects[a]

Dependent Variables	Constant		Race		Potential		Race by Potential		R^2	ΔR^{2b}
	b	s.e.	b	s.e.	b	s.e.	b	s.e.		
Homophily	0.46***	.07	0.62***	.04	−0.06	.04			.83***	
	0.52***	.08	0.52***	.06	−0.22**	.07	0.22**	.08	.86***	.03**
Intimacy	0.21*	.08	0.08†	.06	0.00	.04			.13	
	0.20*	.09	0.09	.06	0.02	.08	−0.02	.09	.13	.00
Range	1.32**	.50	−0.85**	.29	−0.30	.25			.31**	
	1.53**	.47	−1.28***	.45	−1.23*	.52	1.18*	.57	.37**	.05*
Status	1.83***	.17	0.02	.10	0.10	.09			.16	
	1.73***	.18	0.18	.14	0.34*	.17	−.033†	.19	.21	.05†
Multiplexity, social	0.23	.51	0.44	.31	−0.13	.27			.14	
	−0.06	.52	0.92*	.39	0.70	.52	−1.10†	.59	.20	.06†
Multiplexity, career	1.09*	.48	−0.01	.29	−0.15	.25			.24†	
	1.13*	.57	0.08	.38	−0.27	.50	0.16	.58	.24†	.00
Multiplexity, task	−0.03	.50	0.45	.29	−0.04	.26			.20	
	−0.01	.59	0.43	.39	−0.08	.52	0.05	.59	.20	.00

[a] $N = 63$. Control variables are included in the models but not reported.

[b] ΔR^2 indicates the change relative to the model (not reported) without race by potential interaction term.

† $p < .10$

* $p < .05$

** $p < .01$

*** $p < .001$

(insignificant interaction terms are not reported).

The second model in Table 21.4 tested Hypotheses 7–9 for task utility. Predictions were not supported: Range had similarly negative effects on perceptions of task utility for whites and minorities, and the interaction term (not reported) was not significant. Neither the main nor the interaction effect for status or intimacy was significant.

Discussion

This study produced three sets of findings. First, when human capital variables, such as tenure and graduate education, and positional resources, such as rank and potential for advancement, were held constant, minority and white middle managers in comparable jobs differed in the homophily and intimacy of their organizational network ties. I viewed these findings as evidence of structural constraints on network patterns. Since potential for advancement was held constant, differences in ability or performance were not considered to be plausible alternative explanations for the race difference obtained. Second, evidence for the role of individual strategies, as well as support for the pluralist, rather than assimilationist, perspective was obtained from the finding that high-potential minorities differed from high-potential whites and non–high-potentinl minorities in the range, status, and multiplexity of their network ties. These results are consistent with the notion that strategies for managing structural constraints explain a variety of race differences in informal net-

Table 21.4
Results of Regression Analysis[a]

Variables	Dependent Variables			
	Career Utility		Task Utility	
	b	s.e.	b	s.e.
Race	−3.44*	1.70	0.46	0.73
Potential	−0.30	0.24	−0.22	0.25
Gender	−0.72**	0.26	−0.17	0.25
Education	0.12	0.26	0.23	0.26
Tenure	−0.01	0.02	0.01	0.02
Range	−0.37†	0.21	−0.34*	0.14
Status	−0.07	0.56	0.17	0.37
Homophily	−1.36	1.04	−1.23	1.07
Intimacy	0.20	0.76	0.65	0.80
Multiplexity, career	0.32*	0.13		
Multiplexity, task			0.29*	0.13
Race × range	0.48†	0.28		
Race × status	1.95*	0.77		
Constant	1.06	0.49	−0.09	1.07
R^2	0.43**		0.31*	
Adjusted R^2	0.29		0.17	
ΔR^{2b}	0.11*			

[a] $N = 63$. Race is coded as 0 = minority, 1 = white. Potential is coded as 0 = high-potential, 1 = non–high-potential. Company dummies were removed after a test of their contribution to model fit indicated no company effects.

[b] ΔR^2 indicates change resulting from the inclusion of interaction terms.

† $p < .10$
* $p < .05$
** $p < .01$

works. Third, the race-based variation in the effects of range and status on perceptions of career utility provide additional support for a pluralist rather than an assimilationist perspective on career strategies. These effects also suggest that homophily constraints may produce unique tradeoffs for minority managers that lead them to view certain network characteristics as producing fewer benefits than are produced in the view of white managers. . . .

Limitations

The most important methodological limitation of this study is that its cross-sectional design precludes statements about causal relationships. As discussed above, the direction of the relationship between network structure and potential for advancement is difficult to determine. Further, given the apparent role of racial identity, future research is needed to explore how individual differences in developmental tasks and self-con-

Figure 21.1

Conditional Effects of Status on Perceived Career Utility of Network[a]

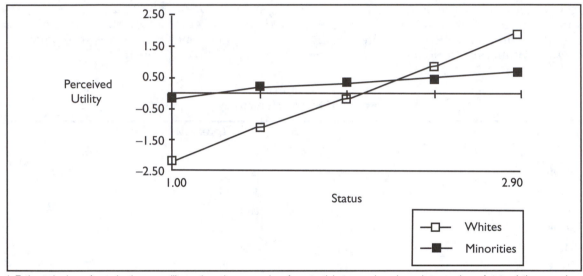

* Estimated values of perceived career utility are based on zero values for potential, race, and gender and mean values of status, intimacy, and career multiplexity.

Figure 21.2

Conditional Effects of Range on Perceived Career Utility of Network[a]

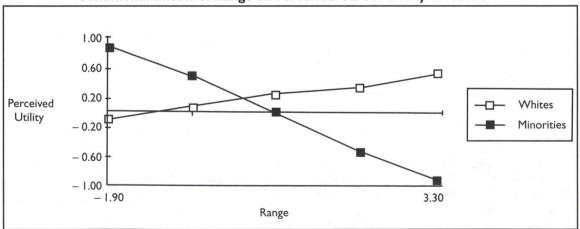

* Estimated values of perceived career utility are based on zero values for potential, race, and gender and mean values of range, intimacy, and career multiplexity.

cepts shape relationship networks (Kram & Isabella, 1985). Longitudinal designs and richer qualitative data are also needed to examine differences in strategies and approaches over time. . . .

The investigation of whether similar constraints and strategies distinguished between male and female managers would also be productive but was beyond the scope of this study. The social network literature suggests common constraints (Ibarra, 1993), but important differences may produce different empirical patterns. For example, in U.S. firms the numbers of female managers are currently greater than the numbers of minority managers, and the numbers of minority women in management are even fewer (Morrison & Von Glinow, 1990); thus, homophily-related effects may not be as pronounced for women. With respect to the development of intimate relationships, norms for cross-sex interaction are more fully established than norms for interracial interaction, which is characterized by greater uncertainty (Dickens & Dickens, 1982). This effect may be mitigated, however, by uniquely gender-related issues, including sexual dynamics (Kanter, 1977; Kram, 1988). Overall, although this study may inform research on gender differences in networks, additional empirical and conceptual work is necessary before these conclusions can be so generalized.

Few network studies including significant numbers of minority group members in managerial positions have been conducted to date, and most studies of the effects of race on organizational experiences have either lacked theoretical underpinnings (Cox & Nkomo, 1990a) or been conducted within a narrowly defined paradigm that fails to cast race as an integral part of a "complicated web of socially constructed elements of identity formation" (Nkomo, 1992: 507). The alternative perspective advocated here confirms the pervasiveness of structural constraints but also emphasizes the role of strategic action and indicates a critical role for social identity. Although the present results are only a starting point, research on the unique opportunities and constraints minority managers face in developing useful networks of organizational relationships may prove a promising area for future inquiry.

References

Alderfer, C. P. 1986. An intergroup perspective on group dynamics. In J. Lorsch (Ed.), *Handbook of organizational behavior:* 190–222. Englewood Cliffs, NJ: Prentice-Hall.

Allport, G. W. 1954. *The nature of prejudice.* Cambridge, MA: Addison-Wesley.

Bell, E. L. 1990. The bicultural life experience of career-oriented black women. *Journal of Organizational Behavior,* 11: 459–477.

Berger, J., Fisek, N. H., Norman, R. Z., & Zelditch, M., Jr. 1977. *Status characteristics and social interaction: An expectation states approach.* New York: Elsevier.

Blau, J. R., & Alba. R. D. 1982. Empowering nets of participation. *Administrative Science Quarterly,* 27: 363–379.

Blau, P. M. 1977. *Inequality and heterogeneity: A primitive theory of social structure.* New York: Free Press.

Brass, D. J. 1984. Being in the right place: A structural analysis of individual influence in an organization. *Administrative Science Quarterly,* 29: 518–539.

———. 1985. Men's and women's networks: A study of interaction patterns and influence in an organization. *Academy of Management Journal,* 28: 518–539.

Burt, R. S. 1984. Network items and the General Social Survey. *Social Networks,* 6: 293–339.

———. 1992. *Structural roles: The social structure of competition.* Cambridge, MA: Harvard University Press.

Campbell, K. E., Marsden, P. V., & Hurlbert, J. S. 1986. Social resources and socioeconomic status. *Social Networks,* 8: 97–117.

Cox, T., Jr. 1991. The multicultural organization. *Academy of Management Executive,* (5)2: 34–47.

Cox, T., Jr., & Nkomo, S. M. 1990a. Invisible men and women: A status report on race as a variable in organization behavior research. *Journal of Organizational Behavior,* 11: 419–431.

———. 1990b. Factors affecting the upward mobility of black managers in private sector organizations. *Review of Black Political Economy,* 18(3): 39–48.

Davis, G., & Watson, G. 1982. *Black life in corporate America.* Garden City, NY: Anchor Books.

Dickens, F., Jr.. & Dickens, J. B. 1982. *The black manager: Making it in the corporate world.* New York: AMACOM.

DiMaggio, P. 1992. Nadel's paradox revisited: Relational and cultural aspects of organizational structure. In N. Nohria & R. G. Eccles (Eds.), *Networks and organizations: Structure, form and action:* 118–142. Cambridge, MA: Harvard Business School Press.

DiTomaso. N., Thompson, D. E., & Blake, D. H. 1988. Corporate perspectives on the advancement of minority managers. In D. E. Thompson & N. DiTomaso (Eds.), *Ensuring minority success in corporate management:* 119–136. New York: Plenum Press.

Fernandez, J. P. 1991. *Managing a diverse workforce.* Lexington, MA: Lexington Books.

Freeman, L. C., Romney, A. K., & Freeman, S. C. 1987. Cognitive structure and informant accuracy. *American Anthropologist,* 89: 310–325.

Granovetter, M. 1973. The strength of weak ties. *American Journal of Sociology,* 6: 1360–1380.

Granovetter, M. 1982. The strength of weak ties: A network theory revisited. In P. V. Marsden & N. Lin (Eds.), *Social structure and network analysis:* 105–130. Beverly Hills, CA: Sage.

Harlan. A., & Weiss, C. L. 1982. Sex differences in factors affecting managerial career advancement. In P. A. Wallace (Ed.), *Women in the workplace:* 59–100. Boston: Auburn House.

Holland, P. W., & Leinhart, S. 1973. The structural implications of measurement error in sociometry. *Journal of Mathematical Sociology,* 3: 85–111.

Ibarra, H. 1992. Homophily and differential returns: Sex differences in network structure and access in an advertising firm. *Administrative Science Quarterly,* 37: 422–447.

Ibarra, H. 1993. Personal networks of women and minorities in management: A conceptual framework. *Academy of Management Review,* 18: 56–87.

Irons, E., & Moore. G. 1985. *Black managers: The case of the banking industry.* New York: Praeger.

Jaccard J., Turrisi, R., & Wan, C. K. 1990. *Interaction effects in multiple regression.* Newbury Park, CA: Sage.

Kanter, R. M. 1977. *Men and women of the corporation.* New York: Basic Books.

Kaplan, R. E. 1984. Trade routes: The manager's network of relationships. *Organizational Dynamics,* 12: 37–52.

Kotter, J. P. 1982. *The general managers.* New York: Free Press.

Kram, K. E. 1988. *Mentoring at work: Developmental relationships in organizational life.* New York: University Press of America.

Kram, K. F,. & Isabella, L. A. 1985. Mentoring alternatives: The role of peer relationships in career development. *Academy of Management Journal,* 28: 110–132.

Lin, N. 1982. Social resources and instrumental action. In P. V. Marsden & N. Lin (Eds.), *Social structure and network analysis:* 131–145. Beverly Hills, CA: Sage.

Lincoln, R., Jr., & Miller, J. 1979. Work and friendship ties in organizations: A comparative analysis of relational networks. *Administrative Science Quarterly,* 24: 181–199.

Mainiero, L. A. 1986. Coping with powerlessness: The relationship of gender and job dependency to empowerment-strategy usage. *Administrative Science Quarterly,* 31: 633–653.

Marsden, P. V. 1988. Homogeneity in confiding relations. *Social Networks,* 10: 57–76.

Marsden, P. V. 1990. Network data and measurement. In J. Blake (Ed.), *Annual Review of Sociology,* vol. 16: 435–463. Palo Alto, CA: Annual Reviews, Inc.

McPherson, J. M., & Smith-Lovin, L. 1987. Homophily in voluntary organizations: Status distance and the composition of face-to-face groups. *American Journal of Sociology,* 52: 370–379.

Moore, G. 1990. Structural determinants of men's and women's personal networks. *American Sociological Review,* 55: 726–735.

Morrison, A. M., & Von Glinow, M. V. 1990. Women and minorities in management. *American Psychologist,* 45: 200–208.

Nkomo, S. 1992. The emperor has no clothes: Rewriting "race in organizations." *Academy of Management Review,* 17: 487–513.

O'Reilly, C. A., III, Caldwell, D. F., & Barnett, W. P. 1989. Work group demography, social integration, and turnover. *Administrative Science Quarterly,* 34: 21–37.

Rogers, E. M., & Kincaid. D. L. 1981. *Communications networks.* New York: Free Press.

Smith-Lovin, L., & McPherson, M. J. 1993. You are who you know: A network approach to gender. In P. England (Ed.), *Theory on gender/feminism on theory:* 223–251. New York: Aldine.

South, S. J. Bonjean, C. M., Markham, W. T., & Corder, J. 1982. Social structure and intergroup interaction. Men and women in the federal bureaucracy. *American Sociological Review,* 47: 587–599.

Thomas, D. A., & Alderfer, C. P. 1989. The influence of race on career dynamics: Theory and research on minority career experiences. In M. B. Arthur, D. T. Hall, & B. S. Lawrence (Eds.), *Handbook of career theory:* 133–158. Cambridge: Cambridge University Press.

Thomas, D. A. 1990. The impact of race on managers' experiences of developmental relationships (mentoring and sponsorship): An intra-organizational study. *Journal of Organizational Behavior,* 2: 479–492.

Thomas, D. A. 1993. The dynamics of managing racial diversity in developmental relationships. *Administrative Science Quarterly,* 38: 169–194.

Tsui, A. S., Egan, T. D., & O'Reilly, C. A., III. 1992. Being different: Relational demography and organizational attachment. *Administrative Science Quarterly,* 37: 549–579.

Tsui, A. S., & O'Reilly, C. A., III. 1989. Beyond simple demographic effects: The importance of relational demography in superior-subordinate dyads. *Academy of Management Journal,* 32: 402–423.

U.S. Bureau of the Census. 1993. *Statistical abstract of the United States.* Washington, DC: U.S. Government Printing Office.

Wharton, A. S. 1992. The social construction of gender and race in organizations: A social identity and group mobilization perspective. In P. Tolbert & S. Bacharach (Eds.), *Research in the sociology of organizations,* vol. 10: 55–84. Greenwich, CT: JAI Press.

Chapter 22

The Effects of Organizational Demographics and Social Identity on Relationships Among Professional Women

Robin J. Ely

Increasing percentages of women in the work force mean that women have more opportunities to work for other women now than in the past. Analyzing data she collected from a sample of women lawyers, Robin Ely examines women's relationships with other women in the workplace. Do women who work for other women view their superiors positively? Do more senior women become role models for those who are more junior? Are women more likely to compete or cooperate with other women in their workplace?

Ely finds that hierarchical relationships between women in the workplace are complicated, as their quality depends not simply on the personal characteristics of the individual women but on the features of the organizations that employ them. Women viewed other women more positively in some of the firms she studied, and more negatively in others. Women's relationships with other women were enhanced in organizations where one's status as a woman was not perceived as a liability.

Changes in the demographic composition of the labor force are creating more opportunities than ever before for professional women to work with and for other women. If similarity on attributes such as sex makes communication easier and fosters relationships of trust and reciprocity, as some research suggests (Lincoln and Miller, 1979; McPherson and Smith-Lovin, 1987), then these relationships have the potential to provide women with an important source of emotional and instrumental support (Kram, 1986; Ibarra, 1992), Yet research investigating the quality of women's same-sex work relationships has yielded inconsistent results (for a review, see O'Leary, 1988). These studies support one of two competing stereotypes about women's relationships. According to one stereotype, women are insecure, overcontrolling, and unable to engage in team play (e.g., Hennig and Jardim, 1977; Briles, 1987; Madden, 1987); their relationships are therefore competitive and difficult. According to the other stereotype, women are relationship-oriented, non-hierarchical, and interested in sharing power and information (e.g., Helgesen, 1990; Rosener, 1990), which reinforces the notion of solidarity among women and portrays their relationships as mutually supportive. In light of these inconsistencies, further research is needed on work relationships among women and how they might contribute to women's career success.

Proponents of both views rely on women's sex-role socialization to explain the personality traits and behavior patterns they attribute to women, largely ignoring the sociocultural contexts within which women work. These accounts assume that role socializations based on sex are always activated and that they are activated in psychologically similar ways for all women (Wharton, 1992). In addition, researchers focusing on women's sex-role socialization compared with men's may attribute sex differences in patterns of relationships to dispositional differences between men's and women's orientations toward interpersonal relationships when social structural explanations may be more valid (Moore, 1990). These person-centered explanations reinforce constraining, often negative stereotypes about women and their capacity to work productively with one another (Kanter, 1977; Riger and Galligan, 1980; Keller and Moglen, 1987).

Two theoretical perspectives relevant to this topic that may be more promising than sex-role socialization are social identity theory (Tajfel, 1978, 1982) and organizational demography (Martin, 1985; Konrad and Gutek, 1987; Zimmer, 1988; Yoder, 1991). This paper unites work in these two areas and extends each to address questions about relationships among women at work. Social identity theory explicates how social structure informs the meaning people attach to their membership in identity groups, such as sex, and how this in turn shapes their social interactions with members of their own and other identity groups. Research on organizational demography investigates the disproportionate representation of some identity groups over others as an important factor in the social structure of the work environment that may influence these processes (Wharton, 1992). Taken together, these two perspectives offer a psychological account of how demographic structure influences the kinds of work relationships women establish with other women.

A widely documented finding in the social identity literature is that people prefer to interact with members of their own identity group than with members of other groups (Tajfel, 1982; Abrams and Hogg, 1990). This line of research has focused largely on situations in which in-group favoritism serves to enhance a person's positive self-image. This paper extends this research by exploring intragroup relationships in those situations in which clear and abiding status differences between groups create negative or ambivalent feelings in members of low-status groups about their group identity. Under these conditions, members of low-status groups are more likely to engage in self-enhancing strategies that undermine solidarity within their groups (Lambert et al., 1960; Tajfel, 1981). Work relationships among women thus are likely to be negatively affected when there are large status disparities between men and women.

While research on organizational demography provides the basis for operationalizing intergroup status differences and defining the organizational conditions that give rise to different group identity and interaction processes, this paper moves beyond traditional demographic research on status differences between men and women, such as work on women's representation in occupations, jobs, or work groups, to focus on women's differentiated representation across levels of the organization's hierarchy. Though some researchers interested in demographic processes have recognized that proportional representation in the upper echelons of organizations is important theoretically (Konrad and Gutek, 1987; Ridgeway, 1988; Pfeffer, 1989), few studies have examined its impact empirically, and none considers its impact on work relationships). According to this approach, if there are few women at higher organizational levels, gender may continue to be a negative status indicator for women, despite balanced representation at lower organizational levels (Ridgeway, 1988). Women's proportional representation in senior positions of an organization may signal to junior women the extent to which positions of power are attainable by women. This helps to shape the meaning and significance women attach to being female in that organization which, in turn, may influence the nature and quality of their work relationships with other women.

This study examined the relationship between women's proportional representation in organizational positions of authority and the quality of hierarchical and peer relationships among professional women. I investigated these relationships from the perspective of women lawyers working as associates in law firms in which there was a low proportion of women partners (male-dominated firms) and in law firms in which there was a higher proportion of women partners (sex-integrated firms).

Conceptual Background

Social and Gender Identity

Cognitive social psychologists developed social identity theory (Tajfel, 1978, 1982; Tajfel and Turner, 1985; Turner, 1987), which researchers have recently begun to apply to organizations (Ashforth and Mael, 1989; Kramer, 1991; Tsui, Egan, and O'Reilly, 1992; Wharton, 1992). According to this perspective, "identity" represents "the location of a person in social space" (Gecas, Thomas, and Weigert, 1973: 477). Identity has two components: a personal component derived from idiosyncratic characteristics, such as personality and physical and intellectual traits, and a social component derived from salient group memberships, such as sex, race, class, and nationality (Ashforth and Mael, 1989). The social component of identity involves processes of self-categorization and attaching value to particular social categories (Pettigrew, 1986), such that "an individual's knowledge of his or her memberships in social groups together with the emotional significance of that knowledge" constitute social identity (Turner and Giles, 1981: 24). Social identity acquires meaning through comparison with other groups when status differences between groups are salient. How favorably a group member perceives his or her group compared with other relevant groups determines the adequacy of the person's social identity in that setting.

A basic assumption of social identity theory is that people have a need for and are therefore motivated to achieve and maintain a favorable self-image. When possible, people sustain this image by drawing intergroup comparisons that favor their own group over other groups, and they show a preference for in-group over out-group interactions. Here, the self-enhancement motive operates at the group level and promotes in-group solidarity, cooperation, and support (Hogg and Abrams, 1990).

Though social identity research has mostly been conducted in settings in which group members are able to sustain positive feelings toward their group, it has shown that when there are clear and abiding status differences between groups, members of low-status groups find it difficult to maintain positive in-group distinctiveness and hence find in-group interactions less attractive (for a review, see Hinkle and Brown, 1990). Under these circumstances, members of low-status groups may engage in personal self-enhancing strategies. Williams and Giles (1978) have suggested that such people may actively dissociate from members of their group by attempting to distinguish themselves as exceptional or uncharacteristically worthy in comparison with other group members. When intergroup comparisons prove unsatisfactory, in-group rather than out-group members thus become the referents for self-enhancing comparisons. Under these circumstances, the self-enhancement motive threatens in-group solidarity, cooperation, and support (Williams and Giles, 1978).

Another aspect of social identity, which has implications for relationships among members of a group, is group identification. According to social identity theory, identification with a group is "a perceptual cognitive construct . . . not necessarily associated with any specific behaviors or affective states" but, rather, based in a sense of oneself as "psychologically intertwined with the fate of a group" (Ashforth and Mael, 1989. 21). Members' identification with their group is strong to the extent that they perceive their own capacity to succeed in any given setting as dependent on how well other group members are doing. Identification with the group involves an emotional investment in both the successes and failures of one's group (Ashforth and Mael, 1989) and positive, negative, or ambivalent feelings toward the group and its members, depending on whether group membership bodes well or poorly for one's well-being (Tajfel, 1981).

Women's gender identity is one aspect of their social identity and refers to the meaning women attach to their membership in the category "female." Based on the assumption, well-documented in the research literature, that our society accords men dominant status over women (Webster and Foschi, 1988), social identity theory posits that women construct their gender identity by drawing comparisons between their own group and men (Williams and Giles, 1978). Such comparisons strengthen women's identification with women by reinforcing a perception of their own individual fates as interdependent with the fate of women as a group. In settings in which women can perceive their group favorably relative to men, as when there is evidence of women's advancement, women's identifying with women will be a positive experience and can serve to strengthen relationships among them. In settings in which women perceive little basis for drawing favorable comparisons and, instead, view their sex as a liability, as when there is little evidence of women's advancement, women's identifying with other women will be a negative experience and may actually interfere with the development of constructive relationships among them.

Organizational Demography

Demographic characteristics of organizations, such as race and sex segregation and group composition, help to shape the meaning people attach to their identity group memberships at work (Wharton, 1992). This, in turn, structures people's relationships to their groups and, by extension, to members of their groups. While organizational demographics may thus be related to the nature and quality of work relationships among members of the same identity group, research linking organizational demographics to the development of work relationships has focused largely on interactions between members of different groups, such as relationships between men and women (e.g., Gutek and Morasch, 1982; South et al., 1982; Fairhurst and Snavely, 1983) and blacks and whites (Alderfer et al, 1983; Thomas and Alderfer, 1989). Kanter's (1977) analysis of the "queen bee syndrome" (Staines, Jayaratne, and Tavris, 1974) explicates the only direct theoretical link between an organization's demographic structure and the nature of work relationships between members of the same group. Queen bees are token women in traditionally male-dominated settings whom male colleagues reward for denigrating other women and for actively working to keep other women from joining them.

Kanter's focus on token status as the critical explanatory factor in these relationships constitutes an important theoretical shift from the person-centered explanations of socialization theorists. Building on Kanter's approach, others have argued that additional aspects of demography, such as a predominance of one group over others in organizational positions of authority, also deserve consideration (Gutek, 1985; Yoder, 1991). In particular, some researchers have speculated that white men's extreme over-representation in organizational positions of authority may have a negative impact on women and nonwhite subordinates (Konrad and Gutek, 1987; Ridgeway, 1988; Pfeffer, 1989). Ridgeway (1988) has suggested that the disproportionate representation of men over women in senior organizational positions may highlight for women their limited mobility and reinforce their lower status as women, even in work groups composed entirely of women. When this occurs, women form lower expectations for the positions women, and they, as women, are likely to achieve in the organization. Hence the extent to which power differentials exist along sex lines may help to shape the meaning women attach to their membership in the category "female."

Hypotheses

Hierarchical relationships between women. A correlation between identity and hierarchical group membership, such that men tend to predominate in positions of authority while women tend to occupy more junior positions, may communicate to junior women that membership in their gender group is incompatible with membership in more powerful organizational groups. In these male-dominated organizations, senior women, as members of these two ostensibly incompatible groups, may present a dilemma for junior women as they assess their own prospects for promotion. To make sense of a woman's rise to the top, junior women may come to view the possibility of success as available only to women who shed their feminine identity and are not truly women because they act like men or who have attained their positions of authority illegitimately. This tension may make it difficult for junior women to respect senior women and to use gender-based identification with them as a source of support, rendering the development of productive, developmental relationships with them unlikely. Identifying with senior women is a negative experience, since women's scarcity in senior positions bodes poorly for the fate of other women in the organization.

By contrast, when women perceive that the boundary to top positions is permeable, and it is credibly so, their gender identity is less likely to create problems, because they are less likely to perceive their sex as incompatible with success and promotion. Rather than presenting a dilemma, senior women in these sex-integrated organizations are likely to represent to junior women evidence of women's capacity to succeed, and identifying with women is likely to be a positive experience. Able to draw on shared gender, as well as benefit from differences in experience, knowledge, and skill, junior women are more likely to construct satisfying developmental relationships with their senior women counterparts.

According to this perspective, the relative presence or absence of senior women signals the compatibility between female gender and organizational success, making gender identification a more or less positive experience for junior women. This, in turn, has implications for women's hierarchical relationships. I expect that junior women in firms with few women in senior positions (i.e., male-dominated firms) will be more critical of senior women than will junior women in firms with a relatively high proportion of senior women (i.e., sex-integrated firms). More specifically,

Hypothesis 1a (H1a): Junior women in male-dominated firms will be less likely to identify with senior women as a source of validation and support than will junior women in sex-integrated firms.

Hypothesis 1b (H1b): Junior women in male-dominated firms will be less likely to view senior women's authority as legitimate than will junior women in sex-integrated firms.

Hypothesis 1c (H1c): Junior women in male-dominated firms will be less likely to view senior women as good role models than will junior women in sex-integrated firms.

Peer relationships among women. If women seeking to advance in the organization perceive their gender as a barrier to upward mobility—a barrier signaled by a scarcity of women in senior positions—they may perceive links to other women as detrimental to their careers and thus may attempt to create distance between themselves and their women peers. Kanter (1977) reported that the men in her study often initiated and reinforced this tendency by setting up invidious comparisons between women in which one was characterized as superior and the other as inferior, exaggerating traits in both cases. The "successful" woman, relieved to be so judged, was then reluctant to enter an alliance with the identified failure, for fear of jeopardizing her own acceptance. Instead she had an interest in maintaining the distance by reinforcing the perceived differences in their capabilities (for example, by comparing herself favorably with the other in front of her senior colleagues). Such attempts to maintain positive identity by differentiating oneself from fellow group members undermine solidarity within the subordinate group (Abrams and Hogg, 1990). In this situation, women identify with one another in that they perceive themselves as interdependent because one's evaluation is contingent on the other's, but it is a negative experience. Kanter predicted that with larger numbers of women, supportive alliances would be more likely to develop. This study tests whether that predicted outcome may also be contingent on the degree to which women are represented in positions of formal organizational authority.

It follows that when resources and opportunities are scarce for women, relationships between women may also be more competitive. Keller and Moglen (1987) have suggested that in these circumstances women tend to compare themselves with one another, rather than with men, in their assessments of whether and how they will make it to the top. A perception that only one or two women will succeed may promote rivalries among women, pitting them against one another. This observation is consistent with Broder's (1993) finding that female reviewers for the National Science Foundation's Economics Program were harsher critics of women's proposals than were male reviewers. She attributed her finding to the small percentage of women academics in economics, which may lead women to compete with one another for what they perceive to be a fixed number of "female slots." Again, this is a situation in which women identify with one another because they perceive their fates to be interdependent, but the experience is a negative one.

By contrast, women in firms with higher proportions of senior women may experience their working environment as more hospitable to women, and it may easier for them to identify with women peers as positive sources of support, rather than as competitors for limited resources. This leads to the following hypotheses:

Hypothesis 2a (H2a): Junior women in male-dominated firms will characterize more of their relationships with women peers as competitive than will junior women in sex-integrated firms.

Hypothesis 2b (H2b): Junior women in male-dominated firms will characterize fewer of their relationships with women peers as supportive than will junior women in sex-integrated firms.

Method

Sample

The main criteria for selecting the organizational domain from which to draw a sample of participants for this research were (1) variability across organizations in the proportional distribution of women and men in senior positions and (2) comparability across organizations in hierarchical structure (i.e., what was a senior position in one was comparably senior in the other), overall size, type of work, and proportional distribution of women and men in junior positions. Law firms, with easily identifiable partners and associates and with status and job responsibilities relatively similar across firms for people in these positions, met these criteria. In addition, law firms have structures similar to other organizations of professionals, including accounting firms, management consulting firms, and universities, in which up-or-out policies typically govern career paths and women encounter similar barriers to top positions (Chamberlain, 1988; Morrison and Von Glinow, 1990).

I identified eligible law firms from the 1987 *NALP Law Directory*, which presents demographic and other descriptive data over 1,000 law firms in the U.S. In the top 251 U.S. law firms, the proportion of women partners averages 11.1 percent and ranges from zero (in one firm) to 23 percent (in two firms) (Epstein, 1993). I defined a sex-integrated firm operationally as one in which at least 15 percent of the partners were women, because using a higher percentage would have yielded an inadequate number of firms from which to select. I further restricted the pool of eligible firms to those with at least 40 attorneys, since smaller firms were likely to introduce more variability in firm culture (Epstein, 1993). In the geographic area from Boston to Washington, D.C. (the area to which limited finances confined my data collection), eight firms of sufficient size met the sex-integrated criterion. I randomly selected four firms from this group. Three of these firms were large, employing at least 100 attorneys, and one was about half this size. The proportion of women associates ranged from 38 percent to 47 percent. Their legal work varied, but primarily involved litigation and corporate, real estate, and labor law.

To control for the potentially confounding effects of these firm characteristics, I created a procedure for matching male-dominated firms with the sex-integrated firms. My operational definition of a male-dominated firm depended on firm size. For the larger firms, the criterion was no more than 5 percent women partners; for the smaller firms, it was not more than two women partners (or somewhat more than 5 percent). Using a uniform criterion of 5 percent women partners proved too restrictive, because I could not find a firm to match the small sex-integrated firm. This would have required finding a small male-dominated firm with only one woman partner, and there was none. I thus expanded the criterion for inclusion in this category to include small firms with no more than two women partners, while retaining the 5-percent rule for the larger firms. There were 66 male-dominated firms of sufficient size (at least 40 attorneys). From this set I selected four firms, one to match each of the four sex-integrated firms in overall size, geographic location, ratio of male to female associates, and types of legal work.

Table 22.1 summarizes the sex composition of the eight firms in the study. . . .

I randomly selected four women from each of the six large firms in the study and three women from each of the two smaller firms. This process yielded a total sample of 30 women attorneys working as associates in these firms: 15 in male-dominated firms and 15 in sex-integrated firms. All partici-

Table 22.1
Percentage of Women in Firms

Matched pairs of firms*	Percent women in partnership		Percent women in associateship	
	Male-dominated	Sex-integrated	Male-dominated	Sex-integrated
A	.05	.15	.40	.38
B	.04	.18	.40	.40
C	.05	.16	.41	.47
D†	.11	.29	.50	.43

* Firms in pairs A, B, and C employed between 100 and 200 attorneys; the firms in pair D employed approximately 50 attorneys.

† The relatively higher proportions of women partners in pair D reflects the smaller size of the partnerships in these firms. In absolute numbers of women partners, the male-dominated firm in this pair was similar to the other male-dominated firms in the study, whereas the sex-integrated firm had fewer women partners than the other sex-integrated firms.

Table 22.2
Characteristics of Participants

Characteristics	Male-dominated firms	Sex-Integrated firms
No. married	9	10
No. with at least one child	5	5
No. in corporate practice	4	1
No. in litigation	6	8
No. in other practice area	5	6
Mean age	32.0	32.3
Years of practice	4.9	5.0

pants were white, but one also identified herself as Hispanic. Table 22.2 provides further information about the participants.

Data Sources

Interviews. Following Kram and Isabella's (1985) method for studying peer relationships in career development, I conducted two in-depth, semistructured interviews with each participant. The first interview oriented participants to the study and was dedicated primarily to collecting personal history data and perceptions about the role, if any, gender played in their work lives. The second interview session was dedicated to collecting data on women's relationships with their coworkers. At the start of this session, to focus the participant's attention on her significant relationships, I asked each participant to draw a diagram, or relational map, to represent graphically her relationships to significant coworkers. Significant relationships were those based on work or social ties without which her work life would be changed significantly for better or worse. . . .

Questionnaires. I developed a questionnaire as a second source of data to corroborate findings from the interviews. The questionnaire items paralleled the thematic categories I used in the content analysis and thus served as alternative measures of the constructs in the hypotheses. These complementary methods produce more valid results than either method alone (Jick, 1979). I also included questionnaire items to measure other dimensions of women's relationships that participants discussed during their interviews but that hypotheses did not address directly. . . .

Data Analysis

I used the data I collected in this study to examine the same phenomena from different methodological perspectives, in the spirit of triangulation (Webb et al., 1966; Jick, 1979). The content analysis and questionnaire responses served as alternative measures of the constructs relevant to my hypotheses. From these two methods, I was able to construct parallel statistical comparisons of women's relationships in male-dominated and sex-integrated firms. In particular, to test hypotheses about hierarchical relationships, I performed generalized least squares (GLS) and logit regressions using mean questionnaire responses and dummy-coded variables from the content analysis, respectively, as the dependent variables. . . .

[N]either the content analysis which classifies experience into relatively broad categories, nor the questionnaire, which restricts experience to single, simple dimensions, was adequate to capture the nuance contained in people's own accounts. These accounts provide deeper insights into the psychological aspects of women's relationships. Hence, as part of this analysis, I also drew on excerpts from interviews and interpreted them directly to provide "a more complete, *holistic*, and contextual portrayal" of women's workplace relationships (Jick, 1979: 603). These excerpts serve to illustrate and further inform finding is from the content and questionnaire analyses.

Results

Hierarchical Relationships

I based hypotheses concerning women's hierarchical relationships on the notion that women in male-dominated firms may perceive a contradiction between being female and being successful in their firms. I had expected that this perceived contradiction would lead women to believe that success was available only to women who shed their feminine identity or who had attained their positions of authority illegitimately and, moreover, that these beliefs would compromise their ability to develop constructive relationships with the senior women in their firms.

Conversely, I had expected that in sex-integrated firms, the presence of a significant number of senior women would demonstrate to junior women that being female is not a barrier to success. I expected that this greater sex-integration at senior levels would create the conditions for more positive identification experiences, and hence more constructive relationships, between junior and senior women.

As expected, compared with participants in sex-integrated firms, those in male-dominated firms rated women partners more negatively on the 18-item scale designed to assess women's overall attitudes toward women partners. Results from separate analyses of interview themes and corresponding questionnaire items, shown in Tables 22.3 and 22.4, respectively; provide some support for each of the more specific hypotheses concerning women's hierarchical relationships. Table 22.5 summarizes the statistically significant results from these two data sources.

Positive gender identification. There was strong support for hypothesis 1a, that junior women in male-dominated firms would be less likely to identify with senior women as a source of validation and support than would women in sex-integrated firms. One indicator of such identification was whether or not participants reported feeling a bond of mutual understanding with women partners based on shared experiences as women. As expected, results from both the interview and questionnaire data showed that women in sex-integrated firms were more likely than their counterparts in male-dominated firms to report such feelings.

Participants in sex-integrated firms routinely attributed positive aspects of their relationships with women partners to their shared identity as women. One participant

Table 22.3
Content Analysis of References to Women Partners by Women Associates in Male-dominated and Sex-integrated Firms*

| Theme | Proportion of women who cited the theme | | t |
	Male-dominated firms	Sex-integrated firms	
Gender as a source of shared experiences/ understanding	.40	.80	2.40**
Act like men	.33	.13	−1.98**
Competent	.93	1.00†	.57
Incompetent	.27	.13	−.68
Inappropriate expressions of sexuality	.33	.07	−1.67*
Good role models	.20	.40	1.41*
Poor role models	.27	.00‡	−2.38**

* $p < .10$; **$p < .05$; one-tailed tests.

* Dependent variable is a dummy variable; 1 designates participants who cited the theme, 0 designates those who did not.

† One observation set equal to .999 to produce variance required for calculating coefficient estimates.

‡ One observation set equal to .001 to produce variance required for calculating coefficient estimates.

referred to the "identification factor" in her relationship with a woman partner; "We have times when we interact like women typically do when they're in a more social situation. Something strikes us as funny and we begin to giggle, to have a sort of telepathy that escapes the men in the room." Another said she had "a rapport with [a woman partner] because she was a woman" and, as a result, found her to be "very open, very supportive." Still another emphasized the empathy she felt from women partners who could identify with the experiences women encountered. The women partners "understand that when you send me out on a meeting alone, I'm as likely as not to be across the table from somebody who's 'dearing' me or something like that." Unlike their counterparts in male-dominated firms, these participants often stated that women partners went out of their way to assist the women associates in their firm:

> [The women partners] know more of what you're going through so when you are doing a good job [they will be] the ones who will be actively trying to foster your career. . . . [Among the women partners] there's more of a sense of, "Well, if this really is a good person then maybe the sources of support for a male associate are not available to her, so I have to be out front, and I have to do these things to make sure that she doesn't get lost in the shuffle."

Participants in male-dominated firms not only provided significantly fewer such accounts of their women partners; several expressed explicitly their disappointment and frustration with women partners for failing to meet their expectations in this regard. One participant described a woman partner in her firm as "just the opposite of why I described I like women. It doesn't seem to me that she's accessible at all as a person." Another said she expected "women partners to be nice to women because, gee, we're all in this together," and was sorely disappointed that this had not been the case in her firm.

As expected, the interview data showed that participants in male-dominated firms were more likely to criticize women partners for acting too much like men. One woman complained that the women partners in her firm were women "whose femaleness is not noticed" and who are "modeling more on men." Participants' perceptions of women partners in this regard contributed directly

Table 22.4
Mean Questionnaire Ratings of Attitudes toward Women Partners by Women Associates in Male-dominated and Sex-integrated Firms*

	Male-dominated firms Mean (s.d.)	Sex-integrated firms Mean (s.d.)	*t*
Attitudes toward women partners (18-term scale)	3.69 (.57)	4.05 (.30)	193*
Item pairs			
High/low identification based on gender	3.20 (.84)	3.64 (.79)	2.78**
Act like men/do not act like men	4.10 (.63)	4.14 (.72)	.17
Competent/incompetent	4.03 (.79)	4.45 (.39)	.99
Appropriately/inappropriately sexual	4.03 (.97)	4.62 (.49)	1.81*
Good/poor role models	3.47 (.79)	4.04 (.37)	2.46*
Portray positive/negative image of women	3.60 (.66)	4.32 (.32)	3.71***
Personalities pleasant/difficult	3.32 (.64)	3.86 (.41)	1.94*
Helpful/unhelpful	3.20 (.77)	3.32 (.70)	.44
Politically powerful/powerless	3.57 (.96)	3.61 (.71)	.23

* p < .05; **p < .01; ***p < .001; one-tailed tests.
* A high score indicates an affectively positive rating on a 5-point Likert-type scale.

Table 22.5
Summary of Statistically Significant Findings: Hierarchical Relationships*

Theme	Direction	Statistical evidence	
		Interviews	Questionnaires
Gender as source of shared experiences/understandings with partners	SI > MD	+	+
Partners act like men	SI < MD	+	0
Partners inappropriately express sexuality	SI < MD	+	+
Partners good role models	SI > MD	+	+
Partners poor role models	SI < MD	+	+[†]
Partners' personalities pleasant	SI > MD	NA	+
Partners portray positive image of women	SI > MD	NA	+
Overall positive view of partners	SI > MD	NA	+

* SI = Sex-integrated, MD = Male-dominated firms; + = Differences between firm types reached statistical significance at, minimally, p < 10; 0 = Differences between firm types were not statistically significant; NA = Statistical analysis not conducted because category was excluded from content analysis of interview data.

† Corresponding positive and negative thematic categories in interview data were combined into single mean response to pair of questionnaire items.

to their sense that they would receive little support from them. One participant explained, the women who are going to become partners here are going to be women who act pretty much like men. They're not going to make things more tolerable for me, or change my chances of becoming partner." Items on the questionnaire designed to tap this theme did not yield significant results; however, consistent with the expectation that women in male-dominated firms will have problems with the way senior women behave as women, questionnaire data did show that these participants were more critical of the image of women their senior colleagues portrayed.

Legitimacy of authority. There was some support for hypothesis 1b, that women in male-dominated firms would be less likely than women in sex-integrated firms to view senior women's authority as legitimate. Although there were no significant differences in either the interview or questionnaire data between women's perceptions of women partners' competence (a legitimate basis for authority), women in male-dominated firms were more likely in their interviews to describe women partners as having relied on sexual attraction as an illegitimate strategy for achieving success. Likewise, on the parallel questionnaire items there was a marginally significant difference ($p = .053$) showing that women in male-dominated firms were more critical of their women partners for using their sexuality instrumentally.

Participants' accounts of women partners are especially illustrative of the problems sexuality posed for women's hierarchical relationships in male-dominated firms. One woman described two of the women partners in her firm as "horrible examples" for junior women:

> [They are] very, very deferential to men. I don't like that. And maybe its not true. I mean, they must be good lawyers to have made it, I'll grant them that. But their demeanor is just very flirtatious. One of them, everyone feels, is a manipulative bitch who has no legal talent. . . . She's talked about all the time as having slept with numerous partners. It doesn't even matter if it's not true, if that's the way she's perceived, she's a bad role model.

This participant went on to describe the women partners in her firm as having "done it the wrong way . . . by pandering to men in a sort of base way." Similarly, another participant described one of the women partners in her firm as "a twitty little flirt" with a reputation for having "brown-nosed her way into her position . . . by using disgustingly typically feminine wiles." Junior women's focus on women partners' sexuality in their criticisms suggested that they did not perceive the status differences between them and women partners to be fully legitimate.

Unprompted, one participant summarized how the delegitimation of women's authority inhibited constructive hierarchical relationships between women. She observed that while there was some truth to the stereotype that women do not get along with one another at work, women's tenuous status within her firm was largely responsible for the problems they encountered in this regard:

> When someone is more advanced than you, enough so that you naturally take direction from them because of their superior experience, then you get along with them a lot better. So far [those people have] always been men. . . . So it's very unfair to say, "Well, women are always fighting with each other, they're not getting along with each other," when it's the nature of the situation that you're never dealing with a woman who is so firmly entrenched in her authority that you follow her lead with the same degree of deference that you would follow a man in that position. There just aren't any; there aren't enough of them So, it's just terribly unfair.

Women partners as role models. As expected by hypothesis 1c, women in male-dominated firms were more likely in their interviews to criticize women partners for being poor role models, whereas those in sex-integrated firms were more likely to praise them for being good role models. Questionnaire data provided corroborating evidence for this result: Women in male-dominated firms rated women partners less positively on the role-model dimension than did women in sex-integrated firms. Women's accounts sharply illustrate these differences. One woman in a male-dominated firm expressed it this way: "[The women partners are] just such lousy role models in one way or another. There's one who worked herself to death. And there's one who got there—it doesn't matter if it's not true, if that's the way she got there, she's a bad role model—her reputation is that she got there by laughing at all these guys' jokes and just submitting to that." And another woman in a male-dominated firm commented, "There are very few role models around here. Very few women partners that you could point to and say, 'Look, that could be me.'" By contrast, the comments of women in sex-integrated firms were more positive: "By and large, [the women partners] are really nice people-good role models, professional, stylish, friendly, down-to-earth, accessible, encouraging." And "Having a lot of senior women here affects all the women associates because they're such good role models and because they're such good standard bearers. Because of their success, we're perceived [by the men in the partnership] as having the ability to be successful."

Peer Relationships

I based hypotheses about women's peer relationships on the notion that a scarcity of women in senior positions may signal to women lower down in the organization that their gender is a liability. I expected that this would foster competitiveness among women and inhibit alliances of support. As expected, compared with participants in sex-integrated firms, those in male-dominated firms rated women associates more negatively on the 10-item scale designed to assess women's overall attitudes toward women associates. Interview data confirmed the specific hypotheses about these relationships: questionnaire data were consistent with the hypotheses, but did not directly support them. Tables 22.6 and 22.7, respectively, report these results. Table 22.8

summarizes the statistically significant results from these two data sources.

Competitiveness. Although women discussed on average the same number of peer relationships during their interviews (4.5 in both types of firms), participants in male-dominated firms characterized more of their relationships with women peers as competitive in ways that inhibited their ability to work together than did participants in sex-integrated firms, supporting hypothesis 2a. In their accounts of competition with other women, participants in male-dominated firms often focused on feelings of envy or jealousy. The following excerpts provide examples of this from three women:

> It's very complicated because some of it is very rational and you can identify what you have to do to get certain places, and some of it is just green-eyed monster stuff. Sometimes I just feel envious of her political connections, and I do these irrational things like wishing I could do everything she can do.

Table 22.6

Content Analysis of Peer Relationships Reported by Women in Male-dominated and Sex-integrated Firms*

	Male-dominated firms Mean (s.d.)	Sex-integrated firms Mean (s.d.)	t
Distressed due to competitiveness	.50 (.75)	.27 (.59)	−1.68*
Supportive	1.43 (1.16)	2.47 (1.68)	3.70**

* p < .10; **p < .001; one-tailed tests.

† Dependent variable is the number of relationships that fell into the category.

Table 22.7

Mean Questionnaire Ratings of Attitudes toward Women Peers by Women Associates in Male-dominated and Sex-integrated Firms*

	Male-dominated firms Mean (s.d.)	Sex-integrated firms Mean (s.d.)	t
Attitudes toward women peers (10-item scale)	3.95 (.48)	4.15 (.29)	1.98*
Item pairs			
Supportive/ unsupportive	4.00 (.53)	4.14 (.36)	.84
Distressful/ nondistressful competition	3.93 (.60)	4.05 (.51)	.58
Competent/ incompetent	4.15 (.61)	4.16 (.50)	.05
Appropriately/ inappropriately sexual	3.83 (.59)	4.32 (.54)	2.32*
Portray positive/ negative image of women	3.83 (.67)	4.07 (.58)	1.73*

* p < .05; one-tailed tests.

† A high score indicates an affectively positive rating on a 5-point Likert-type scale.

Table 22.8
Summary of Statistically Significant Findings: Peer Relationships*

Theme	Direction	Statistical evidence	
		Interviews	Question-naires
Relationships supportive	SI > MD	+	0
Relationships distressed due to competitiveness	SI < MD	+	0
Peers portray positive image of women	SI > MD	NA	+
Peers inappropriately express sexuality	SI < MD	NA	+
Overall positive view of peers	SI > MD	NA	+

* SI = Sex-integrated, MD = Male-dominated firms; + = Differences between firm types reached statistical significance at, minimally, *p* < .10; 0 = Differences between firm types were not statistically significant; NA = Statistical analysis not conducted because category was excluded from content analysis of interview data.

With women, it's like being jealous over a man . . . [whereas] I feel that if I'm being competitive with a man, it's just good clean fun. I really want to kick his ass, I just don't feel that kind of malicious aspect to it that I do with [a woman].

[Competition with women has] more of a personal element [compared with men]. I'm jealous of her looks. . . . And she's very self-confident and I'm jealous about that also.

Another woman from a male-dominated firm offered the following description of competitiveness in one of her relationships with a woman associate who was slightly senior to her:

[Working with a woman] both helps and hurts. It cuts both ways. It helps because I think it makes her feel protective of me against the outside world. It becomes a sort of sisterly or familial relationship. The way it hurts is both of us say things to each other that we would never say to other lawyers in a similar situation. . . . There are just things that make the atmosphere tense. On the one hand, she uses me for ideas and she cultivates me thinking on my own. But then, when she wants to be the boss [because she has had more years of experience], she just wants me to turn it off. . . . And it's terrible. You feel like all of a sudden your dignity has been taken away from you. And that's a prob-

lem. She just doesn't like to give up that little power. And then I've hurt her feelings several times, too, because she's very sensitive about the fact that I'm bright and I'm her friend. She seems threatened by my intelligence or by the fact that I might be competent too.

According to this account, in order for each woman to express her competence, the other was required to give up a piece of herself: The respondent gave up dignity; her colleague had to give up power.

This account, like those above, suggests that women in male-dominated firms had difficulty perceiving their work accomplishments and competencies as independent of one another. In each, one's strengths (e.g., political connections, self-confidence, dignity, power) fostered in the other feelings of inadequacy or insecurity or, at the very least, a sense that there could be only one winner (as in a competition "over a man"). In male-dominated firms, this construction of competition as zero-sum was a consistent theme in women's more troubled accounts of competition. One participant attributed competitiveness among women directly to the law firm's promotion structure and to the fact that it had yielded few senior women: "It probably is more true in a law firm that has an up or out policy that women would have more problems with each other because there isn't that layer of senior women. . . . Your relationships with women are all people that are conceivably competitors." Others in male-dominated firms corroborated the view that limited access to senior positions may foster these kinds of competitive experiences:

It's a divide and conquer strategy on the part of men. . . . I can see it starting to happen in terms of the women who are thinking about how the men perceive them vis à vis the other women, and thinking that we can't all quite make it— that being a woman is going to be a factor in their decision, so what kind of woman do they want? It's very subtle. . . . And I'm very concerned about that because I think that means we're going to modify our own self-concepts and the way we treat each other. I'm not so sure that isn't going to be somewhat painful.

Two other participants described this dynamic in action. They had observed women being especially critical of other women and questioned whether this was a strategy they might be using to gain a comparative advantage:

> She does little things to me that I think are not fair. She will jokingly sort of disparage me in front of the partner. . . . And she's laughing the whole time and I don't know if she's trying to sabotage me, or if she really doesn't know [what she's doing].

> Some people say she destroys people whom she sees as a threat to her. . . . She's done things that subtly may be undermining so that [another woman and I] are less of a threat. [For example,] she has characterized [a woman peer] to the partners as "fru-fru"—too feminine, too emotional, organized but maybe not the highest caliber brain. . . . A little bit like she is too flirty.

Accounts from other women in male-dominated firms suggested that senior men sometimes fuel women's competitive feelings by drawing comparisons between them. When relating a particularly painful experience of competitiveness, one woman described an event in which a male partner criticized her publicly for being less "lady-like" than her female colleague. "He played us off one another," she explained. Another woman from a male-dominated firm described "a rivalry" between another woman and her, generated by their shared dependence on a male partner for whom they were both working. She criticized her coworker as a woman who "exudes a lot of sexuality" and resented the attention she received from this partner when she flirted with him.

The repeated references to sexuality in these excerpts—the comparison between competition with women and "being jealous over a man," the competitiveness generated from jealousy over another woman's looks, and the criticisms that other women associates are "too flirty" or too sexual—suggest the variety of ways in which issues of sexuality were a source of disturbance in peer relationships among women in male-dominated firms. Questionnaire results supported this observation: Women in male-dominated firms were more likely to criticize their women peers for expressing sexuality in inappropriate ways and were more critical of the image of women their peers portrayed than were women in sex-integrated firms.

By contrast, women in sex-integrated firms encountered fewer problems in their relationships with women peers. In particu-

lar, they were less likely to experience distress in their relationships as a result of competitive feelings. A story one woman told of an incident with a woman peer with whom she felt competitive exemplifies the way competition operated in these relationships. When she was a junior associate, a partner had assigned her to a project with another woman associate who was in her same class year, a situation that assigning partners try to avoid because associates in the same class tend to compete at the same time for partnership. Due to a previous, unrelated misunderstanding about the project, the assigning partner and the interviewee were angry with each other. Consequently, the partner interacted only with the other woman associate throughout the project "So she was in the position of having to handle [giving me work assignments] without making me feel like she was giving me orders," the interviewee explained. They arrived at a tacit agreement that forestalled conflict The interviewee was careful always to solicit direction so that her colleague did not have to give her work assignments. In addition, each was careful to consult with the other throughout the project. Despite the discomfort they both felt, their shared understanding that the competitive situation was potentially divisive and unproductive led them to handle it so that it worked out well: "And she was good at handling the politics of the situation. She complained a lot about [the partner], which was something that was meant to make me feel better. So, we got it done. And she couldn't have done it alone at that level. But the two of us sort of advising each other could." These two women were able to divide the task and authorize each other to do their parts. In this way, the two were able to differentiate from one another, each bringing her own strengths to their task, without the emergence of envy or sense of loss evident in relationships among their counterparts in male-dominated firms.

A woman from another sex-integrated firm described a similar situation in which she and her friend were both eligible for early promotion to the same partnership slot. The interviewee was not chosen. The competitive feelings that ensued were channeled productively, however, into a win-win resolution. While this woman felt hurt at not being chosen and described feelings of competitiveness with her colleague, she was able to compare their strengths and weaknesses and the differences between them in the kinds of work they each preferred to do. On this basis, she was able to recognize, or at least rationalize, the decision as a just one After her colleague was promoted, they worked together to gain an understanding of why the interviewee had not been chosen to fill the position. As a partner, her colleague was now privy to information that could help the interviewee understand and reverse the perceptions that had kept her from receiving the partnership offer. By sharing this information, her colleague made the interviewee's future candidacy for partnership much more viable.

These stories exemplify the way competitiveness tended to operate in sex-integrated firms. In both incidents, women recognized the structural realities of competitiveness in their relationships with other women associates. Moreover, they seemed able to use this understanding to turn potentially threatening situations with other women, in which a zero-sum orientation might have been dysfunctional both for the relationship and for the work, into shared gain through mutual support, i.e., positive-sum outcomes.

Supportiveness. As hypothesized (H2b), women in male-dominated firms characterized fewer of their relationships with women peers as supportive than did women in sex-integrated firms. Data from the interviews presented above suggest that the nature of competition in male-dominated firms inhibited the development of supportive relationships among women in those firms, whereas the nature of competitiveness in sex-integrated firms did not.

Discussion and Conclusions

This analysis demonstrates how structural features of a firm may affect the nature and quality of interpersonal relationships at work, casting doubt on wholly person-centered explanations for the difficulties often observed in workplace relationships among women. This study shows, instead, that social identity plays a critical role.

Social Identity and Women's Hierarchical Relationships

The results of this study suggest that women partners as women were a matter of special interest and concern for interviewees regardless of their firm affiliation. In this sense, women appeared to identify with women partners on the basis of shared gender group membership. The nature of interviewees' interests and concern varied, however, according to the sex composition of their firm's partnership.

I had reasoned that a scarcity of women in senior positions may signal to women lower down in the organization that their gender is a liability, making it difficult for them to identify positively with senior women. Such problems would then interfere in the development of constructive, developmental relationships that could help to elevate more women in the firm. Results showed, as expected, that shared gender provided little basis for validation and support for firms that appeared to restrict women's access to those positions. As expected, women's criticisms of their senior colleagues centered on their credentials both as women and as partners. Women partners not only failed to be the kind of women on whom junior women could rely for support but failed as well to be the kind of partner whose authority junior women could respect. Not surprisingly, these women were less satisfied with the image of women their partners portrayed and found them difficult to emulate as role models. The negative associations with women's gender in these firms, communicated by the scarcity of women in senior positions, seemed to remove gender as a potentially positive basis for identification and relationship.

By contrast, in firms that appeared not to restrict women's access to senior positions, women were able to use their identification with women partners as a source of validation and support. Interviewees in these firms raised far fewer concerns about the legitimacy of women partners' authority and, instead, viewed the success of some women as a signal of the possibility of their own. For these associates, the entry of women into the partnership seemed to indicate that they too could become partners and that their sex per se would not pose a barrier. Thus perceived inconsistencies between one's identity as a woman, on the one hand, and success, on the other, were diminished for women in sex-integrated firms, which helped them establish constructive developmental relationships.

Social Identity and Women's Peer Relationships

The concept of social identity is also useful for understanding the link between the relative presence of women in senior positions and relationships among women lower down in the organization. In particular, the degree to which women were represented in senior positions influenced the nature of women's identification with other women. This, in turn, shaped how they experienced competition and support in relation to one another.

The most striking difference in women's accounts of their competitive experiences centered on whether they constructed competition as zero-sum or positive-sum. Zero-sum constructions made for more problematic encounters and were more evident in reports by women in male-dominated firms; positive-sum constructions generated more constructive outcomes and were more evident among women in sex-integrated firms. A related difference was the tendency of women in male-dominated firms to compare themselves directly with other women associates as a way of gauging their own success and relative opportunities for advancement. Women in sex-integrated firms did not show this tendency.

These findings resonate with clinical research that suggests that underlying these different constructions of competition may be differences in the way women identify with their women peers (Lindenbaum, 1987). As described above, identification in this context refers to women's sense of being "psychologically intertwined with the fate of [women as] a group" (Ashforth and Mael, 1989: 21). Identification can make empathy and support possible, as it did for interviewees and their women peers in sex-integrated firms. Women in male-dominated firms, however, may have perceived their fate to be too closely aligned with the group's, causing them to lose their sense of individual identity. Ironically, this situation may call for excessive efforts to differentiate oneself from others in the group. Such overidentification and overdifferentiation may explain women's dual tendency in male-dominated firms to construct other women's strength as evidence of their own weakness and, at the same time, to defend against this construction by denigrating other women. Hence, when group identification is a source of vulnerability, intragroup competition is a threatening experience.

By contrast, women in sex-integrated firms seemed able to use identification as a positive source of support in both their hierarchical and their peer relationships, and competition was constructive. According to Lindenbaum (1987: 203), this form of competition "requires two people, each of whom has a sufficiently separate identity to risk measuring herself against the separate identity of the other." Rather than feeling threatened by the strengths of their women colleagues, women in sex-integrated firms affirmed such strengths and, in the process, affirmed themselves.

The research presented here suggests that by shaping the relative value people attach to their group memberships, different demographic structures foster different manifestations of these identification processes. In male-dominated firms, women may perceive their gender group membership as less valued and become overly invested in the adequacy of other women as representatives of their group. The psychological boundary between self and group becomes blurred, leading women to take a hypercritical stance with one another and to differentiate themselves as better than their peers (Kanter, 1977). In sex-integrated firms, where promotion appears less tied to gender group affiliation, identification processes are balanced by less pejorative assessments of difference. Women are able both to identify with other women and to draw on differences that are constructive to their relationship and their work. Consequently, women are better able to manage their competitive feelings in productive ways and build supportive relationships. These kinds of relationships are more likely to grow out of conditions that allow women to compete legitimately with one another for promotion—conditions structured in part by women's greater representation at senior levels.

Limitations of the Study

The statistical results showing relationships between the presence of women in senior positions and junior women's experiences in their firms are necessarily associational rather than causal. Consequently, it is unclear whether the presence of women in senior positions per se makes a difference in women's experiences or whether other factors in organizations' internal environments lead both to increased proportions of women partners and to more positive relationship experiences. . . .

Implications for Theory and Practice

This study makes three theoretical contributions. First, it helps to clarify contradictory results and theories in previous research on women's relational versus competitive orientation with one another at work. While that research has tended to rely on women's socialization as a primary explanation, this study challenges these individual-level explanations by offering support for women's proportional representation in senior positions as a structural variable influencing their workplace relationships. The result is a more complex, contextual understanding of the impact of gender on women's organizational experiences.

Second, this study demonstrates the usefulness of social identity theory as a framework for understanding how demographic arrangements help people socially construct the meaning and consequences of their identity group memberships. This paper thus lays the groundwork for future research into the workplace experiences of members of other identity groups that have been traditionally underrepresented in positions of organizational authority, such as racial and ethnic minorities. In particular, these results add to our understanding of the organizational conditions that may enhance or undermine in-group solidarity. In addition, although researchers have traditionally used social identity theory to understand competition between groups, this study shows that the theory is also useful for understanding competition within groups.

Third, this study extends the developing literature on organizational demography to include the impact of demographic composition across hierarchical levels of the organization by moving beyond the literature on tokenism to highlight the distribution of power within organizations as an important consideration in demographic research. Unexamined variability in groups' representation at senior organizational levels may explain Tsui, Egan, and O'Reilly's (1992) findings that women and minorities were generally unaffected by their demographic status in their work units.

This study also has practical implications. At the organizational level, removing barriers keeping women from top positions may go a long way toward easing the stresses and facilitating more productive working relationships for women lower down in the organization. In addition, once they are aware of identification processes and their effects, women themselves will be better able to manage their interpersonal relationships at work and develop the constructive alliances and mentoring relationships with women that allow them to realize their potential.

References

Abrams, Dominic, and Michael A. Hogg. 1990. *Social Identity Theory: Constructive and Critical Advances*. New York: Harvester Wheatsheaf.

Alderfer, Clayton P. 1968. "Comparison of questionnaire responses with and without preceding interviews." *Journal of Applied Psychology*, 52: 335–340.

Alderfer, Clayton P., Robert C. Tucker, David R. Morgan, and Fritz Drasgow. 1983. "Black and white cognitions of changing race relations in management." *Journal of Occupational Behavior*, 4: 105–136.

Ashforth, Blake E., and Fred Mael. 1989. "Social identity theory and the organization." *Academy of Management Review*, 14: 20–39.

Briles, Judith. 1987. *Woman to Woman: From Sabotage to Support*. Far Hills, NJ: New Horizon Press.

Broder, Ivy E. 1993. "Review of NSF economics proposals: Gender and institutional patterns." *American Economic Review*, 83: 964–970.

Chamberlain, Mariam K. 1988. *Women in Academe*. New York: Russell Sage Foundation.

Ely, Robin J. 1989. "An intergroup perspective on relationships among professional women." Unpublished doctoral dissertation, Yale University.

———. 1990. "The role of men in relationships among professional women." *Best Papers Proceedings of the Academy of Management*: 364–368. San Francisco: Academy of Management.

———. 1992 "Organizational demographics and women's gender: Identity at work." *Working Paper Series, R93-21*. Cambridge, MA: J. F. Kennedy School of Government, Harvard University.

Epstein, Cynthia Fuchs. 1993. *Women in Law*. New Haven, CT: Yale University Press.

Fairhurst, Gail T., and B. Kay Snavely. 1983. "Majority and token minority group relationships: Power acquisition and communication." *Academy of Management Review*, 8: 292–300.

Gecas, Viktor, Darwin L. Thomas, and Andrew J. Weigert. 1973. "Social identities in Anglo and Latin adolescents." *Social Forces*, 51: 477–484.

Gutek, Barbara A. 1985. *Sex and the Workplace*. San Francisco: Jossey-Bass.

Gutek, Barbara A., and Bruce Morasch. 1982. "Sex-ratios, sex-role spillover, and sexual harassment of women at work." *Journal of Social Issues*, 38: 55–74.

Helgesen, Sally. 1990. *The Female Advantage: Women's Ways of Leadership*. New York: Doubleday.

Hennig, Margaret, and Anne Jardim. 1977. *The Managerial Woman*. New York: Pocket Books.

Hinkle, Steve, and Rupert J. Brown. 1990. "Intergroup comparisons and social identity: Some links and lacunae." In Dominic Abrams and Michael A. Hogg (eds.), *Social Identity Theory: Constructive and Critical Advances*: 48–70. New York: Harvester Wheatsheaf.

Hogg, Michael A., and Dominic Abrams. 1990. "Social motivation, self esteem and social identity." In Dominic Abrams and Michael A. Hogg (eds.), *Social Identity Theory: Con-*

structive and Critical Advances: 28–47. New York: Harvester Wheatsheaf.

Ibarra, Herminia. 1992. "Homophily and differential returns: Sex differences in network structure and access in an advertising firm." *Administrative Science Quarterly*, 37: 422–447.

Jick, Todd D. 1970. "Mixing qualitative and quantitative methods: Triangulation in action." *Administrative Science Quarterly*, 24: 602–611.

Kanter, Rosabeth Moss. 1977. *Men and Women of the Corporation*. New York: Basic Books.

Keller, Evelyn Fox, and Helene Moglen. 1987. "Competition: A problem for academic women." In Valerie Miner and Helen E. Longino (eds.), *Competition: A Feminist Taboo?*: 21–37. New York: Feminist Press.

Konrad, Alison, and Barbara A., Gutek. 1987. "Theory and research on group composition: Applications to the status of women and ethnic minorities." In S. Oskamp and S. Spacapan (eds.), *Interpersonal Processes*: 85–121. Newbury Park, CA: Sage.

Kram, Kathy E. 1986. *Mentoring at Work: Developmental Relationships in Organizational Life*. Glenview, IL: Scott Foresman.

Kram, Kathy E., and Lynn A. Isabella. 1985. "Mentoring alternatives: The role of peer relationships in career development." *Academy of Management Journal*, 28: 110–132.

Kramer, Roderick M. 1991. "Intergroup relations and organization dilemmas: The role of categorization processes." In L. L. Cummings and Barry M. Staw (eds.), *Research in Organizational Behavior*, 13: 191–228. Greenwich, CT: JAI Press.

Lambert, W. E., R. C. Hodgson, R. Gardner, and S. J. Fillenbaum. 1960. "Evaluative reactions to spoken languages." *Journal of Abnormal and Social Psychology*, 60: 44–51.

Lincoln, James R., and John Miller. 1979. "Work and friendship ties in organizations: A comparative analysis of relational networks." *Administrative Science Quarterly*, 21: 181–199.

Lindenbaum, Joyce P. 1987. "The shattering of an illusion: The problem of competition in lesbian relationships." In Valerie Miner and Helen E. Longino (eds.), *Competition: A Feminist Taboo?*: 195–208. New York: Feminist Press.

Madden, Tara Roth. 1987. *Women Versus Women: The Uncivil Business War*. New York: AMACOM.

Martin, Patricia Y. 1985. "Group sex composition in work organizations: A structural-normative model." In Samuel B. Bacharach and Stephen M. Mitchell (eds.), *Research in the Sociology of Organizations*, 4: 311–349. Greenwich, CT: JAI Press.

McPherson, J. Miller, and Lynn Smith-Lovin. 1987. "Homophily in voluntary organizations: Status distance and the composition of face-to-face groups." *American Sociological Review*, 54: 365–381.

Miner, Valerie, and Helen E. Longino (eds.). 1987. *Competition: A Feminist Taboo?* New York: Feminist Press.

Moore, Gwen. 1990. "Structural determinants of men's and women's personal networks." *American Sociological Review*, 55: 728–735.

Morrison, Anne M., and Maryanne Von Glinow. 1990. "Women and minorities in management." *American Psychologist*, 45: 200–208.

O'Leary, Virginia E. 1988. "Women's relationships with women in the workplace." In B. Gutek, A. H. Stromberg, and L. Larwood (eds.), *Women and Work: An Annual Review*, 3: 189–213. Newbury Park, CA: Sage.

Pettigrew, Thomas F. 1986. "The intergroup contact hypothesis reconsidered." In Miles Hewstone and Rupert Brown (eds.), *Contact and Conflict in Intergroup Encounters*: 169–195. New York: Basil Blackwell.

Pfeffer, Jeffrey. 1989. "A political perspective on careers: Interests, networks, and environments." In Michael B Arthur, Douglas T Hall, and Barbara S. Lawrence (eds.), *Hand-*

book of Career Theory: 380–396. Cambridge: Cambridge University Press.

Ridgeway, Cecilia L. 1988. "Gender differences in task groups: A status and legitimacy account." In Murray Webster, Jr., and Martha Foschi (eds.), *Status Generalization: New Theory and Research*: 188–206. Stanford, CA: Stanford University Press.

Riger, Stephanie, and Pat Galligan. 1980. "Women in management: An exploration of competing paradigms." *American Psychologist*, 35: 902–910.

Rosener, Judy. 1990 "Ways women lead." *Harvard Business Review*, Nov–Dec: 118–125.

South, Scott J., Charles M. Bonjean, William T. Markham, and Judy Corder. 1982. "Social structure and intergroup interaction: Men and women of the federal bureaucracy." *American Sociological Review*, 47: 587–599.

Staines, Graham L., Toby E. Jayaratne, and Carol Tavris. 1974. "The queen bee syndrome." *Psychology Today*, 7 (Jan.): 55–60.

Tajfel, Henri. 1978. "Social categorization, social identity and social comparison." In Henri Tajfel (ed.), *Differentiation between Social Groups*: 61–76. New York: Academic Press.

———. 1981. *Human Groups and Social Categories*. Cambridge: Cambridge University Press.

———. 1982. *Social Identity and Intergroup Relations*. Cambridge: Cambridge University Press.

Tajfel, Henri, and John C. Turner. 1985. "The social identity theory of intergroup behavior." In S. Worchel and W. G. Austin (eds.), *Psychology of Intergroup Relations*: 7–24. Chicago: Nelson-Hall.

Thomas, David, and Clayton P. Alderfer. 1989. "The influence of race on career dynamics: Research and theory in minority career experiences." In Michael B Arthur, Douglas T. Hall, and Barbara S. Lawrence (eds.), *Handbook of Career Theory*: 133–158. Cambridge: Cambridge University Press.

Tsui, Anne S., Terri D. Egan, and Charles A. O'Reilly III. 1992. "Being different: Relational demography and organizational attachment." *Administrative Science Quarterly*, 37: 549–579.

Turner, John C. 1987. *Rediscovering the Social Group: A Self-Categorization Theory*. Oxford: Basil Blackwell.

Turner, John C., and Howard Giles. 1981. *Intergroup Behavior*. New York: Basil Blackwell.

Webb, Eugene J., Donald T. Campbell, Richard D. Schwartz, and Lee Sechrest. 1966. *Unobtrusive Measures: Nonreactive Research in the Social Sciences*. Chicago: Rand McNally.

Webster, Murray, Jr., and Martha Foschi. 1988. *Status Generalization: New Theory and Research Stanford*. CA: Stanford University Press.

Wharton, Amy S. 1992. "The social construction of gender and race in organizations: A social identity and group mobilization perspective." In Pamela S. Tolbert and Samuel B. Bacharach (eds.), *Research in the Sociology of Organizations*, 10: 55–84. Greenwich, CT: JAI Press.

Williams, J., and H. Giles. 1978. "The changing status of women in society: An intergroup perspective." In Henri Tajfel (ed.), *Differentiation between Social Groups*: 431–449. London Academic Press.

Yoder, Janice D. 1991. "Rethinking tokenism: Looking beyond numbers." *Gender and Society*, 5: 178–192.

Zimmer, Lynn. 1988. "Tokenism and women in the workplace: The limits of gender-neutral theory." *Social Problems*, 35: 64–77.

Chapter 23
(In)voluntary Association

A Multilevel Analysis of Gender Segregation in Voluntary Organizations

Pamela A. Popielarz

The final chapter in this section moves us from the paid workplace to voluntary organizations. Pamela Popielarz documents the high levels of gender segregation in these groups, and considers some of the factors that contribute to these patterns. This chapter also explores some of the larger societal implications of highly gender segregated voluntary groups and the differential impact of group membership on women and men.

Gender segregation in organizations facilitates the unequal distribution of rewards to men and women. Although recent efforts in sociology document the persistently high level of gender segregation in the labor market (Petersen and Morgan 1995; Reskin 1984), we know much less about the same phenomenon in voluntary associations. My strategy here is to develop a comprehensive description of segregation in voluntary associations. I use a unique data set to investigate the typical characteristics of voluntary group members, members of groups segregated by gender, and gender-segregated organizations themselves. I then discuss the implications of these new findings, outlining how gender segregation affects societal integration, social movements, and personal networks and stratification outcomes.

Voluntary Associations and Gender Segregation

Voluntary associations are formal and informal social groups that are not directly part of family, government, religion, or economic firms. This includes church-related groups, but not church memberships (Knoke and Thomson 1977). As defined here, voluntary associations include some social movement organizations, or their local chapters, as well as a wide array of social groups with, for example, charity, civic, sports, and fraternal aims. Such groups primarily involve face-to-face contact at local meetings.

In this article, a gender-segregated voluntary association consists of either 90 to 100 percent female members (in which case the group is called female-dominated) or 0 to 10 percent female members (in which case the group is male-dominated).[1] In integrated voluntary associations, women make up between 10 and 90 percent of the membership. These cutoff points reflect previous work on gender segregation and tokenism (Jacobs 1989).

To completely describe gender segregation in voluntary associations, three broad questions need attention. Answering each necessitates a different level of empirical analysis. First, who belongs to voluntary associations? Studying affiliation patterns among a sample of individuals will help to answer this question. Next, what traits differentiate members of gender-segregated organizations from members of integrated organizations? This inquiry necessitates studying a sample of people who belong to voluntary associations. Last, what are the typical traits of gender-segregated and integrated organizations? Because gender segregation is a characteristic of an organization, not of an individual, this task demands a sample of organizations for study. Without organizational-level data, one cannot distinguish between the following two scenarios: (1) Men and women belong to the same organizations but have different experiences, in which case internal organizational processes probably explain those differences, and (2) men and women have different experiences because they belong to different organizations, in which case the demographic makeup of organizations should also be a focus of research. As we will see, men and women do typically belong to different organizations. Furthermore, the existence of gender segregation makes other demographic traits of these organizations interesting to study, particularly patterns of segregation and integration on age and education. This study is uniquely able to document connections between gender segregation and segregation on age and education. Before describing the data necessary to answer the three research questions, I briefly review some of the voluntary association literature.

Decades of research on voluntary association affiliation rates show how membership is related to various demographic characteristics (see Smith and Freedman 1972 for a review). Although some studies imply that men participate more than women do (Booth 1972), it seems that after controlling for education and other influences, men and women have the same affiliation rates (Gustafson, Booth, and Johnson 1979). As for other demographic traits, organizational participation increases until the middle-age years and then decreases (Knoke and Thomson 1977). For education, a similar pattern of increasing then decreasing participation is evident, with the peak between 12 and 16 years of education (McPherson and Rotolo 1996). Affiliation is also positively linked with employment (Gustafson, Booth, and Johnson 1979) and social network size (McPherson, Popielarz, and Drobnič 1992).

Little research focuses on the differences between members of gender-exclusive associations and members of integrated associations. The most in-depth study on the subject to date indicates "little support for the sex integration hypothesis" (McPherson and Smith-Lovin 1986, 61). Indeed, in that study, 68 percent of voluntary association memberships were in gender-exclusive groups. Women were significantly more likely than men to belong to these associations. Single people and those with low education were more likely to belong to segregated groups. Involvement in marriage or full-time work decreased the chance of a woman belonging to a female-dominated organization, as did extremely high or low education. Membership in all-male groups was most likely for men who were not highly educated, worked full-time, and were either single or married (as opposed to widowed, separated, or divorced).

The organizational and environmental correlates of gender segregation also receive little research attention other than studies indicating that gender-integrated voluntary organizations occur more often in larger cities and that women's organizations are smaller than other types of groups (McPherson and Smith-Lovin 1982, 1986).

In sum, a complete description of organizational gender segregation depends on the ability to address the three research questions delineated above by doing empirical analysis at multiple levels; the individual, the member, and the organization. The next section introduces the data set I use to analyze these three levels of inquiry.

Data

Data for this study come from the Niches and Networks project, collected in the summer and fall of 1989. This multilevel, multistage survey drew respondents from 1.0 size-stratified towns in the same state. The towns included in the study ranged in size from a very small community (population 1,318) to the largest city in the state (population 350,000). The first stage of the project provides data appropriate for answering the first two research questions. Organizational-level data from a later stage of the project helps answer the third question.

The first stage of the project surveyed a stratified random sample of respondents spread roughly equally across the 10 towns. Respondents provided such demographic information as gender, race, religion, age, years of education, employment, and marital status. The instrument also included questions about the respondents' memberships in each of 17 types of voluntary associations.[2] For each membership, respondents reported various characteristics of the organization, including gender composition. In addition, respondents completed a version of the General Social Surveys social network instrument (Davis and Smith 1988), in which they were asked to name up to 5 persons with whom they had "discuss[ed] important matters" over the past six months.

Data from this stage of the survey permit analysis on both the individual and the member level. For the individual-level data set, there is one observation corresponding to each respondent in the survey. Analyzing this data set will help answer the first research question, Who belongs to voluntary associations? For the member-level data set, each of the organizational memberships mentioned by each respondent constitutes one observation. Thus, a respondent reporting memberships in four voluntary associations contributes four observations to the member-level data set, and a respondent reporting no memberships contributes no observations. The member-level data set will be used to answer the second research question, What traits differentiate members of gender-segregated organizations from members of gender-integrated organizations?

A later stage of the survey used hypernetwork sampling (McPherson 1982) to gather data on a sample of voluntary organizations. The hypernetwork technique generates a sample of organizations by asking a random sample of individuals about their memberships and using the resulting list of organizations as a sampling frame. Once the sample of voluntary associations was identified, all members present at actual meetings of the chosen organizations were surveyed with a questionnaire asking for basic demographic data (gender, age, years of education) as well as information about their organizational involvement (e.g., when they joined the group). Aggregating the data on members of each of the specific organizations results in an organizational-level data set that contains such information as group size and gender composition. Analyzing this organizational-level data set will provide answers to the final research question, What are the typical traits of gender-segregated and integrated organizations? I now turn to the results.

Who Belongs to Voluntary Associations?

The task in this first section of the analysis is to briefly identify some of the personal characteristics associated with voluntary organization involvement. The data set contains information on 1,047 respondents, 57.9 percent of whom were women. Of these respondents, 79.6 percent belonged to one or more voluntary associations. The number of memberships per respondent ranges from 0 to 20, with a mean of 2.83.

According to Table 23.1, there is scant evidence that women are more likely than men to belong to one or more voluntary associa-

tions ($\chi^2 = 3.99, p = .05$). Although women in the sample have an average of 2.87 memberships, and men average 2.78 memberships, the difference in number of memberships is not statistically significant ($t = 0.48, p = .68$).

The lack of difference between men and women in voluntary association membership becomes clearer in a multivariate context. Panel A of Table 23.2 displays the results of a logistic regression model for belonging to one or more voluntary associations. Membership is significantly related to several demographic traits but not to gender. The results indicate that, although men and women have the same propensity for membership, voluntary associations in general are less likely to include nonwhites and young people as well as people with no religious preference, low education, and/or small personal networks.

This brief description of the demographic characteristics associated with voluntary organization membership gives us an idea of who is included in the voluntary world, but it does not distinguish between affiliations in gender-segregated and integrated groups. For this task, I turn to the member-level data set.

Who Belongs to Gender-Segregated Voluntary Associations?

What distinguishes the typical characteristics of persons involved in segregated and integrated voluntary organizations? To address this question, I use the member-level data set, containing 1,421 observations coded by the gender type of the organization to which the member belonged. Table 23.3 demonstrates that the majority of memberships (64.5 percent) are in segregated voluntary organizations, and most of those are in female-dominated organizations. Women are significantly less likely to belong to integrated groups than are men (30.4 percent and 44.1 percent, respectively, $Z = 5.21, p =$

Table 23.1

Cross-Tabulation of Membership in One or More Voluntary Associations by Gender (column percentages in parentheses)

	Male	*Female*	*Total*
No memberships	103 (23.4)	111 (18.3)	214 (20.4)
One or more memberships	338 (76.6)	495 (81.7)	833 (79.6)
Total	441	606	1,047

.00). Even among those who belong to segregated organizations, there is evidence of asymmetry. The percentage of women claiming membership in female-dominated groups is significantly higher than the percentage of men who are members of male-dominated groups (66.9 percent and 53.8 percent, respectively, $Z = 4.85$, $p = .00$). These results not only confirm the existence of gender segregation in voluntary associations but also imply that the voluntary association experience is an isolating one for most women involved. Of course, these differences may be due to the influences of other traits confounded with gender.

Panel B of Table 23.2 displays the results of a logistic regression model for belonging to a gender-integrated voluntary association. The independent variables include demographic characteristics of the member as well as one variable unique to the intersection of individual and group: membership duration. The results indicate that, even controlling for many other factors, women are significantly less likely than men to belong to integrated voluntary associations. In addition, members who are older and more stable (longer duration of membership) are less likely to belong to integrated than to segregated organizations. Integrated groups are likely to incorporate members from the residual employment category (unemployed, in school, other) and unlikely to have members who keep house or who were never married.

An even more detailed picture of the different traits associated with membership in male- and female-dominated groups appears in Table 23.4, where I present the results of a multinomial logistic regression model predicting the gender type of the group to which a member belongs. Not surprisingly, women rarely belong to male-dominated groups and are less likely to belong to integrated groups than to female-dominated ones. More interesting are the effects of other demographic traits.

Reading across the rows of Table 23.4, one can see that older members are significantly

Table 23.2
Logistic Regressions of Membership in Voluntary Associations

Independent Variable	A Membership in One or More Voluntary Associations		B Membership in an Integrated Voluntary Association	
	Parameter Estimate	$\chi 2$ (1 df)	Parameter Estimate	$\chi 2$ (1 df)
Female	0.1430	0.62	−0.3214**	5.41
Nonwhite	−1.1788**	5.44	0.4281	0.48
Age	0.0203***	8.08	−0.0122**	4.09
Years of education	0.1944***	23.04	0.0350	2.18
Catholic	−0.0318	0.03	−0.1976	1.84
No religious preference	−0.6226**	5.22	0.3099	0.79
Never married	0.0915	0.13	−0.5501**	4.85
Divorced/separated	−0.0232	0.01	−0.0923	0.13
Widowed	−0.1572	0.28	0.0039	0.00
Part-time	0.1533	0.28	−0.3898	3.20
Retired	0.0732	0.05	−0.2990	1.77
Housekeeping	0.2269	0.65	−0.6612***	10.18
Unemployed/in school/other	−0.4881	2.39	0.8450**	5.76
Network size	0.1464**	6.61	0.0303	0.60
Membership duration	—	—	−0.0020***	17.53
Intercept	−2.4124***	11.94	0.5637	1.20
Model χ^2	66.022 with 14 df ($p = .00$)		140.29 with 15 df ($p = .00$)	

NOTE: Omitted categories are religion (Protestant), marital status (married), and employment (full-time).

** $p < .05$.   *** $p < .01$.

more likely to belong to male-dominated groups than to female-dominated groups or integrated ones. Never-married members are more likely to appear in male-dominated organizations than integrated ones in part because many integrated groups are clearly organized around married couples. Members who work part-time, are retired, or keep house are significantly more likely to be found in female-dominated groups than in either male-dominated or integrated ones. Members in the residual category of employment status (unemployed, in school, or other) are more likely to belong to integrated associations than to male-domi-

nated ones. Last, longer memberships are more common in female-dominated organizations than in integrated ones.

These results aggregate across many specific organizations. As such, they reveal the traits of the average group member, but they make it impossible to fully interpret some of the effects. For instance, there appears to be no association between level of education and belonging to a segregated organization. However, we do not yet know whether each segregated organization incorporates a mix of members with high and low education or whether there are some gender-segregated

Table 23.3
Cross-Tabulation of Membership in a Female-Dominated, Male-Dominated, or Integrated Voluntary Association by Gender (column percentages in parentheses)

	Male	Female	Total
Membership in a female-dominated organization	11 (2.1)	599 (66.9)	610 (42.9)
Membership in a gender-integrated organization	232 (44.1)	272 (30.4)	504 (35.5)
Membership in a male-dominated organization	283 (53.8)	24 (2.7)	307 (21.6)
Total	526	895	1,421

Table 23.4
Multinomial Logistic Regression of Membership in Female-Dominated, Male-Dominated, and Integrated Voluntary Associations

Independent Variable	Male-Dominated vs. Female-Dominated		Integrated vs. Female-Dominated		Male-Dominated vs. Integrated	
	Parameter Estimate	χ^2 (1 df)	Parameter Estimate	χ^2 (1 df)	Parameter Estimate	χ^2 (1 df)
Female	−3.1221***	240.59	−1.8243***	118.25	−1.2978***	92.21
Age	0.0244**	4.82	−0.0046	0.39	0.0290***	9.62
Years of education	−0.0456	1.15	0.0140	0.17	−0.0596	3.79
Catholic	−0.1246	0.91	−0.1761	3.32	0.0515	0.26
No religious preference	0.1663	0.25	0.2459	0.80	−0.0796	0.14
Never married	0.2264	1.07	−0.1770	1.14	.04034**	5.62
Divorced/separated	0.4259	3.68	0.1569	0.76	0.2690	2.87
Widowed	−0.2330	1.31	−0.0190	0.03	−0.2140	1.24
Part-time	−0.3638	2.73	−0.2939**	5.93	−0.0699	0.12
Retired	−0.6071***	9.79	−0.3926***	7.86	−0.2145	1.82
Housekeeping	−0.6889***	5.35	−0.4270***	14.79	−0.2619	0.77
Unemployed/in school/other	−0.3795	1.29	0.1981	0.65	−0.5776**	5.67
Membership duration	−0.0016	3.77	−0.0027***	20.75	0.0011	2.44
Network size	0.0190	0.07	0.0323	0.41	−0.0133	0.06
Intercept	−1.4190	1.74	1.0785	1.81	−2.4975***	9.63

NOTE: Omitted categories are religion (Protestant), marital status (married), and employment (full-time).

**$p < .05$. ***$p < .01$.

groups that cater exclusively to people with high education and others that specialize in members with low education. Making such a distinction necessitates analyzing the distributions of members' demographic traits within groups, as is done in the next section.

What Traits Characterize Gender-Segregated Voluntary Associations?

This section examines the organizational characteristics that best describe segregated and integrated voluntary associations, using the organizational-level data set. Table 23.5 presents ample evidence that voluntary organizations are heavily segregated by gender. Of the 233 groups in the sample, 152 (67.9 percent) are gender segregated. The majority of these segregated groups (44.2 percent of the total) are female dominated. The last column of the table demonstrates that the gender distributions within the different types of organizations are extremely skewed. The mean percentage of women in female-dominated groups is 99.5 percent. Similarly, the mean percentage of women in male-dominated organizations is less than 1 percent. We may safely conclude that not only are the majority of voluntary organizations gender segregated, but they are almost completely gender exclusive.

The next problem involves discovering the traits that distinguish segregated and integrated organizations from one another, aside from their gender distributions. Most important, I am concerned with whether there is an association between the gender distribution in a group and the distributions on age and education. I concentrate on these variables because they each exhibit consistent relationships with voluntary association membership. The question is whether gender-segregated groups specialize in members having particular levels and ranges of age and education. In other words, are gender-segregated groups themselves segregated by either age or education? There are two elements to this problem: the average age (education) of a group's members and the spread of members' ages (education) within the group.

Results of this investigation appear in Table 23.6, in which I used multinomial logistic regression to model organizational gender type. Contrary to results in previous research, male-dominated organizations are smaller than other types of organizations, and the size of the town in which a group meets has no significant impact on its gender composition. Long memberships are equally common in both types of segregated associations. Segregated and integrated groups do not differ in mean age, but both male- and female-dominated groups have significantly lower mean education than do integrated organizations.

The parameter estimates for the standard deviations of members' ages and education measure the relationship between the variability of members' characteristics and group gender composition. Both variables are significantly related to group gender composition. The variability in members' ages is significantly higher in male-dominated and integrated groups than in female-dominated ones. Evidently, the range of members' ages is severely restricted within women's groups. Similarly, the standard deviation of members' education is significantly higher in integrated organizations than in either type of segregated organization. In other words, individual segregated associations bring together members who vary very little in education. Armed with these results, and those of the previous two sections, we can now draw a comprehensive picture of gender segregation in voluntary associations.

Table 23.5
Frequency of Organizational Gender Type (233 voluntary associations)

Organizational Gender Type	Raw Frequency	Weighted Percentage	Weighted Mean Percentage of Women Members
Gender-integrated	81	32.0	56.4
Gender-segregated	152	67.9	—
Female-dominated	104	44.2	99.5
Male-dominated	48	23.7	0.5

NOTE: Organizations are weighted by the inverse of their number of members. . . .

Table 23.6
Multinomial Logistic Regression of Voluntary Association Gender Type

Independent Variable	Male-Dominated vs. Female-Dominated		Integrated vs. Female-Dominated		Male-Dominated vs. Integrated	
	Parameter Estimate	χ^2 (1 df)	Parameter Estimate	χ^2 (1 df)	Parameter Estimate	χ^2 (1 df)
Log (number of members)	−0.6052**	5.73	0.1617	0.39	−0.7669**	6.58
Town size ÷ 10,000	−0.0114	0.36	0.0013	0.01	−0.0101	0.23
Mean duration of membership	−0.0071	0.08	−0.1492***	18.75	0.1422***	15.01
Mean age	−0.0306	2.52	−0.0178	0.99	−0.0128	0.34
Mean education	−0.0960	0.46	0.3469**	6.14	−0.4429***	7.51
Standard deviation of age	0.0921***	6.83	0.0788*	3.70	0.0133	0.11
Standard deviation of education	0.1525	0.46	0.6397***	6.87	−0.4872*	3.37
Intercept	2.4050	1.11	−5.2452**	5.05	7.6502***	8.26

NOTE: Organizations are weighted by the inverse of their number of members. . . .

*p < .10. **p < .05. ***p < .01.

Synthesis: The Main Characteristics of Gender Segregation in Voluntary Associations

Overall, the majority of the voluntary association experience is one of demographic homogeneity. Most memberships are in gender-segregated organizations, and most organizations have only male or female members. Furthermore, the evidence amassed here indicates that segregated and integrated voluntary associations differ by more than just gender composition.

Both male- and female-dominated voluntary groups exhibit low average education and low range in education, indicating that gender segregation coincides with educational segregation in the voluntary world. In segregated voluntary associations, membership turnover is very low, making the half-life of such organizations extraordinarily long (cf. McPherson, Popielarz, and Drobnič 1992, 166). Even after controlling for these patterns, women are less likely to belong to integrated associations than are men.

Women's voluntary organizations outnumber men's groups by approximately two to one and are larger than men's groups. These groups tend to include women from traditionally disadvantaged employment statuses: part-time work, retirement, and keeping house. Most important, women's groups are highly restricted in the range of members' ages. This segregation by age, coupled with the link between gender segrega-tion and educational segregation, exposes involvement in women's voluntary associations as an extremely narrow experience.

In sum, work and marital status appear closely linked to organizational gender type. Age and education are related to voluntary group affiliation in general, but more important, they are bases on which members become sorted across different gender-segregated organizations. Women not only belong to groups with other women but are further confined to groups of women with the same age and education level as their own. Highly educated women belong to organizations with men or with other educated women. Women (and men) with very low education tend not to affiliate at all. Women with intermediate levels of education belong to groups that are finely sorted by age and employment status.

Overall, the multilevel analysis in this article offers a unique description of segregation. With organizational-level data, it is possible to see more precisely the links between segregation by gender, age, and education in voluntary associations. Many questions remain, including how it is that segregation comes about and is perpetuated (Popielarz 1992; Popielarz and McPherson 1995). Nonetheless, the results of this analysis have clear implications for individuals, organizations, and society at large. . . .

Conclusion

The prospects for voluntary association integration are not entirely clear. The differential speed of membership turnover in segregated and integrated organizations favors segregation. Indeed, integration may only be a fleeting state in some voluntary groups, not only because turnover is relatively high but because the specific pattern of turnover increases group homogeneity (Popielarz 1992; Popielarz and McPherson 1995). In addition, low turnover in segregated groups makes them very slow to change. As women enter the labor force in increasing numbers, the well-documented work-family time crunch may make them less likely to join voluntary associations (Hochschild 1989). However, they may be more likely to join professional groups, which tend to be integrated by gender. As a result, we may see either disparate organizational experiences put increasing distance between women in and out of the labor force or increasing gender segregation in professional organizations.

This article provides new details regarding not only the existence of gender segregation but also the asymmetry in the disadvantage resulting from it. Women's groups offer very limited contact with persons of different ages, education, and marital and work statuses. When women only come into contact with similar women in organizational settings, all of the resources that flow across these connections remain segregated as well. This is undesirable in and of itself, but it is even more worrisome given that it contributes to the "pervasive ordering of human activities, practices, and social structures in terms of differentiations between women and men" (Acker 1992, 567). Thus, gender segregation in voluntary associations not only reflects but also helps to maintain a system of gendered institutions. The pervasiveness of organizations as the institutional arbiters of success in so many spheres of life (Coleman 1982) makes organizational gender segregation an especially vexing problem.

Notes

1. I mean the word *dominated* in the numerical sense only; neither formal nor de facto governance of the group is a concern here.

2. These types included church related, professional, veterans/patriotic, recreational, social, youth fraternal/service, union, farm, civic, and other.

References

Acker, Joan. 1992. Gendered Institutions: From sex roles to gendered institutions. *Contemporary Sociology* 21:565–69.

———. 1995. Feminist goals and organizing processes. In *Feminist organizations: Harvest of the new women's movement*, edited by M. M. Ferree and P. Y. Martin. Philadelphia: Temple University Press.

Aldrich, Howard E. 1989. Networking among women entrepreneurs. In *Women-owned businesses*, edited by O. Hagan, C. Rivchun, and D. Sexton. New York: Praeger.

Booth, Alan. 1972. Sex and social participation. *American Sociological Review* 37:183–92.

Campbell, Karen E. 1988. Gender differences in job-related networks. *Work and Occupations* 15:179–200.

Coleman, James S. 1982. *The asymmetric society*. Syracuse, NY: Syuracuse University Press.

Davis, James A., and Thomas W. Smith. 1988. *General social surveys, 1972–88*. Chicago: National Opinion Research Center.

Gustafsom, Kathleen, Alan Booth, and David Johnson. 1979. The effects of labor force participation on gender differences in voluntary association affiliation: A cross-national study. *Journal of Voluntary Action Research* 8:51–56.

Hochschild, Arlie Russell. 1989. *The second shift*. New York: Avon.

Jacobs, Jerry A. 1989. *Revolving doors: Sex segregation and women's careers*. Stanford, CA: Stanford University Press.

Knoke, David, and Randall Thomson. 1977. Voluntary association membership trends and the family life cycle. *Social Forces* 56:48–65.

Liao, Tim Futing. 1994. *Interpreting probability models: Logit, probit and other generalized linear models*. Sage University Paper Series on Quantitative Applications in the Social Sciences, 97–101. Thousand Oaks, CA: Sage.

McPherson, J. Miller. 1982. Hypernetwork sampling: Duality and differentiation among voluntary organizations. *Social Networks* 3:225–49.

McPherson, J. Miller, Pamela A. Popielarz, and Sonja Drobnič. 1992. Social networks and organizational dynamics. *American Sociological Review* 57:153–70.

McPherson, J. Miller, and Thomas Rotolo. 1996. Testing a dynamic model of social composition: Diversity and change in voluntary groups. *American Sociological Review* 61:179–202.

McPherson, J. Miller, and Lynn Smith-Lovin. 1982. Women and weak ties: Differences by sex in the size of voluntary organizations. *American Journal of Sociology* 87:883–904.

———. 1986. Sex Segregation in voluntary associations. *American Sociological Review* 51:61–79.

Petersen, Trond, and Laurie A. Morgan. 1995. Separate and unequal: Occupation-establishment sex segregation and the gender wage gap. *American Journal of Sociology* 101:329–65.

Popielarz, Pamela A. 1992. Connection and competition: A structural theory of sex segregation in voluntary associations. Ph.D. diss., Cornell University, Ithaca, NY.

———. 1994. Do weaker bridges span longer distances? Paper presented at the International Social Networks Conference, New Orleans, Louisiana.

Popielarz, Pamela A., and J. Miller McPherson. 1995. On the edge or in between: Niche position, niche overlap and the duration of voluntary association memberships. *American Journal of Sociology* 101:628–720.

Reskin, Barbara. 1984. *Sex segregation in the workplace: Trends, explanations, remedies*. Washington, DC: National Academy Press.

SAS Institute. 1989. *SAS/STAT User's guide, version 6*. 4th ed. Cary, NC: SAS Institute.

Smith, Constance, and Anne Freedman. 1972. *Voluntary associations: Perspectives on the literature*. Cambridge, MA: Harvard University Press.

Smith-Lovin, Lynn, and J. Miller McPherson. 1993. You are who you know: A network approach to gender. In *Theory on gender/feminism on theory*, edited by P. England. New York: Aldine de Gruyter.

Pamela A. Popielarz, "(In)Voluntary Association: A Multilevel Analysis of Gender Segregation in Voluntary Organizations." In *Gender & Society* 12:234–250. Copyright © 1999. Reprinted with permission. ✦

Part III

Organizations and Environments

The Creation of

Organizational Forms

Chapter 24
The Iron Cage Revisited

Institutional Isomorphism and Collective Rationality in Organizational Fields

Paul J. DiMaggio and
Walter W. Powell

What factors determine the structure and form of an organization? DiMaggio and Powell argue against those who claim that efficiency concerns are the driving force here. Instead, they call attention to the process of isomorphism—a set of pressures in the organizational field that push organizations toward homogeneity in their basic forms and structures. Unlike many other researchers motivated to explain variation in organizations or organizational processes, DiMaggio and Powell are interested in the factors that push organizations to be more alike. These factors reside for the most part in the broader organizational field; that is, they are largely external to the organization.

Organizations can become like one another through several different processes. DiMaggio and Powell introduce three of those processes here, and attempt to identify some conditions under which isomorphic change is likely to occur. Most important, however, is their call for researchers to pay more attention to the role of external forces in shaping organizational structures and the pressures for similarity that those external factors induce.

In *The Protestant Ethic and the Spirit of Capitalism,* Max Weber warned that the rationalist spirit ushered in by asceticism had achieved a momentum of its own and that, under capitalism, the rationalist order had become an iron cage in which humanity was, save for the possibility of prophetic revival, imprisoned "perhaps until the last ton of fossilized coal is burnt" (Weber, 1952:181–82). In his essay on bureaucracy, Weber returned to this theme, contending that bureaucracy, the rational spirit's organizational manifestation, was so efficient and powerful a means of controlling men and women that, once established, the momentum of bureaucratization was irreversible (Weber, 1968).

The imagery of the iron cage has haunted students of society as the tempo of bureaucratization has quickened. But while bureaucracy has spread continuously in the eighty years since Weber wrote, we suggest that the engine of organizational rationalization has shifted. For Weber, bureaucratization resulted from three related causes: competition among capitalism firms in the marketplace; competition among states, increasing rulers' need to control their staff and citizenry; and bourgeois demands for equal protection under the law. Of these three, the most important was the competitive marketplace. "Today," Weber (1968:974) wrote:

> it is primarily the capitalist market economy which demands that the official business of administration be discharged precisely, unambiguously, continuously, and with as much speed as possible. Normally, the very large, modern capitalist enterprises are themselves unequalled models of strict bureaucratic organization.

We argue that the causes of bureaucratization and rationalization have changed. The bureaucratization of the corporation and the state have been achieved. Organizations are still becoming more homogeneous, and bureaucracy remains the common organizational form. Today, however, structural change in organizations seems less and less driven by competition or by the need for efficiency. Instead, we will contend, bureaucratization and other forms of organizational change occur as the result of processes that make organizations more similar without necessarily making them more efficient. Bureaucratization and other forms of homogenization emerge, we argue, out of the structuration (Giddens, 1979) of organizational fields. This process, in turn, is effected largely by the state and the professions, which have become the great rationalizers of the second half of the twentieth century. For reasons that we will explain, highly structured organizational fields provide a context in which individual efforts to deal rationally with uncertainty and constraint often lead in the aggregate, to homogeneity in structure, culture, and output.

Organizational Theory and Organizational Diversity

Much of modern organizational theory posits a diverse and differentiated world of organizations and seeks to explain variation among organizations in structure and behavior (e.g., Woodward, 1965; Child and Kieser, 1981). Hannan and Freeman begin a major theoretical paper (1977) with the question, "Why are there so many kinds of organizations?" Even our investigatory technologies (for example, those based on least-squares techniques) are geared towards explaining variation rather than its absence.

We ask, instead, why there is such startling homogeneity of organizational forms and practices; and we seek to explain homogeneity, not variation. In the initial stages of their life cycle, organizational fields display considerable diversity in approach and form. Once a field becomes well established, however, there is an inexorable push towards homogenization.

Coser, Kadushin, and Powell (1982) describe the evolution of American college textbook publishing from a period of initial diversity to the current hegemony of only two models, the large bureaucratic generalist and the small specialist. Rothman (1980) describes the winnowing of several competing models of legal education into two dominant approaches. Starr (1980) provides evidence, of mimicry in the development of the hospital field; Tyack (1974) and Katz (1975) show a similar process in public schools; Barnouw (1966–68) describes the development of dominant forms in the radio industry; and DiMaggio (1981) depicts the emergence of dominant organizational models for the provision of high culture in the late nineteenth century.

What we see in each of these cases is the emergence and structuration of an organizational field as a result of the activities of a diverse set of organizations; and, second, the homogenization of these organizations, and of new entrants as well, once the field is established.

By organizational field, we mean those organizations that, in the aggregate, constitute a recognized area of institutional life: key suppliers, resource and product consumers, regulatory agencies, and other organizations that produce similar services or products. The virtue of this unit of analysis is that it directs our attention not simply to competing firms, as does the population approach of Hannan and Freeman (1977), or to networks of organizations that actually interact, as does the heterorganizational network approach of Laumann et al. (1978), but to the totality of relevant actors. In doing this, the field idea comprehends the importance of both *connectedness* (see Laumann et al., 1978) and *structural equivalence* (White et al., 1976).[1]

The structure of an organizational field cannot be determined a priori but must be defined on the basis of empirical investigation. Fields only exist to the extent that they are institutionally defined. The process of institutional definition, or "structuration," consists of four parts: an increase in the extent of interaction among organizations in the field; the emergence of sharply defined interorganizational structures of domination and patterns of coalition; an increase in the information load with which organizations in a field must contend; and the development of a mutual awareness among participants in a set of organizations that they are involved in a common enterprise (DiMaggio, 1982).

Once disparate organizations in the same line of business are structured into an actual field (as we shall argue, by competition, the state, or the professions), powerful forces emerge that lead them to become more similar to one another. Organizations may change their goals or develop new practices, and new organizations enter the field. But, in the long run, organizational actors making rational decisions construct around themselves an environment that constrains their ability to change further in later years. Early adopters of organizational innovations are commonly driven by a desire to improve performance. But new practices can become, in Selznick's words (1957: 17), "infused with value beyond the technical requirements of the task at hand." As an innovation spreads, a threshold is reached beyond which adoption provides legitimacy rather than improves performance (Meyer and Rowan, 1977). Strategies that are rational for individual organizations may not be rational if adopted by large numbers. Yet the very fact that they are normatively sanctioned increases the likelihood of their adoption. Thus organizations may try to change constantly; but, after a certain point in the structuration of an organizational field, the aggregate effect of individual change is to lessen the extent of diversity within the field.[2] Organizations in a structured field, to paraphrase Schelling (1978: 14), respond to an environment that consists of other organizations responding to their environment which consists of organizations responding to an environment of organizations' responses.

Zucker and Tolbert's (1981) work on the adoption of civil-service reform in the United States illustrates this process. Early adoption of civil-service reforms was related to internal governmental needs, and strongly predicted by such city characteristics as the size of immigrant population, political reform movements, socioeconomic composition, and city size. Later adoption, however, is not predicted by city characteristics, but is related to institutional definitions of the legitimate structural form for municipal administration. Marshall Meyer's (1981) study of the bureaucratization of urban fiscal agencies has yielded similar findings: strong relationships between city characteristics and organizational attributes at the turn of the century, null relationships in recent years. Carroll and Delacroix's (1982) findings on the birth and death rates of newspapers support the view that selection acts with great force only in the early years of an industry's existence. Freeman (1982:14) suggests that older, larger organizations reach a point where they can dominate their environments rather than adjust to them.

The concept that best captures the process of homogenization is *isomorphism*. In Hawley's (1968) description, isomorphism is a constraining process that forces one unit in a population to resemble other units that face the same set of environmental conditions. At the population level, such an approach suggests that organizational characteristics are modified in the direction of increasing compatability with environmental characteristics; the number of organizations in a population is a function of environmental carrying capacity; and the diversity of organizational forms is isomorphic to environmental diversity. Hannan and Freeman (1977) have significantly extended Hawley's ideas. They argue that isomorphism can result because nonoptimal forms are selected out of a population of organizations *or* because organizational decision makers learn appropriate responses and adjust their behavior accordingly. Hannan and Freeman's focus is almost solely on the first process: selection.

Following Meyer (1979) and Fennell (1980), we maintain that there are two types of isomorphism: competitive and institutional. Hannan and Freeman's classic paper (1977), and much of their recent work, deals with competitive isomorphism, assuming a system rationality that emphasizes market competition, niche change, and fitness measures. Such a view, we suggest, is most relevant for those fields in which free and open competition exists. It explains parts of the process of bureaucratization that Weber observed, and may apply to early adoption of innovation, but it does not present a fully adequate picture of the modern world of organizations. For this purpose it must be supplemented by an institutional view of isomorphism of the sort introduced by Kanter (1972:152–54) in her discussion of the forces pressing communes toward accommodation with the outside world. As Aldrich (1979:265) has argued, "the major factors that organizations must take into account are other organizations." Organizations compete not just for resources and customers, but for political power and institutional legitimacy, for social as well as economic fitness. The concept of institutional isomorphism is a useful tool for understanding the politics and ceremony that pervade much modern organizational life.

Three Mechanisms of Institutional Isomorphic Change

We identify three mechanisms through which institutional isomorphic change - occurs, each with its own antecedents: 1) *coercive* isomorphism that stems from political influence and the problem of legitimacy; 2) *mimetic* isomorphism resulting from standard responses to uncertainty; and 3) *normative* isomorphism, associated with professionalization. This typology is an analytic one: the types are not always empirically distinct. For example, external actors may induce an organization to conform to its peers by requiring it to perform a particular task and specifying the profession responsible for its performance. Or mimetic change may reflect environmentally constructed uncertainties. Yet, while the three types intermingle in empirical setting, they tend to derive from different conditions and may lead to different outcomes.

Coercive isomorphism. Coercive isomorphism results from both formal and informal pressures exerted on organizations by other organizations upon which they are dependent and by cultural expectations in the society within which organizations function. Such pressures may be felt as force, as persuasion, or as invitations to join in collusion. In some circumstances, organizational change is a direct response to government mandate: manufacturers adopt new pollution control technologies to conform to environmental regulations; nonprofits maintain accounts, and hire accountants, in order to meet tax law requirements; and organizations employ affirmative-action officers to fend off allegations of discrimination. Schools mainstream special students and hire special education teachers, cultivate PTAs and administrators who get along with them, and promulgate curricula that conform with state standards (Meyer et al., 1981). The fact that these changes may be largely ceremonial does not mean that they are inconsequential. As Ritti and Goldner (1979) have argued, staff become involved in advocacy for their functions that can alter power relations within organizations over the long run.

The existence of a common legal environment affects many aspects of an organization's behavior and structure. Weber pointed out the profound impact of a complex, rationalized system of contract law that requires the necessary organizational controls to honor legal commitments. Other legal and technical requirements of the state—the vicissitudes of the budget cycle, the ubiquity of certain fiscal years, annual reports, and financial reporting requirements that ensure eligibility for the receipt of federal contracts or funds—also shape organizations in similar ways. Pfeffer and Salancik (1978:188–224) have discussed how organizations faced with unmanageable interdependence seek to use the greater power of the larger social system and its government to eliminate difficulties-or provide for needs . They observe that politically constructed environments have two characteristic features: political decisionmakers often do not experience directly the consequences of their actions; and political decisions are applied across the board to entire classes of organizations, thus making such decisions less adaptive and less flexible.

Meyer and Rowan (1977) have argued persuasively that as rationalized states and other large rational organizations expand their dominance over more arenas of social life, organizational structures increasingly come to reflect rules institutionalized and legitimated by and within the state (also see Meyer and Hannan, 1979). As a result, organizations are increasingly homogeneous within given domains and increasingly organized around rituals of conformity to wider institutions. At the same time, organizations are decreasingly structurally determined by the constraints posed by technical activities, and decreasingly held together by output controls. Under such circumstances, organizations employ ritualized controls of credentials and group solidarity.

Direct imposition of standard operating procedures and legitimated rules and structures also occurs outside the governmental arena. Michael Sedlak (1981) has documented the ways that United Charities in the 1930s altered and homogenized the structures, methods, and philosophies of the social service agencies that depended upon them for support. As conglomerate corporations increase in size and scope, standard performance criteria are not necessarily imposed on subsidiaries, but it is common for subsidiaries to be subject to standardized reporting mechanisms (Coser et al., 1982). Subsidiaries must adopt accounting practices, performance evaluations, and budgetary plans that are compatible with the policies of the parent corporation. A variety of service infrastructures, often provided by monopolistic firms—for example, telecommunications and transportation—exert common pressures over the organizations that use them. Thus, the expansion of the central state, the centralization of capital, and the coordination of philanthropy all support the homogenization of organizational models through direct authority relationships.

We have so far referred only to the direct and explicit imposition of organizational models on dependent organizations. Coercive isomorphism, however, may be more subtle and less explicit than these examples suggest. Milofsky (1981) has described the ways in which neighborhood organizations in urban communities, many of which are committed to participatory democracy, are driven to developing organizational hierarchies in order to gain support from more hierarchically organized donor organizations. Similarly, Swidler (1979) describes the tensions created in the free schools she studied by the need to have a "principal" to negotiate with the district superintendent and to represent the school to outside agencies. In general, the need to lodge responsibility and managerial authority at least ceremonially in a formally defined role in order to interact with hierarchical organizations is a constant obstacle to the maintenance of egalitarian or collectivist organizational forms (Kanter, 1972; Rothschild-Whitt, 1979).

Mimetic processes. Not all institutional isomorphism, however, derives from coercive authority. Uncertainty is also a powerful force that encourages imitation. When organizational technologies are poorly understood (March and Olsen, 1976), when goals are ambiguous, or when the environment creates symbolic uncertainty, organizations may model themselves on other organizations. The advantages of mimetic behavior in the economy of human action are considerable; when an organization faces a problem with ambiguous causes or unclear solutions, problemistic search may yield a viable solution with little expense (Cyert and March, 1963).

Modeling, as we use the term, is a response to uncertainty. The modeled organization may be unaware of the modeling or may have no desire to be copied; it merely serves as a convenient source of practices that the borrowing organization may use. Models may be diffused unintentionally, indirectly through employee transfer or turnover, or explicitly by organizations such as consulting firms or industry trade associations. Even innovation can be accounted for by organizational modeling. As Alchian (1950) has observed:

> While there certainly are those who consciously innovate, there are those who, in their imperfect attempts to imitate others, unconsciously innovate by unwittingly acquiring some unexpected or unsought unique attributes which under the prevailing circumstances prove partly responsible for the success. Others, in turn, will attempt to copy the uniqueness, and the innovation-imitation process continues.

One of the most dramatic instances of modeling was the effort of Japan's modernizers in the late nineteenth century to model new governmental initiatives on apparently successful western prototypes. Thus, the imperial government sent its officers to study the courts, Army, and police in France, the Navy and postal system in Great Britain, and banking and art education in the United States (see Westney, forthcoming). American corporations are now returning the compliment by implementing (their perceptions of) Japanese models to cope with thorny productivity and personnel problems in their own firms. The rapid proliferation of quality circles and quality-of-work-life issues in American firms is, at least in part, an attempt to model Japanese and European successes. These developments also have a ritual aspect; companies adopt these "innovations" to enhance their legitimacy, to demonstrate they are at least trying to improve working conditions. More generally, the wider the population of personnel employed by, or customers served by, an organization, the stronger the pressure felt by the organization to provide the programs and services offered by other organizations. Thus, either a skilled labor force or a broad customer base may encourage mimetic isomorphism.

Much homogeneity in organizational structures stems from the fact that despite considerable search for diversity there is relatively little variation to be selected from. New organizations are modeled upon old ones throughout the economy, and managers actively seek models upon which to build (Kimberly, 1980). Thus, in the arts one can find textbooks on how to organize a community arts council or how to start a symphony women's guild. Large organizations choose from a relatively small set of major consulting firms, which, like Johnny Appleseeds, spread a few organizational models throughout the land. Such models are powerful because structural changes are observable, whereas changes in policy and strategy are less easily noticed. With the advice of a major consulting firm, a large metropolitan public television station switched from a functional design to a multidivisional structure. The stations' executives were skeptical that the new structure was more efficient; in fact, some services were now duplicated across divisions. But they were convinced that the new design would carry a powerful message to the for-profit firms with whom the station regularly dealt. These firms, whether in the role of corporate underwriters or as potential partners in joint ventures, would view the reorganization as a sign that "the sleepy nonprofit station was becoming more business-minded" (Powell, forthcoming). The history of management reform in American government agencies, which are noted for their goal ambiguity, is almost a textbook case of isomorphic modeling, from the PPPB of the McNamara era to the zero-based budgeting of the Carter administration.

Organizations tend to model themselves after similar organizations in their field that they perceive to be more legitimate or successful. The ubiquity of certain kinds of structural arrangements can more likely be credited to the universality of mimetic processes than to any concrete evidence that the adopted models enhance efficiency. John Meyer (1981) contends that it is easy to predict the organization of a newly emerging nation's administration without knowing anything about the nation itself, since "peripheral nations are far more isomorphic—in administrative form and economic pattern—than any theory of the world system of economic division of labor would lead one to expect."

Normative pressures. A third source of isomorphic organizational change is normative and stems primarily from professionalization. Following Larson (1977) and Collins (1979), we interpret professionalization as the collective struggle of members of an occupation to define the conditions and methods of their work, to control "the production of producers" (Larson, 1977:49–52), and to establish a cognitive base and legitimation for their occupational autonomy. As Larson points out, the professional project is rarely achieved with complete success. Professionals must compromise with nonprofessional clients, bosses, or regulators. The major recent growth in the professions has been among organizational professionals, particularly managers and specialized staff of large organizations. The increased professionalization of workers whose futures are inextricably bound up with the fortunes of the organizations that employ them has rendered obsolescent (if not obsolete) the dichotomy between organizational commitment and professional allegiance that characterized traditional professionals in earlier organizations (Hall,

1968). Professions are subject to the same coercive and mimetic pressures as are organizations. Moreover, while various kinds of professionals within an organization may differ from one another, they exhibit much similarity to their professional counterparts in other organizations. In addition, in many cases, professional power is as much assigned by the state as it is created by the activities of the professions.

Two aspects of professionalization are important sources of isomorphism. One is the resting of formal education and of legitimation in a cognitive base produced by university specialists; the second is the growth and elaboration of professional networks that span organizations and across which new models diffuse rapidly. Universities and professional training institutions are important centers for the development of organizational norms among professional managers and their staff. Professional and trace associations are another vehicle for the definition and promulgation of normative rules about organizational and professional behavior. Such mechanisms create a pool of almost interchangeable individuals who occupy similar positions across a range of organizations and possess a similarity of orientation and disposition that may override variations in tradition and control that might otherwise shape organizational behavior (Perrow, 1974).

One important mechanism for encouraging normative isomorphism is the filtering of personnel. Within many organizational fields filtering occurs through the hiring of individuals from firms within the same industry; through the recruitment of fast-track staff from a narrow range of training institutions; through common promotion practices, such as always hiring top executives from financial or legal departments; and from skill-level requirements for particular jobs. Many professional career tracks are so closely guarded, both at the entry level and throughout the career progression, that individuals who make it to the top are virtually indistinguishable. March and March (1977) found that individuals who attained the position of school superintendent in Wisconsin were so alike in background and orientation as to make further career advancement random and unpredictable. Hirsch and Whisler (1982) find a similar absence of variation among *Fortune* 500 board members. In addition, individuals in an organizational field undergo anticipatory socialization to common expectations about their personal behavior, appropriate style of dress, organizational vocabularies (Cicourel, 1970; Williamson, 1975) and standard methods of speaking, joking, or addressing others (Ouchi, 1980). Particularly in industries with a service or financial orientation (Collins, 1979, argues that the importance of credentials is strongest in these areas), the filtering of personnel approaches what Kanter (1977) refers to as the "homosexual reproduction of management." To the extent managers and key staff are drawn from the same universities and filtered on a common set of attributes, they will tend to view problems in a similar fashion, see the same policies, procedures and structures as normatively sanctioned and legitimated, and approach decisions in much the same way.

Entrants to professional career tracks who somehow escape the filtering process—for example, Jewish naval officers, woman stockbrokers, or Black insurance executives—are likely to be subjected to pervasive on-the-job socialization. To the extent that organizations in a field differ and primary socialization occurs on the job, socialization could reinforce, not erode, differences among organizations. But when organizations in a field are similar and occupational socialization is carried out in trade association workshops, in-service educational programs, consultant arrangements, employer-professional school networks, and in the pages of trade magazines, socialization acts as an isomorphic force.

The professionalization of management tends to proceed in tandem with the structuration of organizational fields. The exchange of information among professionals helps contribute to a commonly recognized hierarchy of status, of center and periphery, that becomes a matrix for information flows and personnel movement across organizations. This status ordering occurs through both formal and informal means. The designation of a few large firms in an industry as key bargaining agents in union-management negotiations may make these central firms pivotal in other respects as well. Government recognition of key firms or organizations through the grant or contract process may give these organizations legitimacy and visibility and lead competing firms to copy aspects of their structure or operating procedures in hope of obtaining similar rewards. Professional and trade associations provide other arenas in which center organizations are recognized and their personnel given positions of substantive or ceremonial influence. Managers in highly visible organizations may in turn have their stature reinforced by representation on the boards of other organizations, participation in industry-wide or inter-industry councils, and consultation by agencies of government (Useem, 1979). In the nonprofit sector, where legal barriers to collusion do not exist, structuration may proceed even more rapidly. Thus executive producers or artistic directors of leading theatres head trade or professional association committees, sit on government and foundation grant-award panels, or consult as government- or foundation-financed management advisors to smaller theatres, or sit on smaller organizations' boards, even as their stature is reinforced and enlarged by the grants their theatres receive from government, corporate, and foundation funding sources (DiMaggio, 1982).

Such central organizations serve as both active and passive models; their policies and structures will be copied throughout their fields. Their centrality is reinforced as upwardly mobile managers and staff seek to secure positions in these central organizations in order to further their own careers. Aspiring managers may undergo anticipatory socialization into the norms and mores of the organizations they hope to join. Career paths may also involve movement from entry positions in the center organizations to middle-management positions in peripheral organizations. Personnel flows within an organizational field are further encouraged by structural homogenization, for example the existence of common career titles and paths (such as assistant, associate, and full professor) with meanings that are commonly understood.

It is important to note that each of the institutional isomorphic processes can be expected to proceed in the absence of evidence that they increase internal organizational efficiency. To the extent that organizational effectiveness is enhanced, the reason will often be that organizations are rewarded for being similar to other organizations in their fields. This similarity can make it easier for organizations to transact with other organizations, to attract career-minded staff, to be acknowledged as legitimate and reputable, and to fit into administrative categories that define eligibility for public and private grants and contracts. None of this, however, insures that conformist organizations do what they do more efficiently than do their more deviant peers.

Pressures for competitive efficiency are also mitigated in many fields because the number of organizations is limited and there are strong fiscal and legal barriers to entry and exit. Lee (1971:51) maintains this is why hospital administrators are less concerned with the efficient use of resources and more concerned with status competition and parity in prestige. Fennell (1980) notes that hospitals are a poor market system because patients lack the needed knowledge of potential exchange partners and prices. She argues that physicians and hospital administrators are the actual consumers. Competition among hospitals is based on "attracting physicians, who, in turn, bring their patients to the hospital." Fennell (p. 505) concludes that:

> Hospitals operate according to a norm of social legitimation that frequently conflicts with market considerations of efficiency and system rationality. Apparently, hospitals can increase their range of services not because there is an actual need for a particular service or facility within the patient population, but because they will be defined as fit only if they can offer everything other hospitals in the area offer.

These results suggest a more general pattern. Organizational fields that include a large professionally trained labor force will be driven primarily by status competition. Organizational prestige and resources are key elements in attracting professionals. This process encourages homogenization as organizations seek to ensure that they can provide the same benefits and services as their competitors.

Predictors of Isomorphic Change

It follows from our discussion of the mechanism by which isomorphic change occurs that we should be able to predict empirically which organizational fields will be most homogeneous in structure, process, and behavior. While an empirical test of such predictions is beyond the scope of this paper, the ultimate value of our perspective will lie in its predictive utility. The hypotheses discussed below are not meant to exhaust the universe of predictors, but merely to suggest several hypotheses that may be pursued using data on the characteristics of organizations in a field, either cross-sectionally or, preferably, over time. The hypotheses are implicitly governed by *ceteris paribus* assumptions, particularly with regard to size, technology, and centralization of external resources.

A. *Organizational-level predictors.* There is variability in the extent to and rate at which organizations in a field change to become more like their peers. Some organizations respond to external pressures quickly; others change only after a long period of resistance. The first two hypotheses derive from our discussion of coercive isomorphism and constraint.

Hypothesis A-1: *The greater the dependence of an organization on another organization, the more similar it will become to that organization in structure, climate, and behavioral focus.* Following Thompson (1957) and Pfeffer and Salancik (1978), this proposition recognizes the greater ability of organizations to resist the demands of organizations on whom they are not dependent. A position of dependence leads to isomorphic change. Coercive pressures are built into exchange relationships. As Williamson (1979) has shown, exchanges are characterized by transaction-specific investments in both knowledge and equipment. Once an organization chooses a specific supplier or distributor for particular parts or services, the supplier or distributor develops expertise in the performance of the task as well as idiosyncratic knowledge about the exchange relationship. The organization comes to rely on the supplier or distributor and such transaction-specific investments give the supplier or distributor considerable advantages in any subsequent competition with other suppliers or distributors.

Hypothesis A-2: *The greater the centralization of organization A's resource supply, the greater the extent to which organization A will change isomorphically to resemble the organizations on which it depends for resources.* As Thompson (1967) notes, organizations that depend on the same sources for funding, personnel, and legitimacy will be more subject to the whims of resource suppliers than will organizations that can play one source of support off against another. In cases where alternative sources are either not readily available or require effort to locate, the stronger party to the transaction can coerce the weaker party to adopt its practices in order to accommodate the stronger party's needs (see Powell, 1983).

The third and fourth hypotheses derive from our discussion of mimetic isomorphism, modeling, and uncertainty.

Hypothesis A-3: *The more uncertain the relationship between means and ends the greater the extent to which an organization will model itself after organizations it perceives to be successful.* The mimetic thought process involved in the search for models is characteristic of change in organizations in which key technologies are only poorly understood (March and Cohen, 1974). Here our prediction diverges somewhat from Meyer and Rowan (1977) who argue, as we do, that organizations which lack well-defined technologies will import institutionalized rules and practices. Meyer and Rowan posit a loose coupling between legitimated external practices and internal organizational behavior. From an ecologist's point of view, loosely coupled organizations are more likely to vary internally. In contrast, we expect substantive internal changes in tandem with more ceremonial practices, thus greater homogeneity and less variation and change. Internal consistency of this sort is an important means of interorganizational coordination. It also increases organizational stability.

Hypothesis A-4: *The more ambiguous the goals of an organization, the greater the extent to which the organization will model itself after organizations that it perceives to be successful.* There are two reasons for this. First, organizations with ambiguous or disputed goals are likely to be highly dependent upon appearances for legitimacy. Such organizations may find it to their advantage to meet the expectations of important constituencies about how they should be designed and run. In contrast to our view, ecologists would argue that organizations that copy other organizations usually have no competitive advantage. We contend that, in most situations, reliance on established, legitimated procedures enhances organizational legitimacy and survival characteristics. A second reason for modeling behavior is found in situations where conflict over organizational goals is repressed in the interest of harmony; thus participants find it easier to mimic other organizations than to make decisions on the basis of systematic analyses

of goals since such analyses would prove painful of disruptive.

The fifth and sixth hypotheses are based on our discussion of normative processes found in professional organizations.

Hypothesis A-5: *The greater the reliance on academic credentials in choosing managerial and staff personnel, the greater the extent to which an organization will become like other organizations in its field.* Applicants with academic credentials have already undergone a socialization process in university programs, and are thus more likely than others to have internalized reigning norms and dominant organizational models.

Hypothesis A-6: *The greater the participation of organizational managers in trade and professional associations, the more likely the organization will be, or will become, like other organizations in its field.* This hypothesis is parallel to the institutional view that the more elaborate the relational networks among organizations and their members, the greater the collective organization of the environment (Meyer and Rowan, 1977).

B. *Field-level predictors.* The following six hypotheses describe the expected effects of several characteristics of organizational fields on the extent of isomorphism in a particular field. Since the effect of institutional isomorphism is homogenization, the best indicator of isomorphic change is a decrease in variation and diversity, which could be measured by lower standard deviations of the values of selected indicators in a set of organizations. The key indicators would vary with the nature of the field and the interests of the investigator. In all cases, however, field-level measures are expected to affect organizations in a field regardless of each organization's scores on related organizational-level measures.

Hypothesis B-1: *The greater the extent to which an organizational field is dependent upon a single (or several similar) source of support for vital resources, the higher the level of isomorphism.* The centralization of resources within a field both directly causes homogenization by placing organizations under similar pressures from resource suppliers, and interacts with uncertainty and goal ambiguity to increase their impact. This hypothesis is congruent with the ecologists' argument that the number of organizational forms is determined by the distribution of resources in the environment and the terms on which resources are available.

Hypothesis B-2: *The greater the extent to which the organizations in a field transact with agencies of the state, the greater the extent of isomorphism in the field as a whole*. This follows not just from the previous hypothesis, but from two elements of state/private-sector transactions: their rule-boundedness and formal rationality, and the emphasis of government actors on institutional rules. Moreover, the federal government routinely designates industry standards for an entire field which require adoption by all competing firms. John Meyer (1979) argues convincingly that the aspects of an organization which are affected by state transactions differ to the extent that state participation is unitary or fragmented among several public agencies.

The third and fourth hypotheses follow from our discussion of isomorphic change resulting from uncertainty and modeling.

Hypothesis B-3: *The fewer the number of visible alternative organizational models in a field, the faster the rate of isomorphism in that field*. The predictions of this hypothesis are less specific than those of others and require further refinement; but our argument is that for any relevant dimension of organizational strategies or structures in an organizational field there will be a threshold level, or a tipping point, beyond which adoption of the dominant form will proceed with increasing speed (Granovetter, 1978; Boorman and Leavitt, 1979).

Hypothesis B-4: *The greater the extent to which technologies are uncertain or goals are ambiguous within a field, the greater the rate of isomorphic change*. Somewhat counterintuitively, abrupt increases in uncertainty and ambiguity should, after brief periods of ideologically motivated experimentation, lead to rapid isomorphic change. As in the case of A-4, ambiguity and uncertainty may be a function of environmental definition, and, in any case, interact both with centralization of resources (A-1, A-2, B-1, B-2) and with professionalization and structuration (A-5, A-6, B-5, B-6), Moreover, in fields characterized by a high degree of uncertainty, new entrants, which could serve as sources of innovation and variation, will seek to overcome the liability of newness by imitating established practices within the field.

The two final hypotheses in this section follow from our discussion of professional filtering, socialization, and structuration.

Hypothesis B-5: *The greater the extent of professionalization in a field, the greater the amount of institutional isomorphic change*. Professionalization may be measured by the universality of credential requirements, the robustness of graduate training programs, or the vitality of professional and trade associations.

Hypothesis B-6: *The greater the extent of structuration of a field, the greater the degree of isomorphics*. Fields that have stable and broadly acknowledged centers, peripheries, and status orders will be more homogeneous both because the diffusion structure for new models and norms is more routine and because the level of interaction among organizations in the field is higher. While structuration may not lend itself to easy measurement, it might be tapped crudely with the use of such familiar measures as concentration ratios, reputational interview studies, or data on network characteristics.

This rather schematic exposition of a dozen hypotheses relating the extent of isomorphism to selected attributes of organizations and of organizational fields does not constitute a complete agenda for empirical assessment of our perspective. We have not discussed the expected nonlinearities and ceiling effects in the relationships that we have posited. Nor have we addressed the issue of the indicators that one must use to measure homogeneity. Organizations in a field may be highly diverse on some dimensions, yet extremely homogeneous on others. While we suspect, in general, that the rate at which the standard deviations of structural or behavioral indicators approach zero will vary with the nature of an organizational field's technology and environment, we will not develop these ideas here. The point of this section is to suggest that the theoretical discussion is susceptible to empirical test, and to layout a few testable propositions that may guide future analyses.

Implications for Social Theory

A comparison of macrosocial theories of functionalist or Marxist orientation with theoretical and empirical work in the study of organizations yields a paradoxical conclusion. Societies (or elites), so it seems, are smart, while organizations are dumb. Societies comprise institutions that mesh together comfortably in the interests of efficiency (Clark, 1962), the dominant value system (Parsons, 1951), or, in the Marxist version, capitalists (Domhoff, 1967; Althusser, 1969). Organizations, by contrast, are either anarchies (Cohen et al., 1972), federations of loosely coupled parts (Weick, 1976), or autonomy-seeking agents (Gouldner, 1954) laboring under such formidable constraints as bounded rationality (March and Simon, 1958), uncertain or contested goals (Sills, 1957), and unclear technologies (March and Cohen, 1974).

Despite the findings of organizational research, the image of society as consisting of tightly and rationally coupled institutions persists throughout much of modern social theory. Rational administration pushes out nonbureaucratic forms, schools assume the structure of the workplace, hospital and university administrations come to resemble the management of for-profit firms, and the modernization of the world economy proceeds unabated. Weberians point to the continuing homogenization of organizational structures as the formal rationality of bureaucracy extends to the limits of contemporary organizational life. Functionalists describe the rational adaptation of the structure of firms, schools, and states to the values and needs of modern society (Chandler, 1977; Parsons, 1977). Marxists attribute changes in such organizations as welfare agencies (Piven and Cloward, 1971) and schools (Bowles and Gintis, 1976) to the logic of the accumulation process.

We find it difficult to square the extant literature on organizations with these macrosocial views. How can it be that the confused and contentious bumblers that populate the pages of organizational case studies and theories combine to construct the elaborate and well-proportioned social edifice that macrotheorists describe?

The conventional answer to this paradox has been that some version of natural selection occurs in which selection mechanisms operate to weed out those organizational forms that are less fit. Such arguments, as we have contended, are difficult to mesh with organizational realities. Less efficient organizational forms do persist. In some contexts efficiency or productivity cannot even be measured. In government agencies or in faltering corporations selection may occur on political rather than economic grounds. In other contexts, for example the Metropolitan Opera or the Bohemian Grove, supporters are far more concerned with

noneconomic values like aesthetic quality or social status than with efficiency per se. Even in the for-profit sector, where competitive arguments would promise to bear the greatest fruit, Nelson and Winter's work (Winter, 1964, 1975; Nelson and Winter, 1982) demonstrates that the invisible hand operates with, at best, a light touch.

A second approach to the paradox that we have identified comes from Marxists and theorists who assert that key elites guide and control the social system through their command of crucial positions in major organizations (e.g., the financial institutions that dominate monopoly capitalism). In this view, while organizational actors ordinarily proceed undisturbed through mazes of standard operating procedures, at key turning points capitalist elites get their way by intervening in decisions that set the course of an institution for years to come (Katz, 1975).

While evidence suggests that this is, in fact, sometimes the case—Barnouw's account of the early days of broadcasting or Weinstein's (1968) work on the Progressives are good examples—other historians have been less successful in their search for class-conscious elites. In such cases as the development of the New Deal programs (Hawley, 1966) or the expansion of the Vietnamese conflict (Halperin, 1974), the capitalist class appears to have been muddled and disunited.

Moreover, without constant monitoring, individuals pursuing parochial organizational or subunit interests can quickly undo the work that even the most prescient elites have accomplished. Perrow (1976:21) has noted that despite superior resources and sanctioning power, organizational elites are often unable to maximize their preferences because "the complexity of modern organizations makes control difficult." Moreover, organizations have increasingly become the vehicle for numerous "gratifications, necessities, and preferences so that many groups within and without the organization seek to use it for ends that restrict the return to masters."

We reject neither the natural-selection nor the elite-control arguments out of hand. Elites do exercise considerable influence over modern life and aberrant or inefficient organizations sometimes do expire. But we contend that neither of these processes is sufficient to explain the extent to which organizations have become structurally more similar. We argue that a theory of institutional isomorphism may help explain the observations that organizations are becoming more homogeneous, and that elites often get their way, while at the same time enabling us to understand the irrationality, the frustration of power, and the lack of innovation that are so commonplace in organizational life. What is more, our approach is more consonant with the ethnographic and theoretical literature on how organizations work than are either functionalist or elite theories of organizational change.

A focus on institutional isomorphism can also add a much needed perspective on the political struggle for organizational power and survival that is missing from much of population ecology. The institutionalization approach associated with John Meyer and his students posits the importance of myths and ceremony but does not ask how these models arise and whose interests they initially serve. Explicit attention to the genesis of legitimated models and to the definition and elaboration of organizational fields should answer this question. Examination of the diffusion of similar organizational strategies and structures should be a productive means for assessing the influence of elite interests. A consideration of isomorphic processes also leads us to a bifocal view of power and its application in modern politics. To the extent that organizational change is unplanned and goes on largely behind the backs of groups that wish to influence it, our attention should be directed to two forms of power. The first, as March and Simon (1958) and Simon (1957) pointed out years ago, is the power to set premises, to define the norms and standards which shape and channel behavior. The second is the point of critical intervention (Domhoff, 1979) at which elites can define appropriate models of organizational structure and policy which then go unquestioned for years to come (see Katz, 1975). Such a view is consonant with some of the best recent work on power (see Lukes, 1974); research on the structuration of organizational fields and on isomorphic processes may help give it more empirical flesh.

Finally, a more developed theory of organizational isomorphism may have important implications for social policy in those fields in which the state works through private organizations. To the extent that pluralism is a guiding value in public policy

deliberations, we need to discover new forms of intersectoral coordination that will encourage diversification rather than hastening homogenization. An understanding of the manner in which fields become more homogeneous would prevent policy makers and analysts from confusing the disappearance of an organizational form with its substantive failure. Current efforts to encourage diversity tend to be conducted in an organizational vacuum. Policy makers concerned with pluralism should consider the impact of their programs on the structure of organizational fields as a whole, and not simply on the programs of individual organizations.

We believe there is much to be gained by attending to similarity as well as to variation among organizations and, in particular, to change in the degree of homogeneity or variation over time. Our approach seeks to study incremental change as well as selection. We take seriously the observations of organizational theorists about the role of change, ambiguity, and constraint and point to the implications of these organizational characteristics for the social structure as a whole. The foci and motive forces of bureaucratization (and, more broadly, homogenization in general) have, as we argued, changed since Weber's time. But the importance of understanding the trends to which he called attention has never been more immediate.

Notes

1. By *connectedness* we mean the existence of transactions tying organizations to one another: such transactions might include formal contractual relationships, participation of personnel in common enterprises such as professional associations, labor unions, or boards of directors, or informal organizational-level ties like personnel flows. A set of organizations that are strongly connected to one another and only weakly connected to other organizations constitutes a *clique*. By *structural equivalence* we refer to similarity of position in a network structure: for example, two organizations are structurally equivalent if they have ties of the same kind to the same set of other organizations, even if they themselves are not connected: here the key structure is the *role* or *block*.

2. By organizational change, we refer to change in formal structure, organizational culture, and goals, program, or mission. Organizational change varies in its responsiveness to technical conditions. In this paper we are most interested in processes that affect organizations in a given field: in most cases these organizations employ similar technical bases; thus we do not attempt to partial out the relative importance of technically functional versus other forms of organizational change. While we shall cite many examples of organizational change as we go along, our purpose here is to identify a widespread class of organizational processes relevant to a broad range of substantive problems, rather than to identify deterministically the causes of specific organizational arrangements.

References

Alchian, Armell. 1950. "Uncertainty, evolution, and economic theory." *Journal of Political Economy* 58:211–21.

Aldrich, Howard. 1979. *Organizations and Environments*. Englewood Cliffs, NJ: Prentice-Hall.

Althusser, Louis. 1969. *For Marx*. London: Allan Lane.

Barnouw, Erik. 1966–68. *A History of Broadcasting in the United States*, 3 volumes. New York: Oxford University Press.

Boorman, Scott A. and Paul R. Levitt. 1979. "The cascade principle for general disequilibrium dynamics." Cambridge/New Haven: Harvard-Yale Preprints in Mathematical Sociology. Number 15.

Bowles, Samuel and Herbert Gintis. 1976. *Schooling in Capitalist America*. New York: Basic Books.

Carroll, Glenn R. and Jacques Delacroix. 1982. "Organizational mortality in the newspaper industries of Argentina and Ireland: An ecological approach." *Administrative Science Quarterly* 27: 169–98.

Chandler, Alfred D. 1977. *The Visible Hand: The Managerial Revolution in American Business*. Cambridge: Harvard University Press.

Child, John and Alfred Kieser. 1981. "Development of organizations over time." Pp. 28–64 in Paul C. Nystrom and William H. Starbuck (eds.), *Handbook of Organizational Design*. New York: Oxford University Press.

Cicourel, Aaron. 1970. "The acquisition of social structure: Toward a developmental sociology of language." Pp. 136–68 in Jack D. Douglas (ed.), *Understanding Everyday Life*. Chicago: Aldine.

Clark, Burton R. 1962. *Educating the Expert Society*. San Francisco: Chandler.

Cohen, Michael D., James G. March and Johan P. Olsen. 1972. "A garbage can model of organizational choice." *Administrative Science Quarterly* 17:1–25.

Collins, Randall. 1979. *The Credential Society*. New York: Academic Press.

Coser, Lewis, Charles Kadushin and Walter W. Powell. 1982. *Books: The Culture and Commerce of Book Publishing*. New York: Basic Books.

Cyert, Richard M. and James G. March. 1963. *A Behavioral Theory of the Firm*. Englewood Cliffs, NJ: Prentice-Hall.

DiMaggio, Paul. 1981. "Cultural entrepreneurship in nineteenth-century Boston. Part I: The creation of an organizational base for high culture in America." *Media, Culture and Society* 4:33–50.

———. 1982. "The structure of organizational fields: an analytical approach and policy implications." Paper prepared for SUNY-Albany Conference on Organizational Theory and Public Policy. April 1 and 2.

Domhoff, J. William. 1967. Who Rules America? Englewood Cliffs, NJ: Prentice-Hall.

———. 1979. *The Powers That Be: Processes of Ruling Class Domination in America*. New York: Random House.

Fennell, Mary L. 1980. "The effects of environmental characteristics on the structure of hospital clusters." *Administrative Science Quarterly* 25: 484–510.

Freeman, John H. 1982. "Organizational life cycles and natural selection processes." Pp. 1–32 in Barry Staw and Larry Cummings (eds.), *Research in Organizational Behavior*. Vol. 4. Greenwich, CT: JAI Press.

Giddens, Anthony. 1979. *Central Problems in Social Theory: Action, Structure, and Contradiction in Social Analysis*. Berkeley: University of California Press.

Gouldner, Alvin W. 1954. *Patterns of Industrial Bureaucracy*. Glencoe, IL: Free Press.

Granovetter, Mark. 1978. "Threshold models of collective behavior." *American Journal of Sociology* 83:1420–43.

Hall, Richard. 1968. "Professionalization and bureaucratization." *American Sociological Review* 33:92–104.

Halperin, Mortin H. 1974. *Bureaucratic Politics and Foreign Policy*. Washington, D.C.: The Brookings Institution.

Hannan, Michael T. and John H. Freeman. 1977. "The population ecology of organizations." *American Journal of Sociology* 82:929–64.

Hawley, Amos. 1968. "Human ecology." Pp. 328–37 in David L. Sills (ed.), *International Encyclopedia of the Social Sciences*. New York: Macmillan.

Hawley, Ellis W. 1966. *The New Deal and the Problem of Monopoly: A Study in Economic Ambivalence*. Princeton: Princeton University Press.

Hirsch, Paul and Thomas Whisler. 1982. "The view from the boardroom." Paper presented at Academy of Management Meetings, New York, NY.

Kanter, Rosabeth Moss. 1972. *Commitment and Community*. Cambridge, MA: Harvard University Press.

———. 1977. *Men and Women of the Corporation*. New York: Basic Books.

Katz, Michael B. 1975. *Class, Bureaucracy, and Schools: The Illusion of Educational Change in America*. New York: Praeger.

Kimberly, John. 1980. "Initiation, innovation and institutionalization in the creation process." Pp. 18–43 in John Kimberly and Robert B. Miles (eds.), *The Organizational Life Cycle*. San Francisco: Jossey-Bass.

Knoke, David. 1982. "The spread of municipal reform: temporal, spatial, and social dynamics." *American Journal of Sociology* 87:1314–39.

Larson, Magali Sarfatti. 1977. *The Rise of Professionalism: A Sociological Analysis*. Berkeley: University of California Press.

Laumann, Edward O., Joseph Galaskiewicz and Peter Marsdell. 1978. "Community structure as interorganizational linkage." *Annual Review of Sociology* 4:455–84.

Lee, M. L. 1971. "A conspicuous production theory of hospital behavior." *Southern Economic Journal* 38:48–58.

Lukes, Steven. 1974. *Power: A Radical View*. London: Macmillan.

March, James G. and Michael Cohen. 1974. *Leadership and Ambiguity: The American College President*. New York: McGraw Hill.

March, James C. and James G. March. 1977. "Almost random careers: The Wisconsin school superintendency, 1940–72." *Administrative Science Quarterly* 22:378–409.

March, James G. and Johan P. Olsen. 1976. *Ambiguity and Choice in Organizations*. Bergen, Norway: Universitetsforlaget.

March, James G. and Herbert A. Simon. 1958. *Organizations*. New York: Wiley.

Meyer, John W. 1979. "The impact of the centralization of educational funding and control on state and local organizational governance." Stanford, CA: Institute for Research on Educational Finance and Governance, Stanford University, Program Report No. 79-B20.

———. 1981. Remarks at ASA session on "The Present Crisis and the Decline in World Hegemony." Toronto, Canada.

Meyer, John W. and Michael Hannan. 1979. *National Development and the World System: Educational, Economic, and Political Change*. Chicago: University of Chicago Press.

Meyer, John W. and Brian Rowan. 1977. "Institutionalized organizations: Formal structure as myth and ceremony." *American Journal of Sociology* 83:340–63.

Meyer, John W., W. Richard Scott and Terence C. Deal. 1981. "Institutional and technical sources of organizational structure explaining, the structure of educational organizations." In Herman Stein (ed.), *Organizations and the Human Services: Cross-Disciplinary Reflections*. Philadelphia, PA: Temple University Press.

Meyer, Marshall. 1981. "Persistence and change in bureaucratic structures." Paper presented at the annual meeting of the American Sociological Association, Toronto, Canada.

Milofsky, Carl. 1981. "Structure and process in community self-help organizations." New Haven: Yale Program on Non-Profit Organizations, Working Paper No. 17.

Nelson, Richard R. and Sidney Winter. 1982. *An Evolutionary Theory of Economic Change*. Cambridge: Harvard University Press.

Ouchi, William G. 1980. "Markets, bureaucracies, and clans." *Administrative Science Quarterly* 25:129–41.

Parsons, Talcott. 1951. *The Social System*. Glencoe, IL: Free Press.

———. 1977. *The Evolution of Societies*. Englewood Cliffs, NJ: Prentice-Hall.

Perrow, Charles. 1974. "Is business really changing?" *Organizational Dynamics,* Summer:31–44.

———. 1976. "Control in organizations." Paper presented at American Sociological Association annual meetings, New York, NY.

Pfeffer, Jeffrey and Gerald Salancik. 1978. *The External Control of Organizations: A Resource Dependence Perspective.* New York: Harper & Row.

Piven, Frances Fox and Richard A. Cloward. 1971. *Regulating the Poor: The Functions of Public Welfare.* New York: Pantheon.

Powell, Walter W. Forthcoming. "The Political Economy of Public Television." New Haven: Program on Non-Profit Organizations.

———. 1983. "New solutions to perennial problems of bookselling: Whither the local bookstore?" Daedalus: Winter.

Ritti, R. R. and Fred H. Goldner. 1979. "Professional pluralism in an industrial organization." *Management Science* 16:233–46.

Rothman, Mitchell. 1980. "The evolution of forms of legal education." Unpublished manuscript. Department of Sociology, Yale University, New Haven, CT.

Rothschild-Whitt, Joyce. 1979. "The collectivist organization: an alternative to rational bureaucratic models." *American Sociological Review* 44:509–27.

Schelling, Thomas. 1978. *Micromotives and Macrobehavior.* New York: W. W. Norton.

Sedlak, Michael W. 1981. "Youth policy and young women, 1950–1972: The impact of private-sector programs for pregnant and wayward girls on public policy." Paper presented at National Institute for Education Youth Policy Research Conference, Washington, D.C.

Selznick, Philip. 1957. *Leadership in Administration.* New York: Harper & Row.

Sills, David L. 1957. *The Volunteers: Means and Ends in a National Organization.* Glencoe, IL: Free Press.

Simon, Herbert A. 1957. *Administrative Behavior.* New York: Free Press.

Starr, Paul. 1980. "Medical care and the boundaries of capitalist organization." Unpublished manuscript. Program on Non-Profit Organizations, Yale University, New Haven, CT.

Swidler, Ann. 1979. *Organization Without Authority: Dilemmas of Social Control of Free Schools.* Cambridge: Harvard University Press.

Thompson, James. 1967. *Organizations in Action.* New York: McGraw-Hill.

Tyack, David. 1974. *The One Best System: A History of American Urban Education.* Cambridge, MA: Harvard University Press.

Useem, Michael. 1979. "The social organization of the American business elite and participation of corporation directors in the governance of American institutions." *American Sociological Review* 44:553–72.

Weber, Max. 1952. *The Protestant Ethic and the Spirit of Capitalism.* New York: Scribner.

———. 1968. *Economy and Society: An Outline of Interpretive Sociology.* Three volumes. New York: Bedminster.

Weick, Karl. 1976. "Educational organizations as loosely coupled systems." *Administrative Science Quarterly* 21:1–19.

Weinstein, James. 1968. *The Corporate Ideal in the Liberal State, 1900–1918.* Boston, MA: Beacon Press.

Westney, D. Eleanor. Forthcoming. *Organizational Development and Social Change in Meiji, Japan.*

White, Harrison C., Scott A. Boorman and Ronald L. Breiger. 1976. "Social structure from multiple networks. I. Blockmodels of roles and positions." *American Journal of Sociology* 81:730–80.

Williamson, Oliver E. 1975. *Markets and Hierarchies, Analysis and Antitrust Implications: A Study of the Economics of Internal Organization.* New York: Free Press.

———. 1979. "Transaction-cost economics: the governance of contractual relations." *Journal of Law and Economics* 22:233–61.

Winter, Sidney G. 1964. "Economic 'natural selection' and the theory of the firm." *Yale Economic Essays* 4:224–72.

———. 1975. "Optimization and evolution in the theory of the firm." Pp. 73–118 in Richard H. Day and Theodore Graves (eds.), *Adaptive Economic Models.* New York: Academic.

Woodward, John. 1965. *Industrial Organization, Theory and Practice.* London: Oxford University Press.

Zucker, Lynne G. and Pamela S. Tolbert. 1981. "Institutional sources of change in the formal structure of organizations: the diffusion of civil service reform, 1880–1935." Paper presented at American Sociological Association annual meeting, Toronto, Canada.

Chapter 25
The Demographic Perspective

Glen R. Carroll and
Michael T. Hannan

Demography is typically thought of in terms of human populations—their births, deaths, age distributions, and so forth. A demographic perspective can also be applied to the study of organizations. In fact, many of the same concepts can be used regardless of whether the unit in question is a person or a firm. Carroll and Hannan introduce some basic demographic principles and illustrate their application to understanding organizational populations. They show that a demographic perspective can help us make sense of many of the kinds of issues of interest to organizational scholars.

This [chapter] looks at corporations and other kinds of organizations from a demographic perspective. It presents theories, methods, and empirical findings that exemplify a demographic approach. Although the demographic perspective figures prominently in much recent theory and research on organizations, the connections with the broader discipline of demography have not received much attention. We think that there is much to be gained by emphasizing these linkages.

For organizational studies, exploiting the models and methods of demography promises to generate new ways of studying corporations. It should increase rigor in organizational theory and research as well. For demography, a new subfield can be developed, one that brings demographic theory and methods to bear on issues of growing importance: the dynamics of organizational change and their socioeconomic consequences. The new substantive problems encountered in studying corporations will also likely spur innovation in demographic theory and methods.

Unfortunately, the demographic perspective of social science often gets misunderstood and underestimated. Too many social scientists and other analysts subscribe to the view that demography amounts to little more than an accounting system for populations. Demography is commonly considered as just a methodology, and an established boring methodology at that. While we admit that demography (like all domains of social sciences) has its share of uninspiring efforts, we believe that this general characterization is grossly inaccurate. Demography has, to be sure, an institutionalized set of methodological procedures, usually involving aspects of counting. Yet, these methods are not ends in and of themselves. Instead, they serve as tools for producing reliable empirical facts that inform a particular way of looking at research questions and developing theory. When used properly, demography yields unique and deep insights into social phenomena. . . .

Basic Demography of Business Organizations

Although demographic intuition about the human population might be fairly elementary, it appears to be reasonably accurate. For example, we would venture that many Americans know that the population of the United States consists of approximately 250 million persons. Many also probably know that the United States ranks as one of the larger countries in the world population-wise but that it falls well behind China and India in terms of sheer size. Most Americans also know of the demographic bulge in the population known as the "baby boomers" (the disproportionately large group of persons born between 1945 and 1955). There is even a sense among the general public that the baby boomer bulge in the population exerts disproportionate effects on the country's cultural, political, and social life.

Demographic intuition about the corporate population appears to be much more limited and more often wrong. What, for instance, is the size of the American corporate population? Its ranking relative to other countries? Its age structure? Or any possible effects of its demographic structure on American society and economy? Although the use of publicly available data imposes severe limitations, we can nonetheless construct estimates of some of these basic demographic facts. For instance, Table 25.1 shows the federal government's estimate of the number of American business entities from 1970 to 1990. It includes a breakdown by three generic organizational forms, corporations (which typically have limited liability) and partnerships and proprietorships (which typically have other levels of liability). Obviously, this population has grown rapidly in recent decades. The number of corporations more than doubled between 1970 and 1990. Partnerships and proprietorships also soared, making the total number of business entities rise rapidly as well. In 1990, the number of business entities stood at roughly 20 million, with roughly one independent business for every 12 or 13 persons.

Table 25.2 gives some basic information on the size distribution of American corporations in 1990. It shows size classes as measured by annual business receipts. As might be expected, a large proportion of these companies were small, with annual receipts below $25,000. Nonetheless, the largest size class by this grouping is for medium-size corporations, those with receipts between $100,000 and $500,000. The substantial size of the largest group also deserves note.

How has organizational size changed over time in the United States? Table 25.3 presents some estimates of average size of business organizations from 1960 to 1990, based on aggregate data on business and the labor force.[1] It indicates clearly that the major trend in firm size over this period runs toward smaller organizations. No matter which of the four "average" size calculations (shown at the top of the table) one prefers, the same pattern appears from 1960 to 1990. Such a decline represents a profound change in the organizational structure of the Ameri-

can economy, one with potentially far-reaching implications, given the close association of size with many other features of organizational life, including especially employment. It must be meaningful, for instance, that many Americans now work in smaller firms. For comparable jobs, small firms typically pay less, offer fewer opportunities for advancement, provide less generous benefits, and experience less stability than large firms. Table 25.3 also reveals that the management structure of American corporations might have changed over this period in that the number of administrative-managerial employees per corporation has declined (but note too that employees per administrator-manager has also dropped).

Table 25.1

Counts (in thousands) of U.S. business organizations, 1970–1990.

	1970	1980	1990
Corporations	1,665	2,711	3,717
Partnerships	936	1,380	1,554
Proprietorships	6,494	9,730	14,783
All business entities	9,095	13,821	20,054

Source: *Statistical Abstract of the United States.*

Table 25.2

Size distribution of U.S. corporations, 1990.

Size-class (by receipts)	Number (thousands)	Percent
Under $25,000	879	23.6
$25,000 to $49,999	252	6.8
$50,000 to $99,999	359	9.7
$100,000 to $499,999	1,162	31.3
$500,000 to $999,999	416	11.2
$1,000,000 or more	649	17.5

Source: *Statistical Abstract of the United States*

Table 25.3

Estimates of average business size in the United States, 1960–1990.

	1960	1970	1980	1990
Economically active persons per corporation	61.2	51.6	39.4	34.0
Economically active persons per business entity	na	10.3	8.2	6.3
Employees per corporation	50.6	46.4	35.7	30.9
Employees per business entity	na	9.2	7.4	5.7
Administrative and managerial employees per corporation	4.8	5.0	4.1	4.0
Employees per administrative and managerial employee	10.5	9.9	8.6	7.8

Note: na means not available.

Sources: Calculations using data from the *International Labor Organization Yearbook* and the *Statistical Yearbook of the United States.*

What about specific industries? Although many commentators on the economy apparently regard their intuition about industrial demographic matters as good, we sense that it usually is not. Complete demographic counts of the number of firms within an industry commonly surprise most people. Consider, for example, the automobile manufacturing industry. Many social scientists are startled to learn that as many as 2,197 producers have operated within the United States sometime during 1885–1981. Figure 25.1 shows their distribution across history. At its peak, in the second decade of the century, this industry was home to 345 automobile manufacturers. Even in the recent era, with a highly concentrated market for the largest automakers, there are many more producers than most people know (mainly because they do not know about small specialist producers making alternative fuel cars, kit cars, vintage cars, and the like).

American society generated more automobile producers than other countries, but it is not unique in spawning what many social scientists find to be a startling abundance of car manufacturers. Figure 25.2 shows historical demographic counts for France and Germany. By our count, during 1885–1980 the French population of automakers included 828 firms and the German population numbered 373. Interestingly, the populations show roughly the same general pattern of growth and decline: as well as peaks around the same period, 1920 to 1925. This type of regularity across different countries constitutes an important empirical fact to be explained. Was there something inherent in automobile technology or production systems that produced it? Or might automobile producers have been—somewhat unexpectedly in these early days of trade—linked socially or economically across countries?

Consider a different example: banking. Figure 25.3 compares two populations of organizations but in this case the two are subsets of a single industry. The figure shows the growth in numbers of two types of commercial banks in Singapore from the time of founding of its first bank in 1840 until 1990. The first type is the *full-license bank*, which can operate in all aspects of commercial banking in Singapore. The second type is the *off-shore bank*, which cannot operate freely in the local commercial market but which specializes in money-center banking for the region. The explosion of off-shore banks in the 1970s and 1980s reflects the effect of regulation: this organizational form was first authorized in 1970 with the establishment of the Monetary Authority of Singapore.

For further comparison, Figure 25.4 presents historical counts of beer brewers in the United States. Notice again a general longterm pattern of population growth to a

Figure 25.1

Number of automobile manufacturers in the United States, 1885–1981.

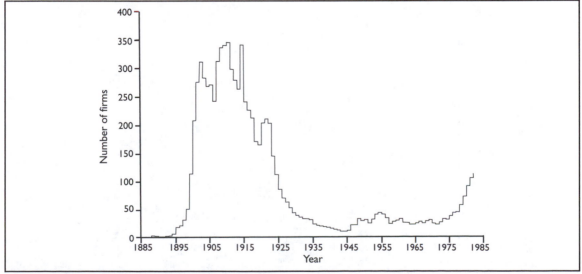

peak and then decline. The decline here is dramatic. However, it is followed in the most recent period by an even more dramatic upsurge in the number of brewers. Against the backdrop of the automobile producers, these observations raise two research questions. First, can some process account for the longterm evolution of organizational populations generally? Second, is there some way to explain the apparent late-stage reversals in the process?

What about "modern" industries? Figure 25.5 shows counts of firms in the worldwide hard-disk drive industry. Despite its short history, this industry shows a pattern of early growth and decline similar to that seen

Figure 25.2

Number of automobile manufacturers in France and Germany, 1885–1981.

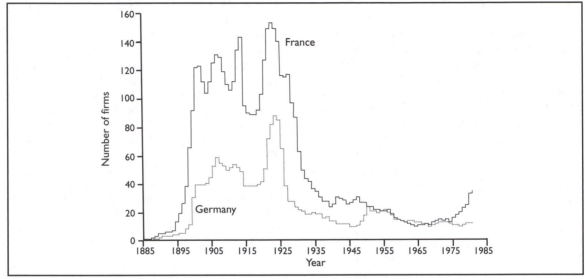

Source: Hannan et al. (1995). Copyright © 1995 by American Sociological Association. Used by permission.

Figure 25.3

Number of full-license (solid line) and off-shore (dashed line) commercial banks in Singapore, 1840–1990.

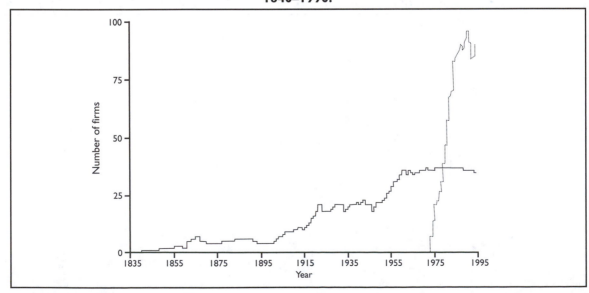

Figure 25.4

Number of brewing firms in the United States, 1633–1995.

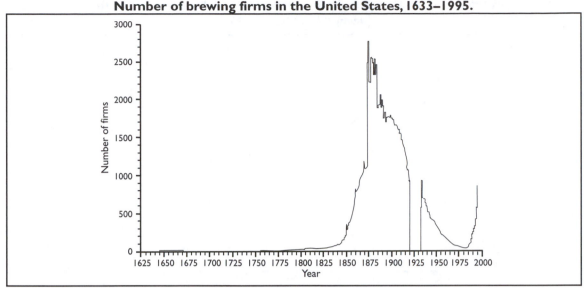

Source: Carroll and Swaminathan (1998). Copyright © 1998 by Glenn R. Carroll and Anand Swaminathan. Used by Permission.

above, except that it occurs over a shorter time frame. Perhaps industrial evolution moves with greater speed in modern high-technology industries. However, no reversal is yet evident.

Organizing Principles of Demography

Demographic facts about corporations and industries might be interesting; but what should we make of such phenomena? How should the empirical facts of corporate demography be analyzed? Before addressing these questions directly, it is instructive to review more generally the way demography looks at the world, its conceptual organizing principles. We identify five principles that arguably constitute demography's core.

Demography adopts a *population perspective*. This means that demographic analysis does not concern itself much with any given individual or even sets of individuals. Instead, demography seeks to explain properties of populations such as their composition (e.g., age distribution) or their dynamics (e.g., growth rates). Except in the case of an extremely homogenous population, it makes little sense to speak of a representative individual from a population. Adequate description of a population almost always entails distributional measures.

Demographic analysis examines the occurrence of events. The central objects of study in demographic analysis are the so-called *vital events* of birth and death. Other kinds of events draw attention insofar as they affect the flow of vital events. So, for instance, events of marriage and divorce frequently get brought into the picture in human demography because they affect rates of natality. For populations with permeable boundaries, rates of emigration and immigration also constitute significant events since they generate population changes.

Formal analysis in demography concentrates on the flows of events in time and the implications of events for population structure. *Age is the master clock* in standard demographic analyses of biological populations. That is, demographers assume that age differences summarize the dominant sources of variation in the outcomes of interest, leading Keyfitz (1977, 1) to proclaim that "age is the characteristic variable of population analysis." Analysis of the vital rates (of natality and mortality) in animal or human populations invariably begins with the calculation of age-specific hazards (or rates). It then proceeds to make comparisons of these rates across time and among various groups.

Events occurring to individuals are related back to the population level by the use of *counting* procedures. The demographic

Figure 25.5

Number of disk drive manufacturers in the world (solid line) and in North America (dashed line), 1957–1996.

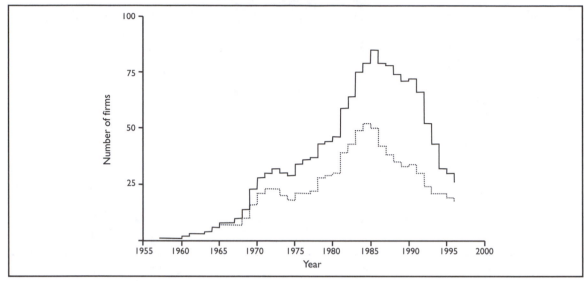

researcher calculates and recalculates population-level measures based on counts of events among individuals in the population. In the simplest case, population size gets incremented or decremented as a result of the simple aggregation of birth and death events. Distributional measures of the population such as the mean and variance in age require more elaborate counting systems. In other analyses, events might be assigned differential weights (special counting rules) based on specific characteristics of the event or those individuals experiencing the events.

Models of demographic systems possess a *coherent and consistent internal logic*. This logic allows demographers to move freely across parts and levels of the system, confident that the consistency of their theories can be checked and that theory fragments can potentially be unified. In a common exercise of this logic, information on vital rates and population characteristics get used in analytical procedures to derive implications for population change and stability.

Formal Demography and Population Studies

Demographers often make a distinction between formal demography and population studies. We think that this distinction provides a useful orientation for understanding how demographic research on corporations might relate to established traditions in demography and organizational studies. In their overview of the discipline, Shryock and Siegel (1971, 2) define formal demography as "concerned with size, distribution, structure and change of populations." This means that formal demographic analysis addresses the flows of vital events in time and develops population-level implications of the flows. Births and deaths (and sometimes migrations) comprise the vital events in biological and human demography. These events occur to individuals in the population, and certain regularities in their timing make it possible to develop mathematical models for their occurrence. From these models, demographers often deduce important information about the population. For example, assuming that birth and death rates do not change, it is straightforward to predict how long it will take a given population to stabilize, meaning that its overall growth or decline rate ceases to vary. It is also possible to derive the age structure of the population at any given time.

What of population studies? According to demographers Hauser and Duncan (1959, 2–3),

Population studies examine not only classic population variables but also the relationships between population changes and other variables: social, economic, political, biological, genetic, geographical, and the like.

This means, of course, that population studies encompass a far broader range of issues and types of research than does formal demography. Population studies is such a broad category that Hauser and Duncan equate the field with the study of the "determinants and consequences of population trends." This definition would include such diverse topics as the impact of war on the population age structure and fertility, the relationship between the automobile and sexual behavior of teenagers, the drinking patterns of middle-aged men during economic depression, the relationship between the strength of familial bonds and the economic incentives to migrate from underdeveloped countries, and the effects of large young cohorts on national consumption, savings, and economic development.

Formal demography and population studies play complementary roles in enhancing our understanding of population processes (Keyfitz 1971). In its classical forms, demography rests on strong assumptions of homogeneity: the only source of variation in vital rates is age (and sometimes sex). This assumption still characterizes much formal demography. It facilitates greatly the development and analysis of mathematical models, which are both elegant and extremely useful. As Kreps (1990, 6–7) has noted, a formal model possesses the advantages of: (1) clarity ("It gives a clear and precise language for communicating insights and contributions."); (2) ease of comparability ("It provides us with general categories of assumptions so that insights and intuitions can be transferred from one context to another and can be cross-checked between different contexts."); (3) logical power ("It allows us to subject particular insights and intuitions to the test of logical consistency."); and (4) analytical precision ("It helps us to trace back from 'observational' to underlying assumptions to see what assumptions are really at the heart of particular conclusions.").

Population studies typically relax the assumption of homogeneity. They might build on the formalisms of demography, but they get much closer to reality by incorporating explicitly information about differences among members of the population. In actual demographic analyses, this heterogeneity is typically linked to individuals, but the source of the heterogeneity might lie at any level, including the environment, the individual's location in the population structure, or intrinsic properties of individuals. Population studies identify the important dimensions of heterogeneity by empirical means, by adding and testing the effects of covariates in models, and by weighting and reweighting various explanatory factors. A population study usually has a more specific concern with the idiosyncratic features of a situation than does a typical formal modeling effort; population studies frequently attempt to explain all the variance in the outcomes of a particular historical context (e.g., fertility rates of Chinese emigrants to California) while formal demography seeks generality. Consequently, population studies might be more informative about any given research problem, but they also tend to be less elegant and less general than formal analyses.

The differences between the orientations of formal analysis and population studies generate some intellectual tension. This can be healthy: formal demography and population studies ideally build on each other in ways that prove productive to each. Population-studies researchers usually find it helpful to have a general model as a point of departure on which to build complexity and heterogeneity, as the specific research context requires. Conversely, formal theorists often look to empirical population studies for facts worth incorporating into their models. In some fields, the interplay between the two orientations spawns a fertile middle ground where beneficial features of both can be found. For example, in the field of evolutionary ecology. . . , theoretical analysis typically results in the development of formal models of the populations of species and their habitats. Much of the information about species behavior (and interrelationships with the environment) used in the model-building enterprise comes from natural-history studies in which researchers have spent years observing and documenting species activity in particular habitats.

Successful research programs in demography typically reflect the orientations of both formal modeling and population studies. Consider again evolutionary ecology. For many research questions, the field contains one or two basic general models of the relevant process along with a series of increasingly detailed models where analysts have built in layers of complexity for certain specified contexts (MacArthur 1972). Such nested series of models develop in research programs whose field investigators uncovered empirical regularities of ever-increasing detail while its theorists devised ways to incorporate these systematic patterns into models of the underlying basic process. This type of theoretically driven, cumulative research program characterizes much demography (Keyfitz 1977).

Demographic Explanation

Demographers and other social scientists often refer to certain explanations as "demographic." What exactly does this mean? For many, it means that outcomes of interest are related to certain types of variables and processes: those related to population characteristics, especially growth and decline. For instance, the argument that China experienced fast economic growth after the reforms of the 1980s because of the vast size of its potential market (approximately 1.2 billion persons) fits this type. For others, a demographic explanation implies mainly a counting of observable indicators. So, in this sense, to explain demographically a firm means to enumerate its employees by age, sex, ethnicity, location in the organizational structure, and the like.

Although neither of these meanings is necessarily misleading, each fails to convey the full analytical potential of demography. In our view, an explanation should be regarded as demographic when it is based on a *decomposition* of the population. An important class of such explanations relates change in the composition of a population to change in social structures and outcomes (Coleman 1964; Stinchcombe 1968). For instance, a simple explanation of this type might be used to explain the trends in firm size discussed above: the longterm decline in size coincides with the dramatic shift of the American economy into the service sector, which is populated by smaller firms (Carroll 1984b).

To give another simple example, consider variations in pension coverage of workers in the United States, which some analysts fear might be declining (thus placing greater pressure on the government's Social Security system). A way to explain this change would be to collect information on a sample of firms and then count those that do and do not provide pensions as part of the employment relation. (We ignore important differences in the types and levels of the pension plan.) Say that 50% of the employees in the whole set of firms have such coverage. Decomposition of the set by various characteristics of firms would typically reveal some large differences in the rate. A demographically inclined decomposition would look first at firm age and size: it would likely show strong associations with rates of pension coverage. For example, firms with more than 1000 employees have coverage rates near 85% while those with fewer than 25 have almost half that level (Reich and Ghilarducci 1997). A finer decomposition would look at such factors as whether the firm's employees are unionized, which would also show a strong association with pension provision (unionized firms have higher rates of coverage across all size classes; the disparity seems greatest for small firms).

Turning back to the original question, why has pension coverage been declining, this type of analysis attempts to explain the decline by examining the growth and decline in groups of firms with differing rates of coverage. In other words, a demographic explanation posits that changes in vital rates alter the compositions of populations; and thereby change features of the social structures based on these populations.

The simplicity of our examples comes in large part from our regarding the vital rates of the various groups of firms composing the population as exogenous. More realistic portrayals relax this assumption and recognize that subgroup vital rates depend upon demographic characteristics of the group or the subpopulation defined by the form. The most interesting of these have to do with population dynamics within and among the compositional elements; these processes tend to be complex and nonlinear.

For example, the figures reviewed above on the historical automobile manufacturers across different countries all show a similar longterm trend of population growth and decline. This regularity reflects in part the operation of endogenous demographic processes of *density dependence* whereby the vital rates depend on the population's size: as population density rises, founding rates climb to apeak and then fall while mortality rates drop and then go up. . . . Similarly, the figures above on the historical number of American beer brewers display a dramatic late upsurge in the population. The increase results wholly from the high founding rates (and low mortality rates) of particular specialist organizational forms (microbrewers, brewpubs, and contract brewers). These form-specific founding rates and mortality rates in turn depend strongly on the extent to which a few organizations in the other population (mass production breweries) dominate the market for beer (in a process called resource partitioning . . .).

Demographic explanations frequently invoke the effects of environmental conditions as well. In organizational demography, researchers analyze the effects of resource abundance, technology, industry structure, sociopolitical institutions, and the presence and scale of other organizational populations in the corporate community. . . . Consideration of these kinds of effects also adds complexity to the analysis. In fact, modern analyses treat these factors as covariates in specifications of (unit-specific) functions of vital rates. . . . For example, estimated mortality models for beer breweries (Carroll and Swaminathan 1992) typically specify effects of variables measuring the size of the potential market (human population), the state of the economy (gross national product), and periods of relevant legislation (the Volstead Act and its later repeal). Other variables (often associated with organizational characteristics) are used as controls (in the case of breweries, organizational size).

From a research-design viewpoint, these specifications represent a middle ground between the approaches of formal demography and population studies. They seek to retain the elegance and generality of a formal model while still incorporating the complexity and specificity of a multivariate analysis.

Figure 25.6 summarizes the general structure of demographic explanations of social structure, using corporate organizations as the focal point. It shows the four general components of argument used in a demographic analysis: the social structure to be explained; the decomposition of the entire set of organizations in the system into constituent organizational populations; the estimation of population-specific vital rates; and the specifications of environmental conditions affecting the rates. The solid arrows depict the dominant flows in the causal structure. Sometimes researchers analyze one or several of these in isolation and treat the causes as exogenous. At other times, analysts consider one or more of the feedback mechanisms in the system, shown by dotted lines in the figure, and build models with endogenous causes.

Finally, there are other, perhaps longer-term feedback mechanisms in the system, shown by the dashed line. Although many theorists agree that these forces operate at some level and over some time frame, they often do not get modeled, explicitly, in part because available theory is not up to the task. . . .

The Demography of the Work Force

Corporate demography is not the only kind of application of demography in organizational settings. A second type involves the demography of the work force of organi-

Figure 25.6

General structure of demographic explanations.

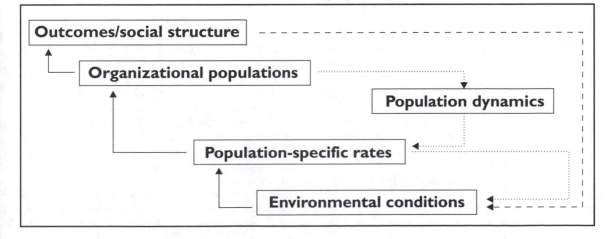

zations, especially its turnover and mobility. Research in this tradition usually adopts an organization-level analysis and posits theory from the perspective of a focal organization. Theoretical arguments often focus on the factors associated with mobility within the organization; however, they obviously have implications for external mobility as well.

Research on mobility within an organization typically focuses on the characteristics and effects of established internal labor markets, which Doeringer and Piore (1971, 1–2) define as:

> an administrative unit, such as a manufacturing plant, within which the pricing and allocation of labor is governed by a set of administrative rules and procedures. The internal labor market . . . is to be distinguished from the external labor market of conventional economic theory where pricing, allocating, and training decisions are controlled by economic variables.

The boundaries between such an enclosed market and the larger labor market mean that the usual effects of sex, ethnicity, social class, industrial sector, and the like will often be muted for internal mobility. That is to say, mobility within an organization with an internal labor market tends to be rationalized according to some personnel plan, be it implicit or explicit (Weber 1968). A person's mobility chances, however, also depend upon his or her location within the structure of the organization itself.

Organizational research on mobility has gone in two directions, one focusing on the work force of the organization and its demographic characteristics, the other based on dimensions of organizational structure. Research on internal work force demography usually involves temporal analysis of career-mobility patterns within a single organization. Studies have demonstrated that rates of mobility within and across organizations are affected by rates of growth and decline of organizations (Keyfitz 1973; Stewman and Konda 1983), the distribution of employee cohorts (Ryder 1965; Brüderl, Preisendörfer, and Ziegler 1989), early career history (Turner 1960; Rosenbaum 1984), vacancy chains (White 1970), and career lines (Spilerman 1977; DiPrete 1987).

Early research on organizational structure and mobility drew pictures of relationships between organizational characteristics, such as the presence of departmen-

tal boundary-spanning units, and average levels of wages and status; Baron (1984) provides a review. Recent work in this tradition addresses issues such as the determinants of internal labor markets, sex segregation in jobs, fragmentation of work, and the opportunity structure within organizations; Carroll et al. (1990) give an overview.

Research on the work force demography of organizations reveals that a wide variety of factors are associated with mobility within and across organizations. Yet very little of this work takes seriously the basic notion that organizational populations change over time and experience demographic pressures of their own. There is, for instance, little consideration given in this literature to the mobility consequences of organizational founding and mortality (for an exception see Haveman and Cohen 1994). Since even a single event might generate massive job turnover and mobility, the demography of corporations and industries deserves consideration in this research context. . . .

Internal Organizational Demography

A third line of demographic research on organizations also goes by the name of organizational demography, but it could more appropriately be labeled as *internal* organizational demography. Most contemporary research on internal organizational demography stems from Pfeffer's (1983) theoretical essay on the topic. In that essay, Pfeffer (1983, 303) defines demography as "the composition, in terms of basic attributes such as age, sex, educational level, length of service or residence, race and so forth of the social unit under study." He adds that "the demography of any social entity is the composite aggregation of the characteristics of the individual members of that entity." Pfeffer makes the straightforward observation that organizations can be readily described this way and he presents a persuasive case for the study of internal organizational demography.

In an approach akin to that of the population-studies tradition, Pfeffer also advances a number of specific theoretical propositions about the causes and consequences of demographic phenomena in organizations. Most of these specific arguments concentrate on the properties of demographic distributions of persons in the focal organization, especially the tenure or length of service (LOS) distribution of members of the organization or its top-management team. The arguments that have attracted the greatest research attention concern the consequences of the LOS distribution on a wide variety of organizational outcomes, including employee turnover, organizational innovation, internal control structures, the power distribution, interorganizational relations, and firm performance (Carroll and Harrison 1998). Although the details of the theorized process depend on the particular outcome, the common general theoretical formulation used in each argument focuses on the unevenness or heterogeneity in the LOS distribution as the demographic variable of primary interest.

In fact, the idea that unevenness (heterogeneity) in the LOS distribution should affect organizational outcomes, such as turnover, constitutes the standard operational framework for virtually all empirical research on internal organizational demography. The framework might seem theoretically stark in that it relies on the statistical association between only two variables: the homogeneity/heterogeneity of the LOS distribution and an organizational outcome. Studies investigating LOS effects, however, usually invoke some kind of social process to motivate the framework theoretically. For example, Wagner, Pfeffer, and O'Reilly (1984, 76) justify investigating the relationship between variation in LOS and turnover with the following explanation:

> Similarity in time of entry into the organization will positively affect the likelihood of persons communicating with others who entered at the same time . . . the more frequent the communication, the more likely it is that those interacting will become similar in terms of their beliefs and perceptions of the organization and how it operates.

Other processes used for explaining LOS-outcome associations include psychological processes of similarity and attraction, social psychological processes of homophily and group dynamics (including especially communication patterns), and sociological processes about norms (Boone and Van Olffen 1997).

Carroll and Harrison (1998) reviewed the 21 major empirical studies conducted within this framework. By most standards, the set of studies is impressive. It includes studies of organizations in the public and private sectors, in a variety of different industries, and in two major national economies (the United States and Japan). Turnover is the most frequently studied outcome; however, various other outcomes have also received attention. Over time, the focus of this research has shifted from entire organizations to work groups within organizations, especially top-management teams. The coefficient of variation in tenure (the standard deviation of tenure divided by the mean of tenure) has also become the most common measure of LOS heterogeneity. Most of the evidence presented in these studies supports theory about the effects of the LOS distribution. By Carroll and Harrison's (1998) count, eleven studies present solid supporting evidence, another four provide weak support, and six offer no support.

So, the main difference among approaches is that we treat the demography *of* corporations and the other two styles of research treat demography *within* corporations. . . .

Note

1. These figures are calculated as the number of relevant persons (counts of the economically active population and major occupational classes taken from the *Labor Yearbook*) over the number of relevant organizations (counts of business entities by major class taken from the *Statistical Abstract of the United States*). That is, they are ratios of independent aggregate counts of persons and organizations. The estimates of size are imprecise in several ways. Most notably, the employee counts include those who work in the public and nonprofit sectors but the firm counts exclude public and nonprofit employers; the numbers also exclude overseas employees of American businesses. Other methods of estimating organizational size sometimes yield radically different estimates.

References

Baron, James N. 1984. "Organizational Perspectives on Stratification." *Annual Review of Sociology* 10:37–69.

Boone, Christophe, and Woody van Olffen. 1997. "The Confusing State of the Art in Top Management Composition Studies: A Theoretical and Empirical Review." Research Memorandum No. 97-11. Netherlands Institute of Business Organization and Strategy, Maastricht.

Brüderl, Joseph, Peter Preisendörfer, and Rolf Ziegler. 1989. "Intraorganizational Career Mobility: The Effects of Individual Characteristics, Hierarchy, Opportunity Structure, Growth, and Cohort Size." Unpublished paper. University of Munich.

Carroll, Glenn R. 1984b. "Organizational Ecology." *Annual Review of Sociology* 10:71–93.

Carroll, Glenn R., and J. Richard Harrison. 1998. "Organizational Demography and Culture: Insights from a Formal Model and Simulation." *Administrative Science Quarterly* 43:637–67.

Carroll, Glenn R., Heather A. Haveman, and Anand Swaminathan. 1990. "Karrieren in Organizationen: Eine ökologische Perspektive." *Kölner Zeitschrift für Soziologie und Sozialpsychologie* (Sonderheft) 31:146–78.

Carroll, Glenn R., and Anand Swaminathan. 1992. "The Organizational Ecology of Strategic Groups in American Brewing Industry From 1975 to 1990." *Industrial and Corporate Change* 1:65–97.

Coleman, James S. 1964. *Introduction to Mathematical Society*. New York: Free Press.

DiPrete, Thomas A. 1987. "The Professionalization of Administration and Equal Employment Opportunity in the U.S. Federal Government." *American Journal of Sociology* 93:119–40.

Doeringer, Peter B., and Michael J. Piore. 1971. *Internal Labor Markets and Manpower Analysis*. Lexington, Mass.: Heath.

Hauser, Philip M., and Otis Dudley Duncan. 1959. *The Study of Population*. Chicago: University of Chicago Press.

Haveman, Heather A., and Lisa E. Cohen. 1994. "The Ecological Dynamics of Careers: The Impact of Organization Founding, Dissolution, and Merger on Job Mobility." *American Journal of Sociology* 100:104–52.

Keyfitz, Nathan. 1971. "Models." *Demography* 8:571–80.

———. 1973. "Individual Mobility in a Stationary Population." *Population Studies* 27:335–52.

———. 1977. *Applied Mathematical Demography*. New York: Wiley.

Kreps, David M. 1990. *Game Theory and Economic Modeling*. Oxford: Oxford University Press.

MacArthur, Robert H. 1972. *Geographical Ecology*. New York: Harper & Row.

Pfeffer, Jeffrey. 1983. "Organizational Demography." Pp. 299–357 in *Research in Organizational Behavior*, Volume 5, edited by L. Cummings and B. Staw. Greenwich, Con.: JAI.

———. 1992. *Managing with Power*. Boston: Harvard Business School Press.

Reich, Michael, and Theresa Ghilarducci. 1997. "Pensions, Unions and Training." Unpublished paper. University of California, Berkeley.

Rosenbaum, James E. 1984. *Career Mobility in a Corporate Hierarchy*. New York: Academic Press.

Ryder, Norman B. 1965. "The Cohort as a Concept of in the Study of Social Change." *American Sociological Review* 30:843–61.

Shryock, H. S., and J. S. Siegel. 1971. *The Methods and Materials of Demography*. Washington: U.S. Bureau of the Census.

Spilerman, Seymour. 1977. "Careers, Labor Market Structure and Socioeconomic Achievement." *American Journal of Sociology* 83:551–93.

Stewman, Shelby, and Suresh Konda. 1983. "Careers and Organizational Labor Markets: Demographic Models of Organizational Behavior." *American Journal of Sociology* 88:637–85.

Stinchcombe, Arthur L. 1968. *Constructing Social Theories*. Chicago: University of Chicago Press.

Turner, Ralph, 1960. "Modes of Social Ascent through Education: Sponsored and Contest Mobility." *American Sociological Review* 25:855–67.

Wagner, W. Gary, Jeffrey Pfeffer, and Charles A. O'Reilly. 1984. "Organizational Demography and Turnover in Top-Management Groups." *Administrative Science Quarterly* 29:74–92.

Weber, Max. 1968. *Economy and Society: An Outline of Interpretive Sociology*. New York: Bedmeister. 3 vols. [Originally published in 1924.]

White, Harrison C. 1970. *Chains of Opportunity*. Cambridge: Harvard University Press.

Chapter 26
Caveat Emptor

The Construction of Nonprofit Consumer Watchdog Organizations

Hayagreeva Rao

What are the main sources of new organizational forms? This chapter continues this theme by considering alternative explanations for the emergence of new social forms, including the role of cultural frames, collective action, and "institutional entrepreneurs." Tracing the historical development of nonprofit consumer watchdog organizations, Hayagreeva Rao explains how this organizational form emerged and became an established part of the organizational landscape in the United States. In Rao's view, new organizational forms emerge out of conflict and politics as contending groups struggle to frame issues, acquire resources, and mobilize for change.

Where new organizational forms come from is one of the central questions of organizational theory. New organizational forms are new embodiments of goals, authority, technology, and client markets. Novel social structures matter because they underpin organizational diversity. The ability of societies to respond to social problems hinges on the diversity of organizational forms, and in the long run, in a fluid environment, diversity can be maintained or increased by the rise of new forms (Hannan and Freeman 1989, p. 3). Moreover, new forms are consequential motors of evolution—indeed, organizational change consists of the replacement of existing organizational forms by new organizational forms (Schumpeter 1950; Astley 1985). Furthermore, since new forms are structural incarnations of beliefs, values, and norms, they emerge in tandem with new institutions and foster cultural change in societies (Durkheim 1950, p. 16; Stinchcombe 1965; Scott 1995).

It is only recently that organizational theorists have begun to analyze the origins of new organizational forms from the standpoint of the random variation, constrained variation, and the cultural-frame institutional perspectives. The *random variation perspective* is premised on biological evolutionary models and holds that realized variations in organizational forms are random. Proponents of this view suggest that new forms arise when search routines lead to modifications of operating routines (Nelson and Winter 1982), or when a small group of competence-sharing organizations is isolated and finds a favorable resource environment (McKelvey 1982). Despite its appeal, the random variation perspective is of limited use since it is difficult to empirically identify competencies and routines. Another major drawback is that it is silent on the specific processes that generate variations and on the content of variations.

The *constrained variation perspective* asserts that conditions in the environment predictably foster or diminish variations in organizational forms. Its different versions emphasize creative destruction through technological innovation (Schumpeter 1950; Tushman and Anderson 1986), environmental imprinting, wherein social conditions at the time of founding limit organizational inventions (Stinchcombe 1965; Kimberly 1975), and existing organizations as producers of new organizational forms (Brittain and Freeman 1982; Lumsden and Singh 1990). A key premise common to all versions of the constrained variation perspective is that the existence of ecospaces unoccupied by other forms is an important precondition for the birth of new organizational forms. Nevertheless, proponents of the constrained variation perspective differ with respect to the antecedents of resource spaces. If models of creative destruction hold that the demise of existing organizations frees resources for new organizations, then models of environmental imprinting stress the importance of political upheavals (Carroll, Delacroix, and Goodstein 1990), entrepreneurs' access to wealth and power, labor markets, and the protective role of the state (see Aldrich 1979). By contrast, those who portray existing organizations as producers of new organizations hold that interrelations among existing organizations influence the branching of new resource spaces (Carroll 1984) and the ability of existing or-

383

ganizations to exploit new resource spaces (Romanelli 1989). Although the constrained variation perspective usefully emphasizes the primacy of resource spaces, its drawback is that resources do not preexist as pools of free-floating assets but have to be mobilized through opportunistic and collective efforts (Van de Ven and Garud 1989). Another defect is that the constrained variation perspective elides how formal structures become imbued with norms, values, and beliefs during the process of resource mobilization by entrepreneurs.

The *cultural-frame institutional perspective* complements the constrained variation perspective and proposes that new organizational forms arise when actors with sufficient resources see in them an opportunity to realize interests that they value highly. A core premise is that the creation of all new organizational forms requires an institutionalization project wherein the theory and values underpinning the form are legitimated by institutional entrepreneurs (DiMaggio 1988, p. 18). In this perspective, institutional projects can arise from organized politics or social movements. When they arise from organized politics, they still also resemble social movements in that the resources and interests of actors are not fixed and the rules governing interaction are contested (Padgett and Ansell 1993; Fligstein 1996a, p. 5). The cultural-frame institutional perspective on the rise of new organizational forms is, as yet, emergent and needs to "pay more attention to preexisting institutional conditions, what the alternative institutional projects are in a given situation, and the political process by which projects win out" (Fligstein 1996a, p. 27) and to "direct attention to the role of professionalization in the institutionalization of new forms, and more generally, to the establishment of fieldwide environments around the forms" (DiMaggio 1991, p. 289).

These gaps in the cultural-frame institutional perspective supply the motivation for this article to analyze the institutional production of nonprofit consumer watchdog organizations (CWOs) in the United States. CWOs are social control specialists who institutionalize distrust of agents by inspecting their performance on behalf of their clients and who sustain social order (Luhmann 1979; Zucker 1986; Shapiro 1987). For-profit CWOs like Morningstar and Lipper Analytical Services inform cus-

tomers by disseminating evaluations of mutual funds. By contrast, nonprofit CWOs such as Consumers Union and the Council for Responsible Genetics evaluate products and technologies, lobby legislators and governmental agencies, and educate consumers about their rights. Unlike for-profit CWOs, nonprofit CWOs do not distribute surpluses as profits to shareholders.

Nonprofit CWOs are a significant outcropping of the social organization of distrust. Since the formation of the first nonprofit CWO, Consumers Research in 1927, the number of national-level nonprofit CWOs in the United States has surged to 200 in 1995 (Bykerk and Manney 1995). Some national nonprofit CWOs are "second-order associations" (composed of other organizations as members), focusing on lobbying legislators and government, whereas other national nonprofit CWOs are "first-order associations," consisting of individual members. In 1995, the largest second-order association, the Consumer Federation of America (started in 1967) consisted of 240 national and regional organizations whose total membership was more than 50 million members. The largest first-order association was Consumers Union with 4.9 million members (Bykerk and Manney 1995). By virtue of their monitoring, lobbying, and educational activities, national nonprofit CWOs have induced American business firms to create special-purpose departments concerned with consumer affairs. Indeed, a new professional group called the Society for Consumers Affairs Professionals in Business was set up in 1973, and by 1988, it had 750 large firms as members (Fornell 1988). Non profit CWOs coexist with watchdogs specializing in environmental, civil rights, child welfare, animal welfare, voter rights, and human rights sectors. In a study of the American nonprofit watchdog community, Meyer and Imig (1993) reported 196 national watchdogs that sought to influence legislation in the consumer, child welfare, animal rights, civil rights, and antipoverty sectors. Although watchdogs in these sectors perform specialized functions, there is some interpenetration. Thus, prominent environmental watchdogs also espouse consumer agendas (Bykerk and Manney 1995); for example, Greenpeace promotes the idea that consumers ought to be environmentally responsible by purchasing "green" goods and disciplines errant firms by organizing consumer boycotts.

Despite their importance, there is a dearth of research on the social origins of nonprofit CWOs. Sociologists have analyzed nongovernmental nonprofit watchdogs such as accrediting bodies (Wiley and Zald 1968) and professional societies (Briloff 1972; Freidson 1986) but have overlooked the cultural origins of nonprofit CWOs. The burgeoning literature on consumerism glosses over how institutional dynamics shape the design of nonprofit CWOs. Brobeck (1990, p. xxxii) surveyed 943 articles on consumer organizations and concluded that there was insufficient empirical research on the cultural origins of nonprofit consumer organizations, their advocacy and interrelationships, and their linkages with other organizations. In their detailed review of consumption, Frenzen, Hirsch, and Zerrillo (1994, p. 410) noted that the "processual linking of producers and consumers is a rich, though still unexplored, research arena for economic sociology, with available archival and contemporary data sources waiting to be mined." If variability in the social organization of distrust is to be understood, as Shapiro (1987) recommends, then the study of the cultural origins of nonprofit CWOs is essential. Below, I begin by elaborating cultural-frame institutional arguments on the rise of new forms, and thereafter, I present a detailed case study of the formation of Consumers Research and Consumers Union to demonstrate cultural-frame institutional arguments.

Institutional Dynamics and the Rise of New Forms

The starting point of cultural-frame institutionalism is that new forms do not arise automatically in resource spaces but have to be constructed from prevalent cultural materials. In turn, detailed attention to the process of the construction of new forms devolves into an analysis of institutional entrepreneurs (Granovetter 1994). Institutional entrepreneurs are ideological activists who combine hitherto unconnected beliefs and norms into an organizational solution to a problem (Becker 1963).

Entrepreneurs, Frames, and Legitimacy

Stinchcombe (1968, p. 194) asserts that the entrepreneurial creation of new forms "is preeminently a political phenomenon" because support has to be mobilized for the goals, authority structure, technology, and clients embodied in the new form. In some cases, resource spaces unoccupied by other forms may exist, but the existence of such unfilled resource spaces does not mean that "free floating" resources are easily available to potential entrepreneurs. Entrepreneurs have to assemble resources, to legitimate the new form, and to integrate it with the prevalent institutional order. In other cases, resource spaces for a new form may not exist, and entrepreneurs have to construct these spaces by defining opportunity, by identifying distinctive resources, and by prying them away from existing uses. Since entrepreneurs are trying to convince others to go along with their view, the formation of new industries and forms resembles social movements (Fligstein 1996b, pp. 663–64).

Social movement theorists propose that institutional entrepreneurs can mobilize legitimacy, finances, and personnel through the use of frames (McAdam, McCarthy, and Zald 1988). Frames define the grievances and interests of aggrieved constituencies, diagnose causes, assign blame, provide solutions, and enable collective attribution processes to operate (Snow and Benford 1992, p. 150). Thus, frames are theories that justify an organizational form—an incarnation of goals, authority, technology, and clients, as indispensable, valid, and appropriate. Frames are tools of unobtrusive influence and can shape people's "perceptions, cognitions, and preferences in such a way that they accept their role . . . either because they see or imagine no alternative to it, or because they view it as natural" (Lukes 1974, p. 24). In "much the same way that pictures are framed, questions and actions are framed, and the context in which they are viewed and discussed determines what gets done . . . setting the context is a critical strategy for exercising power and influence" (Pfeffer 1992, p. 202).

Institutional entrepreneurs create frames by selecting items from a preexisting cultural menu (Meyer and Rowan 1977, p. 345). Swidler (1986, p. 277) suggests that a culture is not a "unified system that pushes action in a consistent direction. Rather it is more of a 'tool kit' or a repertoire from which actors select differing pieces for constructing lines of action." Douglas (1986) points out that bricolage is an important method by which entrepreneurs construct new cognitive models and formal structures. Thus, entrepreneurs can recombine elements from existing repertoires through imitation or consciously revise existing models on the basis of their training in other organizations.

Multiple Frames and Conflict

Politics become obtrusive when an unfilled resource space "calls forth and permit a range of definitions of the situation" (Zald and McCarthy 1980, p. 6) and when rival coalitions of issue entrepreneurs champion incompatible frames. Even as entrepreneurs may draw on a generalized Western cultural account (Meyer, Boli, and Thomas 1987) and justify their actions on the basis of the widely accepted myths of progress and justice, there is a wide scope for conflict over the practical implications of the western cultural account in the construction of new organizational forms. As moderates plead for progress and radicals glorify justice and clash like tectonic plates, interorganizational conflict ensues. Which frame and its organizational embodiment should be chosen to define and organize an activity is a political question (DiMaggio 1994; Tarrow 1989). Friedland and Alford (1991, pp. 240–42) propose that the creation of new organizational forms unfolds at three levels of analysis, with "individuals competing and negotiating, organizations in conflict and coordination, and institutions in contradiction and interdependency. . . . We conceive of these levels of analysis as 'nested,' where organization and institution specify higher levels of constraint and opportunity for individual action."

When multiple frames and forms vie with each other, why one form is chosen and why other roads are not pursued hinge on larger constellations of power and social structure (Brint and Karabel 1991, p. 346). Struggles to produce new meanings and new social structures are, therefore, the motors of cultural change in societies (Tarrow 1989), and these tussles unfold in an organizational field where the state and the professions play an important role (DiMaggio and Powell 1983).

The state constrains the creation of new forms as a collective actor and as an institutional structure (Campbell and Lindberg 1990). As a set of semiautonomous actors, agencies of the state grant charters, allocate finance or monopoly status, and impose taxes and regulatory controls. Baron, Dobbin, and Jennings (1986) showed that personnel offices arose as document providers because firms had to file "manning tables" enumerating manpower needs and jobs in response to employment stabilization policies instituted by the federal government during World War II. As an institutional structure, the structure of the state, whether it is fragmented or centralized, affects organizational structures. Moreover, the executive, legislative, and judicial arms of the state also serve as arenas within which conflicts within and among organizations are adjudicated. Finally, states have the capacity to define and enforce property rights, rules that determine the conditions of ownership and the control of the means of production (Campbell and Lindberg 1990, p. 635).

Professions shape the rise of new organizational forms by providing cognitive frameworks and by spawning formal structures to create and defend jurisdictional claims (Freidson 1986; Abbott 1990). Professionals can be conservatives in organizational roles and simultaneously use field wide organizations to reform the system that employs them. In the case of museums, administrative professionals dominated fieldwide structures and were at the forefront of debate about whether museums were to be structured like libraries, symphony orchestras, or department stores (DiMaggio 1991, p. 287). Professionals such as personnel experts and labor attorneys can also overstate legal threats (Sutton and Dobbin 1996) and can encourage organizations to institute defenses such as grievance procedures. Alternatively, professionals who are sited outside organizations can impel organizations to conform to models dominant in the profession—thus, firms have been shown to dediversify when there is a mismatch between the industries in which the firm competes and the industry coverage of the financial analysts who follow it (Zuckerman 1996).

Apart from the state and the professions, the organizational field also consists of key suppliers, resource and product consumers, regulatory agencies, and other organizations that produce similar goods and services (DiMaggio and Powell 1983; DiMaggio 1994). Some of these actors may support a given frame, others may champion rival frames, and uncommitted organizations may withhold judgment and be neutral. It is in this multiorganizational field that institutional entrepreneurs interpret grievances, exchange evaluations, forge alliances, and joust with antagonists (Klandermans 1992). If alliances provide resources and opportunities for entrepreneurs, antagonists drain resources and restrict opportunities.

Boundaries of Forms

These arguments suggest that both entrepreneurs and frame conflict play a substantial role in bundling goals, authority structure, technologies, and clients into new organizational forms. Although organizational economists assert that technical considerations, especially transaction costs, determine "efficient boundaries" of organizational forms (Williamson 1985), institutional dynamics, as Hannan and Freeman (1989, pp. 43–59) note, play a double-edged role—they can blend differences among organizational forms or segregate activities into distinct organizational forms.

On the one hand, institutional processes can erode distinctions among organizational forms. Thus, bricolage can blur distinctions among organizational forms. Institutional entrepreneurs can recombine elements from existing repertoires by imitation into new theories or frames or by consciously redesigning existing theories of organization (Douglas 1986). Similarly, copying errors can lead to the accumulation of small unintended changes and can blur differences among forms as organizations diverge from common models (Powell 1991). Deinstitutionalization, wherein the rules defining social and technical boundaries are broken by the passage of legislation or by the crossover of personnel can also eliminate distinctions among forms (Oliver 1992).

Arguably, institutional processes are the "important segregating mechanism" (Hannan and Freeman 1989, p. 54). New forms become established when a powerful actor (e.g., the state) endorses the claims of social actors using a form, or when a form becomes taken for granted as the way to organize activities. Collective action by members of a group can also foster distinctions among forms (e.g., the formation of trade associations). Moreover, closure of social networks through inbreeding and replication (Powell 1991) can also encode distinctions among forms.

Hannan and Freeman (1989. p. 60) observe that segregating and blending processes are not stages in an evolutionary process but are subprocesses that simultaneously edit organizational diversity. Rival bands of entrepreneurs can construct incompatible frames through bricolage and can promote structural proposals that are recombinations of preexisting organizational models. When rival blends vie for dominance, politics determine which frame is chosen and how boundaries are imposed on organizational activities. The success of collective action efforts and the endorsement of powerful actors shape the selection of a frame and the concomitant choice of organizational boundaries. Collective action and the endorsement of powerful actors become even more important when technical differences among rival frames and structural proposals are minimal. In cases where the criteria for a good technical solution are contested, political and institutional processes shape not only what organizations can do, but which organizations can exist (Powell 1991, pp. 186–87).

The coalition that garners the greatest political support will find that its frame will be privileged (Brint and Karabel 1991, p. 355; McAdam 1994). Whether a coalition wins or not hinges on its size, the existence of political opportunity, the attitude of state actors, its support from professionals, and its ability to build a political coalition around an identity (Fligstein 1996b, p. 664). Thus, the scope of the form (i.e., the goals, authority structure, technology, and clients subsumed by the form) are outcomes of contending attempts at control and competing quests to impose a preferred definition of the identity of the constituencies that benefit from the form (White 1992).

Nelson and Winter (1982, pp. 109–11) propose that intraorganizational routines become *operative* only when there is a comprehensive truce or when there is a cessation of conflict amongst members of an organization. Analogously, the boundaries of a new organizational form become established and the new form becomes integrated into an community of organizations only when there is a truce amongst the constituents of the organizational field about which frame is used to organize activities. Like truces among nations, truces among rival institutional entrepreneurs can also be unequal, with some winning a larger slice of the cake and as a result, having a privileged position for their frame.

March and Olsen (1989) suggest that conflicts may be resolved through the logic of aggregation and give and take, or the logic of integration wherein one of the parties can learn from the other and even convert to the other's point of view. Those who lose can exit the arena, concentrate on a different niche or even embrace the ascendant frame. When the proponents of a losing frame abandon deviant ideas and capitulate by adopting the ascendant frame, they can "normalize" themselves and become integrated into the social system (Hirsch 1986).

Truces increase the capacity for collective action by reducing comprehensiveness; some points of view arc ignored or suppressed. The terms of a truce among rival institutional entrepreneurs can never be completely explicit. thus, the maintenance of truces depends upon the disincentives for actors for engaging in provocative actions and the defensive alertness of parties keen on preserving the status quo. As a result, just like intraorganizational routines, organizational forms are "confined to extremely narrow channels by the dikes of vested interest. Adaptations that appear 'obvious' and 'easy' to an external observer may be foreclosed because they involve a perceived threat to the . . . political equilibrium" (Nelson and Winter 1982, p. 111).

The Formation of Nonprofit CWOs in America

Historians of the consumer movement recognize three eras: the antiadulteration movement culminating in the passage of the Pure Food and Drugs Act of 1906, the rise of nonprofit consumer watchdogs such as Consumers Research and the Consumers Union in the 1930s, and legal activism commencing with Ralph Nader's crusade for product safety in the 1960s (Hermann 1970).

This article focuses on the second wave of activism because it witnessed the rise of nonprofit CWOs as a new organizational farm. The early history of a new organizational form, as Scott (1995, p. 147) notes, is a period of coevolution in which existing institutional arrangements are delegitimated and new norms and beliefs are being constructed. This article relies on a wide variety of archival and publicly available sources—documents of the Consumers Union, Consumers Research, newspapers, census statistics, and writings of issue entrepreneurs and historians. Historical research on the origins of an organizational form provides greater breadth than conventional ethnography and enables us to derive a historically informed understanding of organizations (DiMaggio 1991, 1994). In order to demonstrate how nonprofit CWOs emerged as a new organizational form, I begin by discussing organizational precursors to nonprofit CWOs: standards and testing organizations and consumer leagues.

Precursor Organizations

Standards and testing organizations were an important organizational precursor to nonprofit CWOs and arose around 1900 as proponents of the idea of removing wasteful variety through standardization. By contrast, consumer leagues that arose in the early part of the 20th century sought to improve standards of living.

Standards and testing organizations.— Standards and testing organizations were mainly extensions of trade associations and professional societies seeking to promulgate common metrics to assist business organizations. In 1894, an association of insurance underwriters (Underwriters Laboratory) received a charter to certify wires and light fixtures as fire resistant in order to build insurable real estate. Other trade associations established standard nomenclatures and performance specifications in the wool blanket and laundry industries.

A professional society of engineers called the Society of Automotive Engineers (SAE) was established in 1906 for the explicit purpose of standardizing the supply of components to automobile manufacturers. Instead of having numerous suppliers making incompatible components, the SAE initially laid down 600 specific standards to ensure the interchangeability of components and thereby increased the size of the potential market for parts manufacturers and ensured reliability for auto producers (Chase and Schlink 1927). Similarly, materials testing experts promulgated standards for paint, and electrical engineers developed standards for electrical components for large business enterprises.

Standard-setting bodies that arose as extensions of trade associations and professional societies induced action by governmental authorities. The National Bureau of Standards (established in 1901) instituted annual national conferences on weights and measures and the *Journal of Weights and Measures* was set up in 1908 for the "benefit of Dealers, Sealers, and the Purchasing Public." During World War I, the War Industries Board pushed producers to standardize products and conserve resources, so much so that colors of typewriter ribbons were reduced from 150 to 6 colors, automobile tires from 287 types to 9, and buggy wheels from 232 sizes to 4 (Cochrane 1966). After the war, the American Standards Association was formed in 1919 and persuaded hundreds of firms to adopt common standards with the active support of the National Bureau of Standards and the then–commerce secretary, Herbert Hoover, in a bid to improve efficiency.

Large private corporations such as General Motors, General Electric, Westinghouse, and American Telephone and Telegraph also set up special purpose departments to establish standards for devices. American Telephone and Telegraph was reputed to have saved a million dollars because of the use of a standardized repeater in long distance lines (Chase and Schlink 1927, p. 235).

Consumer leagues.—Unlike standards and testing organizations that were extensions of professions and trade associations, consumer leagues were loosely modeled on trade unions. If trade unions used the threat of a strike to discipline employers, consumer leagues relied on the threat of a boycott to push for better prices and standards of living. Generally, these consumer leagues had visible involvement from women activists and, on occasion, trade union leaders and often depended on women's groups for support.

The earliest such organization, the National Consumer League, was founded in 1899 to ameliorate the plight of child labor and had many women members. Florence Kelley, the first executive director, a former chief factory inspector and attorney, stated that the major aim of the organization was to "moralize" the demand function of consumer power so that workers received fair living wages, goods were produced under sanitary conditions, and the interests of the community were promoted (Kelley 1899, p. 290). By contrast, other consumer leagues were concerned about the effect of prices on the standard of living. Bureaus of labor statistics in different states had legitimized the linkage between wages, prices, and consumption by conducting cost-of-living inquiries. Massachusetts was the first to create a state labor bureau of statistics, and by 1885, 14 other states had followed suit. By 1910, cost-of-living inquiries referred to the consumer as a category of actors (Samson 1980, p. 114).

Rising food and meat prices motivated attempts to organize consumer leagues. The National Anti-Food Trust League started in 1909, had the president of District of Columbia's Central Labor Union as a member (Samson 1980, p. 152), but it failed to go beyond organizing a few hearings. A consumer boycott of meat in 1910 was organized in Cleveland by the city's central labor union, and 100,000 people signed a pledge not to eat meat for 30 days. Soon, boycotts sprang up in Pittsburgh, Kansas City, and Baltimore, but they failed because of poor organization, the lack of solidarity, and the inability of meat producers to bear lower prices.

By 1910, a few buying clubs consisting of housewives had also begun to appear on the horizon. The same year the Housekeepers Cooperative Association was organized in Pittsburgh with the intent of providing advice on spending and on defeating unscrupulous practices. The Federated Marketing Club was organized in Chicago in 1911 to publish daily lists of bargains and had a board consisting of the presidents of the Illinois Federation of Women's Clubs, the Cook County Federation of Women's Clubs, and the Chicago Federation of Labor. In 1911, a Housewives League was started in New York to ensure accurate weights and measures. A butter boycott was successfully prosecuted, the National Association of Housewives' Leagues was established in 1912, and a magazine called *Housewives League* was rolled out to "represent the consumer in the fight to reduce the cost of living" (Samson 1980, p. 160). The First World War saw the league championing conservation, but by the end of the war, consumer leagues had become moribund due to the lack of support and the waning of inflation.

Distinctiveness of nonprofit CWOs.—Nonprofit CWOs were an important departure from standard-setting organizations and consumer leagues. Unlike standard-setting bodies that were extensions of trade associations and professional societies, nonprofit CWOs were formally separate from the industries they monitored and were explicitly oriented to the needs and interests of consumers. Unlike consumer leagues that were extensions of women's clubs or relied primarily on women for support, nonprofit CWOs served both men and women. If consumer leagues sought to ensure lower prices, nonprofit CWOs aimed to protect consumers (by deterring fraud, promoting product safety), to educate consumers (by providing literacy and decision-making skills), to lobby legislators, and to inform consumers (via best buy recommendations in the consumer goods, health, and consumer finance industries). How was this form established? How did it emerge as a departure from its organizational precursors? How were its boundaries defined? Below, I address these issues by discussing how a resource space or niche initially arose for nonprofit CWOs.

Emergence of a Resource Space for Nonprofit CWOs

Rising expenditures on consumer durables, mounting complexity of product choices, changes in the pattern of advertising, and lack of product liability rules created the social context that made it possible for institutional entrepreneurs to mobilize resources for the establishment of nonprofit CWOs as solutions.

Durable goods expenditures.—Disposable income, in 1970 dollars, registered a fivefold increase from $14.1 billion in 1901 to $74.5 billion in 1930 (U.S. Bureau of the Census 1975). As disposable income grew, individuals were able to purchase a wider array of consumer durables, and they began to account for a greater share of disposable income (Olney 1991). Table 26.1 shows changes in the average allocation of durable goods expenditures. It reveals that the share of transport vehicles jumped from 6.4% in the period 1899–1908 to 28.3% in the period 1919–28. The spurt rise in automobile purchases was spurred by installment buying and by the growth of personal finance companies that allowed individuals to purchase goods through credit. Furniture and household appliances accounted for virtually all other major consumer durable goods spending. Electrification provided an impetus for the purchase of household appliances. In 1907, only 8% of homes in America had electricity, but by 1925, 53.2% had electricity (U.S. Bureau of the Census 1975). Households with electricity were a lucrative market for clothes washers, refrigerators, and radios. Old products like the broom, unchanged since ancient Egypt, were superseded by new products like the vacuum cleaner (Silber 1983, p. 10). Table 26.1 also shows that china, tableware, watches, and jewelry were the most purchased minor consumer durable goods.

Table 26.1
Average Allocation of Durable Goods Expenditures (%), 1900–1928

	1899–1908	*1909–18*	*1919–28*
Transport vehicles	6.4	10.3	28.3
Furniture	30.8	24.8	22.5
Household appliances	3.3	3.7	4.1
Entertainment appliances	1.0	1.3	1.5
All major durable goods	41.6	40.0	56.5
China and tableware	19.5	23.0	14.0
House furnishings	21.1	18.5	14.7
Watches and jewelry	6.9	7.8	5.5
Medical products	1.0	1.9	1.9
Books and maps	7.9	6.6	5.6
Miscellaneous	2.0	2.2	1.9
All minor durable goods	58.4	60.0	43.5
Total	100	100	100

Source—Olney (1991), pp. 37–45.

Note—All estimates are based on constant 1982 price estimates using Bureau of Economic Analysis data.

Table 26.2
Automobile Sales by Price Classes (%), 1903–26

Car Price (in dollars)	1903	1908	1913	1918	1923	1926
Low:						
< 675	4.2	5.0	46.6	41.6	62.2	51.6
Medium:						
676–875	22.1	18.8	.5	11.6	7.5	8.5
876–1,375	42.4	19.5	19.9	33.5	13.2	24.7
High:						
1,376–1,775	6.1	10.6	13.7	6.0	8.8	7.5
1,776–2,275	1.7	10.4	10.2	3.9	5.2	3.2
2,276–2,775	12.0	16.6	3.9	1.1	1.4	2.4
Luxury:						
2,776–3,775	7.6	3.5	2.6	1.7	1.2	1.3
3,776–4,775	2.6	10.4	1.6	.4	.4	.5
> 4,776	1.3	5.2	1.0	.2	.1	.3

Source: The data on percentage of shares by share classes are drawn from Epstein's (1929) survey of auto producers.

As products like the icebox were replaced by automatic electric refrigerators, consumers had to choose technologically complex products with which they had little familiarity. Moreover, individuals with wealth, as Veblen (1919) noted, were able to construct personal styles through the purchase of consumer durables. These styles were imitated by others in the social ladder so that the status conferred by a consumer durable good mattered more than its usefulness. Indeed, products enabled individuals to extend their definition of self and to augment their personal identities as distinctive individuals (Schudson 1978).

Complexity of product choice.—Product comparison became costlier with an increased number of price classes and a rising number of brands within each price class. Table 26.2 shows that consumers could buy cars in four price classes and often had to choose among price categories within a price class. In each price class, a purchase involved a comparison of several producers. In 1918, for example, the medium-priced producers, who accounted for 43.2% of all cars sold, included Willys-Overland, Buick, Dodge, Chevrolet, Maxwell, Studebaker, Saxon, Reo, Regal, Briscoe, Grant, Hupp, Dort, and Mitchell, each of whom allowed consumers to choose a plethora of options (Thomas 1977)

By 1926, annual model changes powered by the doctrine of planned obsolescence led to an emphasis on style and aesthetic appeal rather than mechanical performance. Paid advertising for automobiles exploded from $1 million a year in 1901 to $4 million in 1914 and $41 million in 1926 (1.5% of the wholesale value of industry output; Thomas 1977, p. 236). Thus, consumer choice began to be influenced by style rather than substance.

The changing pattern of advertising.—In 1900, $542 million was spent on advertising through newspapers, radio, outdoor, and miscellaneous media. By 1930, advertising expenditures had grown to $2.6 billion (U.S. Bureau of the Census 1975). Newspapers, especially Sunday newspapers, began to cover fashion, etiquette, beauty, hygiene, and clothing by having special "advice" columns for women on how to use products to acquire social status and to signal it discreetly (Schudson 1978, pp. 100–102). In 1902, *Good Housekeeping*, a Hearst publication, developed a "Seal of Approval" for goods it judged worthy of advertising space in its pages.

Table 26.3, drawn from Pollay (1985) documents changes in the pattern of advertising during the period 1900–1930. It reveals changes in who advertised: The share of direct marketers dropped from 50% in the

1900s to 4% in the 1930s whereas advertisements from manufacturers rose from 48% in the 1900s to 94% in the 1930s. The rhetorical focus of advertising also changed. Advertisements based on appeals to logic shrank from 62% in the 1900s to 35% in the 1930s, and advertisements appealing to emotion (pathos) rose from 27% in the 1900s to 42% in the 1930s. Advertisers sought to manipulate greed, envy, and fear. Listerine evoked the fear of halitosis in its campaign, "even your best friend won't tell you," and in concert with other products, these campaigns led to the discovery of bodily functions as targets of marketing opportunity (Fox 1984). The content of the advertisement also changed as advertisements depicting products and people shot up from 34% in the 1900s to 72% in the 1930s. Celebrity testimonials extolled products: the queen of Romania explained why she entrusted her skin to Pond's cold cream in advertisements, and movie stars like Joan Crawford shared why they used Lux soap. Finally, table 26.3 shows that the tactical focus of advertisements was also transformed. In the 1900s, 59% of advertisements emphasized product features, but by the 1930s, only 20% did so. Instead, the 1930s advertisements began to stress the benefits accruing from the product and the risks that could be avoided by using the product. Taken together, all of these changes suggest that, as Veblen (1919) lamented, the fabrication of consumers had become a routine operation much like a mechanical industry.

The lack of product liability rules.—A 1923 study of 244 advertisements by Stuart Chase found 44 advertisements that were palpably false and 28 cases where harmful products were touted as useful (Vaile 1927). But consumers possessed restricted legal rights and had little recourse when faced with defective or harmful products of poor quality. The period 1860–1920 was dominated by the doctrine of negligence, wherein ideas of privity, contributory negligence, and assumption of risk were applied to deny plaintiffs recovery and to impede consumer rights (Spacone 1985). Under the notion of privity, manufacturers had no obligation to a party to which it was not in direct contract (e.g., passengers in a car could not sue the manufacturer for a defect in the car). Similarly, the assumption of risk meant that consumers had accepted some risk when they purchased a product or used a service. Due to these restrictive ideas,

Table 26.3
Changing Patterns of Advertising, 1900–1930

Dimension	% of Ads Examined			
	1900s	1910s	1920s	1930s
Advertisers:				
Manufacturers	48	80	82	94
Direct marketers	50	17	12	4
All other	2	2	5	2
Rhetorical focus:				
Source (ethos)	11	7	14	24
Tone (pathos)	27	25	30	42
Logic (logos)	62	68	56	35
Depiction:				
Product only	19	21	14	9
People only	29	15	23	17
Product and people	34	57	61	72
Neither	18	7	2	3
Tactical focus:				
Product features	59	43	29	20
Benefits to be gained	40	54	62	63
Risks to be avoided	1	4	8	17

Source—Pollay (1985).

there were very few product liability cases, and the few cases that were decided invariably cited negligence and tort cases to legitimate their claims. Table 26.4 provides a decennial count for the period 1900–1930. It shows that the number of product liability cases was in single digits and that, as the number of cases inched upward, the tendency to cite negligence and tort cases to justify claims of liability diminished. One landmark case, *MacPherson v. Buick Motor Co.*, was decided in 1916 by the New York Court of Appeals, and Justice Cardozo weakened the privity requirement when he ruled that a manufacturer was liable if any product was inherently dangerous or if it was dangerously and negligently manufactured. However, the small number of product liability cases suggests that the idea of liability was not firmly established before 1930. Legal historians suggest that it was only from 1930 onward that scholars, especially Friedrich Kessler and Fleming James, led the movement for tort reform by attacking the premises of contract and negligence law

Table 26.4
Product Liability Cases in American Courts, 1900–1930

Decennial	No. of Product Liability Cases	No. of Negligence/Tort Cases Cited
1900–1910	3	59
1911–20	4	28
1921–30	7	14

Note: Product liability cases are from Madden (1988) and Vandall (1989). Negligence and tort cases cited in the product liability cases come from court reporters (e.g., *Northeast Reporter, Southeast Reporter, Southwest Reporter, Federal Reporter, Pacific Reporter*).

and by inventing the idea of enterprise liability (Priest 1984). It was only in the late 1950s and early 1960s that the *MacPherson v. Buick Motor Co.* case was followed in several jurisdictions and served to undermine the ideas of privity and negligence (Spacone 1985, p. 22).

CWOs as Impartial Testing Agencies: Consumers Research

Sporadic attempts backed by women's organizations to improve the lot of the consumer arose but did not flourish. Thus, attempts by the Federated Marketing Club in Chicago (1911), the Housewives' League in New York (1911), and the National Association of Housewives' Leagues (1912) to provide bulletins of prices failed as inflation declined. It was against this backdrop that two issue entrepreneurs, Stuart Chase and Frederick Schlink, diagnosed the problems facing consumers and framed a new social control mechanism as the solution—the CWO.

The impartial testing frame.—Chase, an accountant by profession who was affiliated with Veblen in Howard Scott's ephemeral Technocratic movement, wrote two polemics entitled *The Challenge of Waste* (1922) and *The Tragedy of Waste* (1925) and castigated the riot of products that were detrimental to man and outside the category of wants. With Frederick Schlink, who was an ex-employee of the National Bureau of Standards and the National Standards Association, Chase in 1927 wrote *Your Money's Worth*, which became an instant best-seller. Chase and Schlink portrayed the consumer as an "Alice" in a wonderland created by advertising and product differentiation. They blamed manufacturers for failing to *serve* the consumer by instead creating wasteful variety. They noted that a "housewife needing a sewing machine needle might as well look for one in a haymow as on a neighbor's machine. Such needles are made in nine diameters . . . and in lengths varying by as little as one thirty-second of an inch" (Chase and Schlink 1927, p. 174). Chase and Schlink (1927, p. 2) attacked advertising for deceiving consumers, deriding the "conflicting claims, bright promises, fancy packages, soaring words, and almost impenetrable ignorance" and asserted that modern marketing practices impeded consumers' access to the benefits of mass production.

Consumers were urged to imitate Schlink's consumer's club established in a church in White Plains, New York. This neighborhood club prepared two "confidential lists"—one carrying "products considered to be of good value in relation to their price; the second, products, one might well avoid, whether on account of inferior quality, unreasonable price, or of false and misleading advertising" (Chase and Schlink 1927, p. 254). The book sparked hundreds of inquiries, and Schlink transformed the neighborhood club into Consumers Research (CR)—an organization that sought to serve as an "economist, scientist, and an accountant" (Silber 1983, p. 18). The list was renamed as the *Consumers Research Bulletin* that would "investigate, test, and report reliably hundreds of commodities" (Silber 1983, p. 18).

The organization embodied a new mechanism for the social control of business (its target) and consumers (its clients). It explicitly stated that its aim was to readjust the "rapidly increasing power of the manufacturer and seller over the mind and judgment of the consumer" (CR 1932, p. 1). As a social control device. CR aimed to promote new norms of consumption. . . .

The new organization sought to reform the system of production so that waste was reduced and producers *served* customers by making goods needed by customers and charging fair prices. The tools of control were product standards and scientific tests. Efficiency was a valued norm and was to be promoted by reducing wasteful variety through standardization. CR also aimed to replace magic in salesmanship with the norm of scientific analysis, so that facts rather than emotions would guide consumption. Consumers were exhorted to be rational and vigilant and to use the information provided by tests to extract the most value for their dollar. Finally, the organization sought to signal its impartiality through its nonprofit structure and its distance from political parties.

Legitimating the Impartial Testing Frame

As an embodiment of a new form of social control, CR encountered very little opposition except some stray attacks, despite its vigorous assaults on manufacturers and advertisers. One writer foresaw a future society in which a man who did not like standard coffee was arrested for buying an unauthorized brand (Stoddard 1928, pp. 117–20). But in the main, CR's attacks evoked little opposition from business firms, advertisers, or even state authorities.

The absence of conflict does not mean that CR's birth was a plain story of an organization emerging to fulfill a need in the marketplace. Instead, it suggests that CR's founders had deftly defused opposition by their creative use of hitherto unconnected cultural elements. Granovetter (1994, p. 484) notes that the assembly of elements into a form is a "good example of the Schumpeterian definition of entrepreneurship, which involves pulling together previously unconnected elements." Biggart (1989) shows that the synthesis of unconnected elements can disarm opposition to innovations—hence, direct-selling organizations seamlessly linked the logics of the family and marketplace and were able to legitimate themselves. Put simply, skillful framing allows entrepreneurs to set the context and to exercise unobtrusive power. Ranson, Hinings, and Greenwood (1980, p. 8) note that "power is most effective and insidious in all its consequences when issues do not arise at all."

CR's founders preempted opposition by seamlessly combining hitherto unrelated cultural elements into a new frame or model of consumption. CR's founders deftly framed their critiques of business and advertising around the ideas of service to the customer and truth in advertising—concepts that businessmen and advertisers had begun to implement in a bid to professionalize their trades. CR's founders also borrowed elements of their solution—standards, testing, and science—from the work of industrial standard-setting bodies and the home economics profession. Below, I suggest that these professional infrastructures shaped the cognitions of CR's founders but shielded them from opposition. By borrowing ideas from these cultural repositories and by aligning themselves with professionalization efforts, CR's founders were also able to insulate themselves from potential attacks.

The professionalization of retailing.—Between 1910 and 1925, numerous business firms adopted codes of ethics that exalted service to the customer (Heermance 1924). A study by Kitson (1922) in the *Journal of Political Economy* reported that advertisements that contained the word "service" increased from less than 5% in 1900 to 24% in 1920. The growth of the service ideal was due to the professionalization of business and competitive pressures on firms.

Schools of retailing blossomed across the country between 1902 and 1920. In 1902, Arthur Sheldon set up a school of scientific salesmanship in Chicago, and by 1921, 20 such schools existed (Samson 1980, p. 204). The American Association of Collegiate Schools of Business was created in 1916, and by 1925, it had 25 members, many of whom instituted courses in retailing and business ethics built around ideas of service. The service idea diffused among businesses also because of the Rotary Clubs. Initially set up in 1905 as a mutual-aid society among individuals from different commercial fields, the Rotarians championed the service ideal after the 1911 convention when their platform, influenced by Arthur Sheldon, stated that "the science of business is the science of service: he profits most who serves best" (*National Rotarian*, March 1912, p. 15). By 1915, the Rotary Club adopted a code of ethics that made service the "Golden Rule," and it became the model for business firms.

The promotion of the service ideal by the retailing profession induced business firms, especially retailers, to implement the service idea as a competitive weapon. A survey by the U.S. Bureau of Education in 1917 found that 50 stores, such as Wanamaker's, Altman's, Macy's, and Grant's, employed teachers of salesmanship. Stores began to rely on one-price selling and money-back guarantees and even employed "service shoppers" to make reports on the quality of service. Store manuals on service such as Wanamaker's exhorted employees to "hold the customer's interest jointly sacred with the interests of business" (Fuld 1916, p. 16). Trade associations such as the National Retail Dry Goods Association spoke of the need for the retailer to serve as a "protector of the consumer" (Letts 1914, p. 7) and the *Journal of Retailing* echoed this sentiment. Schlink published an article in the journal a month before his best-seller with Chase appeared and urged retailers to work as guardians of consumers and to reduce the costs of shopping. It was CR, however, that came to take on the role of a guardian of consumers, devoted to ensuring that business served customers.

The exaltation of the service ideal provided an evaluative yardstick for Chase and Schlink and made it possible for them to expose contradictions between precepts and practices. When Chase and Schlink (1927, p. 12) attacked business for violating norms of service and lamented that "we are deluged with things we don't wear, which we lose, which go out of style, which make unwelcome presents for our friends," businessmen and retailers could not respond with counterattacks because to do so would have meant disowning the ideal of service.

Professionalization of advertising.—Similarly, when Chase and Schlink (1927, p. 12) castigated "the advertiser [who] plays on the essential monkey within us," the advertising community could not respond because its bid to professionalize itself hinged on truth in advertising. After the formation of the Sphinx Club of New York in 1896, numerous advertising clubs sprang up, and in 1904, several clubs merged to form the Associated Advertising Clubs of America (AACA). By 1909, the AACA had established an educational committee to systematize training and to promote honest advertising. In the 1911 convention of the AACA, a proposal initiated by John Romer, the publisher of *Printers Ink*, was introduced wherein it was illegal for an advertisement to contain deceptions or misleading facts. Romer also urged advertising clubs to establish vigilance committees to ascertain the truthfulness of advertisements issued by members, to discipline errant members, or even to take them to court. The National Vigilance Committee was created in 1912, and by 1914, 24 cities had also founded vigilance committees in a bid to signal the advertising community's commitment to probity and professional conduct. In 1916, vigilance committees were renamed as Better Business Bureaus, and by 1930, more than 10,000 businesses were supporting these bureaus in numerous cities (Samson 1980, p. 343). Some of the bureaus instituted programs akin to service shopping, wherein advertising claims were tested by purchasing the products. However, these bureaus lacked any enforcement capability—for example, a resolution banning the use of paid testimonials was rarely honored. Similarly, in 1925 the New York bureau found that the claim made by Macy's that its prices were at least 6% less than other department stores was unjustified. Macy's resigned from the bureau because it did not accept the finding. The Macy's case undermined the credibility of the bureaus and showed that they could not contend with large and influential firms.

Thus, the advertising community sensitized CR's founders to the issues of ethics and truth and laid the foundation for their critique. When CR's founders attacked advertising for deception and characterized it as "largely competitive wrangling as to the relative merits of two undistinguished and often indistinguishable compounds" (Chase 1925, p. 125), advertisers could neither organize any vigorous defense nor launch an offensive. By co-opting elements of the truth-in-advertising movement into their critique of advertising, CR's founders insulated themselves from attack.

Home economics profession and rational purchasing.—A new profession, that of home economics, had emerged around 1908, and its propagation of rational techniques of purchasing provided invaluable protective cover for Chase and Schlink. Ellen Richards, a lecturer in sanitary chemistry at MIT, sought to eradicate inefficiency in home management by organizing conferences of like-minded women at Lake Placid, New York, during the period 1899–1908. These conferences persuaded librarians to put books related to home management under the "economics of consumption" category rather than the category of "production. " In 1908, the American Home Economics Association was created to foster thrift, efficiency, and safety in the "management" of households.

Home economists suggested that poverty also was the result of incompetent spending. In 1910, a number of charitable societies, especially the Cleveland Associated Charities, established separate home economics departments and integrated consumer expertise into social work practice (Zelizer 1994, p. 153). Home economists sought to substitute carelessness and ignorance in home management with systematic budgeting, comparison shopping, and rational techniques to allocate resources to clothes, rent, and food. The emphasis on rational purchasing also induced advertisers to change their techniques; some advertisers began to emphasize paired product comparisons and automobile manufacturers, such as Buick, whose cars won races, built their advertising around the theme "tests tell" (Schudson 1978).

Colleges began to introduce home economics courses in their curricula due to funding from the federal government through the Bureau of Home Economics and Cooperative Extension Services of the Department of Agriculture. The latter organized a large project under which 2,500 home economists involved with numerous land-grant colleges set up demonstration projects—each such project covered 12–35 communities in an area and brought women together once a month to discuss consumption (Sorenson 1941, p. 64). As the number of students enrolled in federally aided home economics programs rose from 31,000 in 1918 to 175,000 in 1930 (U.S. Bureau of the Census 1975), techniques of rational home management and purchasing also spread. Additional support for the home economists' attempt to rationalize purchasing by households received encouragement from the U.S. Commerce Department's National Bureau of Standards, which published pamphlets for housewives. Two pamphlets called *Measures for the Household* and *Materials for the Household* published in 1915 and 1917 urged consumers to rely on standards and tests and contributed to the rise of a new model of purchasing by consumers.

Growth of CR.—The emphasis on testing and standardization disarmed opposition to CR and fueled its growth. Pfeffer (1992, pp. 247–49) says, "Power is most effectively employed when it is fairly unobtrusive. Using rational, or seemingly rational processes of analysis helps render the use of power and influence less obvious. . . . Decisions are perceived to be better and are accepted more readily to the extent they are made following prescribed and legitimate procedures."

CR grew quickly. In 1927, it had 656 subscribers, but by 1933, there were 42,000 subscribers (Silber 1983). The lack of sustained opposition from advertisers and businesses and Chase and Schlink's skillful framing of their cause and solution spurred CR's growth. CR's ideas grew more popular due to the Depression, which forced consumers to be more vigilant about price-quality relationships. For example, as shirts, sheets, and shoes wore out quicker than consumers expected them to, people felt cheated and wanted to remedy the situation (Sorenson 1941, p. 10). A wave of exposés also fostered interest in product testing. *Skin Deep* by Mary C. Phillips, *The American Chamber of Horrors* by Ruth DeForest Lamb, and *100,000,000 Guinea Pigs: Dangers in Everyday Foods, Drugs, and Cosmetics* by Kallett and Schlink, the secretary of CR, called for mandatory disclosure of product ingredients because weak laws rendered "a hundred million Americans . . . as unwitting test animals in a gigantic experiment with poisons, conducted by food, drug and cosmetic manufacturers" (cited in Silber 1983, p. 18). A spate of other books followed, and much like the muckraking journalism, this guinea-pig journalism blended moral indignation with insistent pleas to the public to use objective information in purchasing. As a result, by 1935, CR had a staff of 50 employees and 200 outside consultants, and the readership of the *Consumers Research Bulletin* rose to 55,000.

CWOs as Engines of Radical Change: Consumers Union

As CR grew, other consumer advocates were lured to the organization by its rising stature. Notable recruits included Alexander Crosby (a journalist critical of advertising in newspapers), Dewey Palmer (an engineer seeking relief from college teaching), and Arthur Kallett (a colleague of Schlink's at the American Standards Association). As new activists joined, older activists left CR because of disagreements with Schlink. In 1932, Stuart Chase left the board of CR, and in 1933, two other board members, Bernard Reis and E. J. Lever, resigned due to budgetary disagreements with Schlink. These members were replaced by newcomers such as J. B. Matthews and Mary C. Phillips, who were allied with Schlink.

These budgetary disagreements within CR stemmed from differences about how much money should be spent on testing and how much on advocating reform of labor conditions. Some employees and members of the board, Palmer and Kallett, for example, felt that CR should lobby for the reform of labor conditions. The 1932 edition of the *Consumers Research Bulletin* (p. 3) noted that "CR is desirous of adding union and other labor groups to its subscription list; second, members of CR's board are pretty generally interested in not ignoring the labor conditions under which products are produced." By contrast, Schlink, Matthews, and Phillips thought that social questions concerning wages and working conditions were beyond their scope and could not be studied in an "unbiased" manner (Sorenson 1941, p. 47). Thus, CR was beset with a debate about whether it would be an impartial provider of information for consumers or a journal of radical political economy dedicated to the amelioration of the plight of workers.

These tensions flared during a union recognition drive by CR's employees in August 1935. When 20 or more employees formed a chapter of the Technical, Editorial, and Office Assistants Union and asked for recognition, John Heasty, a chemist and union president, and two other union activists were fired. A strike was called, and the union twice demanded the removal of Mary C. Phillips and J. B. Matthews from the board because they were concerned with "personal aggrandizement" and not with the "real interests of the masses of consumer-workers at heart" (Strike Demands of Workers, cited in Katz 1977, p. 75). Dewey Palmer was dismissed from the board because he opposed Schlink, and Kallett threw in his lot with the striking workers. Frederick Schlink, Mary Phillips. J. B. Matthews, and other board members resorted to strikebreakers, legal injunctions, and armed detectives to retain control of the magazine and the organization. The Association of Subscribers, composed of members sympathetic to labor concerns, was formed to exhort Schlink and his allies to negotiate with the union but had little effect, and as a result, the association demanded a refund of subscriptions.

Attempts to break the deadlock between the management and the strikers were fruitless. An attempt by Reinhold Niebuhr to mediate was rejected by Schlink, who also challenged the jurisdiction of the National Labor Relations Board when it was called in to settle the strike. Schlink and his allies felt that the strikers were "dupes of business" and "communists" (see Silber 1983, p. 21).

As a result, 30 workers led by Kallett established a new organization called Consumers Union (CU), which sought to unite the cause of consumers and workers. Initially, three names were considered—National Consumers Union, Consumers Technical Union, and Consumers Union of the United States. The first was discarded because it was similar to the National Consumer League (which focused on child labor). The use of the word "technical" in the second name created opposition. Finally, the third was chosen as the best description of the new organization. Its publication was to be called *Consumer Union Reports*.

The radical change frame.—CU was more than a breakaway faction of CR and was premised on a strikingly different diagnosis of the problems facing the consumer. The organization's founders felt that a watchdog guarding consumers could not merely provide scientific and impartial information to consumers to make rational purchasing decisions. Instead, the originators of CU defined the consumer as a worker concerned with the standard of living and not just a rational actor seeking to get the best value for his money. The problem facing consumers was not one of variety and deceptive advertising, it was also one of wages and income. The founders opined that "all the technical information in the world will not give enough food or enough clothes to the textile workers' families living on $11 a week. . . . They like the college professor or the skilled mechanic are ultimate consumers. . . . The only way in which any organization can aid them materially is by helping them, in their struggle as workers, to get an honest wage" (*Consumers Union Reports,* May 1930, p. 2).

CU's founders proposed that the new organization "give information and assistance on all matters relating to the expenditure of earnings and family income . . . to create and maintain decent living standards for ultimate consumers." CU was more than an advocacy organization and aspired to be a new method for the social control of business (its target) and consumers (its clients). . . . The new organization viewed socially responsible buying and collective action as tools to improve working conditions and create decent living standards fur consumers. Like its rival, CR, CU also valued the norms of scientific analysis and rational purchasing and was committed to impartial testing. In contrast to CR, however, CU saw buying as a socially responsible act, urged members to picket antiunion stores, and pleaded with them to use labor conditions as a criterion in the purchasing process. CU was also committed to the norm of equity in incomes and saw itself as a critic of companies exploiting their workers. Its founders were careful to signal their commitment to impartial testing by not only having a nonprofit organization but also by decoupling product ratings from evaluations of labor conditions.

The first issue explained why *Consumers Union Reports* was a confidential magazine (because of legal reasons), outlined its rating system (why products were rated as "best buys," "also acceptable," and "not acceptable"), ran an exposé of Alka Seltzer's advertising claims, and compared credit unions and commercial banks. By the end of 1936, CU issued a 240-page buying guide that also discussed labor conditions in firms making consumer products. Subsequent issues analyzed products and labor conditions: for example, *Consumers Union Reports* used blind tests to assess major cigarette brands, found no significant differences in taste, and concluded that it made sense to select the cheapest union-made cigarette. It opined that the big four cigarette manufacturers had labor policies that "ranged from bad to worse. . . . [Their] social policy is transplanted from the Dark Ages" (*Consumers Union Reports,* August 1938, p. 19). In 1936, 11 of its members were arrested picketing Orbachs, the department store in New York. CU supported antifascist boycotts, provided testimony in Federal trade-law hearings, organized promotional drives among the poor, and supported labor movement picketing during 1936–38. It was so involved that, of the 50 employees of CU, only seven were technical employees (Silber 1983, p. 27). CU's board reflected the endorsements of the trade unions and left-leaning intellectuals. It had several radical trade unionists among its officers, and the board was composed of academics (Robert Brady, Charles Marlies), union leaders (Philip Randolph, Rose Schneiderman, Heywood Broun), an accountant, and the staff representative (John Heasty).

Contested Boundaries of the Nonprofit CWO Form

The rival frames promoted by the founders of CR and CU led to divergent definitions of the boundaries of the nonprofit CWO form. CR was focused in its goals and technology and how it served clients: it sought to reduce waste, rely on testing, and catered to one constituency—consumers. By contrast, CU was diversified in its scope—its goals; technologies, and constituencies. It sought to provide information to consumers, to improve standards of living, to rely on testing and boycotts, and to serve two constituencies—consumers and workers.

These contradictory proposals suggested that the support base of the nonprofit CWO form was heterogeneous. Social movement researchers suggest that a heterogeneous potential support base permits a range of definitions of the situation (Zald and McCarthy 1980). If CR drew its support from those committed to professionalizing retailing and advertising and rationalizing home management, CU drew strength from those committed to labor issues. During the period preceding the birth of CU, labor legislation had created a propitious environment for trade unions; in 1932, the Norris–La Guardia Act gave workers the right to join unions, and in 1935, the Wagner Act recognized the right of employees to strike and defined unfair labor practices on the part of employers. Consequently, union membership rose from 1.1 million in 1901 to 3.75 million in 1935. As unions became more militant, work stoppages increased from less than 2,000 to 4,500 in 1937 (U.S. Bureau of the Census 1975). Hence, linking labor and consumer issues was both topical and sensible. For a new organization that sought to espouse a radical agenda, CU grew rapidly—by the end of 1936, it had 20,700 members, and by 1937, it had close to 40,000 members.

Moreover, neither form enjoyed clear-cut technical advantages premised on transaction cost considerations. CR's claim to efficiency hinged on the premise that focus (on a single goal, technology, and constituency) reduced coordination costs. This argument implies that focus on a single issue credibly communicates commitment to a cause (Williamson 1985), reduces conflicts of interest among donors, and precludes adroit managers from exploiting conflicts among donors and from diverting resources toward causes they personally favor (Fama and Jensen 1983). By contrast, CU's claim to efficiency pivoted on the premise that diversification leads to economies of scope in lobbying. When market segments are similar, goals and technologies are related to each other and can augment each other, then, managers can use a dominant management logic and realize efficiency gains (Aldrich et al. 1994).

Since neither definition of form enjoyed any decisive technical advantages, the choice of which frame to use to design non-profit CWOs and what boundaries to impose on their activities hinged on politics and, in particular, endorsements by powerful actors—professions, state authorities, and naturally, the targets of watchdog activity—businesses and advertisers.

Early Supporters of Impartial Testing and Radical Change Frames

At the outset, CU constituted only one instance of the model of a watchdog pursing labor and consumer agendas, and CR was the only instance of an organization incarnating the model of the CWO as an impartial testing agency. However, the scales began to tilt against CU when a new organization, Intermountain Consumers Service, was set up by S. A. Mahood, a chemist affiliated with the U.S. Products Lab and a consumer educator to boot. It had a membership of 3,500 subscribers, and it chose to mimic CR and extol the model of the consumer as a rational decision maker who needed to rely on scientific tests.

The model of the consumer as a rational decision maker, promoted originally by CR, was also diffusing through governmental agencies and professional societies. Thus, the Consumers Advisory Board was established in the National Recovery Administration in 1933, and it sponsored a report by Robert Lynd, the sociologist, which called for the creation of common standards and the allocation of funds for testing. The Consumer Counsel was established in the Department of Agriculture in 1933 that issued a bimonthly publication called *Consumer Guide* with a circulation of over 150,000. Later, when the National Emergency Council set up a consumer's division in 1934 to coordinate all consumer-related activities of the federal government, 200 county consumer councils were established to facilitate two-way communication (Sorenson 1941, p. 16–17).

The concepts of rational decision making, standardization, and scientific testing that were initially promoted by CR also spread in professional circles. The American Home Economics Association set up the Standing Committee on the Standardization of Consumer Goods in 1927, became a member of the American Standards Association in 1928, and organized cooperative standardization projects between women and merchants in several cities (Sorenson 1941, p. 66). Later, other long-established national organizations, such as the National Education Association, the American Federation of Teachers, the American Marketing Association, the MidWestern Economics Association, and others began to devote time to consumer education issues during their annual conferences.

By contrast, small newly founded consumer groups such as the Consumer Conference in Cincinnati (1934), the League of Women Shoppers (1935), the High Cost of Living Conferences (1935), and the Milk Consumers Protective Committee (1939) endorsed CU. The dearth of endorsements only invigorated the desire of CU's founders to increase circulation as a means of jump-starting a bandwagon of support and pushing for radical reform. Resources from increased circulation were essential to fund an expansion of the product-testing program and to reward technical talent. Moreover, CU was wary about creating local groups because it did not want to be legally responsible for their conduct. Additionally, CU's founders had also realized that their bulletin was not reaching low-income workers and felt that boosting circulation could help them to sustain low-price editions of their bulletin.

Opposition to the Radical Change Frame

CU's attempt to increase circulation evoked resistance from diverse institutional actors. For example, in 1937, CU published "The Contraceptive Report," which summarized the efficacy of birth control techniques—it chose this topic given the belief that family planning was important for sustaining standards of living for workers. It was also a shrewd bid to sell more copies of *Consumers Union Reports*. However, the postmaster general of New York banned it in 1939, and CU fought a court case that was only resolved in its favor in 1943. CU sought to advertise itself through mass media but faced a media boycott. Sixty-two newspapers, including the *New York Times*, refused to sell advertising space to CU (Sorenson 1941, p. 37). The *Times* stated that the reason for the refusal was that CU's "services comprised attacks on industries. This the *Times* does not permit" (letter by C. McPuckett to S. Zaslowsky, cited in Katz 1977, p. 170). Attempts to advertise in professional journals such as *Science* met with the reply that "it is not possible for the Consumers Union to supply information that has scientific validity" (letter by J. McCatrell to A. L. Kallett, 1938, cited in Katz 1977, p. 171). Even the *Journal of Home Economics* declined to accept advertisements because they felt that CU was making accusations that could not be substantiated, and home economists rejected invitations to join the board.

Rival entrepreneurs also constructed CWOs that were interpreted as threats by CU's founders. In 1937, Albert Lane began to publish *Consumer Bureau Reports,* which provided favorable ratings in return for free samples from manufacturers. Undeniably, this venture threatened to besmirch the image of all CWOs. However, CU was more concerned than CR because Lane's publication had a name that could be confused with CL's own *Consumers Union Reports.* Moreover, Lane's publication also copied CU's breezy format and may have confused readers because it praised products that CL had rated as unacceptable. Another entrepreneur, William Foster, established the Consumers Foundation as a research organization advising consumers. mobilized money, and even succeeded in drafting Robert Lynd as a supporter. CU raised questions about the new organization's sources of funds, and it was found that the Institute of Distribution, a trade association of chain stores, had supported it. Attempts such as these tarnished the image of all CWOs, but CU was concerned about spillover effects.

CU was also attacked by other publications, especially the Hearst newspapers. In its second issue, CU asked its readers to support a strike against Hearst's *Wisconsin News,* and from 1936 to 1939, it issued articles that exposed Hearst's Good Housekeeping Institute (so much so, that the Federal Trade Commission launched an investigation against the institute). As a result, Hearst became a bitter enemy and charged that CU was a Communist-front organization. The *Women's Home Companion* also accused CU of undermining the American way of life.

The attacks reached their zenith in 1938 when a House committee on subversive activities chaired by Congressman Dies sought to investigate whether CU was engaged in un-American activities harmful to the national interest. J. B. Matthews, an associate of Schlink's at CR, served as counsel for the Select Committee on Un-American Activities (the Dies Committee) and Matthews suggested that Kallett's writings and the fact that a CU ex-employee, Susan Jenkins, had admitted to being an employee of a Communist newspaper (the *Daily Worker*) were proof that the organization was a Communist front. Matthews labeled CU as a "red transmission belt"—the Hearst newspapers printed Matthews's accusations in full, and *Good Housekeeping* distributed the Matthews report in the November-December issue of its Consumer Information Service. However, the Dies Committee did not challenge the credibility of CU's rival, CR.

One reason why CR did not face problems from the Dies Committee is that Matthews was an associate of Schlink. Another reason is that the very existence of CU may have made CR more acceptable. Haines (1984) suggests that "radical" organizations by their sheer existence make "moderate" organizations more acceptable and enable them to acquire support and resources. It is possible that CR may have been shielded from criticism from business corporations and newspapers.

Narrowing Boundaries: Adaptation of CU

CU sued Albert Lane not only because he was deemed to be a copycat using a similar name and style but also because suing Lane may have positioned CU as a defender of not just its own integrity but the standing of the nonprofit CWO form. Rising to the defense of a form was a credible method of signaling CU's commitment to independence and impartiality at a time when its standing was being impugned by CR and the business press. CU won the suit. It secured some protection from the damage done by the Dies Committee when Eleanor Roosevelt rushed to its defense in a variety of public statements. The Dies Committee was running out of money, and some members of the committee, especially Representative Voorhis, attacked Chairman Dies for the conduct of the hearings. The Dies Committee was a select committee, which later, in 1945, was made a standing committee—the House Un-American Activities Committee. Although there was no systematic investigation of the charges leveled at CU, the fact that CU's name was on the committee's shortlist of targeted Communist organizations was a matter of concern to the founders and potential supporters. Later, these charges would be revived during the McCarthy era when CU's founders were forced to testify.

Nevertheless, the pressure exerted by hostile activists (such as Matthews), elements of the media (the Hearst publications), and politicians (such as Dies and others on the Select Committee on Un-American Activities), impelled CU's founders to disengage from radical advocacy. Kallett and some other officers of CU recognized that the organization would be shielded from external attacks if it developed its testing program and concentrated on rating products. The adaptation of CU was a gradual process of disengaging from the labor agenda.

During the second annual meeting in 1938, three resolutions urging a focus on ratings and a disavowal of interest in labor and the threat of fascism or other "ideologies" were introduced but not approved. A founder and board member, Charles Marlies, tendered his resignation (Sorenson 1941, p. 49). In 1938, CU decided to "lapse" its coverage of labor conditions in its buying guide because "detailed information and numerous qualifications were usually necessary to give a fair picture of labor relations in a given industry or plant, labor notes are not included. In addition, the very swift changes continually taking place in labor relations make it impossible to include in annual publication, annual data that would remain up to date and reliable" (CU 1938, p. 9).

CU's management rationalized their retreat by noting that a truce between labor and business was essential in combating the specter of fascism in Europe. CU's management justified product testing for its "trickle-down effects"—the work of the testers would improve the lot of the workers indirectly by enhancing the quality of all merchandise and by promoting legislation benefiting all consumers. In a turnabout in 1939, CU began to assert that "just the ordinary products bought each day can save members $50 to $300 a year" (*Consumers Union Reports*, April 1939, p. 14).

In 1939, Arthur Kallett and Colston Warne, the president, sought to derive support from the scientific community and arranged a meeting with the Cambridge-Boston chapter of the American Association of Scientific Workers (AASW), a fledgling organization

that was created in 1938 by a group of biologists at Woods Hole, Massachusetts. At this meeting, CU members confessed to the inadequacy of their testing, and the AASW agreed to provide expert advice and testing for certain products. In 1940, the board rejected an attempt by the editor of *Consumers Union Reports* to recruit union members as subscribers. In 1940, the National Advisory Committee, composed of academics, was also created to establish linkages with colleges and universities.

World War II forced CU to adapt to a war economy, where shortages rather than abundance and inflation rather than quality became the problems. Product testing made sense in an economy of abundance but not in an economy of rationing. In 1939, CU began to publish a section on war and prices that was expanded in 1940 into a weekly newsletter called *Bread and Butter*. This publication distanced itself from labor issues but sought to assist low-income consumers by acting as an early warning system designed to help consumers cope with shortages and to buy goods likely to be hit with price increases by profiteers. *Bread and Butter* exhorted consumers to unite against profiteers—the Council of Organized Consumers was established in 1942 but was unsuccessful. The war economy, however, forced CU to shrink its payroll and the length of its bulletins and took a toll on membership.

In 1942, CU sought to invite Robert Lynd to join their board. but he demurred even as he denied that he was a "red-baiter" (Katz 1977, p. 201). The legacy of the Dies Committee's allegations convinced Kallett and his colleagues that they needed to more formally distance themselves from a labor agenda. In 1942, the name of the magazine was changed from *Consumers Union Reports* to *Consumer Reports* to ostensibly avoid confusion in the mind of the public about whether a company's labor policies influenced the ratings of its products.

Kallett and his colleagues were concerned about the tendency of some of CU's employees to espouse radical agendas through *Bread and Butter*. Even at the time of the formation of the newsletter, there were divisions in the board between whether to forewarn consumers of price increases or to educate them about product maintenance. As resource constraints impelled Kallett to downgrade the paper quality of *Bread and Butter*, its advocates within CU accused

Kallett of curtailing resources for the newsletter. In 1944, Kallett persuaded the board that *Bread and Butter* and *Consumer Reports* ought to be delinked, and as a result, consumers were not to be forced to take both publications simultaneously. In 1946, with the end of the war, *Bread and Butter* outlined a six-point postwar reconstruction proposal that included price controls, rationing, food subsidy programs, rent control, subsidized housing, and health care. At this time, the business community was lobbying Congress for an end to rationing and price controls. Influenced by the legacy of the Dies Committee, Kallett was concerned about ideological conflict and the advocacy of *Bread and Butter* and in 1947, persuaded the board to collapse *Bread and Butter* into a feature of *Consumer Reports* under the title "Economics for Consumers." In June 1948, Leland Gordon, an economist at CU, asked the organization to reinstate reports on labor conditions, but Kallett and Isserman (a prolabor sympathizer) objected on the grounds that it might compromise CU.

The containment of advocacy proceeded within CU. In 1947, Kallett changed CU's bylaws so that subscribers could be distinguished from members and thereby sought to deflect criticism that members might be Communists. In the same year, the union of CU's workers lamented that its board representative was a second-class citizen and asked that the position be terminated. The board agreed with alacrity. This was a radical turnabout for an organization that had prided itself on being a collectivist enterprise at the time of its creation and was, for the first year or so, structured as an egalitarian organization.

The postwar years also saw the rise of Keynesian economics, and some of CU's leaders felt that a marriage of consumer reform goals with the Keynesian philosophy of full employment and the importance of consumption would best situate CU in a regulated free-enterprise economy. Indeed, as early as 1943, some of the more radical elements at CU, working with *Bread and Butter*, wanted to work for the establishment of a consumer democracy, but Kallett and others concerned more with CU, felt that accepting Keynes's ideas meant that the organization would not be labeled un-American.

Hence, CU's conversion was not one dramatic event but a slow and gradual process of repositioning and reconstruction. CU slowly ceased to be an engine of political, social, or moral activism and reinvented itself as an impartial testing agency. Over time, CU began to recognize products as conditionally acceptable even if they were not best buys and expanded its testing to ensure that it was clone in-house instead of subcontracting it out as CR did. Its evaluations and options appeared in the form of tables and charts with numerical results of tests. Annual surveys of its members enabled it to respond to its subscribers' needs. For example, CU provided ratings of cars on the basis of speed after it learned that consumers valued speed as a criterion in purchasing cars. Even after introducing a segment on health and medicine in 1945 and providing careful summaries of medical research on smoking, *Consumer Reports* provided information on how to "roll your own" cigarettes during the cigarette famine of 1945.

By emphasizing testing and science and disavowing radical labor advocacy, Kallett and his colleagues not only shielded CU from external attack but transformed it into a scientific conservative to fit with the prevailing beliefs about science, rigor, and objectivity. The price of viability for the organization was abstinence from advocacy.

CR may have won the struggle over what a nonprofit watchdog ought to be, but it was outdistanced in the battle for circulation. By joining the media and politicians in critiquing CU, CR may have sown the seeds for its own decline because its embrace of scientific conservatism proved advantageous to CU. By 1949, with 500,000 subscribers, CU rated 1,793 brands spanning 116 products, and its technical division was divided into electronics, textiles, automobiles, special projects, chemistry, and foods. By contrast, CR had made little progress and refused to publicize its circulation details (Thorelli and Thorelli 1974). CU's gradual adaptation to political pressure and its concurrent adjustment to the demands of a postwar economy fueled a rise in CU's membership base. Figure 26.1 chronicles CU's growth from its inception to 1971. After an initial rise from 1936 to 1938, the circulation of *Consumers Union Reports* decreased due to World War II and slowly picked up after 1945. After the war, CU received the endorsement of prestigious universities and the federal government. The Home Economics Department of Cornell University assisted in the testing of sewing machines and the Department of Agriculture allowed an employee to work under its supervision on the grading of canned food.

In 1951, the Dies Committee's allegations were revived by Better Business Bureaus in Akron, Cincinnati, Dayton, and Detroit, and the school boards in these cities threatened a ban on CU's magazines in the school libraries. CU avoided publicity on the bannings to the extent possible and denied allegations directly when asked. Its restraint stemmed from concern because its name was still on the list of un-American organizations compiled by the House Un-American Activities Committee. J. B. Matthews joined McCarthy's investigative staff in 1953 and resurrected the charges. A Hearst columnist, E. F. Tompkins, publicized them, and CU's board stated that "in the present period of ideological conflict, the Board of Directors of Consumers Union reaffirms its faith in democratic society in which the production of goods and services is guided by the free choice of consumers" (CU 1952, pp. 1–2).

CU's leaders testified before the House Un-American Activities Committee, and after a long hearing, the organization's name was finally struck off the list of un-American organizations in 1954.

By 1955, William Whyte noted that *Consumer Reports* and *Consumers Research Bulletin* had an impact over and above their actual circulation—both magazines were produced by organizations that institutionalized distrust of advertising and aimed to create impersonal trust by providing scientific, objective, and impartial evaluations. By 1956, the ratings of CU could spell good fortune or doom for a company: spokesmen for Maytag washers and Volkswagen cars attributed their penetration of hitherto oligopolistic markets to favorable ratings (Samson 1980). In 1959, the *New York Times*, an erstwhile critic noted that "what Dr. Spock is to freshman parents, the Consumers Union is to bewildered housewives" (Silber 1983, pp. 30–31). By 1958, psycholo-

Figure 26.1

Consumers Union Reports' and *Consumer Reports'* circulation, 1936–71

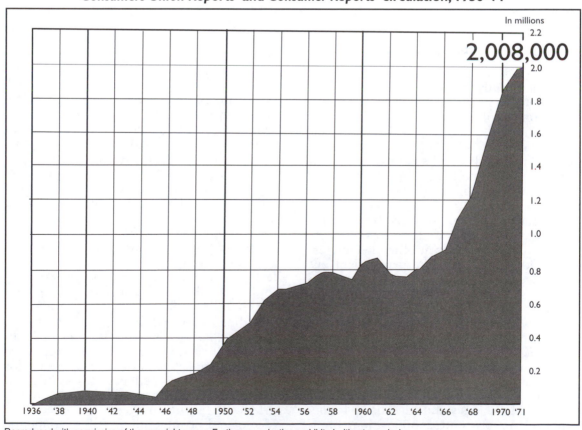

gists and marketing experts opined that consulting the scientific ratings provided by CWOs had become a buying ritual in an age of science that enabled consumers to think of themselves as rational, logical, and informed consumers (Sargent 1958). So established was the identity of CWOs as meticulous scientific conservatives that the ratings techniques used by them were lampooned by magazines. A British comedy group even had a skit entitled *"Consumer Reports* looks at religion."

However, the transformation of CU into a scientific conservative was a double-edged sword. If it strengthened the legitimacy of CU, it also inhibited it from espousing radical causes and thereby provided an opening for other issue entrepreneurs to articulate fresh grievances and create new nonprofit CWOs. Ralph Nader's (1965) *Unsafe at Any Speed,* an expose of General Motors, was initially offered by him to CU, but the book was disparaged by its automotive division as unscientific and biased. Nader called CU a sleeping giant, and later his best-seller enabled the formation of new groups dedicated to the enforcement of the legal rights of consumers.

Discussion

This study responds to Scott's (1995, p. 147) call to study the emergence of new organizational forms and to illuminate the co-evolution of culture and organizations. One implication of this study is that organizational forms are structural conveyances for cultural materials that become infused with norms, values, and beliefs as entrepreneurs use frames to mobilize resources. When entrepreneurs use frames to legitimate the new form, they inject an organizational form with cultural content and serve as conduits by which cultural rules are encoded into organizations. The infusion of prevalent but unconnected cultural elements into the watchdog form was not an apolitical act. Rather it exemplified the use of unobtrusive power, wherein problems of consumption and solutions were framed in much the same way that a picture is framed (Pfeffer 1992). CR's founders, Schlink and Chase, deftly co-opted the ideas of service and truth in advertising in their critique of business for wasteful inefficiency and advertising for deception and preempted opposition. Similarly, the prevalence of industrial standards and home economics training enabled Chase and Schlink to present their solution—an independent testing agency designed to aid rational decision making by consumers. In sharp contrast, CU's founders, Kallett and his colleagues, strove to frame their organization as a champion of downtrodden workers and as a crusader for decent and just living standards. Thus, as both groups of founders relied on the Western cultural account with its themes of progress and justice (Meyer, Boli, and Thomas 1987), they generated conflict about the practical implications of that cultural account. By showing how entrepreneurs are skillful political operatives employing frames as mobilization devices (Swidler 1986; Biggart 1989; Snow and Benford 1992), this article addresses DiMaggio and Powell's (1991, p. 30) lament that neoinstitutional accounts of new organizational forms say little about "how skillful entrepreneurs put multiple institutional logics to strategic use" and creates a bridge between social movement theory and the literature on the creation of new forms (Fligstein 1996a).

The case study of the origins of nonprofit CWOs illustrates how the boundaries of organizational forms are defined by institutional processes rather than by transaction cost considerations. Organizational economists insist that transaction cost considerations determine the "efficient boundaries" of organizational forms (Williamson 1985). However, Powell (1991) notes that institutional processes shape the boundaries of forms when technical differences among rival forms are ambiguous or when the criteria to evaluate technical excellence are disputed. Institutional processes, as Hannan and Freeman (1989) point out, can erode or establish boundaries. Bricolage by entrepreneurs, copying errors, and deinstitutionalization can efface boundaries among forms. By contrast, closure of social networks, collective action, endorsement by powerful actors. and taken-for-grantedness can secure the boundaries of organizational forms.

Although complexity of product choice, deceptive advertising, and the lack of product liability rules created the resource space for nonprofit CWOs and made it possible for quality assurance activities to be bundled into a new organizational form, the boundaries of the form emerged as an outcome of ideological competition. CR's founders, Schlink and Case, borrowed the idea of scientific testing from standard-setting bodies and the idea of reducing the cost of product comparisons from discussions in the retailing profession. They sought to erode the boundaries between nonprofit CWOs and standard-setting organizations. By contrast, CU's founders, Kallett and his allies, strove to import characteristics of trade unions into the consumption sector and sought to make nonprofit CWOs the counterparts of unions. These rival combinatorial attempts represented two potential ways of bundling the activities of the nonprofit CWO form. Neither model enjoyed a decisive technical advantage—if CR's focus reduced its coordination costs, then CU's diversified emphasis led to economies of scope in lobbying.

Each model was premised on a different notion of the identity of the consumer. Chase and Schlink defined a consumer as a decision maker keen on getting the best value for the money, promoted norms of efficiency, rationality, and scientific analysis, and extolled watchdogs as impartial testers. By contrast, Kallett and his allies viewed the consumer as a worker keen to better his or her standard of living, promoted norms of socially responsible buying and equity, and portrayed watchdogs as engines of radical change. CR and CU, therefore, represented alternative models for the social control of industry, premised on different ideals of identity.

Sustained hostility from the Hearst publications, especially *Good Housekeeping,* and politicians such as Congressman Dies forced CU to scale back labor-related activism and emphasize scientific testing. Thus, the dikes of vested interest prevented the rise of the consumer-as-worker model and instead confined consumers and CWOs into a narrower channel of activity. By emphasizing how a contest over the identity of the consumer delineated the boundaries of the form, this article reveals how consumers and consumption were produced by processes other than industrialization (see DiMaggio 1994), shows how struggles over identity (White 1992) are the mechanisms by which forms are imbued with meaning and constituted as cultural objects, and speaks to DiMaggio's (1991) call to incorporate agency and interest in the creation of new forms.

Another implication of this article is that, just as routines become operative only when there is a cease-fire agreement among organizational members (Nelson and Winter 1982), new organizational forms become operative only when they embody a truce among contending social factions. Had conflict over who a consumer was and what consumption was persisted, given the precarious interpersonal relationships between the founders of CR and CU, the energies of both organizations would have been sapped by internecine warfare. Conceivably, an opening may have been created for business firms, newspapers, and advertisers to discredit the notion of nonprofit CWOs. When CU's founders bowed to pressure by embracing the model of an impartial tester and disavowed sociopolitical advocacy, there was a cessation of hostilities and a moratorium on the debate about the identity of consumers and nonprofit CWOs. This truce on the contours of the nonprofit CWO form was maintained because CU's founders were keen to avoid the risks of political pressure from Congress and the defensive alertness of actors opposed to sociopolitical advocacy. The absence of debate about the role of nonprofit CWOs made it possible for them to rationalize consumption and to become influential monitors of big business. Although nonprofit CWOs embodied an implicit truce, truces can also be explicit and encoded in legislation. For example, there was intense debate about the scope of commercial banks, insurance firms, investment banks, and securities firms before the passage of the Glass-Steagall Act of 1933; the enactment of this law codified a truce among the proponents of the interests of these constituencies. Explicit or implicit truces can be breached by new issue entrepreneurs who strive to take advantage of new technologies and the emergence of new constituencies with grievances. Thus, Nader breached the truce on nonprofit CWOs by exploiting the issue of product safety and contributed to the rise of nonprofit CWOs as legal activists.

The study of nonprofit CWOs also speaks to DiMaggio's (1991) call to shed light on the role of professionals in the birth of new forms. Attempts to professionalize occupations delegitimate the existing social order and create openings for institutional entrepreneurs to build new forms. For example, museum directors launched a reform movement that discredited existing museums and spawned new organizational models. In the case of nonprofit CWOs, attempts by sales experts to train retailers in customer service sought to professionalize retailing but delegitimated the existing system of managing customer relationships. Similarly, the truth-in-advertising movement aimed to professionalize advertising but discredited prevalent modes of advertising. Thus, both movements provided an opening for Chase and Schlink to launch their critique of business and advertising and to legitimate nonprofit CWOs as desirable and appropriate social control mechanisms.

The saga of nonprofit CWOs also illuminates how the state can be an arena for disputes about the boundaries of an organizational form. Just as Congress and the courts can be audiences for jurisdictional disputes between professions (Abbott 1990), they can also serve as audiences for jurisdictional contests between rival coalitions of entrepreneurs. The debate between the faction that saw CWOs as engines of radical change and the opposing faction that preferred CWOs to serve as impartial testers spilled into Congress when J. B. Matthews, a critic of the radical change model (and CU), and a one-time board member at CR, exploited his role as a counsel to the Dies Committee in investigating CU. These investigations tainted the reputation of CU, led to its inclusion in a roster of un-American organizations, and induced CU to scale back advocacy. The specter of Congressional investigation continued until the McCarthy hearings, forced CU to embrace the model of the watchdog as impartial tester, and maintained the truce about the contours of nonprofit CWOs.

The story of CU also demonstrates that mimicry can be an outcome of coercion. Neoinstitutionalist accounts treat the state and the professions as engines of coercive and normative isomorphism and portray mimicry as the unthinking adoption of peer group practices (DiMaggio and Powell 1983). Neoinstitutional accounts of mimicry paint cultural change as a process of diffuse social learning and neglect how conflict underlies the assimilation of new models into the general culture (see Tarrow 1989). Our case study suggests that vested interests can foist coercive cultural expectations on an organization and can create inducements for it to imitate its peers. March and Olsen (1989) suggest that conflicts may be resolved through the logic of aggregation and give and take or the logic of integration, wherein one of the parties can learn from the other and even convert to the other's point of view.

In our case study, the logic of integration prevailed—CU responded to withering political attacks by discarding its founding beliefs, by embracing the ascendant logic, and by converting itself into a scientific conservative.

A related implication that flows from the conversion of CU is that resistance may be followed by acquiescence. Neoinstitutionalist researchers generally describe acquiescence, compromise, avoidance, defiance, and manipulation as alternative strategic responses to institutional pressures (Oliver 1991). However, these responses may also be sequential and shaped by strategic considerations. CU began as an insurrection against the prevailing frame, and when its attempt to resist failed, its founders complied to external pressure and copied the ascendant model of nonprofit CWOs. An alternative was to concentrate on a narrow, subscriber base. The founders of CU chose to acquiesce because they were concerned about the survival of the organization and its long-term prospects.

Some limitations of this study also deserve elaboration and point to future research possibilities. This study analyzed a phase of the consumer movement characterized by the existence of two ideological frames and two main organizational embodiments. One frame became ascendant because it enjoyed greater political support. The organization backing the losing frame embraced the ascendant frame, thereby making it unquestionably dominant. However, when multiple frames and multiple organizational embodiments exist, the process by which one frame becomes dominant may be more path dependent (Powell 1991) or may be shaped by density-dependent processes of legitimation and competition (Hannan and Freeman 1989).

As a historical analysis, this study only looked at the origins of nonprofit CWOs during their formative phases in the United States but not at their transformation by Ralph Nader and environmental activists. Tarrow (1989) suggests that collective action unfolds in cycles of protest and urges that the idea of structural stability needs to be replaced with the notion of dynamic stability—the successive realizations in different forms of the same principle. Cycles of protest are characterized by heightened conflict across the social system, diffuse in specific ways from the center to the periphery, possess peaks and troughs, and are the crucibles from which new social repertoires evolve. Since their origins, CWOs have been profoundly influenced by cycles of protest—for example, the Civil Rights and antiwar movements provided an ideological context for Nader and other issue entrepreneurs to undermine the model of CWOs as scientific conservatives and to transform them into legal activists seeking to enforce the legal rights of consumers. Later, the environmental movement also led to an expanded notion of corporate social responsibility and the ethics of consumption. Clearly, the question of how protest cycles underpin the structural transformation of nonprofit CWOs merits scrutiny. One payoff may well be a more nuanced account of how social movement industries evolve and how interorganizational relationships within a social movement industry are transformed through time (Zald 1992).

This study lacked a comparative thrust and confined its attention to the United States. Nonprofit CWOs have diffused across the world since the establishment of the first CWOs in the United States (1927 and 1935), Germany (1925), and Finland (1939). In 1995, Consumers International, the international association of nonprofit CWOs, had 200 members from 90 countries (Consumers International Bulletin 1997). The international evidence reveals considerable diversity in the origins of nonprofit CWOs. In France, Belgium, the Netherlands, and Austria, for instance, CWOs were affiliated with labor organizations. By contrast, CWOs were created as distinct entities but were affiliated with women's guilds in Finland, Canada, Denmark, and Switzerland. Except the Swiss CWO, other CWOs evolved to focus exclusively on consumer issues and roots in women's guilds atrophied. In Norway, product testing began in 1939 with support from state authorities, and now several state-sponsored CWOs flourish in Asia and Africa—many of these are government affiliate members of Consumers International. The birth of nonprofit CWOs in other developed and newly industrializing countries needs to be chronicled in order to understand the international trajectory of this social control mechanism.

Additionally, the relationships between nonprofit watchdogs and forprofit watchdogs also merit scrutiny. Although this study did discuss the antagonism between CU and

Good Housekeeping during the early history of nonprofit CWOs, detailed analyses of the interdependencies between nonprofit CWOs and for-profit counterparts are needed. When do nonprofit CWOs spawn for-profit rivals? When do nonprofit CWO publications such as *Consumer Reports* and for-profit organizations such as J. D. Powers play complementary roles? Do issue entrepreneurs bear the risks of legitimating new social control arrangements only to see forprofits engage in successful free riding? The systematic analysis of such questions is needed to not only extend our grasp of CWOs but also to promote a better understanding of the division of labor between the for-profit and the nonprofit sector.

This study focused on the process by which nonprofit CWOs came to be injected with norms and beliefs. It is also necessary to analyze how these social control mechanisms influence culture. Just as cultural theories spur structural innovation, social structures also contribute to the rationalization of society. As noted earlier, nonprofit CWOs embodying the model of scientific conservatives played a part in rationalizing the purchasing decisions of individuals, making them logical and systematic (Sargent 1958). Future research needs to delineate how environmental watchdogs have influenced conceptions of environmental risk and have rationalized the management of environmental disasters. Similarly, the analysis of how human rights watchdogs have influenced conceptions of rights and have formalized oversight of nation-states also deserves scrutiny.

Moreover, this article has confined its attention to one type of nonprofit policing organization—the nonprofit CWO. Other nonprofit watchdogs also clamor for attention. The analysis of human rights watchdogs (epitomized by Amnesty International) and watchdogs that monitor corruption in nation-states (such as Transparency) might shed light on the social processes fostering the rise of control mechanisms that issue report cards on modern states. An irony of all watchdog organizations is that, like other social control mechanisms that institutionalize distrust, they are also vulnerable to the abuse of trust (Shapiro 1987). For example, the Clean Water Act permits environmental watchdogs to act as a private attorney general and to sue polluters who break the law. Many such suits are settled before they are brought to court; polluters agree to halt the flow of effluents and to make charitable donations to environmental groups not involved in the suit, ostensibly, to repair the damage done by the polluter. Although a judge authorizes such consent decrees, environmental watchdogs have been known to divert resources to satellite organizations, which may pursue projects unrelated to the consent decree. Even when contested by the Justice Department, such settlements between an environmental watchdog and its targets have been upheld by courts as consistent with the provisions of the Clean Water Act (Felten 1991). Who polices watchdogs? Do failures of watchdogs promote the growth of new social control mechanisms? Is the price of impersonal trust an iron cage, as forecasted by Weber?

References

Abbott, A. 1990. *The System of the Professions.* Chicago: University of Chicago Press.

Aldrich, Howard E. 1979. *Organization and Environments.* Englewood Cliffs, N.J.: Prentice-Hall.

Aldrich, Howard E., Catherine R. Zimmer, Udo H. Staber, and John J. Beggs. 1994. "Minimalism, Mutualism, and Maturity: The Evolution of American Trade Associations in the 19th Century." Pp. 223–39 in *Evolutionary Dynamics of Organizations,* edited by J. Baum and J. V. Singh. New York: Oxford University Press.

Astley, W. G. 1985. "The Two Ecologies: Population and Community Perspective on Organizational Evolution." *Administrative Science Quarterly* 30:224–41.

Baron, J. N., F. R. Dobbin, and P. D. Jennings. 1986. "War and Peace: The Evolution of Modern Personnel Administration in U.S. Industry." *American Journal of Sociology* 92:350–83.

Becker, Howard. 1963. *Outsiders: Studies in the Sociology of Deviance.* New York: Free Press.

Biggart, Nicole W. 1989. *Charismatic Capitalism: Direct Selling Organizations in America.* Chicago: University of Chicago Press.

Briloff, A. J. 1972. *Unaccountable Accounting.* New York: Harper & Row.

Brint, Steven, and Jerome Karabell. 1991 "Institutional Origins and Transformations: The Case of American Community Colleges." Pp. 337–60 in *The New Institutionalism in Organizational Analysis,* edited by W. W. Powell and Paul DiMaggio. Chicago: University of Chicago Press.

Brittain, W. J., and John Freeman. 1982. "Organizational Proliferation and Density Dependent Selection." Pp. 291–338 in *The Organizational Life Cycle,* edited by J. R. Kimberly and R. H. Miles. San Francisco: Josey-Bass.

Brobeck, Stephen. 1990. *The Modern Consumer Movement: References and Resources.* Boston: G. K. Hall.

Bykerk, L., and A. Manney. 1995. *U.S. Consumer Interest Groups: Institutional Profiles.* Greenwich, Conn.: Greenwood.

Campbell, John L., and Leon Lindberg. 1990. "Property Rights and the Organization of Economic Activity by the State." *American Sociological Review* 55: 634–47.

Carroll, Glenn R. 1984. "Organizational Ecology." *Annual Review of Sociology* 10: 71–93.

Carroll, Glenn R., Jacques Delacroix, and Jerry Goodstein. 1990. "The Political Environment of Organizations: An Ecological View." Pp. 61–100 in *Evolution and Adaptation of Organizations,* edited by Barry Staw and Larry L. Cumming. Greenwich, Conn.: JAI Press.

Chase, Stuart. 1922. *The Challenge of Waste.* New York: New York League for Industrial Democracy.

———. 1925. *The Tragedy of Waste.* New York: Macmillan.

Chase, Stuart, and Frederick Schlink. 1927. *Your Money's Worth.* New York: Macmillan.

Cochrane, Rexmond C. 1966. *Measures for Progress: A History of the National Bureau of Standards.* Washington, D.C.: Department of Commerce.

Consumers International. 1997. *Consumers International Fact Book.* New York: Consumers International.

CR (Consumers Research). 1932, "Bylaws." New York: Consumers Research.

CU (Consumers Union). 1936. "Certificate of Incorporation." New York: Consumers Union.

———. 1938. *Consumers Union Buying Guide.* New York: Consumers Union.

———. 1952. "Minutes of the Board of Directors." New York.

DiMaggio, Paul. 1988. "Interest and Agency in Institutional Theory." Pp. 3–21 in *Institutional Patterns and Organizations: Culture and Environment,* edited by L. G. Zucker. Cambridge, Mass.: Ballinger.

———. 1991. "Constructing an Organizational Field as a Professional Project: U.S. Art Museums 1920–1940." Pp. 267–92 in *The New Institutionalism in Organizational Analysis,* edited by W. W. Powell and Paul DiMaggio. Chicago: University of Chicago Press.

———. 1994. "Culture and Economy." Pp. 27–57 in *Handbook of Economic Sociology,* edited by N. J. Smelser and R. Swedberg. New York: Russell Sage.

DiMaggio, Paul J., and Walter W. Powell. 1983. "The Iron Cage Revisited: Institutional Isomorphism and Collective Rationality in Organizational Fields." *American Sociological Review* 48:147–60.

———. 1991. Introduction to *The New Institutionalism in Organizational Analysis,* edited by Walter W. Powell and Paul DiMaggio. Chicago: University of Chicago Press.

Douglas, Mary. 1986. *How Institutions Think.* Syracuse, N.Y.: Syracuse University Press.

Durkheim, Emile. 1950. *The Rules of Sociological Method.* Glencoe, Ill.: Free Press.

Edwards, Bob, and Sam Marullo. 1995. "Organizational Mortality in a Declining Social Movement: The Demise of Peace Movement Organizations in the End of the Cold War Era." *American Sociological Review* 60 (6):908–27.

Epstein, Ralph C. 1928. *The Automobile Industry: Its Economic and Commercial Development.* Chicago: A. W. Shaw.

Fama, Eugene, and Michael Jensen. 1983. "Separation of Ownership and Control." *Journal of Law and Economics* 24:301–23.

Felten, Eric. 1991. "Money from Pollution Suits Can Follow a Winding Course." *Insight* 7:18–20.

Fligstein, Neil. 1996a. "How to Make a Market: Reflections on the Attempt to Create a Single Market in the European Union." *American Journal of Sociology* 102:1–33.

———. 1996b. "Markets as Politics: A Political Cultural Approach to Market Institutions." *American Sociological Review* 61:656–73.

Fornell, C. 1988. "Corporate Consumers Affairs Departments: Retrospect and Prospect." Pp. 595–620 in *Frontiers of Research on Consumers Interest,* edited by E. Scott Maynes. Columbia, Mo.: American Council on Consumer Interest.

Fox, William. 1984. *The Mirror Makers.* New York: William Morrow.

Frenzen, J., Paul Hirsch, and Phillip Zerrillo. 1994. "Consumption, Preferences, and Changing Lifestyle." Pp. 403–25 in *Handbook of Economic Sociology,* edited by Neil Smelser and Richard Swedberg. New York: Russell Sage.

Friedland, Roger, and Robert R. Alford. 1991. "Bringing Society Back In: Symbols, Practices, and Institutional Contradictions." Pp. 232–66 in *The New Institutionalism in Organizational Analysis,* edited by Walter W. Powell and Paul J. DiMaggio. Chicago: University of Chicago Press.

Friedson, Eliot. 1986. *Professional Powers: A Study of the Institutionalization of Formal Knowledge.* Chicago: University of Chicago Press.

Fuld, Leonhard Felix. 1916. *Service Instructions of American Corporations.* Washington, D.C.: U.S. Department of the Interior, Bureau of Education.

Granovetter, Mark. 1994. "Business Groups." Pp. 454–76 in *Handbook of Economic Sociology*, edited by N. J. Smelser and R. Swedberg. New York: Russell Sage.

Haines, Herbert H. 1984. "Black Radicalization and the Funding of Civil Rights: 1957–1970." *Social Problems* 32:31–43.

Hannan, Michael T., and John Freeman. 1989. *Organizational Ecology*. Cambridge, Mass.: Belknap Press.

Hechter, Michael T. 1990. "The Emergence of Cooperative Social Institutions." Pp. 13–34 in *Social Institutions: Their Emergence, Maintenance, and Effects*, edited by Michael Hechter, Karl-Dieter Opp, and Reinhard Wippler. New York: Aldine de Gruyter.

Heermance, Edgar L. 1924. *Codes of Ethics: A Handbook*. Burlington, Vt.: Free Press.

Hermann, Robert O. 1970. "Consumerism: Its Goals, Organizations and Future." *Journal of Marketing* 34 (October):55–60.

Hirsch, Paul M. 1986. "From Ambushes to Golden Parachutes: Corporate Takeovers as an Instance of Cultural Framing and Institutional Integration." *American Journal of Sociology* 91:801–37.

Kallet, Arthur, and Frederick Schlink. 1933. *100,000,000 Guinea Pigs: Dangers in Foods, Drugs, and Cosmetics*. New York: Grosset & Dunlap.

Katz, Norman. 1977. "Consumers Union: The Movement and the Magazine." Ph.D. dissertation. Rutgers University.

Kelley, Florence. 1899. "Aims and Principles of the Consumers' League." *American Journal of Sociology* 5 (3):289–304.

Kimberly, J. R. 1975. "Environmental Constraints and Organizational Structure: A Comparative Analysis of Rehabilitation Organizations." *Administrative Science Quarterly* 20:1–14.

Kitson, Harry. 1922. "The Growth of the 'Service Idea' in Selling." *Journal of Political Economy* 30 (June):417–19.

Klandermans, B. 1992. "The Social Construction of Protest and Multi-Organizational Fields." Pp. 77–103 in *Frontiers in Social Movement Theory*, edited by Aldon Morris and Carol Mueller. New Haven, Conn.: Yale University Press.

Lamb, Ruth deForest. 1936. *American Chamber of Horrors: The Truth about Food and Drugs*. New York: Farrar & Rinehart.

Letts, Arthur. 1914. "Progressive Methods in Dry Goods Retailing." *Dry Goods Economist* 68 (April):7.

Luhmann, Niklas. 1979. *Trust and Power: Two Works*. Chichester, N.Y.: Wiley.

Lukes, S. 1974. *Power: A Radical View*. London: Macmillan.

Lumsden, C., and Jitendra Singh. 1990. "The Dynamics of Organizational Speciation." Pp. 145–63 in *Organizational Evolution: New Directions*, edited by Jitandra V. Singh. San Francisco: Sage.

Madden, M. Stuart. 1988. *Product Liability*. St. Paul, Minn.: West.

March, James. and Johan Olsen. 1989. *Rediscovering Institutions*. New York: Free Press.

McAdam, D. 1994. Culture and Social Movements. Pp. 36–57 in *New Social Movements*, edited by Enrique Larana, Hank Johnston, and Joseph R. Gusfield. Philadelphia: Temple University Press.

McAdam, D., J. D. McCarthy, and M. N. Zald. 1988. "Social Movements." Pp. 695–737 in *Handbook of Sociology*, edited by Neil J. Smelser. Beverly Hills, Calif.: Sage.

McKelvey, B. 1982. *Organizational Systematics: Taxonomy, Evolution, Classification*. Berkeley. and Los Angeles: University of California Press.

Meyer, D. S. and D. R. Imig. 1993. "Political Opportunity and the Rise and Decline of Interest Group Sectors." *Social Science Journal* 30:253–70.

Meyer, John W., John Boli, and George M. Thomas. 1987. "Ontology and Rationalization in the Western Cultural Account." Pp. 12–37 in *Institutional Structure: Constituting State, Society, and the Individual*, edited by George M. Thomas, John W. Meyer, Francisco Ramirez, and John Boli. Newbury Park, Calif.: Sage.

Meyer, John, and Brian Rowan. 1991. "Institutional Organizations: Formal Structures as Myth and Ceremony." *American Journal of Sociology* 83:340–63.

Nader, Ralph. 1965. *Unsafe at Any Speed: The Designed-in Dangers of the American Automobile*. New York: Grossman.

Nelson, Richard R., and Sidney G. Winter. 1982. *An Evolutionary Theory of Economic Change*. Cambridge, Mass.: Belknap Press.

Oliver, Christine. 1991. "Strategic Responses to Institutional Processes." *Academy of Management Review* 16:145–79.

———. 1992. "The Antecedents of Deinstitutionalization." *Organization Studies* 13:563–88.

Olney, M. 1991. *Buy Now, Pay Later*. Chapel Hill: University of North Carolina Press.

Oster, Sharon. 1994. *Modern Competitive Analysis*. New York: Oxford University Press.

Padgett, John, and Christopher K. Ansell. 1993. "Robust Action and the Rise of the Medici, 1400–1434." *American Journal of Sociology* 98:1259–1319.

Pfeffer, J. M. 1992. *Managing with Power*. Cambridge, Mass.: Harvard University Press.

Phillips, Mary C. 1934. *Skin Deep*. New York: Vanguard.

Pollay, R. 1985. "The Subsiding Sizzle: A Descriptive History of Print Advertising, 1900–1980." *Journal of Marketing* 49 (3):24–39.

Powell, Walter W. 1991. "Expanding the Scope of Organizational Analysis," Pp. 183–203 in *The New Institutionalism in Organizational Analysis*, edited by Walter W. Powell and Paul J. DiMaggio. Chicago: University of Chicago Press.

Priest, G. 1984. "The Invention of Enterprise Liability: A Critical History of the Intellectual Foundations of Modern Tort Law." Working paper, no. 27. Yale Law School, Yale University.

Ranson, S., C. L. Hinings, and Royston Greenwood. 1980. "The Structuring of Organizational Structure." *Administrative Science Quarterly* 25:1–14.

Romanelli, E. 1989. "Organizational Birth and Population Variety: A Community Perspective on Origins." Pp. 211–246 in *Research in Organizational Behavior*, vol. 11. Edited by Barry Staw and Larry L. Cummings. Greenwich, Conn.: JAI Press.

Samson, Peter. 1980. "The Emergence of a Consumer Interest in America." Ph.D. dissertation. University of Chicago.

Sargent, Hugh. 1958. "The Influence of Consumer Product Testing and Reporting Services on Consumer Behavior." Ph.D. dissertation. University of Illinois.

Schlink, F. 1927. "Tests and Specifications for the Household." *Journal of Home Economics* 19:18–20.

Schudson, Michael. 1978. *Discovering the News*. New York: Basic.

Schumpeter, J. A. 1950. *Capitalism, Socialism and Democracy*. New York: Harper.

Scott, W. R. 1995. *Institutions and Organizations*. San Francisco: Sage.

Shapiro, Susan P. 1987. "The Social Control of Impersonal Trust." *American Journal of Sociology* 93:623–58.

Shepsle, K. 1990. *Perspectives on Positive Political Economy*. Cambridge: Cambridge University Press.

Silber, Norman Isaac. 1983. *Test and Protest: The Influence of Consumers Union*. New York: Holmes & Meier.

Sorenson, Helen. 1941. *The Consumer Movement*. New York: Harper.

Snow, David A., and Robert D. Benford. 1992. "Master Frames and Cycles of Protest." Pp. 133–55 in *Frontiers in Social Movement Theory*, edited by Aldon Morris and Carol Mueller. New Haven, Conn.: Yale University Press.

Spacone, C. A. 1985. "The Emergence of Strict Liability: A Historical Perspective and Other Considerations including Senate 100." *Journal of Product Liability* 8:1–40.

Stinchcombe, Arthur L. 1965. "Social Structure and Organizations." Pp. 142–93 in *Handbook of Organizations*, edited by James G. March. Chicago: Rand McNally.

———. 1968. *Constructing Social Theories*. Chicago: University of Chicago Press.

Stoddard, C. K. 1928. "Your Standard's Worth." *Printers Ink*, August 16, pp. 117–20.

Sutton, J. R., and F. Dobbin. 1996. "The Two Faces of Governance: Responses to Legal Uncertainty in U.S. Firms, 1955–1986." *American Sociological Review* 61: 794–811.

Swidler, Ann. 1986. "Culture in Action: Symbols and Strategies." *American Sociological Review* 51:273–86.

Tarrow, Sidney. 1989. *Democracy and Disorder: Protest and Politics in Italy: 1965–1975.* Oxford: Oxford University Press.

Thomas, Robert Paul. 1977. *An Analysis of the Patterns of Growth of the Automobile Industry, 1895–1929.* New York: Arno Press.

Thorelli, Hans, and Sarah Thorelli. 1974. *Consumer Information Handbook.* New York: Praeger.

Tushman, Michael L., and Philip Anderson. 1986. "Technological Discontinuities and Organizational Environments." *Administrative Science Quarterly* 31:439–65.

U.S. Bureau of the Census. 1975. *Historical Statistics of the United States, Colonial Times to 1970.* Washington, D.C.: U.S. Department of Commerce.

Vaile, R. 1927. *The Economics of Advertising.* New York: Ronald Press.

Vandall, F. 1989. *Strict Liability: Legal and Economic Analysis.* New York: Quorum Books.

Van de Ven, A. H., and R. Garud. 1989. "A Framework for Understanding the Emergence of New Industries." Pp. 195–225 in *Research in Technological Innovation, Management, and Policy,* edited by R. Rosenbloom and R. Burgelman. Greenwich, Conn.: JAI Press.

Veblen, Thorstein. 1919. *The Place of Science in Modern Civilization and Other Essays.* New York: Huebsch.

White, Harrison. 1992. *Identity and Control.* Princeton, N.J.: Princeton University Press.

Wiley, Mary., and Mayer Zald. 1968. "The Growth and Transformation of Educational Accrediting Agencies: An Exploratory Study in the Social Control of Institutions." *Sociology of Education* 41:36–56.

Williamson, Oliver E. 1985. *The Economic Institutions of Capitalism.* New York: Free Press.

Zald, Mayer N. 1992. "Looking Backward to Look Forward: Reflections on the Past and Future of the Resource Mobilization Research Program." Pp. 326–48 in *Frontiers in Social Movement Theory,* edited by Aldon Morris and Carol Mueller. New Haven, Conn.: Yale University Press.

Zald, Mayer, and John D. McCarthy. 1980. "Social Movement Industries: Competition and Cooperation among Movement Organizations." *Research in Social Movements, Conflict, and Change* 3:1–20.

Zelizer, Vivianna A. 1994. *The Social Meaning of Money.* New York: Basic.

Zucker, Lynne G. 1986. "The Production of Trust: Institutional Sources of Economic Structure: 1840–1920." Pp. 53–111 in *Research in Organizational Behavior,* vol. 8. Edited by Barry Staw and Larry L. Cummings. Greenwich, Conn.: JAI Press.

Zuckerman, E. 1996. "Mediating the Corporate Product. Securities Analysts and the Scope of the Firm." Working paper. University of Chicago, Department of Sociology.

Part III

Organizations and Environments

Studies of Organizational

Adaptation and Change

Chapter 27
Autonomy, Interdependence, and Social Control

NASA and the Space Shuttle *Challenger*

Diane Vaughan

In 1986, the shocking explosion of the space shuttle Challenger focused the nation's attention on the great promise and perils of technology in the modern world. As Diane Vaughan explains in this chapter, however, the preoccupation with the technological failures that contributed to this disaster may have been somewhat misplaced. Organizational factors also played a role in this tragedy. In particular, Vaughan argues that serious flaws in organizational policies, procedures, and systems of regulation increase the likelihood of serious accidents.

The tragic loss of the space shuttle *Challenger* on January 28, 1986 sent the nation into mourning and forced a citizenry ordinarily preoccupied with other matters to confront again the risks of living in a technologically sophisticated age. Preceded by the incidents at Three Mile Island and Union Carbide in Bhopal and soon followed by Chernobyl, the *Challenger* accident left in its aftermath a deeply troubling question: Has our ability to create highly developed technological systems exceeded our ability to control and master them in practice? Perrow (1984) addressed this question, arguing that technological complexity has a tendency to result in "normal accidents," accidents that are inevitable for certain technical systems. These accidents initially are caused by technical component failures but become accidents rather than incidents because of the nature of the system. The failure of one component interacts with others, triggering a complex set of interactions that can precipitate a technical system accident of catastrophic potential.

Technology isn't the only culprit, however: The organizations that run these risky enterprises often contribute to their own technological failures. Turner (1976, 1978) has investigated accidents and social disasters, seeking any systematic organizational patterns that might have preceded these events. He found that disasters had long incubation periods characterized by a number of discrepant events signaling danger. These events were overlooked or misinterpreted, accumulating unnoticed. Among the organizational patterns contributing to there "failures of foresight" (Turner, 1978: 51) were norms and culturally accepted beliefs about hazards, poor communication, inadequate information handling in complex situations, and failure to comply with existing regulations instituted to assure safety (Turner, 1976: 391).

Paradoxically, a long incubation period is advantageous. Hypothetically, regulatory agents could intervene, possibly averting a technical system accident. True, some are unavoidable, because they involve multiple errors of design, equipment failure, and systems operation. But for those technical system accidents that are potentially avoidable and whose impending occurrence is obscured by organizational patterns such as those Turner noted, effective regulation may reduce the probability that a technical failure will occur. Unfortunately, regulatory agents are organizations subject to their own failures of foresight.

When regulatory failure occurs in the monitoring of an organization that deals in high-risk technology, the resulting accident may be thought of as an organizational-technical system accident: a potentially avoidable technical system accident resulting from the failure of the technical components of the product, the organization responsible for its production and use, and the regulatory organizations designed to oversee the entire operation. The failures of the producer and regulatory organizations are failures of foresight, arising from organizational patterns that block problem identification and correction in the pre-accident incubation period. Such an accident cannot be explained by the failure of the technical system alone. The organization malfunctions, failing to correct a correctable technical problem. The regulatory organization charged with surveillance of the technical product and the organization's performance fails to resolve the problems in both. The result is an organizational-technical system accident, perhaps of catastrophic proportion.

The *Challenger* disaster was an organizational-technical system accident. The immediate cause was technical failure. The O-rings—two 0.280-inch diameter rings of synthetic rubber designed to seal a gap in the aft field joint of the solid rocket booster—did not do their job. The Presidential Commission (1986, 1: 72) investigating the incident stated that design failure interacted with "the effects of temperature, physical dimensions, the character of the materials, the effects of re-usability, processing, and the reaction of the joint to dynamic loading." The result of these interactive factors was, indeed, a technical system accident similar to those Perrow identified. But there was more. The post-accident investigations of both the Commission (1986, 1: 82–150) and the U.S. House Committee on Science and Technology (1986a: 138–178) indicated that the NASA organization contributed to the technical failure. As Turner might have predicted, the technical failure had a long incubation period. Problems with the O-rings were first noted in 1977 (Presidential Commission, 1986, 1: 122). Thus, NASA might have acted to avert the tragedy. But the organizational response to the technical problem was characterized by poor communication, inadequate information handling, faulty technical decision making, and failure to comply with regulations instituted to assure safety (Presidential Commission, 1986, 1: 82–150; U.S. House Committee on Science and Technology, 1986a: 138–178). Moreover, the regulatory system designed to oversee the safety of the shuttle program failed to identify and correct program management and design problems related to the O-rings. NASA insiders referred to these omissions as "quality escapes": failures of the program to preclude an avoidable problem (Presidential Commission, 1986, 1: 156, 159). NASA's safety system failed at monitoring shuttle operations to such an extent that the Presidential Commission's report referred to it as "The Silent Safety Program" (1986, 1: 152).

My purpose in this paper is to analyze NASA's safety regulatory system and specify the organizational bases of its ineffective-

ness. NASA, like all organizations, is subject to restraint and control that occur as a consequence of interaction with other organizations in its environment acting as consumers, suppliers, competitors, and controllers (Pfeffer and Salancik, 1978: 40–54). In this analysis, I focus only on those organizations with (1) officially designated social control responsibilities, (2) safety assurance as the sole function, and (3) personnel with aerospace technical expertise. Although the uniqueness of this case requires the usual disclaimers about generalization, its uniqueness also allows analysis of a complex technical case perhaps not possible otherwise. The tragedy generated an enormous amount of archival information as well as much conflicting public discourse by people more technically competent than I, leading me to sources and questions that might not have occurred to me.

Over 122,000 pages of documents gathered by the Presidential Commission are catalogued and available at the National Archives, Washington, D.C. I've drawn my analysis from documents pertaining to safety that were generated by NASA, contractors, and safety regulators prior to the disaster. I also relied on volumes 1, 2, 4, and 5 of the 1986 *Report of the Presidential Commission on the Space Shuttle Challenger Accident*, volumes 4 and 5 of which contain 2,800 pages of hearing transcripts from both closed and open Commission sessions; the 1986 Report of the Committee on Science and Technology, U.S. House of Representatives, which includes two volumes of hearing transcripts; and the published accounts of journalists, historians, scientists, and others.

I also conducted interviews. Crucial to my methodology was the use of information from both insiders and outsiders: insiders are participants in the organizations or event being studied; outsiders are individuals informed about the subject matter who, because of position within the organizations being studied, membership in other organizations, ideology, occupation, or even varied proximity to the event or setting, may hold different perspectives on an event than insiders. Outsiders produce additional insights that aid in discovering biases inherent in primary data sources. In this case, the insiders I interviewed were people responsible for regulating safety at NASA and contractor sites; outsiders were whistleblowers, journalists who investigated NASA's safety system following the disaster, and participants in NASA's regulatory environment who were not directly responsible for regulating safety but were knowledgeable about it. I sent selected insiders and outsiders copies of the penultimate draft of this paper, and their comments were taken into account. In the final version, I also used transcripts from 160 additional interviews conducted by 15 experienced government investigators who supported Commission activities, documenting the factual background of the incident and safety activities at NASA and its contractors (totaling approximately 9,000 pages stored at the National Archives). Nearly 60 percent of those interviewed by government investigators never testified before the Presidential Commission or the House Committee on Science and Technology.

Constraints on the Social Control of Organizations

Research on legally empowered agents of social control regulating business firms reveals how interorganizational relations constrain social control. Both the autonomy and interdependence of regulatory and regulated organizations inhibit control efforts (Vaughan, 1983: 88–104). While autonomy and interdependence affect the full range of regulatory activities—discovery, monitoring, investigation, and sanctioning—they each appear to affect particular control activities differentially. Autonomy, or the fact that social control agents and business firms exist as separate, independent entities, seems to be a critical factor in regulatory efforts to discover, monitor, and investigate organizational behavior. All organizations are, to varying degrees, self-bounded communities. Physical structure, reinforced by norms and laws protecting privacy, insulates them from other organizations in the environment. The nature of transactions further protects them from outsiders by releasing only selected bits of information in complex and difficult-to-monitor forms. Thus, although organizations engage in exchange with others, they retain elements of autonomy that mask organizational behavior. While an organization's structure and the nature of its transactions obscure activities from all other organizations in the environment, they pose particular problems for agents of social control.

Autonomous structures in their own right, regulators are mandated to oversee the behavior of other organizations. But the autonomy of regulated organizations obstructs the gathering and interpretation of information necessary for discovery, monitoring, and investigation. Regulators attempt to penetrate organizational boundaries by periodic site visits and/or by requiring the regulated organization to furnish information to them. These strategies allow regulators to examine only limited aspects of organizational life, however. Moreover, even when regulators have access to organizations in these two ways, the size and complexity of this targeted organization, its numerous daily transactions, specialization; and the unique languages that accompany it can be difficult to master. Technology adds to the challenge. Regulators, always under pressure to keep informed of developments in the industries they regulate, find their tasks complicated by scientific advance and the burgeoning use of computer technology in nearly every aspect of routine business activity.

Attempting to surmount these obstacles, regulators tend to become dependent on the regulated organization to aid them in gathering and interpreting information. While certainly the potential exists for a productive relationship, informational dependencies also can undermine social control in subtle ways. First, regulators' definitions of what is a problem and the relative seriousness of problems are shaped by their informants. Second, informational dependencies tend to generate continuing relationships that make regulators vulnerable to cooptation (Selznick, 1966). Regulators may take the point of view of the regulated because they develop sympathy and affinity for them, compromising the ability both to identify and report violations. Finally, the situation is ripe for intentional distortion and obfuscation by the regulated, for informational dependencies prevent regulators from detecting falsification.

Paradoxically, regulatory organizations and the organizations they regulate have the capacity to be autonomous and interdependent simultaneously. Despite being physically separate independent entities, regulator and regulated may become linked such that outcomes for each are, in part, determined by the activities of the other (Pfeffer and Salancik, 1978: 39–61; Vaughan, 1983: 93–104). When organizations are interdependent, the outcomes they reach are determined by the nature and distribution of resources between the two and the way those resources are used. Although interdependence may affect the entire regulatory process, its major impact is on the ability of regulators to threaten or impose meaningful sanctions. Interdependence can be of two types: competitive or symbiotic (Pfeffer and Salancik, 1978: 41). Competitive interdependence exists when two organizations compete for the same scarce resources and when one succeeds, the other, by definition, fails (Pfeffer and Salancik, 1978: 41). Competitive interdependence applies to social control agents and the organizations they regulate in a slightly different sense. Because they are adversaries, the resources of each can be used in ways that interfere with the goals of the other. Regulatory organizations possess resources (investigative and sanctioning powers) that can impose costs and threaten the operation of regulated organizations. At the same time, regulated organizations may possess resources (wealth, influence, information) that can interfere with the successful enactment of tasks necessary to social control (Stone, 1975: 96; Cullen, Maakestad, and Cavender, 1987). Consequently, both regulator and regulated tend to avoid costly adversarial strategies to impose and thwart punitive sanctions; instead, bargaining becomes institutionalized, as negotiation demands fewer resources from both (Vaughan, 1983: 88–104). Hence, sanctions: often are mitigated as a result of the power-mediating efforts of both parties.

Symbiotic interdependence also affects tile sanctioning process. Symbiotic interdependence exists, when resource exchange occurs between social control organizations and those they regulate: different resources are exchanged, one organization's output functioning as the input of the other (Pfeffer and Salancik, 1978: 41). When harm or good fortune befalls one, the well-being of the other is similarly affected. Hence, they rise and fall together. When the exchange is asymmetrical, symbiotic interdependence may either enhance or impede regulatory efforts. On the one hand, when a firm is dependent on the government to supply a critical resource, the probability that the regulated organization will comply with government laws and regulations is increased (Wiley and Zald, 1968: 35–56). On the other hand, when the government is dependent on a firm to supply a critical resource and that firm violates laws or rules,

the probability that a government regulatory agency will invoke stringent sanctions to achieve compliance is decreased (Pfeffer and Salancik, 1978: 58–59).

Situations of mutual dependence (whether symbiotic or competitive) are likely to engender continual negotiation and bargaining rather than adversarial tactics, as each party tries to control the other's use of resources and conserve its own (Yuchtman and Seashore, 1967). To interpret the consequences of this negotiation and bargaining (e.g., the "slap-on-the-wrist" sanction or no sanction at all) as regulatory "failure" is to miss the point. Compromise is an enforcement pattern systematically generated by the structure of interorganizational regulatory relations.

The concepts of autonomy and interdependence are useful analytic tools for research on the social control of organizations. But to restrict inquiry to private sector organizations and legal actors is to make artificial distinctions that impede theorizing. Structural similarities, grounded in the hierarchical nature of organizational forms, allow us to apply concepts, models, and theories in multiple contexts (Vaughan, 1990). Because regulatory difficulties are systematically generated by the structure of relations between organizations, we can use autonomy and interdependence heuristically to guide analysis of official regulatory relations between diverse types of organizations. Further, organizations exist in a hierarchy of organizations and develop an internal hierarchy of their own. Consequently, concepts developed to explain relations between an organization and others in its environment can be used to examine intraorganizational relations (Vaughan, 1990: 3–6). Many organizations are self-regulating, initiating special subunits to discover, monitor, investigate, and sanction in order to control deviant events intraorganizationally. While empirical and theoretical work on the external control of organizations is extensive, we know much less about the organizational dimensions of self-regulation (but see Katz, 1977; Sherman, 1978; Punch, 1985; Braithwaite and Fisse, 1987). By using autonomy and interdependence to explore social control relations intra- and interorganizationally and by varying the type of organizations studied, we may (1) learn more about how the structured relations of organizations affect social control, (2) specify these two concepts more fully, and (3) move toward more broadly based theory on the social control of organizations.

I've used these two concepts to guide my analysis of safety regulatory enforcement at NASA. In contrast to the research tradition of investigating the social control of business firms by legally empowered agents of social control, I explore the regulation of a government agency and one of its contractors. Two internal safety organizations established by NASA and one external safety regulator created by Congress regulated the shuttle program. Consequently, we have the rare opportunity of examining a self-regulating system reinforced by external control. While the strategy at NASA of combining self-regulation with external review would appear to be maximally effective (the advantages of one compensating for the disadvantages of the other), I hypothesize that regulatory effectiveness at NASA was undermined by autonomy and interdependence, reducing the probability that safety hazards would be identified and corrected.

Each regulatory strategy has its own structurally engendered weaknesses. Created to reap the independent review potential of an autonomous structure, NASA's external regulator would tend to experience difficulties in getting access to and interpreting information, perhaps developing informational dependencies that would undermine independent review. If NASA and the external regulator are found to be interdependent, the application of sanctions would tend to be mitigated by negotiation and compromise. We also would expect to find autonomy and interdependence at work intraorganizationally. The advantage of internal regulatory bodies is access to the organization and knowledge of language, specialization, and technology, which allows them a closer purview than external regulators (Bardach and Kagan, 1982: 219, 272). Yet, when organizations are large, internal structure, specialization, and numerous transactions can confound insiders, preserving organizational autonomy. Despite having better access to data, an internal regulator still may encounter barriers to discovery, monitoring, and investigation. Informational dependencies, previously identified only in interorganizational control relations, are a likely result. Moreover, we would expect self-regulating systems to be plagued continuously by symbiotic inter-dependence. When regulatory authority, resources, and time are controlled by the regulated organization, many phases of the regulatory process might be compromised, from issuing warnings to imposing sanctions. Most certainly, these dependencies would tend to subvert objective review.

Exploring the structural contribution to regulatory ineffectiveness at NASA shifts the focus away from individual actors. Undeniably, individuals had a hand in it: those administrators who made critical decisions about regulatory structure and resource allocation to safety over the years, as well as the actions of individual safety personnel on the job. Neither are addressed here. The decisions of NASA administrators that affected the structure of regulation necessarily are recounted, but the explanation behind those decisions requires extensive analysis of the NASA organization and its history. While all three components of NASA's organizational-technical system are essential to understanding the accident, such an examination is beyond the scope of this paper. Clarifying the structural bases of NASA's regulatory ineffectiveness is significant in its own right, however, having implications both for theory and policy concerning the social control of organizations.

Organizations no doubt have failures of foresight more frequently than we realize. Only when these failures lead to harmful consequences that then become public do outsiders have the opportunity to consider the cause. Because official investigations shape what outsiders perceive as cause, and because documents from official investigations are used in this research, consideration must be given to the accounts that result from such investigations. The Presidential Commission and the House Commission on Science and Technology also are part of NASA's safety regulatory environment, both having officially designated social control responsibilities. The extent to which autonomy and interdependence may have affected the documents they produced deserves inquiry. This phase of my research is still in progress. While the conclusions drawn by these official investigations remain to be assessed as a product of the politico-socio-historical environment that produced them, the descriptions of NASA's regulatory environment in general and the three safety units in particular have been corroborated from multiple sources, justifying their use as an example of regulation in an organizational-technical system accident.

NASA's Regulatory Environment: Structure and Process

The foundation of NASA's regulatory system was established by the National Aeronautics and Space Act of 1958 (U.S. Congress, 1959). This act allocated broad oversight responsibilities to two bodies, to the National Aeronautics and Space Council and to Congress, but the responsibility for close surveillance was left to NASA. The space agency, from its inception, was to guide and implement its own regulation. NASA was given the authority "to make, promulgate, issue, rescind, and amend rules and regulations governing the manner of its operations and the exercise of the powers vested in it by law" and "to appoint such advisory committees as may be appropriate for purposes of consultation and advice to the Administrator in the performance of its functions" (U.S. Congress, 1959: sec. 203).

Self-regulation is a frequent solution to the classic dilemma of government: Who controls the controller? But, more significantly, the space agency's self-regulatory responsibilities were designed to complement and assure NASA's central goal: U.S. supremacy in the international competition for scientific advance and military supremacy (McDougall, 1985). To meet both scientific and defense goals, NASA required a regulatory system that would closely monitor technical development and management aspirations to assure safety, reliability, and quality of equipment design and performance. At the same time, the space agency needed to encourage innovation. While safety and innovation are inherently conflicting goals (the former requiring constraint, the latter freedom), both were essential for competitive success. Hypothetically, an independent external body could effect the constraint necessary to assure safety. But would an external regulator have the capability for regular surveillance as well as the ability' to assess NASA's complex technical systems and operations? Moreover, an external regulator might impose constraints that would interfere with innovation or, a related concern, penetrate the secrecy necessary to Department of Defense projects on which NASA cooperated.

What agency was better qualified in the technical expertise necessary to ensure safety than NASA? What agency was better able to encourage and foster innovative space technology and at the same time keep the secrets necessary to national defense? In its self-regulating efforts, NASA created a regulatory structure intended to ensure both safety and innovation by separating oversight responsibilities for these two goals. To encourage innovation, NASA created a system of advisory committees staffed with respected leaders from the aerospace industry, research institutes, and universities, who would shape policy and technological developments. To assure safety, NASA created two intraorganizational regulatory units staffed by NASA personnel: the Safety, Reliability, and Quality Assurance Program and the Space Shuttle Crew Safety Panel. The sole responsibility of these units was to assure safety through intensive scrutiny of both technical design and program management. These two internal safety units were created with the expectation that NASA personnel, informed about its technology, management systems, personnel, and with access to day-to-day activities, were capable of the close monitoring essential to safety. Moreover, these internal units were physically separate from the activities they were to regulate, so they were expected to bring to their task the objectivity necessary for independent review (U.S. House, 1967a, pt. 2: 41).

These safety units existed at the inception of the shuttle program, but there was one addition. Shortly after the 1967 Apollo launch-pad fire that killed three astronauts, Congress supplemented NASA's own advisory committee structure with an advisory committee solely responsible for safety surveillance: the Aerospace Safety Advisory Panel (Rumsfeld and Kriegsman, 1967; U.S. Congress, 1968). The creation of this panel was an explicit attempt by Congress to balance NASA's internal safety system with an independent external regulatory body composed of aerospace experts (Presidential Commission, 1986, 5: 1488–1489; Egan, 1988). Legislative action was guided by the notion that the combination of internal and external regulatory bodies would provide the surveillance essential for preventing future accidents (U.S. House, 1967a, pt. 2: 229).

Legal agents of social control tend to regulate through one of two generic strategies: deterrence or compliance (Reiss, 1984). Reiss (1984) noted that many, if not most, social control systems mix compliance and deterrence strategies of law enforcement, but as ideal types the two models behave quite differently. In a deterrence strategy, punishment is invoked after a violation has occurred. Social control is adversarial: discover, investigate, prosecute, and punish violators. While the entire investigatory process communicates the message that violations will be met with enforcement action, it is ultimately the punishment itself that is believed to affect decision making. But empirical questions about the deterrent effects of punishment aside, some situations exist for which a deterrence strategy is out of the question. Some violations, such as those resulting in accidents at nuclear power plants, have consequences so extreme that to allow the possibility of their occurrence is to take a socially unacceptable risk.

For NASA, the potential result of technical and procedural violations was losses too great to risk. Not only might lives and an expensive vehicle be destroyed, but an in-flight failure could also jeopardize funding from commercial and congressional sources. Moreover, post-accident interruption to space science and military ventures linked to the shuttle program could threaten the U.S. position among world powers. In such situations, a compliance strategy is more appropriate. And the regulatory process of all three NASA safety units was thus characterized by a compliance strategy. Prevention of social harm was the goal. A compliance strategy has regulators monitoring, negotiating, and intervening regularly with target organizations in order to gain compliance with existing standards—thus attempting to avoid violations and the social costs that would ensue (Reiss, 1984: 28). Whereas deterrence systems primarily manipulate punishments, compliance systems principally manipulate rewards. Negotiation gradually begins to incorporate elements of punishment as compliance efforts run into trouble. Although a compliance system also has penalties available, they are used primarily as a threat rather than as a sanction to be carried out. A sanction invoked as a threat during compliance negotiations is intended to stop the inappropriate behavior, the same as a sanction invoked as punishment to be carried out after failed negotiations. When compliance is achieved, typically the sanctions are suspended or withdrawn. To carry out a punishment is a sign that negotiation—the hallmark of the system—has failed (Reiss, 1984: 25). The threat (sometimes to punish by withdrawing a reward) is part of an array of enforcement tactics that are all characterized by a continuing personal contact between regulator and regulated in which social relationships are valued not only as a means of easing the job, but also as a means of assisting in the future discovery of problems (Hawkins, 1984).

NASA's internal and external safety regulatory units were intended to provide the balanced scrutiny necessary to safeguard the shuttle program. Yet this safety system failed to avert the *Challenger* tragedy. Below, I describe the three safety units, their compliance strategies, inadequacies, and the structural constraints on social control, to show how autonomy and interdependence undercut effective discovery, monitoring, investigation, and sanctioning of safety hazards in the NASA system. For this account, I have relied heavily on documents in the National Archives, which are listed in the references, as well as on the interview data I collected.

Barriers to Discovery, Monitoring, and Investigation

The Safety, Reliability, and Quality Assurance Program (SR&QA)

Of the three safety units, SR&QA bore the major responsibility for safety oversight. This internal NASA safety program was headed by the chief engineer at NASA headquarters in Washington. In addition to the staff there, SR&QA had subunits at Johnson, Kennedy, and Marshall space centers (Presidential Commission, 1986, 1: 153). Its responsibilities extended to NASA contractors responsible for shuttle components, which SR&QA monitored from offices located at contractor facilities. Although SR&QA offices were organized differently at each center, their functions and compliance strategies were the same (Bunn, 1986). The compliance strategy of SR&QA included the three monitoring responsibilities indicated by its name, all with direct flight-safety implications. The safety function was carried out by engineers who prepared and executed plans for accident prevention, flight systems safety, and industrial safety requirements. Additionally, safety engineers identified in-flight and post-flight problems, determined and monitored potential hazards, and assessed risk. The reliability engineers' responsibility was to determine that particular components and systems arriving at the centers from contractors could be relied on to work as planned. Quality assurance engineers had the responsibility for procedural controls: assessing inspection programs and identifying and reporting problems (Presidential Commission, 1986, 1: 152–153; NASA, 1986).

Safety standards for these activities were published in a wide-scoped, detailed document that was updated annually (NASA, 1986). SR&QA staff monitored and implemented these standards on a day-to-day basis at all NASA locations and at contractor sites. Contractors were required to create their own internal safety organization and prepare a safety plan complying with all requirements in the document (NASA, 1986: 2–2). SR&QA personnel situated in contractor facilities monitored compliance with written procedures and worked closely with contractor safety personnel. In addition, SR&QA audit teams audited contractor activities periodically. Contractors submitted problem reports and corrective actions to the center monitoring them, which forwarded summary reports to Washington (Quong, 1986: 18–20, 30).

Because O-ring problems were first noted at NASA in 1977, both the Presidential Commission and the House Committee on Science and Technology wanted to know why NASA managers were not better informed about the solid rocket booster joint difficulties. NASA engineers at Marshall were aware; SR&QA staff at both Marshall and Morton Thiokol, Inc. of Utah, the contractor responsible for manufacturing the solid rocket boosters, were monitoring the problem. Yet NASA administrators reported they did not consider the problem hazardous to mission safety. The official *Challenger* incident inquiries found major failures in SR&QA's monitoring and investigating responsibilities, supposedly the primary advantage of internal control. Three principal failures were discovered, involving safety-critical items, trend data, and problem-reporting requirements. (Presidential Commission, 1986, 1: 153–156; U.S. House

Committee on Science and Technology, 1986a: 69, 174–179). Had SR&QA handled these three responsibilities effectively, the probability that NASA administrators would have accurately assessed the O-ring problem would have been increased.

Safety-critical items. SR&QA assigns criticality categories that identify shuttle components by the seriousness of failure consequences. The failure of a component designated Criticality 1 (C 1), for example, results in "loss of life or vehicle" (Presidential Commission, 1986, 1: 153). SR&QA produces a Critical Items List for each component and is responsible for monitoring these items. The solid rocket booster (SRB) joint was originally listed as C 1-R, indicating redundancy (i.e., a back-up existed to prevent failure). But in 1982, the criticality category was changed to the more serious C 1 designation (Marshall Space Flight Center, 1982: A-6A, 6B). After the accident, some internal NASA documents were discovered that still listed the joint as C 1-R after the criticality change, which apparently led some NASA managers wrongly to believe that redundancy existed, and SR&QA failed to identify and rectify this confusion (Presidential Commission, 1986, 1: 155–159).

Trend data. The development of trend data is a standard function of any reliability and quality assurance program. Beginning with the tenth mission of the shuttle in January 1984 and concluding with the twenty-fifth (the *Challenger* flight), more than half the missions experienced O-ring problems. This trend was not identified and analyzed by SR&QA (Presidential Commission, 1986, 1: 155–156). Had SR&QA compiled and circulated trend data on in-flight O-ring erosion, NASA administrators (and SR&QA personnel) would have had essential data on the history and extent of the joint problem.

Problem-reporting requirements. The Presidential Commission found three problem-reporting requirement failures. First, SR&QA did not establish and maintain clear and sufficient requirements for reporting shuttle problems up the NASA hierarchy (Presidential Commission, 1986, 1: 154). As shown in Figure 27.1, the shuttle program management structure consisted of four hierarchical levels. Prior to 1983, Level III was required to report all problems, trends, and problem closeout actions to Level II unless the problem was associated with hardware that was not "flight-critical" (Presidential Commission, 1986, 1: 154). In 1983, the director of SR&QA at Johnson reduced the requirements for reporting problems (Johnson Space Center, 1983). The result was that less documentation and fewer reporting requirements replaced previous directives that all safety problems be reported to upper levels in NASA's hierarchy (Presidential Commission, 1986, 1 : 154).

Second, SR&QA failed to create a concise set of requirements for reporting in-flight anomalies (unexpected events or unexplained departures from past mission experience). Those rules that were in effect were scattered in individual documents and often contradicted each other, causing confusion about which document applied and to which level of management a problem should be conveyed (Presidential Commission, 1986, 1: 154–155).

Finally, SR&QA failed to detect violations of problem reporting requirements. NASA's Level III project managers were required to inform Level II of launch constraints (Presidential Commission, 1986, 1: 138, 159). A launch constraint is issued by Level III managers in response to a serious safety issue. The constraint requires corrective action be taken before the shuttle can fly. Because of the extensiveness of O-ring erosion found after the shuttle launch of April 1985, Level III managers placed a launch constraint against the next six shuttle flights (Presidential Commission, 1986, 1: 137). Each time a launch approached, Level III solid rocket booster project manager Lawrence Mulloy formally waived the constraint, allowing the flight to proceed. Yet neither Level II nor Level I NASA administrators were informed of the constraints or the subsequent waivers, in violation of the launch constraint reporting requirement, and SR&QA did not discover the reporting requirement violations (Presidential Commission,1986, 1: 138–139, 155, 159).

SR&QA was not making trends, status, and problems visible with sufficient accuracy and emphasis. In addition to these shortcomings, the Commission noted that SR&QA staff were absent from key *Challenger* pre-launch decision making: the controversial teleconference between Marshall Space Flight Center and Morton Thiokol personnel the night before the launch, when Thiokol engineers expressed concern about the potential for O-ring erosion and objected

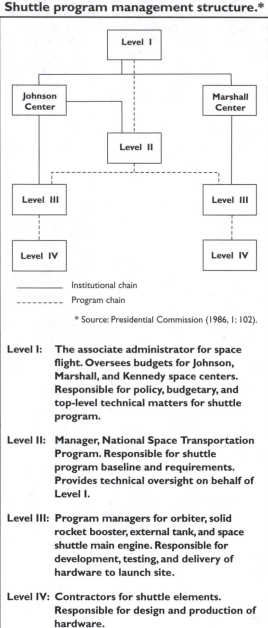

Figure 27.1

Shuttle program management structure.*

——————— Institutional chain

– – – – – – Program chain

* Source: Presidential Commission (1986, 1: 102).

Level I: The associate administrator for space flight. Oversees budgets for Johnson, Marshall, and Kennedy space centers. Responsible for policy, budgetary, and top-level technical matters for shuttle program.

Level II: Manager, National Space Transportation Program. Responsible for shuttle program baseline and requirements. Provides technical oversight on behalf of Level I.

Level III: Program managers for orbiter, solid rocket booster, external tank, and space shuttle main engine. Responsible for development, testing, and delivery of hardware to launch site.

Level IV: Contractors for shuttle elements. Responsible for design and production of hardware.

to launching in the predicted cold weather (Presidential Commission, 1986, 1: 152). Although safety representatives are incorporated into formal pre-flight decision making, "no one thought to invite a safety representative or a reliability and quality assurance engineer" to the hurriedly convened January 27 teleconference, which occurred not only outside the mandated formal review process, but began at 5:45 p.m. EST, after many people at Kennedy had gone for the day (Presidential Commission, 1986, 1: 152). Furthermore, no safety representative was on the Mission Management Team that made key decisions concerning ice and cold during the countdown (1986, 1: 152). The absence of SR&QA staff was another missed opportunity to identify and communicate safety concerns. Supposedly, SR&QA created and maintained exacting and extensive safety procedures during the Apollo program (Presidential Commission, 1986, 1: 152; *Wall Street Journal*, 1986: A-2). What happened is that both autonomy and interdependence were undermining regulation intraorganizationally.

In the mid-sixties, a complex nexus of factors, both international and domestic, resulted in uncertainty about the future direction of the space program and a consequent decline in congressional appropriations for NASA (McDougall, 1985: 420–435). The shuttle program was born in the midst of this decline, with funding struggles as its inalienable birthright (Roland, 1985). Rather than the redundancy that typified the program during Apollo, safety surveillance for the shuttle was characterized by scarcity. The Safety, Reliability and Quality Assurance Program was dependent on NASA decisions that allocated resources to it, and NASA had cut those resources (Diamond, 1986; Presidential Commission, 1986, 1: 159–161; *Wall Street Journal*, 1986). In 1982, the shuttle was officially declared operational, signifying that the developmental phase was over: after four test flights, the shuttle had proven ready to fulfill the tasks for which it had been designed (Presidential Commission, 1986, 1: 161). At that time, NASA either reorganized SR&QA offices or continued them with reduced personnel. Between 1970 and the *Challenger* tragedy, NASA trimmed 71 percent of its safety and quality control staff (U.S. House Committee on Science and Technology, 1986a: 176–177; Magnuson, 1986: 17). SR&QA staff at Marshall, which had NASA responsibility for the solid rocket booster project, had been cut from about 130 to 84. (U.S. House Committee on Science and Technology, 1986b, 1: 655; Quong, 1986: 27). At the time of the accident, total SR&QA personnel numbered about 500; total NASA employees were about twenty-two thousand (U.S. House Committee on Science and Technology, 1986a: 176–177).

Even before staff reductions, we might expect SR&QA to be handicapped by the autonomy generated by the NASA/contractor system's size, complexity, and enormous amounts of highly technical paperwork. But staff reductions made it all but impossible to monitor adequately a system as complex as NASA's (Presidential Commission, 1986, 1: 153; U.S. House Committee on Science and Technology, 1986a: 177). One example of an SR&QA failure cited by the official investigations was its confusion over the criticality rating of the SRB joint. In 1982 when the SRB joint's criticality category was changed from C 1-R to C 1, only one reliability engineer was monitoring paperwork for problem reporting and close-out at NASA headquarters (Quong, 1986: 17). SR&QA staff members themselves often mistakenly labeled individual problem reports on the SRB joint as C 1-R rather than C 1 (Bunn, 1986: 13). Apparently, the reliability engineer did not catch the errors (Quong, 1986: 17). The summaries of problem reports on the solid rocket motor, solid rocket boosters, external tank, and main engine were compiled into books three inches thick. Although the SR&QA director and deputy director at NASA headquarters received these summaries, they did not notice the SRB joint criticality change (Quong, 1986. 16). Not only did the amount of information being conveyed obscure the discrepancies, but both the director and the deputy director had other responsibilities, each spending, respectively, 10 percent and 25 percent of their time on the shuttle program, leaving meager time for safety concerns (Quong, 1986: 30–32). Given that overburdened SR&QA directors and staff members were not able to identify and correct their own misunderstandings on the SRB joint criticality rating, it is not surprising that they were not able to identify and rectify the confusion among NASA administrators.

Like their external counterparts, internal social control agents develop informational dependencies that circumvent the structural barriers to discovery, monitoring, and investigation. Staff reductions are likely to increase reliance on formalized dependency relations, however, as increased workloads force regulators from proactive to reactive oversight. Although there are no data on how these dependencies affected regulation overall, one example shows how dependency relations were pertinent to the O-ring problem. In the SR&QA unit permanently situated at Thiokol, staff members monitored problem reports submitted by the contractor, compliance with written procedures, and worked closely with contractor safety personnel. Although they did pursue safety issues with some of the Thiokol employees, staff size undermined comprehensive surveillance. Roger Boisjoly, the Morton Thiokol engineer in charge of the O-ring Seal Task Force who vigorously protested launching *Challenger*, reported that he never had a safety person ask him about the workings of the solid rocket booster joint (Boisjoly, 1986: 44). Although this omission cannot be linked to any of the specific SR&QA failures cited by official investigations, one must wonder about the effects that information dependencies had on what SR&QA staff defined as problems and the seriousness attributed to those problems.

SR&QA was dependent on NASA in another important way that could have had a telling impact, even when resources were abundant. SR&QA offices at Kennedy and Marshall space centers were under the supervision of the parts of the organization and activities they were to check (Presidential Commission, 1986; 1: 160). Dependence on the management structure to act on recommendations compromised SR&QA's ability to act in the interest of safety. Boisjoly noted, "SR&QA was relegated to honor status only, as demonstrated by how they reported organizationally" (personal communication, 19 September 1989). As the Presidential Commission (1986, 1: 153) stated, "The clear implication of such a management structure is that it fails to provide the kind of independent role necessary for flight safety."

The Space Shuttle Crew Safety Panel (SSCSP)

In addition to the Safety, Reliability and Quality Assurance Program, NASA created a second internal unit in 1974 to be responsible solely for crew safety (Johnson Space Center, 1974). The panel was composed of 20 people from Johnson, Kennedy, and Marshall space centers, Dryden (the NASA facility at Edwards Air Force Base, California), and the Air Force (Hammack, 1986: 2–3). Forestalling accidents—the goal of a compliance strategy—was to be achieved by (1) identifying possible hazards to shuttle crews, and (2) advising shuttle management about these hazards and their resolution. To assure communication and coordination on all crew safety issues, panel members were selected from throughout the NASA/contractor system, representing engineering, project management, and the Astronaut Office, which trains astronauts and provides flight crews for space vehicles (Presidential Commission, 1986, 1: 161; 5: 1411). Their responsibilities on this panel were additions to the responsibilities normally associated with their positions. The panel was chaired by Scott H. Simpkinson, manager for flight safety, an experienced NASA "troubleshooter" (Maley, 1986: 1).

In meetings, the Space Shuttle Crew Safety Panel (SSCSP) identified potential problem areas, developed solutions, and reviewed schedules (Hammack, 1986: 2–3). Often, the chair assigned individual problems to members for detailed investigation, negotiation, and resolution. The panel relied on its own working groups when practical but established subpanels or employed subsystem managers and technical specialists to supplement panel expertise when necessary. The panel prioritized safety issues for NASA's attention, submitting a formal report to the Space Shuttle Program manager after each meeting (Maley, 1986). From 1974 through 1979, the SSCSP met 26 times, addressing such issues as mission-abort contingencies, crew escape systems, and equipment acceptability (Hammack, 1986: 5; 9–19).

Although the O-ring problem was first noted at NASA in 1977, my review of SSCSP meeting summaries gives no indication the O-ring problem was addressed by this panel (Hammack, 1986: 12–19). Was this omission a consequence of intraorganizational autonomy? Available data do not allow us to explore the precise effects of the NASA system's structure, specialization, and transactions on the crew safety panel. On the one hand, the strategy of drawing members from representative parts of the organization would tend to reduce these problems. On the other hand, a twenty-member panel could not cover all the bases in so vast a system, as evidenced by its dependence on other technical experts. As with SR&QA, inadequate staff numbers tend to increase the problems associated with discovery, monitoring, and investigation of safety issues in complex organizations. But this panel had additional handicaps. Responsibilities for their own jobs restricted the amount of work each person could do for the panel, limiting the number of problems panel members could investigate, as well as the depth of their investigations. Thus, while the parts of the organization that panel members represented may have received adequate attention, other parts may have received inadequate attention, or none.

As expected in a self-regulating system, symbiotic interdependence manifested itself in several forms that curtailed the effectiveness of the SSCSP. First, the crew safety panel was dependent on NASA management for resources essential to its inquiries. Members had to provide "the necessary details" analyses, manpower, and plans required to fulfill task resolutions assigned by the panel chairman and must be authorized by their parent organization to commit necessary resources" (Johnson Space Center, 1974: 2). Second, all panel recommendations for change were subject to management approval and designation of necessary resources. Finally, the panel was dependent on NASA for its very existence. This was true of SR&QA, too, of course, but the consequences for the crew safety panel were more extreme.

The NASA document that created the panel stated that the panel would function only "during the design development and flight test phases of the shuttle" (Johnson Space Center, 1974: 1). In 1981, as the shuttle began moving from its developmental to its operational stage, discussions were held about whether the panel should or should not continue (Hammack, 1986: 6). A decision was made to combine it with another panel. The attempt was unsuccessful due to "lack of program interest, appropriate subjects, program maturity, lack of SSCSP membership support and differences in panel purposes" (Hammack, 1986: 7). Significant to this denouement was the retirement of Simpkinson, the troubleshooting flight safety manager, who was not replaced. Without a mandate to continue in the operational phase of the shuttle program, SSCSP went out of existence with Simpkinson's retirement in 1981 (Maley, 1986: 2).

With the panel's demise went an important formal mechanism for interjecting information about danger to crew and the value of human life into the NASA decision-making structure. The panel's elimination did not mean crew safety was no longer on NASA's agenda, however. The Astronaut Office and the astronauts themselves were vitally concerned with crew safety, thus possibly compensating for the loss of the SSCPS. The Astronaut Office, although not an officially designated safety regulator, might have prevented the *Challenger* tragedy by refusing to provide a crew until the O-ring erosion problem was solved. But, like SR&QA and the crew safety panel, the Astronaut Office's ability to act on technical issues was constrained by NASA's internal structure and specialization, which resulted in informational dependencies. The Astronaut Office had many responsibilities directly relevant to flight operations (Presidential Commission, 1986, 5: 1414–1415; U.S. House Committee on Science and Technology, 1986b, 1: 544–624). Because of preoccupation with flight operations generally and the specifics of each flight, the Astronaut Office (like the flight crew and the commander responsible for the final "go") was dependent on others to supply information about design problems (Presidential Commission, 1986, 5: 1420, 1423, 1424). The Astronaut Office was not informed of early solid rocket booster design and test problems in any "formal organizational way" (Presidential Commission, 1986, 5: 1416–1418). Nor did the Astronaut Office gain this critical information informally as awareness and concern about the O-rings grew among some personnel at both NASA and Morton Thiokol.

At the time of the *Challenger* launch, the Astronaut Office had 91 astronauts who participated in many phases of the program. In addition to their own flight training, many astronauts did more than one job (Presidential Commission, 1986, 5: 1467–1470). Despite the contacts with various parts of the shuttle program that the astronauts' multiple responsibilities incurred, information about the seriousness of the SRB joint problem did not reach the Astronaut Office through astronauts' connections with other parts of the organization (U.S. House Committee on Science and Technology, 1986b, 1: 565). Not that the Office or the astronauts were uninformed about technical matters. Rather, their ability to assess flight safety issues was impaired by their other responsibilities and their position in NASA's information structure, both of which assigned them to a reactive stance where design problems were concerned (U.S. House Committee on Science and Technology, 1986a: 152–154). They were reliant on others both for problem identification and assessment (U.S. House Committee on Science and Technology, 1986b, 1: 557–563). When questions about the O-rings arose in other parts of the organization, they were either resolved and not conveyed or else were conveyed as nonserious problems (Presidential Commission, 1986, 2: H 1–3). Neither the Astronaut Office nor the astronauts were informed of the teleconference between Marshall Space Flight Center and Thiokol personnel the night before the launch (Presidential Commission, 1986, 5: 1415–1416; U.S. House Committee on Science and Technology, 1986b, 1: 557–563).

The Aerospace Safety Advisory Panel (ASAP)

The Aerospace Safety Advisory Panel was created to supplement NASA's internal safety system with an external regulatory body capable of independent surveillance of safety hazards. The dilemma Congress faced in constituting it was finding people with the technical training and experience necessary to do the job (U.S. House, 1967b: pt. 16: 21807). Congress turned to aerospace industry leaders (Presidential Commission, 1986, 5: 1488) . Panel membership was set by statute at "no more than nine members, of whom up to four may come from NASA" (U.S. Congress, 1968: sec. 6). Each would serve a three-year term. The NASA participants were included to circumvent the problems of autonomy confronted by external regulatory bodies. They were to act as liaisons between the five aerospace experts and internal NASA operations, informing them about operations, design, and other internal matters. The panel members were joined by the NASA chief engineer as an ex-officio member and a small staff of full-time NASA employees. The panel's duty, according to statutory definition, was to be responsive to the NASA administrator's definition of problems (U.S. Congress, 1968: sec. 6).

In keeping with NASA's own mandate (U.S. Congress, 1959: sec. 303), the agency was actively involved in outlining the limits of the Aerospace Safety Advisory Panel's domain. Immediately following ASAP's creation, senior NASA officials set to work determining the panel's role (NASA, 1967: 163–165). The NASA administrator approved ASAP's charter and appointed its members and chair (NASA, 1968: 147–148).

As the shuttle program matured, changes improved its ability to discover, monitor, and investigate in the evolving program. The domain of the panel was expanded to include assessment of the safety implications of programs and their management, rather than being limited to surveillance of technical risks (Presidential Commission, 1986, 1: 160). The term of membership was increased: to six years to take advantage of the expertise panel members developed. The panel became increasingly proactive, pursuing its own leads based on its own judgments (Aerospace Safety Advisory Panel, 1973: 2).

Beginning in 1980, the original requirement that four NASA members serve on the panel was changed. With the exception of the ASAP staff director, no NASA representatives participated on the panel. During the course of a six-year term, panel members grew knowledgeable about NASA personnel and activities and developed informal contacts. Consequently, NASA people were no longer needed to provide insights that the aerospace experts didn't have (Interview, staff director, Aerospace Safety Advisory Panel, 2 March 1988). In addition, the panel's membership expanded. To cope with the panel's increased responsibilities, the NASA administrator appointed five non-NASA members as consultants (propulsion, rocketry, human factors, and nuclear specialists). Sometimes consultants later moved into active panel membership; sometimes former panel members became consultants after their six-year terms. The logic behind these rotations was acquired expertise: once these specialists understood NASA activities, the NASA administrator and ASAP staff director were reluctant to let them go. As a result, the entire panel consisted of experts (most were retired CEOs of aerospace firms) who had become familiar with NASA activities and personnel. These changes, along with ASAP's compliance strategy, created what was thought to be a qualified and influential unit for protecting safety in the program.

ASAP's compliance strategy included conducting fact-finding sessions at NASA centers and contractor sites to investigate safety issues. These issues came to panel members' attention in various ways. The NASA administrator requested investigations. The ASAP staff director learned of safety problems while attending meetings at centers and with contractors, referring them to panel members to investigate in on-site visits. Occasionally, congressional committees requested specific information from the panel. Sometimes ASAP members discovered problems at an investigative site. In 1985, the year preceding the accident, the full panel conducted seven fact-finding sessions, and individual panel members conducted forty-seven, meeting at NASA headquarters, seven NASA centers, six contractor sites, Vandenberg Air Force Base, and three other locations (Aerospace Safety Advisory Panel, 1986, 1: 25–28). Panel members attempted to negotiate safety issues at the lowest possible level, then went to the top, as necessary: the contractor vice president or chief engineer, then the NASA program manager, associate administrator, or administrator.

ASAP members gave personal feedback to the people with whom they had contact. The panel sent formal statements of findings and recommendations to the centers and contractors, who responded in writing to each recommendation. These statements were forwarded to NASA headquarters. ASAP annually conveyed findings and recommendations to Congress and the NASA administrator orally and in an annual report (Presidential Commission, 1986, 5: 1488). Created by Congress rather than NASA, ASAP reported to Congress as part of the annual congressional authorization of NASA required by the 1958 Space Act. The process of authorization itself was a form of social control frequently leading to hearings on controversial issues. NASA's responses to ASAP recommendations were conveyed to Congress in the following year's annual report.

Although the role of ASAP expanded and changed over the years, and its annual reports (1984, 1985, 1986) indicate an active exploration of problems and risks, the Presidential Commission found no indication that the solid rocket booster joint design or associated flight anomalies were assessed by ASAP (1986, 1: 161). The Commission attributed this failure of foresight to the panel's "breadth of activities" (1986, 1: 161). This panel did have vast oversight responsibilities. The limitations of a nine-member panel (working on average 30 days per year, aided by five consultants called in sporadically) on discovering all problems in the NASA enterprise are obvious. To attribute the panel's failure to discover the problematic O-rings to breadth of activities alone, however, suggests time and system size were the only constraints. Such a conclusion overlooks the effects of interorganizational relations on social control.

Dependencies on NASA that were incorporated into ASAP's original design compromised independent review. ASAP's status was strictly advisory and under the authority of the NASA administrator (Presidential Commission, 1986, 1: 161; Egan, 1988). The administrator appointed panel members, suggested concerns and specific interests for panel inquiry, and ultimately made decisions about panel recommendations. Because the panel was primarily guided by the concerns and interests of the NASA administrator, the staff director, and Congress, the amount of time remaining for original discovery could not have been much. Moreover, the panel experienced the obstacles normally encountered in external control of an autonomous structure. In the beginning, ASAP members were qualified in aerospace but were not experts on NASA or the shuttle program. This obstacle apparently was overcome, as evidenced by the eventual elimination of NASA members from the panel. But this alteration coincided with panel members' development of informal associations that were important to penetrating the maze of NASA life. The development of informal connections between the aerospace experts on the panel and NASA and contractor personnel no doubt increased the panel's ability to investigate and negotiate in a manner essential to an effective compliance strategy. Still, ASAP members were not involved in day-to-day activities, and much of what went on eluded them. The result was that the panel remained dependent on NASA and contractor personnel for information.

While informational dependencies partially resolved the difficulties resulting from ASAP's externality, they curtailed the panel's fact-finding capability in another way. What constituted a problem and the panel's definition of the seriousness of the problem were shaped by the information that was given to them and by the definitions of seriousness held by NASA and contractor personnel. With little opportunity for proactive investigation and not receiving a formal request from NASA administrators to investigate the solid rocket booster joint anomalies, ASAP was dependent on Thiokol and NASA personnel to alert them to the O-ring problem. As the ASAP staff director commented on the

Challenger tragedy, "Sometimes people don't tell the whole story. Morton Thiokol didn't tell us the whole story. Marshall Space Flight Center didn't. If people aren't forthcoming, we are limited" (Interview, 2 March 1988).

The extent and direction of the effects of interdependence on the monitoring and investigating of the Aerospace Safety Advisory Panel are unknown, though the economic importance of the space program may have had an effect on safety regulation. Economists generally agree that the space program is vital to the technological standing of U.S. industry (Congressional Budget Office, 1988: 68–74). Panel members were drawn primarily from the aerospace industry, but, as noted, interdependence between industry and government may either enhance or impede regulatory efforts. Informal associations with NASA and Thiokol personnel also may have affected ASAP's safety surveillance. Like interdependence at the macro-level, informal organization either may subvert or advance the goals of an organization (Roethlisberger and Dickson, 1947). Whether these informal associations coopted or improved ASAP's monitoring and investigation remains open to conjecture. What is certain is that ASAP, like the other regulatory units, had little authority to sanction when inappropriate behavior continued.

Barriers to Effective Sanctioning

Sanctions are an important resource, and, whether invoked or not, they increase the power of regulators and thus the potential to achieve compliance (Hawkins, 1983: 68). Interdependence, however, bears importantly on the ability of regulators to threaten or impose meaningful sanctions. Although NASA adopted a compliance strategy—negotiation and regular monitoring to secure conformity, rather than an adversarial stance—the capacity to reward and punish, necessary to a compliance system as a lever to persuade, was not written into the charters of the regulatory units. Instead, all three were dependent on NASA to invoke sanctions in their behalf. Subordinate positioning plus the absence of an independent sanctioning capability meant that the setting of priorities and the resolution of safety issues were not likely to be joint, but a function of hierarchy (Blau, 1964; Wilson and Rachal, 1977).

The efficacy of a compliance strategy in a self-regulating system in which regulatory units are dependent on the regulated organization for formal sanctions (among other resources) deserves inquiry. The goal of a compliance system is to achieve compliance and avoid sanctioning; nonetheless, the threat of sanction imposition is considered an important enforcement tool. Although researchers have explored how the characteristics of sanctions and variation in their use affect compliance when legally empowered agents are in an adversarial position toward potential violators (Hawkins, 1984; Reiss, 1984; Manning, 1989), we know little about the use and efficacy of sanctions in compliance systems in which regulators are reliant on the regulated organization to enforce in their behalf.

Without sanctions of their own, these safety units' ability to achieve compliance would be affected by (1) NASA and contractor willingness to comply voluntarily with suggested changes and (2) absent voluntary compliance, the effectiveness of the sanctions to which they had access, however indirectly, to serve as a lever to persuade. No doubt NASA and its contractors voluntarily complied on many of the problems that safety regulators recommended they address. Symbiotically interdependent, NASA, contractors, and the safety regulatory units were linked by a common goal: to prevent accidents. NASA and its contractors were joined in continuing buyer-seller arrangements due to NASA's need for shuttle components and the contractors' reliance on NASA as a lucrative source of income. NASA and shuttle contractors depended on the safety units for information critical to accident prevention and, thus, attainment of the space shuttle's scientific and military goals. The regulatory units, NASA, and the contractors all stood to benefit from the shuttle's success by prestige, increased resources, expanded domain, or simply continued functioning; in the case of failure, one or more might suffer from funding cutbacks or even program demise.

Symbiotic interdependence guaranteed cooperation in furtherance of shared interests. NASA and its contractors would strive for compliance on problems that both regulator and regulated defined as serious safety issues. When disagreement occurred about whether or not a problem should receive attention or about prioritizing those problems that should, however, NASA administrators would determine the outcome. One possible result might be concerted noncompliance: NASA administrators disagree with the regulators and so do not invoke sanctions to alter noncompliant behavior. Should NASA administrators agree with regulators and invoke sanctions, however, then compliance would turn upon the effectiveness of NASA's sanctions at converting noncompliance into compliance. To explore sanction effectiveness, one must consider the deterrent potential of penalties invoked as threats in a compliance system. Deterrence research, which explores the relationship between punishment and individual behavior, stresses the importance of the perceived and actual certainty and severity of sanctions imposed rather than their statutory existence (Williams and Hawkins, 1986). The assumption is that behavior is guided by the probability of punishment being meted out and the severity of that punishment. The certainty and severity of punishment meted out is considered here: when NASA administrators invoke sanctions on behalf of regulators as a threat to achieve compliance, what is the likelihood that the threat will be fulfilled, and, if so, what is the nature of the punishment?

Compelling Compliance

Contracts are mechanisms for control of both individual and organizational behavior (Heimer, 1985; Stinchcombe, 1985). NASA exerts formal control over both NASA employees and contractors responsible for shuttle components through contracts, and behavior is subject to periodic formal review. These evaluations affect financial remuneration as specified in the contract as well as its continuation. When sanctions are directed at the financial well-being of individuals and organizations in a symbiotic relationship with the sanctioning authority, the harshness of sanctions tends to be mitigated by negotiation and compromise. NASA management's use of contracts on the safety regulators' behalf reveals the constraints of interdependence on the regulators' ability to control safety problems.

Sanctioning employees. Key to understanding contracts as a mechanism for control of employees is that promotion, raises, and contract renewal are status system rewards (Stinchcombe, 1985: 133–134). Status

systems with these incentives are intended to encourage careers and, thus, commitment and discipline. Consistent with a premonitory compliance strategy, the employee contract offers the possibility of both positive and negative sanctions, contract termination being one option. NASA's use of these sanctions for all employees is unknown, but other research and NASA's postaccident treatment of executives suggests the safety units' regulatory efforts would not have been well-served by them. Katz (1977) argued that self-regulating organizations tend to practice nonenforcement or to punish so discreetly that the internal actions being sanctioned are condoned rather than condemned. Organizations solidify internal authority and deflect external regulatory authorities from intervening by covering up internal deviance. Further, superordinates tend not to respond to deviance officially because of enforcement tradeoffs. Decisions not to enforce safety rules are commonly traded for compliance with production standards, for example (Katz, 1977: 10). Certainly the tendency toward nonenforcement and discreet punishment will vary with the questionable behavior as well as with an organization's dependence on the employee. Position, skills, experience, competence, integration, and replaceability will bear upon the latter. NASA's postaccident treatment of executives closely associated with the controversial decision to launch *Challenger* confirms Katz's argument: Some managers took voluntary retirement, some received lateral transfers, some remained in their positions, but none were terminated or even publicly castigated by NASA.

Sanctioning contractors. NASA monitored contractors by "incentive/award fee contracts" (U.S. House Committee on Science and Technology, 1986a: 179). These contracts primarily manipulated rewards, although negative sanctions in the event of component failure were also written into them. The amount of the incentive fee was based on contract costs (lower costs yield a larger incentive fee), timely delivery, and successful launch and recovery. The award fee focused on the safety record of the contractor. Two facts lead to skepticism about NASA's ability to employ sanctions effectively when necessary to secure contractor compliance on safety issues.

First, NASA's incentive/award fee contract itself prioritized cost saving and meeting deadlines over safety (U.S. House Committee on Science and Technology, 1986a: 179–180): The incentive fee, rewarding cost savings and timely delivery, could total as much as 14 percent of the value of the contract; the award fee, rewarding the contractor's safety record, could total a maximum of 1 percent. No provisions existed for performance penalties or flight anomaly penalties. Absent a major mission failure. which entailed a large penalty after the fact, the fee system reinforced speed and economy rather than caution (U.S. House Committee on Science and Technology, 1986a: 179). Although in traditional deterrence research the characteristics of sanctions as defined by statute are regarded as less significant than perceptions of their use, the characteristics of sanctions as defined in contracts appear to have had significant implications for contractor safety compliance at NASA. As the House Committee on Science and Technology (1986a: 182) commented on the contracting-fee system,

> . . . so long as [contractor] management is convinced that a festering problem like the [O-ring] seal problem is not likely to cause mission failure, there is little incentive for the company to spend resources to fix the problem. In fact, if the solution involves significant delays in delivery, there may be a strong financial dis-incentive for the company to pursue a short-term solution aggressively.

Even the possibility of contract loss appears to have reinforced production interests at Thiokol, not safety. Post-accident investigations suggest that Thiokol managers approved the launch over engineering objections because launch delay might jeopardize the company's ongoing contract negotiations to continue producing the solid rocket booster for NASA (Presidential Commission, 1986, 1: 104; McConnell, 1987: 180–181).

Second, while NASA's use of the contracting-fee system with all contractors is unknown, no evidence exists that sanctions were used to enhance safety compliance at Morton Thiokol prior to the *Challenger* launch. There had been more than twenty-five occurrences of O-ring erosion and related SRB anomalies at the time of the accident. Thiokol had never been penalized, nor was there evidence that punishment had been threatened (U.S. House Committee on Science and Technology, 1986a: 181). Rather, at the time of the *Challenger* acci-

dent; Thiokol was eligible to receive a near-maximum incentive fee of approximately $75 million. Furthermore, safety and procedural violations occurred at Thiokol's Utah facilities over the years, several resulting in fires and/or explosions. Again, the persistence of the problem indicates the failure to achieve compliance either through negotiation or sanctions invoked as threat. Even after these violations became public, Thiokol was not penalized, as is customary upon negotiation failure in compliance systems (U.S. House Committee on Science and Technology, 1986a: 181). NASA contracts presented two standards that sometimes could not be met simultaneously: (1) cost savings and timely delivery and (2) safety. When rewards were great for cost savings and meeting deadlines and punishment was not forthcoming for safety infractions, contractors would tend to alter their priorities accordingly. Thiokol did comply, but with NASA production interests, not with safety standards.

NASA's failure to punish past safety violations bears importantly on any NASA attempts to negotiate contractors' compliance with safety standards, for historic sanctioning patterns may affect contractors' willingness to comply during a current negotiation. If punishment has not been imposed in the past in response to violations that resulted in harm that became public knowledge, then why should contractors be quick to respond to punishment invoked as threat in early phases of negotiation? A resource dependence perspective would predict that, absent an equally attractive alternative supplier, punishment would be mitigated by NASA's dependence on the contractor for the shuttle component. Symbiotically interdependent, both would be harmed. In the event that punishment had to be inflicted, NASA would also experience consequences if that punishment interfered with the quality of the product or the contractor's ability to produce it on schedule. The harsher the punishment. the greater the probability that NASA would also incur costs. The tendency, then, would be for NASA to mitigate those costs by not punishing, or, if punishment were inflicted, to minimize costs if possible.

This hypothesis is confirmed by NASA's post-accident treatment of Thiokol. Terminating Thiokol's contract was the harshest sanction available to NASA. But NASA did not terminate the contract. To have done so would have resulted in costs for NASA's shuttle program. Johnsrud (1988) found that many companies in the defense and aerospace industries develop structural and operational congruencies and complementarities with the federal government because government (including NASA) represents such a stable and often lucrative market for products. Congruencies are similarities in workgroup organization, operating procedures, and communication patterns that aid in joint endeavors. Complementarities are differences between these factors that facilitate the achievement of shared interests. Congruencies and complementarities affect the awarding of prime and subcontracts for products and services, creating continuing mutual interdependencies for resource exchange (Johnsrud, 1988: 5–6). Terminating Thiokol's contract and beginning with a new SRB contractor would have created shuttle program delays and perhaps new safety hazards while the kinks got worked out of the interface problems between both organizational and technical systems.

Instead, NASA imposed the penalty for component failure that was written into the contract. The designated penalty was altered in subsequent negotiations between NASA and Thiokol, however. While certainly the cost to Thiokol was great, it was not as great as it might have been. According to Thiokol's contract with NASA, a reduction of $10,000,000 in incentive fee earned would ensue if failure of the solid rocket motor/motors resulted in loss of life and mission (U.S. House Committee on Science and Technology, 19868: 181). Further, any contractor responsible for component failure must sign a document admitting responsibility for the resulting accident, adding social stigma and legal liability to the financial loss. Admission of legal liability might result in other financial repercussions, such as limiting a contractor's ability to compete successfully for future government contracts and vulnerability to suit by private parties. Thiokol was unwilling to accept the "full contractual penalties" due the manufacturer of a failed component (U.S. House Committee on Science and Technology, 1986a: 181). Thiokol was willing to forfeit the money but unwilling to sign the document and was prepared to litigate the issue. The willingness to take adversarial action raised the specter of additional costs for both symbiotic interdependence would be joined by competitive interdependence if each began to use resources to thwart the litigation goals of the other.

Both organizations were concerned with conserving resources and maintaining established routines. NASA and Morton Thiokol made an agreement in order to "avoid litigation and keep priority on returning the shuttle to flight, and bypasses [*sic*] the question of the company's liability for the accident" (*Aviation Week and Space Technology*, 1987: 28). Instead of the $10,000,000 contract penalty for the failure, NASA and Morton Thiokol agreed that Thiokol would "voluntarily accept" the $10,000,000 reduction in the incentive fee it had earned under the contract at the time of the accident (1987: 28). By voluntarily forfeiting $10,000,000 of its profits in lieu of the contract penalty, Thiokol avoided signing the document admitting legal liability. Thus, Thiokol remained eligible to bid on future government contracts. Thiokol did agree to perform at no profit approximately $505 million worth of work required to redesign the field joint, rework existing hardware to include the redesign, and replace the reusable hardware lost in the *Challenger* accident (Marshall Space Flight Center, 1988).

With the bargaining and compromise characteristic of both competitive and symbiotically interdependent regulatory relationships, the outcome was negotiated in the interest of each organization and shared program goals. Bargaining is a consequence of interdependence, but it may have an independent effect on sanctioning under contractual agreements that require cooperation in the doing of the contracted work and/or in the regulation of it. When bargaining becomes institutionalized between parties, adversarial strategies would violate the norms of the relationship and so would tend to be constrained. In addition, adversarial strategies might alter the future character of the working relationship, thus posing potential additional costs for one or both organizations. Stinchcombe (1986: 234) noted that when an exchange relationship is continuous, current exchange is modified by the expectation of future exchange. Because of institutionalized bargaining as well as interdependence, then, the full contractual promise regarding harshness of penalties to be carried out is not likely to be fulfilled.

Alternative sources of sanctions. Available alternatives can alter power-dependence relations (Blau, 1964). SR&QA and the

Space Shuttle Crew Safety Panel had no alternative sources of official sanctions besides those NASA management controlled. The Aerospace Safety Advisory Panel did, however. ASAP reported, its findings annually to Congress. Congressional response to these findings ultimately manifested itself in budget appropriations. It was through the budget that Congress could respond to ASAP's concerns by sanctioning both NASA's internal activities and contractor relations, but congressional invocation of sanctions on behalf of ASAP would be uncertain.

As an external regulator subject to the limitations of autonomy, Congress would have difficulty making judgments concerning technical controversies between NASA and ASAP because its members lack aerospace engineering training. Historically, NASA had authority, bestowed by Congress, over ASAP recommendations. In addition, on both organizational and technical matters, NASA was consulted by the agencies regulating commercial space ventures to such an extent that it was NASA's terms and conditions that shaped government regulatory policies (Levine, 1986). In a dispute between NASA and ASAP, the tendency would be for the agency's expertise and experience to carry the day or a controversial issue. This conclusion is supported by my analysis of ASAP recommendations for action on safety matters submitted to NASA and Congress in annual reports and NASA's item-by-item responses published in those reports.

If Congress did invoke sanctions, they would not be likely to threaten seriously the progress or survival of the American space program. NASA and Congress were symbiotically interdependent. Congress (as well as other branches of government) was dependent on NASA's monopoly in meeting U.S. goals for space science and military supremacy; NASA was dependent on Congress as its primary source of funding. As previously noted, symbiotic interdependence can enhance social control, and the space agency's extreme vulnerability to budgetary fluctuations would suggest a readiness to comply (Presidential Commission, 1986, 1: 164–177; U.S. House Committee on Science and Technology, 1986a: 116–131). Yet such readiness may not always result in compliance, for a government agency can deny and avoid the authority of government regulators. An agency's tasks are legislatively mandated, and it can defend itself by mobilizing allies elsewhere in government who share a stake—material or ideological—in the agency's well-being (Wilson and Rachal, 1977).

But symbiotic interdependence also can inhibit social control Regulators are often constrained in penalty use because the regulated organization is thought to be acting in the interest of the public at large (Vaughan, 1983: 47–50). When that organization is the major or only supplier of a service to a large population, it is even less vulnerable to social control (Zald, 1978: 92). Yet this tendency may not be consistently realized, for in the face of uncooperative behavior, the regulator must resort to using sanctions, not only to assure compliance but also to protect its credibility as a watchdog against symbolic assaults on its authority (Hawkins, 1983: 40).

The consequences of autonomy and symbiotic interdependence between NASA and Congress would be the mitigation of ASAP's efforts to bring a recalcitrant NASA into compliance. This conclusion, while speculative, can be reinforced theoretically by shifting the analytical focus, in keeping with the idea that the hierarchical nature of organizational forms allows us to apply concepts, models, and theories in multiple contexts (Vaughan, 1990). If we consider the U.S. government as the organizational unit of analysis and one of its goals as U.S. military and space supremacy in the international arena, Congress and NASA can then be viewed as subunits of the larger organization. Congress becomes an internal regulator with oversight responsibilities for the space agency, itself an internal unit. From this perspective, the U.S. government is a self-regulating organization, and Katz's (1977) insight applies: Self-regulating organizations tend to practice nonenforcement or to punish so discreetly that those internal activities that are sanctioned are condoned rather than condemned. Despite the availability of an alternative source of sanctions that would appear to increase ASAP's power over NASA, interdependence between NASA and Congress would tend to mitigate use of those sanctions. Resource exchange affected the sanctioning capabilities of all three safety units, with the result that NASA, designed to be self-regulating, remained so.

Autonomy, Interdependence, and Social Control

Accident prevention was essential to NASA's competitive success; consequently, multiple strategies and systems were employed to assure safety. The extensive program for crew training, the 122,000 pages of documents pertaining to safety now stored at the National Archives, the four volumes of items routinely checked in each pre-launch countdown, and even the midnight-hour teleconference on the eve of *Challenger's* launch are a few of NASA's many formal and informal precautionary measures. NASA's safety regulatory structure also reflected the space agency's concern with safety. It was designed to provide the balanced scrutiny necessary to safeguard the shuttle program: internal and external review units using a compliance strategy. The internal units, staffed by NASA personnel, would be capable of close monitoring. To assure objective review, they would be physically separate from the programs they were to regulate. The external unit would, by definition, be separate. To provide a close monitoring capability, it would be guided by NASA personnel formally appointed to the panel. While an analysis of NASA's entire safety system is beyond the scope of this research, my investigation of the three safety units indicates that just as caution was designed into the NASA system, so was failure. Autonomy and Interdependence interfered with regulatory ability to discover, monitor, investigate, and sanction in the interest of safety, decreasing the probability that developing problems would be identified and corrected.

The NASA/contractor system's autonomy obstructed discovery, monitoring, and investigation of safety hazards. Size, structure, changing technology, specialized language, and numerous transactions created barriers for both internal and external regulatory units. The external regulator, the Aerospace Safety Advisory Panel, did not discover the O-ring problem. Even when ASAP became sufficiently attuned to NASA and contractor activities not to require NASA members on its staff, this change did not eliminate the constraints autonomy placed on the panel. The panel's surveillance capability was still limited by its absence from daily NASA activities, so it remained dependent on informal relations with NASA-contractor personnel for the information necessary to regulate. Despite being located internally, SR&QA and the crew safety panel also had problems in discovery, monitoring, and investigation, due to the size, complexity, and burdensome technical paperwork of the NASA/contractor system. The crew safety panel did not address the O-ring problem in its meetings. SR&QA identified the problem but failed at other monitoring and investigative responsibilities that led to insufficient, contradictory, and sometimes inaccurate information about the O-rings being circulated throughout the NASA system. Informational dependencies, previously noted only in research on interorganizational regulatory relations, existed in all three cases, although data are insufficient to understand their effects. Also, the data do not allow us to investigate the possibility of cooptation, frequently a consequence of continuing regulatory relations.

Regulatory ineffectiveness at NASA cannot be attributed only to problems associated with autonomy, however. Although interdependence primarily affects regulators' ability to threaten and impose meaningful sanctions, here it also affected surveillance. Symbiotically interdependent with NASA, both internal regulators relied on the NASA organization for resource allocation and legitimacy, which impaired their ability to discover, monitor, and investigate hazards. NASA eliminated the crew safety panel five years before the *Challenger* tragedy, and its budget cuts and personnel transfers depleted the resources SR&QA required for effective surveillance. The external regulator, ASAP, never became the independent problem-defining entity Congress intended; its original mandate made it dependent on the direction of the NASA administrator, its staff director, and Congress. Moreover, all three regulatory units reported to the parts of the NASA organization they were intended to regulate. Consequently, all three were dependent on the NASA management structure for transferring information and recommendations about safety problems throughout the organization and for implementing suggested changes. Thus, interdependence also reduced the probability that risky technical and managerial systems would be identified and corrected.

The dependent condition of these units was reinforced not only by the reporting system, but by the fact that none of the units had sanctions of its own to impose. When threat of sanctions or sanction imposition was necessary to compel compliance; regulators were dependent on NASA to use contracts to achieve safety goals. Although we have little information on the effects of social control at NASA on its employees, the effectiveness of the NASA/Thiokol contract as a lever to compel safety compliance was undermined not only by symbiotic interdependence, but also by the incentives NASA encoded in the contracts. In the Space Shuttle Program, the power advantage lay with the regulated, not the regulators. Here we see not only the regulatory contribution to this technical failure, but also NASA's. The space agency created a regulatory structure and controlled its operation. Over time, however, NASA administrators altered that structure. By so doing, they altered the information available to them about hazards in the Space Shuttle Program, hence altering the bases on which still other critical decisions were made. One of them was the decision to launch the Space Shuttle *Challenger*.

In addition to clarifying the organizational contribution to this technical system accident, this analysis demonstrates the analytic utility of the concepts of autonomy and interdependence for both intra- and interorganizational regulatory relations. Moreover, it raises the possibility that autonomy and interdependence, formerly associated only with official regulatory relations between legally empowered agents of social control and business firms, may systematically inhibit regulation, regardless of the nature of the regulated enterprise. Consequently, we might benefit from research using these concepts in intra- and interorganizational settings that diverge from the traditional legal actor/public enterprise model, so that we may understand regulatory relations better. From these data, we may begin to develop a general theory of the social control of organizations.

The uniqueness of the *Challenger* incident limits making broad claims on the basis of this case study. In addition, available data limit what can be concluded about this organizational-technical system accident. We can conclude that the organizational patterns uncovered were correlated with the accident, but no direct evidence exists that allows us to assert that these organizational patterns caused the accident. Even the conclusions about correlation must be accompanied by a caveat. Studying a specific technological failure obscures those instances in which autonomy and interdependence of regulators and regulated may have forestalled an accident. How many times did the externality of ASAP result in discovery and investigation of a problem that insiders would hesitate to reveal to NASA administration? How many times did internal regulators identify and pursue a problem that only NASA employees closely involved in daily activities could identify? How often did contractual ties between organizations represented by ASAP members and NASA, or informal ties between individuals in the two organizations, result in an investigation that otherwise would not have occurred?

The precise trade-off between the negative and positive effects of autonomy and interdependence on safety regulation at NASA are uncertain. The possible benefits suggested above, however, are threatened by the comparative powerlessness that results when the regulators are dependent on the regulated organization for information, financial resources, personnel, communicating information about hazards, implementing suggested changes, or imposing sanctions. Quality negotiation and investigation brought to bear on a particular problem deserve less celebration if many other problems go untended because of inadequate resources, if members of the regulated organization don't receive warnings about hazards, or if recommendations for change aren't heeded.

Regulation itself appears to be risky business, subject to uncertain trade-offs that result from autonomy and interdependence. Strategies of social control selected for their potential to increase regulatory effectiveness are likely to be undermined in subtle, complex ways by the disadvantages. This is not to argue that failure is inevitable. The probability of failures of foresight clearly decreases as regulatory resources increase. Personnel changes and/or increasing resources to strengthen surveillance and sanctioning capabilities may result in efficiency and effectiveness in regulating a specific problem. But the structure of regulatory relations will continue to generate patterned obstacles to social control. Autonomy and interdependence are fundamental to the interaction of social control agents and regulated organizations, so they inhibit the social control of organizations regardless of available skills, resources, and commitment to fulfill the regulatory mandate.

All of the above leads to the conclusion that if both negative and positive consequences are systematically associated with intra- and interorganizational regulatory relationships, then regulators cannot be relied upon to prevent accidents. Clarke (1988: 30) noted that "closer attention to interorganizational relations should provide valuable insights into assessment, distribution, mitigation, and acceptability of risk." In designing strategies for the social control of risky technology, intraorganizational relationships also need to be taken into account. A logical assumption is that organizations producing high-risk technological products will play an active role in their own regulation, if for no other reason than because they have the technical knowledge to do so. Self-regulating systems, however, are "fundamentally suspect" (Shapiro, 1987: 646). Any organizational system that, like NASA, regulates resources and their exchanges, in effect, concentrates influence over those resources (Pfeffer and Salancik, 1978: 51). As a consequence, self-regulation of risky technical enterprise may, by definition, be accompanied by dependencies that interfere with regulatory effectiveness, despite what may be well-intentioned attempts to create a regulatory system with the capacity to regulate vigorously and effectively (Hall, 1982: 132). Of particular concern are high-risk technological products produced and regulated by government (Wilson and Rachal, 1977).

Many advocates of policy for regulating risk focus on technical failure. Morone and Woodhouse (1986) and Perrow (1984), for example, first distinguish technical systems by their potential for failure and catastrophe, assign them to categories according to risk potential, then suggest policy that varies according to the risk category to which a particular technical system has been assigned. Assessment of risk is fundamental to policy development, but policy advocates err in suggesting policy based on definitions of risk derived from technology alone (Freudenburg, 1988). Clearly, a technical explanation is insufficient to explain the *Challenger* tragedy. The existence of organizational patterns that contribute to failures of foresight increases risk. Moreover, any system runs a risk of failure when human actors are involved. Policy makers and advocates need to take into account the organizational contribution to technical system accidents when defining technical systems as more or less risky for the purpose of selecting strategies of social control.

This case study does not generate the sort of comparative information on which definitive policy statements can be made, however. While autonomy and interdependence between regulatory and regulated organizations predictably will mitigate social control efforts, we do not know the dynamics of arrangements other than those observed here, so we do not know which arrangements offer the greatest or least potential for reducing organizational-technical system accidents. Until we systematically assemble data on the relationship between autonomy, interdependence, and social control in diverse types of regulatory settings, we have no basis for distinguishing regulatory systems by their potential for failure or success or for assigning them to categories according to risk potential, as Morone and Woodhouse (1986) and Perrow (1984) have done with technical systems. Furthermore, even when comparative data are available, difficulties in measuring variation in autonomy and interdependence may mean our assessments necessarily will be imprecise. Finally, both preventive strategies and post-accident attempts to correct the organizational contribution to technical system accidents are handicapped by our lack of skill at converting research findings into diagnostic recommendations for organizations.

While we cannot make precise recommendations from this research, we safely can conclude that intra- and interorganizational relations are characterized by structurally engendered weaknesses that contribute to technical system accidents. Because the sophisticated formulas used to estimate risk in technical systems do not acknowledge the possible organizational contribution to technical failures, risk is always underestimated, creating unwarranted confidence in all risky technological systems. Decisions to design, manufacture, and use sophisticated technological products should be guided by this knowledge.

References

Aerospace Safety Advisory Panel (ASAP). 1973. "Responsibility in the Space Shuttle Program." Internal mimeo. Washington, DC: Aerospace Safety Advisory Panel.

———. 1984. *Annual Report Covering Calendar Year 1983.* Washington, DC: Aerospace Safety Advisory Panel.

———. 1985. *Annual Report Covering Calendar Year 1984*. Washington, DC: Aerospace Safety Advisory Panel.

———. 1986. *Annual Report Covering Calendar Year 1985*. Washington, DC: Aerospace Safety Advisory Panel.

Aviation Week and Space Technology. 1987. "Morton Thiokol will forfeit $10 million in lieu of contract penalty." 2 March: 28.

Bardach, Eugene, and Robert A. Kagan. 1982. *Going by the Book: The Problem of Regulatory Unreasonableness*. Philadelphia: Temple University Press.

Blau, Peter M. 1964. *Exchange and Power in Social Life*. New York: Wiley.

Boisjoly, Roger. 1986. Interview transcript, 2 April Morton Thiokol. Inc. files. National Archives.

Braithwaite, John, and Brent Fisse. 1987. "Self-regulation and the control of corporate crime." In Clifford D. Shearing and Phillip C. Stenning (eds.), *Private Policing*: 221–246. Newbury Park, CA: Sage.

Bunn, Wiley. 1986. Interview transcript, 17 April. Marshall Space Flight Center files, National Archives.

Clarke, Lee. 1988. "Explaining choices among technological risks." *Social Problems*, 35:22–35.

Congressional Budget Office. 1988. *The NASA Program in the 1990's and Beyond*. Washington, DC: Congressional Budget Office.

Cullen, Francis T., William J. Maakestad, and Gray Cavender. 1987. *Corporate Crime under Attack: The Ford Pinto Case and Beyond*. Cincinnati: Anderson.

Diamond, Stuart. 1986. "NASA cut or delayed safety spending." *New York Times*, 2:4 April: A-1, B-4.

Egan, Daniel F. 1988. "The origins of the Aerospace Safety Advisory Panel." Unpublished manuscript, Department of Sociology, Boston College.

Freudenburg, William R. 1988. "Perceived risk, real risk, social science and the art of probabilistic risk assessment." *Science*, 242 (7 October): 44–49.

Hall, Richard H. 1982. *Organizations: Structure and Process*, 3d ed. Englewood Cliffs, NJ: Prentice-Hall.

Hammack, J. B. 1986. "Space Shuttle Crew Safety Panel history." Internal mimeo for Presidential Commission on the Space Shuttle Challenger Accident, National Archives.

Hawkins, Keith. 1983. "Bargain and bluff: Compliance strategy and deterrence in the enforcement of regulation." *Law and Policy*, 5: 15–73.

———. 1984. *Environment and Enforcement: Regulation and the Social Definition of Pollution*. Oxford: Oxford University Press.

Heimer, Carol A. 1985. *Reactive Risk and Rational Action: Managing Moral Hazard in Insurance Contracts*. Berkeley: University of California Press.

Johnson Space Center. 1974. Space Shuttle Program Directive 4A, 14 April. National Archives.

———. 1983. Space Shuttle Program Requirements Control Board Directive, PRCBD S21701R2, 7 March. National Archives

Johnsrud, Cristy S. 1988. "Conflict, complementarity and congruence: The administration of cross-sector organizational linkages." Paper presented at the 1988 American Anthropological Association Annual Meeting, Phoenix.

Katz, Jack. 1977. "Cover-up and collective integrity: On the natural antagonisms of authority internal and external to organizations." *Social Problems*, 25: 3–17.

Levine, Arthur L. 1986. "Commentary: Space technology and societal regulation." *Science, Technology, and Human Values*, 2: 27–39.

Magnuson, Ed. 1986. "Fixing NASA." *Time*, 9 June. 14ff.

Maley, Patrick James. 1986. Memorandum to Alton G. Keel, Jr., Executive Director, Presidential Commission on the Space Shuttle Challenger Accident, 18 April. National Archives.

Manning, Peter K. 1989. "Managing uncertainty in the British nuclear installations inspectorate." *Law and Policy*, 11: 350–369.

Marshall Space Flight Center. 1982. "SRB Critical Items List." 17 December. National Archives.

———. 1988. Press release 88-58, 12 May.

McConnell, Malcolm. 1987. *Challenger: A Major Malfunction*. New York: Doubleday.

McDougall, Walter A. 1985. *The Heavens and the Earth: A Political History of the Space Age*. New York: Basic Books.

Morone, Joseph G., and Edward J. Woodhouse. 1986. *Catastrophe: Strategies for Regulating Risky Technology*. Berkeley: University of California Press.

National Aeronautics and Space Administration (NASA). 1967. Eighteenth Semiannual Report to Congress. July 1–December 31, 1967. Washington, DC: NASA.

———. 1968. *Nineteenth Semiannual Report to Congress*. January 1–June 30, 1968. Washington, DC: NASA.

———. 1986. *Reliability and Quality Assurance Publications*. NHB 53004 (1 D-2). Washington, DC: NASA.

Perrow, Charles B. 1984. *Normal Accidents: Living with High-Risk Technologies*. New York: Basic Books.

Pfeffer, Jeffrey, and Gerald R. Salancik. 1978. *The External Control of Organizations: A Resource Dependence Perspective*. New York: Harper and Row.

Presidential Commission on the Space Shuttle Challenger Accident. 1986. *Report of the Presidential Commission on the Space Shuttle Accident*, 5 vols. Washington, DC: U.S. Government Printing Office.

Punch, Maurice. 1985. *Conduct Unbecoming: The Social Construction of Police Deviance and Control*. London: Tavistock.

Quong, Harry. 1986. Interview transcript, 11 April. NASA Headquarters files, National Archives.

Reiss, Albert J., Jr. 1984. "Selecting strategies of social control over organizational life." In Keith Hawkins and John M. Thomas (eds.), *Enforcing Regulation*: 23–35. Boston: Kluwer-Nijhoff.

Roethlisberger, F. J., and William J. Dickson. 1947. *Management and the Worker*. Cambridge, MA: Harvard University Press.

Roland, Alex. 1985. "The shuttle: Triumph or turkey." *Discover*, 6: 35–48.

Rumsfeld, Donald, and William E. Kriegsman. 1967. "A proposal for an aerospace advisory panel: A way to close the hazard evaluation gap." *National Safety News*, October: 44–47.

Selznick, Phillip. 1966. *TVA and the Grass Roots: A Study in the Sociology of Formal Organization*. New York: Harper and Row.

Shapiro, Susan P. 1987. "The social control of impersonal trust." *American Journal of Sociology*, 93: 623–658.

Sherman, Lawrence W. 1978. *Scandal and Reform: Controlling Police Corruption*. Los Angeles and Berkeley: University of California Press.

Stinchcombe, Arthur L. 1985. "Contracts as hierarchical documents." In Arthur L. Stinchcombe and Carol A. Heimer (eds.), *Organization Theory and Project Management: Administering Uncertainty in Norwegian Offshore Oil*: 121–171. Oslo: Norwegian University Press.

———. 1986. "Norms of exchange." In Arthur L. Stinchcombe, *Stratification and Organization: Selected Papers*: 231–267. Cambridge: Cambridge University Press.

Stone, Christopher D. 1975. *Where the Law Ends: The Social Control of Corporate Behavior*. New York: Harper and Row.

Turner, Barry M. 1976. "The Organizational and Interorganizational development of disasters." *Administrative Science Quarterly*, 21: 378–397.

———. 1978. *Man-Made Disasters*. London: Wykeham.

U.S. Congress. 1959. National Aeronautics and Space Act of 1958. (P.L. 85-568 72 Stat. 426, July 1958). U.S. Statutes at Large 85th Congress. 2nd Session. Vol. 72. Washington, DC: U.S. Government Printing Office.

———. 1968. National Aeronautics and Space Administration Authorization Act of 1968. (P.L 90-67 81 Stat. 168. August 1967). U.S. Statutes at Large. 90th Congress, 1st Session. Vol. 81 Washington, DC: U.S. Government Printing Office.

U.S. House of Representatives. 1967a. Hearings before the House, Committee on Science and Astronautics on H.R. 4450, H.R. 6470 (Superseded by HR. 10340). 90th Congress, 1st Session. Washington, DC: U.S. Government Printing Office.

———. 1967b. House, Congressional Record. 90th Congress, 1st Session. Vol. 113. Washington, DC: U.S. Government Printing Office.

U.S. House of Representatives, Committee on Science and Technology. 1986a. *Investigation of the Challenger Accident Report*. Washington, DC: U.S. Government Printing Office.

———. 1986b. *Investigation of the Challenger Accident, Hearings*, 2 vols. Washington, DC: U.S. Government Printing Office.

Vaughan, Diane. 1983. *Controlling Unlawful Organizational Behavior: Social Structure and Corporate Misconduct*. Chicago: University of Chicago Press.

———. 1990 "Organization theory. A method of elaboration." Paper presented at "A Symposium on Basic Social Science Precepts: What is a Case?" Northwestern University, March 2–3.

Wall Street Journal. 1986. "Shuttle disaster puts spotlight on safety: Trade-off for performance is a critical question." 4 February: A-2, A-26.

Wiley, Mary G., and Mayer N. Zald. 1968. "The growth and transformation of educational accrediting agencies: An exploratory study of the social control of Institutions." *Sociology of Education*, 41: 36–56.

Williams, Kirk R., and Richard Hawkins. 1986. "Perceptual research on general deterrence: A critical review." *Law and Society*, 20: 545–572.

Wilson, James Q., and Patricia Rachal. 1977. "Can the government regulate itself?" *Public Interest*, 146: 3–14.

Yuchtman, Ephraim, and Stanley Seashore. 1967. "A system resource approach to organizational effectiveness." *American Sociological Review*, 32: 891–903.

Zald, Mayer N. 1978. "On the social control of industries." *Social Forces*, 57: 79–102.

Chapter 28
Institutional Pressures and Strategic Responsiveness
Employer Involvement in Work-Family Issues

Jerry D. Goodstein

Organizations must continually adapt to changes taking place in their environments. One important change that has taken place over the last few decades is the increasing percentage of dual-earner households with children. This change has shaped all organizations to some degree, as they have had to adapt to the changing demographics of the larger labor force. Some organizations responded to this change by adopting policies designed to reduce their employees' work-family conflict, while others have resisted such policies.

Goodstein aims to make sense of these divergent responses. He identifies the conditions under which we might expect an organization to respond to changes in its environment by adding new programs and those that might lead an organization to pursue a different strategy. Goodstein argues that organizations do not always passively comply with external demands, nor do they always resist them. Instead, organizations must balance the competing costs and benefits of compliance and resistance as they adapt and change over time.

The development of institutional theory has led to significant insights regarding the importance of institutional environments to organizational structures and actions. In particular, institutional theorists have attempted to identify various mechanisms, such as professional norms and state regula-

tions, that motivate organizations to respond to institutional pressures in similar ways (DiMaggio & Powell, 1983; Meyer & Rowan, 1977; Meyer & Scott, 1983).

A number of theorists have argued that this broad emphasis on processes of conformity to institutional pressures has led to a downplaying of the role of interest and agency in organizational adaptation to institutional environments (Covaleski & Dirsmith, 1988; DiMaggio, 1988; Powell & DiMaggio, 1991; Elsbach & Sutton, 1992; Mezias, 1990; Oliver, 1991; Powell, 1991; Scott, 1987). Oliver summarized these critiques, noting, "Institutional theorists, by virtue of their focus, have tended to limit their attention to the effects of the institutional environment on structural conformity and isomorphism and have tended to overlook the role of active agency and resistance in organization-environment relations" (1991: 151). A narrow focus on processes of conformity has deflected theoretical interest away from accounting for the circumstances in which institutionalization is contested or incomplete (Powell, 1991: 195).

This broad critique has engendered a recognition that institutional environments are not "iron cages" (DiMaggio & Powell, 1983). As Scott argued, "Just as is the case within their technical environments, organizations may be expected to exercise 'strategic choice' (Child, 1972) in relating to their institutional environments and responding to institutional pressures" (1991: 170). Reflecting this important insight, Oliver (1991) elaborated a continuum of strategic responses to institutional pressures. She theorized that, depending on a number of factors, such as the characteristics of institutional constituencies and the congruence of institutional norms and organizational goals, organizations may respond to institutional pressures in a variety of modes ranging from passive compliance with institutional norms to direct and active defiance of an institutional environment. . . .

Institutional Pressures and Strategic Responsiveness

A central concern for organizational researchers has been the degree of strategic choice organizations can exert in response to environmental conditions (Aldrich, 1979; Aldrich & Pfeffer, 1976; Child, 1972; Hannan & Freeman, 1977). Over time, this large and diverse literature has been synthesized into two dominant theoretical perspectives. One perspective emphasizes external control (Romanelli & Tushman, 1986) and the importance of environmental constraints, including industry, economic, and social characteristics, in limiting strategic responses. In contrast, the strategic choice perspective (Child, 1972) emphasizes the ability of organizations to interpret and select their environments, responding to relatively fixed constraints and actively modifying other environmental elements (Hitt & Tyler, 1991). Organizations can then both adapt to environmental conditions and actively determine strategic responses to them (Hitt & Tyler, 1991). Over time, there has been a growing recognition that both perspectives are critical to understanding organizational adaptation and strategic decisions (Hitt & Tyler, 1991; Hrebiniak & Joyce, 1985).

The elaboration of the external control and strategic choice perspectives has highlighted organizational adaptation primarily with respect to companies' competitive, or task, environments (Pfeffer & Salancik, 1978). Organizations must, however, not only meet technical, or task, constraints, but must also respond to a variety of institutional pressures and demands embodied in regulations, norms, laws, and social expectations (Meyer & Rowan, 1977). These institutional pressures and demands emanate from a number of sources, including the state, via regulatory and governmental agencies, the professions, and public and private interest groups (DiMaggio & Powell, 1983; Meyer & Rowan, 1977; Meyer & Scott, 1983; Scott, 1987).

Historically, institutional theorists have emphasized the control exerted by institutional environments and direct or symbolic compliance and conformity to environmental demands (DiMaggio & Powell, 1983; Meyer & Rowan, 1977). More recently, institutional theorists have argued that the choice of conformity or resistance to institutional pressures is a strategic choice that is affected by organizational interests (Covaleski & Dirsmith, 1988; DiMaggio, 1988; Powell, 1991; Scott, 1991). Further, either conformity or resistance to institutional pressures is likely to reflect both institutional and technical concerns. Organizations do not necessarily blindly conform to institutional pressures but rather, may actively assess the extent to which conformity

allows them to enhance technical concerns, such as efficiency or the acquisition of resources (Covaleski & Dirsmith, 1988; Powell, 1991; Scott, 1991). Although this line of theoretical development has moved away from earlier concerns with isomorphism and conformity, it has opened up the possibility of addressing a number of important questions that have received limited attention within organizational theory: How do organizations strategically respond to institutional pressures and what factors affect organizational responses?

These questions are at the core of Oliver's (1991) insightful examination of strategic responses to institutional pressures. Oliver elaborated a theoretical framework that explicitly adopts the assumption that organizational responsiveness to institutional pressures is a strategic choice. Oliver posited that organizations may pursue five broad strategies in responding to institutional processes. First, organizations may *acquiesce* and fully conform to institutional pressures and expectations. Second, organizations may *compromise* by partially complying with institutional demands. Third, they may *avoid* institutional pressures through such means as concealing nonconformity, responding symbolically, and buffering themselves. Fourth, they may actively reject institutional norms or expectations in *defiance* of institutional pressures. Fifth, organizations may adopt an aggressive posture toward institutional agents and, through *manipulation*, attempt to actively change or exert power over institutional pressures. These types of strategic responses "vary in active agency by the organization from passivity to increasing active resistance" (Oliver, 1991: 151). Oliver (1991) acknowledged the importance of institutional and technical determinants to this choice by defining institutional pressures in terms of five factors: cause, constituents, content, control, and context.

Cause refers to the underlying rationale or expectations associated with institutional pressures. When institutional demands can enhance the legitimacy of an organization, it will be motivated to conform to those demands, and resistance will be difficult (Dowling & Pfeffer, 1975; Meyer & Rowan, 1977).

Strategic responses will be affected by the characteristics of the constituent groups, such as public agencies and employees, creating institutional pressure on an organization. When there are multiple *constituents* with potentially conflicting objectives, the potency of institutional pressures may be weaker (Powell, 1991) and organizational resistance may be easier. Conflicting institutional pressures and multiple constituents call create fragmentation within an institutional environment and reduce the degree of consensus among institutional actors (D'Aunno, Sutton, & Price, 1991; Jepperson, 1991; Oliver, 1991; Powell, 1991): Resistance to institutional pressure is also more likely when an organization has low dependence on institutional constituents. The greater the extent to which institutional constituents control the allocation or availability of critical resources for the organization, the more difficult resistance to the expectations of those constituents will be (DiMaggio & Powell, 1983; Pfeffer & Salancik, 1978).

The *content* of institutional demands is a critical determinant of organizational responsiveness. When institutional pressures conflict with organizational goals or constrain the ability of an organization to reach its goals—for instance, by forcing the allocation of resources to meeting institutional requirements—resistance is more likely. Covaleski and Dirsmith (1988) demonstrated how a university was able to reject an institutionalized budgetary process when the process became inconsistent with the goals and interests of the university.

The nature of institutional *control* can determine how organizations respond. Oliver (1991) emphasized two important processes through which institutional pressures are exerted on organizations: legal coercion and voluntary diffusion. The imposition of institutional demands by powerful institutional actors is likely to meet with little resistance (Scott, 1987). Organizational conformity to institutional demands is also more likely when norms and expectations have been voluntarily adopted and diffused among organizations within al given field or sector (DiMaggio & Powell, 1983; Scott, 1987).

Finally, an organization's environmental *context*—specifically, the extent of environmental uncertainty and interconnectedness—shapes organizational responses. High environmental uncertainty motivates organizations to attempt to reduce uncertainty by acquiescing to institutional pressures or compromising with key constituent groups. When there is a high degree of interconnection among organizations, the diffusion of institutional norms and demands is widespread and the likelihood of conformity is high (DiMaggio & Powell, 1983; Meyer & Rowan, 1977).

The Institutional Context of Employer Involvement in Work-Family Issues

To illustrate and amplify these determinants of institutional conformity and resistance, this article explores organizational responsiveness to institutional pressures related to work and family issues. In particular, I focus on employer adoption of work-family initiatives and examine the determinants of varying levels of employer responsiveness. The discussion emphasizes two primary areas of employer involvement in work-family issues: (1) the adoption of child care benefits and (2) the adoption of benefits that enhance workplace flexibility (Auerbach, 1988; Galinsky & Stein, 1990; Kamerman & Kahn, 1987). Employer involvement in child care typically assumes one of three major forms: (1) providing fully or partially subsidized on-site child care, (2) directly financing employee child care expenses, for example by contracting with external organizations or making benefit contributions, or (3) providing child care information and referral services that link employees to child care providers (Auerbach, 1988; Burud, Aschbacher, & McCroskey, 1984; Kahn & Kamerman, 1987; Kamerman & Kahn, 1987). Employers may also adopt benefits that enhance workplace flexibility. Researchers have identified workplace options such as flextime, voluntary shifts to part-time work, job sharing, and flexible leaves as important benefits that provide flexibility for working parents (Auerbach, 1984; Burudet al., 1984; Galinsky & Stein, 1990; Kamerman & Kahn, 1987).

Organizational involvement in work-family issues has evolved as a function of a number of important social, economic, and political changes. As Kanter (1977) suggested, historically organizations have varied in how they have viewed work and family issues. Early in the 20th century, corporations tended to "swallow the family and take over its functions" by making workplaces into more or less total institutions via company towns and company lodging (Kanter, 1977). Later, organizations attempted to separate the work and family spheres in order to "exclude or neutralize particularistic ties that might compete with loyalty to the system as a whole" (Kanter, 1977: 9). Rather than incorporating and co-opting families, modern organizations have tended to approach them as a competing loyalty that has to be "pushed aside and excluded from business" (Kanter, 1977: 15).

More recently, there has been increased pressure on employers to acknowledge that family life and work have changed and that they are no longer separable as aspects of working parents' lives (Auerbach, 1988; Hewlett, 1991; Kamerman & Kahn, 1987; Kanter, 1977). Changes in the demography of the work force, such as the rapid increases in the numbers of working mothers and dual income–career families (Cook, 1989; Hewlett, 1991; Kamerman & Kahn, 1987; Kanter, 1977), have increased the interdependence of work and family spheres and intensified the conflicting demands of work and family. In 1980, an estimated 43 percent of U.S. women with children under age six were in the work force; but by 1986, 51 percent of mothers with children under six worked outside the home (Kahn & Kamerman, 1987). In 1980, both the husband and wife worked in 52 percent of families; by 1988, that proportion had risen to 63 percent (Hyland, 1990). Finally, the number of single-parent households has risen 23 percent since 1980 (Hyland, 1990).

As the salience of work and family issues has intensified with these demographic changes, public attention to these issues has also increased and heightened institutional pressure on employers to respond by adopting work-family options (Hewlett, 1991; Kamerman & Kahn, 1987). Work and family issues, and in particular, employer involvement in child care, have been featured in business publications as well as in the popular media (Milliken, Dutton, & Beyer, 1990). In addition, a variety of organizations, including industry and labor-related groups like the Conference Board and the Bureau of National Affairs, national women's organizations, and professional personnel associations, have devoted significant attention to work and family concerns (Kamerman & Kahn, 1987).

Accompanying these broad social changes were the Reagan administration's efforts to implement a program of privatization and reduce the federal government's level of social expenditures. These political changes had important implications for employer involvement in work-family issues, particularly with regard to child care. The federal government attempted to motivate greater private sector involvement in child care by creating new tax legislation. In 1981, as part of the Economic Recovery Tax Act, the federal government provided employers with the opportunity to create "dependent care assistance plans" (DCAPs). This legislation permitted an exclusion from gross income for the value of employer-provided child care services. In addition, the legislation provided for an increase in the credit available to taxpayers for day-care expenses necessary to their employment and created depreciation benefits for employers creating on-site or nearby child care centers for employees' children. A second tax change was passed to foster the development of flexible benefit plans. These plans specifically allowed employers to set aside part of an employee's salary and place those pretax dollars into an account that could be used to pay for various benefits, including child care.

As a result of these social and political forces, institutional pressure on employers intensified. The federal government strongly urged employers to assume more responsibility for providing human services programs, such as child care. Social welfare professionals and other researchers began to urge employers to assume a more active role in providing key social programs, such as child care, and to initiate other flexible workplace options that would help employees better balance work and family demands (Fernandez, 1986; Hewlett, 1991; Kahn & Kamerman, 1987; Kamerman & Kahn, 1987).

Given the pervasiveness of these institutional pressures, it is surprising that little systematic empirical research has been directed toward understanding either the variety of organizations' strategic responses to these pressures or the relative influences of institutional and economic factors on organizational responsiveness (see Morgan and Milliken [1993] for an exception). A weakness characterizing prior research is the lack of an overarching theoretical framework, such as the one provided by Oliver (1991) and other organizational researchers, that would allow for specifying the nature of strategic responses and the causal determinants of these responses.

Hypotheses

Organizational responsiveness to work-family issues can be understood as a specific example of the general organizational processes outlined above. More specifically, I posited that the strategies employers adopt to respond to institutional pressures will depend on five primary factors that define the nature of these pressures: cause, constituents, content, control, and context (Oliver, 1991). The hypotheses: outlined below specify the effects of each of these considerations on levels of responsiveness to institutional pressures for employer adoption of work-family initiatives.

Cause

Underlying some of the pressures institutional constituents are placing on employers is a set of normative beliefs whose central theme is that employers should assume a more active role in helping employees balance work and family demands (Kamerman & Kahn, 1987). Advocates of employer adoption of work-family initiatives argue that employers who provide these benefits help address a critical societal concern and enhance their legitimacy and social fitness (Oliver, 1991).

Considerations of legitimacy and social fitness are particularly salient for large organizations. By virtue of their size and visibility, large organizations are subject to much attention from the state, media, and professional groups (Dowling & Pfeffer, 1975; Meyer, 1979; Powell, 1991). Although theorists have pointed out the importance of the acquisition of legitimacy and social fitness to smaller firms in overcoming the initial liability of newness (Aldrich & Auster, 1986; Hannan & Freeman, 1989; Stinchcombe, 1965), legitimacy and social fitness may be even more important for large organizations. As firms grow and become involved in industry activities and dense networks of exchange, the institutionalized expectations of other firms, consumers, and the state exert greater influence on them (Powell, 1991). These organizations become increasingly accountable (Hannan & Freeman, 1989) to external constituencies and more vulnerable to public pressure (Freeman & Gilbert, 1988; Mintzberg, 1983).

Because large organizations are visible and accountable to various constituencies, they have a strong incentive to take actions to ensure their legitimacy (Mintzberg, 1983). In a number of empirical studies, researchers have found a consistent relationship between organization size and level of corporate social responsibility (Buehler & Shetty, 1976; Lentz & Tschigiri, 1963; Miles, 1987). Miles argued that within many of the large insurance firms he studied there was an awareness that "a large, complex corporation not only has a duty to adapt its policies and practices to changes in society, but also that because of the scope and pervasiveness of its operations, such a corporation can exert nontrivial influences on society" (1987: 276). Miles found that large firms adopting this perspective were more likely to be socially responsive in that they took a problem-solving, collaborative approach to regulatory agencies and developed strong internal organizations devoted to community relations.

These arguments apply directly in the case of employer involvement in work-family issues. Large companies typically have been the most proactive in developing and adopting employee benefits, including work-family benefits (Kamerman & Kahn, 1987; Morgan & Milliken, 1993). Through providing a broad range of work-family benefit options, large employers and public organizations signal their responsiveness to institutional pressures (Dowling & Pfeffer, 1975; Meyer, 1979; Pfeffer, 1982) and enhance their social legitimacy (Carroll, 1979; Kamerman & Kahn, 1987).

Hypothesis 1: The greater the size of an organization, the greater its level of responsiveness to institutional pressures for employer involvement in work-family issues.

Constituents

Critical constituents also play an important role in employer involvement in work-family issues. Of specific concern in this study was the degree of employer dependence on important institutional constituents. One of the most important groups influencing employers to adopt work-family initiatives are working women (Auerbach, 1988; Burud et al., 1984; Kamerman & Kahn, 1987; Magid, 1983; Milliken et al., 1990; Morgan & Milliken, 1993). Women currently constitute 45 percent of the U.S. labor force, and it is projected that women will account for two-thirds of the net increase in the labor force over the next ten years (Hyland, 1990). Kamerman and Kahn (1987) noted that more than 70 percent of the women in the work force are in their prime childbearing years (18–44), and 80 percent of those women will become pregnant at some point in their working lives.

Working women face particularly strong work-family pressures as typically the responsibility for securing child care and taking care of other demands at home falls on them (Auerbach, 1988; Emlen & Koren, 1984; Kamerman & Kahn, 1987). The ability of working women to influence organizational policies regarding work and family is likely to be a function of the dependence of employers on female employees (Auerbach, 1988; Burud et al., 1984; Cook, 1989; Hyland, 1990; Kamerman & Kahn, 1987). The greater this dependence, the more responsive industry employers must be to the values and expectations of female employees regarding employer responsibility for helping them balance work and family demands.

In conjunction with these trends has been growth in the number of working parents and some broadening of the discussion of work-family issues to include men as well as women (Auerbach, 1988). Labor force statistics suggest that the number of dual earner families increased dramatically over the period 1970–86 (Cook, 1989; Hayghe, 1988). By 1987, both spouses were working in 57 percent of married-couple families in the United States (Wiatrowski, 1990). Many of those parents are part of the baby boom generation, born between 1946 and 1964, a group that has placed increasing pressure on organizations to meet the needs of employees who must balance the demands of work and family life (Hall & Richter, 1990; Kamerman & Kahn, 1987).

To the extent that an organization must depend on women specifically and on working parents in general, they become influential groups in motivating employer responses to pressures for child care services.

Hypothesis 2: The greater the dependence of an organization on female employees, the greater its level of responsiveness to institutional pressures for employer involvement in work-family issues.

Hypothesis 3: The greater the dependence of an organization on employees who are par-

ents, the greater its level of responsiveness to institutional pressures for employer involvement in work-family issues.

Content

A third factor Oliver (1991) emphasized is the content of institutional pressures. Organizational conformity to institutional expectations may be a function of the consistency and congruence of those expectations with the organization's existing goals and policies.

In the domain of work-family issues, this congruence is likely to be particularly strong for public sector organizations. Federal, state, and local governments can use their power to authorize or legitimate policies and structures (Scott, 1987) that other organizations within the public sector will adopt. As Scott suggested, subordinate organizations responding to the influence of the state are "not compelled to conform but voluntarily seek out the attention and approval of the authorizing agent" (1987: 502). By contrast, in the private sector conformity to institutional pressures may be precluded by organizational goals that give greater weight to "technical and economic standards against which firm performance is primarily assessed" (Oliver, 1991: 165).

These processes have contributed to the wide adoption within the public sector of personnel policies such as affirmative action and due process procedures (Baron, Dobbin, & Jennings, 1986; DiMaggio & Powell, 1983; Dobbin, Edelman, Meyer, Scott, & Swidler, 1988). With regard to work-family issues, there are also efforts at the federal and state level to promote child care and flexible workplace options in the public sector. The federal government adopted flextime policies in 1974, the first major organization to do so (Fernandez, 1986). The General Services Administration gave an appointed federal official the specific task of creating more child care facilities for government employees (Hayghe, 1988). California mandated all state agencies to provide information and referral services to employees. Other states, including Michigan and New York, have introduced important initiatives to foster public sector support of child care for state employees and to carry out the states' role in fostering socially responsive policies (Hayghe, 1988).

Hypothesis 4: Public sector organizations will be more responsive than private sector organizations to institutional pressures for employer involvement in work-family issues.

Control

The mechanisms through which institutional pressures are enforced are important determinants of organizational responses to those pressures. In the absence of any legal requirements mandating work-family benefits, the primary mechanism through which influence occurs is voluntary diffusion (Oliver, 1991). As similar organizations adopt norms and practices, they are increasingly legitimated throughout a given organizational field or sector (Fligstein, 1985; Tolbert & Zucker, 1983). Early adopters become models for other organizations and reduce the uncertainty associated with a specific innovation. As norms diffuse throughout a given sector, organizations will increasingly incorporate those norms in an effort to enhance their legitimacy, secure critical resources, and remain competitive with similar organizations.

Failure to incorporate practices widely adopted by other organizations may be perceived as a risk to an organization's legitimacy and hence its ability to secure needed resources (DiMaggio & Powell, 1991). In turn, organizations that fail to adopt specific norms or practices may also be at a competitive disadvantage vis-à-vis other organizations that are viewed as more innovative or responsive. This process is particularly important in the context of employer involvement in work-family issues. Writers have noted that organizations are particularly sensitive to their competitors' provision of employee benefits (Hewlett, 1991; Kamerman & Kahn, 1987; Morgan & Milliken, 1993). Organizations' decision makers recognize that, despite the absence of rigorous studies supporting the economic benefits of work-family initiatives (Aldous, 1990; Kamerman & Kahn, 1987; Raabe, 1990), the level of an employer's responsiveness to work-family issues may affect its legitimacy, ability to secure critical resources, and competitiveness.

Hypothesis 5: The greater the number of other organizations within an organization's sector adopting work-family benefits, the greater its level of responsiveness to institutional pressures for employer involvement in work-family issues.

Context

The diffusion of institutional norms and practices is greatly facilitated by a high level of interconnectedness (Oliver, 1991) within the institutional environment. Highly interconnected environments provide relational channels that facilitate consensus on institutional norms (DiMaggio & Powell, 1983; Galaskiewicz, 1991; Meyer & Rowan, 1977). Such consensus in turn increases the strength of institutional norms and their potential influence on organizational responses (Powell & DiMaggio, 1991; Oliver, 1991).

Institutional environments are more likely to be interconnected when they contain many business, professional, and other membership organizations, such as political organizations and civic groups (DiMaggio & Powell, 1983; Powell & DiMaggio, 1991). These membership organizations provide a "vehicle for the definition and promulgation of normative rules about organizational and professional behavior" (Powell & DiMaggio, 1991: 71). They are also particularly valuable because they provide an informal mechanism for diffusing institutional norms and expectations. Thus,

Hypothesis 6: The greater the pervasiveness of business, professional, and membership organizations in a given organization's environment, the greater its level of responsiveness to institutional pressures for employer involvement in work-family issues.

It is clear that technical as well as institutional considerations are important in understanding strategic responses to institutional pressures for employer adoption of work-family initiatives. In deciding on their level of involvement, employers are likely to consider the impact of various work-family options on organizational outcomes (Morgan & Milliken, 1993). In particular, employers will consider the costs of work-family initiatives and the expected organizational benefits of providing those services.

Although technical concerns are potentially relevant to both flexible workplace options and child care policies, they are particularly critical to the adoption of child care services. Programs such as flextime or work at home are often viewed as low-cost accommodations to institutional pressures (Burud et al., 1984; Fernandez, 1986; Galinsky & Stein, 1990). Studies suggest that employers are, however, resistant to adopting child care services because of their perceived cost in terms of both direct expenses and potential liability (Auerbach, 1988; Kahn & Kamerman, 1987; Kamerman & Kahn, 1987). These services represent a type of fixed cost that can be perceived as constraining organizations, particularly those in industries that are subject to cyclical fluctuations (Auerbach, 1988). Therefore,

Hypothesis 7: The lower the perceived cost of child care services, the greater an organization's level of responsiveness to institutional pressures for employer involvement in work-family issues.

In part because of concerns with liability and expenses, employers are particularly interested in the potential benefits of child care. Researchers have pointed out that child care services benefit organizations in a variety of ways: enhancing the recruitment and retention of employees, lowering employee stress, improving employee morale, and increasing productivity (Burud et al., 1984; Emlen & Koren, 1984; Fernandez, 1986). Employers may be more likely to resist adopting child care policies when the perceived benefits are minimal (Auerbach, 1988; Burud et al., 1984; Kamerman & Kahn, 1987; Raabe, 1990).

Hypothesis 8: The greater the perceived benefits of child care services to an organization, the greater its level of responsiveness to institutional pressures for employer adoption of work-family benefits.

The hypotheses outlined above identify both institutional and technical factors (Meyer, Scott, & Deal, 1983; Scott, 1983) that are likely to affect the level of organizational responsiveness to work and family issues. Although I have treated these influences separately, it is important to consider the relationships between institutional and technical factors and specifically, how those relationships predict the strategic responses of employers. Figure 28.1 outlines a framework that identifies strategic responses to institutional pressures as a function of (1) the strength of those pressures and (2) their effects on technical outcomes, such as productivity and turnover.

When institutional pressures for responsiveness are strong and responsiveness to those pressures is perceived as having a positive effect on technical outcomes, organizations are likely to acquiesce to the institutional pressures. Under such conditions, acquiescence is an institutionally and technically rational adaptation. By contrast, when institutional pressures for responsiveness are weak and responsiveness is perceived as having a negative effect on technical outcomes, defiance is the strategy most likely to be adopted.

When institutional pressures are strong but perceived as having a negative effect on technical outcomes, an organization can pursue a compromise strategy that allows for balancing the competing pressures or take actions that allow it to avoid the pressures. Whether a compromise or avoidance strategy is chosen will depend primarily on

Figure 28.1

Framework for Predicting Strategic Responses to Institutional Pressures

		Perceived Effects of Responsiveness on Technical Outcomes	
		Positive	Negative
Strength of Institutional Pressures	High	Acquiescence	Compromise/ Avoidance
	Low	Manipulation	Defiance

the dependence of the organization on critical institutional constituents. When such dependence is high, the strategy of avoidance can be risky, particularly when efforts to avoid public evaluation and assessment raise suspicions and jeopardize the ability of the organization to secure critical resources (Oliver, 1991: 155).

Finally, when institutional pressures are comparatively weak and there are perceived technical benefits, manipulation may be a viable strategy. For example, organizations can coopt institutional actors to gain political support and legitimacy (Pfeffer, 1974; Selznick, 1949). Organizations can also use influence tactics to shape public perceptions or lobby government regulators in efforts to influence important legislation (Oliver, 1991).

This framework can be extended to the specific context of employer involvement in work-family issues. The five institutional factors outlined above determine the strength of institutional pressures. Institutional pressures are hypothesized to be strongest when an organization is large, highly dependent on female employees and working parents, part of the public sector, and part of sectors in which many other organizations provide work-family benefits and professional, trade, and membership organizations are numerous. The technical outcomes are reflected in the measures of the perceived benefits and costs of providing child care services. The following hypotheses follow from the framework depicted in Figure 28.1 and the related discussion.

Hypothesis 9: Organizations will be most likely to pursue an acquiescence strategy when institutional pressures for employer involvement in work-family issues are strong, the perceived benefits of providing child care services are high, and the perceived costs of providing child care services are low.

Hypothesis 10: Organizations will be most likely to pursue a compromise strategy when institutional pressures for employer involvement in work-family issues are strong, the perceived benefits of providing child care services are low, and the perceived costs of providing child care services are high.

Hypothesis 11: Organizations will be most likely to pursue an avoidance strategy when institutional pressures for employer involvement in work-family issues are gen-erally strong (moderated by low dependence on female employees and working parents), the perceived benefits of providing child care services are low, and the perceived costs of providing child care services are high.

Hypothesis 12: Organizations will be most likely to pursue a defiance strategy when institutional pressures for employer involvement in work-family issues are weak, the perceived benefits of providing child care services are low, and the perceived costs of providing child care services are high.

Methods

The hypotheses were tested with a combination of archival and survey data. The survey was designed to examine the extent of employer involvement in work-family issues, focusing in particular on child care and flexible workplace options. The survey also addressed factors facilitating or hindering employer involvement in work-family issues. The Washington State Employment Security Department, an agency of the U.S. Department of Labor, administered the survey in the summer of 1989, sending it out to a stratified random sample of 3,225 private and public sector establishments with ten or more employees. An effort was made to develop a representative sample in terms of both employer size and industry group. . . .

Dependent Variable

To develop a variable to assess the nature of employers' strategic responses to institutional pressures for involvement in work-family issues, I used information on their adoption of child care services and options affording flexibility to employees.

The adoption of a child care service was noted if an organization indicated that it provided to employees at least one of three child care benefits: on-site child care, financial assistance with child care expenses, such as direct subsidies or contracting with an external provider, or child care resource and referral services to link employees with child care providers (Auerbach, 1988; Burud et al., 1984; Kamerman & Kahn, 1987). The adoption of flexible workplace options was noted if an organization indicated that it provided employees at least one of the following benefits: flextime, voluntarily reduced work time, job sharing, work at home, flexible leave, or parental leave. Researchers have pointed out that these benefits provide critical flexibility in workplaces for employees (Auerbach, 1988; Burud et al., 1984; Cook, 1989; Hayghe, 1988; Kamerman & Kahn, 1987; Kanter, 1977). Benefits such as flextime and job sharing provide day-to-day flexibility, and leave policies allow employees to take off significant amounts of time without losing their jobs. To minimize differences in definitions of these benefits across organizations, the survey administrators provided respondents with specific definitions for each of the child care services and flexible workplace options identified above.

From these data, the following measures of strategic responses were developed:

Acquiescence. Researchers have argued that organizations are most responsive to institutional pressures when they provide both dependent care and flexibility options (Auerbach, 1988; Galinsky & Stein, 1990; Kamerman & Kahn, 1987; Raabe, 1990). Organizations that provided one child care benefit or more and one flexibility benefit or more were categorized as pursuing an acquiescence strategy in response to institutional pressures.

Compromise. Organizations that offered only one major type of work-family benefit, either child care or flexibility, but provided multiple options within that area were categorized as pursuing a compromise strategy. These organizations do not fully meet institutional expectations about child care and workplace flexibility but do comply in a meaningful way to institutional norms. . . .

Avoidance. Organizations that offered only one work-family benefit were defined as pursuing an avoidance strategy. These organizations provided neither both child care and workplace flexibility benefits nor multiple benefits of one type. Providing only one benefit can be viewed as a strategy that allows organizations to avoid both the financial and administrative costs associated with the provision of a more comprehensive set of work-family options. . . .

Defiance. Not providing either child care or workplace flexibility benefits represents a dismissal or ignoring of institutional norms and values regarding employer responsiveness to work-family issues.

The dependent variable was then created by assigning the following values to the strategic responses: acquiescence, 3; compromise, 2; avoidance, 1; defiance, 0. I limited analyses to these four strategic responses.

Unfortunately, I did not have data that allowed for determining actions taken by employers to actively manipulate (Oliver, 1991) their institutional environments, for example through co-optation or other influence tactics.

Independent Variables

The critical factors characterizing institutional pressures—cause, constituents, content, control, and context—were measured as follows:

Cause

Organization size. To assess cause, I measured size as the natural logarithm of the total number of an organization's employees.

Constituents

Percentage of female employees. Because establishment-level data were not collected in 1989, I used data from a follow-up 1991 survey to measure the proportion of female employees in each organization, a measure of constituents. I assumed that the demographic composition of these firms had not changed significantly during the two-year period 1989–91. Each respondent was asked to indicate whether the proportion of total female employees was under 20 percent, 20–39 percent, 40–59 percent, 60–79 percent, or 80 percent or more. A 1–5 scale was created from these responses (1 = under 20%). This measure reflects the extent to which an organization depends on a single resource.

Percentage of working parents. For a second constituents measure, respondents similarly indicated the proportion of total employees who were parents of children under age 18, and the variable was coded like the female employees measure.

Content

Public sector organizations. I used data provided by the Washington State Employment Security Department to identify employers associated with federal, state, or local governments. A public-private dichotomous variable was created to reflect this distinction between institutional sectors, thus measuring content.

Control

. . . I included three variables that take both industry and geographic area into account to measure the institutional characteristic of control: same industry–same county diffusion was the proportion of employers in the same industry group and in the same county as a focal organization adopting both child care services and workplace flexibility benefits. Other industries–same county diffusion was the proportion of employers in other industry groups but in the same county adopting both child care services and workplace flexibility benefits. Same industry–other counties diffusion was the proportion of employers in the same industry group but in other counties adopting both child care services and workplace flexibility benefits. . . .

Context

Total business, professional, and membership organizations. In order to measure the degree of interconnectedness within an institutional environment as an assessment of context, I used data provided by the Washington State Employment Security Department to specify the number of business, professional (including labor unions), and membership organizations in a particular county. Membership organizations included civic, social, and fraternal associations, political organizations, and religious organizations.

Technical Determinants

Perceived child care benefits. Each employer was asked to indicate the perceived effects of child care services with respect to nine different outcomes: recruitment, retention, absenteeism, tardiness, employee stress, employee morale, employee loyalty, employee training costs, and employee productivity. Responses were coded as follows: "positive effects," 3; "uncertain effects," 2; "no effects," 1; "negative effects," 0. Responses were then summed to create a total benefits scale.

Perceived child care costs. Employers were asked to indicate the extent to which concerns about expense or liability represented an obstacle to their adoption of child care services. The following four response categories were offered: "not an obstacle," 0; "not sure," 1; "minor obstacle," 2; and "major obstacle," 3. A summary scale was also created from these responses.

Control Variables

Employer knowledge. To the extent that employers remain unknowledgeable about work-family initiatives, there is a greater likelihood that they will resist institutional pressures to adopt those benefits (Auerbach, 1988). Although the survey did not address employer knowledge of both child care and workplace flexibility benefits, it did address five aspects of child care services: (1) tax deductions for employers who provide child care benefits, (2) nontaxability of employer-provided child care assistance, (3) costs of providing various child care benefits, (4) research indicating the effects of child care assistance on productivity and other work-related behaviors, and (5) employer assessment of child care needs. Possible responses were "no knowledge," 1; "low degree of knowledge," 2; and "high degree of knowledge," 3. I developed a total employer knowledge scale by summing the responses to the five categories. . . .

Analysis

Because ordinary-least-squares (OLS) analyses are based on assumptions requiring an interval level of measurement for the dependent variable, I used an ordered multinomial "probit" procedure (McKelvey & Zavoina, 1975; Pindyck & Rubinfeld, 1981) to examine the effects of the independent variables on four levels of employer responsiveness to work-family issues. The multinomial probit procedure explicitly takes into account the ordered categorical nature of the dependent variable. Maximum likelihood methods were used to obtain estimates of the parameters of the model.

A secondary set of analyses was conducted to test the effects of the independent variables on the probability of an organization's adopting each of the four specific strategies. I created four dichotomous dependent variables and included them in separate "logit" models. Logistic regression is a more appropriate procedure when the ordering of a dependent variable is not critical. Because my dependent variable was dichotomous and OLS assumptions were violated (Aldrich & Nelson, 1984), I once again used maximum likelihood procedures to estimate the parameters of the model. . . .

Results

Table 28.1 presents the descriptive statistics for the dependent and independent variables.

I also examined variations in strategic responses across industry groups. Table 28.2 shows findings indicating that important differences exist in the kinds of strategic responses employers have adopted.

The more detailed analysis presented in Table 28.3 indicates some of the important

Table 28.1
Descriptive Statistics and Pearson Product-Moment Correlations[a]

Variables	Means	s.d.	1	2	3	4	5	6	7	8	9	10	11	12	13	14	15	16	17
Dependent variables																			
1. Level of organizational responsiveness	2.45	0.98																	
2. Acquiescence	0.11	0.31	.55																
3. Compromise	0.49	0.50	.54	-.34															
4. Avoidance	0.15	0.36	-.19	-.15	-.41														
5. Defiance	0.25	0.43	-.86	-.20	-.57	.25													
Control variables																			
6. Female unemployment	0.03	0.02	-.22	-.13	-.11	.04	.18												
7. Employer knowledge of child care benefits	12.22	3.08	.19	.27	-.05	-.06	-.10	.06											
Cause																			
8. Organizational size	2.99	2.21	.13	.16	-.05	.06	-.11	-.02	-.15										
Constituents																			
9. Percentage of female employees[b]	2.92	1.47	.29	.18	.15	-.09	-.23	-.41	-.11	.05									
10. Percentage of working parents[b]	2.67	1.28	.05	.09	-.03	-.01	-.02	.06	-.05	.14	.02								
Content																			
11. Public sector	0.08	0.28	.14	.13	-.01	.03	-.12	-.18	-.14	.21	.08	.09							
Control																			
12. Same industry–same county diffusion	12.82	13.57	.24	.36	-.09	-.01	-.14	.26	-.17	.11	.21	.06	.25						
13. Other industries–same county diffusion	11.59	7.68	.21	.19	.01	.02	-.17	-.37	-.15	.19	.31	.12	.62	.40					

Table 28.1 (continued)
Descriptive Statistics and Pearson Product-Moment Correlations[a]

Variables	Means	s.d.	1	2	3	4	5	6	7	8	9	10	11	12	13	14	15	16	17
14. Same industry–other counties diffusion	12.71	7.33	-.02	.01	-.02	-.04	.05	.09	.04	-.01	-.09	-.11	-.13	.14	-.29				
Context																			
15. Total business, professional, and membership organizations	287.49	290.33	.02	.11	-.07	-.03	.02	-.01	-.03	-.03	-.02	-.14	-.10	.31	-.14	.55			
Technical determinants																			
16. Perceived child care benefits	19.98	3.57	.23	.19	.07	-.04	-.18	-.13	-.22	.13	.19	.14	.12	.14	.20	-.03	.04		
17. Perceived child care costs	4.92	1.08	-.05	-.03	-.07	.01	.06	.01	-.04	.11	.03	.08	.06	.01	.03	.05	.02	.06	

[a] All correlations greater than .06 are significant at $p < .05$.
[b] Statistics are not actual percentages; they are based on coding from survey.

institutional determinants that underlie the broader industry group patterns of responsiveness indicated in Table 28.2. The multinomial probit analysis the table reports relates each independent variable to the varying levels of employer adoption of work-family policies. The defiance response was the reference category in this analysis.

Considerations of social fitness and legitimacy appear to be important motivators of employer adoption of work-family benefits. As hypothesized, large organizations are more likely than small ones to pursue responsive strategies. The nature of dependencies on key institutional constituents, in particular female employees, is also a critical determinant of employer adoption of work-family benefits. Finally, as other studies (Fligstein, 1985; Tolbert & Zucker, 1983) have suggested, the diffusion of norms or structures across organizations increases the likelihood that nonadopters will conform to prevailing practices. The presence of a high proportion of other organizations within a given industry group and county adopting both types of work-family benefits significantly increased employer responsiveness to work-family issues.

A number of hypotheses were not confirmed. The proportion of parents in an organization did not affect employer responsiveness to institutional pressures. I also argued that public sector organizations would be more likely to have goals congruent with the expectations of institutional constituencies promoting employer involvement in work-family issues and hence, would be more likely to conform to institutional pressures. The results did not support this hypothesis. The interconnectedness of the institutional environment, defined in this research as the number of business, professional, and membership organizations present, was also not a significant determinant of employer responses. The lack of significant results associated with this measure of -interconnectedness may be the result of its coarseness. A finer-grained measure may have better captured the importance of environmental interconnectedness in fostering employer involvement in work and family issues.

Table 28.2
Distribution of Organizations

Organizational Characteristics	Percentage	Strategic Response			
		Acquiescence	Compromise	Avoidance	Defiance
Size					
0–49	58.3	4.2	53.8	12.5	29.5
50–249	16.9	10.5	41.1	19.1	29.2
250+	24.8	27.4	41.7	18.2	12.7
Industry					
All industries	100	11	48	15	26
Services	30.5	16.7	52.8	12.5	18.0
Public sector	8.5	24.8	48.6	18.1	8.6
Construction and mining	6.8		35.7	15.5	48.8
Durable goods	5.5	10.3	39.7	20.6	29.4
Nondurable goods	10.2	4.0	34.1	23.8	38.1
Transportation and public utilities	4.8	11.9	42.4	10.2	35.6
Wholesale trade	8.9	3.6	43.6	23.6	29.1
Retail trade	19.6	2.9	61.2	8.7	27.3
Finance, insurance, and real estate	5.3	25.8	47.0	15.2	12.1

The analysis further suggests a number of important determinants of employer strategies. The expectation of significant benefits from offering child care services and a high level of knowledge about such services motivate employers to conform to institutional pressures. These results are consistent with the findings of Morgan and Milliken (1993), who found that organizations were most likely to be responsive to work-family issues when they perceived that broadening employees' work-family options would have a significant impact on productivity. Finally, the results indicate that conformity to institutional pressures is more likely to occur in industry groups in which unemployment among women is relatively low.

The logit analysis results presented in Table 28.4 indicate the relative importance of the institutional and technical factors studied on the choice of specific strategic responses (acquiescence, compromise, avoidance, defiance) to institutional pressures for employer involvement in work-family issues. The first model indicates that, as Hypothesis 9 predicts, organizations are most likely to select an acquiescence strategy when institutional pressures are strong and responsiveness to institutional pressures is perceived as having a positive effect on technical outcomes. The coefficients of the variables associated with institutional cause, constituents, control, and context are all positive and significant. In addition, the results support the importance of high perceived benefits and low costs in conjunction with the institutional factors just noted. Surprisingly, the results suggest that private, not public, organizations have a greater probability of pursuing an acquiescence strategy. This finding may reflect the effects of market forces that are reinforcing institutional pressures on private sector organizations to provide work-family benefits.

The adoption of compromise and avoidance strategies was predicted to be most likely when institutional pressures are comparatively strong and responsiveness to those pressures is perceived as having a negative effect on technical outcomes. The second and third models generally provide weak support for these arguments. Institutional considerations do seem to influence the pursuit of a compromise strategy (Hypothesis 10), although the pattern of results presented in the second model is not consistent with a particularly strong set of institutional pressures. Larger organizations and those that employ a relatively high proportion of women are more likely to pursue a

Table 28.3
Results of Ordered Probit Analysis

Variables	b	s.e.
Control variables		
Female unemployment	−4.926*	1.977
Employer knowledge of child care benefits	.051***	.011
Technical determinants		
Perceived child care benefits	.045***	.010
Perceived child care costs	−.012	.031
Cause		
Organizational size	.035*	.016
Constituents		
Percentage of female employees	.153***	.026
Percentage of working parents	.023	.027
Content		
Public sector	.093	.164
Control		
Same industry–same county diffusion	.015***	.003
Other industries–same county diffusion	.002	.007
Same industry–other counties diffusion	.001	.005
Context		
Total business, professional, and membership organizations	.001	.001
Intercept 1	.215	.323
Intercept 2	.682	.323
Intercept 3	2.358	.329
χ^2	104.853***	

* $p < .05$
** $p < .01$
*** $p < .001$

compromise strategy. Contrary to expectations, organizations are significantly less likely to pursue a compromise strategy when there is a high level of diffusion of work-family benefits among similar organizations within the local environment. As Hypothesis 10 predicts, organizational decision makers who adopt a compromise strategy perceive that a moderate level of involvement in work-family issues has important benefits and low costs. Finally, although the results presented in model 3 are generally weak, they do provide some support for the relative importance of institutional dependence in determining whether organizations will pursue a compromise or avoidance strategy (Hypothesis 11). Organizations with a comparatively low proportion of female employees are significantly more likely to pursue an avoidance strategy.

The fourth model in Table 28.4 provides partial support for the predicted (Hypothesis 12) effects of institutional pressures and technical factors on the adoption of a defiance strategy. The probability of adopting a defiance strategy is significantly greater for small organizations, those with a low proportion of female employees, and those in local environments in which adoption of child care and workplace flexibility benefits by other organizations in their industry is low. Employers adopting a defiance strategy are also significantly more likely to perceive few benefits associated with adopting child care benefits.

In summary, the empirical analyses suggest that organizations vary in the strategies they pursue to adapt to institutional pressures and that the level of organizational responsiveness to institutional pressures is significantly related to a set of institutional and technical factors.

Table 28.4
Results of Logit Analysis

	Strategic Response							
	Acquiescence		Compromise		Avoidance		Defiance	
Variables	b	s.e.	b	s.e.	b	s.e.	b	s.e.
Control variables								
Female unemployment	11.773	11.069	−8.995*	3.639	3.206	4.675	7.690*	3.760
Employer knowledge of child care benefits	.190***	.032	.038†	.021	−.056†	.031	−.027	.025
Technical determinants								
Perceived child care benefits	.069*	.029	.043*	.018	−.017	.025	−.091**	.023
Perceived child care costs	−.182†	.102	−.160**	.057	.035	.076	.089	.065
Cause								
Organizational size	.134**	.046	.051†	.029	.097*	.041	−.071*	.036
Constituents								
Percentage of female employees	.258**	.096	.193***	.047	−.196**	.066	−.232***	.055
Percentage of working parents	.227**	.091	−.048	.049	−.061	.069	.022	.057
Content								
Public sector	−.843†	.506	.088	.304	.285	.393	−.773	.472
Control								
Same industry–same county diffusion	.057***	.008	−.020***	.006	.004	.007	−.017*	.007
Other industries–same county diffusion	.032	.027	−.001	.012	.007	.017	.003	.014
Same industry–other counties diffusion	.009	.023	.012	.011	−.018	.016	.001	.013
Context								
Total business, professional, and membership organizations	.010*	.049	−.004	.003	−.001	.010	.004	.003
Intercept	3.724	1.103	1.967	.603	1.498	.855	1.395	.708
χ^2	235.931***		70.217***		27.051**		108.017**	
Pseudo R^2	.167		.064		.028		.083	

$^{\dagger}p < .10$
$^*p < .05$
$^{**}p < .01$
$^{***}p < .001$

Discussion

This research is among the first to examine the strategies organizations adopt in response to institutional norms and pressures. Its findings are generally consistent with the broad thesis advanced earlier. Organizations do not respond uniformly to institutional pressures but rather, adopt varying strategies that depend on the nature of the institutional pressures impinging on them (Oliver, 1991).

The results of this study lend strong support to several fundamental explanations of conformity to institutional pressures. A finding consistent with previous theorizing and research was that the extent of preexisting employer involvement in work-family issues within an organization's sector was strongly related to its conformity to institutional pressures:, suggesting that the more broadly diffused an institutional practice, the higher the likelihood that an organization will adopt it (Fligstein, 1985; Tolbert & Zucker, 1983; Zucker, 1987). The study's findings also support the importance of organizational size and the motivation to secure legitimacy (Dowling & Pfeffer, 1975; Meyer, 1979; Pfeffer, 1982; Powell, 1991) and dependence on influential institutional constituents (Pfeffer & Salancik, 1978; Tolbert, 1985) in shaping the likelihood that organizations will conform to institutional pressures and expectations.

The robust relationship between organizational size and responsiveness to institutional pressures supports the observations of researchers who have argued that large firms, because of their size and visibility, are likely to be under greater pressure to maintain their social legitimacy by responding to institutional demands (Dowling & Pfeffer, 1975; Meyer, 1979; Miles, 1987; Mintzberg, 1983). The adoption of child care and workplace flexibility benefits is a tangible accommodation to institutional pressures that signals important constituents (Meyer, 1979) that an organization is responsive. Insofar as employer involvement in work-family initiatives represents an important discretionary domain of corporate social responsibility (Carroll, 1979), these results support existing research linking corporate size with social responsibility (Mintzberg, 1983). One weakness in the study was the inability to control directly for the effects of organizational slack on the adoption of work-family benefits. Larger organizations might have more organizational slack and resources to devote to the adoption of employee benefits, particularly relatively expensive benefits such as employer-supported child care (Morgan & Milliken, 1993). Morgan and Milliken also argued that large organizations might have large, specialized human resource staffs that can direct greater attention to work-family issues than is possible in small organizations. These are important alternative explanations that I could not directly address in this research.

The present findings also provide strong empirical confirmation that the presence of women in a workplace and heightened demand for child care services and workplace flexibility are important forces motivating employer involvement in work-family issues (Auerbach, 1988; Cook, 1989; Kamerman & Kahn, 1987). In organizations that employ many women, employers' dependence on this important constituency compels them to adopt child care services, flexible workplace options, or both. This relationship appears to be a much stronger factor than the broader parental measure used in this study. These findings may provide additional evidence that institutional pressure for employer involvement in work-family issues is influenced primarily by women, who tend to assume a greater role than men in handling child care and other family concerns (Auerbach, 1988; Emlen & Koren, 1984; Kamerman & Kahn, 1987). . . .

To summarize, this study underscores the importance of researchers' beginning to attend to the multiple strategies that organizations employ to respond to institutional pressures. It will be important for future studies to build on frameworks such as that provided by Oliver (1991) to specify the organizational and environmental factors that condition those strategic choices. As this research progresses, an important focus will be how strategic responses to institutional pressures may be similar to or differ from strategic responses to task and technical environments. Academic knowledge about strategic choice in technical environments is relatively well developed, but there is great potential in beginning to explore the causal dynamics of strategic choice in contexts in which institutional pressures are critical.

References

Aldous, J. 1990. Specification and speculation concerning the politics of workplace family policies. *Journal of Family Issues,* 11: 355–367.

Aldrich, H. E. 1979. *Organizations and environments.* Englewood Cliffs. NJ: Prentice-Hall, Inc.

Aldrich, H. E., and Auster, E. R. 1986. Even dwarfs started small: Liabilities of age and size and their strategic implications. In B. M. Staw & L. L. Cummings (Eds.), *Research in organizational behavior,* vol. 8: 165–198. Greenwich, CT: JAI Press.

Aldrich, H. E., & Pfeffer, J. 1976. Environments of organizations. In A. Inkeles, J. Coleman, & N. Smelser (Eds.), *An-*

nual review of sociology, vol. 2: 79–105. Palo Alto, CA: Annual Reviews.

Aldrich, J. H., & Nelson, F. D. 1984. *Linear probability, logit, and probit models.* Newbury Park. CA: Sage.

Auerbach, J. D. 1988. *In the business of child care.* New York: Praeger.

Baron. J. P., Dobbin. F., & Jennings, P. D. 1986. War and peace: The evolution of modern personnel administration in U.S. industry. *American Journal of Sociology,* 92: 250–283.

Buehler, V. M.. & Shetty, Y. K. 1976. Managerial response to social responsibility challenge. *Academy of Management Review,* 18: 66–78.

Burud, S., Aschbacher, & McCroskey, J. 1984. *Employer-supported child care: Investing in human resources.* Boston: Auburn House.

Carroll. A. B. 1979. A three-dimensional conceptual model of corporate performance. *Academy of Management Review,* 4: 497–505.

Child, J. 1972. Organizational structure, environment, and performance: The role of strategic choice. *Sociology,* 6: 1–22.

Cook, A. H. 1989. Public policies to help dual-earner families meet the demands of the work world. *Industrial and Labor Relations Review,* 42: 201–215.

Covaleski, M. A., & Dirsmith, M. W. 1988. An institutional perspective on the rise, social transformation, and fall of a university budget category. *Administrative Science Quarterly,* 33: 562–587.

D'Aunno, T., Sutton, R. I., & Price, R. H. 1991. Isomorphism and external support in conflicting institutional environments: A study of drug abuse treatment units. *Academy of Management Journal,* 34: 636–661.

DiMaggio, P. J. 1988. Interest and agency in institutional theory. In L. G. Zucker (Ed.), *Institutional patterns and organizations: Culture and environment:* 3–21. Cambridge, MA: Ballinger.

DiMaggio, P. J., & Powell, W. W. 1983. The iron cage revisited: Institutional isomorphism and collective rationality in organizational fields. *American Sociological Review,* 48: 147–160.

Dobbin, F. R., Edelman, L., Meyer, J. W., Scott, W. R., & Swidler, A. 1988. The expansion of due process in organizations. In L. G. Zucker (Ed.), *Institutional patterns and organizations: Culture and environment:* 71–101. Cambridge, MA: Ballinger.

Dowling, J., & Pfeffer, J. 1975. Organizational legitimacy: Social values and organizational behavior. *Pacific Sociological Review,* 18: 122–135.

Elsbach, K., & Sutton, R. 1992. Acquiring organizational legitimacy through illegitimate actions: A marriage of institutional and impression management theories. *Academy of Management Journal,* 35: 699–738.

Emlen, A. C., & Koren, P. E. 1984. *Hard to find and difficult to manage: The effects of child care on the workplace.* Unpublished manuscript, Regional Research Institute for Human Services. Portland State University, Portland, OR.

Fernandez, J. P. 1988. *Child care and corporate productivity: Resolving family-work conflicts.* Lexington, MA: Lexington Books.

Fligstein, N. 1985. The spread of the multidivisional form among large firms, 1919–1979. *American Sociological Review,* 50: 377–391.

Fligstein, N. 1991. The structural transformation of American industry: An institutional account of the causes of diversification in the largest firms, 1919–1979. In W. W. Powell & P. J. DiMaggio (Eds.), *The new institutionalism in organizational analysis:* 311–336. Chicago: University of Chicago Press.

Freeman, R. E., & Gilbert. D. R. 1988. *Corporate strategy and the search for ethics.* Englewood Cliffs, NJ: Prentice Hall.

Galaskiewicz, J. 1991. Making corporate actors accountable: Institution building in Minneapolis-St. Paul. In W. W. Powell & P. J. DiMaggio (Eds.), *The new institutionalism in organizational analysis:* 293–310. Chicago: University of Chicago Press.

Galinsky. E., & Stein. P. J. 1990. The impact of human resource policies: Balancing work and family life. *Journal of Family Issues,* 11: 368–383.

Hall, D. T.. & Richter, J. R. 1990. Career gridlock: Baby boomers hit the wall. *Executive,* 4(3): 7–22.

Hannan, M. T., & Freeman. J. 1977. The population ecology of organizations. *American Journal of Sociology,* 82: 929–964.

Hannan, M. T., & Freeman. J. 1989. *Organizational ecology.* Cambridge, MA: Harvard University Press.

Hayghe, H. V. 1988. Family members in the work force. *Monthly Labor Review,* March: 14–19.

Hewlett, S. A, 1991. *When the bough breaks: The cost of neglecting our children.* New York: Basic Books.

Hitt, M. A., & Tyler, B. B. 1991. Strategic decision models: Integrating different perspectives. *Strategic Management Journal,* 12: 327–351.

Hrebiniak, L., & Joyce, W. F. 1985. Organizational adaptation: Strategic choice and environmental determinism. *Administrative Science Quarterly,* 30: 336–349.

Hyland, S. L. 1990. Helping employees with family care. *Monthly Labor Review,* September: 22–26.

Jepperson, R. L. 1991. Institutions, institutional effects, and institutionalism. In W. W. Powell & P. J. DiMaggio (Eds.), *The new institutionalism in organizational analysis:* 143–163. Chicago: University of Chicago Press.

Judge, W. Q., & Zeithaml, C. P. 1992. Institutional and strategic choice perspectives on board involvement in the strategic decision process. *Academy of Management Journal,* 35: 766–794.

Kahn, A. J., & Kamerman, S. B. 1987. *Child care: Facing the hard choices.* Dover, MA: Auburn House.

Kamerman, S. B., & Kahn, A. J. 1987. *The responsive workplace.* New York: Columbia University Press.

Kanter, R. M. 1977. *Work and family in the United States: A critical review and agenda for research and policy.* New York: Russell Sage Foundation.

Lentz, A., & Tschigiri, H. 1963. The ethical content of annual reports. *Journal of Business,* 6: 387–393.

McKelvey, R. D., & Zavoina, W. 1975. A statistical model for the analysis of ordinal level dependent variables. *Journal of Mathematical Sociology,* 4: 103–120.

Magid, R. Y. 1983. *Child care initiatives for working parents.* New York: American Management Association.

Meyer, J. W., & Rowan, B. 1977. Institutional organizations: Formal structure as myth and ceremony. *American Journal of Sociology,* 83: 340–363.

Meyer, J. W., & Scott, W. R. 1983. *Organizational environments: Ritual and rationality.* Beverly Hills, CA: Sage.

Meyer, J. W., Scott, W. R., & Deal, T. R. 1983. Institutional and technical sources of organizational structure: Explaining the structure of educational organizations. In J. W. Meyer & W. R. Scott (Eds.), *Organizational environments: Ritual and rationality:* 45–70. Beverly Hills, CA: Sage.

Meyer, M. W. 1979. Organizational structure as signaling. *Pacific Sociological Review,* 22: 481–500.

Mezias, S. I. 1990. An institutional model of organizational practice: Financial reporting at the Fortune 200. *Administrative Science Quarterly,* 35: 431–457.

Miles, R. H. 1987. *Managing the corporate social environment: A grounded theory.* Englewood Cliffs, NJ: Prentice-Hall.

Miles, R. H., & Snow, C. C. 1978. *Organizational strategy, structure, and process.* New York: McGraw-Hill.

Milliken, F. J., Dutton, J. E., & Beyer, J. M. 1990. Understanding organizational adaptation to change: The case of work-family issues. *Human Resource Planning,* 13: 91–107.

Mintzberg, H. 1983. *Power in and around organizations.* Englewood Cliffs, NJ: Prentice-Hall.

Morgan, H., & Milliken, F. 1993. Keys to action: Understanding differences in organizations' responsiveness to work-and-family issues. *Human Resource Management Journal,* 31: 227–248.

Oliver, C. 1988. The collective strategy framework: An application to competing predictions of isomorphism. *Administrative Science Quarterly,* 33: 543–561.

Oliver, C. 1991. Strategic responses to institutional processes. *Academy of Management Review,* 16: 145–179.

Pfeffer, J. 1974. Cooptation and the composition of electric utility boards of directors. *Pacific Sociological Review,* 17: 333–363.

Pfeffer, J. 1982. *Organizations and organization theory.* Boston: Pitman.

Pfeffer, J., & Salancik, G. R. 1978. *The external control of organizations.* New York: Harper & Row.

Pindyck, R., & Rubinfeld, D. 1981. *Econometric models and economic forecasts.* New York: McGraw-Hill.

Powell, W. W. 1991. Expanding the scope of institutional analysis. In W. W. Powell & P. J. DiMaggio (Eds.), *The new institutionalism in organizational analysis:* 183–204. Chicago: University of Chicago Press.

Powell, W. W., & DiMaggio. P. J. 1991. *The new institutionalism in organizational analysis.* Chicago: University of Chicago Press.

Raabe, P. H. 1990. The organizational effects of workplace family policies. *Journal of Family Issues,* 11: 477–491.

Romanelli, E., & Tushman. M. L. 1986. Inertia, environments, and strategic choice: A quasi-experimental design for comparative longitudinal research. *Management Science,* 32: 608–621.

Rowan, B. 1982. Organizational structure and the institutional environment: The case of public schools. *Administrative Science Quarterly,* 27: 259–279.

SAS Institute. Inc. 1985. *SAS users' guide: Basics, version 5 edition.* Gary, NC: SAS Institute, Inc.

Scott, W. R. 1983. The organization of environments: Network, cultural, and historical elements. In J. W. Meyer & W. R. Scott (Eds.), *Organizational environments: Ritual and rationality:* 155–178. Beverly Hills, CA: Sage.

Scott, W. R. 1987. The adolescence of institutional theory. *Administrative Science Quarterly,* 32: 493–511.

Scott, W. R. 1991. Unpacking institutional arguments. In W. W. Powell & P. J. DiMaggio (Eds.), *The new institutionalism in organizational analysis:* 164–182. Chicago: University of Chicago Press.

Selznick, P. 1949. *TVA and the grass roots.* Berkeley: University of California Press.

Stinchcombe, A. L.1965. Social structure and organizations. In J. G. March (Ed.), *Handbook of organization:* 142–193. Chicago: Rand McNally.

Tolbert, P. S. 1985. Resource dependence and institutional environments: Sources of administrative structure in institutions of higher education. *Administrative Science Quarterly,* 20: 229–249.

Tolbert, P. S., & Zucker, L. G. 1983. Institutional sources of organizational culture in major law firms. In L. G. Zucker (Ed.), *Institutional patterns and organizations: Culture and environment:* 101–113. Cambridge, MA: Ballinger.

Wiatrowski, W. J. 1990. Family-related benefits in the workplace. *Monthly Labor Review,* March: 28–33.

Zucker, L. G. 1987. Institutional theories of organization. In J. Coleman (Ed.), *Annual review of sociology,* vol. 13: 443–464. Palo Alto, CA: Annual Reviews.

Chapter 29
Breaking the Iron Law of Oligarchy

Union Revitalization in the American Labor Movement

Kim Voss and Rachel Sherman

By almost all measures, labor unions in the United States have lost ground over time. These organizations have faced difficulties recruiting new members and making inroads into previously nonunionized industries and work settings. Although multiple factors explain declines in unionization, many suggest that the fault lies partly with unions themselves. But can struggling organizations reverse course? Voss and Sherman suggest that such change is possible, even for what they describe as "bureaucratically conservative" organizations like labor unions. In taking up these issues, Voss and Sherman highlight the role of social movements in helping produce organizational change.

Introduction

Until recently, the American labor movement seemed moribund, as unions represented ever-smaller proportions of the workforce and their political influence dwindled. Long estranged from their radical roots, local unions confined their efforts primarily to enforcing contracts for members on the shop floor. Organizing drives, which occurred with decreasing frequency, were conducted according to long-standing routines and rarely involved significant disruption. Overall, organized labor had become more like an institutionalized interest group than a social movement.

In recent years, however, some unions have started to change. They have begun to organize new members, using a wide variety of confrontational tactics, including massive street demonstrations, direct action, worker mobilization, sophisticated corporate campaigns, and circumvention of the National Labor Relations Board (NLRB) election process. These organizing and contract struggles look very different from the routinized contests that have typified labor's approach since the 1950s. In the wake of an unprecedented leadership turnover in 1995, the AFL-CIO, long fabled for its inertia and rigidity, actively supports this aggressive stance.

This revitalization of the American labor movement presents a paradox for social movement scholars. The union movement is an unlikely place to find the use of new disruptive tactics. Unions, after all, have existed for many years and are formal, bureaucratic organizations. Since Michels ([1915] 1962), both movement scholars (Piven and Cloward 1977; Staggenborg 1988; Fischer 1994) and activists (Epstein 1991, pp. 114, 118) have considered these features antithetical to the use of confrontational tactics in the pursuit of radical goals. The labor movement in particular exemplified the entrenched leadership and Conservative transformation associated with Michels's iron law of oligarchy. Thus the current revitalization of the movement raises the question of how some organizations have been able to break out of this bureaucratic conservatism. . . .

Breaking Out of Oligarchy: The Social Movement and Organizations Literatures

Scholars have rarely taken up the question of how social movement organizations *reverse* conservatism in goals and tactics. We address literature in the fields of both social movements and organizations, looking at how sociologists have approached the question of organizational change and highlighting particular studies with implications for our question.

Based largely on his study of European socialist parties, Michels claimed that all organizations have a natural tendency to develop oligarchical leadership and conservative goals, as officials gain power and organizational maintenance becomes their highest priority. Jenkins (1977) notes that this "iron law of oligarchy" thesis contains two major components. First, over time, organizations tend to develop oligarchical leadership, despite formal democratic practices. Increasing numbers of professionalized staff become indispensable to the organization, and a growing distance between staff and members allows leaders to mold the organization in their interests rather than in those of the members. Second, goals and tactics are transformed in a conservative direction as leaders become concerned above all with organizational survival.

Several studies supported one or both of these claims (Selznick 1948; Messinger 1955; Lang and Lang 1961; Schmidt 1973), but the most influential for social movement scholars was Piven and Cloward's (1977) study of poor people's movements. Piven and Cloward, especially concerned with disruptive protest, argued that social movements became less contentious once they built formalized organizations, for exactly Michels's reasons: with organization came leaders who were vulnerable to cooptation and increasingly concerned with organizational maintenance rather than disruption. Piven and Cloward's highly influential analysis cemented the association between organization and conservative tactics in the minds of many analysts.

Scholars also critiqued elements of the iron law, beginning with its universality (Clemens 1993; Duffhues and Felling 1989). Several researchers disputed the contention that organizations will inherently develop oligarchical leadership structures (Lipset, Trow, and Coleman 1956; Rothschild-Whitt 1976; Edelstein and Warner 1976). Others challenged the assertion that organizations necessarily become more conservative in goals and tactics over time, suggesting that this happens only under particular conditions (Zald and Ash 1966; Gusfield 1968; Rothschild-Whitt 1976; Gamson 1990; Gamson and Schmeidler 1984; Jenkins 1977, 1985; Schutt 1986; Greenstone 1969). Still others contested the purported association between goals and tactics, arguing that social movement organizations have used radical tactics to achieve conservative goals (Zald and Ash 1966; Gillespie 1983) and that they have pursued radical goals using conservative tactics (Beach 1977).

However, almost all this critical research was devoted to showing how oligarchy or its consequences could be avoided. Rarely did anyone ask whether change is possible once conservative goal transformation has taken place and disruption has been abandoned. A partial exception is Jenkins (1977), who studied the National Council of Churches (NCC), a social service organization that transformed itself into a radical protest group. Jenkins argued that in the NCC, oligarchy permitted professional staff members to change organizational goals in a radical direction. This transformation happened, he claimed, because the clergy who made up the staff had been radicalized in divinity schools, where liberation theology exerted increasing influence. The NCC was expanding at the time and adding staff positions, and this growing, professionalized staff enjoyed relative autonomy from the more conservative membership. Thus, in this case, the capture of the organization by its staff, a condition usually associated with conservative goal transformation, had the opposite effect.

In recent years, most social movement scholars have turned away from organizational analysis and from explicit efforts to confirm or challenge Michels's iron law thesis. Instead, attention has shifted to contentious events analysis as a way to investigate movement origins and effects more historically and comparatively (Tilly 1972, 1982, 1986, 1995; McAdam 1982; Kriesi et al. 1995; Tarrow 1989; Costain 1992; White 1995; Rucht 1998). Along with this focus on events, scholars have come to highlight the importance of external factors like political opportunities rather than internal organizational dynamics when accounting for movement tactics (McAdam 1983; Tilly 1995).

To the extent that contemporary scholars talk at all about social movement organizations, they tend to reinforce Michels's claim that bureaucratized, established organizations are more conservative in goals and tactics, though usually without explicitly engaging the iron law debate. For example, many scholars contrast informal and formal social movement organizations, indicating that only informal organizations have the flexibility to pursue innovative and disruptive tactics (Morris 1981; Staggenborg 1988; Whittier 1995; Jenkins and Eckert 1986; Smith 1996, pp. 108–31). Others highlight the formative moments of social movements—when organizations are most likely to be informally organized—and suggest that the inventiveness of the early period is directly tied to the lack of bureaucratic organization (Koopmans 1993; Kriesi et al. 1995, pp. 134–39).

A few recent studies have inquired specifically about changes in existing social movement organizations. Minkoff (1999) suggests, based on data from 870 women's and racial minority groups, that organizational transformations of all types are more likely to occur when political opportunities and resources are expanding, and in older, more professionalized groups. Tarrow (1989) claims that protest cycle dynamics often trigger changes in contending groups, and especially when cycles peak, established organizations can become radicalized as they compete for attention and support (see also Kriesi et al. 1995, chap. 5). Useem and Zald (1987) argue that countermovements frequently spur organizational changes, as happened when the pronuclear lobby they studied responded to antinuclear protest (see also Zald and Useem 1987; Staggenborg 1991; Meyer and Staggenborg 1996).

While the return to organizational analysis is a welcome step, these studies emphasize factors that are unlikely to account for our case of organizational transformation. Minkoff's study includes very few cases of organizations becoming more disruptive, which suggests that her conclusions may not apply to the revitalization of the union movement. Indeed, during the 1980s and 1990s, when revitalization began, political opportunities and resources for the labor movement were contracting, not expanding, as we show below. Moreover, the United States was not experiencing a protest cycle, as Tarrow might lead us to expect. Finally, while employer countermobilization has certainly eroded labor's position, much as early antinuclear protest undermined government support for nuclear power, oppositional activity by employers has been directed against most of the private sector labor movement, and thus cannot explain the differences between transformed and nontransformed local unions.

In general, then, the debate over the iron law in the social movement literature has remained focused on a single and seemingly final trajectory of movement organizations, rather than on the possibility that movements, once they have become oligarchical, will radicalize their goals. Likewise, the recent emphasis on emerging organizations as sources of disruptive tactics does not explain the appearance of such tactics in an established movement characterized by highly institutionalized, and relatively inflexible organizations. And the few studies that have begun to investigate organizational transformation highlight the importance of factors that were not present when the labor movement began to change.

The organizations literature is another place one might look for explicit theorizing about the type of organizational transformation currently under way in the American labor movement. Here, too, however, the causal mechanisms underlying radical change in existing organizations have received far less attention than the reasons for conservative transformation, inertia, and the standardization of organizational forms.

As in the social movement field, many early theorists of organizations highlighted internal organizational dynamics in accounting for conservative transformation in the goals, structure, and tactics of organizations. Simon (1957), Blau (1963), and Selznick (1943, 1957) all argued, like Michels, that organizational changes can often be understood as growing out of a natural tendency for operational goals to supplant purposive ones, and that such changes would be in a conservative direction.

In recent years, some organizational theorists have jettisoned the question of conservative transformation altogether, because in their view, organizations are unadaptable (Hannan and Freeman 1984; Singh and Lumsden 1990; Barnett and Carroll 1995). Once founded, organizations are subject to strong inertial pressures; hence, change occurs primarily at the population level, through demographic processes of organizational births and deaths. In the few studies of change done by these scholars, the key issue is usually whether change increases the risk of failure rather than the reasons for change, as we are inquiring about here (Singh, Tucker, and Meinhard 1991; Delacroix and Swaminathan 1991; Amburgey, Kelly, and Barnett 1993).

New institutionalist organizational theorists, in contrast, see organizations as mutable (DiMaggio and Powell 1991a; Scott 1995). However, researchers in this tradition have focused on identifying the mechanisms by which organizations become more similar over time, rather than on analyzing why organizations might adopt new, not-yet institutionalized forms (DiMaggio and Powell 1991b; see also Zucker 1991). Thus, only rarely do studies within, this tradition address organizational transformation. One such study is Fligstein's (1985, 1991) research on the multidivisional form in large American firms, which examines why existing business organizations sometimes adopt new forms. He discovers that organizational change rarely happens when the organizational field is stable; instead, adoption of the new multidivisional form takes place in the early periods leading up to the establishment of a new organizational field, and when a shock, such as a new federal antitrust policy, is delivered to a stable organizational field. When shocks occur, organizational change happens in one of three ways: well-positioned actors in existing organizations offer new interpretations of the shock and use this interpretation to push for a changed strategy within the organization; new firms arise in the organizational field; or, in the later periods, the forces of institutionalization come into play as actors in noninnovative organizations begin to follow the lead of successful innovators. Fligstein's language of "turbulence" and "shocks" suggests that adverse institutional changes are more likely than favorable ones to lead existing organizations to adopt new forms.

In a similar vein, Singh, Tucker, and Meinhard (1991) directly compare the effects of positive and negative environmental shifts on the rate and extent of organizational change. Examining organizational change in voluntary social service organizations in metropolitan Toronto, they find that both expanding and contracting political opportunities spur organizational change, but that contracting opportunities prompt faster and more extensive changes (see also Ikenberry 1989). . . .

Labor Movement Revitalization

Although it has deep roots in the 19th century, the contemporary labor movement in the United States is generally considered to have originated in the 1930s, when hundreds of thousands of industrial workers joined unions. During this period, union organizers used radical tactics, most famously the sit-down strike, to pursue the radical goals of bringing workers of all skill levels into unions to seek social justice. As many contemporary social movement scholars would predict, in this period inventive tactics and novel organizational forms were associated with emergent organizations: the organizing committees and industrial unions of the new Congress of Industrial Organizations (CIO). The established craft unions, affiliated with the hidebound and conservative American Federation of Labor (AFL), refused to change their organizations to accommodate the needs and desires of industrial workers.

In the postwar period, routine industrial relations procedures came to govern interactions among the state, employers, and both AFL and CIO unions. As this occurred, the labor movement became subject to the processes Michels described: limited leadership turnover, increasingly conservative goals, and correspondingly nonconfrontational tactics. Some commentators see this development as a paradigmatic illustration of the iron law (Piven and Cloward 1977), while others emphasize external constraints, particularly the Taft-Hartley Act of 1947, which limited unions' tactical possibilities and encouraged purging radicals in unions (Fantasia 1988). Whatever the cause, the labor movement lost much of its oppositional edge, modifying its disruptive tactics and reducing its primary. goals to gaining better contracts for members and influencing routine politics through regular channels. The prevailing method of representing members was "business unionism," in which union business agents "serviced" workers, resolving shop-floor and other problems for them.

From about 1950 until the 1980s, unions did organize new members, but with some notable exceptions (particularly public-sector unions), most labor organizations focused on expanding their existing memberships through conventional tactics. These included organizing "hot shops" (firms where workers are enthusiastic about unionizing because of an immediate workplace grievance); focusing primarily on economic issues, especially wages and benefits; conducting top-down campaigns from union headquarters, with minimal participation by bargaining-unit members; reaching out to workers through gate leafleting, letters, and similar kinds of nonpersonal contact; and dropping campaigns that did not develop quickly enough (Green and Tilly 1987; Perry 1987; Bronfenbrenner 1993). Recognition was usually gained through the process established by the NLRB (National Labor Relations Board).

These organizing strategies were often successful in the period between the 1950s and the 1970s, when the climate was relatively favorable to unions. However, beginning in the mid-1970s and accelerating after President Reagan broke the air traffic controllers strike in 1981, corporate leaders stopped playing by the rules. Employers began aggressively to oppose new organizing and refused to concede to union demands in strikes. They began to contest and delay NLRB elections, fire union activists, hire antiunion consulting firms on a regular basis, and stall in negotiating first contracts (Goldfield 1987; Fantasia 1988; Peterson, Lee, and Finnegan 1992; Bronfenbrenner et al. 1998; Friedman et al. 1994). They also began to resist union demands by threatening to shut down or relocate operations. The traditional tactics of organizing were feeble against the onslaught of corporate opposition. And without employer cooperation, state regulations governing labor relations were revealed to be extremely ineffective; the NLRB was slow to investigate claims of legal violations, and penalties for breaking the law were weak.

Other economic changes also contributed to union decline, including the transition to services from manufacturing, the relocation of industrial production to less developed countries or to nonunion regions of the United States, increasing global competition, and corporate consolidation (Freeman 1985; Troy 1990; Boswell and Stevis 1997; Western 1997). Union organizing efforts shrank significantly in this period; while 1.5% of the private sector workforce was organized through NLRB elections in 1950, only .5% was organized in 1970, only .25% in 1980, and only .1% in 1985 (Bronfenbrenner et al. 1998, p. 5). As a result, unions' share of the workforce dropped from a high of 37% in 1946 (Bronfenbrenner et al. 1998, p. 2) to less than 14% today, with 9.5% in the private sector (Greenhouse 1999).

In the last several years, however, some unions have begun fighting back. They have begun to pursue new members, developing a strategic repertoire of increasingly aggressive and disruptive methods to counteract virulent employer opposition. They are focusing on workers who have traditionally been excluded from organizing efforts, such as women, minorities, and immigrants. In addition to organizing more workers and mobilizing the existing membership, the goals of this revitalized movement include broader social justice ends. Thus some unions have become increasingly involved in struggles for civil rights, immigrant rights, and economic justice for nonmembers. Since the election of a pro-organizing slate

of officers in 1995, the AFL-CIO has actively supported these changes.

The revitalized repertoire comprises tactics used in the heyday of the CIO as well as more recent innovations. These include actively mobilizing workers to confront their employers; focusing on issues such as dignity and fairness in addition to material concerns; using "corporate campaigns," which involve interfering in the employer's relations with lenders, clients, shareholders, and subsidiaries; strategically targeting industries and workplaces to be organized; staging frequent direct actions; pressuring public officials to influence local employers; allying with community and religious groups; using the media to disseminate the union's message; and circumventing the NLRB election process to demand "card-check recognition," in which the union is recognized when it has collected 50% plus one of union authorization cards. These strategies make up a repertoire of tactics and are often used together in "comprehensive campaigns." Organizers stress the need to use multiple tactics simultaneously, because it is never clear from one case to another which will prove most effective. Hence, rather than the introduction of a single new tactic into the movement, there is a gradual adoption of a range of tactics and a strategic way of thinking that is focused on challenging the employer's advantage and preventing employers from conducting "business as usual."

Researchers have found these tactics to be successful, especially when used together (Bronfenbrenner and Juravich 1998). Bronfenbrenner and Juravich (1994) found that union tactics accounted for more variation in the outcomes of NLRB representation elections than any other factor, thus suggesting that unions' approaches have significant consequences for the possibility of gaining members. More important, unions that innovate in general and in terms of organizing in particular are more successful in recruiting members—including formerly excluded minority and gender groups—than unions that do not (Fiorito, Jarley, and Delaney 1995; Sherman and Voss 2000).

Significant organizational changes in local unions have accompanied this radicalization of goals and tactics. The new organizing campaigns require resources. Unions need full-time researchers to find company vulnerabilities for corporate campaigns and to locate strategic organizing targets. Organizing departments, complete with full-time staff and directors, are necessary for many of the intensive rank-and-file techniques associated with worker mobilization. Bilingual organizers are key in sectors with many immigrant workers. Thus, unions that adopt the new tactical repertoire must devote more resources to organizing; consequently, they have fewer left over for servicing current members. The shift to organizing, therefore, has signified a decreased role for business agents and field representatives.

This shift has also transformed the role of current union members, promoting new levels of commitment and participation (Fletcher and Hurd 1999). First, they have been asked to allocate resources to aggressive organizing programs. They are also encouraged to do more of the hard work of organizing, including identifying potential organizing targets, visiting unorganized workers in their homes, and engaging in civil disobedience. Second, the shift of resources away from servicing has led innovative unions to train members to resolve their own problems on the shop floor. For instance, some locals have begun to teach members to handle grievances by enlisting the aid of a shop steward rather than a field representative. They may also encourage members to initiate solidarity actions, such as circulating petitions or collectively approaching management, in order to confront problems in the shop. This approach contrasts with long-standing custom in business unionism, in which union staff took responsibility for resolving grievances and work site problems.

Thus in some ways the labor movement has come to resemble more closely its predecessor of the 1930s. But now, deeply institutionalized, bureaucratic organizations, rather than new, emergent unions, form the core of the movement. As we have seen, these changes fly in the face of conventional theorizing about social movements, which indicates that once institutionalized, movements remain conservative. So we ask, first, how has this revitalization—the radicalization of goals and tactics—been able to occur?

Furthermore, union revitalization, while increasingly widespread, has not by any means come to characterize all unions. Many local and international unions still do not pursue significant organizing of new members. Of those that do, most remain wedded to old tactics or use new tactics in a piecemeal fashion (Bronfenbrenner and Juravich 1998), rather than adopting the entire repertoire described here. Even in the few international unions that have fully endorsed the new approach to organizing, many locals continue to rely on old tactics or eschew new organizing altogether. Hence, the second major question of this inquiry asks, why have some local unions taken on a social movement cast while others have remained conservative?

Research Design

In the American labor movement, which has a federated structure, local unions have a great deal of autonomy from international unions. They decide on matters ranging from the number of officers and how they are selected to the frequency of union meetings, to if and when to conduct organizing campaigns. Because local leaders and staff usually decide whether to innovate and implement new organizing tactics, variation in our dependent variable occurs at the local level. Yet very little recent research features in-depth comparative analysis of particular locals; most investigators choose as the unit of analysis either organizing campaigns (Bronfenbrenner 1993) or the international union (Delaney, Jarley, and Fiorito 1996). Therefore, we took local unions as our unit of analysis. Our research strategy was to study both locals that have been revitalized and those that have not, so we could discover through comparison what differentiates more and less transformed locals. . . .

We began by consulting with labor leaders and labor scholars in Northern California to find out which international unions active in the region had affiliated locals doing significant amounts of organizing. We started with international unions because we did not want to choose locals based on prior knowledge that they were revitalized or not, as this would constitute sampling on the dependent variable; but we did want to choose a sample in which locals were "at risk" of being revitalized. Our informants identified three international unions that met our criteria: SEIU (Service Employees International Union), HERE (Hotel and Restaurant Employees), and the UFCW (United Food and Commercial Workers). We then focused on the local affiliates of these international unions. . . .

We conducted interviews of approximately two hours with union staffers and organizers in almost all the major Northern California locals affiliated with SEIU, HERE, and the UFCW, a total of 14 locals. We conducted 29 interviews in all—23 of them with organizers and staff members. We also interviewed six people affiliated with other labor movement institutions (including one local labor council, the AFL-CIO, two building trades unions, and a labor law firm). . . .

Findings

Fully and Partially Revitalized Locals

Five of the 14 locals were fully revitalized. They include HERE locals A and B and SEIU locals F, G, and H. These locals had all established major organizing programs, beginning between 1989 and 1994. Organizers understood the strategic organizing model, articulated it clearly, and had used it more than once. Locals had made significant organizational changes in order to be able to pursue aggressive organizing. They reported establishing organizing departments, including full-time researchers and sizeable staffs of full-time bilingual organizers. These locals also had instituted new programs to train current union members to take on some of the tasks involved in organizing and to handle some of their own problems on the shop floor. . . . As a result of these shifts, they had all been able to carry out significant organizing involving strategic targeting, worker mobilization, non-NLRB recognition, civil disobedience, public pressure, and community alliances. . . .

Nine of the 14 locals were partially revitalized. They include HERE locals C, D, and E, UFCW locals X, Y, and Z, and SEIU locals J, K, and L. All the locals in this group reported an increased emphasis on organizing new workers, beginning between 1994 and 1997. All had launched more organizing campaigns than they had previously, and all had experimented tactically. However, none of the locals in this group had initiated and carried out a disruptive, comprehensive organizing campaign. Nor had they made the organizational shifts necessary to put their rhetorical commitment to organizing into practice. They had smaller organizing departments than the fully revitalized locals and smaller ratios of organizing to servicing staff. Several locals in this group lacked bilingual organizing staff even when most of their potential organizing targets had immigrant workforces. Few of these locals hired researchers. For the most part, these locals had made few efforts to mobilize their members in support of organizing, either in terms of helping with membership drives or in resolving more of their own grievances. The few that trained shop stewards had much less developed programs than those of the more innovative locals. In terms of tactics, these locals had adopted a few of the new techniques and combined these with more traditional strategies. Few had attempted to avoid the NLRB process or use corporate campaigns; some failed to involve workers in campaigns; and several eschewed disruptive direct action. . . .

The Process of Change: Overcoming Member and Staff Resistance

In order to comprehend how transformation occurs, it is important to understand why members and staff of the organization resist change. We asked our informants about resistance to change and how they dealt with this resistance. Informants in both types of locals indicated that the traditional servicing model was convenient to both members and union staff and that both groups resisted change. They described changing "the culture of the union" as the most important hurdle to transforming the priorities and practices of the local. Fully revitalized locals made more attempts to change and were more successful than partially revitalized locals.

One organizer in a fully revitalized local called member resistance to becoming more active on and off the shop floor the local's "single biggest problem" in implementing the shift to organizing. Revitalization requires directly challenging the old mentality of servicing, in which members pay dues in exchange for a union staff that acts like "an insurance agent," as one organizer put it, by processing grievances and taking care of members' problems for them. As another organizer who had worked with both fully and partially revitalized locals said, "Part of it is just the orientation that the members have. They have this culture that 'we pay our dues, the local union hires representation staff, and therefore they take care of my needs. And therefore they file grievances for me.'

It's . . . a third-party mentality. It's 'the union office will deal with work site problems for me,' as opposed to, 'we're the union here and we oughta be able to work out our problems directly with the supervisor' " (Rosa: SEIU, Local H). One organizer described member resistance this way:

> There's also a lot of pressure from the membership to do things the old way. They don't want to get involved, in large part, they don't want to have to take responsibility; they'd much rather have someone that comes in and takes care of their problems for them. And if that's their experience, and that's how they're used to having things done, if someone new comes in and says, "No, you have to do it. You pay your dues, yeah, but you have to stand up to the boss, that's not my job," their initial reaction is "Geez, service has just gone down the hill. Now we have a union rep that has no backbone or that's a wimp or that won't stand up for us or take care of my problems. What do I pay my dues for?" So it's not just laziness or complacency or conservatism on the part of the union staff. There is a real resistance that you have to fight through. (Mike: HERE, Local B)

Staff resistance is another major obstacle to implementing organizational change, largely because staff tasks are redefined as the shift is made to organizing. An AFL-CIO organizing leader called local staff "the major cause of resistance to institutional change" (George: AFL-CIO). As Michels predicted, longtime staff members fear losing power, or even losing their jobs. They also resist having to perform unfamiliar and daunting tasks, as organizing means working harder and being more confrontational than they are accustomed to as business agents. As one organizing director of a fully revitalized local said about her staff:

> For most field reps, it scares them 'cause it means they have to give up a little power. . . . I've had comments from local staff [who] say, "Well, if we train our shop stewards to be able to process grievances, what are we gonna do?" . . . It means working differently. It also means . . . longer hours, 'cause to build up an internal structure at a work site, that's a lot of one on ones [meetings with workers]. You've really gotta know what your unit is like and know who the leaders are. And it's also doing a fight. Taking on the boss, where you may have kind of a decent relation-

ship with the boss, right? So I think it's a real challenge. (Rosa: SEIU, Local H)

An informant in a partially revitalized local explicitly invoked oligarchical reasoning for staff resistance:

> In these small locals, you get elected to this job, and it's every three years, and after a while you don't feel like going back and tending bar anymore. Well, you start bringing in real sharp, young people [the stewards]. And [the officers] say, "wait a minute, they might want my job." So I think that's one of the reasons it's kind of slow to change some of this stuff. In the past it's been very difficult to bring young people along without making people nervous that they're going to lose their jobs over it because it's not like a tenure situation. (Peter: HERE, Local C)

Another organizer also saw oligarchy as promoting resistance to change, particularly in terms of increasing members' participation: he said, "Once you start to move people into activity, they're going to want to know a little more about the union, right? This could be a little bit problematic to your control" (Phil: SEIU, Local F).

Other organizers pointed out the rewards union staff gained from resolving people's problems for them. The following comments were typical:

> There's also kind of a natural resistance from people who are doing the field staff kind of stuff. They want to help people. They want to do for people. It's a lot easier to take care of someone's problem than it is to train them how to take care of their own problem. (Josh: SEIU, Local J)

> The reps get a lot out of doing grievances, a lot of personal worth. When you're knocking on doors in new organizing and you don't see anybody for two days, you begin to wonder what you're doing, and there's a lot of inherent ego things in business unionism. . . . It's pretty easy to get into, "Oh, I'm competent doing grievances." (Mark: HERE, Local B)

Clearly both members and staff had become attached to the servicing model and had difficulty understanding the need for change. The fully revitalized locals approached this resistance primarily through major educational efforts, including membership conventions and training, to demonstrate to members the importance of organizing to their own contracts and standard of living.

These efforts included the active participation of the members in role plays and small group discussions. They involved communicating to members the idea that the labor movement is facing a crisis and that without augmenting the membership and the shop-floor strength of local unions, they will cease to exist. In cases when the local itself was in decline, leaders illustrated the need for change with local examples; when it was not, educators spoke of the decline of the movement as a whole and the eventual effects of that decline on the members themselves. As one organizer put it:

> My experience has been that we [have to] have the discussions with the rank-and-file leadership, like the executive board, give them the political framework. "Here is the labor movement in the United States. And here is what we represent. And here are 100 million people who ain't got a union, folks, and we have to organize them in order to maintain the standards that we've been able to get, and it's in your best interests to take a look at those 100 million people and get 'em into unions so that we don't lose our standards;' " It's just kind of giving them that political framework. . . . For the most part, [members] view power as the union being successful in filing grievances and negotiating good contracts. And that's one part of it. But then I ask folks, "What's the power within your department? Do you have power in your department? Does the boss deal with your chief shop steward directly? And does your chief shop steward deal directly with the supervisor?" Then I get a blank stare, 'cause that's not what happens. So it's having that discussion. (Rosa: SEIU, Local H)

These efforts have largely been successful in the fully revitalized locals. In some cases, members of these locals have defined their self-interest as new organizing and prioritized that over traditional concerns such as increasing their own wages or benefits, or augmenting their strike fund. In 1996, for instance, HERE Local A members voted overwhelmingly to redirect the $2 each member paid every month for a strike fund into an organizing fund, despite their recent experience of a major strike. In HERE Local B, workers at one restaurant chain temporarily gave up their employer's contribution to the pension fund in exchange for his guarantee of neutrality in organizing drives at his future restaurants. At the same local's membership convention in 1997, members signed pledges to spend at least two hours a month participating in union activities outside their own workplaces.

The fully revitalized locals have dealt with staff resistance much as they have dealt with member resistance: education and retraining. As one organizer described it:

> There's definitely resistance from reps here who don't understand what organizing is, who think it's gonna be so much harder—it's new, so they're freaked out by it. [In] all staff meetings, let's talk about the fears. Let's get people trained—and the answer has been not to fire people . . . but [to] get people the training to make sure they feel comfortable with it, and to explain why we have to do it. If you work for the union, you work for the union. You aren't a grievance handler; you have to help build power, and that takes many different forms. (Steve: SEIU, Local G)

However, when retraining has not worked, resistant staff in some of the fully revitalized locals have been let go or encouraged to quit. Significantly, though, these locals have not faced as much staff resistance as have partially revitalized locals because they have experienced more leadership turnover of a particular kind, which we discuss below.

Partially revitalized locals, in contrast, had made fewer systematic efforts to counter member and staff resistance. Except for Local J, these locals did not have fully functioning member or staff education programs. Nor had they brought in new organizers to replace intransigent business agents. The organizers we interviewed in these locals were often in the minority in their commitment to organizing, and they lacked the expertise and the institutional support to implement strategies for changing organizational culture. As an organizer in one partially revitalized local expressed:

> In reality, [the amount of resources devoted to organizing] is so low it's almost embarrassing. . . . We're lucky if we're doing three [percent]. But then again three years ago, five years ago, there was nothing. . . . I mean even though [the local's president] professes an interest in organizing, and he actually does have more of an interest in organizing than his predecessor, it's still not something to go into the red because of. That's something, if that's gonna make us go into the red we're not gonna do it. Even though if I

was president, we would be in the red to organize. (Anonymous)

Another local staff member said of getting organizers on board, "I don't see any way to [bring in new staff] unless somebody dies, or quits, or something" (Peter: HERE, Local C).

In addition to problems of explicit staff and member resistance, these organizers described deeply entrenched cultural and practical obstacles to organizing. For example, one organizer noted,

We plan to activate our stewards and get them to be doing more stuff, but I don't see them handling grievances. That is a lot our philosophy. I mean, it is mine. . . . I've been pushing it for years, but the predominant feeling at least in California locals [of this union] is that business agents handle grievances, not the members. . . . So the stewards that we have, their job is pretty much to disseminate information and maybe observe if there's contract violations, and so on. (Bob: UFCW, Local Y)

This informant and another UFCW organizer also saw contract provisions as an obstacle to increasing member participation, as contract language fails to protect stewards and does not give them the right to handle grievances, which makes them reluctant to become active on the shop floor.

Other informants in the partially revitalized locals cited lack of time and resources as a barrier to change:

You just can't do it automatically. We don't have the money to just go out and hire three people and say, let's go organize. So we are trying to get the situation where everybody would say, okay, two days a week you'll do nothing but organizing. So if you got a grievance, handle it Monday, Wednesday, and Friday, or something like that. And we've still got a problem that we've got to collect about 20% of the dues by hand because we don't have checkoffs in these small houses. So you're running around, and people don't pay their dues, and it just is a lot of time that you've got to do it. . . . It's been difficult to just draw a line, say, "you can't do anything two days a week except organize: because you've got these grievances come up seven days a week, 24 hours a day, and you can't tell a guy, "well, I can't talk to you for three days because it's my organizing day," so you can't really schedule that. . . . You've got city council meetings and things that you've got to attend,

or unemployment hearings, or workmen's comp problems. I mean you're sort of at the mercy of somebody else to try and squeeze this stuff in. (Peter: HERE, Local C)

This local is much like any other local, in that they believe in organizing, but it's just so hard to put the resources in. And so I think they've always wanted to do it but not really been able to bite the bullet and make it happen. I mean I know that the [half-time] organizer who was on staff before me, even though he was [only] a half-time rep, spent most of his time doing rep work. So, he was able to run only like one campaign in a couple of years. (Donna: SEIU, Local K)

Organizers in fully revitalized locals did not identify such entrenched cultural obstacles, largely because they had already resolved these problems. Because leaders in these locals were committed to changing to organize, they had overcome institutional impediments and had surmounted resistance to transformation. They had changed the culture of the union. Organizers in partially revitalized locals lacked knowledge and institutional power to make these shifts. What explains the difference, then, between these two types of locals?

Causes of Transformation: Political Crisis, Outside Activists, and Centralized Pressure

Our data show that three factors in conjunction distinguish the fully revitalized locals from the others: the experience of an internal political crisis, which facilitated the entrance of new leaders into the local, either through international union intervention or local elections; the presence in the local of staff with social movement experience outside the labor movement; and support from the international union. Any one of these factors alone was not enough to spur full revitalization; only in combination do they explain why fully revitalized locals both had staff committed to making changes and were successful in making those changes, while others did not. . . .

Political Crisis

First, fully revitalized locals had all experienced political crises, ranging from disastrous strikes to mismanagement of the local.

These crises were important primarily because they resulted in a change in leadership. Sometimes locals were temporarily taken over by the international union (placed under "trusteeship"), while in other cases, electoral shake-ups occurred.

As one organizer described the process prior to the trusteeship: "What had happened . . . was a lot of concession bargaining and general chaos, things just not being together, having no administrative systems, you know, contracts lapsing for not being reopened. . . . One [problem] was mismanagement of the union, cronyism, you know, different stuff like that" (Phil: SEIU, Local F).

Another organizer described how a series of strike defeats meant that a new slate of elected leaders committed to organizing came into power:

> In 1984, there was rather a disastrous turn, in that we had a strike in the restaurants and clubs, which the union lost. . . . And it really demonstrated a lot of other organizational problems in the union. . . . [Before that] organizing existed in a vacuum, primarily. So, that kind of non-broader organizing mentality came home to roost in 1984 [in the strike], which the union lost, and in the worst case, in certain restaurants and private clubs, the union not only lost the strike, they broke the union. So out of that, in 1985 there were elections for leadership of the union, and [new people] became the elected leadership of the local. And . . . the important thing was [the new president] understood organizing. Not just organizing in the nonunion sense, but organizing for union power. (Paul: HERE, Local A)

Similar political upheaval occurred in Local B: "[The challenging president] had been brought on staff with the old group and was really just sort of discouraged and put off by how they did things. How they didn't do things, basically. So she ran a campaign against the current leadership at that time and was successful. And then asked the international to come in and assist in rebuilding the local" (Mike: HERE, Local B).

The partially revitalized locals had not experienced the same kinds of political turmoil. None of the informants in this group described major political crises leading to innovative leadership. Only one of the partially revitalized locals was placed under trusteeship, and in this case, the trustee was not interested in new organizing programs

using disruptive tactics. And when electoral turnover occurred in these locals, new leaders were not committed to organizing.

Individual Innovators and Outside Experience

The political crisis, then, facilitated the presence of new leaders in the local. And these were not just any new leaders—they were people with a particular interpretation of the situation of the movement: that it required organizing in order to survive. These individuals had the knowledge, vision, and sense of urgency required to use confrontational strategies and take organizational chances. One AFL-CIO organizing department leader suggested, "I think that it's people who have a vision and who are willing to take political risks. . . . They were individuals who were in authority, who were willing to take a chance, and most other union leaders haven't been" (George: AFL-CIO).

We found that these individuals understood and supported alternative models largely because they had worked in other social movements. In all the locals we identified as full revitalizers, at least half the organizing staff had been hired from outside the rank and file, and almost all arrived with prior experience in other movements. Many leaders over 40 had had experience in community or welfare rights organizing or the United Farm Workers (UFW). Younger informants (in their twenties and early thirties) had also participated in community organizing or in student activism, particularly in Central American solidarity groups and anti-apartheid struggles on college campuses. Thus there are two types of experience, related to age: the organizers who came out of 1960s and 1970s organizing and political activism and those who were trained in campus activism and identity politics in the 1980s and 1990s.

Informants from all fully revitalized locals saw outside activism as an important force for change. One HERE organizer, when asked what differentiated unions that had innovated fully from those that had not, replied:

> I would say a big part of it is a lot of activists from the sixties. . . . Similar to John Lewis saying, "let's bring in the Communists 'cause they know how to organize." . . . I think SEIU realized that let's bring in these activists who were involved in the

Civil Rights movement, the antiwar movement . . . some sort of political organization, some sort of socialist organization, even, who are actively committed to building the union movement, and have some new ideas about how to do that, and will use the strategies developed in the Civil Rights movement, and the welfare rights organizations, the women's rights movement, all these different organizations, and get them plugged in and involved. . . . And where unions have done that, there's been more militancy. (Mike: HERE, Local B)

Another local organizer echoed this comment, when asked what had driven changes within SEIU: "I would say that a lot of the people that are now in leadership positions within, let's say, the international, within different locals, I think a lot of people were kind of steeped in the struggles of the sixties, you know, in terms of civil rights, the women's movement, probably the movement against the war in Vietnam, the fight against racism, all that stuff, so I think a lot of today's activists, they're leading the locals and also in leadership positions in the international" (Phil: SEIU, Local F).

These experiences contributed in several ways to these individuals, developing and embracing a revitalized vision of the labor movement. First, the experience gave them a broader perspective on social injustice and helped them see beyond the universe of unionized workers, thus leading them to consider organizing crucial to the movement's survival. One international staff member described the worldview of people from outside the movement:

[They] don't have a world vision that everything's okay. We haven't been encapsulated in the rather safe union world, we've been out in the rest of the completely nonunionized world. And bringing in people I think with that kind of vision and energy has really driven some of our [growth]. . . . [For example, one organizer] is really driven to organize, and it's not because he was a bellman or a dishwasher somewhere, he just got a certain worldview of poverty and power, and he worked for [a community organizing group], I mean, he has not been out talking to unionized workers! He's out talking to people on the threshold of total disaster. So his world vision is really different than a UFCW retail clerk investing in his vacation home for 15 years. . . . And that's how he came into this and said "We

gotta organize, man. I like what unions have, I've never had it, I've been talking to people that don't have anything." (Pamela: HERE, International Union)

As one AFL-CIO leader pointed out:

The leaders that I can think of have an ideological commitment, not ideological like, "I have some sectarian left ideology," but they have a fanatical belief in building power for working people and also that organizing is the way to do it, and they have it in their guts, and it's what drives them. It's what drove them to become leaders of their unions. It wasn't like careerism, and it wasn't so they could preside over something. It's because they wanted to organize and build real power. . . . I just think people are doing it from a political-moral belief as opposed to they got into the labor movement and they advanced. (George: AFL-CIO)

Second, these organizers were less caught up in traditional models of unionism and were familiar with alternative models of mobilization. They were not accustomed to the servicing model prevalent in the labor movement; rather, they saw organizing people as the way to build union power. One organizer described the worker-centered approach to organizing he and several colleagues implemented at HERE Local A: "We didn't know any different. We all came out of the Farmworkers [with] a lot of experience. . . . So the idea of, like, 'if you're gonna win, you're gonna involve workers' . . . we never thought there was any other way to do it" (Paul: HERE, Local A).

Third, these activities gave organizers the skills they need to mobilize workers. One HERE organizer described how he learned to build committees when he worked in community organizing: "Yeah, that's where I learned to build committees, and what a committee does and how it functions. . . . It really came from that training . . . you have to have committees because you don't have money. You can't pay staff. . . . So getting people to do it themselves. Also, it's the philosophy of empowering people. That comes more from the community organizing than the labor movement, unfortunately" (Mark: HERE, Local B). Another organizer described a similar dynamic: "So [community organizing] was an experience that was very formative. . . . Just getting exposure to role-playing, raps, door-knocking, going door to door, trying to agitate people around issues, identifying people who had some leadership, pushing people to do things, you know, all the sort of skills that you need in union organizing are very similar in community organizing" (Mike: HERE, Local B). An SEIU organizer saw herself as learning particular skills from community activism: "When I did Filipino community work . . . [I got] a lot of training in terms of . . . political analysis. And [another organizer] taught me a lot in terms of how to pull together big events, 'cause we organized these festivals where 500 people would come. And then we organized a West Coast-wide convention of Filipino activists, so I learned good skills there" (Rosa: SEIU, Local H).

Fourth, union staff said that outside experience had influenced how they thought about tactics. One organizer said that because there was "less to lose" in community organizing, "there was more creativity, more pushing the limits," which she and others imported into their union organizing (Brenda: SEIU, Local G). One labor lawyer renowned for using creative tactics attributed his understanding of the need for nonroutine approaches to his experience in the antiwar movement:

> The entire labor movement was like that, it followed proper channels. Just exactly what we learned during the Vietnam war does not work. That the proper channels are laid down to defuse energy that's directed at the ruling class, not to impair that class's interests. And that's one of the ways that I, working in the antiwar movement was so helpful to me, because I realized as a result of the experiences there that reason and proper channels are only for defusing energy, not for channeling it. And you have to act outside those structures if you intend to get anything done. (Oliver)

Speaking specifically of the use of corporate campaign tactics, which target employers' corporate structure and particular corporate leaders, in the pioneering J. P. Stevens organizing campaign during the 1970s and 1980s, he said:

> I can't minimize the influence of the Vietnam War on [the corporate campaign]. One of the things that we did during the antiwar struggle was to start understanding how corporations were making a huge amount of money off the war. . . . Most of the major U.S. corporations were making money on the war. . . . And that

was a part of the war that the teach-ins were all about. The teach-ins weren't just to tell about the atrocities being committed, but to explain the economics behind the war. So then of course we started thinking about things like that. And remember that the Berrigans were very big on these invasions that they did, the pig's blood invasions. And they didn't just go to the headquarters, they would go to the directors too. So they were doing the same type of corporate structure analysis. (Oliver)

Finally, organizers described more tangible benefits to outside activism in terms of making alliances and bringing new kinds of resources into the local. An SEIU organizer said that outside activists were important "just in terms of building community ties" (Rosa: SEIU, Local H). One HERE organizer described staff participation in other movements as "totally crucial. Absolutely crucial. Because you bring that with you. The union completely benefits by having people that work with it that have their own base, their own community, and that have their own networks. Because if you run the kind of program that we're running, those networks need to be tapped into" Michelle: HERE, Local B).

In contrast, the partially revitalized locals hired few organizers from outside the labor movement, or even from outside the local. As a consequence, leaders in these locals did not interpret their situation as requiring a shift to organizing. Instead, in the face of employer attacks, they decided to try to protect the members they still represented. Respondents from two UFCW locals, despite having lost almost all their power in the retail sector, still spoke of "not having to worry about market share" because they had simply decided to think of themselves as representing only grocery workers. One leader of a HERE partially revitalized local described a typical approach to declining power in the 1980s: "We probably made an unconscious decision, which was to [say], 'look, let's batten down the hatches, circle the wagons, see what we got here, let's try [to] keep what we got inside the fold, by the time this tornado is through maybe we'll not have lost half our membership.' And so that was probably an unconscious decision from the mid-80s 'til early in the '90s to try to do that. And even as a result of that, we dropped a thousand members. Just circling the wagons" (Maurice: HERE, Local E).

In addition, leaders in these locals were clearly not as committed to the idea of mobilizing workers, or as familiar with tactics and strategies of doing so. One local leader described the local's relation to the worker committee in an organizing drive as "keeping them updated" and "utilizing" them in public events, rather than empowering them on the job (Scott: UFCW, Local Z). Another informant described the process of house-visiting workers being organized, which was clearly new to him, highlighting its difficulty and his own resistance:

The only way to successfully organize, *it appears*, is to go to people's houses and talk to them because you can't get them on the job. So you've got a hotel . . . and there's four or five hundred people you've got to interview and *try and convince them to be union or back us or whatever or at least tell them what's going on*. It's a lot of houses you've got to hit. Then you can't catch them at night because nobody wants people after dark walking up to their house. . . . You can't catch them on Monday nights during football season. You've got to time all this stuff. A lot of people don't want to be bothered on weekends. You know, you're not sure of their schedules. *It's real difficult*. That's just after you find their address out, you try and catch up to them. Well, if it's a woman, you don't want two guys walking up to the house, and maybe you walk up there and you find out—they open the door and *maybe nobody speaks the same language* so you've got to—you're talking probably hitting every house four or five times before you get the thing going. If you can do two or three a day and you've got five people, you know, *it's a slow process*. (Peter: HERE, Local C; emphasis added)

The reluctance to hire from the outside is related in some cases to generalized resistance to change. One interviewee described how an organizer from outside the rank and file had been met with suspicion in the local: "And he came on board and . . . he just was always doing so much more work than we paid him for, and he was really into it, and scared the shit out of the other people in the local. 'How come he's doin' all this stuff for free? There must be somethin' wrong with him! What's his agenda?' " (Anonymous).

Union culture also stands in, the way in the partially revitalized locals:

I have to say, [hiring only from the rank and file] is something we have to get away from also. There's been a mindset for years that you have to be a member of a local union to go to work for the UFCW. . . . Locally, you still see by and large representatives coming out of the ranks. Some of it is political, they're on your e-board, they're vice-president, an opening occurs, they have the qualifications, [they might as well] go there. Could you find more qualified people if you went outside? Probably. And that has to be done. . . . But the UFCW was somewhat parochial in that area, "this is our organization, we come from within." And I think that's detrimental to the organization. (Scott: UFCW, Local Z)

In sum, activists with experience outside the labor movement brought broad visions, knowledge of alternative organizational models, and practice in disruptive tactics to the locals that became fully revitalized. Much like Jenkins's radicalized clergy and Fligstein's actors with new points of view, these individuals interpreted the local's political crisis as a mandate to change, and they had the know-how and vision to develop new programs to aggressively organize the unorganized.

International Union Influence

A third major factor in full revitalization, which we have already touched on, is the activity of the international union (IU). In the cases of the fully revitalized locals, IU activity came together with the situation of crisis in the local to facilitate innovation. The IU helped ameliorate local oligarchical tendencies by placing people with a commitment to organizing in locals that were under trusteeship or had new leadership. The IU also gave IU-trained organizers and financial resources to these locals, and thus provided them with the know-how and the capability to carry out innovative organizing. In the partially revitalized locals, IU influence was not as great.

The three international unions relevant to this study differ in how much and how consistently they press locals to organize. Each has a history of business unionism, and they vary in the extent to which they have overcome this organizational legacy. The SEIU is the most institutionally committed to organizing and has now mandated that locals develop an organizing program. The IU itself is currently directing more than 30% of its resources to organizing and has been actively promoting a model of militant organizing longer than most other unions. For many years, the international regularly sent its own organizers to locals to lead organ zing drives and now directs national campaigns. The renewed commitment to organizing came during the presidency of John Sweeney and was further institutionalized under Andy Stern, the former organizing director who became president when Sweeney moved to the AFL-CIO.

Organizing has not become as fully institutionalized in HERE, which has not undertaken significant nationwide campaigns; nor has the IU mandated organizing officially. However, the IU is directing increasing resources to locals that organize and provided major support to intensive organizing campaigns in Las Vegas in the 1990s, which it hopes will provide a model for future HERE campaigns. As in SEIU, the rise through the IU hierarchy of individual leaders committed to organizing has contributed to its growing importance. Particularly notable in this respect is the 1998 ascension to the union's presidency of John Wilhelm, the architect of the union's organizing program in Las Vegas.

UFCW organizers did not relate as clear a narrative as SEW and HERE organizers about their IV's stance on organizing, but in the wake of major loss of market share in the Midwest in the mid-1980s, the IU began to pay more attention to organizing. In 1994, the IV instituted the SPUR (Special Projects Union Representative) program, in which the IU pays the expenses of member organizers temporarily taken off their regular jobs. Furthermore, the former organizing director became the IU president, which at least two interviewees saw as favorable to organizing. Yet the initiative seems to rest primarily with the locals; one organizer characterized his IU's attitude as "if you show me you're gonna do something, I'll match you" (Milo: UFCW, Local X). This program appears less comprehensive: than SEW's, and interviewees did not mention particular leaders who strongly influenced organizing. Other labor movement informants were also skeptical about the depths of the UFCW IU's commitment to organizing.

The fully revitalized locals have clearly been connected to the organizing efforts of their internationals. Two of the three SEW fully revitalized locals were trusteed. In the case of Local F, new leaders were brought in as a result of the trusteeship, which allowed the organizing model to be implemented:

> [Before the trusteeship], those were . . . much more old school locals, you know, just entrenched leadership that didn't represent the workforce, that couldn't speak Spanish, that was just holding onto this dying thing. So there was a real housecleaning when [the new local president] came in . . . he came in first as a trustee and then was elected president. That laid the ground work for doing this kind of organizing. . . . [He] is very strategic and has a clear understanding of this industry and what that takes, and he saw that this was the way to go. He had tried to make some of these changes earlier on and been unsuccessful. So he was really important in that and also having the international support for what was at that time a pretty small local. I don't think the campaign, the organizing, could have happened without those things. (Julie: SEIU, Local F)

Another organizer from the local said that the drive to organize was, "in a lot of ways, coming from the international staff that were embedded in the local. . . . There were certain people in place that were driving the program. . . . [The IU] hired people based on their compatibility with the program" (Phil: SEIU, Local F). Another former IU staffer described how this process worked:

> I [used to work] for the international. . . . [At one local], I worked with them to develop and organize; [at another local], I worked with them to get up an organizing program, to get involved. So there was a big emphasis, and we would go back and have our meetings and talk about which locals had our program, how to get them on the program, and what we could do to help. Part of it was just going in and doing campaigns and winning and saying it can be done, and part of it was engaging in the political conversations. (Josh: SEIU, Local J)

Local F continues to receive large subsidies from the international as well as some staff. Local H also received major support from the international, including organizing directors and organizing staff, as well as assistance from the IU president on how to target their organizing strategically.

In SEIU, Local G, IU influence was less direct but still crucial. As in the other fully revitalized locals, organizing began as a result of the opening generated by a trusteeship. But in this case, the local split with the international over conflicts arising from the takeover, so innovation continued in the absence of the international rather than as a result of extended international involvement. However, even here, the IU's commitment to innovative organizing spurred local innovation, because local leaders were determined to reestablish their independence and beat the IU at its own game.

Fully revitalized locals A and B of HERE benefited from their contact with the pro-organizing sector of the international, in a process that was similar to what happened in SEIU locals F and H. Vincent Sirabella, an organizing pioneer in the international, worked with staff at Local A in the early 1980s, so they learned from his organizing focus and experience. Later in the decade, international organizers again came to the aid of the local after it had developed its organizing focus and was facing difficult contract negotiations. Several times, the international also provided funds to the local for organizing. At Local B, when internal crisis led to a change in the elected leadership, the IU furnished an organizer, now president of the local. This organizer had himself worked previously with several of the more experienced IU organizers and went on to become the trustee of a nearby local that was merged into Local B. The international has continued to support the local with organizers and resources.

In the partially revitalized locals, the IU was less influential. As we have seen, the IU did not intervene significantly in these locals, in part because they had not experienced the local political crisis that paved the way for change. Only one of the eight locals was trusteed. In the one that was—partially revitalized HERE Local D—the trustee was not committed to innovative strategies, so while the local has added members, this has occurred primarily through negotiated recognition agreements with employers rather than through the use of disruptive tactics. In other HERE locals, the IU did attempt to spur change, but local resistance and lack of consistency on the part of the international prevented comprehensive change. For ex-

ample, international organizers in one of the HERE partially revitalized locals remained marginalized, because no one in the local was part of the sector of the IU committed to militant organizing. A leader of a third partially revitalized local, asked how the organizing emphasis had begun there, described the IU's influence in terms of changing his interpretation of the situation:

> I'd say probably in the early '90s the awareness came from leaders within our international union, who came to visit us. We had an industry-wide negotiation in 1989, and the employers here, who used to negotiate as one group, broke up individually. And so we had negotiations that were going to be going on with 12 hotels at the same time. And so we had help from the international, and during that time I was able to see a different side of what needs to be implemented within the local in order to turn around some of the stuff that we had been experiencing during the '80s. So that's probably where the first idea came that "look, there's another part of the program that you need to incorporate into a local, or else you're gonna be heading south." (Maurice: HERE, Local E)

However, the presence of the IU in this local diminished after the contract negotiations, and the local did not implement a real organizing program until 1997, after sustained IU support reemerged.

The SEIU partially revitalized locals did not experience sustained IU intervention until recently. Yet leaders explicitly attribute their increasing revitalization to IU influence; these locals were responding to the SEIU international's aforementioned mandate. In SEIU Local J, this process is more advanced than it is in the other locals because of the local leader's participation in SEIU's Committee on the Future, an IU-coordinated effort to discuss and disseminate organizing, which led to the IU mandate. The other two locals have begun more recently to respond to the mandate. As one organizer described her local's situation:

> In terms of organizing, our local is just starting to get a statewide program off the ground. . . . There's never been any statewide-run program throughout the entire local. And there's never been a lot of money dedicated to organizing. And this past year, the international union . . . has set some standards, and [is] requiring locals to spend a certain percentage

of our per capita. So we were actually spending closer to 5% in 1996, and we're taking a leap to 15% in '97. And so we're taking a huge jump in terms of the amount of money that we're putting into organizing, and we're absolutely starting from scratch, pretty much. (Donna: SEIU, Local K)

The UFCW locals had not been particularly influenced by their international. No UFCW organizer mentioned a major influence of IU personnel or philosophical influence. Nor had the IU taken advantage of opportunities to intervene in these locals at moments of organizational change, such as the 1992 merger that created Local X. The IU had sometimes supported these locals by subsidizing the SPUR program. However, this support clearly followed initiative taken by the local, rather than the IU's actively promoting change.

Overall, international union leadership was crucial in leading to full revitalization. The international initiated or supported much of the change in local unions; this process was not one of "bottom-up," local innovation that later reached the top echelons of the bureaucracy. Rather, progressive sectors of the international exerted varying degrees of influence over locals in crisis, which led to full revitalization. Furthermore, IU influence helps explain the differences among the partially revitalized locals; those that have made more changes, in particular HERE Local E and SEIU Local J, acknowledge significant influence by the IU, as do the other SEIU locals, which are responding to the SEIU mandate. The UFCW locals did not experience major IU intervention, and the other HERE partially revitalized locals were either not receptive to the organizing emphasis of the IU or did not experience IU intervention that attempted to promulgate an organizing focus.

The three factors we have identified—crisis, outside activists, and international union influence—are related in complicated ways. In most cases, the pattern was that the local was opened up to outside influence by a political crisis, which allowed particular elements of the international to encourage innovation through trustees, other staff, training, and material resources. Leaders with new interpretations of the situation of the labor movement and new strategies for increasing union power, who had often developed these views in other social move-

ments, came to wield influence through these openings. In some cases, though not all, the outside activists within the local arrived there because of this opening to the international. In any event, these factors in combination were crucial to transformation; locals that did not have crisis, sustained IU intervention, and outside activists did not revitalize fully.

Future Possibilities for Overcoming Oligarchy

So far, we have focused on the factors that led some locals to change more comprehensively and earlier than others. But given the shift to a more pro-organizing climate generally in the labor movement, these factors are unlikely to converge in the same way again. So, what implications do our findings have for locals that have not yet innovated completely? Organizations theory suggests that they may not follow the same path to revitalization, as the dynamics of organizational change are likely to be different in the organizations that adopt innovative forms early and those that adopt them late (see Tolbert and Zucker 1983; DiMaggio 1988).

In particular, DiMaggio and Powell's (1991b) discussion of organizational fields is useful for thinking about what might happen to unions that cling, even partially, to traditional organizations and tactics. They identify three types of institutional forces that encourage organizational change. We see "coercive isomorphism," which refers to the pressure dominant organizations and cultural expectations exert, in the increased commitment of the HERE and SEIU internationals to organizing. In SEIU in particular, the mandate to organize and the refusal to give resources to locals that do not is clearly the major reason for change in the partially revitalized locals. Two of our HERE interviewees believed that it would soon be more difficult for people who had not made the commitment to organizing to ascend in the union's hierarchy. Our finding that the influence of the IU is crucial to change suggests that locals affiliated with international unions that have begun to push for organizational and tactical changes will probably innovate sooner than locals affiliated with international unions that have been slower to transform themselves.

The AFL-CIO's call to organize is another example of a pressure likely to lead to coercive isomorphism, although the organization has no power to force unions to change. The AFL-CIO's endorsement of the strategic model suggests that the "cultural expectations" within the labor movement are shifting, and that unions that do not innovate will be held in lower regard as innovation becomes more widespread. In that respect, the AFLCIO's mandate to organize may also prove to be a major force in convincing international and local unions of the necessity of transformation. As one organizer who faces resistance in his local said of the AFL-CIO shift: "I think it's the greatest thing to happen in a long time. Because even though [to] some people it's penetrating very slowly, it's there. And it's a constant bug up their ass that this is something you know you should do, and if you don't remember, we're gonna remind you. And if they don't remind him, I'm gonna remind him. And I'm gonna constantly pound on you about the 30%. And if you don't hear it from me, you're gonna hear it from [John] Sweeney" (Milo: UFCW, Local X). An AFLCIO leader said, "What we're trying to do is move it past these heroic leaders and say there's an institutional formula that can be developed out of this. . . . Now it's beginning to change because of the culture of the labor movement and the language within the labor movement says, 'if you do these things you can be successful. So people who in the past maybe hung back a little bit can now take this risk, but it's not such a big risk because it's becoming sort of the norm" (George: AFL-CIO). The increase in the sheer numbers of organizations pursuing a strategic model and restructuring themselves accordingly may also lead to greater legitimacy and therefore to reproduction of the form (Minkoff 1994).

"Mimetic isomorphism," a process in which organizations copy other organizations, may also encourage innovation. Several of our interviewees remarked that earlier-innovating locals provided a model for them. One UFCW organizer said, "Y'know, HERE has done a lot to keep me going. I've always watched their tenacity, and it started out with [a major hotel campaign]. 'Cause I worked right next to that building, and I was out there a lot with those guys, and I admired that tenacity; and it gave me the realization that this is what it takes. And it's not been easy for me to transfer that to myself and to here, 'cause they're a whole different level than I am, 'cause they came from a different

place" (Milo: UFCW, Local X). However, it is unlikely that this type of mimesis will be unconscious, as DiMaggio and Powell say it may be, given the high level of explicit discussion of the model in labor organizations, as well as the major changes needed for its implementation. These quotations suggest that later-innovating locals consciously reflect on the experience of earlier innovators in designing their own approaches.

Finally, DiMaggio and Powell's "normative isomorphism," which occurs primarily through professionalization processes, is also present in the labor movement. What they call "the filtering of personnel" (1991b, p. 71) is now occurring through new channels, in particular the AFL-CIO's Organizing Institute (OI), which recruits both rank-and-file and other activists into the labor movement. The training provided by the OI and international unions will presumably produce organizers and staff committed to the strategic model. The changing recruiting practices of particular locals will also encourage a different kind of professional, as will the redefinition of organizing as a higher-prestige occupation within a local. Furthermore, organizers suggest that as the culture and the outward face of the labor movement change, unions will attract young people with a more activist orientation. As one organizer noted, "I think increasingly there's people who are getting into labor who might have taken the route that I took 10 years ago [via other activist organizations] but who are now getting straight into labor. It seems to me there's a lot more of a direct path at this point. . . . There's a lot of recruitment, for one thing, and I think the labor movement is becoming a little more dynamic, so young, progressive activists think that's a cooler thing to do than maybe was true at another time" (Julie: SEIU, Local F).

It seems likely that the conjunction of the three factors we have identified as leading to revitalization will not be necessary to spur change in the future. Specific local crises will probably diminish in importance as the interpretation of generalized crisis requiring innovation takes hold. The new staff of labor unions may eventually have less experience outside the movement, as the training model becomes more developed and such activism becomes less necessary. We can already see in the SEIU partial revitalizers that, given a mandate, locals may not need to have either a situation of crisis or individual, independent innovators present in order to change. Our evidence suggests, rather, that the role of the international will increase in importance as more of these centralized organizations pressure their locals to revitalize.

It is possible, of course, that in response to pressure from above unions will adopt the rhetoric of the model without making concrete organizational and tactical changes, or without making them comprehensively. The SEIU partially revitalized locals appeared not to be doing this, as their leaders articulate a comprehensive program, which is not surprising given the amount of support they have from the IU. In contrast, it seems likely that the UFCW locals will continue to use some aspects of the model without using all of them, as the IU does not appear to be encouraging the kind of total transformation advocated by SEIU. In HERE, locals receiving more attention from the pro-organizing sector of the IU, which is growing, are likely to make comprehensive changes, while others may languish or implement the model only partially.

Notwithstanding uncertainty about the completeness of their adoption, it seems likely that strategic organizing programs will proliferate, given these increasing isomorphic pressures. However, the impediments of organizational culture we have mentioned—particularly staff and member resistance—may stand in the way more than they have for our fully revitalized locals, in which conditions within the local provided an impetus for change as well. The relationship between diffusion and oligarchic resistance remains to be investigated in this respect.

Conclusion

Recent developments in the American labor movement suggest that highly institutionalized and bureaucratized organizations can sometimes radicalize their goals and tactics. Our analysis of local unions that have overcome oligarchy highlights three factors: localized political crisis resulting in new leadership, the presence of leaders with activist experience outside the labor movement who interpret the decline of labor's power as a mandate for change, and the influence of the international union in favor of innovation. . . .

Our findings also have implications for broader issues related to Michels's theory.

First, and perhaps least surprising, these findings confirm previous research arguing that the iron law is more malleable than Michels believed. Yet, as we have seen, other scholars have primarily argued that organizations can avoid conservatism in their initial development, and thus never become oligarchical. We have contributed to this research by demonstrating that the goals and tactics of formalized, bureaucratic organizations that have become oligarchical can also be transformed in a radical direction. Our findings in this regard indicate that, as Michels's work implies, radical changes necessitate new leadership. Yet his pessimism about this prospect, and the subsequent inattention of other scholars to this possibility, have impeded the specification of how such change arises and the importance of various features of the organization and its context.

Second, this study indicates that entrenched organizational culture, as much as leaders' concern with organizational maintenance, can reinforce bureaucratic conservatism. Leaders were reluctant to risk their own positions in the unions we studied, thus illustrating Michels's view of oligarchical resistance. But beyond these narrow interests of individual leaders, we also found that union culture stood in the way of transformation, as both staff and members had developed and defended symbiotic understandings of their roles as business agents and consumers of services. Revitalized locals had to transform this organizational culture, which they did through participatory education and by emphasizing a new, more expansive model of membership. This new model stresses the development of political skills and a sense of efficacy on the part of members, along with greater rank-and-file activism in the labor movement. The salience of this cultural dimension suggests both that members can grow as habituated to oligarchy as leaders, and that changing organizational culture is an important key to radical transformation.

It is commonly believed that only democratic movements from below can vanquish bureaucratic rigidity. Our research challenges this view, for in the locals we studied, this was not the means by which change happened. Often, as when locals were placed in trusteeship, the change was not democratic at all. In the labor movement, rather than democracy paving the way for the end of bureaucratic conservatism, the breakdown of bureaucratic conservatism paves the way for greater democracy and participation, largely through the participatory education being advocated by the new leaders. Thus, the third implication of our study is that we must reexamine the presumed link between bureaucracy and conservatism. While the locals we studied did make significant organizational shifts, none became less bureaucratic, less professionalized, or less formally organized. And the IU was able to play its crucial role because it was part of a bureaucratic structure, not in spite of that.

Fourth, these conclusions call into question the supposed relation between two basic elements of oligarchy—a concern with organizational maintenance and conservatism. Under conditions of crisis, organizational survival is no longer necessarily best pursued by aiming small and adhering to conventional tactics, as is demonstrated by the locals that tried to do this and continued to decline. Indeed, contra Michels, labor activists in some locals argued that survival could only be achieved by the radical transformation of union goals and tactics. Those are the locals that revitalized and grew. It remains to be seen whether these leaders will become entrenched, and whether, if they do, goals and tactics will once again become more conservative. As we have seen, union activists who believe in organizing are ideologically motivated to give power to working people and see disruption as the only way to accomplish that end, which may ameliorate the development of conservatism (Rothschild-Whitt 1976), as may the new model of membership promoted by revitalized locals.

The tendency for innovative leaders to maintain a radical stance will probably be related to the power of the labor movement in the future. This likelihood brings us to a fifth issue linked to organizational development: the relationship of the organization to its external environment. External circumstances, which Michels neglected (Schutt 1986), played a key role in the growth of new organizational forms and disruptive tactics in the labor movement. The general decline of unions provided the need and justification for change, and the outside experience of activists gave them new visions of what was needed in the labor movement. The role of the international unions, which are internal to the movement but external to the locals under study, also demonstrates how local organizations are subject to external pressures that influence their development.

We have a fascination with the new and the dramatic in the social movement field and are often disdainful of older movements. Yet to limit our focus narrows our theoretical vision. If we are right that the iron law is more malleable than social movement theorists have acknowledged, much remains to be learned about when and how bureaucracy functions in mature social movements. The three factors we have identified provide a useful template with which to examine other institutionalized organizations that innovate in a radical direction or fail to do so. While we do not expect other organizations to pursue exactly the same path to transformation, the elements of crisis, new leaders with novel interpretations, and centralized pressure are likely to be key.

References

AFL-CIO Committee on the Evolution of Work. 1985. "The Changing Situation of Workers and Their Unions." Washington, D.C.: AFL-CIO.

Amburgey, Terry L., Dawn Kelly, and William P. Barnett. 1993. "Resetting the Clock: The Dynamics of Organizational Change and Failure." *Administrative Science Quarterly* 38:51–73.

Barnett, William P., and Glenn R. Carroll. 1995. "Modeling Internal Organizational Change." *Annual Review of Sociology* 21:217–36.

Beach, Stephen. 1977. "Social Movement Radicalization: The Case of the People's Democracy in Northern Ireland." *Sociological Quarterly* 18:305–18.

Blau, Peter. 1963. *The Dynamics of Bureaucracy*. Chicago: University of Chicago Press.

Boswell, Terry, and D. Stevis. 1997. "Globalization and International Labor Organizing." *Work and Occupations* 24:288–308.

Bronfenbrenner, Kate. 1993. "Seeds of Resurgence: Successful Union Strategies for Winning Certification Elections and First Contracts in the 1980s and Beyond." Ph.D. dissertation. Cornell University, Department of Labor and Industrial Relations.

Bronfenbrenner, Kate, et al. 1998. *Introduction to Organizing to Win: New Research on Union Strategies*, edited by Kate Bronfenbrenner, Sheldon Friedman, Richard W. Hurd, Rudolph A. Oswald, and Ronald L. Seeber. Ithaca, N.Y.: ILR Press.

———. 1998. "It Takes More Than Housecalls: Organizing to Win with a Comprehensive Union-Building Strategy." Pp. 19–36 in *Organizing to Win: New Research on Union Strategies*, edited by Kate Bronfenbrenner, Sheldon Friedman, Richard W. Hurd, Rudolph A. Oswald, and Ronald L. Seeber. Ithaca: ILR Press.

Bronfenbrenner, Kate, and Tom Juravich. 1994. "Seeds of Resurgence: The Promise of Organizing in the Public and Private Sectors." Working paper. Institute for the Study of Labor Organizations, Washington, D.C.

Clemens, Elisabeth. 1993. "Organizational Repertoires and Institutional Change: Women's Groups and the Transformation of U.S. Politics, 1890–1920." *American Journal of Sociology* 98:755–98.

Costain, Anne. 1992. *Inviting Women's Rebellion*. Baltimore: Johns Hopkins University Press.

Delacroix, Jacques, and Anand Swaminathan. 1991. "Cosmetic, Speculative, and Adaptive Organizational Change in the Wine Industry: A Longitudinal Study." *Administrative Science Quarterly* 36:631–61.

Delaney, John, Paul Jarley, and Jack Fiorito. 1996. "Planning for Change: Determinants of Innovation in U.S. National Unions." *Industrial and Labor Relations Review* 49: 597–614.

DiMaggio, Paul. 1988. "Interest and Agency in Institutional Theory." Pp. 3–22 in *Institutional Patterns and Organizations*, edited by Lynne G. Zucker. Cambridge, Mass.: Ballinger.

DiMaggio, Paul, and Walter Powell. 1991a. Introduction to *The New Institutionalism in Organizational Analysis*, edited by Walter Powell and Paul DiMaggio. Chicago: University of Chicago Press.

———. 1991b. "The Iron Cage Revisited. Institutional Isomorphism and Collective Rationality." Pp. 63–82 in *The New Institutionalism in Organizational Analysis*, edited by Walter Powell and Paul DiMaggio. Chicago: University of Chicago Press.

Duffhues, Tom, and Albert Felling. 1989. "The Development, Change, and Decline of the Dutch Catholic Movement." Pp. 95–114 in *Organizing for Change*, edited by Bert Klandermans. Greenwich, Conn.: JAI Press.

Edelstein, David, and Malcolm Warner. 1976. *Comparative Union Democracy: Organization and Opposition in British and American Unions*. New York: Wiley.

Epstein, Barbara. 1991. *Political Protest and Cultural Revolution: Nonviolent Direct Action in the 1970s and 1980s*. Berkeley and Los Angeles: University of California Press.

Fantasia, Rick. 1988. *Cultures of Solidarity: Consciousness, Action, and Contemporary American Workers*. Berkeley and Los Angeles: University of California Press.

Fiorito, Jack, Paul Jarley, and John Thomas Delaney. 1995. "National Union Effectiveness in Organizing: Measures and Influences." *Industrial and Labor Relations Review* 48 (4): 613–35.

Fischer, Robert. 1994. *Let the People Decide: Neighborhood Organizing in America*. New York: Wayne Publishers.

Fletcher, Bill, Jr., and Richard W. Hurd. 1999. "Political Will, Local Union Transformation, and the Organizing Imperative." Pp. 191–216 in *Which Direction for Organized Labor?* edited by Bruce Nissen. Detroit: Wayne State University Press.

Fligstein, Neil. 1991. "The Structural Transformation of American Industry: An Institutional Account of the Causes of Diversification in the Largest Firms, 1919–1979." Pp. 311–36 in *The New Institutionalism in Organizational Analysis*, edited by Walter Powell and Paul DiMaggio. Chicago: University of Chicago Press.

Freeman, Richard B. 1985. "Why Are Unions Faring Poorly in NLRB Representation Elections?" Pp. 45–64 in *Challenges and Choices Facing American Labor*, edited by T. A. Kochan. Cambridge, Mass.: MIT Press.

Friedman, Sheldon, Richard W. Hurd, Rudolph A. Oswald, and Ronald L. Seeber, eds. 1994. *Restoring the Promise of American Labor Law*. Ithaca, N.Y.: Cornell University Press.

Gamson, William. 1990. *The Strategy of Social Protest*, 2d ed. Belmont, Calif.: Wadsworth.

Gamson, William A., and Emilie Schmeidler. 1984. "Organizing the Poor." *Theory and Society* 13:567–85.

Gillespie, David P. 1983. "Conservative Tactics in Social Movement Organizations." Pp. 262–75 in *Social Movements of the Sixties and Seventies*, edited by Jo Freeman. White Plains, N.Y.: Longman.

Goldfield, Michael. 1987. *The Decline of Organized Labor in the United States*. Chicago: University of Chicago Press.

Grabelsky, Jeffrey, and Richard Hurd. 1994. "Reinventing an Organizing Union: Strategies for Change." Pp. 84–95 in *Proceedings of the 46th Annual Meeting of the Industrial Relations Association*, edited by Paula S. Voos. Madison, Wisc.: Industrial Relations Research Association.

Green, James, and Chris Tilly. 1987. "Service Unionism: Directions for Organizing." *Labor Law Journal* 38 (August):486–95.

Greenhouse, Steven. 1999. "Labor Revitalized with New Recruiting." *New York Times*, October 19, p. 14.

Greenstone, J. David. 1969. *Labor in American Politics*. New York: Knopf.

Gusfield, Joseph. 1968. "Social Movements; The Study." Pp. 445–52 in *International Encyclopedia of the Social Sciences*, no.14. Edited by David Stills. New York: MacMillan.

Hannan, Michael T., and John H. Freeman. 1984. "Structural Inertia and Organizational Change." *American Sociological Review* 49:149–64.

Howley, John. 1990. "Justice for Janitors. The Challenge of Organizing in Contract Services." *Labor Research Review* 15:61–71.

Ikenberry, G. J. 1989. "Explaining the Diffusion of State Norms: Coercion, Competition, and Learning in the International System." Paper presented at the annual meetings of the International Studies Association, London.

Jenkins, J. Craig. 1977. "Radical Transformations of Organizational Goals." *Administrative Sciences Quarterly* 22:568–86.

———. 1985. *The Politics of Insurgency*. New York: Columbia University Press.

Jenkins, J. Craig, and Craig Eckert. 1986. "Elite Patronage and the Channeling of Social Protest." *American Sociological Review* 51:812–29.

Johnston, Paul. 1994. *Success while Others Fail: Social Movement Unionism and the Public Workplace*. Ithaca, N.Y.: ILR Press.

Koopmans, Ruud. 1993. "The Dynamics of Protest Waves: West Germany, 1965 to 1989." *American Sociological Review* 58:637–53.

Kriesi, Hanspeter, R. Koopmans, J. W. Duyvendak, and M. G. Giugni. 1995. *The Politics of New Social Movements in Western Europe*. Minneapolis: University of Minnesota Press.

Labor Research Review. 1991. Thematic issue. "An Organizing Model of Unionism." *Labor Research Review*, vol. 17.

———. 1991/92. Thematic issue: "Let's Get Moving: Organizing for the 90s." *Labor Research Review*, vol. 18 (fall/winter).

———. 1993. Thematic issue: "No More Business as Usual: Labor's Corporate Campaigns." *Labor Research Review*, vol. 21 (fall/winter).

Lang, Kurt, and Gladys Lang. 1961. *Collective Dynamics*. New York: Crowell.

Lipset, Seymour M., Martin Trow, and James Coleman. 1956. *Union Democracy*. New York: Free Press.

McAdam, Doug. 1982. *Political Process and the Development of Black Insurgency, 1930–1970*. Chicago: University of Chicago Press.

———. 1983. "Tactical Innovation and the Pace of Insurgency." *American Sociological Review* 48:735–54.

———. 1988. *Freedom Summer*. New York: Oxford University Press.

Messinger, Sheldon. 1955. "Organizational Transformation: A Case Study, of a Declining Social Movement." *American Sociological Review* 20:3–10.

Meyer, David S., and Suzanne Staggenborg. 1996. "Movements, Countermovements, and the Structure of Political Opportunity." *American Journal of Sociology* 101:1628–60.

Michels, Robert. (1915) 1962. *Political Parties: A Sociological Study of the Oligarchical Tendencies of Modern Democracy*. New York: Dover.

Minkoff, Debra C. 1994. "From Service Provision to Institutional Advocacy: The Shifting Legitimacy of Organizational Forms." *Social Forces* 72 (4):943–69.

———. 1999. "Bending with the Wind: Strategic Change and Adaptation by Women's and Racial Minority Organizations." *American Journal of Sociology* 104:1666–703.

Morris, Aldon. 1981. "Black Southern Student Sit-In Movement: An Analysis of Internal Organization." *American Sociological Review* 46:744–67.

Perry, Charles R. 1987. *Union Corporate Campaigns*. Philadelphia: Wharton School of Business.

Peterson, Richard, Thomas Lee, and Barbara Finnegan. 1992. "Strategies and Tactics in Union Organizing Campaigns." *Industrial Relations* 31 (2):370–81.

Piven, Frances Fox, and Richard Cloward. 1977. *Poor People's Movements: Why They Succeed, How They Fail*. New York: Vintage.

Rothschild-Whitt, Joyce. 1976. "Conditions Facilitating Participatory-Democratic Organizations." *Sociological Inquiry* 46 (2):75–86.

Rucht, Dieter. 1998. "The Structure and Culture of Collective Protest in Germany since 1950." Pp. 29–58 in *The Social*

Movement Society, edited by David S. Meyer and Sidney Tarrow. Lanham, Md.: Rowman & Littlefield.

Schmidt, Alvin. 1973. *Oligarchy in Fraternal Organizations; A Study in Organizational Leadership*. Detroit: Gale Research Company.

Schutt, R. K. 1986. *Organization in a Changing Environment: Unionization of Welfare Employees*. Albany: State University of New York Press.

Scott, W. Richard. 1995. *Institutions and Organizations*. Thousand Oaks, Calif.: Sage.

Selznick, Philip. 1943. "An Approach to a Theory of Bureaucracy." *American Sociological Review* 8:47–54.

———. 1948. "Foundations of the Theory of Organization." *American Sociological Review* 13:25–35.

———. 1957. *Leadership in Administration*. New York: Harper & Row.

Sherman, Rachel, and Kim Voss. 2000. "Organize or Die: Labor's New Tactics and Immigrant Workers." Pp. 81–108 in *Organizing Immigrants: The Challenge for Unions in Contemporary California*, edited by Ruth Milkman. Ithaca, N.Y.: Cornell University Press.

Simon, Herbert. 1957. *Administrative Behavior*. Glencoe, Ill.: Free Press.

Singh, Jitendra, and Charles Lumsden. 1990. "Theory and Research in Organizational Ecology." *Annual Review of Sociology* 16:161–95.

Singh, Jitendra, David Tucker, and Agnes Meinhard. 1991. "Institutional Change and Ecological Dynamics." Pp. 390–422 in *The New Institutionalism in Organizational Analysis*, edited by Walter Powell and Paul DiMaggio. Chicago: University of Chicago Press.

Smith, Christian. 1996. *Resisting Reagan: The U.S. Central America Peace Movement*. Chicago: University of Chicago Press.

Staggenborg, Suzanne. 1988. "The Consequences of Professionalization and Formalization in the Pro-Choice Movement." *American Sociological Review* 53:585–606.

Tilly, Charles. 1972. "How Protest Modernized France, 1845–1855." Pp. 192–255 in *The Dimensions of Quantitative Research in History*, edited by W. O. Aydelotte, Allan G. Bogue, and R. W. Fogel. Princeton, N.J.: Princeton University Press.

———. 1982. "Britain Creates the Social Movement." Pp. 21–51 in *Social Conflict and the Political Order in Modern Britain*, edited by James Cronin and Jonathan Schneer. New Brunswick, N.J.: Rutgers University Press.

———. 1986. *The Contentious French*. Cambridge, Mass.: Harvard University Press.

———. 1995. *Popular Contention in Great Britain, 1758–1834*. Cambridge, Mass.: Harvard University Press.

Tolbert, Pamela S., and Lynne G. Zucker. 1983. "Institutional Sources of Change in the Formal Structure of Organizations: The Diffusion of Civil Service Reform, 1880–1935." *Administrative Science Quarterly* 28:22–39.

Troy, Leo. 1990. "Is the U.S. Unique in the Decline of Private Sector Unionism?" *Journal of Labor Research* 11:111–43.

Turner, Lowell. 1999. "Revitalizing Labor in the U.S., Britain and Germany: Social Movements and Institutional Change." Unpublished manuscript. Cornell University, Department of Industrial and Labor Relations.

Useem, Bert, and Mayer Zald. 1987. "From Pressure Group to Social Movement: Efforts to Promote the Use of Nuclear Power." Pp. 273–88 in *Social Movements in an Organizational Society*, edited by Mayer N. Zald and John D. McCarthy. New Brunswick, N.J.: Transaction Publishers.

Western, Bruce. 1997. *Between Class and Market*. Princeton, N.J.: Princeton University Press.

White, James W. 1995. *Ikki: Social Conflict and Political Protest in Early Modern Japan*. Ithaca, N.Y.: Cornell University Press.

Whittier, Nancy. 1995. *Feminist Generations: The Persistence of the Radical Women's Movement*. Philadelphia: Temple University Press.

Zald, Mayer, and Roberta Ash. 1966. "Social Movement Organizations. Growth, Decay, and Change." *Social Forces* 44:327–40.

Zald, Mayer, and Bert Useem. 1987. "Movement and Countermovement Interaction: Mobilization, Tactics, and State Involvement." Pp. 247–72 in *Social Movements in an Organizational Society*, edited by Mayer N. Zald and John D. McCarthy. New Brunswick, N.J.: Transaction Publishers.

Zucker, Lynne G. 1991. "The Role of Institutionalism in Cultural Persistence." Pp. 83–107 in *The New Institutionalism in Organizational Analysis*, edited by Walter Powell and Paul DiMaggio. Chicago: University of Chicago Press.

Chapter 30
Institutional Sources of Practice Variation

Staffing College and University Recycling Programs

Michael Lounsbury

The creation and diffusion of new organizational practices is the topic of this chapter by Michael Lounsbury. Lounsbury brings together several strands of organizational theory as he examines staffing practices in college and university recycling programs. He argues that variations in staffing patterns can be explained partly by larger societal trends in recycling practices and by factors operating at the college and university level. Lounsbury's focus on variations in staffing practices reminds us that there are important counter-pressures to the forces of organizational homogeneity discussed in previous chapters. Further, as we have seen, social movements have often acted as critical sources of innovation and change in organizations.

Although neoinstitutionalists have demonstrated how broader cognitive, normative, and regulative forces shape how new practice models emerge and diffuse throughout organizational populations (e.g., Scott, 1995), we have little understanding about why organizational responses to institutional pressures differ (Friedland and Alford, 1991; Powell, 1991; Oliver, 1991). There have been two general approaches to the study of variation in the institutional diffusion of new practices or structures. One line of research has focused on understanding how temporal (Tolbert and Zucker, 1983; Thornton and Ocasio, 1999) or spatial (e.g., Strang and Tuma, 1993; Davis and Greve, 1997) differences in institutional processes

shape diffusion, leading to variation in the organizational adoption of a single or similar practice. Another stream of research, rooted in organizational adaptation perspectives (e.g., Thompson, 1967; Pfeffer and Salancik, 1978), has focused more explicitly on explaining variation in organizational practices (e.g., Kraatz and Zajac, 1996; Westphal, Gulati, and Shortell, 1997). In this second line of research, scholars often distinguish conceptually between institutional pressures for conformity and the more idiosyncratic characteristics and technical demands of organizations, which are theorized as counterposing forces that lead to practice diversity.

Over the past decade, however, there have been a number of efforts to develop more integrative conceptual approaches to the study of institutional and organizational dynamics that focus attention on the interconnections between institutional context and variation in organizational behaviors and practices. Oliver (1991), for instance, has called for the study of how organizations employ different kinds of strategies in response to institutional pressures for both legitimacy and efficiency. In a similar vein, Greenwood and Hinings (1996) developed a framework that aims to extend the neoinstitutional perspective by highlighting how the internal dynamics of organizations may lead some organizations to respond differently than others despite exposure to the same institutional pressures. Ruef and Scott (1998) demonstrated the fruitfulness of a more detailed multilevel approach to institutional and organizational change in their study of how the legitimacy of hospitals with different ownership characteristics shifted in tandem with a transformation in logics. There has been virtually no empirical research, however, directed toward understanding how variation in the content of organizational practices is systematically shaped by institutional forces (see Edelman, 1992, for an exception).

In an effort to shed light on how heterogeneity in organizational practices is institutionally shaped, I report on a study of a population of colleges and universities in the Great Lakes states that varied in how they staffed authorized recycling programs upon adoption. By authorized, I mean that the recycling program is formally sponsored and funded by a school's administration. At some universities, authorized recycling programs were staffed by ecological activists who filled newly created full-time recycling coordinator positions. At other schools, authorized recycling programs were mainly staffed by ecologically ambivalent custodial directors who assumed responsibilities for recycling as an additional, part-time duty.

Focusing on staffing is a useful way to probe differences in organizations' responses to their environments because resource commitments to staffing can provide a visible signal to stakeholders about organizational compliance to demands (Rao and Sivakumar, 1999). For instance, in developing her explanation of organizational variation in the creation of Equal Employment Opportunity/Affirmative Action offices (EEO/AA), Edelman (1992) noted that government agencies, which experienced the greatest degree of normative pressure, created EEO/AA offices with a mean of 7.1 full-time salaried employees, whereas colleges and business organizations, which experienced less normative pressure, staffed offices with an average of two or fewer full-time salaried employees. While variation in staffing was not a central focus for Edelman, her analysis suggests that linkages to field-level organizations may importantly shape the implementation of diffusing practices. I build on the insights of Edelman's work as well as other institutional research that has highlighted how field-level associations and organizations such as professions actively promote specific kinds of practices (e.g., DiMaggio, 1991; Dobbin et al., 1993) by studying how field-level organizations may provide a mechanism by which variation in the content of organizational practices emerges.

In particular, I focus on the role of the Student Environmental Action Coalition (SEAC), a national social movement organization, in generating variation in the staffing of college and university recycling programs. McCarthy and Zald (1977: 1218) defined a social movement organization as "a complex, or formal, organization which identifies its goals with the preferences of a social movement or a countermovement and attempts to implement those goals." While the literature on social movements has highlighted the importance of social movement organizations such as the Student Non-Violent Coordinating Committee and the Congress of Racial Equality in fomenting social change, there have been few attempts to

study how such organizations influence the diffusion of new kinds of organizational practices. In this paper, I examine how the adoption of both kinds of college and university recycling program staffing forms was influenced by the wider societal legitimacy of recycling that had been attained by the late 1980s as well as by the local student environmental activism that the SEAC facilitated. The SEAC provided an important communication and resource infrastructure that facilitated the mobilization of student environmental groups at campuses, while also specifically promoting the creation of recycling programs that would be staffed by full-time recycling activists.

My project unfolded in two stages. Through exploratory fieldwork, I initially uncovered variation in the staffing of college and university recycling programs. I then used event history analyses to test hypotheses that would enable me to explain the variation detected in the initial exploratory research.

Recycling Program Variation

The integration of formalized recycling techniques and technologies into mainstream solid waste practices is a relatively new phenomenon, mainly occurring since the mid- to late-1980s. While only 9.6 percent of the U.S. waste stream was recycled in 1980, by 1990 that figure increased to 16.6 percent, and by 1995 to 27 percent (Environmental Protection Agency, 1997). The most dramatic increases have taken place since the late '80s. The Environmental Protection Agency (EPA), estimates that the number of curbside recycling programs in the U.S. increased from approximately 1,000 in 1988 to 7,500 by 1995, providing 48 percent of the U.S. population (120 million people) with access to curbside recycling collection programs by the mid-1990s. This rapid growth in recycling has been fueled by the rejuvenation of the environmental movement, the development and refinement of recycling technologies, the construction of a recycling infrastructure, and the social legitimation of recycling as an appropriate technological solution for dealing with the collection and disposal of solid waste (Blumberg and Gottlieb, 1989; Seldman, 1995; Hoffman, 1997). Despite the proliferation of recycling practices through the 1990s, however, conflicting claims and evidence about the efficiency and effectiveness of recycling practices continually threaten its legitimacy as a solid waste solution (e.g., Denison and Ruston, 1996; Tierney, 1996). In lieu of clear cost-benefit calculations demonstrating the economic benefits of recycling, the diffusion of recycling practices has been mainly driven by normative pressures stemming from environmental groups' activism and coercive pressures exerted by regulatory agencies such as the EPA and state and municipal governments.

Given the rapid rise of recycling practices since the late 1980s, I began with an interest in trying to understand how organizations responded to institutional pressures that encouraged the adoption of recycling practices. I delimited my investigation by focusing on recycling practices at colleges and universities. Between the late 1980s and mid-1990s, the vast majority of colleges and universities had been reported to have created "authorized" recycling programs (Smith, 1993). Unlike student volunteer recycling programs of the late 1960s and 1970s that often disappeared soon after they were created, authorized recycling programs are sponsored by university administrators and are typically set up and maintained by university staff within physical plant departments. While most student volunteer recycling efforts had died off by the late 1970s due to the lack of markets for recyclables (Strong, 1992), authorized recycling programs are at least symbolically committed to the durability of these efforts, despite market fluctuations. . . .

Through my initial fieldwork, I uncovered systematic variation in how university recycling programs were staffed. The main variation I focus on is that some universities organized recycling programs by establishing a new full-time recycling coordinator position while others just added recycling management duties to an existing work role. This variation is what Stinchcombe (1983: 188), has referred to as "status creation," in contrast to "role accretion." In status creation, "a job description for a role is worked out in the abstract, with corresponding rights and duties" and in relation to other roles, "and this vacancy is filled by recruitment. In the role accretion method of creating roles, various rights and duties are added in small bundles to the 'estate' of a given person" (Stinchcombe, 1983: 188). . . .

Status Creation Versus Role Accretion

Although status creation and role accretion are ideal types (Weber, 1978), they tap into important differences in how organizations go about incorporating new bundles of tasks into organizations (Stinchcombe, 1983). This distinction is particularly revealing in college and university recycling programs. Because authorized recycling programs at colleges and universities emerged during a general institutional shift at the societal level toward the incorporation of recycling into mainstream solid waste practices, the creation of new, full-time recycling coordinator positions can be interpreted as a symbolic act that signals compliance, or even greater commitment, to institutional pressures (Edelman, 1992; Rao and Sivakumar, 1999). In addition, my fieldwork indicated that the variation between status-creation and role-accretion recycling coordinators and programs was related to the amount of effort and energy put into building campuswide recycling programs as well as whether recycling program managers espoused broader ecological ideals and participated in national social movement organizations engaged in recycling advocacy.

A key difference distinguishing status-creation and role-accretion recycling program managers had to do with their occupational identity. In university recycling programs that were staffed through role accretion, management duties were most often given to custodial directors or assistant heads of facilities management departments who had little slack in their existing schedules. These extra responsibilities often came with no reduction in other obligations or resources to build and maintain the campus recycling infrastructure. The occupational identities of role-accretion recyclers were tied to their extant, full-time work roles, and they expressed little interest in or enthusiasm toward their recycling duties. In contrast, status-creation recyclers began to forge a new and distinct occupational identity that was connected to the ideals of the broader environmental movement. In the early 1990s, status-creation recyclers began to identify each other through their joint participation in the National Recycling Coalition (NRC), the main national recycling trade association, which has been a key actor in promoting recycling practices since its founding in 1978. In 1993, a group of full-time recycling coordinators formed the College and University Recycling Coordinators (CURC), occupational association during the annual NRC meeting. This group established procedures to elect officials and developed committees to study measurement standards, "buy recycled" campaigns, cooperation between university operations and academics, and other issues related to the construction of campus recycling programs. The group also established a ListServ on the Internet to facilitate ongoing program management dialogue among organization members. The chairperson of the CURC expressed a common view among CURC members that their collaboration represented a step toward creating a recycling coordinator profession:

> I see CURC and the List Server as the vehicle by which our profession will eventually be formally recognized. This will lead to standards and procedures that will assist in legitimizing and progressing our efforts and our ideas. It is the best way to promote and achieve inroads to business and affect their practice.

Fieldwork also revealed differences between role-accretion and status-creation recycling programs in the extent to which they were actively managed. At many schools that had authorized recycling programs that were staffed through role accretion, there were few efforts to publicize the program to the campus community, measure the effectiveness of the program, develop effective logistical systems for handling recyclables, or train custodial staff. These kinds of activities require a great deal of time and energy that role-accretion recyclers did not have, since they already had full-time duties through their existing jobs. In most cases, recycling programs staffed through role accretion could be considered minimalist in that they consisted of little more than a scattering of blue recycling bins around campus.

Full-time recycling coordinators, in contrast, stressed the importance of creating awareness of the recycling program through publicity and educational outreach, developing measurement standards to assess the effectiveness of recycling efforts, as well as engaging in many other activities having to do with building a recycling infrastructure and managing staff and contracts. Many status-creation recyclers work very closely with student environmental groups on campus, and even hire some students as part-time workers, to help build awareness about the recycling program and to educate students, faculty, and staff about the appropriate ways to participate in the recycling program. Moreover, they go beyond educating people to encouraging them both to reduce their production of waste by reusing materials and to purchase recycled products Role-accretion recycling managers, alternatively, conceptualized recycling much more narrowly as the collection of potential recyclables and rarely worked with student groups or spent time on educating people to "reduce, reuse and recycle."

Role-accretion and status-creation recyclers also differed in their value orientations toward recycling. Part-time recycling manager informants tended to view recycling as either a nuisance or marginal work activity. When I asked questions about why an informant was involved in recycling, I received answers such as "Because I was ordered to do it!" or "I'm recycling because it is in my job description." In addition, these role-accretion recyclers made no connections between their recycling duties and broader ecological ideals. For example, in response to a question about how recycling connects to his life outside of work, Rick, a 45-year-old grounds supervisor from a medium-sized East Coast university who manages his school's recycling program as a part-time duty, said, "It doesn't really. When you deal with real life issues such as death and dying, then the issues of recycling really are not as important as people perceive them to be."

By contrast, status-creation recyclers expressed more holistic views about how recycling was integral to their existence and how their promotion of recycling contributes to the wellbeing of life on the planet. For instance, when asked why she was involved in recycling, Karin, a coordinator from a Pacific Northwest university responded:

> Because we need to establish common ground with people throughout the world so we can actually work together in community to deal with other bigger splinter issues that face us . . . garbage is one thing we *all* have in common, recycling is the inroads to *all* other life issues. . . . [I]t is the first step away from the garbage can, the first place we are getting the message to make bigger connections . . . besides that it's big business and we

have totally screwed up our natural resource base so as long as we consume, recycling will be essential to our lives. . . . [R]ecycling is a safe place where we can institute things like waste reduction which is really tied into the whole multinational corporate structure of manufacturing, money, consumption, pollution, *forest destruction*, cancer . . . etc. . . . etc. . . .

Judy, a recycling coordinator from a Midwestern university, answered the question of why she was involved in recycling by emphasizing its substantive value: "I'm not just gonna do something because I'll make a lot of money as an accountant or working at the board of trade. I do something because I feel like it's important . . . what I'm doing is important and valuable to someone or something." Judy and other full-time recycling coordinators I interviewed passionately embraced recycling as an inherently meaningful activity. Judy rooted her involvement in recycling in a worldview that stresses the delicate interconnectedness of the social and natural realms of existence:

And I think a lot of it . . . is just a general respect for other people, other cultures, you know, other things is sort of intertwined with a respect for the environment. It's just a general respect for things and not wanting to destroy things or people or take care of others in general, whether those others are animals, plants or humans.

Charles, another status-creation recycler from a major Southeastern university, was even more passionate in his views on recycling:

Recycling because the other option is extinction! Unless humans begin living in harmony with nature, we will make Mother Nature too sick and she will eventually heal herself just like the human body heals sickness—it kills off and expels the toxins polluting its system. Right now, humans are the equivalent to the toxins!

Although it is difficult to generalize from the basic differences uncovered in my fieldwork, they highlight that the creation of full-time recycling coordinator positions may involve more than an expression of symbolic commitment to institutional pressures (Edelman, 1992; Rao and Sivakumar, 1999). In fact, college and university recycling program staffing variation may potentially be related to the ultimate effectiveness of recycling programs, although this linkage is extraordinarily difficult to demonstrate. Though there have been a number of generic templates devised to guide the measurement of recycling program effectiveness (e.g., Morris, 1994), both role-accretion and status-creation informants often stressed the underlying complexity of measuring the costs and benefits of recycling. Status-creation recycling coordinators were particularly adamant about this issue, since their ability to demonstrate program effectiveness was crucial to their job assessment and to garnering more resources to expand their programs. Jim, a full-time recycling coordinator for a large, Midwestern university expressed some of the elements of measurement complexity:

What do you include in those numbers? Compost? Are the numbers real or estimates? The savings often do not figure in saving pollution to the environment or the cost of not sending materials to the landfill. We can track revenue generation, but that is only part of the story, especially since the prices paid for recyclable material often fluctuate dramatically.

Interviews with recycling managers indicated that few programs systematically track the costs and benefits of recycling efforts. To the extent that they do, the wide variety of measures used make it virtually impossible to compare the relative effectiveness of those recycling programs. Performance measures mentioned in my interviews with recycling program managers included the comparative cost of recycling a ton versus landfilling a ton of material, the diversity of materials recycled, total weight of materials recycled, the percentage of materials diverted from dumps, remaining within budget, customer satisfaction, custodial hours worked, complaints from custodial staff, as well as revenue generated through recycling.

Given the importance of assessing the effectiveness of their efforts by measuring the costs and benefits of programs, however, status-creation recyclers made the number one goal of the CURC "to develop reporting standards for measuring progress toward waste abatement and to allow for accurate comparisons and analyses between schools" (interview with the CURC chairperson). To develop standardized techniques for measuring and evaluating recycling program productivity, the CURC has organized a measurement standards committee that is trying to create training tools and models that will be made widely available to recycling coordinators. To date, little progress has been made, however, and the lack of measurement standards that could support generally acceptable claims about recycling program effectiveness has not only affected the development of recycling programs on college campuses but has helped to fuel ongoing debates about the overall effectiveness of recycling as a solid waste solution (e.g., Denison and Ruston, 1996; Tierney, 1996).

Over the course of this initial fieldwork, I tried to develop an understanding of why some schools created new full-time positions, while others did not. Through my interviews with recycling coordinators, I discovered that virtually all recyclers in newly created full-time recycling coordinator positions were undergraduates at the school where they now had positions. Full-time recycling coordinators argued that when schools decided to authorize the creation of a recycling program, students who were members of the student environmental group that lobbied administrators provided a natural resource pool from which to staff and manage those efforts. As undergraduates, they were leaders of their student environmental groups, participated in and belonged to national social movement organizations such as the Student Environmental Action Coalition (SEAC), which promoted the diffusion of recycling practices, and were active in pressuring their schools to adopt recycling programs. The link to the SEAC seemed to be significant in many of my interviews with full-time coordinators. The SEAC claims to be the largest student-run organization in the U.S., with members at over 2,200 universities, colleges, and high schools (Strauss, 1995). It sponsors annual student conferences and maintains an elaborate network of experienced student organizers who travel to campuses and hold workshops, provide training, and support work on activities such as campus solid waste audits. The SEAC claims to have helped create over 700 recycling programs at U.S. schools (Smith, 1993: 127). The SEAC is supported by student environmental group memberships as well as by foundations such as the Mary Reynolds Babcock Foundation and other social movement organizations such as the National Wildlife Federation.

The SEAC was also instrumental in promoting the adoption of recycling programs that were staffed with full-time recycling coordinator positions. During my research, I gained access to many documents prepared by college and university student groups in their effort to convince school administrators that it was appropriate for them to sponsor the creation of an authorized recycling program. Documents from different schools often contained similar kinds of arguments and examples about how other socially similar schools had adopted recycling programs staffed with full-time recycling coordinator positions. Interviews suggested that the SEAC provided access to key information such as case studies of other socially similar schools that helped student environmental organizations shape their arguments to administrators. This emphasis on student activism and the SEAC contrasted sharply with my interviews with role-accretion recyclers, who claimed that there was little to no student concern about recycling when their programs were adopted. Even though my initial research revealed variation in how colleges and universities staffed their recycling programs and suggested that student activism importantly motivated the creation of new full-time recycling coordinator positions upon program adoption, it did not allow me to develop systematic claims about the variation in how programs were staffed.

How the SEAC, college and university student activism, and the adoption of status-creation recycling programs were linked seemed to be an important focal point for further analysis. It is theoretically interesting because it draws attention to how broader institutional diffusion processes intersect with organization-level processes involving intraorganizational conflict and connections to field-level actors to produce variation in the practices adopted (Greenwood and Hinings, 1996). Most institutional research on diffusion has focused on how innovations flow through a system as a result of a variety of cognitive, normative, and regulative forces that are exogenous to organizations (Scott, 1995). While the adoption of practices is certainly influenced by an organization's susceptibility to broader institutional forces, we know very little about how intraorganizational dynamics and connections to fieldlevel organizations shape responses to institutional pressures. Hence, I set out to gather more systematic data that would enable me to make stronger claims about the interplay between broader institutional processes and organization-level dynamics by testing hypotheses derived from institutional theory and my initial grounded research investigation.

Hypotheses

Institutional analysis often involves theorizing how processes operating at different levels of analysis are connected (Scott, 1995; Schneiberg and Clemens, 2001). My concern was with how the broader legitimation and diffusion of recycling practices at the societal level and lower school-level processes shaped the temporal and spatial dynamics of the adoption of recycling practices in a population of colleges and universities. I focused on how broader institutional dynamics driving the diffusion of recycling got translated into more specific staffing arrangements in college and university recycling programs: whether newly adopted recycling programs at colleges and universities were staffed by existing employees who assumed recycling duties as an additional responsibility (role accretion), or by full-time employees who filled newly created roles in the organizational chart (status creation). Consistent with most institutional studies of diffusion, I focus on the rates by which schools adopt recycling programs with different staffing forms (Strang and Soule, 1998).

In the organizations literature on the diffusion of innovations, there has been a strong emphasis on processes of organizational isomorphism (DiMaggio and Powell, 1983; Davis, 1991; Haunschild, 1993). Isomorphism has been conventionally explained with reference to adaptive responses related to imitation or mimesis, although in practice, it is very difficult to untangle such cognitively based mechanisms from more normative or regulative forces (Mizruchi and Fein, 1999). While there have been a number of studies that have focused on isomorphism across whole fields of actors, there have also been considerable efforts aimed at parsing social space into relatively homogeneous groupings that can help explain the temporal and spatial variation of diffusing practices (e.g., Burt, 1987; Galaskiewicz and Burt, 1991; Greve, 1996).

The general argument is that different groups of socially similar actors will share information with each other and create group norms that will lead to similar beliefs or the adoption of similar kinds of practices (Festinger, 1954). For instance, Galaskiewicz and Burt (1991) found that evaluations of nonprofits by contributions officers in Minneapolis–St. Paul were not uniformly shaped through mimesis but were influenced by shared social status in a hierarchically stratified professional field.

One conventional way to parse educational organizations into socially similar groups is by selectivity (e.g., Kraatz and Zajac, 1996; Kraatz, 1998; Soule, 1997). Schools that are highly selective share many common elements that lead them to define each other as peers and look to each other for cues about how to respond to institutional pressures. For instance, highly selective schools compete for the same kinds of talented students and share similar degrees of media visibility through national comparison rankings. Schools should therefore respond to institutional pressures by choosing adaptive responses similar to those previously chosen by other schools in their status group:

Hypothesis 1 (H1): The prevalence of adoption of recycling programs in a school's status group will increase a school's probability of program adoption.

Research on colleges and universities has shown that schools that are highly selective also tend to have similar kinds of student bodies that typically have a more liberal political orientation (e.g., Sax et al., 1996; Astin et al., 1997). In addition, it has been consistently shown that elite schools are far more likely to experience activism than non-elite schools (e.g., Lipset, 1971; Bloom, 1987). In my initial fieldwork, status-creation recyclers emphasized the role of student activism in the creation of their campus recycling programs. They claimed that local student activism around environmental issues enabled them to enter into newly created full-time positions to manage and promote recycling practices. Since schools of similar status will tend to look to each other for information about how to respond to institutional pressures, and higher status schools have been shown to be more likely to experience student activism, the most selective schools should be more likely to create new recycling coordinator positions:

Hypothesis 2 (H2): Schools that are highly selective will have a higher rate of adopting recycling programs staffed with new full-time recycling coordinator positions.

Another factor that may facilitate the adoption of programs staffed by full-time as opposed to part-time recycling coordinators is direct connection to regulatory organizations and agencies (e.g., Edelman, 1992; Dobbin et al., 1993; see Scott, 1995, for a review). While such institutional linkages can confer both legitimacy and resources (e.g., Baum and Oliver, 1992), they can also provide important channels through which normative pressures flow. For example, Edelman (1992) showed that organizations that were tied to governmental agencies were more likely to adopt Equal Employment Opportunity/Affirmative Action offices as a way to demonstrate their compliance to the passage of EEO/AA laws. Such connections have been captured in the study of colleges and universities by examining variation between schools whose resources are mostly tied to state versus privately generated budgets (e.g., Tolbert, 1985). This kind of institutional linkage is particularly relevant in the study of recycling practices because state governments provided explicit regulative legitimacy through the passage of recycling mandates beginning in the late 1980s. Public schools, which are more closely tied to state governments than private schools, may therefore be more likely to create new full-time recycling coordinator positions in order to demonstrate their commitment to the efforts of state governments to encourage recycling, despite the ambiguity of those mandates:

Hypothesis 3 (H3): Public colleges and universities will have a higher rate of adopting recycling programs staffed with new full-time recycling coordinator positions.

A complete account of institutional change should also examine how intraorganizational dynamics influence how organizations respond to institutional shifts (Oliver, 1991; Greenwood and Hinings, 1996; Hirsch and Lounsbury, 1997). As has been demonstrated across many organizational contexts, functionally differentiated groups provide a particularly important focal point for the analysis of intraorganizational precipitators of change (e.g., Gouldner, 1954;

Lawrence and Lorsch, 1967). As particular groups or coalitions in an organization become dissatisfied with the superordinate values of an organization or the way their interests are accommodated by the dominant coalition, dissatisfaction with the status quo can accrue, leading to mobilization efforts and pressures for change (Zald and Berger, 1978; Covaleski and Dirsmith, 1988; Palmer, Jennings, and Zhou, 1993). In the case of college and university recycling, it is important to investigate how student groups were able to mobilize effectively to affect the staffing of recycling programs that were adopted. It is plausible to hypothesize that schools that have environmentally related majors may have students that are more likely to get involved in environmental activism on campus. Quite often, the study of campus ecological practices is embedded in environmental curricula through lectures and student projects (Smith, 1993; Strauss, 1995). This allows students in environmental majors to be more reflective about ecological issues and become interested in facilitating the development of ecologically benign practices. Further, faculty teaching such environmentally related courses may be more sympathetic to students' efforts to create recycling programs, providing an important resource to facilitate student mobilization. As a result, a more ecologically aware and active student body may emerge and lobby for the creation of a full-time recycling coordinator position. In turn, school administrators may create a recycling program with a full-time, ecologically committed recycling coordinator in an effort to appease student demands and effectively coopt activist students (Selznick, 1949).

Hypothesis 4 (H4): The existence of environmentally related majors will increase a school's probability of adopting recycling programs staffed with new full-time recycling coordinator positions.

While having an environmentally related major may provide a context conducive to the development of student activism around ecological issues such as recycling, my interviews further suggested a more concrete mechanism by which recycling programs became staffed through the creation of new full-time positions. Specifically, my interviews with full-time recycling coordinators further indicated that student efforts to establish an authorized recycling program were importantly influenced by the SEAC, the national social movement organization that provided resources and energy to local student efforts. The role of field-level organizations and associations in facilitating the diffusion of practices has been a common theme among analysts of institutional processes (e.g., DiMaggio, 1991; Edelman, 1992; Dobbin et al., 1993), although the state and professions, as opposed to actors such as social movement organizations, have been the main focal point of such institutional analyses (Scott, 1995: chap. 5). Field-level organizations can affect intraorganizational dynamics by altering power relations among competing constituencies when some groups draw on the resources of such external organizations to advance their goals at the expense of other groups (Pfeffer and Salancik, 1978). The SEAC's influence on local student activism became manifest through its sponsorship of national networking meetings, its efforts to facilitate contact among student environmental groups from different campuses, and its advice about appropriate tactics to get authorized recycling programs created.

The SEAC's national meetings were particularly instrumental in enabling various student environmental groups to share experiences with each other, including how to structure and make claims when advocating recycling on campus. In contrast, student activism and social movement organizations such as the SEAC were noticeably absent from interviews about recycling program creation at schools that did not establish new full-time recycling management positions. Just as environmental courses of study and associated faculty may provide a resource that facilitates student mobilization around ecological issues such as recycling. the SEAC may have provided important resources to students to help them make effective claims to campus administrators. Hence,

> **Hypothesis 5 (H5):** Student environmental group membership in the SEAC will increase a school's probability of adopting recycling programs staffed with new full-time recycling coordinator positions.

Method

Data for this study come from a variety of archival sources as well as a survey that I conducted in a population of Great Lakes colleges and universities in 1996. I chose states that make up the Great Lakes region to control for multistate cooperation efforts that became popular in the 1980s. In 1983, the states of Minnesota, Illinois, Wisconsin, Indiana, Michigan. Ohio, Pennsylvania, and New York formed the Council of Great Lakes Governors to encourage the development of recycling practices. As an analytical strategy, I decided to further delimit my investigation by analyzing only those colleges and universities with total enrollments of at least five thousand in 1995.

I directed my survey questions to both heads of facilities management departments and people with management responsibilities for the campus recycling program, if one existed. I surveyed schools about if and when they created an authorized recycling program, why it was created, whether students on campus played a role in its establishment, how the program was staffed, including the staffing history, whether and when a new full-time recycling management position was created, whether the person in charge of recycling had other, non-recycling duties, and how much time he or she spent on recycling activities. . . .

Variables

The dependent variable is whether a campus recycling program, if and when created, was staffed by creating a new full-time position within the facilities management department (status creation) or by giving recycling duties to an existing facilities employee as an additional obligation (role accretion). These data were obtained through my survey of Great Lakes colleges and universities.

Independent variables. *Percent of program adoptions by school selectivity group* and *High selectivity school* were constructed based on selectivity data published in *Peterson's Guide to Undergraduate Study* and *Barron's Profiles of American Colleges*. I used two sources for cross-checking purposes. I coded school selectivity on a continuous four-point scale, with four being the most selective, and data were coded annually. . . . The *percent of program adoptions by school selectivity group* variable measures the extent to which schools within each of the four status groups have adopted a recycling program. *High selectivity school* is constructed as a standard dummy variable, coded as one for the most highly selective group and zero otherwise.

Public school is a dummy variable indicating whether a college or university is public or private. *Environmentally related major* captures if and when a college or university created an environmental major. This is a time-varying covariate that was developed by systematically coding whether a school had an official major related to environmentalism as reported in *Peterson's Guide to Undergraduate Study* or *Barron's Profiles of American Colleges* from 1975 to the present. Again, I used two sources for the purpose of cross-checking.

Member of SEAC, the Student Environmental Action Coalition, indicates whether a student environmental group was affiliated with this large national social movement organization through official membership. The SEAC provided me with annual membership data from its inception in 1989. This variable is a time-varying dichotomous variable that captures if and when a college or university student environmental group was a member of the SEAC, providing an objective indicator of a school's propensity to experience student advocacy of recycling.

Control variables. I used periodization to demarcate a shift toward state regulatory involvement in recycling practices. Between 1988 and 1990, each of the states in the Great Lakes region passed rules mandating that an increasing percentage of their waste stream must be recycled. . . .

Counts of recycling articles in Business Week capture the ebb and flow of public attention to the issue of recycling. To do this, I tracked the number of articles that focused on recycling in *Business Week*. . . .

Percent change in recycling articles in Waste Age tracks the extent to which recycling became defined as an important technical solution in the U.S. solid waste field. . . .

School enrollment, a proxy for size, was coded as a time-varying covariate based on data from *Peterson's Guide to Undergraduate Study* and *Barron's Profiles of American Colleges* from 1975 to 1995. Enrollment was scaled by one thousand for the purposes of analysis. . . .

Results

As figure 30.1 indicates, there were very few authorized recycling programs staffed through status creation or role accretion at Great Lakes colleges and universities until the late 1980s, when adoption rates increased. In fact, the majority of recycling programs in the population of schools examined were created between 1989 and 1992. By 1995, all but three schools in the population of 154 had adopted one of those two types of programs: 36 authorized recycling programs adopted were staffed through status creation and 115 were staffed through role accretion.

Table 30.1 reports basic descriptive statistics and correlations. There are no major correlational problems with the variables reported. Table 30.2 reports piecewise exponential competing risk analyses of recycling program adoptions. Model 1 provides a baseline model that includes just control variables for regulatory actions that mandated increasing rates of recycling in the states under consideration, the ebb and flow of recycling popularity in *Business Week*, the rise of recycling as a legitimate technological solution in the solid waste field, and school enrollment size. All independent variables reported are lagged by one year except for the invariant dummy variables that indicate whether a school is public or private and examine schools that are most selective. Although log likelihood results are provided for each model, it is not useful to compare across models unless they are hierarchically nested. Models 2–7, therefore, are nested models that provide tests of specific hypotheses.

Model 1 shows that the adoption rate of both recycling-program staffing forms significantly increased from the pre-regulatory period to the regulatory period that demarcates when state-level recycling mandates began to be enacted in 1988. This is no surprise, given that the observed adoption rates in figure 30.1 indicate that the diffusion process began to unfold quite rapidly around the time that most of these mandates were passed in the late 1980s. The *Business Week* variable, which captures the popularity of recycling, is not significant for either program form, perhaps because the rapid growth in the popularity of recycling practices at the societal level was concomitant with the emergence of actions by state governments to support and encourage the development of recycling practices. As DiMaggio and Powell (1983), Scott (1995), and others have argued, it is often difficult to disentangle normative, cognitive, and regulatory forces, since the processes that lead to the normative popularity of a particular practice are often interpenetrated with efforts to establish rules and guidelines related to that practice.

The variable that tracks the legitimation of recycling as a solid waste solution in *Waste Age* is significant but negative for both status-creation and role-accretion programs. This is mainly because recycling as a tech-

Figure 30.1

Observed status-creation and role-accretion recycling program adoption rates among Great Lakes colleges and universities, 1975–1995.

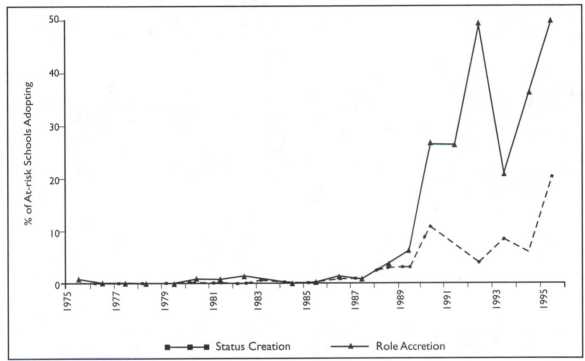

Table 30.1

Means, Standard Deviations, and Correlations for Independent Variables

Variable	Mean	S.D.	1	2	3	4	5	6	7
1. Counts of recycling articles in *Business Week*$_{t-1}$	17.61	12.21							
2. Percent change in recycling articles in *Waste Age*$_{t-1}$	.36	.92	−.08••						
3. School enrollment/1000$_{t-1}$	8.74	7.33	.06••	−.01					
4. Percent of program adoptions by school selectivity group$_{t-1}$	.08	.17	.02	.01	−.04••				
5. High selectivity school dummy	.21	.40	−.01	−.01	.06••	.06••			
6. Public school dummy	.66	.47	−.01	.01	.37••	−.08••	−.25••		
7. Environmentally related major$_{t-1}$	.60	.49	−.02	.04••	.30••	−.03	−.04•	.26••	
8. Member of SEAC$_{t-1}$	.03	.17	.06••	−.10••	.05••	.41••	−.02	.03	.07••
• *p* < .10; •• *p* < .05.									

Table 30.2

Maximum Likelihood Estimates of Piecewise Exponential Competing Risk Models of Status-creation and Role-accretion Recycling Program Adoption (N = 2530)*

Covariate	Model 1		Model 2		Model 3	
	Status creation	Role accretion	Status creation	Role accretion	Status creation	Role accretion
Pre-regulatory period	−7.242***	−5.527***	−7.134***	−5.278***	−7.800***	−5.604***
	(.762)	(.482)	(.745)	(.473)	(.821)	(.492)
Regulatory period	−2.770***	−1.449***	−2.844***	−1.506***	−3.185***	−1.502***
	(.580)	(.329)	(.605)	(.337)	(.596)	(.334)
Counts of articles in	−.039	.023	−.055•	.011	−.033	.025•
Business Week$_{t-1}$	(.028)	(.014)	(.031)	(.016)	(.028)	(.014)
% change in articles in	−.410**	−.293***	−.430**	−.316***	−.419**	−.289***
Waste Age$_{t-1}$	(.183)	(.113)	(.188)	(.117)	(.182)	(.113)
School enrollment/1000$_{t-1}$	.099***	−.040**	.103***	−.040**	.100***	−.041**
	(.016)	(.019)	(.017)	(.019)	(.017)	(.019)
% program adoptions by			.880•	.752**		
school selectivity group$_{t-1}$			(.670)	(.378)		
High select. school					1.173***	.254
dummy					(.345)	(.249)
Public school dummy						
Environmentally related						
major$_{t-1}$						
Member of SEAC$_{t-1}$						
Log likelihood	−425.32		−422.64		−419.74	
Likelihood ratio test			5.36•		11.16***	

• *p* < .10;   •• *p* < .05;   ••• *p* < .01;   tests are two-tailed for control variables and one-tailed for hypothesized effect.

* Standard errors are in parentheses.

nology had been discussed in *Waste Age* throughout the time period under investigation, with the highest rate of increase in the mid-1980s, whereas authorized recycling program adoption rates did not begin to increase until the late 1980s. School size as captured through enrollment is positively significant for status-creation recycling programs and negative and significant for role-accretion programs. This indicates that larger schools, which possess a greater amount of resources, are more likely to create new full-time recycling coordinator positions upon program adoption. The size variable,

however, provides little insight into the underlying mechanisms by which size gets translated into status-creation programs.

The results of model 2 support H1, that the prevalence of recycling programs adopted among socially similar schools, as proxied by selectivity, will increase the rate of recycling program adoption. Results show that social comparison processes were an important component of the recycling program diffusion process, but they do not explain variation in the staffing of adopted programs. Model 3, however, shows that the schools that are most selective have a higher

**Table 30.2
(continued)**

	Model 4		Model 5		Model 6		Model 7	
	Status creation	Role accretion	Status creation	Role accretion	Status creation	Role accretion	Status creation	Role accretion
	−7.189***	−5.619***	−7.555***	−5.575***	−6.960***	−5.625***	−8.081***	−5.647***
	(.790)	(.489)	(.816)	(.489)	(.766)	(.490)	(.952)	(.508)
	−2.710***	−1.539***	−3.146***	−1.496***	−2.980***	−1.461***	−4.027***	−1.789***
	(.624)	(.340)	(.671)	(.338)	(.619)	(.327)	(.798)	(.366)
	−.039	.023	−.038	.024	−.047	.025*	−.038	.013
	(.028)	(.014)	(.029)	(.014)	(.029)	(.014)	(.033)	(.016)
	−.410**	−.298***	−.411**	−.294***	−.238	−.315***	−.254	−.347***
	(.183)	(.113)	(.184)	(.113)	(.200)	(.113)	(.205)	(.118)
	.101***	−.049**	.089***	−.044**	.090***	−.032*	.079***	−.052••
	(.018)	(.021)	(.018)	(.020)	(.018)	(.019)	(.022)	(.023)
							.151	.846**
							(.812)	(.391)
							1.298***	.325
							(.392)	(.272)
	−.114	.254					.148	.373*
	(.455)	(.210)					(.482)	(.229)
			.635*	.130			.744	.171
			(.480)	(.200)			(.488)	(.205)
					1.112***	−.435*	1.031***	−.508**
					(.416)	(.291)	(.417)	(.294)
	−424.55		−424.16		−420.41		−409.79	
	1.54		2.32		9.82**		31.06***	

rate of adopting recycling programs staffed with new full-time recycling coordinators, providing strong support for H2. There was also a positive association between high-selectivity schools and the rate of adopting role-accretion programs, but it was not significant.

Hypothesis 3, which predicted that public schools will have a higher adoption rate of recycling programs that are staffed through status creation, was not supported. Model 4 shows that the public school dummy is in the opposite of the expected direction for status-creation programs and is not significant for either recycling-program staffing forms. Model 5 provides marginal support for H4, that schools with environmentally related majors will have higher rates of adopting re-

cycling programs staffed by full-time recycling coordinators. Schools with environmentally related majors did tend to create recycling programs staffed with new full-time recycling coordinator positions at higher rates, but there was no significant relationship between the existence of an environmentally related major and rates of creating role-accretion programs. Results of model 6 show that having a student environmental group affiliated with the SEAC is positively and significantly related to rates of creating recycling programs staffed through status creation, providing strong support for hypothesis 5. In addition, the relationship between having connections to the SEAC and rates of role-accretion recycling-program adoption is negative and significant, highlighting that recycling program staffing variation was, on the whole, importantly shaped by that field-level organization.

Model 7 provides a complete model that sheds light on the overall processes and mechanisms that explain how variation in the staffing of recycling programs at colleges and universities occurred. The passage of state recycling mandates, as proxied by the regulatory periodization, continues to capture important forces shaping the overall diffusion process. Aside from the period effect, however, the pattern of results for the creation of status-creation and role-accretion recycling programs are remarkably different. For status-creation recycling programs, highly selective schools and membership in the SEAC remain positive and strongly significant, while the percent of programs adopted by school selectivity group and environmentally related major variables are not significant in the full model. For role-accretion recycling programs, all results from previous models remain, with the exception of the public school dummy variable, which became marginally significant. Overall, schools that created new full-time recycling coordinator positions tended to be larger, were more highly selective, and had student environmental groups on campus that were connected to the SEAC. Schools that staffed their recycling programs as a part-time duty with existing staff tended to be smaller, public, influenced by social comparison processes, and lacked connections to the SEAC social movement organization.

While organizational characteristics such as size and school selectivity provide insights into the processes by which schools decided on how to staff adopted recycling programs, connections to the SEAC provide a more concrete mechanism that explains the origins of recycling program staffing variation. While extant research shows that schools that are large and more selective experience higher rates of student activism, school size also provides a dimension of social similarity that may guide efforts by school administrators to search for appropriate responses to institutional pressures. Both my initial fieldwork and the empirical results of the broader survey of Great Lakes schools, however, show that student environmental groups' connections to and support from the SEAC were crucial in making

effective claims, leading to variation in recycling program staffing forms. Large size and high selectivity are perhaps better understood as characteristics that help shape what kinds of schools were most susceptible to the normative influences of the SEAC.

Discussion and Conclusion

This study of variation in the staffing of college and university recycling programs showed that schools that staffed their recycling programs through role accretion tended to be public, smaller, and were importantly influenced by social comparison processes among schools of similar selectivity. Schools that created a new, full-time recycling coordinator position upon program adoption were larger, more selective, and had student environmental groups that actively lobbied their administrations to create an authorized recycling program. This local student activism did not occur in a vacuum, however, but was importantly shaped by the Student Environmental Action Coalition (SEAC), a national social movement organization that provided resources and advice to student environmental groups about how to get their schools to adopt an authorized recycling program. In addition, the passage of recycling mandates by state governments was an important aspect of the process of aggregate recycling program diffusion, but it was relatively unhelpful in explaining how and why staffing variation occurred.

Through the sponsoring of national meetings, the SEAC facilitated the development of network connections among student environmental groups from different campuses. Most importantly, though, the SEAC helped local student environmental groups make effective claims about why their school should adopt recycling programs staffed with full-time, dedicated recycling coordinators. They provided student groups with evidence from comparable schools that emphasized that it was normatively appropriate to create a full-time staff position since the creation and management of a recycling program required full-time attention and a set of skills that was orthogonal to that of managing garbage collection and hauling. This evidence was communicated in formal documents created by student environmental groups that were presented to school administrators in support of their claims. The overall development of such documents was also shaped by interactions with the SEAC and student environmental groups from other campuses.

The role of the SEAC in facilitating the staffing of college and university recycling programs through status creation highlights the general importance of investigating how broader field-level actors and organizations such as governmental agencies, trade associations, and social movement organizations shape the content of organizational practices (Scott, 1995). The case of the Americans with Disabilities Act (ADA), passed in 1990, provides a related non-social-movement organization example. Consistent with institutional arguments that the passage of laws often leaves the specification of how organizations are supposed to respond to the law ambiguous (e.g., Edelman, 1992), ten regional technical assistance centers were created across the country to promote the organizational adoption of specific disability-friendly practices. These technical assistance centers, in turn, provided an important mechanism by which practices adopted in response to that legislation varied-with some organizations adopting more committed responses, such as hiring ergonomic specialists and creating special budget lines for disability accommodation costs, while others adopted more symbolic practices that were much less helpful for people with disabilities (Balser, 1999). A focus on how such fieldlevel organizations like the SEAC or ADA technical assistance centers shape differences in the practices of organizations, therefore, promises to contribute to our understanding of the sources of organizational heterogeneity. . . .

By highlighting the role of a social movement organization in shaping variation in practice implementation, this study also contributes to the growing interest in combining the study of social movements with organizational analysis (e.g., Zald and Berger, 1978; Davis and Thompson, 1994; Clemens, 1997; Rao, 1998). While neoinstitutionalists generally have not highlighted social movement activity as a major factor driving institutional change, student activism should not necessarily be viewed as an explanatory mechanism that is contradictory to new institutional analysis. Social movement organizations provide a mechanism that is consistent with standard neoinstitutional arguments about the influence of broader interorganizational linkages

through organizations such as state agencies and professional bodies (Strang and Meyer, 1993; Scott and Meyer, 1994). What is somewhat different from standard accounts of institutional process, however, is that social activism was responsible for creating institutional variation but not for driving the overall process. This paper indicates that as institutionalists aim to revise their theories of social change to highlight conflict and heterogeneity, variation tied to social activism and movements should receive more attention (e.g., Strang and Soule, 1998; Moore, 1999). . . .

In general, we need more studies that connect institutional change to variation in the content of organizational practices. To uncover institutional sources of practice variation, however, researchers may have to employ more eclectic methodologies that combine large-scale archival analysis with more grounded ethnographic research strategies. By understanding how the content of organizational practices is shaped by broader institutional forces, we may develop new insights about the sources of organizational heterogeneity and gain significant leverage in identifying why organizational diversity exists in some fields but not in others. Finally, by studying practice variation, institutional theorists may be able to identify some boundary conditions that demarcate when and where isomorphic processes are expected to operate and the degree to which certain practices will become more or less institutionalized.

References

Abbott, A. 1988. *The System of Professions*. Chicago: University of Chicago Press.

Astin, Alexander W., et al. 1997. *The American Freshman: Thirty Year Trends, 1966–1996*. Los Angeles: Higher Education Research Institute.

Balser, D. B. 1999. "Implementing new employment law: A contested terrain." Unpublished Ph.D. thesis, Cornell University.

Baron, J. N., and W. T. Bielby. 1980. "Bringing the firms back in: Stratification, segmentation, and the organization of work." *American Sociological Review*, 45: 737–765.

Baum, J. A. C., and C. Oliver. 1992 "Institutional embeddedness and the dynamics of organizational populations." *American Sociological Review*, 57: 540–559.

Bloom, J. M. 1987. *Class, Race, and the Civil Rights Movement*. Bloomington, IN: Indiana University Press.

Blumberg, L., and R. Gottlieb. 1989. *War on Waste*. Washington, DC: Island Press.

Borgatti, S. P., M. G. Everett, and L. C. Freeman. 1999. *UCINET 5 for Windows: Software for Social Network Analysis*. Natick, MA: Analytic Technologies, Inc.

Burt, R. S. 1987. "Social contagion and innovation. Cohesion versus structural equivalence." *American Journal of Sociology*, 92: 1287–1335.

Campbell, J. L., J. R. Hollingsworth, and L. N. Lindberg. 1991. *Governance of the American Economy*. Cambridge: Cambridge University Press.

Clemens, E. S. 1997. *The People's Lobby: Organizational Innovation and the Rise of Interest Group Politics in the United States, 1890–1925*. Chicago: University of Chicago Press.

Covaleski, M. A., and M. W. Dirsmith. 1988. "An institutional perspective on the rise, social transformation, and fall of a university budget category." *Administrative Science Quarterly*, 33: 562–587.

Davis, G. F. 1991. "Agents without principles? The spread of the poison pill through the intercorporate network." *Administrative Science Quarterly*, 36: 583–613.

Davis, G. F., and H. R. Greve. 1997. "Corporate elite networks and governance changes in the 1980s." *American Journal of Sociology*, 103: 1–37.

Davis, G. F., and T. Thompson. 1994. "A social movement perspective on corporate control." *Administrative Science Quarterly*, 39: 141–173.

Denison, R. A., and J. F. Ruston. 1996. "Anti-recycling myths: Commentary on 'recycling is garbage.' " White paper, Environmental Defense Fund, Washington, DC.

DiMaggio, P. J. 1991. "Constructing an organizational field as a professional project: U.S. Art Museums, 1920–1940." In W. W. Powell and P. J. DiMaggio (eds.), *The New Institutionalism in Organizational Analysis*: 267–292. Chicago: University of Chicago Press.

DiMaggio, P. J., and W. W. Powell. 1983. "The iron cage revisited: Institutional isomorphism and collective rationality in organizational fields." *American Sociological Review*, 48: 147–160.

Dobbin, F., J. R. Sutton, J. W. Meyer, and W. R. Scott. 1993. "Equal opportunity law and the construction of internal labor markets." *American Journal of Sociology*, 99: 396–427.

Edelman, L, B. 1992 "Legal ambiguity and symbolic structures: Organizational mediation of civil rights law." *American Journal of Sociology*, 97: 1531–1576.

Eisenhardt, K. M. 1989. "Building theory from case study research." *Academy of Management Review*, 14: 532–550.

Environmental Protection Agency. 1997. *Municipal Solid Waste Factbook*. Washington, DC: EPA.

Festinger, L. 1954. "A theory of social comparison processes." *Human Relations*, 7: 117–140.

Friedland, R., and R. R. Alford. 1991. "Bringing society back in: Symbols, practices, and institutional contradictions." In W. W. Powell and P. J. DiMaggio (eds.), *The New Institutionalism in Organizational Analysis*: 232–266. Chicago: University of Chicago Press.

Galaskiewicz, J., and R. S. Burt. 1991. "Interorganizational contagion in corporate philanthropy." *Administrative Science Quarterly*, 36: 88–105.

Giugni, M. 1998. "Was it worth the effort? The outcomes and consequences of social movements." *Annual Review of Sociology*, 98: 371–393. Palo Alto, CA: Annual Reviews.

Giugni, M. D., McAdam, and C. Tilly. 1999. *How Movements Matter*. Minneapolis, MN: University of Minnesota Press.

Gouldner, A. W. 1954. *Patterns of Industrial Bureaucracy*. New York: Free Press.

Greenwood, R., and C. R. Hinings. 1996. "Understanding radical organizational change: Bringing together the old and the new institutionalism." *Academy of Management Review*, 21: 1022–1054.

Greve, H. R. 1996. "Patterns of competition: The diffusion of a market position in radio broadcasting." *Administrative Science Quarterly*, 41: 29–60.

Hannan, M. T., and J. Freeman. 1989. *Organizational Ecology*. Cambridge, MA: Harvard University Press.

Haunschild, P. R. 1993. "Interorganizational imitation: The impact of interlocks on corporate acquisition activity." *Administrative Science Quarterly*, 38: 564–592.

Haveman, H. A., and L. E. Cohen. 1994. "The ecological dynamics of careers: The impact of organizational founding, dissolution, and merger on job mobility." *American Journal of Sociology*, 100: 104–152.

Hirsch, P, M., and M. Lounsbury. 1997 "Ending the family quarrel: Towards a reconciliation of 'old' and 'new' institutionalism." *American Behavioral Scientist*, 40: 406–418.

Hoffman, A. J. 1997. *From Heresy to Dogma: An Institutional History of Corporate Environmentalism*. San Francisco: New Lexington Press.

Jenkins, C. J. 1977. "Radical transformation of organizational goals." *Administrative Science Quarterly*, 22: 568–586.

Kraatz, M. S. 1998. "Learning by association? Interorganizational networks and adaptation to environmental change." *Academy of Management Journal*, 41: 621–643.

Kraatz, M. S., and E. J. Zajac. 1996. "Causes and consequences of illegitimate organizational change." *American Sociological Review*, 61: 812–836.

Lawrence, P. R., and J. W. Lorsch. 1967. *Organization and Environment*. Boston: Harvard Business School Press.

Leblebici, H., G. R. Salancik, A. Copay, and T. King. 1991. "Institutional change and the transformation of interorganizational fields: An organizational history of the U.S. radio broadcasting industry." *Administrative Science Quarterly*, 36: 333–363.

Lipset, S. M. 1971. *Rebellion in the University*. Boston: Little, Brown.

Lounsbury, M. 2001. "Institutional transformation and status mobility: The professionalization of the field of finance." *Academy of Management Journal*, vol. 44 (in press).

Lounsbury, M., and W. N. Kaghan. 2001. "Organizations, occupations and the structuration of work." In S. P. Vallas (ed.), *Research in the Sociology of Work*, 10. New York: JAI/Elsevier Science (forthcoming).

McCarthy, J. D., and M. N. Zald. 1977. "Resource mobilization and social movements: A partial theory." *American Journal of Sociology*, 82: 1212–1241.

Meyer, J. W., and B. Rowan. 1977. "Institutionalized organizations: Formal structure as myth and ceremony." *American Journal of Sociology*, 83: 340–363.

Miner, A. S. 1990. "Structural evolution through idiosyncratic jobs. The potential for unplanned learning." *Organization Science*, 1: 195–209.

——. 1991. "Organizational evolution and the social ecology of jobs." *American Sociological Review*, 56: 772–785.

Mizruchi, M. S., and L. Fein. 1999. "The social construction of organizational knowledge: A study of the uses of coercive, mimetic, and normative isomorphism." *Administrative Science Quarterly*, 44: 653–683.

Moore, K. 1999. "Political protest and institutional change: The anti-Vietnam War movement and American science." In M. Giugni, D. McAdam, and C. Tilly (eds.), *How Social Movements Matter*: 97–118. Minneapolis, MN: University of Minnesota Press.

Morris, J. 1994. "Does recycling pay?" *World Wastes*, 37: 56–58.

Oliver, C. 1991. "Strategic responses to institutional processes," *Academy of Management Review*, 16: 145–179.

Palmer, D. A., P. D. Jennings, and X. Zhou. 1993. "Late adoption of the multidivisional form by large U.S. corporations: Institutional, political, and economic accounts." *Administrative Science Quarterly*, 38: 100–131.

Pfeffer, J., and G. R. Salancik. 1978. *The External Control of Organizations*. New York: Harper & Row.

Podolny, J. M. 1993. "A status-based model of market competition." *American Journal of Sociology*, 98: 829–872.

Powell, W. W. 1985. *Getting into Print: The Decision-making Process in Scholarly Publishing*. Chicago: University of Chicago Press.

——. 1991 "Expanding the scope of institutional analysis." In W. W. Powell and P. J. DiMaggio (eds.), *The New Institutionalism in Organizational Analysis*: 183–203. Chicago: University of Chicago Press.

Rao, H. 1998. "Caveat emptor: The construction of nonprofit consumer watchdog organizations." *American Journal of Sociology*, 103: 912–961.

Rao, H., and K. Sivakumar. 1999. "Institutional sources of boundary-spanning structures: The establishment of investor relations departments in the Fortune 500 industrials." *Organization Science*, 10: 27–42.

Ruef, M., and W. R. Scott. 1998. "A multidimensional model of organizational legitimacy: Hospital survival in changing institutional environments." *Administrative Science Quarterly*, 43: 877–904.

Sax, L. J., et al. 1996. *The American Freshman*. Los Angeles: Higher Education Research Institute.

Schnaiberg, A., and K. A. Gould. 1994. *Environment and Society*. New York: St. Martin's Press.

Schneiberg, M., and E. S. Clemens. 2001. "The typical tools for the job: Research strategies in institutional analysis." In W. W. Powell and D. Jones (eds.), *Bending the Bars of the Iron Cage*. Chicago: University of Chicago Press (forthcoming).

Schwartzman, H. B. 1993. *Ethnography in Organizations*. Newbury Park, CA: Sage.

Scott, W. R. 1965. "Reactions to supervision in a heteronomous professional organization." *Administrative Science Quarterly*, 10: 65–81.

———. 1994. "Conceptualizing organizational fields." In H. Derlien, U. Gerhardt, and F. W. Scharpf (eds.), *Systemrationalität und Partialinteresse*: 203–221. Baden Baden, Germany: Nomos Verlagsgesellschaft.

———. 1995. *Institutions and Organizations*. Newbury Park, CA: Sage.

Scott, W. R., and J. W. Meyer. 1994. *Institutional Environments and Organizations*. Thousand Oaks, CA: Sage.

Scott, W. R., M. Ruef, P. Mendel, and C. Caronna. 2000. *Institutional Change and Healthcare Organizations From Professional Dominance to Managed Care*. Chicago: University of Chicago Press.

Seldman, N. 1986. "The United States recycling movement 1968–1986: A review." Unpublished manuscript, Institute for Local Self-Reliance. Washington, DC.

———. 1995. "Recycling—History in the United States." In A. Bisio and S. Boots (eds.), *Encyclopedia of Energy Technology and the Environment*: 2352–2367. New York: Wiley.

Selznick, P. 1949. *TVA and the Grass Roots*. New York: Harper and Row.

Smith, A. A. 1993. *Campus Ecology*. Los Angeles: Living Planet Press.

Soule, S. A. 1997. "The student divestment movement in the United States and tactical diffusion: The shantytown protest." *Social Forces*, 75: 855–883.

Stinchcombe, A. L. 1965. "Social structure and organizations." In J. G. March (ed.), *Handbook of Organizations*: 142–193. Chicago: Rand McNally.

———. 1983. *Economic Sociology*. New York: Academic Press.

Strang, D., and J. W. Meyer. 1993. "Institutional conditions for diffusion." *Theory and Society*, 22: 487–512.

Strang, D., and S. A. Soule. 1998. "Diffusion in organizations and social movements: From hybrid corn to poison pills."

Annual Review of Sociology, 24: 265–290. Palo Alto, CA: Annual Reviews.

Strang, D., and N. B. Tuma. 1993. "Spatial and temporal heterogeneity in diffusion." *American Journal of Sociology*, 99: 614–639.

Strauss, A. 1987. *Qualitative Analysis for Social Scientists*. New York: Cambridge University Press.

Strauss, B. H. 1995. *The Class of 2000 Report: Environmental Education, Practices, and Activism on Campus*. New York: Nathan Cummings Foundation.

Strong, D. L. 1992. *Recycling in America*. Santa Barbara, CA: ABC-CLIO.

Thompson, J. D. 1967. *Organizations in Action*. New York: McGraw-Hill.

Thornton, P. H., and W. Ocasio. 1999. "Institutional logics and the historical contingency of power in organizations: Executive succession in the higher education publishing industry, 1958–1990." *American Journal of Sociology*, 105: 801–843.

Tierney, J. 1996. "Recycling is garbage." *New York Times*, June 30: 24–29.

Tolbert, P. S. 1985. "Resource dependence and institutional environments: Sources of administrative structure in institutions of higher education." *Administrative Science Quarterly*, 30: 1–13.

Tolbert, P. S., and L. G. Zucker. 1983. "Institutional sources of change in the formal structure of organizations: The diffusion of civil service reform, 1880–1935." *Administrative Science Quarterly*, 28: 22–39.

Weber, M. 1978. *Economy and Society*. Berkeley: University of California Press.

Westphal, J. D., R. Gulati, and S. M. Shortell. 1997. "Customization or conformity? An institutional and network perspective on the content and consequences of TQM adoption." *Administrative Science Quarterly*, 42: 366–394.

Zald, M. N., and M. A. Berger. 1978. "Social movements in organizations: Coup d'etat, insurgency, and mass movements." *American Journal of Sociology*, 83: 823–861.

Part III

Organizations and Environments

The Twenty-First Century

Organization

Chapter 31
The Capitalist Firm in the Twenty-First Century

Emerging Patterns in Western Enterprise

Walter W. Powell

What will the capitalist firm look like as the twenty-first century unfolds? In this chapter, Powell presents his view on what has changed and what is likely to change in the future. Powell suggests that the uncertainty and disruption that marked the global economy in the latter decades of the twentieth century signaled that a fundamental shift in economic organization was occurring. This shift is marked by changes in how work is "organized, structured, and governed," and Powell contends that a new era of decentralized capitalism has arrived. The implications of these changes are just beginning to be realized. Future generations of organizational sociologists will confront a different world than their predecessors.

The past decade was a confusing period for citizens, policymakers, and pundits alike. The pace of economic and technological change appears relentless, but the direction is unfamiliar. Joseph Schumpeter (1934) was one of the first analysts to observe that innovation brings with it the winds of creative destruction, but few were prepared for the gales of the 1990s. Consider just a few of the discordant trends in the U.S. and global economy.

Alongside the tremendous upsurge of startup companies, created in the United States and abroad as well, we see the creation of global giants in a number of key industries. The startups are regaled for their swiftness, their impressive array of new products and services, and their new business practices. But in banking, oil, autos, and telecommunications, we see the making of global corporate behemoths, the product of mergers such as Exxon and Mobil, Travelers Group and Citibank, Vodaphone Group and Air Touch, and Daimler Benz, Chrysler, and Mitsubishi, which are among the largest deals in history. And corporations continue to acquire and grow even as evidence accumulates that the hoped-for synergies and integration are seldom achieved. Moreover; many of the startups continue the founding and acquisition cycle. In the e-commerce field, the dream of many founders has been to grow large enough to be noticed and bought up. Of course, some startups eventually grow large, and companies like America Online, Microsoft, or Cisco Systems have acquired hundreds of other firms along the way.

But which companies represent the old economy and which ones the new? Cisco Systems had only 250 or so employees back in 1989, but by January 2000 it had more than 26,000 and a market capitalization in excess of $320 billion, one of the largest of any company in the world. Cisco is a designer and maker of computer networking equipment, much of which it sells to traditional companies that are developing Internet services. In so doing, Cisco makes the lines between the new and old economy much blurrier. And the growing reshaping of corporate purchasing through business-to-business e-commerce renders the distinction between the old and the new economy even less meaningful.

Are the new-economy companies in computers, wireless communications, electronic commerce, the life sciences, and genomics creating a new industrial transformation or just a phenomenal amount of speculative excess? *Red Herring* magazine and its Web site, one of many new business publications that has grown fatter and fatter with dot-com ads, routinely warns that Internet company valuations are completely unrealistic even as it touts a new company or the latest technological application. Thus the speculative frenzy increases, and even though caution is warranted, people everywhere are afraid of being left out of the game, falling behind as others make their fortunes, and getting stuck in the "old world" as the "new world" companies ascend. People know that most of the new ventures are unrealistic, but the problem is they do not know which ones are and which ones are not.

Wages and employment offer another puzzle. Unemployment is presently at a thirty-year low, but job security appears tenuous to many employees. Despite impressive performance, many U.S. companies continue to revamp jobs and organizational structures as if the economy were in a tailspin. More jobs were lost to downsizing in 1999 than in any previous year during the 1990s.[1] On the upside, nearly twenty-two million new jobs were created in the United States in the 1990s.[2] Some organizations now complain about the lack of corporate loyalty as employers have become buyers in a seller's market, forgetting that it was their practices of downsizing and contracting out that eroded worker loyalty. Consequently, both voluntary and involuntary departures from jobs have increased (Bernhardt et al. 1998; Capelli et al. 1997; Farber 1996; Osterman 1999, ch. 2).

Despite economic growth, productivity gains, and tight labor markets, there is widening income disparity as growth in the incomes of the winners far outpaces the modest wage gains of others. Moreover, the success of the winners is more and more tied to the fluctuations of the stock market. Industry sources estimate that 48 percent of the U.S. population now has money invested in stocks or stock funds, and roughly ten million workers hold equity in their own companies.[3] But for those whose jobs do not offer such opportunities, the gap grows wider. Silicon Valley is the epitome of these contradictions. In Palo Alto, the local mantra in 1999 was that sixty-four millionaires were created daily, and this success drove the cost of housing to stratospheric levels, making it harder and harder for policemen, school teachers, fire fighters, and assistant professors, not to mention administrative or service workers, to be able to afford to live in the valley.

Finally, consider the emerging political resistance that has coalesced against the specter of globalization and international economic integration. The amalgam of left and right that has brought together environmentalists and dockworkers, French farmers and American steelworkers, has highlighted a backlash against economic change. Anxiety and uncertainty are growing at the same time that more newcomers,

from Ireland to Finland to Israel to Bangalore to Taiwan, prosper from the internationalization of production. In sum, economic change has been so rapid and so profound that few seem to understand its dynamics and shape, and much traditional social science is hard pressed to measure its scope and consequence.

The core claim of this chapter is that, behind the confusion and divergent trends of recent years, we can discern the outlines of a fundamental change in the way work is organized, structured, and governed. This transformation, I suggest, is sufficiently far-reaching that looking back from the twenty-first century to the end of the twentieth, many will view the struggles of the 1990s as a disruptive and costly period of adjustment to a new logic of organizing. Just as the shift to the era of the assembly line, vertical integration, and mass production brought with it a great transformation, so will the change to what today we inarticulately term the "new economy" or decentralized capitalism. . . .

Downsizing and Restructuring

Unquestionably, one of the most dramatic changes of the past fifteen years has been the willingness of large corporations to downsize, shedding themselves of thousands of formerly "safe" white-collar employees. Although downsizing was first regarded as a response to the economic downturn of the late 1980s, it continued throughout the 1990s even as the economy surged. And companies that had long histories of employment security joined the trend. For example, back in January of 1996, on the first business day of the new year, AT&T—a highly profitable company that was known for its job security—announced it would layoff forty thousand employees. The Vice President for Human Resources at AT&T, James Meadows, subsequently opined to the *New York Times* (13 February 1996) that

> People need to look at themselves as self-employed, as vendors who come to this company to sell their skills. In AT&T, we have to promote the concept of the whole work force being contingent [i.e., on short-term contract, no promises], though most of our contingent workers are inside our walls. Jobs are being replaced by projects and fields of work, giving rise to a society that is increasingly "jobless but not workless."

In tandem with the downsizing wave has been a rapid increase in various forms of contingent employment. Benner (1996) dubs temporary employees the shock absorbers of the flexible economy. Various forms of contingent employment have grown rapidly (Barker and Christensen 1998; Carnoy, Castells, and Benner 1997). The idea that workers should be employed only when there is immediate need for their services is hardly new, but clearly the use of this practice grew considerably over the 1990s. Just how rapidly is hotly contested and very much contingent on how one defines the employment practice. Does the term include part-time work, self-employment, contract work, home-based work, temporary-help service employment, or a job without long-term security? Regardless of definition, the expansion of such temporary employment firms as Manpower Incorporated is ample proof to many observers that employees are increasingly regarded as another factor in the process of just-in-time production.

There is little doubt that downsizing has exerted a considerable toll on employees and communities. But just how potent a force is it and is the quest for labor-force flexibility the driving force behind organizational change? Despite the headlines, David Gordon (1996, ch. 2) marshals data suggesting that the proportion of managers and supervisors in private nonfarm employment has not shrunk. Moreover, throughout the 1980s, he tells us, the proportion of managerial and administrative employment was more than three times as high in the United States as in Germany and Japan. U.S. management structures, many analysts claimed, were topheavy, flabby, and redundant.

Osterman (1996) concurs with Gordon that managerial ranks are not shrinking rapidly in the United States, but provides a more nuanced picture of changes in the terms of managers' employment prospects. Middle-level managers are experiencing distress from restructuring, he argues. His analyses show a fairly dramatic decrease in rates of management retention, greater than that experienced by blue-collar employees with comparable job tenure (Osterman 1996, 9). In an excellent study of the insurance industry, Elizabeth Scott et al. (1996) finds a substantial flattening of the structure of firms. This "delayering" is accomplished by cutting several levels of middle to lower management, and greatly upgrading and expanding the role of claims adjusters through the use of expert systems and intensive monitoring. In a careful analysis of a nationwide survey of displaced workers, Farber (1996, 33) documents that "older and more educated workers, while continuing to have lower rates of job loss than younger, have seen their rates of job loss increase more than those of other groups." Moreover, he finds that job loss due to position-abolished reasons, as opposed to layoffs or plant closings, has increased, largely among more educated workers. Thus the number of management jobs may not be declining, but job security clearly has lessened.

Similar complications abound concerning contingent employment, and much of the debate turns on what is meant by routine and nonstandard work, and whether labor-market circumstances are voluntary or involuntary.[4] Standard work has long been thought to be continuous, secure, on a preset schedule, and full-time. In return for satisfactory performance and loyalty, the employer provided benefits and abided by government regulations of employment, in particular protection from hazardous conditions and unfair discrimination, and provided some array of benefits for retirement and health care. These benefits in turn are buttressed by government through social security and unemployment insurance. Nonstandard work, which was the most typical form of work probably until the middle of this past century, comes in many guises, ranging from independent contractors (e.g., plumber, storefront lawyer, seamstress, or computer consultant) to part-time shift workers to temporary employees. All such arrangements purportedly involved weak attachment between a worker and a firm.

The basic analytical problem is whether such agreements are voluntary or involuntary, and whether weak attachment is an apt description. Clearly the labor force includes some people who do not choose to seek full-time jobs and others who would prefer them but can find only contingent work. Has the recent surge in downsizing increased the number of people with involuntary contingent work? The available evidence suggests yes, with women and minorities most likely to be rendered worse off by these new circumstances. . . .

We need to be careful, however, that we do not remain fixed on an image of a mythical workplace. Harriet Presser's (1995) work reminds us that the stylized model of the standard workday no longer holds: less than one third of employed Americans over age eighteen worked the "traditional" Monday-through-Friday, nine-to-five workweek in 1991. Consider too that not all temporary work is low wage. Contingent employment now covers every position up to chief executive. Manpower Incorporated placed 750,000 people in temporary jobs in 1995; high-technology was their fastest growing segment. The growth is fueled by a thirst for high-tech specialists whose wages range from $15–50 an hour and who work on short-term projects averaging thirty-six months. Moreover, whose situation is more contingent—an employee who does the same job but over the course of several years sees considerable turnover in her coworkers and supervisors, or an independent contractor or temporary worker with a long-term, stable clientele?

In a poignant series on "The Downsizing of America," the *New York Times* (3–9 March 1996) emphasized the dislocation and sacrifice that has resulted from this profound remaking of employment. In a segment on the job losses accompanying the merger of Chase Manhattan and Chemical Bank, entitled "Farewell, Mother Chase," the reporters described a thirty-five-year-old bank employee who had previously spent several years as an itinerant pianist in New York:

> He never sought security in corporate work, and thus the merger doesn't especially throw him. He has embraced Chase's career assistance and thinks he has sharpened his abilities, become a resilient worker. His background has given him an emphatically 90s outlook on work. "I feel my job is to do the best that I possibly can, but my whole area could look totally different in five years through no fault of Chase. I can't imagine any corporate entity owes anyone a career."
>
> By virtue of his background, Matt Hoffman is perhaps the archetypal corporate man of the future. His introduction to the world of work was a terrain where his paycheck depended on how well he sold himself each day. Nothing was guaranteed past tomorrow.
>
> He has imported that mindset into banking and currently, into Chase, and he has found the fit to be all too perfect. For an odd reality of the new work environment is that the turbulent world of the freelance classical pianist is more like than unlike the world of the corporate

> employee. He, too, has to sell himself every day, and he, too, doesn't know if the gig will be there tomorrow. (*New York Times*, 4 March 1996).

The reporter conceptualized this new form of employment as a game of musical chairs, an aberrant alternative to a steady, life-long job with clear career prospects. But perhaps the fact that working for a bank now resembles the challenges of "gigging" practiced by freelance musicians is no longer aberrant and instead represents a labor practice that is becoming the norm. Sociologists have long studied "craft-based work" in which workers labored on short-term projects and were paid for specific performances (Stinchcombe 1959; Eccles 1981; Faulkner and Anderson 1987—see the review of this literature in Powell 1990, 306–9). But we treated work in such fields as construction and the film industries as exceptions to a more "standard" organizational structure in which jobs and careers were tied to a single organization. I next argue that the set of social arrangements we label a job are fast disappearing as work is being packaged in a different form and the conditions that once gave rise to a career of performing repeated tasks for a single employer are now disappearing.

For now, three observations seem salient. First, if jobs as a way of organizing work are no longer adaptive, then cutting jobs is not necessarily an effective response. Downsizing reduces head count and creates turmoil, but seldom addresses the idea that work no longer needs to be organized into neat packages called jobs. Consequently, downsizing efforts fail to deliver on expectations, often leading to even further cuts, which in turn leave gaps in corporate memory, diminished reputation, and dissatisfied customers. The American Management Association's survey of downsized companies reports few productivity enhancements in the wake of cutbacks and a host of problems; a *Wall Street Journal* cover story dubbed the trend "dumbsizing."[5]

Second, in companies where rapid technological change is commonplace and tightly defined job ladders are not viable, a project-based model for organizing work has evolved. These companies have the advantage of having never developed career structures and management systems that defined work as a steep vertical ladder, hence there are fewer transition costs to a new form of organizing. At Intel, the largest maker of microchips for computers, the corporate hierarchy is so flat that there are few upper positions to vie for. A horizontal employment model makes sense in areas of semiconductors where each new generation of microprocessors requires a different mix of skills. Intel invests more than $120 million a year on training, or nearly $3,000 per worker, with a goal to redeploy employees as fast as a new generation of chips emerges. The expectation is that workers will redeploy themselves, finding new jobs within the company. But if they are not successful, they are out of work.

Third, by holding fast to the idea of work organized around well-defined jobs and lamenting the loss of job security, we neglect to evaluate the range of options necessary in a world in which the focus should be more on employability and less on preserving dead-end jobs. Access to universal health coverage, portable pension plans, and a form of unemployment benefits for independent contractors and contingent workers are much-needed steps in an environment where work is more likely to consist of short-term projects. A focus only on job preservation leaves workers alone to grapple with the risks of the new workplace. In the labor movement there are clear signs of recognition of these new circumstances. The Justice for Janitors campaigns in Silicon Valley reflect the development of new multi-employer collective bargaining strategies. Benner (1996) points to the Alliance of Motion Picture and Television Producers as one collective response to an industry based on flexible production, craft and technical work, and short-term contracts. The alliance takes on administrative functions formerly done by management and protects the income of "members" directly without necessarily protecting their jobs. Similar innovations are underway in the building and garment trades, where new efforts are afoot to respond to the competitive success of the industry as a whole. In sum, we need more creative responses to the fluidity of project-based work, arrangements possibly like guilds for independent contractors that provide opportunities for professional community and learning, as well as financial security.

Globalization

In the minds of many people, global competition costs workers in advanced industrial nations their jobs and contributes to financial uncertainty as capital flows freely around the globe. Citizens and politicians alike contend that foreign competition robs jobs at home. Corporations now locate their activities according to the logic of a global market. Moreover, fickle international financial markets have become the judge and jury of policymaking, and central banks no longer have the capacity to intervene and stabilize currencies. But is global economic interdependence actually responsible for job loss, declining wages, and changes in the organization of work? The evidence is much less compelling than the heated rhetoric suggests.

The great bulk of our trade imbalance is with Japan (about two-fifths of the total trade deficit) and with Western Europe. In both cases, hourly wages in manufacturing are higher than ours, in Japan by 25 percent and in much of Europe by 10 to 15 percent.[6] The sharpest impact of import competition is in manufacturing, but there has not been a steep decline in wages in this sector. In his analysis of wage decline between 1979 and 1994, Gordon (1996, 191) shows that production-worker wages fell most rapidly in mining, construction, transportation, public utilities, and retail trade—sectors not heavily exposed to competition from abroad. Indeed, immigration into the United States may be more responsible than global competition for wage stagnation in these sectors.

Viewed broadly, today's global economy is not even particularly new. Economic historians remind us that the half century before World War I was roughly comparable in economic integration (J. Williamson 1995, 1996; O'Rourke, Taylor, and Williamson 1996). Trade in goods and services is only slightly larger now, as a fraction of gross world product, than it was in 1914. Measured against GDP, United States imports are somewhat bigger now (11 percent) than they were in 1880 (8 percent). But labor mobility was probably higher in the late nineteenth century. Migrants left Europe for Australia and the United States in extraordinary numbers and investment from the "Old World" followed labor into the New. We also forget that a substantial foreign corporate presence in the United States is not novel either. In 1913 the United States pharmaceutical business was largely German-dominated, and Bayer aspirin the most common medicine of the day. On the other hand, there was scant manufacturing located in the less developed world, and product markets were not global in the pre–World War I period.

What is different today, dramatically so, is the speed with which massive amounts of information can be transmitted and received, making it possible to react to shifts in demand faster. And the content of much of what is traded internationally has high value. The fields most influenced by global competition—accounting, banking, computers, construction, consulting, legal services, semiconductors—are high-wage industries. Thus, globalization does not appear to be the chief culprit for wage decline and job loss in the United States. In a survey of the impact of globalization of wages, labor economist Richard Freeman (1995, 30) concluded that "we lack compelling evidence that trade underlies the problem of the less skilled."

Global economic interdependence is fundamental in an altogether novel respect, however. The speed with which information and certain commodities move around the globe reshapes production in powerful ways. A decade or two ago, new pharmaceutical drugs were initially released in the United States and Western Europe, and after a five- to even 10-year period of sales in the home market, they were sold abroad in less developed countries at cost, while newer medicines were released at home. Now there is demand for new medical interventions from all corners of the globe. Similar product life-cycle stories, with different time lines, could be told for such diverse industries as autos, electronics, or movies. Today, development times are vastly speeded up for almost every product, but especially for these regarded as innovative or fashionable. Whether we are talking about a new CD, cell phone, computer, or clothing, consumers in Mexico City, Helsinki, or Singapore want it at the same time. Sun Microsystems offers round-the-clock technical services at a single phone number, drawing on staffers around the globe who electronically hand work off as each shift comes on line. Such changes in demand press firms to recast their internal organization in a manner that stresses speed and learning. And when competition is based on ideas, the costs of creating additional copies of a conceptual product are low. The advantages of selling in many countries are considerable, provided that the firm is first to market.

The traditional multinational firm's strengths were its wealth and concomitant influence and the economies of scale it reaped in global production. But high tariffs, transportation costs, and local politics often necessitated that a multinational firm set up redundant "full-service" operations in most of the countries in which they sold products. Thus the economies of production were greatly offset by costs of administration. In contrast, an emerging focus on faster product development, combined with sensitivity to local tastes, rewards speed rather than sheer size. The model transnational firm today is no longer Coca-Cola, IBM, or Royal Dutch Shell, but Asea Brown Boveri (ABB), the Swiss-Swedish energy and engineering firm, organized as a "constellation" with more than 65 business areas, 1,100 companies, and 4,500 profit centers, coordinated by a corporate staff in Zurich of less than 200 (Taylor 1991; Bartlett and Ghoshal 1993).

In the United States, General Electric has evolved to a radically decentralized organization with thousands of parts connected not by centralized control but by a passionate commitment to organizational learning. Rather than standardization, GE relies on relentless efforts at knowledge transfer, of moving successful organizational practices and processes across highly disparate units. The aim, then, is diversification and local experimentation, complemented by rapid diffusion of new ideas.[7] These radically decentralized corporations are remaking both the geography of production and the administration of large-scale organization.

But ABB or GE are not here, there, and everywhere at once. They do not shift operations from one site to another in search of lower labor costs as do smaller global firms such as Nike. The United Nations Conference on Trade and Development, which keeps a watchful eye on multinational firms, distinguishes between simple and complex integration. The Nike strategy of chasing cheap labor and switching production exemplifies the simple strategy. In contrast, firms like ABB or GE, which pursue the complex strategy, must rethink all of the activities and strategies that multinationals have long pursued. In trying to be both global and local simultaneously, these firms find that region matters more than ever before. To begin with, subsidiaries are no longer regarded as distant back offices, but may have responsibility for global functions or products. Thus, if the Canadian subsidiary masters cost competitiveness best, it is given the reins of that program throughout a firm's global operations. Or if Hewlett Packard decides the office products market is most appealing in Europe, it relocates responsibility for that business unit in France and serves the United States from abroad. In turn, European firms like Glaxo, Thomson, and Unilever migrate to the United States and set up primary operations here. Far from being oblivious to locale and in search only of low-cost labor, most multinationals are reorganizing into complex internal networks that compete with one another.

Region looms large in several other respects as well. Many of the recognized centers of excellence around the world are found in industrial districts—the Prato region in northern Italy for fashion and design, Seattle for software, Japan for electronics miniaturization, Hollywood for filmmaking, to name only a few. Companies in these industries have no choice but to locate in or have access to these centers in order to stay abreast and draw upon the best talent. Finally, most foreign investment still clusters around the home country—Western Europe moves into Eastern Europe, Japan into Southeast Asia, the United States, into Canada, Mexico, and South America. And the huge growth in many service industries, such as health care, day care, financial services, and the like, represent sectors that are not moveable. These fields must locate where the customers are. . . . Thus, despite much popular talk about globalization location still matters a great deal.

Technological Change

Another common explanation for recent workplace changes is that technological innovations have failed to deliver dramatic increases in productivity and instead have replaced workers rather than enlarged their skills. In this respect, 1990 was a watershed year—one in which, according to the U.S. Department of Commerce, capital spending on the information economy (i.e., computers and telecommunications equipment) was greater than on all other aspects of the country's industrial infrastructure (Zuboff 1995, 202). By 1996 the information technology sector—defined as including computing and telecommunications but not semiconductors or electronic games—was the largest industry in the United States, according to Commerce Department data, employing 4.3 million people and generating 6.2 percent of the nation's output.[8] Has there been a related substitution of machines for hands and minds? Chrysler, for example, produced 1.72 million cars in 1995, the same number as in 1988, but with seven thousand fewer workers. Former Secretary of Labor Robert Reich frequently argued that there is a mismatch between the skills Americans have and the skills the economy requires. Wages are falling for various categories of workers, so the argument goes, because they have become technologically obsolete. Obviously, computing capability once viewed as astounding is now trivial. My son's Nintendo 64 runs on a higher performance processor than the original 1976 Cray supercomputer, which was accessible back then only to an elite team of physicists. Surely, then, one answer to why organizations are restructuring is that there is a mismatch between worker skills and organizational needs.

But not so fast. Hasn't the increase in computing power also allowed workers to produce more? Bound and Johnson (1995), two influential proponents of the skills mismatch view, recognize that evidence in favor of the argument that technology has rendered classes of workers obsolete is "largely circumstantial." Perhaps, then, the explanation is not a misfit in worker skills but a disconnect between organizational form and the new technologies. The canonical twentieth-century bureaucracy was designed to meet the business needs of increasing throughput and lowering unit costs. As Alfred Chandler (1962, 1977) has shown in his magisterial studies of the rise of first a functional hierarchy, then a multidivisional structure, the proliferation of mass production entailed a detailed division of labor and the simplification and delegation of administrative tasks. The role of a manager "evolved as guardian of the organization's centralized knowledge base" (Zuboff 1995, 202). Dramatic gains in computing power were initially harnessed to reinforce hierarchical, centrally controlled organizational structures—to watch, control, detect, and duplicate. Managers fought hard to hold onto the information on which their power rested, even as the new information technologies opened up novel possibilities for broad distribution of information. The organization of General Motors in the 1960s was a complicated analog of a mainframe computer. But, as I later argue, the economy today resembles a web, not a hierarchy, and to force technologies that enhance "networking" into a pyramidal form serves only to constrain their effectiveness. If there is a mismatch, then, I contend it is between the capabilities of information technology to handle information and problems whenever and wherever necessary, and the older organizational arrangements that force decisions to be made by a central managerial hierarchy (see also C. Freeman 1994; Zuboff 1995).

The coevolutionary process by which technologies and institutions adapt to one another entails experimentation and learning, therefore it takes time for fundamentally new technologies to be debugged, widely diffused, and become productive. Thus the long-expected gains in productivity from information technology do not flower until older, centralized organizational arrangements are abandoned and new ways of organizing are institutionalized, and until new methods of measuring productivity, which capture gains in speed and innovation, are developed. Consider how slowly we are adjusting to a world in which companies low on physical capital but extraordinarily high on intellectual capital are in ascendance. We still measure the economy with indicators created for a mass production era. Intellectual assets do not appear anywhere on a balance sheet. The ability to generate new discoveries, to make dramatic improvements in design, service, or customization are not easily measured. But we are moving to a regime where the speed at which individuals and organizations learn may prove to be the only sustainable advantage. The evolution and spread of new information technologies that enhance collaborative work hold the possibility for remaking work practices in radical ways (Brynjolfsson et al. 1994). Achieving results from investments in intellectual capital, that is, winning in a learning race, requires new organization arrangements that allow information to flow freely.

A "Winner-Take-All" System?

There is considerable evidence of a growing disparity in income, in which people in the top one-fifth of the income distribution have grown much wealthier, while those in the lowest fifth have become poorer, and those in between have largely failed to keep pace with inflation. Moreover, the real wages of many blue- and pink-collar workers did not increase in tandem with the economy's resurgence in the 1990s. Thus, to many, capitalism has grown both leaner and meaner, exacerbating social inequality. Wall Street investment banker Felix Rohatyn puts the case vividly, arguing that "advanced capitalism" and its harsh and cruel climate "imposes stringent discipline on its participants." "What is occurring," he claims, "is a huge transfer of wealth from lower skilled, middle-class American workers to the owners of capital assets and to a new technological aristocracy with a large element of compensation tied to stock values."[9]

Bennett Harrison (1994) is more direct, arguing that the global economy is increasingly dominated by large firms that have become skilled in "lean production," which utilize cross-border alliances and extensive networks of subcontracting to maximize their advantage. "Dressed in new costumes—and armed with new techniques for combining control over capital allocation, technology, government relations, and the deployment of labor with a dramatic decentralization of the location of actual production—the world's largest companies, their allies, and their suppliers have found a way to remain at the center of the world stage" (Harrison 1994, 12). Dubbing the process "'concentration without centralization," Harrison argues that firms that have mastered global network production have four key components: (1) core-ring structures, typified by the auto industry's lean manufacturing process, in which there is a center of high-paid, high-skill employees and the rest of production is relegated to a lower-paid periphery; (2) new uses of computerized manufacturing and information management to coordinate far-flung activities according to principles of "just-in-time" production; (3) extensive use of subcontracting and strategic alliances, especially across national borders; and (4) attempts by management to elicit more active collaboration on the part of their most expensive-to-replace employees. Harrison is deeply concerned that these practices exacerbate labor market inequality and free firms from oversight and regulation by national governments.

Critics agree that a new and more flexible mode of organizing has been adopted by many capitalist firms, but they maintain that this new form is a concerted effort to differentiate sharply workers and managers with different levels and types of skills. The much-vaunted lean production system, developed by Japanese automakers, "dramatically lowers the amount of high-wage effort needed to produce a product . . . , and it keeps reducing it through continuous incremental improvement" (Womack et al. 1990, 260). In a similar vein, Vallas and Beck's (1996) research on the introduction of programmable control systems and new process technologies in the paper-making industry shows that these innovations undercut the experience of established manual workers and contributed to the hegemony of well-educated engineers as production decisions came to be based on engineering criteria. More broadly, the massive upsurge in reengineering efforts places considerable power in the hands of those who control the relevant software and computer technologies that guide workplace reorganization.

Changes in the design of work, in tandem with growing reliance on outsourcing and contract manufacturing, have indeed altered the landscape of work. Semi-skilled, decent-paying jobs in manufacturing and transportation have fallen sharply, and this decline has been especially devastating for low-skilled African-American men at the end of the employment queue (Bound and Freeman 1992; Kasarda 1995; Wilson 1996). Combined with the shrinkage in the size and clout of organized labor in manufacturing and the overall evaporation of job security, there has been an erosion in the kind of jobs for blue-collar workers that used to provide a steady, reliable income. Employees who have fallen from semi-skilled positions into low-wage and/or temporary jobs find not only that their incomes and benefits have dropped, but that their work conditions have worsened as well. No longer is work predictable and routine. Even those who secure employment find themselves treated like yo-yos, yanked from part-time work to full-time and back, from the day shift to the night shift.

But treating the labor supply like a spigot to be turned on and off as market conditions dictate is by no means unique to the United States. In West European nations, where the greater power of labor unions makes wholesale restructuring less of an option for employers, more and more manufacturing has moved to the model of the "breathing factory," in which work and hours expand to meet rising demand and contract when conditions slacken. The transformation of production to a system that responds much more rapidly to changes in markets is a global phenomenon. Why, then, is growing income-polarization more pronounced in the United States?

The answer turns on a combination of political, institutional, and technological factors. The comparative weakness and decline of the United States labor movement vis-à-vis its relative strength in West European nations (and the broadly diffused system of seniority-based wages in Japan) means that in those industries most affected by economic changes, managers in the United States dominate labor to an extent unprecedented in the latter half of the twentieth century. Moreover, wage inequality is but one key component of overall inequality. The sparseness of the U.S. social safety net— unemployment, retraining, and welfare— and the more general reliance on the private sector rather than on government for health care and pensions means that changes in the private sector exacerbate inequalities.

But there is a reverse side to the structural change that the United States is undergoing. The United States has been in the forefront of economies creating new jobs and making the shift in its industrial structure to a hightech, knowledge-based economy. The very dynamism and flexibility that creates volatility and renders groups of workers less employable also fosters the development of new industries and new companies that spur job growth. In many of these new fields, pay and other benefits are tied directly to company performance, and so successes result in even greater rewards. The very success of the high-tech sector, however, generates inequality by widening the gap between winners and losers, by closing off opportunities to those experienced in the older system and who are unable to make the transition, and by narrowing the points of entry for unskilled workers.

The shift to the so-called "new economy" widens polarization in several other respects as well. There is, clearly, a dramatic difference between the extraordinary success of a relatively small number of employees at a firm like Microsoft, who are millionaires many times over from their gains on stock options, and the larger number of workers left with only low-wage options. Successes at Microsoft or throughout Silicon Valley contribute to a growing winner-take-all ethic (Frank and Cook 1995), in which success creates increasing returns; that is, the capabilities, skills, and experiences of those who have prospered rebound such that they are vastly better positioned and qualified than those left behind. This reinforcing cycle is virtuous for the winners, vicious for the losers. Moreover, an added consequence of this transformation is that labor conflict has been altered. Unlike the traditional antagonisms between management and labor, conflicts generated by new forms of production disperse laterally: between full-time and part-time workers, between insiders and outsiders, and between knowledge workers and the unskilled. But it is wrong, I believe, to argue that the new system is just a kind of decentralized Fordism or a wolf in sheep's clothing. We are undergoing a period of "creative destruction," in which the established practices of one regime are being replaced by new ones. Income polarization is a clear outcome of the turbulent transition from one system to another, but it is not at all clear that these inequalities are a necessary component of the new form. I have argued previously that the contradictory pulls of integration and disintegration, of collaboration and cut-throat competition, are built into the very nature of how network forms of organization grow and develop (Powell 1990). . . .

I turn now to a fuller analysis of this emergent system, beginning at the level of what used to be called a job, moving to the firm, and then industry level. My aim is not a detailed account of all the components; rather I want to stress how jobs are increasingly constituted as projects, firms as networks, and industries as capabilities, and sketch just how interconnected these changes are.

A New Logic of Organizing

New systems of organizing production do not arrive on the scene ready-made and announce their availability. The historian David Hounshell (1984) showed how the model of mass production emerged piecemeal in the United States in the latter half of the nineteenth century, beginning with the use of interchangeable parts in rifles made at the armories. Subsequently, the manufacture of sewing machines and then bicycles, and later meatpacking and beer brewing all played a critical role in the eventual development of the assembly line by Henry Ford. Similarly, what I term a new logic of network production has emerged incrementally, in fits and starts, but is now visible in a variety of guises.

We need a language to describe profound institutional change. The unraveling of the older system of bureaucratic employment in the large firm is now widely recognized, but how do we ascertain whether a new set of understandings about the nature of work and organization has emerged? In their superb study of the transformation of health care in the Bay Area, Scott, Reuf, Mendel, and Caronna (2000, ch. 6) identify a set of factors that are key components of institutional change. Scott et al. (2000) stress the multidimensional nature of organizational change, noting that governance structures, organizing logics, and the key actors involved shift in tandem with one another. They stress that institutional change is both multilevel and discontinuous, involving new mechanisms of governance, as well as new types of actors. Novel meanings are developed to account for behaviors, and new relationships are forged among key participants. A core aspect of strategic management now involves leading and assessing the various probes in which organizations are engaged, as they explore new technologies, new partners, and new markets (Eisenhardt and Brown 1999). Consequently, the boundaries of organizations are redrawn and the status order of fields is remade. Measured against these metrics, it is possible to talk about a new logic of organization. The developments I discuss next are thoroughly multilevel in nature, involving a transformation in the ordering of work at the point of production, a profound change in the linkages among organizations, and a remaking of relations with competitors. These developments are discontinuous, I argue, because there is no clear stopping point in the process and no road back to the previous system. Performance is replacing seniority as the condition of employment. Learning and speed are replacing quantity as the metrics for evaluating organizations. These shifts bring new actors and identities and new business models to the fore, and push aside incumbents. Entrepreneurs, innovators, venture capitalists, IPOs, new products, new search engines, knowledge management, network managers, information technology officers, and the like become the talk of the day.

More concretely, empirical research shows significant change in the boundaries of organizations, most notably in the area of research and development (R&D). A recent National Research Council analysis of trends in industrial R&D reports that the innovation process has undergone a significant transformation in the past decade, a change that is both "substantial" in magnitude and consequential to economic performance (Merrill and Cooper 1999). There are four components of this reorienting of R&D: (1) a shift in the industries and sectors that dominate R&D toward new emerging technologies and nonmanufacturing industries; (2) a change in the time horizons of R&D, with industry focusing more on shorter-term development and relying more on universities for basic research; (3) a change in the organizational structure of R&D, with greater decentralization of research activities and increased reliance on both outsourcing and collaboration among firms, universities, and government laboratories; and (4) changes in the location of R&D, with successful research increasingly dependent on geographic proximity to clusters of related organizations. A companion National Research Council survey of eleven industries, purposefully diverse in character and technology but all resurgent in the 1990s, notes that common to each industry is an increased reliance on such external sources of R&D as universities, consortia, and government laboratories; and greater collaboration with domestic and foreign competitors, as well as customers, in the development of new products and processes (Mowery 1999, 7).

Thus I think it is possible to theorize about a new logic of organizing, the outlines of which we see in three key interrelated developments. One of my goals is to illuminate the connections among these three components and to flesh out how each contributes to an emerging "system."

From Jobs to Projects

For much of the last half of the twentieth century, we took the social arrangements that constituted work as a job largely for granted, forgetting the enormous effort and power it took to organize work into jobs. E. P. Thompson (1971) vividly illustrated the many struggles around the introduction of time clocks into the workplace. Hounshell (1984, 259) captured the dislocation wrought by the innovations of Henry Ford and his far-reaching mechanization of work in this quote from a letter to Ford written by the housewife of an assembly-line worker:

> The chain system you have is a *slave driver! My God!*, Mr. Ford. My husband has come home and thrown himself down and won't eat his supper—so done out! Can't it be remedied? . . . That $5 day is a blessing—a bigger one than you know but *oh* they earn it.

Jobs emerged in the late nineteenth and early twentieth centuries as a way to package work in settings where the same task was done repeatedly. But what we consider as work today is evolving in terms of how it is conducted, and it is changing into short-term projects often performed by teams. Consequently, the future organization of work is likely to be much less frequently honeycombed into a pattern of highly specified jobs. To be sure, jobs always represented rigid solutions to solving tasks. The ubiquitous phrase "that's not my job" captured the reality that formal structures did not fit readily into a field of work. But in the postwar system, new opportunities and new statuses were typically treated as occasions to create more job categories. Efforts at job-rotation or cross-training were responses to the proliferation of job categories, but such efforts were piecemeal when compared with emerging forms of work organization.

Work is more and more commonly organized around a team or work group charged with responsibility for a project. Sabel (1994) terms this process of joint exploration "learning by monitoring." The activities of work teams are coordinated by a process of iterated goal setting. General projects, such as the design of a new car, are initially determined by thorough study of best practices and prospects for competing alternatives. Then broad plans are in turn successively decomposed into tasks for work groups. The goals are subsequently modified as work groups gain experience in executing the required tasks. Through these revisions, changes in the parts lead to modifications in the conception of the whole, and vice versa. The same procedure of monitoring decentralized learning, moreover, allows each party to observe the performance of the other collaborators closely enough to determine whether continued reliance on them, and dedication of resources to the joint projects, are warranted.

This form of production integrates conception and execution, with design and production running on parallel tracks. With concurrent design and development, participants constantly evaluate one another's work. If project groups decide who supplies their inputs, they need not choose the traditional internal unit but instead may turn to outside suppliers if they provide better value. This reconceptualization of work is designed to reduce and expose fixed costs, to make the expenses of all units dependent on their contribution, and to fuse the knowledge housed in different parts of the organization.

In its most naked form, the new system approaches a form of pay for productivity, with little recourse to loyalty or seniority—in essence, a modern variant on the old putting-out system. In a cover story on the new labor concept, *Fortune* magazine (13 June 1994, p. 44) described the changes bluntly:

> There will never be job security. You will be employed by us as long as you add value to the organization, and you are continuously responsible for finding ways to add value. In return, you have the right to demand interesting and important work, the freedom and resources to perform it well, pay that reflects your contribution, and the experience and training needed to be employable here or elsewhere.

These new arrangements are deeply corrosive of the old system of sequential steps, linear design, and vertical integration that provided worker and manager alike with security. Hence workers are increasingly the authors of their own work. These new methods, designed for a world of rapid changes and product customization, utilize technologies to speed product development in a manner that greatly enhances the contribution of frontline technical workers. Employees forced to transfer their talent from project to project, however, also find they can move readily from employer to employer. In these new circumstances, managers constantly fret about the devolution of their control, worrying that project groups may pursue their own interests rather than those of top management. But, then, when the goals are shaped by success in pushing a technology frontier, whose goals are the appropriate ones? Barley and Orr (1997) refer to work groups that specialize in technically skilled, project-based work as "communities of practice," recognizing the extent to which both work and organization structures are increasingly guided by initiative and skill, and signaling that loyalty to a professional or technical community may be stronger than attachment to a firm. This broadened conception of knowledge and the locus of innovation remakes not only work but organizations as well.

Some commentators initially saw in the merging of conception and execution a renaissance of an earlier craft tradition of organizing work. But as Sabel (1994) points out, this imagery does not do justice to the continuous efforts at exploring new possibilities and the subsequent formalizing of these efforts so that they can be perfected and communicated to others. The combination of methods and tasks, that is, the use of benchmarking, various error-detection correcting systems, just-in-time inventory, and very short product cycles involving intricate steps renders it impossible too rely on the older craft system of informal coordination of work. And it is precisely on this point that critics charge that the new system is really just hyper-Fordism, obscured behind participatory language, resulting in more intensive and stressful work (Pollert 1988; Kenney and Florida 1993; Sayer and Walker 1992). Job intensification, these critics assert, does not constitute the remaking of work.

The various criticisms of the new system are on target in several key respects, as I Will soon discuss, but they are wide off the mark in failing to see just how autonomous many work teams are. In terms of the scope of their efforts and responsibilities, Sabel (1994) points out that some teams approximate the effective rights of independent firms. Teams can determine their own internal organization, communicate horizontally within the organization instead of up a hierarchy, and build close relationships with suppliers, sharing information rather than hoarding it. Teams choose, within broad parameters, the necessary tools, services, and inputs needed to execute a task. Teams intensively monitor their own activities, thus in a key respect, they are self-managed. Critics, however, are right when they point out that supervision, responsibility, and even discipline, is often shifted from managers to peers, without any parallel increase in compensation or security. Thus in many situations, workers are asked to do much more without any increase in pay.

My aim is not to resolve whether this new flexibility is liberating or imprisoning; clearly elements of both are present, and which aspect is more potent depends on specific political and social conditions at the workplace. Instead, I want to highlight how sharply the conception of work has changed from a focus on narrow and specific tasks carried out by individuals, constrained by rules and procedures, to a collective effort conducted by teams with diverse skills, working with considerable discretion, judged on results and outcomes. The hallmark of the old was the compartmentalization of jobs; the core features of the new are interdependence and involvement. A key consequence of the remaking of the division of labor is that important tasks no longer need be performed inside the boundaries of the organization. This change remakes not only the organization of work but also the work of organizations.

Flattening of Hierarchies, Spread of Networks

Just as the changed conception of work, as organized around project teams, transforms firms internally, the growing involvement of firms in an intricate latticework of collaborations with "outsiders" blurs the boundaries of the firm, making it difficult to know where the firm ends and where the market or another firm begins. The former step redraws internal lines of authority, while the latter spreads the core activities of the firm across a much wider array of participants, with an attendant loss of centralized control. Astute observers of these developments, such as Richard Rosenbloom and William Spencer (1996), suggest that industrial competition today resembles less a horse race and more a rugby match in which players frequently change uniforms.

Various forms of interorganizational collaboration have grown rapidly in recent years (Hergert and Morris 1988; Hagedoorn 1995; Gomes-Casseres 1996; Doz and Hamel 1998; Mowery and Nelson 1999). So intensive are these partnering efforts that it may be more relevant to regard the interorganizational network as the basic unit of analysis. To be sure, collaboration does not dampen rivalry but instead shifts the playing field to sharp competition among rival networks with fluid membership. But changes inside the large corporation in the United States, and Europe as well, go way beyond simple agreements to pursue research and development in new fields or to pursue joint ventures to tap new markets. The growth of alliances and partnerships entails novel forms of complex collaboration with suppliers, end-users, distributors, and even former competitors.

The motives for the upsurge in collaborations are varied. In one form, they are an effort to reshape the contours of production by relying more on subcontractors, substituting outside procurement for in-house production. The subcontractors work under short time frames, provide considerable variety of designs, spend more on R&D, and deliver higher quality, while the "lead" firm affords reciprocal access through data-sharing and security through longer-term relationships (Helper 1993; Dyer 1996a and b). There is no natural stopping point, however, in this chain of decisions to devolve centralized control. Thus fixing the boundaries of an organization becomes a nearly impossible task, as relationships with suppliers, subcontractors, and even competitors evolve in unexpected ways. As these network ties proliferate and deepen, it becomes more sensible to exercise voice rather than exit. A mutual orientation between parties may be established, based on knowledge that the parties assume each has about the other and upon which they draw in communication and problem solving. Fixed contracts are thus ineffectual, as expectations, rather than being frozen, change as circumstances dictate. At the core, then, of this form of relational contracting are the "entangling strings" of reputation, friendship, and interdependence (Macneil 1995).

A revolution in the organization of supply chains, such that Chrysler can be considered to have formed its own *keiretsu* (Dyer 1996a), is only one facet of the changes underway. Equally strong are efforts to access diverse sources of technological knowledge. Simply put, companies have awakened to the idea that the best sources of ideas are no longer located internally. Access to relevant centers of knowledge is critical when knowledge is developing at a rapid pace. In attending to dispersed sources of knowledge, firms try to enhance their "absorptive capacity" (Cohen and Levinthal 1989, 1990; Powell et al. 1996). A firm with a greater capacity to learn becomes more adept at both internal R&D and external R&D collaboration, thus enabling it to contribute more to a collaboration and to learn more extensively from such participation.

A good portion of sophisticated technical knowledge is tacit in character (Nelson and Winter 1982)—an indissoluble mix of design, process, and expertise. Such information is not easily transferred by license or purchase. Moreover, passive recipients of new knowledge are less likely to appreciate fully its value or be able to respond rapidly. In our research on biotechnology, an industry rife with all manner of interorganizational collaborations, we have argued that learning is closely linked to the conditions under which knowledge is gained (Powell 1996; Powell et al. 1996). Thus regardless of whether collaboration is driven by calculative motives, such as filling in missing pieces of the value chain, or by strategic considerations to gain access to new knowledge, network ties become admission tickets to high-velocity races. Connectivity to an interorganizational network and competence at managing collaborations have become the drivers of the new logic of organizing.

We have shown that centrality in the biotech industry network enhances a firm's reputation and generates access to resources. Firms so positioned attract new employees, participate in more new ventures, and develop deeper experience at collaborating with other parties. Put colloquially, a firm grows by becoming a player; it does not become a player by growing. Growth and financial success result from centrality in industry networks (Powell, Koput, Smith-Doerr 1996; Powell, Koput, Smith-Doerr, and Owen-Smith 1999). And once firms experience initial success, they typically restart the process by pursuing new avenues of collaborative R&D and deepening their ties

to their partners. By developing more multiplex ties with individual partners, either through pursuing multiple collaborations or expanding an existing R&D partnership into clinical development or manufacturing, biotech firms increase the points of contact with their collaborators. When relationships are deepened, greater commitment and more thorough knowledge-sharing follow. Organizations with both multiple and/or multifaceted ties to others typically develop better protocols for the exchange of information and the resolution of disputes (Powell 1998).

This new knowledge-based conception of a firm (Brown and Duguid 1998; Grant 1996; Powell et al. 1996) views organization and networks as the vehicles for producing, synthesizing, and distributing ideas. The core task of both firms and networks is to access sources of knowledge rapidly and turn the "partial, situated insights of individuals and communities" into tangible products (Brown and Duguid 1998). In tandem with this new model for organizing innovation, a dense, transactional infrastructure of lawyers, financiers, and venture capitalists has emerged to facilitate, monitor, and adjudicate network relationships. These professional-service firms have become the "Johnny Appleseeds" and marriage counselors for relational contracting. In law, these firms deal with intellectual property and dispute resolution more than perform litigation. In venture capital, investors provide money, counsel, and managerial experience to early-stage companies. They offer information and advice, monitor performance, arrange connections, and lend enhanced credibility to small firms (Lerner 1995; Black and Gilson 1998; Gompers and Lerner 1999).

Venture capitalists and financiers have become extremely savvy about valuing the worth of different network ties. Indeed, there is experimentation with altogether different financial conceptions of a firm. To wit, an established biotech company may spin off as a separate entity a promising research team in a newly emerging therapeutic area. Were this group to remain inside the existing firm, its steep R&D expenditures would cause the firm's financial picture to look bleak. But by setting the operation up as a separate legal entity, while retaining partial control, the firm enables the new organization to compete for federal research grants, issue stock, attract new investors, and raise capital much as a startup firm would. The established firm is also buffered in terms of legal liability, as the new entity's assets are treated separately if any legal issues arise. In short, these subsidiary spin-offs are a network alternative to the multidivisional firm, with attendant financial and legal advantages. And by holding the subsidiary's "feet to the fire," its activities are closely tied to both the relevant technical communities and the marketplace. The arms-length relational tie means the new entity must succeed on its own, but with considerably more assistance than if it were a stand-alone operation.

Thus we see the growth of interfirm networks driven by a variety of motives and pursued by a diverse array of organizations. Large firms are relying on more nimble, smaller companies for key components or critical R&D. Large firms ally with oilier large firms to take on projects too risky or expensive for one firm to pursue alone. And clusters of small firms collaborate, cohering into a production network to create what no single small entity could on its own. In sum, firms are coming to resemble a network of treaties because these multistranded relationships encourage learning from a broad array of collaborators and promote experimentation with new methods, while at the same time reducing the cost of expensive commitments. These developments do not mean that competition is rendered moot. Instead we find that the success of firms is linked to the nature and depth of their ties to organizations in diverse fields.

Cross-Fertilization Among Industries

At the industry level, one consequence of the blurring of organizational boundaries is increased effort to deploy competence with a key technology or skill across a range of fields. For example, Microsoft builds on its expertise with computer operating systems to sell software, consumer electronics, corporate-information systems, and news broadcasting. Honda employs its skill with power trains to build lawn mowers, motorcycles, and autos. While efforts to leverage skills across industries are hardly new, what is unusual are the evolving patterns of friend and foe: a competitor in one market is often a collaborator in another. As the rules of competition shift (Powell and Smith-Doerr

1994, 385–91), customers become competitors and vice versa. Thus one does not seek to vanquish opponents, but to outrace them.

At times, the growing fertilization across industries seems all too trendy. The fascination of bankers with neural network models and genetic algorithms seems fanciful and far-removed from the world of customer service, mortgages, and currency exchange. But consider the example of Silicon Graphics, ostensibly a company formed to develop computer-aided lasers, in which Defense Department funding for the Star Wars project led to the special effects of the film *Jurassic Park*. Contract work for the Defense Department, NASA, and the CIA enabled Silicon Graphics to develop technology used in medicine to create virtual surgery for medical training purposes, as well as new "intelligent" designs for such manufacturers as Ford, GM, BMW, Volvo, and Boeing. One of the company's biggest successes has come in the entertainment field, with Nintendo, LucasArts, and Time-Warner, where cutting-edge knowledge has been employed to create vivid special effects for video games and movies. Certainly this was not the intended effect of Star Wars funding, but perhaps a former movie-star-turned-President would approve. The idea is simple: leverage distinctive capability across fields. The execution—compete and collaborate with a dazzling array of rivals and partners—is complex indeed. Beneath the interdependencies, however, are a myriad of new and mixed motives—learning, positioning, supply, and distribution, all bundled together in a process of cooperative competition. Again, my aim at this point is not to comment on whether these developments are harmful or positive for consumers or creators. We cannot address these questions adequately until we recognize how radically the units of analysis, the firm and the industry, have changed.

On The Scope of the Network Form: Toward Convergence or Diversity?

The argument as presented thus far has been largely adaptationist: new competitive pressures, along with changed economic conditions and emergent business ideologies, have given rise to new forms of organizing. In our empirical work on interorganizational collaboration, my colleagues and I have attempted to specify the conditions under which network arrangements arise, arguing that the more rapidly knowledge develops, and the more diverse its sources, the more firms will turn to relational contracting and collaboration (Powell et al. 1996). Such contingency-based arguments imply an unusually high freedom of choice, however. I have argued that the origins and development of network forms of organizing seldom reveal a simple causal story (Powell 1990). The immediate causes, to the extent that they can be discerned, reveal a wide variety of reasons for the proliferation of relational contracting practices. Strategic considerations—efforts to access critical resources or to obtain skills that cannot be produced internally—loom large. But so do concerns with cost minimization, speeding up work, and increasing productivity. And in a world of sharper competition, more vigilant investors, and enhanced efforts and ability to measure just about everything, intensive search efforts are triggered to find ways to cut product development times. Given this constant experimentation, new ideas and new models are readily generated.

The reception and diffusion of these new models, however, is a much more complex story. In some cases, the formation of networks anticipates the need for this particular form of exchange; in other situations, there is a slow pattern of development that ultimately justifies the form; and in still other circumstances, networks are a response to the demand for a mode of organizing that resolves exigencies that other forms are ill-equipped to handle. The evolutionary development of network practices is a complicated and contingent process, one that is also tempered by adjustment to social and political conditions. To account for the diffusion of this new logic, I begin at the level of firms and industries, focusing largely on the United States. I offer an initial assessment of where the new logic of organizing has most firmly taken hold, discuss the difficulties faced by established organizations in responding to new challenges and models, and analyze the role of carriers of management practice in the diffusion process. I then briefly mention several counter trends that either delay or retard diffusion. I then turn to the nation-state, and discuss cross-national responses. The central questions are clear: will each nation find its own accommodation to a new logic of organization, modifying alliance capitalism to its own institutional milieu? Or will some nations more rapidly embrace the new form, while others resist such change? Answers to these questions are much contested. I cannot resolve them here; instead I offer several propositions concerning which nations will be more or less receptive to new forms of organizing.

Diffusion Across Firms

There is wide variation across firms and industries on the three dimensions of change identified above. With respect to changes in the nature of jobs, Osterman (1994) reports that many large corporations in the United States have altered their work practices, but just how deeply these changes go is a matter of contention (Applebaum and Batt 1994). In a series of studies of work practices in the mid-90s, Osterman (1999) finds evidence that a range of reforms, including forms of profit-sharing and greater employee involvement, have been adopted by high-performing firms. Similarly, most large firms are now increasingly reliant on subcontractors, strategic alliances, and joint ventures for one or more key business functions, but again the evolutionary consequences of these collaborative activities are not well understood. Finns also differ in their involvement in multiple industries based on the extent to which their key technologies or capabilities can be exploited in different domains. And in regard to all these dimensions, separating cause and consequence is difficult.

But rather than look cross-sectionally among firms and industries, a better measure of the changes underway comes from a longitudinal view that examines changes over time in established organizations, the emergence of a new cohort of firms and industries, and the development and articulation of new ideas and models of business practice. Viewed in this fashion, the three sets of Organizational changes are quite extensive. Consider what is now taught in business schools, recommended by the leading consultancies and discussed by the business press. These carriers of management practices (Engwall 1997) promote a new model of organizing today, one in which compensation is contingent upon performance and competitiveness is crucially dependent upon the development of core competencies and many basic organizational functions are either outsourced or done collaboratively with outsiders. The basic skeleton of a firm is different, too, with a model of a flatter organization, entailing very different relations with employees, now commonplace.

To be sure, what is championed by business schools, the media, and consultants can represent a good deal of hype, showcasing only the latest fashions from the salons of business couture. But this criticism misses the extent to which a new set of ideas and skills have become part of both managers' and employees' tool kits. The skills and knowledge base of relational contracting and project-based work are now part of this repertoire to an unprecedented degree. As those skills spread and become normatively sanctioned-built into a growing institutional infrastructure in universities, consulting firms, the financial community, and law and venture capital firms-a new model of organizing takes root. Consequently, current and future generations of managers are exposed to a very different set of ideas regarding what a firm should look like.

Simultaneously, as the economies of advanced industrial countries undergo a transition from a manufacturing to a service base, a new set of knowledge-intensive industries (in fields such as information technology, software, artificial intelligence, and biotechnology) become the leading-edge sites where these new ideas about organizing are developed, honed, and eventually transferred to other fields. These knowledge-based fields are either populated entirely by newly formed organizations, which are not tethered to older models of organizing, or by established firms undergoing significant-to-radical changes in their modus operandi.

For established firms, change entails considerable costs. The existing mode of organizing was at one time a recipe for success, and so there is both more resistance to new ways of doing things and greater difficulty in creating novel practices than in a new organization built from scratch. As a result, skepticism, bargaining, persuading, and confusion are often the order of the day. To be sure, Ford Motor Company does not come to resemble Dell, or IBM become like Yahoo, or Eli Lilly like Genentech. Measured in those terms, the extent of change in large, established organizations is only piecemeal and incremental. But much more dramatic is the simple fact that the reference groups for large firms have changed fundamentally.

In this respect, established firms now borrow "best practices" from a much broader set of organizations than they did two decades ago. Again, the repertoire of practices and models has shifted. Moreover, the growing reliance of established firms in all industries on outside parties for nearly every stage in the research, design, and production process has become very strong. Indeed, the direction of change in established companies is as much external as internal. Recognizing that when products and competencies change, old skills may become obsolete, firms look externally for new capabilities and utilize outsiders for tasks that cannot be done effectively internally. The destructive part of this form of learning is the calculation by many firms that it takes too long to retrain and redeploy existing employees; it is cheaper and quicker to fire them and hire new ones.

In an important respect, the disposing of employees rather than redeveloping them may represent a contrary trend. In earlier work I stressed the distinction between the "low road" of cheap labor, usage competition, and costcutting, and the "high road" of reconstituting work and skills without rendering the employees the victim (Powell 1990). Outsourcing and subcontracting can represent a double-edged sword: on the one side, a move toward draconian cost-cutting and sweating labor; on the other, a step toward relational contracting in which trust and joint problem-solving are key. In knowledge-intensive fields, we have argued that the latter strategy is essential because the quality of what you learn externally is crucially dependent upon your internal "absorptive capacity" (Powell et al. 1996). If a firm outsources only in search of cheaper costs, it loses the ability to assess the quality of the services it has procured. But knowledge-based industries are only a part, albeit a highly significant one, of the overall economy.

Variation Across Nations

Turning to cross-national comparisons, there are abundant reasons to expect that this new logic of organizing will diffuse globally. On the other hand, compelling rationales are also offered that suggest national-level institutions have a resilient quality that both refracts global competitive pressures and produces divergent responses. (See the essays in Berger and Dore 1996 for both viewpoints). The world of industry does display considerable uniformity because it develops through global connections: finance moves from country to country, firms set up operations in many lands, international organizations set standards, and consultants offer their counsel around the globe. Thus it is very hard to be immune to transnational developments. Yet there clearly are divergent national systems of production, or put differently, diverse models of capitalism. Recent political developments in France highlight these distinctions, with Prime Minister Jospin referring to "Anglo-Saxon" economics as "ultra-capitalism," and arguing that the French prefer security and equality to efficiency. But even as he speaks, French firms such as Renault and Parabis are undergoing extensive restructuring, and the chemical giant Rhône Poulenc's branch, Rhône Poulenc Rorer, is busy helping establish and bankroll a confederation among some thirty-odd competing, small gene-therapy firms in the United States in order to speed the advancement of this technology.

Still, there is abundant empirical evidence that national differences do matter. Research on the diffusion of lean production systems in autos finds important national-level differences in performance (Womack et al. 1990). Various studies of ostensibly successful companies in different nations making similar products with comparable technologies find that the organization of work is carried out in fundamentally different ways (Dore 1973; Maurice et al. 1986; Jaikumar 1986; Streeck 1992). Moreover, taking a very broad view, the advanced industrial nations appear to have distinctive competencies in quite different fields: German firms excel at high-quality engineering, Japanese at electronics and miniaturization, Italian at fashion and design, British at advertising and publishing, U.S. at software, biotechnology, and filmmaking.

These differences point to the importance of national systems of innovation (Porter 1990; Lundvall1992; Nelson 1993; Freeman 1995). These systems provide the broad institutional context for economic organization, building on the influence of national education systems, industrial relations policy, technical and scientific institutions, government policies, and cultural traditions. Posed abstractly, these ensembles of institutional practices cohere in different ways. Thus, as Boyer (1996) suggests, while global

economic pressures may signal common problems and create an impetus for change, economic forces alone do not provide clear clues about the pathways of change or which policies should be altered and which solutions implemented.

To account for the responses of different national systems to growing international economic interdependence, we need to theorize about the diffusion process in a manner that accounts for both receptivity and resistance. Drawing upon Whitley (1994), I offer a first approximation of the interaction of national-level factors and international influences. Consider, as a start, that the industrial democracies vary markedly in terms of their degree of internal institutional cohesion and interdependence. Thus, the more tightly integrated and cohesive the dominant institutions of the home country, the more resistant that nation will be to forms of organizing that are regarded as foreign. Similarly, strong interdependencies among dominant political, financial, labor, and cultural institutions will deter the spread of non-national forms of organizing. Conversely, the likelihood of adopting new models of organizing is increased to the extent that international organizations (be they financial, political, legal, or cultural) dominate national institutions. Moreover, the degree to which national institutions are fragmented rather than interdependent will render a nation more likely to be susceptible to external models. Finally, as I stressed earlier, new and emergent industries are considerably less dependent on traditional forms of organizing. Consequently, the centrality of new industries to national economies will be a critical factor in determining the pace of adoption of new forms of organizing. Thus the speed of industrial change in Finland and Ireland may seem startling, but the dominance there of the new fields of wireless communications and software, respectively, usher in new business models while stimulating rapid growth.

In sum, explaining the diffusion of a new logic of organizing requires understanding how various national-level practices (e.g., the role of financial markets, labor-management relations, and university-industry linkages), mesh with factors in the international system. Since few nations possess an identical combination of institutional practices and cultural legacies, the diffusion of a new mode of organizing is likely to be uneven and partial throughout the industrial democracies. Rather than convergence, I suggest that we will see distinctive strengths and weaknesses as national elements either combine with or fail to articulate key elements of the new model. But such variety is likely to be useful over the long haul, as each national system may flourish or lag under different economic and political circumstances.

Summary and Conclusion

I have argued that a series of changes are well underway in how work is constituted, organizations are structured, and competition is conducted. These changes are responses to different pressures, and stem from experimentation with divergent ideas. But I contend that they are converging to produce a distinctive and novel logic of organizing that is built around project-based work and team organization; flatter, more horizontal organizations that rely on long-term interdependent relations with external parties; and extensive efforts to leverage capabilities across a wide range of activities. One consequence is that the activities of many organizations are now more interdependent, and selection increasingly operates at the network level as rivalry shifts from firm-versus-firm to coalition-versus-collaboration. This system seems to combine the give and take of long-term relational contracting with a short-term focus on results and market discipline. The transition to this new system is rocky, and there are both considerable gains for the winners and steep losses for the losers. At present, it appears the flexibility of the new model is well suited to an era of rapid technological change. Whether the new system will prove adaptive for the long haul, or be as robust as the post–World War II system was for nearly four decades, is not clear. But what is apparent is how rapidly the social technology for organizing work has changed. Our shared understandings about how work and organization are to be carried out now involve fundamentally different recipes than existed previously.

We need, I suggest, to think much more deeply about the social and political consequences of this transformation. Richard Sennett (1998) has argued that there are considerable costs to individuals when attachment and loyalty are replaced by flexibility and constant change. Although he provides evidence mostly from older workers, he shows poignantly that connection to a larger purpose is hard to sustain in a world of projects and perpetual change. We need to ask who has been harmed the most by this transition, and what social policies might ease the burdens of the shift? What kinds of institutional supports—public, private, and civic—are needed both to cushion and sustain new forms of organizing? What actions might push more organizations to follow the high road of continuous learning for their employees rather than the low road of intensified and insecure work? A key transition is underway, and organizations have, in many respects, become much more productive and responsive. We now know a good deal about the organizational consequences of this transformation; but our understanding of its social ramifications is murky. This chapter is an effort to start these conversations by sketching the outline of the new system and arguing that our current thinking has not kept pace.

Notes

1. Reported in "Career Evolution," *The Economist* (29 January 2000): 89–92.

2. Reported in "The Great American Jobs Machine," *The Economist* (15 January 2000): 25.

3. Reported in Carolyn Lochhead, "Old World Discovers New Economy's Money," *San Francisco Chronicle*, 12 December 1999, sec. A1, p. 23.

4. Indeed, estimates of the size of the contingent workforce vary widely. In 1995 the Bureau of Labor Statistics reported that "contingent and alternative" employment represented five percent of the U.S. work force. The National Association of Part-Time and Temporary Employees, taking a very broad view and including full-time workers employed by temporary agencies and permanent part-time workers, estimates that twenty-four percent of the work force is contingent. (Reported in Elena Bianco, "Temporary Workers Gaining Market Share, Statistics Show," *Los Angeles Times*, 31 December 1996, p. A5.) And whatever the "correct" size of the contingent labor force, there has been another key change: many more workers now pass through temporary agencies on their way to permanent jobs.

5. See "Fire and Forget?" *The Economist*, 20 April 1996: 51–52 for discussion of AMA survey; see "Call It Dumbsizing: Why Some Companies Regret Cost-Cutting," *Wall Street Journal*, 14 May 1996, pp. A1, A8.

6. According to the United States Bureau of Labor Statistics, in 1994 dollars, manufacturing employees in the United States averaged $17.10 an hour, $27.31 in Germany, and $21.42 in Japan. The industrial nations with appreciably lower wages than the United States were Canada at $15.68 and the United Kingdom at $13.62 (Gordon, 1996, 29).

7. Remarks of Steve Kerr, Chief Knowledge Officer, General Electric, at "fireside chat," Organization Science Winter Conference, Keystone, Colorado, 12 February 2000.

8. The study, "Cybernation: The Importance of the High-Technology Industry to the American Economy," was reported in Steve Lohr, "Information Technology Field Is Rated Largest U.S. Industry, *New York Times*, 18 November 1997.

9. In a speech entitled "Requiem for a Democrat," delivered at Wake Forest University, 17 March 1995, quoted in Simon Head (1996, 47).

References

Barker, Kathleen, and Kathleen Christensen, eds. 1998. *Contingent Work: Employment Relations in Transition*. Ithaca, N.Y.: ILR Press.

Barley, Stephen L., and Julian E. Orr. 1997. *Between Craft and Science: Technical Work in U.S. Settings*. Ithaca, N.Y.: ILR Press.

Bartlett, Christopher, and Sumantra Ghoshal. 1993. "Beyond the M-Form." *Strategic Management Review* 14: 23–46.

Benner, Chris. 1996. "Shock Absorbers in the Flexible Economy: The Rise of Contingent Employment in Silicon Valley." Manuscript, Department of City and Regional Planning, University of California, Berkeley.

Berger, Suzanne, and Ronald P. Dore, eds. 1996. *National Diversity and Global Capitalism*. Ithaca: Cornell University Press.

Bernhardt, Annette, Martina Morris, Mark Handcock, and March Scott. 1998. "Summary of Findings: Work and Opportunity in the Post-Industrial Labor Market." Report to the Russel Sage and Rockefeler Foundations, New York.

Black, Bernard S., and Ronald J. Gilson. 1998. "Venture Capital and the Structure of Capital Markets." *Journal of Financial Economics* 47:243–77.

Bound, John, and Richard B. Freeman. 1992. "What Went Wrong? The Erosion of the Relative Earnings of Young Black Men in the 1980s." *Quarterly Journal of Economics* 107: 201–333.

Bound, John, and George Johnson. 1995. "What Are the Causes of Rising Wage Inequality in the United States?" Federal Reserve *Bank of New York Economic Policy Review* (January).

Boyer, Robert. 1996. "The Convergence Hypothesis Revisited: Globalization but Still the Century of Nations?" In *National Diversity and Global Capitalism*, edited by Suzanne Berger and Ronald P. Dore. Ithaca: Cornell University Press.

Brown, John Seeley, and Paul Duguid. 1998. "Organizing Knowledge." *California Management Review* 40 (3):90–111.

Brynjolfsson, Erik, Thomas Malone, Vilay Gurbaxani, Ajit Kambil. 1994. "Does Information Technology Lead to Smaller Firms?" *Management Science* 40, 12: 1628–44.

Capelli, Peter, with L. Bassi, H. Katz, D. Knoke, P. Osterman, and M. Useem. 1997. *Change at Work*. New York: Oxford University Press.

Carnoy, Martin, Manuel Castellis, and Chris Benner. 1997. "Labor Markets and Employment Practices in the Age of Inflexibility: A Case Study of Silicon Valley." *International Labor Review* 136(1): 27–48.

Chandler, Alfred A., Jr. 1962. *Strategy and Structure: Chapters in the History of the American Industrial Enterprise*. Cambridge: MIT Press.

Cohen, Wesley, and David Levinthal. 1989. "Innovation and Learning: The Two Faces of R&D." *Economic Journal* 99:569–96.

———. 1990. "Absorptive Capacity: A New Perspective on Learning and Innovation." *Administrative Science Quarterly* 35:128–52.

Dore, Ronald P. 1973. *British Factory Japanese Factory: The Origin of National Diversity in Industrial Relations*. Berkeley: University of California Press.

Doz, Yves L., and Gary Hamel. 1998. *Alliance Advantage: The Art of Creating Value Through Partnering*. Boston: Harvard Business School Press.

Dyer, Jeffrey H. 1996a. "How Chrysler Created an American *Keiretsu*." *Harvard Business Review* (July–August):42–56.

———. 1996b. "Specialized Supplier Newtworks as a Source of Competitive Advantage: Evidence from the Auto Industry." *Strategic Management Journal* 17, 4:271–91.

Eccles, Robert. 1981. "The Quasifirm in the Construction Industry." *Journal of Economic Behavior and Organization* 2: 335–57.

Eisenhardt, Kathleen M., and Shona Brown. 1999. "Patching: Restitching Business Portfolios in Dynamic Markets." *Harvard Business Review* 77:72–82.

Engwall, Lars. 1997. "The Creation of European Management Practice." Research proposal, Department of Business Studies, University of Uppsala, Sweden.

Farber, Henry S. 1996. "The Changing Face of Job Loss in the United States." Working paper 5596, National Bureau of Economic Research.

Faulkner, Robert R., and Andy Anderson. 1987. "Short-Term Projects and Emergency Careers: Evidence from Hollywood." *American Journal of Sociology* 92: 879–909.

Frank, Robert H., and Phillip J. Cook. 1995. *The Winner-Take-All-Society*. New York: Free Press.

Freeman, Christopher. 1994. "The Economics of Technical Change." *Cambridge Journal of Economics* 18: 463–514.

———. 1995. "The National System of Innovation in Historical Perspective." *Cambridge Journal of Economics* 19: 5–24.

Freeman, Richard B. 1995. "Are New York Wages Set in Beijing?" *Journal of Economic Perspectives* 9:15–32.

Gomes-Casseres, Benjamin. 1996. *The Alliance Revolution: The New Shape of Business Rivalry*. Cambridge: Harvard University Press.

Gompers, Paul, and Josh Lerner. 1999. *The Venture Capital Cycle*. Cambridge: MIT Press.

Gordon, David M. 1996. *Fat and Mean: The Corporate Squeeze of Working Americans and the Myth of Managerial Downsizing*. New York: Free Press.

Hagedoorn, John. 1995. "Strategic Technology Partnering during the 1980s." *Research Policy* 24:207–231.

Harrison, Bennett. 1994. *Lean and Mean: The Changing Landscape of Corporate Power in an Age of Flexibility*. New York: Basic Books.

Helper, Susan. 1993. "An Exit-Voice Analysis of Supplier Relations: The Case of the U.S. Automobile Industry." In *The Embedded Firm: On the Socioeconomics of Industrial Networks*, edited by G. Grabher, 141–60. London: Routledge.

Hergert, Michael, and Deigan Morris. 1988. "Trends in International Collaborative Agreements." In *Cooperative Strategies in International Business*, edited by F. Contractor and P. Lorange, 99–109. Lexington, Mass.: Lexington Books.

Hounshell, David. 1984. *From the American System to Mass Production 1900–1932: The Development of Manufacturing Technology in the U.S.* Baltimore: Johns Hopkins University Press.

Jaikumar, Ramchandran. 1986. "Postindustrial Manufacturing." *Harvard Business Review* 64:69–76.

Kassarda, John D. 1995. "Industrial Restructuring and the Changing Location of Jobs." In *State of the Union: America in the 1990s*, vol. 7, edited by Reynolds Farley. New York: Russell Sage Foundation.

Kenney, Martin, and Richard Florida. 1993. *Beyond Mass Production: The Japanese System and Its Transfer to the U.S.* New York: Oxford University Press.

Lerner, Josh. 1995. "Venture Capitalists and the Oversight of Private Firms." *Journal of Finance* 50:301–18.

Lundvall, Bengt-Ake, (ed.). 1992. *National Systems of Innovation: Towards a Theory of Innovation and Interactive Learning*. London: Pinter.

Macneil, Ian. 1995. "Relational Contracts: What We Do and Do Not Know." *Wisconsin Law Review* 3:483–526.

Maurice, Marc, François Sellier, and Jean-Jacques Silvestre. 1986. *The Social Foundations of Industrial Power*. Cambridge: MIT Press.

Merrill, Stephen A., and Ronald S. Cooper. 1999. "Trends in Industrial Research and Development: Evidence from National Data Sources." In *Securing America's Industrial Strength*, edited by National Research Council Board on Science, Technology, and Economic Policy, 99–116. Washington, D.C.: National Academy Press.

Mowery, David C. 1999. "America's Industrial Resurgence?: An Overview." In *U.S. Industry in 2000: Studies in Competitive Performance*, edited by National Research Council Board on Science, Technology, and Economic Policy, 1–16. Washington, D.C.: National Academy Press.

Mowery, David C., and Richard R. Nelson, eds. 1999. *Sources of Industrial Leadership: Studies of Seven Industries*. New York: Cambridge University Press.

Nelson, Richard, ed. 1993. *National Innovation Systems: A Comparative Analysis*. New York: Oxford University Press.

Nelson, Richard, and Sidney G. Winter. 1982. *An Evolutionary Theory of Economic Change*. Cambridge: Harvard University Press.

O'Rourke, Kevin, Alan Taylor, and Jeffrey Williamson. 1996. "Factor Price Convergence in the Late 19th Century." *International Economic Review* 37 (3): 499–530.

Osterman, Paul. 1999. *Securing Prosperity*. Princeton, N.J.: Princeton University Press.

———, ed. 1996. *Broken Ladders: Managerial Careers in the New Economy*. New York: Oxford University Press.

Pollert, Anna. 1988. "The 'Flexible Firm': Fixation or Facts?" *Work, Employment, and Society* 2 (3): 281–316.

Porter, Michael. 1990. *The Competitive Advantage of Nations*. New York: Free Press.

Powell, Walter W. 1990. "Neither Market nor Hierarchy: Network Forms of Organization." In *Research in Organizational Behavior*, edited by Barry Staw and Lawrence L. Cummings, 295–336. Greenwich, Conn.: JAI Press.

———. 1996. "Inter-Organizational Collaboration in the Biotechnology Industry." *Journal of Institutional and Theoretical Economics* 120 (1): 197–215.

———. 1998. "Learning from Collaboration: Knowledge and Networks in the Biotechnology and Pharmaceutical Industries." *California Management Review* 40 (3): 228–40.

Powell, Walter W., Kenneth Koput, and Laurel Smith-Doerr. 1996. "Technological Change and the Locus of Innovation." *Administrative Science Quarterly* 44 (1): 116–45.

Powell, Walter W., and Laurel Smith-Doerr. 1994. "Networks and Economic Life." In *Handbook of Economic Sociology*, edited by N. J. Smelser and R. Swedberg, 368–402. Princeton: Princeton University Press.

Presser, Harriet B. 1995. "Job, Family, and Gender: Determinants of Nonstandard Work Schedules among Employed Americans in 1991." *Demography* 32 (4): 577–98.

Rosenbloom, Richard S., and William J. Spencer. 1996. "The Transformation of Industrial Research." *Issues in Science and Technology* 12 (3): 68–74.

Sabel, Charles F. 1994. "Learning by Monitoring: The Institutions of Economic Development." In *The Handbook of Economic Sociology*, edited by N. J. Smelser and R. Swedberg, 137–65. Princeton, N.J.: Princeton University Press.

Sayer, Andrew, and Richard Walker. 1992. *The New Social Economy: Reworking the Division of Labor*. Cambridge, Mass.: Blackwell.

Schumpeter, Joseph. 1934. *The Theory of Economic Development*. Cambridge: Harvard University Press.

Scott, Elizabeth D., K. C. O'Shaughnessy, and P. Capelli. 1996. "Management Jobs in the Insurance Industry: Organizational Deskilling and Rising Pay Inequity." In *Broken Ladders*, edited by P. Osterman, 124–54. New York: Oxford University Press.

Scott, W. Richard, Martin Reuf, Peter J. Mendel, and Carol Caronna. 2000. *Institutional Change and Health Care Organizations*. Chicago: University of Chicago Press.

Sennett, Richard. 1998. *The Corrosion of Character*. New York: Knopf.

Stinchcombe, Arthur L. 1959. "Bureaucratic and Craft Administration of Production." *Administrative Science Quarterly* 4: 194–208.

Streeck, Wolfgang. 1992. *Social Institutions and Economic Performance*. London: Sage Publications.

Taylor, William. 1991. "The Logic of Global Business: An Interview with ABB's Percy Bavenick." *Harvard Business Review* 69(2): 91–105.

Thompson, E. P. 1971. "Time, Work, and Discipline." *Past and Present* (December): 56–97.

Vallas, Stephen Y., and John P. Beck. 1996. "The Transformation of Work Revisited: The Limits of Flexibility in American Manufacturing." *Social Problems* 43(3): 339–61.

Whitley, Richard. 1994. "The Internationalization of Firms and Markets: Its Significance and Institutional Structuring." *Organization* 1 (1): 101–24.

Williamson, Jeffrey. 1995. "The Evolution of Global Labor Markets since 1830: Background Evidence and Hypotheses." *Explorations in Economic History* 32: 141–196.

Wilson, William Julius. 1996. *When Work Disappears*. New York: Knopf.

Womack, James P., Daniel T. Jones, and Daniel Roos. 1990. *The Machine That Changed the World: The Story of Lean Production*. New York: Harper and Row.

Zuboff, Shoshana. "The Emperor's New Workplace." *Scientific American* 273: 202–204.

Chapter 32
Corporations, Classes, and Social Movements After Managerialism

Gerald F. Davis and
Doug McAdam

The "new economy" is the topic of our final chapter by Gerald Davis and Doug McAdam. Like Powell in the previous chapter, these authors attempt to make sense of recent changes in global economic organization and consider the implications of these changes for society and organizations in the future. Davis and McAdam are not only interested in understanding social change, however, they are also concerned with organizational theory. What kinds of perspectives will be needed to make sense of corporations in the new economy? Davis and McAdam argue that the traditional view of corporations held by organizational scholars is not well-suited to the twenty-first century corporation. They urge us to consider alternative perspectives, including social movement theory.

Introduction

There is widespread agreement among social scientists that the United States is witnessing the emergence of a new economy borne through a 'third industrial revolution'. Aspects of this have been described in terms of a breakdown of the mass-production paradigm, the dissolution of traditional labor market institutions, and the emergence of globally expansive and hyper-vigilant capital markets led by institutional investors. High velocity labor markets coupled with protean production structures create a sense of ongoing flux in the arrangements disciplining economic life. The American system of corporate governance in which these other institutions are embedded has come to be a model for the world, at least in the eyes of some commentators (Useem, 1998). There is also general recognition that the transition to a new economy is accompanied by enormous social dislocation, and policy recommendations range from meliorative (e.g. Reich, 1991) to Malthusian (e.g. Jensen, 1993). The stakes are high, as evidenced by events following the East Asian financial crisis of the late 1990s.

How these changes are implemented—how the new economy comes to have a particular institutional structure—is by rights a central topic on the agenda of economic sociologists, and particularly for theorists of organization. But the broad contours of the new economy undermine efforts to theorize the world in terms of social entities such as 'organizations'. Organization theory imagines society as an urn filled with balls called organizations: a 'high modernist' conception of boundary-maintaining bodies with relatively centralized control (cf. Scott, 1998). Yet economic production increasingly implicates shifting networks of actors and identities that appears more to resemble a vat of polymer goo, in Harrison White's (1992: 4) memorable terminology. In this chapter, we argue that the core problem facing organizational theory is that it uses a vocabulary and ontology rooted in an image of a mass production, managerialist economy that was roughly apt for the 30 years following World War II in the U.S. but has become inapplicable to the current institutional structure of the economy. . . .

What Is New About 'The New Economy'?

Proclamations of epochal shifts deserve skepticism. But there is substantial agreement among social scientists of various stripes that the 'post-industrial' economy in the U.S. is something different from its predecessor, and that this is realized in different ways of organizing production and different ways of organizing ownership. We first discuss these elements for the post-War U.S. economy and then describe recent changes.

The transition from competitive to monopoly capitalism has been amply documented, accomplished over the course of the twentieth century through mergers that consolidated oligopolistic producers with national scope and tall managerial hierarchies. In broad strokes, the post-War U.S. economy was populated by large, vertically integrated mass producers. Employment and economic power were disproportionately concentrated in a few hundred major corporations. By the early 1980s, 55.3% of non-governmental employees worked for the 750 largest U.S. firms, and the 200 largest non-financial corporations accounted for 35% of the assets of all non-financial corporations (Davis, 1994). Large corporations such as these were said to reflect a separation of ownership and control; that is, they were owned by thousands of dispersed and disorganized investors, but controlled by professional managers who attained their positions through bureaucratic processes and owned little of the firm themselves. This situation of 'managerialism' was argued to change the nature of class relations, from a Marxian society-wide conflict of workers vs. owners to a Weberian conflict of workers vs. managers within the enterprise (see Dahrendorf, 1959). Moreover, unshackling professional managers from the demands of organized investors was believed to free them from the strict dictates of profit maximization, enabling a 'soulful corporation' that balanced the interests of various 'stakeholders'.[1] The aptness of this description was challenged (Zeitlin, 1974), but empirical ownership patterns supported it, as few large firms had a single family owning as much as 10% of their stock.

In a society where employment and economic resources are concentrated within a relatively small number of large corporations, making sense of the corporate sector is a central—perhaps the paramount—task for social theory. Charles Perrow writes:

> [T]he appearance of large organizations in the United States makes organizations the key phenomenon of our time, and thus politics, social class, economics, technology, religion, the family, and even social psychology take on the character of dependent variables . . . organizations are the key to society because *large organizations have absorbed society*. They have vacuumed up a good part of what we have always thought of as society, and made organizations, once a part of society, into a surrogate of society (Perrow, 1991: 725–726).

By this account, to explain the structure of society entails explaining the configuration of organizations we have, as the U.S. has become a society of organizations. This synoptic view of social structure made organization theory (the branch of sociology concerned with formal organizations) the queen of the social sciences. The attainments of individuals are shaped by the reward structures and career ladders (Baron, 1984) and birth and death rates (Hannan & Freeman, 1989) of the organizations in which they work; thus, stratification should be a sub-field of organizational sociology. Creating formal organizations becomes the cover charge for participation in politics (Laumann & Knoke, 1987), and those running large organizations become distinctively influential over state policy, particularly when acting in concert with their colleagues (Useem, 1984); thus, political sociology (for the U.S.) can also be subsumed. In *The Sociological Imagination*, C. Wright Mills cast the role of social science as making sense of the intersection of biography and history in social structure. In a society of organizations, organization theory holds the master key to social structure.

But the corporate structures associated with the post-War U.S. economy have been substantially transformed in the past two decades, and with them the prospects for theories of social structure. For the sake of brevity, we emphasize two broad trends. The first is a shift in the social structures of production away from bounded organizations and toward unbounded network forms (what Sabel [1991] calls 'Moebius-strip organizations'). The second is the hyperdevelopment of capital markets and the marginalization of financial intermediaries such as commercial banks.

Early inklings about the changing shape of production structures came from the surprising resurgence of industrial districts in Italy and elsewhere, which—coupled with the superior performance of vertically disintegrated manufacturers in autos compared to American-style firms—came to be characterized as the breakdown of the mass production paradigm (Piore & Sabel, 1984). Organizations oriented to long production runs that made sense in a world of mass markets were disadvantaged when markets were segmented and tastes changed rapidly. Housing all or most steps of production within a single organizational boundary was not an end-state of industrial development. Alternative ways to divide labor among specialist firms, households, and individuals came to prominence.

As Sabel & Zeitlin (1996) put it, "It is as though the prehistoric and imaginary creatures in the industrial bestiary had suddenly come to life," coexisting as a strange pastiche of economic forms. Some (e.g. industrial districts; home working; project work, as in construction or film production; short-run production networks linking small specialist firms, as in the garment industry) had existed for some time or were newly revived. Others were decidedly new. Nike represents one approach: the firm designs and markets sneakers from a base in Oregon but contracts out for virtually all production with East Asian manufacturers. Ingram Micro uses the same production line to assemble computers for archrivals Compaq, IBM, Hewlett-Packard, Apple, and Acer, which it also distributes. A vice president at Hewlett-Packard explained "We own all of the intellectual property; we farm out all of the direct labor. We don't need to screw the motherboard into the metal box and attach the ribbon cable" for the computer to be a Hewlett Packard product. And Volkswagen's facility in Resende, Brazil represents perhaps a first: an assembly plant run almost entirely by multinational subcontractors, referred to as a 'modular consortium'. Units of Rockwell and Cummins from the U.S., Eisenmann from Germany, and Delga from Brazil each have shops along the assembly line, along with suppliers headquartered in Japan and elsewhere; Volkswagen employees perform R&D, marketing, and quality control. The large majority of workers on site work not for VW but for the other multinational participants. Assembly workers are paid one-third what autoworkers in Sao Paulo make; union leaders are reportedly perplexed by the web of employers at Resende. (The perplexity around the relevant bargaining unit was almost certainly part of VW's plan.) Shortly after the Resende plant opened, GM announced plans for a similar mini-car factory in Brazil, to house 20 multinational suppliers in what is seen as a prototype for future manufacturing facilities for appliances, VCRs, and other consumer goods.

If these were mere anomalies, they would hold little interest. But there is systematic evidence of a global proliferation of various network forms, described by Bennett Harrison as "the signal economic experience of our era" (1994: 127). Due in large part to advances in information technology, the basic calculus of the make-or-buy decision has been altered for tasks from payroll to manufacturing to product design, and even down to naming the organization. In effect, almost everything that a firm might do has a ready market comparison in the form of a specialist contractor. The result is that it is difficult to identify what is 'core' to an organization, and thus what needs protection from uncertainty (cf. Thompson, 1967). We have instead global production chains (McMichael, 1996) in which the boundaries around individual firms are provisional and highly permeable. Even basic facts about an organization's identity, such as whether it is a manufacturing or service business, are labile. Sara Lee Corporation, a large and diversified producer of food and clothing, announced plans in September 1997 to effectively abandon being a manufacturer in favor of being a marketer of its various brands, which range from Ball Park Franks to Hanes underwear to Coach leather goods. Its CEO, with the prodding of Wall Street analysts, came to realize that the firm's 'core competence' was not in making things but in managing their promotion and distribution, and thus the firm planned to shed most of its production capacity ('de-verticalize'). The increasing ambiguity around terms like 'manufacturing' and 'service' was reflected in 1995, when Fortune Magazine changed the definition of the Fortune 500 list from the 500 largest manufacturers to the 500 largest businesses overall.

Changes in the social organization of production have profound implications for theory about organizations, understood as boundary-maintaining systems. Network production systems no longer map onto discrete, bounded entities such as organizations, and social structures of production increasingly elude description using the traditional theoretical vocabulary of organizational sociology. But another change is perhaps even more consequential for the nature of social structure. It is the enormous global expansion of capital markets and the changing nature of the intermediaries that operate in them. The renowned 'triumph of markets' is in important ways the triumph of *capital* markets, both as a mechanism to finance (and discipline) corporations and as an outlet for the savings of households. In the United States during the 1990s, the number of public corporations doubled (to over 11,000), the number of mutual funds tripled (to roughly 9,000), and the proportion of households reporting stock ownership reached a historic high of 42% (double the figure of 30 years earlier). With the encouragement of a well-developed venture capital industry, organizations are increasingly founded with an expectation that they will eventually go public, by floating shares on a stock exchange (Black & Gilson, 1997). What has happened, in short, is that financial markets have largely supplanted alternative mechanisms (such as private ownership and bank lending) for channeling savings from households to firms in the U.S. (Davis & Mizruchi, 1999).

The shift from embedded ties to market-based transactions changes the basic nature of corporate decision making. By hypothesis, markets assign prices to financial instruments (stocks and bonds) according to the expected future income associated with their ownership, adjusted for risk. Thus, managers of firms that care about share price will seek to demonstrate their fitness to the capital markets by adhering to the standards of the most substantial market participants (Useem, 1996; cf. Meyer & Rowan, 1977). Demonstrating fitness to a dispersed financial market is rather different from managing interdependencies with exchange partners, as it requires discerning and acting on intersubjectively-held mental models of appropriate practice that are 'out there' in the market (Shiller, 1990). Indicators of fitness range from appointing CEOs of well-regarded firms to the board of directors (Davis & Robbins, 1998) to adopting particular kinds of incentive compensation systems and rationalizing them in appropriate ways (Westphal & Zajac, 1998) to streamlining the mix of industries in which the firm operates (Zuckerman, 1999). The most substantial market participants also prize liquidity, that is, the ability to sell a financial asset at any moment on a market for a known prevailing price. The marketability of a security is aided by the transparency of what it represents, which helps reduce intersubjective uncertainty about its value. Markets favor the overt over the tacit, and accounting rules and corporate strategies are designed to increase this transparency (Useem, 1996).

Who owns the U.S. corporation has changed substantially in the last decades of the 20th century, thus altering the audience for corporate decisions from individual owners to institutions. Financial assets in the U.S. are owned primarily by financial institutions rather than households. Upwards of 60% of the shares of the largest 1000 corporations is owned by institutions (pension funds, mutual funds, banks, insurance companies, and others), and this proportion has been increasing over time. Individuals are the ultimate beneficiaries of this ownership, of course, but decisions about what financial assets to buy and sell are made by professionals trained in financial analytic techniques and rewarded based on tangible measures of the performance of the assets under their management.[2] In other words, the process by which capital is allocated and accumulated in the U.S. is largely in the hands of employees of institutions, not wealthy individuals acting on their own behalf. The last vestige of the human touch in corporate finance—loans made by commercial banks, which must be approved by individuals who are willing to put a price on a loan based on their judgment—has been all but abandoned by large corporations, which can raise money more cheaply through money markets (Davis & Mizruchi, 1999). The implication, again, is that corporate decision making is oriented toward market-based evaluations.

In markets, disparate producers are compelled to make themselves comparable and thereby susceptible to ranking and valuation by buyers (White, 1992). The range of instruments traded on financial markets, and thus the set of competitors for favorable evaluation, has expanded dramatically during the past two decades through the practice of 'securitization' (that is, turning income-producing entities into tradeable securities such as bonds). Since Fannie Mae entered the mortgage-backed securities business in 1981, for instance, this market has expanded from $25 billion to over $4 trillion outstanding. In principle, almost anything that has future income associated with it can be securitized: a financial institution could bundle together a set of home mortgages, student loans, credit card receivables, or other loans it has made, divide them into shares, and sell them. The price of a share would reflect various factors likely to change the flow of income (e.g. changes in interest rates that influence whether individuals payoff mortgages early or default). Cheap computing power and new financial analytic techniques make it possible to place a value on such securities quickly in ways that would have been prohibitively expensive 25 years ago. Variations on this basic theme have become extravagant. In 1997, pop star David Bowie received $55 million for selling 10-year bonds to be paid from the anticipated royalties generated through future album sales. The entire issue was purchased by Prudential Insurance, and a unit of Nomura Securities subsequently established a division to specialize in creating securities backed by future revenues generated by music, publishing, film, and television products. Insurance companies sell 'disaster bonds' that pay attractive returns to their investors unless rare natural disasters (hurricanes; earthquakes) require the insurers to make large payouts to those they insure, in which case bondholders lose some or all of their investment. The large fees associated with underwriting these securities propel frantic innovation on the part of investment banks seeking to securitize anything with a potential income (or loss) associated with it. Again, these securities are generally purchased by institutions, not individuals. Institutions, moreover, have no inherent reason to prefer owning shares in a corporation to owning David Bowie bonds or bundles of Citibank credit card receivables sold as securities: what they own is a financial asset for which the only relevant evaluations concern risk and return. As the range of entities traded as securities expands from home mortgages to insurance claims of the terminally ill to municipal settlements with tobacco companies, corporations (understood as financial entities) face increasingly exacting standards of evaluation by financial markets.

How American corporations organize production and how they are financed have undergone a substantial transition toward decentralization. Social structures of production do not readily map onto the boundaries of formal organizations, and corporations operate in a world of disembedded, universalistic financial markets that discipline how they look and what they do. Further, the financial intermediaries that dominate these markets have little reason to prefer investing in the securities of American corporations to investing in other flavors of securities. To paraphrase Perrow (1991), financial markets are the key to soci-

ety because financial markets have absorbed society. It is organizational strategies and structures that have become the dependent variables.

Prospects and Problems for Theories of Organization in the New Economy

Organization theory is the branch of sociology concerned with formal organizations, typically construed as entities constructed to pursue specific goals. The classic text defines organizations as "assemblages of interacting human beings [that are] the largest assemblages in our society that have anything resembling a central coordinative system . . . [This] marks off the individual organization as a sociological unit comparable in significance to the individual organism in biology" (March & Simon, 1958: 4). In this approach, "it is durable, coherent entities that constitute the legitimate starting points of . . . sociological inquiry" (Emirbayer, 1997: 285). If organizations are taken as basic units of analysis analogous to actors or organisms, the domain of the discipline follows readily. Organization theory studies the origin, structure, persistence, change, and disappearance of organizations, as well as the relations constructed among them and the impacts they have on individuals and the broader society. The basic imagery is of organizations as meaningfully bounded units responding to various pressures prompting adaptation or, failing that, selection.

The difficulty of applying this approach to the new economy will be evident from the previous discussion. What might have made perfect sense in discussions of vertically integrated managerialist firms in the 1960s has come to be nearly irrelevant to the current structure of the corporate sector, as several studies document. We illustrate this with two theories that are considered to be among the crown jewels of the field: resource dependence theory and population ecology. In each case, two problems arise: they can't account for empirical patterns in the nature of American corporations since 1980, and they show little prospect of being able to do so into the future.

Resource Dependence Theory

Resource dependence theory (RDT) builds a general framework for organizations from the base of a very parsimonious theory of exchange and power (Pfeffer & Salancik, 1978; Burt, 1983; see Davis & Powell 1992 for a review of the empirical research). Emerson's well-known approach sees actor A's power over actor B flowing from A's control over resources valued by B. To the extent that B values what A has and can't get it elsewhere, A has power over B and B is dependent on A. The greater B's dependence, the greater its vulnerability to A's whims and the greater the incentive to take steps to reduce the dependence by changing its structural position. RDT applies this approach to making sense of organizations as actors that seek autonomy and avoid uncertainty but are embedded in webs of exchange that create power and dependence relations. The prototype is a firm that relies on a supplier of a specialized input that it can't easily get elsewhere (such as the relation of General Motors to Fisher Body before GM acquired it). The supplier can hold up the buyer by seeking to change the terms of the contract during a crunch period when the buyer is vulnerable. Organizations can respond to this condition either by maintaining alternatives (using more than one supplier of the specialized input), co-opting the supplier (e.g. by placing one of the suppliers executives on the board of directors to cultivate empathy, which GM did with Fisher), or buying the supplier (which GM also eventually did with Fisher). If none of these are possible or sufficient to reduce vulnerability, perhaps because of unavoidable conditions in the industry, organizations seeking to evade dependence will diversify, operating across a number of industries. Diversification across industries reduces the dependence and uncertainty associated with operating in any one.

Organizations thus deploy a repertoire of actions to respond to dependence that form in essence a Guttman scale: the greater the dependence, the more intense the response (from evasion to interlocking to outright merger). Evidence at the industry level appeared to support this account: the greater the uncertainty one industry posed for another, the more likely industry participants were to share directors, and the more likely were mergers between firms in the two in-dustries (Pfeffer & Salancik, 1978). Firm-level analyses purported to show similar effects (Burt, 1983). The problem is that from about 1980 onwards, this approach fails to account for virtually anything that large corporations did. Essentially, there was little variance left to explain. First, mergers and acquisitions by large firms did not map onto 'problematic dependencies'. Between 1986 and 1990, the 500 largest manufacturers in the U.S. (the 'Fortune 500') collectively make roughly 450 acquisitions. Among these firms, only about 5% bought a firm in an industry with significant vertical relations (that is, a potentially substantial buyer or supplier). In other words, vertical integration had largely disappeared in favor of alternatives like contracting out, at least in the manufacturing sector. Unrelated diversification has also all but disappeared as a tactic: only 3% of these firms did more than one unrelated acquisition during the late 1980s, and diversifiers tended not to be the most dependent organizations, but the *least* dependent, like GE and AT&T (Davis, Diekmann & Tinsley, 1994). Conversely, about one-third of these firms sold off some businesses; usually shedding units outside their primary industries in order to focus on a 'core competence' (Galvin, 1994). In other words, very few large corporations engaged in acquisitions to manage their exchange-based dependence.

The same holds true for board interlocks (that is, cases where an executive of one firm serves on the board of directors of another firm). At one point, interlocks were feared as a device for collusion, with competing firms sharing directors in order to maintain a cartel. But since the Clayton Act of 1914 prohibiting such ties, few have appeared, and in 1994 there were no observed cases of competing major manufacturers appointing the same individual to their board. There were also few potentially co-optive interlocks: no more than 5% of large industrial firms had an executive of a firm in a major buyer or supplier industry on the board in 1994 (Davis, 1996). Ties to financial institutions followed the same pattern: among the Fortune 1000 firms in 1999 that were not commercial banks, only about one out of twenty had an interlock created via an executive of a major bank. Moreover, while 25% of firms had an executive serving on a major bank board in 1982, this number had dropped to 16% in 1994 and to under 11% in 1999, as money markets had replaced banks as sources of short-term debt for major corporations (Davis & Mizruchi, 1999).

It is possible that global markets enabled by information technology have reduced the general level of dependence of anyone business on any other, thus mooting the need for the repertoire described by RDT. But it is not the case that organizations don't merge or interlock; it is that they do not do so in the way described by resource dependence theory or for the reasons it hypothesizes. The top executives of major corporations make sense of their actions almost entirely in terms of 'creating shareholder value', and actions that contradict the prevailing theories of how to create shareholder value (such as vertically integrating, or operating in several industries rather than focusing on one) are sanctioned. Strategies once construed as serving the organization's interest in stability are now seen as serving only the interests of the executives who run it. Pfeffer & Salancik (1978: 114) described their organizational rationale for acquisitions: "We will present data which suggest that merger is undertaken to accomplish a restructuring of the organization's interdependence and to achieve stability in the organization's environment, rather than for reasons of profitability or efficiency as has sometimes been suggested." Compare *The Economist's* account for the conglomerate merger wave of the 1960s: "Synergies from diversification did not exist . . . This was a colossal mistake, made by the managers, for the managers" (*The Economist*, 1991: 44). What RDT describes as an empirical regularity driven by the organization's drive to reduce uncertainty is subsequently recognized as a pathology driven by poorly aligned managerial incentive structures.

Notions of power and exchange are certainly still useful, but they get played out in a historical context that conditions how applicable they are. RDT's greatest strength—its topicality—is also its greatest weakness, because the phenomena it meant to explain are by and large absent today. One might argue that an empirical critique focusing on the Fortune 500 is simply sampling an unrepresentative tail of the distribution. But the largest firms historically accounted for such a disproportionate amount of the assets and employment of the manufacturing sector that it matters little whether the findings generalize to the remaining smaller firms.

One might also argue that the problematic dependency that firms seek to manage now comes not from buyers and suppliers but from shareholders. Thus, corporate action is now oriented toward pleasing shareholders. But to the extent that the main motivation of organizational action becomes equivalent to making profits for shareholders, rather than organizational stability and survival then the need for a theory that is not simply the economic theory of the firm is not obvious.

Population Ecology

Much of the weakness of resource dependence theory comes from the fact that it focused on topical actions that were prevalent at the time the approach was being constructed but that subsequently disappeared. Problems with being overly topical are far less of a concern for population ecology, which seeks a general and trans-historical theory of organizations ranging from Finnish newspapers to American labor unions to German breweries to European universities. Ecology follows Perrow's 'society of organizations' thinking to its logical conclusion: if organizations are the basic units of society, then we should be able to explain the structure of society by explaining the demography of organizational forms, much as one would explain the composition of an urn full of balls by counting the number of balls of each size and color that came into or out of the urn. If we are in fact a society of organizations, what explains the proportions we have? Why are there only three U.S. automakers but dozens of hotels in Manhattan? The answer turns on the relative birth and death rates of organizations having these forms—presumably, over time selection processes insure that we end up with the number and proportions of organizations we have now (see Hannan & Freeman, 1989 for a comprehensive account). A crucial assumption of this approach is that organizations don't change in important ways over time: if balls changed colors and sizes after they were dropped into the urn, then counting which ones went in and came out couldn't tell us the composition of the urn. Thus, ecological research focuses primarily on birth and death rates of organizations sharing a form (where 'form' is generally defined by industry rather than detailed information about organizational structure).

Early studies documented that there were liabilities of newness (younger organizations are more likely to fall than older ones) and smallness (small firms fail more often than big ones; see Davis & Powell, 1992 for a review). Subsequent research has explored a pair of empirical regularities called 'density dependence'. The basic finding is that across a wide spectrum of 'populations', there is a curvilinear relation between the number of organizations in existence at any given time and the rates of birth and death of organizations of that type. That is, when there are few organizations in an industry (say, labor unions), the chances that any given one will fail are fairly high, but as more organizations enter the industry, the probability of failure for each of them goes down. After a certain point, however, the effect reverses such that with each new entrant, the probability of failure goes up: Graphically, plotting probability of failure on number of organizations in the population yields a U-curve. The explanation is that there are two competing effects: *legitimacy* (the more organizations sharing a form there are, the greater their legitimacy), which dominates first, and *competition* (the more organizations there are, the less resources available for anyone), which dominates later. The effects are reversed for births: greater density increases birth rates up to a point, after which it decreases them (see Hannan & Carroll, 1992 for a full elaboration).

At first blush, it appears that density dependence conflates causes and consequences: the thing to be explained (the number of organizations of a given type) is explained by the number of organizations of a given type. Of course, when this quantity is on the right-hand side of the equation, it is an indicator (simultaneously) of the constructs of legitimacy and competition, whereas when it is (figuratively) on the left-hand side, it is the construct itself. But the deeper problem is an ontological one: across much of the manufacturing and service economy in the U.S., it simply no longer makes sense to count organizations as meaningful entities that are born and die in a fashion analogous to organisms. In a social world that looks less like an urn filled with balls than a vat of polymer goo, explanation through counting misses the major dynamics of the new economy. Locating boundaries around firms and even industries becomes an increasingly fruitless task.

Biotech and the culture industries provide shopworn examples, but even the large bureaucratic organizations that motivated the initial ecological arguments about structural inertia (see Hannan & Freeman, 1984 on the inertial effects of age and size) prove to be protean when it pleases financial markets. The recent history of the entity formerly known as Westinghouse shows how: a century-old industrial conglomerate that dabbled in media and employed well over 100,000 people, its CEO was forced out by investor pressure in 1993 and replaced with an executive from Pepsi. Within five years, the former Pepsi executive sold off dozens of businesses, bought CBS and other properties, and after initially proposing to split the company in two chose instead to liquidate its remaining industrial operations. On December 1, 1997, Westinghouse ceased to exist, and CBS became the new identity of the remaining corporation, which abandoned its traditional home in Pittsburgh for New York City. Its 1997 revenues and employment were less than half those of 1990, while its profits were more than doubled.

One example that strains the biological metaphor of ecology may not be proof, but the systematic evidence points in the same direction. Between 1980 and 1990, 28% of the Fortune 500 largest American manufacturers were subjected to takeover bids, which were usually 'hostile' (that is, outsiders sought to buy the company against the wishes of its current management) and usually ended up in the sale of the company. A large proportion of these takeovers were motivated by the fact that diversified companies operating across several industries could be bought for far less than one could get for dismembering them and selling off the component parts, which was what usually happened following the sale (Davis et al., 1994). In light of this, those running large corporations began dismembering their own organizations, although not usually as dramatically as Westinghouse. Within a decade, one-third of the largest corporations ceased to exist as independent organizations (almost none through business failure), and those that remained operated in half as many industries on average as they had at the start (Davis et al., 1994). The manufacturing economy of the U.S. was driven to a radical restructuring by financial concerns, through processes bearing no relation to 'birth' and 'death'. This trajectory continued without letup through the first seven years of the 1990s and showed every sign of continuing into the future, as 'creating shareholder value' had become the only acceptable rhetoric for those that run corporate America. The end state of manufacturing organization when capital markets are dominant appears to be hyper-specialization coupled with production through networks (Davis & Robbins, 1999).

There are of course contexts where organizations do seem to be born and die, and the biological imagery still seems apt. When competitors are dividing a fixed pie of demands (e.g. geographically bounded areas with a stable base of consumers, such as day care centers or hotels in a metropolitan area), ecological models apply fairly well (e.g. Baum & Mezias, 1992). But finding those (increasingly rare) contexts where the model applies is like looking for one's lost keys under the streetlight. Organizations that are elements of small-firm production networks may have readily-defined birth and death dates (e.g. the buttonhole sewing specialists that sub-contract work in the New York garment industry), but their life chances are utterly bound up in the production networks of which they are a part (Uzzi, 1997). One could bump up the unit of analysis such that the network itself is the thing that is born and dies. But new networks are born and die with utter predictability as the fashion 'seasons' change. The Procrustean bed of ecological theorizing would thus obscure rather than clarify the dynamics of the industry. . . .

Problems for Conventional Theories of Class

Although we cannot develop the theme at length here, it is worth noting that problems for theories that take organizations as basic units of analysis have analogues in theories of class. Critiques of Marxian class categories appeared in fairly short order after the discovery of a 'managerial revolution' separating ownership and control, and Ralf Dahrendorf stated case most boldly. The post-war economy was dominated by vast mass production organizations owned by dispersed and powerless shareholders and controlled by professional managers who attained their positions through higher education and demonstrated merit. These high-level bureaucrats may clash with the production workers over the exercise of authority, and they may earn stratospheric salaries, but they do not constitute a capitalist class rooted in control of property. "A theory of class based on the division of society into owners and non-owners of means of production loses its analytical value as soon as legal ownership and factual control are separated" (Dahrendorf, 1959: 136). The managerial revolution replaced the fixed boundaries of old classes rooted in property ownership with the mobility of a meritocracy; thus, ". . . the participants, issues, and patterns of conflict have changed, and the pleasing simplicity of Marx's view of society has become a nonsensical construction" (57). There were surely strata based on income, but there were no longer politically meaningful classes whose interactions provided a trajectory to history.

Not everyone was convinced. Even if one conceded the separation of ownership and control, a variety of devices compelled managers to act in the interests of owners (who were often well-hidden wealthy families; Zeitlin, 1974). More importantly, owners and managers were mutually socialized through elite institutions that allowed them to develop and act on common class interests. Research on these institutions sought to document how members of the 'corporate elite' came to form a self-recognized class capable of exercising unique power over government policy. Various mechanisms were argued to make class cohesion more likely, including board interlocks, living in Greenwich, Connecticut, going to Bohemian Grove to network, or forming associations like the Business Roundtable (Useem, 1984).

But the danger of lumping together owners and managers as a common interest group became evident during the 1980s. The advent of the hostile takeover highlighted the fundamentally conflicting interests of those who ran corporations and those who owned them: corporate executives typically ended up stigmatized and unemployed following a successful takeover, while shareholders commonly got 30–50% premiums for selling their shares to those doing the takeover. To defend their turf against errant owners, managers and boards adopted an array of devices to make it difficult to take their firms over, such as 'poison pills' , and 'golden parachutes' to ensure that they were well-compensated if they lost their jobs after a takeover (Davis & Greve, 1997).

Owners protested vigorously the encroachment on their property rights and the potential losses from unconsummated takeovers. Notably, the most vocal owners were not wealthy families but pension funds such as the College Retirement Equities Fund (CREF) and the California Public Employees Retirement System (CalPERS). The ambiguity of the class interests at play in takeovers was highlighted by the rhetoric of the contending parties when managers and owners disagreed on issues of corporate control. When adopting poison pills or lobbying state legislatures for legal protection, corporate managers routinely cited the devastation wrought by hostile takeovers and their obligations to protect employees, communities, and other 'stakeholders' in the corporation. Pension funds were not swayed by such sentimentality and argued—with some success in the policy arena—that their property rights came first (Davis & Thompson, 1994). The period of owner irrelevance described by Dahrendorf had been replaced by owner hegemony. Yet the hegemons are largely pension fund administrators and other fund managers, not elites with inherited wealth. Because the performance of the funds they manage is fairly objective, almost anyone in their positions would articulate the same interests. It takes no special enlightenment for them to recognize the interests associated with their role, or to construct devices for pursuing them. But most importantly, they can in no sense be identified with the corporate executives to whom their funds are entrusted, nor can they be identified with the wealthy individuals who live off the fruits of their own investments. Their class location may be contradictory, but their influence on the course of business is substantial.

Why the Economic Theory of the Firm Is Not Much Help

We have argued thus far that economic activities are not meaningfully bounded within corporations, and pressures from financial markets—both from institutional investors and more disembodied sources—drive the decisions of those who run corporations. Both shifts create problems of relevance for organization theory.

There exists a theoretical approach with a surprising amount of surface relevance for approaching these problems. It is the agency theory or contractarian approach to the corporation, which developed primarily within the school known as law and economics. The approach begins with the assertion that the "separation of ownership and control" described by Berle & Means (1932) cannot have the consequences they attributed to it, that is, managers with substantial discretion to run corporations in ways harmful to investors. Rational investors (principals) would shun corporations without safeguards against self-dealing managers, and thus such corporations would be selected out. Managers (agents) know this and thus create organizational structures that demonstrate their corporations' fitness as an investment vehicle (Easterbrook & Fischel, 1991). Indeed, the structure of the corporation and the institutions in which it is embedded (corporate and securities law; financial markets; the 'market' for takeovers) embody attempts to resolve the divergence of interests between shareholders and managers. Some practices are voluntary adaptations to demonstrate fitness (e.g. appointing a hard-headed former Secretary of State to the board of directors to be a credible watchdog), while others are devices evolved to institutionalize the resolution of conflicts (e.g. corporate law; the takeover market). But understanding institutional resolutions of the inherent conflict between owners and managers is the central agenda of the approach.

The contractarian approach also has an ontological appeal, as it questions the meaningfulness of the boundaries of organizations rather than assuming firms to be bounded units. Initially, this was stated as a critique rooted in methodological individualism (that is, the view that theoretical explanations must ultimately be reducible to the actions of individuals):

> . . . most organizations are simply *legal fictions which serve as a nexus for a set of contracting relationships between individuals.* . . . Viewed in this way, it makes little or no sense to try to distinguish those things which are 'inside' the firm (or any other organization) from those that are 'outside' of it. There is in a very real sense only a multitude of complex relationships (i.e. contracts) between the legal fiction (the firm) and the owners of labor, material and capital inputs and the consumers of output. . . . We seldom fall into the trap of characterizing the wheat or stock market as an individual, but we often make this error by thinking about organizations as if they were persons

with motivations and intentions (Jensen & Meckling 1976: 310–11, emphasis in original).

This view of the organization as nothing but a set of contracting relations matches well with the types of network organizational structures we described previously. In the contemporary economy, "The question is not when is a nexus-of-contracts *a firm*, but when is it more *firm-like*" (Demsetz, 1991). Rather than "assuming an organization," this approach assumes a set of markets instead.

Strong selection pressures from both product and capital markets insure that corporate structures are reasonably efficient, if not optimally so. Thus, the most prevalent institutional features of the corporate economy can be assumed to serve some discernible economic function (Easterbrook & Fischel, 1991). The separation of ownership and control, long regarded as an unavoidable cost of large size, was re-interpreted as an efficient division of labor between those who were good at managing but had little capital and those who didn't know how to manage but were good at owning. Moreover, tile fact that the corporate equivalents of elections are run by management and the board and typically yield nearly unanimous support for the policies of the incumbent board is not a problem but a virtue. The costs to shareholders of gathering the information to vote intelligently are not outweighed by the benefits, and thus "investors in public firms often are ignorant and passive" for good reason (Easterbrook & Fischel, 1991: 11). If the prospective benefit of gathering more information outweighed the cost, someone would do it. Moreover, passive shareholders are protected by a phalanx of mechanisms that protect their investment without their active intervention. Managers compete among themselves to 'add value', and are rewarded appropriately. This competition in the managerial labor market redounds to the benefit of shareholders (Fama, 1980). Managerial labor markets are complemented by director labor markets, where those most vigilant and talented at finding worthy managers to promote are rewarded (Fama & Jensen, 1983). If all else fails, poorly run firms will be punished with low share prices, inviting takeover by more talented managers (a process known as the 'market for corporate control'; Manne, 1965). The end result is that we dwell in the best of all possible worlds, where only fit firms survive a Darwinian competition for capital (see Easterbrook & Fischel, 1991: Chapter 1 for a compact summary).

Recognizing that considerations of corporate finance (how corporations get the money to fund what they do) provide the motor of institutional development is a useful first step in making sense of the governance of American corporations. But it is crucial to recognize that politics and social structures hold the steering wheel. An extensive critique has appeared elsewhere (Davis & Thompson, 1994), but we want to highlight the centrality of 'contentious politics' (McAdam, Tarrow & Tilly, 1996) to the evolution of the corporation.

Even the most basic structural feature of the American corporation—the separation of ownership and control—is best explained by political struggles that resulted in the fragmentation of financial intermediaries. In contrast to banks in other industrialized nations, American banks have been relatively small, weak, and prohibited from intervening in the affairs of corporations. Allowing banks to expand nationally (rather than only within states) and to own shares in corporations would most likely have created institutions with the wherewithal to hold influential stakes in even the largest corporations. But small town bankers (who didn't want the competition), populists (who didn't trust concentrated economic power), and professional managers (who appreciated the autonomy afforded by dispersed shareholders) repeatedly induced legislators to prevent such developments (Roe, 1994).

Political events of the late 1980s caused even the most devoted contractarians to re-evaluate their faith in the efficacy of American corporate governance and in the causal primacy of markets in shaping corporate structures (see Jensen, 1993). The agency approach requires a selection mechanism to ensure that the strong survive and the weak perish, and the favored institution is the so-called market for corporate control. By hypothesis, firms that don't live up to their promise suffer low share prices, giving incentives to more talented managers to buy and rehabilitate these undervalued assets. The existence of predators (corporate raiders) is argued to keep the prey on their toes, while the consequences of allowing firms to avoid deserved takeovers (e.g. by enabling boards to adopt poison pills) are dire. Thus, "Protected by impenetrable takeover defenses, managers and boards are likely to behave in ways detrimental to shareholders . . . The end result, if the process continues unchecked, is likely to be the destruction of the corporation as we know it" (Jensen, 1988: 347). It would be as if gazelles learned how to erect electric fences to keep out the lions. Yet this electric fence scenario happened on a vast scale, as more than 40 states passed laws making it difficult to take over local corporations; in virtually every instance, at the behest of groups of the managers of local corporations, typically making common cause with labor organizations through an impromptu social movement (Davis & Thompson, 1994).

The most contentious case, and also most informative, was the Pennsylvania statute of 1990. In late 1989 the Belzberg brothers, notorious corporate raiders from Canada, threatened Armstrong World Industries with a takeover. Pennsylvania had been hard-hit by takeovers in the 1980s, most notably when Chevron acquired Gulf in 1984, closing Gulf's Pittsburgh headquarters and eliminating thousands of jobs. Thus, there was considerable sympathy when Armstrong's management sought restrictive anti-takeover legislation that would have made it essentially impossible to take over a Pennsylvania firm without seeking its board's approval. As happened in other states, Armstrong was joined by the Pennsylvania Chamber of Commerce and Industry as well as by labor representatives and local public officials in supporting the bill. Faced with such support, the bill sailed through the state Senate with little debate and a final vote of 45–4. However, hearings in the state House mobilized substantial opposition from investors, academic lawyers and economists, newspaper editorialists, and the Chairman of the Securities and Exchange Commission. *Wall Street Journal* editorialists accused the state of 'expropriation'; the *New York Times* stated the law "intimidates legitimate challengers by penalizing them if their buyout offers fail"; and a local attorney stated "The law undermines and erodes free markets and property rights. From this perspective, this is an anti-capitalist law."

Recognizing that they were sure to lose a clash perceived as 'communities vs. markets', the Belzbergs hired The Analysis Group, a consulting organization with academic affiliates, to research and explain the potential impact of the law using economic science. Legislators received a letter denouncing the bill signed by a group of law and economics scholars organized by an Analysis Group affiliate. The Belzbergs successfully ran Michael Jensen (a noted agency theorist at Harvard Business School and Analysis Group affiliate) as a dissident for the Armstrong board. But the most interesting opposition to the law came from institutional investors. Officials of the two major Pennsylvania public pension funds strongly opposed the bill, with the chairman of the Public School Employees' Retirement System labeling it a 'disaster' that would "lower the stock values of Pennsylvania corporations," and other pension funds voicing similar concerns. And in what was perhaps a first, institutional investors threatened a 'capital strike'—that is, to systematically divest ownership in Pennsylvania corporations if the law were to pass.

Legislators, however, were more swayed by local business and labor leaders than by non-local academics and investors, and the bill passed the House 181–11. Researchers attributed a roughly $4 billion loss in the stock market value of Pennsylvania corporations to the bill. And in part as a result of such laws, the prevalence of hostile takeovers declined substantially during the 1990s: whereas there were 83 takeover bids for Fortune 500 firms from 1981–1986 (most hostile), there were 17 from 1991–1996, and only five could be considered hostile (Davis & Robbins, 1999). In short, the gazelles had erected their fence.

The implications of organized contention among management, labor, and capital are many. For the contractarian approach, it is evident that selection regimes are themselves political choices, and that those running corporations can be well-organized and effective in influencing these choices. We can't understand why we have the corporations we do without unpacking the politics. But politics is embedded in social structures that shape whether, when, and how collective action occurs, and how effective it is (Tilly, 1978). It is here that the relevance of social movement theory becomes apparent for the study of the new economy.

Using Social Movement Theory to Understand the New Economy

We have argued that changes in the organization of production and the expanding scale and scope of financial markets create fundamental problems for organization theory as it applies to the contemporary American economy. Approaches such as resource dependence theory and population ecology take organizations to be basic units of analysis. As units, organizations are born, they manage interdependence with other organizations, and eventually they die. Their inner workings and vital rates structure the careers and life chances of their members. Building on this notion, Perrow (1991) envisions a 'society of organizations' in which economy and society consist of (large) organizations. Of course, organization theorists have recognized that treating organizations as bounded units was a form of reification, as organizations rarely encompass their members fully (see Pfeffer & Salancik, 1978: 29–32). Such reification was simply a justifiable cost of doing business as an organization theorist. But we have argued that the imagery of organizations-as-units has finally become more misleading than enlightening, leading one to ask the wrong kinds of questions and use the wrong kinds of mechanisms to make sense of the social structure of the economy. The contractarian approach to the corporation, widely embraced in law and economics, has some appeal but misses essential processes of social change. This is particularly the case when one considers times of economic upheaval, when institutional structures themselves (such as 'selection regimes') are in flux.

The challenge, then, is to find an appropriate theoretical vocabulary to describe and explain the types of economic structures that the new economy has brought us. Making sense of the constitution of new social structures during times of economic and social upheaval is familiar turf for students of social movements. Much of the work has been on the first two industrial revolutions, but there is no obvious reason why the so-called third industrial revolution currently underway cannot be understood using the same tools. The dynamics of episodic collective action, for instance, seem to us to be precisely parallel to those of episodic economic production. Participants are not 'members' bound by inclusion and subject to the authority of a leader, but 'citizens' who may be persuaded to act in concert voluntarily. Thus, the conceptual kit bag of social movement scholars (e.g. mobilizing structures, framing processes, perceived opportunities and threats, repertoires of contention) is equally relevant to an analysis of the emerging forms of economic action. Moreover, the assumptions characteristic of much social movement theory are consistent with the previous critique: boundaries around social units are problematized; interests and grievances are to some degree socially constructed rather than transparent; and the kinds of mobilizing structures are emergent and path dependent. And the questions that arise in understanding social movements are analogous to those concerning new forms of organization: how is collective action coordinated when participation by 'members' is impromptu and impermanent; what are the characteristic routines of collective action likely to be shared by potential participants; and how do pre-existing social structures (such as networks) influence when and where collective action will occur.

We see, in short, a strong analogy between the processes of mobilization for collective action in social movements and in contemporary business organizations. Mayer Zald & Michael Berger (1978) drew a similar parallel over 20 years ago in their pathbreaking analysis of social movements *in* organizations. Our focus is somewhat different: we see much contemporary economic activity as akin to social movements, that is, more-or-less episodic forms of more-or-less coordinated collective action. We argue that contemporary theory about social movements provides constructs and a vocabulary attuned to the types of actions and actors that we have described:

> Actors, in this view, are not neatly-bounded, self-propelling entities with fixed attributes, but concentrations of energy that interact incessantly with surrounding sources of energy, and undergo modifications of their boundaries and attributes as they interact. Actions consist not of self-deliberated emissions of energy but of interactions among sites. Identities do not inhere in fixed attributes of such sites, much less in states of consciousness at those sites, but in representations of interactions and of connections between those sites and the interactions in which they are involved.

Contentious politics does not simply activate pre-existing actors and their fixed attributes, but engages a series of interactive performances that proceed through incessant improvisation within broadly-defined scripts and organizational constraints (Tilly, 1998: 3).

Theories about organizations and social movements share a common agenda of making sense of more-or-less routinized collective action: its sources, structures, and outcomes. Thus, there has been some interchange among these two traditions (see Zald & Berger, 1978; Clemens, 1993; Minkoff, 1997; and particularly Koput, Powell & Smith-Doerr, 1997). To the extent that economic action comes to look like contentious politics, we expect that theory about social moments will be applicable to the traditional domain of organization theory. . . .

The Origins of Social Movements

A fairly strong consensus has emerged among scholars of social movements around the question of how social movements arise. Increasingly, one finds scholars emphasizing the importance of the same broad sets of factors in analyzing the origins of collective action. These three factors are: (1) an expansion in the political opportunities or threats confronting a given challenger; (2) the forms of organization (informal as well as formal) available to insurgents as sites for initial mobilization, and (3) the collective processes of interpretation, attribution and social construction that mediate between opportunity/ threat and action. We will refer to these three factors by their conventional shorthand designations: political opportunities/threats, mobilizing structures, and framing processes.

Expanding Political Opportunities or Threats

Movement scholars have come to believe that under conditions of relative political stability, excluded groups, or challengers, rarely mobilize. Instead movements arise when broader change processes serve to either significantly threaten the interests of challengers or render the existing regime newly vulnerable or receptive to challenger demands. Expansions in political opportunity or threat accompany any broad change process that serves to significantly undermine the calculations and assumptions on which the political status quo rests. Among the events and processes especially likely to destabilize the status quo are wars, rapid industrialization, international political realignments, economic crises of various sorts, and mass migrations or other disruptive demographic processes.

Extant Mobilizing Structures

If destabilizing changes to the structure of institutionalized politics shapes the likelihood of collective action, the influence of such changes is not independent of the various kinds of mobilizing structures through which groups seek to organize and press their claims. The term mobilizing structures refers to those collective vehicles, informal as well as formal, through which people mobilize and engage in collective action. These include groups, formal organizations, and informal networks that comprise the collective building blocks of social movements. The shared assumption among movement scholars is that changes in the system of institutionalized politics only afford challengers the *stimulus* to engage in collective action. It is the organizational vehicles available to the group at the time the opportunity or threat presents itself that conditions its ability to respond to this environmental stimulus. In the absence of such vehicles, the challenger is apt to lack the capacity to act even when motivated to do so.

Framing or other Interpretive Processes

If a combination of opportunity/threat and mobilizing structures affords a potential challenger a certain structural potential for action, they remain, in the absence of one final factor, insufficient to account for emergent collective action. Mediating between opportunity/threat and action are the shared meanings and cultural understandings that people bring to an episode of incipient contention. At a minimum people need to feel aggrieved and/or threatened by some aspect of their life and at least minimally optimistic that, acting collectively, they can redress the problem. Conditioning the presence or absence of these perceptions is that complex of social psychological dynamics—collective attribution, social construction—which David Snow and various of his colleagues (Snow et al., 1986; Snow & Benford, 1988) have referred to as *framing processes*. When the cognitive and affective byproducts of these processes are combined with opportunity/threat and sufficient organization, chances are very good that collective action will develop.

Though there is consensus among movement scholars regarding the basic factors that condition the initial mobilization of a social movement, such a framework does not by itself constitute a dynamic model of movement origins. How these factors combine to trigger initial mobilization and by what intervening mechanisms is less clearly specified in contemporary movement theory. To redress this deficiency, the second author has recently proposed a modified version of this basic framework in which this somewhat static list of factors has been replaced by a set of dynamic relationships which are thought to predict the onset of 'episodes of contention' (McAdam, 1999). This modified framework is sketched in Fig. 32.1.

Figure 32.1 depicts movement emergence as a highly contingent outcome of an ongoing process of interaction involving at least one set of state actors and one challenger. But while McAdam focuses on state-oriented social movements, we think the perspective can be usefully adapted to analyzing emergent innovation within any relatively coherent system of institutionalized power (e.g. an industry, a single firm, etc.). In Fig. 32.2 we have adapted the model to fit the case of innovative economic action within an industry.

Applying Social Movement Theory: Industry Emergence

Figure 32.2 attributes innovative economic action—such as industry emergence—to a highly contingent process in which destabilizing changes (typically exogenous to the field in question) set in motion a

Figure 32.1

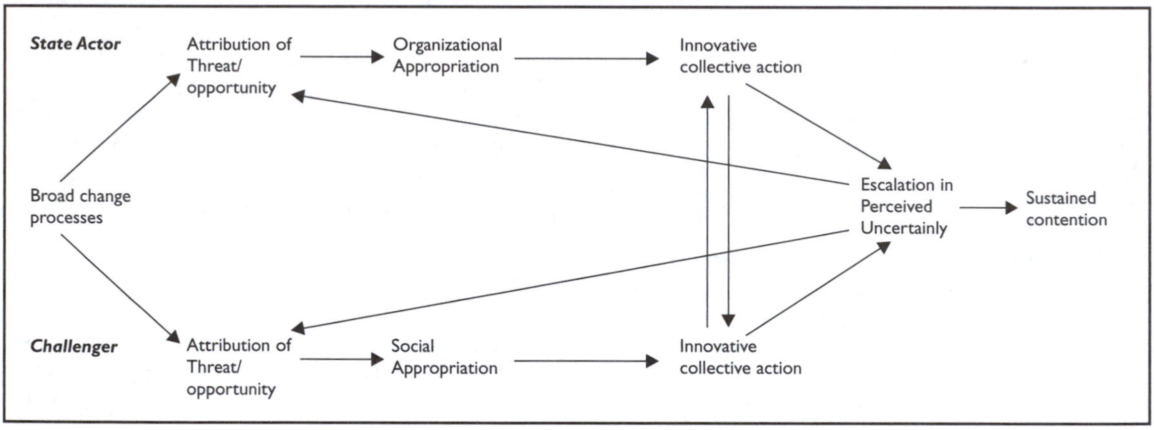

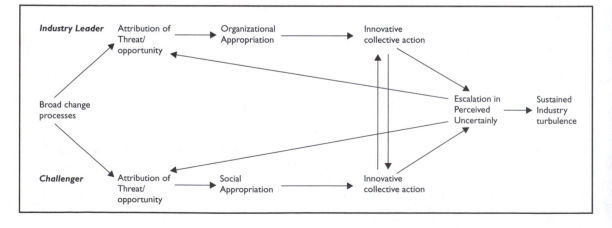

Figure 32.2

sequence of linked mobilization dynamics. The remainder of this section is given over to a discussion of this general sequence. To make the discussion less abstract, we will use a single case—the emergence of the contemporary media industry—to illustrate the more general analytic claims being advanced.

Referring to the media as an industry is something of an act of reification, as some analysts count at least seven separate industries as constituents of the 'communications' industry: television broadcasting, film studios, cable TV, telecommunications, computers, consumer electronics, and publishing (Auletta, 1998). The identities of the core players are remarkably labile, and their web of affiliations is dense and tangled. We mentioned Westinghouse's transformation from old-line industrial conglomerate to broadcaster. GE entered the broadcasting industry via its purchase of NBC, and Disney through its purchase of Capital Cities/ABC. Seagram, the venerable purveyor of alcoholic beverages, became a filmmaker and amusement park operator through its purchase of Universal, and expanded its presence in the music industry through its acquisition of Polygram. Sony expanded from consumer electronics to music and movies. Formerly clear distinctions between industries and media have collapsed as television shows spawn movies (and vice versa), newspapers publish on the World Wide Web, and characters created for movies are merchandised through toys, software, books, fast food, theatrical productions, and other forms of branded merchandise (Disney's film *The Lion King*, for instance, was merchandised through 186 different products and turned into a Broadway show).

What is occurring is the emergence of a global meta-industry out of the confluence of new communication and computing technologies, deregulation in the United States, and privatization elsewhere. The identities and dominance ordering of the core players in the sector are subject to dramatic variations as long-established participants from constituent industries are overshadowed by new challengers, often from previously adjacent industries. To take a shopworn example, the World Wide Web did not exist in 1990 yet has helped spawn a vast outpouring of new businesses and new mini-industries. The market capitalization of Amazon.com,

an on-line bookstore that began operations in 1994, exceeded those of Barnes & Noble and Borders combined four years later. The list of new billion-dollar communications companies is long. Conversely, older players (such as the three broadcast networks) fall further behind as the new economic order takes shape.

Currently there is an inherent and irreducible unpredictability that undermines the calculations of participants tenured under the old regime in the media industry. Figuring out what to do and how to structure oneself in order to succeed appear to hinge more on blind luck than high-level strategizing. Technological advances undermine traditional sources of monopoly power and erode industry boundaries. Television programming can be delivered over phone lines; phone calls can be sent over the Internet; Internet connections can be achieved through television cables; 'cable' programming can be delivered via satellite. Even such basic matters as morphology elude description: an initially helpful parsing of the communications industry into 'channels' (or 'distribution') and 'content' (or 'software') began to lose its analytical value as content providers (such as Disney) integrated into channels and channels (such as Microsoft) integrated into content. There is no settled model of what a 'communications' corporation should look like due to the pervasive uncertainty around the industry, and thus the shifting portfolios of the major participants (chosen from among film studios, newspapers, amusement parks, satellite delivery systems, sports teams, broadcast networks, and so on) represent diverse models of appropriate corporate practice.

Television broadcasting had perhaps the most stable dominance ordering among the constituent industries going into the 1980s. Three incumbents formed an oligopoly capturing upwards of 90% of the total viewing audience, and challengers were peripheral. For these broadcasters, a fundamental exogenous change came with the spread of cable television, which offered alternative means of distribution for 'content', and thus an opportunity for challengers. The rhetoric of challengers seeking to take advantage of this opening at times took on a populist tone: in appearing before Congress in 1976 to seek support for launching a national 'superstation', Ted Turner said:

You have to remember there are three supernetworks . . . that are controlling the way this nation thinks and raking off exorbitant profits . . . They have an absolute, a virtual stranglehold, on what Americans see and think, and I think a lot of times they do not operate in the public good. I came into the independent television station business because I believe there should be more voices heard than the network voices out of New York . . . (quoted in Guthey, 1997: 191).

The threat from cable initially roused little concern from the established broadcasters. The offerings seemed laughable: a 24-hour news channel with no-name anchors and bargain-basement production values; a station that showed promotional videos for rock bands around the clock; an outlet where hawkers sold merchandise via a toll-free number. Within a few years, of course, CNN, MTV, and QVC grew enormously, largely at the expense of the broadcast networks. By 1997, the parents of these three (Time Warner, Viacom, and TCI) each far outstripped the venerable CBS in revenue and influence. Thus, what challengers recognized as opportunities went unrecognized as threats by incumbents until well into the process. By June 1998, more people tuned in to cable programming than the offerings of the four largest broadcast networks combined (CBS, NBC, ABC, and Fox).

How was this upheaval accomplished? The empirical literature documenting the emergence of social movements suggests that movements most commonly arise through the appropriation of existing organizations for new purposes rather than through the founding of entirely new organizations. The most famous instance of this was the transformation of the black church in the South from a generally conservative institution into a key mobilizing structure in the civil rights movement. This required a shift in the churches' missions, from an orientation to the afterlife to a focus on social justice. Similar processes occur in the media, as porous boundaries among communications industries allowed organizations in one industry to launch entries into other industries. Biographies of some of the most successful communications companies demonstrate this organizational 'appropriation'. Rupert Murdoch parlayed a small Australian newspaper that he inherited from his father into the $11 billion News Corpora-

tion, which owns 20th Century Fox, the Fox Network, numerous newspaper, magazine, and book publishers, several sports teams, satellite broadcasting systems covering much of the globe, and interests in over 90 television channels. Ted Turner used his father's billboard business as a vehicle to buy a UHF station that begat the 'superstation', CNN, and other successful cable ventures (see Guthey, 1997 for a critical recounting of the Turner legend). Edgar Bronfman Jr. turned his family business, Seagram, from a purveyor of beverages to a media behemoth through acquisitions and divestitures.

The result of the ongoing re-configuration of the largest media firms has been that organizational boundaries are resolutely tentative, essentially fictions. Where conglomerates have all but disappeared in American manufacturing, deregulation in the U.S. has allowed the construction of global media 'conglomerates' stretching across conventional industry and geographic boundaries. Moreover, because each of the largest participants in the media industry maintain eclectic portfolios of 'channels', 'software', and 'hardware', it is quite common to see corporations that are fierce competitors in one domain creating alliances in another. For example, the film *Titanic* was co-produced by Fox and Viacom's Paramount and spawned a sound track by Sony, a behind-the-scenes book by News Corporation's HarperCollins, and was broadcast on Time Warner's HBO (Rose, 1998). The television series *Buffy, the Vampire Slayer* was produced by News Corporation's Twentieth Century Fox, broadcast on Time Warner's WB, and spawned a sound track CD released by Sony and a series of 'novelizations' published by Viacom's Simon and Schuster. An analyst at Paine-Webber noted that "These companies no longer make films or books. They make brands," lumps of content that can be exploited through a set of their own and other's distribution channels (*The Economist*, May 23 1998). Ken Auletta describes the resulting skein of interconnected communications firms as a 'global keiretsu' of mutual back-scratching (1998: 286). Just as shifting coalitions of movement organizations routinely mobilize to bring off protest actions, the relevant unit of analysis for the media industry is the *project*: a onetime production (broadly defined) created by temporary alliances that may or may not be followed by similar productions, according to circumstance.

Thus, the emergence of the late twentieth century media industry parallels the emergence of a social movement in several important respects. It evolved from a relatively stable configuration of powerful incumbents through a period of turbulence in which challengers took advantage of exogenous shifts in the industry's opportunity structure to launch their alternatives. Challengers, often using organizational vehicles in adjacent industries (billboards, newspaper publishing, film production, and others) ultimately brought about the reshaping of the media industry and the constitution of new rules of engagement rooted in innovation through collaboration. In this way, the media industry came to share important similarities with industrial districts, in which the 'project' rather than the organization is often the more relevant unit of analysis when making sense of episodic production structures.

Routine Movement Activity

In their preoccupation with explaining the rise of broad national movements (Costain, 1992; McAdam, 1999), 'protest cycles' (Tarrow, 1989), or revolutions (Goldstone, 1991; Skocpol, 1979), theorists of social movements could well be accused of focusing on the exceptional, rather than typical, in the study of collective action. Thus, one might argue that technological revolutions of the sort that have transformed the entertainment industry are rare events that are hardly typical of 'normal' economic life. What, critics may ask, about more 'routine' economic activity?

In the contemporary democratic West, the modal form of movement activity looks very different from the broad, highly dramatic, often consequential episodes of national contention that scholars of social movements and revolutions have tended to study. In fact, against the backdrop of these exceptional episodes, one can discern a steady stream of more routine local movement activity. Drawing on recent literature, we briefly sketch an analytic framework for describing this general class of efforts. In our view, such a framework should include a concern with: (a) the nature of local mobilizing structures; (b) the importance of culturally available collective action repertoires; and (c) the typical spurs to local movement activity. We take up each of these topics in turn and then seek to apply them to the study of more routine forms of economic activity.

Local Mobilizing Structures

One of the keys to the emergence of national social movements or revolutions is what we have termed 'social appropriation'. By social appropriation we mean the processes through which previously organized, but non-political groups come to be defined as appropriate sites for mobilization. For example, in the case of the U.S. civil rights movement, it was the mobilization of black churches (and later black colleges) that keyed the movement's rise. But routine local mobilization does not depend upon or generally feature this kind of social appropriation. More often, local movement activity turns on the periodic activation of loose personal networks of 'career activists'. These networks are very likely to have arisen during a peak period of national mobilization of the sort we described in the previous section. But long after that 'protest cycle' has run its course, these loose networks; survive, providing the mobilizing structure within which most local activism gets generated. At times the nominal vehicle through which action gets generated will be a formal social movement organization (SMO), but more often than not these SMOs are little more than 'paper' organizations with few members outside the network of 'career activists' mentioned previously.

This loose activist network is typically well known to city officials and other institutionalized segments of the community. So, for example, left activist networks in the U.S. will generally have fairly strong ties to liberal churches, social service agencies, local unions, and whatever institutions of higher education may exist in a community. Right-wing activist networks are also hooked in to local institutional spheres, but of a very different mix than those of their liberal/left counterparts. Right-wing networks can be expected to have fairly strong ties to conservative churches, veterans groups, and certain kinds of service organizations.

We mention these overlapping network/organizational spheres because they constitute the fields within which most local mobilization takes place. The initial stimulus to action generally arises within the activist networks themselves, with the related organizational spheres providing available pools within which the activists can seek to assemble the 'transitory team' (McCarthy & Zald, 1973) needed to stage whatever march, protest, vigil, petition campaign, or other collective action they have in mind. The contrast with the broad national movements or 'protest cycles' discussed above is stark indeed. Whereas the latter constitute a clear departure from normalcy, the kind of periodic local mobilization we are discussing here is very much 'business as usual', embedded as it is in fairly stable interpersonal/organizational networks and well understood cultural/behavioral routines.

Culturally Available Collective Action Repertoires

A second key element in social movements is what Tilly has (1995a: 41) called the 'repertoire of contention', that is, "the ways that people act together in pursuit of shared interests." Although straightforward sounding, there is an interesting cultural problematic inherent in the selection and application of forms of contention. As Tilly put it back in 1978 (p. 151): "[a]t any point in time, the repertoire of collective actions available to a population is surprisingly limited. Surprisingly, given the innumerable ways in which people could, in principle, deploy their resources in pursuit of common ends. Surprisingly, given the many ways real groups have pursued their own common ends at one time or another." When it comes to real world collective action; the seeming vast variety of action forms turns out to be quite limited. In the final analysis, all groups are constrained in their choice of tactics by the forms of contention culturally available to them. By culturally available we mean two things: (1) that the group has some working knowledge of the form, and (2) that the form enjoys a certain cultural legitimacy within the group. The first of these constraints—what might be termed the informational constraint— has been noted by any number of analysts (Tarrow, 1998; Tilly, 1978, 1995), but the second has been largely absent from writings on the concept of repertoire. But, in our view, illegitimacy constrains as surely as a lack of knowledge (cf. Meyer & Rowan, 1977). Thus, even if a group knows of a tactic and perceives it to be effective, it will avoid using it if it sees it as culturally beyond the pale.

Routine Mobilization of Organized Economic Activity

What do local mobilizing structures and culturally available action repertoires have to do with economic production? We argue that episodic collective action rooted in the social networks of local players and taking the characteristic forms given in the local repertoire describes much contemporary economic activity as practiced in, for instance, Silicon Valley. 'Industrial district' was Alfred Marshall's term for the spatially clustered networks of (mostly small) firms that concentrated on a specific industry or set of related industries. Sheffield had steel, Lyon had silk, and Santa Clara County, California has microelectronics. Industrial districts are distinguished by the fact that geographic boundaries supercede organizational ones in analytical importance. Piore & Sabel (1984: 32) describe the system in Lyon:

> The variability of demand meant that patterns of subcontracting were constantly rearranged. Firms that had underestimated a year's demand would subcontract the overflow to less well situated competitors scrambling to adapt to the market. But the next year the situation might be reversed, with winners in the previous round forced to sell off equipment to last year's losers. Under these circumstances, every employee could become a subcontractor, every subcontractor a manufacturer, every manufacturer an employee.

The ability to size up the character of potential partners was regarded as critical to an individual's (or firm's) success. But perhaps more importantly, the district relied on a set of rules of fair behavior that constrained participants from taking short-term advantage of each other and favored the long-term vitality of the district. Such rules are not laws, and thus are not literally a property of a municipality. But nor are they properties of firms. Rather, they are more like an institution that provides mutual benefits to participants.

Silicon Valley has many characteristics of an industrial district, as described in AnnaLee Saxenian's (1994) book *Regional Advantage*. In the computer industry (broadly construed), rapid changes in technology and markets made it impractical for vertically-integrated firms to maintain a technical edge across all components. Specialist firms have little choice but to keep abreast of their area of specialization, both technically and in terms of price. According to Intel CEO Andy Grove, "Anything that can be done in the vertical way can be done more cheaply by collections of specialist companies organized horizontally" (Saxenian, 1994: 142). Thus, computer firms in the 1980s created collaborative relationships with their most important suppliers, all of which had a mutual interest in the success of the final product. Being located in the same geographical region facilitated frequent face-to-face contact and the development of trust. As in Lyon, the ability to size up potential partners effectively was critical for success. Again, shared understandings of the rules of the game (the local culture) made the construction of production networks feasible. The relatively short lifespan of any given project (e.g. a particular generation of a computer line) implied that partners were likely to meet again on the next round, further bolstering the incentives for consummate cooperation (cf. Axelrod, 1984). "The system's decentralization encourages the pursuit of multiple technical opportunities through spontaneous regroupings of skill, technology, and capital. Its production networks promote a process of collective technological learning that reduces the distinctions between large and small firms and between industries or sectors" and largely dissolves the boundaries between firms (Saxenian, 1994: 9). For instance, in creating Sun's workstations, ". . . it was difficult and somewhat pointless to determine where Sun ended and Weitek or Cypress [two of its suppliers] began. It was more meaningful to describe Sun's workstations as the product of a series of projects performed by a network of specialized firms" (Saxenian, 1994: 145). Nearly any new firm can claim the advantage of state-of-the-art manufacturing simply by 'buying' this function from a contractor, arguably creating a virtuous cycle of innovation.

This project-based dynamic extends even to manufacturing: to a surprising degree, high technology 'manufacturers' contract out much of the actual assembly of their products to firms specializing in manufacturing. Formerly known as 'board stuffers', firms such as Flextronics, SCI Systems, and Solectron do much of the assembly for 'original equipment manufacturers' (sic) such as Hewlett Packard and Sun Microsystems and enable start-ups to grow rapidly by providing a ready manufacturing base. Contractors routinely manufacture products for competing OEMs, but this is seen as having a collective benefit for the larger community as well as individual firms: "All of Solectron's customers benefited from learning that would formerly have been captured only by individual firms. Moreover, lessons learned in manufacturing for firms in one sector were spread to customers in other sectors, stimulating the diffusion of process innovation from industry to industry" (Saxenian, 1994: 154). Considering again Demsetz's question "when is a nexus-of-contracts *more firm like?*," some commentators are driven to ask whether all of Silicon Valley itself (rather than any of its constituent) is properly thought of as a 'firm' (Gilson & Roe, 1993). By Saxenian's account, it is this boundarylessness that is largely responsible for the economic success of Silicon Valley, whereas the bounded firm, mass production culture of Route 128 in Massachusetts is to blame for that region's waning performance in high technology.

The high technology production networks of Silicon Valley might have taken on any number of forms. In practice, however, these networks follow a relatively constrained set of repertoires. As Mark Suchman's work shows, local law firms, particularly Wilson Sonsini Goodrich & Rosati in Palo Alto, acted to compile "pre-processed infusions of relevant know-how." "Such information intermediaries act as interorganizational pollinators—monitoring various pools of constitutive information, determining which structures are 'appropriate' for whom, and compiling summary conclusions in the form of neat, cognitively coherent templates for action" (Suchman, 1998: 49). Law firms acted as veritable computer dating services, matching entrepreneurs, managers, technical talent, and capital suppliers for new ventures from within the broader social network of the Valley. The governance structures of these projects (as indicated by venture capital financing contracts) became increasingly homogeneous over time, particularly within Silicon Valley compared to other locations (Suchman, 1995).

In short, the recurrent mobilization of episodic production through networks of economic 'activists', following locally familiar (and legitimate) repertoires, directly parallels the routine mobilization of sporadic protest events or campaigns by local activists.

Like the production of local movement activity, the origins of routine economic initiative takes the form of routinized, episodic collective action.

Conclusion

The traditional focus in organization theory on corporations as bounded, sovereign, countable units of social structure (Scott's [1998] 'high modernism') is a poor fit with the emerging nature of the new economy. We identified two trends in particular as undermining the applicability of traditional organization theory: the increasingly 'boundaryless' nature of production processes, and the expanding scale and scope of financial markets and the resulting hegemony of their evaluative standards. Our critique of resource dependence theory and population ecology demonstrates the limits of describing the contemporary corporate sector in the United States using the vocabulary of organizations-as-units. Old constructs and mechanisms—such as organizational birth, death, structural inertia, and managing interdependence through mergers and interlocks—provide little explanatory leverage in a world of fluid production structures and hypertrophied financial markets. We also find the new (contractarian) theory of the firm in economics to be remarkably weak in characterizing changes in the American corporate sector. Although there can be little doubt that financial concerns are the North Star of corporate decision making, it is equally evident that the structure and evolution of the corporation result from political choices and social processes that the contractarian approach is ill-equipped to theorize. Making sense of the evolving structures of the new economy requires an approach that does not end with either organizations or markets alone.

We have argued that social movement theory provides an approach that is more fitting for the post-industrial economy. Like contemporary production structures, the boundaries around social movements are fluid, and impromptu productions follow regular processes of mobilization among participants choosing from among culturally familiar and legitimate forms of collective action. We compared the emerging media industry to the emergence of a national social movement, and everyday workings of the network economy of Silicon Valley to the routine mobilization of local movement activity. We found striking parallels. As anticipated by Zald & Berger (1978), forms of coordinated collective action, whether through 'organizations' or 'movements', are ultimately susceptible to the same forms of analysis. As collective economic action becomes increasingly episodic and network based, rather than rooted in, and dependent upon, the traditional practices of the integrated organization, the explanatory balance tilts in favor of social movement theory. . . .

References

Auletta, K. (1998). *The Highwaymen: Warriors of the Information Superhighway.* San Diego: Harcourt Brace.

Axelrod, Robert, M. (1984). *The Evolution of Cooperation.* New York: Basic Books.

Baron, J. N. (1984). Organizational perspectives on stratification. *Annual Review of Sociology* 10, 37–69.

Baum, J. A. C., & Mezias, S. J. (1992). Localized competition and organizational failure in the Manhattan hotel industry, 1898–1990. *Administrative Science Quarterly*, 37, 580–604.

Black, Bernard S., & Gilson, R. J. (1997). Venture capital and the structure of capital markets: Banks versus stock markets. Unpublished, Stanford Law School.

Burt, R. S. (1983) *Corporate Profits and Cooptation: Networks of Market Constraints and Directorate Ties in the American Economy.* New York: Academic.

Clemens, E. S. (1993). Organizational repertoires and institutional change: Women's groups and the transformation of U.S. politics, 1890–1920. *American Journal of Sociology,* 98, 755–798.

Costain, A. W. (1992). *Inviting Women's Rebellion: A Political Process Interpretation of the Women's Movement.* Baltimore: Johns Hopkins Press.

Dahrendorf, Ralf. (1959). *Class and Class Conflict in Industrial Society.* Stanford, CA: Stanford University Press.

Davis, G. F. (1994). The corporate elite and the politics of corporate control. In: C. Prendergast & J. D. Knottnerus (Eds), *Current Perspectives in Social Theory,* Supplement 1, (pp. 245–268). Greenwich, Conn.: JAI Press.

Davis, G. F. (1996). The significance of board interlocks for corporate governance. *Corporate Governance,* 4, 154–159.

Davis, G. F., Diekmann, K. A., & Tinsley, C. H. (1994). The decline and fall of the conglomerate firm in the 1980s: The de-institutionalization of an organizational form. *American Sociological Review,* 59, 547–570.

Davis, G. F., & Greve, H. R. (1997). Corporate elite networks and governance changes in the 1980s. *American Journal of Sociology,* 103, 1–37.

Davis, G. F., & Mizruchi, M. S. (1999). The money center cannot hold: Commercial banks in the U.S. system of corporate governance. *Administrative Science Quarterly,* 44, 215–259.

Davis, G. F., & Powell, W. W. (1992). Organization-environment relations. In: M. D. Dunnette & L. M. Hough, (Eds), *Handbook of Industrial and Organizational Psychology,* (2nd ed.), 3, (pp. 315–375). Palo Alto, Cal.: Consulting Psychologists Press.

Davis, G. F., & Robbins, G. E. (1999). The fate of the conglomerate firm in the United States. In: W. W. Powell, & D. L. Jones (Eds), *How Institutions Change.* (Forthcoming, University of Chicago Press).

Davis, G. F., & Thompson, T. A. (1994). A social movement perspective on corporate control. *Administrative Science Quarterly,* 39, 141–173.

Davis, G. F., & M. Useem. (1999). Top management, company directors, and corporate control. In: A. Pettigrew, H.

Thomas, & R. Whittington (Eds), *Handbook of Strategy and Management* (forthcoming, Sage).

Demsetz, H. (1991). The theory of the firm revisited. In: O. E. Williamson, & S. G. Winter (Eds.), *The Nature of the Firm: Origins, Evolution, and Development* (pp. 159–78). New York: Oxford University.

Easterbrook, F. H., & Fischel, D. R. (1991). *The Economic Structure of Corporate Law.* Cambridge, MA: Harvard University Press.

Emirbayer, M. (1997). Manifesto for a relational sociology. *American Journal of Sociology, 103, 281–317.*

Fama, E. (1980). Agency problems and the theory of the firm. *Journal of Political Economy, 88, 288–307.*

Fligstein, N. (1990). *The Transformation of Corporate Control.* Cambridge, Mass. Harvard University Press.

Galvin, T. (1994). Social influences on restructuring activity. Unpublished, Northwestern University.

Gilson, R. J., & Roe, M. J. (1993). Understanding the Japanese keiretsu: Overlaps between corporate governance and industrial organization. *Yale Law Journal, 102, 871–906.*

Goldstone, J. (1991). *Revolution and Rebellion in the Early Modern World.* Berkeley: University of California Press.

Gould, R. (1993). Collective action and network structure. *American Sociological Review, 58, 182–96.*

Gould, R. (1995). *Insurgent Identities: Class, Community, and Protest in Paris from 1848 to the Commune.* Chicago: University of Chicago Press.

Guthey, E. (1997). Ted Turner's media legend and the transformation of corporate liberalism. *Business and Economic History, 26, 184–199.*

Hannan, M. T., & Carroll, G. R. (1992). *Dynamics of Organizational Populations: Density, Legitimation, and Competition.* New York: Oxford University Press.

Hannan, M. T., & Freeman, J. (1984). Structural inertia and organizational change. *American Sociological Review, 49, 149–164.*

Hannan, M. T., & Freeman, J. (1989). *Organizational Ecology.* Cambridge, MA: Harvard University Press.

Harrison, B. (1994). *Lean and Mean: The Changing Landscape of Corporate Power in the Age of Flexibility.* New York: Basic Books.

Helper, S., MacDuffie, J. P., & Sabel, C. (1997). The Boundaries of the Firm as a Design Problem. Unpublished, National Bureau of Economic Research, Cambridge, Mass.

Jensen, M. C. (1988). The takeover controversy: Analysis and evidence. In: J. C. Coffee, Jr., L. Lowenstein, & S. Rose-Ackerman (Eds.), *Knights, Raiders, and Targets: The Impact of the Hostile Takeover* (pp. 314–354). New York: Oxford University Press.

Jensen, M. C. (1993). The modern industrial revolution, exit, and the failure of internal control systems. *Journal of Finance, 48, 831–880.*

Jensen, M. C., & Meckling, W. H. (1976). Theory of the firm: Managerial behavior, agency cost and ownership structure. *Journal of Financial Economics, 3, 305–360.*

Koput, K. W., Powell, W. W., & Smith-Doerr, L. (1997). Interorganizational relations and elite sponsorship: Mobilizing resources in biotechnology. Unpublished, University of Arizona.

Laumann, E. O., & Knoke, D. (1987). *The Organizational State: Social Choice in National Policy Domains.* Madison, WI: University of Wisconsin Press.

Manne, H. G. (1965). Mergers and the market for corporate control. *Journal of Political Economy, 73, 110–120.*

March, J. G., & Simon, H. A. (1958). *Organizations.* New York: Wiley.

McAdam, D. (1982). *Political Process and the Development of Black Insurgency 1930–1970.* Chicago: University of Chicago Press.

McAdam, D. (1986). Recruitment to high-risk activism: The case of freedom summer. *American Journal of Sociology, 92, 64–90.*

McAdam, D. (1995). 'Initiator' and 'spinoff' movements: Diffusion processes in protest cycles'. In: M. Traugott (Ed.), *Repertoires and Cycles of Collective Action,* (pp. 217–39) Durham, N.C.: Duke University Press.

McAdam, D. (1999). *Political Process and the Development of Black Insurgency, 1930–1970,* second edition. Chicago: University of Chicago Press.

McCarthy, J. D., & Zald, M. N. (1973). *The Trend of Social Movements in America: Professionalization and Resource Mobilization.* Morristown, N.J.: General Learning Press.

McMichael, P. (1996). *Development and Social Change: A Global Perspective.* Thousand Oaks, CA: Pine Forge Press.

Meyer, J. W., & Rowan, B. (1977). Institutionalized organizations: Formal structure as myth and ceremony. *American Journal of Sociology, 83, 340–363.*

Minkoff, D. C. (1997). The sequencing of social movements. *American Sociological Review, 62, 779–799.*

Perrow, C. (1991). A society of organizations. *Theory and Society, 20, 725–762.*

Pfeffer, J., & Salancik, G. R. (1978). *The External Control of Organizations: A Resource Dependence Perspective.* New York: Harper & Row.

Piore, M. J., & Sabel, C. F. (1984). *The Second Industrial Divide: Possibilities for Prosperity.* New York: Basic Books.

Reich, R. (1992). *The Work of Nations: Preparing Ourselves for 21st Century Capitalism.* New York: Vintage.

Roe, M. J. (1994). *Strong Managers, Weak Owners: The Political Roots of American Corporate Finance.* Princeton: Princeton University Press.

Rose, F. (1998). There's no business like show business. *Fortune* (June 22): 87–104.

Sabel, C. F. (1991). Moebius-strip organizations and open labor markets: Some consequences of the reintegration of conception and execution in a volatile economy. In: P. Bourdieu, & J. S. Coleman, (Eds), *Social Theory for a Changing Society,* (pp. 23–54). Boulder, CO: Westview.

Sabel, C. F., & Zeitlin, J. (1996). Stories, strategies, structures: Rethinking historical alternatives to mass production. In: C. F. Sabel, & J. Zeitlin (Eds), *Worlds of Possibility: Flexibility and Mass Production in Western Industrialization.* Cambridge: Cambridge University Press.

Saxenian, A. (1994). *Regional Advantage: Culture and Competition in Silicon Valley and Route 128.* Cambridge, MA: Harvard University Press.

Scott, J. C. (1997). *Seeing Like a State: How Certain Schemes to Improve the Human Condition Have Failed.* New Haven: Yale University Press

Shiller, R. J. (1990). Speculative prices and popular models. *Journal of Economic Perspectives, 4, 55–65.*

Skocpol, T. (1979). *States and Social Revolutions.* Cambridge: Cambridge University Press.

Snow, D. A., & Benford, R. D. (1988). Ideology, frame resonance, and participant mobilization. In: B. Klandermans, H. Kriesi, & S. Tarrow (Eds.), *From Structure to Action: Social Movement Participation Across Cultures,* 197–217. Greenwich, CT: JAI Press.

Snow, D. A., & R. D. Benford. (1992). Master frames and cycles of protest. In: A. Morris, & C. M. Mueller (Eds.), *Frontiers in Social Movement Theory* (pp. 133–55). New Haven, CT: Yale University Press.

Snow. D. A., Rochford, E. B. Jr., Worden, S K., & Benford, R. D. (1986). Frame alignment processes, micromobilization, and movement participation. *American Sociological Review, 51, 464–81.*

Suchman, M. C. (1995). Localism and globalism in institutional analysis: The emergence of contractual norms in venture finance. In: W. R. Scott, & S. Christensen (Eds.). *The Institutional Construction of Organizations* (pp. 39–63). Thousand Oaks, CA: Sage.

Suchman, M. C. (1998). On advice of counsel: The role of law firms in the institutional ecology of Silicon Valley. Unpublished, University of Wisconsin.

Thompson, J. R(1967). *Organizations in Action.* New York: McGraw-Hill.

Tarrow, S. (1989). *Democracy and Disorder: Protest and Politics in Italy, (1965–1975).* Oxford: Oxford University Press.

Tarrow, S. (1998). *Power in Movement,* (2nd ed.). Cambridge: Cambridge University Press.

Tilly, C. (1978). *From Mobilization to Revolution.* New York: Random House.

Tilly, C. (1995a). *Popular Contention in Great Britain, 1758–1834.* Cambridge, MA: Harvard University Press.

Tilly, C. (1995b). Cycles of collective action: Between moments of madness and the repertoire of contention. In: M.

Traugott (Ed.), *Repertoires and Cycles of Collective Action* (pp. 89–116). Durham, N.C.: Duke University Press.

Tilly, C. (1998). Actors, actions, and identities. In: D. McAdam, S. Tarrow, & C. Tilly. (Eds), *Dynamics of Contention*. Unpublished, Center for Advanced Study in the Behavioral Sciences.

Useem, M. (1984). *The Inner Circle*. New York: Oxford University Press.

Useem, M. (1996). *Investor Capitalism: How Money Managers are Changing the Face of Corporate America*. New York: Basic Books.

Useem, M. (1998). Corporate leadership in a globalizing equity market. *Academy of Management Executive*, 12 (4), 43–59.

Uzzi, B. (1997). Social structure and competition in interfirm networks: The paradox of embeddedness. *Administrative Science Quarterly*, 42, 35–67.

Westphal, J. D., & Zajac, E. J. (1998). The symbolic management of stockholders: Corporate governance reforms and shareholder reactions. *Administrative Science Quarterly*, 43, 127–153.

White, H. (1992). *Identity and Control: A Structural Theory of Social Action*. Princeton: Princeton University Press.

Zald, M. N., & Berger, M. A. (1978). Social movements in organizations: Coup d'etat, insurgency, and mass movements. *American Journal of Sociology*, 83, 823–861.

Zeitlin, M. (1974). Corporate ownership and control: The large corporation and the capitalist class. *American Journal of Sociology*, 79, 1073–1119.

Zuckerman, E. W. (1999). The categorical imperative: Securities analysts and the illegitimacy discount. *American Journal of Sociology*, 104, 1398–1438.